Dictionaries are shaped by editors, and the editors of *Dictionary of Christianity and Science* have created a resource unlike anything available. Here the reader will find fair-minded summaries of crucial scientific categories, diverse viewpoints that will surely satisfy and dissatisfy everyone, sketches of schools of thought that become mini-classroom experiences, and a breadth of learning that demonstrates that evangelicalism is coming of age in the discussion about science and faith. Gone are old-fashioned dismissals of science in favor of the Bible. Instead, what we find is rigorous thinking about some of our faith's most difficult challenges. Every Christian studying science will want a copy of *Dictionary of Christianity and Science* within arm's reach.

Scot McKnight, Julius R. Mantey Professor
of New Testament, Northern Seminary

Zondervan's new *Dictionary of Christianity and Science* sparkles with passion, controversy, and diverse perspectives. Contributors cover the many intersections of Christianity and science, and the thinkers who work there. The embattled terrain of evangelicalism receives special emphasis, with contributions from competing thinkers. The result is an engaging, useful volume that belongs in the library of anyone thinking seriously about science and Christian belief.

Karl Giberson, Professor of Science and Religion,
Stonehill College

I am pleased to recommend this dictionary edited by Paul Copan, Tremper Longman, Chris Reese, and Michael Strauss. From the beginning article on Adam and Eve, it is clear that the editors have labored earnestly to include differing perspectives on many issues involving science and Christianity. Although I do not agree with every position, particularly theistic evolution, there is value in challenging readers to examine these issues carefully for themselves.

Dr. Henry F. Schaefer III, Graham Perdue Professor of Chemistry; director,
Center for Computational Quantum Chemistry, University of Georgia

In this unusual dictionary, over a hundred evangelical Christian scholars vigorously (and variously) defend biblical insights in dialogue with and confronting contemporary science (and scientism). From the early Genesis stories of creation, accepting Adam as historical and representative, to Darwinian natural history and genetics, to Jesus's resurrection, to human nature seen theologically and in social science, here is conservative Christianity at its reasoned best.

Holmes Rolston III, University Distinguished Professor,
Colorado State University Templeton Prize Laureate

Zondervan's *Dictionary of Christianity and Science* is an impressive resource that presents a broad range of topics from a broad tent of evangelical scholars. I appreciate that it often presents multiple views. For example, we find entries defending both old-earth and young-earth views of creation as well as one defending a historical Adam and Eve and one not so committed to that view. I look forward to having this reference work on my shelf.

Michael R. Licona, Associate Professor of Theology, Houston Baptist University

Books on the relationship of Christianity and science are, by their very nature, controversial, and this one will be no exception. However, the editors and authors have assembled a substantial amount of material on this topic, including not only terms and definitions but multiple-view discussions that explain various views on many of the more controversial subjects. The sheer number of terms, ideas, concepts, and discussions included in this dictionary make this book an extremely unique and helpful "first step" for anyone interested in the subjects included. This volume is the place to begin when questions dealing with the relationship of Christianity to science are broached.

K. Scott Oliphint, Westminster Theological Seminary, Philadelphia, Pennsylvania

Science and Christianity are the two great forces that have shaped the modern world. This wide-ranging dictionary offers thorough coverage of numerous points at which they have intersected historically, mapping the intellectual landscape. Any serious reader who turns to it for reference or for more thorough study will learn a great deal.

Timothy McGrew, Professor and Chairman, Department of Philosophy, Western Michigan University

As a pastor, I'm called to speak God's word about God's world to God's people. This means connecting Scripture to a whole range of contemporary issues—many of which are outside the training or expertise of the pastor. As a result, I'm always on the lookout for resources to help me wisely shepherd my congregation. That's why I'm thrilled to see the *Dictionary of Christianity and Science*. What pastor has the time to be up to speed on all the issues at the intersection of Christianity and science? Yet what pastor can avoid the need to have something thoughtful to say? Our congregations look to us for this kind of intellectual leadership—and this one-of-a-kind resource makes that job a whole lot easier. A wealth of articles on an array of topics, written with both scholarly acumen and pastoral grace. I can't recommend this resource highly enough.

Todd Wilson, Senior Pastor, Calvary Memorial Church; cofounder and chairman of The Center for Pastor Theologians

This is an invaluable resource that belongs in every Christian's library. Pastors and others will find themselves consulting it frequently for its insightful and helpful entries. I will be keeping my copy close by when I'm writing.

Lee Strobel, author of *The Case for Christ* and the Elizabeth and John Gibson Chair of Apologetics, Houston Baptist University

Since the mid-1990s, an exciting development has arisen within scholarly circles of what many people have termed the "New Academic Dialogue between Science and Religion." There has been a dramatic increase in the number of books moving away from the common perception that modern scientific discoveries and Christian faith are entrenched in a never-ending conflict. The *Dictionary of Christianity and Science* is a welcome addition to this growing body of literature. The excellent selection of entries covers all the major topics and debates that are relevant today. The remarkably clear writing style and balanced presentation of differing views make this dictionary accessible to both specialists in the field and the general public. I am certain that this dictionary will serve the church for many years in leading many to demonstrate that modern science can glorify our Creator and honor his creation.

Denis O. Lamoureux, DDS, PhD (Theology), PhD (Biology), Associate Professor of Science and Religion, St. Joseph's College, University of Alberta

I am very grateful to the editors and contributors for this incredible resource. They have wisely sought advocates of the differing positions and have throughout sought to be comprehensive, informative, and, above all, fair. "Dictionary" is too humble a label for what this is! I anticipate that this will offer valuable guidance for Christian faithfulness.

C. John Collins, Professor of Old Testament, Covenant Theological Seminary

DICTIONARY OF CHRISTIANITY AND SCIENCE

DICTIONARY OF CHRISTIANITY AND SCIENCE

Paul Copan, Tremper Longman III, Christopher L. Reese, Michael G. Strauss, General Editors

THE DEFINITIVE REFERENCE FOR THE INTERSECTION OF CHRISTIAN FAITH AND CONTEMPORARY SCIENCE

ZONDERVAN

Dictionary of Christianity and Science
Copyright © 2017 by Paul Copan, Tremper Longman III, Christopher L. Reese, Michael Strauss

This title is also available as a Zondervan ebook.

Requests for information should be addressed to:
Zondervan, 3900 *Sparks Drive SE, Grand Rapids, Michigan 49546*

ISBN 978-0-310-49605-2

The Bible versions quoted in this book are listed on page 17.

Cover imagery: Elena Korn/Shutterstock
Interior design: Kait Lamphere

Printed in the United States of America

17 18 19 20 21 22 23 24 25 26 27 /DCI/ 20 19 18 17 16 15 14 13 12 11 10 9 8 7 6 5 4 3 2 1

Introduction

Biblical faith and science have been allies and combatants throughout Western history. From Copernicus's heliocentric model to Blaise Pascal's meditations on the mysteries of God, from Darwin's agnosticism to school board disputes over intelligent design, conversation between the two has been both fraught with emotion and fruitful for exploration. Today various scientific theories and discoveries continue to raise questions for Christian views of cosmology, anthropology, and philosophy—and for Bible study and public witness. Possibly more than at any other time in history, views about the relationship between science and Christianity in Western culture are both polarizing and confusing. Thus reasonable dialogue about the intersection of these two topics and clarification of their respective concepts and implications is essential.

The *Dictionary of Christianity and Science* is just such a contemporary investigation of the interaction between Christian faith and science. It is not meant to be exhaustive—much more could be written about each of its entries—but it is wide ranging and accessible. Virtually all of the contributors are evangelical Christians who are experts in their respective fields of study. All entries have been thoroughly peer reviewed by the general editors. It is our hope that the *Dictionary*'s readers will be informed and challenged throughout by accurate summaries and even-handed analysis.

Evangelical Christianity does not have a shared mind regarding science. Well-established camps, often with their own publications, organizations, and events, disagree on fundamental issues. While no book can claim perfect objectivity, the aim of this volume is to represent various evangelical camps and viewpoints as fairly as possible on their own terms. Such an approach will not please everyone. Readers who would prefer settled conclusions might be disappointed. Yet the goal of this dictionary is to chart the outlines of evangelical thought on science and to suggest a framework for future discussions, not to bring such discussions to an end.

This dictionary contains three types of entries.

Introductions. These shorter pieces outline the central facts about a topic in summary form. Where interpretive questions exist, simple explanations of the most viable options are presented, with equal treatment given to each option. The goal of *Introductions* is a quick and easily grasped overview.

Essays. These longer entries begin with the same information as the *Introductions* entries but include further exploration of the implications and significance of the topic under discussion. References to important figures or works related to the topic are often included, as is relevant supporting information. The goal of *Essays* is a thorough introductory synopsis of a consequential subject.

Multiple-View Discussions. Unlike other entries in the *Dictionary*, ***Multiple-View Discussions*** are not meant to be dispassionate. Instead, on key subjects that have stimulated ongoing disagreement and have bearing on the broader relationship between Christian and scientific thought, representatives of significant viewpoints have written pieces that vigorously yet charitably propose their point of view. Argumentation against and anticipation of opposing views' critiques are included. It should be noted that the viewpoint authors did not read one another's entries prior to publication. These viewpoint pieces rely on current research and attempt to present other views accurately, yet the thrust of each piece is to persuade rather than merely to inform. The goal of ***Multiple-View Discussions*** is a debate that delineates the different viewpoints, better equipping readers to come to their own well-informed conclusions. As such, the general editors do not agree with all of the views expressed in these articles. Instead, the editors have tried to promote accuracy but have allowed for a principled dialogue of viewpoints even when controversial. At times there is a fine line between accuracy and opinion.

Entries of all types include a final heading titled "References and Recommended Reading," listing the main sources referenced in each piece and/or further suggested reading.

As the general editors, we have been challenged and enlightened as we have reviewed the many submissions for this dictionary. We believe that you will have the same experience as you interact with the articles and topics included in this volume.

As with any reference work, we are aware that certain important topics or viewpoints may have been omitted. We invite the readers of this dictionary to send suggestions regarding topics that could be incorporated in future editions to dcs@harpercollins.com.

April 2017
Paul Copan, Tremper Longman,
Chris Reese, Michael G. Strauss

Contributors

Joe Aguirre (BS, Biola University) is Editorial Director of Reasons to Believe in Covina, California.

Benjamin H. Arbour is a PhD student at the University of Bristol.

Bruce Ashford (PhD, Southeastern Baptist Theological Seminary) is Professor of Theology and Culture, Provost and Dean of Faculty, and Fellow for the Bush Center for Faith and Culture at Southeastern Baptist Theological Seminary.

Justin L. Barrett (PhD, Cornell University) is Professor of Psychology and Chief Project Developer in the Office for Science, Theology, and Religion Initiatives at Fuller Theological Seminary.

Todd S. Beall (PhD, Catholic University of America) is Professor of Old Testament Literature and Exegesis at Capital Bible Seminary.

Francis J. Beckwith (PhD, Fordham University) is Professor of Philosophy and Church-State Studies, Associate Director of the Graduate Program in Philosophy, and Codirector of the Program in Philosophical Studies of Religion in the Institute for Studies of Religion at Baylor University.

Michael Behe (PhD, University of Pennsylvania) is Professor of Biological Sciences at Lehigh University and a Senior Fellow at the Discovery Institute's Center for Science and Culture.

James Beilby (PhD, Marquette University) is Professor of Biblical and Theological Studies at Bethel University in Saint Paul, Minnesota.

Robert C. Bishop (PhD, University of Texas) is Professor of Physics and Philosophy and the John and Madeleine McIntyre Endowed Professor of Philosophy and History of Science at Wheaton College.

Darrell L. Bock (PhD, University of Aberdeen) is Executive Director of Cultural Engagement and Senior Research Professor of New Testament Studies at Dallas Theological Seminary.

Kenneth Boyce (PhD, University of Notre Dame) is Assistant Professor of Philosophy at the University of Missouri.

Jefrey Breshears (PhD, Georgia State University) is a former Professor at Georgia State University and Reformed Theological Seminary and Founder of The Areopagus, a Christian study center.

Ardel B. Caneday (PhD, Trinity Evangelical Divinity School) is Professor of New Testament Studies and Greek at University of Northwestern in Saint Paul, Minnesota.

Erica Carlson (PhD, University of California at Los Angeles) is Professor of Physics at Purdue University.

Richard F. Carlson (PhD, University of California at San Diego) is Director of the Department of Terrestrial Magnetism at Carnegie Institution for Science.

Stephen Case (PhD, University of Notre Dame) is Professor of Chemistry and Geoscience and Planetarium Director at Olivet Nazarene University.

Graham Cole (ThD, Australian College of Theology) is Dean and Professor of Biblical and Systematic Theology at Trinity Evangelical Divinity School.

Stephen A. Contakes (PhD, University of Illinois) is Assistant Professor of Chemistry at Westmont College.

Paul Copan (PhD, Marquette University) is Professor and Pledger Family Chair of Philosophy and Ethics at Palm Beach Atlantic University's School of Ministry.

Winfried Corduan (PhD, Rice University) is a former Professor of Philosophy and Religion at Taylor University.

William Lane Craig (PhD, University of Birmingham; DTheol, Ludwig-Maximilliéns-Universität München) is Research Professor of Philosophy at Talbot School of Theology and Professor of Philosophy at Houston Baptist University.

Andrew D. Cuthbert is a student in Wheaton College Graduate School's Doctoral Psychology program.

Gregg Davidson (PhD, University of Arizona) is Chair and Professor of Geology and Geological Engineering at the University of Mississippi.

Edward B. ("Ted") Davis (PhD, Indiana University) is Professor of the History of Science at Messiah College.

Ward B. ("Ward") Davis (PsyD, Regent University) is associate professor of psychology at Wheaton College.

Gary Deddo (PhD, University of Aberdeen) is President of Grace Communion Seminary.

William Dembski (PhD, University of Illinois at Chicago) is a former Professor and Research Fellow at the Discovery Institute's Center for Science and Culture.

James Dew (PhD, University of Birmingham) is Associate Professor of the History of Ideas and Philosophy at Southeastern Baptist Theological Seminary and Dean of the College at Southeastern.

Garry DeWeese (PhD, University of Colorado) is Professor at Large at Biola University's Talbot School of Theology.

Calvin B. DeWitt (PhD, University of Michigan) is Professor of Environmental Studies Emeritus at the Gaylord Nelson Institute for Environmental Studies at the University of Wisconsin-Madison.

Travis Dickinson (PhD, University of Iowa) is Associate Professor of Philosophy and Christian Apologetics at Southwestern Baptist Theological Seminary.

Stephen Dilley (PhD, Arizona State University) is Associate Professor of Philosophy at St. Edwards University.

Michael Egnor (MD, Columbia University) is Professor of Neurological Surgery and Pediatrics at Stony Brook University.

Milton Eng (PhD, Drew University) is an Adjunct Professor at William Paterson University and East Coast Project Director at the Institute for the Study of Asian American Christianity.

Martin Erdmann (PhD, Brunel University) is Founding Director of the Verax Institute.

Winston Ewert (PhD, Baylor University) is Senior Researcher at the Evolutionary Informatics Lab.

Darrel R. Falk (PhD, University of Alberta) is Professor Emeritus of Biology at Point Loma Nazarene University and Senior Advisor for Dialogue at BioLogos.

Edward Feser (PhD, University of California at Santa Barbara) is Associate Professor of Philosophy at Pasadena City College.

Chris Firestone (PhD, University of Edinburgh) is Professor of Philosophy and Chair of the Philosophy Department at Trinity International University.

Jonathan Howard Fisher (PhD, Alabama A&M University) is an independent scholar.

Michael Flannery (MLS, University of Kentucky) is Associate Director for Historical Collections at Lister Hill Library of the Health Sciences at the University of Alabama at Birmingham and a Fellow at the Discovery Institute's Center for Science and Culture.

Laurie Furlong (PhD, University of California at Santa Barbara) is Department Chair and Professor of Biology at Northwestern College.

Logan Paul Gage (PhD, Baylor University) is Assistant Professor of Philosophy at Franciscan University of Steubenville.

Ann Gauger (PhD, University of Washington) is a Senior Research Scientist at Biologic Institute and a Senior Fellow at the Discovery Institute's Center for Science and Culture.

R. Douglas Geivett (PhD, University of Southern California) is Professor of Philosophy at Biola University's Talbot School of Theology.

David H. Glass (PhD, Queen's University Belfast) is Senior Lecturer at the School of Computing and Mathematics at the University of Ulster.

Guillermo Gonzalez (PhD, University of Washington) is Assistant Professor of Astronomy at Ball State University and a Senior Fellow at the Discovery Institute's Center for Science and Culture.

Bruce L. Gordon (PhD, Northwestern University) is Scholar in Residence and Associate Professor of History and Philosophy of Science at Houston Baptist University and a Senior Fellow at the Discovery Institute's Center for Science and Culture.

Paul Gould (PhD, Purdue University) is Assistant Professor of Philosophy and Christian apologetics and Chair of Philosophy and Cultural Studies at Southwestern Baptist Theological Seminary.

Tyler S. Greenway (MDiv, Calvin Theological Seminary) is a research assistant at Fuller Theological Seminary's Thrive Center for Human Development and a PhD student in Fuller's psychological science program.

Douglas Groothuis (PhD, University of Oregon) is Professor of Philosophy at Denver Seminary.

Bradley J. Gundlach (PhD, University of Rochester) is Professor of History and Director of the Humanities Division at Trinity International University.

Deborah Haarsma (PhD, Massachusetts Institute of Technology) is President of BioLogos and was previously a Professor and Chair of Physics and Astronomy at Calvin College.

Gary R. Habermas (PhD, Michigan State University) is Distinguished Research Professor of Apologetics and Philosophy at Liberty University's School of Divinity.

Kevin W. Hamlen (PhD, Cornell University) is Associate Professor of Computer Science at the University of Texas at Dallas.

Dominick D. Hankle (PhD, Capella University) is Department Chair and Associate Professor of Psychology at Regent University.

James Hannam (PhD, University of Cambridge) is an author and blogger at BioLogos.

Eric R. Hedin (PhD, University of Washington) is Associate Professor of Physics and Astronomy at Ball State University.

Van Herd (PhD, University of Oklahoma) is an Adjunct Professor at the University of Texas at Austin and Minister of Adult Education at the Congregational Church of Austin.

Rodney Holder (DPhil, University of Oxford) is former Course Director of the Faraday Institute for Science and Religion at St. Edmund's College, Cambridge, where he is a Bye Fellow.

Ryan G. Hornbeck (DPhil, University of Oxford) is a Research Faculty Member at Fuller Theological Seminary's Graduate School of Psychology.

Eric Jones (PhD, Florida Atlantic University) is Associate Professor of Psychology at Regent University.

Michael Keas (PhD, University of Oklahoma) is Professor of the History and Philosophy of Science at Southwestern Baptist Theological Seminary and a Senior Fellow at the Discovery Institute's Center for Science and Culture.

Craig S. Keener (PhD, Duke University) is the F. M. and Ada Thompson Professor of Biblical Studies at Asbury Theological Seminary.

Steward E. Kelly (PhD, University of Notre Dame) is Professor of Philosophy at Minot State University.

P. C. Kemeny (PhD, Princeton University) is Professor of Religion and Humanities at Grove City College.

Jeffrey Koperski (PhD, Ohio State University) is Professor of Philosophy at Saginaw Valley State University.

Maurice Lee (PhD, Yale University) is Assistant Professor of Religious Studies at Westmont College.

David R. Legates (PhD, University of Delaware) is Associate Professor of Geography at the University of Delaware.

James LeMaster (PhD, Southern Baptist Theological Seminary) is a Speaker with the University of Louisville International Medical Ministry.

R. Keith Loftin (PhD, University of Aberdeen) is Assistant Professor of Philosophy and Humanities and Assistant Dean at Southwestern Baptist Theological Seminary.

Tremper Longman III (PhD, Yale University) is Robert H. Gundry Professor of Biblical Studies at Westmont College.

Jonathan Loose (PhD, University of Exeter) is Senior Lecturer in Philosophy and Psychology and Director of Learning and Teaching at Heythrop College, University of London.

Casey Luskin (JD, University of San Diego) previously served as Program Officer in Public Policy and Legal Affairs and as Research Coordinator for the Discovery Institute's Center for Science and Culture.

Hans Madueme (PhD, Trinity Evangelical Divinity School) is Assistant Professor of Theological Studies at Covenant College.

Kerry Magruder (PhD, University of Oklahoma) is Associate Professor of the History of Science and Curator and John H. and Drusa B. Cable Chair of the History of Science Collections at the University of Oklahoma.

Samuel E. Matteson (PhD, Baylor University) is Distinguished Teaching Professor at the University of North Texas.

Lydia McGrew (PhD, Vanderbilt University) is an independent scholar.

Jonathan McLatchie is a PhD student at Newcastle University.

Jennifer Powell McNutt (PhD, University of St. Andrews) is Associate Professor of Theology and History of Christianity at Wheaton College.

Chad Meister (PhD, Marquette University) is Professor of Philosophy at Bethel College in Indiana.

Angus J. L. Menuge (PhD, University of Wisconsin-Madison) is Professor of Philosophy at Concordia University Wisconsin.

Teri R. Merrick (PhD, University of California at Irvine) is Professor of Philosophy and Chair of the Department of Theology and Philosophy at Azusa Pacific University.

Stephen C. Meyer (PhD, University of Cambridge) is Program Director and a Senior Fellow of the Discovery Institute's Center for Science and Culture.

C. Ben Mitchell (PhD, University of Tennessee) is Graves Professor of Moral Philosophy, Provost, and Vice President for Academic Affairs at Union University.

J. P. Moreland (PhD, University of Southern California) is Distinguished Professor of Philosophy at Biola University's Talbot School of Theology.

Paul K. Moser (PhD, Vanderbilt University) is Professor of Philosophy at Loyola University Chicago.

Stephen O. Moshier (PhD, Louisiana State University) is Professor of Geology, Black Hills Science Station Director, and Chair of the Department of Geology and Environmental Science at Wheaton College.

Michael J. Murray (PhD, University of Notre Dame) is Senior Vice President of Programs at the John Templeton Foundation.

Mark Nelson (PhD, University of Notre Dame) is Monroe Professor of Philosophy at Westmont College.

Paul Nelson (PhD, University of Chicago) is a Fellow of the Discovery Institute and Adjunct Professor at Biola University.

Byron Noordewier (PhD, University of Utah) is Professor of Biology at Northwestern College.

Mark Pichaj (MA, Talbot School of Theology) is Assistant Professor of Physical Science at Biola University.

Alexander H. Pierce (MDiv, Trinity Evangelical Divinity School) is an Independent Researcher for the Carl F. H. Henry Center for Theological Understanding.

Jeff Ploegstra (PhD, University of Iowa) is Associate Professor of Biology at Dordt College.

Scott B. Rae (PhD, University of Southern California) is Professor of Christian Ethics and Dean of the Faculty at Biola University's Talbot School of Theology.

Jason M. Rampelt (PhD, University of Cambridge) is an Adjunct Professor at the University of Pittsburgh and a Fellow in Christianity and Science at Greystone Theological Institute.

Christopher L. Reese (ThM, Talbot School of Theology) is a writer, editor, and independent scholar. He previously served as marketing manager for B&H Academic and as associate publisher at Moody Publishers. He is cofounder of the Christian Apologetics Alliance.

Naomi Noguchi Reese (PhD, Trinity Evangelical Divinity School) is Adjunct Professor of Religion at Belmont University.

Victor Reppert (PhD, University of Illinois) is Adjunct Professor of Philosophy at Glendale Community College in Glendale, Arizona.

John Mark Reynolds (PhD, University of Rochester) is Founding President of the Saint Constantine School, a Senior Fellow in the Humanities at the King's College in New York, New York, and a Fellow of the Discovery Institute's Center for Science and Culture.

Brandon L. Rickabaugh (MA, Biola University) is an Adjunct Professor in the Department of Philosophy at Azusa Pacific University.

Warren Rogers (PhD, University of Rochester) is Professor of Physics at Westmont College.

Hugh Ross (PhD, University of Toronto) is President and Founder of Reasons to Believe.

Marcus R. Ross (PhD, University of Rhode Island) is Professor of Geology and Assistant Director of the Center for Creation Studies at Liberty University.

Wayne Rossiter (PhD, Rutgers University) is Assistant Professor of Biology at Waynesburg University and an Adjunct Professor at the University of North Carolina at Wilmington.

Kenneth Richard Samples (MA, Talbot School of Theology) is Senior Research Scholar at Reasons to Believe and an Adjunct Professor at Biola University.

Jeffrey P. Schloss (PhD, Washington University) is Distinguished Professor of Biology, T. B. Walker Chair of Natural and Behavioral Sciences, and Director of the Center for Faith, Ethics, and Life Sciences at Westmont College.

Frederick A. Schneider (PhD, Moscow State Institute of International Relations) is Senior Fellow of the Rivendell Institute at Yale University.

George Schwab (PhD, Westminster Theological Seminary) is Professor of Old Testament at Erskine Theological Seminary.

Scott Shalkowski (PhD, University of Michigan) is Senior Lecturer at the University of Leeds.

Kevin Sharpe (PhD, Purdue University) is Associate Professor in the Philosophy Department at St. Cloud University.

Robert B. Sheldon (PhD, University of Maryland) teaches high school astronomy at Covenant Christian Academy in Huntsville, Alabama.

Bradley L. Sickler (PhD, Purdue University) is Assistant Professor of Philosophy and Program Director for the Master of Arts Program in Theological Studies at the University of Northwestern in Saint Paul, Minnesota.

David Snoke (PhD, University of Illinois at Urbana-Champaign) is Professor of Physics and Astronomy at the University of Pittsburgh.

John Soden (PhD, Dallas Theological Seminary) is a Professor and Program Director of the Master of Arts in Bible Program at Lancaster Bible College.

James S. Spiegel is Professor of Philosophy and Religion at Taylor University.

Ralph Stearley (PhD, University of Michigan) is Professor of Geology at Calvin College.

Michael G. Strauss (PhD, University of California at Los Angeles) is David Ross Boyd Professor of Physics at the University of Oklahoma.

J. B. Stump (PhD, Boston University) is Senior Editor at BioLogos.

Brendan Sweetman (PhD, University of Southern California) is Department Chair and John J. and Laura Sullivan Chair of Philosophy at Rockhurst University.

James E. Taylor (PhD, University of Arizona) is Department Chair and Professor of Philosophy at Westmont College.

Matthew S. Tiscareno (PhD, University of Arizona) is Senior Research Scientist at the Carl Sagan Center for the Study of Life in the Universe at the SETI Institute.

Sara Sybesma Tolsma (PhD, Northwestern University) is Professor of Biology at Northwestern College.

Todd Tracy (PhD, Colorado State University) is Professor of Biology at Northwestern College.

Dennis R. Venema (PhD, University of British Columbia) is Associate Professor at Trinity Western University and a Fellow of Biology at BioLogos.

Donald Wacome (PhD, Duke University) is Professor of Philosophy at Northwestern College.

Matthew Walhout (PhD, University of Maryland) is Professor of Physics and Astronomy and Dean for Research and Scholarship at Calvin College.

John H. Walton (PhD, Hebrew Union College) is Professor of Old Testament at Wheaton College.

John G. West (PhD, Claremont Graduate University) is Vice President of the Discovery Institute and a Senior Fellow at its Center for Science and Culture.

Peter S. Williams (MPhil, University of East Anglia in Norwich; MA, Sheffield University) is Assistant Professor in Communication and Worldview at Gimlekollen School of Journalism and Communication at NLA University College in Norway.

Ken Wolgemuth (PhD, Columbia University) is an Adjunct Professor at the University of Tulsa.

Davis A. Young (PhD, Brown University) is Professor of Geology Emeritus at Calvin College.

Fred Zaspel (PhD, Free University of Amsterdam) is Associate Professor of Christian Theology at Southern Baptist Theological Seminary.

Jeff Zweerink (PhD, Iowa State University) is Research Scholar at Reasons to Believe.

Acknowledgments

We general editors would like to thank Zondervan for the opportunity to edit a volume that we believe to be an important, up-to-date contribution to the Christianity-science discussion. We are especially grateful to Zondervan editor Madison Trammel. He has been a wise, gracious guide — ever open to our suggestions while offering his own good counsel over the several years required to bring this project from proposal to publication.

We would also like to thank Michael Murray, John Churchill, and Alex Arnold of the Templeton Foundation for their helpful suggestions in the early stages of this project.

Bible Versions

All Scripture quotations, unless otherwise indicated, are taken from The Holy Bible, New International Version®, NIV®. Copyright © 1973, 1978, 1984, 2011 by Biblica, Inc.® Used by permission of Zondervan. All rights reserved worldwide. www.Zondervan.com. The "NIV" and "New International Version" are trademarks registered in the United States Patent and Trademark Office by Biblica, Inc.®

Scripture quotations marked ESV are from the ESV® Bible (Holy Bible, English Standard Version®). Copyright © 2001 by Crossway, a publishing ministry of Good News Publishers. Used by permission. All rights reserved.

Scripture quotations marked ISV are from *The Holy Bible: International Standard Version.* Copyright © 1995 – 2014 by ISV Foundation. All rights reserved internationally. Used by permission of Davidson Press, LLC.

Scripture quotations marked KJV are from the King James Version. Public domain.

Scripture quotations marked NASB are from the New American Standard Bible®. Copyright © 1960, 1962, 1963, 1968, 1971, 1972, 1973, 1975, 1977, 1995 by The Lockman Foundation. Used by permission. (www.Lockman.org)

Scripture quotations marked NJB are from *The New Jerusalem Bible.* Copyright © 1985 Darton, Longman & Todd, Ltd. and Doubleday, a division of Bantam Doubleday Dell Publishing Group, Inc., Garden City, NY.

Scripture quotations marked NKJV are from the New King James Version®. © 1982 by Thomas Nelson. Used by permission. All rights reserved.

Scripture quotations marked NLT are from the Holy Bible, New Living Translation. © 1996, 2004, 2007, 2013 by Tyndale House Foundation. Used by permission of Tyndale House Publishers, Inc., Carol Stream, Illinois 60188. All rights reserved.

Scripture quotations marked NRSV are from the New Revised Standard Version Bible. Copyright © 1989 National Council of the Churches of Christ in the United States of America. Used by permission. All rights reserved.

Scripture quotations marked WEB are from the World English Bible™. Public domain.

A

ABORTION. Abortion is the premature termination of a pregnancy, virtually always resulting in the death of the unborn human organism. An abortion can either occur naturally, as in a miscarriage, or intentionally, as in the case of when a pregnant woman procures one. The latter is usually accomplished by procedures performed by physicians or other health care professionals. It is this type of abortion, elective abortion, that is the focus of this entry.

The Christian church has rejected the moral permissibility of elective abortion from its very beginning, even though the Bible does not explicitly condemn it. Nevertheless, the Scriptures' understanding of the human being as made in God's image, combined with the text's prohibition of unjust killing, explains the church's consistent message on the sanctity of nascent human life. In, for example, the earliest extrabiblical book on Christian practice, the *Didache* (c. AD 80–100), we read: "You shall not murder a child by abortion nor kill that which is begotten." Although throughout church history Christian philosophers and theologians have differed over the question of when precisely the developing life in the womb acquires a human soul (or what Thomas Aquinas called "a rational soul"), that disagreement had no bearing on whether abortion was morally permissible. In other words, the moment of rational ensoulment did not determine whether abortion is unjust homicide.

These debates over ensoulment faded away after the onset of modern embryology, when it was discovered that the unborn human is from conception the same being that emerges from the womb at birth, albeit much more fully developed (Haldane and Lee 2003). Once continuity from conception to birth was established, with the born child manifesting the maturation to which the nature of the early embryo was ordered, it became clear to most Christian thinkers that the early embryo had a human soul. However, some maintain that the embryo is not a unified individual organism in the first two weeks or so after conception, since it consists of a cluster of identical totipotent cells (up to the first four days) and pluripotent cells (after the first four days) that seem like independent cells and not the parts of a single organism (Corcoran 2006). Others have disputed this account, arguing that the early embryo is in fact a unified individual organism from conception, since its totipotent and pluripotent cells seem to function in concert in a goal-directed fashion for the good of the whole (George and Tollefsen 2011).

For some thinkers, especially outside the church, the unborn's humanity is not relevant to the moral permissibility of abortion. Some argue that the unborn, though human, are not "persons," since they have not acquired those characteristics we typically attribute to persons, for example, the ability to reason, have a self-concept, and so on (Tooley 1983). Others argue that the unborn, even though persons, may be killed by abortion since no person, born or unborn, has a right to use another's body against her will (Boonin 2002). Christian philosophers have critiqued both sorts of arguments that defend abortion (Beckwith 2007; Kaczor 2014; Lee 2010).

Francis J. Beckwith

REFERENCES AND RECOMMENDED READING

Beckwith, Francis J. 2007. *Defending Life: A Moral and Legal Case against Abortion Choice*. Cambridge: Cambridge University Press.
Boonin, David. 2002. *A Defense of Abortion*. Cambridge: Cambridge University Press.
Corcoran, Kevin J. 2006. *Rethinking Human Nature: A Christian Materialist Alternative to the Soul*. Grand Rapids: Baker.
George, Robert P., and Christopher Tollefsen. 2011. *Embryo: A Defense of Human Life*. 2nd ed. Princeton, NJ: Witherspoon Institute.
Haldane, John, and Patrick Lee. 2003. "Aquinas on Ensoulment, Abortion, and the Value of Human Life." *Philosophy* 78:255–78.
Kaczor, Christopher. 2014. *The Ethics of Abortion: Women's Rights, Human Life, and the Question of Justice*. 2nd ed. London: Routledge.
Lee, Patrick. 2010. *Abortion and Unborn Human Life*. 2nd ed. Washington, DC: Catholic University of America Press.
Tooley, Michael. 1983. *Abortion and Infanticide*. Oxford: Oxford University Press.

ADAM AND EVE (First-Couple View). A book titled *Did Adam and Eve Really Exist?* (Collins 2011) asks a question that for many in evangelical circles might seem self-evident. Of course Adam and Eve really existed, they might say, since without an actual fall as described in Genesis 3, there would be no need for a Savior to redeem mankind from their fallen state. Such has been the near-unanimous view of Christians throughout the first 18 centuries of the church. As William VanDoodewaard observes, "Nearly the entirety of Christendom held to an Adam and Eve who were the first human pair, without ancestry or contemporaries at their point of origin. Almost every Christian theologian, whether in the Roman Empire, the Eastern or Western church, Roman Catholicism or Reformation Protestantism — even most through the **Enlightenment** era — understood Adam and Eve as literally created in the manner described in Genesis 2:2 and Genesis 2:21–22" (VanDoodewaard 2015, 281).

In recent years, however, many evangelical scholars have expressed doubts about a literal Adam and Eve as the first humans created by God and the universal ancestors of all human beings. More recent contributions from genetic analysis that suggests that the original population of humans was at least 10,000 people, not two, have fueled further doubts (Collins 2006, 207). The result is that some scholars see Adam and Eve as (1) historical persons, though if there were many humans around at the same time, they would be chieftains of a tribe specially selected by God (Collins 2011, 121); (2) archetypes but historical people, though not necessarily the first or only humans (Walton 2015, 96–103); (3) literary figures who may or may not be historical (Longman 2013, 122); or (4) not historical at all, though Paul thought they were (Enns 2012, 120–22, 138).

These scholars are to be commended for their labors, as they reinterpret the text of Genesis in an attempt to harmonize the Bible with modern scientific theory. But none of these reinterpretations is ultimately satisfying. As the remainder of this article argues, the best interpretation is that Adam and Eve are real, historical persons, created uniquely by God as the first human pair and the universal ancestors of the rest of humanity.

Adam and Eve in Genesis

The creation of man and woman is mentioned in Genesis 1:26–27, though they are not given proper names until later in the narrative. The word for man (Heb., *adam*) used in Genesis 1:26–27 is identical to the proper name Adam, but the proper name itself is not used until Genesis 2:20b (where the article is not used in the Masoretic text, thus distinguishing Adam from "the man" [Collins 2011, 55–56]). All in all, "Adam" is used nine times in Genesis 1–5 (2:20b; 3:17, 21; 4:25; 5:1 [2], 3, 4, 5), but it seems to be used interchangeably with "the man" (used 22 times in Gen. 1–5) to designate the first human being. Elsewhere in the Old Testament, the proper noun "Adam" occurs only unambiguously in 1 Chronicles 1:1. The name "Eve" (meaning "life") occurs only in Genesis 3:20 (where Adam names his wife Eve because she is "the mother of all the living")

and in Genesis 4:1. She is designated simply as "the woman" 18 times in Genesis 2–5.

All in all, the text of Genesis 1–5 seems clear that Adam is the first human being created by God in his image (Gen. 1:26–27) from the dust of the ground (Gen. 2:7), and that Eve is the first woman, fashioned by God from Adam's rib (Gen. 2:21–22). Theirs is the first marriage (Gen. 2:24); Adam is given a specific command concerning a tree in the garden of **Eden** (Gen. 2:16–17); Eden itself is identified by four named rivers (Gen. 2:10–14); Eve and Adam then disobey God's command (Gen. 3:6); and God expels them from the garden (Gen. 3:22–24). In Genesis 4:1–2 Adam and Eve have sexual relations and bear two children, the oldest of whom (Cain) kills the other (Abel). Cain then builds a city named after his son Enoch, and the **genealogy** of Cain is then given in detail (11 specific names are listed), with the various accomplishments (good and bad) of Cain's descendants listed (4:17–24). Another son (Seth) is born to Adam and Eve in Genesis 4:25–26 as a replacement for Abel.

The last mention of Adam is in Genesis 5:1–5, where the text indicates that Adam had many sons and daughters (thus answering, for some, the perennial question, "Where did Cain get his wife?") in addition to the three mentioned in Genesis 4. The exact age of Adam when he begat Seth is given (130 years old), as is Adam's age at his **death** (930 years old).

All of these specific details demonstrate that the text presents Adam and Eve as historical individuals who lived in a particular place and had a real family with its own real problems (including sibling rivalry and murder) (see also Barrick 2013, 210–11). Adam is created specially by God from "the dust of the ground" (a nonliving entity), not from living hominids or other creatures. The act of God breathing into man's nostrils "the breath of life" (Gen. 2:7) distinguishes man's creation from the creation of the animals. Similarly, Eve's origin is depicted as a direct creation of God from the first man, Adam (Gen. 2:21–22).

Hermeneutical problems with a figurative approach to Adam and Eve in Genesis

All of the details given above support the conclusion that the text of Genesis presents a historical Adam and Eve specially created by God as the first human beings and the ancestors of all future human beings (see **Genesis, Interpretation of Chapters 1 and 2**). Yet many take portions of Genesis 1–11 as figurative or "literary," not necessarily literal in all details. It is impossible (given space considerations) to discuss each of the figurative views, but **John Walton**'s will suffice as a representative. Primarily on the basis of the genealogies and the New Testament discussion of **the fall**, he (rightly) acknowledges that Adam and Eve are historical persons, not merely mythological or legendary. However, since Walton sees their roles as archetypal, he believes that there may be elements "that are not intended to convey historical elements": they present truths about Adam and Eve "rather than historical events" (Walton 2015, 101). Walton concludes that "one can accept the historical Adam without thereby making a decision about material human origins. This has the advantage of separating scientific elements (material human origins) from exegetical/theological elements, with the result that conflict between the claims of science and the claims of Scripture is minimized without compromise" (Walton 2015, 103).

But this approach is problematic. There are many statements about Adam's direct creation from God and his function in Genesis 1–5 (more than 20 are listed in the preceding discussion). How is the reader to determine which are historical and which are not? How can some of the details be accurate and others be nonhistorical, when all are presented as historical? Similar questions could be raised about **the flood**, Babel, Abraham, and so forth. No internal marker exists to indicate that the text of Genesis 1–5 or Genesis 1–11 should be taken figuratively. The structure of Genesis revolves around the phrase *elleh toledoth* ("This is the account of …"). This phrase is used 10 times in the book: twice in Genesis 1–5 (2:4 and 5:1), four more times in Genesis 6–11, and four times in the rest of the book (Kaiser 1970, 59–61).

While some try to argue that Genesis 1 or Genesis 1–3 or Genesis 1–11 is a separate genre, such is not the case. Virtually all of Genesis 1–11 is straightforward narrative prose. The standard form for consecutive narrative prose is the *waw*-consecutive imperfect (wci). The creation account in Genesis 1:1–2:3 contains 55 wci forms in its 34 verses, or an average of 1.6 per verse. Similarly, all of Genesis 1:1–5:5 (from creation through the narrative concerning Adam and Eve) contains 155 wci forms, or an average of 1.4 per verse. By contrast, the poetic section of Genesis 49:1b–27 contains only 8 wci forms, or an average of only 0.30 per verse (Beall, Banks, and Smith 2000, 1–4, 46). The inescapable conclusion is that Genesis 1–5 (and Gen. 1–11, for that matter) is written in standard Hebrew narrative form, not poetry (Westermann 1984, 80). There is therefore no hermeneutical or structural basis for regarding portions of

Genesis 1–2 (concerning creation) or Genesis 1–5 (creation, Adam, Eve, fall) as figurative rather than straightforward historical narrative.

Genealogies

Another strong evidence for the historicity of Adam is found in the **genealogy**. Some scholars attempt to separate Genesis 1–11 from the remainder of Genesis, considering Genesis 1–11 as primeval history, while Genesis 12–50 reflects genuine history (e.g., Westermann 1984, 1–5), but such a separation is not warranted. In addition to the structural marker *elleh toledoth* mentioned above, the genealogies found in Genesis 1–11 are foundational for Genesis 12. The first mention of the great patriarch Abram is not in 12:1 but in 11:26, as part of a long genealogy that stretches all the way back to Noah's son Shem. But the mention of Shem connects it back to the genealogy of Genesis 10, the flood account in Genesis 6–9, and the genealogy of Genesis 5, where Noah and his sons are first mentioned (Gen. 5:29–32). In turn, Genesis 5 contains a genealogy that begins with Adam himself, going right back to creation when God created "male and female" (Gen. 5:1–2). If Adam is simply "everyman," as some attest, then one wonders why Genesis 5:3–5 gives Adam's age when begetting Seth and at Adam's own death.

The same formula is continued throughout the genealogies of Adam. Whether some generations are "skipped" in the genealogies of Genesis (see Sexton 2015) is irrelevant: the genealogies appear to be of real people, each of whom lived a specific number of years before he died. It is difficult to see any hermeneutical justification for taking Abraham and the patriarchs as historical people, but not Adam, Noah, and Noah's sons: all are presented as historical people who lived a certain age and then died (except for Enoch [Gen. 5:24]).

Nor are the Genesis genealogies unique. The last book of the Old Testament (according to the Masoretic text), Chronicles, begins with a lengthy genealogy. This genealogy includes the patriarchs and the sons of Israel but begins with Adam. Similar to Genesis, the genealogy goes through Seth's line to Noah and his sons, gives a limited genealogy of Ham and Japheth, and provides a more extensive genealogy of Shem, leading right to Abraham (1 Chron. 1:1–28). Similarly, in the New Testament, Luke 3:23–38 traces the genealogy of Jesus all the way back to Adam, ending with these words: "the son of Enosh, the son of Seth, the son of Adam, the son of God."

Because of this last phrase, Longman argues that Luke's genealogy is "ultimately a theological statement and not a purely historical" one (Longman 2013, 123), but in fact the last phrase seems to tie Adam directly to God, as one created in God's image, reaffirming exactly what Genesis 1:26–27 proclaims. Yes, the genealogy is a theological statement, but it is historical as well. Seventy-five names are mentioned in the genealogy, including David and Abraham. These are real people, presented as ancestors to Christ. Is Adam the only nonhistorical name in the list? Such a view strains credibility (see Beall 2008, 148). As Walton observes, "Genealogies from the ancient world contain the names of real people who inhabited a real past. Consequently there would be no precedent for thinking of the biblical genealogies differently. By putting Adam in ancestor lists, the authors of Scripture are treating him as a historical person" (Walton 2015, 102).

New Testament References to Adam

In addition to the text of Genesis and the genealogies, the New Testament provides strong evidence that Adam and Eve were historical persons, created by God as the first human beings (see **Adam in the New Testament**). In fact, the New Testament treats all of Genesis 1–11 in a historical, nonfigurative manner (see Matt. 19:4–6; 24:37–38; Mark 10:6–8; Luke 3:38; 17:26–27; Rom. 5:12–20; 8:19–22; 1 Cor. 11:8–9; 15:22; 2 Cor. 4:6; 1 Tim. 2:13–14; Heb. 4:4; 11:3–7; 1 Peter 3:20; 2 Peter 2:5; 3:5–6; and 1 John 3:12; Beall 2008, 146–49). But with specific reference to Adam, Eve, and creation, the following passages are especially pertinent.

The Gospels. When questioned concerning the issue of divorce, Jesus cites Genesis 1:27 and 2:24 as authoritative Scripture (Matt. 19:4–6; Mark 10:6–8). Not only does he reference the creation of man and woman in Genesis 1, noting that "from the beginning of creation, 'God made them male and female'" (Mark 10:6 ESV), but he follows up by citing the statement made after the creation of Eve in Genesis 2 that "the two shall become one flesh" (10:8 ESV).

Acts. In his sermon to the Athenians in Acts 17, Paul first states that God "made the world and everything in it" (v. 24) and then explains further: "From one man he made all the nations, that they should inhabit the whole earth" (v. 26). Here Paul clearly says that all of the rest of humanity descended from one man, just as Genesis states.

Pauline letters. In his letters, Paul gives details about the creation of Adam and Eve and the fall. In 2 Corinthians 11:3 Paul refers to **the serpent** tempting Eve; and in 1 Timothy 2:11–14, Paul says that "Adam was formed first,

then Eve" (v. 13, referring to Gen. 2:20–23), and that "it was the woman who was deceived" (v. 14, referring to Gen. 3:1–13). Similarly, in 1 Corinthians 11:8–9 Paul explains that the woman was created from the man and for the man, just as Genesis 2:18–23 describes. In all of these cases, Paul draws from specific details of the creation and fall narratives in order to make his point.

Two very important passages that contrast Adam and his sin with Christ and his redemption are 1 Corinthians 15:20–23, 45–49 and Romans 5:12–19. In 1 Corinthians 15:21–22, Paul says, "For since death came through a man, the resurrection of the dead comes also through a man. For as in Adam all die, so in Christ all will be made alive." In 1 Corinthians 15:45 Paul states that "the first man Adam became a living being," and in verse 47 Paul observes that Adam was made "of the dust of the earth." Both phrases are taken from the creation narrative of Genesis 2:7. Furthermore, when Paul says in Romans 5:12 that "sin entered the world through one man," he is referencing the fall in Genesis 3 as well as viewing Adam as the ancestor of all people. Paul continues in verse 14, saying that "death reigned from the time of Adam to the time of Moses," thus linking Adam with another historical figure, Moses. The remainder of the passage contrasts Adam's sin and disobedience (leading to death) with Christ's obedience and righteousness (leading to life).

As Douglas Moo cogently writes, "It is difficult to see how Paul's argument in Rom. 5:12–21 hangs together if we regard Adam as mythical. For Adam and Christ are too closely compared in this passage to think that one could be 'mythical' and the other 'historical.' We must be honest and admit that if Adam's sin is not 'real,' then any argument based on the presumption that it is must fall to the ground" (Moo 1996, 325; for a more extensive treatment, see Collins 2011, 78–90).

Conclusion

The evidence throughout the Scripture is that Adam and Eve are historical persons created uniquely by God as the universal ancestors of mankind. The data from the **Human Genome Project** does not contradict that: the starting pool of 10,000 humans is an *inference* from the data—an inference made using the evolutionary assumptions of **common ancestry**, gradual change over long periods of time, and **natural selection** (Carter 2011). Could not God have designed a multitude of genetic variants in Adam and Eve right from the start (Sanford and Carter 2014)? One wonders as well about the ramifications of God's intervention at the **Tower of Babel**: could genetic differentiation have been introduced at the same time as the confusion of languages?

Trying to reinterpret Adam simply on the basis of the inferences of evolutionary geneticists, especially given the newness of the field (witness the rise and fall of "junk DNA" [Sanford and Carter 2014]), does not seem wise, and it does not work. **Peter Enns** rightly comments on those who try to introduce some sort of first pair in the evolutionary process in order to preserve Paul's theology: "The irony, however, is that in expending such effort to preserve biblical teaching, we are left with a first pair that is utterly foreign to the biblical portrait" (Enns 2012, xvii). Scripture's portrayal of Adam and Eve as the first couple uniquely created by God is consistent, clear, and correct.

Todd S. Beall

REFERENCES AND RECOMMENDED READING

Barrick, William D. 2013. "A Historical Adam: Young-Earth Creation View." In *Four Views on the Historical Adam*, ed. Matthew Barrett and Ardel B. Caneday. Grand Rapids: Zondervan.

Beall, Todd S. 2008. "Contemporary Hermeneutical Approaches to Genesis 1–11." In *Coming to Grips with Genesis: Biblical Authority and the Age of the Earth*, ed. Terry Mortenson and Thane Ury. Green Forest, AR: Master.

Beall, Todd S., William A. Banks, and Colin Smith. 2000. *Old Testament Parsing Guide*. Nashville: B&H.

Carter, Robert W. 2011. "The Non-Mythical Adam and Eve! Refuting Errors by Francis Collins and BioLogos." August 20. www.creation.com/historical-adam-biologos.

Collins, C. John. 2011. *Did Adam and Eve Really Exist?* Wheaton, IL: Crossway.

Collins, Francis S. 2006. *The Language of God*. New York: Free Press.

Enns, Peter. 2012. *The Evolution of Adam*. Grand Rapids: Baker.

Kaiser, Walter C., Jr. 1970. "The Literary Form of Genesis 1–11." In *New Perspectives on the Old Testament*, ed. J. Barton Payne. Waco, TX: Word.

Kulikovsky, Andrew. 2009. *Creation, Fall, Restoration: A Biblical Theology of Creation*. Fearn, Ross-shire, Scotland: Mentor.

Longman, Tremper, III. 2013. "What Genesis 1–2 Teaches (and What It Doesn't)." In *Reading Genesis 1–2: An Evangelical Conversation*, ed. J. Daryl Charles. Peabody, MA: Hendrickson.

Moo, Douglas. 1996. *The Epistle to the Romans*. The New International Commentary on the New Testament. Grand Rapids: Eerdmans.

Mortenson, Terry, and Thane Ury, eds. 2008. *Coming to Grips with Genesis: Biblical Authority and the Age of the Earth*. Green Forest, AR: Master.

Sanford, John C., and Robert Carter. 2014. "In Light of Genetics ... Adam, Eve, and the Creation/Fall." *Christian Apologetics Journal* 12 (2): 51–98.

Sarfati, Jonathan D. 2015. *The Genesis Account: A Theological, Historical, and Scientific Commentary on Genesis 1–11*. Powder Springs, GA: Creation Books.

Sexton, Jeremy. 2015. "Who Was Born When Enosh Was 90? A Semantic Reevaluation of William Henry Green's Chronological Gaps." *Westminster Theological Journal* 77:193–218.

VanDoodewaard, William. 2015. *The Quest for the Historical Adam: Genesis, Hermeneutics, and Human Origins*. Grand Rapids: Reformation Heritage.

Walton, John. 2015. *The Lost World of Adam and Eve*. Downers Grove, IL: InterVarsity.

Westermann, Claus. 1984. *Genesis 1–11*. Continental Commentary. Minneapolis: Fortress.

↬ ADAM AND EVE (Representative-Couple View)

Adam and Eve in the Old Testament

The opening chapters of the **book of Genesis** present Adam and Eve as the first human beings created by God. The first creation account (1:1–2:4a) describes the creation of humanity on the sixth day. Genesis 1:27 could theoretically be translated "God created Adam in his own image ...," but since the Hebrew word *'adam* means humanity, it is more likely that here the word is not the personal name since the verse goes on to inform the reader that God created them "male and female."

Indeed, it is possible, even likely, that the personal name Adam does not occur in the second creation account either (2:4b–25; see NRSV). However, the narrator in this section does speak of "the man" as an individual, and since the first man is called Adam at least by Genesis 4:25 (Eve is first named in 3:20), many translations (e.g., NIV) will translate the Hebrew as Adam in Genesis 2 and 3. The rest of this article will identify the man and the woman in Genesis 1–3 as Adam and Eve, reading that name back from Genesis 4 and 5.

The first creation account speaks of humans, male (Adam) and female (Eve), as created on the climactic sixth day of the creation week. God creates them in his image (see **Image of God**) and charges them to have dominion, or to rule, over the rest of the creatures that he has created. He also tells them to multiply and fill the earth and subdue it (1:28). He gives them vegetation for food.

The second creation account presents a more detailed telling of the story of the creation of the first man (Adam) and the first woman (Eve). After creating the world and before he creates vegetation, God breathes into the dust of the ground to form the first man ("The LORD God formed a man [or Adam] from the dust of the ground and breathed into his nostrils the breath of life, and the man became a living being," 2:7).

After the creation of Adam, God then planted a garden, named **Eden**, which means "abundance," and placed man in it. The narrator highlights two trees in Eden, the tree of life and the tree of the knowledge of good and evil. God prohibits Adam from eating the fruit of the latter tree; if he does, he will die. He also commissions Adam to "work" the garden and to "take care" of it (2:15). "Take care" can also be rendered "guard" (*shamar*), and Adam's task is analogous to the later role of the priests in the Holy Place. As with the later sanctuary, God makes his presence known in Eden, and Adam, like the Levites, must guard the holy place.

Adam is in a harmonious relationship with God and lives in a place of abundance. Thus it is surprising that God then announces: "It is not good for the man to be alone. I will make a helper suitable for him" (2:18). The Hebrew term "helper" (*'ezer*) does not denote subordination as some might believe on a surface reading. Indeed, God is later called the "helper" of Israel (Pss. 10:14; 27:9; 118:7), and he is certainly not their servant. Perhaps a better translation of *'ezer* is "ally," in that both of them are charged with protecting the garden from predators (like the "serpent," who appears in Gen. 3:1). After parading the animals before Adam and finding none to be fitting companions, God then creates the first woman (Eve) who will be a helper suitable for Adam.

The way God forms the woman emphasizes her equality and mutuality with the man. She is created not from his head or from his feet, but from his side (or rib). After her creation, the man praises her and the intimacy they share. She is "now bone of my bones and flesh of my flesh" (2:23). The narrator then gives a pronouncement that has since been understood to constitute the institution of marriage ("That is why a man leaves his father and mother and is united to his wife, and they become one flesh," 2:24). Harmony in the garden is signaled by the fact that they can stand naked before each other and not feel shame.

Radical change takes place in the next chapter beginning with the appearance of the **serpent**, a well-known ancient Near Eastern symbol of evil. The serpent addresses the woman (Eve) with a provocative question, "Did God really say, 'You must not eat from any tree in the garden'?" (3:1). His question is ridiculous because, if true, the man and the woman would starve. The serpent, though, here adopts a crafty strategy, because rather than guarding the garden and ignoring the serpent or chasing the serpent from the garden, the woman wrongly engages the serpent in a discussion. She thus is the first apologist or defender of God, but this approach leads to trouble. In her response, she reveals that she is also the first legalist, adding to the prohibition of God by saying not only did God instruct them not to eat from the tree, but also that God prohibited them from touching it.

The serpent disputes God's warning, telling her that she won't die if she eats the fruit of the tree. He entices her with the promise of wisdom ("your eyes will be opened," 3:5). She eats the fruit from the tree and gives some to her husband (Adam), who eats it without discussion or argument. Their eyes are indeed opened, and the consequences are disastrous, destroying the harmony between them and God with ramifications for the relationship between them and also between them and the rest of creation.

Before continuing, I need to comment on the significance of rebelliously eating the fruit of the forbidden tree, the tree of the knowledge of good and evil. Of course, Adam and Eve already knew what was good and what was evil (eating the fruit of the forbidden tree); so eating it did not give them intellectual knowledge or awareness of what is right and wrong. Modern readers need to know that "knowledge" in Hebrew is not simply intellectual apprehension, but includes experience. In other words, by eating the fruit, Adam and Eve arrogate to themselves the right to decide what is right or wrong. They reject God's authority and replace it with their own. By eating of the fruit, they assert their own moral autonomy.

As a result, God punishes them. The serpent will no longer walk, but will slither. In my opinion, the serpent is symbolic of evil (see **Serpent**); so the purpose of this story is not to tell readers the reason why serpents move the way they do, but rather to speak about the humiliation of evil. God also announces that the serpent will be destroyed by the offspring of the woman. The latter is often understood as an anticipation of Christ's defeat of Satan based on the testimony of the New Testament (Rom. 16:20; Rev. 12:9). God punishes the woman by bringing increased pain to her relationships, both physical pain in childbirth and emotional pain in her relationship with her husband. God punishes the man by making work more frustrating. God also ejects the couple from Eden.

God had warned Adam and Eve that rebellion meant death. Spiritual death came immediately after their rebellion (separation from God), and eventually they would die physically as well. Even so, God extends to the man and woman a token of grace (by providing them with clothing now that their nakedness brought shame), showing that he will stay involved with them.

Adam and Eve play a foundational role in the biblical story, but surprisingly, they barely appear in the rest of the Old Testament. Before they physically die, Adam and Eve give birth to two sons, Cain and Abel (4:1–2), and when Cain kills Abel, we hear that Adam and Eve give birth to Seth (Gen. 4:25). But after this, Adam is mentioned only one more time in the Old Testament, at the beginning of the genealogies of the book of Chronicles (1 Chron. 1:1). In the Old Testament, Adam is not only the name of a **person**, but also of a geographical location, according to Joshua 3:16, and though some believe that the reference to Adam in Hosea 6:7 is to the man, it is certainly rather speaking of a geographical location as is made clear by the locative "there" in the second colon: "As at Adam, they have broken the covenant; they were unfaithful to me there." Hosea 6:7 thus is not relevant to a discussion of Adam the person.

Adam and Eve in the New Testament

Adam and Eve appear in the New Testament several times. The **genealogy** of Jesus in Luke extends back to Adam, who is then called "the son of God" (Luke 3:38), indicating that not only is Jesus fully human, he is also fully divine. As John Nolland insightfully comments, "Luke would have us see that Jesus takes his place in the human family and thus in its (since Adam's disobedience) flawed sonship; however, in his own person, in virtue of his unique origin (Luke 1:35) but also as worked out in his active obedience (4:1 – 13), he marks a new beginning to sonship and sets it on an entirely new footing. In this human situation Jesus is the one who is really the Son of God" (Nolland 1989, 173). A second appearance of Adam takes place in the book of Jude, when, quoting Enoch, Jude calls him "the seventh from Adam" (Jude 14), a reference back to the genealogy we find in Genesis 5.

Paul makes the most theological use of Adam and Eve in the New Testament. In his pastoral letter to Timothy, Paul argues that a woman should "learn in quietness and full submission" and should not "teach or assume authority over a man" with reference to the Adam and Eve story. First, he argues from the fact that Adam was created before Eve and, second, that the woman was the one who was deceived by the serpent and not the man (1 Tim. 2:11 – 15).

While the meaning and application of the Timothy passage is much contested, another debate focuses on Adam's role in Romans 5:12 – 19. In this passage, Paul makes an analogy between Adam and Christ. Adam introduced sin and death into the world, and Jesus brought grace into the world. The comparison is based on the fact that one man brought sin and death into the world and the other brought grace into the world, but no analogy is perfectly equal (the point of vv. 15 – 17). Paul makes a similar point in his first letter to the Corinthians, "For since death came through a man, the resurrection of the dead comes also through a man" (15:21), and "So it is written: 'The first man Adam became a living being'; the last Adam, a life-giving spirit" (15:45). These analogies between Adam and Jesus contrast Adam as the one through whom sin and death come into the world and Jesus through whom life and grace come into the world.

Before continuing, we should address a common misunderstanding of these passages, particularly the one in Romans, since it has been used to put forward a specific view of why all humans are sinners. We first note that though Paul attributes to Adam the introduction of sin and death into the world, he never says that people are guilty because of Adam's sin. Nowhere in the Bible is Adam blamed for anyone else's guilt. Paul says, "Therefore, just as sin entered the world through one man, and death through sin, and in this way death came to all people, *because all sinned*" (Rom. 5:12, emphasis added). Our guilt is due to our own sin, not Adam's sin.

The usually insightful **Augustine** thrust interpretation in an unhelpful direction because he mistranslated the Greek preposition *'eph hô* ("because") into Latin as *in quo* ("in whom"). Thus Adam became, according to Augustine, the one man who made us all guilty because we sinned in him. If Augustine was right, then it would be necessary that we would all physically descend from a historical figure named Adam (see below), but he was not correct in his understanding nor in his idea that **original sin** was inherited from Adam like a disease (Hays and Herring 2013). Rather, it seems best to understand Paul as saying that when Adam sinned, he showed what we were all like (we are all sinners). Adam did what we would do if we were in his place. Further, human rebellion so disrupted creation and social relationships that it is not possible not to sin. As John Walton puts it, "Humanity was supposed to continue God's process of moving the cosmos from nonorder to order. With the failure of humanity all creation was stuck in a ripple effect of sin and the disorder it brought" (Walton 2012, 11).

We should also mention certain passages in the New Testament that don't mention Adam and Eve by name, but which do refer to the account of Adam and Eve. In Matthew 19:1 – 12 Jesus instructs his disciples about marriage and divorce and in the process cites Genesis 1:27 ("'Haven't you read,' he replied, 'that at the beginning the Creator "made them male and female"?,'" Matt. 19:4) and Genesis 2:24 ("For this reason a man will leave his father and mother and be united to his wife, and the two will become one flesh," Matt. 19:5) to argue that marriage, between a man and a woman, is to be permanent and divorce should not be easy or common. Paul also cites the latter Genesis text in his discussion of marriage in Ephesians 5:31.

The Historical Adam and Eve

Recent developments in evolutionary theory have raised questions about the historical status of Adam and Eve. Since the mapping of the human genome about two decades ago, evidence indicates to the vast majority of biologists that humanity does not go back to a single couple but rather to an original breeding population of perhaps 5,000 to 10,000 individuals (Venema 2010), raising the now hotly debated question, at least in evangelical Protestant circles, of whether there was a historical Adam and Eve. "If the consensus of biology is correct, is the Bible wrong?" Or, to put the same question in another way, "If the Bible is true, is biology wrong?" For those of us who believe that the Bible is God's Word and thus not misleading, it goes without saying that this is a crucial question.

As we address this question, we need to remember that an evangelical Protestant understanding of the Bible insists that the Bible is true *in all that it intends to teach*. Thus we must ask if it was God's intention in the Bible to teach us how God created humanity in a literal and precise fashion. After all, the two accounts we have of creation (Gen. 1:1 – 2:4a; 2:4b – 25) conflict in terms of the sequence of creation, there is a demonstrable use of figurative language in these chapters as well as interplay with ancient Near Eastern creation stories (for details, see **Genesis, Book of**; **Creation**). These signals indicate that the book of Genesis does not seem interested to tell us how God created creation, but to celebrate that he was the creator of everything. When it comes to humanity, the Bible is not interested in telling us the details of how he created humans, but that he did it.

That said, in Genesis 1 – 2, the foundational story of Adam and Eve, there certainly are historical claims (most noted by the *toledot* structure of the book of Genesis as a whole [see **Genesis, Book of**]). What are those historical claims? First, that God created humanity and that when he created them, they were capable of choice and morally innocent. Second, Genesis 3 clearly teaches that humans rebelled against God and thus, in the words of Paul, brought sin and death into the world.

God created humans, not by literally breathing into dust; after all, God does not have lungs and this description is suspiciously similar to (and likely a polemic against) the account of the creation of the first humans in the ***Enuma Elish*** and ***Atrahasis***. When humanity emerges from their primate past, God then confers the status of **image of God** on them, indicating their special status and relationship

among God's creatures. Who then are Adam and Eve? There are two ways of thinking about them: perhaps they are a representative couple in the original population (or even a representative couple tens of thousands of years after the original population, Wright 2014), or perhaps Adam and Eve simply stand for original humanity. Genesis 3 thus teaches that original humanity (perhaps first the representative couple, perhaps the entirety of original humanity) then rebelled against God and thus, as we mentioned above, not only represented what all humans would do (and actually do do) in their place, but also so affected the social system that it is ever after impossible not to sin.

But what about the New Testament, particularly Paul in Romans 5? Doesn't Paul have to think that Adam is a historical figure to make his analogy work? Not at all (contra Enns 2012), as we suggested above, and here we add a helpful comment from James Dunn:

> It would not be true to say that Paul's theological point here depends on Adam being a "historical" individual or on his disobedience being a historical event as such. Such an implication does not necessarily follow from the fact that a parallel is drawn with Christ's single act: as act in mythic history can be paralleled to an act in living history without the point of comparison being lost. So long as the story of Adam as the initiator of the sad tale of human failure was well known, which we may assume (the brevity of Paul's presentation presupposes such a knowledge), such a comparison was meaningful. Nor should modern interpretation encourage patronizing generalizations about the primitive **mind** naturally understanding the Adam stories as literally historical. It is sufficiently clear for example from Plutarch's account of the ways in which the Osiris myth was understood at this period that such tales told about the dawn of human history could be and were treated with a considerable degree of sophistication with the literal meaning largely discounted. (Dunn 1988, 289 – 90)

Cunningham is also helpful when he points out that in Romans 5, "Paul was not interpreting the story in and for itself; he was really interpreting Christ through the use of images from the story" (Cunningham 2010, 384).

Conclusion

As stated above, the question of the historical Adam and Eve is hotly contested today. Over against those who believe that the entire structure of Christian theology will collapse if

Adam and Eve are not the first (and only) humans at creation (see Versteeg and Phillips; see Collins for a more measured viewpoint), it may be that science has helped us understand the truth claims of the Bible better. Theologians should at least have the humility to consider this as a possibility.

Tremper Longman III

REFERENCES AND RECOMMENDED READING

Barrett, Matthew, and Ardel B. Caneday, eds. 2013. *Four Views on the Historical Adam*. Grand Rapids: Zondervan.

Collins, C. J. 2011. *Did Adam and Eve Really Exist? Who They Were and Why You Should Care*. Wheaton, IL: Crossway.

Cunningham, C. 2010. *Darwin's Pious Idea: Why the Ultra-Darwinists and Creationists Both Get It Wrong*. Grand Rapids: Eerdmans.

Dunn, J. D. G. 1988. *Romans 1–8*. Word Biblical Commentary. Dallas: Word.

Enns, P. 2012. *The Evolution of Adam: What the Bible Does and Doesn't Say about Human Origins*. Grand Rapids: Brazos.

Hays, C. M., and S. L. Herring. 2013. "Adam and the Fall." In *Evangelical Faith and the Challenge of Historical Criticism*, ed. By C. M. Hays and C. B. Ansberry. Grand Rapids: Baker.

Nolland, J. 1989. *Luke 1–9:20*. Word Biblical Commentary. Dallas: Word.

Phillips, R. D., ed. 2015. *God, Adam, and You: Biblical Creation Defended and Applied*. Phillipsburg, NJ: P&R.

Postell, S. D. 2012. *Adam as Israel: Genesis 1–3 as the Introduction to the Torah and Tanakh*. Cambridge: James Clarke.

Venema, D. R. 2010. "Genesis and the Genome: Genomics Evidence for Human-Ape Common Ancestry and Ancestral Hominid Population Sizes." *Journal of the American Scientific Affiliation* 62:166–78.

Versteeg, J. P. 2012. *Adam in the New Testament: Mere Teaching Model or First Historical Man?* Phillipsburg, NJ: P&R.

Walton, J. 2012. "Human Origins and the Bible." *Zygon* 47:875–89.

———. 2015. *The Lost World of Adam and Eve*. Downers Grove, IL: InterVarsity.

Wright, N. T. 2014. *Surprised by Scripture: Engaging Contemporary Issues*. New York: HarperCollins.

ADAM IN THE NEW TESTAMENT. The name *Adam* appears in three writers (Luke, Paul, and Jude) of the New Testament, with the majority of references tied to the apostle. Adam is an important figure representing the prototype human as the first human figure mentioned in the Hebrew Scripture. Jesus also makes allusion to marriage through the picture of **Adam and Eve** in discussions about divorce (Matt. 19:4–6; Mark 10:6–9).

Adam in Luke. Adam is noted in the **genealogy** of Jesus in Luke 3:38. Unlike Matthew's genealogy, which only goes back to Abraham, Luke traces Jesus's origin to the first human generation to picture the universal scope of Jesus's ministry. This fits a larger Lucan theme that shows how the gospel was given to all the world and was to be taken to the ends of the earth. Another interesting note about Luke's use is that in the listing after Adam comes the description of him as "Son of God." This alludes to Adam

as the prototype human, made in God's image and created by him. Of course, the roots for this teaching are in Genesis 1–2. Luke's listing makes no distinction in the generations that precede Abraham from those that follow.

Adam in Jude. Jude 14 mentions Adam briefly and in passing as seven generations removed from Enoch. Enoch is said to point to judgment of the ungodly. Other than a kind of temporal marker looking back to the earliest of times, Jude makes nothing more of Adam.

Adam in Paul's writings. Three texts about Adam are noted in Paul's epistles: Romans 5:14 in a section comparing the first and last Adams in terms of their impact on humanity, sin, and salvation; 1 Corinthians 15:22, 45, and 47, where again the contrast is between the first and last Adam as Paul develops the resurrection as the reversal of death; and 1 Timothy 2:13–14 that declares that Adam was formed first before Eve, with Eve being the one deceived. In all three texts, Adam is presented as the first human and serves as a prototype for humanity in one way or another.

In 1 Timothy the reference to Adam being formed is a direct allusion to God's creation of Adam in Genesis 2:7–8, 15, and 19, using the Greek verb *plassō*. In this pastoral epistle, Paul is explaining the roles of males and females in the church. The primacy of Adam is part of his argument for distinguishing male and female roles. Males and females have each been given different primary roles: the man is to teach, and the woman is to bear children.

In 1 Corinthians 15 Paul is defending resurrection and explaining its significance. Adam brought death to humanity, with verse 22 explaining that "in Adam all die." This sets up the contrastive typology where it is said that in Jesus all are made alive, an allusion to the path of life Jesus creates for anyone who takes advantage of what he offers in salvation. This is a reverse typology. While Adam brought death to humanity in his sin failure, Jesus brings life with the success of his death and resurrection. This superior kind of life is seen in verse 45 in the contrast of what their springing to life means for people. Adam was "a living being," another citation of Genesis 2:7, but Jesus, the last Adam, is a life-giving spirit. The next two verses explain that the natural existence preceded the spiritual existence, as the first man was made from dust but the last is from heaven. So people will share one day in the heavenly existence of the second Adam. Paul is emphasizing how what Jesus brings reverses everything that was lost with Adam.

Romans 5:12–21 goes in a similar direction. Here in verse 14 death is said to have reigned from Adam until

Moses, even among those whose sin was not like that of Adam. **Death** was present before the law and the accounting of sin, which is why Moses is mentioned. The verse also calls Adam "a pattern of the one to come." The gift that comes with Christ as the second Adam reverses the arrival of death with life in the canceling of sins. In the canceling of many sins leading to justification is seen the superiority of the gift. In Christ many are made righteous, just as in Adam all were brought into a world of sin.

All of Paul's uses see Adam as a foundational figure. In Romans and 1 Corinthians Adam's presence is placed on contrastive footing with Jesus. The Savior or his resurrection undo what Adam introduced into the creation for humanity. This fits the way Jews of the second temple period appear to have seen Adam. In 2 Esdras 7 there is a long discussion of the pain Adam introduced into the world. That pain is so profound the writer speculates it would have been better if Adam had never existed or had not sinned (verses 116–18; verses 46–48 in the shorter version). These portraits both in the New Testament and in second temple Judaism point to a genuine historical figure through whom God began the human story.

Allusion to Adam and Eve in Discussing Marriage. In Matthew 19:4–6 (par. Mark 10:6–9), Jesus is dealing with questions about divorce. Rather than going directly to the grounds for divorce, Jesus begins with the design for marriage and cites Genesis 2:24 as showing that when marriage takes place, God is forming a man and woman into a new social unit. Behind that text stands the picture of Adam and Eve. What God forms in this new unit is not to be broken apart. Adam and Eve are also seen here as human prototypes for what God has done in the structure of the creation.

Summary. Everything about the way the New Testament uses Adam points to a figure who forms a base for understanding what God is doing with humanity. As a prototype figure, Adam is seen as the origin of certain human patterns of life, and in some cases dysfunction that has led to a need for the creation to be redeemed. What Adam was with regard to sin and death, Jesus is with regard to forgiveness and life. The history of salvation is wrapped up in the contrast and reversal.

Darrell L. Bock

REFERENCES AND RECOMMENDED READING

Barrett, Matthew, and Ardel B. Caneday, eds. 2013. *Four Views on the Historical Adam*. Grand Rapids: Zondervan.

Carson, D. A. "Adam in the Epistles of Paul." 1980. In *In the Beginning: A Symposium on the Bible and Creation*, ed. N. M. de S. Cameron. Glasgow: Biblical Creation Society.

Collins, C. John. 2011. *Did Adam and Eve Really Exist? Who Were They and Why Should We Care?* Wheaton, IL: Crossway.

Metzger, B. M. 1983. "The Fourth Book of Ezra." In *The Old Testament Pseudepigrapha*, ed. James Charlesworth, 1:540–41. Garden City, NY: Doubleday.

☙ AGE OF THE UNIVERSE AND EARTH
(Billions-of-Years View). The vast majority of evangelical scholars have asserted that the biblical record does not give any **information** about the age of the earth or of the universe. For instance, C. I. Scofield wrote, "Scripture gives no data for determining how long ago the universe was created" (Scofield 1967, 1). A primary reason for this opacity is that the context of Genesis 1 does not require the six **days of creation** to be six consecutive 24-hour days. In fact, Gleason Archer, a principal Old Testament translator of the New American Standard Bible, wrote, "On the basis of internal evidence, it is this writer's conviction that *yôm* in Genesis one could not have been intended by the Hebrew author to mean a literal twenty-four-hour day" (Archer 1994, 199).

Although Holy Scripture does not answer any questions about when God created the heavens and the earth, the record of nature gives an unambiguous and consistent answer that the universe is nearly 14 billion years old and the earth is about 4.5 billion years old. We are told that "the heavens declare the glory of God; the skies proclaim the work of his hands" (Ps. 19:1) and that "since the creation of the world God's invisible qualities—his eternal power and divine nature—have been clearly seen, being understood from what has been made, so that people are without excuse" (Rom. 1:20). Thus we can expect the record of nature to give an accurate representation of God's character and the timing of his creative works.

If there were only one or two methods of dating the age of the earth or the universe, then their age might be ambiguous. However, there are many independent, mutually reinforcing methods for determining ages in the cosmos, solar system, and the earth. When carefully compared, these methods give consistent ages. With so many complementary dating methods, the ages determined are completely unequivocal.

Perhaps the most straightforward methods for setting a lower limit on the age of the earth involve simple counting. For instance, because trees add an annual growth ring, counting the rings on a tree will give an exact age for that tree. The oldest individual trees have rings that date back nearly 5,000 years. Yet even that date is not the oldest possible date using tree rings. Because the size and spacing of tree rings vary from year to year, it is possible to match rings from different trees to find the years in which the life of the two trees overlapped. For instance, the pattern of rings of one tree during its two-hundredth year of life may match the pattern of another tree during its tenth year of life. Thus, using these overlapping patterns, an unbroken record of tree rings can be traced using dead and petrified trees much farther back in time than the lifetime of any single tree. Currently, unbroken tree ring patterns from the same geographical area show the age of the earth to be over 12,400 years old (Friedrich et al. 2004, 1111–22).

Certain lakes, particularly those fed by glaciers, have annual layers of deposited sediment. The annual layers, called varves, can be counted to give a minimum lifetime of the lake. Lake varves have shown a continual history of sedimentation, and Lake Suigetsu in Japan has over 60,000 annual varves of accumulated sediment at its bottom (Ramsey et al. 2012, 370). In polar regions, snow falls in the winter, and with exposure to sunlight in the summer, geologists find an ice core record with annual layers clearly visible. This ice core data shows a record of climate in Greenland back to slightly over 100,000 years (Alley 2014) and in Antarctica to about 800,000 years (Luthi et al. 2008). Finally, in certain caves with seasonal changes in temperature or humidity, speleothems that form will contain discernible annual layers that can be counted. Certain cave formations show over 200,000 years of annual laminations (Wang et al. 2008). These four counting methods all rely on different types of annual recording caused by very different processes, yet they all show a record of consistent and continual earth history for tens to hundreds of thousands of years.

Radiometric dating comprises another class of dating methods involving measurements of the radioactivity of unstable isotopes in a sample material. Certain naturally occurring nuclear isotopes are unstable and decay at a rate that can be experimentally measured and verified. The half-life of an isotope is defined as the time it takes for half of the radioactive nuclei to decay. The rate of decay is essentially a constant value and has been shown to be independent of all external factors, including temperature, pressure, presence of electromagnetic fields, and chemical environment. There are dozens of radiometric decay chains, and all of them give consistent values for the age of the earth and universe.

The most well-known radiometric decay is probably the decay of carbon-14 (C-14) to nitrogen-14 (N-14). This method of dating can only be used for something that was once alive and has died, and it gives the time since the **death** of the plant or animal. A C-14 nucleus has 6 protons and 8 neutrons, while a N-14 nucleus has 7 protons and 7 neutrons. The C-14 nucleus is unstable and decays to N-14 with a half-life of 5,370 years. Most of the carbon in the atmosphere of the earth is carbon-12 (C-12), with 6 protons and 6 neutrons, but a very small fraction of the carbon is C-14. The atmosphere has had approximately the same small proportion of C-14 atoms to C-12 atoms for at least 100,000 years, since C-14 is primarily produced through the collision of cosmic rays with nitrogen high in the earth's atmosphere. Consequently, anything that interacts with the atmosphere (i.e., is alive) will have a similar proportion of C-14 to C-12 as the atmosphere. When that plant or animal dies and ceases to exchange carbon with the atmosphere, the proportion of C-14 will diminish as it decays away. C-14 dating methods have been used to date items as far back as its effective limit of about 40,000 to 60,000 years, depending on the quality of the samples.

This calculation based on C-14 half-life has the known uncertainty of the C-14 percentage in the atmosphere because of variations of production high in the earth's atmosphere, since the cosmic ray bombardment from the sun varies with time. To precisely calibrate this known uncertainty, radiocarbon specialists develop calibration curves based on the counting of tree rings and the counting of sedimentary varves. Tree rings from ancient trees are counted from a few hundred years ago to over 12,400 years ago, and the carbon-14 is measured in those rings (Davidson and Wolgemuth 2010). Likewise the carbon-14 is measured in the organic material in varves that comes from layers between a few hundred years ago to 50,000 years ago (Kitagawa and van der Plicht 1998).

The general correlation between counting of tree rings, counting of sedimentary varves, and radiometric dating gives credence to the accuracy of the dating methods. The best possible age can be determined by measuring the carbon-14 in a sample of unknown age and obtaining the calendar years from counting tree rings and varves. When done in this manner, the half-life need not be used in determining calendar years from this calibration curve. (See the figure in the essay on **Radiometric Dating**).

Because C-14 dating can only be used on samples with carbon from plants or animals that were once alive, and because of its relatively short half-life, it cannot be used to date the oldest objects on earth. However, many methods can be used to date igneous rocks that formed from lava or magma. When molten magma cools, the atomic structure is set up, and any radioactive nuclei are trapped in the rocks. The radioactive isotopes then decay to produce other elements. In one of the most-used dating methods, radioactive potassium-40 will decay to argon-40. Since argon is a gas, there is little or no argon in the initially formed rock, because the gas can escape from the molten magma before the rock cools. Once the rock cools, the argon nuclei that are produced from the potassium decay are trapped in the crystal lattice of the rock and a measurement of the ratio of potassium to argon can be used to determine the age of the rock.

There are many other radioactive decay processes with quite different half-lives that give accurate ancient dates. These various processes all use different methods with different parent (initial) and daughter (decay) elements but give the same ancient dates. For instance, rocks from the Fen Complex in Norway have been dated by at least seven different methods, all to approximately 580 million years ago with uncertainties on the order of a few tens of million years. Rocks in western Greenland have been dated to between 3.5 and 3.8 billion years old using five independent radiometric dating techniques (Wiens 2002). The consistency of the dates from multiple methods with multiple half-lives is only possible because the rocks did actually form at the times indicated. Minerals from western Australia date to between 4 and 4.2 billion years ago. Radiometric dating of moon rocks and meteorites give consistent dates for the formation of our solar system, between 4.4 and 4.6 billion years ago (Head 1976, 265).

Every radiometric technique has a time-scale range in which the technique is reliable. Using the technique to try to find dates for objects with origins outside of the reliable range will give values that lie near the extreme ends of the range. For instance, carbon-14 dating can date objects that lived up to about 60,000 years ago, or in particular circumstances, perhaps 10,000 years older. Thus an object that died longer ago than 60,000 years will give a carbon-14 date of near 60,000 years. Potassium-argon dating can be used to date objects from a few hundred thousand years old to the age of the earth. Some labs, using less sophisticated techniques, have a lower limit for potassium-argon dating of a few million years. Therefore a rock formed within the last few years (say, from the eruption of Mount St. Helens) will be found to have a date near the threshold, maybe a couple of million years old or so.

To correctly use radiometric dating, the limits of reliability must be considered. It would be foolish to assume, for instance, that the potassium-argon method of dating would give a reliable date for a rock formed recently. However, potassium-argon will give a reliable date for a rock formed a few billion years ago.

Astronomical measurements can also be used to give an accurate date for the origin of the universe. Observations of the red shift of light from other galaxies show that the universe is expanding. To understand this, consider the sound of a siren from a police car as the car is moving away from you or toward you. The pitch of the siren will sound higher when the car is moving toward you and lower when the car is moving away from you. This change in pitch, called the Doppler effect, is caused because the wavelength of sound entering your ear will depend on how the source of the sound is moving with respect to you.

In the same way, the wavelength of light that we receive depends on whether an object is moving toward us or away from us. When we look at distant galaxies, we see that wavelengths of light characteristic of particular elements—hydrogen, for instance—are shifted in such a way that it indicates their source is moving away from us. We can correlate the speed by which the objects are moving away from us with their distance, and when we do so we observe that the farther away an object is from us the faster it is moving away from us.

One of the ways that the distance to an object can be determined is by using a "standard candle." An example of a standard candle might be a 100-watt lightbulb. As the bulb is moved farther away, its apparent brightness diminishes. By knowing that you are observing a 100-watt lightbulb and by measuring its apparent brightness, you can determine how far away the bulb is from you. For astronomical scales, certain exploding stars called supernovae type Ia (SNIa) serve as a standard candle. We know precisely the light output from such a supernova, so we can tell how far away any SNIa is by how bright it appears. By comparing the recession speed of distant galaxies using red shift with their distance using standard candles, we observe that farther galaxies are moving away from us faster than close galaxies. Measurements of the rate of expansion and the distance to the cosmological objects show that at one time, about 14 billion years in the past, all the objects were localized into one small region of space where the expansion began. That is, the universe had its origin about 14 billion years ago.

Radioisotopes can also be measured in stars to determine the ages of the individual stars. The process, called nucleocosmochronology, uses the relative abundances of elements in a radioactive decay chain to establish the age of the star. A number of different processes are used, including thorium to europium ratios and uranium-238 decay chains. These measurements have an uncertainty of a few billion years. Nevertheless, the age of the universe determined by these methods ranges from about 12 to 16 billion years (Cowan et al. 1999, 194; Cayrel et al. 2001, 691), with the variance compatible with the uncertainty of the measurement.

The accepted cosmological model of the development of the universe also provides a precise measurement of the age of the universe. Within this model, we expect to observe residual heat from the origin of the universe. Indeed, we measure the cosmic microwave background radiation (CMB) with a temperature of about 2.7 K exactly as predicted by the model. This radiation gives a measurement of what the universe was like approximately 400,000 years after it began, which is like looking at "baby pictures" of the universe on the time scale of its age. The most precise measurement of the age of the universe can be inferred by comparing calculations of the expected CMB spectrum with the observed spectrum. It is remarkable that the theoretical calculations and the observed spectrum agree with each other to about 1 part in 10,000 and give an age for the universe of about 13.82 billion years (Ade et al. 2014).

There are so many other methods of determining the ages of the universe and earth materials that an article of this length cannot address them all. These include counting annual coral growth layers, thermoluminescence measurements of crystalline minerals, electron spin resonance measurements of archaeological material, observations of the age of star clusters and the age of white dwarf stars, and observations of continental drift movement rates with repeated patterns of island formation. All these methods give consistent dates for the age of the universe and the earth. The first three are able to date events on the earth back about 300,000 years. Star cluster and white dwarf dates give consistent ages of the universe between 11 and 15 billion years ago.

In sum, all of the dozens of unique methods for determining the age of the universe and the earth give consistent results within their respective ranges of applicability, and there are no exceptions to the timeline of the universe determined by these different methods. Some Christians have proposed that God created a universe that looks old but is actually young, on the order of a few thousand years. This view has extreme problems. Perhaps foremost is that the universe does not just have an appearance of age, but an appearance of history.

As an example of the difference between appearance of age and appearance of history, suppose God created a tree fully grown. For that tree, the appearance of age might include its large size or uniform tree rings. However, the appearance of history might include things like holes drilled apparently by woodpeckers, scars on the tree apparently caused by fire or lightning, broken limbs that seem to be caused by wind, and varying width of the tree rings that seem to come from unusually dry and wet periods.

Observations of the universe show not just that it appears old but that it has a history. If that observed history is not an actual history, then it could be argued that God has created a deceptive history, and God himself, then, is a deceiver. Since God does not deceive and does not lie, the most straightforward reading of the history of the universe is that it has actually occurred.

Some Christians who believe that the universe is only a few thousand years old have presented supposed evidence that supports a young earth or have tried to refute the evidence for the scientifically accepted age of the universe (see, e.g., Batton 2009). In such cases the presented evidence for a young earth can be refuted by reading the original scientific articles or by investigating the claims in more detail, realizing that young-earth arguments tend to pick and choose portions of articles that might support a preconceived belief while ignoring other evidence. In many cases, the supposed evidence for a young earth distorts the conclusions of the original article. In almost all cases, arguments that support a young earth rely on fallacious reasoning (Tiscareno 2000).

Given that the Bible does not indicate the age of the earth or universe, that there are multiple, varied observations and techniques that give a consistent age for the universe and the earth, that God would not provide a record from nature that distorts its actual history, and that supposed contrary evidence is easily shown to be a distortion of the actual facts and observations, we can confidently affirm that the universe is about 14 billion years old and that the earth is about 4.5 billion years old.

Michael G. Strauss

REFERENCES AND RECOMMENDED READING

Ade, P. A. R., N. Aghanim, et al. 2014. "Planck 2013 Results." *Astronomy and Astrophysics* 571 (November).

Alley, Richard B. 2014. *The Two-Mile Time Machine: Ice Cores, Abrupt Climate Change, and Our Future.* Princeton Science Library. Princeton, NJ: Princeton University Press.

Archer, Gleason. 1994. *A Survey of Old Testament Introduction.* Rev. and exp. ed. Chicago: Moody.

Batton, Don. 2009. "Age of the Earth: 101 Evidences for a Young Age of the Earth and the Universe." http://creation.com/age-of-the-earth.

Becker, B., and B. Kromer. 1993. "The Continental Tree-Ring Record—Absolute Chronology, 14C Calibration and Climatic Change at 11 Ka." *Palaeogeography Palaeoclimatology Palaeoecology* 103 (1–2): 67–71.

Cayrel, R., V. Hill, T. C. Beers, and F. Primas, 2001. "Measurement of the Stellar Age from Uranium Decay." *Nature* 409, no. 6821 (March): 691–92.

Cowan, J., B. Pfeiffer, K.-L. Kratz, F.-K. Thielemann, Christopher Sneden, Scott Burles, David Tyler, and Timothy C. Beers. 1999. "R-Process Abundances and Chronometers in Metal-Poor Stars." *Astrophysical Journal* 521 (April 9): 195–204.

Davidson, Gregg, and Ken Wolgemuth. 2010. "Christian Geologists on Noah's Flood: Biblical and Scientific Shortcomings of Flood Geology." BioLogos Foundation. July. http://biologos.org/uploads/projects/davidson_wolgemuth_scholarly_essay.pdf.

Friedrich, Michael, Sabine Remmele, Bernd Kromer, Jutta Hofmann, Marco Spurk, Klaus Felix Kauser, Christian Orcel, and Manfred Kuppers. 2004. "The 12,460-Year Hohenheim Oak and Pine Tree-Ring Chronology from Central Europe—A Unique Annual Record for Radiocarbon Calibration and Paleoenvironment Reconstructions." *Radiocarbon* 46 (3): 1111–22.

Head, J. W., III. 1976. "Lunar Volcanism in Space and Time." *Reviews of Geophysics and Space Physics* 14 (2): 14.

Kitagawa, H., and J. van der Plicht. 1998. "A 40,000-Year Varve Chronology from Lake Suigetsu, Japan: Extension of the 14C Calibration Curve." *Radiocarbon* 40 (1): 505–15.

Luthi, Dieter, Martine Le Floch, et al. 2008. "High-Res Carbon Dioxide Concentration Record 650,000–800,000 Years before Present." *Nature* 453:370–82.

Meert, Joe. 2000. "Consistent Radiometric Dates." Web page of Dr. Joseph Meert. January 6. http://gondwanaresearch.com/radiomet.htm.

Ramsey, C., Richard A. Staff, et al. 2012. "A Complete Terrestrial Radiocarbon Record for 11.2 to 52.8 KYR B.P." *Science* 338:370–74.

Scofield, C. I., ed. 1967. *The New Scofield Reference Bible.* New York: Oxford University Press.

Tiscareno, Matthew. 2000. "Is There Really Scientific Evidence for a Young Earth?" http://chem.tufts.edu/science/Geology/OEC-refutes-YEC.htm.

Wang, Yongjin, Hai Cheng, et al. 2008. "Millennial- and Orbital-Scale Changes in the East Asian Monsoon over the Past 224,000 Years." *Nature* 451:1090–93.

Wiens, Roger C. 2002. "Radiometric Dating: A Christian Perspective." American Scientific Affiliation. www.asa3.org/ASA/resources/Wiens.html.

↪ AGE OF THE UNIVERSE AND EARTH (Thousands-of-Years View).

The modern scientific consensus is that the age of the universe is between 13 and 14 billion years old, while the age of the earth is between 4 and 5 billion years old. While many Christians accept these dates as valid, there is strong biblical evidence that the universe and the earth are far younger, between 6,000 and 10,000 years old. This article will highlight the biblical support for a young earth and then briefly discuss some of the scientific data.

Biblical Evidence for a Young Earth

A number of passages in Scripture point to a young earth. These will be discussed in turn.

Genesis 1. Genesis 1:1–2:3 describes the creation of "the heavens and earth" in six days. This creation included the earth's vegetation on day 3, the sun, moon, and stars on day 4, the sea creatures and birds on day 5, and the rest of the animals and man on day 6. If the **days of creation** are normal 24-hour days and if there are no time gaps (e.g., between Gen. 1:1 and 1:2), then the universe, the earth, the sun, the moon, the stars, and the first man and woman were all created by God within the same week.

To harmonize Scripture with an old earth and universe, some posit large time gaps between Genesis 1:1 and 1:2 (gap theory). However, Genesis 1:2 describes the earth at the time of creation, not a subsequent action. Furthermore, Genesis 1:1 must also be regarded as part of the first creation day. The identical phrase, "the heavens and the earth," used in Genesis 1:1 is used in Exodus 20:11: "For in six days the LORD made *the heavens and the earth*, the sea, and all that is in them" (emphasis added; see also Ex. 31:17). The only place in Genesis 1 that the creation of the heavens is mentioned is in Genesis 1:1, and according to Exodus 20:11 and 31:17, the creation of the heavens is a part of the six days of creation, not outside of it. So it is not possible to separate Genesis 1:1 from the rest of the creation account in order to allow for a large period of time between Genesis 1:1 and the following verses (see further, **Creationism, Old-Earth**).

Others seek to harmonize Genesis 1–2 with an old earth by viewing the "days" of Genesis 1:1–2:3 as sequential periods of thousands or millions of years (day-age view). The primary difficulty with this view is that the predominant meaning of *yôm*, the Hebrew word for "day," is a 24-hour day (the word has this meaning 2,239 out of 2,304 occurrences, or 97 percent of the time). Furthermore, the phrase "evening and morning," used six times in Genesis 1, reinforces the idea of a 24-hour day. Passages such as Psalm 90:4 and 2 Peter 3:8 (which compare a thousand years in God's sight to a day) cannot be used as valid arguments for the day-age theory, since they are simply teaching that God's view of time is different from man's. Finally, the entire text of Exodus 20:8–11, speaking of the human workweek in terms of God's six-day creation (using *yôm* six times in the passage), is a strong indication that the heavens, the earth, and everything in them were created in six literal days (for further discussion, see **Days of Creation**).

Finally, some see Genesis 1 as a literary framework, not as historical narrative. Advocates of this view (the framework hypothesis) see a literary pattern with the "forms" created on the first three days and then correspondingly "filled" or populated in the final three days. Since the days are simply providing a literary framework, it is argued that neither the days nor the details of what is created in each day are to be taken literally or sequentially. But one wonders why so many details are provided in Genesis 1 if the author is simply saying that "God did it." The text gives no indication of being a literary device; in fact, the verb forms indicate that Genesis 1 is narrative sequential prose, not poetry (where one might expect such a literary device). In addition, if a figurative approach is taken in Genesis 1:1–2:3, how does one determine where in Genesis the text is to be taken as historical narrative? There is no basis for an exegetical or hermeneutical "switch" between Genesis 1–2 and the rest of the book (Beall 2008, 144–58; Kulikovsky 2009, 155–62) (for further discussion, see **Days of Creation**).

Genealogies. The genealogies of Genesis 5, 10, and 11 similarly indicate a recent creation of mankind. The **genealogy** in Genesis 5 begins with Adam and continues through Noah and his sons. Genesis 10–11 continues with the genealogy of Noah's sons, with Genesis 11 tracing Shem's line through Abraham. Even if the genealogies skip some generations, there is a finite limit to the number of generations skipped, meaning that man was created between 6,000 and (at most) 10,000 years ago. While these genealogies may contain gaps of names, no actual chronological gaps exist, since the genealogies indicate the actual age of the parent or grandparent when the child was born (Sexton 2015, 195–205). Since Genesis 1 states that man was created on the sixth day, while the universe and earth were created on the first day, neither the universe nor the earth can be over 10,000 years old.

Universal flood. Genesis 6–8 details a universal flood, which God sent in order to judge the sin of mankind. Noah and his family were the only humans spared. All land animals and birds except those in **Noah's ark** were killed (Gen. 7:21–23). Rain fell nonstop for at least 40 days, with the effects of **the flood** lasting over a year. Genesis 7:20 states that "the waters rose and covered the mountains to a depth of more than fifteen cubits."

While some would insist that the flood was only local ("How Should We Interpret the Genesis Flood Account?"), and others say that it affected all mankind but was still not global (Ross 2009), the narrative of Genesis 6–8 makes it clear that the flood was global in scope and effect. An ark of the size given in Genesis 6:15 would not have been needed for a local deluge, nor would Noah have had to build an ark in the first place, since he could simply have moved. Responding to those who deny the Lord's coming and assert that everything has continued unchanged since

creation, Peter writes: "They deliberately forget that long ago by God's word the heavens came into being and the earth was formed out of water and by water. By these waters also the world of that time was deluged and destroyed. By the same word the present heavens and earth are reserved for fire, being kept for the day of judgment and destruction of the ungodly" (2 Peter 3:5–7). Just as there was a universal flood in Noah's day, destroying the entire earth, so there will be a universal destruction by fire in the end time.

Another indication that the flood was global is that there are over 150 flood stories from nearly every part of the world (Beall 2015, 98, 102). While most modern geologists hold to the assumption of uniformitarian gradualism in their interpretation of the geological evidence, Genesis 6–8 indicates that there was a universal catastrophic flood that likely caused most of the geological features that are often perceived as the end result of a process lasting millions of years (Kulikovsky 2009, 223–37; for detailed geological discussion, see Snelling 2009).

Jesus's statement in Mark 10:6. Jesus's statement in Mark 10:6 that "at the beginning of creation God 'made them male and female'" strongly implies that the earth had not been around for millions of years before **Adam and Eve** were created: they were created at the "beginning of creation," i.e., on the sixth day. The same phrase, "the beginning of creation," is used similarly in Mark 13:19 and 2 Peter 3:4. Jesus states that mankind was created at the beginning of creation, not millions of years later (Kulikovsky 2009, 175; Mortenson and Ury 2008, 318–25). Once again this statement ties together the age of the universe (and the earth) and the age of mankind: there are not millions or billions of years separating the two.

Death before sin? Romans 5:12 states that death had not entered the world until Adam's sin: "Therefore, just as sin entered the world through one man, and death through sin, and in this way death came to all people, because all sinned" (see also 1 Cor. 15:21). While it may be argued from these verses that only human death entered the world because of Adam's sin, Romans 8:21–22 seems to preclude that possibility: "The creation itself will be liberated from its bondage to decay and brought into the freedom and glory of the children of God. We know that the whole creation has been groaning as in the pains of childbirth right up to the present time." The "groaning" of creation began after Adam's fall, with all of creation feeling its effects (Gen. 3:14–19).

Since God's creation was originally declared "very good" by the Lord himself (Gen. 1:31), it was only after **the fall** that death and corruption entered the world. According to 1 Corinthians 15:20–28, Christ's death and resurrection defeated death, and his return will usher in the final restoration of creation where the effects of the curse will be reversed and there will be no more death (see also Isa. 11:6–9; Acts 3:21; Col. 1:15–20; Rev. 21:3–5; 22:3). There is no room in the Scripture for millions of years of death and corruption prior to Adam's sin.

Scientific Issues

Given the strong evidence from Scripture that the universe is young, it may seem surprising that some Christians still hold that the universe is 13–14 billion years old, and the earth is 4–5 billion years old. But they do so because they are persuaded by the scientific arguments for an old universe and earth.

Cosmology, the big bang, and the nature of science. Unfortunately, some Christians do not distinguish properly between empirical science (sometimes called "operational science") and origins science (also called "historical science"). Cosmology, the study of the origin and development of the universe, fits squarely into origins science. With empirical science, a hypothesis is tested and proved by repeated experimentation. But such an empirical process is simply not possible for cosmology or any origins science. As Kate Land explains, "The main problem with cosmology is our sample size—that of just one universe" (Cho 2007, 1848). James Gunn, professor of **astronomy** at Princeton University, observes, "Cosmology may look like a science, but it isn't science. A basic tenet of science is that you can do repeatable experiments, and you can't do that in cosmology" (Cho 2007, 1850).

Yet the age of the universe (13–14 billion years old) is based on the standard cosmological model, the so-called **big bang theory**. This model in turn relies on the cosmological principle, which states that "the distribution of matter throughout the universe is homogeneous (or uniform) and isotropic (the same in all directions)" (Hartnett 2014, 220). The problem is, as **Stephen Hawking** states, "we have no scientific evidence for or against that assumption" (cited in DeWitt 2007, 147).

Richard Lieu similarly states that all the principal assumptions in cosmology "are unverified (or unverifiable) in the laboratory, and researchers are quite comfortable with inventing unknowns to explain the unknown" (Lieu 2007). He states that explanations of various phenomena involve making up other unknowns (such as "**dark matter**" and "**dark energy**"), none of which is based on laboratory experiments or verifiable in any way.

Reporting on a conference titled "The First Crisis in Cosmology Conference," Hilton Ratcliffe concludes that the papers presented at that conference "by some of the world's leading scientists showed beyond doubt that the weight of scientific evidence clearly indicates that the dominant theory on the origin and destiny of the Universe is deeply flawed. The implications of this damning consensus are serious indeed" (Ratcliffe 2005, 24). Given all the problems and unproved (and unprovable) assumptions of the big bang cosmology, one wonders why one should accept a date for the universe that is based on such a questionable theory.

Catastrophism, uniformitarianism, and radiometric dating. Another argument for an old earth comes from the field of **geology**. But like the big bang theory, old-earth geology is based on a number of unprovable assumptions, chief of which is uniformitarianism. Until the early nineteenth-century, geologists held to catastrophism, postulating that the present earth was shaped by major catastrophic events (with Noah's flood playing a central role).

Under the influence of James Hutton and Charles Lyell, the idea of uniformitarianism became the dominant model in geology. Uniformitarianism is the idea that given sufficient time, processes now at work can account for all the geological features of the globe. In his *Principles of Geology* (1830–33), Lyell argued that "no causes whatever have from the earliest time to which we can look back, to the present, ever acted but those now acting; and that they never acted with different degrees of energy from that which they now exert" (Lyell 1881, 1:234).

This change from catastrophism to uniformitarianism was not caused by any new data; rather, it was a philosophical shift, driven by Lyell's desire to "free the science from Moses" (Lyell 1881, 1:268; see also Mortenson 2004, 226). Yet uniformitarianism is directly contradicted by Scripture. Peter writes that scoffers will say, "Ever since our ancestors died, everything goes on as it has since the beginning of creation" (2 Peter 3:4). Peter's answer is that these scoffers "deliberately forget that long ago by God's word the heavens came into being and the earth was formed out of water and by water. By these waters also the world of that time was deluged and destroyed" (2 Peter 3:5–6; see also Heb. 11:3, which implies that one cannot explain the origin of the created universe from what one currently sees).

In addition, there are all kinds of scientific problems with uniformitarianism. For example, fossil graveyards, fossil jellyfish, and polystrate fossils all give evidence of rapid burial and fossilization, not uniformitarianism (see Snelling 2009, 467–610; Walker 2014, 155–91). As geologist Warren Allmon observes, "Lyell also sold geology some snake oil.... This extreme gradualism has led to numerous unfortunate consequences, including the rejection of sudden or catastrophic events in the face of positive evidence for them, for no reason other than that they were not gradual. Indeed, geology appears at last to have outgrown Lyell" (Allmon 1993, 122).

Another method used to determine the earth's age is **radiometric dating**. Yet, as one scientist has noted, "Radiometric dates are some of the trickiest, most delicate and most disputed measurements on Earth" (Hand 2012, 422). Certain assumptions must be made in radiometric dating, one of which is that the rate of decay (the half-life) of the parent isotope being analyzed has remained constant at today's rate throughout the existence of the object (Mason 2014, 197–98; Snelling 2009, 800).

But that involves the uniformitarian assumption once again, something that would not be true if there were a catastrophic universal flood, as Genesis 6–8 describes (see Snelling 2009, esp. 467–76). As Snelling observes, "This is uniformitarianism in the extreme, because it is assumed that decay rates measured in the present (over the past century) have been constant for millions and billions of years, an extrapolation of up to seven orders of magnitude" (801). And radiometric dates have been found to be wildly inaccurate. To cite only one example, radiometric ages for the lava dome formed at Mount St. Helens in 1984 ranged from 350,000 years to 2,800,000 years, rather than the correct age of less than 10 years (Mason 2014, 197).

It is often stated that distant starlight is proof of an old universe, since if a star is millions of light-years away, then it took millions of years for the light of that star to reach the earth. But among the assumptions made using this methodology is that the **speed of light** has remained a constant—uniformitarianism once again. In fact, some astrophysicists have actually proposed that the speed of light was much faster in the past (Davies et al. 2002, 602–3; see also DeWitt 2007, 129–32).

Conclusion

All of these dating methodologies contain assumptions that are either scientifically unprovable or are actually refuted by a global catastrophe such as the flood. At a minimum, when dealing with origins from a scientific standpoint, a large dose of humility is in order: after all, we weren't there at creation. As the Lord reminds Job, "Where were you when I laid the earth's foundation? Tell me, if you understand" (Job 38:4). The biblical record and true science can never be in conflict, but empirical science has its limitations when it comes to origins. It seems wisest to stick with the consistent testimony of Scripture rather than the questionable assumptions of current scientific theory. The Scripture is clear that the universe, the earth, and mankind were all created thousands, not billions, of years ago.

Todd S. Beall

REFERENCES AND RECOMMENDED READING

Allmon, Warren D. 1993. "Review: Post-Gradualism." *Science* 262 (5130): 122–23.

Beall, Todd S. 2008. "Contemporary Hermeneutical Approaches to Genesis 1–11." In *Coming to Grips with Genesis: Biblical Authority and the Age of the Earth*, ed. Terry Mortenson and Thane Ury. Green Forest, AR: Master.

———. 2015. "Noah's Flood: Just Another Pagan Myth?" *Bible and Spade* 28 (4): 98–102.

Cho, Adrian. 2007. "A Singular Conundrum: How Old Is Our Universe?" *Science* 317 (5846): 1848–50.

Davies, P. C. W., Tamara M. Davis, and Charles H. Lineweaver. 2002. "Black Holes Constrain Varying Constants." *Nature* 418:602–3.

DeWitt, David A. 2007. *Unraveling the Origins Controversy.* Lynchburg, VA: Creation Curriculum.

Hand, Eric. 2012. "Planetary Science: The Time Machine." *Nature* 487 (7408): 422–25.

Hartnett, John. 2014. "Cosmology." In *Evolution's Achilles' Heels*, ed. Robert Carter. Powder Springs, GA: Creation Ministries.

"How Should We Interpret the Genesis Flood Account?" BioLogos Foundation. (Accessed August 26, 2016) http://biologos.org/common-questions/biblical-interpretation/genesis-flood.

Kulikovsky, Andrew. 2009. *Creation, Fall, Restoration: A Biblical Theology of Creation.* Fearn, Ross-shire, Scotland: Mentor.

Lieu, Richard. 2007. "ËCDM Cosmology: How Much Suppression of Credible Evidence, and Does the Model Really Lead Its Competitors, Using All Evidence?" (Accessed May 17, 2016) http://arxiv.org/pdf/0705.2462v1.pdf.

Lyell, Katharine M., ed. (1881) 2010. *Life, Letters, and Journals of Sir Charles Lyell, Bart.* Cambridge: Cambridge University Press.

Mason, Jim. 2014. "Radiometric Dating." In *Evolution's Achilles' Heels*, ed. Robert Carter. Powder Springs, GA: Creation Ministries.

Mortenson, Terry. 2004. *The Great Turning Point: The Church's Catastrophic Mistake on Geology—Before Darwin.* Green Forest, AR: Master.

Mortenson, Terry, and Thane Ury, eds. 2008. *Coming to Grips with Genesis: Biblical Authority and the Age of the Earth.* Green Forest, AR: Master.

Ratcliffe, Hilton. 2005. "The First Crisis in Cosmology Conference." *Progress in Physics* 3:19–24.

Ross, Hugh. 2009. "Exploring the Extent of the Flood: What the Bible Says: Part Two." Reasons to Believe. April 1. www.reasons.org/articles/exploring-the-extent-of-the-flood-what-the-bible-says-part-two.

Sarfati, Jonathan D. 2015. *The Genesis Account: A Theological, Historical, and Scientific Commentary on Genesis 1–11.* Powder Springs, GA: Creation Books.

Sexton, Jeremy. 2015. "Who Was Born When Enosh Was 90? A Semantic Reevaluation of William Henry Green's Chronological Gaps." *Westminster Theological Journal* 77:193–218.

Snelling, Andrew A. 2009. *Earth's Catastrophic Past: Geology, Creation and the Flood.* 2 vols. Dallas: Institute for Creation Research.

Walker, Tasman. 2014. "The Geologic Record." In *Evolution's Achilles' Heels*, ed. Robert Carter. Powder Springs, GA: Creation Ministries.

ALCHEMY. Alchemy is a mixture of craft traditions and ideas about matter that flourished in China and the West from antiquity until modern times. Alchemists worked with medicines, gold, silver, precious stones, and dyes. Eastern alchemists tended to be more concerned with medicines, including the Elixir of Life, which was believed to confer health, longevity, or immortality. Western alchemists were more preoccupied with commercial products. Many sought gold by transmuting base metals, sometimes by pursuing the elusive transmutation-catalyzing Philosopher's Stone, itself an alchemical product.

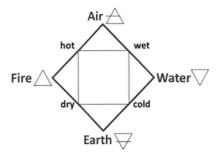

Figure 1. The earth-air-fire-water theory of matter.

Unlike pure artisans, alchemists used matter theories to guide their work. Chinese alchemists sought immortality in reversing the differentiation of Taoist cosmology. They hoped to convert ordinary mercury and lead into their "true" counterparts (associated with yin and yang); these could then be rejoined into the original unity, enabling the alchemist to transcend time. Western alchemists adapted classical Greek ideas, most importantly the **monist** notion that materials consist of "prime matter" infused with qualities. For example, in the "earth, air, fire, and water" theory, real materials consist of mixtures of these four elements. The "elements" in turn can be thought of as consisting of prime matter combined with the two qualities shown adjoining each element's vertex in figure 1. For example earth is prime matter infused with "cold" and "dry." The "mercury-sulfur" theory added the philosophical elements "mercury" and "sulfur." It held that these combine in various proportions in the earth to give metals. Furthermore, since base metals like lead are "unstable" and "decompose" (i.e., rust) they

can ripen in the earth as the proportion of sulfur adjusts to the gold's more stable value. This scheme suggested that base metals could be transmuted to gold, if only alchemists could separate their "mercury" and "sulfur" and recombine them in the correct amounts.

Alchemy was often esoteric in practice and involved secrecy pledges, code names, and allegory imagery known only to the initiated. This, along with the elusiveness of transmutation, facilitated the activities of alchemist-frauds and led to unflattering depictions of alchemists in literature and theater. As with modern gold-plated and costume jewelry today, however, most alchemical fakery was done for legitimate purposes.

After the decline of Greco-Roman civilization, Western alchemy was preserved by Arabs who developed it into the form transmitted to Christian Europe in the twelfth century. Although some medieval Christian thinkers were skeptical about transmutation, mundane alchemical processes were accepted. Scholastics even used alchemy as a measure of the limits of what humanity could achieve in the absence of supernatural intervention, although they debated whether alchemical and natural products were equivalent. Alchemy came to be regarded as a "gift of God," at least in the sense that God inconspicuously guided alchemists' investigations. It became common for alchemists to use Christ's crucifixion, burial, and resurrection as allegories for alchemical processes; in return religious thinkers used transmutation as a metaphor for spiritual transformation.

Alchemy contributed to modern chemistry by classifying chemical reactions, developing useful apparatus, and foreshadowing contemporary chemistry's combining of experiment and theory. Many early modern scientists (including **Isaac Newton** and **Robert Boyle**) employed alchemical ideas, although Boyle's rigorous prioritizing of experimental results over theory would eventually lead to the replacement of alchemical matter theories with those of modern chemistry. Today alchemy is considered a **pseudoscience**, although its ideas continue to be used in popular culture and the teachings of a few occult societies, and are even held by a few remaining practitioners.

Stephen Contakes

REFERENCES AND RECOMMENDED READING

Knight, David M. 1992. *Ideas in Chemistry: A History of the Science*. New Brunswick, NJ: Rutgers University Press.
Levere, Trevor Harvey. 2001. *Transforming Matter: A History of Chemistry from Alchemy to the Buckyball*. Johns Hopkins Introductory Studies in the History of Science. Baltimore: Johns Hopkins University Press.

Newman, William R. 2004. *Promethean Ambitions: Alchemy and the Quest to Perfect Nature*. Chicago: University of Chicago Press.

Predagio, Fabrizio. 2012. *The Way of the Golden Elixir: A Historical Overview of Taoist Alchemy*. Mountain View, CA: Golden Elixir.

Principe, Lawrence. 2013. *The Secrets of Alchemy*. Chicago: University of Chicago Press.

ALTRUISM. Altruism, commonly understood as sacrificially unselfish investment in the welfare of others, is a fundamental issue in both Christian and scientific understandings of **life**. In the Christian tradition, altruism or *agapē* love is construed as the ultimate *telos* of human existence and is epitomized in the self-emptying life and **death** of Jesus Christ. In biology "altruism" has been described as the "central theoretical problem" in the application of biology to social behavior (Wilson 2000): How could **natural selection** favor or even allow sacrifice for others at the cost of the actor (see **Psychology, Evolutionary**)? Note that this question is legitimate even if one doubts the evolutionary origin of humanity: as long as one believes that there are some natural, biologically rooted dispositions to behavior (e.g., the desire of parents to care for their children), if there were a heritable inclination to sacrifice one's own reproductive success for others, it would be weeded out over time.

It is important to make an often-overlooked distinction between two uses of the word *altruism*. Moral or psychological altruism refers to motives: giving without expectation of return. However, biological altruism refers to consequences: increasing another's fitness (reproductive success) at the expense of the actor. Crucially, the latter does not imply that what is natural is intrinsically "selfish." One could have genuinely other-oriented motives—as most parents do for their children—that nevertheless benefit fitness.

But not all investment in others is for offspring, and there are several accounts for how biology could support this. "Kin selection" points out that a sacrifice on behalf of not just offspring but genetically related kin is sustainable by heredity. (As J. B. S Haldane famously said, "Would I lay down my life to save my brother? No, but I would to save two brothers or eight cousins.") Reciprocity theory illuminates how investment in others can "pay off" even if not immediately returned by formation of ongoing supportive relationships or (in the case of "indirect reciprocity") by enhancing the moral reputation of the actor and therefore willingness of others to help when needed. All of these aid the individual or his or her genes. The still-debated theory of "group selection" goes beyond this, proposing that individuals may make net sacrifices on behalf of others' fitness, in situations where there is competition between groups and such sacrifice helps group (and the individual's) survival (Wilson 2015). Think of a basketball player giving up Most Valuable Player status to provide assists, which help earn the championship bonus for all on the team.

These theories have often been used to suggest that all behavior is motivationally "selfish" nepotism or favoritism. But this wrongly conflates motives with consequences, and may just as reasonably but less pejoratively be thought of as genuine love for kin and kindred—even viewed as a manifestation of common grace. However, it remains the case that none of these accounts explain net consequential altruism: radical sacrifice that has no biologically compensatory benefit, like "enemy love." In recognition of this, some biologists have controversially proposed that humans are unique in their ability to transcend or "resist the tyranny" of our biological dispositions (Dawkins 2006; see **Memes**).

These ideas have manifold interactions with Christian faith. Current scientific debates over the extent to which altruism is *rooted in*—versus *opposed to*—human nature are presaged by different theological conceptions of **the fall**, and by Thomistic and Augustinian or agapeist perspectives on grace completing nature or transforming nature (Post et al. 2002). Moreover, the Christian emphasis on *agapē* (Lat., *caritas*) goes beyond acknowledging the importance of sacrifice by affirming not just investment in, but genuine compassion and care for, others. Indeed, it is possible but of no profit to "give all I possess to the poor and give over my body to hardship that I may boast but … not have love" (1 Cor. 13:3). Finally, these theories illuminate the singular distinctiveness of the kind of love affirmed in the Sermon on the Mount. While theories of altruism do not controvert Christian theology, they do illuminate love as the most compelling aspect of Christian witness.

Jeffrey P. Schloss

REFERENCES AND RECOMMENDED READING

Dawkins, Richard. 2006. *The Selfish Gene: 30th Anniversary Edition*. Oxford: Oxford University Press.

Post, Stephen, Lynn Underwood, Jeffrey Schloss, and William Hurlbut, eds. 2002. *Altruism and Altruistic Love: Science, Philosophy and Religion in Dialogue*. Oxford: Oxford University Press.

Wilson, David Sloan. 2015. *Does Altruism Exist? Culture, Genes, and the Welfare of Others*. New Haven, CT: Yale University Press.

Wilson, E. O. 2000. *Sociobiology: The New Synthesis*. 25th ann. ed. Cambridge, MA: Belknap.

AMERICAN SCIENTIFIC AFFILIATION. The American Scientific Affiliation (ASA) is an organization of Christian professional scientists, broadly defined to include disciplines in the natural and **social sciences**, medicine, engineering, **mathematics**, and archaeology, as well as philosophy and theology. The ASA provides a forum for discussion of science and theology among its approximately 2,000 members who are generally committed to mainstream science (that is, the consensus of the broader scientific community).

The ASA statement of faith comprises acceptance of the divine inspiration, trustworthiness, and authority of the Bible in matters of faith and conduct; confession of the triune God affirmed in the Nicene and Apostles' creeds, accepted as brief, faithful statements of Christian doctrine based on Scripture; belief that in creating and preserving the universe God has endowed it with contingent order and intelligibility, the basis of scientific investigation; and recognition of the responsibility, as stewards of God's creation, to use science and **technology** for the good of humanity and the whole world.

The ASA holds annual meetings, publishes a peer-reviewed journal called *Perspectives on Science and Christian Faith*, hosts a website (ASA3.org) with educational resources and an Internet magazine, *God and Nature*, and supports several local chapters and disciplinary interest groups, such as Christian Women in Sciences and the Affiliation of Christian Geologists. Some annual meetings are held with international counterparts in Canada and Europe.

The origin of the ASA is linked to early twentieth-century evangelical and fundamentalist Christian concerns about science. The ASA was founded in 1941 by a small group of science educators and industry scientists invited by Moody Bible Institute president Will H. Houghton to consider organizing annual conferences to help pastors and students better understand the relationship between science and religion. World War II delayed the first national meeting of the ASA until 1946 at Wheaton College in Illinois. After the 1925 Scopes trial over public teaching of evolution, many "Bible-science" groups had emerged to either provide a scientific Christian alternative to evolution or to promote **scientific proof**s of the Bible's veracity, generally advocating a particular understanding of the Bible and science.

The founders of the ASA determined that the organization would not represent any particular approach to faith and science matters beyond its core beliefs. The ASA quickly became the principal evangelical forum for debating evolution, flood geology, and the age of the earth. Early contributors to the ASA journal included **Bernard Ramm**, Carl F. H. Henry, Wilbur Smith, Lawrence Kulp, and Russell Mixter. Two books by ASA authors, *Modern Science and Christian Faith* (1948) and *Evolution and Christian Thought Today* (1959), were widely read in evangelical circles. Historian **Ronald Numbers** (2006) has observed that the ASA devoted more time to appraising than to opposing evolution, which instigated the establishment of overtly creationist organizations such as the **Institute for Creation Research** (see also **Morris, Henry**).

Beyond creation and evolution, topics of interest to members of the ASA in recent years—as reflected in journal articles, meeting themes, and presentations—include medical and **environmental ethics**, technology and sustainable development, **psychology**, **neuroscience**, and history of science.

Stephen O. Moshier

REFERENCES AND RECOMMENDED READING

Everest, F. Alton. 2010. *The American Scientific Affiliation: Its Growth and Early Development.* Ipswich, UK: ASA Press.
Hart, D. G. 1991. "The Fundamentalist Origins of the American Scientific Affiliation." *Perspectives on Science and Christian Faith* 43:238–48.
Numbers, Ronald L. 2006. *The Creationists: From Scientific Creationism to Intelligent Design.* Exp. ed. Cambridge, MA: Harvard University Press.

ANGELS AND DEMONS. The existence of angels and demons forms part of the Christian **worldview** since they appear and are discussed in the Bible. Any attempt to demythologize this material dishonors both the texts and the church's creeds and confessions. While the doctrine of angelology is not as developed as, say, Christology, there is enough biblical material for a coherent account, even if some desired details are missing. The relative paucity of **revelation** about angels is instructive, since mankind's chief concern should be for their Creator, not immaterial spirits. The book of Revelation records that the apostle John began to worship an angel, who rebuked him by saying, "Don't do that! I am a fellow servant with you and with your fellow prophets and with all who keep the words of this scroll. Worship God!" (Rev. 22:9; see also Col. 2:18).

Scripture concerns itself with the narrative and doctrine of human beings far more than it does with angels. While both humans and angels are created beings with agency (mind and will), our knowledge of angels, unlike that of humans, is more inferential than direct. Angels, both good and evil, play a more prominent role in the New Testament than in the Hebrew Bible, but there is no contradiction between the two testaments on their nature and operation. Moreover, angelology is a standard topic in systematic theology.

Angels are created beings who possess supernatural power not available to human beings. Unfallen angels worship God (Isa. 6:2–3), minister to God's people (Pss. 34:7; 91:11–12; Heb. 1:14), are messengers of God (Luke 1:11; Rev. 1:1), and are engaged in spiritual warfare (Rev. 12:7). Fallen angels (demons) rebelled against God (Jude 6; 2 Peter 2:4) and are under the direction of Satan, the chief fallen angel. The redemptive work of Christ dealt the demonic world a fatal blow (Col. 2:15; 1 John 3:8), which will be culminated at the end of history.

Secularism to the contrary, modern science does nothing to contradict the biblical account of angels and demons. The **epistemology** of **Scientism** (which is a corollary of the **metaphysics** of **materialism**) argues that knowledge only comes through scientific observation and theory. Since angels and demons are not subject to such empirical procedures, there is no reason to believe in them. But scientism is self-contradictory, since its claim to monopolize knowledge is itself not a deliverance of any scientific observation or scientific theory. If scientism is false, then it is possible that knowledge comes from other sources, such as rational **intuition** (Rom. 2:14–15) and biblical revelation (2 Tim. 3:16; 1 Peter 1:21).

By definition, the hard sciences (chemistry, biology, and **physics**) are not able to formulate laws or research programs about angelic activity, since any angelic intervention in human affairs stems from their personal agency and is not describable according to impersonal laws. Moreover, angelic behavior is supernatural and thus not under the tutelage of **natural law** (see **Methodological Naturalism**). That, of course, does not mean that angelic activity is logically contradictory or meaningless; it is simply not subject to scientific analysis any more than is the activity of the immaterial human mind (see **Mind-Body Problem**; **Soul**).

Douglas Groothuis

REFERENCES AND RECOMMENDED READING

Dickason, C. Fred. 1995. *Angels: Elect and Evil.* New ed. Chicago: Moody.
Montgomery, John W., ed. 1973. *Principalities and Powers: The World of the Occult.* Minneapolis: Bethany House.

ANIMAL PAIN. In recent years, the existence, nature, and extent of nonhuman animal (henceforth, "animal") pain has been increasingly discussed by philosophers and theologians because it represents a form of evil that is not easily explained by traditional theodicies. Why does animal pain present this unusual challenge to **theism**, and how might the theist account for God's permission of it?

If God were not all-knowing or all-powerful, it might be that such pain and suffering exist because God cannot prevent it (see **Evil, Problem of**). However, here we consider responses to the problem of the existence of animal pain on the assumption of the classical understanding of God.

The first type of response seeks to deny the existence of the problem. If animals do not in fact experience pain and suffering, there is no evil to explain. This response to the problem is often traced to the writings of **René Descartes** (Descartes 1991, 148). For Descartes and his more recent defenders, animals are complex machines that lack the mental states required to support states like pain and suffering (Lewis 1962, 162; Harrison 1989). More recent defenders have argued that work in both philosophy of mind and animal behavior and cognition support this view as well. Murray (2008, chap. 2), for example, examines contemporary theories of phenomenal **consciousness**—the sort of consciousness associated with mental states that "feel" a certain way to those who have them—and notes that on some of these, animals might not have a phenomenal conscious awareness of pain.

One such view is based on a theory of consciousness according to which mental states have phenomenal character (that element that makes them "feel like" something when we have them) when those mental states are the object of another mental state called a "higher order thought" (or HOT). On this view, when I step on a tack, this induces a mental state in me; and when I direct a higher order thought at or toward that mental state, then, and only then, does the mental state "feel" like something (Rosenthal 2002; Lau and Rosenthal 2011). Advocates of this view argue that it can explain certain strange phenomena like blindsight. In blindsight, patients claim that they cannot see anything at all, even though they are able to perform behaviors that clearly require sight (like navigating through a hallway filled with objects without any assistance). HOT theorists argue that blindsight patients have visual mental states, but those states don't "feel like" anything to them, and so they do not have any "awareness" that they have them (thus describing themselves as blind).

If animals lack higher order thoughts, and this theory of consciousness is right, then animals have no conscious awareness of their pains, even though they have pain states. They have, in the case of pain, something analogous to blindsight.

Others have argued that even if animals have pain states with some phenomenal "feel" to them, this might not by itself count as bad or evil. The reason for that is that we know that even human beings with phenomenally conscious pain states sometimes regard those states as not being unpleasant. In the mid-twentieth century, neuroscientist Walter Freeman developed a procedure that came to be known as the lobotomy, in which portions of patients' prefrontal cortices were destroyed or disrupted.

The procedure was sometimes used with patients with chronic pain. Afterward these patients would sometimes express relief, not because the pain was gone but because, according to their reports, they did not "care about" the pain any longer. More recent work in **neuroscience** shows that pain is mediated by two pathways: one that detects the injurious stimuli and one that moderates the level at which we care about it (for more recent work, see Damasio et al. 1990). Since almost all animals lack a part of the brain that is associated with "caring about" our mental states (Markowitsch and Pritzel 1979; Preuss 1995), one possibility that presents itself is this: animals have conscious pain states, but having them does not "bother" them.

Of course, animals would still display all of the behaviors that we associate with unpleasant pain. Presumably those behaviors evolved because they are adaptive behaviors to enact when we are injured, not because they necessarily signal discomfort. So we are left to wonder: *Is that what animal mental states are like when it comes to pain?* The answer is we do not know. But if any of these proposals is correct, it would seem that animal pain and suffering are not a problem to be solved in the first place. And the problem of animal pain and suffering thus evaporates.

Not surprisingly, these views are not popular since animals seem to display behaviors in response to painful stimuli just as humans do. It is thus natural to infer that animals feel pain just like we do. This line of response has been defended recently by Francescotti (2013) and by Dougherty (2014). However, in both cases, Francescotti and Dougherty point to behaviors displayed by animals that are analogous to those displayed by humans and infer that animals must then also be experiencing phenomenally conscious pain. Such reasoning fails to recognize that the behaviors associated with pain (withdrawing one's limb from a painful stimulus, for example) would be likely to evolve even if there were no phenomenally conscious states (see **consciousness**). So if these behaviors evolve for adaptive reason, it is an open question whether the corresponding phenomenal conscious

mental states would have to evolve as well, and if so, why (see Murray 2015).

Other responses to the problem of animal pain accept that the phenomenon is real but argue that God's permission of such pain is morally justified as a necessary condition for securing outweighing goods. What follows is a brief review of the main positions that have been defended along these lines.

Christian thinkers have often argued that all evil states of affairs are to be explained as consequences for the moral wrongdoing of an original human pair created by God (see **Adam and Eve**). This event (**the fall**) is taken to be the causal origin of all moral and natural evils. On this view, the fall and its consequences are justifiably permitted by God as a necessary condition for allowing creaturely free will. Perhaps the existence of animal pain and suffering should thus be understood as a consequence of the fall.

Young-earth creationists often defend such a position and indeed find any other view incompatible with divine goodness (Morris 1973, 72–73; see **Creationism, Young-Earth**). However, such views have come under increasing pressure as the scientific evidence seems to confirm that the existence of animals long predates the existence of human beings. In response, some have argued that the existence of animal pain is to be accounted for as a result of the wrongdoing of Satan prior to the creation of organic life (Boyd 2001), while others have argued that the fall has something like a backward causal impact on the natural world that existed prior to the advent of human beings (Dembski 2009).

While these views more plausibly accommodate the fact that animals predate humans, they face the challenge of explaining why an all-good God would create a world where the permission of pain and suffering of innocent animals can be the consequence of a single act of human moral disobedience. Such a world seems to put innocent animals at an objectionably high level of risk for no apparently good reason.

Others have argued that animal pain and suffering are permitted by God not as a result of the misuse of free will by human agents, but rather as a result of God conferring on the physical cosmos itself a freedom to develop in directions that might lead to the occurrence of evil states of affairs. On this view, creation itself, like the human beings it contains, has a "freedom to wander" which necessarily leaves open the possibility that it will wander in directions that involve natural evil. In defending this view, **John Polkinghorne** affirms that "God has created this amazing universe so that life can evolve and come into being, endowed with the true freedom required for love. This entails giving a certain amount of freedom to the physical processes, and a process of 'creative destruction' via evolution" (Polkinghorne 2005).

Explanations based on the "freedom of creation" face three significant objections. First, despite the label, nonconscious creation is not free in the sense that humans are. Rather, at best, nature displays contingent or unpredictable behaviors. We might be tempted to think of the contingency or unpredictability as a sign that nature as a whole is also free, but this would be to fall prey to what seems to be an objectionable form of anthropomorphism.

Second, even if the cosmos were free to wander, it is not clear why God would allow it to contain as much evil as it does, persisting for so long. A universe created fully formed, in just the way hypothesized by the **young-earth creationists**, could be equally "free to wander." But it would not include the massive suffering that is part of our evolutionary heritage. This gives us reason to doubt that this explanation satisfies the demand that the permitted evil be a "necessary condition" for securing the outweighing good.

Finally, even if we can resolve these two problems, we are still left with the problem that the good of a cosmos that is "free to wander" does not seem to outweigh the resulting evil: all of the billions of organisms that suffer and die horribly. Is the good of a creation "free to wander" worth the price? It is hard to see why one would accept this.

Some have argued that the existence of animal pain and suffering is a result of the fact that God desires to bring creation about by means of a natural and law-like process in ways that entail the existence of potentially suffering animals. On one such view, evolution is the *only* way to bring about the existence of human beings through such a process. However, such a process would require the existence of organisms that are precursors to conscious human beings, and given the incremental nature of evolutionary change, this would require the existence of animals that can experience pain and suffering (Southgate 2008).

Others have argued that even if gradual evolutionary processes are not the *only way* that God could bring about the existence of human beings, the evolutionary process itself manifests something that God values, namely, bringing about desirable states in creation by a process that moves from chaos to order over time. On this view, the cosmos is analogous to a machine-making machine, which in part because of that fact, manifests the intelligence and ingenuity of its creator (Beecher 1885). As with the above view, the gradual evolutionary process involved in bringing about

human beings would require precursor organisms that can experience pain and suffering.

Another approach to the problem of animal pain and suffering argues that the ability to experience such states is necessary for organisms that are embodied and live in a world governed by law-like regularities, and that the existence of such organisms is sufficiently good to justify their potential pain. In such a world, animal bodies are susceptible to injury and as such require some sort of alarm mechanism that warns them when their bodily integrity is compromised or at risk (see Yancey and Brand 1997).

One might argue that views along this line are unsatisfying since it would seem that God could create animals with the ability to react to injurious stimuli through something like nonconscious reflex reactions, rather than through behaviors that are mediated by pain states. However, if animals act on intentions—if they *intend* to do things when they act—there must be some mechanism that allows them to balance their desires to achieve an intended goal and the risks that the intended goals pose to their bodily integrity. There is good reason to think that the only sort of tool that can provide the proper counterbalance is pain. If there were no such mechanisms, animals would be unable to balance the risks of physical injury from their actions against the strength of their desire to achieve some intended goal.

Of course one might still wonder why that countervailing motivation has to be *pain*. Here the work of Paul Brand (cited above) provides some hints at an answer to this question. Brand worked with patients suffering from Hanson's disease, an illness that causes loss of pain in one's limbs and digits. Brand tried a variety of mechanisms to signal to patients that their bodies were being subjected to injurious stimuli (lights that would flash on the lens of their glasses or tones that would sound in their ears). However, the only mechanism that seemed to prevent patients from injuring themselves when they had a strong desire to achieve some goal was the induction of pain in ways that the patient could not override. According to Brand, pain is not just one way to keep intentional agents from injuring themselves; it is either the only way or the most effective way.

Finally, some argue that the capacity of animals to experience pain and suffering is necessary for them to be able to display the great good of noble intentional action. Richard Swinburne (1998, 171–75, 189–92), for example, argues that absent the capacity to experience loss, either through **death** or through real pain and suffering, animals could not possibly have the sorts of mental states required for their actions to count as instances of sympathy, affection, courage, patience, and so on. In addition, for animals to be capable of engaging in intentional action of this sort, they need to know the consequences their actions are likely to have.

For an animal to intend to rescue its offspring, it must believe or otherwise have available to it an awareness of the fact that acting in a certain sort of way will probably yield the intended outcome. Thus, for animals to act courageously or sympathetically, for example, they must know that some of their actions will prevent or forestall the occurrence of certain evils. And to know this they will have to have beliefs or an awareness of the fact that certain conditions will cause other animals harm. Having these beliefs (or coming to such an awareness) will, however, involve animal suffering.

Accounts of this sort encounter two sorts of difficulties. First, it is not clear that pain is in fact necessary for animals to engage in noble actions of this sort. While acting on behalf of other organisms in ways that are meritorious might require that those other organisms are capable of experiencing some loss, it is not clear why those losses must sometimes, or ever, involve pain. Second, in order for these accounts to constitute good reasons for God to permit animal pain and suffering, it must be the case that the goodness of the actions outweighs the pain and suffering that is required for them. It is not clear that this is the case.

Michael J. Murray

REFERENCES AND RECOMMENDED READING

Beecher, H. W. 1885. *Evolution and Religion*. New York: Fords, Howard, and Hurlburt.

Boyd, Gregory. 2001. *Satan and the Problem of Evil*. Downers Grove, IL: InterVarsity.

Damasio, Antonio, Daniel Tranel, and Hanna Damasio. 1990. "Individuals with Sociopathic Behavior Caused by Frontal Damage Fail to Respond Autonomously to Social Stimuli." *Behavioural Brain Research* 41:81–94.

Dembski, William. 2009. *The End of Christianity: Finding God in an Evil World*. Nashville: B&H Academic.

Descartes, René. 1991. *The Philosophical Writings of Descartes*. Vol. 3. *The Correspondence*. Ed. John Cottingham, Robert Stoothoff, Dugald Murdoch, and Anthony Kenny. Cambridge: Cambridge University Press.

Dougherty, Trent. 2014. *The Problem of Animal Pain: A Theodicy for All Creatures Great and Small*. New York: Palgrave Macmillan.

Francescotti, Robert. 2013. "The Problem of Pain and Suffering." In *The Blackwell Companion to the Problem of Evil*, ed. Justin P. McBrayer and Daniel Howard-Snyder. Malden, MA: Blackwell.

Harrison, Peter. 1989. "Theodicy and Animal Pain." *Philosophy*. 64:79–92.

Lau, Hawkwan, and David Rosenthal. 2011. "Empirical Support for Higher-Order Theories of Conscious Awareness." *Trends in Cognitive Science* 15 (8): 365–73.

Lewis, C. S. 1962. *The Problem of Pain: How Human Suffering Raises Almost Intolerable Intellectual Problems*. New York: Collier.

Markowitsch, H. J., and M. Pritzel. 1979. "The Prefrontal Cortex: Projection Area of the Thalamic Mediodorsal Nucleus?" *Physiological Psychology* 7 (1): 1–6.

Morris, Henry M. 1973. "The Day-Age Theory." In *And God Created*, ed. Kelly L. Segraves. San Diego: Creation-Science Research Center.

Murray, Michael J. 2008. *Nature Red in Tooth and Claw*. Oxford: Oxford University Press.

———. 2015. "Review of Trent Dougherty, *The Problem of Animal Pain: A Theodicy for All Creatures Great and Small*." *International Journal of the Philosophy of Religion* 78 (1): 137–41.

Polkinghorne, John. 2005. *Exploring Reality: The Intertwining of Science and Religion*. New Haven, CT: Yale University Press.

Preuss, T. M. 1995. "Do Rats Have Prefrontal Cortex? The Rose-Woolsey-Akert Program Reconsidered." *Journal of Cognitive Neuroscience* 7 (1): 1–24.

Rosenthal, David. 2002. *Consciousness and the Mind*. Oxford: Oxford University Press.

Southgate, Christopher. 2008. *The Groaning of Creation: God, Evolution, and the Problem of Evil*. Louisville, KY: Westminster John Knox.

Swinburne, Richard. 1998. *Providence and the Problem of Evil*. Oxford: Oxford University Press.

Yancey, Philip, and Paul Brand. 1997. *The Gift of Pain*. Grand Rapids: Zondervan.

ANSWERS IN GENESIS. Headquartered in Petersburg, Kentucky, and with a sister ministry in the United Kingdom, Answers in Genesis (AiG) is an evangelical nonprofit organization and is the largest apologetics ministry in the world. Its cofounder and CEO, **Ken Ham**, is perhaps the most well-known creationist alive today. In addition to the speaking tours, books, lecture videos, magazines, and other materials produced by AiG, it also operates the Creation Museum and the Ark Encounter, both located in Kentucky.

In 1993 Creation Science Ministries was founded by Ken Ham, Mark Looy, and Mike Zovath, and rebranded as Answers in Genesis in 1994. From its inception, there was a close partnership with Australia-based Creation Science Fellowship, which also adopted the AiG name in 1994. These two organizations were legally and financially separate but shared a website and content resources, partnered for speaking tours, and jointly published numerous books. The combined AiG ministries grew beyond Australia and the United States, forming satellite branches in New Zealand, South Africa, Canada, and the United Kingdom. In 2006 internal tensions between the US and Australian ministries' leadership resulted in a split. The US and UK offices retained the AiG name, while the remaining groups rebranded as Creation Ministries International.

AiG's influence on the creation-evolution debate is immense. Its website averages more than 400,000 unique visits per month, among the highest of any evangelical ministry. AiG's multiday conferences typically draw hundreds of attendees, and their speakers frequently present at churches, Christian schools, homeschool conventions, and other venues. In 2014 Ken Ham debated Bill Nye ("The Science Guy," a popular science program host) over the merits of the young-earth creation model of earth history. The debate drew more than 3 million viewers during airtime and a total YouTube viewership of over 5 million as of 2015. Furthering its influence, AiG's Creation Museum attracts 300,000 visitors each year, and the Ark Encounter (an attraction featuring a full-sized replica of Noah's ark) is anticipated to welcome 1.5–2 million visitors in its first year alone.

AiG's main audience is church laity, with most of its materials (lectures, conferences, web articles, magazines, and books) written with this group in mind. Overall, the ministry favors a presuppositional approach to apologetics over, but not to the exclusion of, evidential approaches. More academically oriented is *Answers Research Journal*, an open-access peer-reviewed journal published by AiG and dedicated to **young-earth creationist** scholarship. AiG also maintains a research division that employs several staff members who possess doctorates in science and theology.

AiG affirms evangelical Christian beliefs in their statement of faith (including the eternal and triune nature of God, deity of Christ, **virgin birth**, inspiration of Scripture, etc.; see website), along with others more pertinent to young-earth creation. Notable points for the latter include:

- The early passages of Genesis (e.g., chaps. 1–11) represent a true historical account of events and people.
- The whole of creation was formed in six consecutive 24-hour days followed by one day (24 hours) of rest.
- This creation was accomplished about 6,000 years ago.
- Adam and Eve were historical individuals, the first people, and created by God. Their sin introduced **death** (physical and spiritual) into the world.
- The original animals and plants were created by God according to their kinds, not via evolutionary processes.
- Noah's flood was a global event in extent and effect, and it produced the majority of fossil-bearing sedimentary rocks.

Marcus R. Ross

REFERENCES AND RECOMMENDED READING

Answers in Genesis homepage: www.answersingenesis.org
Ark Encounter homepage: www.arkencounter.org
Creation Ministries International homepage: www.creation.com
Creation Museum homepage: www.creationmuseum.org

ANTHROPIC PRINCIPLE. Physicist Freeman Dyson expressed the anthropic principle in personal terms with this comment: "The more I examine the universe and study the details of its architecture, the more evidence I find that the universe in some sense must have known we were coming" (Dyson 1979, 250). In other words, the universe appears to have been engineered to make possible the existence of human beings. This observation is referred to as the *anthropic principle*.

Astronomer Marcelo Gleiser has pointed out that in the astronomical literature, however, the anthropic principle almost always amounts to nothing more than a "prebiotic principle" (Gleiser 2010). Researchers tend to focus on the minimum preconditions necessary for the possible and brief existence of the most primitive life-forms, such as the simplest imaginable bacterium. Targeting prebiotic, as opposed to anthropic, essentials has led scientists to underestimate the design requirements for humanity's existence in the universe. An additional underestimation occurs when the anthropic principle is considered only in the context of the universe as a whole. Fine-tuning for life, and particularly for human life, may be seen on all size scales, from vast to minute—the universe, the Virgo supercluster of galaxies, the Local Group of galaxies, the Milky Way galaxy, the solar system, Earth, Earth's crust and atmosphere, and even to fundamental particles.

Scientists are able to assign numerical values to several hundred of nature's physical features (e.g., the density of protons and neutrons in the universe, the local density of dwarf galaxies, the number and sizes of galactic spurs and feathers, the orbital shapes and masses of partner planets, the Earth-moon mass ratio, strength and duration of Earth's magnetic field, the quantity, diversity, and duration of sulfate-reducing bacteria), all of which must fall within a specific range for humans to have any chance of existence (Ross 2010). These numerical values can then be compared with the best examples of human engineering. Such comparisons imply that the cosmic Creator is a great many orders of magnitude more intelligent, creative, and capable than the most brilliant, skillful, and well-funded human craftspeople and engineers ("creators"). Given that intellect, creativity, and intentionality are attributes that only personal beings possess, the evidence powerfully implies that the cosmic Creator is a personal being.

In their book *The Anthropic Cosmological Principle*, astrophysicists **John Barrow** and **Frank Tipler** (Barrow and

Tipler 1986, 16–23, 305–60, 503–70, 637–77) develop four distinct philosophical interpretations of the anthropic principle:

1. WAP (weak anthropic principle): Conscious beings can only exist in an environment with characteristics that allow for their habitation.
2. SAP (strong anthropic principle): Nature *must* take on those characteristics that allow somewhere, sometime the existence of conscious beings.
3. PAP (participatory anthropic principle): Conscious observers are necessary to bring the universe into existence, and the universe is necessary to bring observers into existence.
4. FAP/OPT (final anthropic principle; the omega point): God does not yet exist. However, life, the universe, and all inanimate resources in the universe together have evolved and will continue to evolve to become an omnipotent, omnipresent, omniscient being with the power to create in the past.

As a subset of the broader anthropic principle, the biological (anthropic) principle expresses the notion that for humans to have any possibility of existence, the events surrounding the origin of life and subsequent history of life must have been extraordinarily fine-tuned. Both scientists and philosophers have inferred that if the architecture of the universe reveals a high level of design precision, then the complex intricacies of biology must reveal much more careful fine-tuning.

Yet another subset of the anthropic principle addresses the "amazing coincidence" of cosmic observability. Research indicates that humanity came on the cosmic scene at a unique moment and in a unique location—sufficiently distant from our galaxy's core, from its spiral arms, and from bright nebulae—that allow observation and measurements of the entire history of the universe, all the way back to the cosmic beginning.

Hugh Ross

REFERENCES AND RECOMMENDED READING

Barrow, John D., and Frank J. Tipler. 1986. *The Anthropic Cosmological Principle.* New York: Oxford University Press.

Dyson, Freeman J. 1979. *Disturbing the Universe.* New York: Basic.

Gleiser, Marcelo. 2010. "Drake Equation for the Multiverse: From the String Landscape to Complex Life." *International Journal of Modern Physics, D* 19 (10): 1299–1308.

Ross, Hugh, 2010. RTB Design Compendium. Reasons to Believe. November 17. www.reasons.org/fine-tuning.

ANTHROPIC PRINCIPLE INEQUALITY. Cosmologist Brandon Carter (Carter 1983) was the first to name the glaring disparity between the time required for intelligent life to come on the cosmic scene and the time such life can remain on the scene: the anthropic principle inequality. He recognized that given the laws of **physics** that govern the operation of the universe, it takes a very long time to prepare a habitat in which humans can possibly exist, yet the maximum time during which humans can survive in a civilized state is very brief.

By taking into account the laws of physics, the characteristics of the universe, and the required properties and long progressive history of life, two physicists (Barrow and Tipler 1986) demonstrated that a minimum of 13–15 billion years is required before the universe is able to sustain intelligent life while the maximum time such intelligent life can exist in a civilized state is 41,000 years or less. Civilized state was defined as an intelligent **species** globally occupying their planet where specialization and trading occurs, roughly akin to the Neolithic revolution, which began about 12,000 years ago.

Factors confirming this calculation would include the supply of fossil fuels and concentrated metal ores, the planet's rotation rate history and plate tectonics history, and the planet's host star's luminosity history and stability. The need for an ice-age cycle and for a warm interglacial with climate stability within an ice-age cycle likely would shorten the time for intelligent life's existence in a civilized state by as much as 20,000 years. Thus the inequality is extreme. The universe takes nearly a million times longer to become ready for intelligent life than the maximum time span that life can survive in a civilized state.

What are the implications of this inequality? Given the quantity of time and quality of design required to prepare a home for even one sentient species that can exist in a civilized state for such a brief time span, an argument can be made for the high value and significant purpose for that species' existence. A useful analogy may be found in the marriage ceremonies of various cultures around the world. In the United States, a typical wedding ceremony, wherein vows are exchanged, lasts barely 20 minutes. The average cost of this typical wedding, including ceremony and celebration, exceeds $20,000. The average preparation time invested in this typical event is equivalent to several months of full-time labor by more than one person. In other cultures, these numbers tend to be higher.

The financial and labor investment by the bride and groom and their families may seem ridiculously disproportionate to the length of the ceremony itself, and yet the parties involved consider their resources well spent because of the significance of what is established in that brief exchange. Similarly, one can reasonably infer that the one who planned, prepared, and provided for civilized human existence considered the investment of some 13.8 billion years of extraordinary fine-tuning worth the investment. The anthropic principle inequality testifies to the extremely high value, purpose, and destiny of human beings.

Hugh Ross

REFERENCES AND RECOMMENDED READING

Barrow, John D., and Frank J. Tipler. 1986. *The Anthropic Cosmological Principle.* New York: Oxford University Press.
Carter, Brandon. 1983. *Philosophical Transactions of the Royal Society of London, A* 310 (December 20): 347–63.

ANTHROPOLOGY. Anthropology is the study of humankind, past and present, and is commonly divided into four subfields: biological anthropology, sociocultural anthropology, linguistics, and archaeology. A new, fifth subfield, cognitive anthropology, draws on insights from the other four and the **mind science**s to account for how cultural forms and human thought mutually inform each other.

Biological anthropology, also known as physical anthropology, is the comparative study of humans as a biological **species**, *Homo sapiens*, relative to other animals, particularly primates. Marquee research agendas include identifying what is unique about humans versus what is continuous with other primates, reconstructing causal factors and timelines informing hominid evolution, and understanding the evolutionary significance of human traits and behaviors. Biological anthropology is not characterized by any single or unique methodology but, rather, employs a diverse range of research tools drawn from **paleontology**, genetics, archaeology, **ecology**, physiology, epidemiology, osteology, and primatology, among others. Biological anthropology is committed to the evolutionary origins of humankind and has spawned evolutionary anthropology as a sub-area that uses evolutionary insights to address questions concerning human behavior in particular, such as mating and parenting strategies.

Sociocultural anthropology is the comparative study of different forms of human social life and cultural experience. The discipline is defined in large part by its focus on long-term fieldwork, participant observation methods, and descriptive ethnographies that give detailed and situated accounts of specific cultures. A premium on intensive involvement with people in their cultural environments for long periods of time has tended social anthropology toward research outputs that offer more holistic and longitudinal treatments of a social group's shared practices, meanings, and contexts, and the interrelations between them, than is found in other academes.

Linguistics is the study of language as a human phenomenon. Like biological anthropology, linguistics is a global discipline and encompasses an expansive range of research on language and form, language and meaning, and language in context. Within anthropology, linguistics data are typically trained on uncovering cultural knowledge and on understanding cognitive and social processes that inform and constrain language development over time.

Archaeology is the study of the ancient and recent human past through the excavation and analysis of material remains, including artifacts (e.g., tools, clothing, dwellings) and waste and remains from human activities.

Cognitive anthropology is a relatively new subfield that seeks to understand causal dialectics between culture and mind—between the symbols, narratives, rituals, ideologies, motivations, historical events, languages, visions, and so forth that constitute cultural practice, on the one hand, and the architectures of mind that enable and constrain these cultural forms, on the other. Toward these ends, cognitive anthropology utilizes a wide range of perspectives and methods from wider anthropology and the mind sciences, cognitive and developmental **psychology** foremost.

According to a Carnegie Foundation survey, anthropology is composed of the most secular professoriate in American universities. Such a distinction may be owed to anthropology's strong reliance on epistemologies associated with social relativism and Darwinian evolution. A 2006 article by Dean Arnold titled "Why Are There So Few Christian Anthropologists? Reflections on the Tensions between Christianity and Anthropology," outlines some key challenges facing Christians who would work in anthropology (Arnold 2006, 266–82).

Ryan G. Hornbeck

REFERENCES AND RECOMMENDED READING

Arnold, Dean E. 2006. "Why Are There So Few Christian Anthropologists? Reflections on the Tensions between Christianity and Anthropology." *Perspectives on Science and Christian Faith* 58 (4): 266–82.

AQUINAS, THOMAS. Under the inspiration of **Aristotle**, Thomas Aquinas (1224–74) produced a great synthesis of Aristotelian philosophy and Christian theology that had enormous influence on Western thinking. Like Aristotle, Thomas believed that science (*scientia*) studies the nature of things, especially in the natural world, in an attempt to arrive at first principles and knowledge of essences, and he adapted Aristotle's metaphysical categories of being and becoming, substance, form and matter, and the **four causes** into his Christian philosophy. He regarded the universe as intelligible and nature as good, and he held that we should use the tools God has given us, especially reason, to investigate God's creation. In this way, reason in general, and philosophy, theology, and science (**natural philosophy**) in particular complement **revelation**. Thomas divided the sciences into two categories, the theoretical (**physics**, **mathematics**, and **metaphysics**) and the practical (economics, ethics, and politics).

Aquinas accepted the principle that "all truth is one," the idea that if a claim is established as true in one discipline (e.g., theology or science), it must therefore be true in all disciplines. This basic principle of **logic** was accepted by many medieval thinkers and defined the way they approached theological questions. It meant, for example, that if a scientific theory came along that seemed to contradict the Bible or certain theological doctrines, the conflict was only apparent and could be resolved by further reflection (a view first developed by **Augustine**).

Thomas is best known for his arguments in the "Five Ways" (*Quinque Viae*) that our study of the natural world leads us to the **existence of God**. It is reasonable to believe in God through **natural theology**, that is, by examining the evidence in the natural world, including from **causation**, change, and order, and working back to the conclusion that there must be a necessary being behind the universe. God is a necessary, eternal being, because this is what the arguments for the existence of God show—one must invoke a necessary being to explain contingent being; otherwise, one cannot explain contingent being. The "articles of faith," however, such as the **incarnation** and **the Trinity**, can only be known through revelation and faith.

Thomas's analysis of causation appealed to the distinction between primary and secondary causes as a way of explaining how God acts in his creation. God is the primary cause of the universe and life because he created them out of a set of initial ingredients, together with the laws of science, and built

in certain goals at the beginning of the process. Secondary causation refers to the fact that everyday physical events in the universe are governed by scientific laws. Although God does not normally intervene in the day-to-day operation of physical events (the secondary causes), God can perform miracles whenever he wishes and often does so, especially by responding to **prayer** (see **Miracles**). God is also immanent in creation in several ways, according to Thomas.

The notions of primary and secondary **causation** have proved very helpful to philosophers and theologians trying to think about the difference between local causes and ultimate causes and the topic of **divine action** in the world. But Thomas's views on these matters have been challenged in recent times by **process philosophy**, atheistic **naturalism**, and even by **intelligent design** theory.

Brendan Sweetman

REFERENCES AND RECOMMENDED READING

Aquinas, Thomas. 1998. *Selected Writings,* ed. Ralph McInerny. New York: Penguin.

Artigas, Mariano. 2000. *The Mind of the Universe.* Philadelphia: Templeton.

McInerny, Ralph. 2004. *Aquinas.* Cambridge, MA: Polity.

Sweetman, Brendan. 2007. *Religion: Key Concepts in Philosophy.* New York: Continuum.

ARCHAEOPTERYX. *Archaeopteryx* is the term for an archaic **species** of organisms that shared many characteristics of modern birds but also had features believed to be transitional between classical **dinosaurs** and modern birds. For example, it had teeth rather than a horned beak and a full-length tail rather than the little nubbin found in modern birds. It also had three distinct clawed fingers and did not have the broad keel at the sternum that characterizes modern birds. On the other hand, like modern birds, it had broad pinnate feathers on its forelimb, which could have provided the necessary air resistance to provide lift for take-off and sustained flight. Whether it would have had the muscular wherewithal for sustained flight as opposed to gliding, however, is not known.

Archaeopteryx's existence is known through 12 fossils found in limestone quarries in Southern Germany believed to be about 145 million years old. The first fossil of archaeopteryx was reported in 1861 only two years after the publication of **Darwin**'s *Origin of Species*. At the time of its discovery, the existence of archaeopteryx was widely considered to confirm predictions laid out by Darwin. Indeed, in a later edition of the book, he noted its existence and discussed its significance.

Although archaeopteryx has long been considered to be an important transitional species between birds and reptiles, throughout the following 130 years, it was surprising that other similar species were not discovered.

Beginning in the 1990s, however, that changed dramatically with the exploration of various geological formations, especially in China. As a result of these studies, it is now well recognized that feathers were not a feature of birds only. Thirty different dinosaur species have now been shown to have had feathers. Paleontologists believe that feathers had other functions than flight in the earliest days, likely, depending on the species, they were important for insulation and/or sexual display.

Although archaeopteryx is still recognized as one of the species that most closely resembles modern birds, other related species have been discovered, and there is a succession of transitional characteristics between extinct dinosaurs and modern birds. This does not mean, however, that evolutionary biologists have identified a clearly marked evolutionary trajectory for bird evolution. Given the rarity of fossilization for any species, the fossils in hand are believed to represent only a tiny fraction of the species that have actually existed. Still, the collection as a whole is considered to be consistent with birds having been created through an evolutionary process. As for archaeopteryx itself, both the timing of its presence (145 million years ago) and the transitional characteristics it had are considered to be consistent with it either having been in the lineage or (more likely) closely related to species that were on the trajectory that gave rise to birds.

Although the overwhelming consensus of biologists and paleontologists is that archaeopteryx and/or its cousin species are transitional species on the lineage from dinosaurs to modern birds, some Christians are hesitant to accept this. One of the alternative views is that a specific "archaeopteryx-like kind" was created according to the creation command and that archaeopteryx and its cousin species are examples of "micro-evolution" — changes within a created "kind." According to this particular view, that "kind" is now extinct. Other Christians accept the transitional body forms associated with birdlike characteristics as evidence that God's creation command was realized through the evolutionary process.

Darrel R. Falk

REFERENCES AND RECOMMENDED READING

Padian, Kevin. 2015. "Paleontology: Dinosaur Up in the Air." *Nature* 521:40–41.
Shipman, Pat. 1999. *Taking Wing: Archaeopteryx and the Evolution of Bird Flight.* New York: Simon & Schuster.

ARISTOTLE. The thought of Aristotle (384–322 BC), one of the most influential philosophers in history, is of enormous significance for the history of science and for its eventual relationship with Christianity. A versatile thinker, Aristotle pursued "**natural philosophy**," a study of nature that today would be called science and a subject he distinguished from **mathematics** and **metaphysics**. Natural philosophy is aimed at finding objective knowledge, which can be obtained by means of inductive logical arguments rooted in our experience of the operations of nature. Inductive reasoning about causes and effects helps the mind to grasp the essence or nature of things by a process of **intuition**. In this way, we come to know first principles, especially of essences, and also gain knowledge of their causes.

Aristotle approached questions about the natures of things through a study of the concept of substance, which he used to describe individual things that exist, such as this man, this horse, this dog. He defined a substance as that which has properties but is not itself a property (e.g., a dog has properties, such as a shaggy coat, but is not itself a property). Aristotle developed his view of substance by introducing his famous account of the four causes. He identified the material, formal, efficient, and final causes of an object (see **Aristotle's Four Causes**).

The notion of a final cause was especially significant because it raised the question of the purpose of an object, in addition to asking who made it or how it was made. Aristotle therefore introduced the notion of **teleology** into philosophy and science. We need to know why things exist, a question that can be asked of everything in nature, including plants and other **species** but also about man, an approach that led to the development of Aristotle's influential virtue theory of ethics. Moreover, it is a question we can study empirically.

The empirical nature of teleological inquiry is one of the reasons the concept became so interesting. Unlike Aristotle himself, later Christian thinkers developed the overall question raised by the concept of final cause, the question of design in the natural world and in the universe, the question of why nature exhibits teleological goals. It wasn't until 1,500 years later, after the development of the **scientific method** in **Galileo** and **Newton**, that final causes began to drop out of the discipline of science. But the teleological question, of course, did not go away, and it led eventually to clashes with the theory of evolution, especially to atheistic or naturalistic interpretations of it.

Aristotle's metaphysical views and his understanding of **causation** found further expression in his understanding of the nature of God. He argued that we need a cause to account for the eternity of motion in the world, and this cause is God, an argument that was a forerunner of the **cosmological argument**. He further held that God is the final cause of the universe rather than the efficient cause, because efficient causes are acted on and so are subject to change, but God (the "Unmoved Mover") is a perfect, unchanging being. He concluded that God must be a nonphysical or incorporeal being, because if God were made of matter, he would be subject to change and would also need a cause.

Later thinkers, including Thomas Aquinas, took up Aristotle's ideas, and consequently his views became very influential in the historical development of various Christian concepts, especially concerning the nature of God, design in nature, and the nature of the moral life.

Brendan Sweetman

REFERENCES AND RECOMMENDED READING

Aristotle. *Ethics; Metaphysics; Physics* (any edition).

Barnes, Jonathan. 2001. *Aristotle: A Very Short Introduction.* New York: Oxford.

Gilson, Etienne. *God and Philosophy.* New Haven, CT: Yale University Press.

Sweetman, Brendan. 2010. *Religion and Science: An Introduction.* New York: Continuum.

ARISTOTLE'S FOUR CAUSES. Aristotle's (384–322 BC) ideas on **causation** had a great influence on Western approaches to science, religion, and ethics. The metaphysical question "What is being?" or "What is substance?" led him to make a detailed study of the natures or essences of things. He asked commonsense questions about the nature of substances and their properties, how substances come into and go out of existence, how they change, and what their purpose is. Individual substances, he argued, consist of matter (the material out of which they are made) and form (the "arrangement" of the matter). For example, a table is made out of wood arranged in the form of a table. Change then is the process of bringing a potentiality in a substance to fulfillment; for example, an acorn has the potentiality to become an oak tree.

Aristotle then developed an account of the four causes as a way of elaborating his insights into the nature of things. The matter out of which an object is made is the material cause, and the arrangement of the matter can be said to be the formal cause. In addition, that which brings the object into existence is the efficient cause. There is also a final cause, which is the purpose (*telos*) of the object or what it is for. For example, the material cause of a vase is the clay, the efficient cause is the potter, the formal cause is the arrangement of the clay, and the final cause is a holder of liquid.

The notions of efficient cause and final cause were especially interesting in Aristotle's approach. While the question of efficient cause forces us to realize the contingency of all events in our universe, the notion of final cause focuses on the fact that all objects have a purpose, natural objects (a man, an acorn) as well as artificial objects (a table or a musical instrument). We can discover the purpose by examining objects empirically. Even though we may sometimes disagree about the *telos*, it is still true that there is a telos, and this is a key fact about nature.

The notion of **teleology** has important implications for our understanding of ourselves as human beings and of the universe. First, it raises the question of design in the universe, how things came to be the way they are and how they got their purpose. In addition, the notion of an efficient cause laid the groundwork for the argument that the universe cannot be the cause of itself, nor can its ultimate explanation come from within itself, a prominent argument in the Christian tradition. Instead, the universe needs an outside sustaining cause that is responsible for its existence, and this is God (though Aristotle himself concluded that God is the final, not the efficient, cause of the universe). Second, the question of everything having a nature prompted Aristotle to argue that there is a human nature consisting of traits and characteristics that, although part of our essence, are not merely biological. These traits include reason, free will, and the moral virtues; although latent, they must be brought to fruition by instruction, training, and the wisdom that comes with experience. This approach proved attractive because it provided a philosophical foundation for the moral life, which inspired many Western systems of education.

Aristotle's account of causation gradually slipped out of science after Newton, especially the formal and final causes, but the questions his account raises have remained among the most interesting in philosophy and theology. His account of human nature, also championed by Thomas Aquinas, was very influential in the development of **Christian ethics**. It led to clashes with later materialistic or reductionistic views of human nature and with various views of biological **determinism**, which became more prominent in the twentieth century in such thinkers as **Daniel Dennett** and **E. O. Wilson**.

Brendan Sweetman

REFERENCES AND RECOMMENDED READING

Aristotle. *Ethics; Metaphysics; Physics* (any edition).

Dudley, John. 2013. *Aristotle's Concept of Chance.* Albany: SUNY Press.

Gilson, Etienne. 1984. *From Aristotle to Darwin and Back Again.* San Francisco: Ignatius.

Johnson, M. R. 2008. *Aristotle on Teleology.* New York: Oxford University Press.

Sweetman, Brendan. 2010. *Religion and Science: An Introduction.* New York: Continuum.

ARTIFICIAL INTELLIGENCE. Artificial intelligence (AI) is a branch of computer science that seeks to develop computer systems and algorithms that replicate or mimic cognitive tasks typically ascribed to humans. Examples of such tasks include speech recognition (translation of spoken sounds to words), natural language processing (generation and comprehension of human-written languages), expert systems (computers that can answer questions about specialized knowledge areas), computer vision (comprehension of visual images), and data mining (discovery of patterns within large data sets).

Automation of such tasks has many practical advantages, including improving the usability of computers by humans, facilitating repetitive tasks for which humans are inaccurate or slow, and assisting humans with disabilities. Advances in AI have led to smartphones that accept voice commands, expert medical systems that help doctors diagnose diseases, and computer vision systems that assist the blind.

The goals of artificial intelligence as a field can be divided into those of *artificial general intelligence* (also known as "Strong AI") and those of *applied artificial intelligence* (also known as "Narrow AI"). Artificial general intelligence seeks to create thinking machines that can succeed in arbitrary cognitive tasks, effectively emulating all aspects of human cognition. In contrast, applied artificial intelligence more narrowly focuses on developing automated proficiency in specialized domains, such as chess playing or medicine. Applied artificial intelligence is widely viewed to be easier to define and has historically seen more decisive successes than the much more difficult problem of artificial general intelligence.

Artificial general intelligence was the original motivating inspiration for artificial intelligence as a field. One of its earliest characterizations comes from computer scientist Alan Turing, whose famous 1950 article titled "Computing Machinery and Intelligence" posed the question "Can machines think?" (Turing 1950). Since there continues to be no universally accepted scientific definition of exactly what comprises "intelligence," Turing adopted a more pragmatic approach, suggesting that if a machine's behavior is indistinguishable from a human's, it can be considered "intelligent" for practical purposes. He then challenged computer scientists to build a machine that demonstrates such "intelligence" by winning a game now known as the **Turing Test**.

In a Turing Test, a human interrogator types arbitrary questions into a computer terminal, which are answered by a human or a machine. The interrogator must decide whether or not the respondent is human. To pass the test, a computer respondent must successfully convince interrogators that it is human more than half the time. While there has been debate over whether any computer has ever passed such a test, and whether any computer that passes can actually be considered "intelligent," the test has nevertheless been a driving force in the development of new artificial intelligence advances since the 1950s.

Six years after Turing posed his challenge, computer scientist John McCarthy's 1956 Dartmouth Summer Research Project on Artificial Intelligence convened, birthing the term *artificial intelligence* and launching AI as a scientific discipline. Artificial general intelligence continued to be aggressively pursued throughout the 1960s; but in the 1970s and '80s, proponents suffered significant setbacks in public perception when overoptimistic predictions of their success went unfulfilled. For example, a 1970 *Life* magazine article quoted prominent AI researchers as predicting the creation of machines with general intelligence equal to humans in under two decades (Darrach 1970).

When it became clear that scientists had significantly underestimated the difficulty of achieving these objectives, the public became disillusioned with AI research, leading to underfunding of research for periods of time in the late 1970s, late '80s, and early '90s. These setbacks motivated many AI researchers to set and promote more attainable, pragmatic goals for AI research, leading to surges in applied artificial intelligence research.

Some prominent successes in applied artificial intelligence over the past few decades include the 1997 victory of IBM's chess-playing supercomputer, Deep Blue, over then-reigning world champion Garry Kasparov; the 2010 VisLab Intercontinental Autonomous Challenge, in which four driverless cars successfully drove from Parma, Italy, to Shanghai, China, with little or no human assistance; and the 2011 televised victory of IBM's *Jeopardy!*-playing supercomputer, Watson, over former human winners Brad Rutter and Ken Jennings. In each case, a machine demonstrated human-like "intelligence" in a specialized domain (chess, driving, and trivia, respectively). Artificial Intelligence advances have also yielded numerous successful commercial applications, such as the Siri voice-recognition **technology** introduced in Apple iPhones in 2010, Amazon's data mining–based product suggestion system, and the page-ranking algorithm behind Google's Internet search engine. After its *Jeopardy!* win, IBM's Watson was subsequently repurposed as an expert medical system that now offers diagnostic advice to doctors and nurses.

The engineering foundations for most artificial intelligence algorithms are based on the **mathematics** of **probability**, **statistics**, and search. For instance, artificial neural networks use probability to approximate data streams as compositions of functions. As the network observes more data, the functions adapt to better predict future data. As its predictions improve, it effectively learns new concepts for which it was not preprogrammed. For example, if the data are pictures or speech, the network might learn to recognize certain objects or words. Search algorithms take an alternative (but complementary) approach, exhaustively exploring a space of possible solutions in a manner that resembles traversing a maze. For example, **logic** programs answer queries by searching a knowledge base of inference rules. Given the query "Do pigs fly?" a logic program whose knowledge base contains the rules "Pigs lack wings," and "Flying animals have wings" would infer that "Pigs do not fly." Some learning algorithms, such as artificial neural networks, are inspired by known biological processes, while others have purely mathematical bases that do not necessarily resemble any methodology by which humans solve problems.

Since the late 1800s, fiction writers and filmmakers have more narrowly associated the term *artificial intelligence* with artificial consciousness or *self-awareness*. Samuel Butler's "Darwin among the Machines" (1863) hypothesized that machines might one day develop **consciousness**. Isaac Asimov's influential Robot series of short stories (c. 1939–1990, later adapted to the 1999 and 2004 films *Bicentennial Man* and *I, Robot*) explored various philosophical and moral implications of self-aware machines. Philip K. Dick's 1968 novel *Do Androids Dream of Electric Sheep?* (later adapted to the 1982 film *Blade Runner*), depicts dangerous, self-aware androids nearly indistinguishable from humans. The television series *Star Trek: The Next Generation* (1987–94) featured a self-aware android named Data (played by Brent Spiner) as one of the star characters.

In the sciences, the nature and definition of consciousness (in humans or machines) continues to be a subject of considerable debate among philosophers, cognitive psychologists, and neurologists. Philosopher David Chalmers distinguishes the "easy problem of consciousness," which defines consciousness purely in terms of functional input-output behaviors expressible as computations, from the "hard problem of consciousness," which considers subjective experience (phenomenology) as an essential ingredient in consciousness (Chalmers 1995). While computers can presently be programmed to address the "easy problem" by imitating humans to various degrees, it remains unclear whether machines will ever have the subjective experiences pursuant to the "hard problem of consciousness."

Kevin W. Hamlen

REFERENCES AND RECOMMEND READING

Chalmers, D. J. 1995. "Facing Up to the Problem of Consciousness." *Journal of Consciousness Studies* 2 (3): 200–219.
Darrach, B. 1970. "Meet Shaky: The First Electronic Person." *Life* November 20:58B–68.
Turing, A. M. 1950. "Computing Machinery and Intelligence." *Mind* 59:433–60.

ASTROLOGY. Astrology is a belief system that holds that the fates of individuals and the course of human events are determined or strongly influenced by the position and motion of various celestial bodies. According to this **paradigm**, an astrologer can predict future human affairs by calculating the location of the stars and planets in the sky. However, most scientists regard astrology—even though it is an ancient and highly developed theory, claiming millions of present-day adherents—as at best a pseudoscience or at worst a superstition.

This is in contrast to **astronomy**, which is accepted by the scientific community as a valid science that has been verified by rigorous testing (Eysenck and Nias 1982). Moreover, astrology is repudiated by many Christian faith traditions that identify astrology with the practice of divination, a sin that is expressly prohibited by Old Testament commandments (see, e.g., Deut. 4:19; 18:10) and disparaged in the New Testament as well (Acts 16:16).

Nevertheless, some practitioners continue to insist that astrology is both a science (Gauquelin 1955) and a practice embedded in the Bible that is compatible with Christian faith. The scientific claims are based on reported correlations of celestial phenomena with sampled terrestrial events, studies that have been severely criticized by mainstream scientists as lacking any statistical validity. Astrology, furthermore, has the appearance of scientific rigor because its practice requires the precise computation of the position of the sun and planets relative to the zodiacal houses of the 12 constellations that lie around the ecliptic along which the sun and planets appear to move in the sky.

Despite this astrological connection with celestial mechanics and astronomy, scientists have verified only the extremely weak effect of gravity on terrestrial objects such as that which causes the ocean tides. No other creditable influence of celestial bodies on human affairs has been established.

Most critiques of astrology on biblical grounds decry the lack of faith in God's **providence** that underlies any desire to predict the future by special astral knowledge. Moreover, the fatalistic **determinism** that is a fundamental premise of astrology, in which our destinies are written in the stars, undermines hope and treats **prayer** as a futile activity since all human events are fated.

Notwithstanding scriptural opprobrium, the Bible does document evidence of ancient astrology that was not "regarded as separate [from astronomy] before the end of the Renaissance and certainly not in Ancient Mesopotamia" (Koch-Westenholz 1995, 21). Various "signs in the heavens" were freighted with portent, often ominous, both in the Old Testament and the New. In Acts 2:20 Peter quotes in his Pentecost sermon the dire prophecy found in Joel 2:31, "The sun will be turned to darkness and the *moon to blood* before the coming of the great and glorious day of the Lord." The phrase "moon turned to blood" generally is understood to refer to a lunar eclipse.

In the first century AD, Jewish historian Philo of Alexandria (Yonge 1854) discussed astrological beliefs: "Our Rabbis taught, When the sun is in eclipse it is a bad omen for idolaters; when the moon is in eclipse, it is a bad omen for Israel" (Babylonian Talmud Sukkah 29a). Humphreys and Waddington (1989) underscored the significance of the blood moon in their chronology of the crucifixion of Jesus of Nazareth. They argued that on one of the most probable dates for the crucifixion, the moon rose partially eclipsed in Jerusalem, as the gospel narrative implies.

In Matthew 2 magi "from the east" follow a "star" to Judea seeking the one born King of the Jews. Many scholars argue that these magi are identical to the Chaldean astronomers/astrologers mentioned repeatedly in the book of Daniel during Israel's captivity in Babylon (Ferrari-D'Occhieppo 1989). Thus, while not embraced as a means of divination, ancient astrology seems to be accepted as a cultural given in the Bible. Moreover, modern astronomy owes much to the ancient Babylonian practice of observational astrology in which meticulous celestial almanacs on durable clay tablets recorded the correlation between hepatoscopy (liver examinations of sacrificial animals), notable heavenly alignments, and the occurrence of unwelcome terrestrial events.

Samuel E. Matteson

REFERENCES AND RECOMMENDED READING

Babylonian Talmud. Sukkah 29a. Judeo-Christian Research. (Accessed August 26, 2016) http://juchre.org/talmud/sukkah/sukkah2.htm#29a.

Eysenck, H. J., and D. K. B. Nias. 1982. *Astrology: Science or Superstition?* New York: Penguin.

Ferrari-D'Occhieppo, Konradin. 1989. "The Star of the Magi and Babylonian Astronomy." In *Chronos, Kairos, Christos: Nativity and Chronological Studies Presented to Jack Finegan*, ed. Jerry Vardaman and Edwin M. Yamauchi. Winona Lake, IN: Eisenbrauns.

Gauquelin, Michel. 1955. *L'influence des astres* (The Influence of the Stars). Paris: Du dauphin.

Koch-Westenholz, Ulla. 1995. *Mesopotamian Astrology: An Introduction to Babylonian and Assyrian Celestial Divination*. Copenhagen: Tusculanum, University of Copenhagen. www.academia.edu/441807/Mesopotamian_astrology_an_introduction_to_Babylonian_and_Assyrian_celestial_divination.

Humphreys, Colin J., and W. G. Waddington. 1989. "Astronomy and the Date of the Crucifixion." In *Chronos, Kairos, Christos: Nativity and Chronological Studies Presented to Jack Finegan*, ed. Jerry Vardaman and Edwin M. Yamauchi. Winona Lake, IN: Eisenbrauns.

Yonge, C. D. 1854. In "De Providentia II, Book 39." *The Works of Philo Judaeus*. London: H. G. Bohn. www.earlychristianwritings.com/yonge/book39.html.

ASTRONOMY. Astronomy is the physical science that describes the identity, nature, and physical interactions of heavenly bodies such as planets, stars, galaxies, and other celestial objects. From ancient times to the present, people have attempted to make sense of what they observe in the heavens. In the Bible one finds allusions to contemporaneous ancient astronomical concepts.

A literalistic reading of the text using the **worldview of Aristotle** led many within the church to conclude that the earth is the center of the universe. In the sixteenth century, **Copernicus** proposed a sun-centered cosmic model; a century later, **Galileo** corroborated this model based on his celestial observations. His championing of this view infamously brought him into conflict with the hierarchy of the Catholic Church.

Some today challenge the doctrine of the Bible's inerrancy because they see Galileo's historic struggle as symptomatic of a wide disparity between the message of the Bible and the results of astronomy. Many astronomers who adhere to the Christian faith, however, assert that different knowledge is found in the book of science and the book of faith; the "two books" are thus complementary, not contradictory.

Astronomy has been criticized by some Christians because

it is a "historical" science in which very few directly controlled experiments can be performed. In such a discipline, one proceeds to hypothesize a mechanism for a celestial phenomenon and to infer what one should observe. The predictions, often quantitative—when compared to observations—assess the validity of the hypotheses. For example, the size of the visible universe can be deduced by a sequence of observations: the size of the earth was determined in antiquity by observing the difference in the angle of sunlight at two different points on the earth at the same time.

From this **information**, astronomers determined the diameter of the earth, a fact that provided a baseline for astronomers to compute the distance to the sun using the method of parallax (i.e., different observational positions or angles to arrive at these precise measurements). Subsequently, knowledge of the diameter of the earth's orbit permitted scientists to calculate the distance to the nearest stars by their parallax, but many "fixed" stars are too far away to exhibit measurable parallax, and their distances were unknown until variable stars like those in the constellation Cepheus provided an alternative method of estimating their intrinsic brightness and thus distance. This information provided the "measuring stick" to extend measurements to ever greater distances.

When Edwin Hubble observed that the spectra of the light from galaxies was "red shifted" due to their motion, he was able to work out the relationship between their "red shift" and their distance. He was astonished to conclude that the universe is of immense size and of astounding age. Refinements in Hubble's methods made over the decades suggest that the universe's size is about 13.8 billion light-years, that is, the light has been traveling to us for billions of years.

These conclusions do indeed challenge certain interpretations of Scripture that hold that the universe is only a few thousand years old, in the same way that the Copernican crisis challenged geocentric interpretations 500 years ago.

Samuel E. Matteson

REFERENCES AND RECOMMENDED READING

Hummel, Charles E. 1986. *The Galileo Connection*. Downers Grove, IL: InterVarsity.
Ross, Hugh. 2008. *Why the Universe Is the Way It Is*. Grand Rapids: Baker.

ATOMISM. Atomism holds that matter consists of small particles (atoms) instead of being infinitely divisible. Greek atomism arose when Leucippus and Democritus (fifth century BC) postulated that the cosmos consists of indivisible uncreated atoms randomly moving in a void. Epicurus later added the concept of a random swerve, and he embedded atomism in a materialist philosophy intended to free men from religion by holding that the **soul**, comprised of atoms, dissociates at **death**.

Because ancient atomism was speculative and associated with **providence**-denying **materialism**, some early Christian writers tended toward dismissing atomism when critiquing the materialism of which it formed a part. Nevertheless, all avoided tying Christianity to particular material conceptions of matter, and some (Justin Martyr, Lactantius) were open to a suitably modified atomism.

Thus the church preserved and never condemned atomism, but it fell into disfavor relative to two things: first, **Aristotle**'s hylomorphism (the view that substance [*ousia*] was comprised of matter [*hylē*] and form [*morphē*]—for example, the soul is the form of the body, and the body, the soul's matter) and, second, his five-element theory (earth, water, air, fire, and ether). Atomism was not seriously considered by Christians in the early Middle Ages, during which time Islam developed a philosophical or dialectical argument (kalam) that defended God's existence and character using an atomism of matter and time.

The late medieval resurgence of learning renewed European interest in atoms and void, primarily in relation to God's power in creation and the world's eternality. Scholastic efforts to theologically rehabilitate atomism, the anti-Aristotelianism of Étienne Tempier's 1227 condemnation, and Henry of Harclay's refutation of Aristotle's antiatomism arguments promoted consideration of atomism while defining theologically appropriate limits.

Early modern atomists include **Copernicus**, **Francis Bacon**, **Galileo**, and Daniel Sennert, who applied atomism to chemistry. Pierre Gassendi theologically rehabilitated atomism while promoting a Christianized Epicureanism; Gassendi's atoms accommodated providence, free will, and divine creation. **Robert Boyle**'s corpuscular (divisible atom) view of matter also distinguished between the material and spiritual. Gassendi's and Boyle's atoms were passive, with God being the primary cause of their motion and chemical properties. Later **Isaac Newton** reconceptualized atoms as centers of force, and Roger Boscovitch proposed that atoms attract at intermediate distances and repel at short ones, an idea the Unitarian chemist Joseph Priestley transformed to obliterate material-spiritual distinctions altogether.

Boyle's emphasis on quantitative measurements proved

decisive when Antione Lavoisier, Joseph Proust, and John Dalton discovered the laws of mass conservation, constant proportions, and multiple proportions. Dalton employed these to argue that hard indivisible atoms combine to give compounds. In associating atom types with elements, Dalton rejected simple primordial atoms that generate elements by combination. Proust, who looked to natural simplicity as evidence of divine design, in turn proposed that atoms were aggregates of hydrogen (1834).

Chemists tended to regard atoms as useful fictions even after Dalton's 1803 proposal, until work in electrolysis, organic stereochemistry, and the periodic table (following the acceptance of Avogadro's hypothesis that equal volumes of gases contain equal numbers of particles) lent credence to their real existence. In addition, **Einstein**'s 1903 explanation of Brownian motion in terms of molecular motions convinced scientists of atoms' reality.

By then, J. J. Thompson's experiments with cathode rays had already indicated that atoms were divisible. Rutherford's gold foil experiment shortly led to the recognition that atoms consist of a nucleus surrounded by electrons, while **Niels Bohr** and others developed a quantum mechanical model that described the electrons' behavior using probabilistic wavelike orbitals—an idea that itself occasioned philosophical and theological reflection.

Atomic-molecular theory currently is central to science even as particle physicists continue probing matter's subatomic structure. It is rarely accorded theological significance, in part ironically because of John Tyndall's unsuccessful attempt to use atomism to promote **conflict thesis** thinking, pitting religion against science (1874; Turner 1993), and despite physicist **Victor Stenger**'s (2013) claim it validates atheism.

Stephen Contakes

REFERENCES AND RECOMMENDED READING

Ashworth, William B., Jr. 2003. "Christianity and the Mechanistic Universe." In *When Science and Christianity Meet*, ed. David C. Lindberg and Ronald L. Numbers, 61–84. Chicago: University of Chicago Press.

Aurélien, Robert. 2011. "Atomism." In *Encyclopedia of Medieval Philosophy: Philosophy between 500 and 1500*, ed. Henrik Lagerlund, 122–25. Dordrecht and New York: Springer.

Berryman, Sylvia. 2011. "Ancient Atomism." In *Stanford Encyclopedia of Philosophy*, ed. Edward N. Zalta. Winter. http://plato.stanford.edu/archives/win2011/entries/atomism-ancient/.

Brush, Stephen G. 1983. *Statistical Physics and the Atomic Theory of Matter: From Boyle and Newton to Landau and Onsager*. Princeton Series in Physics. Princeton, NJ: Princeton University Press.

Chalmers, A. F. 2009. *The Scientist's Atom and the Philosopher's Stone: How Science Succeeded and Philosophy Failed to Gain Knowledge of Atoms*. Boston Studies in the Philosophy of Science. Dordrecht and New York: Springer.

Chalmers, Alan. 2012. "Atomism from the 17th to the 20th Century." *Stanford Encyclopedia of Philosophy*, ed. Edward N. Zalta. Winter. http://plato.stanford.edu/archives/win2012/entries/atomism-modern/.

Charleton, Walter, Pierre Gassendi, and Robert Hugh Kargon. 1966. *Physiologia Epicuro-Gassendo-Charltoniana*. New York: Johnson Reprint.

Clericuzio, Antonio. 2000. *Elements, Principles, and Corpuscles: A Study of Atomism and Chemistry in the Seventeenth Century*. Archives Internationales D'histoire Des Idées (International Archives of the History of Ideas). Dordrecht: Kluwer Academic.

Danton, B. Sailor. 1964. "Moses and Atomism." *Journal of the History of Ideas* 25 (1): 3–16.

Dijksterhuis, E. J. 1969. *The Mechanization of the World Picture* [in English]. London and New York: Oxford University Press.

Fisher, Saul. 2005. *Pierre Gassendi's Philosophy and Science: Atomism for Empiricists*. Brill's Studies in Intellectual History. Leiden: Brill.

Funkenstein, Amos. 1986. *Theology and the Scientific Imagination from the Middle Ages to the Seventeenth Century*. Princeton, NJ: Princeton University Press.

Furley, David J. 1987. *The Greek Cosmologists*. Vol. 1. *The Formation of Atomic Theory and Its Earliest Critics*. Cambridge: Cambridge University Press.

Gregory, Joshua Craven. 1931. *A Short History of Atomism, from Democritus to Bohr*. London: A. & C. Black.

Grellard, Christophe, and Robert Aurélien. 2009. *Atomism in Late Medieval Philosophy and Theology*. History of Science and Medicine Library. Leiden: Brill.

Haas, Jack W., Jr. 2007. "Atoms and Atheism: The Changing Ways That Christians Have Viewed the Nature of Matter." American Scientific Affiliation. June. www.asa3.org/ASA/topics/Physical%20Science/atomism.html.

Henry, John. 1982. "Atomism and Eschatology: Catholicism and Natural Philosophy in the Interregnum." *British Journal for the History of Science* 15 (3): 211–39.

———. 2000. "Atomism." In *The History of Science and Religion in the Western Tradition: An Encyclopedia*, ed. G. Ferngren, E. J. Larson, and D. W. Amundsen. New York: Garland.

Hunter, Michael Cyril William. 2010. *Boyle: Between God and Science*. New Haven, CT: Yale University Press.

Jacob, H. R. 1978. "Boyle's Atomism and the Restoration Assault on Pagan Naturalism." *Social Studies in Science* 8 (2): 211–33.

Kaiser, Christopher B. 1991. *Creation and the History of Science*. The History of Christian Theology. Grand Rapids: Eerdmans.

Kargon, Robert Hugh. 1966. *Atomism in England from Hariot to Newton*. Oxford: Clarendon.

Kubbinga, Henk. 1998. "Atomisme, Molécularisme Et Déterminisme." In *The Interplay between Scientific and Theological Worldviews*, ed. Niels Henrik Gregersen, Ulf Görman, and Christoph Wassermann. Studies in Science and Theology, 2:100–109. Geneva: Labor et Fides.

Leucippus and Democritus. 1999. *The Atomists, Leucippus and Democritus: Fragments: A Text and Translation with a Commentary*, trans. C. C. W. Taylor. The Phoenix Presocratics. Toronto: University of Toronto Press, 1999.

Lüthy, Christoph Herbert, John Emery Murdoch, and William R. Newman. 2001. *Late Medieval and Early Modern Corpuscular Matter Theories*. Medieval and Early Modern Science. Leiden: Brill.

Newman, William Royall. 2006. *Atoms and Alchemy: Chymistry and the Experimental Origins of the Scientific Revolution*. Chicago: University of Chicago Press.

Osler, Margaret J. 2002. *Divine Will and the Mechanical Philosophy: Gassendi and Descartes on Contingency and Necessity in the Created World*. Cambridge: Cambridge University Press.

Prout, William. 1834. *Chemistry, Meteorology, and the Function of Digestion, Considered with Reference to Natural Theology*. The Bridgewater Treatises on the Power, Wisdom and Goodness of God as Manifested in the Creation. London: Pickering.

Pullman, Bernard. 1998. *The Atom in the History of Human Thought* [trans. from the French, *L'atome dans l'histoire de la pensée humain*]. New York: Oxford University Press.

Pyle, Andrew. 1997. *Atomism and Its Critics: From Democritus to Newton*. Bristol: Thoemmes.

Sedley, D. N. 2007. *Creationism and Its Critics in Antiquity*. Sather Classical Lectures. Berkeley: University of California Press.

Stenger, Victor J. 2013. *God and the Atom*. Amherst, NY: Prometheus.

Turner, Frank M. 1993. "Ancient Materialism and Modern Science: Lucretius among the Victorians." In *Contesting Cultural Authority : Essays in Victorian Intellectual Life*, 262–83. Cambridge: Cambridge University Press.

Tyndall, John. 1874. *Address Delivered before the British Association Assembled at Belfast*. Rev. ed. New York: Appleton.

Whyte, Lancelot Law. 1961. *Essay on Atomism, from Democritus to 1960*. Middletown, CT: Wesleyan University Press.

ATRAHASIS. *Atrahasis* is an ancient Mesopotamian myth that, like Genesis 1–11, contains both a creation account as well as a flood story. As such, it, along with **Enuma Elish** has provided **information** to re-create the cultural background to the biblical text. The name *Atrahasis* (meaning "exceedingly wise") comes from the name of the flood hero in the story.

The story is known from cuneiform tablets dated to the Old Babylonian period in the first half of the second millennium BC (which are copies of even earlier sources that we do not have) and then from tablets from the neo-Assyrian period about 1,000 years later. We do not have the entire story, but what we have is of immense importance for the study of the early chapters of Genesis, particularly the creation and flood accounts.

When the narrative opens, the lesser gods were digging irrigation canals. The work was hard, and they decided to go on strike, refusing to work and complaining to their divine foreman, the god Enlil. After some hesitation, Enlil then orders the divine midwife, Belet-ili, to create human beings who will replace the lesser gods in their dreary labor. She enlists the god of wisdom Enki (also known as Ea), who then orders the **death** of a god, Aw-ilum. He then mixes the blood of the slaughtered god with clay from the earth, after which all the gods spit in the mixture, thus creating humanity.

From this first creation, humanity multiplies, and their noise disturbs the gods, who try to reduce their population. Enlil then decides to take the extreme measure of sending a flood to destroy all humans. The flood story that follows is brief and fragmented but seems to be similar to the longer account given in the **Gilgamesh Epic**. The god Ea warns his devotee Atrahasis and instructs him to build an ark and bring the animals on board, and thus he survives the flood. After the flood, the gods, now hungry after being deprived of the food supplied by the animal sacrifices of humans, are relieved that Enlil's impulsive action is not successful. The text ends by considering less extreme methods by which the gods can control human population.

The story of *Atrahasis* has piqued the interest of biblical scholars because of its connection with the primeval history of Genesis 1–11, particularly the accounts of the creation of humans and the flood story. Indeed, the very combination of a creation and a flood story in a single composition has drawn comparison between the two.

There are both similarities and differences between *Atrahasis* and its biblical parallel. Both describe the creation of human beings from both a divine component as well as an earthly one. While the latter is very similar (the dust in Gen. 2:7 and the clay in *Atrahasis*), the difference in the divine component is significant. While the biblical account describes God breathing on the dust to produce the first human, *Atrahasis* speaks of the blood of a lesser god and the spit of the assembly of gods. The former thus has a dignified portrait of humanity's origins, while the latter is one of contempt. In both, humans were created to work, but again in the biblical account work is exalted since God instructs humans to "work" and "take care of" (or "guard") the garden (Gen. 2:15), while in *Atrahasis* the gods create humans to do the job of digging the irrigation ditches, which the lesser gods found undesirable.

When it comes to **the flood** story, again there are similarities and differences. *Atrahasis* (like the *Gilgamesh Epic*) provides different divine motivations for the flood. In the biblical text, it is human sin (Gen. 6:5–7), and in *Atrahasis* the problem is overpopulation and disturbing noise. Contra the Babylonian version, God in the Bible does not want to completely eradicate humanity, but to start again from the righteous Noah and his family.

Perhaps the most dramatic and important difference between *Atrahasis* and the biblical accounts of creation and flood is on their respective understanding of deity. In *Atrahasis*, there are multiple gods often working at cross-purposes or in open conflict. In the biblical account, there is only one God, and he creates humans and then judges them for their moral sin.

Scholars debate over why there are similarities and differences between the biblical and ancient Near Eastern creation and flood stories. The written account of *Atrahasis* is older (and Sumerian flood stories are even older) than the written account in Genesis, though both are likely based on even older oral and perhaps written sources. Perhaps all of these accounts go back to an original event of a major deluge (see

Genesis Flood and Geology, The; also see **Genesis Flood** on the debate whether the biblical account is based on a global or local flood), and traditions descended from the event in more than one tradition history. Of course, many Jews and Christians would defend the idea that the biblical account is reliable, especially from a theological point of view. Others might suggest that the ancient Near Eastern creation and flood tradition provided a template for the biblical account's own theological interpretation of these events.

Tremper Longman III

REFERENCES AND RECOMMENDED READING

Foster, B. R. 1997. "The Epic of Creation." In *The Context of Scripture*, 1:450–53. Leiden: Brill.
Lambert, W. G., and A. R. Millard. (1969) 1999. *Atra-Hasis: The Babylonian Story of the Flood*. Winona Lake, IN: Eisenbrauns.
Sparks, K. L. 2005. *Ancient Texts for the Study of the Hebrew Bible: A Guide to the Background Literature*, 314–15. Peabody, MA: Hendrickson.
Wenham, G. J. 2015. *Rethinking Genesis 1–11: Gateway to the Bible*. Eugene, OR: Cascade.

AUGUSTINE. Arguably the greatest of the church fathers, Augustine of Hippo (AD 354–430) lived more than 1,000 years before the emergence of the **Scientific Revolution** in Europe. Yet he addressed a number of critical philosophical and theological issues in his voluminous writings that anticipated historic Christianity's relationship to science.

Creation ex Nihilo

"Therefore you must have created them from nothing, the one great, the other small. For there is nothing that you cannot do. You are good and all that you make must be good, both the great Heaven of Heavens and this little earth. You were, and besides you nothing was. From nothing, then, you created heaven and earth" (Augustine 1992, 384–85 [7.7]).

Augustine reasoned that God created the world ex nihilo (Lat., literally "out of nothing" or "from nothing"). This means that God created the universe without recourse to anything but his infinite wisdom and awesome power. God called the world into existence not from preexistent matter, energy, or some other "stuff," but literally out of or from nothing. There was nothing but God, and he alone created the universe (including matter, energy, space, and time). Augustine's fifth-century cosmological thinking concerning the universe's origin seems amazingly similar to twenty-first-century big bang cosmology.

Theory of Time

"You are the Maker of all time. If, then, there was any time before you made heaven and earth, how can anyone say that you were idle? You must have made that time, for time could not elapse before you made it" (Augustine 1992, 263 [11.13]).

Augustine developed a thought-provoking concept of time. He argued that time itself is part of the created order and is uniquely apprehended through the human mind (the past in memory, the present in recognition, and the future in expectation). Philosophical skeptic **Bertrand Russell** once said Augustine's theory of time was superior to that of **Immanuel Kant**'s subjective theory. The idea that time began simultaneously with the beginning of the physical universe is again remarkably consistent with the view held by most modern cosmologists.

Two-Books Revelation

"In your great wisdom you, who are our God, speak to us of these things in your Book, the **firmament** made by you" (Augustine 1992, 326 [13.18]).

Augustine utilized the common phraseology known in Christian theology as the two-books theory. This dual view of **revelation** asserts that God is the author of both the figurative book of nature (God's created world) and the literal book of Scripture (God's written Word). Augustine insisted that when properly interpreted, the two books cohere. Yet he warned in his work the *Literal Meaning of Genesis* of the danger of non-Christians hearing Christians who affirm the book of Scripture nevertheless talking nonsense about matters relating to the book of nature. This cautionary note of the need to integrate the two books has implications today for Christians engaged in science-faith dialogues.

Faith Seeking Understanding

"Therefore do not seek to understand in order to believe, but believe that thou mayest understand" (Augustine 1995, 184).

Augustine's *Crede, ut intelligas* (Lat., "Believe in order that you may understand") influenced centuries of Christian thinkers on the relationship between faith and reason. For Augustine, faith (trust in a reliable source) is an indispensable element in knowledge. He argued that one must believe in something in order to know anything. Knowledge begins with faith, which provides a foundation for knowledge. Faith in itself is indirect knowledge (like testimony or authority). While faith comes first in time, knowledge comes first in importance. Faith and reason do not conflict but instead complement each other.

Augustine saw the natural world as real and objective, a notion that was not lost on later Christian thinking when it came to the natural sciences.

Kenneth Richard Samples

REFERENCES AND RECOMMENDED READING

Augustine. 1992. *Confessions.* New York: Barnes & Noble.
———. 1995. "Tractates on the Gospel of John." In *Nicene and Post-Nicene Fathers*, ed. Philip Schaff. Peabody, MA: Hendrickson.
Fitzgerald, Allan D. 1999. *Augustine through the Ages.* Grand Rapids: Eerdmans.

AYALA, FRANCISCO. Francisco Ayala (1934–) is a leading American evolutionary geneticist. Ordained as a Dominican priest in Madrid, Spain, in 1960, Ayala went on to study for a PhD under Theodosius Dobzhansky at Columbia University. Dobzhansky was one of the leading geneticists responsible for the "**neo-Darwinian synthesis**." When Ayala began his work, the basic elements of the "synthesis" had been put firmly in place. Ideas from disparate subdisciplines of biology had been brought together along with mathematical theory to provide a framework that coherently demonstrated the basic mechanics of the evolutionary process. The next stage in evolutionary biology as Ayala started off was to develop the scientific tools to extend studies of the evolutionary mechanism to the level of molecules — **DNA** and proteins. His success in this work contributed significantly to the understanding of evolutionary biology at increasingly sophisticated levels.

Besides being a leading biologist — he is a member of the National Academy of Science, the American Academy of Science, a former president of the American Association for the Advancement of Science, and the winner of the National Medal of Science — Ayala has been a leading spokesperson at the interface between science and religion. He has long argued that there need not be a conflict between religion and science. "Science and religion are two different ways of looking at the world. Science deals with the constitution of matter and the expansion of the galaxies and the origin of **species** and adaptation. Religion has to do with a belief in a supreme being and our values and how we should relate to one another. So they deal with different matters, which are definitely compatible in principle" (Loose 2013).

Ayala has been particularly outspoken in his view that **intelligent design** is not compatible with good Christian theology. He suggests many examples of cases where the structure of components of the human body is poorly designed. The human jaw, for example, is not big enough for our teeth, hence the need to remove the wisdom teeth. The process of cell division, he further points out, is so inefficient that it results in the spontaneous abortion of about 20 percent of all human pregnancies. He calls the notion of intelligent design blasphemy (Ayala 2006) and justifies this assertion based on the many cases of poor design. An all-loving Creator would not design life in this way, he reasons. He also considers the work of proponents of the intelligent design movement to be unscientific.

Ayala served as an expert science witness in two of the most important trials that tested the legality of creationism in the science classroom in the twentieth century. One was in the state of Arkansas (1981) and the other in Louisiana (1987). In response to events surrounding the Arkansas trial, he said, "What was at stake was not a particular branch of science, but the survival of rationality in this country. If we allowed the **Book of Genesis** to be taught as science, that would be as bad for science as it would be for religion" ("Fact Sheet—Francisco J. Ayala" 2010).

In 2010 Ayala was awarded the highly prestigious Templeton Award, given annually to "a living person who has made an exceptional contribution to affirming life's spiritual dimension, whether through insight, discovery, or practical works."

Darrel R. Falk

REFERENCES AND RECOMMENDED READING

Ayala, Francisco J. 2006. "The Blasphemy of Intelligent Design." *History and Philosophy of the Life Sciences* 28:409–21.
———. 2007. *Darwin's Gift to Science and Religion.* Washington, DC: Joseph Henry.
———. 2010. *Am I a Monkey? Six Big Questions about Evolution.* Baltimore: Johns Hopkins University Press.
Ayala, Francisco J., and John C. Avise, eds. 2014. *Readings in Evolutionary Biology.* Baltimore: Johns Hopkins University Press.
"Fact Sheet—Francisco J. Ayala." 2010. Templeton Prize. www.templetonprize.org/pdfs/2010_prize/A-FactSheet.pdf.
Loose, Terrence. 2013. "Interview with Francisco J. Ayala." *Coast Magazine.* February 27. www.coastmagazine.com/articles/ayala–2459—.html.

B

BACON, FRANCIS. Sir Francis Bacon (1561–1626) was the Lord Chancellor under King James I of England before he was dismissed for corruption. He wrote voluminously on philosophy and politics. Although his scientific methods were of little practical value, he enjoyed considerable repute as a founding father of the empirical tradition of science.

Life

Bacon was born to well-to-do parents in London and trained as a barrister. Under the reign of Elizabeth I, he was not successful in his ambitions to achieve high office but became a favorite of her successor, James I, who created him Viscount St. Alban in 1621. However, even though he eventually became Lord Chancellor, Bacon's wealth never matched his lifestyle. In 1621 he was convicted of taking bribes to supplement his income in the cases where he was a judge. This led to him being stripped of his office. Thereafter, he devoted himself to his philosophical writing and was very heavily in debt when he died in 1626. It is likely that he died from pneumonia, although the story that he contracted the illness from an experiment to find out if snow might preserve a chicken is apocryphal (Henry 2008, 41).

Works

Bacon's most famous work was *New Atlantis*, part of the genre of Utopian writing that set out the workings of a perfect society. *New Atlantis* was supposed to be a society based on reason and empirical science, but like many such visions, it would have been decidedly illiberal in practice.

His scientific method consisted of gathering a vast amount of data from which general principles were supposed to be distilled. However, his own investigations tended to be unfocused and his methodology has not been influential as a way of generating new knowledge. Nonetheless, his insistence that science must be based on empirical investigation and not just dry theorizing meant that he was celebrated by early members of the Royal Society in London. It was this lionization by the generation of Newton, Boyle, and Hook that has preserved Bacon's own reputation to the present day. He was also one of the first to recognize that science could produce considerable material benefits even though he lived in an era when it lacked many practical applications.

Bacon's *Novum Organum* (New Method) was intended to be a complete program for the scientific investigation of the world. It was written in deliberate opposition to the rationalism of **Aristotle**'s logical works (collectively called the *Organum*) and provided an empirical alternative. The *Novum Organum* formed a part of a much larger scientific manifesto called the *Great Instauration,* which was left unfulfilled at Bacon's death.

Like many of his contemporaries, Bacon found ample evidence for the work of God in nature. He was a trenchant critic of atheism, noting that a "little philosophy inclineth man's mind to atheism; but depth in philosophy bringeth men's minds about to religion" (Bacon 2008, 371). He also railed against Catholicism and believed that one of the reasons that science was a useful servant to Christianity was because it could debunk "popish superstition." In this vein, Bacon disparaged the Middle Ages and was among the earliest proponents of the myth that the medieval church taught that the earth is flat.

James Hannam

REFERENCES AND RECOMMENDED READING

Bacon, Francis. 2008. *The Major Works*. Oxford: Oxford University Press.
Henry, John. 2008. *Knowledge Is Power: How Magic, the Government and an Apocalyptic Vision Helped Francis Bacon to Create Modern Science.* London: Icon.
Peltonen, Markku, ed. 1996. *The Cambridge Companion to Bacon.* Cambridge: Cambridge University Press.

BARBOUR, IAN. Ian Barbour (1923–2013) arguably did more than anyone else to create the modern dialogue between science and religion. His groundbreaking book, *Issues in Science and Religion* (Barbour 1966), showed scientists and scholars how to think about science and religion both historically and in our own day, while identifying major points of contact and fairly evaluating alternative perspectives on each.

He famously delineated four approaches to "relating science and religion" (Barbour 1990, 3) that have inspired mountains of scholarly work by others and helped a generation of thinkers come to grips with questions and topics that otherwise would have been all but forbidden in the academic community. Courses about science and religion are now taught at hundreds (perhaps thousands) of colleges, universities, and seminaries around the world. Although financial support and encouragement from the **John Templeton Foundation** is partly responsible for the explosion of interest in such courses, the influence of Barbour ultimately lies behind it: he made it academically respectable to speak about science and religion in the same breath.

Barbour was born in Beijing, China, where his Presbyterian father and Episcopalian mother taught at Yenching University—an institution that the Communists closed in 1952 because of its Christian roots, folding parts of it into Peking University and Tsinghua University. His much-traveled youth included three years at a Quaker boarding school in England. He earned a degree in **physics** at another Quaker institution, Swarthmore College, and spent an influential summer at a Quaker work camp. Graduating in the middle of World War II, Barbour registered as a conscientious objector and devoted three years to alternative service. During the Cold War, he completed a doctorate in physics at the University of Chicago, studying with Enrico Fermi and Edward Teller. He later added a degree from Yale Divinity School.

Yearning to teach the liberal arts, Barbour taught both physics and religion at Carleton College, where he also developed highly interdisciplinary courses in the field he essentially created himself. Although he typically presented other viewpoints accurately alongside his own, Barbour's commitments to **critical realism** and a correspondence theory of truth, coupled with much enthusiasm for process theology—which is closely linked with his affirmation of a nonviolent, noncoercive God—substantially shaped his work (Hallanger 2012). His work is accessible to nonspecialists and indispensable to scholars.

Edward B. Davis

REFERENCES AND RECOMMENDED READING

Barbour, Ian G. 1966. *Issues in Science and Religion*. Englewood Cliffs, NJ: Prentice-Hall.

———. 1990. *Religion in an Age of Science*. Gifford Lectures 1989–91. Vol. 1. San Francisco: Harper & Row.

———. 2004. "A Personal Odyssey." In *Fifty Years in Science and Religion: Ian G. Barbour and His Legacy*, ed. Robert John Russell, 17–28. Aldershot, UK: Ashgate.

Hallanger, Nathan J. 2012. "Ian G. Barbour." In *The Blackwell Companion to Science and Christianity*, ed. J. B. Stump and Alan G. Padgett, 600–610. Malden, MA: Wiley-Blackwell.

BARROW, JOHN D. John David Barrow, FRS (1952–), has had an extraordinary career in the fields of cosmology, mathematics, and theoretical **physics**. After earning a PhD in astrophysics at Oxford in 1977, he held academic positions at Oxford, the University of California, Berkeley, and the University of Sussex. In 1999 Barrow was appointed as professor of mathematical sciences at Cambridge University.

Just nine years after receiving his doctorate degree, Barrow with **Frank Tipler** published *The Anthropic Cosmological Principle* (1986), which has been widely influential and informative in discussions on the religious implications of scientific discoveries about the universe. In contemplating the specific values of the ensemble of constants of nature that were fixed at the beginning of the universe, it has become apparent that they are often finely tuned to within a very narrow range, such that life as we know it can exist.

Barrow has authored more than 17 books and 400 articles on physics, cosmology, and mathematics. In recognition of his role in exploring the overlap between **science** and human thought and religion, Barrow received the prestigious Templeton Prize in 2006 "for progress toward research or discoveries about spiritual realities." His nomination cited that in Barrow's writings there is a "deep engagement with those aspects of the structure of the universe and its laws that make life possible.... The vast elaboration of that simple idea has led to a huge expansion of the breadth and depth of the dialogue between science and religion" (Templeton Prize 2006).

Addressing the common question "Why would the universe be so old and vast?" Barrow brings things into focus by observing that "the Universe needs to be billions of light years in size just to support one lonely outpost of life." Rather than viewing the universe as life-averse and meaningless, he maintains that the study of the universe "breathes new life into so many religious questions of ultimate concern and never-ending fascination" (Templeton Prize 2006). The ongoing popularity of Barrow's works demonstrates that widespread interest in understanding the connection between scientific discoveries and questions relating to the meaning of human life continues today.

In his 1998 book, *Impossibility*, Barrow brings to light the interesting thesis that "only those cultures for whom there existed a belief that there was a distinction between the possible and the impossible provided natural breeding grounds for scientific progress." A biblical **worldview** is congruent with this distinction. Barrow summarizes that early Hebrews viewed nature as distinct from God, and that the natural world itself is not a "temperamental deity" but "an artefact of the Creator to be respected, admired, and husbanded by His appointed stewards" (Barrow 1988).

Throughout his writings, Barrow adopts an evolutionary **paradigm**, often postulating inventive scenarios relating to ancient man's evolutionary development into the advanced thinkers of today. However, he also observes that "the human brain was not evolved with science in mind" (Barrow 1998). And yet human scientific achievements, including Barrow's, have been stunningly impressive. Within theories of science, Barrow observes a "strikingly recurrent" pattern that "suggests to us that we can recognize mature scientific theories by their self-limiting character" (Barrow 1998). Perhaps considering the scientific limits of the theory of evolution might catalyze further scientific advancements pertaining to important questions surrounding human origins and the relation between humans and the universe.

Eric R. Hedin

REFERENCES AND RECOMMENDED READING

Barrow, John D. 1988. *The World within the World*. New York: Oxford University Press.
———. 1991. *Theories of Everything: The Quest for Ultimate Explanation*. New York: Oxford University Press.
———. 1994. *The Origin of the Universe*. New York: HarperCollins.
———. 1998. *Impossibility: The Limits of Science and the Science of Limits*. New York: Oxford University Press.
———. 2000. *The Book of Nothing: Vacuums, Voids, and the Latest Ideas about the Origins of the Universe*. London: Random House.
Barrow, John D., and Frank J. Tipler. 1986. *The Anthropic Cosmological Principle*. Oxford: Oxford University Press.
Barrow, John D., Simon C. Morris, Stephen J. Freeland, and Charles L. Harper Jr., eds. 2008. *Fitness of the Cosmos for Life: Biochemistry and Fine-Tuning*. New York: Cambridge University Press.
Gresham College. "Professor John D. Barrow FRS." Gresham College. Accessed October 10, 2015. www.gresham.ac.uk/professors-and-speakers/professor-john-d-barrow-frs.
"John D. Barrow." *Encyclopaedia Britannica Online*. Accessed October 10, 2015. www.britannica.com/biography/John-D-Barrow.
Templeton Prize. 2006. "Prof. John D. Barrow: 2006 Templeton Prize Laureate." www.templetonprize.org/pdfs/Templeton_Prize_Chronicle_2006.pdf.

BAYES' THEOREM. Bayes' theorem is a probabilistic formula that can be used to model the relationship between some evidence and a hypothesis to which that evidence is relevant. The prior **probability** of a hypothesis is its probability considered apart from some particular piece or set of evidence in question. This piece or set of evidence is often designated by the letter E.

If other **information** relevant to the hypothesis is already known, the prior probability of the hypothesis should include its impact. The posterior probability is the probability of the hypothesis when the particular evidence designated as E is taken into account. A likelihood (discussed below) is

the probability of the evidence given a hypothesis. If we call the hypothesis H and the evidence E, we can express their relationship by saying that the posterior probability of H equals the ratio of two quantities: On the top of the ratio is the product of the prior probability of H and the probability of the evidence E given H. On the bottom of the ratio is the prior probability of the evidence—that is, the probability of the evidence on general considerations before we definitely learn it.

$$P(H|E) = \frac{P(H)P(E|H)}{P(E)}$$

If we learn some evidence E, the new probability of the hypothesis H after receiving the evidence will be equal to $P(H|E)$ as given in Bayes' theorem. This process of taking evidence into account is called "updating." If the probability of H given E is higher than the prior probability of H, then E confirms H; if it is lower than the prior probability of H, then E disconfirms H.

Because it separates the prior probabilities of H and $\sim H$ from the likelihoods, a version of Bayes' theorem known as the odds form is useful for isolating and considering the impact of some particular evidence. The odds form says that the ratio of the posterior probability of the hypothesis to the posterior probability of its negation is equal to the ratio of their prior probabilities times the ratio of the likelihoods:

$$\frac{P(H|E)}{P(\sim H|E)} = \frac{P(H)}{P(\sim H)} \times \frac{P(E|H)}{P(E|\sim H)}$$

The last ratio in this equation is known as a Bayes factor or likelihood ratio and is seen by many Bayesians as an important expression of the impact of the evidence on H and $\sim H$.

One contentious issue concerning the use of Bayes' theorem is the famous "problem of the priors." The evidence on which the prior probability of H is based, which should be all our evidence *other* than E, may be vast, complex, and varied, making it difficult to estimate a prior. The prior probability of H should also reflect the impact of any considerations of the inherent simplicity or **complexity** of H. Different people may have widely differing personal prior probabilities for some hypothesis as a result of both their different previous evidence and their own biases.

It is often easier to evaluate the ratio of the likelihoods. Is the evidence more or less to be expected if H is true than if H is false, or is it about equally expected in either case? Can we get a sense of how many times more or less it is to be expected given one hypothesis or the other? Such a focus allows us to get a sense of the impact of the evidence on H even if we do not estimate the prior probability of H. Estimating a likelihood ratio for H and $\sim H$ is relevant to the question of what we should believe; if we can reasonably estimate that Bayes factor, we can see whether a case based on this evidence is strong enough to overcome even a very low prior probability for H. This is the strategy employed by Lydia and Timothy McGrew (2009) in their Bayesian analysis of the evidence for the **resurrection of Jesus**.

Michael Licona (2010) doubts that prior probabilities can be accurately estimated. He also questions the use of probability theory in history altogether, regarding it as inappropriate for studying the acts of personal agents, and he expresses skepticism about applying concepts of probability to divine acts. He prefers to think of the argument for an event such as a miracle as an inference to the best explanation without the use of probability (see also McGrew 2012). Whether inference to the best explanation can be accurately modeled independent of probability theory is a long-standing controversy in the **philosophy of science**, but whatever one concludes on that issue, extreme skepticism about the use of probabilistic concepts in reasoning about the acts of God threatens to undermine the conclusion that a miracle is the *best* explanation of the evidence.

The use of Bayes' theorem has been an important corrective in **philosophy of religion** to a tendency to place too much emphasis on one's **worldview** and hence on prior probabilities. John Earman (2000), who is not a Christian, has used Bayes' theorem to demonstrate the failure of the work of eighteenth-century skeptic **David Hume**, who argued that no merely finite evidence can overcome the rational presumption against the miraculous. Bayes' theorem shows that even an extremely low prior probability can be overcome by sufficiently strong evidence, especially by multiplied independent lines of evidence, which can form an extremely strong cumulative case with surprising rapidity. These probabilistic facts have helped to revive interest in evidence for **miracles** as evidence for Christianity.

The single philosopher of religion who has made the greatest use of Bayes' theorem is Richard Swinburne. Swinburne has argued both for the **existence of God** based on **natural theology** aside from miracles (2004) and for Christianity itself (2003) using Bayesian inference, and he has not hesitated to tackle the problem of the priors. He argues (2001) that the use of simplicity as a criterion of theory choice is necessary for nondeductive inference generally, including scientific reasoning, and is relevant to the prior probability of a hypothesis even aside from all specific evidence. Swinburne argues that the existence of God is at least as probable as not on the basis of **natural theology** and of general **religious experience** and that the evidence for Jesus's resurrection makes the probability of **theism** much higher than 0.5.

Bayes' theorem has also been relevant to the subject of **design argument**s. The argument for the design of the universe from the apparent fine-tuning of the fundamental constants and laws has been given a Bayesian treatment by Swinburne and by Robin Collins (2009). In this they reflect the treatment of the argument in the scientific literature, where fine-tuning is sometimes used to argue for multiple universes rather than for **intelligent design**.

In the biological arena, **William Dembski** (1998) advocates a non-Bayesian approach that seeks to eliminate competitors to intelligent design rather than to confirm intelligent design. McGrew (2005) recommends a Bayesian approach to biological design inferences.

It is important to remember that Bayes' theorem is a model of well-done historical, scientific, and other explanatory and statistical inferences, not a substitute for them. Nor is it necessary to have high-level mathematical skills to benefit from a deeper understanding of probability. The benefits of an explicit use of Bayesian probability come from its ability to sort out various types and lines of evidence and to show how to incorporate that evidence into one's rational corpus. At its best, probabilistic reasoning, including Bayesian reasoning, makes explicit the epistemic judgments of rational agents.

Lydia McGrew

REFERENCES AND RECOMMENDED READING

Collins, Robin. 2009. "The Teleological Argument: An Exploration of the Fine-Tuning of the Universe." In *The Blackwell Companion to Natural Theology*, ed. W. L. Craig and J. P. Moreland, 202–81. Oxford: Wiley-Blackwell.

Dembski, William. 1998. *The Design Inference: Eliminating Chance through Small Probabilities*. Cambridge: Cambridge University Press.

Earman, John. 2000. *Hume's Abject Failure*. Oxford: Oxford University Press.

Licona, Michael. 2010. *The Resurrection of Jesus: A New Historiographical Approach*. Downers Grove, IL: InterVarsity.

McGrew, Lydia, and Timothy McGrew. 2009. "The Argument from Miracles: A Cumulative Case for the Resurrection of Jesus of Nazareth." In *The Blackwell Companion to Natural Theology*, ed. W. L. Craig and J. P. Moreland, 593–662. Oxford: Wiley-Blackwell.

McGrew, Timothy. 2005. "Toward a Rational Reconstruction of Design Inferences." *Philosophia Christi* 7:253–98.

———. 2012. "Inference, Method, and History." *Southeastern Theological Review* 3:27–39.

Swinburne, Richard. 2001. *Epistemic Justification*. Oxford: Clarendon.

———. 2003. *The Resurrection of God Incarnate*. Oxford: Oxford University Press.

———. 2004. *The Existence of God*. Oxford: Oxford University Press.

BEAUTY. Beauty is one of the joys of human life and a primary concern in philosophical aesthetics. One of the perennial debates about the subject concerns whether beauty is an objective quality in the world or merely exists "in the eye of the beholder." The latter view, known as *aesthetic subjectivism*, was famously defended by **David Hume** (1965), who held that "beauty is no quality in things themselves: it exists merely in the mind which contemplates them." In support of their view, subjectivists such as Hume and, later, Santayana, appealed to the variety of aesthetic opinions and the close association of aesthetic judgments with personal pleasure. *Aesthetic objectivists* insist that beauty and other aesthetic qualities are real features of things. Objectivists grant that while human *responses* to beauty (and ugliness) are subjective, there nonetheless remain public facts when it comes to beauty.

While the subjectivist view has had many proponents and retains popular appeal, objectivism accounts for some common-sense **intuition**s, such as broad critical consensus about the quality of certain artworks. This consideration prompted **Kant**'s compromise account, that our aesthetic judgments are grounded in a common aesthetic sense that explains the subjective necessity we attribute to our judgments of taste. Even Hume was reluctant to eschew all **objectivity** concerning beauty, as he insisted that there are "standards of taste" according to which a person may be a more or less skilled aesthetic judge.

But if beauty is real, what is it exactly? *Idealist* accounts ground beauty in transcendent ideas, whether existing as eternal Platonic forms (see **Plato**) or in the mind of God (**Augustine**, Bonaventure, Hegel). *Realist* approaches (as variously found in **Aristotle**, **Aquinas**, and Burke) analyze beauty in terms of proportionality—a pleasing order, balance, symmetry, or ratio among the elements of an object. Some aestheticians taking this approach (e.g., Frances Hutcheson and Clive Bell) emphasize the pleasure-inducing capacity of such formal qualities to the degree that they incline in the direction of subjectivism. Still others (e.g., Jerrold Levinson) opt for a *contextualist* view, which conceives of beauty and other aesthetic facts in terms of their historical or generative contexts.

The concept of beauty has appeal and practical impact far beyond the realm of the arts. Eminent scientists from Poincaré to **Einstein** have emphasized the role of beauty in their research and theorizing. And many historians of science have argued that beauty, elegance, and other aesthetic qualities have been decisive when it comes to theory selection in science. Conversely, a burgeoning area of contemporary research concerns the scientific analysis of judgments of beauty, specifically in terms of mathematical and geometrical proportionality. Thus some research strongly suggests that people find those human faces most attractive which most closely conform to the "golden ratio" in **mathematics** (i.e., 1.61803399). In these ways, the relationship between science and beauty is surprisingly significant.

James S. Spiegel

REFERENCES AND RECOMMENDED READING

Bell, Clive. 1914. *Art*. London: Chatto & Windus.
Hume, David. 1965. *Of the Standard of Taste and Other Essays*. New York: Prentice Hall.
Kant, Immanuel. 1987. *Critique of Judgment*, trans. Werner S. Pluhar. Indianapolis: Hackett.
Plato. 1961. *Symposium*. In *Collected Dialogues*, ed. Edith Hamilton and Huntington Cairns. Princeton, NJ: Princeton University Press.
Plotinus. 1952. "Ennead 1." In *The Six Enneads*, trans. Stephen McKenna and B. S. Page. Chicago: Encyclopedia Britannica.
Santayana, George. 1896. *The Sense of Beauty*. New York: Scribner.
Scruton, Roger. 2009. *Beauty*. New York: Oxford University Press.

BEHAVIORISM. Behaviorism is a family of psychological and philosophical theories that arose in the early twentieth century as a response to the Cartesian view of the mind as an inherently private, subjective entity that is best studied through introspection. In an effort to replicate the success of the natural sciences, psychological behaviorists sought to establish **psychology** as a proper empirical science by restricting it to the study of publically observable behavioral data. In prohibiting any reference to private states of **consciousness** or internal mental processes, the central idea was to provide an explanation of human behavior solely in terms of sensory stimuli, physically specifiable responses, and patterns of reinforcement.

Early forms of psychological behaviorism focused on relatively unsophisticated forms of the stimulus-response mechanisms characteristic of classical conditioning (e.g., Watson 1913, 1930). Like John B. Watson, B. F. Skinner thought that behavior was best explained by stimulus-response mechanisms, but he went beyond Watson in appealing to the concept of reinforcement. In doing so, Skinner drew on Edward Thorndike's work on the law of effect, according to which the likelihood that a response will follow a stimulus is increased if the response is followed by reinforcement (Skinner

1953, chap. 5). Skinner called the behavioral response that is strengthened by reinforcement an "operant" and the process of shaping behavior by means of reinforcement "operant conditioning."

Most famously, Skinner (1938) used the process of operant conditioning to explain a rat's learning to press a lever in an experimental setup (sometimes called a "Skinner Box"), in which pressing the lever would release food and thereby reinforce the lever-pressing behavior. While this represents a relatively simple form of learning, Skinner held that operant conditioning could explain all forms of learning and behavior, human and nonhuman. This conviction rested on a pair of assumptions: (1) a human person is a blank slate shaped by patterns of stimulus, response, and reinforcement, and (2) there is no principled difference between explaining human and nonhuman behavior. While operant conditioning remains a fundamental concept in contemporary psychology, both of these assumptions have proven to be deeply problematic, and psychological behaviorism has subsequently failed to provide an adequate explanation of the rich **complexity** of human behavior.

In addition to facing long-standing difficulties in accounting for certain kinds of animal behavior, including learning that occurs without reinforcement (e.g., latent learning) and behaviors that are contrary to prior reinforcement (e.g., spontaneous alternation), the most notable failure concerned human linguistic behavior. The linguist Noam Chomsky subjected Skinner's treatment of language (Skinner 1957) to criticism that is widely regarded as decisive (see Chomsky 1959, esp. sec. 11). He argued that operant conditioning could not explain key elements of our linguistic behavior, including our ability to create and understand, without any prior reinforcement, new and novel sentences.

As Chomsky argued, children internalize a set of rules that enable them to recognize and generate grammatical sentences (a grammar), and they do so at a very early age and with relative ease. Not only does this disconfirm the reinforcement hypothesis, an internalized grammar constitutes exactly the sort of representational structure behaviorists eschewed. Far from being the blank slates posited by behaviorists, humans possess a rich, highly structured cognitive architecture that underlies our linguistic behavior and intentional action.

Additionally, behaviorism is at odds with foundational truths of Christian **anthropology**: that we are moral agents created in the **image of God** who are able to freely pursue fellowship with God. In virtue of being created in the image of God, we are endowed with an intellect and will through

which we have control over and responsibility for our actions. Yet this account of human nature presupposes what Skinner (1971) calls "autonomous man"—a free agent who is the source of her or his actions. For Skinner, "autonomous man" is a prescientific illusion used to explain behaviors for which we currently lack a proper scientific explanation, by which he means an operant behavioral explanation (14, 19–20, 200).

As a science of behavior develops, "autonomous man" will be replaced by the environmental conditions that shape and maintain human behavior. Only by locating the source of human action in the environment, rather than free agency, do we discover the "real causes of human behavior" (201). As Skinner puts it, "Scientific analysis of behavior dispossesses autonomous man and turns the control he has been said to exert over to the environment" (205). Because they preclude human agents from being the source of their actions, operant behavioral explanations are incompatible with Christian anthropology, as well as key Christian doctrines in which human agency plays a central role, such as sin, redemption, and sanctification. (See Timpe 2015 for an extensive discussion of the role of free agency in Christian theology.)

Kevin Sharpe

REFERENCES AND RECOMMENDED READING

Chomsky, N. 1959. "A Review of B. F. Skinner's *Verbal Behavior*." *Language* 35:26–58. Repr. in Ned Block. 1980. *Readings in Philosophy of Psychology*. 1:48–63.

Skinner, B. 1938. *The Behavior of Organisms*. New York: Appleton-Century.

———. 1953. *Science and Human Behavior*. New York: Macmillan.

———. 1957. *Verbal Behavior*. New York: Appleton-Century-Crofts.

———. 1971. *Beyond Freedom and Dignity*. New York: Knopf.

Timpe, K. 2015. *Free Will in Philosophical Theology*. London: Bloomsbury Academic.

Watson, J. 1913. "Psychology as the Behaviorist Views It." *Psychological Review* 20. Repr. in William Lyons. 1995. *Modern Philosophy of Mind*, 24–42. London: Orion.

———. 1930. *Behaviorism*. Chicago: University of Chicago Press.

BEHE, MICHAEL. Michael Behe (1951–) is a professor of biochemistry at Lehigh University and senior fellow of the **Discovery Institute**. He completed a PhD in biochemistry from the University of Pennsylvania in 1978 with a dissertation on the gelation of sickle cell hemoglobin. Following postdoctoral work on structural transitions in **DNA** at the National Institutes of Health, he began his academic career at Queens College in 1983 and moved to Lehigh three years later, where he was tenured after establishing a research program in DNA structural biochemistry. Since 1995 his work has increasingly shifted to the development of biochemical **intelligent design** proposals.

Though he saw no conflict between evolution and his Roman Catholicism, Behe began doubting evolution's ability to explain biochemical structures after reading **Michael Denton**'s *Evolution: A Theory in Crisis*, and he became associated with the intelligent design movement centered around Philip Johnson after criticizing a negative review of Johnson's *Darwin on Trial* (Behe 1991).

He subsequently debated scientific materialists at Southern Methodist University (Buell and Hearn 1994; Witham 2003, 151) and participated in the Pajaro Dunes Intelligent Design conference, where he first presented the ideas expounded in his 1995 bestseller, *Darwin's Black Box: The Biochemical Challenge to Evolution* (Behe 1995). In this book, Behe argued that biochemical systems such as the blood-clotting cascade, intracellular transport, immune system, and bacterial flagellum are evidence for the activity of a purposeful intelligent designer because they are irreducibly complex, a term he coined to mean they contain too many "well-matched, interacting parts" to have arisen via Darwinian processes.

While some religious believers welcomed Behe's ideas for their apologetics potential, critics questioned Behe's apparent assumption that evolution is incompatible with Christianity (Pennock 2001a, 2001b) or worried his argument could lead to "**god of the gaps**" theologies (Alexander 2011). Moreover, because Behe rejected **methodological naturalism** (Behe 1995, 243), his invocation of a designer was dismissed as unscientific even as biologists criticized his assumptions about how evolution works, challenging his claims that the blood-clotting cascade and flagellum were irreducibly complex (Dembski and Ruse 2004; Doolittle 1997; Miller 1999), or alleging he imposed unreasonable criteria (Behe 2001) for acceptable evolutionary accounts (Boudry 2010).

Behe participated in the 2005 Dover, Pennsylvania, *Kitzmiller v. Dover* trial that led to several embarrassing admissions about intelligent design's scientific status, including its lack of peer-reviewed publications (Transcript 2005; Slack 2007). However, Behe and David Snoke had previously published a theoretical model indicating that **gene** duplication and point mutations alone are extremely unlikely to produce novel protein functions when multiple point mutations are needed (Behe and Snoke 2004), although their results were controversial (Lynch 2005) and could only mean that more complex evolutionary pathways should be considered (Behe and Snoke 2005).

Behe refined his arguments in his second book, *The Edge of Evolution: The Search for the Limits of Darwinism* (Behe 2007). Using chloroquine resistance in malaria as a yardstick,

he argued that Darwinian mechanisms cannot account for multisubunit protein complexes and suggested the **complexity** of cellular development pushed the origin of kingdoms and phyla beyond "the tentative edge of evolution" (Behe 2007, 218). Critics complained that Behe misrepresented molecular evolution and ignored "experimental data that directly contradicts his faulty premises" (Carroll 2007, 1427; Miller 2007). Behe continues to defend and develop his views on the Discovery Institute's Evolution News and Views website.

Stephen Contakes

REFERENCES AND RECOMMENDED READING

Alexander, Denis R. 2011. *The Language of Genetics: An Introduction*. Templeton Science and Religion Series. West Conshohocken, PA: Templeton Press.

Behe, Michael J. 1991. "Understanding Evolution." *Science* 253, no. 5023 (August 30): 951.

———. 1995. *Darwin's Black Box: The Biochemical Challenge to Evolution*. New York: Free Press.

———. 2000. "A True Acid Test: Response to Ken Miller." Discovery Institute. July 31. www.discovery.org/a/441.

———. 2001. "A Reply to My Critics: A Response to Reviews of *Darwin's Black Box: The Biochemical Challenge to Evolution*." *Biology and Philosophy* 15 (5): 685–709.

———. 2007. *The Edge of Evolution: The Search for the Limits of Darwinism*. New York: Free Press.

Behe, Michael J., William A. Dembski, Stephen C. Meyer, and Wethersfield Institute. 2000. *Science and Evidence for Design in the Universe: Papers Presented at a Conference Sponsored by the Wethersfield Institute, New York City, September 25, 1999*. The Proceedings of the Wethersfield Institute. San Francisco: Ignatius.

Behe, M. J., and D. W. Snoke. 2004. "Simulating Evolution by Gene Duplication of Protein Features That Require Multiple Amino Acid Residues." *Protein Science* 13 (10): 2651–64.

———. 2005. "A Response to Michael Lynch." *Protein Science* 14:2226–27.

Beznoussenko, Galina V., and Alexander A. Mironov. 2002. "Models of Intracellular Transport and Evolution of the Golgi Complex." *The Anatomical Record* 268:226–38.

Blair, David F., and Kelly T. Hughes. 2012. "Irreducible Complexity? Not!" In *Microbes and Evolution: The World That Darwin Never Saw*, ed. R. Kolter and S. Maloy, 275–80. Washington, DC: ASM.

Boudry, Maarten. 2010. "Irreducible Incoherence and Intelligent Design: A Look into the Conceptual Toolbox of a Pseudoscience." *Quarterly Review of Biology* 85 (4): 473–82.

Buell, Jon, Virginia Hearn, Foundation for Thought and Ethics, Dallas Christian Leadership, and C. S. Lewis Fellowship. 1994. *Darwinism, Science or Philosophy? Proceedings of a Symposium Entitled "Darwinism, Scientific Inference or Philosophical Preference?"* Southern Methodist University, Dallas, Texas, March 26–28, 1992. Richardson, TX: Foundation for Thought and Ethics.

Carroll, Sean B. 2007. "God as Genetic Engineer." *Science* 316 (5830): 1427–28.

Dembski, William A., and Michael Ruse. 2004. *Debating Design: From Darwin to DNA*, ed. Robert B. Stewart. New York: Cambridge University Press.

Doolittle, Russell. 1997. "A Delicate Balance." *Boston Review* 22 (1). http://new.bostonreview.net/BR22.1/doolittle.html.

Lynch, Michael. 2005. "Simple Evolutionary Pathways to Complex Proteins." *Protein Science* 14, no. 9 (September): 2217–25.

McGrath, Alister E. 2011. *Darwinism and the Divine: Evolutionary Thought and Natural Theology*. The Hulsean Lectures. Oxford and Malden, MA: Wiley-Blackwell.

"Michael J. Behe, Ph.D." Lehigh University. Accessed August 26, 2016. www
.lehigh.edu/~inbios/Faculty/Behe.html.

Miller, Kenneth R. 1999. *Finding Darwin's God: A Scientist's Search for Common
Ground between God and Evolution.* New York: Cliff Street.

———. 2007. "Falling over the Edge." *Nature* 448, no. 28 (June): 1055–56.

Numbers, Ronald L. 2006. *The Creationists: From Scientific Creationism to
Intelligent Design.* Exp. ed. Cambridge, MA: Harvard University Press.

Pennock, Robert T. 2001a. *Intelligent Design Creationism and Its Critics: Philosophical, Theological, and Scientific Perspectives.* Cambridge, MA: MIT Press.

———. 2001b. "Whose God? What Science? Reply to Michael Behe." *Reports
of the National Center for Science Education* 21 (3–4): 16–19.

Slack, Gordy. 2007. *The Battle over the Meaning of Everything: Evolution, Intelligent Design, and a School Board in Dover, PA.* San Francisco: Jossey-Bass.

Transcript of *Tammy Kitzmiller, et al. v. Dover Area School District, et al.* 2005.
(400 F.Supp.2d 707 M.D.Pa.). The trial documents are available at the
National Center for Science Education website, http://ncse.com/creationism/
legal/kitzmiller-trial-transcripts.

Travis, John. 2009. "On the Origin of the Immune System." *Science* 324 (May
1): 580–82.

Witham, Larry. 2003. *By Design: Science and the Search for God.* San Francisco:
Encounter.

Woodward, Thomas. 2003. *Doubts about Darwin: A History of Intelligent Design.*
Grand Rapids: Baker.

BIBLICAL CHRONOLOGY. The events in the Old Testament narrative can be assigned absolute dates and correlated to nonbiblical sources back to the beginning of the divided monarchy in the tenth century BC. Before that time, the lack of external material and precise durations in the Bible itself make establishing a chronology more difficult. For the New Testament, a high degree of certainty is possible about the date of Jesus's death and some significant episodes in the book of Acts.

The Divided Monarchy

The historical books of the Bible, especially 1 Kings, 2 Kings, 1 Chronicles, and 2 Chronicles, provide a list of rulers and the lengths of their reigns for the kingdoms of Israel and Judah. This is typical of the records discovered by archaeologists in respect to other civilizations. The biblical list can be correlated to these nonbiblical sources using events that are mentioned in both. The most famous of these is the siege of Jerusalem by the Assyrian king Sennacherib mentioned in 2 Kings 18:13–19:36 and 2 Chronicles 32:1–21, as well as in Assyria's own annals. Two hundred years earlier, the Egyptian pharaoh Sheshonq I carried out a raid that took in several Canaanite and Judean cities. This is mentioned in the Bible at 1 Kings 14:25 and commemorated by Sheshonq in inscriptions on his temple at Karnak in Egypt.

The durations the Bible gives for the reigns of the kings of Israel and Judah do give rise to some difficult questions of detail. For example, when 2 Kings 21:19 says that King Amon of Judah ruled for two years, it may be that this includes both the first and last year of his reign or neither. This would mean that one year could be double counted or undercounted with that of his predecessor or successor. So Amon might have reigned for barely a year or almost four. Using correlations within the Bible and with events mentioned in extrabiblical sources, it is possible to establish that double counting was common in the northern kingdom but probably abandoned in the southern kingdom in the seventh century BC. Judah and Israel also seem to have marked the new year six months apart, in spring in Judah and in fall in Israel. By taking such complications into account, the accuracy of the biblical king lists can be better established and events in the Bible synchronized with those in other ancient Near Eastern civilizations.

The king lists are known as "floating" or "relative" chronologies by historians because they tell us what happened relative to other events but do not provide absolute dates. Thus, for example, we can say with confidence that King Hoshea of Israel ascended the throne four years before Shalmaneser V of Assyria because we know Shalmaneser captured Samaria in his fifth year, which was the ninth year of Hoshea. But we cannot, from this **information** alone, tell in which year Hoshea's reign started.

To provide absolute dates, historians depend on rare references to astronomical events that can be dated precisely due to the regular movements of the stars. On June 15, 763 BC, a near total eclipse of the sun was visible over a swath of the Near East. The event was noted in the official list of Assyrian high officials, providing the earliest absolute and uncontroversial date in ancient history. By counting from this event through the king lists, historians can provide absolute dates to all the other episodes recorded in Hebrew, Egyptian, and Assyrian chronicles. Thus we know Hoshea's reign started in 732 BC, Shalmaneser's reign started in 727 BC, and Samaria fell in 722 BC.

These dates are relatively uncontroversial. A minority of chronologists, such as Peter James, have attempted to construct other chronologies that differ from the mainstream reconstructions. Although some of these alternative models are superficially attractive, they have received little wider assent. Correlation of biblical events to particular archaeological remains has also proven difficult. The examination of potsherds and carbon dating are not presently accurate enough to provide absolute dates to archaeological finds, and they require external calibration in any case. It may well be that dendrochronology (dating from counting tree rings) and ice cores will eventually allow absolute dates to be assigned to some of the remains dug up in the Levant.

The United Monarchy and Earlier

Prior to the invasion of Canaan by the pharaoh Sheshonq in 925 BC, there are no external sources that corroborate events described in the Bible. Indeed, precisely dating the raid of Sheshonq is only possible by using biblical evidence. Thus chronology prior to this date can only be established using internal evidence in the Bible itself. This means that dates for the reigns of the kings Saul, David, and Solomon cannot be determined precisely since there is no external control to mediate questions such as the "double counting" described above. However, uncertainties for this period are unlikely to be more than a few years in either direction.

The lack of external sources is in no way surprising. The thirteenth to tenth centuries BC are known as the Bronze Age collapse, when several ancient Near East civilizations went into decline or disappeared completely. This is precisely the environment in which an upstart kingdom such as David's Israel could enjoy a period of expansion as the power of its neighbors waned. However, the collapse means that very few written sources pertaining to Canaan exist for this time.

These issues become even more acute for events before the United Monarchy. The dates provided by the biblical authors themselves become less precise for the period of the Judges and previously. External sources remain scarce. Furthermore, as the Hebrews did not at this time form an identifiable kingdom, there is less reason for them to be mentioned in the official documents of other civilizations. It is also unfortunate that Exodus does not give the name of the Pharaoh who released the Israelites. While he is traditionally identified with Rameses II, there is no way to be sure.

In recent years, ice cores and improved carbon dating have caused the entire chronology of the second millennium BC to be revised. The eruption of the volcano Thera in the eastern Mediterranean Sea, previously thought to have happened after 1500 BC, has now been redated to approximately 1620 BC. With all chronology before 1200 BC so fluid, it is not possible to assign absolute dates to biblical events.

Internal evidence in the Bible dates the exodus to before 1400 BC, in which case Joseph probably lived in about 1800 BC and Abraham left Ur a couple of centuries earlier. In the mid-twentieth century, the archaeologist William Albright suggested that the exodus took place rather later, in the thirteenth century BC. His dating, which was based on destruction layers and artifacts that he had uncovered in

Palestine, enjoyed considerable assent, not least because it coincided with the reign of Rameses II, traditionally identified as the pharaoh of the exodus. However, in more recent years, Albright's work has fallen out of favor, and the evidence he used to date the exodus has been called into question.

The New Testament

Unlike many other biblical authors, Luke is concerned to provide his readers with precise dates, and other authors in the New Testament make reference to outside events. However, though most events in the New Testament can be dated to within a year or two, there are still areas of controversy. For example, the nativity narratives are difficult to reconcile, and most scholars prefer Matthew's date for the birth of Jesus of around 6 BC. At Luke 3:1 the evangelist tells us that John the Baptist's ministry began in the fifteenth year of the emperor Tiberius while Pontius Pilate was governor of Judea. This is likely to mean AD 26. The Gospel of John, preferred by many scholars for being an eyewitness account, dates the cleansing of the temple in Jerusalem to 46 years after it was completed, which would be AD 28.

All the Gospels agree that Jesus was crucified at Passover on a Friday. This means he must have died on AD April 7, 30, although AD 33 also has its partisans. The events in the Acts of the Apostles occurred through the 30s to the 50s and conclude with Paul a prisoner in Rome in about AD 62. Both he and Peter were executed during the persecutions of Nero shortly thereafter and are known to have taken place in AD 64.

James Hannam

REFERENCES AND RECOMMENDED READING

Cogan, Mordechai. 1992. "Chronology. The Hebrew Bible." In *Anchor Bible Dictionary*, ed. D. N. Friedman, 1:1002–11. New York: Doubleday.
Jamesones, Peter. 1991. *Centuries of Darkness*. London: Jonathan Cape.
Kitchen, K. A. 2003. *On the Reliability of the Old Testament*. Grand Rapids: Eerdmans.
Meier, John P. 1991. *A Marginal Jew: Rethinking the Historical Jesus*. New York: Doubleday.
Ramsey, C. B., Sturt W. Manning, and Mariagrazia Galimberti. 2004. "Dating the Volcanic Eruption at Thera." *Radiocarbon* 46 (1): 325–44.
Renfrew, C., and P. Bahn. 2012. "Dating the Thera Eruption." *Archaeology: Theories, Methods and Practice*. London: Thames & Hudson.

BIG BANG THEORY. The most widely accepted explanation for the origin, history, and structure of the universe—an explanation consistent with all the available observations of the universe—is called the big bang.

The word *bang* tends to create confusion. *Bang* conjures images of a bomb blast with its associated chaos and destruction. By contrast, the cosmic "bang" was (and is) an immensely powerful yet carefully orchestrated burst of creation—a sudden release of power from which the universe was unfurled in an exquisitely controlled manner. The evidence indicates that in a single moment, matter, energy, time, and space, along with the physical laws governing them, burst into existence—the "effect" of a "cause" from beyond.

In broad outline, the big bang theory describes the universe as a measurable system that expands from a singular beginning of matter, energy, space, and time under pervasive and constant laws of **physics**. This ongoing expansion from a space-time beginning (see **Space and Time**) under unchanging laws, including the law of entropy, implies that the universe started off at a nearly infinitely hot temperature and has progressively cooled in a highly specified way as the universe has aged (just as an engine's piston chamber cools as it expands after the moment of ignition). Because the entire universe has been expanding from the cosmic "ignition" event under the influence of entropy (the law of decay), it becomes progressively colder over time (see **Natural Laws**; **Second Law of Thermodynamics**).

Credit for the discovery of these big bang properties goes primarily to five twentieth-century physicists and astronomers: **Albert Einstein**, **Georges Lemaître**, Edwin Hubble, Arno Penzias, and Robert Wilson. Einstein's theory of general relativity predicted the universe has expanded from a beginning. Lemaître and Hubble demonstrated the reality of cosmic expansion. Penzias and Wilson's measurements showed that the universe has been cooling from its ultrahot origin.

It is worth noting that Scripture speaks about the transcendent beginning of physical reality, including time itself (Gen. 1:1; John 1:3; Col. 1:15–17; Heb. 11:3); about continual cosmic expansion, or "stretching out" (Job 9:8; Ps. 104:2; Isa. 40:22, 45:12; Jer. 10:12); about unchanging physical laws (Jer. 33:25), one of which is the pervasive law of decay (Eccl. 1:3–11; Rom. 8:20–22). These descriptions fly in the face of ancient, enduring, and prevailing assumptions about an eternal, static universe—until the twentieth century.

The obvious Christian implications of big bang cosmology—a transcendent Cause and a beginning that traces back only billions of years—explain why nontheistic astronomers resisted the model for decades. Sir **Arthur Eddington** expressed the following concern regarding the idea of creation's finite timeline, "We [must] allow evolution an infinite time to get started" (Eddington 1931, 672). Later he added, "Philosophically, the notion of a beginning of the present order of Nature is repugnant" (Eddington 1931, 450). Sir **Fred Hoyle** contended, "It seems against the spirit of scientific enquiry to regard observable effects as arising from 'causes unknown to science,' and this in principle is what creation-in-the-past implies" (Hoyle 1948, 72). John Gribbin complained, "The biggest problem with the big bang theory of the origin of the Universe is philosophical—perhaps even theological—what was there before the bang?" (Gribbin 1976, 15–16).

Eventually, however, with the development of increasingly advanced measuring **technology** and techniques, the physical and observational evidence for the big bang became overwhelming. For example, astronomers developed the ways and means (via millimeter wave detectors) to determine the temperature of the cosmic background radiation (CBR), the radiation left over from the cosmic origin event. Because of the finite and constant velocity of light, distance in astronomical observation represents time. Thus, by taking measurements at differing distances, astronomers can determine conditions at differing times in the history of the universe. Research showed that CBR temperatures were higher in direct proportion to the distance at which they were measured. The cosmic cooling curve observed across cosmic history proves consistent with continuous cosmic expansion under unchanging physical laws from a cosmic origin event some 13.8 billion years ago (Muller et al. 2013).

As more powerful instruments allowed them to be seen, distant galaxies (representing earlier epochs in cosmic history) appeared closer together and less mature (seen in earlier developmental stages) in direct proportion to their distance from Earth. Ongoing research has yielded a growing accumulation of supporting evidence, including the following:

- the observed abundances of helium, deuterium, and lithium observed in the universe can best be explained by a 13.8 billion-year-old universe that continues to expand from an initial state of near-infinite density and temperature;
- the angular sizes and amplitudes of temperature variations recorded in maps of the CBR precisely fit what a big bang scenario predicts;
- the observed orbital stability of stars, planets, and moons under the influence of gravity is possible only if the spatiality of the universe is defined by three large space dimensions that have expanded rapidly for 10–20 billion years;

- the spatial distribution of galaxy clusters, galaxy superclusters, and cosmic voids documented in observational studies fit the spatial distribution of hot and cold spots in our CBR maps.

More than a dozen additional pieces of evidence (Ross 2015, 135–60) establish beyond reasonable doubt that we do, indeed, reside in a big bang universe that arose from a beginning of matter, energy, space, and time—a cosmic creation event.

Today research efforts focus specifically on determining what particular version of the big bang model best fits the observations. The Planck satellite recently confirmed the set of inflationary big bang models as the most precise (see **Inflationary Universe Theory**). Galaxy maps such as the Sloan Digital Sky Survey prove consistent with the ËCDM big bang model, a big bang universe dominated by dark energy (see **Dark Matter and Dark Energy**) wherein most matter is exotic matter and most of this exotic matter is in a cold state, that is, with exotic matter particles moving at velocities much lower than the velocity of light.

Future research efforts will help determine what kind of inflation, or inflationary event, the universe experienced. They will also seek to determine more precisely the specific proportions of dark energy, cold exotic matter, warm exotic matter, and ordinary matter that comprise the universe. We have barely begun to understand the mysterious nature of **dark matter and dark energy**.

Long ago the book of Job hinted that darkness is something much more than merely the absence of light. Job 38:19–20 quotes God asking Job and his friends, "What is the way to the abode of light? And where does darkness reside? Can you take them to their places? Do you know the paths to their dwellings?"

No other measured characteristic of the universe is as precisely fixed for the possibility of life as the cosmic expansion rates, and "dark energy" is one of the two parameters governing this expansion. Mass, made up almost entirely by dark matter, is the other.

Hugh Ross

REFERENCES AND RECOMMENDED READING

Eddington, Arthur S. 1931. "The End of the World from the Standpoint of Mathematical Physics." *Nature* 127 (March 21): 447–53.
Gribbin, John. 1976. "Oscillating Universe Bounces Back." *Nature* 259 (January 1): 15–16.
Hoyle, Fred. 1948. "A New Model for the Expanding Universe." *Monthly Notices of the Royal Astronomical Society* 108.
Muller, S., A Beelen, J. H. Black, et al. 2013. "A Precise and Accurate Determination of the Cosmic Microwave Background Temperature at z = 0.89." *Astronomy and Astrophysics* 551 (March 4). www.aanda.org/articles/aa/abs/2013/03/aa20613–12/aa20613–12.html.
Ross, Hugh. 2015. *A Matter of Days.* 2nd exp. ed. Covina, CA: RTB Press.

BIOETHICS. Bioethics is an interdisciplinary endeavor primarily involving the study of moral issues in health care and the life sciences for the purpose of providing ethical guidance for practitioners in clinical and research settings.

Work in bioethics can be found in a variety of academic and professional fields, including medicine, philosophy, biology, theology, **psychology**, and law. The reason for this is that so many of the questions in bioethics overlap several fields of inquiry. For example, the question of whether a physician may assist in a patient's suicide is not merely a medical or biological question, even though a physician is a medical doctor trained in the biological sciences and may use certain medicines to carry out his patient's wishes. Rather, it is primarily a moral question about the rightness or wrongness of intentionally willing another's **death**, even when the one being killed is requesting it. Thus, answering this moral question requires the conceptual tools of philosophy and/or theology.

Other disciplines also play a part in the making of such judgments. For example, whether a patient is competent to choose a particular course of treatment requires the insights of psychology (or psychiatry), and whether there are governmental statutes or regulations on what a physician may or may not do to her or his patient requires the assistance of legal counsel. However, because bioethics is primarily concerned with answering *moral* questions—rather than medical, legal, or biological ones—all of the answers, even when they are inconsistent with each other, either employ the categories of philosophy and/or theology or they presuppose those categories in one way or another. This can be seen in the debates about some of the most contested questions in bioethics.

Beginning of Human Life

What one thinks about the **morality** of **abortion**, human **cloning**, **embryonic stem cell research**, or reproductive technologies will often be determined by what one thinks about the nature of nascent human life and/or the proper function of our sexual powers. If, for example, one believes that a human embryo or fetus lacks full moral status because it cannot engage in certain types of mental activities (e.g., have a self-concept, desire a right to life, have a life plan; Tooley 1983), then practices such as abortion and embryonic stem cell research, which virtually always result in the death of prenatal human subjects, will not seem to be serious moral wrongs (or even wrongs at all). Of course, a different view of nascent human life, one consistent with Christian anthropology, entails that these acts are gravely immoral (George and Tollefson 2011). The latter position, unlike the former, connects a human being's full moral status to his nature (what he is) rather than to the maturation of those powers that flow from his nature (what he does).

Alternatives to ordinary human reproduction (e.g., cloning, in vitro fertilization, surrogate motherhood, artificial insemination) often raise additional questions, though they are no less philosophical or theological than the question of the prenatal human being's full moral status. For example, is it morally right (and/or consistent with God's plan for marriage) to bring children into being apart from the marital act and in ways that seem more like manufacturing than begetting? Christians offer differing answers to this type of inquiry because they take contrary positions on the moral permissibility of extramarital reproductive technologies. Some argue that none of them are licit (Austriaco 2012), while others maintain that some are not immoral (Rae 1996).

End of Human Life

Bioethical decisions at life's end primarily involve answering questions about what constitutes appropriate treatment, the withdrawing or withholding of it, and proper administration of palliative care. For virtually all Christian bioethicists (Austriaco 2012; Keown 2002), a physician may not intentionally kill her patient. However, that does not mean that one is obligated to keep a patient alive at all costs. A physician may act in a way that advances her patient's good by relieving substantial burdens even if she knows that such action will shorten whatever time remains in the patient's life. So, for example, a physician may increase her patient's intake of morphine in order to better manage his pain, even though the physician knows that it will likely hasten death.

There are, however, some secular bioethicists who maintain that because a patient's autonomy and understanding of what is in his best interests are paramount in assessing a physician's responsibility to her ailing patient, there are cases in which physician-assisted suicide is justified if the patient is rational, fully informed, and freely consents (Quill 1991; Smith 2012). This is not to say that Christian bioethicists deny that patient autonomy should play any role in bioethical decision-making. Rather, they argue that patient autonomy cannot be exercised in a way that requires the physician to cooperate with immoral ends (Austriaco 2012; Keown 2002).

Conscience Protection and Professional Responsibility

As secular bioethics increasingly becomes the dominant way that medicine understands its moral obligations, conscientious objection among religiously observant health professionals will likely increase. This is because secular bioethics relies heavily on a school of thought known as *principlism* (Beauchamp and Childress 2013). It maintains that health professionals should assess the morality of their clinical judgments on the basis of four principles—autonomy, nonmaleficence, benevolence, and justice—while at the same time excluding from their judgments contested metaphysical beliefs about the nature of the human person that are usually tightly tethered to religious traditions. Thus a patient's good is determined almost exclusively on what he chooses to believe is in his interests and what fulfills his preference satisfaction.

Under a medical establishment shaped by *principlism*, there will be religiously observant health professionals who will decline for reasons of conscience to participate in, or refer a patient to physicians who are willing to provide certain procedures (e.g., abortion, euthanasia, sex reassignment surgery) that the patient believes are necessary for his well-being as he understands it. Some argue that such health professionals, with limited exceptions, should be viewed as acting in an unethical manner (Dickens 2009). Others, however, argue they should be accorded strong conscience protection, since the procedures are not contested for medical reasons, but rather for reasons having to do with deep and differing philosophical and theological positions for which the architects of modern liberal societies had promised tolerance (Kaczor 2012).

Francis J. Beckwith

REFERENCES AND RECOMMENDED READING

Austriaco, Nicanor Pier Giorgio. 2012. *Biomedicine and Beatitude: An Introduction to Catholic Bioethics.* Washington, DC: Catholic University of America Press.

Beauchamp, Tom L., and James F. Childress. 2013. *Principles of Biomedical Ethics.* 7th ed. Oxford: Oxford University Press.

Dickens, Bernard M. 2009. "Legal Protection and Limits of Conscientious Objection: When Conscientious Objection Becomes Unethical." *Medicine and Law* 28:337–47.

George, Robert P., and Christopher Tollefsen. 2011. *Embryo: A Defense of Human Life.* 2nd ed. Princeton, NJ: Witherspoon Institute.

Kaczor, Christopher. 2012. "Conscientious Objection and Health Care: A Reply to Bernard Dickens." *Christian Bioethics* 18:59–71.

Keown, John. 2002. *Euthanasia, Ethics and Public Policy.* Cambridge: Cambridge University Press.

Quill, Timothy. 1991. "Death and Dignity: A Case of Individualized Decision Making," *New England Journal of Medicine* 324:691–94.

Rae, Scott B. 1996. *Brave New Families: Biblical Ethics and Reproductive Technologies.* Grand Rapids: Baker.

Rae, Scott B., and Paul Cox. 1999. *Bioethics: A Christian Approach in a Pluralstic Age.* Grand Rapids: Eerdmans.

Smith, Stephen S. 2012. *End-of-Life Decisions in Medical Care: Principles and Policies for Regulating the Dying Process.* Cambridge: Cambridge University Press.

Tooley, Michael. 1983. *Abortion and Infanticide.* Oxford: Oxford University Press.

BIOLOGOS FOUNDATION, THE. BioLogos is a Christian ministry founded in 2007 by **Francis Collins**, a leading geneticist who directed the **Human Genome Project**. Collins shared his evangelical testimony and explained the evidence for evolution in his bestselling book *The Language of God: A Scientist Presents Evidence for Belief.* The BioLogos website launched in 2009 to address common questions Collins received about the book from both Christians and skeptics. A few months later, Collins became director of the National Institutes of Health, and the presidential appointment required him to step away from BioLogos. Leadership passed to physicist Karl Giberson, geneticist Darrel Falk, and in 2013 to astronomer Deborah Haarsma.

The mission statement reads, "BioLogos invites the church and the world to see the harmony between science and biblical faith as we present an evolutionary understanding of God's creation." In contrast to secular scientists, the group "embraces the historical Christian faith," stating, "We believe the Bible is the inspired and authoritative word of God. By the Holy Spirit it is the 'living and active' means through which God speaks to the church today, bearing witness to God's Son, Jesus, as the divine Logos, or Word of God." In contrast to views like young-earth creation, old-earth creation, and **intelligent design**, the group supports the view of evolutionary creation. "We believe that the diversity and interrelation of all life on earth are best explained by the God-ordained process of evolution with common descent. Thus, evolution is not in opposition to God, but a means by which God providentially achieves his purposes" (all quotations from BioLogos Foundation homepage).

BioLogos conducts workshops for evangelical thought leaders, pastors, and Christian high school science teachers, and has hosted online dialogues with Southern Baptist scholars and old-earth creationists. Leading evangelicals such as Tim Keller, N. T. Wright, and Philip Yancey have endorsed their work.

The organization also produces a daily blog featuring scientists, theologians, pastors, and students, and in 2012 BioLogos began a three-year competitive grants program. The program's 37 grants across North America and Europe support "projects and network-building among scholars, church leaders, and parachurch organizations to address theological and philosophical questions commonly voiced by Christians about evolutionary creation in a way that is relevant to the church."

Deborah Haarsma

REFERENCES AND RECOMMENDED READING

BioLogos Foundation homepage. http://biologos.org.

Collins, Francis. 2006. *The Language of God: A Scientist Presents Evidence for Belief.* New York: Free Press.

Haarsma, Deborah B., and Loren D. Haarsma. 2011. *Origins: Christian Perspectives on Creation, Evolution, and Intelligent Design.* Grand Rapids: Faith Alive Christian Resources.

BOEHME, JACOB. Jacob Boehme (Jakob Böhme, 1575–1624) was a German thinker who influenced the content and development of later Continental **science** and philosophy. Boehme was born in 1575 in the Lusatian village of Alt Seidenberg (now Sulików, Poland) to Jakob (d. 1618) and Ursula (d. c. 1606) Boehme, who were Protestants and free peasants. At 14 his parents apprenticed him to a local shoemaker. In 1592 he entered upon his career as a professional cobbler, moving to Görlitz in Oberlausitz to open a shop in that city. Shortly thereafter, he was wed to Katherina Kuntzschmann, the daughter of a local butcher.

Görlitz was a mere 90 miles west of Prague and the Court of Rudolf II, to whom **Tycho Brahe** and **Johannes Kepler** served as imperial astronomers in succession during this period. As a consequence, many notable religious and scientific figures passed through Görlitz. In 1600 the Pietist Martin Möller became pastor of Boehme's parish church, Sts. Peter and Paul, and under his ministry revival broke out in Görlitz. Boehme places his conversion during this period. In his testimony, Boehme reveals a Protestant intellectual mystical orientation, founded strongly on Scripture, in which the boundary between creature and Creator retains a definite distinction:

> In my resolved zeal I gave so hard an assault, storm, and onset upon God and upon all the gates of hell, as if I had more reserves of virtue and power ready, with a resolution to hazard my life upon it (which assuredly were

not in my ability without the assistance of the Spirit of God), suddenly my spirit did break through the gates of hell, even into the innermost moving of the Deity, and there I was embraced in love as a bridegroom embraces his dearly beloved bride.... My spirit suddenly saw through all, and in and by all, the creatures ... it knew God, who he is and how he is and what his will is.

Despite persecution by Möller's Gnesio-Lutheran successor, Georg Richter, Boehme attributes fully his experiences to the grace of God *descending to* him, rather than his *ascending to* God. Boehme's conversion was not his first mystical experience, nor was it his last. Combining philosophical, scientific, scriptural, and spiritual insight, Boehme recounts his most scientifically consequential vision in one of his voluminous correspondences:

> For I saw and knew the Being of all beings, the ground and the unground; the birth of the holy trinity; the source and origin of this world and all creatures in divine Wisdom (Sophia).... I saw all three worlds in myself, (1) the divine, angelical, or paradisiacal; ... (2) the dark world ...; (3) the external, visible world ...; and I saw and knew the whole Being in evil and in good, how one originates in the other ... so that I not only greatly wondered but also rejoiced.

This vision was syncategorematic for his eponymous *Mysterium Magnum* of 1622, an immense, two-volume, philosophical and scientific commentary on Genesis. Its importance lies in its introduction of the term *Ungrund* ("abyss" or "unground"). *Ungrund* is properly translated as "absolutely nothing." Francis Schaeffer (1972, 19) captures well Boehme's outlook: "Once there was absolutely nothing (neither mass nor motion nor energy nor personality). This position (never) has ... been propounded seriously by anyone and the reason for this is clear. For this explanation to be true, *nothing* really must be *nothing*—totally nothing." Boehme *does*, however, adopt this position in an acosmic fashion, positing the following theological cosmology and cosmogony:

Absolutely Nothing (*Ungrund*) ➔ God (eternally begetting) ➔ Cosmos (created out of nothing)

After Boehme's death in 1624, it was this uniquely Christian and scientific view that was to exert great influence on thinkers as disparate as **Isaac Newton**, **Robert Boyle**, and a host of spiritual heirs, including George Fox and the embryonic Quaker movement in England.

Van Herd

REFERENCES AND RECOMMENDED READING

Bach, Jeff, and Michael Birkel. 2010. *The Genius of the Transcendent: Mystical Writings of Jacob Boehme.* Boston: Shambhala.

Berdyaev, Nicolai. 1958. Introduction. *Six Theosophic Points and Other Writings [of Jakob Boehme].* Ann Arbor: University of Michigan Press.

Erb, Peter. 1977. *Jacob Boehme: The Way to Christ.* Classics of Western Spirituality Series. New York: Paulist.

Hartmann, Franz. (1891) 1977. *The Life and Doctrines of Jacob Böhme: The God-Taught Philosopher.* Blauvelt, NY: Steiner.

Herd, Van. 2014. "Mathematicopoeisis Nihilo: The Metanarrative of (Boehmean) Creativity." Unpublished manuscript.

Hessayon, Ariel, and Sarah Apetrei, eds. 2014. *An Introduction to Jacob Boehme: Four Centuries of Thought and Reception.* Routledge Studies in Religion Series. New York: Routledge.

Kelley, James L. 2011. *Anatomyzing Divinity: Studies in Science, Esotericism, and Political Theology.* Walterville, OR: TrineDay.

Nicolescu, Basarab. 1991. *Science, Meaning, and Evolution: The Cosmology of Jacob Boehme*, trans. Rob Baker. New York: Parabola.

Schaeffer, Francis A. 1972. *Genesis in Space and Time: The Flow of Biblical History.* Downers Grove, IL: InterVarsity.

Stoudt, John Joseph. 1957. *Sunrise to Eternity: A Study of Jacob Boehme's Life and Thought.* Philadelphia: University of Pennsylvania Press.

Weeks, Andrew. 1991. *Böhme: An Intellectual Biography of the Seventeenth-Century Philosopher and Mystic.* SUNY Series in Western Esotericism. Albany: SUNY Press.

Whyte, Alexander. 1895. *Jacob Behmen: An Appreciation.* Edinburgh: Oliphant, Andersen, and Ferrier.

BOHR, NIELS. Niels Henrik David Bohr (1885–1962) was born in Copenhagen, Denmark. He is widely recognized as one of the greatest physicists of the twentieth century. After completing his PhD at Copenhagen University in 1911, he worked with Ernest Rutherford investigating alpha particle interactions with gold atoms, concluding that atoms consisted of a small heavy nucleus surrounded by its electrons.

Bohr further advanced this idea by suggesting that an atom's electrons traveled in discrete orbits around its nucleus, and that the chemical properties of a given atomic **species** are determined largely by the electrons in the orbits furthest from the nucleus. He also proposed that an electron could make transitions from lower energy orbits to higher energies by the electron's gaining energy from some source, and could subsequently make a transition to a lower energy orbit while emitting a photon (a quantum of light) of energy equal to the difference in electron energies in the two orbits. This work (in the 1910s) was among the first advancements in the new fields of quantum mechanics, the **physics** of the microworld, and nuclear physics.

Early in the twentieth century, experimental evidence showed that under certain conditions light exhibited particle-like characteristics. All previous studies had given results that were consistent with light being understood as a wave. In addition, Clinton Davisson and Lester Germer demonstrated in 1927 that the electron, heretofore always understood to be a particle, could be made to exhibit unmistakable wave properties. Three years earlier Louis-Victor deBroglie postulated that all entities in nature had both particle-like and wave characteristics, for which he received the Nobel Prize in 1929 after confirmation of his proposal by the Davisson-Germer experiment.

From these results, Niels Bohr developed his principle of **complementarity**, which had a direct bearing on the newly discovered dual character of both light and electrons. This principle states that all particles have certain properties that cannot be accurately measured simultaneously. One manifestation of the principle is that every subatomic entity displays both wave and particle characteristics, as deBroglie, Davisson, and Germer had established.

It seems as if these entities, such as light and electrons, require contradictory characteristics for their full understanding. Earlier in the nineteenth century, another Dane, Søren Kierkegaard, had developed the idea of the absolute **paradox** as he had pondered the implications of the dual natures of Jesus Christ, being both fully human and fully divine, as the patristic Christian theologians had concluded at Chalcedon in AD 451. There is no agreement on the extent of Kierkegaard's influence on Bohr, but Bohr read Kierkegaard and found his work worth considering. In any event, Bohr's principle of complementarity appears to be almost an exact analogue to Kierkegaard's absolute paradox.

Other early notable work in quantum mechanics included Bohr's advocacy of an interpretation of quantum mechanical results in terms of **probability**, replacing the strict **determinism** of classical physics by a certain amount of indeterminacy. This interpretation, known as the Copenhagen interpretation, was (and still is) strongly opposed by a number of physicists, including **Albert Einstein**. Discussions of the interpretations of Quantum mechanics continue to this day (see **Quantum Theory, Interpretations of**).

In recognition of his work in advancing knowledge of the atom, Bohr was awarded the Nobel Prize in 1922.

Richard F. Carlson

REFERENCES AND RECOMMENDED READING

Bohr, Niels. 1934. *Atomic Theory and the Description of Nature.* Cambridge: Cambridge University Press.
Cushing, James T. 1998. *Philosophical Concepts in Physics—The Historical Relation between Philosophy and Scientific Theories.* Cambridge: Cambridge University Press.
Loder, James E., and W. Jim Niedhardt. 1992. *The Knight's Move—The Relational Logic of the Spirit in Theology and Science.* Colorado Springs: Helmers & Howard.

BORDE-GUTH-VILENKIN SINGULARITY THEOREM.

As its name suggests, the Borde-Guth-Vilenkin singularity theorem arises from the efforts of three physicists—Arvind Borde, Alan Guth, and Alexander Vilenkin—who dedicated years (1994–2003) to exploring the limits and implications of the space-time theorems developed by **Stephen Hawking** and Roger Penrose (Hawking and Penrose 1970). According to those theorems, *if* the universe contains mass and *if* general relativity reliably describes the dynamics of bodies within the universe, *then* everything in the universe—matter, energy, and even the cosmic space-time dimensions—traces back to a singular boundary or beginning.

Given the significance of this *if-then* conclusion, especially its obvious implication that some causal agent beyond **space and time** must be responsible for initiating space and time, the community of physicists, led by this trio, set out to explore the possibility of reasonable exceptions to Hawking and Penrose's space-time theorems.

In their 10-year search, Borde and Vilenkin published five papers, the final one of which they coauthored with Alan Guth. In these papers the researchers were able to hypothesize several "loophole" models that would avoid a beginning of space and time. However, these models invoked bizarre concepts (such as the reversal of time's direction, violations of the second law of thermodynamics, and negative energies and forces) that would essentially eliminate the possibility of **life**'s existence anywhere in the universe.

Their fifth paper spelled out the conclusion they eventually came to and which became the theorem that bears their name: Any universe that expands on average throughout its history must possess an actual beginning in finite time that includes the beginning of space and time (Borde, Guth, Vilenkin 2003). This theorem applies to *all* inflationary **big bang** models that the laws of **physics** will allow (see **Inflationary Universe Theory**). It says that cosmic inflation demands a beginning in the *finite* past, not in *eternity* past. The theorem applies also to **multiverse** models that posit our universe may be one of many, perhaps an infinite number of, universes, given observations now confirming that our universe has expanded continuously throughout its history.

In Vilenkin's words, "With the proof now in place, cosmologists can no longer hide behind the possibility of a past-eternal universe. There is no escape, they have to face the problem of a cosmic beginning" (Vilenkin 2006, 176).

On the strength of the Borde-Guth-Vilenkin theorem,

the implication of a first cause, or causer, beyond space and time cannot be dismissed. The first tenet of **deism**, which says that reason and observation of the natural realm are sufficient to determine the existence of a creator, seems firmly established. Ironically, the deistic rejection of any and all supernatural events, or effects, beyond the cosmic creation event seems contradicted. The discernible origin of matter, energy, space, and time represents what some may consider the greatest miracle scientists could ever hope to discover. Such a great miracle opens up the **probability** that a creator may have acted many times thereafter.

Hugh Ross

REFERENCES AND RECOMMENDED READING

Borde, Arvind, Alan H. Guth, and Alexander Vilenkin. 2003. *Physical Review Letters* 90 (April): id. 151301.
Hawking, S. W., and R. Penrose. 1970. *Proceedings of the Royal Society of London, A* 314 (January): 520–49.
Vilenkin, Alexander. 2006. *Many Worlds in One.* New York: Hill and Wang.

BOYLE, ROBERT. Only a handful of Christian scientists have matched the combination of intense piety, deep theological reflection, and important scientific accomplishments found in Robert Boyle (1627–91). A brilliant experimentalist who made fundamental contributions to physical science and the **philosophy of science**, he also published about three quarters of a million words on various theological topics, including **natural theology** and other aspects of science and religion—works that were reprinted multiple times in several languages for many decades after his death. In short, he was thoughtful, prolific, and widely read. No early modern thinker was more influential on subsequent thinking about God and nature, not even **Galileo Galilei**, **René Descartes**, or **Isaac Newton**.

Boyle was almost universally regarded by his contemporaries as the greatest natural philosopher in England, until Newton (who was influenced by Boyle on several fronts) superseded him. Although best known today for publishing what we now call "Boyle's law," he actually credited others for this law's precise formulation. Nevertheless, his original scientific contributions were numerous. He discovered many physical and chemical properties of diverse liquids, solids, and gases, including phosphorus, the atmosphere, and the oceans, while contributing key insights to matter theory. He proved that fire, animals, and bioluminescence all need air, and that sound cannot travel through a vacuum.

A pioneer of chemical analysis (indeed he may have been

the first to speak of "analysis" in this context), he refined the use of chemical indictors and other specific tests, isolated hydrogen gas, and invented the match. Above all, Boyle helped establish the modern scientific laboratory and the methods it employs—to design an experiment to test a hypothesis, build the apparatus, supervise the experiment, and publish the results, including meticulously detailed descriptions of the equipment, materials, and procedures, so that others could reproduce it.

Before turning to science in his early twenties, Boyle had already written several devotional works on **morality**, theology, and biblical interpretation. A desire to benefit humanity by improving medicinal chemistry, coupled with his belief that the divinely created book of nature augmented the other two divine books of Scripture and conscience, motivated him to become a scientist. In his view, God had given us a mandate to study nature, and the knowledge gained pointed unambiguously to the creator. It is "very probable," Boyle noted, "that the world was *made*, to manifest the existence, and display the attributes of God; who … made the world for the same purpose, for which the pious philosopher studies it" (Hunter and Davis 1999–2000, 12:483).

Ironically, Boyle's abiding interest in the **design argument** as a powerful foil against unbelief echoed his own lifelong struggle with religious doubt. Not long after his conversion to Christianity during a frightful thunderstorm, the adolescent Boyle fell into melancholic ravings, leading him to contemplate suicide, before "at last it pleas'd God one Day he had receiv'd the Sacrament, to restore unto him the withdrawne sence of his Favor." Although he came through that difficult period, "never after did these fleeting Clouds [of doubt], cease now & then to darken the clearest serenity of his quiet" (Hunter 1994, 25). As he said on another occasion, "Of my own Private, & generally unheeded doubts, I could exhibit no short Catalogue" (Hunter and Davis 1999–2000, 13:180). Consequently, Boyle devoted hundreds of pages to answering the questions that dogged his **soul**, whether they touched on science or not.

In this context, Boyle used the design argument to change lives and hearts, not just minds. His main target was the immorality of certain "baptised infidels," who were "not so fully persuaded, that really *there is* [a God], as, out of regard to him, to deny themselves a much beloved, or very profitable sin, or undergo any considerable hardship, or run any great danger" (Hunter and Davis 1999–2000, 12:482).

In his most systematic work on natural theology, *A Disquisition about the Final Causes of Natural Things* (1688), Boyle expressed the wish "that my Reader should not barely observe the Wisdom of God, but be in some measure Affectively Convinc'd of it." The best way to achieve that, in his opinion, was "by Knowing and Considering the Admirable Contrivance of the Particular Productions of that Immense Wisdom," by which "Men may be brought, upon the same account, both to *acknowledge* God, to *admire* Him, and to *thank* Him" (Hunter and Davis 1999–2000, 11:145 and 95, italics in original). Therefore Boyle endowed a lectureship for "proving the Christian Religion against notorious Infidels [and] Atheists," including Jews and Muslims," while avoiding "any Controversies that are among Christians themselves" (Hunter 2010, 241).

Boyle believed that biblical **miracles**, not arguments from nature, offered the best evidence for the truth of Christianity: we could experience them vicariously through the reliable witnesses who recorded them, establishing the divine origin of the Gospels. A serious student of the Bible, he read it daily in the original languages and underwrote translations into Welsh, Irish, Turkish, and Malayan. He also served very effectively as governor of the Company for the Propagation of the Gospel in New England, under whose auspices John Eliot prepared his famous Algonquin Bible for the Indians in Massachusetts.

In perfect step with his piety and devotion to Scripture—both of which were often noted unambiguously by contemporary commentators—Boyle energetically rejected courtly mores. In a licentious age in which many in high places were given to vanity, promiscuity, and greed, he cultivated humility, chastity, and charity. While giving large sums anonymously, he also aimed to live and work generously in spirit. At a time when leading natural philosophers often hurled verbal assaults, he fervently sought "to speak of Persons with Civility, though of Things with Freedom," instead of "railing at a man's Person, or wrangling about his Words," for "such a quarrelsome and injurious way of writing does very much mis-become both a Philosopher and a Christian" (Hunter and Davis 1999–2000, 2:26).

Overall, Boyle considered himself a "priest" in the "temple" of nature. Although he often spoke of nature in just that way, he actually favored a far more impersonal metaphor: the world was "a great piece of Clock-work" (Hunter and Davis 1999–2000, 8:75), the bodies of living things were "watches," and God was the designing clock maker—a conception only encouraged by the work of contemporary artisans, who built diverse clockwork mechanisms, large and small, of great **complexity**. Boyle compared the universe to the great cathedral clock at Strasbourg, "where all things are so skilfully contriv'd, that the Engine being once set a Moving, all things proceed according to the Artificers first design … by vertue of the General and Primitive Contrivance of the whole Engine" (10:448).

It is easy to see how, in the hands of less pious **Enlightenment** authors a generation or two later, the clock metaphor would become the poster child for **deism**. For the deeply Christian Boyle, however, mechanistic science actually had obvious theological advantages over the Aristotelian conceptions it replaced. By denying the existence of a quasi-divine "Nature" that seemed to function autonomously with a mind of its own, it underscored God's sovereignty and focused our attention on the Creator, not the creation. And by advancing our knowledge of intelligible, mechanical properties of created matter, it empowered us to obey the Genesis mandate to use the creation for our benefit. Boyle's basic rhetorical strategy—that these machine-like "contrivances" in nature were far too complex to have been assembled by "blind **chance**," without a designer—was deeply influential on **William Paley** and modern proponents of **intelligent design**.

Edward B. Davis

REFERENCES AND RECOMMENDED READING

Davis, Edward B. 2007. "Robert Boyle's Religious Life, Attitudes, and Vocation." *Science and Christian Belief* 19:117–38.

Hooykaas, Reijer. 1997. *Robert Boyle: A Study in Science and Christian Belief*, trans. V. D. Dyke. Lanham, MD: University Press of America.

Hunter, Michael, ed. 1994. *Robert Boyle: By Himself and His Friends*. London: Pickering & Chatto.

———. 2010. *Boyle: Between God and Science*. New Haven, CT: Yale University Press.

Hunter, Michael, and Edward B. Davis, eds. 1999–2000. *The Works of Robert Boyle*. 14 vols. London: Pickering & Chatto.

BRADLEY, WALTER L. Walter L. Bradley (1943–), emeritus distinguished professor of mechanical engineering (Baylor University, Texas A&M University), is a prominent advocate of viewing the universe and life as the result of "divine creating activity" (Smarr 2012). He is a fellow of the American Society for Materials, of the **American Scientific Affiliation**, and of the Center for Science and Culture of the **Discovery Institute**. He is author of numerous technical articles relating to his professional specialization of materials engineering as well as many works on the interface between Christianity and science.

Bradley came to prominence in creation science with the appearance of the book *The Mystery of Life's Origin: Reassessing Current Theories* (Thaxton, Bradley, and Olsen

1984), in which he and his coauthors strenuously critiqued explanations of the origins of life that appeal to spontaneous abiogenesis from inanimate organic compounds. His book has been called "a seminal work for the theory of intelligent design" (Discovery Institute 2014). Furthermore, in numerous public lectures he has called attention to the congruence of the findings of science with the accounts in Genesis, notably the **big bang**, which implies a created rather than an eternal physical universe, the **fine-tuning** of the physical constants of **physics** that suggest a nonrandom universe, and the nature of the earth and its natural history that appear uniquely suited for life to exist. Thus he has been characterized as an "old-earth creationist."

Bradley is one of the founding professors of Faculty Commons, the faculty ministry of Campus Crusade for Christ. He has been called "an outstanding role model, excelling in academics while actively pursuing opportunities to share Christ. He pioneered faculty ministry and continues to encourage professors all over the world" ("Zero Out of 50" 2011).

In recent years, Bradley has shifted his research interests to applications of materials engineering "to helping the poorest people in under-developed parts of the world by providing them with useful technologies." In particular, he, with collaborators in Papua New Guinea, has developed a composite for automobile panels that employ coir, a by-product of coconut processing.

Since his retirement from his university position, Bradley has resided in Georgetown, Texas, with his wife, Carol Ann Bradley. He also has continued to participate in research and to present guest lectures throughout the United States.

Samuel E. Matteson

REFERENCES AND RECOMMENDED READING

Discovery Institute. 2014. www.discovery.org/scripts/viewDB/index.php?command=view&printerFriendly=true&id=3594.

"Zero Out of Fifty." 2011. *Frontlines.* Newsletter of Faculty Commons, Campus Crusade for Christ. September. www.facultycommons.com/wp-content/uploads/2010/11/Frontlines-Newsltr-Sept.pdf.

Smarr, Jessica. 2012. "Ratio Christi Lecture Blends Science and Faith." *The Battalion* (Texas A&M). November 20.

Thaxton, Charles B., Walter L. Bradley, and Roger L. Olsen. 1984. *The Mystery of Life's Origin: Reassessing Current Theories.* New York: Philosophical Library.

BRAHE, TYCHO. Though not as well-known today as **Nicolaus Copernicus** or **Johannes Kepler**, Tycho Brahe (1546–1601) was a key figure in the historical development of the scientific revolution of the seventeenth century. He was a Danish astronomer who compiled the most complete, systematic, and precise observations of the planets and stars before the invention of the telescope. His observations cast doubt on the older geocentric view of the universe and paved the way for the Copernican revolution. He also proposed an influential model of the universe known as geoheliocentrism.

Brahe was born in Knudstrup, Denmark (now in Sweden), in 1546 of a prominent Lutheran noble family. He began his studies in law at the University of Copenhagen but early on became interested in **astronomy**. He continued his studies at a number of universities throughout Germany and Switzerland but returned home in 1570 at the request of his ailing father. In 1576 King Frederick II offered Brahe the island of Hven (now called Ven) along with generous funding to establish an observatory there. Uraniborg, as it was called, became the finest observatory and research institution in all of Europe, with its own printing press, paper mill, laboratories, and library. There Brahe and his assistants recorded the positions of the planets and stars for more than 20 years. In 1599 he found a new patron in the Holy Roman emperor Rudolph II and continued his work in Prague. In Prague an assistant joined him whose name was Johannes Kepler.

Brahe's astronomical observations were important in undermining the geocentric model of the universe constructed by **Aristotle** and **Ptolemy**. This model had prevailed for more than 1,000 years. In 1572 he observed a new star in the constellation of Cassiopeia, thereby disproving Aristotle's notion that the heavens above the moon were constant and unchanging.

In 1577 Brahe observed a spectacular comet. With his precision instruments, he determined that the comet was passing through the orbit of Venus. Aristotle had taught that the planets were embedded in solid, crystalline-like spheres that rotated about the earth. If comets could pass through such spheres, they must not exist. Perhaps Brahe's greatest contribution is the vast amount of precise observational data he left behind for his assistant Johannes Kepler to use. Kepler used this data to develop his three laws of planetary motion. These laws added further support for the Copernican model of the universe.

Though Brahe admired the work of Copernicus, he never became an adherent of heliocentrism. For many astronomers of the time, the idea of a moving earth did not accord well with physical sense experience nor with Holy Scripture. In the battle over Gibeon, for example, Joshua commands the sun to be "still"—not the earth (Josh. 10). Though

Brahe was a devout Lutheran, however, it was the lack of a complementary theory of motion (which **Galileo** and Newton would later add) and other empirical complications that finally dissuaded Brahe from the Copernican **worldview**. Instead, he proposed a hybrid geoheliocentric model where the earth remains motionless at the center of the universe with the moon and the sun revolving about it. Then, the five planets (known at the time) revolve about the sun. This geoheliocentric view had the beauty of incorporating Copernicus's superior mathematical modeling of planetary motion while maintaining the **physics** (and scriptural support) of the Aristotelian and Ptolemaic view of an earth-centered universe.

Milton Eng

REFERENCES AND RECOMMENDED READING

Christianson, J. R. 2000. *On Tycho's Island: Tycho Brahe and His Assistants, 1570–1601.* Cambridge and New York: Cambridge University Press.
Danielson, Dennis, and Christopher M. Graney. 2014. "The Case against Copernicus." *Scientific American* 310 (1): 72–77.
Thoren, Victor E., and J. R. Christianson. 1990. *The Lord of Uraniborg: A Biography of Tycho Brahe.* Cambridge and New York: Cambridge University Press.

BROOKE, JOHN HEDLEY. John Hedley Brooke (1944–), the first Andreas Idreos Professor of Science and Religion at Oxford University, is arguably the most accomplished historian of Christianity and science. He has been editor of the *British Journal for the History of Science*, president of both the British Society for the History of Science and the International Society for Science and Religion, and a Gifford lecturer (Brooke and Cantor 1998). As an undergraduate at Cambridge, Brooke studied both chemistry and the history of science. He remained at Cambridge to complete a doctorate on the development of organic chemistry in the nineteenth century, but he has also written extensively about British **natural theology** from the seventeenth to the nineteenth century, various aspects of **Charles Darwin**'s life and work, science and **secularization**, and the intersection of science and religion in diverse religious cultures and contexts.

Brooke's interest in Christianity and science is longstanding. Early on, he wrote several units for the superb correspondence course offered by the Open University, "Science and Belief: from **Copernicus** to Darwin," including an insightful study of God, nature, and mechanical philosophy (Brooke 1974). Several dozen articles and book chapters followed, but his most important work is *Science and Religion: Some Historical Perspectives*, a magisterial study

stressing the great complexity of the historical landscape. No single conceptual model will do, especially not the conflict model: "science" and "religion" have simply meant too many different things to different people at different times. As he says, "Serious scholarship in the history of science has revealed so extraordinarily rich and complex a relationship between science and religion in the past that general theses are difficult to sustain. The real lesson turns out to be the complexity" (Brooke 1991, 5).

His personal religious position is no less complex—and virtually impossible to discern from his publications. According to a recent interview, as a teenager he was "exposed to a certain kind of evangelical Christianity" that "reinforced my interest in **philosophy of science**," but his own position "was always at the very liberal end of the evangelical spectrum." Questions about science and biblical interpretation led him to serious study of theology, in which he is widely read. At this point, Brooke does not see himself "in any way as an orthodox practicing Christian," but he remains "deeply uncomfortable … when I hear scientists sounding off about religion in ways that I consider ill-informed and based on whatever particular anti-religious culture they've been exposed to" (Sanderson 2013, 48–49, 51).

Edward B. Davis

REFERENCES AND RECOMMENDED READING

Brooke, John Hedley. 1974. "Newton and the Mechanistic Universe." In *Towards a Mechanistic Philosophy*. Science and Belief, from Copernicus to Darwin, Unit 2. Milton Keynes, UK: Open University Press.
———. 1991. *Science and Religion: Some Historical Perspectives.* Cambridge: Cambridge University Press.
Brooke, John Hedley, and Geoffrey Cantor. 1998. *Reconstructing Nature: The Engagement of Science and Religion.* Edinburgh: T&T Clark.
Sanderson, Katharine. 2013. "Science's Spiritual Side." *Chemistry World* 10:48–51.

BRUNO, GIORDANO. Giordano Bruno (1548–1600) was an occult thinker from Naples, Italy. He is best known as an early supporter of **Copernicus**'s theory that the earth orbits the sun. He was burned at the stake in Rome in 1600 by the inquisition due to his heretical philosophy.

Life

Bruno was born in 1548 and began his career as a Dominican friar at the age of 15. However, he tired of the structures of a regular life and so absconded from the order to travel Europe in 1576. He appears to have been a gregarious fellow who was able to quickly make friends and also enemies wherever he went. In 1583 Bruno arrived in Oxford, England, where he began delivering lectures that directly contradicted the Aristotelian philosophy of the local professors. On his return to Italy in 1591, Bruno was arrested by the Venetian inquisition after being betrayed by a local aristocrat with whom he was staying. He was extradited to Rome and spent many years in prison as his voluminous writings were investigated for heresy. Eventually he was invited to recant a list of eight heretical statements by Cardinal Robert Bellarmine. His refusal to do so saw him condemned as a recalcitrant heretic, and he was sentenced to death.

Thought

Today Bruno is best known for his support of the proposal by Nicolas Copernicus that the earth orbits the sun. He made his most explicit statements on the topic in his book *The Ash Wednesday Supper* (Bruno 1995), published in England in 1584. Whereas Copernicus based his theory on hard **mathematics**, Bruno argued from his religious veneration of the sun its rightful center of the universe. There is no evidence that this aspect of his thought or his belief in an infinite universe were instrumental in his conviction for heresy. Rather, Bruno's many books provided ample evidence of heterodoxy for the inquisition to pick over. His philosophy appears to have been an amalgamation of neo-Platonism and occult thought derived from the recently translated works attributed to Hermes Trismegistus. Unlike most other occultists of the time, Bruno was explicitly pagan in his religious beliefs. In no sense was he a scientist, although he was happy to use scientific theories as evidence for his mystical speculation.

Legacy

In 1889 Italian rationalists erected a statue of Bruno in the Campo de' Fiori, the square in Rome where he was executed. A shortage of more suitable candidates has lent Bruno the mantle of a martyr for science, although most historians now doubt that this is deserved. His real significance remains a matter of controversy. In the 1960s, Frances Yates (Yates 1964) portrayed him as a magician, while other scholars, led by Hilary Gatti (Gatti 2002), have strained to recast him as a philosopher of note or at least a freethinker. John Bossy's book *Giordano Bruno and the Embassy Affair* (Bossy 1991) found a role for him in the murky world of Tudor espionage. Whatever he may or may not have stood for, Bruno's fame today rests on his terrible death at the stake rather than anything he achieved in his life.

James Hannam

REFERENCES AND RECOMMENDED READING

Bossy, John. 1991. *Giordano Bruno and the Embassy Affair*. New Haven, CT: Yale University Press.
Bruno, Giordano. 1995. *The Ash Wednesday Supper*, trans. Lawrence S. Lerner and Edward A. Gosselin. Toronto: Toronto University Press.
Gatti, Hilary. 2002. *Giordano Bruno and Renaissance Science*. Ithaca, NY: Cornell University Press.
Yates, Frances. 1964. *Giordano Bruno and the Hermetic Tradition*. Chicago: University of Chicago Press.

BURIDAN, JEAN. Jean Buridan (b. before 1300, d. before 1361) taught **logic** and **natural philosophy** at the University of Paris. His widely read commentaries on the works of **Aristotle** made Buridan one of the most influential masters of arts of the fourteenth century. Buridan's significance for science is particularly evident in his development of the theory of impetus, his emphasis on empirical evidence, his use of probable arguments, and his theory of the formation of the earth.

Buridan employed the term *impetus* to refer to an impressed force that acts at a level determined by a combination of the mover's speed and quantity of matter, and which endures in its effect within the moving body unless countered by another force. For Buridan, impetus explains the cause of the motion of projectiles without recourse to the continuing action of air. Buridan also used impetus to explain the acceleration of falling bodies. Weight cannot be the cause of the increase of velocity, since the weight of a falling body remains constant. Rather, acceleration must be due to the addition of increments of impetus. For Buridan, a body continues to accumulate impetus as long as it continues to fall, so the velocity of fall increases according to the time of fall.

Buridan posed a thought experiment to challenge the commonsense assumption of the immobility of the earth. If the earth were once started in motion around its axis, its rotation would be maintained indefinitely by impetus. Buridan then argued that alleged astronomical proofs of the immobility of the earth were inconclusive. One may not determine, by such sensory experience, whether the sphere of fixed stars spins around the earth once a day or whether the earth turns on its axis once a day, because the same observations would result in either case. Although Buridan concluded on other grounds in favor of the immobility of the earth, his arguments for the relativity of motion were influential.

Finally, Buridan articulated a theory of the formation of the Earth. Assuming that the far side of the earth is a watery hemisphere, Buridan hypothesized that sediment eroded from the dry hemisphere would be gradually deposited in layers on the sea floor. As new layers accumulate on the far side, earthquakes uplift the dry side as the earth periodically adjusts to a new center of gravity. Gradually the sea-born layers become buried and rise through the entire body of the earth, eventually to become exposed on the surface of the dry hemisphere. This ongoing cycle of erosion, deposition, and uplift explains why the earth is made of rock layers and why marine fossils occur on the tops of mountains, on the assumption of the antiquity of the earth and without recourse to Noah's **flood**. Buridan's ideas, elaborated by **Nicole Oresme**, Leonardo da Vinci, and others, remained influential into the seventeenth century (Clagett 1959; Moody 1941).

In addition to his work in natural philosophy, Buridan's contributions in logic and **metaphysics** were also significant. His reputation was such that even his donkey achieved legendary status. Spinoza relayed the story that, trained by the master in the **principle of sufficient reason**, Buridan's donkey found himself halfway between two equally appetizing haystacks and therefore starved to death.

Historians of science have scrutinized how a fourteenth-century emphasis on divine omnipotence and the contingency of the natural order facilitated logical thought experiments, probable arguments, and empirical investigations. By employing impetus to explain projectile motion, the acceleration of falling bodies, and the possible rotation of the earth, Buridan and his contemporaries provided a starting point for **Galileo**'s investigations nearly two centuries later. The medieval critique of Aristotelian natural philosophy exemplified by Buridan provides an intriguing historical example of how theology, logic, and empirical considerations combined in a rigorous and fruitful reformation of natural science.

Kerry Magruder

REFERENCES AND RECOMMENDED READING

Clagett, Marshall. 1959. *The Science of Mechanics in the Middle Ages*. Madison: University of Wisconsin Press.
Grant, Edward. 1996. *The Foundations of Modern Science in the Middle Ages*. Cambridge: Cambridge University Press.
Kaiser, Christopher. 1997. *Creational Theology and the History of Physical Science: The Creationist Tradition from Basil to Bohr*. Studies in the History of Christian Thought. Leiden: Brill Academic.
Moody, Ernest A. 1941. "John Buridan on the Habitability of the Earth." *Speculum* 16:415–25.
Sylla, Edith. 2000. "*Ideo quasi mendicare oportet intellectum humanum*: The Role of Theology in John Buridan's Natural Philosophy." In *The Metaphysics and Natural Philosophy of John Buridan*. Medieval and Early Modern Science, ed. J. M. M. H. Thijssen and Jack Zupko, 244–45. Leiden: Brill.

C

CALVIN, JOHN. The sixteenth century was a period fraught with change, from the unfolding of the Protestant **Reformation** to the Copernican Revolution (see **Copernicus, Nicolaus**). From the sphere of theology to **astronomy**, the Aristotelian **worldview** was under pressure. In the midst of newly emerging dynamics for European society and thought, the Reformer John Calvin (1509–64) grew to become one of the most significant and enduring voices of the early modern era. As pastor and lecturer in the city of Geneva for nearly half of his life, Calvin's theology developed as he preached, lectured, and published copiously. His writings, particularly his *Institutes of the Christian Religion*, engaged the topic of Christianity and science in a number of notable regards.

Consistent with a medieval mind-set, Calvin regarded the branches of the liberal arts as the "maidservants" of theology, and he cautioned against elevating them to the level of "mistress." Distinction was, therefore, maintained between knowledge of earthly matters and knowledge of heavenly matters, the latter of which was the greatest wisdom of all to Calvin. By maintaining the fundamental difference between creature and Creator, Calvin denied that human wisdom could ever wholly penetrate the heights of heavenly knowledge in his commentary on 1 Corinthians 1:20: "Man with all his cunning is as capable of understanding by his own powers the mysteries of God as a donkey is capable of understanding a concert" (Holder 2006, 38).

Scholarship has at points interpreted Calvin's cautions toward human reason more polemically than he seemingly intended. Although Calvin affirmed that the revealed wisdom of the gospel was greater than all human philosophy and, in fact, was the true foundation of **epistemology**, this notion did not impede his advocacy of liberal arts learning insofar as that knowledge did not seek pride of place.

Critical to the issue is Calvin's teaching on the doctrine of **the fall**, whereby the **original sin** of Adam rendered human perception of the world distorted and blinded in a hereditary manner though the inherent goodness of creation was never lost. Calvin elevated special **revelation** by explaining that apart from the "spectacles" of Scripture, humanity was susceptible to the traps of idolatry and confusion to the point of inexcusability before God. Yet limited human understanding in no way rendered the universe less of a "mirror" of the invisible God or less of a "theater" of God's glory, particularly in terms of its **beauty** and order. Nevertheless, only those with faith rooted in Jesus Christ and grounded in the revelation of Scripture could then rightly perceive the general revelation of God as Creator and truly appreciate the wonder of God's **providence**.

Meanwhile, Scripture's role in explaining the natural world is best understood in light of Calvin's overarching principle of accommodation. Because Scripture is written for the "common folk" so that they might receive a sufficient knowledge of salvation, God accommodates heavenly wisdom according to human capacities much as a "nurse" communicates to a child. Consequently, Calvin denied that a precise explanation of the natural world is the intention of Scripture; in contrast, Calvin taught that Scripture recounts the world according to common perceptions. Nonetheless, Calvin encouraged unequivocally the advancement of knowledge in terms of astronomy, medicine, and all the natural sciences as an avenue for developing a greater appreciation for God's glory and providence as well as for bettering human life.

Due to Calvin's supportive attitude toward **natural philosophy**, his fundamental affirmation of the created goodness of creation, and his belief that all truth is a gift of God, scholars have increasingly regarded Calvin's thought as playing a role in paving the way for the flourishing of the sciences in subsequent centuries.

Jennifer Powell McNutt

BIBLIOGRAPHY AND RECOMMENDED READING

Gamble, Richard, ed. 1992. *Calvin and Science.* New York: Garland.
Holder, R. Ward. 2006. *John Calvin and the Grounding of Interpretation: Calvin's First Commentaries.* Leiden: Brill.
Schreiner, Susan E. 1995. *The Theater of His Glory: Nature and the Natural Order in the Thought of John Calvin.* Grand Rapids: Baker.
———. 2009. "Creation and Providence." In *The Calvin Handbook*, ed. Herman J. Selderhuis, 267–75. Grand Rapids: Eerdmans.
Zachman, Randall C. 2009. "The Beauty and Terror of the Universe: John Calvin and Blaise Pascal." In *Reconsidering Calvin: Current Issues in Theology*, 6–34. Cambridge: Cambridge University Press.

CAMBRIAN EXPLOSION. The Cambrian Explosion refers to the relatively rapid increase in the diversity of animals that occurred during the Cambrian geological period a little more than a half billion years ago.

Based on the geological record, most scientists believe that life arose about 3.5 billion years ago. The early cells in the **fossil record** resemble simple bacteria, and there is no sign of the more sophisticated, multicompartmental cells known as eukaryotes until about 1.8 billion years ago. Roughly 300 million years later, according to fossil findings, multicellular eukaryotes arose, but likely there was little diversification of these cell-colonies until much later. By about 750 million years ago, however, at least eight different groups of multicellular eukaryotes had come into existence (Erwin and Valentine 2013, 4). Evidence for the **creation** of animals related to modern sponges, as well as others of unidentified affinity, have been found in rocks dated within a geological period known as the Ediacaran at 550 to 575 million years. Rocks of this age also contain beautifully preserved animal embryos. Furthermore, independent molecular evidence suggests the origin of both sponges and cnidarians (a grouping that includes jellyfish) by this time as well.

The Cambrian period is officially dated as beginning 541 million years ago, and it is characterized by the rapid diversification of animals that manifest bilateral symmetry. As the University of California's Museum of **Paleontology** website puts it: "The fastest growth in the number of major new animal groups took place during the second and third stages of the early Cambrian, a period of about 13 million years. In that time, the first undoubted fossil annelids, arthropods, brachiopods, echinoderms, mollusks, onychophorans, poriferans, and priapulids show up in rocks all over the world." Although 13 million years is not a short time, it *is* short relative to the length of time that life has existed on earth.

Why animal diversity appeared so rapidly at that time is not known for certain, but there is strong evidence that this was preceded by a period of rapid increase in oceanic oxygen, so many investigators believe this increase may have been an important factor stimulating animal diversification. Furthermore, there is considerable evidence that some of the key genetic **information** needed to build more sophisticated multicellular organisms was being slowly assembled over the preceding 200 million years.

Interestingly, land plants had a similar "explosion" associated with new plant groups and growth forms, but it occurred about 140 million years later during the Devonian geological period. This rapid diversification in terrestrial plants was followed in turn by a rapid diversification in arthropods, like insects.

The history of life is characterized by episodic "mini-explosions" in new body forms, and this is often associated with some type of ecological change (e.g., the diversification of mammals that occurred soon after the **dinosaurs** went extinct). The Cambrian explosion is especially noteworthy though, because the different animal forms that arose at that time were very different from each other, and almost without exception no other major innovation in animal body plan was ever developed again. Today, and apparently for the past 500 million years or so, it appears that genetic changes that modify the embryo in a manner that would bring about a major change in morphology either have not occurred or, if they have, they are less viable and subsequently lost.

One of the current mysteries in biology is what was different at the time of the Cambrian explosion such that genetic change enabled major new body plans to be developed. Although unanswered at this point, it is a question of great interest and active investigation. The **mystery** associated with the rapidity and uniqueness of the Cambrian explosion has caused many Christians to propose that God's design activity is especially apparent during this period of time. Others stress that the entire evolutionary process occurs in response to the creation command and occurs through God's ongoing presence. According to this view, one need not look for specific times when science does not yet have an explanation of a phenomenon.

Darrel R. Falk

REFERENCES AND RECOMMENDED READING

Erwin, Douglas, and James Valentine. 2013. *The Cambrian Explosion: The Construction of Animal Biodiversity.* Englewood, CO: Roberts and Company.
Meyer, Stephen. 2013. *Darwin's Doubt: The Explosive Origin of Animal Life and the Case for Intelligent Design.* New York: HarperOne.

CARNAP, RUDOLF. Rudolf Carnap (1891–1970) was a highly influential, German-born analytic philosopher who made important contributions in logic, philosophy of language, and **philosophy of science**.

Carnap was born in 1891 in what is now Wuppertal, Germany. Just before the outbreak of World War I, Carnap studied philosophy and **mathematics** at the University of Freiburg and the University of Jena (where he was a pupil of Gottlob Frege). Having finished his military service, Carnap returned to Jena where he completed a dissertation on the philosophical foundations of geometry.

By 1926 he was a member of Moritz Schlick's (1882–1936)

famed Vienna Circle, a group of philosophers and scientists attempting to work out a "scientific" conception of the world—which in their eyes was equivalent to a scientific materialist **worldview**. This group of logical positivists is perhaps best known for its verifiability principle, which claimed that all cognitively meaningful statements must be either analytically true (i.e., true in virtue of the meaning of the terms) or empirically verifiable through observations of the senses. Importantly, because they thought they could not be verified by experience, the positivists dismissed the claims of aesthetics, ethics, theology, and traditional **metaphysics** as meaningless pseudostatements that are neither true nor false. The **verification principle** has primarily been criticized for not meeting its own criterion: the principle itself is neither analytically true nor empirically verifiable.

In 1931 Carnap took a position at Prague's German University. But seeing Europe's growing darkness, Carnap emigrated to America in 1935. There he influenced many notable philosophers as a professor at the University of Chicago and UCLA.

By 1936 Carnap was arguing that scientific or empirical statements are not subject to verification but to *confirmation*. Because empirical hypotheses can always be overturned by further sense experience, Carnap thought that they are subject to increasing probabilistic confirmation or disconfirmation (in light of our evidence) rather than verification. Thus began his lifelong pursuit of an adequate inductive logic, a **logic** of **probability**.

One common way to think of probability is in terms of frequencies. In this view, if three-fourths of all sea turtles fail to survive their first year, then the probability that a randomly chosen baby sea turtle will survive its first year is 0.25. But notice that we often want to know the probability of an event's occurrence *given certain evidence*. Given that a major scientific study reported that half of all sea turtles die their first year, on the degree-of-confirmation interpretation of probability advocated by Carnap, the probability that a randomly chosen newborn sea turtle will die this year is 0.5—even if this doesn't match the actual frequency. In this latter view, probability is a measure of the degree to which a set of evidence confirms a given empirical hypothesis.

One major benefit of Carnap's inductive logic is its potential for solving **David Hume**'s (1711–76) **problem of induction**, in which causes cannot be said to lead certainly to effects. A persistent problem for Carnap's logic, however, was that the probability of universal scientific laws is always zero.

Still hard at work on an adequate system of inductive logic, Carnap died on September 14, 1970.

Logan Paul Gage

REFERENCES AND RECOMMENDED READING

Friedman, Michael, and Richard Creath, eds. 2007. *The Cambridge Companion to Carnap*. Cambridge Companions to Philosophy. Cambridge: Cambridge University Press.
Schilpp, Paul Arthur, ed. 1963. *The Philosophy of Rudolf Carnap*. Library of Living Philosophers. Vol. 11. La Salle, IL: Open Court.

CARTWRIGHT, NANCY. Nancy Cartwright (1944–), a prolific and highly influential contemporary philosopher of science, is perhaps best known for her books *How the Laws of Physics Lie* and *The Dappled World: A Study of the Boundaries of Science*.

She sees her views as flowing out of an empirical methodology that turns to actual scientific practice, as opposed to armchair theorizing, to deliver our picture of the world. Somewhat ironically, she rejects the **empiricism** of **David Hume**, with its disavowal of things like nonoccurrent powers and its associated regularity account of laws, because, in her view, that is not what science delivers.

In *How the Laws of Physics Lie*, Cartwright argues that physicists employ theoretical laws that apply only to highly idealized situations that seldom or never obtain. Taken as descriptions of real-world situations, therefore, these laws are either false or merely vacuously true. For this reason, she concludes that a traditional, covering-law account of scientific explanation cannot be correct. She proposes instead a "simulacrum account." Scientific explanation proceeds not by subsuming real-world phenomena under theoretical laws, but by constructing false, idealized, "prepared descriptions" of those phenomena, to which (approximations of) theoretical laws are then applicable.

However, Cartwright's antirealism concerning theoretical laws does not extend to theoretical entities such as quarks or electrons. She maintains that science often produces successful *causal explanations* by invoking those entities, and that accepting causal explanations requires believing that the entities cited as causes exist.

In *The Dappled World*, Cartwright continues these themes (as well as themes developed in her book *Nature's Capacities and Their Measurement*), but with different emphases. She argues against what she calls a "fundamentalist" view of laws, according to which the universe is governed by fundamental laws that are universal in scope.

The natural world, she maintains, presents us with a patchwork, with different principles applying to different domains. She concedes for the sake of argument that we might correctly regard so-called "fundamental" laws as reporting truths. But if we do, we should regard them not as expressing universally applicable regularities, but in neo-Aristotelian fashion as claims about the natures or capacities of things. Coulomb's law, for example, does not tell us what the actual forces between charged particles are because it ignores other factors, such as the influence of gravitation. Rather, according to Cartwright, it reports the *tendency* of such particles to attract or repel one another *qua charged*.

The regularities associated with these laws apply, Cartwright maintains, only to what she refers to as "nomological machines"—systems, often artificially constructed, in which various capacities are exhibited in the absence of interfering factors. By learning about these capacities, we may construct other kinds of nomological machines with their own associated regularities. She takes this view of laws to have important practical upshots, insofar as it suggests strategies for gaining and applying scientific knowledge for the purpose of manipulating the world, not only in domains such as **physics**, but also in domains such as economics.

Kenneth Boyce

REFERENCES AND RECOMMENDED READING

Cartwright, Nancy. 1983. *How the Laws of Physics Lie.* Oxford: Oxford University Press.
———. 1989. *Nature's Capacities and Their Measurement.* Oxford: Oxford University Press.
———. 1999. *The Dappled World: A Study of the Boundaries of Science.* Cambridge: Cambridge University Press.

CAUSATION. Two names stand out among Christians who hold distinctive views on causation: **John Polkinghorne** affirms upward causation, whereas **Nancey Murphy** supports downward causation.

The idea of causality, by which we mean—in this case—*efficient* or *productive* causality, presumes that one thing leads to another, and deals with whether, why, and how one thing makes another happen. Causality presumes that the antecedent precedes and also makes the incident occur. Other categories of causation exist—final, formal, and material, in addition to efficient. In addition, there is state-state causation, but also agent-state causation. **Divine action** is also a form of causation (see **Aristotle's Four Causes**; **Divine Action**).

Polkinghorne bases his support of upward causation (also referred to as bottom-up thinking or **reductionism**) on his desire to gain understanding based on a careful assessment of phenomena as the guide to physical reality. He distinguishes between the two types of causation: "The world of thought divides into top-down thinkers, who place reliance upon general principles and pursue their clear and discriminating evaluation, and bottom-up thinkers, who feel it is safest to start in the basement of particularity, and then generalize a little" (Polkinghorne 1994, 11).

The upward causation approach begins with the suggestion that everything in our universe is made of matter and everything can be reduced to the elementary particles that are the basic constituents of matter. Elementary particles comprise atoms, atoms make molecules, molecules make cells, and cells comprise the brain. The ultimate cause of all of this is always the interactions between the elementary particles. Upward causation means that all physical causes originate in the elementary particles and move upward. The result is that the behavior of a whole or a system is completely determined by the behavior of its parts, elements, or subsystems. If one knows the laws governing the behavior of the parts, one should be able to deduce the laws governing the behavior of the whole.

In the 1970s Donald Campbell developed an idea from systems theory, noting that in many instances the whole is greater than the sum of the parts, for the whole has emergent properties that cannot be reduced to properties of the parts. **Emergence** is an ambiguous concept, so some people would rather express this in terms of the more precise concept of downward causation, which can be specified as a converse of the reductionist upward causation principle: the behavior of the parts is determined by the behavior of the whole, and so determination moves downward rather than upward. Here determination is not complete, so that a more complete statement of the principle of causation could be formulated this way: "The whole is to some degree constrained by the parts (upward causation), but at the same time the parts are to some degree constrained by the whole (downward causation)."

Nancey Murphy (2000) presents an example first given by Donald Campbell in his explanation of the optimal design of the jaws of worker ants or termites. How did this come about? The bottom-up account gives part of the answer—the termite's genes give instructions for protein formation, in particular for the jaw structure. But how is it that the termite has this particular **DNA** instead of the myriad of other possibilities? The answer is **natural selection**. Bottom-up causation accounts for the production of the optimal macromolecules, and top-down causation has selected from the countless variants the useful ones for the task at hand and hence for survival to reproduce.

A more complete understanding of physical causation must include both bottom-up and top-down approaches.

Richard F. Carlson

REFERENCES AND RECOMMENDED READING

Murphy, Nancey. 1997. *Anglo-American Postmodernity*. Boulder, CO: Westview.
———. 2000. "Downward Causation." Counterbalance. www.counterbalance.org/evp-mind/downw-frame.html.
Polkinghorne, John. 1994. *The Faith of a Physicist: Reflections of a Bottom-Up Thinker*. Princeton, NJ: Princeton University Press.

CHANCE. The concept of chance has been at the center of a debate about religion and its relationship with science, especially in recent times. This is particularly true in the discipline of biology (but less so in **physics**), and especially with regard to the theory of evolution.

A number of leading atheistic thinkers (sometimes called evolutionary naturalists), such as **Richard Dawkins**, **Carl Sagan**, and **Daniel Dennett** have interpreted the biological process of evolution as being governed by a large element of chance, especially at the level of mutations in **DNA**, and hence have argued that evolution is a haphazard, random process that has no overall direction or goal. Their understanding of chance is not the claim that mutations have no causes, but rather that they occur without regard to the benefit, fitness, or "design" of the organism. The coming into being of any **species** (including *Homo sapiens*), as well as the nature of that species, is therefore an unplanned, unsupervised process, and hence they argue that there is no designer guiding the process, no God who directs evolution. This argument is often presented as a critique of certain forms of the **design argument**, especially that of eighteenth-century thinker **William Paley**.

Christian philosophers have offered a number of important criticisms of this general position. First, process thinkers have offered various arguments for the view that it is quite possible for God to include an element of both design and chance in the process of **causation** in the natural world and yet to be directing the final outcomes. A second response is that there is an *underlying* order in the universe, expressed in the laws of physics, which makes science (including evolution) possible. Third, many evangelical thinkers in particular have directly criticized the theory of evolution itself in various ways. Some

defend a creationist viewpoint, arguing that the evidence does not warrant acceptance of the theory; others contend that the claim that evolution operates by chance is not part of the official theory but is a metaphysical assumption by those who have co-opted the theory as a means of defending their atheism. Still others hold that while we must judge the theory of evolution as we would any scientific theory, the **emergence** of rational, conscious, self-aware observers with free will and moral agency, who also have some control over the process of evolution, is very good evidence of an overall design, and therefore of a designer.

Fourth, in the past two decades, advocates of **intelligent design** theory have argued that there are "irreducible complexities" in nature, especially at the molecular level, which the thesis of **natural selection** is unlikely to be able to explain. These complexities suggest a designer. Fifth, some thinkers deny that there is any chance operating in biology, or in any part of the natural world, contending instead that the process of cause and effect that we find in science operates in a deterministic manner. This means that the end results of evolutionary processes are the intended outcomes of God, who set up the initial ingredients of the universe and the laws of physics. Once common confusions in the discussion are cleared up, especially between chance and randomness, and the notions of predictability and **probability**, it is much harder to see a significant role for chance in evolution, and so all atheistic arguments that appeal to chance are considerably undermined.

Brendan Sweetman

REFERENCES AND RECOMMENDED READING

Dembski, W., and M. Ruse, eds. 2004. *Debating Design: From Darwin to DNA*. New York: Cambridge University Press.
Peacocke, Arthur. 1993. *Theology for a Scientific Age*. Minneapolis: Fortress.
Sweetman, Brendan. 2015. *Evolution, Chance and God*. New York: Bloomsbury.
Van Till, Howard. 1986. *The Fourth Day*. Grand Rapids: Eerdmans.

CHAOS THEORY. The success of physical science in the seventeenth through nineteenth centuries left people with the impression that the universe worked as clockwork, operating under deterministic physical laws. In referring to the success of Newtonian **physics** to seemingly account for all motion of objects, big and small, it was suggested that given knowledge of initial conditions and the forces acting on all entities of the universe, the complete determination of all subsequent motion of these entities would be possible. Further, it was thought that as a result there was no such thing as free will, with all future events in the universe having been predetermined.

The twentieth century has seen that viewpoint discredited with the development of quantum theory (including **Heisenberg's uncertainty principle**) and recently with the advent of chaos theory. Even though quantum theory yields definite results (such as eigenvalues and eigenfunctions), the predictions of the theory are understood to yield only probabilistic results, according to the majority viewpoint. The result is that for certain physical processes, the world has become profoundly unpredictable, and at the same time profoundly open and endowed with true becoming. This rather surprising state of affairs is not simply a result of our ignorance.

Chaos theory may be somewhat misnamed, for this aspect of physics does not apply only to chaotic systems but rather to any kind of complex system, for its evolution in time depends exquisitely on precisely knowing its initial conditions—precise to a degree that is unobtainable, at least to us humans. The consequence of this lack of knowledge is that the evolution of the system is completely unknown after a certain time has elapsed, in some cases a small fraction of a second. Such a system can be correctly described by precise deterministic physical laws and hence is a deterministic system. But because of the lack of infinite precision in specifying the system's initial conditions, there are limitations to what can be calculated about its development. Chaos is thus the result. And because the requisite precision of the initial conditions is unobtainable, chaotic behavior is built into the nature of complex (real) systems. Such behavior may represent the true status of many physical systems, and therefore some conclude that this is an ontological status rather than a result of **epistemology**.

This leaves open a possible avenue for God's providential action, for the future is not necessarily rigidly (i.e., causally) predetermined, but rather its development is contained only within finite limits. This results in the possibility of not only bottom-up **causation** but also top-down causation by which God can guide the course of events in a somewhat hidden way by working though chaotic (or even microscopic quantum) events. **Chance** or accidental events do not conflict with divine **providence**.

The net result is that the twentieth century has seen the rigid deterministic clockwork operations of nature (the sixteenth- to nineteenth-century viewpoint) replaced by a more open future, governed by God who rules in a way consistent with the **laws of nature** that have been implemented

by him, but laws that exhibit some inherent openness. The reality of chaos theory is a component contributing to the open character of our universe and world.

Richard F. Carlson

REFERENCES AND RECOMMENDED READING

Polkinghorne, John. 1995. *Serious Talk.* Valley Forge, PA: Trinity Press International.
Russell, Robert John, Nancey Murphy, and Arthur R. Peacocke. 1995. *Chaos and Complexity: Scientific Perspectives on Divine Action.* Vatican City and Berkeley: Vatican Observatory Publications and The Center for Theology and the Natural Sciences.

CHINESE ROOM ARGUMENT. Formulated by the American philosopher **John Searle** in his influential and widely discussed 1980 article "Minds, Brains and Programs," the Chinese Room Argument utilizes a thought experiment to show the impossibility of true **artificial intelligence**. The argument asks us to imagine a native English speaker sitting in a room following English instructions for manipulating strings of Chinese symbols. People outside the room send in other Chinese symbols, which, unknown to the person in the room, are questions in Chinese. By following the instructions for manipulating strings of Chinese symbols, the man in the room is able to pass out Chinese symbols that correctly answer the questions.

According to one popular mark of understanding suggested by **Alan Turing** (1950), the person in the room understands Chinese. But the man does not understand a word of Chinese. The point is, if the man in the room doesn't understand Chinese on the basis of manipulating the correct string of Chinese symbols, then neither does any digital computer possess understanding by following syntactic rules for the manipulation of symbol strings. Thus, while suitably programmed computers might appear to possess understanding and intelligence, they in fact do not.

Searle's Chinese Room highlights the serious problems we face in understanding the nature of meaning and **consciousness** as well as the role of **intuition** in thought experiments. Searle's larger point is that you cannot get semantics (meaning) from syntax (formal symbol manipulation). In reply, critics argue that computers are not "merely syntactical" but are complex causal engines that get content from the various causal connections that hold among other states of the system (internalism) or through the external reality they represent (externalism). Searle rejects computational theories of meaning that depend on these complex causal connections, arguing instead that only the mind has intrinsic intentionality (and intrinsic semantic content). Computers, and whatever content they may possess, exhibit "derived intentionality" and hence neither meaning nor consciousness.

Many replies to the Chinese Room Argument accept the "no understanding" intuition and try to show how, despite appearances, the man in the room, or some other entity in the situation, meets the computationalist criteria for understanding. Another gambit is to argue that Searle's pretheoretical intuition, while widely shared by proponents and opponents of artificial intelligence, is simply wrong and, in light of current science, ought to be rejected. Just as it is an empirical fact that water is essentially H_2O, so too it is an empirical fact that symbol manipulation is the essence of understanding (Wakefield 2003).

While Searle himself is a naturalist, the theist has additional reason to think the no understanding intuition is sound and the Chinese Room Argument successful, and further, that it is not just computer programs that lack understanding and intelligence, but any purely physical machine. Mental phenomena are nonphysical entities, entities that are at home within and provide evidence for a broadly theistic universe (Adams 1987; Moreland 2008). Thus Searle, but not the theist, is saddled with the problem of how to locate mental phenomena in a physical world.

Paul M. Gould

REFERENCES AND RECOMMENDED READING

Adams, Robert. 1987. "Flavors, Colors, and God." *The Virtue of Faith and Other Essays in Philosophical Theology*. New York: Oxford University Press.
Damper, Robert. 2006. "The Logic of Searle's Chinese Room Argument." *Minds and Machines* 16:163–83.
Hauser, Larry. 1997. "Searle's Chinese Box: Debunking the Chinese Room Argument." *Minds and Machines* 7:199–226.
Moreland, J. P. 2008. *Consciousness and the Existence of God*. New York: Routledge.
Searle, John. 1980. "Minds, Brains and Programs." *Behavioral and Brain Sciences* 3:417–57.
———. 1984. *Minds, Brains and Science*. Cambridge, MA: Harvard University Press.
———. 1990. "Is the Brain's Mind a Computer Program?" *Scientific American* 262 (1): 26–31.
Turing, Alan. 1950. "Computing Machinery and Intelligence." *Mind* 59:433–60.
Wakefield, Jerome. 2003. "The Chinese Room Argument Reconsidered: Essentialism, Indeterminacy, and Strong AI." *Minds and Machines* 13:285–319.

CLAYTON, PHILIP. Philip Clayton (1956–) is a contemporary American philosopher and theologian and the Ingraham Professor of Theology at Claremont School of Theology. He holds four graduate degrees: one from Fuller Theological Seminary and three from Yale University, including a joint PhD in Religious Studies and Philosophy. He has taught or held research professorships at Williams College, California State University, Harvard University, Cambridge University, and the University of Munich.

Clayton began his doctoral work under the preeminent German theologian **Wolfhart Pannenberg**, completing that work at Yale University. Over the tenure of his teaching and research career, his interests have evolved from philosophy to the science-religion controversies to, most recently, what he calls "constructive theology," a Christian theology in dialogue with contemporary **metaphysics**, philosophy, and science. His work is expansive and includes publications in **epistemology**, **philosophy of science**, evolutionary biology, **neuroscience**, comparative theology, and constructive metaphysics. His research has focused primarily on biological **emergence**, religion and science, process studies, and contemporary issues in metaphysics, **ecology**, religion, and ethics.

He has also been a preeminent voice in the internationalization of the science-religion dialogue, including being the principal investigator of the Science and the Spiritual Quest Program involving over 120 distinguished senior scientists in dialogue at the intersections of science and spirituality. In addition, he has been a leading advocate for multicultural and multireligious approaches to the field, including from Muslim, Jewish, Christian, Hindu, and Southeast Asian religious traditions.

Theologically, Clayton holds to a dialogical and pluralistic form of process theology. He denies traditional **theism**, or what he calls "classical Christian theism," and champions panentheism, affirming the transcendence of God while denying the separation of God and the world. His panentheism entails a nonreductionistic, nondualistic, emergent and evolving universe, and he maintains that this model provides a more plausible account of **divine action**, ethics, metaphysics, and the **problem of evil** than traditional theism.

Clayton is also a pioneer and leading proponent of strong emergence—an innovative and far-reaching theory with regard to the natural sciences and the human mind and its relevance to religion. He has been deeply involved in the Christian emerging church movement and has lectured throughout the United States and abroad on the evolving understanding of Christian faith in the twenty-first century, including new and imaginative approaches to being the church. He is the head of the TransformingTheology.org project, and he launched the "Big Tent Christianity" movement with Brian McLaren and Tony Jones. Professor

Clayton is the recipient of numerous research grants and international lectureships, and he has published more than 20 books and hundreds of popular and academic articles.

Chad Meister

REFERENCES AND RECOMMENDED READING

Clayton, Philip. 2000. *The Problem of God in Modern Thought.* Grand Rapids: Eerdmans.
———. 2006. *The Oxford Handbook of Religion and Science.* Oxford: Oxford University Press.
———. 2008. *The Re-emergence of Emergence: The Emergentist Hypothesis from Science to Religion.* Oxford: Oxford University Press.
———. 2010. *Transforming Christian Theology: For Church and Society.* Minneapolis: Fortress.
Clayton, Philip, and S. Knapp. 2011. *The Predicament of Belief: Science, Philosophy, and Christian Minimalism.* Oxford: Oxford University Press.

CLIMATE CHANGE (Global-Warming View).
"Christianity and the ideas which lay behind it is a religion and a philosophy of creation" (Glacken 1967). Christianity is this and more because of its wide embrace of God's **revelation** both in creation and Scripture. As such, it is dedicated to holding all God's truth together and consequently makes major contributions to understanding creation and **providence**, including the integrity of the biosphere and the unity of knowledge.

In this it celebrates God's provisions for a habitable earth, including its climes—"inclinations" that "incline" it to be warmer or cooler at various sun angles with the earth's surface. These climes interplay with planetary energy exchange, joining with atmospheric and oceanographic processes, biogeographic and trophic dynamics, biogeochemical cycles, carbon cycling, and fossil carbon sequestration conceptually to emerge as "earth's climate system"—a system that is inseparably integrated within the wholeness of "the earth system" (Steffen et al. 2004).

Early American colleges were dedicated to this wholeness of God's truth and designed to promote "the essential synergy between science and religion" (Roberts and Turner 2000). This changed in the 1870s, however, as specialization and **reductionism** became broadly endorsed, with division and subdivision of knowledge into disciplines, including breaking off seminaries as separate institutions.

Reductionism fragmented the sciences—soon linking them "to skepticism as an operative principle," thereby limiting "the opportunity for religious truths to be 'grounded' in scientific claims." This made it difficult to maintain knowledge of earth as an integral system, much less to express

gratitude for it. No longer would a scientific treatise conclude as did astronomer Frank W. Very's *Atmospheric Radiation* in 1900: "We find the atmosphere playing the part of a conservator of thermal energy, and must gratefully admire the beneficent arrangement which permits the Earth to be clothed with verdure and abundant life." Soon thereafter the atmosphere would simply be taken for granted, without awe, wonder, or appreciation.

Dedication to holding all God's truth together resurged with remarkable strength on June 18, 2015, in a broadly integrative treatise, *Laudato Si'—On Care for Our Common Home.* This encyclical letter from Pope Francis published worldwide in a single day embraced God's revelation both in creation and Scripture with clear purpose: "Faced as we are with global environmental deterioration, I wish to address every person living on this planet." Grounded biblically and scientifically, it addressed climate change, biodiversity loss, ocean degradation, atmospheric pollution, and social degradation in 246 paragraphs—reintegrating disciplines and specialties created in the twentieth century.

In proposing an "integral ecology" the pope asserted that "fragmentation of knowledge and the isolation of bits of **information** can actually become a form of ignorance, unless they are integrated into a broader vision of reality" (¶138). Each specialty promotes its "isolation and the absolutization of its own field of knowledge"—all of which "prevents us from confronting environmental problems effectively" (¶201).

Importantly, Pope Francis confronted "an excessive anthropocentrism" handed us as "a Promethean vision of mastery over the world, which gave the impression that the protection of nature was something that only the fainthearted cared about" (¶116). Contrary to such mastery, he cited the biblical commission of Genesis 2:15 that "should be understood more properly in the sense of responsible stewardship" (¶116)—as a "culture of care" (¶14). Such a caring relationship opens us to awe and wonder, speaks of fraternity and **beauty**, and unites us intimately with all that exists (¶11). It sees earth's climate system as "a common good, belonging to all and meant for all ... a complex system linked to many of the essential conditions for human life" (¶23).

The largest organization of professional ecologists, the Ecological Society of America (ESA), commended Pope Francis—"clearly informed by the science underpinning today's environmental challenges"—for his "insightful encyclical on the environment ... an eloquent plea for responsible Earth Stewardship."

The largest US environmental religious consocation, the

National Religious Partnership for the Environment, also commended Pope Francis. Similarly, the Christian Reformed Church released a statement titled "Christian Reformed Church Celebrates Pope's Call to Climate Action," in which they "welcome[d] Pope Francis's encyclical on environmental stewardship, integral ecology, and climate change." Affirming that "human-induced climate change is a moral, social justice and religious issue," the CRC statement calls on "its institutions, churches, and individual members to take steps to address it" and in accord with the pope's focus on Genesis 2:15, this CRC release says "a central component of this task includes taking seriously God's command in Genesis 2:15 to serve and to protect the rest of the created order and to exercise responsible stewardship."

The Biblical Stewardship Commission

The pope's encyclical states that God's command in Genesis 2:15 fosters a "culture of care" (¶231) that implies a reciprocal relationship—"a relationship of mutual responsibility between human beings and nature" (¶67). This conception expects human beings to return the services of the garden with services of their own, practicing stewardship as "con-service." But this reciprocal relationship can be broken by excessive anthropocentrism, circumstance, or specialization, resulting in carelessness, indifference, and consequent degradation. Stewardship thus is a practice not reducible to a single word, but is rather a realm of stewardship. Both "to till" and "not to till" (as in no-till agriculture) may serve the garden. Beyond con-service, the commission of Genesis 2:15 requires "guardening"—providing a realm of safeguarding. The realm of stewardship incorporates the realms of con-serving and safeguarding as a comprehensive stewardship, while keeping in mind that "realities are more important than ideas" (¶110).

Atmospheric Providence

In dealing with realities, measurement is important. One such measurement is the temperature at the top of earth's atmosphere (TOA). My colleague Verner Suomi, who first used radiometers on earth-orbiting satellites to measure outgoing TOA radiation, found, along with later scientists, this to be 240 watts per square meter (240 w/m^2). The Stefan-Boltzmann law computes this as equivalent to -18°C (0.4°F). Yet earth's surface on average is about 15°C (59°F), which computes as outgoing radiation of 390 w/m^2. The reason for this difference? Earth's atmosphere. Clearly a life-sustaining gift of God's providence, earth's atmosphere makes life on earth possible and sustains it.

How is this achieved? "A great deal has been written on the influence of the absorption of the atmosphere upon the climate," wrote Arrhenius in 1896. "The selective absorption of the atmosphere is, according to the researches of John Tyndall, not exerted by the chief mass of the air, but in a high degree by aqueous vapour and carbonic acid [i.e., carbon dioxide], which are in the air in small quantities" (Arrhenius 1896). Absorption of sunlight by the atmosphere is "comparatively small" but is great for outgoing infrared radiation (IR), and this keeps the earth warmer than it would be otherwise.

Thirty-seven years earlier, in 1859, physicist John Tyndall gave a lecture at London's Royal Institution titled "On the Transmission of Heat of different qualities through Gases of different kinds." He showed that passing light through a prism of rock salt onto a screen elevated screen temperatures across the visible spectrum and surprisingly also in the invisible area below red (infrared, or IR). He next described constructing a three-foot tube sealed at both ends with plates of polished rock salt through which he projected visible light—finding it to pass freely when filled with nitrogen, oxygen, water vapor, or carbon dioxide. IR light also passed freely with the tube filled with nitrogen or oxygen, but was blocked when filled with water vapor or carbon dioxide. "The bearing of this experiment upon the action of planetary atmospheres is obvious," he said. "The solar heat possesses ... the power of crossing an atmosphere; but, when the heat is absorbed by the planet, it is so changed in quality that the rays emanating from the planet cannot get with the same freedom back into space. Thus the atmosphere admits of the entrance of the solar heat, but checks its exit; and the result is a tendency to accumulate heat at the surface of the planet" (Tyndall 1859).

Selective Absorption

In 1865 Tyndall noted, "If you open a piano and sing into it, a certain string will respond. Change the pitch of your voice; the first string ceases to vibrate, but another replies." Modern physical chemists measure these ringing frequencies or resonances for gas molecules as they respond to various frequencies of IR. Acting much like tiny springs, bonds that hold atoms together as gas molecules vibrate both by "stretching" and "bending" as they absorb IR at specific resonant frequencies. Di-atomic molecules have only a "stretching vibration" and are IR active only if the two atoms are different—thus the most abundant atmospheric gases, nitrogen (N=N) and oxygen (O=O) are IR inactive. The element argon has no bonds, thus also is IR inactive.

All gas molecules with three or more atoms are IR active—like atmospheric carbon dioxide (O=C=O) and water vapor (H-O-H), whose central "elbow" allows "bending vibrations" that flex above or below the "normal" angle of 180 degrees for carbon dioxide and 105 degrees for water vapor. Others with three or more atoms are methane (CH_4), nitrous oxide (NO_2), ozone (O_3), and chlorofluorocarbons (CFCs). Veerabhadran Ramanathan's research on CFCs at the Scripps Institution found some CFC molecules about 10,000 times more absorptive than CO_2 (Ramanathan and Xu 2010). These five contribute about 5 percent of atmospheric IR absorption of which methane leakage from wells and pipelines can be prevented and manufacture of CFCs can be eliminated, leaving two major IR active gases, carbon dioxide and water vapor.

The "Offices" of Water Vapor and Carbon Dioxide

These two major atmospheric IR-active gases differ greatly in their respective "offices." Carbon dioxide has a steady and continuous carbonic presence throughout the atmosphere at all temperatures. But water vapor varies widely in time and place from very high concentrations above tropical oceans to very low concentrations in polar climes where it can reach zero. Water vapor is a condensing gas and it has a temperature-dependent physical "cap"—a "saturation capacity" that compels it to condense into liquid when it reaches this temperature limit. Water vapor's "cap" is cut approximately in half for every 10°C (18° F) fall in temperature. In grams of water vapor per kilogram (g/kg) of dry air, it is about 49 at 40°C, 15 at 20°, 3.8 at 0°, 0.75 at -20°, 0.1 at -40°, and 0.01 at -60°C. In polar air it may drop below this cap to zero g/kg (Bloch and Karasiński 2014). In contrast, carbon dioxide does not condense, has no cap, and is everywhere present in the earth's atmosphere.

Atmospheric water dynamics and dramatics

Thus water vapor concentration increases to higher levels in warmer air, and as it moves upward and is blown to cooler places, it condenses into liquid water, releasing its latent heat and forming mists, clouds, and precipitation. The energy released—its "latent heat of condensation"—is equal to its "latent heat of evaporation" that earlier was required for its transformation from liquid to vapor: 540,000 calories per kilogram. Once water vapor is thus removed, it is soon restored by more evaporation into air that again moves upward and is blown to cooler areas—its water vapor moving towards its temperature-dependent saturation cap.

Water vapor thus serves as a powerful heat pump, moving immense amounts of energy from warmer to cooler places. In this movement, atmospheric and water vapor dynamics are often boisterous—in thunderstorms, rushing winds, pelting rains, and bouncing hail—and calming in gentle dewfall, ascending vapor, and rising mists. Remove this vapor from the atmosphere and it comes back; add water vapor and it condenses out, with an average atmospheric residence time of about 10 days. By contrast, the other major IR-active gas—carbon dioxide—is steady and consistent with residence time ranging about 4–10 years.

Atmospheric carbon dioxide for 250, 2,000, and 10,000 years

Carbon dioxide is measured at observatories—as at Mauna Loa, Hawaii, where "flask measurements" began in 1958—and from gas inclusions in ice. An ice core from Law Dome, Antarctica, shows average CO_2 concentration of 43 records for 0 to AD 1600 (pre–Industrial Revolution) as 279.5 parts per million (range: 276 to 284 ppm). Antarctic Vostoc cores show 7 measurements from 2,342 to 10,123 years ago between 254.6 to 284.7 ppm (average: 266.2 ppm). These data show CO_2 maintained with remarkable regularity during recorded human history—near 280 ppm.

This regularity gave human civilization climatically what physiological regulation gives bodily: the freedom not to have to think about it. Over some 250 years of the Industrial Revolution, however, the atmosphere took on a much larger role as a sink for airborne wastes and by-products of human industry, including carbon dioxide and nitrogen oxides. Measurements of atmospheric carbon dioxide concentrations, begun in 1958 by Charles Keeling, found a largely unexpected continual increase. March 2015 became the first month in recorded human history that CO_2 concentration rose above 400 ppm at observatories around the globe.

"Integral Ecology"—Getting It All Together

The consequences of these atmospheric additions were coming to be understood at the turn of the century, assisted by successively improved physical climate models that crossed relevant disciplines. Assessment reports by the Intergovernmental Panel on Climate Change in 1990, 1995, 2001, 2007, 2014 (continuing at six- to seven-year intervals) gave an "up-to-date view of the current state of scientific knowledge relevant to climate change" (IPCC 2015).

These physical models were joined in 2010 by a "scenario approach" that extended their scope by creating a framework that integrated physical with societal aspects called "representative concentration pathways" (RCPs). Four RCPs were published by 19 researchers of the Netherlands Environmental Assessment Agency in 2011, one of which (RCP2.6) held global average temperature increase below 2°C (36°F) — thereby meeting a principal goal of the 2010 international Cancun Agreements (Van Vuuren et al. 2011). This scenario reduced global IR-active gas emissions by 70 percent from 2010 to 2100 and by more than 95 percent in 2100 — a "technically feasible goal." The Institutional Investors Group on Climate Change (IIGCC) — representing US$24 trillion in assets — supported this goal in its "Global Investor Statement on Climate Change" September 2014 (IIGCC 2011; Symon 2013). This was paralleled by two other major initiatives that integrated "human ecology" with "natural ecology": the ESA's "Earth Stewardship" initiative (Chapin 2015) and *Laudato Si'*.

Laudato Si'

With these and other significant actions, world **ecology** and economy have been moving toward global "decarbonization" and a "culture of care" in the early twenty-first century as Christianity and science revitalized the long-standing Stewardship Tradition (DeWitt 1995). The transition has been in many ways a stormy one, described well by Sir John Houghton's *In the Eye of the Storm* (2015). Yet society is coming to understand the earth's climate system and its inseparable integration within the earth system, and is working seriously toward restoration of earth's long-standing atmospheric carbonic temperature regulation. This transition in knowledge and action has made Pope Francis's *Laudato Si'* required reading as the only comprehensive treatise on understanding and caring for the earth system as our common home. And its title invites every person on earth to "gratefully admire the beneficent arrangement which permits the Earth to be clothed with verdure and abundant life."

Calvin B. DeWitt

REFERENCES AND RECOMMENDED READING

Arrhenius, Svante. 1896. "On the Influence of Carbonic Acid in the Air upon the Temperature of the Ground." *Philosophical Magazine and Journal of Science* 41:237–76.

Barnola, J.-M., D. Raynaud, C. Lorius, and N. I. Barkov. 2003. "Historical CO_2 Record from the Vostok Ice Core." In *Trends: A Compendium of Data on Global Change*. Oak Ridge, TN: Carbon Dioxide Information Analysis Center, Oak Ridge National Laboratory, U.S. Department of Energy. http://cdiac.ornl.gov/trends/co2/vostok.html.

Bloch, Magdalena, and Grzegorz Karasiński. 2014. "Water Vapor Mixing Ratio Profiles over Harnsund, Arctic." *Acta Geophysica* 52 (2): 290–301.

Blunden, Jessica, and Derek S. Arndt, eds. 2015. "2015: State of the Climate in 2014." Special Supplement to the *Bulletin of the American Meteorological Society* 96 (7): S1–S267. http://journals.ametsoc.org/doi/10.1175/2015BAMSStateoftheClimate.1.

Carbon Dioxide Information Analysis Center (CDIAC). "Global Carbon Project." U.S. Department of Energy. http://cdiac.ornl.gov/GCP/.

Chapin, F. Stewart. 2015. "Earth Stewardship: An Initiative by the Ecological Society of America to Foster Engagement to Sustain Planet Earth." In *Earth Stewardship: Linking Ecology and Ethics in Theory and Practice*, ed. R. Rozzi et al., 2:173–94. Dordrecht: Springer.

Christian Reformed Church. 2012. *Creation Stewardship Task Force Report*. www.crcna.org/sites/default/files/creationstewardship.pdf.

Comeau, S., R. C. Carpenter, C. A. Lantz, and P. J. Edmunds. 2015. "Ocean Acidification Accelerates Dissolution of Experimental Coral Reef Communities." *Biogeosciences* 12 (2): 365–72. www.biogeosciences.net/12/365/2015.

Daly, Herman E. 1968. "Economics as a Life Science." *Journal of Political Economy* 76 (3): 392–406.

DeWitt, C. B. 1995. "Ecology and Ethics: Relation of Religious Belief to Ecological Practice in the Biblical Tradition." *Biodiversity and Conservation* 4:838–48. https://www.academia.edu/6704422/Ecology_and_Ethics_Relation_of_Religious_Belief_to_Ecological_Practice_in_the_Biblical_Tradition.

———. 1998. "Science, Ethics, and Praxis: Getting It All Together." In *Ecology and Religion: Scientists Speak*, ed. John Carroll and Keith Warner, 53–70. Quincy, IL: Franciscan.

———. 2003. "Biogeographic and Trophic Restructuring of the Biosphere: The State of the Earth under Human Domination." *Christian Scholar's Review* 32:347–64.

———. 2007. "The Professor and the Pupil: Addressing Secularization and Disciplinary Fragmentation in Academia." *Perspectives on Science and Christian Faith* 59 (2): 119–27.

———. 2008. "To Strive to Safeguard the Integrity of Creation and Sustain and Renew the Life of the Earth." In *Mission in the Twenty-First Century: Exploring the Five Marks of Global Mission*, ed. Andrew Walls and Cathy Ross, 84–93. London: Darton, Longman and Todd.

———. 2011a. *Earth-Wise: A Guide to Hopeful Creation Care*. 3rd ed. Grand Rapids: Faith Alive.

———. 2011b. "Going for 'Broke' (Pembroke) — The Keystone XL Pipeline in Global Petroarchitecture." http://faculty.nelson.wisc.edu/dewitt/docs/keystone_xl.pdf. Another version is available as "The Earth Is the Lord's (and Just Look What We're Doing with It)." June 2014. https://sojo.net/magazine/june-2014/earth-lords-and-just-look-what-were-doing-it.

———. 2012a. "Climate Care: Our Profound Moral Imperative." *The Banner* 142 (4): 18–20.

———. 2012b. "The Deadly Misnomer of 'Fossil Fuels.'" September–October. https://sojo.net/magazine/september-october-2012/deadly-misnomer-fossil-fuels.

Francis (Pope). 2015. *Encyclical Letter Laudato Si' of the Holy Father Francis on Care for Our Common Home*. Vatican: Libreria Editrice Vaticana. Also www.papalencyclicals.net.

Glacken, Clarence J. 1967. *Traces on the Rhodian Shore: Nature and Culture in Western Thought from Ancient Times to the End of the Eighteenth Century*. Berkeley: University of California Press.

Global Carbon Atlas. www.globalcarbonatlas.org.

Henderson, Lawrence J. 1913a. "The Fitness of the Environment: An Inquiry into the Biological Significance of the Properties of Matter." *American Naturalist* 47 (554): 105–15.

———. 1913b. *The Fitness of the Environment: An Inquiry into the Biological Significance of the Properties of Matter*. New York: Macmillan.

Houghton, John T. 2015. *In the Eye of the Storm: The Autobiography of Sir John Houghton*. Oxford: Lion.

IIGCC. 2011. *Investment-Grade Climate Change Policy*. London: Institutional Investors Group on Climate Change (IIGCC). http://www.unepfi.org/fileadmin/documents/Investment-GradeClimateChangePolicy.pdf.

IPCC. 2015. Assessment Reports. Geneva: Intergovernmental Panel on Climate Change. www.ipcc.ch/publications_and_data/publications_and_data_reports.shtml.

Lacis, Andrew A., James E. Hansen, Gary L. Russell, Valdar Oinas, and Jeffrey Jonas. 2013. "The Role of Long-Lived Greenhouse Gases as Principal LW Control Knob That Governs the Global Surface Temperature for Past and Future Climate Change." *Tellus B*: 65:19734. http://dx.doi.org/10.3402/tellusb.v65i0.19734.

Lacis, Andrew A., Gavin A. Schmidt, David Rind, and Reto A. Ruedy. 2010. "Atmospheric CO_2: Principal Control Knob Governing Earth's Temperature." *Science* 330, no. 6002 (October 15): 356–59.

MacDougall, Andrew H., and Pierre Friedlingstein. 2015: "The Origin and Limits of the Near Proportionality between Climate Warming and Cumulative CO_2 Emissions." *Journal of Climate* 28:4217–30.

MacFarling Meure, C., D. Etheridge, et al. 2006. "The Law Dome CO_2, CH_4 and N_2O Ice Core Records Extended to 2000 Years BP." *Geophysical Research Letters* 33 (14). ftp://ftp.ncdc.noaa.gov/pub/data/paleo/icecore/antarctica/law/law2006.txt.

Moss, Richard H., Mustafa Babiker, Sander Brinkman, et al. 2008. *Towards New Scenarios for Analysis of Emissions, Climate Change, Impacts, and Response Strategies*. Technical Summary. Geneva: Intergovernmental Panel on Climate Change.

Moss, Richard H., Jae Edmonds, Kathy A. Hibbard, et al. 2010. "The Next Generation of Scenarios for Climate Change Research and Assessment." *Nature* 463:747–56.

New York City Panel on Climate Change. 2015. NPCC 2015 Report. Executive Summary. *Annals of the New York Academy of Science* 1336 (2015): 9–17. http://onlinelibrary.wiley.com/doi/10.1111/nyas.12591/epdf.

Planck, Max. 1937. "On Religion and Science." Repr. in trans. as appendix A in Aaron Barth, *The Creation in Light of Modern Science*, 147. Jerusalem: Jerusalem Post Press, 1968.

Ramanathan, Veerabhadran, and Yangyang Xu. 2010. "The Copenhagen Accord for limiting global warming: Criteria, constraints, and available avenues." Proceedings of the National Academy of Sciences 107(18): 8055–8062.

Roberts, Jon H., and James Turner. 2000. *The Sacred and the Secular University*. Princeton, NJ: Princeton University Press.

Steffen, W., A. Sanderson, P. D. Tyson, et al. 2004. *Global Change and the Earth System*. Berlin: Springer. www.igbp.net/publications/igbpbookseries/igbpbookseries/globalchangeandtheearthsystem2004.5.1b8ae20512db692f2a680007462.html.

Symon, Carolyn. 2013. *Climate Change: Action, Trends and Implications for Business*. Cambridge: Judge Business School, University of Cambridge. https://europeanclimate.org/documents/IPCCWebGuide.pdf.

Timmermans, Steven. 2015. "Christian Reformed Church Celebrates Pope's Call to Climate Action." http://network.crcna.org/creation-matters/christian-reformed-church-celebrates-pope's-call-climate-action.

Tyndall, John. 1859. "On the Transmission of Heat of Different Qualities through Gases of Different Kinds." In *Notices of the Proceedings of the Royal Institution of Britain, Abstracts of the Discourses Delivered at the Evening Meetings*, vol. 3 (1858–62). London: William Clowes and Sons.

UNFCCC. 2010. *Cancun Agreements. Cancun, Mexico: United Nations Framework Convention on Climate Change. Sixteenth Conference of the Parties* (COP–16).

Van Vuuren, D. P., E. Stehfest, M. G. J. den Elzen, et al. 2011. "RCP2.6: Exploring the Possibility to Keep Global Mean Temperature Increase Below 2°C." *Climatic Change* 109 (November): 95–116.

Very, Frank W. 1900. *Atmospheric Radiation: A Research Conducted at the Allegheny Observatory and at Providence, R.I.* Washington: Government Printing Office. https://archive.org/details/atmosphericradia00veryrich.

Vonder Haar, Thomas H., and Verner E. Suomi. 1971. "Measurements of the Earth's Radiation Budget from Satellites during a Five-Year Period. Part I: Extended Time and Space Means." *Journal of Atmospheric Science* 28:305–14.

☙ CLIMATE CHANGE (Natural-Variations View).

Few debates have received greater worldwide attention over the last two decades than anthropogenic (i.e., human-induced) global warming. While views vary from believing it to be a hoax to believing it to be a threat to the very survival of the planet, most scientists hold a myriad of intermediate positions. But what are the facts, and what are we to make of them?

Establishing common ground is important. Our climate has always changed, and it always will. There never has been a period in the earth's history when the climate has been "stable," and there likely never will be. Moreover, humans certainly can and do influence the earth's climate. Estimates of global air temperature have largely increased over the past 160 years (i.e., the observational record). These issues are not at the forefront of the discussion.

Where climate scientists—and Christian scientists—disagree is on the more complex questions. To what extent are humans responsible for the climate change we have observed? What are the future consequences of climate change, from both natural and anthropogenic sources? How should we, as Bible-believing Christians, respond? Indeed, the answers to the second and third questions hinge on the answer given to the first question.

But for a more basic question, what is climate? Many attempts have been made to formulate a concise answer (see Legates 2012), and the worst is probably the one that is the most widely used: climate is simply *average* weather. This definition implies that climate should be viewed as static and not dynamic, particularly on timescales of a century or smaller; hence short-term *climate change* is neither natural nor desirable. Many other representations trivialize climate to simply the radiative characteristics of the atmosphere. For example, statements such as "The earth's atmosphere acts like a blanket" or "Carbon dioxide causes the earth to warm like the windows heat a car on a hot afternoon" ignore most climate processes and focus only on the radiative effects of greenhouse gases, most notably, carbon dioxide.

In reality, it is nearly impossible to fathom just how utterly complex our climate system is. Weather and climate vary on a variety of space- and time-scales and, as a result, on a myriad of factors that influence the earth's climate. Unfortunately, many important climate processes occur at resolutions far below those of most climate models, which usually provide the impetus for arguing for catastrophic anthropogenic climate change. For example, climate models simulate precipitation poorly since they generate rain too frequently with too little moisture (i.e., light showers every day over most of the planet) and do not exhibit the full range of precipitation-forming mechanisms that have been observed (Legates 2014). That is, modeled precipitation is usually limited to convective showers while frontal mechanisms are largely absent. Furthermore, these effects are not trivial—an error of only 5mm in simulating liquid rainfall is equivalent to the energy required to heat the entire troposphere by 1.56°C. Climate models typically exhibit differences between the simulated and observed precipitation greater than 5mm of precipitation *per day*. Thus, climate models lack the ability to simulate adequately fundamental climate processes.

The Basic Science of Climate Change

In a recent letter to me, a Christian climate scientist defined the basics of climate change as follows:

> The basic science of climate change is incredibly simple. We've been burning an increasing amount of fossil fuels, when burned they produce carbon dioxide (CO_2), carbon dioxide traps heat, more carbon dioxide equals more heat being trapped in the atmosphere, and if climate were being controlled by natural factors right now, we'd be cooling.

Fossil fuel use has indeed been increasing in recent years, and carbon dioxide, produced by burning fossil fuels, is a significant greenhouse gas that causes the earth to be warmer than it would be if it were not present in the atmosphere. But such a presentation misses two important points.

The first misconception is that the earth's climate can simply be explained by the concentration of carbon dioxide in the earth's atmosphere. In fact, the fundamental compound that is responsible for most of the variability in climate and climate change is not carbon dioxide; it is water (H_2O). Not only is water vapor the most important greenhouse gas; the fact that it exists in all three states (gas, liquid, and solid) on the earth's surface and in its atmosphere causes water to have a predominant effect on the climate. Water vapor in the atmosphere tends to scatter sunlight and can form highly reflective clouds when it condenses. When it lies on the earth's surface, either in liquid or solid form, it changes the amount of solar energy absorbed. Ice and snow are highly reflective, and oceans, which comprise nearly three-quarters of the planet's surface, greatly dictate the planet's surface albedo (i.e., the amount of reflected solar energy).

As the most important greenhouse gas, water vapor is responsible for about 62 percent of the total greenhouse effect if acting alone (clouds account for about 36 percent), while the decrease in longwave (i.e., heat) absorption would be only about 14 percent if carbon dioxide were removed from the atmosphere. (Total contributions from the various constituents in the atmosphere sum to more than 100 percent because relative contributions of the various gases are difficult to ascertain owing to their overlapping longwave absorption bands—Schmidt et al. 2010.) Storage and transfer of energy by evaporated water (i.e., latent heat) is about 80 Wm^{-2}, or one-half of the total exchange of energy from the earth's surface to the atmosphere (Trenberth et al. 2009). Thus, water is an important component in determining the amount of solar radiation reaching and absorbed by the earth's surface and the amount of heat energy emitted between the earth's atmosphere and the surface (i.e., the greenhouse effect) and transferred to the atmosphere through the evaporation of water. Indeed, water affects virtually every component of the earth's energy budget (Trenberth et al. 2009). It is truly the most important chemical compound in any study of climate or climate change.

A second misconception is that the earth would be cooling if atmospheric carbon dioxide concentrations were not increasing. A strong correlation exists between total solar irradiance (TSI—energy from the sun received by the earth) and global air temperatures (see figure 1), and TSI is near a long-term maximum (e.g., Shapiro et al. 2011; Soon et al. 2011; Breitenmoser et al. 2012; Soon and Legates 2013; Velasco Herrera et al. 2015). Arguments that the recent increase in global air temperature is caused by carbon dioxide are undermined when air temperatures and solar activity are examined over the last millennium. Indeed, satellite and ground-based observations both show that warming has ceased since 1998, consistent with trends in TSI, despite the fact that carbon dioxide concentrations have risen.

Climate Extremes—Are They Becoming More Frequent?

Virtually nothing responds to mean global air temperature. It is the climate extremes (e.g., droughts, floods, and hurricanes) that cause the most deaths, lead to the biggest economic impacts, and, indeed, make the biggest impact in the international media. Usually, a discussion of these events is preceded by the term *unprecedented* or the use of the phrase "the new normal," in reference to the characterization of a "normal" climate. Despite a tenuous connection that is often made to anthropogenic climate change, it still must be demonstrated that a change in climate extremes is linked to a warming climate. While the coverage of such events has increased due to the globalization of the news media and proliferation of global news coverage, have climate extremes really become more frequent?

We understand that global circulation is driven by the equator-to-pole temperature gradient (EPTG); that is, because the equator is warm and the pole is cold, there is a net transfer of energy toward the pole that is manifested in the global circulation of the atmosphere and the oceans. With warming, the EPTG decreases because (1) colder air warms more with the same energy input (i.e., the temperature derivative of the Stefan-Boltzmann radiation law), (2) cold, dry air warms more than warm, moist air (since water vapor has a higher specific heat than other gases in the atmosphere), and (3) a change in albedo from melting ice creates a positive feedback on rising air temperatures in polar regions. Observationally, this was demonstrated by Soon and Legates (2013), who found a strong correlation between the change in the EPTG and solar irradiance (figure 1), which argues for a strong sun-climate interaction.

Thus a warmer world implies a decrease to the EPTG (both from a theoretical and an observational point of view) and a concomitant decrease in the degree of storminess (Hayden 1999) due to the diminished interaction of cold versus warm air masses. Indeed, Chris Huntingford and colleagues (2013, 327) concluded that "many climate models predict that total variability will ultimately decrease under high greenhouse gas concentrations ... our findings contradict the view that a warming world will automatically be one of more overall climatic variation" (see also Kim et al. 2013).

Hydrologic drought is defined as streamflow or reservoir levels that fall below a given threshold, and it depends on the amount (lack) of precipitation, urbanization (i.e., increased water demand), and a change in water-intensive activities. Indeed, increased urbanization—an anthropogenic effect—has led to an increase in drought frequencies in populated areas. To explicitly avoid human influences on water supply and demand, climatologists use a number of indices; for example, Hao et al. (2014) documented a slight decrease in the proportion of the globe in drought since 1982. Sheffield et al. (2012, 435) examined data for the past 60 years and concluded that using "more realistic calculations, based on the underlying physical principles that take into account changes in available energy, humidity, and wind speed, suggest that there has been little change in [global] drought over the past 60 years ... the results have implications for how we interpret the impact of global warming on the hydrological cycle and its extremes."

Even the IPCC (2012), in their publication focusing on extreme climate events, has agreed that "there is medium confidence that some regions of the world have experienced more intense and longer droughts ... but in some regions droughts have become less frequent, less intense, or shorter, for example, in Central North America."

Hydrologically, a flood occurs when streamflow exceeds a certain threshold. Its frequency depends on the amount and timing of precipitation (enhanced by snowmelt and

Figure 1. Total solar irradiance in Wm^{-2} (solid black line) and the annually average mean northern hemisphere anomaly of the equator-to-pole temperature gradient (EPTG) in °C per degree latitude (lighter dashed line—five-year moving average shown in the darker dashed line). Note that positive values of the EPTG indicate a weakened equator-to-pole temperature gradient (i.e., less cooling per degree of latitude). (From Soon and Legates 2013)

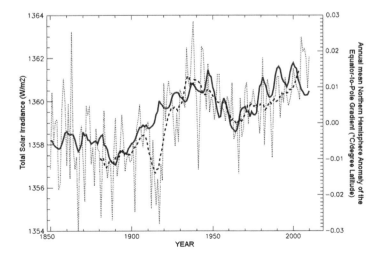

antecedent moisture conditions), urbanization (i.e., creating more runoff and less infiltration), and channelization of streams and rivers through levees, dredging activities, or bank reinforcement. Increasing asphalt and concrete in urban areas has led to increased flooding and, as with droughts, this is a direct effect of anthropogenic change but is not a climate change. Lins and Slack (1999, 227) evaluated 395 rural streams and concluded that "hydrologically, [the] results indicate that the coterminous [United States] is getting wetter, but less extreme."

The US Geological Survey showed that bankfull streamflow—defined as the highest daily mean streamflow value expected to occur, on average, once every 2.3 years—has not changed since 1950 (Pielke 2013). And the IPCC (2012) concluded that "there is limited to medium evidence available to suggest climate-driven observed changes in the magnitude and frequency of floods at regional scales ... thus overall low confidence at the global scale regarding even the sign of these changes." Indeed, Legates (2016) demonstrated that the oft-cited trend in extreme one-day precipitation events in the United States Climate Extremes Index is due entirely to a discontinuity introduced by a change in the rain gauge design resulting from the US Weather Service's modernization program.

Despite much fanfare to the contrary, tropical cyclone (i.e., hurricane) activity is not increasing. Maue (2009, 2011, and updates) evaluated the accumulated cyclone energy (ACE) for all storms in the northern hemisphere and the globe and showed that there has been no long-term trend since 1972. The ACE is a measure of tropical cyclone activity and is calculated by summing the square of the estimated maximum sustained velocity (39 mph or higher) at six-hourly intervals. Neither has the global number of tropical storms and tropical cyclones changed (Maue 2009 and updates), nor has the global number of tropical cyclone landfalls (Weinkle et al. 2012). The IPCC (2012) concluded that "the uncertainties in the historical tropical cyclone records, the incomplete understanding of the physical mechanisms linking tropical cyclone metrics to climate change, and the degree of tropical cyclone variability provide only low confidence for the attribution of any detectable changes in tropical cyclone activity to anthropogenic influences." Indeed, enhanced tropical cyclone activity is more often associated with colder conditions (e.g., Boose et al. 2001; Liu et al. 2001; Mock 2002, 2008).

Due to the limitations in climate models and, in particular, their inability to demonstrate adequate skill in simulating the current climate and its variability, their prognostications of impending catastrophic anthropogenic climate change are not likely scenarios. Furthermore, the observations do not support that climate is changing in a dramatic or dangerous way; nor does the theory suggest that carbon dioxide concentrations are the major component of recent climate variability. A warmer world is more conducive for life, and carbon dioxide enhances plant growth. We can never "stabilize" the climate (whatever that entails or however an optimal climate can be defined) through human actions to limit greenhouse gases—the climate is too complex to be driven simply by atmospheric concentrations of carbon dioxide.

A Christian Response: Prudent and Informed

I believe in God, and I believe that humans have affected our environment. However, after careful study of the science behind anthropogenic climate change, I have concluded that natural climate variations outweigh human-induced effects. Most human impacts on climate center on land-use/ land-cover changes, which exacerbate floods and droughts, and on the well-known urban heat island effect. A doubling of carbon dioxide concentrations is likely to increase global air temperatures by no more than 1°C, and their impact on other aspects of the climate is likely to be even less noticeable. But while we are exhorted to be good stewards of all of creation (Gen. 1:26–28; 2:15), we also are commanded to "examine everything carefully; hold fast to that which is good" (1 Thess. 5:21 NASB). Policies must be based on the best-available science and in accordance with the reality of the current human condition.

Attempts to "control" future global temperatures by reducing carbon dioxide and other greenhouse gas emissions will cause more harm than good. Precious resources must not be squandered, nor should our environment be harmed, but neither should we focus on "solving" nonproblems. The negative consequences of fighting climate change will fall disproportionately on those who are without clean water and adequate sanitation, who must rely on dung or other biomass for indoor cooking and heating, or who are oppressed. This is because they will be most adversely affected by harmful policies designed to solve this exaggerated problem.

Reducing use of fossil fuels would have very little impact on global air temperatures. As evangelical climate scientist Dr. John R. Christy noted in his congressional testimony (Christy 2012, 19), a reduction of greenhouse gas emissions "will not produce a measurable climate effect that can be attributable or predictable with any level of confidence, especially at the regional level." But reliable, affordable, and abundant energy is critical to economic development, especially so in the developing world. If the cost of energy is allowed to skyrocket or if energy is rationed, those in need will be impacted disproportionally.

Energy is an effective tool to combat poverty, disease, hunger, and oppression. The quest for "climate stabilization" will adversely affect over a billion people who lack adequate electricity by continuing their dependence on wood, dried dung, and other biomass as principal heating and cooking fuels. This dependence causes hundreds of millions to suffer from upper-respiratory diseases and leads to over 4 million premature deaths annually in the developing world, primarily among women and young children (World Health Organization 2014). We cannot condemn the world's poorest citizens to brutal conditions because of the severe energy restrictions imposed by climate "stabilization" efforts.

I am reminded of the parable of the talents (Matt. 25:14–30), wherein Jesus told of a master who gave "talents" to three servants. The one to whom was given a single talent was condemned for *hiding it in the earth* and not putting it to use. While we usually think of talents as money or ability, Chenoweth (2005, 61) has argued that the talents in the parable refer to "the knowledge of the secrets of the kingdom of heaven." Through the concept of the talents in this parable, Jesus is most likely emphasizing the stewardship of his disciples to make the most of the knowledge given to them by God. This point could be fairly extended to emphasize the responsible application of any resource—including natural resources, especially as it bears on our responsibility to care for the poor (Prov. 19:17). None of the three servants lost their talents; indeed, every talent handed out by the master was returned. But the slovenly servant was condemned when he returned his unused talent with the statement, "See, you have what is yours" (Matt. 25:25 NASB).

I firmly believe that if we do not use the resources God has set before us to care for those in need, we will stand condemned by our Creator for keeping buried in the ground what we have been given. Failure to use resources to care for the poor, the hungry, the sick, and the oppressed will yield us the same fate as the servant called by his master "wicked, lazy slave" (Matt. 25:26 NASB). While being efficient with our natural resources is part of our Christian calling, caring for what is truly the "second greatest gift" that God has given to us—our human companions—means we must protect the poor from the harms of climate change alarmism.

David R. Legates

REFERENCES AND RECOMMENDED READING

Boose, E. R., K. E. Chamberlin, and D. R. Foster. 2001. "Landscape and Regional Impacts of Hurricanes in New England." *Ecological Monographs* 71 (1): 27–48.

Breitenmoser, P., J. Beer, S. Bronnimann, D. C. Frank, F. Steinhilber, and H. Wanner. 2012. "Solar and Volcanic Fingerprints in Tree-Ring Chronologies over the Past 2000 Years." *Palaeogeography, Palaeoclimatology, Palaeoecology* 313–14: 127–39.

Chenoweth, Ben. 2005. "Identifying the Talents: Contextual Clues for the Interpretation of the Parable of the Talents (Matthew 25:14–30)." *Tyndale Bulletin* 56 (1): 61–72.

Christy, J. A. 2012. *Testimony to the Senate Environment and Public Works Committee, US Senate.* August 1. http://www.epw.senate.gov/public/_cache/files/66585975-a507-4d81-b750-def3ec74913d/8112hearingwitnesstestimonychristy.pdf.

Hao, Z., A. AghaKouchak, N. Nakhjiri, and A. Farahmand. 2014. "Global Integrated Drought Monitoring and Prediction System." *Scientific Data* 1 (140001).

Hayden, B. P. 1999. "Climate Change and Extratropical Storminess in the United States: An Assessment." *Journal of the American Water Resources Association* 35 (6): 1387–97.

Huntingford, C., P. D. Jones, V. N. Livina, T. M. Lenton, and P. M. Cox. 2013. "No Increase in Global Temperature Variability Despite Changing Regional Patterns." *Nature* 500: 327–30.

Intergovernmental Panel on Climate Change (IPCC). 2012. *Managing the Risks of Extreme Events and Disasters to Advance Climate Change Adaptation.* Ed. C. B. Field, V. Barros, T. F. Stocker, et al. Cambridge: Cambridge University Press.

Kim, O.-Y., B. Wang, and S.-H. Shin. 2013. "How Do Weather Characteristics Change in a Warming Climate?" *Climate Dynamics* 41:3261–81.

Legates, D. R. 2012. "Applications of Climatology." In *Geography for the 21st Century*, ed. J. P. Stoltman, 1:67–76. Thousand Oaks, CA: SAGE Publications.

———. 2014. "Climate Models and Their Simulation of Precipitation." *Energy and Environment* 25 (6–7): 1163–75.

———. 2016. "One-Day Precipitation Extremes in the United States Revisited." *International Journal of Climatology*, submitted.

Lins, H. F., and J. R. Slack. 1999. "Streamflow Trends in the United States." *Geophysical Research Letters* 26 (2): 227–30.

Liu, K.-B., C. Chen, and K.-S. Louie. 2001. "A 1,000-Year History of Typhoon Landfalls in Guangdong, Southern China, Reconstructed from Chinese Historical Documentary Records." *Annals of the Association of American Geographers* 91 (3): 453–64.

Maue, R. N. 2009. "Northern Hemisphere Tropical Cyclone Activity." *Geophysical Research Letters* 36 (L05805), doi:10.1029/2008GL035946.

———. 2011. "Recent Historically Low Global Tropical Cyclone Activity." *Geophysical Research Letters* 38 (L14803). doi:10.1029/2011GL047711.

Mock, C. J. 2002. "Documentary Records of Past Climate and Tropical Cyclones from the Southeastern United States." *PAGES News* 10 (3): 20–21.

———. 2008. "Tropical Cyclone Variations in Louisiana, U.S.A., Since the Late Eighteenth Century." *Geochemistry, Geophysics, and Geosystems* 9 (5): doi:10.1029/2007GC001846.

Pielke, R. A., Sr. 2013. *Testimony to the Committee on Science, Space, and Technology.* US House of Representatives, December 11. https://science.house.gov/sites/republicans.science.house.gov/files/documents/HHRG–113-SY18-WState-RPielke–20131211.pdf.

Schmidt, G. A., R. A. Ruedy, R. L. Miller, and A. A. Lacis. 2010. "Attribution of the Present-Day Total Greenhouse Effect." *Journal of Geophysical Research* 115 (D20106). doi:10.1029/2010JD014287.

Shapiro, A. I., W. Schmutz, E. Rozanov, M. Schoell, M. Haberreiter, A. V. Shapiro, and S. Nyeki. 2011. "A New Approach to the Long-Term Reconstruction of the Solar Irradiance Leads to Large Historical Solar Forcing." *Astronomy and Astrophysics* 529 (A67).

Sheffield, J., E. F. Wood, and M. L. Roderick. 2012. "Little Change in Global Drought over the Past 60 Years." *Nature* 491:435–38.

Soon, W., K. Dutta, D. R. Legates, V. M. Velasco, and W. Zhang. 2011. "Variation in Surface Air Temperature of China during the 20th Century." *Journal of Atmospheric and Solar-Terrestrial Physics* 73:2331–44.

Soon, W., and D. R. Legates. 2013. "Solar Irradiance Modulation of Equator-to-Pole (Arctic) Temperature Gradients: Empirical Evidence for Climate Variation on Multi-decadal Timescales." *Journal of Atmospheric and Solar-Terrestrial Physics* 93 (2): 45–56.

Trenberth, K. E., J. T. Fasullo, and J. Kiehl. 2009. "Earth's Global Energy Budget." *Bulletin of the American Meteorological Society* 90 (3): 311–23.

Velasco Herrera, V. M., B. Mendoza, and G. Velasco Herrera. 2015. "Reconstruction and Prediction of the Total Solar Irradiance: From the Medieval Warm Period to the 21st Century." *New Astronomy* 34:221–33.

Weinkle, J., R. N. Maue, and R. A. Pielke Jr. 2012. "Historical Global Tropical Cyclone Landfalls." *Journal of Climate* 25 (13): 4729–35.

World Health Organization. 2014. "Household Air Pollution and Health." Fact Sheet No. 292. http://www.who.int/mediacentre/factsheets/fs292/en/.

divine governance of the creation, thereby anticipating how deists would later use it. However, the deeply pious **Robert Boyle**, a strong believer in **miracles** and divine sovereignty, did more than anyone else to promote it, especially in **natural theology**: the exquisite mechanical "contrivances" of living creatures, he argued, were far too complex to have been assembled by "blind **chance**." Mathew Hale went even further in 1677, originating the famous fiction of finding a watch in a field and wondering from whence it came—the very same idea with which **William Paley** later opened his book, *Natural Theology* (1802). Contemporary proponents of **intelligent design** follow closely in the footsteps of Cicero, Boyle, and Paley.

Edward B. Davis

REFERENCES AND RECOMMENDED READING

Cicero, Marcus Tullius. 1933. *De Nature Deorum*, trans. H. Rackham. Cambridge, MA: Harvard University Press.

Davis, Edward B. 1996. "Newton's Rejection of the 'Newtonian World View': The Role of Divine Will in Newton's Natural Philosophy." In *Facets of Faith and Science, vol. 3: The Role of Beliefs in the Natural Sciences*, ed. Jitse M. van der Meer, 75–96. Lanham, MD: University Press of America.

Koestler, Arthur. 1967. "Kepler, Johannes." In *Encyclopedia of Philosophy*, ed. Paul Edwards, 4:329–33. New York: Macmillan.

Macey, Samuel L. 1980. *Clocks and the Cosmos: Time in Western Life and Thought.* Hamden, CT: Archon.

Price, Derek J. de Solla. 1959. "On the Origin of Clockwork, Perpetual Motion Devices, and the Compass." *United States National Museum Bulletin* 218:81–112.

CLOCKWORK METAPHOR. Mechanical clocks were probably unknown before the eighth century in China, or the late thirteenth century in Europe, but machines capable of mimicking planetary motion certainly existed before the time of Christ. Remarkably, one such device was recovered from the sea bottom near the Greek island of Antikythera in 1900.

According to Cicero, the Romans plundered a bronze planetarium made by Archimedes when they captured Syracuse, and Cicero himself compared the heavens to this machine. "When we see something moved by machinery, like an orrery or clock … we do not doubt that these contrivances are the work of reason." Likewise, the "marvelous velocity" and "perfect regularity" of the heavenly motions leaves no "doubt that all this is effected not merely by reason, but by a reason that is transcendent and divine" (Cicero 1933, 217–19). At least two prominent medieval natural philosophers, John of Sacrobosco and Nicole d'Oresme, also spoke of the world as a "machine" or "clockwork."

During the **Scientific Revolution**, when clocks and watches were ubiquitous, mechanical metaphors became commonplace, not only for the heavens but for almost everything else as well—angels, God, and the human **soul** were the only exceptions. Nature and its components came to be seen as inert, impersonal machines, rather than living organisms capable of acting purposefully.

As **Johannes Kepler** told a friend in 1605, "My aim is to show that the heavenly machine is not a kind of divine, live being, but a kind of clockwork" (Koestler 1967, 331). Contrary to what is often said, **Isaac Newton** actually rejected the clock metaphor, which (in his opinion) effectively denied active

CLONING. Cloning is an artificial process by which the genetic copies of living organisms or their parts are brought into being. Thus a gene, cell, plant, animal, or human being may be cloned. Cloning is fairly common in agriculture and horticulture, and scientists have been cloning human and animal genes for many decades. The idea of cloning whole animals has its roots in the work of embryologist Hans Spemann (1938).

Whole organisms can be cloned in one of two general ways. Embryonic cloning (EC) is the artificial replication of what occurs naturally in monozygotic twinning. Because the very early embryo's cells are totipotent, which means they can develop into any one of the body's cell types, one can be separated from the others and become a whole new embryo. The first known EC occurred in 1885, when a two-celled sea urchin embryo was divided and each cell then developed into an individual sea urchin. In 1993 EC was first successfully conducted on an embryonic human, though each embryo died soon after cell division because the ovum used in the experiment was intentionally fertilized, in vitro, by two sperm.

Nuclear transfer cloning (NTC) occurs when an ovum's nucleus is removed, replaced by the nucleus of a donor's non-germ cell, and this renucleated ovum is electrically stimulated to begin cellular division like an ordinary conception. Early successful experiments on amphibians and mammals used the nuclei of totipotent and pluripotent embryonic cells. Somatic cells (those that are differentiated for specific parts of the body) were first used in cloning a frog in 1958 and in cloning a mammal in 1997. The latter, a sheep named Dolly, raised the prospect of cloning whole human beings by somatic cell nuclear transfer (SCNT).

Infertility and organ donation are the most popular reasons suggested for cloning human beings via SCNT (Kahn 1989). Although such cloning has support (Pence 1998), there is also opposition (Beckwith 2002; Kass 1997). Some argue that if cloning human beings were to become an acceptable practice, it would subtly change our perception of human reproduction from children begotten of their parents' bodily union and love to children manufactured and whose genomes are selected by the will of their makers.

Others argue that because a clone is literally the identical twin of the person whose genome was used to bring the clone into being, widespread use of cloning would contribute to the continued unraveling of ordinary notions of family and property that have served civilization well for millennia. For example, the wife who carries in her womb her husband's SCNT clone that resulted from his genome and her ovum, is literally gestating her brother-in-law. When this child is born and becomes an adult, may he clone himself? Or should his "father" have a say, since it was from his **DNA** that this child was cloned? And what about the child's "paternal" grandparents, who now have another heir, since he is literally the identical twin of their son?

According to critics, cloning human beings to use or harvest their parts for the good of others not only treats these human clones as mere commodities but also unjustly denies them the bodily and personal goods to which they are entitled and to which their development is ordered (Beckwith 2002).

Francis J. Beckwith

REFERENCES AND RECOMMENDED READING

Beckwith, Francis. 2002. "Cloning and Reproductive Liberty." *Nevada Law Journal* 3:61–87.
Kahn, Carol. 1989. "Can We Achieve Immortality? The Ethics of Cloning and Other Life-Extension Technologies." *Free Inquiry* (2): 14–18.
Kass, Leon. 1997. "The Wisdom of Repugnance." *The New Republic* 2:17–26.
Pence, Gregory. 1998. *Who's Afraid of Human Cloning?* Lanham, MD: Rowman & Littlefield.
Spemann, Hans. 1938. *Embryonic Development and Induction.* New Haven, CT: Yale University Press.

COGNITIVE SCIENCE. Cognitive science is the interdisciplinary study of the mind, emphasizing thought, feelings, intelligence, and problem solving over behavior (Barrett 2011; Thagard 2005). The target of cognitive science, then, is cognition, which can be understood as all the thoughts and processes that occur within the human mind (see also **Cognitive Science of Religion**). An example of cognition is the conscious thoughts that we are aware of at this moment, but other examples include the unconscious processes that are present in the mind without our awareness, such as memory formation and face recognition.

The topics studied by cognitive scientists are therefore as various as the different domains of human thought, although these domains are commonly grouped according to some of the general cognitive processes that are most central. Common examples of these groupings include attention, conceptualization, decision making, imagery, imagination, language, learning, memory, perception, and sensation. Topics often overlap, and the relationships between various processes are also of interest to cognitive scientists. For instance, a cognitive scientist may be interested in language development, memory formation, or perhaps the relationship between the two.

A variety of disciplines contribute to cognitive science. For this reason, cognitive science may be better understood as an interdisciplinary field, rather than an academic discipline of its own. An influential text defines it as "the interdisciplinary study of mind and intelligence, embracing philosophy, **psychology**, **artificial intelligence**, **neuroscience**, linguistics, and **anthropology**" (Thagard 2005, ix). Anthropologists may raise questions about why certain behaviors and instincts are present universally in humanity or how cultural systems may influence decision making. Linguists may wonder how language has developed over **time** and how it facilitates problem solving. Computer scientists may investigate how artificial intelligence can be developed or model possible ways that human perceptual systems work.

In recent years, religious studies scholars are even turning to cognitive science to argue that belief in gods, spirits, and afterlives are partially explicable in terms of how well these concepts resonate with the natural tuning of cognitive systems (McCauley 2011). Philosophers and theologians are beginning to discuss whether such cognitive scientific explanations of religious beliefs undercut such beliefs (Trigg and Barrett 2014). All of these questions intersect with cognitive science, allowing each of these disciplines to contribute to this field and learn from one another. "What earns them all the title 'cognitive scientists' … is that they bring scientific evidence to bear on claims and predictions about how humans think and the character of the human mind, and attempt to discover naturalistic explanations for the phenomena the data reveal" (Barrett 2011, 12).

A distinction should also be made between cognitive science and neuroscience, though each may contribute to the other in helpful ways. Neuroscience aims to understand the mechanics of the brain as revealed in the nervous system, while cognitive science focuses on the processes of the mind as revealed in cognition. These two sciences represent two different levels of explanation. If asked how memory works, a neuroscientist might point to different parts of the brain that are distinctively active when a person is thinking about memories and the neurons and neurotransmitters that work to make memory happen. If asked the same question, a cognitive scientist might reference different processes in the mind, such as the perception of the potential memory, the encoding of this **information**, and its recall.

Justin L. Barrett and Tyler S. Greenway

REFERENCES AND RECOMMENDED READING

Barrett, Justin L. 2011. *Cognitive Science, Religion, and Theology: From Human Minds to Divine Minds.* West Conshohocken, PA: Templeton.
McCauley, Robert N. 2011. *Why Religion Is Natural and Science Is Not.* New York: Oxford University Press.
Thagard, Paul. 2005. *Mind: Introduction to Cognitive Science.* 2nd ed. Cambridge, MA: MIT Press.
Trigg, Roger, and Justin L. Barrett, eds. 2014. *The Roots of Religion: Exploring the Cognitive Science of Religion.* Surrey, UK: Ashgate.

COGNITIVE SCIENCE OF RELIGION. As **cognitive science** is the scientific study of minds and mental processes, cognitive science of religion (CSR) is the science of understanding how mental processes and religious expression interact. That is, CSR is an approach to the scientific study of religious expression that uses theories and findings from the cognitive sciences to predict, explain, and understand religious thoughts and actions that recur across cultures (Barrett 2007, 2011, 2012a). For instance, the wide recurrence of belief in gods is accounted for by detailing how ordinary processing tendencies of human minds interact with typical environmental factors to make belief in the **existence of god**s attractive to human minds (e.g., Guthrie 1993; Pyysiäinen 2009). Its moniker notwithstanding, CSR did not emerge from cognitive science but from anthropological and comparative studies of religion (Barrett 2011; see also Lawson and McCauley 1990; Whitehouse 1995).

CSR does not explain everything about religion or even every facet of it (Barrett 2007). CSR attempts to identify the basic cognitive structures that characterize or explain religious thought and action, leaving other disciplines to more thickly describe **religious experience**s and expression. Further, CSR shows relatively little concern with defining "religion" or treating "religion" as a single coherent whole (Barrett 2011; Taves 2010). Instead, CSR identifies different thoughts and actions that seem to occur across cultures and are generally considered religious. Examples include belief in supernatural agents and an afterlife, and actions such as ritual and **prayer** directed at supernatural agents.

Across cultures and different faith traditions, these types of thoughts and actions are generally present in some shape or form. CSR recognizes these occurrences and studies the cognition involved in them. CSR's examination of religion is methodologically pluralistic (Barrett 2007, 2012a), using various research methods to understand religious expression. These methods have included experiments, interviews, ethnographies, computer modeling, archaeology, and historiography.

CSR has begun research on many topics related to religion, including children's ideas about the design and origin of the natural world (Evans 2001; Kelemen 2004), **death** and afterlife beliefs (Astuti and Harris 2008; Bering et al. 2005), the development of concepts of God and gods (Barrett 2012a), magic (Sørensen 2005), prayer (Barrett 2001), religious ritual and ritualized behaviors (Liénard and Boyer 2006, McCauley and Lawson 2002), religious social and moral regulation (Norenzayan 2013), religious systems' social and political formation (Whitehouse 2004), use of Scriptures (Malley 2004), and spirit possession (Cohen and Barrett 2008).

CSR as it is typically practiced tends to favor theories in cognitive science that emphasize pan-human tendencies in how human minds work, rejecting a view of human thought as merely the result of cultural factors (Barrett 2011; McCauley 2011). In other words, CSR generally dismisses the idea that the human mind is a blank slate at birth that is then filled in over time. The reason for this dismissal is the existence of clear biases in the human mind that attend to and process certain kinds of **information** over others and arise as an ordinary part of early development (Barrett 2012a). These early developing, cross-culturally recurrent tendencies in how human minds work encourage people to engage various religious ideas and practices. The general framework of religious thought is largely "maturationally natural" according to Robert McCauley, and the particulars of any given tradition are supplied by cultural input (McCauley 2011). Its emphasis on how minds make some ideas more or less recurrent means that CSR generally has little to say about any idiosyncratic religious ideas or mystical experiences.

CSR is closely allied with evolutionary studies of religion, the area that takes findings and theories from evolutionary studies and applies them to religious thought and practice. The two approaches have many methodological and theoretical similarities and can be complementary (e.g., Bering 2011; Norenzayan 2013). Nevertheless, these two approaches may be helpfully distinguished. Evolutionary studies of religion need not make any reference to cognitive mechanisms or to how the mind works and, therefore, are not necessarily cognitive. Likewise, one may cognitively approach the study of religion with little or no reference to evolution or adaptation (e.g., Whitehouse 1995). Commonly, however, CSR accounts of religion draw on evolutionary **psychology** to frame their identification of cognitive mechanisms relevant to religious expression and typically present their work in terms of cultural evolution (e.g., Atran 2002; Boyer 2001).

Because CSR sheds light on the cognition involved in religious thought and actions, some individuals may perceive CSR as a threat to **theism** or other religious commitments. Popular polemics against religions and some more scholarly treatments of cognitive and evolutionary approaches move seamlessly from CSR to critiques of the rationality of religion and back (e.g., Bering 2011; Dawkins 2006).

This fear of CSR "explaining away" religion, however, appears to be largely unnecessary. That certain features of the mind make people receptive to particular beliefs or practices that we identify as religious does not directly speak to the rationality or truth of such beliefs or the goodness of such practices. Numerous philosophical treatments of CSR's implications for theism (and other religious beliefs) have appeared in recent years, and no consensus has emerged that CSR is problematic for rational religious beliefs (e.g., Schloss and Murray 2009). Indeed, it has even been suggested that CSR, on balance, may be supportive of some theological doctrines such as the *sensus divinitatis*—the idea that all people have an inchoate sense that the supernatural exists (Clark and

Barrett 2010, 2011), or may even be mildly problematic for atheism (Barrett and Church 2013).

CSR may have further implications for religious education and teaching. Evidence suggests that theological concepts that deviate too far from how minds ordinarily, intuitively construe the world (termed *counterintuitive*) are difficult for people to understand or hold consistently (Barrett 1999; Slone 2004). These counterintuitive ideas, such as the notion of God being omnipresent, for instance, may require extra instruction, rehearsal, and other scaffolding. Research on children, however, suggests that children may be less conceptually restricted than previously thought. Even before schooling years, children show signs of being able to make accurate predictions about some of God's superproperties such as superknowledge and superperception, opening the possibility of very early theological education (Barrett 2012a). Understanding how human minds typically receive religious ideas, then, may be valuable information for religious educators.

Justin L. Barrett and Tyler S. Greenway

REFERENCES AND RECOMMENDED READING

Astuti, Rita, and Paul L. Harris. 2008. "Understanding Mortality and the Life of the Ancestors in Rural Madagascar." *Cognitive Science* 32:713–40.

Atran, Scott. 2002. *In Gods We Trust: The Evolutionary Landscape of Religion.* Oxford: Oxford University Press.

Barrett, Justin L. 1999. "Theological Correctness: Cognitive Constraint and the Study of Religion." *Method and Theory in the Study of Religion* 11:325–39.

———. 2001. "How Ordinary Cognition Informs Petitionary Prayer." *Journal of Cognition and Culture* 1:259–69.

———. 2007. "Cognitive Science of Religion: What Is It and Why Is It?" *Religion Compass* 1:768–86.

———. 2011. "Cognitive Science of Religion: Looking Back, Looking Forward." *Journal for the Scientific Study of Religion* 50:229–39.

———. 2012a. *Born Believers: The Science of Children's Religious Belief.* New York: Free Press.

———. 2012b. "Toward a Cognitive Science of Christianity." In *The Blackwell Companion to Science and Christianity*, ed. J. B. Stump and Alan G. Padgett, 317–34. Chichester, UK: Wiley.

Barrett, Justin L., and Ian M. Church. 2013. "Should CSR Give Atheists Assurance? On Beer-Goggles, BFFs, and Skepticism Regarding Religious Beliefs." *The Monist* 93:311–24.

Bering, Jesse M. 2011. *The Belief Instinct: The Psychology of Souls, Destiny, and the Meaning of Life.* New York: W. W. Norton.

Bering, Jesse M., C. Hernández-Blasi, and D. F. Bjorkland. 2005. "The Development of 'Afterlife' Beliefs in Secularly and Religiously Schooled Children." *British Journal of Developmental Psychology* 23:587–607.

Boyer, Pascal. 2001. *Religion Explained: The Evolutionary Origins of Religious Thought.* New York: Basic Books.

Clark, Kelly J., and Justin L. Barrett. 2010. "Reformed Epistemology and the Cognitive Science of Religion." *Faith and Philosophy* 27:174–89.

———. 2011. "Reidian Epistemology and the Cognitive Science of Religion." *Journal of the American Academy of Religion* 79:639–75.

Cohen, Emma, and Justin L. Barrett. 2008. "Conceptualising Possession Trance: Ethnographic and Experimental Evidence." *Ethos* 36:246–67.

Dawkins, Richard. 2006. *The God Delusion.* Boston: Mariner.

Evans, E. Margaret. 2001. "Cognitive and Contextual Factors in the Emergence of Diverse Belief Systems: Creation versus Evolution." *Cognitive Psychology* 42:217–66.

Guthrie, Stewart E. 1993. *Faces in the Clouds: A New Theory of Religion.* New York: Oxford University Press.

Kelemen, Deborah. 2004. "Are Children 'Intuitive Theists'? Reasoning about Purpose and Design in Nature." *Psychological Science* 15:295–301.

Lawson, E. Thomas, and Robert N. McCauley. 1990. *Rethinking Religion: Connecting Cognition and Culture.* Cambridge: Cambridge University Press.

Liénard, Pierre, and Pascal Boyer. 2006. "Whence Collective Ritual? A Cultural Selection Model of Ritualized Behavior." *American Anthropologist* 108:814–27.

Malley, Brian. 2004. *How the Bible Works: An Anthropological Study of Evangelical Biblicism.* Walnut Creek, CA: AltaMira.

McCauley, Robert N. 2011. *Why Religion Is Natural and Science Is Not.* New York: Oxford University Press.

McCauley, Robert N., and E. Thomas Lawson. 2002. *Bringing Ritual to Mind: Psychological Foundations of Cultural Forms.* Cambridge: Cambridge University Press.

Norenzayan, Ara. 2013. *Big Gods: How Religion Transformed Cooperation and Conflict.* Princeton, NJ: Princeton University Press.

Pyysiäinen, Ilkka. 2009. *Supernatural Agents: Why We Believe in Souls, Gods, and Buddhas.* New York: Oxford University Press.

Schloss, Jeffery, and Michael J. Murray, eds. 2009. *The Believing Primate: Scientific, Philosophical, and Theological Perspectives on the Evolution of Religion.* New York: Oxford University Press.

Slone, D. Jason. 2004. *Theological Incorrectness: Why Religious People Believe What They Shouldn't.* New York: Oxford University Press.

Sørensen, Jesper. 2005. *A Cognitive Theory of Magic.* Lanham, MD: Rowman & Littlefield.

Taves, Ann. 2010. *Religious Experience Reconsidered: A Building-Block Approach to the Study of Religion and Other Special Things.* Princeton, NJ: Princeton University Press.

Whitehouse, Harvey. 1995. *Inside the Cult: Religious Innovation and Transmission in Papua New Guinea.* Oxford: Clarendon.

———. 2004. *Modes of Religiosity: A Cognitive Theory of Religious Transmission.* Walnut Creek, CA: AltaMira.

COLLINS, C. JOHN. C. John "Jack" Collins (1954–) is professor of Old Testament at Covenant Theological Seminary (Presbyterian Church in America) in Saint Louis, Missouri, where he has taught since 1993, and a Fellow of the Center for Science and Culture at **Discovery Institute** in Seattle, Washington. He holds SB and SM degrees in computer science and systems engineering from the Massachusetts Institute of **Technology**, an MDiv from Faith Evangelical Lutheran Seminary, and a PhD in Hebrew linguistics from the School of Archaeology and Oriental Studies at the University of Liverpool. He has worked as a research engineer and a church planter but has been a teacher and academic since 1993.

A well-respected Old Testament scholar, his early work (1988) focused on Hebrew grammar, but he also writes on biblical theology and New Testament uses of the Old Testament (2000, 2003a, 2004, 2008, 2009a), and is best known for his defense of an "analogical days" exegesis of Genesis 1 and 2 (1994, 1995, 1999a, 1999b, 2003c, 2006, 2009b, 2013b), his defense of the historicity of **Adam and Eve** in the context of an old-earth creationist understanding of Scripture (1997, 2001, 2006, 2010a, 2011, 2012b, 2013a, 2014), his exposition of **C. S. Lewis**'s views on the relationship between science and faith, his defense of **natural law theory** as accounting for a universal moral sense, and his advocacy of **intelligent design** as a research program in the sciences (2000, 2003a, 2003b, 2010b, 2012a, 2016). Collins was also the Old Testament chairman for the *English Standard Version* translation of the Bible, and the Old Testament editor for the *English Standard Version Study Bible*.

The analogical-day view of Genesis 1 and 2 is distinct from the day-age, intermittent-day, literary-framework, revelatory-day, cosmic-temple-inauguration, and literal 24-hour-day interpretations (see **Biblical Chronology**; **Days of Creation**; also Gordon 2014; Lennox 2011; Parry 2014; Poythress 2006, 79–85, 107–47; and Walton 2009). Collins finds precedent for his view in the writings of the American Presbyterian theologian William Shedd (1820–94) and the Dutch Reformed theologian Herman Bavinck (1854–1921). The analogical-day position holds that "the [creation] days are God's workdays, their length is neither specified nor important, and not everything in the account needs to be taken as historically sequential" (Collins 2006, 124). Collins argues that Genesis 1:1 is best interpreted as a summary of God's activity prior to the first day of creation in Genesis 1:3, which allows for an unspecified period of time to have passed prior to God's beginning to shape the earth for habitability.

Collins develops his analogical understanding in light of the following considerations: (1) the ongoing nature of the seventh "day" that *lacks* an evening and a morning (Gen. 2:2); (2) the expansion of the sixth "day" in the second creation account (Gen. 2:5–25); (3) a lexico-grammatical resolution of the problem of the fourth "day" in which—since God here tasks the sun, moon, and stars to *govern* the day and night (Gen. 1:14–16)—the Hebrew allows God's action to be that of appointing these *previously created* heavenly bodies (Gen. 1:1) to their function of marking time for sentient life (Collins 2006, 56–58); and (4) the poetic parallelism correlating "days" one to three as a triad with "days" four through six (the literary-framework observation), which indicates that day length and chronology are not primary considerations in the creation account.

Collins also defends the historicity of a literal Adam and Eve in the context of an old-earth chronology (see **Adam and**

Eve; **Biblical Chronology**; **Creationism, Old-Earth**; **Creationism, Young-Earth**; **Death**; **Evolutionary Creationism**; **Fall, The**; and **Genealogies**) in contrast with nonhistorical, archetypal, and young-earth views (in addition to Collins's works, see Barrett and Caneday 2013; Enns 2005, 2010; Gordon 2014; Halton 2015; Lamoureux 2008; Madueme and Reeves 2014; Walton 2015). In particular, for the story line of the Bible to have maximal coherence, he argues that all of humanity needs to have one set of ancestors and constitute a family, that God must have acted in some appropriate supernatural sense to create our first parents, and that our first ancestors, by their disobedience, must be the ultimate source of sin, dysfunction, and spiritual **death** in human history.

While he allows for the possibility of a circumscribed polygenesis (Adam as the chieftain of an aboriginal human population, with Eve as his wife), Collins has a strong preference for monogenesis, a position he regards as biblically preferable and historically defensible. In light of the ancestral focus of the biblical genealogies, which are indicative of lines of descent but demonstrably include many gaps, he allows great flexibility in the time frame for God's creation of humanity, remarking that he knows "of no way to figure out whether there is even an upper limit to the number of possible gaps" in the biblical genealogies (2003c, 109).

In summary, while recognizing that the ancient literary forms and conventions of the biblical text introduce metaphorical and dischronologous elements into the story, Collins offers a vigorous and cogent defense of the view that the early chapters of Genesis provide a record of things that, in an appropriate historical sense, actually happened.

Bruce L. Gordon

REFERENCES AND RECOMMENDED READING

Barrett, Matthew, and Ardel B. Caneday, eds. 2013. *Four Views on the Historical Adam*. Grand Rapids: Zondervan.

Collins, C. John. 1988. *Homonymous Verbs in Biblical Hebrew: An Investigation of the Role of Comparative Philology*. PhD diss. University of Liverpool.

———. 1994. "How Old Is the Earth? Anthropomorphic Days in Genesis 1:1 – 2:3." *Presbyterion* 20:109 – 30.

———. 1995. "The *Wayyiqtol* as 'Pluperfect': When and Why." *Tyndale Bulletin* 46 (1): 117 – 40. www.tyndalehouse.com/tynbul/library/TynBull_1995_46_1_08_Collins_WAYYIQTOL_Pluperfect.pdf.

———. 1997. "A Syntactical Note on Genesis 3:15: Is the Woman's Seed Singular or Plural?" *Tyndale Bulletin* 48:141 – 48.

———. 1999a. "Discourse Analysis and the Interpretation of Gen. 2:4 – 7." *Westminster Theological Journal* 61:269 – 76.

———. 1999b. "Reading Genesis 1:1 – 2:3 as an Act of Communication: Discourse Analysis and Literal Interpretation." In *Did God Create in Six Days?* ed. J. Pipa and D. Hall, 131 – 51. Taylors, SC: Southern Presbyterian Press.

———. 2000. *The God of Miracles: An Exegetical Examination of God's Action in the World*. Wheaton, IL: Crossway.

———. 2001. "What Happened to Adam and Eve? A Literary-Theological Approach to Genesis 3." *Presbyterion* 27:12 – 44.

———. 2003a. "Galatians 3:16: What Kind of Exegete Was Paul?" *Tyndale Bulletin* 51:75 – 86.

———. 2003b. "Miracles, Intelligent Design, and God-of-the-Gaps." *Perspectives on Science and the Christian Faith* 55:22 – 29.

———. 2003c. *Science and Faith: Friends or Foes?* Wheaton, IL: Crossway.

———. 2004. "The Eucharist as Christian Sacrifice: How Patristic Authors Can Help Us Read the Bible." *Westminster Theological Journal* 66:1 – 23.

———. 2006. *Genesis 1 – 4: A Linguistic, Literary, and Theological Commentary*. Phillipsburg, NJ: P&R.

———. 2008. "The Theology of the Old Testament." In *The ESV Study Bible*, ed. L. T. Dennis et al. Wheaton, IL: Crossway.

———. 2009a. "Proverbs and the Levitical System." *Presbyterion* 35:9 – 34.

———. 2009b. "The Refrain of Genesis 1: A Critical View of Its Rendering in the English Bible." *Technical Papers for the Bible Translator* 60 (3). www.ubs-translations.org/fileadmin/publications/tbt/technical/TBT_TP_Collins_Jul_09.pdf.

———. 2010a. "Adam and Eve as Historical People, and Why It Matters." *Perspectives on Science and Christian Faith* 62 (3): 147 – 65. www.asa3.org/ASA/PSCF/2010/PSCF9 – 10Collins.pdf.

———. 2010b. "Echoes of Aristotle in Romans 2:14 – 15: Or, Maybe Abimelech Was Not So Bad After All." *Journal of Markets and Morality* 13 (1):123 – 73. www.marketsandmorality.com/index.php/mandm/article/download/112/106.

———. 2011. *Did Adam and Eve Really Exist? Who They Were and Why You Should Care*. Wheaton, IL: Crossway.

———. 2012a. "A Peculiar Clarity: How C. S. Lewis Can Help Us Think about Faith and Science." In *The Magician's Twin: C. S. Lewis on Science, Scientism, and Society*, ed. J. G. West, 69 – 106. Seattle: Discovery Institute Press.

———. 2012b. "Replies to Reviews of *Did Adam and Eve Really Exist?*" *Journal of Creation, Theology, and Science, Series B: Life Sciences* 2:43 – 47. www.coresci.org/jcts/index.php/jctsb/article/download/32/50.

———. 2013a. "A Historical Adam: Old-Earth Creation View." In *Four Views on the Historical Adam*, ed. Matthew Barrett and Ardel B. Caneday, 143 – 95. Grand Rapids: Zondervan.

———. 2013b. "Reading Genesis 1 – 2 with the Grain: Analogical Days." In *Genesis 1 – 2: An Evangelical Conversation*, ed. J. Daryl Charles, 73 – 92. Peabody, MA: Hendrickson.

———. 2014. "Adam and Eve in the Old Testament." In *Adam, the Fall, and Original Sin: Theological, Biblical, and Scientific Perspectives*, ed. H. Madueme and M. Reeves, 3 – 32. Grand Rapids: Baker Academic.

———. 2016. "Freedoms and Limitations: C. S. Lewis and Francis Schaeffer as a Tag Team." In *Firstfruits of a New Creation: Essays in Honor of Jerram Barrs*, ed. M. Ryan and J. E. Eubanks. Forthcoming.

Enns, Peter. 2005. *Inspiration and Incarnation: Evangelicals and the Problem of the Old Testament*. Grand Rapids: Baker Academic.

———. 2010. *The Evolution of Adam: What the Bible Does and Doesn't Say about Human Origins*. Grand Rapids: Brazos.

Gordon, Bruce L. 2014. "Scandal of the Evangelical Mind: A Biblical and Scientific Critique of Young Earth Creationism." *Science, Religion and Culture* 1:144 – 73.

Halton, Charles, ed. 2015. *Genesis: History, Fiction, or Neither? Three Views on the Bible's Earliest Chapters*. Grand Rapids: Zondervan.

Lamoureux, Denis O. 2008. *Evolutionary Creation: A Christian Approach to Evolution*. Eugene, OR: Wipf and Stock.

Lennox, John C. 2011. *Seven Days That Divide the World: The Beginning According to Genesis and Science*. Grand Rapids: Zondervan.

Madueme, Hans, and M. Reeves, eds. 2014. *Adam, the Fall, and Original Sin: Theological, Biblical, and Scientific Perspectives*. Grand Rapids: Baker Academic.

Parry, Robin A. 2014. *The Biblical Cosmos: A Pilgrim's Guide to the Weird and Wonderful World of the Bible*. Eugene, OR: Cascade.

Poythress, Vern S. 2006. *Redeeming Science: A God-Centered Approach*. Wheaton, IL: Crossway.

Walton, John H. 2009. *The Lost World of Genesis One: Ancient Cosmology and the Origins Debate*. Downers Grove, IL: IVP Academic.

———. 2015. *The Lost World of Adam and Eve: Genesis 2–3 and the Human Origins Debate*. Downers Grove, IL: IVP Academic.

COLLINS, FRANCIS. Francis S. Collins (1950–) is a leading geneticist, the former head of the **Human Genome Project**, and the current director of the National Institutes of Health. Collins, a former atheist, became a Christian while he was a medical student in North Carolina.

His conversion was triggered initially following a conversation with an older female patient who, having shared her personal Christian beliefs, asked him what he believed. He was embarrassed by his inability to answer the question, and this constituted the beginning of his quest to find an answer. After doing some reading about world religions, and feeling thoroughly confused, he visited a Methodist pastor in a neighborhood church. The pastor passed along his copy of **C. S. Lewis**'s *Mere Christianity*. Realizing that "his own constructs against the plausibility of belief were those of a schoolboy," he began the quest that eventually led to his decision to become a Christian. He describes the moment of his conversion as occurring during a hiking expedition in the Cascade Mountains of Washington:

> I turned the corner and saw in front of me this frozen waterfall, a couple of hundred feet high. Actually, a waterfall that had three parts to it—also the symbolic three in one. At that moment, I felt my resistance leave me. And it was a great sense of relief. The next morning, in the dewy grass in the shadow of the Cascades, I fell on my knees and accepted this truth—that God is God, that Christ is his son and that I am giving my life to that belief. (Collins 2006, 225)

Collins was raised on a small farm in Virginia's Shenandoah Valley. The farm had no running water and few other physical amenities, but he writes that "these things were more than compensated for by the stimulating mix of experiences and opportunities that were available to me in the remarkable culture of ideas created by my parents" (Collins 2006, 11). He was homeschooled until the sixth grade.

Initially in his high school years and then on to university, he aspired to be a chemist and had little interest in the "messy" field of biology. He earned a BS in chemistry at the University of Virginia in 1970 and a PhD in physical chemistry at Yale University in 1974. It was at Yale, though, that he took a course in biochemistry, and this sparked his interest in the molecules that hold the blueprint for life: **DNA** and RNA. He subsequently changed fields, enrolling in medical school at the University of North Carolina, where he earned an MD in 1977.

After completing his residency in North Carolina, Collins returned to Yale in 1981 as a Fellow in Human Genetics. It was there that he developed a powerful method to cross large stretches of DNA to identify disease genes. The technique, called chromosome jumping, became widely used as a method for isolating genes. In 1984 he joined the medical school faculty at the University of Michigan. His experiments there led to pioneering work on the successful isolation of the **gene** responsible for cystic fibrosis through a technique he called positional **cloning**. This was followed by his work on the successful isolation of other medically important genes, including those for Huntington's disease and neurofibromatosis.

In 1993 Collins was asked to replace the codiscoverer of the structure of DNA, James Watson, to head up the highly ambitious and somewhat controversial project to determine the sequence of the 3 billion code letters that make up the human genome. This was "an adventure," he said, "that beats going to the moon or splitting the atom" (NIH 2015). Indeed, it was by far the single largest project in the history of biology. In 2003, two years ahead of schedule and $400 million under budget, the project was completed.

Although Collins had spoken frequently about his Christian faith in various evangelical forums, such as the annual meeting of the **American Scientific Affiliation** (ASA) and Veritas Forums on university campuses, his position as an evangelical Christian became especially well known after the publication of his *New York Times* bestseller, *The Language of God*. This book outlined the basis of his Christian faith as well as addressing various aspects of the interrelationship between science and the Christian faith. Especially noteworthy in that book is his strong stance on God having created all of life through the evolutionary process and his criticism of various more traditional creationist positions, including the **intelligent design** movement.

The book led to much affirmation from Christians who were in science and led to many personal inquiries about his beliefs regarding various aspects of the connection between science, the Bible, and Christian faith. This in turn resulted in his decision to form the **BioLogos Foundation** to more thoroughly address this interrelationship and to better inform Christians of his belief that science and Christianity are not in conflict but rather share a deep coherence. BioLogos was founded in 2007, and beginning in April 2009 the foundation launched a public website and ministry with Collins as its president.

In the summer of 2009, Collins was tapped for the directorship of the National Institutes of Health, a position that he still holds at this writing, but which required relinquishing any role with BioLogos, although the organization continues to thrive and is highly influential on the science–Christian faith conversation. He has received numerous awards, including membership in the National Academy of Sciences and the Institute of Medicine. In 2007 President George W. Bush awarded Collins the President's National Medal of Freedom, the highest civilian award in the United States, and in 2009 President Barack Obama presented Collins with the National Medal of Science, the highest honor bestowed by the United States government on scientists. Francis Collins is one of only nine persons in history to receive both awards.

Darrel R. Falk

REFERENCES AND RECOMMENDED READING

Collins, Francis. 2006. *The Language of God.* New York: Free Press.
———. 2010. *Belief: Readings on the Reason for Faith.* New York: HarperOne.
———. 2011. *The Language of Life: DNA and the Revolution in Personalized Medicine.* New York: Harper Perennial.
Collins, Francis, and Karl Giberson. 2011. *The Language of Science and Faith.* Downers Grove, IL: InterVarsity.
NIH. 2015. "Francis S. Collins, M.D., Ph.D." National Human Genome Research Institute. Updated September 25. www.genome.gov/10001018/former-nhgri-director-francis-collins-biography.

COMMON ANCESTRY. Most scientists think that all living organisms, including *Homo sapiens*, have been formed through a process of gradual modification from preexisting **species**, so that all living things share common ancestors. In the case of humans, the evidence for this, as they see it, is largely threefold.

1. The gradual increase in sophistication of archaeological artifacts correlated with established geological ages of the sedimentary rock in which they are found.

2. The gradual changes in the skeletal remains of ancient humanlike species found in rock sediment. In general, the younger the fossil-containing rock, the more closely the skeletal remains resemble those of modern humans.

3. The pattern of genetic features shared by humans and the great apes. The genetic features that are indicative of common ancestry fit into three broad classes:

a. *Mutation rate.* Scientists now know quite precisely how many changes (mutations) occur in the 3 billion bits of coding **information** in the **DNA** we each inherit from our two parents—it is about 70. If one extrapolates from these 70 changes in one generation to the number of generations since chimpanzees and humans are believed to have had a common ancestor (about 120,000), one can estimate the number of differences in the DNA that one would expect if chimpanzees and humans share a common ancestor. That number comes close to being 70 changes x 120,000 generations.

b. *Genetic scars.* Just as our bodies accumulate scars that are the telltale signs of old skin abrasions, so also our genome (i.e., our DNA) accumulates cuts that are subsequently healed. Moreover, just as we can "map" the location and shape of each abrasion onto the surface of our body (e.g., tip of left index finger or right side of upper lip), so also we can map the location of sealed cuts in the genome.

The cuts in DNA, like the cuts to our skin, are known to be largely random. We share many sealed cut sites with chimpanzees, indicating that the cut occurred in the DNA of a common ancestor and has been preserved in the genome ever since. Furthermore, we and chimpanzees share many healed cut sites with gorillas, albeit fewer in number. And as we look at the results of damage events even deeper in time, we find that humans, chimpanzees, and gorillas share many of these "scars" with orangutans, although the number of shared scars is reduced even further. This pattern of shared "genetic scars" is considered to be strongly indicative of shared ancestry.

c. *Frequency of synonymous and nonsynonymous differences between closely related species.* Words that mean the same thing are said to be synonyms. For example, in describing the shape of a ball, *circular* and *round* mean the same thing. Just as there may be two or more ways of saying the same thing in describing the shape of a ball, so also there are different ways of saying the same thing in the DNA code for building the body of a human and a chimpanzee.

If descent from a common ancestor were true, then changes in the instructions for building important body parts could be altered through mutation over time as long as those changes were synonymous. Given these ongoing mutational events, the longer it has been since two organisms are believed to have shared a common ancestor, the more synonymous changes that would be expected to have accumulated. Furthermore, it would be expected that nonsynonymous changes in the building of important body parts would be found at a much lower frequency—presumably because when they have occurred, they caused damage that resulted in decreased viability and loss from the lineage. This pattern of genetic change (preservation of synonyms but loss of nonsynonyms) is precisely what one would expect if these species were related to each other through descent from a single previously existing ancestral species.

Darrel R. Falk

REFERENCES AND RECOMMENDED READING

Finlay, Graeme. 2013. *Human Evolution: Genes, Genealogies, and Phylogenies.* Cambridge: Cambridge University Press.
Lieberman, Daniel. 2014. *The Story of the Human Body: Evolution, Health, and Disease.* New York: Vintage.

COMPATIBILISM. Philosophical **naturalism** holds that all of reality is physical in nature, consisting of configurations of matter and energy, and so all things that exist have a scientific explanation in terms of causes and their effects, at least in principle. However, the existence of human free will is regarded by many as a strong argument against this view. Compatibilism in the philosophy of mind was developed as a response to the problem of how to reconcile free will with a thoroughly scientific, and therefore deterministic, account of physical reality. It has been defended by A. J. Ayer, Harry Frankfurt, John Mark Fischer, and Kadri Vilvelin, among others.

Free will involves a genuine choice between alternatives—for example, concerning whether or not to accept a job offer—and though an individual may have reasons in favor of a particular option, the decision is up to the individual or self and so is not caused in the scientific sense. In other words, it is not the end result of a causal chain (i.e., efficient causality) that originates in the brain and the person's environment. In this sense, free will is incompatible with scientific causal explanations (see **Aristotle's Four Causes**). If, however, human beings are completely physical beings, we would appear to be subject to causal **determinism**, the view that together with the laws of **physics**, every event or happening in the universe is caused by antecedent events. So this view would seem to rule out the existence of free will.

Compatibilism is the view that causal determinism and free will are compatible, despite appearances to the contrary. Compatibilists argue that free actions should be understood as those that are not coerced, such as in cases where an individual is hypnotized, brainwashed, duped, or subject to force by an external agent or event. Any action performed after a "process of deliberation" and absent outside influences of this type can be said to be "free." This is because the individual reasons to a decision and then decides to act, even though she or he still would not have a genuine choice between alternatives because of causal determinism. Central to this argument is the compatibilist claim that despite our commonsense understanding of **morality**, one does not need a genuine choice between alternatives in order to be acting freely and therefore to be morally responsible for one's decisions.

Yet compatibilist proposals have never come to terms with the serious objection that if causal determinism holds, then all current events are determined by past events and the **laws of nature**, including human beliefs, reasoning processes, logical inferences, and "decisions." The only difference between the actions of a hypnotized person and those of a deliberative person is the chain of causes involved. Indeed, since all of our decisions would still be subject to physical causes, there really are no deliberative decisions arrived at freely if determinism is true. In general, the indispensability of free will and moral agency, and their crucial connection to moral responsibility, punishment, and even democracy, are regarded by many Christian theists as strong arguments against not only compatibilism but naturalistic accounts of reality in general (see **Naturalism**). Moreover, free will strongly suggests that a **soul** or incorporeal self exists, which strikes against a naturalistic **worldview** (see **Dualism**; **Mind-Body Problem**).

Brendan Sweetman

REFERENCES AND RECOMMENDED READING

Honderich, Ted. 1988. *A Theory of Determinism.* Oxford: Clarendon.
Howard-Snyder, Daniel, and Jeff Jordan, eds. 1996. *Faith, Freedom, and Rationality.* Lanham, MD: Rowman & Littlefield.
van Inwagen, Peter. 1983. *An Essay on Free Will.* Oxford: Clarendon.
Vihvelin, Kadri. 2013. *Causes, Laws and Free Will.* New York: Oxford University Press.

COMPLEMENTARITY PRINCIPLE. The "absolute **paradox**" (Søren Kierkegaard) and complementarity (Niels Bohr) form a closely related conceptual pair (see **Paradox**). In the eighteenth century, Kierkegaard (1813–55) was trying to resolve the paradox of the nature of Jesus Christ, whose nature was affirmed by the Council of Chalcedon (451) to be a unity and yet fully divine and fully human, these natures existing in one person without confusion in unchangeable union (see **Incarnation**).

Kierkegaard realized that this understanding had continued to be the standard for Christian orthodoxy since Chalcedon, and he fully accepted this specification of the nature of Jesus Christ. Furthermore, this formulation comprised the starting point for Kierkegaard's Christology as he developed what he called the absolute paradox.

Some speculation exists regarding the possible influence Kierkegaard had on his fellow Dane, Niels Bohr, in his formulation of the principle of complementarity for application to **physics**. It is true that Bohr's father, Christian Bohr, was an interested follower of Kierkegaard's thought, perhaps through the work of Harold Hoffding. And it is apparent that Bohr's principle of complementarity has a structure that closely resembles Kierkegaard's absolute paradox.

In physics—until early in the twentieth century—entities in nature had rather well-defined properties. For example, evidence pointed to light exhibiting behavior that clearly classified it as an electromagnetic wave, which could be thought of as extending over great spans of space. In contrast, objects like electrons were seen as well localized, with almost a point-like extension and certainly not having properties that could be associated with a wave.

Near the end of the eighteenth century, a new phenomenon was discovered: the photoelectric effect, whereby light could cause electrons to be ejected from certain metals. It was **Einstein** in 1905 who first proposed that this could be understood in terms of light being composed of compact particles of energy, and that a wave understanding of light was completely inconsistent with this effect. A consequence is that light exhibits a dual nature—sometimes wavelike, but in other circumstances particle-like. Einstein's photoelectric analysis, not his work on special and general relativity, earned him the Nobel Prize in 1921.

Shortly thereafter, in 1924, Louis Victor de Broglie proposed that the wave-particle duality seen in light should apply to all entities in nature, and that those entities that had been understood as particles, like electrons, would show wavelike properties under the right conditions. In 1927 Clinton Davisson and Lester Germer devised an experiment by which electrons were seen to behave in a wavelike manner, and de Broglie soon thereafter received the Nobel Prize for his wave-particle proposal.

Also in 1927 Niels Bohr received a letter from the early quantum physicist Werner Heisenberg, informing Bohr of his newly discovered and unpublished uncertainty principle (see **Heisenberg Uncertainty Principle**). In subsequent discussions, Bohr convinced Heisenberg that his principle was a manifestation of the deeper concept of complementarity, which Bohr introduced in September of that year.

There are two main aspects to the concept of complementarity. First, complementarity refers to the concept that the underlying properties of entities (e.g., subatomic particles) may reveal themselves in contradictory forms at different times, depending on the conditions of observation. As a result, a physical model of an entity exclusively in terms of one form or the other will be necessarily incomplete. For example, describing an electron only in terms of its particle nature is incomplete. This principle implies the crucial point that there is no sharp separation between the behavior especially of subatomic entities and their interaction with the experimental apparatus that serves to specify the particular aspect of the entity that will be displayed.

Second, complementarity implies the Heisenberg uncertainty principle and the randomness that is associated with the Copenhagen interpretation of quantum mechanics. This interpretation maintains that physical systems generally do not have definite properties prior to being measured, and that quantum mechanical calculations can only predict a range of probabilities of outcomes of such measurements (see **Quantum Theory, Interpretations of**).

Richard F. Carlson

REFERENCES AND RECOMMENDED READING

Loder, James E., and W. Jim Neidhardt. 1992. *The Knight's Move: The Relational Logic of the Spirit in Theology and Science.* Colorado Springs: Helmers & Howard.

Polkinghorne, John. 2002. *Quantum Theory: A Very Short Introduction.* Oxford: Oxford University Press.

COMPLEXITY. Complexity is a general term for physical systems that not only have many parts but also have many different types of interactions between parts. For example, a gas with billions of atoms is not considered complex because the interactions between the atoms are all the same; a living cell is considered complex because there are many different types of interactions between different groups of atoms. Other examples of complex systems are human societies, computer networks, and environmental ecosystems. Examples of types of complex interactions are hierarchy, feedback, and nonlinearity.

In a hierarchical system, groups of parts connect to each other to make subsystems, which then combine with other subsystems to make even larger subsystems, and so on, sometimes up to dozens of levels of hierarchy. In a system with feedback, the interactions themselves are altered depending on what is happening in the system and what inputs it receives from outside. Nonlinearity is a general term for interactions that can be amplified or weakened as more or fewer parts of the system participate.

Complexity theory is closely connected to the broad-based program of **physics** research started in the 1970s associated with Nobel–prize winner Ilya Prigogine, which sought to explain the origin of life as a physical phenomenon that naturally arises in nonequilibrium systems with energy input and dissipation. In general, the appearance of new structures in systems with many parts is known as **emergence**. In the 1970s and 1980s, several simple emergent phenomena were demonstrated, such as the appearance of orderly stripes of clouds in the sky and orderly patterns of vortices. By the 1990s, however, hope began to fade for showing emergence of higher-level complex behaviors like those seen in living organisms. Many in the complexity-theory community then switched to a different approach of taking existing complex systems and analyzing how they work.

The first type of complexity research, associated with the soft-condensed-matter physics community, can be called a "bottom-up" approach, looking for emergence of complex behavior in systems that have well-understood rules of interactions. Such systems are sometimes called "toy models" because they do not actually represent real living systems or other real complex systems; they have a very limited degree of complexity. The hope with these studies is that general principles may be deduced, which then apply to more complicated systems like living cells. The second type of complexity research, associated with the systems biology and biophysics communities, can be called a "top-down" approach, in which existing living organisms or ecosystems are studied to see how they work. This is sometimes called reverse engineering, as it is similar to how engineers sometimes take devices made by other companies and take them apart to learn how they function.

Complexity theory also has strong connections to systems engineering, a field of engineering in which complex machines and designed systems are studied. In these systems, all the interactions are known, being put in by design, but optimizing the efficiency and predicting the behavior of a whole system can be very difficult. Complexity theory has also been applied to *economics*, a subset of the complicated behavior of human societies. This has led to controversy as human interactions are taken to be random or deterministic (see **Social Sciences**). However, the use of rule-based models for human interactions can be seen as just a way of averaging the behavior of many people.

David Snoke

REFERENCES AND RECOMMENDED READING

Pearcey, Nancy, and Charles B. Thaxton. 1994. *The Soul of Science*, chap. 10. Wheaton, IL: Crossway.
Snoke, David. 2014. "Systems Biology as a Research Paradigm for Intelligent Design." *Bio-complexity* 3:1.

CONCORDISM. *Concordism* refers to the position that the teaching of the Bible on the natural world, properly interpreted, will agree with the teaching of science (when it properly understands the data), and may in fact supplement science. The concordist not only believes that nature and Scripture will harmonize, but sees specific references in the Bible to current scientific understanding of the universe. The concordist, then, looks for those close parallels in order to show that Scripture concords or agrees with scientific conclusions.

Because the concordist holds Scripture as entirely truthful, there cannot be any ultimate contradiction between Scripture rightly interpreted and nature rightly interpreted. In both Scripture and nature, of course, there is the potential for error in the interpretation. Concordism, however, assumes that correlations can be made, believing in a degree of accuracy of interpretation (though not infallibility) in current science and in showing how Scripture supports clear scientific conclusions.

Building from the increasing recognition of Copernican **astronomy** (beginning in the seventeenth century) and the argument that God was accommodating himself to man using man's common language to explain theological truths, the growing authority of the sciences going into the nineteenth century paved the way for science to have a recognized impact on the interpretation of Scripture and for the growing desire to show the harmony of the two disciplines (Davis 2003, 35–42). This desire to show harmony led to the reexamining of Scripture and the championing of views that allowed that harmony, such as the *day-age* view of creation in Genesis 1. Those who find strong specific parallels between science and Scripture present a strong concordist position. More recent concordists see fewer specific parallels and argue for a more general correlation, promoting a moderate concordism.

The young-earth position adheres to a similar fundamental principle and so is sometimes considered concordist, but adherents approach the issue from the reverse direction. Young-earth theorists also presuppose that Scripture and science cannot contradict each other if rightly understood. The young-earth proponents begin with Scripture, however, supposing the accuracy of their interpretation of Scripture. They then reexamine science to try to show that it actually accords with their recent view of creation. At the core, the same conviction that both Scripture and the natural world are from God and must ultimately accord drives both systems of concordism.

An alternative view in the origins debate agrees that in the end science and Scripture will accord in what they affirm. However, this position believes that we are missing the point when we try to read Genesis in light of modern science or to interpret scientific data in light of Genesis. Instead, we need to read the text in light of its ancient context for its original intent. In this view, the Genesis creation account does not affirm a position on modern scientific questions and so does not speak to the expected scientific issues directly (Miller and Soden 2012). Since Genesis 1 does not present scientific claims, such things as the age of the earth can be left to scientific investigation without needing to demonstrate specific correlation.

John Soden

REFERENCES AND RECOMMENDED READING

Davis, Edward B. 2003. "The Word and the Works: Concordism and American Evangelicals." In *Perspectives on an Evolving Creation*, ed. Keith B. Miller, 34–58. Grand Rapids: Eerdmans.

Miller, Johnny V., and John M. Soden. 2012. *In the Beginning ... We Misunderstood: Interpreting Genesis 1 in Its Original Context*. Grand Rapids: Kregel.

Ross, Hugh. 2006. *Genesis One: A Scientific Perspective*. Pasadena, CA: Reasons to Believe.

CONFIRMATION. The term *confirmation* refers to the relationship between a hypothesis and the evidence that supports it or counts in its favor. Despite the important role evidence plays in assessing hypotheses not only in science but also in other fields of study as well as in everyday life, it turns out to be rather difficult to spell out exactly what it means for evidence to support a hypothesis. The goal of confirmation theory is to clarify the nature of this relationship.

One popular account of confirmation is known as *hypothetico-deductivism* (HD). The general idea is straightforward. A hypothesis *h* is confirmed by evidence *e* if *h* entails *e* and it is disconfirmed by *e* if *h* entails that *e* is false. For example, the discovery of the Higgs boson particle would seem to confirm the **standard model** of particle **physics** that predicted it. In this case, the HD approach gets things right, but a well-known problem is that of *irrelevant conjunction*. If a hypothesis *h* entails *e*, then combining *h* with an irrelevant hypothesis will also entail *e*. This means that the discovery of the Higgs boson also confirms the combined hypothesis consisting of the standard model *and* that there is life on Mars.

While various modifications can be made to the HD approach, the leading approach to confirmation is Bayesian confirmation theory (see **Bayes' Theorem**), according to which the degree of confirmation of hypothesis *h* by evidence *e*, denoted *c(h,e)*, satisfies the following conditions:

$$c(h,e) \{mt\} \ 0 \text{ if } P(h|e) \{mt\} \ P(h)$$
$$c(h,e) = 0 \text{ if } P(h|e) = P(h)$$
$$c(h,e) \{lt\} \ 0 \text{ if } P(h|e) \{lt\} \ P(h)$$

That is, the degree of confirmation of *h* by *e* is positive if the **probability** of *h* given *e*, denoted *P(h|e)*, is greater than the probability of *h* and similarly for the other cases. In other words, evidence confirms a hypothesis if it increases its probability. This approach takes into account the insights of the HD approach but avoids the problem of irrelevant conjunction and can handle statistical hypotheses. There are also various ways to quantify the degree of confirmation, which enable two or more hypotheses to be compared quantitatively.

Carl Hempel drew attention to the famous raven **paradox**. It seems sensible to say that an observation of a black raven confirms the hypothesis that all ravens are black. However, it also makes sense to say that if evidence confirms a given hypothesis, it also confirms any equivalent hypothesis. Since the hypothesis that all nonblack things are nonravens is equivalent to the hypothesis that all ravens are black, this means that observing a nonblack object that is not a raven, such as a white shoe, confirms the hypothesis that all ravens are black. The standard Bayesian solution to the paradox accepts that observing a white shoe does in fact confirm the hypothesis that all ravens are black, even if only to a small extent, but it goes on to argue that the hypothesis receives greater confirmation from observing a black raven.

Finally, Bayesian confirmation theory plays an important role not only in **philosophy of science** but in many modern discussions about evidence for God's existence. Rather than arguing that some feature of our universe, such as its order, proves God's existence, the theist can argue that it provides confirmation of God's existence by increasing its probability. This can then be used as part of a cumulative case. The clearest example of this approach is found in the work of Richard Swinburne (2004).

David H. Glass

REFERENCES AND RECOMMENDED READING

Crupi, Vincenzo. 2014. "Confirmation." In *Stanford Encyclopedia of Philosophy*, ed. Edward N. Zalta. Fall. http://plato.stanford.edu/archives/fall2014/entries/confirmation/.
Swinburne, Richard. 1973. *An Introduction to Confirmation Theory*. London: Methuen.
———. 2004. *The Existence of God*. 2nd ed. Oxford: Oxford University Press.

CONFLICT THESIS. The conflict thesis is the overarching view on the history of science that maintains an inescapable and inherent conflict between science and religion. The most influential exponents of the conflict thesis were **John William Draper** (1811–82) and **Andrew Dickson White** (1832–1918). Draper presented a paper at the British Association meeting of 1860 on the intellectual development of Europe with relation to Darwin's theory, just seven months after the publication of **Charles Darwin**'s *On the Origin of Species* (Darwin 1859). It was at this meeting that the famous confrontation between **Thomas Huxley** and Samuel Wilberforce took place.

In the early 1870s, Draper was asked by Edward Livingston Youmans, an American popularizer of science, to write a book titled *A History of the Conflict between Religion and Science* (Draper 1874). Draper's preface stated, "The history of Science is not a mere record of isolated discoveries; it is a narrative of the conflict of two contending powers, the expansive force of the human intellect on one side, and the compression arising from traditionary faith and human interests on the other."

White published his thesis in *Popular Science Monthly* (White 1874), and in his book *The Warfare of Science* (White 1876). White further published *A History of the Warfare of Science with Theology in Christendom* (White 1896), in which he criticized what he considered to be dogmatic and restrictive forms of Christianity. White's perspective drew criticism from James Joseph Walsh, who argued in *The Popes and Science: The History of the Papal Relations to Science during the Middle Ages and Down to Our Own Time* (Walsh 1908) that White's view was antihistorical. Walsh argued that "the story of the supposed opposition of the Church and the Popes and the ecclesiastical authorities to science in any of its branches, is founded entirely on mistaken notions" (1908, 19).

Today historians of science generally no longer favor a conflict model. Colin Russell, formerly the president of Christians in Science, criticized the conflict model, noting that "Draper takes such liberty with history, perpetuating legends as fact that he is rightly avoided today in serious historical study. The same is nearly as true of White, though his prominent apparatus of prolific footnotes may create a misleading impression of meticulous scholarship" (Russell 2000, 15).

One affair that is commonly used to support the conflict thesis is that of **Galileo Galilei** and his condemnation by the Roman Catholic Inquisition in 1633 for his support of the heliocentric system of **Nicolaus Copernicus**. It is commonly believed that Galileo was imprisoned for his work; in truth he was placed under house arrest, and the situation was rather more complex than it is often portrayed. Also, criticisms of the heliocentric system at the time included scientific as well as philosophical and theological objections.

A study conducted on scientists at 21 universities across America revealed that the majority did not see any conflict between science and religion (Ecklund and Park, 2009). In fact, there was a correlation between those who perceived such a conflict and a limited exposure to religion. Nonetheless, there are some prominent defenders of the conflict thesis, including University of Chicago biologist Jerry Coyne (Coyne 2015) and retired University of Oxford zoologist **Richard Dawkins** (Dawkins 2006).

Jonathan McLatchie

REFERENCES AND RECOMMENDED READING

Coyne, J. A. 2015. *Faith vs. Fact*. New York: Viking and London: Penguin.
Darwin, C. 1859. *On the Origin of Species*. London: John Murray.
Dawkins, R. 2006. *The God Delusion*. London: Transworld.
Draper, J. W. 1874. *A History of the Conflict between Religion and Science*. New York: Appleton.
Ecklund, E. H., and J. Z. Park. 2009. "Conflict between Religion and Science among Academic Scientists?" *Journal for the Scientific Study of Religion* 48:276–92.
Russell, C. A. 2000. "The Conflict of Science and Religion." In *Encyclopaedia of the History of Science and Religion*. New York: Routledge.
Walsh, J. J. 1908. *The Popes and Science: The History of the Papal Relations to Science during the Middle Ages and Down to Our Own Time*. New York: Fordham University Press.
White, A. D. 1874. "Scientific and Industrial Education in the United States." *Popular Science Monthly* 5:170–91.
———. 1876. *The Warfare of Science*. New York: Appleton.
———. 1896. *A History of the Warfare of Science with Theology in Christendom*. New York: Appleton.

CONSCIOUSNESS. Consciousness is an extraordinary and unique feature of the world, especially as found in human beings. It seems to be an essential characteristic of the nature of the self and is at the heart of personal identity, self-awareness, subjectivity, free will, and moral agency. It involves our ordinary subjective, perceptual, and rational experiences, including our thoughts, feelings, memories, imagination, and capacity to feel pain. Such experiences are often called **qualia** and would include the experience of seeing a sunset, of smelling a rose, of having confidence when taking an exam, of feeling a pain like a toothache, and perhaps of understanding a concept and of thinking about the game tonight.

Our experience of consciousness is also said to involve other unusual properties such as intentionality and introspection. Intentionality refers to the "aboutness" or "of-ness" of our mental states, the fact that our thinking is often "about" an object outside the mind—for example, in thinking about your car parked in the driveway. Introspection refers to our ability to look inside our own minds and to report (in an incorrigible way) on our conscious states, images, and feelings, to which we have privileged access. Consciousness is also intimately related to the experience of free will in which our decision-making involves many of the above features; moreover, our decisions, if they are to be truly free, are not fully subject to scientific explanations in terms of cause and effect.

Many philosophers, most famously **René Descartes**, argued that consciousness is so unique that it is best understood as a mental or spiritual substance that exists in its own right (see **Dualism**). Its essence is thinking, and, though related to the brain, it is a separate entity and has causal power over the brain—for example, when we act on our decisions. More recently, philosophers such as **Thomas Nagel** and Robert Adams have argued that there is a subjectivity involved in consciousness that cannot be explained in physical or scientific terms. This is because a scientific explanation would need to be an objective, third-person explanation, but such an account would necessarily exclude our personal experience of subjectivity, which involves a first-person point of view.

There is "something it is like to be us," according to Nagel, and it seems that in principle this experience of subjectivity cannot be captured in a scientific explanation. Adams has also criticized attempts to explain consciousness in terms

of brain activity by appealing to physical causes and effects involving matter and energy. He has argued that even if we could plausibly show that (1) an experience of A (e.g., of seeing red) was correlated with a brain state B, and even if (2) B causes A, this would still not be an explanation of the nature and content of A (the *experience* of seeing red). This essential feature would still be missing from the explanation. These arguments convey well the notoriously difficult problem that confronts attempts to explain consciousness and the mental in purely physical terms.

The unique nature of consciousness has been noted by Christian philosophers, with many regarding it as either the essence, or a significant part of the essence, of human nature. It has also been identified with the **soul** by some thinkers, while others have suggested that it may be part of the soul. Christian philosophers have often argued that the existence of consciousness constitutes a more general argument for the **existence of God** and of the supernatural realm. This is because, since consciousness is nonphysical, not only might it be the case that other nonphysical things could exist, such as God, but it would also follow that atheistic **naturalism** is false. The independent nature of consciousness also suggests that the survival of consciousness after **death** is a possibility, and this is a way to defend the notion of immortality. The survival of consciousness would also be a way of safeguarding our personal identity in the afterlife (see **Life after Death**). Another argument against naturalism is provided by the phenomenon of free will, a significant part of consciousness.

Materialists about the mind have presented a variety of positions as alternatives to nonmaterial existence of consciousness, including **eliminative materialism**, **reductionism**, and **functionalism**, among several others. In general, the materialist view proposes that consciousness depends for its existence in some way on the brain and is likely produced as a by-product of the brain during its initial development. There is disagreement over whether once consciousness arises it is physical or nonphysical, about whether it is reducible to, or can be fully explained in terms of, brain properties, and also about whether it can have causal power over the brain.

Many materialist arguments are motivated by atheistic naturalism. These arguments have run into difficult problems concerning free will and moral agency. This is because if one claims that consciousness is produced by the brain and can be fully explained in terms of the causes and effects of brain activity, this view would appear to leave no room for genuine free will, and so **morality**, punishment, and moral responsibility would be compromised. Some materialists have (reluctantly) embraced such conclusions, and others have developed counterintuitive compatibilist theories of free will and causal **determinism** as a way to try to address these difficulties.

The existence of consciousness also raises questions in relation to evolution. There are no good explanations for how consciousness emerged from the evolutionary process, a process that appeals to physical explanations in terms of cause and effect, but which, at least in its contemporary interpretations, is also supposed to be able to account for every feature of organisms (including consciousness). Consciousness must have emerged at some point in evolutionary history, but how would it have originated from a specific arrangement of matter and energy, especially with its unusual properties of self-awareness, subjectivity, reason, intentionality, and free will? More generally, how is it that beings evolved from a material process with a highly sophisticated form of consciousness that allows them to understand and think about the process that gave rise to them, and also to achieve a growing measure of control over it?

Many Christian thinkers have argued that a purely materialist explanation of evolution, which also holds that the process is unguided and is subject to a significant element of **chance**, is counterintuitive and that inventing stories to suggest how evolution may have given rise to unusual features of humanity (as in the work of **Richard Dawkins**, **Daniel Dennett**, and **Michael Ruse**) is far from convincing and that such unique developments as consciousness, morality, and free will suggest the guidance of a (divine) intelligence. Materialists often operate with an assumption that consciousness must be physical and hold that we will eventually discover how it works and originated by means of science. This is why the problem of qualia, and the problem of the subjective nature of consciousness, are difficult ones for **materialism** and interesting for the topic in general, because they suggest that in principle a scientific explanation for the nature of consciousness may not be possible. Moreover, Christian theists point to mental phenomena, including free will and moral agency, as part of the cumulative case for a theistic view of reality.

Brendan Sweetman

REFERENCES AND RECOMMENDED READING

Adams, Robert. 1992. "Flavors, Colors and God." In *Contemporary Perspectives on Religious Epistemology*, ed. R. Douglas Geivett and Brendan Sweetman, 225–40. New York: Oxford University Press.

Blackmore, Susan. 2010. *Consciousness: An Introduction*. London: Routledge.

Goetz, Stewart, and Charles Taliaferro. 2011. *A Brief History of the Soul*. Oxford: Wiley.

Lowe, E. J. 2000. *An Introduction to the Philosophy of Mind*. Cambridge: Cambridge University Press.

Nagel, Thomas. 2012. *Mortal Questions*. New York: Cambridge University Press.

CONSERVATION OF ENERGY. Conservation of energy is the principle in **physics** that the energy of an isolated system cannot change. It is conserved. An isolated system is a system that does not allow matter or energy to be transferred into or out of the system. The universe is considered to be a physically isolated system.

Energy within an isolated system can be transformed from one form to another. For instance, when a ball is dropped near the surface of the earth, gravitational potential energy is transformed to kinetic energy (energy of motion) as the ball falls and its speed increases. **Einstein**'s famous equation $E=mc^2$ (energy = mass times the **speed of light** squared) indicates that mass is one form of energy. Consequently, in an isolated system mass can change into other forms of energy like kinetic energy and vice versa.

It is nearly impossible to make a truly isolated system in any part of the universe. So for most defined systems the energy of the system may change as energy is transferred into or out of the system. This does not violate the principle that energy is always conserved in an isolated system.

Like all principles in physics, the principle of the conservation of energy has been developed by careful observation and experimentation. There has never been any observed violation of this principle. A few key events paved the way for the development of this idea. In 1798 Benjamin Thompson (Count Rumford) noticed that metal being bored to make cannons seemed to continually heat up by friction without any limit. This observation contradicted the prevailing "caloric theory" that proposed heat was a substance that flowed from hotter objects to colder objects.

Thompson's observations fit better with the idea that heat was a transfer of energy due to a difference in temperature. In the mid-nineteenth century, James Joule did a number of experiments that showed that the potential energy of a falling weight could be transferred into water by a paddle inserted into the water and connected to the falling weight by a string. Thus he showed that the higher temperature of the water was due to an increase in the internal energy of the water that was identical to the decrease in the potential energy of the falling weight. Energy could be transformed from one form to another but was not created or destroyed.

The principle of conservation of energy is important

when discussing the origin of this universe. Some scientists believe that the total energy of our universe is exactly zero with the kinetic energy and mass energy of all objects (which is a positive value) exactly balanced by the potential gravitational energy of all objects (which can be a negative value). This leads to the proposed idea that our universe could spontaneously come from nothing without violating the principle of the conservation of energy.

Theologians have discussed the relationship between **miracles** and the laws of physics, like the conservation of energy. The most common postulate is that God supersedes the laws of physics in order to perform a miracle. Some theologians believe that God works within the **laws of nature** to perform miracles or that our understanding of the laws of physics are simply incomplete and insufficient to understand the mechanism God uses to perform miracles.

Michael G. Strauss

REFERENCES AND RECOMMENDED READING

Giancoli, Douglas. 2014. *Physics: Principles with Applications.* 7th ed. Cambridge, UK: Pearson.

Larmer, Robert. 1996. *Water into Wine? An Investigation of the Concept of Miracle.* Montreal: McGill-Queen's University Press.

CONWAY MORRIS, SIMON. Simon Conway Morris (1951–) is a Christian (Anglican) invertebrate paleontologist and professor of paleobiology at Cambridge University. Educated at Bristol University (BS, geology, 1972) and Cambridge University (PhD, 1976), Conway Morris first came to prominence through his interpretations of the fossils of the Burgess Shale, a Middle Cambrian formation in British Columbia characterized by the exquisite preservation of a wide variety of invertebrate phyla.

Under the mentorship of his Cambridge PhD adviser Harry Whittington (1916–2010), Conway Morris reanalyzed Cambrian fossils originally discovered by Smithsonian paleontologist Charles Walcott (1850–1927), leading to a series of technical papers in the late 1970s and 1980s on such genera as *Nectocaris* and *Wiwaxia*, work described for a general audience in Conway Morris's first book *Crucible of Creation* (1998) and recounted in the late paleontologist Stephen Gould's popular science book *Wonderful Life* (1989). Notably, in 1977 Conway Morris named and described the extinct genus *Hallucigenia*, whose oddities much impressed Gould, although it was later determined that Conway Morris had reconstructed the taxon upside down.

Elected a Fellow of the Royal Society in 1990 and appointed professor of paleobiology at Cambridge University in 1991, Conway Morris soon began to take issue with Gould's "historical contingency" view of evolution (a view Gould had supported in part by citing Conway Morris's fossil interpretations) under which evolutionary outcomes on earth derive fundamentally from unique and unrepeatable—"contingent"—circumstances. The "tape" of evolution, if replayed, would not produce *Homo sapiens* or any other **species**.

Conway Morris countered this reading of evolution by arguing that the ubiquity throughout all terrestrial life of *convergence*—namely, the appearances in multiple independently arising lineages of the "same" solution (whether molecular or anatomical)—pointed to an inherent directionality in the evolutionary process. His second and third books, *Life's Solution: Inevitable Humans in a Lonely Universe* (2003) and *The Runes of Evolution: How the Universe Became Self-Aware* (2015), present Conway Morris's case for evolutionary mechanisms from which the appearance of sentient, moral beings is "a near-inevitability," wherein later developments draw on potentialities prepared at earlier stages, a concept Conway Morris dubs "evolutionary inherency." An evolutionary process thus channeled, he argues, while neither proving nor presupposing God's existence, is fully "congruent" with **theism** and creation.

Conway Morris maintains a website dedicated to explicating convergence and its implications (https://mapoflifeblog. wordpress.com/about/), funded by the **John Templeton Foundation**, with whom he has been an active collaborator, grant recipient, and program referee. Although strongly persuaded of the truth of Darwinian evolution, both in terms of the cogency of its primary causal process, **natural selection**, and the overall branching tree of life described by Darwin, Conway Morris is outspokenly critical of the **materialism** and **reductionism** espoused by leading evolutionary biologists.

Paul Nelson

REFERENCES AND RECOMMENDED READING

Conway Morris, S. 1977. "A New Metazoan from the Burgess Shale of British Columbia." *Palaeontology* 20: 623–40.

———. 1998. *Crucible of Creation: The Burgess Shale and the Rise of Animals.* New York: Oxford University Press.

———. 2003. *Life's Solution: Inevitable Humans in a Lonely Universe.* New York: Cambridge University Press.

———. 2006. "Darwin's Dilemma: The Realities of the Cambrian 'Explosion.'" *Philosophical Transactions of the Royal Society, B* 361:1069–83. www.ncbi .nlm.nih.gov/pmc/articles/PMC1578734/.

———. 2007. *Darwin's Compass: How Evolution Discovers the Song of Creation.* Gifford Lectures. Edinburgh: University of Edinburgh. www.ed.ac.uk/arts-humanities-soc-sci/news-events/lectures/gifford-lectures/archive/archive–2006–2007/prof-conway (six lectures recorded as mp3 files).

———. 2012. "Creation and Evolutionary Convergence." In *The Blackwell Companion to Science and Christianity*, ed. J. B. Stump and A. G. Padgett, 258–69. Oxford: Wiley.

———. 2015. *The Runes of Evolution: How the Universe Became Self-Aware.* West Conshohocken, PA: Templeton Press.

CO-OPTION. Co-option, also called co-optation or exaptation, is a model of evolution in which the function of a trait shifts during its evolution. This model stands in contrast to adaptation, where a trait's function remains constant while being refined by **natural selection**. Under co-option, a biological component is borrowed or "co-opted" from one system to perform a new function in another.

One famous co-option hypothesis is that bird feathers and wings initially evolved to provide insulation or trap insects and were later co-opted for flight (Ostrom 1974, 1979; Gould 1980). Another noteworthy example is the giant panda's radial sesamoid bone, which is said to have been co-opted into a "thumb," used for stripping bamboo leaves (Gould 1978).

At the biochemical level, co-option is often cited as a mechanism for recruiting new genes or evolving irreducibly complex systems. One paper proposes that the bacterial flagellum arose through co-option, or "mergers between several modular subsystems," which initially performed other nonflagellar functions (Pallen and Matzke 2006). Another paper argues that thrombin—crucial to the blood clotting cascade—has multiple functions and might have originally arisen for a different purpose before being co-opted into the cascade (Forrest and Gross 2007).

The raw data backing co-option explanations typically entails homology, or sequence similarity, between different proteins. Little detail is provided, other than to assert that homologous parts were co-opted, retooled, and redeployed to form a new system. As two evolutionary biologists note, "Little is known about the mechanisms by which co-option of **gene** function takes place," but it is supported by "broad distribution of conserved proteins and motifs across the tree of life" (True and Carroll 2002).

Critics of co-option proffer multiple reasons why it cannot explain irreducible **complexity**. First, many parts are unique and unavailable to be borrowed from other systems (e.g., orphan genes) (Meyer 2013). Second, even if homologous proteins exist for all components of an irreducibly complex system, at most this suggests **common ancestry**; mere sequence similarity does not constitute a stepwise evolutionary explanation (Behe 1996). Third, machine parts are not necessarily easily interchangeable, or "modular." Grocery carts and motorcycles both have wheels, but one could not be borrowed from the other without significant modification. In biology, where many changes may be necessary to convert a protein to a new function, this problem can be severe (Gauger and Axe 2011). Fourth, even if all necessary parts were available to be borrowed and were compatible, co-option does not explain the assembly instructions needed to construct the system. Fifth, co-option relies on sheer luck, where the starting system just happens to be "preadapted" to the final system's function, making the explanations sound teleological.

Angus Menuge argues that any co-option account must explain the following:

1. Availability of parts (e.g., homology).
2. Synchronization, where parts are available at the same time.
3. Localization, where parts are available at the same location.
4. Coordination, where part production is coordinated for assembly.
5. Interface compatibility, where parts are "mutually compatible, that is, 'well-matched' and capable of properly 'interacting.'" (Menuge 2004)

Critics claim co-option accounts virtually never explain anything beyond element (1). They seek examples where co-option observably produced new systems via unguided material mechanisms. **William Dembski** notes that none are known: "What is the one thing in our experience that co-opts irreducibly complex machines and uses their parts to build a new and more intricate machine? Intelligent agents" (Dembski and Witt 2010).

Casey Luskin

REFERENCES AND RECOMMENDED READING

Behe, Michael J. 1996. *Darwin's Black Box: The Biochemical Challenge to Evolution.* New York: Free Press.

Dembski, William A., and Jonathan Witt. 2010. *Intelligent Design Uncensored.* Downers Grove, IL: InterVarsity.

Forrest, Barbara C., and Paul R. Gross. 2007. "Biochemistry by Design." *Trends in Biochemical Sciences* 32:301–10.

Gauger, Ann, and Douglas Axe. 2011. "The Evolutionary Accessibility of New Enzyme Functions: A Case Study from the Biotin Pathway." *BIO-Complexity* 2011 (1): 1–17.

Gould, Stephen Jay. 1978. "The Panda's Peculiar Thumb." *Natural History* 87:20.

———. 1980. "Is a New and General Theory of Evolution Emerging?" *Paleobiology* 6:119–30.

Menuge, Angus. 2004. *Agents under Fire: Materialism and the Rationality of Science.* Oxford: Rowman & Littlefield.

Meyer, Stephen. 2013. *Darwin's Doubt: The Explosive Origin of Animal Life and the Case for Intelligent Design.* New York: HarperOne.

Ostrom, John. 1974. "*Archaeopteryx* and the Origin of Flight." *Quarterly Review of Biology* 49:27–47.

———. 1979. "Bird Flight: How Did It Begin?" *American Scientist* 67:45–56.

Pallen, Mark J., and Nicholas J. Matzke. 2006. "From the Origin of Species to the Origin of Bacterial Flagella." *Nature Reviews Microbiology* 4:784–90.

True, John R., and Sean B. Carroll. 2002. "Gene Co-option in Physiological and Morphological Evolution." *Annual Review of Cell and Developmental Biology* 18:53–80.

COPERNICAN PRINCIPLE. The Copernican principle, more often called the cosmological principle (Chaisson and McMillan 2014, 669), is an empirical discovery that there are no special places in the cosmos and no special directions of observation at the largest distance scales. The kinds of matter and energy and their density are the same everywhere in the universe when we average over large enough distance scales. Moreover, every direction we turn our telescopes we observe that the universe looks the same over large enough distance scales.

This "no special place" idea is usually motivated by the myth that **Copernicus** removed humanity from its "special place" at the center of the solar system, an idea Copernicus and no one else in his time ever endorsed (Danielson 2009). It has been developed as a principle for the universe in the following way. Astronomers discovered in the nineteenth century that the sun was a fairly average star. In the twentieth century, they discovered that the Milky Way galaxy contains about 200 billion stars. Furthermore, our solar system is located on the edge of the Milky Way and our galaxy is just one among 100 billion or more galaxies. Everywhere we look, there are stars and galaxies, hydrogen, helium and other gasses, the same **laws of nature**, and so forth.

As a strictly scientific principle, the Copernican principle is an expression of our best understanding of the uniformity of nature. However, it has also been developed into a metaphysical/value principle: humans do not live in a special place, so there is nothing particularly special about human beings (Gingerich 2006). This is often called the principle of mediocrity (Freedman 1996).

The mediocrity principle contributes nothing to our understanding of **astronomy** or cosmology because it is an ideologically driven interpretation of astronomy. Moreover, this unwarranted extension of the Copernican principle does not hold up under inspection. For example, we have discovered that our solar system occupies a life-affirming patch of the Milky Way, one of the "special places" where the right conditions exist for life to originate and be sustained.

Finally, as with the myth that Copernicus "demoted" the place of human beings in the universe, the mediocrity principle suffers from an ambiguity on the idea of "special place." On the one hand, a place could be special in terms of location (e.g., a Park Avenue address). On the other hand, we often speak of humanity's special place in God's plans and purposes. There is nothing particularly special about spatial location that has any connection with what special role humanity may play in God's plans and purposes. The mediocrity principle confuses a physical feature with a meaning feature of reality to draw a false conclusion about humanity.

Robert C. Bishop

REFERENCES AND RECOMMENDED READING

Chaisson, Eric, and Steve McMillan. 2014. *Astronomy Today.* San Francisco: Pearson Education.

Danielson, Dennis R. 2009. "Myth 6. That Copernicus Demoted Humans from the Center of the Cosmos." In *Galileo Goes to Jail and Other Myths about Science and Religion,* ed. Ronald L. Numbers, 50–58. Cambridge, MA: Harvard University Press.

Freedman, David H. 1996. "The Mediocre Universe." *Discover Magazine* (February 1). http://discovermagazine.com/1996/feb/themediocreunive694/.

Gingerich, Owen. 2006. *God's Universe.* Cambridge, MA: Belknap.

COPERNICUS, NICOLAUS. Nicolaus Copernicus (1473–1543) was a Polish clergyman and astronomer who was the first in modern times to argue that the earth was not the center of the universe but instead orbited the sun. His book *Revolutions of the Heavenly Spheres* (1543) presented a comprehensive mathematical model of the solar system. Although he knew his ideas were controversial, he suffered from no religious pressure to suppress them.

Copernicus was born Nikolaj Kopernik and brought up by his uncle, the bishop of Ermeland in Poland. He initially studied at the University of Cracow but, in 1496, traveled to Italy to spend time at the universities of Bologna and Padua before receiving a degree in canon law at Ferrara. On his return to Poland, Copernicus's uncle appointed him as a canon of Frombork Cathedral, which provided him with a good income for the rest of his life. His duties as a canon were sufficiently undemanding, which gave him plenty of time to devote to his passion for **astronomy**.

Copernicus began to circulate his theory that the earth

orbits the sun to a small number of correspondents in 1507. He continued to work on his ideas, eventually offering a complete model of the solar system to rival **Claudius Ptolemy**'s system of an earth-centered cosmos. It is likely that Copernicus indirectly drew some of his geometrical theorems from medieval and Muslim mathematicians, although he makes no mention of them in his work.

In 1543 Copernicus finally allowed his theory to be published. The resulting book, *Revolutions of the Heavenly Spheres*, was presented to him shortly before he died. Copernicus believed that his theory represents physical reality and that the earth really is moving through space around the sun at high speed. However, Andreas Osiander, a friend of Copernicus who saw the book through the press, added an unsigned preface stating that the theory was only meant to be a hypothesis rather than a fact. Most readers assumed that Copernicus himself had written the preface, leading to widespread misunderstanding of his own views.

Copernicus was fully aware that his ideas were intellectually controversial and insisted that he be judged only by those able to understand the dense mathematical synthesis that he had put forward. His book was discussed by astronomers, but very few people thought that he was right to posit that the earth orbited the sun. Nonetheless, his mathematical achievement was widely recognized. He had no fear of ecclesiastical censure: a cardinal was among those who urged him to publish, and his book was dedicated to Pope Paul III. It was not until 1616 that the Roman Catholic Church formally condemned heliocentricism, and even then it only required that some trivial corrections were made to Copernicus's book, rather than banning it altogether. In the meantime, the church was happy to use Copernicus's cutting-edge **mathematics** for its own reform of the calendar, completed in 1582.

Once the heliocentric system became widely accepted from the mid-seventeenth century, Copernicus was celebrated as a scientific pioneer as well as a gifted mathematician. Today the publication of *Revolutions of the Heavenly Spheres* in 1543 is often cited as the beginning of modern **science**.

James Hannam

REFERENCES AND RECOMMENDED READING

Copernicus, Nicolaus. 1995. *On the Revolutions of the Heavenly Spheres*. Amherst, NY: Prometheus.
Henry, John. 2001. *Moving Heaven and Earth: Copernicus and the Solar System*. Cambridge, UK: Icon.
Saliba, George. 2007. *Islamic Science and the Making of the European Renaissance*. Cambridge, MA: MIT Press.
Westman, Robert. 1986. "The Copernicans and the Churches." In *God and Nature: Historical Essays on the Encounter between Christianity and Science*, ed. David Lindberg and Ronald Numbers, 76–113. Berkeley: University of California Press.
———. 1990. "Proof, Poetics and Patronage: Copernicus's Preface to *De Revolutionibus*." In *Reappraisals of the Scientific Revolution*, ed. David Lindberg and Robert Westman, 167–205. Cambridge: Cambridge University Press.

COSMOLOGICAL ARGUMENT. The cosmological argument is a piece of **natural theology** that seeks to demonstrate a Sufficient Reason or First Cause of the existence of the cosmos. Its proponents include many of the most prominent figures in the history of Western philosophy: **Plato**, **Aristotle**, Ibn Sina, al-Ghazali, Maimonides, Anselm, Aquinas, Scotus, **Descartes**, Spinoza, Leibniz, and Locke, to name but some.

Exposition

We can distinguish three basic types of cosmological argument: the Kalam cosmological argument for a First Cause of the beginning of the universe, the Thomist cosmological argument for a sustaining Ground of Being of the world, and the Leibnizian cosmological argument for a Sufficient Reason why anything at all exists.

The Kalam cosmological argument derives its name from the Arabic word designating medieval Islamic scholasticism, which helped to advance this version of the cosmological argument. The argument aims to show that the universe had a beginning at some moment in the finite past. Although medieval proponents of the argument pressed philosophical arguments against the infinitude of the past, the stunning discoveries of astrophysical cosmology related to the origin of the universe in a **big bang** some 14 billion years ago have especially reignited contemporary interest in the argument. If the universe began to exist, then, since something cannot come out of nothing, the universe must have a transcendent cause, which brought it into being.

The Thomist cosmological argument, named for the medieval philosophical theologian Thomas Aquinas, seeks a cause that is first, not in the temporal sense, but in the sense of rank. On Aquinas's Aristotelian-inspired metaphysic, every existing finite thing is composed of essence and existence and is therefore radically contingent. If an essence is to be instantiated, there must be conjoined with that essence an act of being. The instantiation of an essence involves a continual bestowal of being by an external cause, or the thing would be annihilated. Although Aquinas argued that there cannot be an infinite regress of causes of being and that therefore there must exist a First Uncaused Cause of being, his actual view was that there can be no intermediate causes of being at all, that any finite substance is sustained in existence immediately by the Ground of Being. This must be a being who is not composed of essence and existence and hence requires no sustaining cause. It is, as Thomas says, *ipsum esse subsistens*, the act of being itself subsisting. Thomas identifies this being with the God whose name was revealed to Moses as "I AM" (Ex. 3:14).

The Leibnizian cosmological argument is named for the seventeenth-century German polymath **Gottfried Wilhelm Leibniz**, who sought to develop a version of the cosmological argument from contingency without the Aristotelian metaphysical underpinnings of the Thomist argument. "The first question which should rightly be asked," he wrote, "is this: why is there something rather than nothing?" ("The Principles of Nature and of Grace, Based on Reason"). Leibniz meant this question to be truly universal, not to apply merely to finite things.

On the basis of his **principle of sufficient reason** (PSR) that "no fact can be real or existent, no statement true, unless there be a sufficient reason why it is so and not otherwise" ("The Monadology"), Leibniz held that this question must have an answer. It will not do to say that the universe (or even God) just exists as a brute fact. There must be an explanation for why it exists. He went on to argue that the Sufficient Reason cannot be found in any individual thing in the universe, nor in the collection of such things which is the universe, nor in earlier states of the universe, even if these regress infinitely. Therefore, there must exist an ultramundane being that is metaphysically necessary in its existence, that is to say, its nonexistence is impossible. It is the Sufficient Reason for its own existence as well as for the existence of every contingent thing.

Discussion

Undoubtedly, the most controversial premise in the Leibnizian cosmological argument is the PSR. Not every fact can have an explanation, it has been said, for there cannot be an explanation of what we might call the big contingent conjunctive fact (BCCF), which is itself the conjunction of all the contingent facts there are; for if such an explanation is contingent, then it, too, must have a further explanation; whereas if it is necessary, then the fact explained by it must also be necessary.

Some Leibnizians have either challenged the assumption that there is a BCCF or sought to provide an acceptable explanation of it. This debate, though fascinating, is somewhat academic, since the argument does not depend on anything as strong as Leibniz's own version of the PSR. The proponent of the Leibnizian cosmological argument could hold, for example, that for any contingently existing thing, there is an explanation why that thing exists. Or again, he could assert that everything that exists has an explanation of its existence, either in the necessity of its own nature or in an external cause. Or, more broadly, he might maintain that in the case of any contingent state of affairs, there is either an explanation why that state of affairs obtains or else an explanation of why no explanation is needed. All of these are more modest, nonparadoxical, and seemingly plausible versions of the PSR.

The nontheist may retort that while the universe has an explanation of its existence, that explanation lies not in an external ground but in the necessity of its own nature. That the universe is a metaphysically necessary being is an extremely bold suggestion. We have, one can safely say, a strong **intuition** of the universe's contingency. We generally trust our modal intuitions on other matters with which we are familiar; if we are to do otherwise with respect to the universe's contingency, then the nontheist needs to provide some reason for such skepticism other than his desire to avoid **theism**.

Still, having some stronger argument for the universe's contingency than our modal intuitions alone would be desirable. Could the Thomist cosmological argument help us here? If successful, it would show that the universe is a contingent being causally dependent on a necessary being for its continued existence. The difficulty with the Thomist argument, however, is that it is very difficult to show that things are, in fact, contingent in the special sense required by the argument. Certainly things are naturally contingent in that their continued existence is dependent on a myriad of physical factors, but this natural contingency does not suffice to establish things' metaphysical contingency in the sense that being must continually be added to their essences lest they be spontaneously annihilated. Indeed, if Thomas's argument does ultimately lead to an absolutely simple being whose essence is existence, then one might well be led to deny that beings are metaphysically composed of essence and existence if, as most Christian philosophers think, the idea of such an absolutely simple being proves to be unintelligible.

The aim of the Kalam cosmological argument is to show that the universe is not sempiternal (everlasting) but had a beginning. It would follow that the universe must therefore be contingent in its existence. Not only so, but the Kalam argument shows the universe to be contingent in a very special way: it came into existence without a cause. The nontheist who would answer Leibniz by holding that the existence of the universe is a brute fact, an exception to the PSR, is thus thrust into the awkward position of maintaining not simply that the universe exists eternally without explanation, but rather that for no reason at all it magically popped into being out of nothing, a position that might make theism look like a welcome alternative.

Space does not permit here a review of the arguments and evidence for the finitude of the past. Suffice it to be said that the idea of an infinite past remains deeply perplexing philosophically and the evidence of astrophysical cosmology continues to accumulate in support of the universe's beginning at some time in the finite past.

William Lane Craig

REFERENCES AND RECOMMENDED READING

Beck, W. David. 2000. "The Cosmological Argument: A Current Bibliographical Appraisal." *Philosophia Christi* 2:283–304.
Burrill, Donald R. 1967. *The Cosmological Arguments.* Garden City, NY: Doubleday.
Craig, William Lane. 1979. *The* Kalam *Cosmological Argument.* London: Macmillan. Repr., Eugene, OR: Wipf and Stock, 2000.
———. 1980. *The Cosmological Argument from Plato to Leibniz.* New York: Barnes & Noble.
Craig, William Lane, and James Sinclair. 2009. "The *Kalam* Cosmological Argument." In *The Blackwell Companion to Natural Theology,* ed. William Lane Craig and J. P. Moreland, 101–201. Oxford: Wiley-Blackwell.
Davis, Stephen T. 1997. *God, Reason, and Theistic Proofs.* Grand Rapids: Eerdmans.
Gale, Richard M. 1991. *On the Existence and Nature of God.* New York: Cambridge University Press.
Harrison, Jonathan. 1999. *God, Freedom, and Immortality.* Avebury Series in Philosophy. Burlington, VT: Ashgate.
Hick, John. 1971. *Arguments for the Existence of God.* London: Macmillan.
Leibniz, Gottfried Wilhelm. 1951. *Leibniz Selections,* ed. P. Wiener. New York: Scribner's.
———. 1989. *Philosophical Essays,* trans. R. Ariew and D. Garber (Hackett Classics). Indianapolis: Hackett Publishing Company.
Mackie, John L. 1982. *The Miracle of Theism.* Oxford: Clarendon.
Martin, Michael. 1990. *Atheism: A Philosophical Justification.* Philadelphia: Temple University Press.
Pruss, Alexander. 2005. *Ex Nihilo Nihil Fit: A Study of the Principle of Sufficient Reason.* Cambridge: Cambridge University Press.
———. 2009. "The Leibnizian Cosmological Argument." In *The Blackwell Companion to Natural Theology,* ed. William Lane Craig and J. P. Moreland, 24–100. Oxford: Wiley-Blackwell.
Rowe, William L. 1975. *The Cosmological Argument.* Princeton, NJ: Princeton University Press.
———. 1997. "Circular Explanations, Cosmological Arguments, and Sufficient Reasons." *Midwest Studies in Philosophy* 21:188–99.
Sobel, Jordan Howard. 2004. *Logic and Theism: Arguments for and against Beliefs in God.* Cambridge: Cambridge University Press.
Swinburne, Richard. 1991. *The Existence of God.* Rev. ed. Oxford: Clarendon.
Vallicella, William. 1997. "On an Insufficient Argument against Sufficient Reason." *Ratio* 10:76–81.
Wright, Crispin, and Bob Hale. 1992. "Nominalism and the Contingency of Abstract Objects." *Journal of Philosophy* 89:111–35.

COSMOLOGICAL CONSTANTS.

(For a description of what is most often referred to as *the* Cosmological Constant, see **Dark Matter and Dark Energy**.)

Cosmological constants are measurable parameters of the universe that are fixed (or nearly so) over the **space and time** of the universe.

In Jeremiah 33:19–26, God compares his immutable promises to his people to the fixity of the laws that govern heaven and earth. The comparison focuses on observed physical constancy, the laws that pervasively govern the operation of the physical world. Many of these laws are described by the fundamental cosmological constants of **physics**.

Observed examples of fixed patterns in nature in Jeremiah's context would have included the constancy of gravity's effect, the movements of the sun, moon, and stars, seasonal patterns, and more. Examples today include Planck's constant, the velocity of light, the charge of the electron, the mass of the proton, and certain ratios like the fine-structure constant, the ratio of the proton mass to the electron mass, and the ratio of the electromagnetic force to the gravitational force. The constancy of these laws permits scientific investigation and advance. It also makes possible life's survival.

Laboratory tests repeated over many years show certain cosmological constants to vary fewer than 4 parts in 100 quadrillion per year (Rosenband et al. 2008). Astronomical tests—for example, observations of the operations of atoms barcoded in the spectra of light arriving from galaxies billions of light-years away—reveal that the physical constants of the universe have varied no more than 2 parts in 10 quadrillion per year over the past 10 billion years (Thong et al. 2010). The first data released from the Planck satellite observations, which studied the radiation left over from the **big bang** creation event (the cosmic background radiation), indicate that the fine-structure constant varies in no measurable way over the entire spatial extent of the universe (O'Bryan et al. 2013).

Not only is this physical constancy an essential for life, but also, according to ongoing research, these physical constants appear to have been fine-tuned to make life possible. The slightest change in the value of any of these constants would disturb the stability of life-essential chemistry, thermodynamics, and more (see **Anthropic Principle**). Physicists have determined that if the ratio of the electromagnetic and gravitational force constants were altered by as little as 1 part in 10,000 trillion trillion trillion, stars would either never form at all, or they would form and then instantly explode. Either way, physical life would not exist.

From a historical perspective, confidence in the constancy of physical laws provided essential foundational support for scientific advance. The temporal and spatial constancy of the laws governing the physical universe suggested that scientific research could discover truth about the natural realm—and that these truths, or facts, could be counted on to apply consistently and universally. It seems no wonder, then, that **scientific revolution** grew out of Western Europe where God was understood to be the creator of a rational universe that obeyed consistent and comprehensible laws.

Hugh Ross

REFERENCES AND RECOMMENDED READING

O'Bryan, Jon, et al. June 2013. eprint arXiv:1306.1232.
Rosenband, Till, et al. 2008. "Frequency Ratio of Al+ and Hg+ Single-Ion Optical Clocks; Metrology at the 17th Decimal Place." *Science* 319 (March 28): 1808–12.
Thong, Le Duc, et al. 2010. "Constraining the Cosmological Time Variation of the Fine-Structure Constant." *Astrophysics* 53 (July): 446–52.

COSMOLOGICAL SINGULARITY, THE. Current astronomical evidence consistently shows that the universe has been undergoing a continual expansion of space since its beginning about 13.8 billion years ago. This evidence is primarily based on the redshift of the spectral lines of light coming from distant galaxies, revealing the property now known as Hubble's law, which states that the further away a galaxy is the faster it is receding from us. The expansion of space is consistent with and even predicted by **Einstein**'s **general theory of relativity**. Tracing the expansion of space backward in time leads to an initial state of the universe in which all matter and energy existed in an extremely dense, hot, and small volume.

Hard as it may be to imagine, the laws of **physics** tell us that the initial size of our entire visible universe was in the beginning smaller than a single atom! The moment of the beginning of the universe, when it began to rapidly expand in size and cool from its initial incandescent temperature has become known as the big bang (see **Big Bang Theory**). Suggestive of a random explosion, the term is a misnomer, and the event is better characterized as a highly orchestrated

expansion. The forces and constants of nature fixed in the beginning are such that the matter and energy unfolding over eons of time crafted a universe of galaxies, stars, and planets capable of sustaining life on planet Earth.

In discussing the beginning of the universe, the evidence is clear that all stars and galaxies, and even space itself, had a beginning in the finite past. A subtler question is whether time came into being at the same moment as the physical universe, since time and space are interdependent on each other. Einstein's general theory of relativity not only predicts the expansion of the universe (leaving off a "fudge factor" that Einstein initially included when he published the theory in 1919 to satisfy the mistaken views of the academic community of his day), but it concomitantly predicts the beginning of time at the moment of the big bang.

The beginning of **space and time**, or "space-time," when the universe was almost infinitely small, hot, and dense has become known as the cosmological *singularity*. The significance of this is the implication that **the singularity** represents "an absolute origin *ex nihilo*" (Craig 2011), consistent with the biblical statement, "By faith we understand that the universe was formed at God's command, so that what is seen was not made out of what was visible" (Heb. 11:3).

Space-time singularity theorems proved by Penrose, Hawking, Ellis, and others in the 1960s and '70s demonstrated that "the occurrence of singularities in cosmological models is the rule rather than an exception" (Heller 2009). And yet more recent and speculative theories have attempted to circumvent a true singularity at the origin of the universe, thus negating a beginning of time (Hawking 1988; Hawking and Mlodinow 2010). Hawking's theorems have been criticized by other cosmologists, stating that "Hawking has failed to show that the universe did not have a beginning" (Holder 2013, Gordon 2011). A cosmological theorem proved by Borde, Guth, and Vilenkin in 2003 (Borde et al. 2003) showed that space *and* time must have a beginning under conditions of rapid inflation of the early universe (see **Borde-Guth-Vilenkin Singularity Theorem**). Even if future variations of general relativity to include quantum gravity possibly modify these conclusions, it is safe to say that the universe as we know it had a beginning out of nothing that currently exists.

Eric R. Hedin

REFERENCES AND RECOMMENDED READING

Borde, Arvind, Alan H. Guth, and Alexander Vilenkin. 2003. "Inflationary Spacetimes Are Incomplete in Past Directions." *Physical Review Letters* 90:151301.

Craig, William Lane. 2011. "Naturalism and the Origin of the Universe." In *The Nature of Nature: Examining the Role of Naturalism in Science*, ed. Bruce L. Gordon and William A. Dembski, 506–34. Wilmington, DE: ISI Books.

Ellis, George F. R., and Stephen W. Hawking. 1975. *The Large-Scale Structure of Space-Time.* Cambridge: Cambridge University Press.

Gordon, Bruce L. 2011. "Balloons on a String: A Critique of Multiverse Cosmology." In *The Nature of Nature: Examining the Role of Naturalism in Science*, ed. Bruce L. Gordon and William A. Dembski, 558–93, Wilmington, DE: ISI Books.

Guth, Alan H. 1997. *The Inflationary Universe: The Quest for a New Theory of Cosmic Origins.* London: Jonathan Cape.

Hawking, Stephen. 1988. *A Brief History of Time.* London: Bantam.

Hawking, S. W., and G. F. R. Ellis. 1968. "The Cosmic Black-Body Radiation and the Existence of Singularities in Our Universe." *Astrophysical Journal* 152:25–36.

Hawking, Stephen, and Leonard Mlodinow. 2010. *The Grand Design: New Answers to the Ultimate Questions of Life.* London: Bantam.

Heller, Michael. 2009. *Ultimate Explanations of the Universe.* Berlin: Springer-Verlag.

Holder, Rodney. 2013. *Big Bang, Big God: A Universe Designed for Life?* Oxford: Lion Hudson.

Liddle, Andrew. 2015. *An Introduction to Modern Cosmology.* 3rd ed. Chichester, UK: Wiley.

COSMOLOGY, ANCIENT. Literature from the ancient Near East (ANE) features numerous texts that can be classified as cosmology texts, but many more texts of various genres provide **information** for understanding the cosmological perspectives of the ancient world. Lines in hymns, myths, wisdom literature, incantations, divination texts, and temple building accounts all contribute to a larger picture, just as Old Testament cosmology is found not only in Genesis but also in Psalms, Job, and the prophets. The charts in this article survey the most important ANE texts.

Ontology

Creation pertains to the transition from nonexistence to existence at any number of different levels. *Ontology* is the philosophical term that pertains to what it means for something to exist. *Cosmology* pertains to the study of the cosmos, particularly with regard to its origins and its nature. *Cosmic ontology* therefore asks what characterizes the existence of the cosmos. The cosmology texts of any culture express how that culture understands existence and the events that brought the cosmos into existence.

In modern Western culture, cosmic ontology customarily focuses on the origins of the material universe. We struggle to imagine any different way of thinking. Nevertheless, substantial information from the texts of the ANE indicates that their cosmic ontology focused on order rather than material. In such an ontology, something did not truly exist until it

had a role and a purpose in an ordered system. "Creation," then, involved activities that brought order (such as separating and naming, observable both in Genesis and in the ANE), rather than an act or process that merely produced something material. Israelite thinking and biblical texts reflect this ontology. Consequently, an ancient account of cosmic origins would naturally relate the origins of order rather than the origins of the material cosmos.

Nonexistence

Once we understand this characteristic of their cultural way of thinking, we can begin to read the texts in a new light, now comprehending how the ancient audience would have understood them. In both Egyptian and Babylonian texts, something that is nameless does not exist. Egyptian texts label the desert and its exotic animals as nonexistent (Allen 1988, 57; Assmann 2002, 206; Hornung 1982, 173–83). In Babylon the most famous cosmology, ***Enuma Elish***, begins when nothing is yet named, including the gods. In Israel's cosmology, the nonordered state is described by the Hebrew words *tohu wabohu* in Genesis 1:2. When the usage of these words in the Hebrew text is examined, we find that they do not pertain to the shapelessness of material objects but to the absence of order, role, or function (Walton 2009, 46–52). Thus the Genesis 1 cosmology begins with no order and then recounts the establishment of order.

Causation/Purpose

Throughout the ancient world, the gods were viewed as agents of causation in cosmic origins. The ancients had no category of "natural" laws or causes and drew no distinctions between levels of causation as we are inclined to do. They would not distinguish between the activity of the gods and levels of origins that could be explained "naturally." In Hebrew, a word such as *'asa* (often translated "do" or "make") simply indicates a role in causation without clarifying whether that role was direct or indirect.

Since the gods are always involved as causative agents, creation is carried out with purpose. In Genesis the purpose of God can be easily inferred, but it is not always so clear in the rest of the ancient world, largely because the gods there were not in the habit of communicating their purposes. One distinction, however, is that the gods of the ANE tended to focus their activities on themselves and their needs rather than on people. Despite that distinction, cosmology in the ancient world is driven by the gods' purposes, even when their purposes are unknown.

Ancient Cosmology

CHART 1: Summary of Features Appearing in Ancient Cosmological Accounts

Primary Sources	Pre-creation Condition	Separating Heaven and Earth	Theogony Mixed with Cosmogony	Theo-machy	Naming as act of Creation	Separating as act of Creation	Creation of people	Temple Connection	Rest
Egyptian									
Hermopolitan: pBremner-Rhind BM 10188	X		X			X			
Hermopolitan: CT spell 76–80	X	X	X				X		
Heliopolitan: CT 335/ Book of the Dead, 17	X	[X]	X			X	X		
Theban: Papyrus Leiden I 350	X		X						
Memphite Theology			X		X			X	X
Instruction of Merikare				X			X	X	
Sumerian									
Huluppu Tree	X	X			X		X		
Ewe and Wheat			X		[X]				
Bird and Fish									
E'engura Hymn							X	X	
Song of the Hoe		X					X	X	
Enki and World Order	X							X	
Enki and Ninhursag			X						
Enki and Ninmah	X	(X)			X		X	X	
Eridu Genesis							X	X	
NBC 11108	X	[X]							
KAR 4	X	X					X		

(X) = implied   [X] = stated as not yet having occurred

CHART 1: Summary of Features Appearing in Ancient Cosmological Accounts (continued)

Primary Sources	Pre-creation Condition	Separating Heaven and Earth	Theogony Mixed with Cosmogony	Theo-machy	Naming as act of Creation	Separating as act of Creation	Creation of people	Temple Connection	Rest
Akkadian									
Atrahasis				X			X		
Enuma Elish	X	(X)	X	X	X		X	X	X
Dunnu Theogony			X	X					
Worm and Toothache									
Two Insects									
Tamarisk and Palm									
Great Astrological Treatise									
VAT 17019							X		
Seleucid Foundation Prayers	X	X	X		X		X	X	

(X) = implied   [X] = stated as not yet having occurred

CHART 2: Summary of Elements Appearing in Ancient Cosmological Accounts

Primary Sources	Gods	Heaven and Earth	Sky	Waters	Dry land	Plants Fecundity	Birds/fish	Animals	Society or civilization	Celestial Bodies
Egyptian										
Hermopolitan: pBremner-Rhind BM 10188	X	X			X					
Hermopolitan: CT spell 76–80	X	X	X		X		X	X		
Heliopolitan: CT 335/ Book of the Dead, 17	X									X
Theban: Papyrus Leiden I 350	X	X								X
Memphite Theology	X	X							X	
Instruction of Merikare	X	X				X	X	X	X	

CHART 2: Summary of Elements Appearing in Ancient Cosmological Accounts (continued)

Sumerian	Huluppu Tree		X				X			X	
	Ewe and Wheat						X		X	[X]	
	Bird and Fish		X		X		X	X	X	X	
	E'engura Hymn						X				
	Song of the Hoe		X							X	
	Enki and World Order				X		X	X	X	X	
	Enki and Ninhursag								[X]	X	
	Enki and Ninmah	X	X							X	
	Eridu Genesis								X	X	
	NBC 11108	[X]	[X]	[X]						[X]	
	KAR 4		X		X		X			X	
Akkadian	Atrahasis				X	X					
	Enuma Elish	X	X	X	X						X
	Dunnu Theogony	X		X			X		X		
	Worm and Toothache		X		X						
	Two Insects		X						X		
	Tamarisk and Palm				X	X				X	
	Great Astrological Treatise		X								X
	VAT 17019										X
	Seleucid Foundation Prayers	X	X		X	X	X		X	X	

(X) = implied [X] = stated as not yet having occurred

Note: These charts list the Egyptian, Sumerian, and Akkadian compositions we have that enable us to understand the cosmology of the ANE. The vertical row on the left lists the relevant compositions, while the horizontal row at the very top notes important cosmological features, which are marked if present in the relevant text. This chart originally appeared in *Genesis 1 as Ancient Cosmology* (Eisenbrauns 2011); reprinted with permission.

Order/Roles

In the ancient world, political and social realities were established by decree of the authority (e.g., king, governor, elder). Cosmic realities were similarly established by the decrees of the gods. It is therefore no surprise that even though cosmologies do not often explicitly mention creation by the spoken word, order in the cosmos, in society, in the temple, and at every level of existence was determined by decree. In Akkadian and Sumerian sources, the primary forces of life are all laid down in a process known as the decreeing of the destinies. The roles of gods, people, groups, social institutions, temples, and cosmic entities (the cosmos was full of entities rather than objects) were decreed. A similar perspective can be seen in Genesis generally as the spoken word is used to make decrees bringing order, and specifically as the roles of the sun, moon, and stars are indicated.

Chaoskampf

One of the ideas that is commonly identified as distinguishing Israelite thinking from that of the ANE concerns the role of conflict in creation. Oddly enough, however, conflict in cosmology is not as common as we might think. Egyptian **mythology** features daily conflict as the sun rises and is threatened by the chaos creature, Apophis. In Sumerian literature, the cosmology texts do not feature conflict. In Akkadian, the *Enuma Elish* tells of the battle between Marduk and Tiamat, but even there, the account is of a reorganization of the cosmos under the rule of Marduk (Walton 2011, 68–74). Clearly, however, Genesis gives no indication of such a conflict (though Ps. 74 demonstrates that such an element is not totally absent). Nevertheless, this is not as clear a distinction as is often stated since the concept is the exception rather than the rule throughout ANE cosmologies.

Cosmos and Temple

Since cosmologies focus on establishing order, it is no surprise to find that temples play a significant role in cosmology. The temple in the ancient world was the seat of divine authority. It was from the temple that the god ruled and maintained order in the cosmos. The temple was also a connecting link between heaven and earth. In cosmologies such as *Enki and World Order* and *Enuma Elish*, the cosmology features the establishment of a temple from which the god can assume rule over the cosmos that has been organized under his control.

Cosmic Geography

Cosmology is comprised not only of perspectives on the origins of the world as it is known but also of the shape of the world, known as cosmic geography. Though there are individual variations from culture to culture and time to time, a general commonality pervades the ancient world. The main features of the cosmos were the heavens, the earth, and the seas. The netherworld was a component of the earth. Cosmologies often recounted the initial separation between these components (heaven and earth, earth and seas, waters above and waters below). The gods established boundaries for the sea and to keep the earth and heaven separated as well as to restrain the waters above. An understanding in the ancient world was that there was a single continent surrounded by cosmic waters. Ancient cosmologies also regularly conceived of the sky as solid though many different ideas existed concerning the nature of the dome. Genesis reflects many of the common perspectives of the ancient world.

John H. Walton

REFERENCES AND RECOMMENDED READING

Allen, J. 1988. *Genesis in Egypt.* New Haven, CT: Yale University Press.
Assmann, J. 2002. *The Mind of Egypt.* New York: Metropolitan.
Clifford, R. 1994. *Creation Accounts in the Ancient Near East and the Bible.* Catholic Biblical Quarterly Monograph Series 26. Washington, DC: Catholic Biblical Association.
Hornung, E. 1982. *Conceptions of God in Ancient Egypt.* Ithaca, NY: Cornell University Press.
Horowitz, W. 1998. *Mesopotamian Cosmic Geography.* Winona Lake, IN: Eisenbrauns.
Keel, O. 1978. *The Symbolism of the Biblical World.* New York: Seabury.
Lesko, L. 1991. "Ancient Egyptian Cosmogonies and Cosmology." In *Religion in Ancient Egypt,* ed. B. Shafer, 88–122. Ithaca, NY: Cornell University Press.
Walton, John H. 2006. *Ancient Near Eastern Thought and the Old Testament: Introducing the Conceptual World of the Hebrew Bible.* Grand Rapids: Baker Academic.
———. 2009. *The Lost World of Genesis 1.* Downers Grove, IL: InterVarsity.
———. 2011. *Genesis 1 as Ancient Cosmology.* Winona Lake, IN: Eisenbrauns.

COSMOLOGY, BIBLICAL. Cosmology, while including cosmogony (the origins and structure of the universe), provides the helpful distinction of also including the function and destiny of the universe and informs a culture's **worldview**. Biblical cosmology, then, examines the biblical writers' views of the origin, organization, function, and future of the cosmos, including the role of both God and humanity in it.

Cosmology in the Old Testament

The Bible does not present a clearly ordered cosmology. We must piece together various references to cosmology within the context of theological reflections on creation, the working and power of God, or praises to him. The Old Testament writers often use terminology and images similar to those of the ancient world around them, so it is helpful to understand something of those backgrounds, both to be able to see the similarities, as well as recognize the differences.

Cosmology in the ancient Near Eastern context

The ancient world had broad agreement on basic concepts of the creation and structure of the cosmos, which are reflected in the Old Testament, though many details vary. Of the near neighbors to Israel, more **information** has been provided from archaeology for Mesopotamian and Egyptian views on cosmology than for the various Canaanite states.

Mesopotamian cosmology. While earlier Sumerian texts describe the creation of humans among creation events, only two later (second millennium BC) Akkadian accounts, *Atrahasis* and **Enuma Elish**, give much detail, and neither provides a fully ordered account of all of creation. *Atrahasis* presents the creation of humanity and humankind's near **extinction** by the gods with some general parallels in structure and content to Genesis 2–11. *Enuma Elish* defends the god Marduk's claim to be sovereign over the gods, and includes his creation of the universe and humankind. Marduk created the cosmos after his epic battle with the watery abyss (Tiamat) by splitting the cosmic waters, using half of her for the heavens above and half below. After creating the land and filling it with plants and animals, people are created to relieve the gods of their labor.

The various Mesopotamian accounts provide a fairly consistent structure of the universe, picturing a three-level universe: heaven (in three levels: realms of differing gods, depending on the time period, with the stars in the lowest), earth (in three levels: realm of people, realm of the fresh water [god Ea], and the underworld), and the lower cosmic sea. The inhabited world forms a bubble in the midst of the cosmic waters. Various gods govern all the areas of the cosmos. People were created to serve the gods and do their work for them. The affairs of humanity and humankind's future are determined by these gods.

Egyptian cosmology. No single comprehensive account records Egypt's cosmogony. Nevertheless, the overall picture of creation remains remarkably consistent throughout more than two millennia (Allen 1988, 56). For the Egyptians, creation begins with an infinite dark, watery, chaotic sea. The creator god (Atum, Re, Amun or Ptah, depending on the writer and time) brings himself into being, then creates the rest of the cosmos, beginning with the atmosphere as a bubble of light and order in the middle of the dark chaotic waters. Land, plants, animals, and people all follow. In Egyptian accounts, the main point is really the creation of the gods, which embody the various parts of the cosmos.

The Egyptian world structure includes the sky, land, and the underworld or Duat which float in the endless dark waters like a bubble. The sun was the most important part of creation, and so the chief deity. Cosmic order, or Ma'at, established at creation, was maintained by the Pharaoh, the representative of the gods. Humankind was formed by the gods for their use.

The Genesis creation accounts

The placement of the creation account at the beginning of the Hebrew Bible highlights the importance of cosmology for Israel's worldview and theology. Genesis 1:1–2:3, a theological cosmogony, presents God as the sole sovereign creator, benefactor, and ruler of all creation. The account emphasizes the goodness of God as creator, as well as his sovereign rule. Genesis 2:4–25 focuses on Yahweh's creation of humankind and their role and responsibilities as his image bearers.

The creation account in Genesis 1 holds numerous similarities to the ancient stories around Israel, but with significant differences. There are general similarities with the Mesopotamian accounts, including a watery darkness before creation; light, day, and night before the sun, moon, or stars; waters being separated to create the atmosphere with waters above and waters below; the sun, moon, and stars created for signs, seasons, days, and years; man formed from dust or clay; and God (or the gods) resting after the creation of man. The Egyptian accounts include more specific similarities including a god speaking creation into existence (in some accounts) and the major events of creation in the same order (Miller and Soden 2012, 77–96). The differences are particularly significant, however, for our understanding of cosmology.

In contrast to the other ancient Near Eastern views, God in Genesis is not created, existing independently apart from his creation. He therefore transcends all creation. God exhibits absolute and effortless power, speaking all things into being, without enemy or conflict. All creation obeys God's sovereign bidding. He does not need magic. In fact, Genesis allows no other gods or power, and what the cultures around Israel worshiped as deities appear as subservient objects in God's created world.

God's creation of man and woman as his image bearers and representatives climaxes Genesis 1. God provides for humanity, whom all creation will serve, rather than humanity providing for the gods. In a significant distinction from their neighbors, Israel must enter into God's Sabbath rest, the goal of creation, imitating him and enjoying his provision for them (Ex. 31:12–17). God's rest as the goal of creation directly contrasts a cyclical view of history, with the sun in Egypt, for example, struggling each day to reassert his supremacy, merely to ultimately succumb and return to nothingness.

Genesis 2 adds to the function and responsibilities of humanity, portraying man and woman as the focus of Yahweh's creation, his high priest and priestess placed in his royal temple garden. The account presents mankind with their duties and also their frailty, made of dust. Genesis 3 reveals the cause of humanity's struggle to exercise the dominion for which they were created. Humankind's rebellion squanders the opportunity for life, bringing certain **death** as well as frustration and struggle until that death.

Genesis 1 may sound familiar, but it actually fits into its ancient conceptual context better than a modern one. Things like the separation of the waters to make the atmosphere in Genesis 1:7 do not fit easily into a modern cosmology but are perfectly at home in the world around Israel. The light, day, and night before the luminaries (Gen. 1:3–5, 14–18) also fit the ancient view of the universe, rather than a modern view. The rest of the Old Testament continues to portray the cosmos in ancient terms. The writers' concern is not, however, with the physical structure but with the theological significance and the implications for how Israel must view life, God, and their world, and what they can expect.

Cosmology in the rest of the Old Testament

The rest of the Old Testament devotes little attention to cosmogony, aside from a few poetic accounts of creation that do not provide specific descriptions (Job 38:4–15; Ps. 104; Prov. 8:22–31). The vocabulary used in these passages fits very well into the ancient environment, but it is more difficult to be certain of underlying beliefs.

Origin of the cosmos. The entire Old Testament assumes Yahweh created all things in accordance with the Genesis narratives. Interestingly, the order of creation varies in the Job, Psalms, and Proverbs passages. Yet these passages emphasize that Yahweh created all things, giving good things to all (Ps. 104). He ordered creation in wisdom, founding Israel's wise living (Prov. 8:22–31) and ruling over all from his temple in heaven (Ps. 104:2–3, 13) with absolute control (Job 26, 38).

Structure of the cosmos. The terms and descriptions that we do find in the Old Testament have often been understood to present a three-level universe, similar to the Mesopotamian descriptions (Stadelmann 1970). Jonathan Pennington has helpfully critiqued this view, arguing for a two-part view of the universe, pictured in the common phrase, "heaven and earth" (2004). Even so, the depictions consistently reflect their ancient context.

The "heavens" in the Old Testament describe the atmosphere and realm of the stars and angels (Gen. 1:8, 14–17; 28:12), stretched out like a tent over the earth (Ps. 104:2; Isa. 40:22). The heavens also present a barrier to keep the waters above from the waters below, where the earth is (Gen. 1:6–8). The heavens describe the place where God built his dwelling (Isa. 40:22; Amos 9:6; though sometimes above the heavens, Ps. 113:5–6), which may reflect an ontological cosmology more than a physical one (Pennington 2004).

Theologically, Solomon realized that all of heaven cannot really contain God (1 Kings 8:27), demonstrating the possibly figurative understanding of many of the descriptions. There are waters above the heavens (Ps. 148:4) or stored in the heavens (Ps. 104:13; Jer. 10:12–13), and God lays the beams of his chambers on the waters (Ps. 104:3). This image, along with Psalm 29:10 where Yahweh "sits enthroned over **the flood**," echoes the cosmic ocean imagery of Israel's neighbors. Several passages picture windows or gates in heaven to water the earth (Gen. 7:11; Ps. 104:13; Mal. 3:10), or places to store the wind (Ps. 135:7) or snow and hail (Job 38:22–23).

The Old Testament also describes the earth with language that is at home in the ancient world. The earth and the mountains are described in many passages with footings and a cornerstone (Job 38:6) or foundations (Pss. 18:7; 104:5; Isa. 48:13) or pillars (Job 9:6). These descriptions echo the construction of the temple (Ps. 78:69; Job 38:4–7) because the universe forms God's temple (Isa. 66:1). Yet in other places the earth is spread on the waters (Pss. 24:2; 136:6) and in Job 26:7 it is suspended over nothing. Job 26:7 sounds suspiciously modern, though it may simply be visualizing Genesis 1:2 in a poetic way, describing the desolate waters before creation (using the term for "formless" from Gen. 1:2 in Job 26:7a), or perhaps reflecting another ancient Mesopotamian conception of Shamash, the sun god, suspending the lands from the heavens. The disparate descriptions show greater interest in function and significance than actual structure.

Below the earth, the "deep" (Gen. 49:25) provides water to the springs (Deut. 8:7) or the floodwaters of judgment

(Gen. 7:11). The underworld, typically called Sheol or the pit, also lies below the earth (Num. 16:28–33; Deut. 32:22). Sheol, more than the grave, denotes with negative connotations the place of the dead after life (Ps. 49:14; Johnston 2002, 34, 82–83). The Old Testament does not develop a full theology of the afterlife.

Function and destiny of the cosmos. All creation exists for Yahweh's glory, with humanity intended to exhibit his glory and lead creation in his worship (Pss. 72:19; 96). The prophets in particular envision the cosmos being renewed under the ultimate rule of Yahweh and his Anointed with a new heavens and earth (Isa. 65:17–25) and universal worship of Yahweh (Isa. 66:22–24; Zech. 14:6–9), extending the image of the royal temple garden and bringing healing from the curse (Ezek. 47:1–12). Finally, all creation will acknowledge God's eternal rule (Pss. 96–99; Isa. 45:22–23).

Cosmology in the New Testament

Greek thinkers revolutionized the perceived structure of the universe. In the fourth century BC, **Plato** provided the basis for the classical Aristotelian view of a spherical earth with concentric spheres around it carrying the sun, moon, planets, and stars (Adams 2008, 13–14). We should not assume, then, that the New Testament writers pictured a **flat earth**, for example, even though they refer to "the four corners of the earth" (Rev. 7:1; 20:8). With little devotion to the concrete aspects of origins and structure, the New Testament focuses the reader far more on the underlying function of the universe with attention riveted on God's sovereign plan and the final outworking of that plan in the goal of creation.

Origin and structure of the cosmos

The New Testament writers consistently based their message on the cosmology of Genesis 1, with God external to creation (Rev. 1:4), as sole creator (Rom. 1:20; Eph. 3:9; Rev. 4:11), and Jesus as the agent of all creation (John 1:1–3; Col. 1:15–17; Heb. 1:2). Creation appears ex nihilo or out of nothing (see Rom. 4:17), by God's word (Heb. 11:3; 2 Peter 3:5–6). New Testament writers do not describe its structure clearly, summarizing creation as heaven and earth (Acts 17:24; Eph. 1:10; Heb. 1:10), "the heavens and the earth and the sea" (Acts 14:15), or "heaven … earth and under the earth" (see Phil. 2:10; Rev. 5:3, 13). Paul's reference to the "third heaven" in 2 Corinthians 12:2 may reflect the Jewish terminology of a stratified heaven, though it is uncertain. Similarly, the temple of God sometimes appears above the heavens (Rev. 4:1, 6; 6:14), though the images in **Revelation** do not supply a physical geography.

The New Testament expresses a much more developed theology of the afterlife and ongoing punishment in hell than the Old Testament's shadowy realm of the dead. Underworld names like Hades or Gehenna are supplemented by descriptors like "darkness" and "fire," highlighting the condition rather than the location (Matt. 3:12; 22:13; Rev. 20:13–15). The location is generally down in the depths, following the Old Testament conception of the underworld (Matt. 11:23), also suggested by the use of Hades in passages like Acts 2:25–31, where it translates Sheol from Psalm 16:10. Similarly, "heaven" appears to be "up," as for example, in Christ's ascension (Acts 1:9).

Function and destiny of the cosmos

God, as creator of all things, drives all of history to its consummation (Matt. 25:34; Mark 13:31), for his preordained purpose (Eph. 1:4; 1 Cor. 2:7) planned from the beginning and under his ultimate direction (Matt. 24:3–35; John 17:20–26; Acts 17:24–31). The current world is given over for a time to evil spiritual powers headed by Satan himself (1 Cor. 2:6; Eph. 2:2; 6:11–12; Rev. 12:9, 12), but it will be judged by Jesus (Matt. 13:36–43; Acts 17:31; Rev. 20:11–21:8), reconciled to God (2 Cor. 5:19; Col. 1:20) through redemption in Christ (Rom. 8:18–25) for his glory and ultimate rule (1 Cor. 15:20–28; Eph. 1:10). New Testament writers develop the interplay between the physical heavens and earth and the spiritual heavens and earth from the Old Testament as they contrast the earth or this "world" (including the human and spiritual opposition to God, John 1:10) and the heavens (including God's heavenly realm, John 6:33; Heb. 9:11; Rev. 4; 6:11–17), from which God sends communication, blessing, or judgment.

While Genesis shows the foundational nature of cosmology, Revelation provides the climax and pictures the goal of creation (including Eden-like geography). The temporal portrayal of creation, highlighted with the use of "ages" for the universe (Heb. 1:2; 11:3), emphasizes the goal as the inheritance of the Son (Heb. 1:2), who will reign forever over it (Rev. 11:15). The new ideal creation, following the end of the current corrupted creation (2 Peter 3:10–13; Rev. 21–22), is available to all believers in Christ (2 Peter 3:13), who will reign with Christ (Rev. 20:6; 22:5).

Summary

The biblical writers show far more interest in the God of creation and the implications of his creating for life now than the mechanics of the origin and structure of the universe.

Cosmology grounds theology, leading to a perspective for living and an end to pursue, focusing on God's rule and over-arching plan in creation. While biblical writers consistently use terminology at home in their world, their cosmology shows significant differences that flesh out their vision of a single sovereign King who will bring all of creation back under his absolute benevolent control through his own sac-rifice, ending all corruption in his world.

John Soden

REFERENCES AND RECOMMENDED READING

Adams, Edward. 2008. "Graeco-Roman and Ancient Jewish Cosmology." In *Cosmology and New Testament Theology*, 5–27. New York: T&T Clark.

Allen, James P. 1988. *Genesis in Egypt: The Philosophy of Ancient Egyptian Creation Accounts*. Yale Egyptological Studies 2. New Haven, CT: Yale University Press.

Beale, Gregory K. 2004. *The Temple and the Church's Mission: A Biblical Theology of the Dwelling Place of God*. New Studies in Biblical Theology. Downers Grove, IL: InterVarsity.

Johnston, Philip S. 2002. *Shades of Sheol: Death and Afterlife in the Old Testament*. Downers Grove, IL: Apollos/InterVarsity.

Lambert, W. G. 1975. "The Cosmology of Sumer and Babylon." In *Ancient Cosmologies*, ed. Carmen Blacker and Michael Loewe, 43–65. London: Allen and Unwin.

Miller, Johnny V., and John M. Soden. 2012. *In the Beginning … We Misunderstood: Interpreting Genesis 1 in Its Original Context*. Grand Rapids: Kregel.

Oswalt, John. 2009. *The Bible among the Myths: Unique Revelation or Just Ancient Literature?* Grand Rapids: Zondervan.

Pennington, Jonathan T. 2004. "Dualism in Old Testament Cosmology: Weltbild and Weltanschauung." In *Scandinavian Journal of the Old Testament* 18 (2): 260.

Pennington, Jonathan T., and Sean M. McDonough. 2008. *Cosmology and New Testament Theology*. Library of New Testament Studies. New York: T&T Clark.

Stadelmann, Luis I. J. 1970. *The Hebrew Conception of the World*. Analecta Biblica. Rome: Pontifical Biblical Institute.

Tsumura, David Toshio. 1989. *The Earth and the Waters in Genesis 1 and 2: A Linguistic Investigation*. Journal for the Study of the Old Testament: Supplement Series. Sheffield Academic Press.

Walton, John H. 2006. *Ancient Near Eastern Thought and the Old Testament: Introducing the Conceptual World of the Hebrew Bible*. Grand Rapids: Baker Academic.

COSMOLOGY, CONTEMPORARY.

Cosmology, defined as the study of the origin and structure of the universe, has been a subject of interest for as long as humanity has gazed in wonder at the night sky and pondered how the world came to be. Contemporary scientific cosmology, however, really begins with **Albert Einstein** (1879–1955), whose 1915 **general theory of relativity** replaced the theory of gravity developed by **Isaac Newton** (1642–1727). In Einstein's theory, the presence of matter has gravitational effects that change the structure of space-time around it as gravitational waves ripple outward at the **speed of light**.

As the physicist John Wheeler succinctly put it, in general relativity, matter tells space-time how to curve and space-time tells matter how to move.

A mathematical consequence of general relativity is the extraordinarily well-confirmed **big bang theory** of the origin of the universe. As Roger Penrose and **Stephen Hawking** showed in the late 1960s, regardless of which general-relativistic model of our universe is chosen, every temporal path backward through space-time leads to a beginning point in the finite past—a singularity, to use the technical term—from which not just matter and energy but space-time itself emerged. The big bang predicts the observed expansion of the universe, which, from measurement of the expansion rate, allows a reasonable calculation of its age (13.7 billion years). The model also explains the origin of hydrogen and helium in the early universe and predicts their relative abundances as well as predicting and explaining the observed cosmic microwave background radiation that permeates the cosmos.

These triumphs of explanation give us a good understanding of the universe back to the time right after the strong force holding the nucleus of the atom together separated from the electro-weak force (in the neighborhood of 10^{-32} to 10^{-12} seconds), but **physics** before this point is highly speculative.

All physics breaks down at a singularity, and since quantum effects in the gravitational field should manifest at sizes smaller than the Planck length (10^{-35} meters)—which was the size of the observable universe prior to 10^{-43} seconds—this era in universal history is called the Planck epoch, and speculations pertaining to it form a branch of theoretical physics known as quantum cosmology.

Immediately following is the Grand Unification epoch, which extends from 10^{-43} to 10^{-36} seconds and is understood as the period when gravity separated from the other three fundamental forces (strong, electromagnetic, and weak), which remained unified at this energy scale.

It is then conjectured that the separation of the strong nuclear force from the two remaining unified forces triggered a period of exponential cosmic expansion (see **Inflationary Universe Theory**) that lasted from around 10^{-36} to 10^{-32} seconds and distributed radiation and matter (the latter in the form of a quark-gluon plasma) relatively uniformly throughout the size of the observable universe during this epoch (a volume ranging from 10 centimeters to a meter in diameter, depending on the parameters of the inflationary model). It is from this point in the history of the universe that the well-understood physics of the standard model and big bang theory takes over.

This treatment of contemporary cosmology will be selective because many relevant issues are discussed in other entries in this dictionary. A cursory reading of various ideas about the origin of the universe reveals that much contemporary cosmology is highly speculative. This derives from the fact that our knowledge of the global structure of the universe is underdetermined by the observable universe and from the assumptions that many cosmologists make to overcome this fact.

How do astronomers and cosmologists use what we can see (the observable universe) to make inferences about what we cannot see (the global structure of the whole universe)? Since the speed of light is the limiting signal speed in the universe, we only ever have access to **information** about our local part of space-time—the "past light cone" within which light has had time to reach us.

While the equations of general relativity yield a local relationship between space-time geometry and mass-energy distribution, there are no global constraints warranting an inference from local observations to some "best" global structure (Manchak 2009). Even locally, the current wisdom is that explaining what we see using general relativity requires attributing 96 percent of the universe's mass-energy density to hypothesized entities that cannot be seen directly (see **Dark Matter and Dark Energy**) but whose existence is inferred from effects on observed matter. However, this inference is based on assumptions and extensions in accepted theories that can be questioned, raising the possibility that some alternative gravitational theory could explain what we can see without postulating new entities (Smeenk 2014).

To apply general relativity to the universe as a whole, Einstein assumed something called the cosmological principle: on large scales, space-time geometry is homogeneous (mass-energy is evenly distributed) and isotropic (the universe looks basically the same in every direction from every location). In fact, the degree of homogeneity and isotropy in what we can see is so pronounced that the **inflationary universe theory** was proposed in the 1980s as an explanation for it. The inflationary mechanism works by pushing any inhomogeneities beyond the horizon of what can be seen. In short, calculations of global structure are justified on the basis of an unverifiable assumption that can be challenged but that also provides some predictions that may be observed.

Arguments for the cosmological principle range from its utility as a simplifying assumption to its being a necessary condition for global theorizing (Beisbart 2009), but its status

as a metaphysical assumption used to extend cosmological research beyond the observable should be recognized.

The relatively innocuous cosmological principle has morphed into the **Copernican principle** (Gonzalez and Richards 2004, 247–74) that denies the earth occupies a privileged place in the cosmos. As Jim Baggott (2013, 23) states it, "The universe is not organized for our benefit and we are not uniquely privileged observers." This blatantly metaphysical assumption, proffered under the guise of **methodological naturalism**, is rendered problematic by the singular properties of the earth and its local environment (Gonzalez 2011; Gonzalez and Richards 2004) and by contemporary cosmological discoveries showing we live in a "Goldilocks universe" with just the right initial conditions, laws, and natural constants to support life (Barnes 2011; Barrow and Tipler 1986; Collins 1999, 2003, 2009, 2013; Copan and Craig 2004; Davies 1982; Gordon 2011; Holder 2004).

Much contemporary work in theoretical cosmology is motivated by attempts to mitigate the metaphysical implications of the universe having a beginning (see **Big Bang Theory**; **Borde-Guth-Vilenkin Singularity Theorem**; **Cosmological Arguments**) and being fine-tuned for life (see **Fine-Tuning of Universe and Solar System**). In short, it seems to be resistance to the fact that the transcendent God hypothesis fits the observational data of contemporary cosmology that drives much current speculation.

Since a singular beginning to the universe would make it inaccessible to physical explanation, some theoretical physicists have proposed a "different physics" at the beginning of time. The big bang tells us that the observable universe was once smaller than an atom, which is the scale where **quantum physics** takes effect. Applying quantum theory to this epoch has created a speculative branch of physics called "quantum cosmology."

The most famous quantum cosmologist is Stephen Hawking, who popularized his "no boundary proposal" in the bestselling book *A Brief History of Time* (1988). This model has deep problems (see Gordon 2011; Isham 1993; and Lennox 2011 for more detail).

First, we do not have a consistent account of quantum gravity, and if someday we do, it may not fit with current quantum cosmological models.

Second, Hawking's proposal makes essential use of the problematic many-worlds interpretation of quantum theory (see **Quantum Theory, Interpretations of**).

Third, he mathematically transforms the structure of space-time to make his equations solvable and, while this eliminates **the singularity** at the beginning of time, this singularity reappears when the procedure is reversed to describe the space-time of our universe. Hawking's famous question predicated on a beginningless universe—"What place, then, for a Creator?" (1988, 141)—therefore falls flat on two counts: (a) the requisite reverse transform *does* necessitate a beginning; and (b) even if it didn't, the universe's structural particularity would still mandate a **cosmological argument** from contingency (Koons 1997; Pruss 2009).

Fourth, as quantum cosmologist Alexander Vilenkin admitted, "An observational test of quantum cosmology does not seem possible. Thus … quantum cosmology is not likely to become an observational science" (Vilenkin 2002).

Fifth, quantum cosmological models require an infinite winnowing (fine-tuning) of mathematical structures to produce their technical machinery, establish the right relationship between matter variables and the curvature of space, and render the geometry of our universe typical in accordance with the Copernican principle. But any Copernican typicality of a universe so "explained" is more than nullified by the fine-tuning of the model required to produce it.

Lastly, we still face Hawking's most lucid question (1988, 174): "What is it that breathes fire into the equations and makes a universe for them to describe?" The fact that a mathematical equation can be written down does not mean it describes anything. Even if quantum cosmological equations described something, the existence of what they described would still need explaining and the mathematical models themselves would still be fine-tuned.

While transcendent intelligent agency seems implied by the existence of the universe and its fine-tuned, life-permitting properties, many contemporary cosmologists try to avoid this conclusion through speculative universe-creating mechanisms designed to produce an unlimited number of universes with different properties (initial conditions, laws, and constants). In these **multiverse** scenarios, the life-permitting properties of our universe get explained as "observer selection effects": we must exist in a region of the multiverse having conditions compatible with our existence. The "anthropic string landscape" (Susskind 2003, 2006; Weinberg 2011) is the best known of these proposals, combining the speculations of inflationary cosmology with those of **string theory** in a bid to mitigate fine-tuning in the observable universe. The proposal is fraught with difficulties, however, and on pain of infinite regress, cannot resolve the fine-tuning issues afflicting scientific **materialism**.

We conclude by briefly mentioning some of these

difficulties (see Gordon 2010 and 2011 for a comprehensive discussion). Inflationary cosmology requires fine-tuning that goes far beyond the fine-tuning it was invented to explain (Barnes 2011; Gordon 2011; Penrose 2005; Steinhardt 2011) but swamps all improbabilities by multiplying the number of universes generated without limit. Since anything that can happen does happen somewhere in the inflationary multiverse, invoking inflation to explain away fine-tuning has the consequence of undermining scientific rationality.

The "Boltzmann Brain **Paradox**" (Bousso and Freivogel 2007; Dyson et al. 2002; Linde 2007) and the "Youngness Paradox" (Guth 2011) illustrate this. From a probabilistic standpoint, typical observers in an infinite multiverse will be spontaneous thermal fluctuations with memories of a past that never existed (Boltzmann brains) rather than observers of the sort we take ourselves to be (Overbye 2008). By another measure, postinflationary universes overwhelmingly will have just been formed, so universes as old as ours become extraordinarily improbable. In short, the inflationary string landscape makes our universe infinitely improbable with respect to its age and its observers—so much for the Copernican principle! String theory's contribution to the scenario fares no better (Gordon 2011; Smolin 2006; Woit 2006). Aside from the fact that its mathematical richness can incorporate almost anything—leading to a complete lack of unique and testable predictions—its account of matter requires supersymmetry, which increasingly looks untenable (Wolchover 2012).

Finally, any "universe generator" will have design parameters that require explanation. Postulating a random universe generator to explain the design parameters of a single universe does not remove design from the picture, it merely bumps it up to the next level. Avoiding an infinite explanatory regress requires actual design by a transcendent intelligence existing timelessly and logically prior to any universe or multiverse. Timeless existence is necessary existence and—provided the intrinsic properties of this necessarily existent cause are themselves necessary—puts an end to explanatory demand. So we see that multiverse cosmologies require theistic grounding too (Collins 2007; Page 2008 offers a more idiosyncratic view), which, with perfect irony, undermines the motivation for proposing them in the first place.

Bruce L. Gordon

REFERENCES AND RECOMMENDED READING

Baggott, Jim. 2013. *Farewell to Reality: How Modern Physics Has Betrayed the Search for Scientific Truth.* New York: Pegasus.

Barnes, Luke A. 2011. "The Fine-Tuning of the Universe for Intelligent Life." December 21. http://arxiv-web3.library.cornell.edu/pdf/1112.4647v1.pdf.

Barrow, J. D., and F. J. Tipler. 1986. *The Anthropic Cosmological Principle.* Oxford: Oxford University Press.

Beisbart, Claus. 2009. "Can We Justifiably Assume the Cosmological Principle in Order to Break Underdetermination in Cosmology?" *Journal for General Philosophy of Science* 40:175–205.

Bousso, Raphael, and Ben Freivogel. 2007. "A Paradox in the Global Description of the Multiverse." *Journal of High-Energy Physics* 6 (18). 0706:018. http://arxiv.org/pdf/hep-th/0610132.

Collins, Robin. 1999. "A Scientific Argument for the Existence of God: The Fine-Tuning Design Argument." In *Reason for the Hope Within*, ed. Michael J. Murray, 47–75. Grand Rapids: Eerdmans.

———. 2003. "Evidence for Fine-Tuning." In *God and Design: The Teleological Argument and Modern Science*, ed. N. Manson, 178–99. New York: Routledge.

———. 2007. "The Multiverse Hypothesis: A Theistic Perspective." In *Universe or Multiverse?* ed. Bernard Carr, 459–80. Cambridge: Cambridge University Press.

———. 2009. "The Teleological Argument: An Exploration of the Fine-Tuning of the Universe." In *The Blackwell Companion to Natural Theology*, ed. William L. Craig and J. P. Moreland, 202–81. Oxford: Blackwell.

———. 2013. "The Fine-Tuning Evidence Is Convincing." In *Debating Christian Theism*, ed. J. P. Moreland, Chad V. Meister, and Khaldoun A. Sweis, 35–46. New York: Oxford University Press.

Copan, Paul, and William Lane Craig. 2004. *Creation Out of Nothing: A Biblical, Philosophical, and Scientific Exploration.* Grand Rapids: Baker Academic.

Davies, P. C. W. 1982. *The Accidental Universe.* Cambridge: Cambridge University Press.

Dyson, L., M. Kleban, and L. Susskind. 2002. "Disturbing Implications of a Cosmological Constant." *Journal of High-Energy Physics* 210:11–38. http://arxiv.org/pdf/hep-th/0208013v3.

Gonzalez, Guillermo. 2011. "Habitable Zones and Fine-Tuning." In *The Nature of Nature: Examining the Role of Naturalism in Science*, ed. Bruce L. Gordon and William A. Dembski, 602–38. Wilmington, DE: ISI Books.

Gonzalez, Guillermo, and Jay Richards. 2004. *The Privileged Planet: How Our Place in the Cosmos Is Designed for Discovery.* Washington, DC: Regnery.

Gordon, Bruce L. 2010. "Inflationary Cosmology and the String Multiverse." In *New Proofs for the Existence of God: Contributions of Contemporary Physics and Philosophy*, ed. Robert J. Spitzer, 75–103. Grand Rapids: Eerdmans.

———. 2011. "Balloons on a String: A Critique of Multiverse Cosmology." In *The Nature of Nature: Examining the Role of Naturalism in Science*, ed. Bruce L. Gordon and William A. Dembski, 558–601. Wilmington, DE: ISI Books.

Guth, Alan H. 2011. "Eternal Inflation and Its Implications." In *The Nature of Nature: Examining the Role of Naturalism in Science*, ed. Bruce L. Gordon and William A. Dembski, 487–505. Wilmington, DE: ISI Books.

Hawking, Stephen W. 1988. *A Brief History of Time: From the Big Bang to Black Holes.* New York: Bantam.

Holder, Rodney D. 2004. *God, the Multiverse, and Everything: Modern Cosmology and the Argument from Design.* Burlington, VT: Ashgate.

Isham, Christopher J. 1993. "Quantum Theories of the Creation of the Universe." In *Quantum Cosmology and the Laws of Nature*, ed. R. J. Russell, N. Murphy, and C. J. Isham, 51–89. Notre Dame: University of Notre Dame Press.

Koons, Robert C. 1997. "A New Look at the Cosmological Argument." *American Philosophical Quarterly* 34:171–92.

Lennox, John. 2011. *God and Stephen Hawking: Whose Design Is It Anyway?* Oxford: Lion Hudson.

Linde, Andrei. 2007. "Sinks in the Landscape, Boltzmann Brains, and the Cosmological Constant Problem." *Journal of Cosmology and Astroparticle Physics* 0701:022. http://arxiv.org/pdf/hep-th/0611043.

Manchak, John. 2009. "Can We Know the Global Structure of Spacetime?" *Studies in History and Philosophy of Modern Physics* 40:53–56.

Overbye, Dennis. 2008. "Big Brain Theory: Have Cosmologists Lost Theirs?" *New York Times*, Science Section, January 15.

Page, Donald N. 2008. *"Does God So Love the Multiverse?"* January 17. http://arxiv.org/pdf/0801.0246.

Penrose, Roger. 2005. *The Road to Reality: A Complete Guide to the Laws of the Universe.* New York: Knopf.

Pruss, Alexander. 2009. "Leibnizian Cosmological Arguments." In *The Blackwell Companion to Natural Theology*, ed. William L. Craig and J. P. Moreland, 24–100. Oxford: Blackwell.

Smeenk, Christopher. 2014. "Cosmology." In *The Routledge Companion to the Philosophy of Science*, ed. Martin Curd and Stathis Psillos, 609–20. 2nd ed. New York: Routledge.

Smolin, Lee. 2006. *The Trouble with Physics: The Rise of String Theory, the Fall of a Science, and What Comes Next.* New York: Mariner.

Steinhardt, Paul. 2011. "The Inflation Debate," *Scientific American* 34 (4): 36–43.

Susskind, Leonard. 2003. "The Anthropic Landscape of String Theory." February 27. http://arxiv.org/pdf/hep-th/0302219.

———. 2006. *The Cosmic Landscape: String Theory and the Illusion of Intelligent Design.* New York: Little, Brown.

Vilenkin, Alexander. 2002. "Quantum Cosmology and Eternal Inflation." April 18. http://arxiv.org/pdf/gr-qc/0204061v1.

Weinberg, Steven. 2011. "Living in the Multiverse." In *The Nature of Nature: Examining the Role of Naturalism in Science*, ed. Bruce L. Gordon and William A. Dembski, 547–57. Wilmington, DE: ISI Books.

Woit, Peter. 2006. *Not Even Wrong: The Failure of String Theory and the Search for Unity in Physical Law.* New York: Basic Books.

Wolchover, Natalie. 2012. "Supersymmetry Fails Test, Forcing Physics to Seek New Ideas." *Scientific American.* November 29. www.scientificamerican.com/article.cfm?id=supersymmetry-fails-test-forcing-physics-seek-new-idea.

CRAIG, WILLIAM LANE.

William Lane Craig (1949–) is an analytic philosopher who specializes in **philosophy of religion**. He completed his undergraduate studies at Wheaton in 1971, and in 1973 he entered Trinity Evangelical Divinity School during Norman Geisler's tenure. After completing two master's degrees, Craig matriculated as a PhD student in philosophy at the University of Birmingham, where he wrote under the direction of John Hick. Craig later enrolled at the University of Munich, where he completed a second doctorate in theology under the tutelage of **Wolfhart Pannenberg**.

Currently, Craig holds appointments as a research professor at both Houston Baptist University and Talbot School of Theology.

His primary academic work focuses on the intersection of contemporary **metaphysics** with various issues in philosophy of religion. He is well known for his defenses of the Kalam **cosmological argument** for the **existence of God**. Craig appeals to both science and philosophy while defending key premises of the Kalam argument. Specifically, he appeals to **big bang** cosmology to defend the idea that the universe began to exist, as well as the notion of the impossibility of actual infinites.

In light of Craig's understanding of cosmology and his work on the metaphysics of time, Craig suggests a novel approach to the question of God's relation to time. Craig maintains that time itself came into existence at creation. Therefore, "prior" to creation, God "was" timeless, but at the moment of creation, according to Craig, God changed from being timeless and became a temporal being. This view is sometimes called accidental divine temporalism.

Even though Craig is staunchly committed to traditional articulations of divine omniscience, he defends presentism as the proper ontology of time, which is the same A-theoretic (tensed) approach to time that open theists defend. His defenses of tensed theories of time, and of presentism in particular, involve significant interaction with contemporary **physics**, especially **Einstein**'s two theories of **relativity** (see **Time**). His scientific and philosophical approaches to these questions also factor heavily into his articulation and defense of Molinism as a theory of meticulous divine **providence**.

In addition to his academic work, Craig is the head of Reasonable Faith, a ministry devoted to publicly defending the Christian faith and educating Christians to engage in apologetics at both academic and popular levels. Craig has debated many well-known philosophers and scientists, including Sean Carroll, **Antony Flew**, Christopher Hitchens, **Lawrence Krauss**, Quentin Smith, and Michael Tooley.

Most recently, Craig has been researching divine aseity. He has argued against Christian Platonism (see **Plato**) by suggesting that Platonist understandings of God fail to preserve Nicene orthodoxy in that God is not rightly understood, on Platonist understandings, to be the creator of all things, seen and unseen (which many take to include abstract objects). This research involves the doctrine of *creatio ex nihilo* (creation out of nothing), and his defenses of this component of Christian theology include significant engagement with scientific literature.

Besides this, Craig is well known for defending the historicity of the bodily resurrection of Jesus of Nazareth. His apologetic work usually proceeds by pointing to evidence, but Craig is not committed to evidentialistic epistemologies. In fact, he defends a Plantingian (see **Plantinga, Alvin**) approach to warrant and proper **functionalism**, which is often called Reformed **epistemology**.

Benjamin H. Arbour

REFERENCES AND RECOMMENDED READING

Craig, William Lane. 1977. "The Cosmological Argument and the Problem of Infinite Temporal Regression." *Archiv für Geschichte der Philosophie* 59:261–79.

———. 1978. "A Further Critique of Reichenbach's Cosmological Argument." *International Journal for Philosophy of Religion* 9:53–60.

———. 1979a. "Dilley's Misunderstandings of the Cosmological Argument." *New Scholasticism* 53:388–92.

———. 1979b. "God, Time, and Eternity." *Religious Studies* 14:497–503.

———. 1979c. *The Kalam Cosmological Argument.* London: Macmillan.

———. 1979d. "Kant's First Antinomy and the Beginning of the Universe." *Zeitschrift für philosophische Forschung* 33:553–67.

———. 1979e. "Wallace Matson and the Crude Cosmological Argument." *Australasian Journal of Philosophy* 57:163–70.

———. 1979f. "Whitrow and Popper on the Impossibility of an Infinite Past." *British Journal for the Philosophy of Science* 39:165–70.

———. 1980a. *The Cosmological Argument from Plato to Leibniz.* London: Macmillan.

———. 1980b. "Julian Wolfe and Infinite Time." *International Journal for Philosophy of Religion* 11:133–35.

———. 1981. "The Finitude of the Past." *Aletheia* 2:235–42.

———. 1985. "Professor Mackie and the *Kalam* Cosmological Argument." *Religious Studies* 20:367–75.

———. 1986. "God, Creation, and Mr. Davies." *British Journal for the Philosophy of Science* 37:168–75.

———. 1988a. "Barrow and Tipler on the Anthropic Principle vs. Divine Design." *British Journal for the Philosophy of Science* 38:389–95.

———. 1988b. *The Problem of Divine Foreknowledge and Future Contingents from Aristotle to Suarez.* Leiden: Brill.

———. 1990a. *Divine Foreknowledge and Human Freedom: The Coherence of Theism: Omniscience.* Leiden: Brill.

———. 1990b. "'What Place, Then, for a Creator?' Hawking on God and Creation." *British Journal for the Philosophy of Science* 41:229–34.

———. 1991a. "The *Kalam* Cosmological Argument and the Hypothesis of a Quiescent Universe." *Faith and Philosophy* 8:104–8.

———. 1991b. "Theism and Big Bang Cosmology." *Australasian Journal of Philosophy* 69:492–503.

———. 1991c. "Time and Infinity." *International Philosophical Quarterly* 31:387–401.

———. 1992a. "God and the Initial Cosmological Singularity: A Reply to Quentin Smith." *Faith and Philosophy* 9:237–47.

———. 1992b. "The Origin and Creation of the Universe: A Reply to Adolf Grünbaum." *British Journal for the Philosophy of Science* 43:233–40.

———. 1993a. "The Caused Beginning of the Universe: A Response to Quentin Smith." *British Journal for the Philosophy of Science* 44:623–39.

———. 1993b. "Graham Oppy on the *Kalam* Cosmological Argument." *Sophia* 32:1–11.

———. 1993c. "Smith on the Finitude of the Past." *International Philosophical Quarterly* 33:225–31.

———. 1994a. "Creation and Big Bang Cosmology." *Philosophia Naturalis* 31:217–24.

———. 1994b. "Professor Grünbaum on Creation." *Erkenntnis* 40:325–41.

———. 1994c. "A Response to Grünbaum on Creation and Big Bang Cosmology." *Philosophia Naturalis* 31:237–49.

———. 1994d. "The Special Theory of Relativity and Theories of Divine Eternity." *Faith and Philosophy* 11:19–37.

———. 1996. "Timelessness and Creation." *Australasian Journal of Philosophy* 74:646–56.

———. 1997a. "Adams on Actualism and Presentism." *Philosophia* 25:401–5.

———. 1997b. "Divine Timelessness and Necessary Existence." *International Philosophical Quarterly* 37:217–24.

———. 1997c. "Hartle-Hawking Cosmology and Atheism." *Analysis* 57:291–95.

———. 1997d. "In Defense of the *Kalam* Cosmological Argument." *Faith and Philosophy* 14:236–47.

———. 1997e. "Is Presentness a Property?" *American Philosophical Quarterly* 34:27–40.

———. 1998a. "Design and the Cosmological Argument." In *Mere Creation*, ed. William A. Dembski, 332–59. Downers Grove, IL: InterVarsity.

———. 1998b. "The Tensed vs. Tenseless Theory of Time: A Watershed for the Conception of Divine Eternity." In *Questions of Time and Tense*, ed. Robin LePoidevin, 221–50. Oxford: Oxford University Press.

———. 1998c. "Theism and the Origin of the Universe." *Erkenntnis* 48:47–57.

———. 1999a. "The Presentness of Experience." In *Time, Creation, and World Order*, ed. Mogens Wegener, 107–20. See *Acta Jutlandica* 54:1. Humanities Series 72. Aarhus, Denmark: Aarhus University Press.

———. 1999b. "A Swift and Simple Refutation of the *Kalam* Cosmological Argument?" *Religious Studies* 35: 57–72.

———. 1999c. "Temporal Becoming and the Direction of Time." *Philosophy and Theology* 11:349–66.

———. 1999d. "Tensed Time and Our Differential Experience of the Past and Future." *Southern Journal of Philosophy* 37:515–37.

———. 1999e. "The Ultimate Question of Origins: God and the Beginning of the Universe." *Astrophysics and Space Science* 269–70:723–40.

———. 2000a. "The Extent of the Present." *International Studies in the Philosophy of Science* 14:165–85.

———. 2000b. *Naturalism: A Critical Appraisal*, ed. William Lane Craig and J. P. Moreland. Routledge Studies in Twentieth-Century Philosophy. London: Routledge.

———. 2000c. "Relativity and the 'Elimination' of Absolute Time." In *Recent Advances in Relativity Theory*, vol. 1, *Formal Interpretations*, ed. M. C. Duffy and Mogens Wegener, 47–66. Palm Harbor, FL: Hadronic.

———. 2000d. *The Tensed Theory of Time: A Critical Examination*. Synthese Library 293. Dordrecht: Kluwer Academic.

———. 2000e. *The Tenseless Theory of Time: A Critical Examination*. Synthese Library 294. Dordrecht: Kluwer Academic.

———. 2000f. "Timelessness, Creation, and God's Real Relation to the World." *Laval théologique et philosphique* 56:93–112.

———. 2000g. "Why Is It Now?" *Ratio* 18:115–22.

———. 2001a. "God and the Beginning of Time." *International Philosophical Quarterly* 41:17–31.

———. 2001b. *God, Time, and Eternity*. Dordrecht: Kluwer Academic.

———. 2001c. "McTaggart's Paradox and Temporal Solipsism." *Australasian Journal of Philosophy* 79:32–44.

———. 2001d. "Prof. Grünbaum on the 'Normalcy of Nothingness' in the Leibnizian and *Kalam* Cosmological Arguments." *British Journal for the Philosophy of Science* 52:1–16.

———. 2001e. "Tense and Temporal Relations." *American Philosophical Quarterly* 38:85–97.

———. 2001f. *Time and the Metaphysics of Relativity*. Philosophical Studies Series 84. Dordrecht: Kluwer Academic.

———. 2001g. "Wishing It Were Now Some Other Time." *Philosophy and Phenomenological Research* 62:159–66.

———. 2002a. "Divine Eternity and the Special Theory of Relativity." In *God and Time*, ed. Gregory E. Ganssle and David M. Woodruff, 129–52. Oxford: Oxford University Press.

———. 2002b. "Must the Beginning of the Universe Have a Personal Cause? A Rejoinder." *Faith and Philosophy* 19:94–105.

———. 2002c. "On the Mind-Dependence of Temporal Becoming." In *Time, Reality, and Transcendence in Rational Perspective*, ed. Peter Ohrstrom, 129–45. Copenhagen: Aalborg University Press.

———. 2002d. "Relativity and the Elimination of Absolute Time." In *Time, Reality, and Transcendence in Rational Perspective*, ed. Peter Ohrstrom, 91–127. Copenhagen: Aalborg University Press.

———. 2003a. "Design and the Anthropic Fine-Tuning of the Universe." In *God and Design: The Teleological Argument and Modern Science*, ed. Neil Manson, 178–99. London: Routledge.

———. 2003b. "In Defense of Presentism." In *Time, Tense, and Reference*, ed. Aleksander Jokic and Quentin Smith, 390–408. Cambridge, MA: MIT Press.

———. 2004. *Creation Out of Nothing: A Biblical, Philosophical, and Scientific Exploration*. Grand Rapids: Baker.

———. 2006. "J. Howard Sobel on the *Kalam* Cosmological Argument." *Canadian Journal of Philosophy* 36:565–84.

———. 2009. "Divine Eternity." In *The Oxford Handbook of Philosophical Theology*, ed. Thomas P. Flint and Michael C. Rea, 145–66. New York: Oxford University Press.

———. 2011a. "Divine Eternity and Einstein's Special Theory of Relativity." In *God, Eternity, and Time*, ed. Christian Tapp and Edmund Runggaldier, 145–55. Aldershot, UK: Ashgate.

———. 2011b. "Graham Oppy on the *Kalam* Cosmological Argument." *International Philosophical Quarterly* 51:303–30.

Craig, William Lane, and James Sinclair. 2009. "The *Kalam* Cosmological Argument." In *The Blackwell Companion to Natural Theology*, ed. William L. Craig and J. P. Moreland, 101–201. Oxford: Wiley-Blackwell.

———. 2012. "On Non-singular Spacetimes and the Beginning of the Universe." In *Scientific Approaches to the Philosophy of Religion*, ed. Yujin Nagasawa, 95–142. Palgrave Frontiers in Philosophy of Religion. London: Macmillan.

Craig, William Lane, and Quentin Smith. 1993. *Theism, Atheism, and Big Bang Cosmology*. Oxford: Clarendon.

———. 2007. *Einstein, Relativity, and Absolute Simultaneity*. London: Routledge.

CREATION. Humans have always been curious about origins. Where did the world come from? What accounts for our existence? Thus it is not at all surprising that we have accounts of the creation of the cosmos and humans from many ancient cultures. In this article, we are particularly interested in the biblical account and other ancient Near Eastern creation compositions. Our interest in the ancient Near East (ANE) is because it helps us recover the ancient context of the biblical stories. Modern science also explores questions concerning the origins of the cosmos and humanity in a way that some see as a threat to biblical explanations. This article will describe the different accounts of creation from the Bible, the ANE, and modern science in broad terms and consider the question of the relationship between them.

The Bible opens with two discrete accounts of creation (Gen. 1:1–2:4a; 2:4b–25). The first account focuses on the creation of the cosmos and everything in it. It is a matter of debate whether or not the text speaks of the creation of matter (*creatio ex nihilo*) or begins the story of creation with formless matter already present (Copan and Craig 2004). The Hebrew of Genesis 1:1–2 is not clear on this point, and different English translations support different views (NIV, ESV, and NLT favoring creation from nothing; NRSV favoring the presence of matter at the beginning). The book of Hebrews makes the teaching of creation from nothing explicit (Heb. 11:3). It may be that the original readers of Genesis were not interested in the question of the origin of matter (and assumed that God created it), while the New Testament was written in a Greco-Roman context that was interested in the question.

The creation of the cosmos and humanity over a six-day period may not focus on material creation, but on God's making the cosmos functional for the apex of his creation, humanity (Walton 2011). The nature of the **Days of Creation** is also a matter of controversy. After the creation was complete and pronounced "very good" (Gen. 1:31), God ceased his activities, represented in the creation week as the first Sabbath.

The second creation account focuses on the creation of humanity. Some read this account as a close-up view of the sixth day (Collins 2003), others as a completely separate account. There are apparent differences of sequence between the two accounts (does the creation of vegetation precede or follow the creation of humans?). In the second creation account, the man is created first and the woman second. Debate surrounds whether the description of their creation is literally describing how it happened (from dust and the breath of God [Gen. 2:7] and from the side/rib of the man [Gen. 2:21–23]). But whether literal or not, there is no missing the symbolic significance of the acts. The first man created from the dust shows that he is part of the creation, but the breath of God indicates that humanity has a special relationship with God. The woman's creation shows that her relationship with the man is one of mutuality and equality. The biblical creation account is not only written to tell humans that their existence is the result of God's creative activity but also informs on subjects such as gender, sexuality, marriage, Sabbath, and work.

Genesis 1–2 may be the most important accounts of creation in the Bible, but they are not alone. A number of psalms (e.g., Pss. 8, 19, 24, 33, 74, 104, 136), the book of Proverbs (3:19–20; 8:22–31), and a passage in Job (38:4–11) as well as texts in the New Testament (John 1:1–5; Rom. 1:18–20; Col. 1:15–20) are examples of other passages that describe God's creation of the cosmos and/or humanity. The variation of imagery used to narrate God's creation is striking, raising the question of whether the biblical authors intend us to take any of these descriptions as literal depictions of how God created the world and human beings.

Israel's neighbors also had accounts of creation that provide the background for our reading of the biblical story. While there are creation accounts from Sumer (e.g., the Eridu Genesis, *Song of the Hoe, Enki and Ninhursag*) and Egypt (*Shabaka Stone*), the most relevant creation stories to the biblical texts are written in Akkadian (the language of the Assyrians and Babylonians) and Ugaritic (the language of the Canaanites). The two most important Akkadian creation texts are ***Enuma Elish*** and ***Atrahasis*** (see articles for details and plot summaries), and the most important Ugaritic text is the Baal Epic. Both *Enuma Elish* and the Baal Epic depict creation as the result of a battle between the creator God (Marduk/Baal) and the sea god(dess) (Tiamat/Yam). After the sea is defeated, the creator shapes the carcass of its body into a functional cosmos. In *Enuma Elish* and *Atrahasis*, humans are created from clay and the blood and/or spit of the gods, an interesting similarity to the fact that Adam is created from an earthly component, dust, and a divine one, the breath of God (Gen. 2:7).

Modern science asks questions about the origins of the cosmos and humanity. Most scientists today believe that the cosmos began with a **big bang**, which led to the ultimate formation of the universe through stellar and planetary evolution. When it comes to humanity, evidence persuades the vast majority of biologists and other scientists that humanity emerged through an evolutionary process, most recently sharing a **common ancestry** with primates.

The nature of the relationship between the Bible and science when it comes to creation is hotly contested. Young- and old-earth creationists (creation science) turn to the Bible first and typically contest contrary evidence from the scientific community. Others believe that science discounts the biblical account and consider themselves atheists (**New Atheism**). Still others believe that the Bible, when read in the light of modern science, reveals awareness of the real state of the world as presently understood by scientists (**Concordism; Reasons to Believe**). Still others believe that science cannot explain everything by natural causes and in these gaps of explanation see the hand of God at work (**intelligent design**).

Finally, others see **science and the Bible** as addressing completely different questions, the one concerning physical realities and the other metaphysical; this is known as **nonoverlapping magisteria** (NOMA). A variation of the latter suggests that religion provides the conceptual framework within which science operates, but that religion and science are "partners in theorizing," having "differing competencies" to answer the same questions (Van Till in Carlson 2000, 126, 195). Any Christian reconciliation of the relationship between the Bible and science will ultimately conclude that the two have the same author and give a consistent picture.

Tremper Longman III

REFERENCES AND RECOMMENDED READING

Carlson, Richard F., ed. 2000. *Science and Christianity: Four Views.* Downers Grove, IL: InterVarsity.

Carlson, R. F., and Tremper Longman III. 2010. *Science, Creation, and the Bible,* Downers Grove, IL: InterVarsity.

Collins, C. J. 2003. *Science and Faith: Friends or Foes?* Wheaton, IL: Crossway.

Copan, Paul, and William Lane Craig. 2004. *Creation Out of Nothing: A Biblical, Philosophical, and Scientific Exploration*. Grand Rapids: Baker Academic.
Walton, John H. 2011. *Genesis 1 as Ancient Cosmology*. Winona Lake, IN: Eisenbrauns.

CREATIONISM, INTELLIGENT DESIGN, AND THE COURTS.

American schools took nearly a generation to catch up with **Charles Darwin**, who put forth his theory of evolution in 1859, just two years before the Civil War. There were no textbooks in the unified science of "biology" prior to the early twentieth century, and nineteenth-century textbooks in botany, zoology, and **geology** were thoroughly creationist well into the 1870s or even longer (Larson 2003). Once evolution did arrive, at first it was placed in an explicitly theistic framework; indeed, the term *theistic evolution* was coined no later than 1877, though not in a textbook. By century's end, however, even implicit references to divine agency had all but disappeared, leaving students to wonder exactly what God had to do with the history of life in an evolving world.

At the same time, the number of students enrolled in public high schools exploded. In 1890 there were only about 2,500 high schools across the nation; by 1910 the number had quadrupled, with a further rise of 40 percent over the next decade. For the first time, millions of students were being exposed to evolution, and God was assigned no role in it—even though many scientists at the time believed that evolution is a goal-directed, purposeful process. Furthermore, textbooks increasingly promoted scientific racism, eugenics, and other forms of social **Darwinism**. For example, George W. Hunter's *A Civic Biology*, the book required in Tennessee where it was used by John Scopes, depicted Caucasians as "the highest type of all" (Larson 2003, 21).

Fierce opposition to social Darwinism partly motivated William Jennings Bryan's support for state laws banning the teaching of evolution in public schools and universities. The youngest presidential candidate in American history, Bryan had run unsuccessfully three times as a populist Democrat, advocating progressive reforms, such as Philippine independence, women's suffrage, a graduated income tax, and the abolition of the gold standard. After World War I, shocked by what biologist Vernon Kellogg had written in his book *Headquarters Nights* (1917) about the link between militarism and evolution in pre-war German thought, Bryan led a national campaign against teaching evolution with public funds. To garner political support, he argued that taxpayers themselves, not academic elites, have the right to determine what is taught in public schools: if they don't want evolution, it should be removed. He also believed that evolution is inherently atheistic, so the teaching of evolution with tax dollars violates the religious neutrality required of American government.

Bryan reaped a big harvest. Before the end of the 1920s, more than 20 states considered antievolution laws, five states passed them, and the United States Senate debated a ban on pro-evolutionary radio broadcasts (Numbers 2006, 55). The whirlwind came in 1925 when Tennessee made it a crime "to teach any theory that denies the story of the Divine Creation of man as taught in the Bible, and to teach instead that man has descended from a lower order of animal" (Larson 2003, 54). Immediately the American Civil Liberties Union (ACLU) solicited a teacher who would be willing to break the law in order to put the law itself on trial in a higher court as an infringement on free speech. Local power brokers in Dayton, Tennessee, saw an opportunity to put their small rural town on the map. Acting on instructions from the chair of the school board, rookie teacher John Scopes agreed to stand trial. Ultimately, the Tennessee Supreme Court overturned his conviction on a trumped-up technicality, while finding the law constitutional; it was never tested in federal court and remained on the books until 1967. In the meantime, for three decades schools and textbooks put substantially less emphasis on evolution.

Whereas Bryan's goal was simply to stop the teaching of evolution, creationists since the 1960s have tried to put creationism into science classes without removing evolution. A common argument holds that scientific support can be found for either view, so students ought to be allowed to choose for themselves which one makes more sense—a position that has garnered some popular support and drew favorable comments from President Ronald Reagan (Larson 2003, 157, 173).

However, the type of creationism being promoted today is very different from earlier creationism. Fundamentalist leaders of Bryan's generation almost entirely accepted the evidence for vast geological ages, filled with fossilized creatures now mostly extinct, long before humans were created. In stark contrast, today's young-earth creationists almost entirely reject any science that contradicts their view that the whole universe was created in six literal days no more than about 10,000 to 12,000 years ago, with most fossils resulting from Noah's flood. Not even **big bang** cosmology, which lends itself to theistic interpretations, is acceptable. A more violent collision with modern science is hard to imagine.

Creationism of this new type reached federal courts in the 1980s, in cases originating in Arkansas and Louisiana, with the ACLU claiming that recently enacted state laws requiring the teaching of creationism amounted to an unconstitutional establishment of religion. Two witnesses in the Arkansas case, philosopher **Michael Ruse** and theologian Langdon Gilkey, persuaded the court that creationism is sectarian religion, not science—a conclusion that continues to shape the controversy. When the Louisiana case reached the US Supreme Court in 1987, the ACLU challenge was upheld, but the court also explicitly left the door open for teaching multiple theories about human origins, provided that a clear secular educational purpose was being served.

Intelligent design (ID) was carefully designed by a law school professor, Phillip E. Johnson, to walk through that door. The problem with young-earth creationism, in his opinion, is its close association with the Bible. The real issue ought to be a designing intelligence vis-à-vis purely naturalistic evolution, clearly marking off ID from young-earth creationism (Larson 2003, 186–87).

Johnson's goal of leaving the Bible and young-earth creationism out of the ID conversation failed when some leading proponents of ID cooperated with creationists to publish the first explicitly pro-ID textbook, *Of Pandas and People* (1989), as a supplement to public school biology texts. Previous versions of that book (which had different titles over the years) had been purely creationist works, making frequent use of the words *creation* and *creationists*. Following the Louisiana case, however, those terms were replaced wholesale with "intelligent design" and "design proponents" (Numbers 2006, 375–76). Consequently, when the school board in Dover, Pennsylvania, tried to insert the book into the curriculum, a federal judge ruled against them in 2005, adding that the evidence had shown "that ID is nothing less than the progeny of creationism" (Davis 2006, 11). The decision presently applies only to that federal district; whether other cases will arise elsewhere remains to be seen.

Edward B. Davis

REFERENCES AND RECOMMENDED READING

Davis, Edward B. 2006. "Intelligent Design on Trial." *Religion in the News* 8 (Winter): 8–11, 26.
Larson, Edward J. 1997. *Summer for the Gods: The Scopes Trial and America's Continuing Debate over Science and Religion.* New York: Basic Books.
———. 2003. *Trial and Error: The American Controversy over Creation and Evolution.* 3rd ed. Oxford: Oxford University Press.
Numbers, Ronald L. 2006. *The Creationists: From Scientific Creationism to Intelligent Design.* Exp. ed. Cambridge, MA: Harvard University Press.

↪ CREATIONISM, OLD-EARTH (Critical View).

Old-earth creationism is a general term used to describe those who believe in an old earth yet still in some way hold that God was responsible for creation. Further, old-earth creationists believe that there is no necessary conflict between Scripture and science. In addition, old-earth creationists largely accept the modern geological consensus regarding the antiquity of the earth. However, many old-earth creationists strongly reject macroevolution and believe that God was actively involved in the entire creative process. Others are agnostic on the matter of process (whether evolutionary or not), stating that the text of Genesis says little about the process of creation.

Since the views of old-earth creationists differ widely, it will only be possible to discuss briefly some of the main positions and the weaknesses of each of them.

The Gap Theory

One way of harmonizing the Bible and modern scientific theory is by positing a "gap" between Genesis 1:1 and 1:2. This view, popularized by the *Scofield Reference Bible* (in 1909 and subsequent editions), holds that there were two creations: Genesis 1:1 describes the first creation, after which Satan, the earth's ruler (over pre-Adamic "men"), rebelled. Because of Satan's fall, sin entered the universe and brought God's judgment on the earth in the form of a flood (indicated by the water of 1:2) and then a global ice age. This resulted in the earth's judged condition, indicated by the phrase "without form and void" (Heb., *tohu wabohu*) in Genesis 1:2. The plant, animal, and human fossils on earth today date from this flood and are genetically unrelated to plants, animals, and humans on earth today. Genesis 1:2 thus describes the ruined condition of the earth, while Genesis 1:3–31 describes God's re-creation.

There are several major problems with this view. First, it is full of speculation, since there is not one word about Satan's fall in Genesis 1, nor any "men" prior to Adam, nor any judgment on the earth prior to **the flood** of Genesis 6–8. Second, the Hebrew phrase *tohu wabohu* used in Genesis 1:2 does not always carry the idea of judgment, but simply means that the earth was unformed and unfilled (see Fields 1976, 113–30). Finally, in Genesis 1:2 the Hebrew form used is a *waw* disjunctive, indicating the setting at the **time** the earth was created by God. If the meaning of Genesis 1:2 was "the earth *became* unformed and unfilled," as the gap theory requires, then the *waw* consecutive form would have been used, as it is throughout the remaining verses of Genesis 1. Thus Genesis 1:2 does not describe action subsequent to Genesis 1:1, as required by the gap theory. Consequently, the gap theory is not popular today among evangelical scholars.

The Day-Age View

A second way of harmonizing Genesis 1–2 with modern scientific theory is by viewing the "days" of Genesis 1:1–2:3 as sequential periods of thousands or millions of years (see **Days of Creation, Interpretations**). For the most part, old-earth creationists accept modern **geology** with respect to the age of the earth but reject evolution as a part of the creation process. This view is sometimes called progressive creationism. Yet some who hold to theistic evolution (also called evolutionary creationism) as the mechanism for creation also call themselves old-earth creationists (see **Evolutionary Creationism**). In either case, the central tenet is that the "days" of Genesis 1:1–2:3 are not literal days, but instead represent long periods of time.

Arguments against the day-age theory will be summarized here (though presented more fully in **Days of Creation**). The primary difficulty with this view is that the predominant meaning of *yôm*, the Hebrew word for "day," is a 24-hour day (the word has this meaning 2,239 out of 2,304 occurrences, or 97 percent of its usage). Furthermore, the phrase "evening and morning," used six times in Genesis 1, reinforces the idea of a 24-hour day. Passages such as Psalm 90:4 and 2 Peter 3:8 (that compare a thousand years in God's sight to a day) cannot be used as valid arguments for the day-age theory, since they are simply teaching that God's view of time is different from man's. The comparison in these texts is to a single 24-hour day, with the comparative particle *like* used in these texts, but not in Genesis 1. Finally, Exodus 20:8–11 is a strong argument against the day-age view, since it explicitly links the **days of creation** to the days of the workweek. The term *yôm* is used six times in the passage. It hardly makes sense for the term to mean a literal 24-hour day in the first three usages (describing the workweek) but then to mean an undetermined length of time in the final three usages (dealing with creation).

Nor does the day-age view help harmonize the biblical text with evolutionary theory. The evolution model differs in many details from the order of events presented in Genesis 1. If the days of Genesis 1 were actually long periods of time, it would make little sense to have insects created after the plants (as Genesis 1 states), since insects would have been needed for pollination. In addition, according to evolutionary theory, the simple (insects) should not appear after the more complex animals, but that is exactly what Genesis 1 portrays. This is only one of a host of problems that indicates that the day-age theory does not work from an evolutionary standpoint either (see further Kulikovsky 2009, 152–53).

While the progressive creationism view does not have the difficulties mentioned in the preceding paragraph (since evolution is not regarded as the "mechanism" of creation), it also runs into some scientific difficulties of its own. Since the current scientific model of the solar system necessitates that the sun was formed before the earth, there is a direct conflict with Genesis 1, in which the earth was created on day (or "epoch"!) one, while the sun was created on day-age four. Progressive creationists such as **Hugh Ross** have tried to argue that the sun was created on day-age one, but it only appears visible from the earth's perspective on day-age four (Ross and Archer 2001, 135). But this interpretation appears to bend the Scripture to conform to science, since the text of Genesis 1:16 clearly says that God "made" the sun and the moon on day 4.

The Framework Hypothesis

Another means of interpreting Genesis 1 that allows for an old earth is the framework hypothesis. In this view, the day is a 24-hour day, but the days are literary and not sequential. God's creative week is seen as a literary structure, where the first three days depict the creative kingdoms while the final three days speak of the creature kings that "rule" over the corresponding kingdoms of days 1–3 (e.g., the sun, moon, and stars of day 4 rule over the day and night of day 1). Or, to put it another way, the "forms" are created on the first three days, and they are correspondingly "filled" or populated in the second set of three days. Often the following pattern is noted:

Creation kingdoms	Creature kings
Day 1: light; day and night	**Day 4:** light bearers: sun, moon, stars
Day 2: sea and sky	**Day 5:** sea creatures; birds
Day 3: land and vegetation	**Day 6:** land creatures; man (Irons and Kline 2001, 224)

But there are problems with the framework approach. First, even if such a literary pattern existed, that would still not necessitate a nonliteral approach to the chapter, since the two (literal and literary) are not mutually exclusive. Second, this pattern breaks down in multiple places. For instance, the light of day 1 is not dependent on the sun; so the sun is hardly its ruler. And man (created on day 6) was not to rule over the land and vegetation (created on day 3), but over the land animals (created on day 6) and the sea creatures and birds (created on day 5). In addition, the waters existed on day 1, not just day 2. Furthermore, in verse 14 the "lights" of day 4 are set in the "expanse" created on day 2 (not day 1). Finally, the creatures of day 5 were to fill the "water in the seas," which was created on day 3, not day 2, contrary to the chart above (see Gen. 1:10). The so-called pattern simply isn't there (see further Kulikovsky 2009, 155–62).

Furthermore, the text of Genesis 1 is not poetic (as one would expect with such a literary structural approach as the framework hypothesis), but is a straightforward sequential narrative, with the standard Hebrew narrative *waw* consecutive imperfect form used 50 times in the chapter. In addition, if a figurative approach is taken in Genesis 1–2, where in Genesis should one take the text literally? There is no simple exegetical or hermeneutical "switch" between Genesis 1–2 and the rest of the book (Beall 2008, 144–58).

Biblical problems with old-earth creationism

Irrespective of the particular theory proposed (gap, day-age, or framework), there are a number of biblical problems with old-earth creationism. Some of these (such as the necessity of *yôm* in Gen. 1 referring to a literal 24-hour day) have been discussed above and will therefore not be repeated.

Genesis 1:1 is part of the six-day creation. Often the statement is made that Genesis 1:1 is not a part of the creation week but is merely a title; therefore it is impossible to know when the creation of the earth actually began, since day 1 starts in Genesis 1:3 (so Waltke, cited in Kulikovsky 2009, 109). It is true that Genesis 1:1 is a majestic opening verse that in some sense can serve as a grand introduction to the creation narrative to follow. But Genesis 1:1 must also be regarded as part of the first creation day. Genesis 1:1 says, "In the beginning God created *the heavens and the earth*" (emphasis added). The identical phrase, *the heavens and the earth*, is used in Exodus 20:11: "For in six days the LORD made *the heavens and the earth*, the sea, and all that is in them" (emphasis added; see also Ex. 31:17 for a similar expression).

The only place that the creation of the heavens is men-tioned is in Genesis 1:1, and according to Exodus 20:11 and 31:17, the creation of the heavens is a part of the six days of creation, not outside of it. One cannot resort to separating Genesis 1:1 from the rest of the creation account in order to allow for a large period of time between Genesis 1:1 and the following verses. The entire text of Exodus 20:8–11, speaking of the human workweek in terms of God's six-day creation (using *yôm* six times in the passage), is a strong indication that the heavens, the earth, and everything in it were created in six literal days.

The genealogies in Genesis 5 and 11 indicate a recent creation of mankind. Old-earth creationists generally hold that man was created no earlier than 50,000 years ago (Ross states that man was created between 50,000 and 100,000 years ago. But that amount of time is impossible according to the genealogies in Genesis 5, 10, and 11 (and largely repeated in Luke 3:34–38). The **genealogy** in Genesis 5 begins with Adam and continues through Noah and his sons. Genesis 10–11 continues with the genealogy of Noah's sons, with Genesis 11 tracing Shem's line through Abraham.

Even if the genealogies skip some generations, there is a finite limit to the number of generations skipped, meaning that man was created between 6,000 and (at most) 10,000 years ago. In fact, it is likely that while these genealogies may contain gaps, no actual chronological gaps exist, since the genealogies indicate the actual age of the parent or grandparent when the child was born (Sexton 2015, 195–205). This point is often missed in the discussion of the genealogies of Genesis 5, 10, and 11. If the genealogies in these chapters are to be taken seriously, it is impossible to come up with such long ages of mankind (50,000–100,000) as posited by old-earth advocates.

Jesus's statement that mankind was created at the beginning of creation. Jesus's statement in Mark 10:6 that "at the beginning of creation God 'made them male and female'" strongly implies that the earth had not been around for millions of years before **Adam and Eve** were created: they were created at the "beginning of creation," i.e., on the sixth day. The same phrase, "the beginning of creation," is used similarly in Mark 13:19 and 2 Peter 3:4. Jesus says that mankind was created in the initial creation week, not millions of years later.

Death before sin? Another problem for old-earth cre-ationism is that it necessitates thousands or millions of years of animal death before Adam and Eve's sin in the garden. Yet Scripture states that death had not entered the world until Adam's sin: "Therefore, just as sin entered the world through one man, and death through sin, and in this way death came to all people, because all sinned" (Rom. 5:12; see also 1 Cor. 15:21).

While it may be argued from these verses that only human death entered the world because of Adam's sin, Romans 8:21–22 seems to preclude that possibility: "The creation itself will be liberated from its bondage to decay and brought into the freedom and glory of the children of God. We know that the whole creation has been groaning as in the pains of childbirth right up to the present time." The groaning of the creation began after Adam's fall, with all of creation feeling its effects (Gen. 3:14–19). Since God's creation was originally declared "very good" by the Lord himself (Gen. 1:31), it was only after **the fall** that death and corruption entered the world. It is only Christ's death and resurrection that will usher in the final restoration of creation where the effects of the curse will be reversed and there will be no more death (Isa. 11:6–9; Rev. 21:3–5; 22:3). Scripture has no room for millions of years of death and corruption prior to Adam's sin.

Conclusion

Old-earth creationism has no solid scriptural support. It is a valiant attempt to harmonize Genesis with current scientific theory, but as has been shown above, the various old-earth models are scripturally untenable. Instead of twisting the Scripture to support the current scientific view, it would be preferable to take a closer look at the assumptions behind an old-earth cosmology (see **Age of the Universe and Earth** for further discussion). In particular, one should look at the effects of a global catastrophic flood (as portrayed in Gen. 6–9) that lasted for over a year, in which "all the springs of the great deep burst forth" (Gen. 7:11), producing all kinds of geological havoc on the earth. One should also look at the **radiometric dating** methods that are used, recognizing that the assumption of a uniform rate of decay of a particular isotope is highly questionable, especially in light of a catastrophic flood.

As well, when God created the universe, it had an appearance of age: Adam was not a mere baby, but a fully grown human being. Just as when Jesus turned the water into wine at Cana, and the ruler of the feast thought that the wine had aged for a long time (John 2:1–11), so also the Lord miraculously created a finished universe in a short period of time. Is he not capable of doing so (Heb. 11:3)?

It seems best not to alter our understanding of Scripture to fit with current scientific opinion: after all, as the Lord reminds Job, we weren't there when he laid the earth's foundations (Job 38:4), so it is best to adhere to the account he gives us in his Word.

Todd S. Beall

REFERENCES AND RECOMMENDED READING

Beall, Todd S. 2008. "Contemporary Hermeneutical Approaches to Genesis 1–11." In *Coming to Grips with Genesis: Biblical Authority and the Age of the Earth*, ed. Terry Mortenson and Thane Ury. Green Forest, AR: Master.

Fields, Weston. 1976. *Unformed and Unfilled*. Nutley, NJ: Presbyterian and Reformed.

Hasel, Gerhard F. 1994. "The 'Days' of Creation in Genesis 1: Literal 'Days' or Figurative 'Periods/Epochs' of Time?" *Origins* 21 (1): 5–38.

Irons, Lee, and Meredith G. Kline. 2001. "The Framework View." In *The Genesis Debate*, ed. David Hagopian. Mission Viejo, CA: Crux.

Kulikovsky, Andrew. 2009. *Creation, Fall, Restoration: A Biblical Theology of Creation*. Fearn, Ross-shire, Scotland: Mentor.

McCabe, Robert V. 2000. "A Defense of Literal Days in the Creation Week." *Detroit Baptist Seminary Journal* 5 (Fall): 97–123.

Mortenson, Terry, and Thane Ury, eds. 2008. *Coming to Grips with Genesis: Biblical Authority and the Age of the Earth*. Green Forest, AR: Master.

Pipa, Joseph, Jr., and David Hall, eds. 2005. *Did God Create in Six Days?* 2nd ed. White Hall, WV: Tolle Lege.

Ross, Hugh, and Gleason Archer. 2001. "The Day-Age View." In *The Genesis Debate*, ed. David Hagopian. Mission Viejo, CA: Crux. See also www.reasons.org/rtb–101/ageofadam.

Sarfati, Jonathan D. 2015. *The Genesis Account: A Theological, Historical, and Scientific Commentary on Genesis 1–11*. Powder Springs, GA: Creation.

Sexton, Jeremy. 2015. "Who Was Born When Enosh Was 90? A Semantic Reevaluation of William Henry Green's Chronological Gaps." *Westminster Theological Journal* 77 (2015): 193–218.

✧ CREATIONISM, OLD-EARTH (Supportive View).

Old-earth creationism seeks to marry the scientific consensus that the earth is very old with the biblical doctrine of creation that arises from Scripture. The Bible provides insight otherwise lacking, such as mankind being created in the image of God. But the overall understanding of how God created everything comes from the study of the physical world. Old-earth creationism interprets the Bible in a way consistent with science. Old-earth creationists are persuaded that the modern consensus is valid and that the universe is about 13.7 billion years old, and they seek ways to read the Bible consistently with that.

Young-Earth Creationism, by contrast, is at odds with the consensus view of every relevant field of science, including stratigraphy, paleontology, astronomy, glaciology, coral reef study, radiometric dating, geochronology, physical cosmology, and even archeology and Egyptology. Young-earthers have argued that for more than a century the vast majority of scientists have been blinded by their assumptions, while the young-earth position views the data clearly because it has rejected the naturalistic assumptions pervading these disciplines.

But historically, it was the young-earth assumption that proved inadequate. The hypothesis that the universe is old gradually became the dominant view among Christian naturalists in the eighteenth and nineteenth centuries, through the study of geological formations and fossils. At first, the idea that fossils were remains of extinct species was rejected, since this seemed to contradict the doctrine of creation. For God to allow extinctions would undermine the whole point of Noah's ark. Because of this, fossils were considered simply minerals with the appearance of skeletons. (**Noah's ark** has since been radically rethought by young-earth and old-earth creationists alike.)

Various attempts to calculate the age of the earth based on salt content in the oceans, or the earth's rate of cooling, surprisingly yielded ages far longer than the six millennia commonly assumed by young-earth creationists. The stratification of rocks seemed inconsistent with a worldwide flood, but rather indicative of cycles of sedimentary deposits. The surface of the earth was recognized as a "formation." Its layers could be counted like tree rings to suggest an age for the earth—which unexpectedly predated human history (by more than six days). Against the researchers' biblical presuppositions, the evidence mounted for a slow gradual geological process over many millions of years, and not to one global catastrophe lasting mere months. By the time **Charles Darwin** published his *Origin of Species* (1859), it was already conceded that the earth was ancient. "The modern view that the Earth is extremely old was developed by Christian men who believed wholeheartedly in creation and the Flood and were opposed to evolution" (Young 1982, 66).

Eventually, a correspondence was noted between fossil types and specific strata. Rocks were loaded with fossil after fossil of extinct creatures, with predictable regularity. Simpler and less developed ones were in older layers, more modern ones in newer. The natural history of the planet seemed to feature species unknown to man that thrived for an age until a sudden demise, only to be replaced by another age with a new suite of species. Distinguishable are the Age of Invertebrates, the Age of Fish, the Age of Amphibians, the Age of Reptiles, and so on.

This repeated cycle is certainly not the picture presented in young-earth interpretations of Genesis. And why would aquatic and marine creatures such as fish and alligators perish early in Noah's flood, while animals that hardly swim, such

as primates, stay above water longer? Can one imagine ferns drowning early, unable to escape the rising tide, while maple trees clawed their way upward to perish later?

Young-earth creationism has no real answer for why plant and animal fossils are consistently arrayed in ascending order, how there could be an ecology with no plant or animal death, how light from distant stars reached earth in 6,000 years, how there could be light and plant life without the sun, how all the species fit in the ark or why they rapidly differentiated afterward (and have since essentially stopped), and so on. To escape critique, some invoke *deus ex machina*, a special creation situation. They also insist on an inflexibly literal hermeneutic, even where that causes inter-biblical contradictions. That same hermeneutic centuries ago caused some to reject Galileo, concluding that telescopes deceive.

Various versions of old-earth creationism are presented below and critiqued. Some seek to find a scientific viewpoint from within Genesis, which no reader would have understood before the mid-twentieth century. Others seek to read Genesis unencumbered by this distinctively modern outlook, and recover an ancient understanding of creation.

Original Chaos

The "Gap" theory supposes that the vast majority of earth history happened between the first two verses of Genesis. Instead of reading, "the earth was formless and void," Gap theorists read, "the earth became formless and void." By this reading, the original earth was not formless and void, but was created habitable (Isa. 45:18). For some reason (through Satan's fall?) it disintegrated and thus required a second creation. Then in six literal days, God refashioned it from billions-old material. But why would the heavenly luminaries—and light itself—need to be remade? The Gap theory advanced in the nineteenth century and was popular into the mid-twentieth century. It is out of favor today, largely supplanted by other models.

Some argue that the earth's formless and void state was its original state, which continued for untold eons. "Creation," properly speaking, is the imposition of a new order on this ancient wasteland, beginning with "Let there be light." Some old-earth theorists, operating with the presupposition of a long prehistory in Genesis, believe they have biblical support in an open-ended chaotic state.

Of course, the creation of light, plants, animals, stars, and so on came after this long era. Thus the fossil record, stuffed with the bones of creatures, cannot be a record of precreation events. Neither can starlight. The problem, for example, is birds—created on Day Five—found in the Mesozoic Era. Eons preceding Creation Week cannot explain this. What then is gained by this view? With respect to the goal of resolving science and Scripture and dating the known universe, the precreation chaos theories are much ado about nothing.

The Day-Age Theory

Another interpretive strategy is the "Day-Age" theory, where each day in Genesis represents long ages in real time. One version of this is the Progressive Creation template advanced by **Hugh Ross** (2004). When God said, "Let there be light," sunlight first penetrated the atmosphere of primordial earth. The sky cleared by Day Four, such that, if anyone stood there, they could have seen sun, moon, and stars. Day Five speaks of birds and "sea mammals." (Fish with gills would have come much earlier.) God continued to create and destroy species until the advent of man on Day Six. Since then, no new forms have arisen. In addition, the verses that say God "stretched out the heavens" (Isa. 42:5) refer to the cosmic expansion of the universe, known today by the observed redshift of galaxies. "No author writing more than 3,400 years ago could have accurately described these events and their sequence, plus the initial conditions, without divine inspiration" (Ross 2004, 235).

But as young-earthers are quick to point out, Genesis clearly speaks of ordinary (what we would call 24-hour) days. Each follows the Jewish calendar, beginning with evening and followed by morning. If the biblical writer intended something other than a regular week, why not say so?

Perhaps it is not so simple. Old-earth creationists argue that the Hebrew word for "day" can mean any number of things. Genesis 2:4 reads, "In the day that God created the heavens and the earth." There and in 5:1, "day" seems to be a synonym for "generations"—eons, long historical ages. Day Seven does not have an evening and a morning and seems to go on forever. Perhaps each of the days also continues on. There was no sun during the first three days, so obviously those "evenings" and "mornings" could not be meant in a strictly literal sense.

Perhaps "evening and morning" is like "heavens and earth" or "springtime and harvest," a figure of speech meaning no time period *per se* but rather the idea of completeness—that is, everything God wanted to have happen in that "day" was accomplished. Thus there is plenty of "wiggle room" in the mornings and evenings to accommodate alternative interpretations.

One way of harmonizing an old cosmos with six literal days is to employ Einstein's theory of relativity. In a strong gravitational field or at high velocity, time is "dilated," or slowed down. Thus, in the gigayears it took for the universe to develop, only six 24-hour days may have occurred relative to some universal frame of reference. (Some young-earth creationists also gravitate to aspects of this approach.)

Toward a Non-Scientific Reading

Young-earthers calculate a short period of human history largely on the basis of a strictly literal understanding of the biblical genealogies. The genealogies of Genesis 5 and 11 add up to fewer than 2,000 years between Adam and Abraham. But Matthew 1:8–9 lists kings in Jesus's line, skipping three generations (1 Chr. 3:10–13). This allows a well-balanced history with three panels of 14 sample generations each—purposely sacrificing historical detail for literary design. But can this method convert 2,000 years into 40,000 or even 130,000 years?

Genesis 10 records humanity spreading out after the flood, developing the great ancient civilizations. By the time of Abraham, the distinctive cultures and languages of Egypt, Babylon, Assyria, and Canaan had developed. Noah's era, the post-flood situation, was long gone. The new era, characterized by diverse nations, had arisen.

But this history is completely undermined if the genealogies are used to calculate the age of the earth, creating the illusion that between Noah and Abraham not one person had died. A young-earth approach to Genesis 11 results in Noah still living when Abraham was born. Obviously, this is not the impression the narrative wants to make. Such a use of the genealogies subverts the Table of Nations (see Gen. 10).

It is better to allow that the genealogies select representatives from the past that are merely illustrative—despite details of birth, death, siring, and naming, that seem an unbroken chain from father to son. They may leap great durations of time. (Genesis 4:22 telescopes antediluvian bronze and iron innovation to one generation, which in postdiluvian history were separated by two millennia.) The original audience probably knew the genealogies in Genesis were conventionalized. Matthew's stylizing was not unusual. (Also, the genealogies only suggest how long humans have existed—not the whole universe.)

Even so, no Israelite reader would have seen in the text a gap of millions of millennia, an expanding universe, punctuated evolution in progressive epochs, or relativistic time dilation. Modern science was unknown to the Hebrews and cannot reasonably be expected in Genesis. Young-earth proponents are correct to critique these attempts to modernize Genesis.

Finding a Theological Message in Genesis 1

But some old-earth approaches consider that science and Scripture do not answer the same sort of questions, and thus one can have an old earth and affirm Genesis also. Answers from Genesis are of one sort, while answers from the physical sciences are quite another. The "Framework Hypothesis" is one such approach. The days of Genesis are regarded as a literary device and not a sequence in time. The first three days set up the spaces or realms within which corresponding creatures are placed in the next three days. God separated light from darkness on Day One. But God also did exactly this again on Day Four. Thus Day One and Day Four are not separate in time, but actually describe the same creative act. Creation week is not describing a succession of events at all, but is using the artificial schema of a week to describe God creating all things decently and in order, culminating on the seventh day. Israelite readers would have seen this and read it accordingly.

Against the background of Genesis are all of the creation accounts of Israel's pagan contemporaries. These mythologies describe creation as the result of cosmic struggle. Although one or another warlike deity might achieve prominence, no single deity—not even the original parents of the gods—was alone responsible for the present shape of the universe. Against this background, it is clear that one significant theological assertion in Genesis is that God alone is Creator and the world works according to his design (see **Biblical Cosmology**).

The ancient creation myths often involve the building of a powerful god's dwelling place. "Without hesitation the ancient reader would conclude that [Genesis 1] is a temple text and that day seven is the most important of the seven days" (Walton 2009, 71). Genesis 1 can be read as a stylized account of the building of God's cosmic temple. God rested on the seventh day. The place of his rest is his temple, the whole of creation (Isa. 66:1). The seven days move thematically through the creation of time and space, filling it with life, culminating in mankind, finally with God himself resting there, sanctifying it (Gen. 2:3).

If this sort of theological doctrine is expected, as opposed to a scientific treatment, then of course the reader can affirm the message of Genesis while also endorsing the scientific consensus of an old earth. Genesis answers who, what, and why; nature tells us how and when.

In the pre-scientific history of the church, interpretations of Genesis tended to read it as having such a spiritual message. In **Augustine**'s *Literal Interpretation of Genesis* (c. AD 394), "Let there be light" meant that God converted and enlightened heaven and earth and made the angels. Augustine believed in instantaneous creation, in fact, based in part on Genesis 2:4, which literally states that God created heaven and earth in a day.

According to the documentary hypothesis and subsequent source critical theory, the first chapter of Genesis is a post-exilic addition. If this is correct, then before the exile, Israel's sacred text may have begun, "In the day that God created heaven and earth ...," with no hint of a seven-day period. Thus Creation Week, added later, would have been interpreted harmoniously with the already established single-day creation enshrined in the pre-exilic Law of Moses.

Augustine's general interpretative method was highly influential, seen reflected in lights such as the Venerable Bede (c. 673–735) and Anselm (c. 1033–1109). Versions of the framework hypothesis can be seen as early as the twelfth century and were advanced by **Thomas Aquinas** (1225–74).

The New Testament seems to have less interest in what Genesis meant to its original Hebrew audience, or as a story in its own right. Instead of interpreting Genesis per se, passages from Genesis are cited to explain aspects of the Gospel.

Paul explicitly says he treats Sarah and Hagar allegorically (Gal. 4:24), and he calls Adam a "type" of Christ (Rom. 5:14). Thus Adam, fashioned from dust (Gen. 2:7), is interesting to Paul as an illustration of Christ and the resurrection (1 Cor. 15:42–49). Adam is called the "son of God" in Luke's stylized genealogy of 77 generations (3:38). This is as far as Luke goes in describing Adam's origins. Paul calls Genesis 2:23 a "profound mystery" about Christ and the church (Eph. 5:32). In day 1, Paul does not see the big bang, light shining through aerosol, time starting up, infusion of energy into the earth, or any other physical process. Instead, he says that "Let light shine out of darkness" relates to the light of the gospel that shines in the hearts of Christians (2 Cor. 4:6).

The writer of Hebrews does not find the seventh day significant as a calendar day, but as a state of being, the Sabbath rest that believers always have in Christ (Heb. 4:1–11). Even "In the beginning" is reassigned to Jesus (John 1:1–14). So a methodology that discovers in the first chapters of Genesis great truths about the Creator, the Gospel, and implications for faith, apart from any reference to modern science, has a model in how New Testament authors referenced Genesis.

It is this brand of old-earth creationism that ultimately satisfies. It exalts the Creator and finds a theological message that the Hebrews would have understood and modern believers can still affirm, while leaving the question of technical detail to the scientists who study such things.

George Schwab

REFERENCES AND RECOMMENDED READING

Ross, Hugh. 2004. *A Matter of Days*. Colorado Springs: NavPress.
Walton, John H. 2009. *The Lost World of Genesis One*. Downers Grove, IL: InterVarsity Press.
Young, Davis. 1982. *Christianity and the Age of the Earth*. Grand Rapids: Zondervan.

↰ CREATIONISM, YOUNG-EARTH (Critical View).

Two primary questions concern us when evaluating the young-earth creationist (YEC) position on the relationship between Scripture and science. The first is whether it is the right way to understand the Bible and, if not, whether a better way is available. This piece will argue that young-earth creationism seriously misunderstands the nature of the biblical account of creation and that another approach is necessary. The second question is whether YEC assumptions offer a tenable approach to doing science. As we shall see, they do not.

Evangelicals share the belief that all of Scripture is inspired by God and—when properly interpreted—is completely trustworthy and authoritative in all it teaches. The key question is one of proper interpretation, which explains the many doctrinal differences among Christians today. These differences are possible even when sound principles of interpretation are followed. Unfortunately, young-earth literalism ignores both the ancient Near Eastern context of biblical **revelation** and the interpretive significance inherent in ancient Hebrew literary devices, social conventions, and literary genres, especially as these relate to the unfolding narrative of salvation history and the broader canonical context by which New Testament theology illuminates our understanding of the Old Testament.

Creation in the Context of History

The biblical creation account and history of humanity in Genesis 1–11, which leads into the story of Abraham and his descendants as progenitors of the Hebrew people and the nation of Israel, was not given in a historical vacuum. It

functions as a theological polemic responding to the polytheistic cosmogonies, cosmologies, and theogonies of the surrounding ancient Near Eastern cultures in the middle of the second millennium BC. It is therefore no surprise that biblical cosmography, as understood by the original recipients of revelation, is ancient Near Eastern in structure. Rather than burdening the ancient Israelites with cosmological details they would not have understood and did not need for theological purposes, God accommodated the cosmological conceptions of that time and place, using them to reveal his identity and purposes in history. The Bible provides a phenomenological description of creation—that is, an account and interpretation of what human beings saw and understood from within their historically and geographically situated perspective.

Let's explore the significance of this in more detail. The first recorded understanding that the earth is spherical dates to Greek antiquity in the sixth or fifth century BC and is attributed variously to Pythagoras, Parmenides, or Hesiod. In the third century BC, Aristarchus of Samos was the first to hypothesize that the earth orbited the sun, but broad recognition of this truth had to await the work of **Copernicus**, **Kepler**, **Galileo**, and Newton almost 2,000 years later. Noting this, we may fairly ask whether the biblical authors believed the earth was spherical and orbited the sun. The answer is that insofar as they even raised such questions, they did not. God spoke to them in a broad Mesopotamian context where the earth was described as a flat disk surrounded by ocean beneath a hemispherical sky.

While it is unclear how much of this the ancient Hebrews took literally (Collins 2006, 260–65), it is clear that we see this cosmography reflected in the Bible. After the opening merism (Gen. 1:1) in which God creates "the heavens and the earth" (i.e., everything that exists), God goes to work forming the earth out of a watery chaos ("the deep" in Gen. 1:2). After creating light and separating it from darkness, God creates a dome (Heb., *raqîaʿ*) that splits the deep in two, with waters above and below the dome (Gen. 1:6–7). This picture of God creating and splitting primordial waters is a theological corrective to creation myths like the Babylonian ***Enuma Elish***, which predates Genesis. *Enuma Elish* divinizes the primeval waters as the god Tiamat, whom the god Marduk slays, splitting her body in two and forming the earth with one half and the sky with the other.

In the biblical corrective, the deification of the primal waters and the battle among nature gods is rejected. The one true God, who is prior to and separate from his creation, brings into being all there is. The primeval waters he creates are subject to his command, and he splits them in two to bring order to chaos and create a home for living things (see Parry 2014 for a good discussion of biblical cosmography in its ancient cultural context; see also Arnold and Beyer 2002; Enns 2005, 2014; Godawa 2011; Lamoureux 2008, 105–47; Seely 1991, 1992, 1997; and Walton 2006; Collins 2006, 249–78 tempers this discussion).

Read literally, the "heavens and the earth" in the biblical account are made from these primordial waters and further partitioned by God. The **firmament** or sky dome (*raqîaʿ*) dividing the waters is supported by the "pillars of the heavens" (see 2 Sam. 22:8; Job 26:10–11) and also divides the biblical heavens (*shâmayim*) into the space below the dome and the space above it. Set in the sky dome are the sun, moon, and stars (Gen. 1:17; Ps.19:4b–6). Immediately over the sky dome are the "waters above the heavens" (Gen. 1:6–8; Ps. 148:3–4), and above these waters are the highest heavens, the dwelling place of God (Deut. 26:15; 1 Kings 8:27, 30, 39; 2 Chron. 30:27; Pss. 104:2–3; 115:16; Lam. 3:66). The sky dome also contains "gates" or "doors" or "windows" (Gen. 7:11b; 8:2; 28:17; Ps. 78:23–25). It is these windows that are opened in the biblical account of Noah's flood to inundate the earth with waters from above the sky dome (Gen. 7:11). These windows are then closed to bring an end to the flooding (Gen. 8:2). Below the sky dome is the heaven across which birds fly and in which weather transpires (Gen. 1:20; 8:2; Josh. 10:11; Job 38:28–29; Ps. 147:8; Isa. 55:9–11).

The waters below the heavens are then gathered into one place at God's command, causing the dry land to appear (Gen. 1:9–10; 2 Peter 3:5) and forming the circle of the earth in the midst of the ocean (Job 26:10; Prov. 8:27–29; Isa. 40:21–22). This expanse of land is flat (Job 28:24; 37:3; 38:13; Ps. 65:5; Isa. 11:12; Jer. 16:19; Dan. 4:10–11; Acts 13:47; Rev. 7:1; consider also the implications of Matt. 4:8 and Rev. 1:7) and supported over the nether deep by pillars that serve as its foundation (1 Sam 2:8; 2 Sam. 22:16; Job 9:6; 38:4; Pss. 75:3; 104:5). The earth, so established, is held in place by God and cannot be moved (1 Chron. 16:30; Pss. 93:1; 96:10; 104:5). Beneath the land are the waters under the earth (Ex. 20:4; Deut. 5:8; Pss. 24:1–2; 33:7; 136:6; Prov. 8:27–29), from which arise the fountains of the deep that spring forth during Noah's flood (Gen. 7:11) and are subsequently closed (Gen. 8:2). Finally, in the uttermost depths of the earth by its pillars is Sheol, the realm of the dead (Deut. 32:22; Job 11:7–8; 26:5–6; Ps. 71:20; Prov. 9:18;

Amos 9:2) and the deepest correlate of the highest heaven that is God's dwelling place (Ps. 139:8; Isa. 7:11).

Given the knowledge of geography at that time and a phenomenological perspective rooted in appearances and responding to ancient paganism, we can understand why biblical cosmography, as the ancient Israelites spoke of it, took this form. Again, just how literally the ancient Hebrews took this world picture is debatable (Collins 2006, 263–65); it is a religious cosmography communicating a **worldview**, not a scientific description of the universe's constitution.

Nonetheless, the YEC approach is to read selective portions of this world picture as literal and a basis for science. YEC interpreters almost universally reject: (1) geocentrism; (2) the idea that the earth is flat and rests on pillars that support it over still extant primordial waters; (3) the conception that the sun, moon, and stars are embedded in a solid sky dome overhead; (4) the idea that this sky dome is itself supported by pillars; (5) the idea that primordial waters not exhausted by the Noahic flood still remain above the sky dome; (6) the conception that the heaven God inhabits is literally located above the celestial waters; and (7) the idea that a netherworld of the dead occupies the very bowels of the earth at the base of its pillars.

While dismissing these cosmological constructs as metaphorical, YEC interpreters nevertheless maintain: (1) a literal 24-hour understanding of the creation days; (2) the idea that the sun, moon and stars (i.e., the rest of the universe) were created *after* the earth on the fourth day of the creation week; (3) a worldwide Noahic flood claimed to explain the phenomena of **geology** and **paleontology**; and (4) the belief that all this happened in the last 6,000 years or so. This selectivity evinces a double standard. Consistency demands either literalness across the board or recognition that a genre-sensitive interpretation of sociohistorically conditioned phenomenological language grounds the truths about history and theology that God is communicating in Scripture. Common sense demands the latter.

To be clear, this recognition does not negate a historical core to the text. The biblical stories of the creation, **the fall**, and **the flood** are based on events that actually happened. But the highly stylized manner in which the opening chapters of Genesis present this history indicates the metaphorical nature of certain features of the narrative as it encounters and overcomes the pagan theogonies and cosmogonies in the surrounding ancient cultures. It is at this point—where historical-critical exegesis meets a broader theological perspective—that other hermeneutical options consistent with an old earth (the day-age interpretation, the framework hypothesis, and the analogical days interpretation) gain their traction (see Collins 2003, 2006, 2011; Futato 1998; Kline 1958, 1996; Rana and Ross 2005; Ross 2006).

Three Problematic Proposed Solutions

While the failure to discern ancient religious cosmography is bad, young-earth science, constructed on arbitrarily chosen aspects of this world picture, is worse (for a more detailed critique, see Gordon 2014, 162–69). Cosmologically, young-earth proponents must deal with the fact that light travels at a finite speed and took 13.7 billion years to reach us from the most distant objects in the visible universe.

Three YEC solutions have been proposed. The first is that light traveled millions of times faster at creation and has since slowed down (Setterfield and Norman 1987); the second is that the earth is in a gravitational well created by a nearby black hole and subject to general relativistic time dilation (Humphreys 1994); and the third is the "mature creationist" proposal that God created the light from distant galaxies already visible.

The first suggestion founders since there is no indication of variability in light speed, and the energy output ($E = mc^2$) from the sun would have incinerated the earth early on if it were millions of times faster. The second conjecture fails for multiple reasons (Conner and Page 1998; Conner and Ross 1999; Fackerell and McIntosh 2000); the easiest to understand are that light falling into a gravity well would be shifted toward the blue end of the spectrum rather than the red due to observed universal expansion, and that the measured cycles of Cepheid variable stars and orbital rates of distant binary star systems would be significantly different. We are not in a gravity well. Since the third option, that of mature creationism, involves more than just astronomical data, it will be confronted at the end of the criticisms of young-earth science.

Suggestions that the decay rate of the earth's magnetic field places an upper boundary of 10,000 years on earth's antiquity (Barnes 1973; Humphreys 1984, 1986, 1988) ignore fluctuations in earth's magnetic field strength (Muscheler et al. 2005) due to the dynamo effect induced by differential rotation speeds of its solid inner and molten outer core (NASA 2003) and field polarity having flipped multiple times. These polarity flips are confirmed by different magnetization directions of the ocean bed correlated with continental drift, the current rate of which is measurable by satellite and shown by **radiometric dating** to have been relatively constant for millions of years (Nelson 2015; USGS

1999). These observations also refute John Baumgardner's (1994) YEC theory that runaway subduction of oceanic plates pushed the oceans onto land to create a universal flood.

Young-earth creationism attempts to discount radiometric dating as inaccurate (DeYoung 2005; Slusher 1973) are also ill conceived. Deviation from the linear in an isochron plot of isotope ratios is a reliable indicator of any age-distorting contamination in a sample, and the fact that there are more than 40 different radiometric dating techniques provides more than enough resources for independent cross-checks of date determinations (Dalrymple 1994; Gordon 2014; Nave 2014; Wiens 2002; Young 1977, appendix; Young and Stearley 2008).

Geological and biological evidence also runs contrary to a global flood, both in terms of a source for the floodwaters and in terms of it having happened. We have seen that Baumgardner's (1994) subduction model fails, but the water canopy hypotheses (Baugh 1992; Dillow 1982; Patten 1966) and hydroplate theory (Brown 2008) are worse. Apart from the physical untenability of such hypotheses and their inconsistency with what we observe, the atmospheric pressures and temperatures associated with the existence and release of such waters would have sterilized the earth of all life (Deem 2007; Gordon 2014).

Furthermore, at no point in human history was the whole earth covered in water (Davidson and Wolgemuth 2010; Gordon 2014): (1) The stratigraphic layering of the Grand Canyon is inconsistent with a global flood, exhibiting instead multiple instances of "fining upward" of sediments only explained by numerous local floods over eons of time and independently corroborated by radiometric dating of the canyon's geological strata. These strata also contain massive layers of limestone that are never present in substantial amounts in flood deposits. (2) Salt beds hundreds of feet thick buried beneath tons of rock on the ocean floor of the Gulf of Mexico cannot be explained, as flood advocates assert, by the evaporation of Noahic floodwaters. These waters could not both evaporate to leave the salt yet remain in sufficient force to bury it under thousands of feet of sediment. (3) Evidence from yearly sedimentation in freshwater lakes like Lake Suigetsu in Japan, which goes back 100,000 years and is independently corroborated by radiocarbon dating for the last 50,000 years, shows there could not have been a global flood during that time. (4) There are currently anywhere from 3 to 5 million **species** of animals populating the earth (May 1988) and, if one adds **dinosaurs** and other extinct species, this number rapidly escalates.

That Noah's story cannot be read literally in many of its details is evident in that fitting seven pairs of every clean animal and one pair of every unclean animal aboard the ark with food supplies is mathematically impossible. Even minus the fish, there is not enough room on a hundred such arks—and what of freshwater fish that cannot live in salt water? This is not remedied by conjecturing that the animal species were restricted to representatives of major kinds. Micro-evolutionary differentiation into present biological diversity and dispersal around the world from one location would require a much longer time frame and leave a different paleontological record. We could multiply such counterevidences indefinitely, but it is clear that a global flood in recent history has no sound evidential basis. The Noahic flood was a local event that, from an ancient phenomenological perspective, covered the earth "under the entire heavens" (Gen. 7:19) understood as the visible vault of the sky (see Gordon 2014, 156–60 for a full defense of this interpretation).

Completeness demands mention of the "Omphalos hypothesis" (Gosse 1857) that God created the world a few thousand years ago with the *appearance* of age for immediate functionality. The oft-made objection that, by this standard, God might have created the world with our memories intact a few seconds ago illustrates how "mature creationist" hypotheses undermine any reliable historical inferences. The very same reasoning involved in defending the historicity of Christ's resurrection using multiple streams of historical evidence is also used in determining the age of the universe (13.7 billion years) and the earth (4.5 billion years) on the basis of independent streams of evidence from the natural world. Sauce for the goose is sauce for the gander, and rightly so, for basic to both inferences is a commitment to using our God-given rationality to discover and defend what is true. Beyond this, mature creationism still affirms a global flood after the creation of humanity, which is rationally untenable.

For better approaches to science within a theistic worldview, see the resources in the recommended reading (Collins 2003, 2011; Copan and Craig 2004; Dembski 1999, 2009; Dembski and Wells 2008; Gauger et al. 2012; Gordon 2013, 2014; Gordon and Dembski 2011; Holder 2004; Lamoureux 2008; Lennox 2007, 2011; Meyer 2009, 2013; Plantinga 2011; Rana and Ross 2005; Ross 2006; Snoke 2006; Walton 2009, 2015; Young 1977; Young and Stearley 2008).

There is good reason to think that YEC literalism regarding the creation account is untenable and that YEC science is impossible. For other and better ways of relating science to Scripture, see **Creationism, Old-Earth**; **Evolutionary Creation**; and **Progressive Creation**. Since educated non-Christians who come across young-earth advocates will equate inaccuracies about the natural world with the teaching of the Bible and thus be less inclined to give credence to the gospel, and since young Christians immersed in YEC doctrine who later discover its untenability may face a crisis that robs them of their faith, it is time for evangelical Christianity to move beyond such obstacles and pitfalls into a comprehensive integration of faith and scholarship. God has given us two books: the book of his words and the book of his works (**Two Books Metaphor**). Properly interpreted, Scripture and nature are not in conflict with each other, and Christians must proceed with grace and wisdom to discern how they are related.

Bruce L. Gordon

REFERENCES AND RECOMMENDED READING

Arnold, Bill T., and Bryan E. Beyer, eds. 2002. *Readings from the Ancient Near East: Primary Sources for Old Testament Study.* Grand Rapids: Baker Academic.

Barnes, Thomas G. 1973. *Origin and Destiny of the Earth's Magnetic Field.* ICR Technical Monograph 4. San Diego: Creation-Life.

Barrett, Matthew, and Ardel B. Caneday, eds. 2013. *Four Views on the Historical Adam.* Grand Rapids: Zondervan.

Barton, John. 1984. *Reading the Old Testament: Method in Biblical Study.* Philadelphia: Westminster.

———. 2007. *The Nature of Biblical Criticism.* Louisville, KY: Westminster John Knox.

Baugh, Carl. 1992. *Panorama of Creation.* Oklahoma City: Hearthstone Publishing, Inc.

Baumgardner, John R. 1994. "Runaway Subduction as the Driving Mechanism for the Genesis Flood." Institute for Creation Research. www.icr.org/research/index/researchp_jb_runawaysubduction/.

Blocher, Henri. 1984. *In the Beginning: The Opening Chapters of Genesis.* Downers Grove, IL: InterVarsity.

Brown, Walt. 2008. *In the Beginning: Compelling Evidence for Creation and the Flood.* 8th ed. Phoenix: Center for Scientific Creation.

Collins, C. John. 2003. *Science and Faith: Friends or Foes?* Wheaton, IL: Crossway.

———. 2006. *Genesis 1–4: A Linguistic, Literary, and Theological Commentary.* Phillipsburg, NJ: P&R.

———. 2011. *Did Adam and Eve Really Exist? Who They Were and Why You Should Care.* Wheaton, IL: Crossway.

Conner, Samuel R., and Don N. Page. 1998. "*Starlight and Time* Is the Big Bang." *CEN Technical Journal* 12 (no. 2): 174–94. http://static.icr.org/i/pdf/news/rh_connpage1.pdf.

Conner, Samuel R., and Hugh Ross. 1999. "The Unraveling of *Starlight and Time.*" Reasons to Believe. March 22. www.reasons.org/articles/the-unraveling-of-starlight-and-time.

Copan, Paul, and William Lane Craig. 2004. *Creation Out of Nothing: A Biblical, Philosophical, and Scientific Exploration.* Grand Rapids: Baker Academic.

Dalrymple, G. Brent. 1994. *The Age of the Earth.* Palo Alto, CA: Stanford University Press.

Davidson, Gregg, and Ken Wolgemuth. 2010. "Christian Geologists on Noah's Flood: Biblical and Scientific Shortcomings of Flood Geology." BioLogos Foundation. July. http://biologos.org/ uploads/projects/davidson_wolgemuth_scholarly_essay.pdf.

Deem, Richard. 2007. "The Water Vapor Canopy Theory: Why the Bible (and Science) Says It Is False." Evidence for God from Science. http://godandscience.org/youngearth/canopy.html.

Dembski, William A. 1999. *Intelligent Design: The Bridge between Science and Theology.* Downers Grove, IL: InterVarsity.

Dembski, William A., and Jonathan Wells. 2008. *Design of Life: Discovering Signs of Intelligence in Biological Systems.* Dallas: Foundation for Thought and Ethics.

Dembski, William A. 2009. *The End of Christianity: Finding a Good God in an Evil World.* Nashville: B&H.

DeYoung, Don. 2005. *Thousands … Not Billions: Challenging an Icon of Evolution, Questioning the Age of the Earth.* Green Forest, AR: Master.

Dillow, Joseph C. 1982. *The Waters Above: Earth's Pre-flood Vapor Canopy.* Chicago: Moody.

Enns, Peter. 2005. *Inspiration and Incarnation: Evangelicals and the Problem of the Old Testament.* Grand Rapids: Baker Academic.

———. 2014. *The Bible Tells Me So … Why Defending Scripture Has Made Us Unable to Read It.* San Francisco: HarperOne.

Fackerell, E. D., and C. B. G. McIntosh. 2000. "Errors in Humphreys' Cosmological Model." *CEN Technical Journal* 14 (2): 77–80. www.trueorigin.org/rh_fackmcin1.pdf.

Fokkelman, J. P. 1975. *Narrative Art in Genesis.* Amsterdam: Van Gorcum.

Frei, Hans. 1974. *The Eclipse of Biblical Narrative: A Study in Eighteenth and Nineteenth Century Hermeneutics.* New Haven, CT: Yale University Press.

Futato, Mark. 1998. "Because It Had Rained: A Study of Gen. 2:5–7 with Implications for Gen. 2:4–25 and Gen. 1:1–2:3." *Westminster Theological Journal* 60:1–21.

Gauger, Ann, Douglas Axe, and Casey Luskin. 2012. *Science and Human Origins.* Seattle: Discovery Institute Press.

Godawa, Brian. 2011. "Mesopotamian Cosmic Geography in the Bible." BioLogos Foundation. http://biologos.org/uploads/projects/godawa_scholarly_paper_2.pdf.

Gordon, Bruce L. 2013. "In Defense of Uniformitarianism." *Perspectives on Science and Christian Faith* 65 (2): 79–86.

———. 2014. "Scandal of the Evangelical Mind: A Biblical and Theological Critique of Young Earth Creationism." *Science, Religion and Culture* 1 (3): 144–73.

Gordon, Bruce L., and William A. Dembski, eds. 2011. *The Nature of Nature: Examining the Role of Naturalism in Science.* Wilmington, DE: ISI Books.

Gosse, Philip. 1857. *Omphalos: An Attempt to Untie the Geological Knot.* London: John Van Voorst.

Green, William Henry. 1890. "Primeval Chronology." *Bibliotheca Sacra* 47:285–303.

Ham, Ken. 2013. *Six Days: The Age of the Earth and the Decline of the Church.* Green Forest, AR: Master.

Hayes, John H., and Carl R. Holladay. 1982. *Biblical Exegesis: A Beginner's Handbook.* Atlanta: John Knox.

Hays, Christopher M., and Christopher B. Ansberry, eds. 2013. *Evangelical Faith and the Challenge of Historical Criticism.* Grand Rapids: Baker Academic.

Herder, Johann G. 1833. *The Spirit of Hebrew Poetry.* Vol. 1. Trans. J. Marsh. Burlington, VT: Edward Smith.

Hill, Carol A. 2003. "Making Sense of the Numbers of Genesis." *Perspectives on Science and the Christian Faith* 55 (4): 239–51.

Hoffmeier, James K., and Magary, Dennis R., eds. 2012. *Do Historical Matters Matter to Faith? A Critical Appraisal of Modern and Postmodern Approaches to Scripture.* Wheaton, IL: Crossway.

Holder, Rodney D. 2004. *God, the Multiverse, and Everything: Modern Cosmology and the Argument from Design.* Burlington, VT: Ashgate.

Humphreys, D. Russell. 1984. "The Creation of Planetary Magnetic Fields." *Creation Research Society Quarterly* 21:140–49.

———. 1986. "Reversals of the Earth's Magnetic Field during the Genesis Flood." *Proceedings of the First International Conference on Creationism* 2:113–26.

———. 1988. "Has the Earth's Magnetic Field Ever Flipped?" *Creation Research Society Quarterly* 25:130–37.

———. 1994. *Starlight and Time: Solving the Puzzle of Distant Starlight in a Young Universe.* Green Forest, AR: Master.

Kitchen, K. A. 2003. *On the Reliability of the Old Testament.* Grand Rapids: Eerdmans.

Kline, Meredith. 1958. "Because It Had Not Rained." *Westminster Theological Journal* 20:146–57.

———. 1996. "Space and Time in the *Genesis* Cosmogony." *Perspectives on Science and Christian Faith* 48 (1): 2–15.

Krentz, Edgar. 1975. *The Historical-Critical Method.* Philadelphia: Fortress.

Lamoureux, Denis O. 2008. *Evolutionary Creation: A Christian Approach to Evolution.* Eugene, OR: Wipf and Stock.

Lang, Bernhard. 1985. "Non-Semitic Deluge Stories and the Book of Genesis: A Bibliographic and Critical Survey." *Anthropos* 80:605–16.

Lennox, John C. 2007. *God's Undertaker: Has Science Buried God?* Oxford: Lion Hudson.

———. 2011. *Seven Days That Divide the World: The Beginning According to Genesis and Science.* Grand Rapids: Zondervan.

Longman, Tremper, III. 1987. *Literary Approaches to Biblical Interpretation.* Grand Rapids: Zondervan.

———. 2005. *How to Read Genesis.* Downers Grove, IL: InterVarsity.

Longman, Tremper, III, and Raymond B. Dillard. 2006. *An Introduction to the Old Testament.* 2nd ed. Grand Rapids: Zondervan.

Madueme, Hans, and Michael Reeves, eds. 2014. *Adam, the Fall, and Original Sin: Theological, Biblical, and Scientific Perspectives.* Grand Rapids: Baker Academic.

May, Robert M. 1988. "How Many Species Are There on Earth?" *Science*, new ser., 241 (4872): 1441–49.

McCarter, P. Kyle, Jr. 1986. *Textual Criticism: Recovering the Text of the Hebrew Bible.* Philadelphia: Fortress.

Merrick, J., and Stephen M. Garrett, eds. 2013. *Five Views on Biblical Inerrancy.* Grand Rapids: Zondervan.

Meyer, Stephen C. 2009. *Signature in the Cell: DNA and the Evidence for Intelligent Design.* New York: HarperOne.

———. 2013. *Darwin's Doubt: The Explosive Origin of Animal Life and the Case for Intelligent Design.* New York: HarperOne.

Moreland, J. P., and John Mark Reynolds, eds. 1999. *Three Views on Creation and Evolution.* Grand Rapids: Zondervan.

Morris, Henry M. 1974. *Scientific Creationism.* Public School ed. San Diego: Creation-Life.

Morris, John. 2007. *The Young Earth: The Real History of the Earth—Past, Present, and Future.* Green Forest, AR: Master.

Muscheler, R., J. Beer, P. W. Kubik, and H. A. Synal. 2005. "Geomagnetic Field Intensity during the Last 60,000 Years Based on ^{10}Be and ^{36}Cl from the Summit Ice Cores and ^{14}C." *Quaternary Science Reviews* 24:1849–60.

NASA. 2003. "Earth's Inconstant Magnetic Field." NASA Science News. December 29. http://science1.nasa.gov/science-news/science-at-nasa/2003/29dec_magneticfield/.

Nave, C. R. 2014. "Radioactive Dating." HyperPhysics. http://hyperphysics.phy-astr.gsu.edu/hbase/nuclear/raddat2.html.

Nelson, Stephen A. 2015. "Continental Drift, Sea Floor Spreading and Plate Tectonics." Tulane University. www.tulane.edu/-sanelson/eens1110/pltect.pdf.

Noll, Mark A. 1991. *Between Faith and Criticism: Evangelicals, Scholarship, and the Bible in America.* 2nd ed. Vancouver: Regent College Publishing.

———. 1994. *The Scandal of the Evangelical Mind.* Grand Rapids: Eerdmans.

Parry, Robin A. 2014. *The Biblical Cosmos: A Pilgrim's Guide to the Weird and Wonderful World of the Bible.* Eugene, OR: Cascade.

Patten, Donald. 1966. *The Biblical Flood and Ice Epic: A Study in Scientific History.* Seattle: Pacific Meridian Publishing Company.

Perrin, Norman. 1969. *What Is Redaction Criticism?* Philadelphia: Fortress.

Plantinga, Alvin. 2011. *Where the Conflict Really Lies: Science, Religion and Naturalism.* New York: Oxford University Press.

Price, George McCready. 1906. *Illogical Geology: The Weakest Point in the Evolution Theory*. Los Angeles: Modern Heretic.

———. 1923. *The New Geology: A Textbook for Colleges*. 2nd ed. Mountain View, CA: Pacific.

Rana, Fazale, and Hugh Ross. 2005. *Who Was Adam? A Creation Model Approach to the Origin of Man*. Colorado Springs: NavPress.

Ratzsch, Del. 1996. *The Battle of Beginnings: Why Neither Side Is Winning the Creation-Evolution Debate*. Downers Grove, IL: InterVarsity.

———. 2000. *Science and Its Limits: The Natural Sciences in Christian Perspective*. Downers Grove, IL: InterVarsity.

Richards, Jay, ed. 2010. *God and Evolution*. Seattle: Discovery Institute Press.

Ross, Hugh. 2006. *Creation as Science: A Testable Model Approach to End the Creation/Evolution Wars*. Colorado Springs: NavPress.

Sarfati, Jonathan. 2004. *Refuting Compromise: A Biblical and Scientific Refutation of "Progressive Creationism" (Billions of Years) as Popularized by Astronomer Hugh Ross*. Green Forest, AR: Master.

Seely, Paul H. 1991. "The Firmament and the Waters Above. Part I: The Meaning of *raqîa'* in Gen. 1:6–8." *Westminster Theological Journal* 53:227–40.

———. 1992. "The Firmament and the Waters Above. Part II: The Meaning of 'The Water above the Firmament' in Gen. 1:6–8." *Westminster Theological Journal* 54:31–46.

———. 1997. "The Geographical Meaning of 'Earth' and 'Seas' in Genesis 1:10." *Westminster Theological Journal* 53:231–55.

Setterfield, Barry, and Trevor Norman. 1987. "The Atomic Constants, Light, and Time." Genesis Science Research. August. www.setterfield.org/report/report.html.

Slusher, Harold S. 1973. *Critique of Radiometric Dating*. ICR Technical Monograph 2. San Diego: Creation-Life.

Snoke, David. 2006. *A Biblical Case for an Old Earth*. Grand Rapids: Baker.

Sparks, Kenton L. 2008. *God's Word in Human Words: An Evangelical Appropriation of Critical Biblical Scholarship*. Grand Rapids: Baker Academic.

Stek, John H. 1970. "Biblical Typology Yesterday and Today." *Calvin Theological Journal* 5:133–62.

USGS (US Geological Survey). 1999. "Magnetic Stripes and Isotopic Clocks." http://pubs.usgs.gov/gip/dynamic/stripes.html.

Vos, Geerhardus. 1948. *Biblical Theology: Old and New Testaments*. Grand Rapids: Eerdmans.

Waltke, Bruce K. 1975. "The Creation Account in Genesis 1:1–3. Part 3: The Initial Chaos Theory and the Procreation Chaos Theory." *Bibliotheca Sacra* 32:216–28.

Walton, John H. 2006. *Ancient Near Eastern Thought and the Old Testament: Introducing the Conceptual World of the Hebrew Bible*. Grand Rapids: Baker Academic.

———. 2009. *The Lost World of Genesis One: Ancient Cosmology and the Origins Debate*. Downers Grove, IL: IVP Academic.

———. 2015. *The Lost World of Adam and Eve: Genesis 2–3 and the Human Origins Debate*. Downers Grove, IL: IVP Academic.

Walton, John H., and D. Brent Sandy. 2014. *The Lost World of Scripture: Ancient Literary Culture and Biblical Authority*. Downers Grove, IL: IVP Academic.

Warfield, Benjamin B. 1911. "On the Antiquity and the Unity of the Human Race." *Princeton Theological Review* 9 (1): 1–25.

Wells, Jonathan. 2011. *The Myth of Junk DNA*. Seattle: Discovery Institute Press.

Wenham, Gordon J. 1978. "The Coherence of the Flood Narrative." *Vetus Testamentum* 28, Fasc. 3:336–48.

———. 1987. *Genesis 1–15*. Word Biblical Commentary 1A. Nashville: Thomas Nelson.

Whitcomb, John C., and Henry M. Morris. 1961. *The Genesis Flood: The Biblical Record and Its Scientific Implications*. Philadelphia: Presbyterian and Reformed.

Wiens, Roger C. 2002. "Radiometric Dating: A Christian Perspective." American Scientific Affiliation. www.asa3.org/ASA/resources/Wiens2002.pdf.

Wright, N. T. 2014. *Surprised by Scripture: Engaging Contemporary Issues*. New York: HarperOne.

Young, Davis A. 1977. *Creation and the Flood: An Alternative to Flood Geology and Theistic Evolution*. Grand Rapids: Baker.

Young, Davis A., and Ralph F. Stearley. 2008. *The Bible, Rocks and Time: Geological Evidence for the Age of the Earth*. Downers Grove, IL: InterVarsity.

☞ CREATIONISM, YOUNG-EARTH (Supportive View)

Introduction

Young-earth creationism (YEC) is a diverse movement of beliefs related to the creation story in Genesis and **the flood** in the days of Noah.

Most contemporary young-earth creationists believe that the entire cosmos is less than 10,000 years old. Some young-earth creationists assert the rest of the cosmos is relatively older (following the majority of scientific opinion) and the earth or **life** on the earth younger. All young-earth creationists believe that **Adam and Eve** were historical persons and that the story of **the fall** has both theological and historical value. Almost all young-earth creationists believe there was a global flood in the days of Noah and that the story of the ark is historical.

Young-earth creationism does not preclude mythological, theological, or mystical further interpretations of Genesis, but asserts that the core of the Genesis story is historical. If all forms of evolutionary ideas and a relatively old earth were shown to be false, YEC would not be proven, merely shown to be possibly true. As a result, YEC has gradually shifted from being mostly "antievolution" to attempting to provide a positive alternative scientific, theological **worldview**.

History

The position of biblical writers on the idea of the age of the earth, creation, or the extent of the flood is contentious. The position of the majority of the church fathers is not. The late Fr. Seraphim Rose wrote an exhaustive survey of the opinions of the church fathers, with a special emphasis on the East, that demonstrates that most early Christian scholars and leaders assumed the earth was relatively young, that Adam and Eve were historical figures, that creation was "out of nothing," and that the flood was global (Rose 2000).

Key dissent from the consensus came from figures influenced by Platonism and the cosmological concerns found in his dialogue, the *Timaeus*. Platonists were, oddly, concerned more about the length of a creation stretched over seven days. Why so long? To a Platonist, such a long time to create seemed to challenge God's power and wisdom. As a result, certain of the Fathers, such as **Augustine**, were willing to read Genesis more metaphorically. On the other hand, interpreting even these Fathers is difficult for a layperson, as ancient writers tended to assume the historicity of the accounts but find them of little interest. They were looking for the theological and in particular the christological meanings of the Old Testament accounts. In any case, outside of a few Fathers such as Basil and Augustine (Augustine 1982), there is no doubt that most of the major figures of the church into the eighteenth century would have been sympathetic to YEC.

Young-earth creationism was not, therefore, born in the twentieth century, but modern YEC is an attempt by scholars and scientists to argue for or sustain a long-held Christian position. Many laypeople and theologians continued to prefer a generally young-earth point of view, but scientific defenses of this view had mostly vanished by the middle of the twentieth century. Skepticism about the general theory of evolution was fairly common in prominent evangelists like Billy Sunday, but also came from more mainstream figures such as G. K. Chesterton (Chesterton 2007). A positive alternative was not proposed (Numbers 2006).

Evangelical academics accepted large elements of old-earth ideas and even some parts of evolutionary theory. As robust a document as *The Fundamentals* included progressive creationist **James Orr**. This changed with an intellectually interesting defense of creation and an attack on evolution by figures in the Seventh-day Adventist movement led by **George McCready Price**.

By the 1960s, evangelical academics such as engineer **Henry Morris** (1918–2006) brought the historic YEC position and Price's geological ideas to a more mainstream evangelical audience. Morris and theologian **John C. Whitcomb** produced a book titled *The Genesis Flood* that spurred widespread popular support for YEC and a revival of interest in some academic circles (Morris and Whitcomb 2011).

Through the 1970s and 1980s, YEC was a popular, legal, and scholarly movement. Many of the popular organizations, such as the **Institute for Creation Research**, began to fade by the turn of the century as advocates aged. Legal cases failed to give creationism equal time in high school biology classes and were unpopular with many creationists themselves, who preferred to wait for more maturity in their movement. Early claims that merely looking at the scientific evidence with an open mind would cause anyone to adopt a YEC point of view failed. There were *reasons*

to assert a YEC view, but those reasons appeared as mere anomalies to someone working in a different explanatory framework.

Meanwhile, in the 1990s, many creationists in academia began to organize conferences such as the International Conference on Creationism with a more robust set of standards and under the leadership of a "new breed" of creationists such as Harvard-trained paleontologist Kurt Wise (Wise and Wood 2003), who criticized bad arguments in the movement and pressed for a more positive alternative to Darwinian ideas.

The movement also began to develop greater philosophical sophistication as contact with the **intelligent design** movement brought some reinforcements. **J. P. Moreland** wrote a seminal defense of creationism as science (Moreland 1999). The "father of the intelligent design movement," Phillip E. Johnson, refused pressure either to adopt a YEC point of view or to remove YEC proponents from the ID movement. YEC and ID philosopher Paul Nelson has been influential in bridging the gap between the two groups and increasing the sophistication of the YEC **philosophy of science**.

The more academic turn of YEC, with fewer debates and more research, led to less public attention and better quality work. Many schools, including Liberty University, have experimented with creationist research centers that have produced new and more scholarly work. This institutionalization of the movement got a popular boost with a Creation Museum that advances both public education in YEC ideas and research by scientists on staff.

Philosophical and Theological Differences in the Movement

The most prominent contemporary American young-earth organization, **Answers in Genesis**, takes a presuppositional approach to the debate. Scholars at the organization and popular speakers such as **Ken Ham** begin with their reading of Scripture and develop scientific theories out of these assumptions. They have been responsible for weeding out the more irresponsible arguments in popular YEC. While supportive of criticisms of evolution coming out of the intelligent design movement, they are critical of any scientific theorizing that does not begin with their interpretation of Scripture.

In contrast, writers such as Paul Nelson and John Mark Reynolds have proposed an "open philosophy of science" and have embraced the intelligent design movement (Moreland 1999). An open philosophy of science allows scientists to consider intelligent agency as a cause for events in every area of science including biology. An open philosophy of science is not *closed* to the existence of immaterial agents and is willing to concede that the scientific method may have important limits if such agents exist.

Contrary to the skeptic who would dismiss divine revelation as irrelevant and the presuppositional approach that begins in **revelation**, many YEC thinkers argue that reason and revelation exist in a biconditional relationship. Both would tell us the same thing if we could hear correctly, but in a fallen world certainty escapes us.

Revelation and scientific interpretation must be held in tension with each other. Our exegesis may be mistaken and must take science into account, but our interpretation of the data may be mistaken as well. Following other changes in the history of science, this YEC position posits that a YEC model will likely incorporate many of the useful insights of evolutionary theory. They concede that working scientists must continue to use evolutionary ideas until YEC has better theories for the scientists to use. False ideas may be useful, after all.

State of the Argument and Best Resources

Most evangelical scholars have found YEC scientifically unpersuasive and the theological case inconclusive. Most evangelical college science departments are not open to young-earth arguments or advocates. The popular YEC movement has shifted with the passing of the leadership from the mid-twentieth century with an increased focus on positive arguments for creationist science and less on antievolution. On the whole, this may have been good for the movement, for it has allowed time and freedom to develop better arguments.

Young-earth scholars argue that while inadequacies in mainstream scientific views do not prove YEC is correct, they do provide a rational basis to explore alternatives. Traditional readings of Scripture provide a sufficient motive to make continuing work in YEC important to evangelicals. Recent books like *Coming to Grips with Genesis* have attacked any purportedly biblical basis for reading the text other than one compatible with YEC (Ury and Mortenson 2008).

Why should a Christian be a young-earth creationist? First, the view has overwhelming support in church history. Second, the view continues to be exegetically defensible. Third, the scientific consensus is real, but adopting it does not mean that one agrees that it is *true*. A Christian in science has adequate reasons in theology and history to look

for an alternative set of scientific explanations that would preserve her or his preferred reading of Scripture. Not only does this out-of-the-box thinking not harm science, but it may generate new tools for science. This was certainly the case in the career of John Baumgardner. His interest in flood **geology** helped motivate him to produce computer modeling tools used by conventional geologists.

The YEC scientific community is tiny compared to mainstream scientific groups, but it has shown a willingness to engage in self-criticism. It develops competing theories and abandons ideas that fail. In short, it shows all the marks of a genuine academic community. If one wishes to do science, there is no evidence that one cannot do so with great success as a young-earth creationist. As critics of YEC like to point out, if the small community can make good on their project, then it would be a revolution in science.

Seventh-day Adventists continue to produce some of the best positive scholarship related to young-earth creationism at the Geoscience Research Institute. Leonard Brand has spent his career examining evidence of a global flood (Brand 2009). Scholars like Andrew Snelling and Steven Boyd have taken the arguments regarding a Genesis flood found in early authors like Morris and Whitcomb to a new level of sophistication (Snelling and Boyd 2014). The *Answers Research Journal* publishes periodic scholarship advancing a YEC model. Scientists like Todd Wood of Core Academy of Science engage in responsible scientific and popular work. Molecular biologist Georgia Purdom has founded and leads several creation study groups. If young-earth creationism is a pseudoscience, then it is a rarity—a pseudoscience that has grown more sophisticated over time.

Young-earth creationism continues to be divided about the necessity of their ideas to Christian faith. *Answers in Genesis* would concede that YEC is not "necessary for salvation," but insists that the YEC position is the only acceptable one for believers. Other YEC advocates argue their position is the best option for Christians but are open to other possibilities.

Finally, young-earth creationists are correct when they argue that if they can make their case, much of the contemporary academic criticism of Christianity would crumble. Darwinian theories may be logically compatible with Christianity, but traditional Christianity is not the most natural conclusion of adopting such theories. The development of a sophisticated alternative able to make predictions in the natural world would be a major achievement in the history of science.

John Mark Reynolds

REFERENCES AND RECOMMENDED READING

Augustine. 1982. *On a Literal Genesis.* Mahwah, NJ: Paulist.

Brand, Leonard. 2009. *Faith, Reason, and Earth History.* Berrien Springs, MI: Andrews University Press.

Chesterton, G. K. 2007. *The Everlasting Man.* Peabody, MA: Hendrickson Publishers.

Moreland, J. P. 1999. *Christianity and the Nature of Science.* Grand Rapids: Baker.

Morris, Henry, and John C. Whitcomb. 2011. *The Genesis Flood. 50th Anniversary Edition.* Phillipsburg, NJ: P&R.

Nelson, Paul, and John Mark Reynolds. 1999. "Young Earth Creationism." In *Three Views of Creation and Evolution,* ed. J. P. Moreland and John Mark Reynolds. Grand Rapids: Zondervan.

Numbers, Ronald. 2006. *The Creationists.* Cambridge, MA: Harvard University Press.

Rose, Seraphim. 2000. *Genesis, Creation, and Early Man: The Orthodox Christian Vision.* Platina, CA: Saint Herman.

Snelling, Andrew, and Steven Boyd. 2014. *Grappling with the Chronology of the Biblical Flood.* Green Forest, AR: Master.

Ury, Thane, and Terry Mortenson. 2008. *Coming to Grips with Genesis Biblical Authority and the Age of the Earth.* Green Forest, AR: Master.

Wise, Kurt, and Todd Wood. 2003. *Understanding the Pattern of Life.* Nashville: B&H.

CRICK, FRANCIS. Francis Harry Compton Crick (1916–2004) was born in Northampton in the United Kingdom, and at age 14, on a scholarship, he entered the religiously nonconformist Mill Hill School, a boarding school in North London. He had ceased attending church services two years earlier and tolerated the religious education that was part of the school. He excelled in **mathematics** and **physics** and completed his undergraduate education at University College London, and then continued as a graduate student there in physics. During WWII, the lab where he worked was closed and his graduate project was ultimately destroyed by a German bomb in 1941. In 1940 he joined the Royal Navy and successfully developed numerous new sea mines and mine-sweeping technologies.

With a growing interest in the physical basis of life, Crick left his stable military research position in 1947 to pursue biological research at the Strangeways lab in Cambridge. Under the auspices of the Medical Research Council, in 1949 he joined a team working on X-ray crystalography. He continued as a doctoral student in 1950, now as a member of Gonville and Caius College. Working with Max Perutz, John Kendrew, and Hugh Huxley in the lab, Crick mastered the skills of interpreting X-ray diffraction patterns of organic molecules and studying their structure through conjectural model building. James Watson joined the lab in 1951, and with him and Maurice Wilkins and Rosalind Franklin at King's College, London, they discovered the double-helical structure of **DNA** in 1953. For the achievement, Crick, Watson, and Wilkins received a Nobel Prize in 1962.

Crick completed his PhD and continued research on the role of DNA in the molecular structure of life. He understood that DNA was a code spelled out in four letters, and that it was responsible for organizing the 20 amino acids into proteins—the sequence hypothesis—essential to cellular function. He also articulated the "Central Dogma," which states that **information** flows in one direction, from DNA, to RNA, to protein. That is, proteins are the product, not the source of biological information, contrary to what had been previously suggested.

Having been a chief participant in the founding of the new discipline of molecular biology, in the late 1960s, Crick shifted his attention to **neuroscience**. In 1977 he retired from the MRC and took up a professorship at the Salk Institute in La Jolla, California, having enjoyed a sabbatical there the previous year. His main interest was human **consciousness**, and he began a collaboration with Christof Koch in 1981. He approached the question of consciousness through a study of the visual system and attention but did not conduct any experiments of his own and made only a modest contribution to the field.

Crick pursued his scientific research in a quest to penetrate some of the deepest human questions: the nature of life and consciousness. In this search, he rejected religion and **revelation** as sources of information. Rather, he regarded religion as an obstacle to knowledge, believing that all would ultimately be subsumed by physics and chemistry, as his earlier discovery of the role of DNA had suggested. "Vitalism," the view that life was a unique nonmaterial principle, was to him a carryover from a former time and should be expurgated from scientific thinking. This included eliminating any discussion of "mind" apart from the physical brain.

Jason M. Rampelt

REFERENCES AND RECOMMENDED READING

Crick, Francis. 1966. *Of Molecules and Men.* Seattle and London: University of Washington Press.

———. 1970. "The Central Dogma of Molecular Biology." *Nature* 227:561–63.

———. 1981. *Life Itself: Its Origin and Nature.* New York: Simon & Schuster.

———. 1988. *What Mad Pursuit: A Personal View of Scientific Discovery.* New York: Basic Books.

———. 1994. *The Astonishing Hypothesis: The Scientific Search for the Soul.* New York: Scribner.

Olby, Robert. 2009. *Francis Crick: Hunter of Life's Secrets.* Cold Spring Harbor, NY: CSH Press.

Watson, James. 1968. *The Double Helix: A Personal Account of the Discovery of the Structure of DNA.* New York: Penguin.

Watson, J. D., and F. H. C. Crick. 1953a. "Genetical Implications of the Structure of Deoxyribonucleic Acid." *Nature* 171:964–67.

———. 1953b. "A Structure for Deoxyribose Nucleic Acid." *Nature* 171:737–38.

CRITICAL REALISM. Critical realism (CR) is a **philosophy of science** with special application in three primary areas: philosophies of perception, the science and religion movement (SRM), and efforts to balance positivism in academic **sociology**. The term was first used by scholars at the University of Würzburg, starting in the 1880s, who were trying to build a philosophy and **psychology** of human perception based on their experiments with human cognition. The first significant philosopher to use the term in the English language was Roy Wood Sellars at the University of Michigan. Between 1908 and 1916, Sellars introduced and defended the concept in a number of important journal articles. In 1916 he published *Critical Realism: A Study of the Nature and Condition of Knowledge.*

Sellars may well have been aware of the earlier group of Germans, but he was breaking new ground as he sought for an **epistemology** that would be free of Kantian transcendental **idealism**, naive realism, and the popular pragmatism of the early twentieth century (see **Kant, Immanuel**; **Quine, W. V. O.**). While Sellars continued to publish, often on topics rooted in his critical realist approach, well into the 1970s, a series of other positions gained the spotlight of philosophical attention to such a degree that by the time **Ian Barbour** raised the issue again in 1966, many felt that Barbour had coined an entirely new term. In fact, Barbour raised the topic at a crucial moment, during a time of **paradigm** shift among theistic philosophers of **science** ready to accept and expand on the *instrumentarium* of the CR approach. From these beginnings grew the science and religion movement.

At this same time, another group of philosophers of social science were also ready to make use of this approach. In 1975 Roy Bhaskar published *A Realist Theory of Science*, and though he did not use the term until the 1980s, he rapidly became (especially after discussion with Margaret S. Archer) a leader in the application of the approach to the philosophy of science and especially to a new discussion of social science methodologies.

These three names—Sellars, Barbour, and Bhaskar—serve as standard bearers for the three main streams of CR. All three, to various degrees, stand in opposition to positivism, idealism, **instrumentalism**, and naive realism in their fields.

All three accept a Kantian skepticism as regards the uncertainty of human perception, but all three oppose its radical extension as an attack on our commonsense experience with arguments from logical coherence and instrumental necessity. SRM adds a supernatural Creator to the picture, allowing us to have greater epistemic confidence rooted in the Creator's implanting of the tools, categories, and machinery of accurate perception in the human mind (see **Reason, Argument from**). Theist followers of Bhaskar (Archer, Collier, Porpora) perhaps unconsciously bridge these two worlds by adding similar arguments to their discussions of social science method (Archer et al. 2004).

The differences between these three streams of CR can at least partially be explained by the movements against which they are arrayed. Sellars fought against pragmatists and early positivists (Bergson, **Whitehead**, Dewey). Bhaskar's followers opposed later versions of these but gradually redeployed the bulk of their work against the positivist inertia of the social science establishment (see **Logical Positivism**). Barbour, with a careful eye on the ongoing dialogue between realism and idealism, argued against efforts to divorce science from theology based on positivism, neoorthodoxy, linguistic analysis, and various branches of liberal theology. As a result, all three streams have argued, in specialized language, for several core ideas.

First, a limited realism. As Sellars put it, "We start from independent things, and not from precepts" (Sellars 1916, 3). Fifty years later, Barbour seconded this core idea in his *Issues in Science and Religion*. He argued that there is an objective reality "out there" that can be known by human observers, even if we may not be able to know it exactly. Mental construction and imaginative activity allow us to form theories, and some of these conform to observations better than others because events have an objective pattern (Barbour 1966, 172).

Barbour, along with a number of important SRM standard bearers like **Arthur Peacocke** and **John Polkinghorne**, argues that the fundamental source of all reality is the Creator God, the Ground of all Being. Physical reality is endowed with objective existence, even if it is contingent on the continual upholding of the Creator. They go on to argue that, because of this unity, science and theology have a deep similarity: both are methods of studying reality, and both are limited by the fallen humans that deploy these tools of knowledge.

Secular CR goes on to posit a "causal criterion of existence." If effects are registered, then their cause has objective existence. While this may not strike the physicist or the theologian as an important postulate, in the **social sciences**, such an idea has long been held up for attack.

Another set of CR battle lines is drawn up against the entrenched bias toward **empiricism** in the social sciences, especially in the United States. While modern physicists must wrestle with a strong bias toward instrumentalism, social scientists often hide behind the epistemic fallacy (if we can't measure it, then it must not exist) to sidestep the challenges raised by Bhaskar and his followers. Though social structures are not directly observable, Bhaskar would say that they have a real ontological existence because "their causal power establishes their reality" (Bhaskar 1998, 25). This is partly in response to movements in the social sciences that accept only measurable social facts or recordable "events." Among many sociologists, nothing else can be directly measured and nothing further can be posited (see **Sociology**). CR argues for a return to a more commonsense understanding of the underlying structures of reality. As Barbour put it, "intelligibility rather than observability is the hallmark of the real" (Barbour 1966, 170).

Of course, CR is not just about realism. It is also critical. First, all three movements are epistemically critical. All three recognize that all perceptions are affected by the human cognitive structures that attempt objective recording and analysis. This is also true about all instruments designed by humans to both collect and analyze data.

Second, CR adherents also accept that most of academic science and theology are both "theory laden" and "value laden." Claims of **objectivity** must be critically appraised. For social scientists (and theologians) this is even more difficult since the objects of their study (society, the **soul**, God, and the Bible) are so deeply connected with the **worldview** (and fallen nature) of the scholar. In fields like modern social science, a "critical" approach has often been associated with "progressive" values. From Comte to Foucault, many in the social sciences have uncritically accepted a philosophical naturalist social agenda that often infects the "Conclusions" sections of peer-reviewed journals and even creeps into the research design of otherwise careful projects (see **Methodological Naturalism**; **Naturalism**).

Third, CR practitioners reject efforts to discover "covering laws" of social behavior and effect (see **Hempel, Carl G.**). They tend to be very critical of any effort to bracket human agency, worldview, or personality from social analysis and prediction.

In all of its manifestations, CR maps out a middle ground between positivism and idealism and encourages a nuanced appreciation of human cognition and personality.

Frederick A. Schneider

REFERENCES AND RECOMMENDED READING
Archer, Margaret S., Douglas V. Porpora, and Andrew Collier. 2004. *Transcendence: Critical Realism and God.* London: Routledge.
Barbour, Ian G. 1966. *Issues in Science and Religion.* New York: Harper & Row.
Bhaskar, R. A. 1975. *A Realist Theory of Science.* London: Verso.
———. 1998 [1979]. *The Possibility of Naturalism.* 3rd ed. London: Routledge.
Losch, Andreas. 2009. "On the Origins of Critical Realism." *Theology and Science* 7 (1): 85–106.
Sellars, Roy Wood. 1916. *Critical Realism: A Study of the Nature and Condition of Knowledge.* Chicago: Rand McNally.

CULTURAL MANDATE. The cultural mandate is the divine injunction given to humanity in Genesis 1:26–28 to take care of God's creation and to draw out, work with, and benefit from its inherent potentialities as God's representatives on earth. The cultural mandate flows from the fact that humans are made in God's image. Humanity is given the privilege of taking care of God's creation because they reflect the **image of God** (v. 26). Analogous to the way God creates, humanity is called not only to "fill the earth" but also to "subdue [Heb., *kabash*] it" (v. 28), which suggests a certain resistance and need for taming.

However, this does not imply humanity's permission to exploit the creation for its own gain. On the contrary, humanity must preserve the creation as God's royal vice-regents who treat it with love and care as a gift from God. Humanity must not only subdue nature but cultivate and maintain it. Indeed, as Genesis 2 indicates, Adam was instructed to work and take care of the garden of Eden (v. 15). This is one way in which humanity glorifies God.

To fulfill this divine commandment, knowledge of how the natural world works is indispensable. Responsible stewardship requires such knowledge to obey God's charge. Hence science as a systematic enterprise for obtaining knowledge of nature is one proper means for responsible stewardship of the creation that contributes to fulfilling the cultural mandate (cf. Isa. 28:23–29).

This view is attested in Christian history. **Galileo Galilei** (1564–1642), in a 1615 letter to the Grand Duchess of Tuscany asserted the importance of studying the Bible and observing natural phenomena for obtaining knowledge of the creation, and argued, "The holy Bible and the phenomena of nature proceed alike from the divine Word, the former as the dictate of the Holy Ghost and the latter as the observant executrix of God's commands" (Galilei 1957). Similarly, Christian and theistic scientists such as **Robert Boyle** (1627–91) and **Isaac Newton** (1642–1727) believed that the study of the created world reveals the wisdom and intelligence of the Creator. They therefore argued that such design establishes God's providential relation to his creation. Hence "The entire enterprise of studying the natural world was embedded in a theological framework that emphasized divine creation, design, and **providence**" (Osler 2009).

Yet those engaged in scientific pursuits must exercise caution. Although the **Scientific Revolution** and industrialization have contributed to human flourishing, the ecological problems arising from this activity cannot be overlooked. Humanity was given dominion over creation as a divine representative. This instruction that is bound up with our being made in God's image indicates that dominion is an essential aspect of our human identity. Thus our destiny and the destiny of the creation are intertwined, and creation should therefore not be perceived as dispensable. Indeed, the very fact that God became incarnate in Christ gives significance to the creation, and reveals its indispensability to the human condition.

The cultural mandate is the mandate that humanity "dwell caringly in the world as faithful stewards of God, bringing forth the fruits of the created order in a way that sustains its well-being in honor of the true Creator king" (Lundberg 2011). Human flourishing is only possible when humanity and creation coexist in harmony.

Naomi Noguchi Reese

REFERENCES AND RECOMMENDED READING

Deane-Drummond, Celia. 2006. "Theology, Ecology, and Values." In *The Oxford Handbook of Religion and Science*, ed., Philip Clayton, 891–907. Oxford: Oxford University Press.

Galilei, Galileo. 1957. "Letter to the Grand Duchess Christina." In *Discoveries and Opinions of Galileo*, ed. Stillman Drake, 173–216. Garden City, NY: Doubleday. http://inters.org/galilei-madame-christina-Lorraine

Gunton, Colin E. 1992. *Christ and Creation*. Eugene, OR: Wipf and Stock.

Hoekema, Anthony A. 1986. *Created in God's Image*. Grand Rapids: Eerdmans.

Lundberg, Matthew D. 2011. "Creation Ethics." In *Dictionary of Scripture and Ethics*, ed. Joel B. Green, 189–92. Grand Rapids: Baker Academic.

Matthews, Kenneth A. 1996. *Genesis 1–11:26*. Vol. 1a. New American Commentary, ed. E. Ray Clendenen. Nashville: B&H.

Middleton, J. Richard. 2011. "The Image of God." In *Dictionary of Scripture and Ethics*, ed. Joel B. Green, 394–97. Grand Rapids: Baker Academic.

Osler, J. Margaret. 2009. "That the Scientific Revolution Liberated Science from Religion." In *Galileo Goes to Jail: And Other Myths about Science and Religion*, ed. Ronald L. Numbers, 90–98. Cambridge, MA: Harvard University Press.

Ratzsch, Del. 2000. *Science and Its Limits: The Natural Sciences in Christian Perspective*. Downers Grove, IL: InterVarsity.

Rolston, Holmes, III. 2006. "Environmental Ethics and Religion/Science." In *The Oxford Handbook of Religion and Science*, ed. Philip Clayton, 908–28. Oxford: Oxford University Press.

Wenham, Gordon J. (1986) 2002. *Genesis 1–15*. Vol. 1. Word Biblical Commentary. Nashville: Thomas Nelson.

D

DARK AGES. The Dark Ages is a term once used by historians to denote the early Middle Ages. It remains in common parlance today, but its use has largely been rejected by scholars.

Origins of the Concept of the "Dark Ages"

In England the Dark Ages were commonly supposed to begin in AD 410 when a plea for reinforcements by the province of Britannia fell on deaf ears in Rome. The period ended with the Norman Conquest of 1066 when England was drawn more closely into the affairs of continental Europe by the French-speaking King William I and his descendants. Elsewhere in Europe, the Dark Ages are said to have started with the deposition of the last western Roman emperor in AD 476 and to have ended with the crowning of Charlemagne as Roman emperor in AD 800. In the United States, it has also been common to use the term "the Dark Ages" to denote the entire Middle Ages from late antiquity until the Renaissance.

Francesco Petrarch (1304–74), an Italian scholar and early humanist, coined the term *the Dark Ages* in the fourteenth century. He was thinking specifically in literary terms, comparing the quality of Latin written in the ancient Roman Empire with that of the intervening period (Russell 1997, 65). In the eighteenth century, English historian Edward Gibbon blamed the decline in learning after the fall of the Roman Empire on Christianity, a view that no serious scholar now entertains. For more recent historians, the darkness of the early medieval period was signified by a lack of written records.

Civilization in the Early Middle Ages

Respectable arguments can be made that there was a sharp fall in the level of civilization in Europe following the barbarian invasion of the Western provinces of the Roman Empire in the fifth century. In some areas, such as Spain and Italy, invading Goths attempted to maintain the Roman administrative apparatus. However, the empire's fragmentation led to a collapse in trade and a general decline in living standards. The replacement of the Roman civilian elite with a caste of foreign military rulers also changed the complexion of society. Education and administrative ability became the

preserve of the church as the aristocracy concentrated on martial prowess.

Some areas, in particular the province of Britannia, suffered a near total collapse. The monetary economy ceased to exist in the British Isles, and even the knowledge of such basic **technology** as the potter's wheel was lost for two centuries (Ward-Perkins 2005). However, from this nadir, the Early Middle Ages were a time of slow but significant technological advance. Machinery, in the form of waterwheels, spread across Europe such that thousands were recorded in England in the eleventh century. Improvements to harness design made horses an efficient beast of burden, while the stirrup, introduced from the East, made them into more effective mounts for knights (White 1966).

During this period, it is not an exaggeration to say that the light of learning was preserved by the Catholic Church, which was the only institution of the late Roman Empire to survive its collapse. The church also ensured the continuation of Latin literacy. Almost all extant ancient Roman literature was copied and recopied by Christian monks who labored to preserve this pagan and secular heritage, together with exclusively Christian writing. As the barbarian tribes were converted to Christianity by Irish monks from the West and Italian missionaries from the South, European civilization was slowly rebuilt.

James Hannam

REFERENCES AND RECOMMENDED READING

Collins, Roger. 2005. *Early Medieval Europe 300 AD – 1000 AD.* 3rd ed. New York: Palgrave Macmillan.

Fletcher, Richard. 1999. *The Barbarian Conversion: From Paganism to Christianity.* Oakland: University of California.

Russell, Jeffrey Burton. 1997. *Inventing the Flat Earth: Columbus and Modern Historians.* Westport: Praeger.

Ward-Perkins, Bryan. 2005. *The Fall of Rome and the End of Civilization.* Oxford: Oxford University Press.

White, Lynn. 1966. *Medieval Technology and Social Change.* Oxford: Oxford University Press.

DARK MATTER AND DARK ENERGY. Although people typically picture the universe as a vast expanse of galaxies, gas cloud nebulae, stars, planets, moons, asteroids, and comets, these heavenly bodies make up only 0.27 percent of all the stuff of the cosmos. The remaining 99.73 percent has been labeled "dark matter" and "dark energy."

There are two kinds of dark matter. Ordinary dark matter (protons, neutrons, and electrons) interacts strongly with photons (light) but exists in concentrations insufficient to emit detectable light. Exotic matter (neutrinos, axions, and other particles) interacts either weakly or not at all with photons and, regardless of concentration, emits no detectable light. According to the latest data from the Wilkinson Microwave Anisotropy Probe (Hinshaw 2013) and Planck satellites (Ade 2013), ordinary dark matter makes up 4.48 percent of the universe and exotic dark matter, 25.23 percent.

One way astronomers can detect the spatial locations of dark matter is by observing its gravitational influence on light-emitting matter, a technique called gravitational lensing. Gravitational lensing measurements have revealed that galaxies are embedded in giant halos of dark matter. These halos play a significant role in maintaining a galaxy's structure. It now appears that certain features of these halos, such as mass, size, and shape, must fall within certain fine-tuned ranges to make possible the existence of advanced life in the universe and in our Milky Way galaxy in particular. Dark matter can also be inferred by observing the rate at which galaxies rotate around their centers.

Dark energy seems even more mysterious than exotic dark matter. Although it makes up 70 percent of the energy density of the universe, it was only first positively detected as recently as 1999. Since then, astronomers have devoted much effort to understanding and describing it. Current understanding says dark energy is uniformly distributed throughout the space-time surface of the universe, and its basic property is to expand the cosmic surface along which all the stuff of the universe is constrained. As the cosmic surface gets larger as the universe grows older, dark energy becomes progressively stronger in its capacity to accelerate cosmic expansion.

This expansion, or "stretching out," of the heavens is a relatively new observation, one that played a significant role in the development of **big bang** cosmology. Yet multiple Old Testament writers depicted the stretching out of the heavens (by God) as similar to the unfurling of a folded-up tent. So these passages of the Bible long ago may be interpreted as providing hints that we reside in an expanding universe. The Bible's oldest book, Job, also tells us that "darkness" is something more than merely the absence of light. According to Job, darkness is something that has a place, a residence, in the universe. Again, this comment may be a unique foreshadowing of the discovery of dark matter.

To date, dark energy yields what may be considered the most spectacular *measurable* evidence for the supernatural, intentional design of the cosmos for the benefit of life. For dark energy to drive cosmic expansion at the just-right rate so that stars and planets form at the just-right time and just-right place for advanced life, it must be fine-tuned to a degree that exceeds by far the best-known examples of human creativity and design. The second most spectacular evidence for divine design may well be the degree of fine-tuning in both the quantity and the specific locations of dark matter. Thanks to dark matter and dark energy, the heavens are shouting the glory of God more loudly than ever.

Hugh Ross

REFERENCES AND RECOMMENDED READING

Ade, P. A. R., N. Aghanim, c. Armitage-Caplan, et al. 2013. "Planck 2013 Results. XVI. Cosmological Parameters." In the Smithsonian/NASA Astrophysics Data System. March. http://arxiv.org/abs/1303.5076.

Hinshaw, G., et al. 2013. "Nine-Year *Wilkinson Microwave Anisotropy Probe (WMAP)* Observations: Cosmological Parameter Results." *Astrophysical Journal Supplement* 208 (October): no. 19.

DARWIN, CHARLES. The name Charles Darwin (1809–82) carries immense symbolic power in the modern world. Typically it stands for scientific rationality over religious credulity, free inquiry over enforced orthodoxy. In 1909 John Dewey wrote that Darwin had effected the greatest intellectual transformation of modern times. Though Darwin himself eschewed outright atheism, his name and the theory of evolution associated with him remain rallying points for unbelief.

Yet Darwin the man does not equate to the theory—or rather theories—that bear his name. The so-called Darwinian revolution of the nineteenth century consisted largely in the turn from creationism to *non*-Darwinian versions of evolution, despite the use of Darwin's name as the generic label. What Darwin did was to present a plausible theory of evolution backed by a mass of scientific detail—and to open wide vistas for new research and further theorizing in **paleontology**, embryology, genetics, biochemistry, and more. After Darwin, broader notions of evolution borrowed the prestige of science: society, culture, and religion now were viewed in terms of natural development from primitive beginnings, a tale of progress that encouraged the rejection or radical reshaping of Christian belief.

Though liberal Christians celebrate Darwin for substituting change for fixity (and so encouraging doctrinal and moral revision), and fundamentalist Christians deplore him as the fount of unbelief, cultural deterioration, and even genocide (the Darwin to Hitler trope), many mediating views of Darwin and evolution exist within the Christian fold (see **Darwinism**).

Biography

Charles Darwin was born February 12, 1809, in Shrewsbury, England, son of Dr. Robert Darwin and grandson of the colorful deist and evolutionist, Erasmus Darwin. Charles's mother was the daughter of the early industrialist and Unitarian Josiah Wedgwood of pottery fame.

Charles's father sent him to study medicine in Edinburgh, where he enjoyed collecting invertebrate specimens, encountered radical materialist ideas, and neglected his medical studies. At Cambridge he trained for the church, in hopes that a country parish would afford respectability, an income, and leisure to pursue his interests in natural science. At this time, he later recalled, he did not doubt "the strict and literal truth of every word in the Bible" (Darwin 1887, 1:45). He found his Cambridge studies uninspiring, except (ironically, in view of later developments) the work of **William Paley**, whose *Natural Theology*, with its famous watchmaker analogy, Darwin found a model of orderly reasoning and right thinking on religion. His love of collecting specimens continued, and on reading Alexander von Humboldt's *Personal Narrative*, he caught a "burning zeal" for science as romantic adventure.

Adventure beckoned in a position as captain's companion on HMS *Beagle*. On its five-year voyage down the coast of South America and around the world, Darwin collected 5,436 specimens, took 1,750 pages of notes, and kept a 770-page diary. His study of volcanoes and the formation of islands convinced him of the uniformitarian theory of **Charles Lyell**. The abundance of tropical forests inspired him, but bizarre, sometimes horrific particulars in the structures and behavior of life-forms unsettled his earlier notions of beneficent divine contrivance. The natives of Tierra del Fuego, trapped in a struggle to survive, appalled him. The world was powerful and beautiful but also cruel and violent.

Soon after his return to England in 1836, Darwin moved to London, entered leading scientific circles, and prepared his *Beagle* journals for publication. Darwin employed the best experts to interpret his specimens—in key cases (such as the Galapagos finches) overturning his first impressions. He found the idea of the mutability of **species** tantalizing, as it presented nature and nature's God in simpler, more sublime terms: God gave natural laws through which life-forms adapted to changing conditions.

Thomas Malthus's *Essay on the Principle of Population* pictured a struggle for existence in human society resulting from overpopulation. As Gertrude Himmelfarb (1959, 163) argues, what Malthus intended as an argument against infinite progress, Darwin made into a mechanism for improvement in the succession of life-forms. Given variation within a population, the struggle for existence would naturally favor those traits better adapted for current conditions, leading to gradual change in the species over time. This struck Darwin as a natural, undirected way of doing what breeders do purposefully—thus "**natural selection**."

Darwin waited 20 years to publish his theory of evolution, spurred finally by a paper by Alfred Russel Wallace. *On the Origin of Species by Means of Natural Selection; or, The Preservation of Favoured Races in the Struggle for Life* appeared in 1859. The public quickly pounced on its implications for human origins, though Darwin had avoided discussing them. At the British Association in 1860, Bishop Samuel Wilberforce ridiculed the theory of human brute ancestry, calling forth **Thomas Henry Huxley**'s spirited defense of science against clerical prejudice. By the time Darwin published *The Descent of Man* (1871), Huxley and others had already applied evolution to humankind, but Darwin shocked many by deriving all human mental and moral powers from animal precursors, placing us in every way on a continuum with the beasts that perish.

The tree of life for Darwin did not thrust upward to the production of man at the pinnacle; it bore many branches rather than a main trunk. Humankind was no more intended, and no further perfected, than any other branch. This decentering of humanity and ascribing of evolution to **chance** especially distinguished Darwin's theory. The American botanist Asa Gray tried to convince Darwin that natural selection still evidenced divine design, but Darwin would have none of it.

From about the age of 30, Darwin suffered chronic bouts of ill health. He retreated to a country house in Kent, carried on a voluminous correspondence, and died so revered that he was buried next to **Isaac Newton** in Westminster Abbey.

Interpretations of Darwin and His Significance

Widely divergent lessons have been drawn from Darwin's life story. Darwin was celebrated as the genius of the age, a great man whose penetrating mind changed the course of history. Alternatively, some have taken the very fact that he was an unremarkable and unpromising student to highlight the **objectivity** of evolutionary science: the data, not the thinker, produced the theory.

Historians of science and of ideas have long rejected the triumphalistic rendering of Darwin and his work, taking care to chart events and changes of opinion, and noting the complex interplay of scientific theory with social, political, and religious developments. They observe the striking parallels between Darwin's theories and his situation in Victorian Britain, a society characterized by overpopulation, fierce competition, the strong dominating the weak, and firm belief in progress. And they counter any reading back of later evolutionary understandings onto Darwin the man, or reducing the panoply of evolutionisms to Darwin's work.

Perhaps most contested has been the significance of Darwin's religious biography. His family background in freethinking, his conventional Anglican schooling, his wife's devout but Unitarian faith, his crisis of belief on the death of his daughter and subsequent ruminations on the orthodox picture of hell for unbelievers like his father and grandfather, and finally his confessed inability to perceive divine design or beneficence in natural history all beckon the interpreter to draw religious or irreligious lessons from his story.

Darwin's own accounts invite the reader to sympathize with his doubts, crises, and loss of faith. B. B. Warfield pictured Darwin's religious life as a tale of warning: Darwin descended gradually into unbelief as his religious sense atrophied from sheer disuse. A very different story gained wide acceptance among believers: that Darwin, saddened by the God-denying effects his theory had produced, renounced evolutionism shortly before he died and converted to evangelical Christianity. The Darwin family vehemently denied the story, and James Moore has thoroughly debunked it.

Bradley J. Gundlach

REFERENCES AND RECOMMENDED READING

Bowler, P. J. 1990. *Charles Darwin: The Man and His Influence.* New York: Cambridge University Press.
Browne, J. 1995. *Charles Darwin: Voyaging.* New York: Knopf.
———. 2002. *Charles Darwin: The Power of Place.* New York: Knopf.
Darwin, C. 1887. *The Life and Letters of Charles Darwin, Including an Autobiographical Chapter,* ed. F. Darwin. New York: Appleton.
Desmond, A., and J. Moore. 1991. *Darwin: The Life of a Tormented Evolutionist.* New York: Warner.
Himmelfarb, G. 1959. *Darwin and the Darwinian Revolution.* Garden City, NY: Doubleday.
Moore, J. 1994. *The Darwin Legend.* Grand Rapids: Baker.
Warfield, B. B. 1888. "Charles Darwin's Religious Life: A Sketch in Spiritual Biography." *Presbyterian Review* 9:569–601.

DARWINISM. Old Princeton theologian **Charles Hodge** (1797–1898) famously concluded, "What is Darwinism? It is atheism" (Hodge 1874, 156). In contrast, Chauncey Wright (1832–75), mathematician and philosopher of science at Harvard University, in his 1871 pamphlet defined Darwinism as metaphysically and religiously neutral. These are just two of the many connotations "Darwinism" has had historically.

Darwinism as a Scientific Account of Evolution

Sometimes Darwinism is used as a synonym for **Charles Darwin**'s (1809–82) scientific theory of evolution. **Thomas Henry Huxley** (1825–95), British biologist and fellow of the Royal Society, first coined the term for just such description (Huxley 1860, 569). In summary, Darwin's theory maintained that a population of organisms in a particular ecological niche faces a number of pressures (e.g., constrained resources such as food and shelter, competition for mates, predation, and disease). The offspring inherit slight variations of their parents' characteristics. Some variations that offspring inherit confer a slight advantage in navigating the ecological pressures, giving them a small differential reproductive advantage. This differential advantage is what Darwin meant by *natural selection*. These reproductive advantages would be passed on to future generations of offspring and eventually spread throughout the population.

The process of natural selection is one of Darwin's important contributions to our understanding of the natural history of organisms. Darwin also allowed for other processes to play roles in evolution, such as sexual selection, correlative variation, and the use or disuse of parts. Nevertheless, for any processes to produce new kinds of **species**, Darwin also had to assume that species could change over time. This assumption contrasted with the dominant belief that species were immutable. The idea that species were fixed and unchanging was rooted in the invariable nature of Platonic and Aristotelian forms (Wilkins 2009). Darwin's theory provided a means and rationale for species being modified over time, producing the tremendous diversity of life we observe.

In 1871 St. George Mivart, also a British biologist and fellow of the Royal Society, defined Darwinism as natural selection alone in his *On the Genesis of Species,* mimicking the title of Darwin's masterwork. Such a reduction of Darwinism—a shrewd though inaccurate rhetorical ploy—proved difficult for Darwin and Huxley to overcome even though neither would qualify as Darwinians under such a narrow construal.

Darwinism as Ateleological Evolution

By 1864 Huxley had developed Darwinism as a rejection of **teleology**, writing, "Far from imagining that cats exist in order to catch mice well, Darwinism supposes that cats exist because they catch mice well — mousing being not the end, but the condition, of their existence" (1864, 569). He clearly articulated Darwin's view that processes in nature such as natural selection led to species diversification over time. The emphasis was on natural processes rather than a designing hand, the latter being the dominant view of the nineteenth century.

Darwinism as Atheistic Evolution

In the 1860s, Darwinism also became associated with an anticreationist **naturalism** that may or may not have involved natural selection as the sole or even chief means for species transformation. This naturalism is what Hodge was objecting to.

While he accepted that some qualified form of diversification of species over time had occurred, Hodge realized that it was an empirical matter whether natural selection could account for such diversification. The heart of his worry about Darwin's ideas, however, was the ruling out of any divine influence in the workings of natural selection: "In using the expression Natural Selection, Mr. Darwin intends to exclude design, or final causes" (Hodge 1874, 41). Hodge had a particular conception of designer in mind; so by Darwinism he meant a metaphysical banishment of that conception of design and purpose from the workings of nature. What he pinpoints as "by far the most distinctive element" of Darwin's theory is "that this natural selection is without design, being conducted by unintelligent physical causes" (1874, 48).

Hodge was clear that no scientific investigations could ever lead to a sound conclusion that God was absent from working in nature. Such a conclusion could only come from atheistic assumptions. Hence Darwin's "atheistic theory" was objectionable on biblical grounds because it excluded design from nature (1874, 177). That species had changed over time and that natural selection might have played a part, Hodge thought were legitimate scientific questions that merited further research. Moreover, he thought these possibly could be compatible with Christianity so long as divine teleology and design were recognized as involved in

these processes. So there could be theistically sanctioned versions of evolution and atheistic versions. Darwin's, Hodge judged, was a species of the latter.

Benjamin Breckenridge Warfield (1851–1921) was another important Old Princeton theologian with complex views on evolution. Like Hodge, he believed that Darwin had fallen into articulating an atheistic account of evolution. So he often treated Darwinism in the same metaphysical sense as Hodge. At other times, however, Warfield seems to refer to Darwinism merely as Darwin's scientific theory minus the metaphysical trappings. Further scientific investigation would clarify and validate or invalidate Darwin's scientific ideas. Meanwhile, Warfield also had a sophisticated conception of how God worked through secondary causes (Noll and Livingstone 2000) and believed that in some form

> all that has come into being since [the original creation of the world-stuff] — except the souls of men alone — has arisen as a modification of this original world-stuff by means of the interaction of its intrinsic forces. Not these forces apart from God, of course … all the modifications of the world-stuff have taken place under the directly upholding and governing hand of God, and find their account ultimately in His will. But they find their account proximately in "secondary causes." (Warfield 1915, 208)

Warfield had a different conception of design from Hodge's, so it is not surprising that Warfield's response to Darwinism — and to evolution in general — is nuanced differently than Hodge's.

Darwinism as Theistic Evolution

There were Christians, such as botanist Asa Gray (1810–88), arguably American's leading and most recognized scientist in the nineteenth century up to his death, who argued that Darwinism should not be understood as atheistic, but theistic (1877, 266–82). James Dwight Dana (1813–95), a noted geologist and editor of the *American Journal of Science*, is another example of a Christian interpreting Darwinism theistically (Sanford 1965).

Following up these interpretations, some have argued that Hodge and Warfield (among others) missed either the implied or explicit teleology in Darwin's *The Origin of Species*. For example, at the end of his masterwork, Darwin writes, "There is grandeur in this view of life, with its several powers, having been originally breathed by the Creator into a few forms or into one; and that, whilst this planet has gone circling on according to the fixed law of gravity, from so simple a beginning endless forms most beautiful and most wonderful have been, and are being evolved" (1876, 429). However, care must be exercised when interpreting what Darwin meant by this vague reference to a creator. And while it is the case that Darwin uses language that might be easily interpreted as teleological, he was often clear in his correspondence that his theory was ateleological.

Darwinism as Worldview

The February 10, 1868, edition of the *Pall Mall Gazette* observed, "Everywhere 'Darwinism' has become a byword, which has gone far to replace 'materialism.'" **Materialism** was generally understood to be a worldview that eschewed the supernatural in any form and maintained that reality was only matter and natural processes. This was Darwinism as a worldview for all of life. Whether a term of derision or a badge of honor, materialism was controversial in the 1860s. Huxley held that it "is as utterly devoid of justification as the most baseless of theological dogmas" (1868, 162) and began to disassociate himself from his neologism, Darwinism, because of this association with materialism.

Meanwhile, Alfred Russel Wallace, who discovered natural selection independently of Darwin, also came to associate Darwinism with a worldview, but one on the opposite end of the spectrum from materialism. Wallace had converted to spiritualism as early as 1866 and by 1871 argued that "matter is essentially force, and nothing but force.... It does not seem an improbable conclusion that all force may be will-force; and thus, that the whole universe, is not merely dependent on, but actually *is*, the will of higher intelligences or of some Supreme Intelligence" (1871, 365–66, 368, emphasis in the original).

Darwinism Today

One of the lessons of the nineteenth-century history of Darwinism is how easy it was for writers to project their own larger concerns into the term. This cacophony of meanings is still the case with Darwinism. Mivart's (1871) reduction of Darwinism's meaning to merely natural selection gained and still has many adherents (aided by Wright's pamphlet critiquing Mivart's *Genesis of Species*). Stephen J. Gould (1941–2002), a paleontologist and evolutionary biologist at Harvard for many years, and Richard C. Lewontin, Alexander Agassiz Professor of Zoology and Professor of Biology at Harvard University, both characterize Darwinism as a scientific theory about the phenomenon of species change.

Yet Gould took it that Darwinism was evolution by natural selection alone, whereas Lewontin does not.

Richard Dawkins, evolutionary biologist and fellow of the Royal Society, argues that Darwinism is natural selection and that selection works only at the level of genes. In contrast, Darwin maintained that selection worked at the level of organisms or groups of organisms. Peter Bowler, historian of science, also has reduced Darwinism to natural selection alone in his work (e.g., 1992).

On the other hand, Dawkins also combines Darwinism as natural selection and worldview in one pithy sentence: "The logic of Darwinism concludes that the unit in the hierarchy of life which survives and passes through the filter of natural selection will tend to be selfish" (2008, 246). Phillip Johnson, a law professor for many years at the University of California at Berkeley and founding member of the **intelligent design** movement, harks back to Hodge's concerns, writing that Darwinism is "fully naturalistic evolution—meaning evolution that is not directed or controlled by any purposeful intelligence" (Johnson 1991, 4n).

Often in books and articles, authors use Darwinism with one or more of these meanings without indicating (or even realizing) that it is a complex term with a rich history. As it was in the nineteenth century, so it is today: People's response to Darwinism depends on their particular understanding of that term as well as how they understand design (e.g., engineering vs. directing an artistic production).

Robert C. Bishop

REFERENCES AND RECOMMENDED READING

Bowler, Peter J. 1992. *The Eclipse of Darwinism: Anti-Darwinian Evolution Theories in the Decades around 1900*. Baltimore: Johns Hopkins University Press.

Darwin, Charles. 1876. *On the Origin of Species by Natural Selection; or The Preservation of Favoured Races in the Struggle for Life, Sixth Edition, with Additions and Corrections to 1872*. London: John Murray.

Dawkins, Richard. 2008. *The God Delusion*. New York: Mariner.

Gray, Asa. 1877. *Darwinia: Essays and Reviews Pertaining to Darwinism*. New York: Appleton.

Hodge, Charles. 1874. *What Is Darwinism?* New York: Scribner, Armstrong, and Co.

Huxley, Thomas Henry. 1860. "The Origin of Species." *Westminster Review*, n.s., 17:541–70.

———. 1864. "Criticisms on 'The Origin of Species.'" *Natural History Review*, n.s., 4:566–80.

———. 1868. "On the Physical Basis of Life." In *Collected Essays* 1:130–65. New York: Appleton.

Johnson, Phillip E. 1991. *Darwin on Trial*. Downers Grove, IL: InterVarsity Press.

Mivart, St. George. 1871. *On the Genesis of Species with Numerous Illustrations*. 2nd ed. London: Macmillan.

Noll, Mark A., and David N. Livingstone, eds. 2000. *B. B. Warfield: Evolution, Science, and Scripture: Selected Writings*. Grand Rapids: Baker.

Sanford, William. 1965. "Dana and Darwinism." *Journal of the History of Ideas* 26:531–46.

Wallace, Alfred Russel. 1871. *Contributions to the Theory of Natural Selection: A Series of Essays.* London: Macmillan.

Warfield, Benjamin B. 1915. "Calvin's Doctrine of Creation." *Princeton Theological Review* 13:190–225.

Wilkins, John. 2009. *Species: A History of the Idea.* Los Angeles: University of California Press.

Wright, Chauncey. 1871. *Darwinism: Being an Examination of Mr. St. George Mivart's "Genesis of Species."* London: John Murray. Reprinted from the *North American Review* (July 1871), with additions.

DAVIES, PAUL. Paul Charles Williams Davies (1946–) is a British-born theoretical physicist, cosmologist, and astrobiologist. The bestselling author of science books that often pursue theological questions, Davies received the 1995 Templeton Prize, the 2001 Kelvin Medal, and the 2002 **Michael Faraday** Prize (from the Royal Society).

After earning his PhD at University College London, Davies conducted postdoctoral research under **Fred Hoyle** at Cambridge. After several academic appointments in England, Davies moved to Australia in 1990 to be professor of mathematical physics at the University of Adelaide. While there, he also helped found the Australian Centre for Astrobiology. Davies is currently Regents' Professor and Director of the Beyond Center for Fundamental Concepts in Science at Arizona State University.

Davies proclaims, "One of the great outstanding mysteries is the origin of life," opining that "nobody has a clue" how it happened (Davies 2006, 35). Davies recognizes that the key issue here is the origin of life's specified **complexity**: "A living cell is distinguished by its immense organized complexity … it is a specific and peculiar state of matter with high **information** content" (Davies 2007, 263). He notes that "the spontaneous appearance of such elaborate and organized complexity seems so improbable" (Davies 1995, 18–19).

To overcome these improbabilities, Davies looks to an as yet undiscovered type of natural law, reckoning that while "Contingency undoubtedly plays a large part in the details of evolution … the general trend from simple to complex … seems to me to be built into the **laws of nature** in a basic way" (54). Davies believes life and **consciousness** are fundamental emergent properties of nature, "outworkings of the laws of **physics**" (70). Hence he predicts that "given the right conditions, life and consciousness should emerge elsewhere" (71). Davies was a forerunner of the theory that life on planet Earth transferred from Mars and suggests Earth might host a shadow biosphere of alternative life forms.

To explain cosmic fine-tuning, Davies favors design over a **multiverse**: "To postulate an **infinity** of unseen and unseeable universes just to explain the one we do see seems like a case of excess baggage carried to the extreme. It is simpler to postulate one unseen God" (Davies 1993, 190). Moreover, "a multiverse is not a complete explanation of existence, because it still requires some unexplained physical laws" (Davies 2007, 250). Davies argues that design needn't mean an appeal to miracle: "*We* can contrive to produce highly non-random processes … without violating any laws of physics, so presumably a purposeful deity could also do this" (Davies 1995, 20). However, while Davies says, "**Occam's razor** compels me to put my money on design" (Davies 1993, 220), he avoids **theism** by appealing to John Wheeler's (self-contradictory) participatory universe model in which "the physical universe bootstraps itself into existence" (224).

Davies recognizes that this "falls short of a complete explanation" (225) and concludes, "The search for … a complete and self-consistent explanation for everything is doomed to failure" (226). Because he conflates the necessity of God's existence with a necessity of his actions, Davies thinks divine design is incompatible with the contingency of the universe (Davies 2007, 231).

Peter S. Williams

REFERENCES AND RECOMMENDED READING

Davies, Paul. 1990. *God and the New Physics.* London: Penguin.

———. 1993. *The Mind of God: Science and the Search for Ultimate Meaning.* London: Penguin.

———. 1995. *Are We Alone? Philosophical Implications of the Discovery of Extraterrestrial Life.* London: Penguin.

———. 2003. *The Origin of Life.* London: Penguin.

———. 2006. "Paul Davies forecasts the future," *New Scientist* (November 15): 35. https://www.newscientist.com/article/mg19225780-078-paul-davies-forecasts-the-future/.

———. 2007. *The Goldilocks Enigma: Why Is The Universe Just Right for Life?* London: Penguin.

———. 2011. *The Eerie Silence: Searching for Ourselves in the Universe.* London: Penguin.

———. 2013. "Are We Alone in the Universe?" *New York Times.* November 18. www.nytimes.com/2013/11/19/opinion/are-we-alone-in-the-universe.html.

Johnson, Phillip E. 1999. "The Fear of God: Review of *The Fifth Miracle: The Search for the Origin of Life,* by Paul Davies." Access Research Network. www.arn.org/docs/johnson/fifthmiracle.htm.

Website

Professor Paul Davies, ASU Department of Physics. Accessed September 8, 2016. https://physics.asu.edu/content/paul-davies.

Audio

The Guardian Science Weekly Extra audio interview, "Paul Davies on the Search for ET." www.theguardian.com/science/blog/audio/2010/mar/15/science-weekly-extra-podcast-paul-davies.

DAWKINS, RICHARD. Richard Dawkins (1941–) is a biologist, ethnologist, noted atheist speaker, author, and public intellectual. He was born in Nairobi, British Kenya, to Jean Mary Vyvyan and Clinton John Dawkins. Both of Dawkins's parents were science enthusiasts and sought to answer Dawkins's questions with scientific answers. Dawkins embraced Anglican Christianity until his midteens, being confirmed in the Church of England at the age of 13. Concluding that the theory of biological evolution by **natural selection** provided a more satisfying explanation for the **complexity** of **life**, Dawkins felt that it "pulled the rug out from under the argument of design," which "left [him] with nothing" (Hattenstone 2003). Dawkins thus permanently lost his belief in God.

As an Oxford undergraduate and graduate student, Dawkins studied under Nobel Prize winner Niki Tinbergen, earning his DPhil in ethology, the study of animal behavior. Dawkins's biggest scientific contribution was his popularization of the **gene** as the principal unit of selection, a view that he articulated in 1976 in his book *The Selfish Gene* (Dawkins 2006b) and his later book *The Extended Phenotype* (Dawkins 1982; see **Selfish Gene**).

Richard Dawkins has been an outspoken public critic of religion and is perhaps most famous for his internationally bestselling book *The God Delusion* (Dawkins 2006a), which was translated into more than 30 different languages and sold more than 3 million copies. Dawkins disagrees with the principle of **non-overlapping magisteria** (NOMA) put forward by **Stephen Jay Gould** and argues instead that the concept of God should be treated like any other scientific hypothesis. In *The God Delusion*, Dawkins puts forward a spectrum of theistic **probability**, from 1 (100 percent belief in God) to 7 (100 percent belief that God does not exist). Dawkins puts himself at a 6.9, representing one who thinks "I cannot know for certain but I think God is very improbable, and I live my life on the assumption that he is not there" (see **Probability**; **Bayes' Theorem**).

In 2006 Dawkins founded the Richard Dawkins Foundation for Reason and Science, headquartered in the United States. In 2008 his foundation supported the Atheist Bus Campaign, which raised funds to place advertisements on London buses bearing the slogan "There's probably no god. Now stop worrying and enjoy your life." In 2011 the foundation also launched The Clergy Project, which is an online community that supports clergy members who have lost their faith. Dawkins is also a patron of the British Humanist Association.

Dawkins's *The God Delusion* has drawn strong criticism from philosophers and theologians. Dawkins has participated in debates and dialogues with Christian theologians, including **John Lennox**, Rowan Williams, and **Alister McGrath**. Dawkins has also drawn criticism for his refusal to debate philosopher **William Lane Craig**, who is regarded by many to be one of the world's top intellectual defenders of Christian belief. Daniel Came, an atheist philosopher at Oxford University, criticized Dawkins's refusal to debate Craig as "cynical and anti-intellectualist" (Came 2011). Dawkins defended his decision not to debate Craig in an article published in *The Guardian*, stating, "This Christian 'philosopher' is an apologist for genocide. I would rather leave an empty chair than share a platform with him" (Dawkins 2011).

Jonathan McLatchie

REFERENCES AND RECOMMENDED READING

Came, D. 2011. "Richard Dawkins's Refusal to Debate Is Cynical and Anti-intellectualist." *The Guardian*. www.theguardian.com/commentisfree/belief/2011/oct/22/richard-dawkins-refusal-debate-william-lane-craig.

Dawkins, Richard. 1982. *The Extended Phenotype*. Oxford: Oxford University Press.

———. 2006a. *The God Delusion*. London: Transworld.

———. 2006b. *The Selfish Gene: 30th Anniversary Edition*. Oxford: Oxford University Press.

———. 2011. "Why I Refuse to Debate with William Lane Craig." *The Guardian*. www.theguardian.com/commentisfree/2011/oct/20/richard-dawkins-william-lane-craig.

Hattenstone, S. 2003. "Darwin's Child." *The Guardian*. www.theguardian.com/world/2003/feb/10/religion.scienceandnature.

☙ DAYS OF CREATION (24-Hour Day View).

One possible means of harmonizing the biblical account of creation in Genesis 1 with the prevailing scientific consensus regarding the age and origin of the earth is to see the days of Genesis 1 as something other than ordinary 24-hour days. In the medieval church, with figurative and allegorical interpretations of the Bible in abundance, the view that the "days" of creation were figurative and not literal was somewhat common (see **Science and the Medieval Church**).

However, since the Protestant Reformation, with its insistence on the supremacy of Scripture and a more literal understanding of the text, the predominant view until recently has been that the creation days were 24 hours. As Luther states, "We assert that Moses spoke in the literal sense, not allegorically or figuratively, i.e., that the world, with all its creatures, was created within six days, as the words read" (Luther 1958, 5), Luther likewise makes clear that the creation day was 24 hours in length (see **Science and the Reformation**).

Yet in recent years, with the increasing acceptance of an old universe and (for some) an evolutionary approach to origins, there has been a renewed desire to see the days of creation in Genesis 1 as something other than literal 24-hour sequential days. While some of these approaches treat the text of Genesis more carefully than others, all the interpretations ultimately fail to be convincing, as will be argued in the remainder of this article.

The Day-Age View

The day-age theory sees each creation "day" as a period of thousands or millions of years. So the six days of creation are "six sequential, long periods of time" (Ross and Archer 2001, 147). Support for this view is seen in that the Hebrew term for "day," *yôm*, may sometimes mean an indefinite period of time.

Second, passages such as Psalm 90:4 ("A thousand years in your sight are like a day that has just gone by, or like a watch in the night") and 2 Peter 3:8 ("But do not forget this one thing, dear friends: With the Lord a day is like a thousand years, and a thousand years are like a day") are alleged to demonstrate that God's days are "not necessarily the same as our days," but can be indeterminate in length (Ross and Archer 2001, 147).

Third, advocates of the day-age view contend that the various events described prior to the creation of Eve in Genesis 2, especially Adam's naming of the animals, had to involve much longer than a portion of a day. As Gleason Archer asks, "who can imagine that all of these transactions could possibly have taken place in 120 minutes of the sixth day?" (Archer 1994, 201).

Finally, day-age advocates see the seventh day as continuing, since there is no formula "evening and morning" statement at the end of the seventh day, and Hebrews 4:3 (citing Ps. 95:11) seems to support that God's rest is not yet finished. Therefore, they surmise that "given the parallelism of the Genesis creation account, it seems reasonable to conclude that the first six days may also have been long time periods" (Ross and Archer 2001, 146).

Yet each of these supports for the day-age theory is problematic. The most basic problem is the meaning of *yôm*. While *yôm* may mean an indefinite period of time in 65 instances in the OT (such as Gen. 2:4), by far the predominant meaning of *yôm* (2,239 times out of its 2,304 occurrences) in the OT

refers to a 24-hour day. In fact, the main exceptions to the literal 24-hour meaning are found with the combination of a preposition plus *yôm* plus a verb following.

That is precisely the construction that is found in Genesis 2:4, where *beyôm* should be translated as "when." Yet none of the 14 instances of *yôm* in Genesis 1:1–2:3 has that construction. In the **book of Genesis** as a whole, the term *yôm* occurs 83 times in the singular, including 72 times in the absolute state. In each of these 72 occurrences, *yôm* means a normal 24-hour day, not an indefinite period of time. In addition, in virtually every passage where a limiting number is attached (first, second, third, etc.), as is the case in 9 of the instances of *yôm* in Genesis 1:1–2:3, the meaning is a 24-hour day.

This construction occurs 30 additional times in Genesis (from Gen. 7:4 through Gen. 50:10), with *yôm* meaning a 24-hour day in each case. Furthermore, the phrase "evening and morning" (used in Gen. 1:5, 8, 13, 19, 23, and 31) reinforces the idea of a 24-hour day. All of the major Hebrew lexicons similarly affirm that *yôm* in Genesis 1 is used to communicate a 24-hour day. The evidence is so conclusive that even many of those who would hold to some form of nonliteral understanding of Genesis 1 still agree that the intended meaning in Genesis 1 is six literal 24-hour days. For example, **John Walton** observes, "It is extremely difficult to conclude that anything other than a 24-hour day was intended. It is not the text that causes people to think otherwise, only the demands of trying to harmonize with modern science" (Walton 2001, 81; see further Hasel 1994).

Second, passages such as Psalm 90:4 and 2 Peter 3:8 have little bearing on the discussion of *yôm* in Genesis 1. In both texts a comparison is made: a thousand years in God's sight are *like* a day. In no case is it suggested that the actual word "day" really stands for a longer period of time. The point is that what might seem a long time for us, given our limited life spans (specifically referenced in Ps. 90:10), is really not a very long time at all from the Lord's standpoint. In Genesis 1 there are no such comparative particles indicating a comparison. In fact, neither Psalm 90:4 nor 2 Peter 3:8 have anything to do with the days of the creation week.

Third, the objection that too many events occur in Genesis 2 for them all to have occurred on the sixth day of creation cannot be sustained. Archer somehow squeezes the events from the creation of man to the creation of Eve into only 120 minutes, but it seems just as likely that God's creation of each entity on day 6 may have taken only a few seconds or even less. The major issue here is Adam's naming of the animals prior to the Lord's creation of Eve. But this could have been done quite readily by Adam in a few hours, since (1) the Lord brought the animals to Adam (Gen. 2:19); (2) only the cattle, beasts of the field, and birds were included, not (for example) insects or fish; and (3) the basic "kinds" would no doubt be broader than **species** (with perhaps only 2,500 or fewer animals being named [Sarfati 2015, 327]). The main point of Adam naming the animals was for him to recognize that there was as of yet no one else corresponding to him.

Finally, the argument for God's "rest" still continuing is also problematic. First, the expression "evening and morning" is a phrase used to mark the end of each day of creation. Since the seventh day was not technically a day of creation, but a day of God's rest, there was no need for the usual expression. Second, even if it were somehow true that the seventh day of rest continues, why would there be any cause to import that concept to the first six days when creation actually occurred? Hebrews 4 does not say that the seventh day of God's rest continues; it simply seems to use God's "rest" as a picture of eternal life or presence with the Lord—entering into his rest means ceasing from one's own labors, simply trusting in the Lord, and being in his blessed presence. The meaning of God's "rest" in Hebrews 4 has no bearing whatsoever on the length of the creation days of Genesis 1:1–2:3 (McCabe 2000, 113–16).

Furthermore, a key problem for the day-age view is the text of Exodus 20:8–11. In this passage, the term *yôm* is used six times. It hardly makes sense for the first three usages to refer to literal 24-hour days (which they clearly do) but for the last three usages (dealing with creation) to refer to some undetermined large period of time.

For those who think that adopting the day-age view enables them to solve the basic tension between evolutionary theory and the biblical text, unfortunately it does not satisfy in that area either. No matter how long one stretches out the "days" of Genesis 1, the order of events depicted in Genesis 1 and those envisioned by the evolutionary model are radically different. According to Genesis 1, plants were created on the third day and marine animals on the fourth. The sun, moon, and stars were created on the fourth day, *after* the plants. The birds were created with fish on the fifth day, but the evolutionary model says that the birds evolved from the fish *after* the reptiles (created on the sixth day). Insects were created on the sixth day, *after* plants. Yet insects would have been needed for pollination, not to mention the problem that the simple (insects) should not

follow the complex animals according to the evolutionary model (see further Kulikovsky 2009, 152–53).

In short, the day-age theory not only proves to be invalid strictly from a biblical sense, but it also does not concur with current evolutionary theory.

The Framework Hypothesis: Literary, Not Literal, Days

The multitude of problems with the day-age theory has led some scholars to alternatives other than a literal six 24-hour day creation, some of which are quite innovative. For example, one scholar believes that the word *eretz* ("earth") in Genesis 1:2 should be translated "land," so that Genesis 1:2–31 refers to the creation of the Promised Land, not the world (Sailhamer 1996, 47–59).

However, this interpretation would require two different meanings for the same word in Genesis 1:1 and 1:2; and nowhere in Genesis 1 is there a hint that only the creation of the Promised Land is in view. Another scholar sees the seven days of Genesis 1 as "the seven days of divine **revelation** to Moses," not the days of creation (Garrett 1991, 193). Yet nowhere in the text does it indicate that these are days of Moses's divine revelation; in fact, Moses is not even mentioned in the book of Genesis. Several other scholars see the seven days as "God's workdays—analogous to human workdays" but of unknown length (Collins 2013, 88); yet the problem with this understanding is that Exodus 20:8–11 says that the seven-day workweek is patterned after the actual creation week of 24-hour days, not some "workday" of God's that was of unknown length.

Another scholar thinks that the seven days of Genesis 1:1–2:3 refer not to the creation of the world but to "seven days of cosmic temple inauguration" (Walton 2009, 95); yet there is not a hint of a temple, cosmic or otherwise, anywhere in Genesis 1–2. All of these proposals require reading into the text something that, frankly, simply is not supported by the context of the passage.

One of the most popular of the relatively recent non-literal views of the days of Genesis 1 is the framework hypothesis. This view addresses one of the major weaknesses of the day-age theory, in that the six days of creation are usually viewed as normal 24-hour days. Yet this picture of God's creative work in a week is not to be taken literally; instead, "it functions as a literary structure in which the creative works of God have been narrated in a topical order" (Irons and Kline 2001, 219). Often the following pattern is noted:

Forms/Creation kingdoms	Fullness/Creature kings
Day 1: light; day and night	**Day 4:** light bearers: sun, moon, stars
Day 2: sea and sky	**Day 5:** sea creatures; birds
Day 3: land and vegetation	**Day 6:** land creatures; man (Irons and Kline 2001, 224)

But the framework hypothesis has many problems. First and foremost, the genre of Genesis 1 is not poetry, but standard Hebrew sequential narrative. The chapter contains 50 *waw* consecutive imperfect forms (the standard marker for consecutive, sequential action), more than all but three of the first 20 chapters of Genesis. There are an average of 1.61 *waw* consecutive imperfect forms per verse in Genesis 1. By contrast, in the poetic section in Genesis 49:1b–27 (Jacob's blessing of his sons), there are only a total of eight *waw* consecutive forms, or 0.30 per verse. To put it another way, Genesis 1 has five times more narrative sequential markers than a comparable poetic section. As Pipa notes, "Is there any way Moses could have more precisely indicated six, normal, sequential days?" (Pipa and Hall 2005, 183).

It is fascinating that the day-age advocates insist (correctly) that Genesis 1 speaks of the days in *sequential* action, while the framework hypothesis advocates insist (correctly) that the days of Genesis 1 are normal *24-hour days*. Only the literal 24-hour-day view holds that the days are both sequential and literal 24-hour periods.

A second objection to the framework hypothesis is that the pattern outlined above breaks down at several points. Even if the pattern held true completely, it would not be an argument for a nonliteral approach to the chapter: just because something is presented according to a pattern does not mean that the pattern should not be taken literally.

But the pattern itself does not hold. A few examples will suffice. First, the light of day 1 is not dependent on the sun, so the sun is hardly the "ruler" of it. If some have a problem with understanding light without the sun, then they should recognize that the same will be true in the eternal state. According to Revelation 21:23 and 22:5, the sun will not be needed at all, since the Lord himself is the light. Why could not the light of day 1 have emanated from God himself? Second, the waters existed on day 1, not just day 2. Third, in verse 14 the "lights" of day 4 are set in the "expanse" created on day 2 (not day 1). Fourth, the sea creatures of day 5 were to fill the "water in the seas," which was created on day 3, not day 2, contrary to the chart above

(see Gen. 1:10); and none of the sea creatures or birds or land creatures other than man were told by God to "rule" anything. Finally, man was created on day 6, not to rule over the land and vegetation (created on day 3), but over the land animals created on day 6 and the sea creatures and birds created on day 5.

Despite the chart presented above, the patterns simply do not hold up under closer scrutiny.

The third objection is that if Genesis 1 is not intended to provide details about creation but rather to demonstrate that God did it in an orderly way, then why are all the details provided? In other words, if the details are not the point of the chapter, then why did the author provide so many of them?

Finally, there is a major hermeneutical issue with the framework hypothesis. Simply put, if one regards Genesis 1 as not literal, but rather figurative language that in essence says that "God did it," then where does one decide that the text of Genesis should be taken literally? Is that done in chapter 3, where **the serpent** tempts Eve, or is that metaphorical as well? And if so, was there an actual historical fall? Similar questions could be raised about the flood, Babel, Abraham, and so forth.

There is no internal marker to indicate that the text of Genesis 1 should be taken figuratively. The New Testament clearly refers to creation in Genesis 1 and 2 and regards the accounts as historically accurate (see Matt. 19:4–6; Mark 10:6–8; Luke 3:38; Rom. 5:12–19; 8:19–22; 1 Cor. 11:8–9; 15:22; 2 Cor. 4:6; 1 Tim. 2:13–14; Heb. 4:4; 11:3; 2 Peter 3:5). As E. J. Young aptly states, "If the 'framework' hypothesis were applied to the narratives of the **virgin birth** or to the resurrection or Romans 5:12ff., it could as effectively serve to minimize the importance of the content of those passages as it now does the content of the first chapter of Genesis" (Young 1964, 99).

Despite all of these alternative proposals, the best approach is to take the days of Genesis 1:1–2:3 as literal, sequential 24-hour days.

Todd S. Beall

REFERENCES AND RECOMMENDED READING

Archer, Gleason. 1994. *A Survey of Old Testament Introduction*. Rev. ed. Chicago: Moody.

Beall, Todd S. 2008. "Contemporary Hermeneutical Approaches to Genesis 1–11." In *Coming to Grips with Genesis: Biblical Authority and the Age of the Earth*, ed. Terry Mortenson and Thane Ury. Green Forest, AR: Master.

Collins, John. 2013. "Reading Genesis 1–2 with the Grain: Analogical Days." In *Reading Genesis 1–2: An Evangelical Conversation*, ed. J. Daryl Charles. Peabody, MA: Hendrickson.

Garrett, Duane. 1991. *Rethinking Genesis*. Grand Rapids: Baker.

Hasel, Gerhard F. 1994. "The 'Days' of Creation in Genesis 1: Literal 'Days' or Figurative 'Periods/Epochs' of Time?" *Origins* 21 (1): 5–38.

Irons, Lee, and Meredith G. Kline. 2001. "The Framework View." In *The Genesis Debate*, ed. David Hagopian. Mission Viejo, CA: Crux.

Kulikovsky, Andrew. 2009. *Creation, Fall, Restoration: A Biblical Theology of Creation*. Fearn, Ross-shire, Scotland: Mentor.

Luther, Martin. 1958. *Commentary on Genesis*. 2 vols. Grand Rapids: Zondervan.

McCabe, Robert V. 2000. "A Defense of Literal Days in the Creation Week." *Detroit Baptist Seminary Journal* 5 (Fall): 97–123.

Mortenson, Terry, and Thane Ury, eds. 2008. *Coming to Grips with Genesis: Biblical Authority and the Age of the Earth*. Green Forest, AR: Master.

Pipa, Joseph, Jr., and David Hall, eds. 2005. *Did God Create in Six Days?* 2nd ed. White Hall, WV: Tolle Lege.

Ross, Hugh, and Gleason Archer. 2001. "The Day-Age View." In *The Genesis Debate*, ed. David Hagopian. Mission Viejo, CA: Crux.

Sailhamer, John. 1996. *Genesis Unbound: A Provocative New Look at the Creation Account*. Sisters, OR: Multnomah.

Sarfati, Jonathan D. 2015. *The Genesis Account: A Theological, Historical, and Scientific Commentary on Genesis 1–11*. Powder Springs, GA: Creation Books.

Walton, John. 2001. *Genesis*. The NIV Application Commentary. Grand Rapids: Zondervan.

———. 2009. *The Lost World of Genesis One: Ancient Cosmology and the Origins Debate*. Downers Grove, IL: InterVarsity.

Young, Edward J. 1964. *Studies in Genesis One*. Philadelphia: P&R.

⚭ DAYS OF CREATION (Day-Age View). Day-age creationists believe God miraculously transformed the earth and created all its life within six literal days—that is, six long but finite time periods. The Hebrew word *yôm*, translated "day," has four distinct definitions, all of which are "literal" in the sense that they fall within the strict, accurate meaning of the word:

1. Part of the daylight hours
2. All the daylight hours
3. One rotation period of Earth
4. A long but finite time period

In biblical Hebrew there is no word other than *yôm* for a long, finite time period.

Three of these definitions are used in the Genesis creation account. Creation day 1 contrasts day and night, using the second definition. Creation day 4 contrasts seasons, days, and years, using the third definition. In Genesis 2:4 *yôm* refers to the entire creation week, using the fourth definition. The day-age view treats the creation days as six sequential, non-overlapping long periods of time.

This perspective holds that God's **revelation**s in both the Bible's words and nature's record can be fully trusted to reveal truth. While the Bible is the only authoritative revelation from God, nature's record remains utterly trustworthy and reliable. The day-age position upholds both a high, literal view of Scripture and a high, literal view of nature. It allows one to fully and joyfully embrace both of God's books.

Biblical Evidence for Long Creation Days

1. *The events of creation day 6 require a long time.* God creates three different kinds of specialized land mammals and *both* **Adam and Eve** on creation day 6. Genesis 2 lists events between Adam's creation and Eve's. God planted a garden in **Eden**, making "all kinds of trees to grow out of the ground." Then Adam tended the garden. Next, Adam named all the *nephesh* ("soulish" creatures—animals endowed by God with mind, will, and emotion). Evidently, Adam thoroughly examined each creature while considering a name to describe how that animal was uniquely designed to serve and please him. Adam had time to discover the joys of interacting with all the *nephesh* creatures and the loneliness of having no equal companion. Finally, God put Adam into a deep sleep, performed "surgery," and, after Adam awoke, introduced him to Eve (see **Adam and Eve**).

Adam's exclamation on seeing Eve is recorded in Genesis 2:23—*happa'am*. This word is usually translated as "now at length" (see Gen. 29:34–35; 30:20; 46:30; Judg. 15:3), roughly equivalent to the English expression "At last!"

Still later on the sixth day, God taught Adam and Eve about their responsibility to manage the earth's resources for the benefit of all life. This instruction would have taken considerable time. In sum, the activities of just this latter portion of the sixth day, regardless of Adam's intellect, would seem to have required many weeks, months, or even years.

2. *The seventh day continues.* Of the first six creation days, Moses wrote, "There was evening, and there was morning—the [X] day." That is, each day had a start time and an end time. However, no such wording is attached to the seventh day—not in Genesis nor anywhere else in the Bible. Given the parallel structure marking the creation days, this distinct change for narrating the seventh day strongly suggests this day has not yet ended.

In Psalm 95, John 5, and Hebrews 4, we learn that God's rest day continues. For example:

> For somewhere he [God] has spoken about the seventh day in these words: "On the seventh day God rested from all his works." … It still remains for some to enter that rest…. There remains, then, a Sabbath-rest for the people of God; for anyone who enters God's rest also rests from their works, just as God did from his. Let us, therefore, make every effort to enter that rest. (Heb. 4:4, 6, 9–11)

These passages establish that the seventh day of Genesis 1 and 2 represents a minimum of several thousand years and a maximum that is open-ended (but finite). It seems reasonable, given the parallelism of the Genesis creation account, that the first six days must also have been long time periods.

3. *God's days need not be the same as our days.* "A thousand years in your sight are like a day that has just gone by, or like a watch [four hours] in the night" (Ps. 90:4). Moses's words remind us that God's days are not our days any more than his ways are our ways (Isa. 55:9).

4. *Scripture makes explicit statements about the earth's antiquity.* Habakkuk 3:6 declares that the mountains are "ancient" and the hills are "age-old." In 2 Peter 3:5 the heavens are said to have existed "long ago." Such adjectives would carry little impact if the universe and the earth's hills were only a few days older than humankind.

5. *Scripture compares God's eternal existence to the mountains and the earth's longevity.* Figures of speech used in Psalm 90:2–6; Proverbs 8:22–31; Ecclesiastes 1:3–11; and Micah 6:2 all depict God's immeasurable antiquity. Compared to 3 billion years, a 3,000-year terrestrial history (at the time these words were written) seems an inadequate metaphor for God's eternality.

6. *Numbered days need not be 24-hour days.* Young-earth creationists argue that *yôm*, when attached to an ordinal (second, third, fourth, etc.) *always* refers to a 24-hour period. That this is often the case for days of human activity does not imply it must also be so for days of divine activity. Furthermore, it is not always the case for human activity days. Hosea 6:2 prophesies that "after two days he [God] will revive us [Israel]; on the third day he will restore us." For centuries Bible commentators have noted that the "days" in this passage (where the ordinal is used) refer to years, perhaps as many as 1,000 or more.

7. *Sabbath day for man and Sabbath year for the land are analogies to God's "work" week.* "For in six days the LORD made the heavens and the earth … but he rested on the seventh day" (Ex. 20:11). This passage is often cited as proof for 24-hour creation days. However, this kind of inference is akin to saying the eight-day celebration of the Feast of Tabernacles proves the wilderness wanderings in Sinai lasted only eight days.

Sometimes the *Sabbath* refers to a full year (cf. Lev. 25:4). Human well-being dictates one day of rest out of every seven days; for the crop-growing land's well-being, one year of rest out of every seven years. Since God has no biological limitations, his rest period is completely flexible. The emphasis in Exodus 20 is on the pattern of work and rest—a ratio of six to one—not on the creation day's length.

8. *Bloodshed before Adam's sin does not alter the atonement doctrine.* The Bible teaches that the shedding of Christ's blood is the one and only acceptable payment for our sin. It does not say *all* bloodshed goes toward the remission of sin.

Hebrews 10:1–4 explains that the blood of animal sacrifices *will not take away sin.* The sacrificial killing of animals was a physical picture (prefiguring the true atonement to come) of the spiritual **death** caused by sin. Since the penalty for sin is spiritual death, no animal sacrifice could ever atone for sin. The crime is spiritual. Thus the atonement must be made by a spiritual being. Upholding the atonement doctrine in no way demands a creation scenario in which none of God's creatures received a scratch or other bloodletting wound before Adam sinned.

Many more biblical evidences for long creation days exist, all described in the book *A Matter of Days* (Ross 2015). Long creation days make the defense of biblical authority, inspiration, and inerrancy straightforward. It is the one view that permits all the Bible's creation texts to be interpreted both literally and consistently.

Benefits of the Day-Age View

In addition to permitting a literally accurate and consistent view of all biblical creation accounts, the old-earth view accomplishes the following.

It credits God, not evolution, for creating life

Competing creation-evolution models require a much more natural process of evolution than the day-age model (see **Evolution, Biological**). For example, young-earth creationist models need herbivores to rapidly evolve into carnivores, including radical alterations in their livers and intestinal tracts, at the time of Adam's fall. Also, the several thousand **species** onboard **Noah's ark** must rapidly evolve into millions shortly after **the flood**.

While young-earth creationists deny these changes are evolution—they prefer to call them diversifications—they, nonetheless, are invoking rates of natural changes in the **DNA** and morphologies of species that are tens of thousands of times more efficient and rapid than what any atheistic Darwinist would dare suggest. As Philip Kitcher, philosopher of science at Columbia University, observes, "The rates of speciation [that] 'creation-science' would require … are truly breathtaking, orders of magnitude greater than any that have been dreamed of in evolutionary theory" (Kitcher 2001, 259).

Evolutionary creationists believe that life progresses from Earth's first life-form all the way to humans through the process of common descent (see **Human Evolution**). This common descent, they claim, is achieved through God directing the mechanisms of **natural selection**, mutation, and **gene** exchange. However, in their model there is no scientific means for distinguishing between directed and undirected biological evolution. As for life's origin, evolutionary creationists agree that no naturalistic explanation currently exists, but they hold to the possibility that one might be forthcoming.

Day-age creationists believe the Bible declares that God miraculously intervened to create life and that science has eliminated any reasonable possibility of a naturalistic explanation for life's origin on Earth. They also point out that the Bible's use of the Hebrew word *min* ("kind") implies that for the higher animals (Lev. 11:14–19; Deut. 14:12–18) natural process evolution is limited, at most, to the species level—and for lower life-forms (Lev. 11:22), at most, to the genus level. They also demonstrate that real-time and long-term evolution experiments and conservation biology studies affirm the biblical restrictions on natural process evolution. Thus the day-age view invokes not just thousands but tens of millions of miraculous creations of new kinds of life throughout Earth's history (see **Evolution, Biological**).

It gets the chronology of creation acts correct

A century ago Bible scholar Friedrich Delitzsch wrote, "All attempts to harmonize our biblical story of the creation of the world with the results of natural science have been useless and must always be so" (Delitzsch 1902, 45). Today a wide range of creationists insist that the Bible got it right and scientists have gotten it dead wrong. Meanwhile, theistic evolutionists and evolutionary creationists insist science got it right and the Bible is largely silent concerning natural history.

The day-age view delivers Christians from such defeatist theologies. It acknowledges that Genesis relates a chronological account of God's miraculous acts in transforming Earth and filling it with life to prepare a home for humans where an uncountable number can receive God's redemption offer. By understanding that the creation days in Genesis 1 are six consecutive long time periods and that the point of view for the six-days account is the surface of Earth's waters (Gen. 1:2), it yields a creation narrative in perfect accord with the established scientific record both in the description of God's creation acts and in the order in which they occur (Ross 2014, 25–108).

Genesis 1 yields another demonstration of the Bible's predictive power. Recent discoveries showing that vegetation on the continents predates the Avalon and **Cambrian explosion**s of animals in the oceans by hundreds of millions of years (Knauth and Kennedy 2009, 728–32; Strother et al. 2011, 505–9) establish that indeed the Bible got it right in stating that God created vegetation on the continents before he created animals in the oceans. Likewise, scientific findings showing that the advanced land mammals most critical for launching civilization appeared after the first birds and sea mammals vindicates the biblical declarations in Genesis 1:20–25 and Job 38–39.

Day-age creationism answers the **fossil record** enigma. The fossil record shows an enormous number and frequency of speciation events throughout all phyla of life before the arrival of humans and a virtual lack occurring afterward, especially for the higher taxa. While evolutionary models grasp for an explanation for this **mystery**, Genesis 1 offers a ready explanation. For six long time periods, God created new kinds of life. During the seventh epoch that followed—the human era—God ceased from his work of creating life.

It gets the story of Noah's flood correct

The church has suffered much abuse and ridicule from Christians' failure to integrate all the Bible's texts pertaining to Noah's flood. Genesis 6–8 says that the flood wiped out the entire world of humanity and all the soulish (*nephesh*) animals associated with humans. Many Christians interpret these chapters to imply that the flood was global in extent.

Two passages in 2 Peter indicate otherwise. According to 2 Peter 2:5, the world of the ungodly was flooded. The following chapter (2 Peter 3:6), says *ho tote kosmos*—the world at the time the event took place—was flooded. The qualifications Peter attached to *kosmos* (world) imply that Noah's flood was not global (see **Genesis Flood, The**; **Genesis Flood and Geology, The**).

This conclusion is confirmed in texts beyond Genesis describing God's works on the third creation day. For example, Psalm 104:6–8 relates God's acts in transforming Earth from a water world into a realm featuring surface continents and oceans. Psalm 104:9, concerning the continents God formed, declares, "You set a boundary they [the waters] cannot cross; never again will they cover the earth." Likewise, Job 38:8–11 and Proverbs 8:29 state that the continents provided the oceans with permanent boundaries.

It retains human exceptionalism

Young-earth creationists believe Neanderthals and *Homo erectus* are fully human. Theistic evolutionists and evolutionary creationists believe humans and Neanderthals are descended from a common ancestor. Day-age creationists believe humans are separate from Neanderthals and *H. erectus* and that all three species are distinct creations of God. They believe all humans are descended from two historical individuals, Adam and Eve, whom God created in his image and independent of any other life-form. The four known rivers meeting in Eden establish that Adam and Eve were created sometime during the last ice age, a date consistent with the best scientific evidence.

Day-age proponents point out the wealth of scientific evidence showing that humans alone, not Neanderthals or *H. erectus*, possess the capacity for symbolic recognition and communication, painting on cave walls, playing musical instruments, and engaging in spiritual activities. Humans alone demonstrate the capacity for technological advance and the development of agriculture and civilization. New evidence shows that even during episodes of extreme climate instability that characterized the last ice age, humans were maintaining small mixed farms and manufacturing flour and clothing.

It adheres to a correct doctrine of death

Romans 5:12 says, "Sin entered the world through one man, and death through sin, and in this way death came to all people." By two qualifications, "death through sin" and "death came to all people," Paul clarifies that Adam's sin inaugurated death to all humans. Not here, and nowhere else in the Bible, does Scripture say that Adam's offense brought death to *all life* or a change in the physical laws of the universe.

Death of nonhuman life provided humanity with a prodigious repository of more than 76 quadrillion tons of biodeposits (e.g., coal, oil, natural gas, clathrates, limestone)—resources that make possible the fulfillment of the Great Commission in just thousands, rather than millions, of years. As Christ's crucifixion and resurrection demonstrate, as baptism illustrates, and as Paul repeatedly writes, only through death can we truly live.

Hugh Ross

REFERENCES AND RECOMMENDED READING

Delitzsch, Friedrich. 1902. *Babel and Bible: Making Sense of the Most Talked About Book of All Time*, trans. Thomas J. McCormack and W. H. Carruth. Chicago: Open Court.

Kitcher, Philip. 2001. "Born-Again Creationism." In *Intelligent Design Creationism and Its Critics: Philosophical, Theological, and Scientific Perspectives*, ed. Robert T. Pennock. Cambridge, MA: MIT Press.

Knauth, L. Paul, and Martin J. Kennedy. 2009. "The Late Precambrian Greening of the Earth." *Nature* 460 (August): 728–32.

Ross, Hugh. 2014. *Navigating Genesis: A Scientist's Journey through Genesis 1–11*. Covina, CA: RTB Press.

———. 2015. *A Matter of Days: Resolving a Creation Controversy*. 2nd ed. Covina, CA: RTB Press, 2015.

Strother, Paul K., et al. 2011. "Earth's Earliest Non-marine Eukaryotes," *Nature* 473 (May): 505–9.

↝ DAYS OF CREATION (Framework-Hypothesis View).

The Bible is God's Word. As such, it bears authority and has a claim on Christians, and those who read are obliged to believe and obey. It is not just an artifact from antiquity, but is infallibly true. This and many other excellences follow logically from the fact that it is inspired—breathed out—by the Holy Spirit himself.

But as a written work of literature, it must be interpreted. And it is precisely here that the genius of the divine Author shines forth. The Bible is also quite human and should not be read as if it were the Qur'an or Joseph Smith's golden plates. We don't have to plumb the infinite mind of God. People with brains—and minds—like ours wrote at a certain time and circumstance to a certain group, and if we want to know what a given text means, we first ask, what did the human author intend? How would the original audience have understood this material? Unless we are sensitive to their mind-set, we will flounder with anachronistic, inappropriate, and downright silly interpretations.

The interpreter must keep in mind that Genesis is an ancient text written for a nation of mostly pastoral people. Any meaning discovered there must be measured against this touchstone. Unfortunately for moderns who are steeped in scientific **paradigm**s, any form of scientific meaning is almost entirely excluded from consideration. Genesis 1 is no more scientific than Genesis 30:37–39, where Jacob controlled genetic traits with sticks of wood. Instead of invoking an expanding cosmos, **Einstein**, **fossils**, entropy, or any scientific idea, one must find meaning in terms of its ancient cultural setting.

The New Testament writers did not interpret Genesis, let alone read it "literally." They treated its stories archetypally and symbolically, as illustrations to help explain Jesus and the gospel. Paul treated the first day this way: "God, who said, 'Let light shine out of darkness,' made his light shine in our hearts to give us the light of the knowledge of

God's glory displayed in the face of Christ" (2 Cor. 4:6). Obviously this is not straightforward exegesis — yet it is his normal procedure. The modern Christian should keep this in mind when reading chapter 1 (see **Creationism, Old-Earth [Supportive View]**; **Creationism, Young-Earth [Critical View]**).

One Day, Genesis 1:3 – 5

Throughout history, interpreters have struggled with the **paradox** of sourceless light. Origen (AD 185 – 254) believed the enigma made any literal interpretation impossible. Basil the Great (AD 330 – 79) suggested that the "nature of light" was created, as opposed to actual lights, what today might be called the laws governing electromagnetic radiation. Actual light came later.

Because this day lacked the sun, the meaning of "evening and morning" is obscure. What sort of morning has no sunrise? This gives the whole of Genesis 1 a surreal quality and may be a purposeful clue to its genre. Perhaps Moses dreamed the chapter or saw it in a prophetic vision. Hence it is symbolic. Or maybe God took a week to reveal it. Thus Moses lived through the six days, and they are not a timescale for creation at all. The best explanation is that the seven days are a literary device, and the light did not ever physically exist apart from sun, moon, and stars.

No ancient reader would have imagined a big bang, or the sky brightening after particulate matter diffused from the stratosphere, or God infusing energy to start chemical reactions. Nor would any relativistic time dilation be envisioned. We do not have to guess the infinite mind of God. We simply have to ask what the people of the land would make of the account of the first day (see **Biblical Cosmology**).

A Second Day, Genesis 1:6 – 8

On the second day of creation, God placed a "**firmament**" (KJV) that separated celestial from terrestrial oceans. The Hebrew word "firmament" is derived from the verb for working metal, and (in Phoenician) is used for metallic bowls. Numbers 16:38 uses a cognate for hammered plates. Job 37:18 claims that the sky is hard like metal. It looks like ice or crystal in Ezekiel 1:22.

The ancient Near East universally believed that the sky was hard like stone and the stars were lights fixed to it. Thus the Bible speaks of the sky having pillars and foundations (Job 26:11; 2 Sam. 22:8), an upper chamber (Amos 9:6) with a reservoir of water (Ps. 148:1 – 4). When God opens its windows and gates, rain comes (Gen. 7:11).

Thus God accomplished two things. He carved out a space in the universe for life to thrive and established a means to regulate and preserve it. Today we can appreciate these things far more than the ancient audience ever could, but we express them in other terms. If the earth were smaller or larger, life could not exist here. If it were closer or further from the sun, if its complement of elements were different, or if hundreds of other known parameters were off just a little bit — including universal constants such as Planck's or the **speed of light** — life could not exist. People of faith today can celebrate how God made a space for life and sustains it, as the ancient audience celebrated this according to their cosmology.

Many modern interpreters are uncomfortable with such a blatantly prescientific assertion in Genesis, translating it "expanse," and relegating the heavenly waters to clouds and vapor. Thus God made clouds in the atmosphere. But this forces a square peg into a round hole — trying to make an ancient cosmological concept conformable to modern meteorology. If one truly wants the text to be scientifically descriptive — with a literal creation week — one must believe a physical dome is really up there.

A Third Day, Genesis 1:9 – 13

The writer of Genesis was well aware that plants come from seed, yet used unscientific language for the first plants: the earth sprouted them. This is probably nontechnical speech that treats seed in the soil as a "given." In other words, it means, "Let seed in the ground germinate." The origin of the seed is unstated.

The grammar of 1:11 suggests that God commanded trees to be entirely made of fruit — down to the bark and wood center. Ancient and medieval rabbis debated this issue. A literalistic, precise approach must explain why the trees did not turn out as commanded.

Today every believer appreciates that God provides life's necessities like food. "Give us this day our daily bread," is the **prayer** Jesus taught his disciples, which captures the essence of this third day. The land's largesse is for man and beast (1:29 – 30). This is what the passage is about. The text, written for ancient tribesmen, is not a scientific thesis. (Although God knew that algae oxygenated the air in the Archean eon, this is not the meaning that Genesis conveyed to them, and thus that is not what it means.)

A Fourth Day, Genesis 1:14 – 19

With sun and moon now circling the earth, there could be actual evenings and mornings without ad hoc explanations.

As with everything in this chapter, including the earth itself, no material origins or stages of formation from prior substance are cited.

With the luminaries, a pattern begins to emerge beyond simple progression. In days 4–6, God adorns the partitions of the first three days with creatures. This analysis is called the framework hypothesis, and it may be the key to reading the six days. They can be seen not as a chronology, but as a thematic review of aspects of creation. Now the second half has begun, and the creative work of the first half is revisited.

Sun and moon separated the day from the night (1:18). Since this had already been done (1:4), day 4 describes the same creative act as day 1. Day 4 reveals how God accomplished day 1—solving the mystery of the missing light source. This is like the double creation account of humanity. First, humans are simply created (Gen. 1:27). Later, this is retold with different emphasis (2:7ff.). Similarly, the six "days" might be nonsequential, a literary device to separate creation into topics. After all, Genesis 2:4 folds the whole week's work into a single day.

The luminaries are not gods. This sets the Genesis account at odds with pagan myths but does not make it concordant with modern science. Psalm 19 describes the sun's tent, from whence he enthusiastically runs his daily course. The kings of Judah may have believed a horse-drawn chariot carried the sun (2 Kings 23:11). The detractors of **Copernicus,** such as Martin Luther, cited Joshua 10:13 to disprove his cosmological model—another illustration of how literalism can produce bad science.

If the universe is only six millennia old, how is it possible to see distant celestial phenomena at all? No solution to this problem has reached a consensus among young-earth theorists. Some suggest the universe was created "mature," with the appearance of great age. Light was created "enroute." Thus we see light of exploding suns that never existed. This argument ends any further scientific discourse on the subject and turns **astronomy** into fiction. Astronomers peer into a past that never happened. The heavens declare a story of fraud.

A Fifth Day, Genesis 1:20–23

God adorns the firmament above and waters below with life. Birds fly beneath the upper sea. Fish swim in the lower sea. He blessed them with the command to multiply and fill the world with their kinds. No comment is made concerning their substance or corporeal origins; they appear propagating naturally.

Young-earth creationists define a "kind" as a basic animal type: the taxonomic rank of a **species** in some cases, in others a genus or family. Young-earth conjecture allows for a few basic prototypes on the ark and very rapid phylogenesis after **the flood**—their development into modern families taking less than 1,000 years. A literal reading of Scripture brings this to Moses, who, according to this theory, should have observed genera change throughout his lifetime. Abraham was born only 297 years after the flood, so our zoology had not yet appeared in his day.

Perhaps the best critique of the literalist, young-earth view, is to simply state what it claims. The flood supposedly happened 2348 BC. That would place it at the end of Early Bronze III, the sixth dynasty of the Old Kingdom, several centuries after Egyptologists date the first pyramids.

The Sixth Day, Genesis 1:24–31

First, God created the domestic and wild brutes that live on land. Specifically, God told the ground to "bring out" the beasts. This might be symbolic for procreation. Psalm 103:14, for example, says this of humans: "we are dust." Psalm 139:15 refers to gestation as being "intricately woven in the depths of the earth" (ESV). Thus the ground causing animals to exist might not be identifying their actual origins at all. It means, "Let creatures be born and hatched." It is in this manner, then, that God made them.

God issues orders in an executive manner, but the text (wisely) has no interest in how, materially and organically, those orders were fulfilled. Light shines from no obvious source, plants appear from tacit seed, sun and moon are unveiled already shining, birds and fish appear teeming, fauna are born and hatched from unstated matrices. The text reads as if the days of creation are a documentary, each episode pointing to cycles of nature readily observable to ancient Israel, saying, "God made that!"

The support systems for life appear in three acts; these are rendered with spawning creatures in another three. Finally, as creation's culmination, God decrees mankind, fashioning male and female in God's image to rule and multiply. Thus the primordial state of being uninhabitable and uninhabited (Gen. 1:2) has been redressed. This is pronounced "very good." Most excellent—the creation is complete, viable, and functioning as intended. The **ecology** works. Life thrives. Humanity rules.

The fact that Genesis 1–2 has two distinct treatments of the creation of humans may be a clue to its literary genre. Focusing on the ordering of days and their events may miss the point. The whole grand story revolves around humanity, and this involves telling it in several different sequences. The point is not about what part of creation came after what or how long it took or how it was done. Creation is about mankind in relationship with God. The universe is a foil for this. The ordering of days in Genesis may be representative or thematic: any number of methods could have been used to express its salient theological ideas. Compare, for example, Psalms 8 and 104, or Proverbs 8:22–31.

But a secular universe is not enough. One sanctifying day remains as the climax of the story, giving meaning to them all.

The Seventh Day, Genesis 2:1–3

The partitions created in days 1–3 are filled in days 4–6. This literary design leaves the seventh day to stand alone and apart. The climax of creation week is where the ultimate purpose of creation is achieved: God takes up his abode in his temple, and this consecrates the universe.

The sanctuaries of the ancient Hebrews (the tabernacle, Solomon's temple, and the second temple) were constructed with three partitions, as the universe has three partitions in Genesis. Within these houses of worship were images of creation: the menorah (a stylized tree with seven lamps like the seven lights in the sky), loaves of bread (made from grain), a wash basin (the sea), and so on. The idea is clear: God's true sanctum is the universe. The manmade sanctuaries symbolize that. Isaiah 66:1 explicitly compares the cosmos as the place of God's rest to an inadequate earthly building.

The six days of creation made the universe orderly and whole, a fit habitation for the holy God. Thus, resting from the work of creation in his new ordered house, God makes it holy—something more than its parts—adding a transcendent dimension. The seventh day makes the universe special. God taking his repose in the holy day is equivalent to saying, "Holy, holy, holy is the Lord Almighty; the whole earth is full of his glory" (Isa. 6:3). It is also equivalent to the presence of God filling the temple at its dedication. In Solomon's words, "The heavens, even the highest heaven, cannot contain you. How much less this temple I have built!" (1 Kings 8:27).

Young-earth creationists insist that the time measurement of "evening and morning" means a 24-hour day (see **Creationism, Young-Earth**). But the seventh day has no such metric. Thus Genesis intentionally places the seventh day outside of the rhythm of the first six days. It seals creation as holy and blessed. The Sabbath rest of God is the beatitude of the universe. The Hebrews celebrated its continuation by resting from their labors every seventh day. By doing so again and again, they treated this timeless day as a state of being, the condition of being sanctified. The fourth commandment states this two ways: remember when God rested (Ex. 20:11), and remember when he rescued Israel from slavery in Egypt (Deut. 5:15). These both speak of the same spiritual reality: Israel keeps Sabbath to enjoy the eternal benediction of God's rest.

Hebrews 3:16–4:11 traces the motif of "resting" from creation week, through the rest of the Promised Land, to resting from one's own works and trusting in Jesus. Thus a true creationist is one who enters day 7 by hearing the gospel and responding in faith and obedience. Believing the gospel is what creation week is all about. This takes the seventh day full circle back to the first. In the words of the apostle Paul, "God, who said, 'Let light shine out of darkness,' made his light shine in our hearts to give us the light of the knowledge of God's glory displayed in the face of Christ" (2 Cor. 4:6).

George Schwab

REFERENCES AND RECOMMENDED READING

Gardner, Paul. 2009. *The New Creationism.* Carlisle, PA: Evangelical Press.
Ross, Hugh. 2004. *A Matter of Days.* Colorado Springs: NavPress.
Walton, John H. 2009. *The Lost World of Genesis One.* Downers Grove, IL: InterVarsity.
Young, Davis. 1982. *Christianity and the Age of the Earth.* Grand Rapids: Zondervan.

DAYS OF CREATION, INTERPRETATIONS.

The meaning and length of the days of creation as recorded in Genesis are among the most discussed topics regarding the account of creation in the Bible. At no time in history has there been a consensus view held by all theologians regarding the length and meaning of the days, though there have been at least 10 to 20 different ideas and proposals. As an example, a report on the days of creation released by the Presbyterian Church of America in 2000 discussed four major views and six minor views regarding the **days of creation** (Presbyterian Church in America 2000).

Historically, interpretations of Genesis have often been influenced by the culture. Both Origen (AD 185–284) and **Augustine** (354–430), in his later writings, were influenced by Greek thinking and believed that the universe was created instantaneously, so they viewed the days of creation in an allegorical manner (Letham 1999). This article will briefly discuss some of the most widely held contemporary views. Three of the more prevailing views are discussed in more length in the accompanying advocacy entries.

The word translated into English as "day" is the Hebrew word *yôm*. Like the English word "day," *yôm* can have many different meanings depending on the context. In the sentence "This is a beautiful day," the word "day" refers to the present moment, for it might have been dark and stormy even a few hours ago. If I write, "In George Washington's day the colonists fought the Revolutionary War," then the word "day" means a certain longer period of time. C. I. Scofield's classic reference Bible says, "The word 'day' is used in Scripture in four ways: (1) that part of the solar day of twenty-four hours which is light ...; (2) a period of twenty-four hours ...; (3) a time set apart for some distinctive purpose, as 'day of atonement' ...; and (4) a longer period of time during which certain revealed purposes of God are to be accomplished.... Cp. Gen 2:4, where the word 'day' covers the entire work of creation" (Scofield 1967).

Some claim that the language and context of Genesis 1 clearly indicate that the days of creation are 24 hours long. However, in the original Hebrew such a conclusion is not necessarily warranted. Some of the most prominent Hebrew scholars have concluded the opposite. Gleason Archer, a renowned scholar of ancient Hebrew and one of the primary translators of *The New American Standard Bible*, writes, "On the basis of internal evidence, it is this writer's conviction that *yôm* in Genesis One could not have been intended by the Hebrew author to mean a literal twenty-four-hour day" (Archer 1994). There are many alternative ideas about the meaning of the days of creation precisely because the Hebrew is not definitive.

Framework Day

Those who advocate the so-called framework hypothesis suggest that the days are used to give a framework or outline to the text (Kline 1958, 1996). There is no chronology or length of time involved, so the days are not necessarily sequential or consecutive. Genesis 1:2 states the two problems that the earth was formless and void (or "desolate" and "empty" [cf. Isa. 34:11]).

The days are outlined in such a way as to address those problems. Days 1 through 3 deal with the formless nature of the earth—or more precisely, the realms God creates—and days 4 through 6 address the problem that the void or realms must be filled. On day 1 light and darkness are separated. On day 2 waters above in the sky are separated from waters below on the earth. On day 3 the dry land and sea are separated, and the vegetation sprouts on the land. Days 4 through 6 parallel and "fill" the first three days. On day 4 the lights in the heaven fill the void that was formed

when God made light and darkness. On day 5 the birds fill the air containing the waters above and the fish fill the sea containing the waters below. Finally, on day 6 land animals and man are created to fill the void that was formed when God made the dry land appear.

24-Hour Day

The days are consecutive days of one earth rotation, approximately 24 hours in length (MacArthur 2006; Mortenson and Ury 2008). Thus God created the entire universe in a span of approximately 144 hours. This view is usually accompanied by the belief that the genealogies of Genesis are basically complete so that the universe is approximately 6,000 years old.

Day-Age

Each of the days is a great length of time, with the days basically proceeding in a sequential fashion. Contemporary day-age interpretations would accept the **big bang** model of the origin of the universe and the long geological ages implied by the **fossil record**. One of the most popular current day-age models proposes that the days of creation give an account of God preparing the earth for mankind as told from a perspective on the surface of the earth (Ross 2004). Each of the days comprises tens to hundreds of millions of years.

Analogical Day

The days of creation describe God's days as he does his work and are analogous to our days of the week in which we do work, but they are not identical in length or in composition (Collins 1994, 1999, 2003). The days are broadly consecutive and sequential, and the length of each day is not specified. God's creative week, of unspecified length, sets the pattern for our week of work and rest.

Unspecified Length Day

Similar to the analogical day view, the length of the day is not specified. Each day could be 24 hours or longer, in contrast to the day-age view, in which every day is considered to be a long eon of time. On this view, the days are sequential and describing straightforward history. This view was held by scholars such as W. H. Green, Herman Bavinck, B. B. Warfield, and E. J. Young.

Gap Idea

The days are usually considered to be 24 hours but after a large gap of time between the events described in Genesis 1:1 and then those described in Genesis 1:2. Proponents of this view may assert that the large gap in time was accompanied by a cataclysmic event, like the fall of Satan, and that Genesis 1:2 might be translated as "the earth became formless and void." The creation then described in the remaining verses of Genesis 1 is a re-creation of the heavens and the earth after the cataclysmic event. The gap theory has been espoused by theologians such as Thomas Chalmers, Arthur Custance, and C. I. Scofield.

Days of Revelation

The days of Genesis 1 are six consecutive 24-hour days, but they are not days in which God created the heavens and the earth. Instead, they are the days that God revealed his creation to the author of Genesis (Wiseman 1958). In this view, nothing is implied in the text about the time scale or chronology of creation. We only know that the events of day 1 were revealed by God to the author on the first day, the events described on day 2 were revealed during the second day, and so on. The actual creation could have taken any length of time and occurred in any sequential order, not necessarily the same order as the days of **revelation**.

Days of Divine Fiat

The days are six consecutive 24-hour days in which God made declarations that the earth and universe be formed and filled (Hayward 1994). The execution of those divine instructions occurred then over an unspecified length of time subsequent to God's commands.

Intermittent Days

The days of creation are normal 24-hour days in which God performed his creative acts, but each day may be separated by a long, unspecified time period. So even though God performed his creative acts in six 24-hour days, the age of the universe is unspecified and could be very long because of the time gaps between each of the days (Newman and Eckelmann 1977).

Days Focused on Palestine

The story of creation as described in Genesis 1:2 and beyond is only describing God's creative acts focused on preparing the land of Canaan for the Israelites (Sailhamer 1996). The length and timing of the days remains unspecified.

God's General Relativity Days

The general-relativity-days view has been proposed by Jewish physicist **Gerald Schroeder** (Schroeder 1990). This view claims that the days of creation are contiguous and are each

24 hours from God's perspective. However, due to time dilation inherent in **Einstein**'s theory of general relativity, those six consecutive 24-hour days appear to an earthly observer as many billions of years. Thus, from God's perspective, the time of creation is about 144 hours, but from our perspective, the universe is billions of years old. From our perspective, each successive day is about half the time of the previous day, with day 1 lasting about 7 billion years, day 2 about 3.5 billion years, and so on. (The lengths of time stated here have been scaled from Shroeder's original work to match the current consensus about the age of the universe.)

Michael G. Strauss

REFERENCES AND RECOMMENDED READING

Archer, Gleason, 1994. *A Survey of Old Testament Introduction.* Chicago: Moody Bible Institute.
Collins, C. John. 1994. "How Old Is the Earth? Anthropomorphic Days in Genesis 1:1–2:3," *Presbyterion* 20, no. 2 (Fall): 109–30.
———. 1999. "Reading Genesis 1:1–2:3 as an Act of Communication: Discourse Analysis and Literal Interpretation." In *Did God Create in Six Days?* ed. Joseph Pipa Jr. and David Hall. Taylors, SC: Southern Presbyterian Press and Kuyper Institute.
———. 2003. *Science and Faith: Friends or Foes?* Wheaton, IL: Crossway.
Hayward, Alan. 1994. *Creation and Evolution: Facts and Fallacies.* 2nd ed. London: SPCK.
Kline, Meredith G. 1958. "Because It Had Not Rained." *Westminster Theological Journal* 20 (May) 146–57.
———. 1996. "Space and Time in the Genesis Cosmogony." *Perspectives on Science and Christian Faith* 48. March: 2–15.
Letham, Robert. 1999. "In the Space of Six Days." *Westminster Theological Journal* 61:149–74.
MacArthur, John. 2006. *The Battle for the Beginning: Creation, Evolution, and the Bible.* Nashville: Thomas Nelson. 2001.
Mortenson, Terry, and Thane Ury. 2008. *Coming to Grips with Genesis.* Green Forest, AR: New Leaf.
Newman, Robert, and Herman Eckelmann Jr. 1977. *Genesis One and the Origin of the Earth.* Downers Grove, IL: InterVarsity.
Orthodox Presbyterian Church. 2004. *Report of the Committee to Study the Views of Creation.* http://opc.org/GA/CreationReport.pdf.
Presbyterian Church of America. 2000. *Report of the Creation Study Committee.* www.pcahistory.org/creation/report.html.
Ross, Hugh. 2004. *A Matter of Days: Resolving a Creation Controversy.* Colorado Springs: NavPress.
Sailhamer, John. 1996. *Genesis Unbound.* Sisters, OR: Multnomah.
Schroeder, Gerald. 1990. *Genesis and the Big Bang.* New York: Bantam.
Scofield, C. I., 1967. *The New Scofield Reference Bible.* New York: Oxford University Press.
Wiseman, Donald J. 1991. "Creation Time—What Does Genesis Say?" *Science and Christian Belief* 3(1): 25–34.
Wiseman, P. J. (1948) 1958. *Creation Revealed in Six Days: The Evidence of Scripture Confirmed by Archaeology.* London: Marshall, Morgan & Scott.
Young, E. J. (1964) 1999. *Studies in Genesis One.* Phillipsburg, NJ: P&R.

DEATH. Death is the cessation of vital functions or, in biblical terms, the withdrawal of spirit and breath (Job 34:14;

Ps. 104:29). The focus of death (and life) in the Old Testament is tangible and physical, while the New Testament highlights the figurative and spiritual aspects of death. The biblical view of death is relevant to issues in the debate over creation and evolution.

Death in the Old Testament

Death initially came into view in Genesis 2, when Yahweh commanded the man not to eat of the fruit of the tree of the knowledge of good and evil or he would "certainly die" (Gen. 2:17). When Eve and Adam ate from that tree, in Genesis 3, death became the certain end for human life (Gen. 3:22–23; Pss. 49:10; 82:7). Yahweh as the Creator of life (Gen. 1) and the one who can pronounce death (Gen. 2:17; 18:25) has ultimate power over life and death (Deut. 32:39; 1 Sam. 2:6). He is able to deliver from death (Ps. 9:13), and he will finally end death (Isa. 25:8). For the Old Testament believers, then, their very existence and perspective on life and death was closely related to their understanding of and connection to Yahweh.

In distinction from Israel's neighbors, who personified death as a deity and understood it as the result of offense against a variety of deities, Israel's Scriptures clearly portray life and death as a result of Israel's response to Yahweh alone (Deut. 4:1; 8:3; 30:15–20; 32:39, 47). Therefore, all of the possible reasons for the fragility of life in the ancient world, drought and famine, disease, enemies, accident, and even wild beasts, are all under the control of Yahweh (Lev. 26; Deut. 28). As such, Israel was to understand Yahweh as just, good, and worthy of their allegiance and praise (Deut. 6:4–5; Ps. 9). Far from being capricious, God treasures life, particularly cherishing the righteous (Ps. 116:15; Ezek. 18:32; 33:11).

Israel does occasionally personify death, but when they do, it is not as a deity, but rather under Yahweh's complete control (Isa. 28:15–19). From man's perspective, death is overwhelming and somewhat incomprehensible. Death is pictured as waves or ropes or a snare that can easily overpower or capture the helpless victim (2 Sam. 22:5–6; Pss. 18:4–5; 116:3; Prov. 13:14). On the other hand, Yahweh can deliver from death because he is the righteous one's life (Deut. 30:20; Ps. 27:1). He is the Creator (1 Sam. 2:6–8), and therefore God, the only God, holding life in his power (Deut. 32:39; 2 Kings 5:7).

Because the Old Testament writers saw death as a certainty (2 Sam. 14:14; Pss. 49:10–12; 82:7), their attention turned to the means, timing, and manner of death. God judged rebellion from Adam (Gen. 3) to every subsequent sinner (Ezek. 18:4, 20). Death necessarily followed specific sins in talionic justice (Ex. 21:23; Lev. 20:9–16), as well as loss of Yahweh's presence (Ps. 13:1–3).

As punishment or disaster, death provoked fear, but death was not always negative. Death was the natural end of life and was described in peaceful terms within the context of the blessing of Yahweh (Gen. 25:8). While Enoch and Elijah show the possibility of escaping death (Gen. 5:24; 2 Kings 2:11), such an opportunity was never the cause for longing or reflection in the Old Testament. Instead, a peaceful end with God's blessing and family around, culminating a long life, consistently pictured the appropriate end of the righteous (Gen. 15:15; Num. 23:10).

The dead inhabit Sheol, with little clear explanation. While popular theology may equate Sheol with hell, scholars have generally understood Sheol as the place of all dead. Sheol does not describe "hell" in the New Testament sense (giving no clear connotation of judgment), but it does occur in predominantly negative contexts, suggesting that there may have been more underlying theology of punishment than the texts express, and was not necessarily the destination of the righteous. The two passages suggesting that it includes both the righteous and the wicked are not conclusive (Ps. 89:48; Eccl. 9:10; Johnston 2002, 82–83). With the relatively small number of references to Sheol in the Old Testament, the afterlife is not a major concern for its writers. Resurrection to an afterlife is even more elusive, with only a few clear references (Isa. 26:19; Dan. 12:2, 13).

Religiously, Israel seemed to be focused on the present and their current relationship with Yahweh: loving God brought life now (Deut. 30:19–20). Out of about 1,000 uses of the general Hebrew root for "death" in the Old Testament (verb and noun), not one of them clearly refers to spiritual death. We may assume, for example, that because Adam does not die "in the day" that he ate from the tree but actually hundreds of years later according to the text (Gen. 5:5), he must have died spiritually. That assumption, however, does not fit the rest of the Old Testament uses. The simplest explanation takes the Hebrew "in the day" with its normal meaning of "when" and the certainty ("certainly die") as referring to the event, not the timing ("you will then have the certainty of death" rather than "you will certainly die then").

Death in the New Testament

Jewish literature between the Old and New Testaments significantly developed the Jewish theology of life and death, including events after death and resurrection. Jesus and the

New Testament authors continued this, directing far more attention to the spiritual than the physical, including the afterlife. The New Testament still refers to physical death most often, but the expressed understanding of death expands significantly to include various figurative ideas, including spiritual death.

Writers in the Old Testament sometimes portrayed the dead as separated from Yahweh because they were no longer experiencing the immediate benefits of his promises: without his wonders or praise (Ps. 88:10–12) and cut off from his care (Ps. 88:5). The New Testament would now describe a second death as separation from God and from all that is eternal and ultimately life (Rev. 2:11; 20:6, 13–15). Death defines the state of the self-indulgent widow (1 Tim. 5:6) or the false teachers (Jude 12), even though they are physically still alive. Death describes the consequences of sin (Rom. 7:8–13), the state of the unbeliever (John 5:24), as well as the final judgment and separation from God (the second death—John 11:25–26; Rev. 20:6). As the final judgment, the second death brings torment (Luke 16:22–25) and suffering (2 Thess. 1:7–10; Rev. 20:14–15).

The New Testament clarifies that death for all mankind, including the potential of second death, originated from Adam's sin (Rom. 5:12–21; 1 Cor. 15:21–22). Some argue from these passages that there was no death for other creatures before **the fall** of mankind in Genesis 3. None of the relevant passages, however, refer to the death of anything other than mankind. Since man was not created immortal, but with the potential of life (the tree of life), why assume other creatures were initially immortal? The stated prohibition to fruit of the tree of the knowledge of good and evil only mentioned death to those who ate (Gen. 2:17). The death effects then pass on to those born in Adam's image (Gen. 5).

Finally, in the ultimate providence of God through Jesus, death itself will be destroyed (1 Cor. 15:26, 50–57). While the New Testament describes the suffering and judgment in death, it also expresses the promise for believers in Jesus; they will live with Christ forever (Phil. 1:21–23), mortality being swallowed up by life (2 Cor. 5:4), and death swallowed up in victory (1 Cor. 15:54). The second death, the final judgment from God, will have no power over those in Christ (Rev. 2:11; 20:6).

John Soden

REFERENCES AND RECOMMENDED READING

Johnston, Philip S. 2002. *Shades of Sheol: Death and Afterlife in the Old Testament*. Downers Grove, IL: Apollos/InterVarsity.

Levenson, Jon Douglas. 2006. *Resurrection and the Restoration of Israel: The Ultimate Victory of the God of Life*. New Haven, CT: Yale University Press.

Miller, Johnny V., and John M. Soden. 2012. *In the Beginning . . . We Misunderstood: Interpreting Genesis 1 in Its Original Context*. Grand Rapids: Kregel.

Routledge, Robin L. 2008. "Death and Afterlife in the Old Testament." *Journal of European Baptist Studies* 9 (1): 22–39.

DEISM. During the **Enlightenment** (1650–1800), deism—from the Latin *Deus* ("God")—rose to prominence. It reached its zenith in the 1790s in England, its country of origin, and in 1794 became France's official national religion under Robespierre.

Many have described this **worldview** as one in which a God who creates and winds up the universe like a clock is not thereafter directly involved in the world's affairs through **miracles** or special **revelation**. Indeed, deists argued, if God acted in the world by performing miracles, this would suggest his not having gotten things right in the first place; the miraculous is tantamount to irrationality. While deistic skeptical philosopher **David Hume** defined miracles as a violation of nature's laws, Voltaire put it more forcefully: "A miracle is the violation of mathematical, divine, immutable, eternal laws. By the very exposition itself, a miracle is a contradiction in terms: a law cannot at the same time be immutable and violated" (Voltaire 1901, 272).

US President Thomas Jefferson exemplified the spirit of deism in his attempt to treat Jesus as a mere enlightened moral teacher of reason rather than the miracle-working Son of God of special revelation. While in the White House in 1804, Jefferson cut out portions of the Gospels and created his own desupernaturalized, Enlightenment "gospel"—a "precious morsel of ethics" sans Jesus's **incarnation**, miracles, authoritative claims, atonement, and **resurrection**. The product was *The Jefferson Bible*, or *The Life and Morals of Jesus of Nazareth Extracted Textually from the Gospels* (2011). He frankly expressed his deism in a letter to John Adams dated April 11, 1823: "The day will come, when the mystical generation of Jesus, by the Supreme Being as His Father, in the womb of a virgin, will be classed with the fable of the generation of Minerva in the brain of Jupiter" (cited in Sanford 1984, 111–12).

A recent example of a Jeffersonian deist was the late philosopher **Antony Flew**, who abandoned his long-held atheism in light of the staggering **complexity** of the universe and biological life (Flew and Varghese 2008).

Deism espoused a "gospel . . . as old as creation," according to deist Matthew Tindal (1730). Another prominent deist, Benjamin Franklin, described this "natural religion" as containing "the essentials of every religion" (Franklin 1962, 80): that there exists one God, who made all things; that he governs the world by his providence; that he ought to be worshiped by adoration, **prayer**, and thanksgiving; that the most acceptable service of God is doing good to man; that the **soul** is immortal; and that God will certainly reward virtue and punish vice, either here or hereafter.

Classical deism was not a monolithic belief system but had different hues. It might emphasize divine withdrawal from humanity or a divine Providence to whom humans may pray. It could stress that God leaves it up to humans to live by a moral system that could be universally known by humanity and affirmed by reason. Or it could be understood more negatively, namely, that a God that does not engage in miracles or reveal himself through particularistic revelation yielding irrational, superfluous, and perhaps even harmful dogmas such as **original sin**, the incarnation/virginal conception, as well as Jesus's atonement and resurrection. And the common **God of the Gaps** argument presupposes more of a deistic view of God than a biblical one, in which God sustains the universe in being and lovingly engages with his creatures by acting in the world through providence, miracles, and revelation.

A contemporary version of deism common among American youth is "moral therapeutic deism": God exists but is not necessarily involved in human lives; the goal of life is to be happy and feel good about oneself; and all humans, whatever their religion, should be good and nice, and if they are, they will go to heaven (Smith and Denton 2005).

Paul Copan

REFERENCES AND RECOMMENDED READING

Byrne, Peter. 1989. *Natural Religion and the Nature of Religion: The Legacy of Deism*. London: Routledge.
Flew, Antony, with Abraham Varghese. 2008. *There Is a God*. New York: HarperOne.
Franklin, Benjamin. 1962. *The Autobiography of Benjamin Franklin*. New York: Collier.
Jefferson, Thomas. 2011. *The Jefferson Bible: The Life and Morals of Jesus of Nazareth*. Washington, DC: Smithsonian Books.
Sanford, Charles B. 1984. *The Religious Life of Thomas Jefferson*. Charlottesville: University of Virginia Press.
Smith, Christian, with Melinda L. Denton. 2005. *Soul Searching: The Religious and Spiritual Lives of American Teenagers*. Oxford: Oxford University Press.
Voltaire. (1764) 1901. *Philosophical Dictionary*. In *The Works of Voltaire*, vol. 11. New York: E. R. DuMont.

DEMARCATION, PROBLEM OF. Modern **science** has made spectacular progress, both in its theoretical understanding of nature and in its practical ability to solve problems. By contrast, other disciplines, like literature and philosophy, show modest innovations, but their major themes are perennial and their basic ideas are resistant to change. The unparalleled growth of scientific knowledge suggests that science has a distinctive method that embodies especially important epistemic virtues. This motivates the problem of demarcation in the **philosophy of science**: Can we establish the criterion that distinguishes between scientific and nonscientific statements and activities so that we can draw a sharp line between the two?

In his *Posterior Analytics*, **Aristotle** (384–322 BC) argued that scientific beliefs "deal with causes, . . . use logical demonstrations, . . . identify the universals which 'inhere' in the particulars" and "must have *apodictic certainty*" (Laudan 1983, 112). Aristotle assumed that science was founded on infallible **intuition**s of natural necessity, governed by essences, but later thinkers questioned his approach. In the medieval period, nominalists like William of Occam (1287–1347) rejected essences as fictional constructs and insisted that the course of nature is not necessary but reflects God's free choices. By the time of the **scientific revolution**, scientists had recovered **Augustine**'s idea that nature is God's other book (Augustine 1987, 32.20; see **Two Books Metaphor**). **Galileo** (1564–1642) wrote that science "is written in this grand book, the universe . . . in the language of mathematics" (Galilei 1957, 237), and **Johannes Kepler** (1571–1630) and **Robert Boyle** (1627–91) agreed (Harrison 2004, 73–74).

Francis Bacon (1561–1626) was clear about how this conception of scientific method disagreed with Aristotle's. Bacon accused the Aristotelians of attempting to anticipate the course of nature through *a priori* **metaphysics** and argued that the growth of scientific knowledge required a better method, one more honest about human limitations and more willing to be surprised by observation and experiment (Bacon 2000). For Bacon, scientists must first recognize and purge themselves of preconceived biases (which he called "idols of the mind"). Then they must collect large amounts of empirical data to discriminate between competing hypotheses.

For Bacon and many others, a rigorous empirical method is what distinguishes science from nonscience. However, Bacon followed Aristotle in looking for causes (he attempts to find the cause of heat), while the **astronomy** of his time was more modest, aiming only to accurately describe the mathematical relations between bodies (kinematics), not their causes (dynamics). One of the most profound controversies in the history of science concerns whether it is enough for science to devise models that "save the appearances," allowing accurate prediction of observable events, or if science must uncover the real causes of phenomena. Certainly, many statements that seem undeniably scientific, like Kepler's laws of planetary motion and Newton's law of gravitation, do not identify the cause of the relationships they describe.

A series of developments in philosophy contributed to a more limited view of the nature of science. **David Hume** (1711–76) argued that the senses may reveal the constant conjunction of events, but not a necessary connection between them, and that there was no logically sound demonstration that the regularities observed in the past would continue in the future (see **Induction, Problem of**). **Immanuel Kant** (1724–1804) attempted to rehabilitate the idea of **causation** as necessary connection by arguing that it reflected categories imposed by us on the phenomena and thus necessarily valid of them. The cost of Kant's solution was that we cannot claim that this connection is valid of things in themselves (*noumena*), and so science is apparently incapable of discovering the *vera causa* (true cause) of things. Indeed, **Pierre Duhem** (1861–1961) argued for *instrumentalism*: a scientific theory is not an attempt to capture reality, but a mere calculating device that maps observable inputs to observable outputs.

This general tendency toward dissociating empirical science from **metaphysics** found its sharpest statement in the **logical positivism** (or logical **empiricism**) of the nineteenth and early twentieth centuries. Important representatives included Auguste Comte (1798–1857), members of the Vienna Circle—such as Moritz Schlick (1882–1936) and **Rudolf Carnap** (1891–1970)—and A. J. Ayer (1910–89). According to the **verification principle** (Ayer 1936), meaningful statements are either analytic (true by definition) or synthetic (they make a claim about the world), and the latter are literally meaningful only if they are verifiable by observation. On this view, there is a strict demarcation between scientific assertions (empirical or definitional ones) and metaphysical assertions (which are synthetic but not empirical). Metaphysical statements are declared literally meaningless, while science is conceived as the inductive **confirmation** of theory by observation.

Logical positivism was roundly rejected by the majority of philosophers. C. E. M. Joad (1891–1953) noted that the verification principle is self-defeating: since neither analytic, nor empirical, "its assertions, being metaphysical, must be nonsensical" (Joad 1950, 72). **Karl Popper** (1902–94) rejected positivism for a number of reasons. Popper recognized that in the *context of discovery* (where we find our hypotheses), nonscientific input—such as dreams, hunches, and philosophies—has often been important for science, and agreeing with Hume, he noted that the universal statements of science are never conclusively confirmed by observations. Popper thus valued unpretentious nonscience like literature and philosophy, and held that the important boundary was between science and *pseudo*sciences (like **psychoanalysis** and Marxism). This boundary emerges in the *context of justification* (where theories are tested): a truly scientific theory must be *falsifiable*.

Critics of Popper noted that it is hard to tell when a scientific theory has been falsified because it is tested only alongside other "auxiliary assumptions," for example, about the reliability of our senses and instruments and the absence of interfering factors. Popper admitted that we cannot tell if a statement is being used scientifically by inspecting its content: what matters is how we use it—"the methods applied" and a "decision" (Popper 1980, 82) not to use a "conventionalist stratagem" (Popper 1972, 37), which saves a theory only by ad hoc assumptions.

However, **Thomas Kuhn** (1922–96) argued that scientists were often justified in making such maneuvers. This is because dominant scientific theories create **paradigm**s defining what counts as normal science (Kuhn 1970). Within normal science, the paradigm is assumed as a research program, and anomalies trigger puzzle-solving but not refutation. This seems particularly rational when the theory has a strong track record of success and there is no credible competitor: when Newtonian predictions conflicted with the observed orbit of Uranus, scientists expected some unknown factor would account for it and were vindicated by discovering Neptune.

Popper conceded that refutation is often contrastive, requiring us to test one theory against another. But Kuhn denied that even this was logically decisive, because proponents of different paradigms see the data differently, making the paradigms incommensurable and causing a communication breakdown. Critics of Kuhn saw this as an attack on scientific rationality, arguing that scientists share a "basic level of observation … related to our genetic inheritance, and our needs and interests as human beings, [which] provides a common ground for communication" (O'Hear 1989).

Nonetheless, most philosophers of science today agree with **Larry Laudan** that we do not possess a credible demarcation criterion: every known attempt to propose necessary and sufficient conditions for scientific activity is vulnerable to counterexamples. Thus, if explanation by law is required, much of historical science is excluded, but if only careful observation is required, Jane Austen's novel writing is included. Laudan argues that this is because science is a family of activities characterized by "epistemic heterogeneity" (Laudan 1983, 124), with different epistemic standards relevant to different contexts. Laudan also suggested that labeling ideas as pseudoscience was largely ideological.

Angus J. L. Menuge

REFERENCES AND RECOMMENDED READING

Augustine. 1987. *Contra Faustum Manichaeum*. In *Nicene and Post-Nicene Fathers*, ser. 1, vol. 4, ed. Philip Schaff. Buffalo, NY: Christian Literature Publishing. Available at Christian Classics Ethereal Library: www.ccel.org/ccel/schaff/npnf104.pdf.

Ayer, A. J. 1936. *Language, Truth, and Logic*. London: Victor Gollancz.

Bacon, Francis. 2000. *The New Organon*, ed. Lisa Jardine and Michael Silverthorne. New York: Cambridge University Press.

Galilei, Galileo. 1957. *The Assayer*. In *Discoveries and Opinions of Galileo*, trans. Stillman Drake. New York: Doubleday.

Harrison, Peter. 2004. "Priests of the Most High God, with Respect to the Book of Nature." In *Reading God's World: The Scientific Vocation*, ed. Angus J. L. Menuge, 59–84. St. Louis, MO: Concordia.

Joad, C. E. M. 1950. *A Critique of Logical Positivism*. Chicago: University of Chicago Press.

Kuhn, Thomas. 1970. *The Structure of Scientific Revolutions*. 2nd ed., enl. Chicago: University of Chicago Press.

Laudan, Larry. 1983. "The Demise of the Demarcation Problem." *Physics, Philosophy, and Psychoanalysis*. Boston Studies in the Philosophy of Science 76:111–27. Dordrecht: D. Reidel.

O'Hear, Anthony. 1989. *An Introduction to the Philosophy of Science*. Oxford: Clarendon.

Popper, Karl. 1972. *Conjectures and Refutations*. 4th ed., rev. London: Routledge and Kegan Paul.

———. 1980. *The Logic of Scientific Discovery*. 10th impression, rev. London: Hutchinson.

DEMBSKI, WILLIAM.

DEMBSKI, WILLIAM. William Dembski (1960–) is a mathematician, philosopher, and theologian and one of the leading theoreticians for the **intelligent design** (ID) movement. He holds doctorates in **mathematics** and philosophy, as well as graduate degrees in theology and **statistics**, and has taught at Baylor University, Southern Baptist Theological Seminary, and Southwestern Baptist Theological Seminary. He is also a research fellow at the **Discovery Institute** in Seattle, Washington, the foremost think tank for the defense and propagation of ID.

Dembski published *The Design Inference: Eliminating Chance through Small Probabilities* in 1998 with Cambridge University Press, a work that provided a sophisticated theoretical basis for ID. (A less technical and more theological work was published in 1999 by InterVarsity.) Design may be reliably detected, Dembski argues, through the use of a "design filter." In brief, if a material state of affairs cannot be explained by natural laws or **chance** events or the combination of both, then that state of affairs (say, a molecular machine inside a cell) must be designed.

These objects exhibit what Dembski calls "**specified complexity**." *Specification* is a pattern that exists independently of the object being considered, such as the face of Abraham Lincoln carved on Mount Rushmore. **Complexity** concerns the improbability of the object in question. The patterns forming the face of Lincoln on Rushmore are extremely improbable. When specification and complexity are found in any object—living or nonliving—it indicates an intelligent cause as the explanation.

Design can be detected in this manner in many areas of science, such as archaeology (determining whether an object is an artifact or a mere rock), cryptography (finding design patterns in codes), and in forensic evidence (determining whether a **death** was accidental or intentional). The discipline of biology, however, resists such inferences, even when the evidence for design is overwhelming. Dembski argues that this refusal is merely ad hoc. Given the cogency of the design inference, it should be applied in the realm of biology and **physics** as well. Only a stubborn commitment to ***methodological naturalism*** (nature must be explained by unintelligent causes) quarantines biology against the design inference.

Dembski has added two books to *The Design Inference* to form an intelligent design trilogy. In 2002 he released *No Free Lunch: Why Specified Complexity Cannot Be Purchased without Intelligence*, published by Rowman & Littlefield. *Being as Communion: A Metaphysics of Information* was released in 2014, published by Ashgate. Dembski has also written numerous books and articles on popular apologetics.

Douglas Groothuis

REFERENCES AND RECOMMENDED READING

Dembski, William A. 1998. *The Design Inference: Eliminating Chance through Small Probabilities*. Cambridge: Cambridge University Press.

———. 2004. *The Design Revolution*. Downers Grove, IL: InterVarsity.

DENNETT, DANIEL.

DENNETT, DANIEL. Daniel Clement Dennett III (1942–) was born in Boston, Massachusetts, to Ruth Marjorie and Daniel Clement Jr. He received his BA in philosophy from Harvard University and his PhD in philosophy from Christ Church, Oxford. He has been awarded a Fulbright Fellowship, two Guggenheim Fellowships, and a Fellowship at the Center for Advanced Study in the Behavioral Sciences.

Dennett's career as an academic has focused on philosophy and science of the mind as well as evolutionary theory. He has written extensively on decision theory and human **consciousness**, including his book *Consciousness Explained* (1992). Dennett is a strong proponent of memetics, where "**memes**" are considered viral ideas that can influence social (and individual) behavior. While not biologically heritable, Dennett argues that memes are subject to the same basic Darwinian principles as genes; **natural selection** preserves and amplifies memes that are successful in establishing and transmitting themselves through populations of minds.

Much of Dennett's public work has been at the interface between science and faith, where he has argued from the perspective of scientific **naturalism**, holding that all phenomena can be reduced to natural processes. In the biological sciences, Dennett sees these processes as Darwinian, and, in his book *Darwin's Dangerous Idea*, he refers to the Darwinian theorem as a "universal acid" that "eats through just about every traditional concept, and leaves in its wake a revolutionized world-view, with most of the old landmarks still recognizable, but transformed in fundamental ways" (1996, 65).

In a later book, *Breaking the Spell* (2006), Dennett made a frontal attack on religion, arguing that religion itself is a natural phenomenon that is explainable in naturalistic terms. Dennett casts faith in the supernatural as a kind memetic complex akin to the *superstition* seen in B. F. Skinner's pigeon experiments (where pigeons memorize and reenact elaborate strings of behaviors under the false pretense that they lead to a food reward). Elsewhere he has voiced concerns about the harmful effects of religion on society, saying, "If religion isn't the greatest threat to rationality and scientific progress, what is?" and "religion is preventing [people] from being as good as they could be."

Philosophically, Dennett claims moral realism and holds to a two-stage decision-making process in human free will. Notably, Dennett has been named one of the "Four Horsemen" of the **New Atheism** (along with **Richard Dawkins**, **Sam Harris**, and the late Christopher Hitchens). As a secular humanist, he has served on the Secular Coalition for America advisory board, and he was named to the Freedom from Religion Foundation's honorary board of distinguished achievers in 2010. More recently he was invited as one of the 15 leading metaphysical naturalists to the "Moving Naturalism Forward" meeting (Stockbridge, MA, 2013). He is currently the Austin B. Fletcher Professor of Philosophy

and codirector of the Center for Cognitive Studies at Tufts University.

Wayne Rossiter

REFERENCES AND RECOMMENDED READING

Dennett, Daniel C. 1991. *Consciousness Explained*. Boston: Little, Brown.
———. 1996. *Darwin's Dangerous Idea: Evolution and the Meaning of Life*. New York: Simon & Schuster.
———. 2003. "The Bright Stuff." *New York Times*. July 12. www.nytimes.com/2003/07/12/opinion/the-bright-stuff.html.
———. 2006. *Breaking the Spell: Religion as a Natural Phenomenon*. New York: Penguin.
Dennett, Daniel, and Robert Winston. 2008. "Is Religion a Threat to Rationality and Science?" *Guardian*. April 22. www.theguardian.com/education/2008/apr/22/highereducation.uk5.

DENTON, MICHAEL. Michael Denton (1943–) is a medical doctor, geneticist, and advocate of a nontheistic teleological understanding of biology who first came to international prominence following the publication of his book *Evolution: A Theory in Crisis* (1985).

Born in Newcastle on Tyne in the United Kingdom, Denton gained a medical degree from Bristol University in 1969 and a PhD (biochemistry) from King's College London in 1974, with stints at the University of Toronto and Hebrew University. From 1990 to 2005, he was a senior research fellow in the Biochemistry Department at the University of Otago, Dunedin, New Zealand. Denton has researched the genetics of human eye diseases, sampling from populations in southern Asia and the Indian subcontinent.

He currently is a senior fellow at the **Discovery Institute**'s Center for Science and Culture. Denton's first book, *Evolution: A Theory in Crisis* (published in the United Kingdom in 1985, and then in an American edition in 1986) was noteworthy for its breadth of coverage of biological and paleontological data, which Denton argued were incompatible with classical neo-Darwinian gradual evolution. He further argued that a phenomenon of "molecular equidistance" in **DNA** and protein sequence patterns was also inconsistent with neo-Darwinian predictions, a claim widely disputed by evolutionary biologists looking at the same patterns.

Denton's overall case against neo-Darwinian evolution was especially distinctive because he did not propose a creationist or **intelligent design** alternative hypothesis, remaining agnostic about the cause of life's origin and diversity, while also holding that biology gave evidence of purpose and **teleology**. This thesis was further articulated in Denton's second book, *Nature's Destiny* (1998), whose subtitle, *How the Laws* *of Biology Reveal Purpose in the Universe*, expressed Denton's belief in a teleological, albeit law-governed, directionality to the evolutionary process (as it unfolded in the common descent of life on the earth). Denton's more narrowly technical scientific publications, such as his 2002 publication on protein folds (Denton et al. 2002), also contend for a law-governed view of biology, wherein functional roles are "clearly secondary modifications of primary 'givens of physics.' "

Most recently Denton has amplified this position in his third book, *Evolution: Still a Theory in Crisis* (2016), in which he revisits the arguments of his 1985 book in the light of new findings, concluding that textbook evolutionary theory still falls short of its explanatory targets, and that a broadly teleological view should be preferred. Denton continues to make his case through his writings, videos, and lectures globally on genetics, evolution, and the anthropic argument for design. He continues to develop a nontheistic but teleology-motivated understanding of biology and science generally, seeing purpose in the most fundamental structures of the universe.

Paul Nelson

REFERENCES AND RECOMMENDED READING

Denton, Michael. 1985. *Evolution: A Theory in Crisis.* London: Burnett.
———. 1998. *Nature's Destiny: How the Laws of Biology Reveal Purpose in the Universe.* New York: Free Press.
———. 2016. *Evolution: Still a Theory in Crisis.* Seattle: Discovery Institute.
Denton, Michael, Craig J. Marshall, and Michael Legge. 2002. "The Protein Folds as Platonic Forms: New Support for the Pre-Darwinian Conception of Evolution by Natural Law." *Journal of Theoretical Biology* 219:325–42.

DESCARTES, RENÉ. Descartes (1596–1650) is considered the "Father of Modern Philosophy," leading the turn from scholasticism, and he developed much of the groundwork for modern scientific thinking. He was educated in a scholastic tradition that combined Christian doctrine with the philosophy of **Aristotle** and Aquinas. However, he abandoned the final cause view of Aristotelianism for a mechanistic view of the world. Descartes also made significant contributions to **mathematics**, developing the Cartesian coordinate system.

Descartes thought the scholastics' view that sensation is the source of all knowledge was susceptible to skepticism. In *Meditations on First Philosophy* (1641), he argued that because our senses can deceive, it is impossible to know with certainty that we are not in a dream or being deceived by an evil demon such that we cannot trust our senses or our reasoning (First Meditation). However, Descartes argued that the one thing that he could not doubt is that he exists. The act of doubting is an act of thinking. In order to think, one must exist (Second Meditation). He then argued that the concept of God cannot be constructed from his own mind, but must come from God, who is the source of truth (Third Meditation). Descartes then argued that because God is not a deceiver, we can trust our ability to know in cases where we have "clear and distinct ideas" (Fourth Meditation).

To further support his argument against skepticism, he offered a version of the ontological argument for the **existence of God** (Fifth Meditation). Ultimately, Descartes argued that "the certainty and truth of all knowledge depends uniquely on my awareness of the true God, to such an extent that I was incapable of perfect knowledge about anything else until I became aware of him" (Fifth Meditation).

Descartes maintained that human persons are comprised of a physical body and a nonphysical mind or **soul** (see, **Dualism**; **Soul**). However, he rejected the dualism of **Plato**, which sees the soul and body as entirely separate. The soul, said Descartes, does not reside in the body "as a pilot resides in a ship" (1641, Sixth Meditation), but rather forms a kind of natural unity. His view has more in common with scholastic theories of soul-body union than is commonly portrayed (Skirry 2005). For Descartes, the soul is not a ghost in the machine (see **Gilbert Ryle**) but a "substantial form" (CSM 3:207–8) of, and "substantially united" (CSM 3:243) with, the body. Nevertheless, contrary to the scholastics, Descartes held a mechanistic view of the body.

Descartes offered a variety of arguments to support substance dualism. He argued that he must be distinct from his body because (1) he can doubt that he has a body, (2) he can conceive of himself without a body, and (3) his body is divisible while he is not (1641, Sixth Meditation). Moreover, Descartes argued that the ability to reason and use language is beyond the abilities of a body, which is merely a stimulus-response machine (1637, part 5). Each argument has been challenged while contemporary versions are still defended.

Brandon L. Rickabaugh

REFERENCES AND RECOMMENDED READING

Beck, L. J. 1965. *The Metaphysics of Descartes: A Study of the Meditations.* Oxford: Oxford University Press.
Clarke, Desmond M. 1982. *Descartes' Philosophy of Science.* Manchester: Manchester University Press.
Cottingham, John G. 1986. *Descartes.* Oxford: Blackwell.
———. 1992. *The Cambridge Companion to Descartes.* Cambridge: Cambridge University Press.
Descartes, René. 1620–c. 1628. *Rules for the Direction of the Mind.* In *The Philosophical Writings of Descartes*, vol. 1. Ed. and trans. J. Cottingham,

R. Stoothoff, D. Murdoch, and A. Kenny. 3 vols. Cambridge: Cambridge University Press. Hereafter CSM.

———. c. 1630–33. *The World*. In CSM, vol. 1.

———.1637. *Discourse on the Method*. In CSM, vol. 1.

———.1641. *Meditations on First Philosophy*. In CSM, vol. 2.

———.1644. *Principles of Philosophy*. Excerpted in CSM, vol. 1.

———.1649. *The Passions of the Soul*. In CSM, vol. 1.

———.1984–91. *The Philosophical Writings of Descartes*, ed. and trans. J. Cottingham, R. Stoothoff, D. Murdoch, and A. Kenny. 3 vols. Cambridge: Cambridge University Press.

Des Chene, Dennis. 1996. *Physiologia: Natural Philosophy in Late Aristotelian and Cartesian Thought*. Ithaca, NY: Cornell University Press.

Doney, Willis. 1967. *Descartes: A Collection of Critical Essays*. Garden City, NY: Doubleday.

Garber, Daniel. 1992. *Descartes' Metaphysical Physics*. Chicago: University of Chicago Press.

Grosholz, Emily. 1991. *Cartesian Method and the Problem of Reduction*. Oxford: Oxford University Press.

Skirry, Justin. 2005. *Descartes and the Metaphysics of Human Nature*. New York: Continuum.

DESIGN ARGUMENT. Ancient Greek philosophers were among the first to draw attention to the apparent order and design in the world and to believe it required an explanation. Later thinkers in the Christian tradition built on their insights and developed the argument for the existence of a designer, or a divine mind, behind the universe.

In recent times, the notion of design has become the center of dispute between Christian theists and atheists in a number of areas, including **natural theology**, evolution and the question of **teleology** in nature, and the question of the overall structure and organization of the universe. We can identify at least four main forms of the design argument in both historical and contemporary discussions.

One of the best known versions is to be found in the work of English philosopher **William Paley** (1743–1805). Paley's basic line of reasoning is common to many forms of the design argument. His premise is that the universe shows evidence of design or order. This order is detectable in ordinary empirical ways. Paley focused on cases of design in nature, such as the physiological structure of living things; for instance, the arrangement of parts in the human eye or the valves of the heart (structures that resemble the intricate workings of a watch, in Paley's famous example). The conclusion of the argument is that order of this sort needs an explanation, so there is likely an intelligent designer who is responsible for the design in nature and in the universe more generally.

The argument is an inductive or probabilistic one; it does not claim that the design in the universe offers conclusive proof of a designer, only that it is a very reasonable conclusion.

The argument is based on a comparison of human artifacts that are designed (such as a watch or a car engine) and are the product of (our) intelligence with the universe and its design that points, analogously, to (God's) intelligence.

Many interpreted **Charles Darwin**'s theory of **evolution** as a refutation of Paley's argument because it proposed a naturalistic explanation for precisely the type of design and order that Paley focused on. The "design" in the complexities of **species** and in the suitability of their habitats is only apparent, according to the theory, and is due to the "blind" process of **natural selection**, which is unguided and operates largely according to **chance**. This is why some have interpreted evolution as an attack on the notion of teleology, at least as it applies to the origin and nature of species (see **Darwinism**). Although some thinkers were only too glad to interpret it in this way, it is by no means clear that it does undermine the view that nature is teleological, since the theory applies only to biological systems.

Despite the exaggerated claims of some contemporary naturalists, such as **Richard Dawkins** and **Daniel Dennett**, evolution is unable to explain (and does not officially claim to explain) the *origin* of matter and energy, nor the physical laws of the universe, nor what caused the process of evolution itself, nor the progressive direction of the process.

Christian philosopher **Richard Swinburne** has pioneered a modern version of the argument from design, sometimes called "the laws of **physics**" or "the laws of science" version. This version avoids problems raised by evolution because it appeals to a different type of order, the underlying order that is present in the laws of the universe. Swinburne appeals to the "regularities" that occur in nature; these are empirically detectable patterns in how nature behaves. They have been discovered and established as the laws of science, such as Newton's laws of motion. He argues that it is a remarkable fact that our universe follows laws consistently, with no exceptions, laws that make life as we know it possible, including **mathematics**, science (including evolution), and medicine. It is not plausible to say that these patterns in nature just happened to come about by accident. This underlying order in the universe, Swinburne argues, is evidence of an intelligence.

The **anthropic argument** for the **existence of God** claims that design can be detected in an analysis of the initial ingredients of the universe that led eventually to the **emergence** of conscious, rational observers that have free will and moral agency. This argument has been advanced by **John D. Barrow**, **Frank J. Tipler**, and **Paul Davies**, among others. The argument appeals to the nature of the **big bang**, specifically to the fact that it appears "fine-tuned" in its initial ingredients to produce a universe that would eventually lead to the emergence and survival of life and to the arrival of conscious observers who can understand many of the processes that gave rise to their existence.

Drawing on recent work in cosmology, **astronomy**, and astrophysics, proponents note that the nature of the processes involved in the big bang (such as the degree of gravitational force, the strong and weak nuclear forces, the isotropic distribution of matter and radiation, and the ratio of matter to antimatter) reveal that the **probability** of the right conditions occurring on earth for the support and sustaining of life is extremely low, so low as to be almost incalculable. The conclusion of the argument is that "fine-tuning" of this sort is an indication of an intelligent mind. The physicist Freeman Dyson has expressed this point by noting that it almost seems as if the universe "in some sense must have known that we were coming."

Many philosophical arguments appeal to analogies, and such arguments are evaluated by judging whether the two things being compared are similar in enough respects for the reasoning to be plausible. Eighteenth-century British philosopher **David Hume** (1711 – 76) questioned whether the analogy with human design that is appealed to in most design arguments is appropriate since the world is very different from human artifacts. Yet many have found Paley's basic point hard to deny: that evidence of design or order (the purposeful arrangement of parts) suggests an intelligence. Hume also suggested that perhaps we should conclude that the designer of the universe is like man, but Swinburne has replied effectively to these types of objections by noting that we can't say the designer of the universe is like man because man cannot make a universe.

In recent years, a new argument has gained a foothold in our intellectual culture called **intelligent design** (ID) theory. Proponents of this view argue that the complexities we come across at the level of molecular biology cannot be explained by the thesis of unguided natural selection, and such complexities are good evidence of a designer. ID gained notoriety not only because this claim is a criticism of the theory of evolution, but also because its proponents argued that it must be regarded as a scientific, and not a theological or philosophical, conclusion. Although this view has met with quite a bit of criticism, including within the Christian scholarly community, ID proponents further proposed that ID should be part of the discipline of science, a thesis that,

if accepted, would have implications not only for the issue of design but for the philosophical debate concerning the definition of science.

Brendan Sweetman

REFERENCES AND RECOMMENDED READING

Dembski, William, and Michael Ruse, eds. 2004. *Debating Design: From Darwin to DNA*. New York: Cambridge University Press.
Dyson, Freeman. 1979. *Disturbing the Universe*. New York: Harper & Row.
Manson, Neil, ed. 2003. *God and Design*. New York: Routledge.
Sweetman, Brendan. 2010. *Religion and Science: An Introduction*. New York: Continuum.
Swinburne, Richard. 1996. *Is There a God?* New York: Oxford University Press.

DETERMINISM. Determinism is the view that for every event there is a cause or sufficient condition for its occurrence. The doctrine dates to the pre-Socratic philosophers, most notably Democritus (c. 460 BC – c. 370 BC). With the advent of Christianity, the determinist thesis eventually rose to the status of a major problem, as theologians from **Augustine** to Aquinas wrestled with the implications of determinism for human freedom and moral responsibility.

By the early modern period, two forms of determinism had emerged. One of these is hard determinism, the view held by Democritus, which says that since all events are caused, humans are not free or morally responsible. Another view, held by **Descartes**, Locke, **Hume**, and most other early modern philosophers, is **compatibilism** (or sometimes "soft determinism"), so named because it affirms that universal **causation** is logically compatible with human freedom and moral responsibility. Among nondeterminist views, there is **indeterminism**, which denies altogether that events of any kind are strictly causally determined, and there is the more moderate position, libertarianism, which affirms the law of causality except regarding the human will. In this view the human will is sometimes characterized as a sort of unmoved mover and, in any case, not compelled by causal factors, be they physical, psychological, social, or otherwise.

Arguments in support of determinism range from the theological to the scientific, with proponents of each dating back to ancient times. Theological determinists such as the Protestant Reformer **John Calvin** and pantheist philosopher **Baruch Spinoza** explained all events, including human choices, in terms of the will or nature of God. Other theological determinists stop short of affirming divine foreordination of all events but nonetheless affirm determinism for the theological reason that since God eternally knows the whole human history, all events must be predetermined or at least cannot be otherwise.

The scientific argument for determinism reasons that since science is predicated on the doctrine of universal causation and humans are a part of the physical world, even human choices must be determined. In support of this claim, scientific determinists appeal to the predictability and explicability of human actions. Most noteworthy are the two leading schools of thought in **psychology** since the mid-twentieth century, both of which are strongly (hard) determinist: Freudian **psychoanalysis** and Skinner's **behaviorism**. Both theoretical approaches seek to subsume human behavior under lawlike generalizations.

Nondeterminists use theological and scientific arguments of their own. Thus some appeal to **morality**, arguing that the biblical presumption of personal responsibility for one's actions implies the so-called "power of contrary choice," which is the capacity to choose otherwise than one actually chooses. On the scientific side, nondeterminists sometimes appeal to quantum indeterminacy in **physics**.

So theology and science alike have been taken to point in either direction regarding the determinist thesis. Accordingly, numerous Christian scholars can be found on either side of the debate over determinism. But where there is near consensus among Christians is in believing that humans are free and have moral responsibility. Since denial of this appears to contradict Scripture, few Christian scholars have endorsed hard determinism.

James S. Spiegel

REFERENCES AND RECOMMENDED READING

Butterfield, Jeremy. 1998. "Determinism and Indeterminism." In *Routledge Encyclopedia of Philosophy*, ed. E. Craig. London: Routledge.
Earman, John. 1986. *A Primer on Determinism*. Dordrecht: Reidel.
Fischer, John Martin, Robert Kane, Derek Pereboom, and Manuel Vargas. 2007. *Four Views on Free Will*. Walden, MA: Blackwell.
James, William. 1956. "The Dilemma of Determinism." In *The Will to Believe and Other Essays in Popular Philosophy*. New York: Dover.
Mele, Alfred R. 2013. *A Dialogue on Free Will and Science*. New York: Oxford University Press.
Pereboom, Derk. 2001. *Living without Free Will*. Cambridge: Cambridge University Press.

DINOSAURS. Dinosaurs are an extinct group of diapsid reptiles. Living diapsids include lizards, snakes, crocodiles, and birds. Dinosaur remains are found in strata deposited during the Mesozoic era, from the Triassic period (approximately 230 million years ago during the Carnian epoch) to the end of the Cretaceous period (approximately 66 million years ago). Their cylindrical, internally open hip socket allowed dinosaurs to move as bipeds or quadrupeds with dominant weight on the hind limbs.

Two taxonomic orders of dinosaurs are distinguished on the basis of pelvic structure. *Saurischia* include sauropodomorphs, mostly herbivore quadrupeds with elongated necks and tails, such as the colossal brachiosaurus; and theropods, mostly carnivorous bipeds such as birdlike ceolophysis and gigantic tyrannosaurus. *Ornithischia* were herbivores that include quadrupedal marginocephalians such as triceratops, quadrupedal thyreophorans such as stegosaurus, and bipedal ornithopods such as iguanodon and edmontosaurus. Herbivorous dinosaurs used rows of interlocking teeth and gastroliths (ingested stones) to process plants for food. Many could defend themselves from predators with body or head armor, spiny or clubbed tails, and skull horns. Predators were muscular, swift, and armed with sharp claws and daggerlike, serrated teeth.

Over 1,500 dinosaur **species** have been identified. Dinosaurs dominated Mesozoic ecology and landscape, and their diversity exceeded contemporaneous terrestrial amphibians, birds, and mammals. Strata preserve not only their skeletal remains, but also trackways and nests of eggs that provide **information** on their movement and social behavior. In contrast to living reptiles, there is evidence that some dinosaurs possessed feathers, and most were probably homoeothermic (warm-blooded). Archaic Mesozoic birds compare to theropod dinosaurs called avepods, leading most paleontologists to believe that modern birds are evolutionary descendants of dinosaurs (see **Archaeopteryx**). The reign of dinosaurs ended with a mass extinction that removed 50 percent of the species of animals and plants on earth (see **Extinction**).

Herodotus (fifth century BC) most certainly described a dinosaur bone deposit in Egypt. Scientific description of dinosaurs commenced in nineteenth-century Britain. In 1824 Rev. William Buckland identified fossil remains (the Stonesfield monster) as a carnivorous reptile and named it megalosaurus. Esteemed anatomist Richard Owen coined the term *Dinosauria* as a new order of reptiles in 1842.

At the same time, in North America, Rev. Edward Hitchcock (president of Amherst College) made a significant collection of dinosaur tracks from early Mesozoic strata of New England, assuming they were bird tracks. A bounty of dinosaurs was discovered in the western United States, leading to the infamous bone wars (1890s to 1920s) between

Othniel Charles Marsh, Edward Dinker Cope, and their protégés who represented different museums competing for the best collections.

Dinosaurs in popular culture often reflect scientific perspectives of the times, from the lumbering, monochromatic beasts of Walt Disney's *Fantasia* (1940) to the agile, cunning, and colorful animals of Steven Spielberg's *Jurassic Park* (1993). Comparisons have been made between dinosaurs and the biblical behemoth (Job 40), but traditionally the behemoth was identified as a hippopotamus or, more recently, mythical creatures known in ancient Near Eastern literature.

Young-earth creationists believe that dinosaurs and humans lived together on Earth, at least until the time of the **Genesis flood**. Suspected human footprints in a dinosaur trackway in the Glen Rose Formation in Texas (exposed in the Paluxy River) are now known to be altered dinosaur prints or hoaxes. Lacking physical evidence for human-dinosaur coexistence, some young-earth creationist authors propose that dragon legends reflect the ancient memory of dinosaurs in human history.

Stephen O. Moshier

REFERENCES AND RECOMMENDED READING

Brett-Surman, M. K., T. R. Holtz Jr., J. O. Farlow, and B. Walters, eds. 2012. *The Complete Dinosaur.* Bloomington: Indiana University Press.
Paul, G. S., ed. 2010. *The Princeton Field Guide to Dinosaurs.* Princeton: Princeton University Press.

DISCOVERY INSTITUTE. Discovery Institute (www .discovery.org) is a nonprofit, nonpartisan educational and research organization whose mission "is to advance a culture of purpose, creativity and innovation." Its guiding philosophy is a belief that "mind, not matter, is ... the wellspring of human achievement" (Discovery Institute, "About Discovery").

Founded by former Reagan administration official Bruce Chapman and futurist George Gilder in 1990, the Institute has a special focus on the impact of science and **technology** on culture. It currently operates programs in a variety of areas, including economics, **bioethics**, citizen leadership, and telecommunications and public policy. However, the institute is best known for its largest program, the Center for Science and Culture (www.discovery.org/id), cofounded by philosopher of science **Stephen Meyer** and social scientist John G. West in 1996. The center serves as the institutional hub for scientists and other scholars identified with the theory of **intelligent design**, which the center defines as the idea that "certain features of the universe and of living things are best explained by an intelligent cause, not an undirected process such as **natural selection**."

The Center for Science and Culture has nearly 40 affiliated research fellows, including biologists **Michael Behe**, Jonathan Wells, and Richard Sternberg; mathematicians **William Dembski** and David Berlinski; astronomer Guillermo Gonzalez; philosophers Jay Richards and Paul Nelson; and historian Richard Weikart.

The center supports research, education, communication, and academic freedom. In the area of research and scholarship, the center supports the writing of books and articles, and funds the lab research of an affiliated organization, the Biologic Institute, directed by molecular biologist Douglas Axe. In the area of education, the center develops curricula and organizes conferences and events, including summer programs for graduate students and professionals.

In the area of communication, the center interacts with journalists, creates educational documentaries, and operates more than 50 websites, an online news service, and social networking sites. In the area of academic freedom, the center defends the right of scientists, teachers, and students to raise critical questions about modern Darwinian theory free from retaliation.

The center opposes requiring the study of intelligent design in K–12 public schools, and it publicly opposed the policy requiring a mention of intelligent design that led to the *Kitzmiller v. Dover* court case (DeWolf et al. 2007). Instead, the center favors policies that encourage students to study the strengths and weaknesses of modern evolutionary theory and that protect the freedom of teachers to discuss scientific controversies in an impartial and pedagogically appropriate manner. A number of states and local school districts have adopted science standards or statutes reflecting the center's educational approach, and none have faced lawsuits.

Discovery Institute is a secular organization, but its work is self-consciously inspired by the Judeo-Christian tradition, and many of its leaders identify with Protestant, Catholic, or Orthodox branches of Christianity. In theological terms, the institute operates within the sphere of what has been called "general **revelation**," seeking to offer ideas and insights based on evidence publicly accessible to all people regardless of their religious beliefs. These ideas (such as intelligent design) may have faith-affirming implications, but they are not themselves based on religious faith.

John G. West

REFERENCES AND RECOMMENDED READING

DeWolf, David K., John G. West, and Casey Luskin. 2007. "Intelligent Design Will Survive *Kitzmiller v. Dover.*" *Montana Law Review* 68:7–57. www.discovery.org/f/1372.

Discovery Institute. "About Discovery." Accessed August 9, 2014. www.discovery.org/about.

———. "A Brief History of Discovery Institute." Accessed August 9, 2014. www.discovery.org/a/9781.

———. "Discovery Institute's Science Education Policy." Accessed August 9, 2014. www.discovery.org/a/3164.

———. "Fellows." Accessed August 9, 2014. www.discovery.org/id/about/fellows.

DISSECTION, HUMAN. Human anatomy is an ancient science and is the foundation of the science of medicine. Pagan societies discouraged human dissection, and most classical knowledge of human anatomy was comparative anatomy, derived from dissections of animals. Although Herophilus of Chalcedon and Erasistratus of Chios dissected human bodies in the third century BC, under Roman law human dissection was forbidden and human dissection was not systematically practiced in the West in antiquity.

The leading classical anatomist—Galen of Pergamon (AD 129–c. 200)—never dissected a human being. Galen dissected animals, including Barbary apes, and extrapolated his investigation of animal anatomy from human beings. Galen's work was seminal; he described the diaphragm's role in breathing, the vacuum in the pleural cavities containing the lungs, and the anatomy of the venous system of the brain. Galen's work, while largely accurate about animal anatomy, was wrong about important aspects of human anatomy (such as the number of lobes of the human liver and the rete mirabile, a blood vessel structure found in sheep and dogs but not in humans), due to unwarranted extrapolation from animal to human anatomy.

After the fall of the Roman Empire, the pagan injunction on human dissection persisted in the chaos of the early Middle Ages. With the High Middle Ages in the thirteenth century, Christian civilization—the first civilization in history to do so—endorsed and promoted the study of anatomy by systematic human dissection.

Medieval Human Dissection

With the widespread Christianization of Europe, European science, tethered for centuries to classical pagan scholarship, began to embrace experimentation and the scientific method. Katharine Park, a Harvard professor of the history of science, observes that human dissection for anatomical study was widely practiced in Christian medieval Europe, beginning no later than the thirteenth century and long before the Renaissance (Park 2006). Christian scholars in the Middle Ages extended the common practice of embalming and autopsy to the scientific study of the human body. There was a particular focus on the reproductive anatomy of women, although all aspects of human anatomy were studied by dissection beginning in the High Middle Ages.

These anatomical studies were supported at Catholic universities and were widely endorsed by the church. Mondino de Liuzzi carried out the first public dissection of a human being for anatomical study in 1315, with the sanction of the church. The church ordered an anatomical study performed on the bodies of conjoined twins Joana and Melchiora Ballestero in Hispanola in 1533 to investigate the relationship between the body and the **soul**.

In the sixteenth century, Andreas Vesalius, a Catholic working at the University of Padua in Italy, revolutionized anatomical science by performing detailed human dissections and demonstrating the inaccuracy of many of Galen's teachings about anatomy. Vesalius's magnum opus, *De humani corporis fabrica*, is widely acknowledged as the first modern anatomy textbook.

Building on the anatomical foundation of medieval Christian scholars, Ambrose Pare, William Harvey, Giovanni Morgagni, John Hunter, and countless Christian scientists made seminal anatomical and physiological discoveries over the next few centuries and created modern medical science.

Christianity and Human Dissection

The science of human dissection was widely practiced in the Christian Middle Ages and was endorsed and supported by the church. In fact, human dissection as a scientific endeavor is uniquely a product of Christian civilization. Other civilizations—pagan antiquity, the Far East, and Islam—never practiced scientific human dissection on any scale and in fact generally proscribed such study.

As with the majority of modern science, Christian civilization was the spark and the fuel of scientific advancement in the study of human anatomy. The myth that Christian civilization impeded the science of human anatomy—a concept that would have astonished medieval and Renaissance scholars like Vesalius, who did their anatomical work in a culture immersed in Christian theology and who worked in Catholic institutions with the support and encouragement of the church—arose in the nineteenth century as a part of now-refuted historical scholarship aimed to advance a narrative of conflict between Christianity and science.

Michael Egnor

REFERENCES AND RECOMMENDED READING

Merrigan, T. 1907. "Anatomy." In *The Catholic Encyclopedia*. New York: Robert Appleton Co. Accessed September 7, 2016. www.newadvent.org/cathen/01457e.htm.

Nuland, Sherwin. 1988. *Doctors: The Biography of Medicine*. New York: Vintage.

Park, Katherine. 2006. *Secrets of Women: Gender, Generation, and the Origins of Human Dissection*. New York: Zone.

Stark, Rodney. 2004. *For the Glory of God: How Monotheism Led to Reformations, Science, Witch-Hunts, and the End of Slavery*. Princeton, NJ: Princeton University Press.

⚓ DIVINE ACTION (Concursus View). Discussions of divine action often focus on the question of whether God needs to intervene—where intervention is understood as working apart from or contrary to the **laws of nature**—to act in the world (e.g., Saunders 2002; Koperski 2015). It is also the case that most discussions of divine action focus on miracles (see **Miracles**). Yet these discussions are typically framed in terms of a fairly abstract **theism** rather than the rich trinitarian nature of God. Trinitarian love reshapes how we think about God's relationship to and action in creation as well as helping us see that God is active in all aspects of creation and not just in special or miraculous events.

Theological Background

There is no *ex nihilo* creation without purpose, and God's purposes are always infused with love. The triune love of God is the foundation for creation. Since the loving community of the Trinity is a freeing love, creation was a free act of Father, Son, and Spirit. The Trinity's freeing love is expressed in faithfulness through creating and sustaining all things (through the Son) and enabling creation to come to perfection in Christ (through the Spirit). God's love for creation is grounded in the trinitarian being of God and the covenantal nature of divine love (see **Trinity**).

If God's relationship to creation is one of freeing love, then the Trinity had no need to create the world either out of the necessity of God's nature or some sense of incompleteness. This means that God made creation for its own sake as an object of love. The Spirit's enablement and energizing of creation to be what the Father called it to be is not only for God's glory but also for the sake of creation. Moreover, the Spirit's work enabling and perfecting creation implies that when creation acts, it is a means through which God acts (Bishop 2011; Gunton 1998).

Divine Action

One upshot of all this is that creation takes its shape through a dynamic relationship with the triune God and ultimately acts to fulfill the purposes of its Creator. A second upshot is that God's action in creation typically is not in the form of special interventions. God does not need to circumvent or suspend laws of nature to act in creation. Nor does God need "indeterministic cracks" within creation to act robustly. Pregnancy and birth are divine actions mediated through regular processes of creation (Ps. 139:13). Springs and streams providing water for plants and animals, trees and crags providing shelter for animals, and cycles of day and night and the seasons are all pictured as God acting in and providing through creation (Ps. 104; Job 38–39). When flowers bloom in springtime, God is working through creation. Similarly, the physical, chemical, biological, and geological processes scientists study can be seen as means through which the Father creates through the superintendence of the Son and the enablement of the Spirit.

This means that God's usual way of acting in creation is *concursus*—acting through and alongside the processes of creation that were all made through the Son. The **incarnation** gives us the best illustration of concursus: everything Jesus did in his life and ministry on earth was a fully human action while also being a fully divine action by the power and enablement of the Spirit as he did the will of the Father (see **Incarnation**). The Spirit conceived Jesus's human body and energized its growth, enabling its being woven together in Mary's womb. Jesus's physical nature was both genuine as well as an important means through which he acted in the world by the enablement of the Spirit.

Similarly, creation's nature is genuine and is an important means through which God accomplishes divine purposes in creation. All created things, whether quarks, cells, organisms, stars, or galaxies, are energized and enabled by the Spirit to be what they are called to be in the Son and to serve the Father's purposes. God works through every created thing in such a way that it fully exhibits its nature and becomes what it is called to be. Furthermore, because this trinitarian relationship to creation is ultimately based on covenant love, it is a freeing relationship of enablement, conferring a relative freedom to all created things. Biblically, this is the main means through which God acts in creation (Gen. 1:24–25; Ps. 104).

This biblical picture of God's relationship to and action in creation contrasts sharply with the deterministic clockwork picture we have received from the seventeenth century. God's sovereignty over creation does not imply that creation is some deterministic machine operating under some kind of necessity that God occasionally intervenes in. The making of creation for its own sake because of God's freeing love grounds the relative freedom creation has to genuinely become what it is called to be. As a loose analogy, parents practice freeing love toward their children when giving them relative freedom to develop and grow. Similarly, the Trinity gives creation relative freedom to develop and grow into what it is called in the Son and enabled by the Spirit to be. Divine covenantal faithfulness is what makes the relative freedom of creation as gift possible. In turn, this relative freedom God gives creation is one of the conditions making human free will possible.

Ordinary and Special Divine Action

Ordinary divine action is often defined as God's preserving or upholding creation, while special divine action is often defined as occasions where God's action makes a difference in the world. The trinitarian view of concursus I have sketched here tends to erase this distinction between ordinary and special divine action. Every event in creation is both a natural and divine event. Langdon Gilkey's (1961) attempt to *objectively* distinguish natural acts and specifically divine acts proves to be incoherent, as there are no instances where creation acts purely or solely on its own. No such objective distinction along these lines can be drawn.

The ordinary/special distinction presupposes a false dilemma that events in creation are due either to (1) God's unmediated divine interventions or (2) natural processes without any divine influence whatsoever. The second horn of the dilemma may be recognized as **deism**. This horn is taken to be the realm of scientific explanation—hence the tremendous difficulty so many accounts of divine action face when trying to reconcile themselves to a scientific **worldview** (Saunders 2002). There seems to be no coherent room for divine action represented by the first horn of the dilemma in a scientific worldview.

However, this is a false choice, as Genesis 1:24–25; Job 38–39; Psalms 104 and 139:13 show: the Father is always acting genuinely through the very processes of nature studied by scientists. These processes are created and sustained through the Son and enabled and guided by the Spirit. Moreover, to settle on scientific accounts and a scientific worldview as the only accounts and worldview is philosophically arbitrary, as there is nothing in the sciences that licenses or forces such choices.

Miracles

This is not to say that God always and only acts through creation, but rather that much of the divine activity revealed in the Bible is mediated through creation (Bishop 2011; Gunton 1998). Certainly some miracles (e.g., resurrections or resuscitations) are interventions in the sense of suspending or circumventing natural laws. But the view I have sketched here implies that such interventionism is neither the only way nor even the primary way God acts in creation. Some miracles may be the result of concursus with exquisite timing (e.g., Israel crossing the Jordan River to enter the Promised Land).

It is a further question as to how many interventions have taken place over the course of creation's history that fit the requirements for suspending or circumventing natural laws. One implication of a robust trinitarian understanding of God's relationship to creation is that only *some* of God's activity in creation takes the form of such interventions.

Explanation

Even though some miracles might occur through concursus, at best we would only be able to give a scientific explanation of the "natural side" of such events. There would be no scientific explanation of the "divine side." Nor is there any reason to expect that a scientific explanation would reveal a "divine causality" that was somehow foreign to scientific explanations (Gunton 1997). A robust trinitarian theology of action implies that scientific explanations are the wrong forms of explanation to apply to divine action. To default to scientific explanations as the only valid explanations, to demand that an account of divine action is only valid if it "intermeshes with the causal language of modern science" (Saunders 2002, 29), is to grasp the second horn of the false dilemma. God's action in creation is confined to be only instances of special divine interventions. Such interventions would break the supposed unbroken network of cause and effect that the sciences study—hence the tensions so many feel over divine action in a modern scientific world.

Instead, we need multiple layers of explanation—scientific and theological, among others—to fully capture the richness of God's activity in creation. A healthy trinitarian understanding of God's relationship to creation provides a framework for seeing scientific investigation as studying God's normal ways of acting in and through creation.

We can interpret natural processes through a theological lens as ordinary means through which the Trinity fulfills divine purposes. Moreover, we can see that there is always more to the story than what the sciences reveal about what is happening in nature. Biblical texts such as Genesis 1:24–25 and Psalm 104 "pull the curtain back" to reveal that the processes at work in creation are forms of mediated divine action. Scientific investigation helps us understand some of the "how" of God's normal ways of working in and through creation. The Bible and theology help us understand some of the "why" of God's intentionality in creation. Much of divine action in the world is seen through *theological* interpretations of scientific explanations of the ordinary ways creation works (Bishop 2011).

What about those cases where God clearly *does* work apart from or override laws of nature, such as resurrections or resuscitations? These clearly are cases going beyond the usual order of creation. In such cases, there is no expectation that we should be able to give a scientific explanation of such singular events. Scientific methods were designed by **Galileo**, Gassendi, Bacon, Boyle, Newton, and others to study repeated events, the functional integrity God gave to creation expressed in the persistent patterns of creation. Scientific methods were not designed to study singular, nonrepeatable events. Scientific explanations can help us understand when we may be facing such unique events, but there is nothing about such divine actions that somehow violates scientific norms and explanations (Koperski 2015)—unless one has adopted a scientific worldview that simply rules out singular events and divine action in the first place. In this event, one's **metaphysics** have gone far beyond anything that scientific investigation could possibly license.

Divine Action and Randomness

What I have been arguing is twofold: Debates about divine action (1) tend to leave trinitarian theology to the side to their detriment, and, as a consequence, (2) focus too narrowly on divine special interventions while missing the vast terrain of God's normal activity mediated through creation's functional integrity. But what about randomness? How does that fit into a rich picture of trinitarian-mediated action? Is not genuine randomness a threat to God's rule in creation?

Two forms of randomness show up in scientific explanations. The first is *apparent randomness*. Such randomness has an underlying deterministic basis, but due to epistemic limitations, we cannot precisely know all the conditions of this basis. Roulette wheels and throwing dice are examples. There is a deterministic basis for the outcomes (e.g., which number the ball will land on), but due to ignorance, we cannot say which outcome will be realized.

The second form is *irreducible randomness*. For such randomness all of the relevant physical factors only determine a fixed **probability** for outcomes, but not the specific outcome itself. Radioactive decay would be an example. Given a sample

of a radioactive isotope, the probability for how many nuclei in the sample will undergo a decay event in a 24-hour period is determined by the relevant physical conditions. Nevertheless, which particular nuclei will undergo decay events is not determined. To be clear, irreducible randomness *is not* lawless chaos. Irreducible randomness *always* conforms to statistical laws. This is part of the regular order of the functional integrity God gave creation.

It is possible that although God established the probabilities for irreducibly random outcomes through creation's functional integrity, God actualizes the particular outcomes such that they always fulfill the laws of nature (Russell 1997). However, if God is continually actualizing all or even most of these outcomes, this would imply that creation's functional integrity is somehow inadequate to fulfill its calling to become what the Father destined through the Son as enabled by the Spirit.

Instead, from the vantage point of the Trinity's freeing love, we can see that even irreducible randomness is part of the nature of the creation that God made for its own sake. And such randomness is enabled by the Spirit to fulfill divine purposes. After all, we work through radioactive processes all the time to accomplish purposes (e.g., radiation therapy, nuclear power). These are ways in which humans genuinely act though mediated through irreducible randomness. It is nothing, then, for God to act in mediated ways through such processes to fulfill divine purposes. Scientists can give a description of such processes, but they really are only describing some of the means through which God works in the world.

Robert C. Bishop

REFERENCES AND RECOMMENDED READING

Bishop, Robert C. 2011. "Recovering the Doctrine of Creation: A Theological View of Science." BioLogos Forum. http://biologos.org/uploads/static-content/bishop_white_paper.pdf.

Gilkey, Langdon. 1961. "Cosmology, Ontology and the Travail of Biblical Language." *Journal of Religion* 41:194–205.

Gunton, Colin. 1997. "The End of Causality? The Reformers and Their Predecessors." In *The Doctrine of Creation*, ed. Colin Gunton, 63–82. Edinburgh: T&T Clark.

———. 1998. *The Triune Creator: A Historical and Systematic Study.* Grand Rapids: Eerdmans.

Johnson, Phillip E. 1999. "The Fear of God: Review of *The Fifth Miracle*: *The Search for the Origin of Life*, by Paul Davies." Access Research Network. www.arn.org/docs/johnson/fifthmiracle.htm.

Koperski, Jeffrey. 2015. *The Physics of Theism: God, Physics, and the Philosophy of Science.* Malden, MA: Wiley-Blackwell.

Russell, Robert John. 1997. "Does 'the God Who Acts' Really Act? New Approaches to Divine Action in the Light of Science." *Theology Today* 54:43–65.

Saunders, Nicholas. 2002. *Divine Action and Modern Science.* Cambridge: Cambridge University Press.

⚡ DIVINE ACTION (Engaged-Governance View).
Theists believe that God has created the universe and continues to sustain it, but what else does God do? In particular, does God sometimes intervene in the natural order to bring about events that would not have otherwise occurred, and sometimes intervene to prevent other events from happening? This is the question of *special divine action.*

From a biblical point of view, the answer seems clear. In the Old Testament, there are acts of God that are contrary to the normal flow of nature. Some are small, like an ax head that floats (2 Kings 6); others are dramatic, such as the plagues against Egypt (Ex. 7–10). In the New Testament, there are **miracles** performed by Jesus, but there are also "signs and wonders" brought about by the power of God working through his followers: Peter healing the lame man (Acts 3) and the spiritual gifts of healing and miracles mentioned by Paul (1 Cor. 12), among others.

More liberally minded theologians have tried to naturalize biblical miracles. Instead of the miraculous feeding of the 5,000 (Matt. 14:13–21), for example, some have proposed that Jesus's teaching prompted his audience to spontaneously share their food with others, thereby feeding everyone. There is also a question of whether miracles should be understood as breaking the **laws of nature** or rather "marvels" that are religiously significant but do not require God to intervene. As William Pollard put it, "Biblical miracles are, like that in the exodus, the result of an extraordinary and extremely improbable combination of **chance** and accident. They do not, on close analysis, involve, as is so frequently supposed, a violation of the laws of nature" (Pollard 1958, 115).

For example, say that the Jews in first-century Jerusalem had fasted and prayed for 40 days to be spared from the Roman general Titus. Say that on day 40, Titus was struck and killed by a meteorite. Was this a miracle? Although those in Jerusalem would have described it that way, it might merely have been a marvel. God might have foreseen these **prayer**s and put this meteor in motion at creation so that it would land on Titus at the appointed time—no intervention required. (Such well-timed "marvels" are sometimes called acts of "extraordinary providence." This is in contrast to "ordinary providence"—providing rain and sunshine and a fruitful earth [Matt. 5:45; Acts 14:17]—and to "miracle," which is discussed below.)

While some events and aspects of design in nature can be accounted as marvels, this is not the case for many biblical miracles. As N. T. Wright has often remarked, for example, ancient people knew that dead people stay dead. The raising of Lazarus required God to intervene. The same is true for many purported answers to prayer through the centuries. Miracles in the New Testament, throughout church history, and across the world in our own day have been ably documented in Craig Keener's two-volume *Miracles* (Keener 2011). With this in mind, I take interventionist divine action to be the default position in this debate. The burden of proof is on the noninterventionist. Therefore, instead of presenting positive arguments in favor of this view, let's consider some noninterventionist objections.

1. *Incompetent.* A powerful analogy presented by the German philosopher Gottfried Leibniz has long shaped this debate. While **Isaac Newton** and others allowed for divine intervention in nature, Leibniz argued that an omniscient deity would not act that way:

> According to [the Newtonian] doctrine, God Almighty wants to wind up his watch from time to time: otherwise it would cease to move. He had not, it seems, sufficient foresight to make it a perpetual motion. Nay, the machine of God's making is so imperfect, according to these gentlemen, that he is obliged to clean it now and then by an extraordinary concourse, and even to mend it, as a clockmaker mends his work. (Leibniz and Clarke 1956, 11–12)

In other words, an omniscient and omnipotent deity would have gotten it right in the first place. An infinite clockmaker, says Leibniz, would make a clock that would keep perfect time forever without winding or making adjustments. The same goes for the universe as a whole. A God who needs to intervene in nature from time to time would be incompetent. To think as the Newtonians do is to "have a very mean notion of the wisdom and power of God."

2. *Inconsistent.* Since the seventeenth century, theists have widely believed that God set the laws of nature in place and continues to uphold them. This presents a problem for divine intervention. Noninterventionists argue that it would be inconsistent for God to intervene in nature and thereby violate the very laws he previously ordained. If God had wanted some event to happen, he could have structured the laws to bring it about or changed the initial conditions at creation. To implement and then break his own laws would involve a kind of divine schizophrenia. Hence God does not violate the decrees that we recognize as natural laws.

3. *God-of-the-gaps.* Newton's theory of gravitation is "universal" in the sense that it applies to everybody in the

universe. Why then, Newton wondered, don't we observe stars falling toward one another over long periods of time? After all, they attract each other. Why don't they move? His answer in the *Opticks* was that God intervenes in order to keep the stars in place (1704, query 31). In time, of course, a naturalistic explanation was found and there was no need to posit divine intervention to account for the fixed stars.

Newton's explanation is an example of what is now called "God-of-the-gaps reasoning": When a given phenomenon doesn't seem possible according to our best theories, one infers that God is responsible, thus filling the gap in our understanding. Noninterventionists argue that this same inference is used whenever divine action is invoked as an explanation. The problem, as the Newton example illustrates, is when science eventually closes the explanatory gaps and God is pushed out. Each time that God is eliminated strengthens the atheistic conclusion that divine action is never needed to explain anything. "Science," the atheist assures us, "will plug all of the gaps in time." Noninterventionists believe this argument can best be undermined by avoiding gap reasoning in the first place. Theists, they say, should not appeal to divine intervention to explain phenomena that they find surprising (see **God of the Gaps**).

4. *Unscientific.* With the possible exception of quantum mechanics, we are told, science has shown that physical reality is made up of an unbroken chain of natural causes. Observations only reveal physical effects produced by physical causes. In other words, many believe that science has proved the *causal closure of the physical*: physical events can only be caused by earlier physical events in conjunction with the laws of nature. Divine intervention is problematic because it breaks the chain of **causation**. Hence atheists and some theists believe that miraculous intervention is contrary to science. In particular, God acting within the universe would require energy to be put into the system. Such an act would violate the **conservation of energy** and is therefore unscientific in the strongest sense: it is an event that science has shown to be impossible.

Insofar as science is considered the gold standard of human knowledge, noninterventionists believe that **theism** ought to avoid any conflict with science. It is better, therefore, for Christians to avoid appeals to divine intervention.

I believe there are good answers to each of these objections. Let's consider them in order.

1. *Bad metaphor.* Leibniz presented his clockmaker analogy at a time when the universe was considered to be a vast machine. And it makes sense that if God were to create a machine, it would work perfectly and without maintenance. But what if God does not view his creation like that? What if God sees creation as something like a garden or perhaps a musical instrument? In those cases, the appeal isn't merely in the making or owning, but rather in the interaction with what has been made. I suggest that rather than a detached deistic god, the creative God of Christianity loves and appreciates what he has made and takes joy in an interactive relationship with it, as he does with us. The acts we understand as divine intervention are not the marks of incompetence, but rather creative genius. In any case, our theology of divine action ought not be driven by a seventeenth-century metaphor.

2. *Laws and God's will.* We ought not forget that the idea that there are laws of nature was developed within a theistic framework (Koperski 2015, 15–20). The claim that God's declaration of the laws is inconsistent with special divine action would have been a great surprise to **Descartes**, Newton, and most of the other scientists who relied so heavily on the idea. Many agreed with **Robert Boyle** that while the laws are what God ordinarily declares or orders, he was free to choose otherwise, as in the case of miracles (1772, 161). Why must this entail a conflict of divine will?

Consider an analogy. When it comes to pain, my will and desire for my dog is clear: I want him not to have it. Nonetheless, I took him to the vet for shots, which I knew in advance would be painful. Was this inconsistent? No, one's will has different layers and often takes into consideration a wide array of circumstances. My general will for Thatcher is that he not be in pain, but I allow it at times in order to bring about a greater good. Likewise, God can have a general will to govern via the laws of nature and yet have special cases/circumstances where he does not. I see no reason to think of this as inconsistency or a conflict of will.

3. *Gap explanations.* It's true that virtually any phenomenon can be "explained" as being an act of God. One might worry, then, that theists will use divine intervention as an explanation for any event that is beyond the reach of current science. Is this a good reason for the blanket rejection of divine intervention?

The history of science is a helpful guide here. Apart from the example of Newton and the stars, does this history contain a long line of theistic scientists routinely appealing to God as an explanation for puzzling events? No. The reason Newton is cited so often is that he is an exception. Theistic scientists prefer naturalistic explanations to supernatural ones. As I mentioned above, however, many of those same scientists also believed that God sometimes intervenes and that miracles do in fact occur. A preference for naturalistic explanations is not the same thing as an absolute rejection of special divine action.

No doubt, some Christians too quickly and unnecessarily reach for supernatural explanations of events. Banning such appeals, though, is a theological overreaction.

4. *Causal closure and* **metaphysics**. Given the claims about causal closure above, one might wonder which scientific observation or theory established that the universe is causally closed. The answer is *none*. Closure is not a claim found in any law, theory, or observation; closure is a metaphysical principle. Now, there is nothing intrinsically wrong with that. Science could not get off the ground without a wide variety of philosophical principles, such as the mind independence of reality and the reliability of reason. While many ontological naturalists—those who believe that natural entities are all that exist—argue that causal closure also belongs on the list of scientifically endorsed principles, this one is far more controversial. In particular, why should anyone who is not an ontological naturalist believe in causal closure? As philosopher Alvin Plantinga rightly argues:

> There is an interesting irony, here, in the fact that the hands-off [=noninterventionist] theologians, in their determination to give modern science its due, urge an understanding of classical science that goes well beyond what classical science actually propounds. Hands-off theologians can't properly point to science—not even to eighteenth- and nineteenth-century classical science—as a reason for their opposition to divine intervention. What actually guides their thought is not classical science **as** such, but classical science plus a metaphysical add-on—an add-on that has no scientific credentials and goes contrary to classical Christianity. (Plantinga 2008, 380)

So let's be clear: While divine intervention violates causal closure, that is not equivalent to it being contrary to science. The most that the naturalist or noninterventionist can rightly claim is that *in the absence of nonphysical causes*, physical effects are produced by physical causes in conjunction with the laws of nature.

As for the conservation of energy, there are two reasons it is a *non sequitur* when it comes to divine action. First, it does not apply to the universe as a whole. Texts on the **general theory of relativity** make it clear that there is no consensus definition for the energy of the whole of space (Wald 2010, 70). (More technically, conservation of energy applies if and only if the laws governing a system are time-translation

invariant, which is not the case in an expanding universe.) Conservation of energy applies only to systems in which energy is defined; hence it cannot be violated by forces originating from beyond our particular space-time.

Second, conservation principles in physics do not forbid the influence of forces from outside of a system. They instead say what happens within a system that is considered closed or isolated. For example, the conservation of momentum will allow a physicist to calculate the trajectories within a closed system of two billiard balls before and after a collision. However, conservation does not prevent a child from grabbing one of the balls off the table at the point of collision. Note that the child does not violate the conservation of momentum in doing so. When an outside force interferes with a "closed system," conservation principles no longer apply. For this reason, it is not possible for divine action to violate the conservation of energy. Such principles do not apply when God acts in nature.

Finally, while I have been defending the legitimacy of divine intervention, this does not preclude models of divine action that allow for God's active governance of creation without breaking the laws of nature. Such models exist (Koperski 2015, chap. 1). My concern has been to defend special divine action from critics whose theology leans uncomfortably toward **deism** and from ontological naturalists who mistake their preferred philosophical views with science.

Jeffrey Koperski

REFERENCES AND RECOMMENDED READING

Boyle, Robert. 1772. "Reason and Religion." In *The Works of the Honourable Robert Boyle*, vol. 4, ed. Thomas Birch. London. J. and F. Rivington.

Keener, Craig S. 2011. *Miracles: The Credibility of the New Testament Accounts.* 2 vols. Grand Rapids: Baker Academic.

Koperski, Jeffrey. 2015. *The Physics of Theism: God, Physics, and the Philosophy of Science.* Malden, MA: Wiley-Blackwell.

Leibniz, Gottfried W., and Samuel Clarke. 1956. *The Leibniz-Clarke Correspondence: Together with Extracts from Newton's Principia and Optics*, ed. H. G. Alexander. Manchester: Manchester University Press.

Newton, Isaac. 1704. *Opticks.* Many editions.

Plantinga, Alvin. 2008. "What Is 'Intervention'?" *Theology and Science* 6 (4): 369–401. doi:10.1080/14746700802396106.

Pollard, William G. 1958. *Chance and Providence: God's Action in a World Governed by Scientific Law.* New York: Scribner.

Wald, Robert M. 2010. *General Relativity.* Chicago: University of Chicago Press.

DIVINE VOLUNTARISM. When God created the world, did he do so freely or out of necessity? Can necessary reasons be given for the existence and natures of specific created things, or was God free to create anything he wished in any way he pleased? Questions such as these have long been central to the doctrine of creation, especially in medieval and early modern conversations about divine will and power (Oakley 1984; Osler 1994). Their relevance to the development of science was underscored by the seminal work of British philosopher Michael Beresford Foster in the 1930s.

Foster identified two contrasting attitudes toward God's creative activity. Rationalist theology "is the doctrine that the activity of God is an activity of reason," so that "there is … nothing mysterious or inscrutable in his nature." Such a theology entails "a rationalist theory of knowledge of nature." Since the world and our minds were both created by divine reason, our minds disclose God's thoughts to us, revealing "the essential nature of the created world." Voluntarist theology, on the other hand, "attributes to God an activity of will not wholly determined by reason," and therefore the created world is contingent, not logically necessary. Since unaided reason cannot attain truth about a contingent reality, evidence from the senses is essential for natural science (Foster 1936, 1, 5n5, 10).

Leading scholars still use similar terms and conceptions, whether or not they accept Foster's view that theological voluntarism leads inevitably to modern empirical science (Harrison 2002; Henry 2009). Historian Reijer Hooykaas wrote about the method of "rational **empiricism**" that "has an open eye for the contingency of the existence and the way of being of things" (Hooykaas 1972, 29), while theologian **Thomas Torrance** spoke of the universe itself as a "contingent order" (Torrance 1981). The issues Foster raised have ongoing relevance, as seen in **Albert Einstein**'s famous statement, "What I'm really interested in is whether God could have made the world in a different way; that is, whether the necessity of logical simplicity leaves any freedom at all" (Holton 1978, xii).

Edward B. Davis

REFERENCES AND RECOMMENDED READING

Foster, Michael. 1934. "The Christian Doctrine of Creation and the Rise of Modern Natural Science." *Mind* 43:446–68.
———. 1935. "Christian Theology and Modern Science of Nature (I)." *Mind* 44:439–66.
———. 1936. "Christian Theology and Modern Science of Nature (II)." *Mind* 45:1–27.
Harrison, Peter. 2002. "Voluntarism and Early Modern Science." *History of Science* 40:63–89.
Henry, John. 2009. "Voluntarist Theology at the Origins of Modern Science: A Response to Peter Harrison." *History of Science* 47:79–113.
Holton, Gerald. 1978. *The Scientific Imagination.* Cambridge: Cambridge University Press.
Hooykaas, R. 1972. *Religion and the Rise of Modern Science.* Grand Rapids: Eerdmans.
Oakley, Francis. 1984. *Omnipotence, Covenant, and Order.* Ithaca, NY: Cornell University Press.
Osler, Margaret J. 1994. *Divine Will and the Mechanical Philosophy: Gassendi and Descartes on Contingency and Necessity in the Created World.* Cambridge: Cambridge University Press.
Torrance, Thomas F. 1981. *Divine and Contingent Order.* Oxford: Oxford University Press.

DNA. Deoxyribonucleic acid (DNA) is the primary molecule carrying genetic **information** in living organisms. Its double-helix structure, discovered in 1953 by James Watson and **Francis Crick** (Watson and Crick 1953), has been compared to a winding staircase, with nucleotide bases cross-linking two helical backbones made of alternating sugars (deoxyribose) and phosphate groups, coiled symmetrically about an axis. All known living organisms use DNA to carry biological information and transmit that information to their offspring. DNA carries information in both digital and analog forms.

DNA's digital information is carried through the sequence of pairs of nucleotide bases along its spine. As a *Nature* paper titled "The Digital Code of DNA" explained: "DNA can accommodate almost any sequence of base pairs—any combination of the bases adenine (A), cytosine (C), guanine (G) and thymine (T)—and, hence any digital message or information" (Hood and Galas 2003). MIT engineer Seth Lloyd elaborates how DNA carries digital information:

> DNA is very digital. There are four possible base pairs per site, two bits per site, three and a half billion sites, seven billion bits of information in the human DNA. There's a very recognizable digital code of the kind that electrical engineers rediscovered in the 1950s that maps the codes for sequences of DNA onto expressions of proteins. (Lloyd 2007)

The biochemical language of DNA uses strings of three nucleotide bases (called codons) to symbolize commands that specify the ordering of amino acids in proteins, as well as other commands, such as "start" or "stop" protein production. Cellular machinery interprets and executes these instructions through a process called transcription and translation.

During transcription, cellular machinery copies the information in a gene-coding section of DNA into messenger RNA (mRNA), a mobile, though less stable molecule also capable of carrying genetic information. Next, mRNA travels to the ribosome, a molecular machine that reads and "translates" the mRNA's instructions to assemble a protein. Another molecule called transfer RNA (tRNA) ferries needed amino acids to the ribosome so that the protein chain can be assembled. Secondary digital codes also exist within DNA to regulate translation speed and protein folding (D'Onofrio and Abel 2014).

DNA's analog information is carried through the continuous shape of supercoiled DNA as a chromosome, which exposes only certain sites along the DNA molecule at certain times to permit transcription, thus regulating protein production (Muskhelishvili and Travers 2013).

Many have recognized the computerlike properties of DNA's language-based code. Bill Gates observes, "Human DNA is like a computer program but far, far more advanced than any software we've ever created" (Gates 1996); **Francis Collins** notes, "DNA is something like the hard drive on your computer" containing "programming" (Collins 2003); and Craig Venter contends that "life is a DNA software system" (Venter 2013). Even **Richard Dawkins** says, "The machine code of the genes is uncannily computer-like" (Dawkins 1995).

DNA's elegant structure for carrying genetic information has confounded attempts to explain its origin. **Intelligent design** theorist **Stephen Meyer** argues that "the information-bearing properties of DNA" show "there is at least one appearance of design in biology that may not yet have been adequately explained by **natural selection** or any other purely natural mechanism" (Meyer 2009). Indeed, decades after codiscovering DNA's structure, Francis Crick acknowledged that "biologists must constantly keep in mind that what they see was not designed, but rather evolved" (Crick 1988).

Casey Luskin

REFERENCES AND RECOMMENDED READING

Collins, Francis S. 2003. "Faith and the Human Genome." *Perspectives on Science and Christian Faith* 55:142–53.

Crick, Francis H. 1988. *What Mad Pursuit: A Personal View of Scientific Discovery.* New York: Basic Books.

Dawkins, Richard. 1995. *River Out of Eden: A Darwinian View of Life.* New York: Basic Books.

D'Onofrio, David J., and David L. Abel. 2014. "Redundancy of the Genetic Code Enables Translational Pausing." *Frontiers in Genetics* 140:1–16.

Franklin, Rosalind E., and R. G. Gosling. 1953a. "Molecular Configuration in Sodium Thymonucleate." *Nature* 171:740–41.

———. 1953b. "Evidence for 2-Chain Helix in Crystalline Structure of Sodium Deoxyribonucleate." *Nature* 172:156–57.

Gates, Bill. 1996. *The Road Ahead.* Rev. ed. New York: Viking.

Hood, Leroy, and David Galas. 2003. "The Digital Code of DNA." *Nature* 421:23.

Lloyd, Seth. 2007. "Life: What a Concept!" *Edge.* www.edge.org/documents/life/lloyd_index.html.

Meyer, Stephen C. 2009. *Signature in the Cell: DNA and the Evidence for Intelligent Design.* New York: HarperOne.

Muskhelishvili, Georgi, and Andrew Travers. 2013. "Integration of Syntactic and Semantic Properties of the DNA Code Reveals Chromosomes as Thermodynamic Machines Converting Energy into Information." *Cellular and Molecular Life Sciences* 70 (23): 4555–67.

Venter, J. Craig. 2013. "The Big Idea: Craig Venter on the Future of Life." *Daily Beast.* October 25. www.thedailybeast.com/articles/2013/10/25/the-big-idea-craig-venter-the-future-of-life.html.

Watson, James D., and Francis H. Crick. 1953. "A Structure for Deoxyribonucleic Acid." *Nature* 171:737–38.

DRAPER, JOHN WILLIAM. John William Draper (1811–82) was an English-born American photochemist known for contributions to early photography, photochemistry, and intellectual history. His *History of the Conflict between Religion and Science* (Draper 1875) is an exemplar of the "**conflict thesis**."

The son of a scientifically inclined Methodist minister, Draper received a thorough early education and completed a "certificate of honors" in chemistry at the University of London. Afterward he immigrated to Virginia to teach at a Methodist College. When travel delays cost Draper the job, he conducted independent research, supported by his sisters who ran a seminary for girls and gave painting and drawing lessons (Fleming 1950). After publishing several scientific papers, he completed an MD degree at the University of Pennsylvania with a thesis on "glandular action" (Chamberlain 1902), arguing (contra vitalism) that respiration can be explained in terms of ordinary physiochemical processes (Fleming 1950).

After a short period on the faculty at Hampton-Sidney College, Draper was appointed professor of chemistry at New York University. His scientific achievements there include one of the first daguerreotype portraits (Fleming 1950; McManus 1995), pioneering work in scientific photography (McManus 1995), successful textbooks (Draper 1846, 1848; Kane and Draper 1842), an early photometer, the Grothuss-Draper law, and discovery of the Draper point (977°F), at which solids become incandescent.

Draper's efforts to explain plant and human physiology (Draper 1844, 1856) in terms of deterministic laws were extended into the field of social history from the 1850s onward. An early outline of his ideas, which then focused on applying Darwinian adaptation to European intellectual history, provided the occasion for the Wilberforce-**Huxley** debate at the 1860 British Association meeting (Fleming 1950). His efforts culminated in his massive *History of the Intellectual Development of Europe* (Draper 1869), in which Draper, taking his cues from nineteenth-century liberalism, presented the intellectual development of Europe as a struggle between the expansion of human inquiry and the blind faith of a repressive Roman Catholicism.

After his history of the American Civil War (Draper 1867) further solidified his reputation as an intellectual historian, he was invited to produce *History of the Conflict between Religion and Science* (Draper 1875). It is primarily a condensed version of the relevant portions of his *History of the Intellectual Development of Europe*, although its tone was shaped by more recent Roman Catholic attempts to resist modernity, interfere in European politics, and make claims for papal infallibility (Fleming 1950, 125–26).

Although he began *History of the Conflict between Religion and Science* with the conflict thesis and presented a picture of religion as locked in a losing struggle with a triumphant science, Draper personally viewed God as a cosmic planner (Fleming 1950, 130–31) and claimed "a reconciliation of the Reformation with Science … would easily take place, if the Protestant Churches would [follow Luther in allowing] private interpretation of the Scriptures" (Draper 1875, 363).

However, given Draper's positivism, this effectively meant a radical reinterpretation of Christianity controlled by science. His book sold wildly even though contemporaries complained that both his historical scholarship and view of science were deeply flawed (Fleming 1950, 80, 134), a conclusion supported by modern scholarship (Brooke 1991; Brooke and Cantor 2000).

Draper served as the first president of the American Chemical Society in 1876 and continued his teaching and scholarly work until shortly before his death in 1882 (Bohning 2001).

Stephen Contakes

REFERENCES AND RECOMMENDED READING

Barker, George F. 1886. "Biographical Memoir of John William Draper." In *National Academy of Sciences Biographical Memoirs, Volume II*, 349–88. Washington, DC: National Academy of Sciences.
Bohning, James J. 2001. "American Chemical Society Founded 1876, John W. Draper First President." Ed. American Chemical Society. Washington, DC: National Historical Chemical Landmarks Program of the American Chemical Society.
Brooke, John Hedley. 1991. *Science and Religion: Some Historical Perspectives.* Cambridge History of Science. Cambridge and New York: Cambridge University Press.
Brooke, John Hedley, and G. N. Cantor. 2000. *Reconstructing Nature: The Engagement of Science and Religion.* Gifford Lectures. New York: Oxford University Press.
Chamberlain, Joshua Lawrence. 1902. "Draper, John William 1811–1882." In *University of Pennsylvania: Its History, Influence, Equipment and Characteristics; with Biographical Sketches and Portraits of Founders, Benefactors, Officers and Alumni*, 2:47–49. Boston: R. Herndon.
Draper, John William. 1844. *A Treatise on the Forces Which Produce the Organization of Plants.* New York: Harper & Brothers.
———. 1846. *A Text-Book on Chemistry: For the Use of Schools and Colleges.* New York: Harper & Brothers.
———. 1848. *A Text-Book on Natural Philosophy.* 3rd ed. New York: Harper & Brothers.
———. 1856. *Human Physiology, Statistical and Dynamical.* New York: Harper & Brothers.
———. 1867. *History of the American Civil War.* 3 vols. New York: Harper.
———. 1869. *History of the Intellectual Development of Europe.* 5th ed. New York: Harper & Brothers.
———. 1871. *Thoughts on the Future Civil Policy of America.* 4th ed. New York: Harper & Brothers.
———. 1875. *History of the Conflict between Religion and Science.* New York: Appleton.
———. 1878. *Scientific Memoirs, Being Experimental Contributions to a Knowledge of Radiant Energy.* New York: Harper & Brothers.
Fleming, Donald. 1950. *John William Draper and the Religion of Science.* Philadelphia: University of Pennsylvania Press.
Flynn, Tom. 2007. "Draper, John William." In *The New Encyclopedia of Unbelief*, ed. Tom Flynn, 265–66. Amherst, NY: Prometheus.
Kalfus, Sly. 2010. "Across the Spectrum." *Chemical Heritage* 28, no. 2 (Summer). www.chemheritage.org/distillations/article/across-spectrum.
Kane, Robert John, and John William Draper. 1842. *Elements of Chemistry.* New York: Harper & Brothers.
McManus, Howard R. 1995. "The Most Famous Daguerreian Portrait: Exploring the History of the Dorothy Catherine Draper Daguerreotype." *The Daguerreian Annual*, 148–71.

DRUMMOND, HENRY. Born to a prosperous Stirling, Scotland, merchant and devout Free Church of Scotland family, Drummond (1851–97) studied for three years at the University of Edinburgh but did not complete a degree. In 1870 he enrolled at the Free Church's New College in Edinburgh to prepare for the ministry. After completing his studies at New College, he was appointed to a lectureship in the sciences at the Free Church College in Glasgow in 1877, and in 1883 to a professorship in theology (Bebbington 2007).

In the face of the Darwinian challenge to conventional nineteenth-century Protestant beliefs, Drummond attempted to synthesize conservative Protestantism with evolution. Drummond's views of science and religion enjoyed widespread approval among many evangelicals at least in part because he was widely admired as an evangelist.

When the American revival team of Dwight L. Moody and Ira Sankey launched a campaign in Edinburgh in 1874, Drummond assisted the effort. Moody recognized that the dashingly handsome and articulate Drummond was so effective as an evangelist that he convinced Drummond to suspend his education for a year in order to assist him on his campaign throughout Britain. Although he declined an invitation to join Moody on a permanent basis, Drummond did work with the evangelist on his campaigns in Great Britain in 1887 and 1892 (Bebbington 2005; Moore 1985). The two, moreover, remained lifelong friends. Drummond's personal piety so impressed Moody that the American evangelist once described him as the most "Christlike man he had ever known" (Smith 1898).

Drummond's 1887 devotional commentary on 1 Corinthians 13, *The Greatest Thing in the World*, quickly became a devotional classic and was translated into 19 different languages (Bebbington 2005; Moore 1985).

In addition to his success as an evangelist, Drummond's work as a scientist added further credibility to his views on evolution, at least among evangelicals. Drummond joined Edinburgh geologist Archibald Geikie on his expedition of the Canadian Rocky Mountains in 1879. The following year, he became a fellow of the Royal Society of Edinburgh. In 1883–84, he explored the region between Lakes Nyasa and Tanganyika for the African Lakes Corporation, which resulted in the publication of *Tropical Africa* in 1888. Although largely viewed as an amateur by his contemporaries, Drummond had enough competence as a scientist to merit deep respect among many Protestants (Bebbington 2005; Moore 1985).

Drummond's *Natural Law and the Spiritual World* (1883) and *The Ascent of Man* (1894) represent his more important publications. Drawing heavily on the atheistic Herbert Spencer's purely naturalistic views of evolution, Drummond argued that the same principles operating in the material world were also directing the spiritual world. In other words, Drummond attempted to harness evolution for the cause of **natural theology** by arguing that evolution was the method God used to create and develop the world. The volume proved to be wildly popular, selling more than 69,000 copies in its first five years after publication. By 1897 it had gone through 29 editions in Britain and 14 pirated editions in America.

Intended as a response to Darwin's *Descent of Man*, Drummond's *The Ascent of Man* argued that the struggle for life that **Darwin** described was then followed by struggle for the lives of others. Because of this altruistic impulse, Drummond argued, both evolution and Christianity were ultimately one because they resulted in love.

Criticized by scientists for his scholarship and conservative theologians for his heterodox views regarding the inspiration of the Bible, the substitutionary atonement, and the bodily resurrection of Christ, Drummond's significance is the fact that he demonstrates that late nineteenth-century evangelical Protestants attempted to harness **Darwinism** by synthesizing evolution with their theology (Bebbington 2005; Moore 1985). Drummond suffered from a bone disease and died prematurely at the age of 45 in 1897 (Bebbington 2007).

P. C. Kemeny

REFERENCES AND RECOMMENDED READING

Bebbington, David W. 2005. "Henry Drummond, Evangelicalism and Science." *Records of the Scottish Church History Society* 28:129–48.
———. 2007. "Orr, James (1844–1913)." *Oxford Dictionary of National Biography.* Oxford: Oxford University Press.
Drummond, Henry. 1888. *Tropical Africa.* London: Hodder and Stoughton.
———. 1890. *Natural Law in the Spiritual World.* London: Hodder and Stoughton.
———. 1894a. *The Ascent of Man.* London: Hodder and Stoughton.
———. 1894b. *The Greatest Thing in the World and Other Addresses.* London: Hodder and Stoughton.
Moore, James R. 1985. "Evangelicals and Evolution: Henry Drummond, Herbert Spencer, and the Naturalisation of the Spiritual World." *Scottish Journal of Theology* 38 (3): 383–417.
Smith, George Adam. 1898. *The Life of Henry Drummond.* New York: Doubleday and McClure.

DUALISM. Dualism is a view in which the universe as a whole, or some central aspect of it, is understood to consist of two fundamental and irreducible kinds of entities or principles. In this sense, dualism contrasts with **monism**, a view in which there is only one fundamental and irreducible kind of entity or principle; and it also contrasts with pluralism, a view in which there are many fundamental and irreducible kinds of entities or principles. In Christian theology, for example, dualism may refer to metaphysical dualism in which a distinction is made between God, who is immaterial spirit, and the universe, which is material stuff. Or it may refer to mind-body dualism in which the physical human body is taken to be distinct from the immaterial **soul**.

Plato (428–348 BC) set forth metaphysical dualism in proposing a distinction between the realm of Forms or Ideas (which are universal, timeless, unchanging, and permanent realities), which is most real, and the realm of visible things (which are particular, temporal, changing, and decaying things), which is less real. This view was in contrast to both Parmenides (c. 515–c. 460 BC), who proposed that reality is one and unchanging, and to Democritus (c. 460–c. 370 BC), who proposed that reality is many, material, and in constant flux. Plato also proposed mind-body dualism, arguing that the human soul belongs to the immaterial realm of the Forms, whereas the body belongs to the material realm of visible and corruptible things.

Within Christian thought, both metaphysical and mind-body dualism have been widely affirmed throughout history. Platonic influence was significant in the early centuries of Christian thought, both in the Eastern and the Western sides of the Roman Empire. To many early Christian theologians, the Christian Scriptures seemed to support metaphysical dualism (cf. John 4:24) and mind-body dualism (cf. Matt.

10:28; 2 Cor. 5:8), though in recent times there are a number of Christian physicalists (in this context, those who deny the existence of an immaterial soul).

In recent philosophical discussions, dualism generally refers to mind-body dualism, such as substance dualism, the view that the soul or mind is distinct from the material body, or to property dualism, the view that while there is only one kind of substance (matter), mental states are distinct properties from physical states. Classical adherents of mind-body dualism include Plato, **Augustine** (AD 354–430), and **René Descartes** (AD 1596–1650).

Mind-body dualism is not a prominent position among philosophers and theologians today, yet it is alive and well. Contemporary adherents include Stewart Goetz, **J. P. Moreland**, Howard Robinson, Daniel Robinson, Charles Taliaferro, and Richard Swinburne.

Chad Meister

REFERENCES AND RECOMMENDED READING

Murphy, Nancey. 2006. *Bodies and Souls, or Spirited Bodies?* Cambridge: Cambridge University Press.
Plato. (c. 360 BC) 1997. *Phaedo.* In *Plato: Complete Works*, ed. John Cooper, 49–100. Indianapolis: Hackett.
Swinburne, Richard. 1997. *The Evolution of the Soul.* Rev. ed. Oxford: Oxford University Press.
Taliaferro, Charles. 1994. *Consciousness and the Mind of God.* Cambridge: Cambridge University Press.

DUHEM, PIERRE. Pierre Duhem (1861–1916) was a French physicist, philosopher, and historian of science. He made lasting contributions in the field of thermodynamics and argued that the field is foundational to the rest of physical theory (including **physics**, chemistry, electricity, and magnetism). In the history of science, Duhem showed that the conventional wisdom about the paucity of original scientific thinking in the Middle Ages was wrong through his massive, multivolume works *Études sur Léonard de Vinci* and *Le système du monde.*

Most relevant to the topic of science and religion is Duhem's work in the **philosophy of science**, chiefly his *Aim and Structure of Physical Theory.* Originally written as a series of articles in the *Revue de philosophie* in 1904–5, *Aim and Structure* was published as a book in 1906, and then a second edition in 1914 included two new articles in an appendix, including "Physics of a Believer." Duhem was a zealous Catholic and made no attempt to veil his religious beliefs. But he was equally zealous in disavowing the claim that his religious beliefs influenced his science. In his view, the task of science is merely to economically summarize and classify the facts discovered by experimenters. It is not the place of the scientist to hypothesize on the underlying causes of experience. That would be to confuse science with **metaphysics**.

Actually, Duhem's thinking about science is subtler than this and allows that correct predictions by scientific theory can point to a "natural classification," which is the reflection of a real order. But Duhem has become the representative of the view that science and metaphysics should remain separate. In the 1990s, the Christian philosopher **Alvin Plantinga** wrote a series of articles on **methodological naturalism** contrasting what he called Duhemian science with Augustinian science. The latter, sometimes called theistic science, is the approach Plantinga favored, whereby one's metaphysical or religious beliefs are taken into consideration when evaluating science. Duhemian science supposedly adheres to the dictates of methodological naturalism.

Perhaps ironically, then, Duhem's work was an important inspiration for the philosophy of science in the middle of the century that argued for the deep entanglement of science and extrascientific values. Duhem had claimed that "the physicist can never subject an isolated hypothesis to experimental test, but only a whole group of hypotheses" (Duhem 1954, 187). This thesis was revived by **W. V. O. Quine** and has come to be known in the literature as the **Duhem-Quine Thesis**. It is the source of the concept of theory-laden observation according to which one's presuppositions and expectations affect what one sees.

A corollary to the Duhem-Quine (or Quine-Duhem) thesis is that it is possible for there to be multiple theories that are consistent with the same set of data. When that is the case, there will inevitably be nonscientific (and perhaps even theological) factors that influence theory selection. This is a central issue of contention in much of the contemporary discussion of science and religion.

J. B. Stump

REFERENCES AND RECOMMENDED READING

Duhem, Pierre. 1954. *The Aim and Structure of Physical Theory.* Princeton, NJ: Princeton University Press.
Plantinga, Alvin. 1996. "Science: Augustinian or Duhemian?" *Faith and Philosophy* 13:368–94.

DUHEM-QUINE THESIS. The Duhem-Quine thesis, named after the French physicist **Pierre Duhem** (1861–1916) and the American philosopher **Willard Van Orman Quine** (1908–2000), is the customary designation for what might better be regarded as a family of three inter-related theses articulated with varying strength. The three theses in question are (1) the holistic contention that no hypothesis or theory is ever tested in isolation, (2) the claim that there is no such thing as a crucial experiment that would decide between two theories, and (3) the thesis that consideration of the available evidence never absolutely determines the truth or falsity of any theory (see **Underdetermination**).

The thesis of holism is variously expressed but has as its central notion the idea that an individual element within a complex whole of interrelated elements has the properties it does in virtue of its multiple connections to everything around it. For Duhem (1954), this meant that no scientific theory entails any observation by itself, but only when conjoined with other theories related to the phenomena, the function of the experimental apparatus, various auxiliary hypotheses, and various background assumptions about the world. For Quine (1980), this holism is semantic, and truth assessments for individual sentences depend on a pragmatic evaluation of their relationships to other sentences in the same language.

The radical nature of Quine's holism is famously expressed in his metaphor of a force field that impinges on experience at its periphery and emanates from central logical and ontological commitments. The equilibrium of this field could be maintained by various means, and "it becomes folly to seek a boundary between synthetic statements, which hold contingently on experience, and analytic statements, which hold come what may. Any statement can be held true come what may if we make drastic enough adjustments elsewhere in the system. Even a statement close to the periphery can be held true in the face of recalcitrant experience by pleading hallucination or amending certain statements of the kind called logical laws. Conversely, by the same token, no statement is "immune to revision" (Quine 1980, 43).

While self-referentially problematic, Quine's suggestion that everything is up for grabs in principle is still fashionable for sociologists of science who understand the acceptance of theories solely in terms of human conventions and social dynamics (Bloor 1976; Woolgar 1988).

Quine's kind of semantic holism also undergirds the "incommensurability thesis" in the **philosophy of science** (Feyerabend 1975; Kuhn 1970; 2000). Strongly stated, this thesis holds that the meanings of theoretical terms and the standards for theory evaluation are theory laden to such an extent that rival theories cannot be compared because they do not mean the same thing or conform to the same evaluative standards, even when their terminology and standards *seem* to overlap.

Obviously, such arguments undermine the idea that science is a cumulative enterprise and the history of science is one of progress in our understanding of the physical world since advocates of different theories occupy incommensurable conceptual worlds. Philosophers of science and language have responded to incommensurability claims by championing causal theories of reference and the role of experiment and observation, by challenging the coherence of conceptual relativism, and by developing alternative accounts of scientific progress (Hacking 1983; Harris 1992; Kripke 1980; Laudan 1977; Putnam 1975).

Needless to say, if two theories are not comparable because their adherents inhabit different conceptual realities, no experiment will be able to decide between them. But the denial that there is such a thing as a crucial experiment falsifying one of two competing theories or hypotheses does not need to rest on so radical a claim.

As mentioned, Pierre Duhem (1954) noted that the more modest thesis of the ambiguity of falsification has the same entailment. If a prediction should turn out to be false, the blame for its failure need not be absorbed by the theory, but may be assigned to auxiliary hypotheses, experimental error, equipment failure or inadequacy, background assumptions, and so on. Nonetheless, most scientists and philosophers of science agree that over the course of time, reasonability and good judgment will prevail in the scientific community as to whether a theory has been adequately tested and deserves acceptance, or has repeatedly failed to be adequate and should be rejected. However, some philosophers, following in Quine's (1975; 1980) footsteps, have advocated the more radical thesis that no experimental evidence or observation can conclusively falsify *any* theory under *any* circumstances (Collins 1981a, 1981b). This radically relativistic underdetermination thesis (see **Underdetermination**) has been roundly critiqued and is widely rejected (Harris 1992; Howson and Urbach 2006; Laudan 1990).

Bruce L. Gordon

REFERENCES AND RECOMMENDED READING

Bloor, David. 1976. *Knowledge and Social Imagery*. London: Routledge.
Collins, Harry M. 1981a. "Stages in the Empirical Programme of Relativism." *Social Studies of Science* 11:3–10.

———. 1981b. "Son of Seven Sexes: The Social Destruction of a Physical Phenomenon." *Social Studies of Science* 11:33–62.

Curd, Martin, J. A. Cover, and C. Pincock, eds. 2013. *Philosophy of Science: The Central Issues.* 2nd ed. New York: W. W. Norton.

Duhem, Pierre. (1906) 1954. *The Aim and Structure of Physical Theory*, trans. Philip P. Wiener. Princeton, NJ: Princeton University Press.

Feyerabend, Paul. 1975. *Against Method: Outline of an Anarchist Theory of Knowledge.* New York: Verso.

Gillies, Donald. 1993. *Philosophy of Science in the Twentieth Century.* Oxford: Blackwell. See esp. pp. 98–116; repr. in Curd, Cover, and Pincock, 2013, 271–87.

Hacking, Ian. 1983. *Representing and Intervening: Introductory Topics in the Philosophy of Natural Science.* Cambridge: Cambridge University Press.

Harris, James F. 1992. *Against Relativism: A Philosophical Defense of Method.* La Salle, IL: Open Court.

Howson, Colin, and Urbach, Peter. 2006. *Scientific Reasoning: The Bayesian Approach.* 3rd ed. La Salle, IL: Open Court.

Kripke, Saul A. 1980. *Naming and Necessity.* Cambridge, MA: Harvard University Press.

Kuhn, Thomas S. 1970. *The Structure of Scientific Revolutions.* Chicago: University of Chicago Press.

———. 2000. "Commensurability, Comparability, Communicability." In *The Road since Structure: Philosophical Essays 1970–1993*, ed. James Conant and John Haugeland, 33–57. Chicago: University of Chicago Press.

Laudan, Larry. 1977. *Progress and Its Problems: Towards a Theory of Scientific Growth.* Berkeley: University of California Press.

———. 1990. "Demystifying Underdetermination." In *Scientific Theories*, ed. C. Wade Savage, 14:267–97. Minnesota Studies in the Philosophy of Science. Minneapolis: University of Minnesota Press. Repr. in *Philosophy of Science Central Issues*, ed. J. A. Cover, Martin Curd, and Christopher Pincock, 2nd ed., 288–320. New York: W. W. Norton, 2013.

Putnam, Hilary. 1975. *Mind, Language, and Reality.* Philosophical Papers, vol. 2. Cambridge: Cambridge University Press.

Quine, Willard Van Orman. 1975. "On Empirically Equivalent Systems of the World." *Erkenntnis* 9 (3): 313–28.

———. (1953) 1980. "Two Dogmas of Empiricism." In *From A Logical Point of View: Nine Logico-Philosophical Essays*, 20–46. 2nd rev. ed. Cambridge, MA: Harvard University Press.

Ratzsch, Del. 2000. *Science and Its Limits: The Natural Sciences in Christian Perspective.* Downers Grove, IL: InterVarsity.

Woolgar, Steve. 1988. *Science: The Very Idea.* New ed. London: Routledge.

DURKHEIM, ÉMILE. Émile Durkheim (1858–1917) was a French sociologist and a professor of science, education, and social science. He is considered to be one of the founding fathers of **sociology**, along with August Comte (1789–1857), Max Weber (1864–1920), and Karl Marx (1818–83). He is known for his analysis of suicide (1970), the influence of the modern division of labor on social change (1964), and the role of religion in social life (1995).

Durkheim was born in Épinal, France, to an eighth-generation Jewish rabbi. Although Durkheim was not an orthodox believer, his Jewishness may have greatly influenced his scholarship as a sociologist, especially in his analysis of the role of religion in society (Fournier 2005). In fact, unlike **Sigmund Freud** (1856–1939), who saw religion as a mental disease, "a symptom of psychic aberration" (Pals 1996), Durkheim perceived religion as a sign of social health, despite the fact that both theories fit "the mold of an aggressively reductionist **functionalism**" (ibid.).

Durkheim's contributions to sociology are many. He attempted to establish sociology as a scientific discipline within academia. He held that to become scientific, sociology must study *social facts*, which are "those emergent properties and realities of a collectivity which could not be reduced to the actions and motives of individuals, and that individuals were shaped and constrained by their external social environment." Durkheim understood society as a *sui generis* reality since social facts existed in their own right (Fish 2008). Further, he was a founder of *L'Année Sociologique*, which published and reviewed many articles from a sociological perspective. The popularity of this journal in France and around the world enabled Durkheim to promote sociology and gave him a significant voice in its development as well as other social-science disciplines.

Among Durkheim's significant contributions are his ideas regarding society, **morality**, and religion. Although there are earlier echoes of these ideas in books and articles prior to 1912, his definitive treatment of the role of religion in society appeared in *The Elementary Forms of Religious Life*, in which Durkheim employed ethnographic data gathered from the Arunta, a primitive Australian tribe, to identify the nature of religion.

In *The Elementary Forms of Religious Life*, Durkheim defined religion as "a system of beliefs and practices that bind a community together around those things which it holds sacred" (1995). Notably, theological ideas such as a transcendent God and the supernatural are not found in Durkheim's definition of religion. For Durkheim, "religion's true purpose is not intellectual but social" (Pals 1996). Thus religion's purpose is not to teach truths about the creation of the world and explain supernatural phenomena. Rather, religion functions as "the carrier of social sentiments, providing symbols and rituals that enable people to express the deep emotions which anchor them to their community" (ibid.). Durkheim argued that although religious beliefs are false and absurd in modern thinking, religious behaviors (e.g., rituals) will endure because they function to support the cohesiveness and unity of society. Consequently, religion retains its vitality since society needs rituals in order to exist in harmony.

Naomi Noguchi Reese

REFERENCES AND RECOMMENDED READING

Durkheim, Émile. (1893) 1964. *The Division of Labor in Society*, trans. George Simpson. Glencoe, IL: Free Press.

———. 1982. *The Rules of Sociological Method and Selected Texts on Sociology and Its Method*, ed. Steven Lukes. Trans. W. D. Halls. New York: Free Press.

———. (1897) 1970. *Suicide: A Study in Sociology*, trans. John A. Spaulding and George Simpson. London: Routledge.

———. (1898–99) 1961. *Moral Education: A Study in the Theory and Application of the Sociology of Education*, ed. Peter Hamilton. Trans. Steven Lukes. London: Routledge.

———. (1912) 1995. *The Elementary Forms of Religious Life*, trans. Karen E. Fields. New York: Free Press.

Fish, Jonathan S. 2008. "Durkheim, Émile." In *International Encyclopedia of the Social Sciences*, ed. William D. Darity Jr., 2:465–67. 2nd ed. Detroit: Macmillan Reference.

Fournier, Marcel. 2005. "Durkheim's Life and Context: Something New about Durkheim?" In *The Cambridge Companion to Durkheim*, ed. Jeffrey C. Alexander and Philip Smith, 41–69. Cambridge: Cambridge University Press.

Luke, Steven. 1973. *Émile Durkheim: His Life and Work*. London: Allen Lane.

Nielsen, D. A. 1999. *Three Faces of God: Society, Religion and the Categories of Totality in the Philosophy of Émile Durkheim*. Albany, NY: State University of New York Press.

Pals, Daniel L. 1996. "Society as Sacred: Émile Durkheim." In *Seven Theories of Religion*, 88–123. New York: Oxford University Press.

Pickering, W. S. F. 2009. *Durkheim's Sociology of Religion: Themes and Theories*. Cambridge: James Clarke.

E

ECCLES, SIR JOHN C. John Eccles (1903–97) said that at the age of 17 or 18 "[I] became enthused by the brain-mind problem, in particular as it related to my own experienced self-consciousness" (Eccles 1975, 158). This enthusiasm led him ultimately to research in Charles Sherrington's lab in Oxford. Sherrington had coined the term *synapse*, which became the subject of Eccles's research and, in his later thought, the central point of contact between the **soul** and the brain (see **Dualism**; **Mind**; **Mind-Body Problem**; **Soul**). In his research labs in Australia and New Zealand, Eccles studied the action of neurons via intracellular electrical recording. He shared a Nobel Prize in 1963 with Alan Hodgkin and Andrew Huxley for his work on the reflex arc in the spinal cord.

By the 1940s, the means of communication between neurons was debated, based on either electric transmission or chemical processes. Eccles resisted the chemical model of synaptic transmission. Through his relationship with the philosopher **Karl Popper**, he came to appreciate the importance of the crucial experiment—one that could falsify a theory. Eccles performed such an experiment in 1951, disproved his own model, and heartily accepted the chemical model of synaptic transmission, which British biochemist Henry Dale styled Eccles's scientific "Damascus Road experience."

Eccles was a Roman Catholic and in 1964 successfully organized a conference under the auspices of the Pontifical Academy of Sciences. The meeting in Rome included the top neuroscientists of his day and was designed to discuss the relations between the brain and **consciousness**. Eccles was frustrated, however, that he was restricted from inviting any philosophers, and the scientists present were permitted to consider consciousness only in a scientific sense, not a religious or moral one.

While he accepted that the human brain was an evolved organ, the soul was an independent special creation of God that acted in "liaison" with the brain. He expressed this view often in his more philosophical publications that followed his retirement from scientific work in the mid-1970s. His views are most explicitly presented in his collaboration with Karl Popper, *The Self and Its Brain*. There he advocated an interactionistic dualism of soul and body, reminiscent of the seventeenth-century philosopher **René Descartes**.

Eccles believed that human freedom and dignity were lost in a strictly physical description of humans, necessitating the dualist position.

Working with others, he continued to pursue the possibility of understanding how the soul might interject its will into the workings of the brain, and he published several papers on the subject near the end of his life. He postulated that the vesicular grid in the presynaptic bouton is so small that quantum effects become relevant considerations within synaptic transmission. This means that while statistically we can predict the overall behavior of the neuron, the actual transmission of a particular synaptic vesicle is unpredictable. This creates "room" for action of the soul yet without our ability to see that action and without violating any laws of physics. In this way Eccles believed science and faith could be reconciled.

Jason M. Rampelt

REFERENCES AND RECOMMENDED READING

Beck, Friedrich, and John C. Eccles. 1992. "Quantum Aspects of Brain Activity and the Role of Consciousness." *Proceedings of the National Academy of Sciences USA* 89, no. 23 (December 1): 11357–61.

Eccles, John Carew. 1953. *The Neurophysiological Basis of Mind: The Principles of Neurophysiology*. Oxford: Oxford University Press.

———. 1964. *The Physiology of Synapses*. Berlin: Springer.

———. 1975. "Under the Spell of the Synapse." In *The Neurosciences: Paths of Discovery*, ed. Frederic G. Worden, Judith P. Swazey, and George Adelman, 158–79. Cambridge, MA: MIT Press.

———. 1979. *The Human Mystery*. Gifford Lectures. 1977–78. University of Edinburgh. Heidelberg: Springer.

———. 1980. *The Human Psyche*. Gifford Lectures. 1978–79. University of Edinburgh. Berlin: Springer.

———. 1986. "Do Mental Events Cause Neural Events Analogously to the Probability Fields of Quantum Mechanics?" *Proceedings of the Royal Society of London, B* 227, no. 1249, 411–28.

Eccles, John C., Masao Ito, and János Szentágothai. 1967. *The Cerebellum as a Neuronal Machine*. Berlin: Springer.

Eccles, John C., and Donald M. MacKay. 1967. "The Challenge of the Brain." *Science Journal* 3, no. 4 (April): 79–83.

Eccles, John, and Karl Popper. 1977. *The Self and Its Brain*. Berlin: Springer.

ECOLOGY. Many historians believe that the foundations for ecology (namely, ecosystems biology) were laid by Baron Alexander von Humboldt (1799). The term *ecology* was first used by Ernst Haeckel (1866) and literally means "household science" (i.e., the study of the dwellings of organisms).

Haeckel defined ecology as "the whole science of the relations of the organism to the environment including, in the broad sense, all the 'conditions of existence.'" Charles Elton (1927) would simply define it as "scientific natural history."

Elton's rendering displays a clear transition from the thinking of the pre-ecology naturalists to a scientific line of enquiry. Whereas Henry David Thoreau (and many prior naturalists) meditated and wrote on the meaningfulness of nature, ecologists would seek to understand the patterns and processes involved in structuring nature as an amoral scientific enterprise. In this sense, it also meant that ecology would not only be descriptive but would establish functional theories that would allow it to be predictive as well.

In his pioneering book *Fundamentals of Ecology*, Eugene Odum defined ecology as "the study of the structure and function of nature" (1959). Building on the definition produced by Herbert Andrewartha, Charles Krebs defined it as "the scientific study of the interactions that determine the distribution and abundance of organisms" (2008). Even this definition is probably too restrictive, and a more basic working definition of ecology is the study of organisms and their interactions with the biotic and abiotic environment.

Given this definition, ecology is largely dedicated to higher-order patterns and processes in nature. As examples, an ecologist might study the metabolic efficiency of a fish **species** in cold-water streams, the competition between two co-occurring species of salamanders, the effects of drought on seed dispersal across a savanna, the microbial diversity of forest soils, nutrient cycles across entire ecosystems, or the formation of ecological communities across island chains. Modifying Theodosius Dobzhansky's claim that "nothing in biology makes sense except in the light of evolution," it might be argued that nothing in biology makes sense outside the context of the organism's ecology. After all, life history traits, species-species interactions (i.e., competition, predation, mutualism, etc.), niche space, and differential reproduction are all ideas properly housed in ecology. For this reason, ecology links nearly all aspects of biology to the level of the organism and its relevant interactions.

Following the rise of modern environmentalism, the field of ecology regained the moral component that many early naturalists had espoused with respect to the relationship between humanity and nature. Species conservation, invasive species biology, toxicology, resource management, and conservation biology are all extensions of ecology into societal behavior and policy. This has also led to some division between basic and applied aspects of ecological science.

Today the field of ecology sits at the confluence of many disparate areas of science and represents a vast and expanding collection of subdisciplines (e.g., ecological physiology, population genetics, community dynamics, biogeography, evolutionary ecology, animal behavior and **psychology**, and climatology).

Wayne Rossiter

REFERENCES AND RECOMMENDED READING

Egerton, Frank N. 2013. "History of Ecological Sciences, Part 47: Ernst Haeckel's Ecology." *Bulletin of the Ecological Society of America* 94:222–44.
Elton, Charles S. 1927. *Animal Ecology*. London: Sidgwick & Jackson.
Krebs, Charles C. J. (1972) 2008. *Ecology: The Experimental Analysis of Distribution and Abundance*. 6th ed. San Francisco: Benjamin Cummings.
Morris, Christopher. *Milestones in Ecology*. Accessed July 28, 2014. http://press.princeton.edu/chapters/s9_m8879.pdf.
Odum, Eugene P. 1959. *Fundamentals of Ecology*. Philadelphia: W. B. Saunders.

EDDINGTON, ARTHUR. British astronomer and astrophysicist Arthur Stanley Eddington (1882–1944) was widely recognized during his lifetime as one of the most important scientists of his generation. Educated at Owens College (now the University of Manchester) for a short time, he won an entrance scholarship to Trinity College, Cambridge, in 1902 and graduated in three years, receiving an appointment in 1905 as chief assistant at the Royal Observatory in Greenwich. Over the course of the next seven years, he began his theoretical work on stellar motion, was part of a 1909 astronomical expedition to Malta, and led an astronomical expedition to Brazil in 1912 to observe a solar eclipse. He was appointed as Plumian Professor of **Astronomy** at Cambridge in 1913, a position he held for 31 years until his death in 1944.

The recipient of numerous honors, most notably the Henry Draper Medal of the U.S. National Academy of Sciences (1924), the Gold Medal of the Royal Astronomical Society (1924), and the Royal Medal of the Royal Society (1928), Eddington was knighted in 1930 and awarded the Order of Merit in 1938. A lifelong Quaker, his Christian faith received expression in regular attendance at meetings of the Society of Friends, in his conscientious objection during the First World War (though he volunteered but was refused for ambulance duty on the front lines), and in the way the mysticism inherent in his Quakerism permeated his thinking about the universe and the interpretation of science, especially in his more philosophical writings (Batten 1994; Cohen 1930; Eddington 1925, 1928, 1929; Seeger 1984).

Eddington's Christian mysticism may come as a surprise to those familiar with his famous remark in response to evidence convincing him of the big bang: "Philosophically the notion of a beginning of the present order of Nature is repugnant to me" (Eddington 1931a, 450). While many Christians find scientific evidence for the doctrine of creation *ex nihilo* in the discovery that our universe had a beginning, the idea of an abrupt start to the universe disturbed Eddington's sense of aesthetic symmetry in physical theory. He preferred a static four-dimensional space-time without temporal beginning, beautifully structured, with God conceived as the ground of its being in a timelessly eternal way. His spiritual sensibilities, tutored by the temporal ambiguities in general relativity, were Augustinian in this respect.

Eddington also resisted formal inferences to purpose or design from observed features of the universe, regarding them as an impoverished and unreliable basis for faith. Instead, in his Swarthmore Lectures, *Science and the Unseen World*, he emphasized mystical apprehension and communication with the divine over academic arguments for God's existence (Eddington 1929, 42–48; see also Seeger 1984). "Mind is the first and most direct thing in our experience," he maintained, and "in the mystic sense of the creation around us, in the expression of art, in a yearning towards God, the **soul** grows upward and finds the fulfillment of something planted in its nature." In our personal experience and our study of both spiritual and physical reality, "the idea of a universal Mind, or Logos, would be, I think, a fairly plausible inference from the present state of theory." Nonetheless, while "religion or contact with spiritual power must be a commonplace of ordinary life," Eddington opined that "primarily it is not a world to be analyzed, but a world to be lived in."

While Eddington is perhaps most famous for being the leader of an expedition to the island of Principe off the coast of West Africa in 1919 to measure the deflection of starlight by the sun's gravitational field during a total eclipse in the first successful test of **Albert Einstein**'s **general theory of relativity** (Dyson et al. 1920; Earman and Glymour 1980), and for his masterful exposition of Einstein's theory (Eddington 1923), it was his work on stellar astrophysics that was revolutionary (see **Relativity, General Theory of**).

His first theoretical investigations dealt with the motion of stars (Eddington 1914), but he began studying their composition in 1916 and established that their interior heat energy was transported to the surface by radiation, not convection, as had previously been thought. He also established that radiation pressure was an important factor maintaining stellar equilibrium, which was achieved by the outward pressure of gas and radiation being balanced by the inward pull of gravitation. He showed that as the pressure of stellar matter increased with interior depth, so did radiative pressure and temperature, and hence the star's luminosity. This led to his discovery of the mass-luminosity law, which demonstrated that the amount of radiative energy produced by a large star depends almost exclusively on its mass. Eddington's work was critical to a proper understanding of stellar astrophysics, and it necessitated a complete revision of our understanding of stellar evolution (Eddington 1917, 1920a, 1926, 1927).

After 1930 Eddington worked on the relationship between relativity and quantum theory (Eddington 1931b, 1935, 1936, 1939b, 1942b), trying to give workable expression to his idea that, without recourse to observation, one could calculate all the values of natural constants that could be expressed as pure numbers (Eddington 1936, 1942a). In his book *Fundamental Theory* (1946), which was published posthumously, he presented his calculations of many of these constants—for example, the number of particles in the universe, the ratio of the gravitational force to the electrical force between a proton and an electron, the fine-structure constant, the recession velocity of galaxies outside our own, and the **speed of light**—defending the idea that these constants were integral and natural to any complete specification for constructing a universe, and that their values were not accidental (Kilmister 1995).

This work, undoubtedly colored by Eddington's Christian mysticism, anticipates later discoveries and discussions of cosmological fine-tuning and the anthropic principle (see **Anthropic Principle**; **Fine-Tuning of the Universe and Solar System**) and fits well within the edifice of his broader philosophy of **science** and its relationship to religion (Eddington 1920b, 1920c, 1925, 1928, 1929, 1939a, 1941; see also Batten 1994; Cohen 1930; and Douglas 1957). Indeed, Eddington's view of the nature of the universe is arguably a form of structuralist idealism (see **Idealism**) that drew on the epistemologies of **Immanuel Kant** (1724–1804) and Edmund Husserl (1859–1938) and was further influenced by **Bertrand Russell** (1872–1970). But while Eddington's transcendental-phenomenological structuralism is ensconced in **naturalism** by modern philosophers of science (French 2003; Ladyman 2014; Ryckman 2005; Yolton 1960), it nonetheless emerges as a corollary of Eddington's appreciation of the metaphysical primacy of mind within the broader context of his mystical Christian **theism**.

Bruce L. Gordon

REFERENCES AND RECOMMENDED READING

Batten, Alan H. 1994. "A Most Rare Vision: Eddington's Thinking on the Relation between Science and Religion." *Quarterly Journal of the Royal Astronomical Society* 35:249–70.

Cohen, Chapman. 1930. *God and the Universe: Eddington, Jeans, Huxley and Einstein. With a Reply by A. S. Eddington.* London: Pioneer.

Douglas, A. V. 1957. *Arthur Stanley Eddington.* New York: Thomas Nelson.

Dyson, F., A. S. Eddington, and C. Davidson. 1920. "A Determination of the Deflection of Light by the Sun's Gravitational Field, from Observations Made at the Total Eclipse of May 29, 1919." *Philosophical Transactions of the Royal Society of London, A* 220:291–333.

Earman, John, and Clark Glymour. 1980. "Relativity and Eclipses: The British Eclipse Expeditions of 1919 and Their Predecessors." *Historical Studies in the Physical Sciences* 11:49–85.

Eddington, Arthur S. 1914. *Stellar Movements and the Structure of the Universe.* London: Macmillan.

———. 1917. "On the Radiative Equilibrium of the Stars." *Monthly Notices of the Royal Astronomical Society* 77:596–612.

———. 1920a. "The Internal Constitution of the Stars." *Scientific Monthly* 11 (4): 297–303.

———. 1920b. "The Meaning of Matter and the Laws of Nature according to the Theory of Relativity." *Mind* 29:145–58.

———. 1920c. "The Philosophical Aspect of the Theory of Relativity." *Mind* 29:415–22.

———. 1923. *The Mathematical Theory of Relativity.* Cambridge: Cambridge University Press.

———. 1925. "The Domain of Physical Science." In *Science, Religion and Reality*, ed. J. Needham, and J. A. Balfour, 187–218. New York: Macmillan.

———. 1926. *The Internal Constitution of the Stars.* Cambridge: Cambridge University Press.

———. 1927. *Stars and Atoms.* Oxford: Oxford University Press.

———. 1928. *The Nature of the Physical World.* Gifford Lectures. Cambridge: Cambridge University Press.

———. 1929. *Science and the Unseen World.* New York: Macmillan.

———. 1931a. "The End of the World: From the Standpoint of Mathematical Physics." *Nature* 127:447–53.

———. 1931b. "On the Value of the Cosmical Constant." *Proceedings of the Royal Society of London, A* 133:605–15.

———. 1935. "On 'Relativistic Degeneracy.'" *Monthly Notices of the Royal Astronomical Society* 95:194–206.

———. 1936. *Relativity Theory of Protons and Electrons.* Cambridge: Cambridge University Press.

———. 1939a. *The Philosophy of Physical Science.* Cambridge: Cambridge University Press.

———. 1939b. "Lorentz Invariant Quantum Theory." *Proceedings of the Cambridge Philosophical Society* 35:186–94.

———. 1941. "Discussion: Group Structure in Physical Science." *Mind* 50:268–79.

———. 1942a. "The Theoretical Values of the Physical Constants." *Proceedings of the Physical Society* 54:491–504.

———. 1942b. "Lorentz Invariant Quantum Theory 2." *Proceedings of the Cambridge Philosophical Society* 38:201–9.

———. 1946. *Fundamental Theory.* Cambridge: Cambridge University Press.

French, Steven. 2003. "Scribbling on the Blank Sheet: Eddington's Structuralist Conception of Objects." *Studies in History and Philosophy of Modern Physics* 34 (2): 227–59.

Kilmister, C. W. 1995. *Eddington's Search for a Fundamental Theory: A Key to the Universe.* Cambridge: Cambridge University Press.

Ladyman, James. 2014. "Structural Realism." In *Stanford Encyclopedia of Philosophy*, ed. Edward N. Zalta. January 10. http://plato.stanford.edu/entries/structural-realism/.

Ryckman, Thomas. 2005. *The Reign of Relativity: Philosophy in Physics 1915–1925.* Oxford: Oxford University Press.

Seeger, Raymond J. 1984. "Eddington, Mystic Seeker." *Journal of the American Scientific Affiliation* 36 (1): 36.

Yolton, John W. 1960. *The Philosophy of Science of A. S. Eddington.* The Hague: Martinus Nijhoff.

EDEN. Eden, the garden into which God placed Adam and Eve to serve after creating them in Genesis 2, provided the first sacred space for God's creation. The name itself, though debated, most likely means something like "bliss, luxurious, or delight" (Tsumura 1989, 136).

While we typically think of Eden as a garden, Eden is actually the larger region in which God placed a garden (Gen. 2:8; Ezek. 28:13), and from which the river flows that waters the garden (Gen. 2:10). The garden then comes to be referred to simply as Eden, taking the name of the larger region (Isa. 51:3). This observation helps us to understand this initial sacred space, pictured in the tabernacle and temple. In ancient terms, Eden portrays God's dwelling (the Holy of Holies) adjoining the garden (the Holy Place) in which the priests serve in worship to God (Beale 2004, 66–80). The sacred temples described later in Scripture correlate with the description here. Ezekiel pictures water flowing out from under the threshold of the temple, producing life (47:1–12), and Revelation 22 pictures the river of life flowing from the throne of God watering the tree of life (vv. 1–2).

Yahweh places Adam and Eve in his garden, then, to "work" (or serve) and "keep" (or protect) the garden (Gen. 2:15). The two Hebrew terms used here consistently refer to priestly service in the tabernacle when used together (e.g., Num. 3:7–8). Genesis alludes to the function of Adam and Eve in the garden as king-priests serving God in his sacred garden.

The picture of Eden as sacred space, similar to the temple or tabernacle later in the Old Testament, helps us to understand the imagery in Ezekiel 28, where Eden is understood in those same ancient Near Eastern terms. The garden in Eden is not Adam's garden, but it is the garden of God (Isa. 51:3; Ezek. 28:13). The garden is on the "holy mount of God" (Ezek. 28:14, 16), which in ancient terms describes God's sanctuary, consistent with the picture of the garden being in a region called Eden. The complex comparison of the power of Assyria to the cedars in Lebanon and the trees in Eden in Ezekiel 31:1–9 expands on the picture of Eden as not only the garden of God (Ezek. 31:8) but a symbol of his control over all the kingdoms of the world.

The imagery of sacred space, the holy mountain, and God's sanctuary raises the question of the relationship of the biblical Eden to physical geography. The traditional view that it was a historical site, with attempts to locate that place, either with reference to modern geography or through assumed changes due to a catastrophic flood, has been challenged by those who would see the description as mythic, symbolic, or utopian. Certainly the geography elicits difficulties, such as how one headwater can become four major rivers and how it correlates with modern geography (including the identity of two of the rivers). Though neither the possibility of symbolic language nor an ambiguous context necessarily denies physical existence, it does provoke necessary interaction with the text.

The imagery of Eden is used by later biblical authors to symbolize the lush provision of the creator of the universe. When Yahweh shows his rule by bringing his day of judgment on his people, the devastation is starkly described as turning the "garden of Eden" before the destroyers into a "desolate wilderness" after them (Joel 2:3 ESV). The description draws on the sanctuary imagery by sounding the "alarm on my holy mountain" (Joel 2:1 ESV). In contrast, when Yahweh restores his people, their land that was desolated by his judgment will flourish like Eden (Ezek. 36:35).

The original placement of mankind in Yahweh's garden, then, shows their intended role before him as well as God's gracious and lush provision for them. This flourishing provision will only be ultimately realized in the end times (Rev. 21:1–4).

John Soden

REFERENCES AND RECOMMENDED READING

Beale, Gregory K. 2004. *The Temple and the Church's Mission: A Biblical Theology of the Dwelling Place of God.* New Studies in Biblical Theology. Downers Grove, IL: InterVarsity.

Tsumura, David Toshio. 1989. *The Earth and the Waters in Genesis 1 and 2: A Linguistic Investigation.* Journal for the Study of the Old Testament: Supplement Series. Sheffield: Sheffield Academic Press.

EINSTEIN, ALBERT. Albert Einstein (1879–1955) is regarded by many as the greatest physicist of the twentieth century, and perhaps the greatest physicist since Sir **Isaac Newton**. He was born in Ulm, Germany. He is best known for his special and general theories of relativity (see **Relativity, General Theory of; Relativity, Special Theory of**), as well as for his development of the photon theory of light, which helped launch the field of quantum mechanics.

Einstein's religious education started very early when his Jewish parents, Pauline and Hermann, who did not embrace Judaism or any of its traditions, placed him in a Catholic school in Munich because of its proximity to their home. He was the only Jewish child among 70 children in his class and apparently enjoyed the required instruction in the Catholic religion. When he was nine he was moved to a high school near Munich that specialized in math and science. Upon receiving instruction in Judaism at that high school, Einstein became very interested in the Jewish traditions and began observing the Sabbath and many dietary restrictions with great passion and discipline, even while his family did not.

Contrary to popular myths, Einstein was quite skilled in **mathematics** from a very early age. He was encouraged and tutored in mathematics by his uncle Jacob Einstein, an engineer. He developed a keen penchant and skill for mathematical problem solving and consistently performed at or near the top of his classes. Einstein began his education in the sciences at age 12, at which point he began to abandon his religious convictions, believing several accounts in the Bible to be untrue and developing a deep suspicion and mistrust of organized religion as well as for authority in general. From that point onward in his life, he avoided all religious practices. When asked to record his religious preference (for job applications and the like), he would write "Mosaic."

Einstein graduated in 1900 from Zurich Polytechnic, and unable to find any jobs in teaching, worked as a clerk at the Swiss patent office in Bern while he pursued his doctoral studies at the University of Zurich. In 1905, at the age of 26, Einstein wrote his doctoral thesis and four additional groundbreaking scientific papers all in a matter of several months, a time often referred to as his *annus mirabilis*, or "miracle year." In March he wrote a scientific paper on a theory of light consisting of individual, discrete packets, or "photons," a view that would feed the development of modern-day quantum mechanics. In April he completed his doctoral thesis (submitted to the University of Zurich in July) on the topic of determining the size of molecules, a topic he chose to be "safe" for acceptance by his thesis committee (compared with some of the more radical ideas he was to publish). In May he wrote a paper outlining a theoretical accounting for Brownian motion, thereby establishing once for all the physical existence of atoms. In June he wrote a paper on his **special theory of relativity**, which completely altered fundamental notions of physical **space and time**. And finally, in September he concluded his *annus mirabilis* by writing a paper on the relationship between mass and energy, captured by what is probably the most celebrated equation in all of science, $E = mc^2$.

By 1908 Einstein was widely recognized as an eminent scientist and was appointed a lecturer at the University of Bern. Between 1911 and 1915, he developed his most ambitious and far-reaching theory, his **general theory of relativity**, which deals with the nature of gravity and its relationship to space-time, with far-reaching consequences for the large-scale structure of the universe. In 1921 he was awarded a Nobel Prize for his work on the photoelectric effect.

After occupying a series of faculty positions in both Switzerland and Germany, Einstein finally emigrated to the United States in 1933 when the Nazis came to power under Adolf Hitler. He was granted a position at the Institute for Advanced Study at Princeton University and spent the latter years of his life serving for the causes of civil rights and pacifism. He continued his affiliation at the institute until his death in 1955.

Throughout his life, Einstein came to embrace, perhaps influenced by his early childhood religious instruction, a belief that the physical universe and the people in it were not the product of a cosmic accident. He lived with a deep reverence for the **beauty** of the cosmos and the mathematical symmetry and simplicity of the laws by which it operated. A driving desire for him in the pursuit of his physical theories of nature was to "know the mind of God."

Warren Rogers

REFERENCES AND RECOMMENDED READING

Isaacson, Walter. 2007. *Einstein: His Life and Universe.* New York: Simon & Schuster.
Pais, Abraham. 1982. *Subtle Is the Lord: The Science and Life of Albert Einstein.* London: Oxford University Press.

ELIMINATIVE MATERIALISM. Eliminative materialism (also eliminativism) is the radical and counterintuitive view that our commonsense understanding of the mind is wrong and that mental states such as beliefs, desires, and perceptions do not exist. Eliminativists such as Patricia and Paul Churchland adopt the so-called theory of mind, taking our commonsense understanding to be a theory of intelligent behavior or "folk **psychology**" (Churchland, 1984; Churchland 1986; Putnam 1960, 148–79; Sellars 1956, 250–329). This theory is not acquired by direct perception of one's inner life but by informal learning from the linguistic and social world within which folk psychology is embedded.

If mind is understood according to a theory, then a better theory may be discovered to replace it. Eliminativists believe that **neuroscience** is explanatorily superior and supersedes folk psychology. The only way to preserve beliefs and other intentional states would be to show that they are *reducible* to neuroscientific categories. Eliminativists hold that this reduction is impossible, and so these states are eliminated. Intentional mental states are "psychological caloric." (Caloric—a postulated weightless, spatially extended fluid identical to heat—was eliminated from explanations in chemistry when it was shown that heat is in fact a form of energy.)

Stephen Stich reaches an eliminativist position from another direction. He articulates folk psychology in terms of the representational theory of mind and thus takes mind to be a general-purpose computing device. On this view, mental states are sentences in an innate language of thought, and mental processes are operations on those statements (Stich 1983). However, the machine's operation will depend on the *syntactic* properties of sentences alone. Hence the *semantic*, intentional content of a mental state plays no causal role in the production of behavior.

This point is made clearly by Searle's **Chinese Room Argument**, and Stich effectively offers that argument in reverse. Taken in the usual way, the Chinese Room demonstrates that thought cannot be attributed to computing machines since they can produce intelligent behavior (such as answering questions in Chinese) while clearly not possessing the relevant intentional states (such as understanding Chinese). Reversing this, Stich argues that the best understanding of folk psychology is that thought is computation, and since computation has no place for intentional states, we must eliminate them from theories of human thought too.

The implausibility and incoherence of eliminativism is commonly expressed in the claim that it is self-refuting. Baker points out that if eliminativism is true, then many of the grounds for accepting it disappear, such that eliminativism is "cognitive suicide" (Baker 1987). The Nobel Prize-winning neuroscientist Sir **John Eccles** asks pointedly, "How do professional philosophers and psychologists think up the notion that there are no thoughts, come to believe that there are no beliefs, and feel strongly that there are no feelings?" (Eccles and Robinson 1985, 53). There is no easy escape from such objections. This is important for other positions too, such as reductive materialism and **Daniel Dennett**'s instrumentalist views (see **Instrumentalism**) that ultimately turn out to be forms of eliminativism themselves.

Jonathan Loose

REFERENCES AND RECOMMENDED READING

Baker, Lynne Rudder. 1987. "The Threat of Cognitive Suicide." In *Saving Belief: A Critique of Physicalism.* Princeton, NJ: Princeton University Press.

Churchland, Patricia Smith. 1986. *Neurophilosophy: Toward a Unified Science of the Mind/Brain.* Cambridge, MA: MIT Press.

Churchland, Paul M. 1984. *Matter and Consciousness.* Cambridge, MA: MIT Press.

Eccles, John Carew, and Daniel N. Robinson. 1985. *The Wonder of Being Human: Our Brain and Our Mind.* Boston & London: Shambhala.

Putnam, H. 1960. "Minds and Machines." In *Dimensions of Mind*, ed. Sidney Hook, 148–79. New York: New York University Press.

Sellars, W. 1956. "Empiricism and the Philosophy of Mind." In *The Foundations of Science and the Concepts of Psychology and Psychoanalysis*, ed. H. Feigl and M. Scriven, 250–329. Minneapolis: University of Minnesota Press.

Stich, Stephen. 1983. *From Folk Psychology to Cognitive Science: The Case against Belief.* Cambridge, MA: MIT Press.

ELLIS, GEORGE F. R.

George F. R. Ellis (1939–) was born in South Africa. He earned a PhD in applied **mathematics** and theoretical **physics** from Cambridge University in 1964 (Templeton Prize 2004). Ellis has served as a visiting professor at several universities around the world, including Boston University, the University of Chicago, and London University. He is currently emeritus professor in mathematics at the University of Cape Town, South Africa. Ellis's reputation as a leading cosmologist, specializing in general relativity theory is undisputed. Together with Stephen Hawking, Ellis published one of a series of important scientific papers demonstrating that general relativity predicted the existence of a singularity in the past history of our universe, which has implications for a unique beginning to **space and time** (Hawking and Ellis 1968). In 1973 Ellis coauthored *The Large Scale Structure of Space-Time* with Stephen Hawking, which among other things provides the mathematical foundation for black holes.

As a renowned physicist, Ellis's interests extend beyond the confines of mathematical equations into the realm of ultimate questions with enduring interest to humans everywhere. In his book *On the Moral Nature of the Universe*, Ellis and coauthor Nancey Murphy present a deeply grounded argument for "the incompleteness of physical sciences apart from a metaphysical superstructure." They analyze multiple approaches to explain ultimate **causation** in cosmology, including random **chance** and necessity, and conclude: "Comparing the different possibilities, it is difficult to avoid the conclusion that the design concept is one of the most satisfactory overall approaches" (Murphy and Ellis 1996, 59). More remarkably, Ellis claims that "the ultimate purpose of the universe is to allow for [an] uncoerced response to the creator" and as such, an important feature of the universe is

"the hidden nature of ultimate reality" (Murphy and Ellis 1996, 209).

While acknowledging that the concept of a **multiverse** is "probably the only scientific answer to this question of fine-tuning," Ellis firmly critiques the multiverse concept by stating, "The only problem with this is that you haven't got the faintest knowledge of what these other universes are like, you have no causal connection with them, you don't actually even know if they exist." Ellis therefore maintains that "the existence of these universes is a metaphysical rather than a scientific presupposition" (Templeton Prize 2004, 17). In his writings, Ellis has argued that human free will is a space-time reality, and that certain humanistic philosophies that deny the reality of **consciousness** and free will are promoting "a completely incoherent position" (Templeton Prize 2004, 18). His argument is based on the **logic** that if consciousness and free choice aren't real, then scientific conclusions aren't reliable. And if this is the case, then one can't take seriously the conclusion that free will is not a reality.

Ellis was awarded the prestigious 2004 Templeton Prize for progress toward research or discoveries about spiritual realities. In his acceptance speech, Ellis stated, "I believe the science and religion dialogue is one of the most important issues we can engage in at the present time" (Templeton Prize 2004, 7). In addition to his academic work in cosmology, Ellis has had his feet firmly planted on the ground, as exemplified through his active opposition to apartheid in South Africa. Ellis also committed half of his Templeton Prize money toward a variety of projects in South Africa to support economic, cultural, and religious development.

Eric R. Hedin

REFERENCES AND RECOMMENDED READING

Ellis, George F. R., and Stephen W. Hawking. 1975. *The Large Scale Structure of Space-Time.* Cambridge: Cambridge University Press.

Ellis, George F. R., and Ruth M. Williams. 1988. *Flat and Curved Space-Times.* New York: Oxford University Press.

Hawking, S. W., and G. F. R. Ellis. 1968. "The Cosmic Black-Body Radiation and the Existence of Singularities in Our Universe." *Astrophysical Journal* 152:25–36.

Murphy, Nancey, and George F. R. Ellis. 1996. *On the Moral Nature of the Universe: Theology, Cosmology, and Ethics.* Minneapolis: Augsburg Fortress.

Templeton Prize. 2004. "Prof. George F. R. Ellis: 2004 Templeton Prize Laureate." Accessed October 10, 2015. www.templetonprize.org/pdfs/Templeton_Prize_Chronicle_2004.pdf.

EMBRYONIC STEM CELL RESEARCH.

Since the late 1990s, when scientists first discovered how to harvest stem cells from human embryos, there has been great excitement about embryonic stem cell research (ESCR) and its potential to aid patients suffering from myriad diseases. Stem cells are being used or are anticipated to be used to treat various cancers, blood diseases, immune system disorders, Parkinson's disease, diabetes, and multiple sclerosis (MS). They can also be used for repair of heart tissue and growth of new blood vessels, and there is hope for using stem cells to treat spinal cord injuries.

Stem cells are *undifferentiated* cells that can be directed in the lab to develop into any of the roughly 200 types of cells and tissues in the body. Some stem cells are completely undifferentiated—that is, they have not begun down the developmental pathway that dictates that they become a certain type of cell, for example, neurological cells or cardiac cells. These are called *pluripotent* stem cells and, in theory, can be engineered in the lab to become any of the cells in the body.

Some stem cells have become somewhat differentiated however. That is, they have begun down their developmental pathway but still can be directed to become cells of a specific type, within boundaries. For example, neurological stem cells can become any neurological cell but not blood cells or any other type of cells outside their initial developmental boundaries. These stem cells are called *multipotent* stem cells and are very useful in treating a variety of diseases but do not have the same *plasticity*, or developmental flexibility, that pluripotent stem cells have.

To be clear, there is a distinction between types of stem cells, depending on the source from which they are derived. Most of the stem cells that are in clinical use at present are what are called *adult stem cells*, meaning that they are derived from sources other than human embryos. Most often they are harvested from the adult patient's own body, the bone marrow, for example. In fact, a bone marrow transplant is a form of stem cell therapy that has been in place for some time. Other sources of stem cells come from the blood (e.g., umbilical cord blood) or other parts of the body. Nonembryonic sources of stem cells are uncontroversial today.

Embryonic stem cells (ESCs) are pluripotent and are derived from several different sources. They can come from embryos left over from in vitro fertilization treatments for infertility—roughly 400,000 embryos remain in storage in infertility clinics in the United States, though very few of them have been designated for research. They can also come from embryos created through a process known as therapeutic cloning, where an identical twin is created in the

lab and its stem cells are harvested. In both these methods, the stem cells are harvested at roughly three to five days after conception, and at present, ESCs harvested from these two sources result in the destruction of the embryo. This raises an acute ethical dilemma for those who hold that embryos are persons from conception forward.

A source of embryonic-like stem cells is through what is called *induced pluripotent stem cells* (iPS). Two different teams of researchers, one in Japan and one in the United States, have successfully "reprogrammed" adult cells and coaxed them to go backward on their developmental pathway, enabling them to produce stem cells that have all the properties of stem cells harvested from human embryos. They have the potential to become, under the right conditions, any of the roughly 200 cell or tissue types in the human body. This is a potentially significant breakthrough enabling researchers to use embryonic-like stem cells that can be harvested without either creating or destroying embryos. This discovery overcomes the most significant moral obstacle to using embryonic stem cells, the destruction of human embryos. There is some debate over what exactly these pluripotent stem cells are "housed" in when the process reaches its end point. Are these embryos themselves, or embryo-like entities? If the latter, this process has the potential to resolve the ethical dilemma in the use of pluripotent stem cells.

The debate over ESCs revolves around the moral status of human embryos outside the womb. If a person does not believe that human embryos have the moral status of persons, then the discussion is over and there is no debate. But those who hold that human embryos are persons with the right to life also hold that human beings are actually being sacrificed for the benefit of others.

At the outset, it is important to see that the moral status of embryos is not fundamentally a scientific question, but a philosophical one. Science cannot conclusively determine philosophical matters by scientific observation alone. What science can tell us is what kind of a biological entity an embryo is, whether it is alive, and even whether it is human (embryos that are the sources of stem cells are both alive and human, even when stored in the lab). But whether or not embryos are *persons* is not a biological question but a philosophical one. It's not fundamentally a theological question, since one could arrive at the same conclusions apart from religious convictions.

Proponents of ESCR argue that the embryos are going to be discarded and that it is immoral not to use them for research and treatment. However, there is a significant problem with patient compatibility, in that most ESCs are not a match for the patient for whom they are intended. This helps explain the success of adult stem cells that are derived from the patient and thus have no compatibility issues. This also explains the early impetus toward therapeutic cloning, to produce embryos that are a match for the patient because they are identical twins to the patient. Further, this underscores the importance of iPS, since the raw material for that process comes from the patient, and any stem cells harvested via iPS will be a match for the recipient patient.

Proponents of ESCR further argue that there is a morally relevant difference between a fetus in the womb and an embryo in the lab. They argue that surely something that must be seen under a microscope cannot be a person. But neither size nor location makes an ontological difference (that is, a difference in what kind of a thing something is). This is analogous to the notion that at birth a fetus becomes a person—objectors rightly suggest that location makes no difference in that instance. The human embryo (more specifically, the fertilized egg) is what is called a *totipotent* cell; that is, it has all it needs to mature into a full-grown adult. The Bible suggests that from the very earliest points of pregnancy (Ps. 139:16 ESV, referring to the unborn as the "unformed substance," and Luke 1–2 referring to Jesus in the womb in the very earliest stage of pregnancy), a divine-image-bearing person exists, with full rights and protectability.

Scott B. Rae

REFERENCES AND RECOMMENDED READING

Green, Ronald M., ed. 2001. *The Human Embryo Research Debates: Bioethics in the Vortex of Controversy.* Oxford: Oxford University Press.
Holland, Suzanne, Karen Lebacqz, and Laurie Zoloth, eds. 2001. *The Human Embryonic Stem Cell Debate: Science, Ethics and Public Policy.* Cambridge, MA: MIT Press.
Waters, Brent, and Ronald Cole-Turner, eds., 2003. *God and the Embryo: Religious Voices on Stem Cells and Cloning.* Washington, DC: Georgetown University Press.

EMERGENCE. Emergence has been variously understood. It is the idea that novel, irreducible features (properties or substances) can arise from sufficiently complex systems of more fundamental elements. The importance accorded to discussions of emergence can be traced to the British emergentists, a group of thinkers including John Stuart Mill (Mill 1882), who rose to prominence in the early twentieth century through the contrasting perspectives of Samuel Alexander and C. D. Broad, each of whom used a distinct idea of emergence to account for the place of mind in the natural world. Whether the processes they described actually characterize observable natural processes remains unclear (Alexander 1920; Broad 1925).

Alexander's work prefigures so-called epistemological emergence: the view that some systems may possess emergent features in the sense that they are either unpredictable from or irreducible to the activity of the more fundamental elements of which the system is composed. Epistemological emergence entails that there are principled limits to knowledge of complex systems. It is thus impossible to predict the presence of certain features before they are observed. These features together constitute an emergent level at which the system may be described, the dynamics of which may be described in terms of emergent laws. These laws are irreducible to those that govern the behavior of the more fundamental elements, and together they constitute a special science.

Epistemological emergence makes sense of the world in terms of system-level features. The world is thus not layered in the fullest sense, but is better described as systematically patterned. Broad followed Mill in adopting a stronger view that is the forerunner of so-called ontological emergence. On this view the world is truly layered. As systems become increasingly complex, novel entities arise that are not only irreducible but also fundamental.

The claim that human persons are emergent entities has been employed to avoid reductive physicalist or eliminativist accounts of mind that would obliterate many commonsense and universally held anthropological beliefs as well as those widely held for theological reasons (see **Eliminative Materialism**). For example, **Nancey Murphy** offers a nonreductive **physicalism** that takes mental properties to be epistemologically emergent (Murphy 2006). Timothy O'Connor goes further, considering human persons to be ontologically emergent individuals: essentially embodied beings that nevertheless exist as fundamental, irreducible entities, thanks to the possession of ontologically emergent "particularities" that unify the complex physical systems in which they participate (O'Connor and Jacobs 2003). Finally, William Hasker has argued that human persons are ontologically emergent **soul**s that are contingently related to the bodies that produce and sustain them (Hasker 1999). Emergence thus explains the enduring connection of a soul to a particular body.

Such theories are problematic. Murphy's epistemological emergence runs into trouble with mental **causation**; O'Connor's notion of a particularized system may not be coherent; and Hasker's emergent **dualism** may recruit the problems of both physicalism and dualism along with their virtues. However, these examples nevertheless illustrate that different interpretations of the seemingly vague notion of emergence remain important to some Christian accounts of the relation between human persons and the natural world.

Jonathan Loose

REFERENCES AND RECOMMENDED READING

Alexander, Samuel. 1920. *Space, Time, and Deity.* 2 vols. London: Macmillan.
Broad, C. D. 1925. *The Mind and Its Place in Nature.* London: Routledge and Kegan Paul.
Hasker, William. 1999. *The Emergent Self.* Ithaca, NY: Cornell University Press.
Mill, John Stuart. 1882. *A System of Logic, Ratiocinative and Inductive.* New York: Harper & Brothers.
Murphy, Nancey C. 2006. *Bodies and Souls, or Spirited Bodies.* Current Issues in Theology. Cambridge: Cambridge University Press.
O'Connor, Timothy, and Jonathan D. Jacobs. 2003. "Emergent Individuals." *Philosophical Quarterly* 53 (213): 540–55.

EMPIRICISM. Empiricism is a philosophical concept that can be contrasted with rationalism; in fact, they are quite the direct opposites of one another. In empiricism the basic idea is that experience, sense perception, and induction are the basis for knowledge, whereas in rationalism the basis for knowledge is innate ideas, thoughts, reason, and deduction.

The word *empiricism* is derived from the Greek *empeiria* meaning "experience," from which we get the word *experiment*, implying empiricism is involved with actual research, experiment, observation.

Empiricists believe that sense perception is the main source of knowledge, and that knowledge is obtained only through experience, and not through innate ideas. Through experience one obtains simple ideas, and these simple ideas can be combined into complex ideas. The key idea is that experience is the source of knowledge, and this means that knowledge depends ultimately on the use of the senses and what is discovered through them.

The traditional view of modern science is that the first step to knowledge is by collecting observational data in a purely objective manner, free from prejudices of a priori notions, free from philosophical or religious constraints or presuppositions. Second, the data are then organized in some appropriate way, again with no a priori conditions, although the process of going from pure raw data to the place where the questions for which the project was designed can be approached may require the use of agreed upon principles and complex calculations. Third, by the use of induction, generalizations and explanatory principles may emerge, including hypotheses related to possible further scientific knowledge or effects for which there has been as yet no satisfactory understanding. This procedure is called the *hypothetical-inductive method* and is based on the crucial first step of acquiring empirical data.

We must add a further word on sense perception and experience. Many topics of scientific interest are not directly observable by the eye. Sizes and distances vary by enormous amounts—cosmological sizes of galaxies, for instance, all the way to the microworld of the molecule, atom, nucleus, and fundamental particle involve the impossibility of direct observations at each end of the size scale, which brings up the question of "sensory extenders." Various types of telescopes aid in cosmological investigations, and the understanding involved with the operation of such devices is well known by many so that it seems that direct observations are possible because of glass lenses or mirrors, and thus it is not too hard to accept these measurements. But the submicroscopic regime is a bit subtler, as highly specialized and complicated devices are employed in these investigations, and the best that one can say is that these procedures contain numerous steps, each one of which can be understood in terms of accepted scientific principles.

The entire cluster of operations leading to what is referred to as "observing" a particular nuclear or particle event make up a self-consistent story, that after many checks and cross-checks the group carrying out the investigation become convinced that what they are actually "seeing" is what they intended to "see" in their experiment. And so, this is empirical evidence obtained in a straightforward but indirect means, given the type of submicroscopic investigations that are being undertaken. The "proof of the pudding" as it were comes at least partly from, for example, the practical uses that nuclear knowledge derived in this way can be used to do successful radiation therapy for cancer victims, can be used to design and construct nuclear reactors for energy production, and has given us understanding to design and construct magnetic resonance imaging (a nuclear process).

Many people believe that restricting science in practice to naturalistic (empirical generated) concepts is valid as long as one realizes that one cannot in the name of science extrapolate scientific principles into metaphysical or religious topics.

Richard F. Carlson

REFERENCES AND RECOMMENDED READING

Ratzsch, Del. 1980. *Philosophy of Science.* Downers Grove, IL: InterVarsity.

ENLIGHTENMENT, THE. The period of roughly 1650–1800 is known as the Enlightenment, and although it is often simplistic and inaccurate to paint with a broad brush, certain defining ideas and themes may be identified as characterizing this period in intellectual history. These include an emphasis on reason and science in thinking through the great questions of human life; a newfound belief in the progress of mankind in religion, **morality**, and political society; and the phenomenon of scientific advancement in a number of areas, including in our understanding of the universe.

These developments were accompanied in the work of some influential thinkers by a questioning of traditional forms of authority and religion, a concern about the close relationship between church and state in many countries, and a general suspicion of establishment thinking. The Enlightenment is also significant for the emergence in the work of some thinkers of materialistic views of the human person and of secular humanist approaches to ethics and politics that tended to clash with traditional religious outlooks.

The beginnings of the Enlightenment period can be traced to the work of **René Descartes** (1596–1650)—specifically, his program of doubt aimed at establishing the discipline of philosophy on a sound, rational footing, although Descartes himself exempted God and ethics from his skeptical questioning, and his desire to move beyond the speculative **metaphysics** of medieval philosophy and theology.

John Locke was also an influential figure with his *Letter Concerning Toleration* (1689), which brought together several ideas that were gaining prominence, including freedom of conscience and of religion. He proposed a limited form of religious freedom in the state but excluded Catholics and atheists. In addition, his famous work *Two Treatises of Government* (1689) introduced some of the foundational ideas of democracy, such as natural rights, including the right to own property, the social contract understanding of political society, and sovereignty of the people. It also laid out a blueprint for the basic structure of democratic government. His ideas were very influential with the US founding fathers, and consequentially the US Constitution and Bill of Rights are often regarded as major legacies of the Enlightenment period.

The American experiment in ordered liberty was a major contributory factor to the continuing influence of Enlightenment ideas, such as the desirability of the democratic form of government, the separation of church and state, freedom of religion, a focus on human rights and individual freedom, and the distinction between rational and revealed religion evident in the writings of Thomas Jefferson and Benjamin Franklin. This period also saw a move away from **theism** toward a more deistic view of the universe in the work of some prominent thinkers. In general, such ideas were regarded by some as a way to encourage the separation of civil and religious power, to move away from theocratic states, and to diminish the possibility of religious intolerance and violence in the wake of the upheaval of the Reformation and the Thirty Years' War (1618–48).

Enlightenment thinking was also influenced by new discoveries in science after **Galileo** (1564–1642) and **Newton** (1642–1746), particularly by the development of the **scientific method**. The scientific method was rightly regarded as a powerful new way of studying the physical world, one that was constantly giving us new insights and discoveries, and this fact contributed to the belief in progress among many intellectuals in such areas as **technology**, medicine, and the study of nature, a belief satirized in the writings of Jonathan Swift (1667–1745).

A pioneering thinker was **Francis Bacon** (1561–1626), whose reflections on inductive reasoning and the nature of **causation** in his *Novum Organum* (1620) drew considerable attention to the potential of the scientific method. Bacon also promoted a practical, utilitarian attitude to knowledge and scientific progress, coupled with a rejection of Aristotelian metaphysics. **Isaac Newton**'s work in **mathematics** and classical mechanics, which often depicted the world as a machine operating according to cause and effect and largely in a deterministic manner, suggested an overall intelligibility in the natural world and placed an emphasis on reason and science as a way of discovering its nature.

It was not too long before a materialist view of nature and of man was proposed, especially in the work of French thinkers Denis Diderot (1713–84) and Julien Offray de La Mettrie (1709–51). Diderot was one of the editors of the influential French *Encyclopédie* of the eighteenth century, which introduced the latest ideas in philosophy, theology, and science and gained notoriety for questioning many of the established views of the time. Diderot's ideas were an early version of atheistic naturalism. He understood nature to be matter in motion and hypothesized a materialist theory of living things, including human beings. He also agreed with Baron D'Holbach (1723–89) and other Enlightenment thinkers that the human mind is but a property of the brain. La Mettrie argued that the soul is really produced from matter, thereby giving metaphysical priority to the body in the study of human life and to science in the study of reality, rather than to philosophy or theology. His book *Man a Machine* (1748) expressed the view that human beings are completely physical beings and that science is the best way to approach the study of human behavior.

Other thinkers of the Enlightenment, such as Voltaire (1694–1778) and Thomas Paine (1736–1809), while not outright atheists, were influential in contributing to the spread of political and social ideas such as freedom of conscience and the separation of church and state that aimed at undermining revealed religion and the influence of the Bible. Voltaire rejected religious dogmas, often ridiculed Christianity, and was critical of the institutional church. A similar approach was to be found in the United States in the writings of Thomas Paine, who supported a form of **deism** but rejected institutional religion and questioned the reliability of revelation.

Although many Enlightenment thinkers remained theists, such as Descartes, Locke, Newton, and **Immanuel Kant** (1724–1804), their ideas contributed to what came to be recognized as an Enlightenment way of looking at the deeper philosophical questions, and these ideas were to have a growing influence on the subsequent development of the modern world. Some would argue that today we are all products of the Enlightenment in the sense that most intellectuals accept some version of the key ideas that emerged out of this period. The influence of Enlightenment ideas is everywhere evident today, including in a growing skepticism concerning the human mind's ability to know reality, a belief in the inadequacy and fallibility of human knowledge, a suspicion of religion, an increased confidence in science, and a defining emphasis on freedom, tolerance, and the autonomy of the individual—all ideas championed by Enlightenment thinkers.

The legacy of the Enlightenment among Christian thinkers in particular is that some agree with secularists in seeing it is a significant intellectual achievement of mankind, while others regard it with a healthy suspicion for opening up tendencies in ethics, politics, and religion whose fruition we see today and which have had the practical effect of leading to skeptical, relativistic, and nihilistic attitudes toward ethics and the meaning of life.

Brendan Sweetman

REFERENCES AND RECOMMENDED READING

Byrne, James. 1997. *Religion and the Enlightenment: From Descartes to Kant.* Louisville, KY: Westminster John Knox.

Kramnick, Isaac. 1995. *The Portable Enlightenment Reader.* London: Penguin.

Pagden, Anthony. 2013. *The Enlightenment: And Why It Still Matters.* New York: Random House.

ENNS, PETER. Peter Enns (1961–) is an evangelical biblical scholar and author or editor of over a dozen books on Old Testament interpretation, the inspiration of Scripture, and the intersection of science and faith. He taught at Westminster Theological Seminary for 14 years (1994–2008) until his controversial departure following the publication of his book *Inspiration and Incarnation: Evangelicals and the Problem of the Old Testament* in 2005. He is currently Abram S. Clemens Professor of Biblical Studies at Eastern University, St. Davids, Pennsylvania.

Enns was born in Passaic, New Jersey, and he graduated from Messiah College in 1982 with a bachelor's degree in behavioral science. He obtained a MDiv from Westminster Seminary in 1989 and a PhD in Near Eastern Languages and Civilizations from Harvard University in 1994. After Harvard he taught at Westminster as a professor of Old Testament and biblical hermeneutics until 2008. From 2009 to 2011, Enns worked as a senior fellow of biblical studies at the **BioLogos Foundation**, writing weekly blogs on science and faith. In 2012 he published *The Evolution of Adam*, which attempted to reconcile the modern theory of evolution with current biblical study of the historical Adam. Enns also maintains an active web presence, writing for his own website and blog and making contributions to the *Huffington Post*.

In *Inspiration and Incarnation*, Enns argued for a revised understanding of biblical inspiration as traditionally understood by evangelicals. According to Enns, the field of modern biblical studies and the phenomena of Scripture itself require this. Consequently, narrative portions of the Old Testament are not "objective historiography," nor is the Bible all that "unique" in its ancient Near Eastern context.

In *The Evolution of Adam* (2012), Enns begins by accepting evolutionary theory as true, arguing that following the completion of the **Human Genome Project** in 2003, headed by BioLogos founder **Francis Collins**, it is "beyond any reasonable scientific doubt that humans and primates share **common ancestry**" (ix). He then goes on to argue for a rereading of key portions of Scripture, namely, the story of Adam (pt. 1) and the apostle Paul's comments on the Adam story (pt. 2).

In the first place, Enns argues that Genesis cannot be read literally, historically, or scientifically. Furthermore, a careful reading of Genesis and of the entire Pentateuch realizes that this material was compiled and shaped with

Israel's self-definition in mind during the exilic and postexilic periods. Enns suggests that the Adam story is not so much a story of human origins but a story of Israel's origins (and ultimate rebellion and exile).

In regard to Paul, Enns admits that the apostle understood Adam in Romans 5 to be historical but proposes that he was merely buttressing a theological truth with the only idiom he could use in the context of his Hellenistic Jewish culture. Paul's use of the historical Adam does not undermine the theological truth it supports any more than the Bible's geocentric **worldview** is essential to its message. Inspired by the radical events of Christ's death and resurrection, Paul added a new dimension to the ancient Jewish understanding of human origins to include not only death but *condemnation*, a unique Pauline interpretive and hermeneutical contribution. Enns further argues that attempts to posit a hominid pair that God infused with the *imago Dei* within the chain of evolution or delegated as some kind of "representative head" are inadequate because they are faithful neither to Genesis nor to Paul.

Milton Eng

REFERENCES AND RECOMMENDED READING

Enns, Peter. 2005. *Inspiration and Incarnation: Evangelicals and the Problem of the Old Testament.* Grand Rapids: Baker Academic.
———. 2011. "Evolution and Our Theological Traditions: Wesleyanism." *Daily Blog* (Peter Enns). The BioLogos Foundation. May 17. http://biologos .org/blogs/archive/evolution-and-our-theological-traditions-wesleyanism.
———. 2012. *The Evolution of Adam: What the Bible Does and Doesn't Say about Human Origins.* Grand Rapids: Brazos.
———. 2014. "The Bible, History, and Storytelling (from *The Bible Tells Me So*)." Rethinking Biblical Christianity." *Patheos.* September 1. http://www .patheos.com/blogs/peterenns/2014/09/the-bible-history-and-storytelling -from-the-bible-tells-me-so/.

ENUMA ELISH. *Enuma Elish* is a Babylonian composition that describes how the god Marduk assumed the kingship of the gods among the Babylonians and the resulting construction of his temple Esagila (for English translation, see Foster 1997). Since Marduk was the city god of Babylon, his rise to dominance in the pantheon is likely coincident with the rise of the city of Babylon to political dominance in the region of Mesopotamia. While some scholars date this to the rise of Babylon under Nebuchadnezzar I (twelfth century BC), others date it as early as the rise of the Old Babylonian kingdom under Hammurapi (eighteenth century BC). Today's interest in *Enuma Elish* is heightened by its account of the creation of the cosmos and humanity and its relationship to biblical descriptions of creation.

The title *Enuma Elish* comes from the opening words of the myth, which translated from Akkadian mean "when on high." These words are followed by a theogony, an account of the birth of gods. The god Apsu (representing the fresh waters) and the goddess Tiamat (the salt water) are there at the beginning. The mingling of their waters produces the next generation of gods and goddesses, the ones whom the original Babylonian readers would have recognized as the ones they worshiped.

The young gods, however, are restless and disturb the sleep of Tiamat and Apsu, leading Apsu to declare his intention to do away with them, even though Tiamat tries to dissuade him from this course of action. Ea, known widely in Babylonian literature as the god of wisdom, learns of Apsu's plot and takes preemptive action. He succeeds in killing Apsu, building his home on his carcass. In that home, Ea and his consort Damkina gave birth to Marduk, who is the central figure of the composition.

Though solving the threat posed by Apsu, Ea's action results in a greater danger. Tiamat had tried to dissuade Apsu from killing their divine children, but now she is angry, and she is much more powerful than her husband. She produces a demonic horde and determines to take up where Apsu failed. She appoints a demon god named Qingu as her new consort and the leader of the horde.

Ea knows that he is no match for Tiamat, but his son Marduk steps forward as the champion of the gods. He announces that he will fight Tiamat, and, if successful, he will claim the kingship of the gods.

Marduk then confronts Tiamat, and the result is a fearsome battle. Eventually Marduk proves victorious. He kills Tiamat and then splits her body in half. With the upper half of her body, he creates the heavens (from which the waters fall in the form of rain), and with the lower half he creates the waters of the world. He places the gods and goddesses in the upper half of her body, and they constitute the sun, moon, and stars. He then pushes back the waters to form land. Finally, he kills Qingu and "from his blood he made mankind, they imposed the burden of the gods on them!" (Tablet VI, 33–34). This account of the creation of humankind and the purpose for their creation is presented in more detail by another Babylonian creation text, **Atrahasis**. *Enuma Elish* ends by extolling the 50 names of Marduk.

Enuma Elish is an important rival account to the biblical creation accounts, and it provides (along with *Atrahasis*) a significant cultural background to the biblical creation stories both in terms of similarities and also differences. In *Enuma*

Elish creation of the cosmos is the result of divine conflict, which is missing in the Bible. While the celestial bodies are deities in *Enuma Elish*, they are God's creation in Genesis. Humanity is created from the blood of a demon god in the Babylonian story and for the purpose of doing menial labor, as opposed to the biblical account in which humans are created from the dust of the ground and the breath of God (Gen. 2:7). Rather than engaging in menial labor, humans "subdue" the earth and "rule over" its creatures (Gen. 1:28). God places them in his paradisiacal garden and orders them to "work it and take care of [or guard] it" (Gen. 2:15).

The biblical creation accounts were not written in a cultural vacuum. The *Enuma Elish* along with other ancient Near Eastern creation stories provides helpful background to our study of creation in the Bible.

Tremper Longman III

REFERENCES AND RECOMMENDED READING

Foster, B. R. 1997. "The Epic of Creation." In *The Context of Scripture* 1:390–402. Leiden: Brill.
Lambert, W. G. 2013. *Babylonian Creation Myths.* Winona Lake, IN: Eisenbrauns.
Sparks, K. L. 2005. *Ancient Texts for the Study of the Hebrew Bible: A Guide to the Background Literature.* Peabody, MA: Hendrickson.

EPIGENETICS. Epigenetics is the field of biology that studies changes in **gene** expression or the cellular phenotype that is caused by factors other than the **DNA** sequence. As defined by the Cold Spring Harbor meeting in 2008, an epigenetic trait refers to a "stably heritable phenotype resulting from changes in a chromosome without alterations in the DNA sequence" (Berger et al. 2009). Epigenetics thus involves functionally relevant alterations to the genome which affect how genes are expressed without any change to the DNA sequence (such alterations include DNA methylation or histone modification). For example, repressor proteins that attach to silencer regions of DNA can influence gene expression without affecting the underlying DNA sequence.

Following fertilization of an egg cell, the resultant zygote undergoes a series of divisions, eventually resulting in the various different cell types of the organism (Mitalipov and Wolf 2009). Totipotent stem cells (i.e., cells with the most differentiation potential) develop into the various pluripotent cell lines of the embryo, which further develop into fully differentiated cells including blood vessels, muscle cells, neurons, epithelium, and endothelium. This occurs by activating and inhibiting gene expression. Differentiated cells are thus able to express only those genes that are required for their own

cell type. When cells divide, epigenetic modifications are preserved (Bird 2002; Jablonka and Raz 2009).

An additional source of epigenetic **information** that affects embryological development is found in the arrangement of sugar molecules on the exterior surface of the cell's plasma membrane (Gabius 2000; Gabius et al. 2004). Sugars can attach to the membrane's lipid molecules to form glycolipids. The cell surface patterns that emerge as a result can be extremely complex, and hence have a high level of information-storage capacity. The ability of these structures to influence the arrangement of cell types during embryogenesis has led to it being referred to as the "sugar code."

Another contributor to morphogenesis is the distribution and spatial arrangement of ion channels in the cell membrane (although these ion channels are themselves encoded by DNA, their spatial distribution is not). These ion channels can establish an electromagnetic field that can influence the form of a developing organism (Levin 2003; Shi and Borgens 1995; Skou 1998; Vandenberg et al. 2011).

A further category of epigenetic phenomena occurs at the cell population level, relating to cases when inductive interactions between two cell populations results in the creation of a third. For example, certain aspects of bone morphology arise as a consequence of interaction between the bone and muscle activity—being completely unpredictable from the intrinsic development of the tissues themselves—and are hence understood to be epigenetic (Allori et al. 2008; Pearson and Lieberman 2004).

Epigenetic phenomena can also be found in species-species interactions or in interactions between members of the same species. For example, in the interaction between predator and prey **species** in plankton, diffusible chemicals from the predator result in the formation of features in the prey that are otherwise not present in the predator's absence (Vaughn 2007).

Proponents of **intelligent design** have argued that the role of epigenetic information in directing the morphogenesis of organismal form represents a significant challenge to the neo-Darwinian evolutionary **paradigm**, since mutating DNA alone may be inadequate to produce a fundamentally new body plan (Wells 2013).

Jonathan McLatchie

REFERENCES AND RECOMMENDED READING

Allori, A. C., A. M. Sailon, J. H. Pan, and S. M. Warren. 2008. "Biological Basis of Bone Formation, Remodeling, and Repair. Part III: Biomechanical Forces." *Tissue Engineering* 14:285–93.

Berger, S. L., T. Kouzarides, R. Shiekhattar, and A. Shilatifard. 2009. "An Operational Definition of Epigenetics." *Genes and Development* 23:781–83.

Bird, A. 2002. "DNA Methylation Patterns and Epigenetic Memory." *Genes and Development* 16:6–21.

Gabius, H. J. 2000. "Biological Information Transfer beyond the Genetic Code: The Sugar Code." *Naturwissenschaften* 87:108–21.

Gabius, H. J., H. C. Siebert, S. Andre, J. Jimenez-Barbero, and H. Rudiger. 2004. "Chemical Biology of the Sugar Code." *ChemBioChem* 5:740–64.

Jablonka, E., and G. Raz. 2009. "Transgenerational Epigenetic Inheritance: Prevalence, Mechanisms, and Implications for the Study of Heredity and Evolution." *Quarterly Review of Biology* 84:131–76.

Levin, M. 2003. "Bioelectromagnetics in Morphogenesis." *Bioelectromagnetics* 24:295–315.

Mitalipov, S., and D. Wolf. 2009. "Totipotency, Pluripotency and Nuclear Reprogramming." *Advances in Biochemical Engineering/Biotechnology* 114:185–99.

Pearson, O. M., and D. E. Lieberman. 2004. "The Aging of Wolff's 'Law': Ontogeny and Responses to Mechanical Loading in Cortical Bone." *Yearbook of Physical Anthropology* 47:63–99.

Shi, R., and R. R. Borgens. 1995. "Three-Dimensional Gradients of Voltage during Development of the Nervous System as Invisible Coordinates for the Establishment of Embryonic Pattern." *Developmental Dynamics* 202:101–14.

Skou, J. C. 1998. "The Identification of the Sodium Pump." *Bioscience Reports* 18:155–69.

Vandenberg, L. N., R. D. Morrie, and D. S. Adams. 2011. "V-ATPase-Dependent Ectodermal Voltage and pH Regionalization Are Required for Craniofacial Morphogenesis." *Developmental Dynamics* 240:1889–1904.

Vaughn, D. 2007. "Predator-Induced Morphological Defences in Marine Zooplankton: A Larval Case Study." *Ecology* 88:1030–39.

Wells, Jonathan. 2013. "The Membrane Code: A Carrier of Essential Biological Information That Is Not Specified by DNA and Is Inherited Apart from It." *Biological Information—New Perspectives*, www.worldscientific.com/doi/pdf/10.1142/9789814508728_0021.

EPISTEMOLOGY.

Epistemology is a subfield of philosophy concerned with the nature of knowledge—what it is, how it is acquired, and the limits of human knowledge. For most of the history of Western philosophy, epistemological debate has concerned the sources of knowledge, with philosophers tending to opt either for *rationalism* (**Plato, Descartes,** and **Spinoza**) or *empiricism* (**Aristotle, Locke,** and **Hume**). The rationalist school emphasized reason as the most reliable source of knowledge and affirmed innate ideas, while empiricists saw sense experience as the ultimate source of all knowledge and thus denied innate ideas.

In the modern period, the divide between rationalists and empiricists widened with the **Scientific Revolution.** Modern science essentially formalized the empirical method, leading to discoveries and applications that transformed Western civilization. Despite the practical successes of science, however, the modern rationalist philosophical systems of **Kant** and **Hegel** were, and continue to be, extraordinarily influential.

The contours of epistemological debate were completely reshaped in 1963 with the publication of Edmund Gettier's critique of the standard definition of knowledge dating back to Plato. The received view until that time was that justified true belief is sufficient for knowledge. But using some compelling counterexamples, Gettier demonstrated that this is not necessarily the case. The last half century of epistemology has largely consisted of debate over various proposals to solve the "Gettier problem." Some have pressed for a fourth ingredient in the definition (e.g., indefeasibility, a causal condition, a reliable belief-forming mechanism, virtue-based factors, etc.).

Some have insisted that the problem is best dealt with by dropping or reconceiving the justification requirement for knowledge, suggesting that in order to know, one need not know *how* one knows. Such an approach is called *externalist*, as it grants that the conditions for knowledge need not be accessible to the knower. This significantly departs from the traditional *internalist* view that the justifying conditions for knowledge must be internally accessible to the knower.

Among internalists, much debate has concerned the logical structure of justification of beliefs. *Foundationalists* maintain that some beliefs are properly basic, such that their justification is not inherited from other beliefs. *Coherentists* deny such basic beliefs, insisting that each belief is only justified in terms of the system of beliefs of which it is a part. Still another approach is offered by *contextualists*, who argue that all justification is relative to social and conversational context.

While epistemologists have tended to the analysis of knowledge and justification, many epistemological issues have occupied scholars at the interface of multiple disciplines. Among the most contentious are those involving science and theology (e.g., biological origins, **intelligent design, consciousness,** and **miracles**). Sharp disagreement on these issues persists even within the Christian community, and a major source of the disagreement has to do with epistemology, specifically pertaining to one's view of scientific knowledge and/or theological knowledge.

James S. Spiegel

REFERENCES AND RECOMMENDED READING

Alston, William. 1989. *Epistemic Justification: Essays in the Theory of Knowledge.* Ithaca, NY: Cornell University Press.

Audi, Robert. 1998. *Epistemology: A Contemporary Introduction to the Theory of Knowledge.* Cambridge: Cambridge University Press.

Dew, James K., Jr., and Mark W. Foreman. 2014. *How Do We Know? An Introduction to Epistemology.* Downers Grove, IL: InterVarsity.

Feldman, Richard. 2003. *Epistemology.* Upper Saddle River, NJ: Prentice Hall.

Gettier, Edmund L. 1963. "Is Justified True Belief Knowledge?" *Analysis* 23:121–23.

Steup, Matthias. 2005. "Epistemology." In *Stanford Encyclopedia of Philosophy*, ed. Edward N. Zalta. http://plato.stanford.edu/entries/epistemology/.

Zagzebski, Linda Trinkaus. 1996. *Virtues of the Mind: An Inquiry into the Nature of Virtue and the Ethical Foundations of Knowledge.* Cambridge: Cambridge University Press.

ERIKSON, ERIK. Erik Homburger Erikson (1902–94) was born near Frankfurt, Germany. His mother was Jewish, and his biological father's identity is unknown. Erikson was three years old when his mother married Dr. Theodor Homburger, a Jewish pediatrician. Erikson believed Dr. Homburger was his biological father for some time. Erikson (1975, 27) later claimed his parents "kept from me the fact that my mother had been married previously and that I was the son of a Dane who had abandoned her before my birth." Erikson was never close to his stepfather or three half-sisters.

Erikson graduated with a basic education, never pursuing any formal academic training. As a gifted sketch artist, he traveled through southern Germany, France, and Italy until he was invited to teach for a Montessori school in Vienna. While in Vienna he met Anna Freud who trained him as a psychoanalyst. This credential led to his acceptance as a member in the Vienna Psychoanalytic Society.

The rise of fascism in Europe convinced Erikson, his wife, and his two children to immigrate to the United States. Erikson was able to accept a research position with Massachusetts General Hospital, Harvard Medical School, and Harvard Psychological Clinic, even though he lacked formal academic and medical credentials.

Erikson continued traveling through the Unites States and lived temporarily among the Sioux Nation, eventually teaching at the University of California-Berkeley. His cultural anthropological studies among the Sioux deeply influenced his psychological theory. During this period, Erikson became an American citizen and officially changed his name to Erik Erikson, associating himself with the great European explorer Leif Ericson (Erikson 1975).

In 1950 Erikson published his first book, *Childhood and Society*, drawing on the work of **Freud** and his own research in **psychology**, cultural **anthropology**, and historical analysis. Erikson saw his work as a means of extending what Freud had started (Erikson 1963, 403). Erikson's work is recognized as foundational for studies of life span and identity development even today.

Erikson left Berkeley and finished his teaching career at Harvard as a professor of human development. Erikson

retired from teaching in 1970 but continued a productive writing, research, and counseling career until he died in 1994, at the age of 91.

Erikson's theory is criticized because it lacks scientific validation. It reflects the same deterministic elements as Freud's theory, downplaying the existence of free will. Similar to the humanistic approach to psychology, the theory overemphasizes the positive nature of people and seldom acknowledges the sinful side of the human condition. While the theory can contribute to a Christian understanding of human development, it should be carefully evaluated.

Dominick D. Hankle

REFERENCES AND RECOMMENDED READING

Erikson, E. H. 1963. *Childhood and Society.* 2nd ed. New York: W. W. Norton.
———. 1968. *Identity: Youth and Crisis.* New York: Norton.
———. 1975. *Life History and the Historical Moment.* New York. W. W. Norton.
———. 1980. *Identity and the Life Cycle.* New York: W. W. Norton.
———. 1982. *The Life Cycle Completed.* New York: W. W. Norton.
Hopkins, J. R. 1995. "Erik Homburger Erikson (1902–1994)." *American Psychologist* 50:796–97.

ESCHATOLOGY. In Christian theology, eschatology describes the ultimate destiny of God's creation, the fate that awaits the entire cosmos and each individual person. It is the study of "last things" and includes doctrines like the general resurrection, heaven and hell, immortality of the **soul**, second coming of Christ, new heaven and new earth, and final judgment. According to the Bible's inaugurated eschatology, the kingdom of God has already broken into our world in Christ's death and resurrection, but God's complete transformation of this world awaits the eschaton (Rev. 21–22). It is precisely this rich, biblical picture that is undermined by standard scientific cosmologies.

The **big bang theory** is the prevailing cosmological model, according to which our universe came into being at a single point in time—about 14 billion years ago—and has been expanding ever since. On the one hand, the "freeze" scenario (the "Big Freeze") of the big bang has a universe that is infinite in size and yet keeps expanding limitlessly, with temperatures that will eventually plummet to absolute zero. The "fry" scenario, on the other hand, suggests a finite universe that is destined to stop expanding in the distant future; it will then contract back down to a singularity, its temperature and density sky-rocketing to **infinity** (Russell 2012). Interestingly, this "fry" scenario (the "Big Crunch") seems less likely given evidence that dark energy is causing the universe to accelerate apart without limit (the "Big Rip"; see Riess et al. 1998 and Weinberg 2008). All of these cosmological scenarios are far removed from the biblical picture of the new heaven and new earth, where the dwelling of God will be with his people (Rev. 21:3).

Christians have offered a range of proposals to resolve this conflict between science and theology (Russell 2008b). Some argue that scientific cosmology and biblical eschatology are independent projects, separate domains of knowledge; in principle there can be no conflict. Others, more radically, have tried to reinterpret eschatology as an instance of physical cosmology (e.g., Tipler 1994). **John Polkinghorne** suggests that distinctive features of the resurrection body of Jesus—e.g., crucifixion marks postglorification—lead us to expect both continuity *and* discontinuity between present cosmology and the new creation. He anticipates that continuity will be manifested in key features of cosmology such as holism, relationality, energy, and pattern (Polkinghorne, 2002). In his groundbreaking work, Robert John Russell analyzes how specific areas of eschatological continuity and discontinuity yield insights for future scientific research programs (e.g., Russell 2012). Other looming issues of eschatological concern include environmentalism and ecotheology (e.g., Northcott 2002).

Evangelicals have largely been absent from this interdisciplinary dialogue, in part because they reject the naturalistic assumptions of modern cosmology. Their eschatological focus instead has historically been limited to interpretative disputes over the millennium (e.g., premillennialism, postmillennialism, and amillennialism; cf. Bock 1999; Grenz 1992). But evangelicals have also analyzed issues of embodiment and its significance for theological **anthropology** and the intermediate state (or afterlife); they are divided between traditional dualists and Christian physicalists (e.g., Cooper 2001; Green and Palmer 2005).

Eschatological disagreements on the significance of scientific cosmologies will persist. Christians must nevertheless retain the promise of a future bodily resurrection, the physical return of the Lord Jesus, and a new heaven and earth.

Hans Madueme

REFERENCES AND RECOMMENDED READING

Bock, Darrell, ed. 1999. *Three Views on the Millennium and Beyond.* Grand Rapids: Zondervan.
Cooper, John W. 2001. *Body, Soul and Life Everlasting: Biblical Anthropology and the Monism-Dualism Debate.* 2nd ed. Grand Rapids: Eerdmans.
Green, Joel, and Stuart L. Palmer, eds. 2005. *In Search of the Soul: Four Views.* Downers Grove, IL: InterVarsity.
Grenz, Stanley. 1992. *The Millennial Maze: Sorting Out Evangelical Options.* Downers Grove, IL: InterVarsity.
Moltmann, Jürgen. 1996. *The Coming of God: Christian Eschatology,* trans. Margaret Pannenberg. Minneapolis: Fortress.
Murphy, George L. 2002. "Hints from Science for Eschatology—and Vice-Versa." In *The Last Things: Biblical and Theological Perspectives on Eschatology,* ed. Carl Braaten and Robert Jensen, 146–68. Grand Rapids: Eerdmans.
Northcott, Michael S. 2002. *A Political Theology of Climate Change.* Grand Rapids: Eerdmans.
Peters, Ted, Robert John Russell, and Michael Welker, eds. 2002. *Resurrection: Theological and Scientific Assessments.* Grand Rapids: Eerdmans.
Polkinghorne, John. 2000. "Eschatology: Some Questions and Some Insights from Science." In *The End of the World and the Ends of God: Science and Theology on Eschatology,* ed. John Polkinghorne and Michael Welker, 29–41. Harrisburg, PA: Trinity Press International.
———. 2002. *The God of Hope and the End of the World.* New Haven, CT: Yale University Press.
Riess, Adam G., Alexei V. Filippenko, Peter Challis, et al. 1998. "Observational Evidence from Supernovae for an Accelerating Universe and a Cosmological Constant." *Astronomical Journal* 116 (3): 1009–38.
Russell, Robert John. 2008a. "Cosmology and Eschatology." In *The Oxford Handbook of Eschatology,* ed. Jerry Walls, 563–80. Oxford: Oxford University Press.
———. 2008b. *Cosmology from Alpha to Omega: The Creative Mutual Interaction of Theology and Science.* Minneapolis: Fortress.
———. 2012. *Time in Eternity: Pannenberg, Physics, and Eschatology in Creative Mutual Interaction.* Notre Dame: University of Notre Dame Press.
Stoeger, William R. 2010. "God, Physics, and the Big Bang." In *The Cambridge Companion to Science and Religion,* ed. Peter Harrison, 173–89. Cambridge: Cambridge University Press.
Tipler, Frank J. 1994. *The Physics of Immortality: Modern Cosmology, God, and the Resurrection of the Dead.* Garden City, NY: Doubleday.
Weinberg, Steven. 2008. *Cosmology.* Oxford: Oxford University Press.

ETHICS, CHRISTIAN.

Christian ethics is a blend of virtues and principles. It is strongly deontological (principle-based) because of the emphasis on God's commands and biblical principles. But it is also significantly virtue-oriented, as virtues provide the proper Christian emphasis on a person's character, as opposed to being solely focused on a person's actions. Christian ethics asks not only "What is the right thing to do?" but also "What kind of person am I becoming?"

In Christian ethics, the ultimate source for **morality** is God's character. God's commands are the penultimate source for morality and are derived from his character. Ultimately, the reason God commands the things he does is because he is a God of a certain type. Christian ethics calls its followers to be loving people, but not primarily because "love makes the world go round" (and even if that were true, that would not be the most compelling reason for becoming a loving person). Christian ethics demands love because that is fundamentally who God is. Similarly, Christian ethics calls for forgiveness, but not primarily because forgiveness heals fractured relationships, though that is certainly true.

The most persuasive reason for forgiveness is because that is intrinsically who God is, and as a result, that is what is to characterize his followers.

Christian ethics is set in the framework of the individual's relationship to God. Though it is true that the ethical demands of God are embedded in the framework of the world and are normative across time and culture (though the application of any ethical virtue or principle may look quite different in different cultures), the Bible sets Christian ethics in the context of a relationship to God. The ethical demands are not simply abstract moral principles but are an expression of one's relationship to God. In Christian ethics, one follows the demands because they are an expression of loyalty to God and love for God.

The Bible further connects the work of the Holy Spirit and moral renewal (Gal. 5:16, 22–25). Adherence to Christian ethics is not something that can be achieved on one's own, but requires the indwelling Holy Spirit to empower the person to live consistently with the demands of Christian ethics. In addition, the Bible strongly affirms the social dimension of Christian ethics (Matt. 25:34–40). It is not for individuals alone, but finds its fulfillment in the life of communities, manifesting the character of God in the way they live their lives together in community. This social dimension is further developed in the repeated mandates to care for the poor and marginalized in one's community.

Christian ethics is known both through how it is revealed in God's Word, as well as how it is revealed in God's world. The latter is commonly known as natural law (Rom. 2:14–15) (see **Natural Law**), or the law that is "written on the heart." Both means of **revelation** are important. The Bible clarifies and specifies further what may be unclear in natural law, but natural law is important for communicating Christian ethics to a post-Christian culture.

Scott B. Rae

REFERENCES AND RECOMMENDED READING

Grenz, Stanley J. 2000. *The Moral Quest: Foundations of Christian Ethics.* Downers Grove, IL: IVP Academic.
Hollinger, Dennis P. 2002. *Choosing the Good: Christian Ethics in a Complex World.* Grand Rapids: Baker Academic.
Rae, Scott B. 2013. *Doing the Right Thing: Making Moral Choices in a World Full of Options.* Grand Rapids: Zondervan.

ETHICS, ENVIRONMENTAL. Environmental ethics is the study of the principles and standards regarding the moral relationship between humans and nature. Environmental ethics can be thought of as how a person (or group of persons) assigns value to nature. Modern views on Christian environmental ethics (often termed "creation care" or "Christian environmental stewardship") are largely rooted in Scripture but are influenced by secular viewpoints as well.

Utilitarian Value of Nature

The instrumental (or utilitarian) value of nature is based on nature providing for human needs. Examples of such provisions (often called *ecosystem services*) include food, fuel, fiber, and building materials; purification of air and water; decomposition of wastes; stabilization and moderation of climate; moderation of floods; nutrient cycling and renewal of soil fertility; pollination of crops; control of pests and disease; and cultural and aesthetic benefits. The modern conservation movement (led by Theodore Roosevelt in the early twentieth century) has been criticized by preservationists for its focus on the instrumental value of nature, specifically on the sustainable use of resources so they can be available for use by future generations.

The instrumental value of nature is probably the most widely understood and embraced purpose for creation among Christians, as there is much support throughout Scripture (beginning with Gen. 1:29) for the argument that God has provided creation for our use. However, this utilitarian value described in Scripture extends beyond humans, as Genesis 1:30 suggests that the same **providence** is given to all animals. Psalm 104:14–15 speaks of a God who not only provides for human and animal needs, but through creation also provides for our enjoyment. Although God provides creation for our needs and enjoyment, this use is not without its limits, as there are several Scripture passages in which God warns us against wastefully destroying creation and overusing creation's resources beyond its capacity to regenerate itself (Deut. 20:19–20; 22:6; Rev. 11:18).

Intrinsic Value of Nature

Value ascribed to creation beyond human utility is typically referred to as "intrinsic value"—value in and of itself, generally connected to the idea that living things have an intrinsic right to exist and to pursue ends and interests of their own. This philosophy is manifested in the New Age–related deep **ecology** movement, which posits that the whole of nature is in a balanced interrelationship, with no part (e.g., humans) having any more importance than any other. Wilderness preservation, population control, and simple living are three main tenets of the deep ecology movement. Deep ecology is closely associated with animism, **pantheism**, and nature worship, so some Christians tend to deem "guilty by association" any sentiments suggesting that we should live simply, care for creation, or save the earth.

Theistic Intrinsic Value of Nature

Many Christian scholars include creation's value *to God* as one aspect of intrinsic value, but since value to God is technically extrinsic, it would be more accurate to use the term *theistic intrinsic value*, coined by Barrett and Bergstrom (1998). On this God-centered account of the value of creation, Bouma-Prediger states, "Individual creatures and the earth as a whole have an integrity as created by God and as such have more than merely instrumental value. Creatures exist to praise God and are valuable irrespective of human utility" (2001, 142). There are myriad examples in Scripture of creation praising its Creator (e.g., Pss. 103:20–22; 148; Isa. 49:13; 55:12), and indeed, when Christians sing the Doxology, they acknowledge that all creatures praise God, not just people.

Scripture describes a God who enjoys and loves *all* of his creation (e.g., Gen. 1; Pss. 104:31; 145:9). In Romans 8:19–22, Paul points to the ultimate redemption of all of creation: "For the creation waits in eager expectation for the children of God to be revealed. For the creation was subjected to frustration, not by its own choice, but by the will of the one who subjected it, in hope that the creation itself will be liberated from its bondage to decay and brought into the freedom and glory of the children of God. We know that the whole creation has been groaning as in the pains of childbirth right up to the present time." Arguments that this passage does not describe the redemption of all of creation typically involve an interpretation that the verses specifically refer to humans. However, "whole creation" in verse 22, and "Not only so, but we ourselves" in verse 23 seem to suggest otherwise. Other Christians believe that the rest of creation will cease to exist, thus ending its groanings, but, as pointed out by Campolo (1992, 58), "annihilation is not deliverance."

Theistic intrinsic value of creation includes God's role for creation in general **revelation**, which involves God using creation to make known his power and divinity, providing the context for special revelation through Scripture (see **Two Books Metaphor**). Psalm 19 speaks of the revelation of God's power, divinity, and creativity as displayed in the heavens. Romans 1:19–20 likewise describes the role of creation in general revelation, as **John Calvin** explains in his *Institutes*

of the Christian Religion: "[God] not only sowed in men's minds that seed of religion of which we have spoken but revealed himself and daily discloses himself in the whole workmanship of the universe. As a consequence, men cannot open their eyes without being compelled to see him.... But upon his individual works he has engraved unmistakable marks of his glory, so clear and so prominent that even unlettered and stupid folk cannot plead the excuse of ignorance" (Calvin 1960, 1.5.1).

Christian Environmental Stewardship

A steward is someone who is called to take care of something that she or he does not own, often while the owner is away. On the secular level, environmental stewardship may be thought of as taking care of the natural world and wisely using resources so we can pass things on to the next generation (along the lines of the phrase, "We are borrowing the earth from our children"). While Christians would generally embrace this idea (loving our future neighbor as ourselves), Christian scholars generally point instead to the directive given by God in Genesis 1:28 and especially Genesis 2:15 to tend to his creation and help maintain its fertility. Furthermore, in Psalm 24:1 ("The earth is the Lord's, and everything in it") and elsewhere in Scripture, God reminds us that all of creation belongs to him, giving further credibility to the creation-care **paradigm**.

Many Christian scholars subscribe to some level of a creation-care paradigm, but Christians in general are less likely to espouse such views for several reasons. These include **eschatology** (believing that the earth will be burned up when Christ returns: 2 Peter 3:10); rejection of the things of "this world" (Rom. 12:2); and rejection of a paradigm that seems too pantheistic (i.e., we should serve the Creator, not the created). Furthermore, many Christians (and many critics of Christianity) believe that Genesis 1:28 gives humans license to dominate, subdue, and vanquish the earth. Taking the verse in isolation, such an interpretation seems plausible, but on consideration of Scripture in its entirety, most Christian scholars conclude that such an interpretation is flawed. Indeed, we find a few verses later (in Gen. 2:15) that God delivers the directive to take care of the garden (and presumably the earth), not to vanquish it. Humans, in fact, share rule of creation with God (Ps. 8), who does not abuse his creation.

Another reason for Christians eschewing a paradigm of creation care is that it seems to elevate the rest of creation to the same level as people. Indeed, some of the most contentious environmental issues among Christians involve disagreements as to how stewardship and creation care should be manifested in public policy when such policies have the potential to negatively impact the poor and downtrodden. For example, while many Christian scholars support international efforts to curb global **climate change**, members of the Cornwall Alliance for the Stewardship of Creation take the position that well-intentioned climate policies restricting the use of fossil fuels will ultimately doom the poor by preventing economic development. Cornwall Alliance founder E. Calvin Beisner espouses the belief that an infinitely wise God has equipped our planet with robust, self-regulating, and self-correcting negative feedback loops that would offset potentially harmful inputs such as increased atmospheric carbon dioxide (see **Climate Change**).

Todd Tracy

REFERENCES AND RECOMMENDED READING

Barrett, Christopher B., and John C. Bergstrom. 1998. "The Economics of God's Creation." *Bulletin of the Association of Christian Economists* 31:4–23.
Berry, Wendell. 1993. "Christianity and the Survival of Creation." In *Sacred Trusts: Essays on Stewardship and Responsibility*, ed. M. Katakis, 38–54. San Francisco: Mercury House.
Bouma-Prediger, S. 2001. *For the Beauty of the Earth: A Christian Vision for Creation Care.* Grand Rapids: Baker Academic.
Calvin, John. 1960. *Institutes of the Christian Religion.* Library of Christian Classics. Vol. 20. Ed. J. McNeill. Trans. F. Battles. Louisville, KY: Westminster.
Campolo, Tony. 1992. *How to Rescue the Earth without Worshiping Nature.* Nashville: Thomas Nelson.
DeWitt, C. B. 1994. "Christian Environmental Stewardship: Preparing the Way for Action." *Perspectives on Science and the Christian Faith* 46:80–89.
Finger, T. 1998. *Evangelicals, Eschatology, and the Environment.* Scholars Circle Monograph #2. Evangelical Environmental Network. www.creationcare.org.
Legates, D., and G. C. van Kooten. 2014. "A Call to Truth, Prudence, and Protection of the Poor: The Case against Harmful Climate Policies Gets Stronger." Cornwall Alliance for the Stewardship of Creation. Burke, VA. September. http://www.cornwallalliance.org/wp-content/uploads/2014/09/A-Call-to-Truth-Prudence-and-Protection-of-the-Poor–2014-The-Case-Against-Harmful-Climate-Policies-Gets-Stronger.pdf.
Petersen, K. 2003. "The Educational Imperative of Creation Care." *Christian Scholar's Review* 32 (4): 433–54.
Stott, J. 2001. *The Birds Our Teachers: Biblical Lessons from a Lifelong Bird Watcher.* Grand Rapids: Baker.
Van Dyke, F., D. Mahan, J. Sheldon, and R. Brand. 1996. *Redeeming Creation: The Biblical Basis for Environmental Stewardship.* Downers Grove, IL: InterVarsity.
Warners, D., M. Ryskamp, and R. Van Dragt. 2014. "Reconciliation Ecology: A New Paradigm for Advancing Creation Care." *Perspectives on Science and the Christian Faith* 66:221–35.

ETHICS, EVOLUTIONARY. Evolutionary ethics is the attempt to provide an evolutionary explanation for the moral sensibilities of human beings and any other animals with highly developed social instincts capable of cooperative behavior. On **Darwin**'s view, any animal with the right social instincts "would inevitably acquire a moral sense or conscience, as soon as its intellectual powers had become as well, or nearly as well developed, as in man" (Darwin 1998, 101). He offered a four-stage account of the origin of our moral sense: (1) social instincts were selected as an aid to survival and reproduction; (2) mental faculties appeared that could judge the superiority of the social instinct to more short-lived instinctual urges like hunger and sexual desire; (3) the emergence of language allowed the community to express the common good and hold individuals accountable; and (4) instruction and practice allowed moral behavior to become habitual, thus reinforcing social instincts.

An important consequence of evolutionary ethics is that the moral sensibilities of human beings are contingent on their natural history. This is a conclusion that Darwin (1998) drew explicitly.

> If … men were reared under precisely the same conditions as hive-bees, there can hardly be a doubt that our unmarried females would, like the worker-bees, think it a sacred duty to kill their brothers, and mothers would strive to kill their fertile daughters; and no one would think of interfering. Nevertheless, the bee, or any other social animal, would gain in our supposed case, as it appears to me, some feeling of right or wrong, or a conscience. For each individual would have an inward sense of possessing certain stronger or enduring instincts, and others less strong or enduring.… In this case an inward monitor would tell the animal that it would have been better to have followed the one impulse rather than the other. The one course ought to have been followed, and the other ought not; the one would have been right and the other wrong. (Darwin 1998, 102–3)

What is not clear in Darwin's account is whether our natural history shapes our moral sense alone, or also determines moral obligations. Suppose we had been raised like hive bees. Is Darwin's view that (1) fratricide and infanticide would then have *been* duties? Or is it merely that (2) we would have *thought* that fratricide and female infanticide were duties?

Consider the first alternative. This claims that moral value and obligations themselves derive from natural history. One difficulty for this view is the famous problem of **altruism**. If **morality** reflects our biological interests, then it seems there can only be moral reasons to aid those with whom we are genetically related. That might include more than our immediate family: as William Hamilton argued, there may be some genetic connection to more distant relatives or *kin selection* (Wilson 1993, 41). Darwin went further, arguing that since the survival and reproduction of individuals is enhanced by their belonging to a cohesive tribe, some traits will be selected because they are good for the tribe (*group selection*).

However, Christopher Boehm argues that neither of these approaches adequately explains altruism: "humans don't merely assist their close or distant blood kin; they also help people who are unrelated to them—even though … such altruistic assistance will be costly to their fitness because there is no shared heredity" (Boehm 2012, 8). Nor is it the case that altruistic actions are confined to people of the same tribe: on 9/11, emergency workers risked their lives to rescue people from many nations trapped in the World Trade Center towers.

Boehm's own theory is that altruism arose due to *social selection*: by making a person's reputation dependent on moral behavior, individuals are more likely to prosper and find mates if they do the right thing. One problem for Boehm's account is that social selection still does not explain why we should value the lives of *all* human beings, including those who have no impact on our reputation. Another problem, common to many theories in evolutionary ethics, is that Boehm conflates explaining our moral faculties with explaining the existence and authority of moral norms, claiming that "morality began with having a conscience" (Boehm 2012, 15). While it is plausible that one cannot be subject to a moral demand one does not recognize, such recognition does not create the demand or explain its authority.

A more general worry is that if morality depends on natural history, moral obligations do not have normative necessity. For even if females are contingently obligated to respect their brothers' lives, had they been raised like hive bees, these females would have no such obligation and would instead be obliged to kill their brothers. This also implies that there are no genuinely inalienable human rights, since a different natural history would mean that some humans would lose those rights. And this same result could also be achieved artificially, through social engineering. Arguably, social organizations that depend on apartheid and slavery are attempts to engineer living conditions so that (it is claimed) the same moral obligations do not apply to some human beings.

It is also highly problematic to base human worth on the historically contingent distribution of natural characteristics. The idea of basic human rights is that all human beings have equal moral worth, but natural advantages (like strength and intelligence) are not uniformly distributed and are degreed properties (some are stronger or smarter than others); so "Why should we treat all people equally in any respect in the face of manifest inequalities among them?" (Moreland 2009, 144). Such thinking allowed the Nazi doctors to exterminate thousands of physically and mentally impaired individuals because they were deemed "unworthy of life" (Lifton 1986).

Now consider the second alternative. In this case our moral sense might have been different (we might have thought fratricide was a duty), but no claim is made about moral reality (fratricide might still be wrong). But if our moral sense is not dependent on moral reality, our moral judgments can only be right by accidental coincidence; so we cannot claim to have moral knowledge.

Indeed, many defenders of naturalistic evolution accept the skeptical implication that moral knowledge is impossible. For example, Michael Ruse and **E. O. Wilson** argue, "Human beings function better if they are deceived by their **genes** into thinking that there is a disinterested objective morality binding upon them, which all should obey" (Ruse and Wilson 1986, 179). Richard Joyce reinforces the point: the fact that it was "systematically useful for our ancestors to form beliefs about moral rightness and wrongness" does not imply "that any actual moral rightness or wrongness existed in the ancestral environment" (Joyce 2007, 183).

Angus J. L. Menuge

REFERENCES AND RECOMMENDED READING

Boehm, Christopher. 2012. *Moral Origins: The Evolution of Virtue, Altruism, and Shame.* New York: Basic Books.
Darwin, Charles. (1871) 1998. *The Descent of Man.* Amherst, NY: Prometheus.
Joyce, Richard. 2007. *The Evolution of Morality.* Cambridge, MA: MIT Press.
Lifton, Robert Jay. 1986. *The Nazi Doctors: Medical Killing and the Psychology of Genocide.* New York: Basic Books.
Moreland, J. P. 2009. *The Recalcitrant Imago Dei: Human Persons and the Failure of Naturalism.* London: SCM.
Ruse, Michael, and E. O. Wilson. 1986. "Moral Philosophy as Applied Science." *Philosophy* 61 (236): 173–92.
Wilson, James Q. 1993. *The Moral Sense.* New York: Free Press.

ETHICS IN SCIENCE. The spectrum of ethical issues scientists face reflects science's aims as a truth-seeking and technology-generating enterprise, its networks of collaborations, and its capital-intensive nature. However, the specific issues scientists face are shaped by the way science functions and its cultural norms.

Contemporary science is to some degree institutionalized (Ravetz 1971). Its overall direction is partly shaped by governments, industries, and private foundations; these work with scientists to suggest promising avenues for research and propose important scientific and technological challenges. Individual investigators and groups of researchers then respond by proposing particular solutions (or, more commonly, partial solutions) to these challenges and by writing grant proposals, which are reviewed by scientific panels (for government grants and most foundations) or business leaders (for industrial research) who determine which proposals will be funded based on their "intellectual merit" and potential "broader impacts" (National Science Board 2011). Successful investigators are then expected to make significant progress on the proposed work as measured by outputs in the form of publications, products, patents, or venture capital, with failure resulting in a loss of competitiveness in future funding cycles or the marketplace.

The whole process is competitive and often involves significant sums; for instance, in 2012 the US National Science Foundation's overall funding rate was 24 percent and its average grant size was $166,000 (National Science Foundation 2013). It is also collaborative in that most scientific work is performed by teams of researchers at different stages of their career, sometimes working at different institutions in geographically disparate locations.

Scientific research can be extremely work intensive and involve high stakes, as successful grants, journal publications, patents, and other outputs are often used as metrics of success for the awarding of degrees, hiring, retention, and promotion decisions. However, the temptation to cut corners is significantly counterbalanced by science's status as a truth-seeking collaborative enterprise and the correspondingly high value the scientific community places on integrity.

Not only is honesty in conducting and reporting research stressed by most scientific organizations' ethical codes, but also many scientific subfields are relatively small communities in which the scientists involved depend on the reliability and honesty of each member's publications and review work. Because honesty is widely valued by scientific communities, blatant "scientific misconduct" in the form of "fabrication, falsification, or plagiarism (FFP) in proposing, performing, or reviewing research, or in reporting research results" (Public Policy Commitee 2009, 3) is relatively rare. Instead, most

ethical quandaries arise in the gray areas where the ideas of others are half remembered or forgotten, exaggerated claims of significance are touted in proposals and papers, studies are designed to promote an expected result, exemplary results are passed off as representative, poorly documented procedures are reconstructed from memory, unwelcome outliers are discarded without statistical cause, data are selectively or suggestively presented, and informal social contracts of workload and credit sharing are negotiated amid a context of disparate power relationships.

Thus in many respects ethical scientific behavior begins at the level of research group leaders, journal editors, and other gatekeepers. The degree of transparency and honesty with which these propose and evaluate projects, recruit collaborators, design studies, keep and manage records, follow data analysis best practices, and disseminate their results determine the climate and ethical norms for workers in their fields. Research group leaders play an especially important role since they are responsible for setting clear expectations for each collaborator's workload, productivity, and requirements for authorship and for creating a climate of ethical responsibility among the junior collaborators who function as workers on the ground. These collaborators are more likely to be aware of unethical behavior at the data collection and analysis level and thus have greater opportunity to correct lapses before they reach the level where injuries and accidents occur or papers need to be retracted, misconduct investigations initiated, and sanctions imposed by institutional or government review boards.

Several special ethical issues occur commonly enough that procedures for handling them have been codified. Studies involving human or animal subjects are typically overseen by institutional review boards to ensure subjects are treated in a humane and ethical manner. Human experimentation in particular is subject to the Nuremburg code, which establishes that investigators are responsible for designing human subject studies responsibly, minimizing the potential for suffering and harm, and ensuring that participation is voluntary and subject to informed consent. Similarly, federal and institutional guidelines have been set up to avoid potential conflicts of interest involving members of review panels, principal investigators, granting and policy agency staff, and other decision makers. These have been strengthened in recent years as increasing numbers of scientists engage in industrial consulting or seek to market their innovations through **technology** transfer startups.

There are a few cases where unethical behavior in science

is recognized but effectively tolerated, typically due to the scientific community's ignorance or inability to resist politically astute, well-funded, and potentially amoral interests. Perhaps the most prominent examples involve industry-funded "mercenary scientists" publishing in and running "captured journals" for the purpose of "manufacturing" doubt for "product defense" purposes; their typical tactics include massaging data or designing studies to give the desired result, often by reducing study population sizes until any harmful effects are statistically insignificant (Michaels 2008; Oreskes and Conway 2010).

Some projects have the potential to generate revolutionary insights or new technologies or have significant social, economic, and public policy implications. In these cases, additional ethical issues can arise due to the work's potential impacts and implications. However, while most scientists pursue projects with the hope that they will produce valuable knowledge or beneficial innovations, relatively few consider the potential adverse impacts of their work.

This is understandable since scientific knowledge and technology typically reach the public and other stakeholders through a complex network of engineers, technicians, business professionals, and politicians; consequently many scientists, few of whom have significant ethical training, are content to leave consideration of the wider ethical implications of their work to others (Wolpe 2006). However, there are several well-accepted instances where scientists generally recognize their responsibility to the wider public. These include protecting the health and safety of coworkers and the public and the need for limits on human **cloning** and other ethically questionable lines of research. Recently there have been efforts to exercise responsible control over the dissemination of dual-use research, namely, that which has the potential to be adapted for harmful purposes by terrorists and other rogue agents.

Similarly, there is a longstanding tradition of recognizing individual scientists' right to conscientiously abstain from work they find objectionable. For instance, a number of scientists conscientiously refused to participate in post–World War II nuclear weapons research; based on their special knowledge of these weapons' destructiveness, some even felt a special social responsibility to protest against nuclear weapons themselves.

Scientists engaged in fields like epidemiology and climate science often have a strong sense of social responsibility due to these fields' implications for human welfare and their potential influence on economic and public policy. Scientists working in these fields face the additional challenge of determining when to publicize the results of their work, a decision that can be complicated due to the need to balance the uncertainty inherent in low-incidence epidemiological studies or predictive climate modeling with the risk of harm due to inaction (Krimsky 2000). Furthermore, because their work can have public policy and legal implications, these scientists sometimes find themselves the target of political and professional attacks from special interest groups or mercenary scientists (Michaels 2008).

On the whole, science's ethic of integrity is consonant with the Christian ethic of integrity; the latter even provides motivation for honest behavior in the gray areas where scientific social norms practically allow for (but don't endorse) unethical behavior. Indeed, it is important for Christians in the sciences to be self-aware of their behavior in these gray areas, as they present opportunities for both practical witness and moral corruption (Hearn 1973).

Sometimes believing scientists choose to work in areas they perceive as consonant with their moral vision; it is easy, for example, to look on medical or environmental research as a form of practical Christian service. Similarly, particular theological outlooks and church cultures can influence scientists' decisions to formally or informally abstain from work they believe is ethically questionable. For example, Christian pacifists typically avoid military research, while **abortion**-conscious evangelicals have been apprehensive over research involving embryonic stem cells (see **Embryonic Stem Cell Research**).

Stephen A. Contakes

REFERENCES AND RECOMMENDED READING

Bennett, George D. 2008. "A Comparison of Green Chemistry to the Environmental Ethics of the Abrahamic Religions." *Perspectives on Science and Christian Faith* 60:16–25.

Brock, Brian. 2010. *Christian Ethics in a Technological Age*. Grand Rapids: Eerdmans.

Carson, Joseph P. 2002. "Should ASA Defend and Advance Professional Ethics in Science and Technology Professions?" *Perspectives on Science and Christian Faith* 54:124–26.

Chalk, Rosemary. 1989. "Drawing the Line: An Examination of Conscientious Objection in Science." *Annals of the New York Academy of Sciences* 577:61–74.

"Chemical Professional's Code of Conduct." 2007. American Chemical Society.

Coates, Joseph F. 1989. "The Ethics of Corporate and Military Research." *Annals of the New York Academy of Sciences* 577:149–53.

Comstock, Gary. 2012. *Research Ethics: A Philosophical Guide to the Responsible Conduct of Research*. Cambridge and New York: Cambridge University Press.

Coppola, Brian P. 2001. "The Technology Transfer Dilemma: Preserving Morally Responsible Education in a Utilitarian Academic Culture." *Hyle— International Journal for the Philosophy of Chemistry* 72 (1): 156–67.

Craven, Bruce. 2006. "Ethics in Research." *ISCAST Online Journal* 2. www .iscast.org/journal/opinion/Craven_B_2006–12_Ethics_In_Research.pdf.

Crouch, Catherine H. 2000. "Scientific Ethics: A Realm for Partnership." *Perspectives on Science and Christian Faith* 52:156–58.

Dabrock, Peter. 2009. "Playing God? Synthetic Biology as a Theological and Ethical Challenge." *Systems and Synthetic Biology* 3:47–54.

Deane-Drummond, Celia. 2006. *Genetics and Christian Ethics*. New Studies in Christian Ethics. Cambridge: Cambridge University Press.

Douglas, Heather E. 2009. *Science, Policy, and the Value-Free Ideal*. Pittsburgh: University of Pittsburgh Press.

Edgar, Brian. 2009. "Biotheology: Theology, Ethics and the New Biotechnologies." *Christian Perspectives on Science and Technology: ISCAST Online Journal* 5. www.iscast.org/journal/articles/Edgar_B_2009–07_Biotheology.pdf.

Ermer, Gayle E. 2008. "Professional Engineering Ethics and Christian Values: Overlapping Magesteria." *Perspectives on Science and Christian Faith* 60 (1): 26–34.

Fischer, Julie Elizabeth. 2005. *Dual-Use Technologies: Inexorable Progress, Inseparable Peril: A Report of the Project on Technology Futures and Global Power, Wealth, and Conflict*. CSIS Series on Technology Futures and Global Power, Wealth, and Conflict. Washington, DC: CSIS Press.

Hatfield, Charles. 1973. *The Scientist and Ethical Decision*. Downers Grove, IL: InterVarsity.

Hearn, Walter R. 1973. "Whole People and Half-Truths." In *The Scientist and Ethical Decision*, ed. Charles Hatfield, 83–96. Downers Grove, IL: InterVarsity.

Imperiale, Michael J. 2012. "Dual-Use Research after the Avian Influenza Controversy." *Bulletin of the Atomic Scientists*. July 11. http://thebulletin .org/dual-use-research-after-avian-influenza-controversy.

Kovac, Jeffrey. 2000a. "Professionalism and Ethics in Chemistry." *Foundations of Chemistry* 2: 207–19.

———. 2000b. "Science, Law, and the Ethics of Expertise." *Tennessee Law Review* 67:397–408.

———. 2004. *The Ethical Chemist: Professionalism and Ethics in Science*. Prentice Hall Series in Educational Innovation. Upper Saddle River, NJ: Pearson Prentice Hall.

Krimsky, Sheldon. 2000. *Hormonal Chaos: The Scientific and Social Origins of the Environmental Endocrine Hypothesis*. Baltimore: Johns Hopkins University Press.

———. 2003. *Science in the Private Interest: Has the Lure of Profits Corrupted Biomedical Research?* Lanham, MD: Rowman & Littlefield.

Kulakowski, Elliott C., Lynne U. Chronister, and Research Enterprise. 2006. *Research Administration and Management*. Sudbury, MA: Jones and Bartlett.

Lonsdale, Kathleen. 1951. "The Ethical Problems of Scientists." *Bulletin of the Atomic Scientists* 7, no. 7 (August): 201–4.

Macrina, Francis L. 2005. *Scientific Integrity: Text and Cases in Responsible Conduct of Research*. 3rd ed. Washington, DC: ASM Press.

Martinson, Brian C., Melissa S. Anderson, and Raymond de Vries. 2005. "Scientists Behaving Badly." *Nature* 435:737–38.

Michaels, David. 2008. *Doubt Is Their Product: How Industry's Assault on Science Threatens Your Health*. Oxford and New York: Oxford University Press.

Mitcham, Carl. 1989. "The Spectrum of Ethical Issues Associated with the Military Support of Science and Technology." *Annals of the New York Academy of Sciences* 577: 1–9.

Mitchell, C. Ben. 2007. *Biotechnology and the Human Good*. Washington, DC: Georgetown University Press.

Moghissi, A. Alan, Betty Love, and Sorin Straja. 2011. *Peer Review and Scientific Assessment: A Handbook for Funding Organizations, Regulatory Agencies, and Editors*. Cambridge and New York: Cambridge University Press.

National Science Advisory Board for Biosecurity. 2007. *Proposed Framework for the Oversight of Dual Use Life Sciences Research: Strategies for Minimizing the Potential Misuse of Research Information*. http://osp.od.nih.gov/office-biotechnology-activities/nsabb-reports-and-recommendations/proposed-framework-oversight-dual-use-life-sciences-research.

National Science Board. 2011. "National Science Foundation's Merit Review Criteria: Review and Revisions." Arlington, VA: National Science Foundation.

National Science Foundation. 2013. *Report to the National Science Board on the National Science Foundation's Merit Review Process Fiscal Year 2012*. Arlington, VA: National Science Foundation.

"Office of Research Integrity." U.S. Department of Health and Human Services. http://ori.hhs.gov.

"Online Ethics Center." National Academy of Engineering. www.onlineethics.org.

Oreskes, Naomi, and Erik M. Conway. 2010. *Merchants of Doubt: How a Handful of Scientists Obscured the Truth on Issues from Tobacco Smoke to Global Warming*. 1st US ed. New York: Bloomsbury.

Public Policy Committee on Science, Engineering, and Public Policy: National Academy of Sciences, National Academy of Engineering, and Institute of Medicine of the National Academies. 2009. *On Being a Scientist: Responsible Conduct in Research*. 3rd ed. Washington, DC: National Academies Press.

Ravetz, Jerome R. 1971. *Scientific Knowledge and Its Social Problems*. Oxford: Clarendon.

Santoro, Michael A., and Thomas M. Gorrie. *Ethics and the Pharmaceutical Industry*. Cambridge: Cambridge University Press.

Schummer, Joachim. 2001. "Ethics of Chemical Synthesis." *HYLE—International Journal for the Philosophy of Chemistry* 7 (2): 103–24.

Schuurman, E. *The Technological World Picture and an Ethics of Responsibility: Struggles in the Ethics of Technology*. Sioux Center, IA: Dordt College Press.

Selgelid, Michael J. 2009. "Governance of Dual-Use Research: An Ethical Dilemma." *Bulletin of the World Health Organ* 87:720–23.

Shinn, Roger L. 1989. "Moral Arguments and the Traditions of Religious Ethics." *Annals of the New York Academy of Sciences* 577:40–46.

Stewart, Gavin. 1999. *The Partnership between Science and Industry: Co-operation or Conflict of Interest?* London: British Library.

van den Belt, Henk. 2009. "Playing God in Frankenstein's Footsteps: Synthetic Biology and the Meaning of Life." *Nanoethics* 3:257–68.

Whitbeck, Caroline. 2011. *Ethics in Engineering Practice and Research*. 2nd ed. Cambridge: Cambridge University Press.

Wolpe, Paul R. 2006. "Reasons Scientists Avoid Thinking about Ethics." *Cell* 125, no. 6 (June): 1023–25.

Zierler, David. 2011. *The Invention of Ecocide: Agent Orange, Vietnam, and the Scientists Who Changed the Way We Think about the Environment*. Athens: University of Georgia Press.

⚡ EVIL, PROBLEM OF (Evolutionary-Creationist View).

I address the problem of evil as an evolutionary creationist. Evolutionary creation (EC) has little connection to some aspects of the problem of evil. For instance, human beings have free will and have thereby caused countless evils. There is robust philosophical discussion about God's role with respect to this kind of evil, but its relationship to EC is indirect, so I will not address it here. Instead, I will focus on those aspects of the problem that are directly related to and perhaps even exacerbated by EC.

For the purposes of this article, I will take it as given that God brought about the diversity of life on earth today through the process of evolution. That's the "evolutionary" part of EC. I also want to clearly affirm the "creation" part of EC: I believe God is the Creator and that he created human beings in his image. I am not taking a stand on whether the mechanisms of genetic mutation and **natural selection** are sufficient for explaining this process in scientific terms, but

I will affirm the theory of **common ancestry** according to which all life today is related.

Furthermore, I accept the interpretations of the genetic evidence that show there cannot have been one human pair from whom all other humans descended. Some versions of EC still appeal to **Adam and Eve** as real people and as representatives (not ancestors) of all humanity. I'm not persuaded by the theological arguments for the necessity of such a postulation, and it is difficult to see how there could be evidence for this in either science or history. So I will work from the standard scientific picture according to which human beings developed from earlier primates and never numbered below about 10,000 individuals. This blocks responses to the problem of evil that pin so much of it on the result of Adam and Eve's sin.

The chief difficulty for this perspective is squaring the characterization of evolution as "nature red in tooth and claw" with a good, all powerful God who is worthy of worship. It is little comfort to say that God knows when a sparrow falls or a gazelle is torn apart by a cheetah or a **species** of hominids goes extinct if God set up the system that guarantees such events will happen—often with gruesome pain and suffering. **Richard Dawkins** paints the picture for us:

> During the minute it takes me to compose this sentence, thousands of animals are being eaten alive; others are running for their lives, whimpering with fear; others are being slowly devoured from within by rasping parasites; thousands of all kinds are dying of starvation, thirst and disease. It must be so. If there is ever a time of plenty, this very fact will automatically lead to an increase in population until the natural state of starvation and misery is restored. (Dawkins 1995, 132)

Take the events of that minute and multiply them by the hundreds of millions of years of animal life on the planet, and you see the problem. Are there reasons that can be given that reconcile the kinds and amount of evil we find in the world with the traditional conception of God? Such reasons are typically called a *theodicy*. In what follows, I offer some brief sketches of the sorts of theodicies that might be given for this problem.

Are the Pain and Suffering Associated with Evolution Really Evil?

The first question we might ask is whether the pain and suffering that attend evolution is really evil. We don't say that the lion itself is evil when it kills a wildebeest (or even a human being). Certainly it causes pain and suffering, and we would do everything we could to stop it if it were loose in a village threatening the people there. But we wouldn't judge the lion to be morally reprehensible like we would a person who did the same thing. So someone might claim that there is no problem of evil that is confined to the pre-human animal world.

But now we have to ask what God's role in this might be. For we don't say that a gun or a knife is evil when it is an instrument used to kill an innocent person. Rather, it is the agent who used them that has caused evil. Is evolution an instrument that God uses? Evolutionary creationists believe so. In the same way he uses volcanoes to create the Hawaiian Islands, he has used evolution to create human beings and other species of life. Does that make God responsible for what seems to be the massive waste of life? In some sense it does. We can't just assert it isn't evil, but must look for a different way of reconciling what we find in nature with the character of God.

Extinction and Essentialism

It seems to me that there is one way of responding to the charge of wastage that is brought against the process of evolution. It is well established that about 99 percent of all species that have ever existed are now extinct. If God has created human beings through this process, does our existence come at the expense of these other species? Doesn't the survival of the weak at the expense of the strong seem to cut against the grain of Jesus's message? We will consider an eschatological response to this charge later. First, I consider the problem from the perspective of **metaphysics**, or more specifically, ontology.

Ontology is the study of existence and of the kinds of things that exist, and the specific question here is what kind of ontological status to give to "species." Do they really exist independently of what we think about them, or are they artificial categories to aid in our thinking about things? We can't get away from using terms that refer to groups of individuals like oak trees, zebras, and blue jays. But what is it that allows us to group such similar individuals together? Traditionally, the concept of species was used and implicitly understood to be a static and unchanging thing. Evolution challenges that. Of course, among individuals with significant differences, we can easily put them into distinct groups. But when the differences are slighter, and especially when we look at a population across time, it is much more difficult.

Offspring bear strong resemblance to their parents, but

after many generations, resemblance to ancestors is considerably smaller. About 50,000 generations before us today, we come to *Homo erectus*—a hominin species that lived around 1 million years ago, possibly living in hunter-gatherer groups using tools and fire. But was this ancestor a human being? Most biologists would say no. But there is no clear line at which *Homo erectus* becomes *Homo sapiens*. The same can be said of the other lines of descent that can be traced back from the organisms alive today. And there are other lines of descent that terminate with no further descendants. This is an "extinction," but if it is hard to define a "species," then it is hard to say what has gone extinct. All we can say is that some group of individuals had no further descendants.

The point is that when we say it is a bad thing for a species to go extinct, we are assuming that there is some entity existing above and beyond the individuals that goes out of existence when all of the individuals in that group go out of existence. But the group in question can only be arbitrarily defined. It is only on the assumption of "essentialism" (that there is some particular essence of what it is to be a cat or a cactus) that this objection about the **extinction** of species in evolution carries any force. The life of an individual cat or cactus is not affected by its "species" going extinct some generations after it lived. There are individual lives, and these have the same sort of life whether or not their descendants lived and prospered.

Now of course, some of those individuals have difficult lives. Dissolving the problem of extinction does not make the problem of **animal pain** and suffering go away. We have already seen that during evolutionary time scales, many, many individuals die prematurely and in gruesome ways. What sense can the Christian make of this process?

Greater Goods and Only Way

Strategies for responding to this problem typically appeal to "greater goods" or "the only way." For example, a world with human free will—even with all the trouble it causes—is thought to be a greater good than a world without it. And natural evils like hurricanes and tornadoes can plausibly be said to be consequences of the only way to maintain a dynamic planet that can support life. Can it be argued that evolution is the only way to bring about greater goods that God desired for his creation? Can we know what those greater goods might be?

Some theists say no. Their position has come to be called *skeptical* **theism**. It is the view that we should be skeptical of our ability to discern and understand the reasons God

might have for allowing the evils we see in the world. God's ways are so far beyond our ways that our inability to come up with good reasons for why there is the kind and amount of evil in the world does not show that God has no good reasons for allowing that evil. Surely there is some truth to the claim that our finite minds cannot fully comprehend the ways of God. But there are troubling implications to taking skeptical theism to the degree needed to answer in full the problem of natural evil. Chief among these is the undermining of all our claims to moral knowledge. Skeptical theism seems to suggest for any instance of natural evil, that for all we know, there could be reasons why that instance is in fact a good thing (or at least better than the alternative). That seems to undermine our ability to make any sort of moral judgment that things ought not to be the way we find them to be. Beyond this, there is the commonly held **intuition** that we ought to be able to offer something more in the way of reasons for why the world is the way it is. So we must keep looking for greater goods and only ways, even if these are only speculative.

One of the greater goods that evolution makes possible might be that God delights in the transformation of chaos into order, and delights in the cooperation of his creation in the process. Genesis does not claim that the created world was perfect and complete. Rather, it was good. But even then, God commissioned his image bearers to subdue the earth, implying that the work of transforming the chaos into order was not complete. If God did not delight in this process, then we would expect God to have created things in a final, perfect form rather than creating over time. Even the young-earth creationist position breaks down here when we ask why God took seven days to accomplish what he could have done instantaneously. God does not seem to be in a hurry, but instead patiently teases order out of chaos. To claim otherwise invites the question of why God even bothered with creating this order of things instead of just starting off with a perfect and eternal heaven.

Few people would think that the process of transformation is enough to justify the eons of animal pain and suffering. To this, though, we might add an "only way" **theodicy**. Perhaps the evolutionary struggle is the only way to develop sentient, moral beings like us. It can be argued that moral maturity is a quality that must be developed through making moral decisions. God can no more create morally mature creatures than he could create free beings who are incapable of sin. So to achieve moral maturity, agents must be involved in their own moral formation by making decisions with moral implications. But then in order to have genuine moral decisions, there must be a challenging environment in which beings are subjected to the kinds of natural evils that force difficult decisions.

When faced with such situations, will creatures opt for their own selfish preservation over doing what is right and good? Until recently, no one studying evolutionary history would have even considered such a question. But now more and more people are taking an interest in the role of cooperation and even **altruism** in the story of the development of more complex animal forms (see Coakley 2016, and Deane-Drummond 2014). In this sense, suffering is a catalyst for greater goods, but not in a crude instrumental way. The suffering and pain are in some sense constitutive of the greater good of moral formation—and the only way to bring it about.

If this line of thinking has merit, we must question whether we would want a world history devoid of the kind of natural evils considered in this chapter. We need not try to force ourselves to think that evil is good, but it seems that God has structured things so that good comes from evil—and the kinds of goods that could come about no other way.

Eschatology

These are interesting theoretical possibilities, but we are still left with the instances of countless individuals in this world who suffered and died without living the fulfilled lives they were intended to. This inescapable truth drives some Christian thinkers to conclude that there may be some sort of existence after death for animals. **Keith Ward** says, "Immortality, for animals as well as humans, is a necessary condition of any acceptable theodicy" (Ward 1982, 201).

This is not just a post-Darwinian innovation in Christian theology. The eighteenth-century founder of Methodism, John Wesley, considered the objection of animal suffering and said, "The objection vanishes away if we consider that something better remains after death for these creatures also; that these likewise shall one day be delivered from this bondage of corruption, and shall then receive ample amends for all their present sufferings" (Wesley 1998, 251). When we understand that the groaning of all creation was addressed in Christ's act of redemption, it is plausible to think that all creatures have the possibility of achieving the ends for which they were intended.

These responses to the pain and suffering we find in the evolutionary picture of the world are speculative, for now we see through a glass darkly. But they are responsible to the data of the natural world and seem consistent with the character of God as revealed through Scripture.

J. B. Stump

REFERENCES AND RECOMMENDED READING

Coakley, Sarah. 2016. *Sacrifice Regained: Evolution, Cooperation and God.* Oxford: Oxford University Press.
Dawkins, Richard. 1995. *River Out of Eden.* New York: Basic Books.
Dean-Drummond, Celia. 2014. *The Wisdom of the Liminal: Evolution and Other Animals in Human Becoming.* Grand Rapids: Eerdmans.
Meister, Chad. 2012. *Evil: A Guide for the Perplexed.* New York: Bloomsbury.
Southgate, Christopher. 2008. *The Groaning of Creation.* Louisville, KY: Westminster John Knox.
Ward, Keith. 1982. *Rational Theology and the Creativity of God.* New York: Pilgrim.
Wesley, John. 1998. "The General Deliverance." In *The Works of John Wesley,* 3rd ed., vol. 6. Grand Rapids: Baker.

❧ EVIL, PROBLEM OF (Progressive-Creationist View).

Atheists, agnostics, and deists cite the problem of evil as a potent challenge to the truth of Christianity. The syllogism for the argument may be stated as follows:

1. The God of the Bible is omniscient, omnipresent, and omnibenevolent.
2. A world created by such a God would not contain evil.
3. The world contains evil.
4. Therefore such a God does not exist.

Christianity rejects the second premise; therefore Christians must provide a rational justification for the existence of evil in the world; that said, *all* **worldview**s—not simply Christians—must grapple with the question of evil (see **Theodicy**).

Two-Creation Model

The premise of the two-creation model is that God has no good purpose for the presently existing evil and suffering. Some belief systems accept this assertion as true. Various major world religions share the tenet that humans arose in an evil-free, paradisiacal state that was soon lost. Where they differ is in their belief that God, gods, or cosmic forces are working to restore humanity to that paradise. In non-Christian belief systems, the present evil is largely gratuitous—it serves no beneficial purpose. In contrast, Christianity proclaims a two-creation model in which both realms are radically different, and evil ultimately serves a purpose.

The first creation is "very good" (Gen. 1:31). It is the best possible realm in which to encourage as many humans as possible to choose something far better, an eternally secure, loving relationship with God. This creation also equips and trains individuals to receive the roles, rewards, and relational fulfillments of the new (second) creation. Part of that equipping and training includes a brief (relative to eternity) exposure to evil and suffering. And yet this present creation also provides the best possible stage on which to bring about a rapid, permanent removal of all evil. Until then, God allows humanity to be briefly exposed to evil because of a greater good such exposure yields.

The second creation is "perfect." Evil will never exist there. Unlike the present creation, no limitations brought on by human sin will restrict anyone's free will. Consequently, love without limits can and will be expressed.

Some skeptics may respond, "Why didn't God place **Adam and Eve** in the new creation to start with?" This two-creation model holds that unless humans are first tested by the greatest possible temptation—the most compelling attraction of evil—then the roles, rewards, and relationships of the new creation cannot be made both perfect and permanent. Either human free will and the capacity for love would be greatly diminished (rather than greatly enhanced) or the return of rebellion against God's authority and the consequent evil would remain an ever-present danger.

Eternal Freedom

Adam and Eve enjoyed a loving relationship with God and one another in **Eden**. God could have kept it that way for all eternity. He had the power to keep temptation away, but his will for humanity did not include an earthly paradise forever. He had better plans.

In Eden Adam and Eve lacked assurance that their relationship with God, one another, and the rest of Eden's creatures would remain permanently pure. God created them as free-will beings. Free will was crucial because, without it, love is impossible. But free will meant that at any time, humans had the potential to go their own way and worship something or someone less worthy.

For people to possess security in a relationship with God, that relationship must be tested. To assure the possibility of an eternally secure relationship, humans had to endure the most difficult test possible.

God left Eden's gate open on purpose. He made certain Satan, and not some lesser demon, tested Adam and Eve. Similarly, God permitted Satan to tempt Jesus of Nazareth as he was about to embark on his public ministry. God deliberately allows every human to be exposed to evil and its source in the spiritual realm.

In granting Satan the opportunity to beguile humanity, God allows each person to face the most difficult of all possible tests. No created being anywhere in God's creation is more powerful, appealing, or clever than Satan. If anyone can endure this most difficult of tests—a test that is too challenging for any human to pass without receiving assistance from God by his grace, or unmerited favor—she or he can rest assured for all eternity that never again will there be a greater challenge than the one already overcome.

Optimized Physics for Overcoming Evil

To some degree humans are equipped to overcome. The human body is biologically designed so that no one enjoys extra work, pain, or wasted time. This trait is so strong that parents, teachers, and governing authorities use extra work, pain, and wasted time as tools to correct unacceptable behavior. God designed the laws of physics such that negative consequences mount as behavior worsens.

Consider the law of decay (i.e, **second law of thermodynamics**) described in Romans 8:20–22. This pervasive law does not discourage humans from creative activity and productive work, because the decay rate is not too high. Conversely, the decay rate is not so low as to let sin and evil go unrestrained.

All other physical laws complement the law of decay by guaranteeing an optimal balance between productive work and avoidance of evil. The universe's space-time dimensions contribute as well. Time for the universe occurs in one dimension only, and the passage of time cannot be reversed or stopped. Cosmic time properties and humans' short life spans limit the damage evil people can perpetrate. An evildoer like Adolf Hitler could commit evil for decades but not centuries.

Additionally, humans are confined to three large space dimensions. Thus travel limitations will prevent the execution of considerable intended evil.

Both natural consequences that arise from the physical laws and justice from human authorities are necessary to adequately rein in humanity's impulse to commit evil. Further, as the Bible reveals and observation verifies, unless human authorities are ever watchful, diligent, and just, and unless the physical laws consistently render consequences for wicked acts, evil will multiply.

Natural Evil?

Given the laws of physics and space-time dimensions, the forces behind natural disasters—sometimes called *natural evil*—are all designed to deliver maximum benefit for humanity. For example, God can eradicate hurricanes. Such elimination, however, would drastically reduce the input of sea-salt aerosols and bacterial and viral particles into the atmosphere. That reduction would lead to a life-threatening decrease in global rainfall. Hurricanes also regulate tropical ocean temperatures and deliver chlorophyll to continental shelf ecosystems. Both the frequency and average intensity of hurricanes are set to maximally benefit humanity and human civilization. Likewise tornadoes, earthquakes, volcanoes, wildfires, ice ages, floods, droughts, and disease are all set at levels that deliver the maximum benefit and minimum damage to humans and their civilization (Ross 2006).

But humans do not always make wise choices about where and how to build their structures (Matt. 7:24–27). Even so, it is stunning to consider the high survival rates in the face of nature's outbursts. There is no way to determine how catastrophic an event "might have been" apart from God's restraint. On some occasions, it appears he miraculously intervenes to rescue people from disaster. However, if God intervened in natural calamities in an overriding way, he would abrogate the disciplinary and virtue-producing benefits of physical laws and space-time dimensions.

New Creation Physics

Because evil will no longer be possible in the new creation, the need for evil-restraining physics will be gone. Revelation 21:4 says there will be no decay or death in the new realm. The thermodynamic laws will have been expunged. In the new creation, structures will exist that require the elimination of gravity. There will be no darkness or shadows, which implies light will arise from a source other than electromagnetism. "The city does not need the sun or the moon to shine on it, for the glory of God gives it light, and the Lamb is its lamp" (21:23).

In the new creation, people will experience continual, intimate fellowship with God and one another. Such relationships imply that humans in the new creation will be released from the constraints of three dimensionality and time into a far more expansive realm.

There will be no grief or regrets. All humans will value and understand why every bit of suffering and evil they experienced on earth was necessary to prepare them for their roles and rewards in the new creation. As Paul says in 2 Corinthians 4:17: "Our light and momentary troubles are achieving for us an eternal glory that far outweighs them all."

Inadequate Evidence for Belief?

Nevertheless, some humans struggle to see evidence for the God of the Bible here and now. A variant of the argument from evil states that God's omnipotence and omnibenevolence mean he would not make it difficult for creatures endowed with theological awareness to discover and relate to him. Since finding evidence for God, let alone gaining a relationship with him, seems difficult, skeptics conclude that the God of the Bible cannot exist.

This argument against God's existence is often expressed with comments like "If God exists and really loves me, why won't he stand before me right now?" Christians over the centuries have developed several responses.

One is based on Hebrews 11:6: "Anyone who comes to him [God] must believe that he exists and that he rewards those who earnestly seek him." Atheists presume that the presence of any amount of evil for any amount of time proves that God is not a rewarder of those who earnestly seek him. But as Romans 1:18–25 explains, this presumption will cause the individual to engage in self-imposed ignorance, blinding him or her to the clear evidence of God's existence and attributes abundantly available in the record of nature.

A second response, also based on Hebrews 11:6, suggests that a halfhearted or apathetic search for God will not suffice. Humans behave irrationally if they do not consider the question of the existence or nonexistence of God as the most worthwhile question in life. To fail to make a diligent search for God is to give up on the meaning of life. Jesus promised in Matthew 7:7, "Seek and you will find." This declaration implies, however, that if one does not seek, one will not find (see **Hiddenness of God**).

A third response argues that if the God of the Bible exists, he must—in most forms and at most times—be invisible and untouchable. As the Bible repeatedly declares and as the space-time theorems prove (see **Borde-Guth-Vilenkin Singularity Theorem**), the beginning of the universe marks the inception of all physical reality—matter, energy, space, and time. The cause of the universe, therefore, must be an agent with the capacity to create independent of or from beyond matter, energy, space, and time. Such transcendent operation points to the personal God revealed in Scripture.

A fourth response is to encourage the nonbeliever to get out of the city and into the countryside and wild parts of nature. Romans 1:20 says, "God's invisible qualities—his eternal power and divine nature—have been clearly seen, being understood from what has been made." This verse implies that examination of the wonders of nature leads to evidence of God's attributes. According to this response, it is no coincidence that most atheists live in urban areas.

Providence

If one can establish that a God who is omniscient, omnipresent, and omnibenevolent exists, then it would follow that God must possess good reasons for the present existence and level of evil. Although humans cannot fully understand those reasons, evil is temporary and, in some sense, beneficial for humans and all other beings God has created (Rom. 8:28). But there is also much good in creation.

In Paul's sermon to the citizens of Lystra, the apostle pointed out (Acts 14:17) that God "has not left himself without testimony: He has shown kindness by giving you rain from heaven and crops in their seasons; he provides you with plenty of food and fills your hearts with joy." To the Athenians, Paul explained (Acts 17:24–28) that God is the giver of life and breath, and he designed earth so that humans could inhabit and prosper over all its landmasses. Paul's point is that the bountiful provision of rain, crops, food, and pleasant places to live only makes sense if there exists a God who is omniscient, omnipresent, and omnibenevolent.

As knowledge and understanding of nature's record continually accrues, the argument for God from **providence** dramatically strengthens. Astronomers now acknowledge that as large, as massive, and as old as the universe measures to be, every bit of its size, mass, and age is necessary for advanced life to exist on earth. Paleontologists and geologists likewise recognize that all the life that has ever existed on earth was needed to launch and sustain global high-technology civilization. Meteorologists add that not only abundant rain but also dew, mist, snow, frost, hail, sheets of ice, and several other outcomes of the water cycle (see Job 37–38) are all required to sustain global civilization. The natural resources the universe, Earth, and Earth's life provide for humanity's benefit boggles the mind. No rational doubt should remain that an omniscient, omnipresent, and omnibenevolent God must exist.

Too Much Evil, Too Much Good

Additionally, skeptics must address their *own* difficulty accounting for evil and good. Atheists, agnostics, and deists attribute both evil and good to the laws of physics and biological evolution. Social norms or "**morality**" evolved as humans learned to cooperate in some cases, or act selfishly in others, in order to survive. However, those explanations fail to explain humanity's more extreme behaviors. For example, the evil that Hitler, Lenin, Stalin, Mao, Pol Pot, and Caligula perpetrated on their own people cannot simply be attributed to natural processes and survival instincts. Such evil is too great and contrary to the despots' best interests.

Likewise, **altruism**, where individuals sacrifice their life, wealth, and/or well-being for the benefit of total strangers or avowed enemies and where no hope of recognition, reward, or payoff exists, defies natural explanations. Humans are depraved beyond what natural processes would ever predict; they also are virtuous beyond what natural processes would ever predict. Naturalists not only have the problem of evil to address, but also the problem of goodness as well; the existence of real evil presupposes a standard of goodness or some design plan, from which evil is a departure.

God's Ultimate Purpose

God's stated purpose for creating was to magnify the expression of his love. Genesis 1:31 proclaims the present creation as "very good." However, only the new creation (Rev. 21–22) is described in terms of ultimate perfection. In one respect, though, the present creation is "perfect." It is the optimally designed creation for the fulfillment of God's plans to rapidly, efficiently, and permanently conquer and remove evil and suffering. At the same time, this creation greatly enhances, for those humans who are willing, free-will capacities to receive and express love. Though this creation is fraught with momentary exposure to evil, the glorified state of humanity promises unfettered love from an infinitely loving Creator.

Hugh Ross

REFERENCES AND RECOMMENDED READING

Ross, Hugh. 2006. *Creation as Science*, 165–74. Colorado Springs: NavPress.

EVOLUTION, BIOLOGICAL. At its most fundamental level, evolution is the change in average characteristics of a population over time. **Darwin** termed this effect "descent with modification." All populations exhibit genetic variation, since **DNA** copying is imperfect and mutations may occur. Recombination in sexually reproducing organisms generates further diversity by producing new combinations of alleles. Thus the genetic makeup of a population may shift over time, leading to a corresponding change in average characteristics. Only the uniform transmission of all genetic variation in a population in stable proportions from generation to generation will prevent change from occurring.

Hence populations of organisms, or even entire species, have an inherent potential to change over time.

This intrinsic possibility of incremental change over time within a population may lead to the formation of new species, and the term *evolution* is often used in this context. If a barrier arises that blocks or hinders the sharing of genetic variation between members of a population, then the process of incremental change runs independently in the two groups and may cause the two groups to diverge in their average characteristics. For example, if a population becomes separated into two subpopulations, then the incremental changes accumulating over time in the two subpopulations are now not averaged across the entire population. This means that incremental change over time may shift the average characteristics of each of the subpopulations away from the other. Over enough time, if the average characteristics of the two subpopulations diverge enough, this effect can lead to subpopulations that do not recognize each other as members of the same species.

Anything that alters the uniform transmission of genetic variation in stable proportions from generation to generation will contribute to the evolution of a **species** over time. One such mechanism, **natural selection**, was Darwin's seminal insight into how descent with modification took place. Darwin reasoned that nature could act in a way analogous to selective breeding performed by humans: from a pool of existing genetic variants within a population (that arise through **random mutation**), those able to leave more offspring over successive generations would, in time, come to predominate. This process, since it is continually selecting those individuals in a population best suited for reproduction in that environment (i.e., with the highest relative *fitness*), over time produces organisms that are well adapted for their ecological niche.

Since Darwin's time, geneticists have come to appreciate that mechanisms other than natural selection also operate to shape the history of species over time. For example, many mutations are neutral—i.e., they have no effect on the evolutionary fitness of a species. Additionally, **chance** events may eliminate genetic variants within a population even if such variants are adaptive; a deleterious variant may increase in frequency over time despite selection against it, and so on. Such changes driven by chance events are examples of what is known as *genetic drift*.

One analogy that may be useful to consider is language change over time. While no analogy is perfect, there are many helpful correspondences between language change over time and biological evolution. A language is spoken by a population

of speakers, and it too can shift its average characteristics over time: words may acquire new spellings or new meanings; new words may be introduced or coined; or words may fall into disuse and disappear. None of these changes is instantaneous. New words (or spellings, or meanings) begin as uncommon variants that then become more common over time. Eventually what was once an uncommon variant may become common; later it may become predominant. So too for genetic variation in a population: new variants enter the population as singular mutation events but then may become more common within the population over time as they are passed on to successive generations. The point is that change within a population—for organisms or for a language—is not a rapid event, but rather plays out over many generations.

Consider the change within the lineage leading to modern English: starting at the present day, working back through Victorian times, on to the period of the King James Bible, and so on, back to Anglo-Saxon times over 1,000 years ago. While modern readers can struggle through King James English with some difficulty, works from the Middle Ages and before are impenetrable to all but scholars. Yet we know that this lineage represents an unbroken series of incremental changes over time. Each generation spoke the "same language" as their parents and taught the "same language" to their children. Still, over time, their language changed—and changed such that no one would claim that Anglo-Saxon and present-day English are equivalent. So too with change within a biological lineage: there is no easy point of demarcation when a lineage changes from one species into another, since the process is a gradient over time.

The formation of new languages over time is also analogous to the formation of new species. If a population is separated through migration, then the incremental shifts in average characteristics between the two groups are uncoupled. Given enough time, these isolated populations may come to speak languages that are different enough from each other to be recognized as distinct. Examples of this are common and form a gradient of differences. American and British English have accumulated only a few differences since their relatively recent (and incomplete) separation, and they remain almost entirely intelligible to each other. Present-day English and West Frisian speakers share a common ancestral population of speakers dating to about 1,600 years ago. Though these two modern languages are not mutually intelligible, they retain a striking number of commonalities reflecting their recent shared ancestry. Similarly, romance languages such as Spanish, Portuguese, and Italian all derive from

Latin following the decline of the Roman Empire and the subsequent fragmentation of its population.

As anyone who has studied more than one of these modern languages knows, learning one is a great boon to learning another due to the large number of shared features—features that reflect their **common ancestry**.

Like languages, what biologists call "species" also form a gradient. Within a species, "varieties" or "subspecies" might be recognized. Closely related species may remain interfertile, despite rarely interbreeding. Species with a more distant common ancestral population are easily recognized as distinct species. Defining a "species," then, is an attempt to draw a line on what is in fact a gradient, just as is distinguishing a dialect from a distinct language. In both cases, we encounter difficulty because the process that produces them—whether species or languages—is incremental.

It is also possible, for languages or species, to determine degrees of relatedness by comparing shared features. Populations that share a more recent common ancestral population will have more shared features than with more distantly related populations. For species, the result is a *phylogeny*: a "family tree" of relatedness between species. Reading from the tips of the phylogeny, which represent species in the present day, phylogenies show which species share a more recent common ancestral population (where two branches converge into one) and so on, reaching further back in time. Current evidence strongly supports the hypothesis that all present-day living things share common ancestors, and that all descend from the last universal common ancestral population, or LUCA. Thus it appears that life originated on earth only once and has diversified over approximately 3.8 billion years to the present day. (See also **Evolutionary Creationism**.)

Dennis R. Venema

REFERENCES AND RECOMMENDED READING

Futuyma, D. J. 2013. *Evolution.* 3rd ed. Sunderland, MA: Sinauer.
Venema, D. R. *Evolution Basics.* Blog series. BioLogos. http://biologos.org/blogs/dennis-venema-letters-to-the-duchess/series/evolution-basics.

⌃ᴥ EVOLUTION, HUMAN
(Evolutionary-Creation View)

Introduction

Few matters are of greater concern to Christians than our own origin as a species. Scientific investigation portrays a human origin that is gradual—not from scratch—through an evolutionary process that is frequently portrayed by certain pundits as atheistic. Christians, however, disagree.

Some exhibit their disagreement by arguing that the science of evolution is deeply flawed, and some also argue that a 4.5-billion-year-old earth and a 13.8-billion-year-old universe is flawed. Others accept that evolution has occurred and that even our own species, *Homo sapiens*, has been created through the evolutionary process from previously existing primate species. The latter, however, maintain that even if humans were formed through evolution, this does not exclude **divine action** from the process (see **Providence**). Furthermore, it does not exclude the existence of a first couple, **Adam and Eve**, as viewed, for example, in the biblical manner laid out so profoundly by **John Walton** (2015; see also Provan 2014). The purpose of this essay is to examine the evidence for God having created humankind through the evolutionary process and to summarize the findings that have emerged from the scientific mainstream.

Humans share a number of traits with the apes that are not found in other primates. Those shared unique characteristics include relatively large brains, absence of a tail, a more erect posture, greater flexibility of the hips and ankles, increased flexibility of the wrist and thumb, as well as changes in the structure and use of the arm and shoulder (Herron and Freeman 2014). In addition, along with the African great apes, they are uniquely characterized by elongated skulls, enlarged brow ridges, short but stout canine teeth, and a few other distinctive features.

Fossil Evidence

Mainstream biologists and paleontologists estimate that the last common ancestor to humans and our closest living relatives, the chimpanzee and bonobo, lived about 5 to 7 million years ago. All **species** that are on the human side of the lineage from that common ancestral species (as opposed to the chimpanzee side) are known as hominins. Although there are only a few partial skeletons that can be dated to the approximate time of the transition, there is a near-complete fossil skeleton of *Ardipithicus ramidus*, which lived in northeastern Africa about 4.5 million years ago.

Ardi, as she is generally known, had several features that suggested strongly that unlike modern-day chimpanzees and gorillas, she was not a knuckle-walker like them but was bipedal like us. Still, her feet had a splayed big toe sticking out sideways in a manner that resembles that of the foot of chimpanzees and gorillas, and she had hands that were well suited for life in the trees as well. Moving forward a bit to the study of species that lived on earth about 3.5 to 2 million years ago, we find that they possess traits that are increasingly like our own. They were bipedal with a gait very much like ours (based, for example, on a stretch of 3.6-million-year-old footprints that show that the big toe was parallel to the other toes, no longer splayed outward). The tibia (shin bone) would have joined the ankle in a manner that resembles ours rather than a chimpanzee, and the structure of the ankle is humanlike. On the other hand, the face was apelike with a flattened nose and strongly protruding lower jaw, and the brain was about one-third the size of ours.

Multiple species have been found that would have existed within this time frame—likely several of them were cousin species not on the direct lineage to *Homo* that subsequently went extinct. Beginning about 2 million years ago, the first species of our own genus, *Homo*, sharing an increased number of our own characteristics came into being. At the beginning of this period, the cranium (brain case) was still apelike in size, but gradually over the next million years or so, the cranium increased to a size that matches our own. For the most part, the later the fossil find, the larger the brain size, until it leveled off about a million years or so ago.

So many fossil species have now been discovered and dated from 5 to 7 million years ago that scientists cannot say with any degree of certainty which ones were on the direct lineage to *Homo sapiens*. However, the key issue at hand for the purposes of this summary of human evolution is that the evolutionary model predicts that there is a set of transitional species that, as time has gone by, have come to increasingly resemble our own species. This prediction is born out in remarkable anatomical detail, likely more so than any other lineages in the entire tree of life. We will return to discuss the specimens in more detail below, but at this point, it is important to emphasize that the fossil data is highly consistent with an evolutionary model for human creation.

Genetic Evidence

Three basic types of genetic evidence indicate that God created humankind through the process of common descent from earlier formed primate species. Here is a summary of that evidence. For more detail, please see the outstanding book by New Zealand geneticist and part-time evangelical pastor, Graeme Finlay (Finlay 2013).

Mutation rate

Children get all of their **DNA** (the instructions for building their bodies) from their two parents. DNA is in the form of

code—with 6 billion units (called *bases*) in the code—3 billion bases from each parent. Although the code is passed from the parents, it does change ever so slightly from one generation to the next. We can measure the rate of change precisely, and an average of 70 base changes (out of 6 billion) occur each generation.

As we go deeper back in time, this means there are more and more genetic differences between our ancestors and us. For example, of your 6 billion bases, there would be 140 alterations not found in any of your four grandparents and, going back even deeper in time, 210 not found in the century or so between your birth and that of each of your great-grandparents. If common descent is true, then one can calculate how many changes (mutations) would have occurred in the 6 million years (60,000 centuries) since the common ancestral species of both chimpanzees and humans existed. When that calculation is done, it turns out that the number of genetic differences is within twofold of the predicted number.

Genetic "scars"

Perhaps sometime during your life, you suffered a cut and still carry the scar of that event. No matter how old you are, the remnants of that event still exist as a mark at a particular location on your body. Sometimes the DNA code is altered not as a single base (as in the previous section), but as the deletion or insertion of a *block* of bases. Since there are 6 billion bases, there are lots of places where a deletion or insertion can take place. The boundaries of such a change can be identified to the exact base on either side. Just as the scar from your cut is still at the exact place that it was when you had the accident, so also the "scar" in the DNA remains in place through the centuries as it gets passed through the lineage. Chimpanzees and humans share many deletions and insertions (the equivalent of scars), and each is at exactly the same location. This implies that they result from a single event in a single ancestor.

One might think that there is a functional reason why chimpanzees' and humans' insertions and deletions are at the same precise locations—perhaps they need to occupy a precise position for the body to function properly. However, an overwhelming amount of evidence indicates that even if the inserted or deleted sequence had functional significance, it could do its job just fine if moved a little bit. There are hundreds of thousands of such "scars," each at a precise location from a single event. Each happened at one time in a common ancestor they both share.

Synonymous versus nonsynonymous coding

Words that mean the same thing are referred to as *synonyms*. For example, I may describe the shape of an object as being circular, or I may say that it is round. The two words *circular* and *round* used in this context mean the same thing. Similarly, the genetic code contains synonyms. Certain parts of the genetic code can be written in alternative ways that mean exactly the same thing to cells. Given that mutations occur (see above), then we might expect that synonymous changes would be tolerated, but nonsynonymous ones — because they change the instructions — would not.

Let's think about that. If chimpanzees and humans really do descend from a single ancestral species, we would expect to find 60,000 centuries later many more synonymous differences in our DNA (since they would have been tolerated) than nonsynonymous differences. Here's one way to think about the concept. You might readily change a sentence from "Pick up that *circular* red object and bring it to me" to "Pick up that *round* red object and bring it to me." It would mean the same thing. However, you wouldn't change it to "Pick up that *white* red object and bring it to me." Such a change in the sentence would result in a meaningless instruction.

There are millions of potential synonyms in the genome, and differences in them are abundant when one compares the chimpanzee DNA sequence to that of the human. There are also many potential nonsynonymous changes, but these differences are much less frequent. This is what one would expect if there were a single ancestral species. Synonymous changes would be tolerated in a lineage. However, when nonsynonymous changes occurred, they would frequently reduce viability or fertility and hence would not be passed on as effectively.

Both the genetic data and the fossil data have emerged with a great deal of force over the past two decades, and the two sets of data together are considered by almost everyone in the field of biology as exceedingly strong evidence for human evolution.

The Hominin Radiation

Initially there were two different ways of thinking about hominin evolution. One was a gradual transition of a single lineage gradually changing to become more and more like modern humans through time: evolution as a ladder. The alternative features not a single upward ladder, but rather a cluster of lineages — evolution as a bush. All branches on the bush eventually end abruptly as an **extinction** except for that one branch leading to *Homo sapiens*. The fossil data

now make it clear that through most of the history since the existence of that common ancestral species that gave rise to both humans and chimpanzees, there have likely been multiple hominin species on earth. Our current situation, with only one for the past 20,000 or so years, is likely almost unprecedented in the past 5 million years of hominin history.

Two specimens, found in Chad and Kenya respectively, are vying for identification as the oldest identified hominin representative — *Sahelanthropis tchadensis* and *Orrorin tugenensis*. Each is identified through partial skeletal remains, and details other than its approximate age (5 to 7 million years) is somewhat scanty. However, that changed with the recent characterization of the almost complete 4.5-million-year-old *Ardipthicus ramidus* specimen. It stood four feet tall, had a brain about the size of a chimpanzee, and as mentioned above, had various distinctive anatomical features that indicated that it would have been a fine upright bipedal walker while also being adapted for climbing and life in the trees.

Beginning with specimens dated at about 4 million years and extending up to a date of about 2 million years, a set of fossils representing at least five species of the genus *Australopithicus* have been found. All have been found in Africa. A number are fairly complete. The five australopithecines identified have small brains, are somewhat barrel-chested, and have dental characteristics associated with the ability to eat fairly tough plant material. Since the **fossil record** is incomplete, it is not possible to say which of these species is on the lineage to *Homo*. Indeed, it is conceivable that none is, and the five identified so far are cousins to the actual precursor. Still it is likely that one or more of these (or at least their very close relatives) are part of a succession that eventually gives rise to members of the *Homo* genus.

About 2 million years ago, several unique species came into existence. They were characterized by robust skeletal features and a jaw with distinctively large teeth. Although clearly closely related to the other more slender (gracile) members of the *Australopithicus* genus, so characteristically different are they, that many investigators put them into their own genus, *Paranthropis*, while others prefer to classify them simply as robust members of the *Australopithicus* genus. Regardless, they are distinctive enough from members of the concomitantly emerging *Homo* genus that they are considered cousin species on the bushy hominin tree, all of which went extinct without contributing directly to the *Homo* lineage.

This illustrates that in paleoanthropology there is a degree of arbitrariness associated with determining the criteria that ought to be used for defining a species or even a genus. This fact is likely no less apparent than is the case for the difficulty of classifying the earliest members of the genus *Homo*, especially since the specimens representing the transition are fragmentary. The earliest members in this category that have been discovered, each found in the central region of eastern Africa and tagged as *Homo habilis* and *Homo rudolfensis*, are dated as living about 2 million years ago. Some investigators would place these specimens in the *Australopithicus* genus, although the adult brain size of both is up to 40 percent larger than australopithecines.

Geological analysis indicates that a significant global cooling trend began about 2.5 million years ago. With that, forests shrank while woodlands, grasslands, and other more arid and more seasonal habitat expanded in Africa. By about 2 million years ago, more of the region was coming to resemble the set of *The Lion King* rather than the jungle of *Tarzan* (Lieberman 2013). As food became scarcer and more restricted to seasonal availability, there was a transition to the hunter-gatherer way of life, and with that a significant change in the hominin body. *Homo erectus*, with fossils dating back to about 1.9 million years ago in Africa, had a long, slender body much like ours, with longer legs, full arches in the feet, shorter toes, a narrow waist, larger hips, as well as larger knee and ankle joints, making the species better adapted for running and walking. In this environment of a scarcer and seasonal food supply, likely *Homo erectus* ate more meat, with its richer caloric content, using tools to process the otherwise difficult-to-chew meat, and cooperated in a manner that enabled them to share food and various tasks.

Interestingly, very soon after *Homo erectus* makes an appearance in the African fossil record, we have the first evidence of hominins in Asia. There is an extensive fossil record at 1.8 million years in the republic of Georgia between the Caspian and Black seas, in Java at about 1.6 million years ago, and in China at about that same time. Hominins are also found in the fossil record of southern Europe at about 1.2 million years ago. Throughout this time there is an ongoing and gradual increase in brain size from 700 cc (compared to about 500 cc for *Australopithecus)* in its earliest days to about 1200 cc in the latest *Homo erectus*, which went extinct about 150,000 years ago (see fig. 10 of Lieberman 2013 and chap. 8 of Begun 2013).

Beginning about 700,000 years ago another *Homo* species, *Homo heidelbergensis*, likely derived from *Homo erectus*, appears in the fossil record. Largely similar in body proportions to *Homo erectus*, but with some structural distinctives, specimens of this species have been found in central and

southern Africa and throughout Europe. Recently its DNA was successfully isolated from approximately 350,000-year-old bones found in a cave in Spain—the oldest specimens for which we actually have genetic **information**. Interestingly, the genetic analysis of the DNA present in these individuals indicates that they were ancestors not of modern humans, but of *Homo neanderthalensis* (Neanderthals)—a cousin species of *Homo sapiens* that existed in Europe and Asia from about 200,000 to 40,000 years ago. Earlier African populations of *Homo heidelbergensis* (about 700,000 years ago) may have been ancestors to modern humans (*Homo sapiens*) as well, but this question remains unclear at present because of the absence of meaningful paleontological data from that key point in time.

The Origin of *Homo sapiens*

The first fossils that are largely indistinguishable from modern humans were found in Africa's Rift Valley and have been dated to approximately 200,000 years ago. Although many archaeological sites from before and after this time period provide artifacts that show details of human activity, none give evidence of symbolic thinking. Beginning about 70,000 to 100,000 years ago, that changed as distinctive cultural activities closely associated with symbolic reasoning began to become apparent. After describing the development of the complex **technology** needed to make certain tool-making material found in 75,000-year-old deposits in South African caves, Ian Tattersall (2015), perhaps America's most noteworthy human evolution expert, writes the following:

> There is a lot of other evidence that the unique human way of viewing the world, and of manipulating information about it, was actively emerging in the African continent after about 100,000 years ago. Before that time, unequivocal evidence for symbolic behaviors is rare or lacking in the record; after it, such evidence gradually accumulates. So what could possibly have happened to spur members of the already-established species *Homo sapiens* to begin using their brains in the radically new way? After all, the transition from the nonsymbolic to the symbolic cognitive condition was, on the face of it, an extremely improbable one; it certainly could not have been predicted from anything that went before. Indeed, the only reason we have for believing such a transition could ever happen is that it so evidently *did* happen. (loc. 3678)

While *Homo sapiens* was emerging as a distinctive species in Africa, *Homo neanderthalensis* was similarly arising in

Europe. Neanderthals thrived in Europe and northern Asia until their extinction about 40,000 years ago. Although there is evidence that Neanderthals buried their dead and cared for their infirm, there is little sign of symbolic thinking. As it relates to the practice of burying their dead, Tattersall (2013, 175) writes:

> Yes, the Neanderthals did invent the practice of burial; and no, there is no really convincing evidence that they ever did so with the ritual that typically accompanies modern human burials.... That they [i.e. the nature of the burials] imply some sort of deep empathetic feeling seems close to certain; but in the broader context of what we know about Neanderthals, it is far less probable that they imply belief in an afterlife—something that would indeed demand symbolic cognitive abilities.

In examining other aspects of Neanderthal activity as evidenced by the archaeological record, Tattersall (2013, 177) goes on to say:

> The upshot of all of this is that we find nothing in the technological record of the Neanderthals to suggest that they were symbolic thinkers. Skillful, yes; complex, certainly. But not in the way that we are.... Behaviorally there was no qualitative break with the past; the Neanderthals were simply doing what their predecessors had done, if apparently better. In other words they were like their ancestors only more. We are not. We are symbolic.

Meanwhile in Africa, our species, *Homo sapiens,* was emerging with clear evidence of symbolic capability. Unfortunately, key attributes like language and a full theory of mind (defined as the ability to recognize that others have a mind with thoughts very much like one's own) do not fossilize. However, most investigators believe that these attributes emerged shortly before and during this time. One aspect of speech that does fossilize is the anatomy of that portion of the skull that produces speech. In *Homo sapiens* the vertical (larynx) and horizontal (mouth) sound-generating "tubes" are nearly equal in length, and the passageway includes an open space between the epiglottis and the soft palate. Having two such tubes of equal length enables the production of vowels whose frequencies are more distinct and that can be pronounced more easily (Lieberman 2013; Tattersall 2013). The sound-generating anatomy of Neanderthals and other early hominins was structured differently in a manner that would not lead to the precision of our sound-generating framework.

Other changes, especially changes in the brain, were also responsible for making language possible. Over the past several years, the genetic instructions (i.e., the DNA) for making the Neanderthal body have been obtained from ancient bones. So as we learn more about how those instructions are involved in physically constructing the brain, it will be increasingly possible to compare our neurological capabilities for language with those of Neanderthals. Indeed, since investigators have obtained the DNA of ancient ancestors to Neanderthals (see above), it is quite possible that it will be feasible to explore the evolutionary changes that took place in the building of the Neanderthal brain in evolutionary time.

For our species, the earliest genome that has been deciphered so far is from an individual who lived in Siberia about 45,000 years ago (Fu et al. 2014). Amazing as this feat is, it would be extremely informative to have the genetic information from individuals who lived even earlier.

Migration Out of Africa

The first paleontological evidence of our own species outside of Africa is the finding of a 100,000 year-old skull, almost indistinguishable from our own, at the Israeli cave site called Jebel Qafzeh (Tattersall 2013). Through genetic analysis, it has been possible to show that the ancestry of modern non-African humans can be traced back to about 1,000 individuals who left Africa roughly 70,000 years ago (Harris 2015). This has been determined by deciphering the code for the Y chromosome and demonstrating that all non-African males have Y chromosomes that are quite similar. In light of our knowledge of mutation rates (see above), the differences that do exist can be readily accounted for by the accumulation of mutations over a 70,000-year time span. Knowing the rate of mutation, one can calculate back to determine how long it has been since there was a single set of Y chromosomes and how many varieties there were at that time. The same type of analysis has been done for the **gene**s found in a part of our cells known as mitochondria, and the results are almost identical.

Finally, the analysis has been done with a set of genes that are found on all the major chromosomes. The various aspects of the entire analysis all suggest the same thing—non-Africans arose from a group of 1,000 or so individuals who left Africa (likely not all at once) about 70,000 to 100,000 years ago. At the time of the migration(s), there were likely about 10,000 or so individuals in Africa itself (see Harris 2015 for a general discussion of the basis of these conclusions).

After migration out of Africa, *Homo sapiens* gradually spread out into the rest of the world. For example, humans arrived at what is now Australia about 50,000 years ago. This spreading of our species throughout the world does not imply a mass migration. For example, if the population spread slowly generation by generation (say, for the point of illustration, 10 miles per generation), this would add up to 1,500 miles in 2,500 years. Still, the arrival in Australia is remarkable. These individuals would have had to cross 50 miles of open ocean—a feat that, according to Tattersall (2013), "would have required not only boats—or at least sophisticated rafts—but excellent navigational skills as well."

Paleontological, archaeological, and genetic data indicate that humans crossed the Bering Strait into Alaska about 20,000 years ago. North and South American natives are most closely related to individuals from northeast Asia. However, recently it has been shown that some Amazonian populations have genetic signs indicating a portion of their genome is of Australasian origin. This suggests that the arrival in the Americas may be more complex than first thought, with some migrating by boat across the Pacific (Skogland et al. 2015).

Ancient DNA

The ability to decipher the code of ancient DNA from old bones is a totally unexpected development. DNA is a fragile thread only a thousandth of the thickness of a human hair. The notion that the code of tiny broken portions of the string could be deciphered and then put back together by a computer was unimaginable until recently. Perhaps no illustration of its power is more poignant than the identification of the formerly unknown species, *Homo denisova* (Denisovans), now known from its DNA, completely deciphered, even though only a single finger bone about the size of a pencil eraser and a few teeth have been discovered. From its genetic code, we now know that representatives of this species interbred with our species.

Today people from Oceana still carry a small percentage (less than 1 percent) of their genes from Denisovans. Furthermore, people from Tibet, are better able to thrive at high elevations because of a gene that originated in Denisovans but was brought into their specific lineage by ancient interbreeding between their ancestors and Denisovans. By analyzing the Denisovan DNA, we find that Neanderthals and Denisovans share a common ancestor from about 550,000 years ago, and that modern humans (*Homo sapiens*) share a common ancestor with both of these two species that lived about 700,000 years ago (Gibbons 2015). The fact that a different *Homo* species was unknown from the fossil record and has only been identified by a molecular remnant emphasizes how incomplete the fossil record is. Just because

we don't have fossil representatives of various intermediates (or cousins of intermediates) does not mean that they never existed. Quite the contrary. Our knowledge is fragmentary on the paleontological details, but investigators need to work with what they have and fill in the gaps in as informed a manner as possible.

Just as it has been possible to show that modern humans interbred with Denisovans, so it is possible to explore what happened when they moved out of Africa into the Middle East and on up into Europe to locations occupied by Neanderthal populations. It has been possible to show unequivocally that interbreeding took place. Indeed, about 2 percent of the DNA of non-Africans is derived from Neanderthals. This raises the question of whether it is possible to identify any Neanderthal—modern human hybrids in the fossil record.

One fossil specimen found in Romania puzzled paleontologists when it was first discovered. Although it had primarily modern human characteristics, it seemed to share some features with Neanderthals and not other *Homo sapiens*. DNA was successfully isolated from one of the bones, and it turns out that it was from a male who contained 6 to 9 percent Neanderthal DNA. In some cases, this Neanderthal component occurred as long, nondisrupted blocks along the chromosome. Based on this analysis, it is apparent that one of his ancestors about four to six generations earlier had been a Neanderthal.

As for the long-term retention of the Neanderthal form of certain genes, there is evidence that at least some have been retained in our lineage because they conferred an advantage, likely in part because of Neanderthals' adaptation to the cool, temperate climate of high latitudes.

Theological Considerations

If humans really were created through the evolutionary process, then any perceived theological problems must be more apparent than real. Indeed, if the evolutionary process was God's way of carrying out his will for our existence, understanding human evolution ought to enrich Christian theology, not denigrate it. This, after all, would be creation's response to God's decree; the active manifestation of that which emanates from the God who above all else is love.

It has become increasingly apparent that the evolutionary success of our species is the result of characteristics that foster cooperation and love. In essence, investigators are realizing that what made us flourish as a species was our ability to function well in community, and thus these were increasingly the traits that the evolutionary process selected for. Consider the following by the nontheist evolutionary biologist David Sloan Wilson (2015, 52):

> In fact, most of the mental attributes that we regard as distinctively human, such as our capacity for symbolic thought (including but not restricted to language) and the ability to transmit learned information across generations (culture), are fundamentally communal activities. This assertion has led to a hypothesis that a *single* shift in the balance between levels of selection led to the *entire package* of distinctively human traits including our ability to cooperate in groups of unrelated individuals, our distinctive cognition, and our ability to transmit culture. (emphasis in original)

Indeed, it has become apparent that with the shift in selection from individual survival to group success, the groups that were most successful were those that operated on the principles of cooperation and love. So important was this shift that a number of investigators prefer to think that groups of individuals functioned almost like a single organism with its many interacting organs as opposed to a disconnected bunch of independent self-centered individuals. Wilson (2015, 143) goes on to say, "The fact that single organisms are societies and functionally integrated societies qualify as organisms—not figuratively but literally—was one of the most important developments of evolutionary thought during the twentieth century."

This shift in emphasis to the group becoming like a functioning organism sounds quite biblical—almost straight out of 1 Corinthians 12 or Ephesians 4—and thus is theologically very satisfying. But there is more. E. O. Wilson (2012) suggests that a war exists within the human mind between two sets of tendencies—one set a product of our ancient prehuman history where there was selection for better and better functioning as individuals, and a second set of tendencies that emerge from the more recent selection for living within cooperating groups: "An unavoidable and perpetual war exists between honor, virtue, and duty, the products of group selection, on one side, and selfishness cowardice, and hypocrisy, the products of individual selection, on the other side" (loc. 808).

Although a number of evolutionary biologists are uncomfortable with certain aspects of E. O. Wilson's discussion of the mechanics of how this comes about, as David Sloan Wilson emphasizes, the *principle* holds and is summarized especially well by E. O. Wilson (2012) himself: "In summary, the human condition is an endemic turmoil rooted in the evolution processes that created us. The worst in our nature coexists with the best, and so it will ever be" (loc. 814).

Finally, it is important to examine one other feature of human evolution that is theologically enriching. If the evolutionary process simply describes the manner in which humans were created in response to God's creation command, then for theological reasons, human evolution must have a teleological component. Scripture makes it clear (e.g., John 1) that humankind was willed into existence from the beginning by God. Is there something about creation as revealed through science that addresses the question of whether our existence is the fulfillment of a specific divine plan?

The fine-tuning of the physical universe is well known. Indeed, it is incorporated into the **anthropic principle** that states that if the physical constants and parameters that govern the cosmos were slightly different, complex molecules and therefore life could not have arisen. Nontheist, Christof Koch (2012, 155) summarizes it this way:

> Take Newton's law of gravity and Coulomb's law, which governs the way electrically charged particles attract and repel each other. Both laws have the same form, stating that the forces decay with the square of the distance between any two particles. Only the constant in front of the quadratic decay term differs. Intriguingly the attraction between two opposite charges must be exactly 10,000 trillion trillion trillion times stronger than their mutual gravitational attraction in order for life as we know it to form. An itsy-bitsy more or less and we would not be around. Another cosmic constraint is that the sum of all positively charged particles in the universe must equal the sum of all negatively charged particles; otherwise electromagnetism would dominate gravity, and stars, galaxies, and planets couldn't form. The number of electrons must equal the number of protons to within one part in a trillion trillion trillion. If the strong nuclear force were slightly stronger or weaker than it actually is, either nothing but hydrogen or no elements heavier than iron would exist. If the universe had expanded too rapidly, protons and neutrons couldn't have bonded into atomic nuclei; if the initial expansion of the universe had been ever so slightly slower, the fiery brew that made up the early universe would have been too hot for nuclei to have formed. In short, an amazing number of "coincidences" had to occur to give rise to a universe that was stable for a sufficiently long time and diverse enough in chemical elements to support complex carbon-based life-forms.

Actually, as Koch points out, the *anthro*pic (*anthro* = human) principle is misnamed. It is a principle that addresses the fine-tuning of various physical parameters that had to line up if life itself (not just human life) was to come into existence. If Christian theology requires that creation began with *us* in God's mind, then perhaps something resembling an anthropic principle might be detected in biology too. So if there is an anthropic principle that emerges from the physical sciences, is there a biological one as well—one that specifically addresses the question of human life? The atheistic biologist E. O. Wilson (2013) answers the question for *human* existence in a manner that resembles how physical scientists address the same question for the likelihood of the physical parameters lining up:

> That the pre-human line made it all the way to *Homo sapiens* was the result of our unique opportunity combined with extraordinarily good luck. The odds opposing it were immense. Had any one of the populations directly on the path to the modern species suffered extinction during the past six million years since the human-chimpanzee split—always a dire possibility—another hundred million years might have been required for a second human-level species to appear. (loc. 945)

Virtually all of the books on human evolution written by secular scientists stress the pure luck of our presence here. Too many highly unlikely events have to line up for it to be anything other than luck that we emerged. However, for the theist, the fact that we are here is wonderfully congruent with that which theists have believed all along. We are here because of Providence. We are here not by sheer unadulterated luck, but as the result of creation's response to the Creator's beckoning. And that makes all the difference.

Darrel R. Falk

REFERENCES AND RECOMMENDED READING

Begun, David. 2013. *A Companion to Paleoanthropology*. Hoboken, NJ: Wiley-Blackwell.

Finlay, Graeme. 2013. *Human Evolution: Genes, Genealogies and Phylogenies*. Cambridge: Cambridge University Press.

Fu, Qiaomei, Heng Li, Priaya Moorjani, et al. 2014. "Genome Sequence of a 45,000-Year-Old Modern Human from Western Siberia." *Nature* 514:445–49.

Gibbons, Ann. 2015. "Cave Was Lasting Home to Denisovans." *Science* 349:1270.

Harris, Eugene E. 2015. *Ancestors in Our Genome: The New Science of Human Evolution*. Oxford: Oxford University Press.

Herron, Jon C., and Scott Freeman. 2014. *Evolutionary Analysis*. 5th ed. New York: Pearson.

Koch, Christof. 2012. *Consciousness*. Cambridge, MA: MIT Press.

Lieberman, Daniel. 2013. *The Story of the Human Body: Evolution, Health and Disease*. New York: Vintage.

Provan, Iain. 2014. *Seriously Dangerous Religion: What the Old Testament Really Says and Why It Matters*. Waco TX: Baylor University Press.

Skoglund, Pontus, Swapan Mallick, Maria Cátira Bortolini, et al. 2015. "Genetic Evidence for Two Founding Populations of the Americas." *Nature* 525:104–8.

Tattersall, Ian. 2013. *Masters of the Planet: The Search for Our Human Origins*. New York: Macmillan.

———. 2015. *The Strange Case of the Rickety Cossack: And Other Cautionary Tales from Human Evolution*. New York: St. Martin's. E-book.

Walton, John. 2015. *The Lost World of Adam and Eve: Genesis 2–3 and the Human Origins Debate*. Downers Grove, IL: IVP Academic.

Wilson, David Sloan. 2015. *Does Altruism Exist? Culture, Genes and the Welfare of Others*. New Haven, CT: Yale University Press.

Wilson, E. O. 2012. *The Social Conquest of the Earth*. New York: Liveright. E-book.

———. 2013. *The Meaning of Human Existence*. New York: Liveright. E-book.

❧ EVOLUTION, HUMAN (Unique-Origin View)

Introduction

How are we to understand who we are and where we came from? What is the nature of our being? In past centuries, these questions were the domain of philosophy or religion, but in the last 150 years, scientists have asserted that new **information** coming from **paleontology** and biology outweighs and even eliminates old answers. Some go so far as to claim that the old answers are harmful (Dawkins 2006).

Dealing with our biological origins has thus become a subject particularly fraught with challenges. Cosmology can be taken to support a theistic view of origins (Richards and Gonzales 2004), and the same can be said of chemistry and astrobiology (Denton 2013). Biology, however, presents a much larger challenge. The biological data dealing with our origins must therefore be critically examined and not taken automatically as leading to one conclusion only.

There are four possible positions one might take with regard to our origins: (1) we are here as the result of a strictly naturalistic unguided process; (2) we are the product of a guided but undetectable evolutionary process; (3) we are the result of a guided, detectable process that used common descent; and (4) we are not the product of common descent and may in fact have a unique origin.

To distinguish among these views, we must first consider whether a purely naturalistic mechanism of evolution is capable of producing what we see in life today. Current evolutionary theories include the standard evolutionary theory, self-organization, natural genetic engineering, structuralism, or some form of heritable **epigenetics** (Dawkins 1986; Denton 1986; Kauffman 1995; Pigliucci 2013; Salthe 1993; Shapiro 2005). Some overlap exists between the theories mentioned.

For example, a structuralist may consider emergent or self-organizational processes to be part of structuralism, and he or she may or may not support **intelligent design**. Likewise, with natural genetic engineering and epigenetics. A particular scientist's stance depends to a large extent on his or her philosophical presuppositions.

Discussion of all these theories requires more space than is allotted for this article. The references cited above, however, can serve as a starting point for those interested. We will focus here on whether the standard evolutionary mechanism is sufficient, since it is accepted by most scientists and, in particular, theistic evolutionists. The evidence for intelligent design and for and against common descent will also be presented.

The standard mechanism proposed for evolution is a combination of random variation (mutation and recombination), **natural selection** (organisms best suited to their environment tend to have the most offspring), and genetic drift (the random events of life affecting survival and reproduction). These things when combined may or may not be sufficient to account for evolutionary change. If they are sufficient, then the natural outcome of these processes will be to produce a branched tree of common descent, as organisms change over the course of millennia.

The mechanism of evolution and the idea of common descent are tightly interwoven but not inseparable. If the proposed evolutionary mechanism outlined above is sufficient to produce the necessary changes in the time available, common descent follows as a natural result. On the other hand, if it can be shown that common descent is false, completely or in part, it follows that the standard evolutionary story is necessarily false, and questions of mechanism become moot. Obviously, this conclusion would require that much scientific thinking be substantially revised.

Perhaps this is why common descent is such a privileged concept in evolutionary biology. Evolutionary biologists are willing to challenge the mechanisms of evolution—indeed, many have (Mazur 2009)—but to preserve common descent in the face of anomalous results (of which there are many), all kinds of alternative explanations and special cases are proposed. This should be viewed with suspicion.

Is Unguided Mutation and Selection Sufficient?

Many scientists now recognize the insufficiency of the classic Darwinian story to account for the appearance of new features or innovations in the history of life. They realize that the traditional story of population genetics (more about this in

a bit) cannot account for "the arrival of the fittest" nor the "survival of the fittest" (De Vries 1904). They acknowledge the insufficiency of **Darwinism** because they know the accounting won't work.

Mutations arise at a particular rate and are propagated from generation to generation, so the number of generations and the population size limit how many mutations can accumulate. Then there is the matter of having those mutations persist and become fixed (universal) in the population. In small populations, like ours would have been, mutations are likely to be lost and have to recur many times before they actually stick, just because of random effects. A particular neutral mutation may have to arise many times before it becomes established in the population. Based on these factors, one can estimate how many years it would take to acquire specific mutations.

As a particular case, a number of population geneticists have examined how long it would take to evolve a **DNA** binding site, a small stretch of DNA that regulates the amount of product its neighboring **gene** makes. This is a serious problem for Darwinian evolution—evolution of binding sites is the main way proposed for evolution of new animal or plant forms. An estimate from a recent paper using numerical simulations is 1.5 million years (Sanford et al. 2015). Our estimated divergence time from chimps (the time we last shared a common ancestor with chimps) is 6 million years.

What if two specific mutations are necessary to make a new binding site and effect a beneficial change? Sanford and others estimate 84 million years, which is well past 6 million years. Other scientists have done this calculation using analytical methods, but their numbers are even worse. One report calculates 6 million years for one specific base change in an eight-base target typical of the size of a DNA binding site to fix (Durrett and Schmidt 2007) and 100 million years to get two specific mutations (Durrett and Schmidt 2008; that work was later amended to 216 million years). Extrapolating from other published data merely confirms the problem (Axe 2010b; Behe and Snoke 2004; Ewert 2015).

It must be acknowledged that another paper came up with much shorter time frames by assuming that any 5- to 10-base-pair binding site could arise anywhere within 1,000 bases of *any* gene promoter within the genome (Behrens and Vingron 2010). That is roughly 20,000 x 400 five-base sequences or 8 million places available for a new binding site to appear. This would appear to shorten considerably the odds of getting a new binding site. But for this to be true, new binding sites in front of any genes at all would need to be beneficial, which is unlikely. Many more than two binding sites would need to change in specific ways to accomplish any significant adaptive change. Genes operate in networks, and to shift a gene regulatory network would require many specific mutations, and not just random ones.

How Much Change Is Required?

We do not know what our putative last common ancestor (LCA) with chimps looked like, but fossils indicate it was apelike, so there had to be numerous changes to get from the LCA to us. We have significant differences from chimps—genetic, anatomical, physiological, behavioral, and intellectual. As for the often quoted 1.2 percent genetic difference between human and chimpanzee genomes, that measure only counts single base changes (Cohen 2007). Add small insertions and deletions and the differences climb to about 3 to 5 percent, depending on whose estimate is used (Britten 2002; Chen et al. 2007). Add another 2.7 percent for large-scale duplications or deletions (Cheng et al. 2005; Hahn et al. 2005), especially in the Y chromosome (Hughes et al. 2010), and some unknown number for large-scale rearrangements of the DNA, and at least 0.7 percent for insertions of mobile genetic elements (Hedges et al. 2004), or new genes (Knowles and McLysaght 2009; Wu et al. 2011), and at least 7.7 percent of our genome differs from chimps.

This number is, of course, disputed by naturalists, but the fact remains that the estimate of 1.2 percent is vastly insufficient. The methods used for that figure do not take into account the differences described above. Gene duplications would likely be missed, as would repetitive DNA sequences and rearrangements. And differences in gene expression would be missed entirely. Just as one example, a recent paper described more than 600 RNA transcripts expressed in humans but not chimps or other species, due to the presence in humans of promoter sequences upstream of these "genes" but absent in the other species. The resulting transcripts could have important functional roles, but because they come from stretches of aligned DNA, they would be counted as having few genetic differences (Ruiz-Orera et al. 2015).

In addition to new promoters, DNA and RNA modifications affect gene expression, especially in the brain (Oldham et al. 2006; Paz-Yaacov et al. 2010; Shulha et al. 2012). These changes may be the most significant of all. By some estimates, as much as 17.4 percent of neural connections in the cortex of the brain are specific to humans compared to chimps (Oldham et al. 2006), due at least in part to modifications to DNA and RNA that are human specific.

Genetic differences help to produce the many morphological and physiological differences that distinguish us from chimps. A partial list of these morphological and physiological differences includes our pelvises, rib cages, shoulders, spines, legs, feet, arms, hands, throats, skulls, neurology, development, and reproductive biology. We walk and run upright, throw, speak, craft fine tools, and think (Bramble and Lieberman 2004; Marks 2009a; Roach et al. 2013).

Our differences are large enough that we don't even get the same diseases as chimps (Varki and Altheide 2005). In terms of what makes us human, not the things that are the same, but the things that are different are what matter (Marks 2009b). It is unlikely that even parallel evolution of many single mutations in many different genes could produce all the above anatomical, physiological, and genetic differences. In fact, if just two or more coordinated mutations that were beneficial only in combination were required in a single, specific gene somewhere along the road to humanity, it could not happen *at all* in the time available, given the 216-million-year estimate of Durrett and Schmidt (2008).

Taken together, too many coordinated changes would be required to have occurred by known naturalistic means. There simply is not enough time or probabilistic resources to make it happen. The standard mechanism proposed to explain evolution is insufficient. This argues against options one and two as an explanation of our origins and in favor of options three and four (see the introduction).

Some may ask, what about the other theories or as yet undiscovered naturalistic explanations? Of course, science is provisional, and new data may overturn or support any existing theory. However, we are only able to discuss and test the presently available evidence for any theory of origins. We cannot discuss or test unknown theories. It is appropriate to come to a conclusion based on the evidence at hand; we should not refuse to draw a conclusion on the grounds that some unknown possibility may yet exist. Second, to allow for unlimited future naturalistic explanations is essentially a promissory note—there is no such explanation now but maybe someday there will be. At what time will the promissory note expire?

Third, and most importantly, the above question is ignoring positive evidence for design. The only known cause in our uniform and repeated experience that is capable of generating information-bearing codes, especially overlapping functional codes like we see in DNA, is intelligence (Meyer 2009). Complex, sophisticated, cellular machines like ATP (adenosine triphosphate) synthase, the flagellum, the ribosome, or the spliceosome are made of many integrated, essential parts, once again the kind of thing that intelligent agents but not emergent properties are likely to generate (Axe 2010a; Behe 1996; Staley and Woolford 2009). Complex, causally circular metabolic networks (Axe and Gauger 2013; Kun et al. 2008) and the integrated, self-sustaining properties of ecosystems (Leisola et al. 2012) also argue for design.

Does Similarity Indicate Common Descent?

We have ruled out the Darwinian mechanism as insufficient, but we have not addressed the question of common descent yet. Evidence for common descent is often taken as evidence against intelligent design. This does not logically follow. Intelligent design could have happened in two ways, one involving a guided **common ancestry** leading to humans and another involving a unique origin for humans. The idea of common descent does affect how we view our origin, however.

Like the argument above using human population genetics, work on the bacterial evolution of new enzyme functions has shown that even apparently simple transitions may require too many coordinated mutations to have happened in an unguided manner (Axe and Gauger 2015; Gauger and Axe 2011; Gauger et al. 2010; Reeves et al. 2014). Even for bacteria, with very large population sizes and rapid generation times, the limit for what is possible may be two or three mutations (Axe 2010b; Reeves et al. 2014). This puts an extreme limit on the kinds of change purely random natural processes can accomplish.

The other lesson to be drawn from this work is that *just because two things appear to be similar does not mean there is an unguided evolutionary path between them*. Or put another way, similarity of structure or sequence does not necessarily indicate common descent by evolutionary processes (Gauger et al. 2012). This rule applies to proteins but also to genomes, fossils, and species, especially humans, and runs directly counter to the common assumption by evolutionary biologists that similarity of sequence or form means common ancestry (Gauger et al. 2012).

In fact, a broad distinction can be made between the assumptions of evolutionary biologists and design biologists. Evolutionary biologists tend to assume randomness and attribute any similarity to common descent; design biologists tend to assume order and purpose and assume any similarity is functional, not necessarily due to common descent.

For example, evolutionary biologists take the fact that similar **species** have a highly similar arrangement of genes along their chromosomes (called *synteny*) as evidence for their common origin. The underlying assumption is that the only explanation for similarity is a common origin. Otherwise, genes should be random in order. Design biologists would say that because the species are similar, they have similar functional and design constraints, which may be reflected in their gene order. The assumption is that order and functionality are the original state, and similarity is evidence of shared design.

Darwinian evolutionists tend to assume that many poorly understood aspects of our genomes (e.g., synonymous codons, pseudogenes, or junk DNA) do not have important functions and are the product of **random mutation**s and/or common descent. In contrast, ID proponents predict that if our genomes were designed, then many of these mysterious features will turn out to have important functions. The problem is to distinguish between the two viewpoints.

Arguments Used to Support Common Descent

Synonymous codon use. One of the evidences offered in favor of common descent is the "reuse" of synonymous codons. Some codons—triplet nucleotide sequences in DNA—specify the same amino acid. For example, lysine may be encoded by four codons, CUU, CUC, CUA, or CUG. The assumption has been that codons truly are synonymous and can be used interchangeably. When there is a choice among possible codons, chimp and human genomes almost always use the same codon. It is therefore argued that this is because the sequences share a common ancestor.

However, it has since been discovered that codons are used for multiple purposes—which codons are used changes the DNA sequence, which in turn can affect gene expression (Stergachis et al. 2013), protein degradation (the controlled destruction of proteins by the cell), or how proteins fold into three-dimensional shapes (Cannarozzi et al. 2010; Li et al. 2012; Tuller et al. 2010; Weygand-Durasevic and Ibba 2010; Zhang et al. 2010).

Codons may therefore be identical because they have to perform multiple jobs that are specific to one codon—none of the others will do. The fact that both humans and chimps use the same codons may be due to this rather than their ancestry. In addition, this is a strong argument for design—the sophistication required to have codes within codes would not arise by simple mutation and **natural selection**.

Synteny refers to how well chromosomal sequences from

different species align with one another. If they align well, that is assumed to indicate they came from a common ancestor. But there is a possible functional explanation—chromosomal structure has a profound effect on gene regulation. Where in the nucleus genes are located affects their expression (Cavalli 2011; Filion et al. 2010; Hoang and Bekiranov 2013; Homouz and Kudlicki 2013; Jachowicz et al. 2013; O'Sullivan 2011; Verdaasdonk et al. 2013).

Synteny is an active area of research, as the preceding list of citations indicates. What is being discovered is that "the association of chromosomes with each other and other nuclear components plays a critical role in nuclear organization and genome function.... Genomes are highly ordered yet dynamic entities in which chromosomal positions, structures and interactions are controlled in order to regulate nuclear processes" (Rodley et al. 2009). Once again, this sophistication argues for design.

Pseudogenes are genes that appear to have been truncated or otherwise changed in their coding sequences so that they cannot make protein. Some appear to be the product of mutation; others appear to be the result of a transposition of processed messenger RNA to a new location. Because they appear to make defective protein, or none at all, they have been thought to be "junk," remnants of the evolutionary process. Because they tend to be located in the same place and have the same "errors" in humans and in chimps, they are taken as evidence for common descent.

Yet those that have been adequately studied often are functional (Balakirev and Ayala 2003; Wen et al. 2012). A pseudogene may only be active in specific tissues during particular stages of development, making identification of their functions difficult. As techniques become more sophisticated, more functional pseudogenes will be discovered (Wen et al. 2012).

One reason to expect functionality is their high degree of DNA sequence conservation between species. With more than 8,000 processed pseudogenes in the human genome, of which 60 percent are highly conserved between mouse and human, some essential function for them is likely (Wen et al. 2012). That conservation would not be expected if these were genetic remnants without function.

Finally, the functioning of these pseudogenes is highly dependent on their precise sequences, so the similarity between chimp and human sequences is not surprising. It is likely they are performing the same function, requiring the same sequence in both genomes.

For more about pseudogenes, see Hirotsune et al. 2003;

Moleirinho et al. 2013; Pink et al. 2011; Poliseno 2012; Poliseno et al. 2010; Tam et al. 2008; and Zheng and Gerstein 2007.

Chromosomal fusion. When chimp and human genomes are compared, our chromosome 2 appears to be a fusion of two chimp chromosomes. The argument is made that this demonstrates our common ancestry with chimps. However, the junction where the supposed fusion took place is not made of typical telomeric sequences. (Telomeres are special sequences found at the end of chromosomes.) Instead, degenerate sequences are found, sequences found elsewhere in the genome but not associated with breaks or fusions (Fan et al. 2002).

The human chromosome 2 may have always been as it appears now. There is no particular reason to propose there was a fusion event except under the assumption of common descent. Therefore it cannot be used as an argument *for* common descent.

The designer as a deceiver. This argument goes something like this, "If there is an intelligent designer, then why did he or she make it look like things evolve? That makes him or her a deceiver."

There is a logical flaw here as well—it is stated as fact that things look like they evolved by natural processes. But things don't look like they evolved. As has been shown, molecular biology provides many good reasons to believe things were designed. There are also many examples from the design of larger-scale structures like the eye or a bird's wing; even the complementary and interlocking nature of the biosphere give evidence of design (Denton 1986; Leisola et al. 2012; Meyer 2009). In fact, biologists are continually told that they must remember that things only *look* designed—they really aren't (Dawkins 1986). That clearly means the designer is not a deceiver. He has made it so that everyone can detect his design.

Critiques of Common Descent

Having considered the arguments made in favor of common descent, let us consider evidence that indicates common descent may not be true. Bear in mind, intelligent design does not require that common descent be false. Only the question of our unique origin and the size of the founding population are affected by these arguments.

Incongruent phylogenetic trees. Quite frequently, when scientists try to draw trees showing the evolutionary relationships between species, inconsistencies emerge, depending on what gene or character is chosen to base the tree. Numerous articles in the mainstream literature acknowledge the problem of incongruent trees (Degnan and Rosenberg 2009; Rokas and Carroll 2006). Many explanations for these problems exist—transfer of genes between species confuses gene histories; loss of traits in some lineages gives a false history; incomplete lineage sorting may produce scrambled gene trees among closely related species; independent evolution of the same traits in different lineages (convergent evolution) could occur. All these explanations are possibilities—but at some point, one has to wonder why common descent deserves such special protection. Might there be another reason why so many problems exist?

For example, it was recently discovered that proteins produced from endogenous retroviruses (ERVS), viruses that permanently reside in our genomes, are involved in placental formation. Placental formation is considered to be the trait that distinguishes all true mammals from other animals. After further study it was found that rats, mice, dogs, cows, rabbits, and primates all require this kind of protein for placental formation. But in all these different groups of mammals, the proteins are different from one another (Lavialle et al. 2013). In other words, different proteins are being used in the placental formation of different orders of mammals. If common descent is true, an argument could be made that this shouldn't be the case, because the method of placental development should have been shared among all these groups. Because this data cannot easily be explained by common descent, evolutionary biologists cite this as an amazing example of convergent evolution (Lavialle et al. 2013). Design biologists feel the evidence more reasonably points to common design.

Patterns and function where there should be none. Short interspersed nuclear elements (SINEs) also pose a challenge to common descent. SINEs are short genetic elements that are believed to be able to spread around the genome. Using another genetic element's enzymes, they copy themselves and then insert into a new location in the genome at random (or so it was assumed) (Doolittle and Sapienza 1980). Thus over time, evolutionary biologists said, our genome has become littered with them, like so much junk (Orgel and Crick 1980). This argument assumes SINEs have no function.

It has been shown that species-specific SINEs, supposedly with independent insertion histories occurring after the divergence of the two species, have almost exactly the same distribution patterns across chromosomes in rats and mice, a distinctly nonrandom pattern (Rat Genome Sequencing Project Consortium 2004). Furthermore, they are found in the vicinity of similar classes of genes in mice and humans, and are involved in regulating their output (Tsirigos and Rigoutsos 2009). Lastly, 6 percent of our genome is human-specific SINEs called *Alu* elements (Hedges et al. 2004), at least some of which regulate DNA methylation and RNA editing in the brain (Paz-Yaacov et al. 2010; Shulha et al. 2012). These things contribute to a substantial difference in gene expression between us and chimps, specifically in the brain (Oldham et al. 2006). Thus at least some Alus in humans are functionally significant. That these elements have a shared nonrandom distribution and function argues for design. That there are some Alus unique to humans that influence gene expression in the brain also suggests design.

The identical insertion patterns in chimps and humans in the presumed absence of function were taken previously as evidence of common descent. But if there are functional reasons for their placement, the argument does not hold up.

Unbridgeable fossil gaps. The genetic, physiological, morphological, functional, social, and intellectual differences between chimps and humans (Varki and Altheide 2005; Varki et al. 2008) are too large to be bridged by evolutionary processes, at least without substantial designer intervention. We do not know what our putative LCA with chimps looked like; if it existed, it would have been essentially apelike based on fossil evidence, so the gap between us and that ancestor is real. There are fossils proposed to be intermediate in form, yet there is a large gap between *Australopithicus* and other fossils supposedly in our lineage, and *Homo erectus*, the first truly human fossil. The absence of transitional fossils that cross the gap is discussed by Casey Luskin in one of this volume's entries on **hominid fossils**.

Population genetics and Adam and Eve. In recent years, there has been much discussion about whether the genetic data indicates that humans could not have descended from an initial couple. Evolutionary biologists often cite population genetics models in this regard. These mathematical methods depend on assumptions about the behaviors of ancient populations that cannot be verified. They are models only, not reproductions of the past, and models are only as good as their assumptions (Hawks 2008). In fact, under some conditions, where the population is broken up into groups and migrating, it is not even possible to determine population size (Sjödin et al. 2005). Of course, the models also depend on the assumption of common descent.

One method used to estimate ancient evolutionary history is to look at genetic polymorphisms. Everyone in the human population has the same basic genome, but some of our genes have more than one version, meaning they are polymorphic. Scientists use the positions of mutations in these variable genes to create models of our genetic history. They use these models to estimate the number of gene variants and the population size at the time of our LCA with chimps, all assuming, of course, that common descent and the other assumptions that go into the model are true.

Francisco Ayala used this technique on a highly variable gene from the immune system in order to show we couldn't have come from just one man or woman. He compared sequences from a number of human, chimp, and macaque DNA genes. From that data, Ayala calculated there must have been 32 separate human versions of the gene and a population of about 100,000 individuals at the time of our LCA with chimps (Ayala 1995). This ruled out the possibility of two first parents, he said.

However, Ayala broke a number of rules in choosing the DNA to compare. For his calculation to work, the sequence he chose should have had only a background rate of mutation, recombination, and selection. The DNA he chose had high rates of all three. Another lab pointed out the problem and redid the comparison using neighboring sequences (not subject to the same problems) from the same gene. Their calculations came up with only seven separate human versions at the time of our LCA (Bergström et al. 1998). They have since redone the calculation using sequence data from the entire gene and found only four versions at the time of our LCA with chimps (von Salome et al. 2007). Ayala's disproof of Adam and Eve has collapsed, since four versions of one gene can be carried by two first parents. (It should be said, this new analysis does not prove the existence of two first parents, but it at least makes it possible.)

Summary

Remember the four possibilities concerning human evolution that were outlined at the beginning. Option one is purely naturalistic. Option two allows for the undetectable action of a designer. Option three says design is detectable, but it posits that the designer used common descent, while option four says universal common descent is not true—there are too many unresolved difficulties—and further, our origin may be unique.

From the evidence presented here, options one and two are unlikely. The mechanism of random mutation and natural selection is not sufficient to accomplish our origin in the time available, so an unguided Darwinian mechanism will not work. While it is true that other naturalistic processes exist (see the introduction), it is not necessary to postulate them—the sophistication and the functionality of things described here and elsewhere (Denton 1986; Meyer 2009; Meyer 2014; Wiker and Witt 2006), plus their intrinsic order, all suggest design. In particular, certain features of life like the genetic code may only be explainable by design. Options three and four, both requiring detectable design, therefore are viable explanations.

The preponderance of the evidence suggests option four, our unique origin, because common descent cannot adequately explain patterns we see in our genomes. If things like synteny, shared codon usage, and pseudogenes can be explained functionally, common descent is undermined, and a unique origin becomes more likely. The fossil evidence for an unbridgeable gap between us and our LCA, and the significant genetic differences between us and chimps further argue for a unique origin. Lastly, population genetics arguments against a unique origin are subject to question because of implicit assumptions of common descent.

All intelligent design proponents agree with the necessity of design; a unique human origin is not essential. However, one of the chief questions asked about human evolution is this: Are we the product of common descent from an apelike ancestor, or are we unique, with a distinct origin? The answer to this question impacts how we see ourselves and the world around us, and how we integrate religion and science. A provisional answer from this analysis is that we are unique. Future scientific work interpreted without bias will no doubt continue to shed light on the subject, at present still a subject of debate. Regardless of the answer, though, we need not fear the truth.

Ann Gauger

REFERENCES AND RECOMMENDED READING

Axe, Douglas D. 2010a. "The Case against a Darwinian Origin of Protein Folds." *BIO-Complexity* 2010 (1): 1–12.

———. 2010b. "The Limits of Complex Adaptation: An Analysis Based on a Simple Model of Structured Bacterial Populations." *BIO-Complexity* 2010 (4): 1–10. doi:10.5048/bio-c.2010.4.

Axe Douglas D., and Ann K. Gauger. 2013. "Explaining Metabolic Innovation: Neo-Darwinism versus Design." In *Biological Information: New Perspectives*, ed. Marks R. J., II, M. J. Behe, W. A. Dembski, B. L. Gordon, and J. C. Sanford, 489–507. Hackensack, NJ: World Scientific.

———. 2015. "Model and Laboratory Demonstrations That Evolutionary Optimization Works Well Only If Preceded by Invention—Selection Itself Is Not Inventive." *BIO-Complexity* 2015 (2): 1–13.

Ayala, Francisco. 1995. "The Myth of Eve: Molecular Biology and Human Origins." *Science* 270: 1930–36.

Balakirev, Evgeniy S., and Francisco J. Ayala. 2003. "Pseudogenes: Are They 'Junk' or Functional DNA?" *Annual Review of Genetics* 37 (1): 123–51.

Behe, Michael J. 1996. *Darwin's Black Box: The Biochemical Challenge to Evolution*. New York: Simon & Schuster.

Behe, Michael J., and David W. Snoke. 2004. "Simulating Evolution by Gene Duplication of Protein Features That Require Multiple Amino Acid Residues." *Protein Science* 13:2651–64.

Behrens, Sarah and Martin Vingron. 2010. "Studying the Evolution of Promoter Sequences: A Waiting Time Problem." *Journal of Computational Biology* 17 (12): 1591–1606.

Bergström, Tomas F., Agnetha Josefsson, Henry A. Erlich, and Ulf Gyllensten. 1998. "Recent Origin of HLA-DRB1 Alleles and Implications for Human Evolution." *Nature Genetics* 18 (3): 237–42.

Bramble, Dennis M., and Daniel E. Lieberman. 2004. "Endurance Running and the Evolution of Homo." *Nature* 432:345–52.

Britten, Roy J. 2002. "Divergence between Samples of Chimpanzee and Human DNA Sequences Is 5%, Counting Indels." *Proceedings of the National Academy of Sciences USA* 99 (21): 13633–35.

Cannarozzi, Gina, Nicol N. Schraudolph, Mahamadou Faty, et al. 2010. "A Role for Codon Order in Translation Dynamics." *Cell* 141 (2): 355–67.

Cavalli, Giacomo. 2011. "From Linear Genes to Epigenetic Inheritance of Three-Dimensional Epigenomes." *Journal of Molecular Biology* 409 (1): 54–61.

Chen, Feng-Chi, Chueng-Jong Chen, Wen-Hsiung Li, and Trees-Juen Chuang. 2007. "Human-Specific Insertions and Deletions Inferred from Mammalian Genome Sequences." *Genome Research* 17 (1): 16–22.

Cheng, Z., M. Ventura, X. She, et al. 2005. "A Genome-Wide Comparison of Recent Chimpanzee and Human Segmental Duplications." *Nature* 437:88–93. doi:10.1038/nature04000.

Cohen, Jon. 2007. "Relative Differences: The Myth of 1%." *Science* 316:1836.

Dawkins, Richard. 1986. *The Blind Watchmaker: Why the Evidence of Evolution Reveals a Universe without Design*. New York: W. W. Norton.

———. 2006. *The God Delusion*. New York: Mariner.

Degnan, J. H., and N. A. Rosenberg. 2009. "Gene Tree Discordance, Phylogenetic Inference and the Multispecies Coalescent." *Trends in Ecology and Evolution* 24 (6): 332–40. doi:10.1016/j.tree.2009.01.009.

Denton, Michael J. 1986. *Evolution: A Theory in Crisis*. Chevy Chase, MD: Adler & Adler.

———. 2013. "The Place of Life and Man in Nature: Defending the Anthropocentric Thesis." *BIO-Complexity* 2013 (1). doi:10.5048/bio-c.2013.1.

De Vries, Hugo. 1904. *Species and Varieties: Their Origin by Mutation*. Chicago: Open Court.

Doolittle, W. Ford, and Carmen Sapienza. 1980. "Selfish Genes, the Phenotype Paradigm and Genome Evolution." *Nature* 284:601–3.

Doxiadis, G. G., N. de Groot, N. G. de Groot, I. I. N. Doxiadis, and R. E. Bontrop. 2008. "Reshuffling of Ancient Peptide Binding Motifs between HLA-DRB Multigene Family Members: Old Wine Served in New Skins." *Molecular Immunology* 45 (10): 2743–51. doi:10.1016/j.molimm.2008.02.017.

Durrett, Richard, and Deena Schmidt. 2007. "Waiting for Regulatory Sequences to Appear." *Annals of Applied Probability* 17 (1): 1–32. doi:10.1214/105051606000000619.

———. 2008. "Waiting for Two Mutations: With Applications to Regulatory Sequence Evolution and the Limits of Darwinian Evolution." *Genetics* 180 (3): 1501–9. doi:10.1534/genetics.107.082610.

Ewert, Winston. 2015. "Overabundant Mutations Help Potentiate Evolution: The Effect of Biologically Realistic Mutation Rates on Computer Models of Evolution." *BIO-Complexity* 2015 (1): 1–11.

Fan, Yuxin, Elena Linardopoulou, Cynthia Friedman, Eleanor Williams, and Barbara J. Trask. 2002. "Genomic Structure and Evolution of the Ancestral Chromosome Fusion Site in 2q13–2q14.1 and Paralogous Regions on Other Human Chromosomes." *Genome Research* 12:1651–62.

Filion, Guillaume J., Joke G. van Bemmel, Ulrich Braunschweig, et al. 2010. "Systematic Protein Location Mapping Reveals Five Principal Chromatin Types in Drosophila Cells." *Cell* 143 (2): 212–24.

Gauger, Ann K., and Douglas D. Axe. 2011. "The Evolutionary Accessibility of New Enzymes Functions: A Case Study from the Biotin Pathway." *BIO-Complexity* 1:1–17. doi:10.5048/bio-c.2011.1.

Gauger, Ann K., Douglas Axe, and Casey Luskin. 2012. *Science and Human Origins*. Seattle: Discovery Institute Press.

Gauger, Ann K., Stephanie Ebnet, Pamela F. Fahey, and Ralph Seelke. 2010. "Reductive Evolution Can Prevent Populations from Taking Simple Adaptive Paths to High Fitness." *BIO-Complexity* 2010 (2): 1–9. doi:10.5048/BIO-C.2010.2.

Hahn, M. W., T. De Bie, J. E. Stajich, C. Nguyen, and N. Cristianini. 2005. "Estimating the Tempo and Mode of Gene Family Evolution from Comparative Genomic Data." *Genome Research* 15 (8): 1153–60. doi:10.1101/gr.3567505.

Hawks, John. 2008. "From Genes to Numbers: Effective Population Sizes in Human Evolution." In *Recent Advances in Palaeodemography*, ed. Jean-Pierre Bocquet-Appel, 9–30. New York: Springer.

Hedges, D. J., P. A. Callinan, R. Cordaux, J. Xing, E. Barnes, and M. A. Batzer. 2004. "Differential Alu Mobilization and Polymorphism among the Human and Chimpanzee Lineages." *Genome Research* 14 (6): 1068–75. doi:10.1101/gr.2530404.

Hirotsune, Shinji, Noriyuki Yoshida, Amy Chen, et al. 2003. "An Expressed Pseudogene Regulates the Messenger-RNA Stability of Its Homologous Coding Gene." *Nature* 423:91–96.

Hoang, Stephen A., and Stefan Bekiranov. 2013. "The Network Architecture of the *Saccharomyces cerevisiae* Genome." *PLOS ONE* 8:e81972.

Homouz, Dirar, and Andrzej S. Kudlicki. 2013. "The 3D Organization of the Yeast Genome Correlates with Co-expression and Reflects Functional Relations between Genes." *PLOS ONE* 8:e54699.

Hughes, J. F., H. Skaletsky, T. Pyntikova, et al. 2010. "Chimpanzee and Human Y Chromosomes Are Remarkably Divergent in Structure and Gene Content." *Nature* 463:536–39. doi:10.1038/nature08700.

Jachowicz, Joanna W., Angèle Santenard, Ambre Bender, Julius Muller, and Maria-Elena Torres-Padilla. 2013. "Heterochromatin Establishment at Pericentromeres Depends on Nuclear Position." *Genes and Development* 27 (22): 2427–32.

Kauffman, Stuart. 1995. *At Home in the Universe: The Search for the Laws of Self-Organization and Complexity*. New York: Oxford University Press.

Knowles, D. G., and A. McLysaght. 2009. "Recent De Novo Origin of Human Protein-Coding Genes." *Genome Research* 19 (10): 1752–59. doi:10.1101/gr.095026.109.

Kun, Ádám, Balázs Papp, and Eörs Szathmáry. 2008. "Computational Identification of Obligatorily Autocatalytic Replicators Embedded in Metabolic Networks." *Genome Biology* 9 (3): 51.

Lavialle, C., G. Cornelis, A. Dupressoir, et al. 2013. "Paleovirology of 'Syncytins,' Retroviral ENV Genes Exapted for a Role in Placentation." *Philosophical Transactions of the Royal Society, London, B* 368 (1626): 20120507. doi:10.1098/rstb.2012.0507.

Leisola M., O. Pastinen, and D. D. Axe. 2012. "Lignin—Designed Randomness." *BIO-Complexity* 2012 (3): 1–11.

Li, G. W., E. Oh, J. S. Weissman. 2012. "The Anti-Shine-Dalgarno Sequence Drives Translational Pausing and Codon Choice in Bacteria." *Nature* 484:538–41.

Marks, Jonathan. 2009a. "Darwin's Ventriloquists." *Anthropology Now* 1 (3): 1–11.

———. 2009b. "What Is the Viewpoint of Hemoglobin, and Does It Matter?" *History and Philosophy of Life Sciences* 31:241–62.

Mazur, Suzan. 2009. *The Altenberg 16: An Exposé of the Evolution Industry*. Berkeley, CA: North Atlantic.

Meyer, Stephen C. 2009. *Signature in the Cell: DNA and the Evidence for Intelligent Design*. New York: HarperCollins.

———. 2014. *Darwin's Doubt: The Explosive Origin of Animal Life and the Case for Intelligent Design*. New York: HarperOne.

Moleirinho, Ana, Susana Seixas, Alexandra M. Lopes, Celeste Bento, Maria J. Prata, and António Amorim. 2013. "Evolutionary Constraints in the ä-Globin Cluster: The Signature of Purifying Selection at the ä-Globin

(HBD) Locus and Its Role in Developmental Gene Regulation." *Genome Biology and Evolution* 5 (3): 559–71.

Oldham, Michael C., Steve Horvath, and Daniel H. Geschwind. 2006. "Conservation and Evolution of Gene Coexpression Networks in Human and Chimpanzee Brains." *Proceedings of the National Academy of Sciences USA* 103 (47): 17973–78. doi:10.1073/pnas.0605938103.

Orgel, Leslie E., and Francis H. C. Crick. 1980. "Selfish DNA: The Ultimate Parasite." *Nature* 284:604–7.

O'Sullivan, Justin M. 2011. "Chromosome Organization in Simple and Complex Unicellular Organisms." *Current Issues in Molecular Biology* 13:37–42.

Paz-Yaacov, N., E. Y. Levanon, E. Nevo, et al. 2010. "Adenosine-to-Inosine RNA Editing Shapes Transcriptome Diversity in Primates." *Proceedings of the National Academy of Sciences USA* 107 (27): 12174–79. doi:10.1073/pnas.1006183107.

Pigliucci, Massimo. 2013. "Between Holism and Reductionism: A Philosophical Primer on Emergence." *Biological Journal of the Linnean Society* 112 (2): 261–67.

Pink, Ryan Charles, Kate Wicks, Daniel Paul Caley, et al. 2011. "Pseudogenes: Pseudo-Functional or Key Regulators in Health and Disease?" *RNA* 17 (5): 792–98.

Poliseno, Laura. 2012. "Pseudogenes: Newly Discovered Players in Human Cancer." *Science Signaling* 5 (242): 5.

Poliseno, Laura, Leonardo Salmena, Jiangwen Zhang, et al. 2010. "A Coding-Independent Function of Gene and Pseudogene mRNAs Regulates Tumour Biology." *Nature* 465:1033–38.

Rat Genome Sequencing Project Consortium. 2004. "Genome Sequence of the Brown Norway Rat Yields Insights into Mammalian Evolution." *Nature* 428:493–521.

Reeves, Mariclair A., Ann K. Gauger, and Douglas D. Axe. 2014. "Enzyme Families—Shared Evolutionary History or Shared Design? A Study of the GABA-Aminotransferase Family." *BIO-Complexity* 2014 (4): 1–16.

Richards, Jay W., and Guillermo Gonzales. 2004. *The Privileged Planet: How Our Place in the Cosmos Is Designed for Discovery.* Washington, DC: Regnery.

Roach, Neil T., Madhusudhan Venkadesan, Michael J. Rainbow, and Daniel E. Lieberman. 2013. "Elastic Energy Storage in the Shoulder and the Evolution of High-Speed Throwing in Homo." *Nature* 498:483–86.

Rodley, C. D. M., F. Bertels, B. Jones, and J. M. O'Sullivan. 2009. "Global Identification of Yeast Chromosome Interactions Using Genome Conformation Capture." *Fungal Genetics and Biology* 46 (11): 879–86.

Rokas, A., and S. B. Carroll. 2006. "Bushes in the Tree of Life." *PLOS Biology* 4 (11): e352. doi:10.1371/journal.pbio.0040352.

Ruiz-Orera, Jorge, Jessica Hernandez-Rodriguez, Cristina Chiva, et al. 2015. "Origins of De Novo Genes in Human and Chimpanzee." *PLOS Genetics* 11 (12): e1005721.

Salthe, Stanley N. 1993. *Development and Evolution: Complexity and Change in Biology.* Cambridge, MA: MIT Press.

Sanford, John, Wesley Brewer, Franzine Smith, and John Baumgardner. 2015. "The Waiting Time Problem in a Model Hominin Population." *Theoretical Biology and Medical Modelling* 12:18.

Ségurel, Laure, Emma E. Thompson, Timothée Flutre, et al. 2012. "The ABO Blood Group Is a Trans-Species Polymorphism in Primates." *Proceedings of the National Academy of Sciences USA* 109:18493–98. doi:10.1073/pnas.1210603109.

Shapiro, J. A. 2005. "A 21st-Century View of Evolution: Genome System Architecture, Repetitive DNA, and Natural Genetic Engineering." *Gene* 345 (1): 91–100. doi:10.1016/j.gene.2004.11.020.

Shulha, H. P., J. L. Crisci, D. Reshetov, et al. 2012. "Human-Specific Histone Methylation Signatures at Transcription Start Sites in Prefrontal Neurons." *PLOS Biology* 10 (11): e1001427. doi:10.1371/journal.pbio.1001427.

Sjödin, P., I. Kaj, S. Krone, M. Lascoux, and M. Nordborg. 2005. "On the Meaning and Existence of an Effective Population Size." *Genetics* 169 (2): 1061–70. doi:10.1534/genetics.104.026799.

Staley, Jonathan P., and John L. Woolford Jr. 2009. "Assembly of Ribosomes and Spliceosomes: Complex Ribonucleoprotein Machines." *Current Opinion in Cell Biology* 21 (1): 109–18.

Stergachis, A. B., E. Haugen, Anthony Schafer, et al. 2013. "Exonic Transcription Factor Binding Directs Codon Choice and Affects Protein Evolution." *Science* 342:1367–72.

Tam, Oliver H., Alexei A. Aravin, Paula Stein, et al. 2008. "Pseudogene-Derived Small Interfering RNAs Regulate Gene Expression in Mouse Oocytes." *Nature* 453:534–38.

Tsirigos, A., and I. Rigoutsos. 2009. "Alu and B1 Repeats Have Been Selectively Retained in the Upstream and Intronic Regions of Genes of Specific Functional Classes." *PLOS Computational Biology* 5 (12): e1000610. doi:10.1371/journal.pcbi.1000610.

Tuller, Tamir, Asaf Carmi, Kalin Vestsigian, et al. 2010. "An Evolutionarily Conserved Mechanism for Controlling the Efficiency of Protein Translation." *Cell* 141 (2): 344–54.

Varki, A., and T. K. Altheide. 2005. "Comparing the Human and Chimpanzee Genomes: Searching for Needles in a Haystack." *Genome Research* 15 (12): 1746–58. doi:10.1101/gr.3737405.

Varki, A., D. H. Geschwind, and E. E. Eichler. 2008. "Explaining Human Uniqueness: Genome Interactions with Environment, Behaviour and Culture." *Nature Review of Genetics* 9 (10): 749–63. doi:10.1038/nrg2428.

Verdaasdonk, Jolien Suzanne, Paula Andrea Vasquez, Raymond Mario Barry, et al. 2013. "Centromere Tethering Confines Chromosome Domains." *Molecular Cell* 52 (6): 819–31.

von Salome, J., U. Gyllensten, and T. F. Bergstrom. 2007. "Full-Length Sequence Analysis of the HLA-DRB1 Locus Suggests a Recent Origin of Alleles." *Immunogenetics* 59 (4): 261–71. doi:10.1007/s00251–007–0196–8.

Wen, Yan-Zi, Ling-Ling Zheng, Liang-Hu Qu, Francisco J. Ayala, and Zhao-Rong Lun. 2012. "Pseudogenes Are Not Pseudo Anymore," *RNA Biology* 9 (1): 27–32.

Weygand-Durasevic, I., and M. Ibba. 2010. "New Roles for Codon Usage." *Science* 329 (5998): 1473–74.

Wiker, Benjamin, and Jonathan Witt. 2006. *A Meaningful World: How the Arts and Sciences Reveal the Genius of Nature.* Downers Grove, IL: InterVarsity.

Wu, D. D., D. M. Irwin, and Y. P. Zhang. 2011. "De Novo Origin of Human Protein-Coding Genes." *PLOS Genetics* 7 (11): e1002379. doi:10.1371/journal.pgen.1002379.

Zhang, F., S. Saha, S. A. Shabalina, and A. Kashina. 2010. "Differential Arginylation of Actin Isoforms Is Regulated by Coding Sequence-Dependent Degradation." *Science* 329:1534–37.

Zheng, Deyou, and Mark B. Gerstein. 2007. "The Ambiguous Boundary between Genes and Pseudogenes: The Dead Rise Up, or Do They?" *Trends in Genetics* 23 (5): 219–24.

EVOLUTION AND PROBABILITY. Regardless of one's position on origins, everyone agrees that complex life is too improbable to have been produced by random **chance** alone. The theory of evolution provides an account for why life is not as improbable as it might initially seem (Dawkins 1986, 1996). **Natural selection** allows for a gradual increase in the **complexity** of life. This gradualness allows the theory of evolution to avoid the extreme improbability of random chance alone. Thus, for advocates of Darwinian theory, the improbability of life is a problem, but one solved by natural selection.

Critics of Darwinian theory disagree that the problem is solved. They argue that despite the effects of natural selection, the evolution of complex life remains prohibitively improbable. Selection is not capable of providing sufficient gradualism to render probable the development of complex life.

However, as frequently pointed out by both critics and supporters of design, improbable events happen all the time (Brigandt 2013; Dembski 1998; Rosenhouse 2005a). Drawing five cards from a well-shuffled deck will produce a very improbable combination of five cards. It will be less probable than winning some lotteries. Yet it is easy to deal cards and hard to win the lottery. Design proponents view the difference as being one of specificity. A specified event is one that adheres to an independent pattern. Your random hand of five cards does not fit any pattern besides itself. The winning lottery ticket fits the independent pattern of the winning number selected by the lottery runner. Critics of evolution argue that biological life exhibits **specified complexity** (Dembski 1998). This means that life is both improbable under Darwinian evolution and is specified, fitting the independent pattern of functional systems.

Defenders of evolution argue that the evolution of these complex adaptations is not as improbable as intelligent design proponents argue. They argue that natural selection will render the evolution of complex forms relatively probable. They also argue that the specifications offered by **intelligent design** advocates are too narrow, focusing on the outcomes actually observed in evolution as opposed to many others that could have been observed instead.

In some cases, defenders of evolution object to the form of this argument. Various criticisms have been offered on the technical details of the formulation of specified complexity (Elsberry and Shallit 2011; Felsenstein 2007; Olofsson 2007). The objections raised are diverse, bringing up a large number of issues. On the basis of these alleged issues, these critics argue that specified complexity is an incoherent concept. In contrast, defenders of intelligent design have argued that these objections misunderstand specified complexity and are engaged in attacking a straw man (Dembski 1999; 2004b; 2005; Ewert 2013a; 2013b; Luskin 2010).

Evolutionists commonly charge that claims that evolution gives a low **probability** for complex life are simply asserted (Brigandt 2013). When probabilities are calculated, critics of evolution calculate the probability under an assumption of random chance alone, ignoring the effect of selection (Bailey 2001; Brigandt 2013; Musgrave 1998; Rosenhouse 2005a). Such calculations ignore the actual processes that are argued to produce complex life and, as a consequence, are irrelevant to the question of whether evolution is true.

Some defenders of **Darwinism** offer arguments that the probability of evolution is high enough to be plausible (Schneider 2000; Wilf and Ewens 2010). Others hold that any such calculation is infeasible (Olofsson 2007; Rosenhouse 2005a). Calculating accurate estimates of the probability of any complex system would require extensive knowledge we don't have. As Rosenhouse writes, "It would require almost God-like knowledge of natural history and the physiologies of long-extinct organisms to produce a meaningful probability calculation for any complex biological system" (Rosenhouse 2005a).

The truth is likely even more problematic. In order to determine an accurate probability, it would not only be necessary to know about long-extinct organisms, but also to evaluate the myriad of organisms that did not actually exist, but could have, if evolution had turned out differently (Bailey 2001).

The calculation of such probabilities is completely infeasible. Rather than relying on flawed probability calculations, Darwinists appeal to evidence in other areas of science such as the fossil record or comparative genomics. It is argued that evidence in these areas is overwhelming, and we can safely conclude that the evolution of complex life must be sufficiently probable. As Rosenhouse writes, "If a mountain of biological evidence says that evolution happened, but a back of the envelope probability calculation says that evolution is impossible, then what you have is evidence that your calculation was based on faulty assumptions" (Rosenhouse 2005b).

Proponents of design argue that this characterization of their probability argument is inaccurate. There are flawed probability arguments made against evolution, but it is mistaken to claim that all arguments fall into this category. Calculations are made that assume random chance alone, but these are typically done to set the stage for arguments about evolution; they are not intended as an argument against the process of Darwinian evolution itself (Lennox 2009; Meyer 2010).

Some arguments made against Darwinian evolution do address the evolutionary process, not simply a straw man of pure random chance. For example, **irreducible complexity** (Behe 1996, 2001; Dembski 2004a) argues for biological situations in which selection cannot help build complex systems. Other work has argued that adaptations will often require multiple mutations before any selective benefit will accrue, and obtaining multiple mutations is prohibitively improbable (Axe 2010; Behe 2007; Gauger and Axe 2011; Sanford et al. 2015).

Critics of design argue that intelligent design proponents are too focused on the actual outcomes of evolution as opposed to other potential outcomes. The individual outcome might be very improbable. However, there are many possible outcomes that could have resulted in evolution besides the one that we observe. If the observed outcome did not happen, some other equally complex and functional outcome would take its place (Bridgham et al. 2009; Harms and Thornton 2014; Zimmer 2009). It is argued that a seemingly improbable event is evidence of many other possibilities that did not occur. Moran argues this point: "When such a triple mutation arises we recognize that it was only one of millions and millions of possible evolutionary outcomes" (Moran 2014).

Design advocates dispute the existence of this multitude of alternative outcomes (Behe 2014). There is no evidence for millions upon millions of alternatives to evolving a flagellum, flight, or eyes. Undoubtedly some other alternatives exist, but in order to resolve evolution's improbability problem, they are forced to appeal to immense numbers of alternatives for which there is no evidence.

In sum, critics of evolution argue that biological life is highly improbable under Darwinian evolution and is highly specified. This demonstrates that evolution is false. The defenders of evolution argue that life is much more probable than the critics contend, and that there are many more possible specified forms than are believed by the design advocates. Defenders of design argue that the probability is correctly deemed to be very low, and the immense numbers of alternative possibilities invoked by Darwinists exist only in the imagination.

Winston Ewert

REFERENCES AND RECOMMENDED READING

Axe, Douglas D. 2010. "The Case against a Darwinian Origin of Protein Folds." *BIO-Complexity* 2010 (1): 1–12. doi:10.5048/BIO-C.2010.1.

Bailey, David H. 2001. "Evolution and Probability." *Reports of National Center for Science Education* 20 (4): 4–7.

Behe, Michael J. 1996. *Darwin's Black Box: The Biochemical Challenge to Evolution*. New York: Free Press.

———. 2001. "Reply to My Critics: A Response to Reviews of *Darwin's Black Box*: The Biochemical Challenge to Evolution." *Biology and Philosophy* 16, no. 5 (November): 685–709.

———. 2007. *The Edge of Evolution*. New York: Free Press.

———. 2014. "Drawing My Discussion with Laurence Moran to a Close." *Evolution News & Views*. August 26. www.evolutionnews.org/2014/08/drawing_my_disc089331.html.

Bridgham, Jamie T., Eric A. Ortlund, and Joseph W. Thornton. 2009. "An Epistatic Ratchet Constrains the Direction of Glucocorticoid Receptor Evolution." *Nature* 461:515–19. doi:10.1038/nature08249.

Brigandt, Ingo. 2013. "Intelligent Design and the Nature of Science." In *The Philosophy of Biology*, ed. Kostas Kampourakis, 1–36. New York: Springer.

Dawkins, Richard. 1986. *The Blind Watchmaker: Why the Evidence of Evolution Reveals a Universe without Design*. New York: W. W. Norton.

———. 1996. *Climbing Mount Improbable*. New York: W. W. Norton.

Dembski, William A. 1998. *The Design Inference: Eliminating Chance through Small Probabilities*. *Mind*. Vol. 112. Cambridge: Cambridge University Press. doi:10.1093/mind/112.447.521.

———. 1999. "Explaining Specified Complexity." *Metaviews*. www.metanexus.net/essay/explaining-specified-complexity.

———. 2004a. "Irreducible Complexity Revisited." Bill Dembski.com. www.billdembski.com/documents/2004.01.Irred_Compl_Revisited.pdf.

———. 2004b. *The Design Revolution: Answering the Toughest Questions about Intelligent Design*. Downers Grove, IL: InterVarsity.

———. 2005. "Specification: The Pattern That Signifies Intelligence." *Philosophia Christi* 7 (2): 299–343.

Elsberry, Wesley, and Jeffrey Shallit. 2011. "Information Theory, Evolutionary Computation, and Dembski's 'Complex Specified Information.'" *Synthese* 178 (2): 237–70. doi:10.1007/s11229-009-9542-8.

Ewert, Winston. 2013a. "Design Detection in the Dark." *Evolution News & Views*. June 6. www.evolutionnews.org/2013/06/design_detectio072931.html.

———. 2013b. "Information, Past and Present." *Evolution News & Views*. April 15. www.evolutionnews.org/2013/04/information_pas071201.html.

Felsenstein, Joe. 2007. "Has Natural Selection Been Refuted? The Arguments of William Dembski." *Reports of National Center for Science* 27 (3–4): 1–12.

Gauger, Ann K., and Douglas D. Axe. 2011. "The Evolutionary Accessibility of New Enzyme Functions: A Case Study from the Biotin Pathway." *BIO-Complexity* 2011 (1): 1–17. doi:10.5048/BIO-C.2011.1.

Harms, Michael J., and Joseph W. Thornton. 2014. "Historical Contingency and Its Biophysical Basis in Glucocorticoid Receptor Evolution." *Nature* 512:203–7. doi:10.1038/nature13410.

Lennox, John. 2009. *God's Undertaker: Has Science Buried God?* Oxford: Lion Hudson.

Luskin, Casey. 2010. "Intelligent Design Proponents Toil More Than the Critics: A Response to Wesley Elsberry and Jeffrey Shallit." Intelligent Design & Evolution Awareness Center. July. www.ideacenter.org/contentmgr/showdetails.php/id/1488.

Meyer, Stephen C. 2010. *Signature in the Cell: DNA and the Evidence for Intelligent Design*. New York: HarperOne.

Moran, Laurence A. 2014. "Understanding Michael Behe." *Sandwalk*. August 22. http://sandwalk.blogspot.ca/2014/08/understanding-michael-behe.html.

Musgrave, Ian. 1998. "Lies, Damned Lies, Statistics, and Probability of Abiogenesis Calculations." December 21. *TalkOrigins Archive*. www.talkorigins.org/faqs/abioprob/abioprob.html.

Olofsson, Peter. 2007. "Intelligent Design and Mathematical Statistics: A Troubled Alliance." *Biology & Philosophy* 23 (4): 545–53. doi:10.1007/s10539-007-9078-z.

Rosenhouse, Jason. 2005a. "Can Probability Theory Be Used to Refute Evolution? (Part One)." *Commitee for Skeptical Inquiry Special Articles*. CSI. September 19. www.csicop.org/specialarticles/show/can_probability_theory_be_used_to_refute_evolution_part_one/&title=.

———. 2005b. "Can Probability Theory Be Used to Refute Evolution? (Part Two)—CSI." *Commitee for Skeptical Inquiry Special Articles*. CSI. September 19. www.csicop.org/specialarticles/show/can_probability_theory_be_used_to_refute_evolution_part_two.

Sanford, John C., Wesley H. Brewer, Franzine Smith, and John R. Baumgardner. 2015. "The Waiting Time Problem in a Model Hominin Population." *Theoretical Biology and Medical Modelling*, 1–28. doi:10.1186/s12976-015-0016-z.

Schneider, Thomas D. 2000. "Evolution of Biological Information." *Nucleic Acids Research* 28 (14): 2794–99. doi:10.1093/nar/28.14.2794.

Wilf, Herbert S., and Warren J. Ewens. 2010. "There's Plenty of Time for Evolution." *Proceedings of the National Academy of Sciences USA* 107 (52): 22454–56. doi:10.1073/pnas.1016207107.

Zimmer, Carl. 2009. "The Blind Locksmith Continued: An Update from Joe Thornton." *Loom*. October 15. http://blogs.discovermagazine.com/loom/2009/10/15/the-blind-locksmith-continued-an-update-from-joe-thornton/#.Vg67MRNVikp.

EVOLUTION AND THEOLOGY. The relationship between theology and **evolution** is both complex and contentious, especially in the context of the Judeo-Christian tradition. While there is a lively debate about whether evolution undermines or supports orthodox theological claims, few thinkers on either side have noted the important role that theology plays in arguments *for* evolutionary theory.

A number of prominent biologists rely on theological claims in some of their arguments for **common ancestry**. These thinkers include Theodosius Dobzhansky (1973), **Stephen Jay Gould** (1980, 2002), Sean Carroll (2009), Niles Eldredge (2000), Douglas Futuyma (1995, 2013), **Francisco Ayala** (2007), Gavin de Beer (1964), Jerry Coyne (2009), **Richard Dawkins** (2009), George Williams (1997), **Francis Collins** (2006), **Kenneth Miller** (1999), and others — not to mention **Charles Darwin** himself (1859). Theology may not appear in all arguments for evolution, yet, at the least, it plays a significant de facto role in the current defense of common ancestry (cf. Dilley 2012, 2013; Hunter 2001, 2007, 2014; Lustig 2004; Nelson 1996; Sober 2008).

Consider three examples. The first comes from Stephen Jay Gould, a prolific biologist of the late twentieth century. He writes:

> Our textbooks like to illustrate evolution with examples of optimal design — nearly perfect mimicry of a dead leaf by a butterfly or of a poisonous species by a palatable relative. But ideal design is a lousy argument for evolution, for it mimics the postulated action of an omnipotent creator. Odd arrangements and funny solutions are the proof of evolution — paths that a sensible God would never tread but that a natural process, constrained by history, follows perforce. (1980, 20–21)

Imperfections are "the proof of evolution" because "a sensible God" would never make such flaws, whereas evolution, which cobbles together organisms over time, allows suboptimal traits (or creatures). For more than 20 years, Gould's favorite example was the panda's thumb (1980, 2002). The thumb is poorly designed, he says, a mere "contraption" that "wins no prize in an engineer's derby" (1980, 24). Gould contends that "a sensible God" would have made the thumb more functional than it is. Accordingly, the alleged imperfection of the thumb serves as strong evidence for evolution.

A second example comes from Jerry Coyne, an award-winning geneticist at the University of Chicago. In his mature work defending evolution, *Why Evolution Is True*, Coyne invokes theology in an array of arguments for evolution (2009, 12, 13, 18, 26–58, 64, 71–72, 81–85, 96, 101, 108, 121, 148, 161). Most poignantly, he identifies the **fossil record** as offering the best evidence for evolution (79). He argues:

> There is no reason why a celestial designer, fashioning organisms from scratch like an architect designs buildings, should make new species by remodeling the features of existing ones. Each species could be constructed from the ground up. But natural selection can act only by changing what already exists. It can't produce new traits out of thin air. **Darwinism** predicts, then, that new species will be modified versions of older ones. The fossil record amply confirms this prediction. (54)

Coyne's argument that the fossil record supports evolution rather than divine design hinges in part on a crucial theological claim about a "celestial designer." This designer fashions "organisms from scratch" rather than making "new **species**" by remodeling the features of existing ones." In other words, God would create each new species afresh, constructing each one entirely and independently from the ground up. He would not borrow from previous designs, modifying them for each new species.

A final and more complex example comes from Richard Dawkins, perhaps the most vocal evolutionist of the early twenty-first century. His mature defense of evolutionary theory, *The Greatest Show on Earth*, relies heavily on theology (2009, 270, 296–97, 315, 321–22, 332, 341, 351, 354, 356, 362, 364, 369, 371, 375, 388–89, 390–96). His best argument is no exception: "The **DNA** code is invariant across all living creatures, while the individual **genes** themselves vary. This is a truly astounding fact, which shows more clearly than anything else that all living creatures are descended from a single ancestor" (315). This fact supports evolution in part because of a *theological* reason: phylogenetic analysis of animal genes shows that "every gene delivers approximately the same tree of life. Once again, this is exactly what you would expect if you were dealing with a true family tree. It is not what you would expect if a designer had surveyed the whole animal kingdom and picked and chosen — or 'borrowed' — the best proteins for the job, wherever in the animal kingdom they might be found" (322).

According to Dawkins, analysis of each animal gene individually reveals the *same* pattern of ancestor-descendant relationships across all animal genes. This single, consistent tree of life is exactly what one would expect on the common ancestry thesis. But why wouldn't a divine designer create the same pattern?

Dawkins's answer is that a designer would only select the "best proteins" to optimize each new species' adaptation (322). More fully, a "creator" would act like "any sensible human designer" who "is quite happy to borrow an idea from one of his inventions, if it would benefit another" (297). So God would create a new species by surveying older species and *borrowing their genes piecemeal* in order to best benefit a given new species. Thus there would be no consistent tree of life from gene to gene. The deity would not create new species and genes from scratch. God also would not create "variations on a theme" by modifying a universal **DNA** code for each new species. (Doing so might produce a single pattern of ancestor-descendant relationships from gene to gene.) Thus gene studies support evolution in part because of particular claims about God.

Observations about These Arguments

Stepping back, a few features emerge from these examples.

First, all these arguments are positive arguments for evolution. They are not simply critiques of creationism or **intelligent design**, but part of the evidential case in favor of descent with modification.

Second, the theology in these arguments is indispensable. In each case, if God-talk is removed, then the conclusion no longer follows from the empirical data.

Third, Coyne, Dawkins, and Gould rely on sectarian ideas about God. They don't use creationist or creedal theology, for example, but instead invoke their own partisan ideas about what God would do.

Fourth, they offer minimal justification for their particular theology.

Fifth, the trio self-report that these arguments are their best single arguments for evolution, respectively.

Sixth, the arguments of a number of other biologists exhibit these same five features (see References and Recommended Reading below).

Finally, and more generally, theology-laden arguments repeatedly appear not just in polemical works defending evolution and attacking creationism or intelligent design, but even in "neutral" or "purely scientific" contexts, such as encyclopedia entries or textbook descriptions of the evidence for evolution (e.g., Ayala 1988; Belk and Maier 2010; Futuyma 2013; Herron and Freeman 2014; Reece et al. 2011).

Ongoing Questions

Open questions remain. First, to what extent does the doctrine of **the fall**, which holds that the natural world is marred, counter Gould's claim that God would never allow imperfection? Second, which theology is correct? Recall that Dawkins held *inter alia* that God would always borrow from previous designs, never fashioning new species from scratch. By contrast, Coyne averred that God would create from scratch, never borrowing from older species. Both biologists cannot be correct. Third, are theology-laden arguments for evolution compatible with compartmentalism, complementarity, or **methodological naturalism** (see **Science and Religion, Models of Relating**)? All three of these positions typically hold (or imply) that the propositional content of theology cannot affect the epistemic justification of a given scientific hypothesis or theory. Yet in the arguments just surveyed, theology plays precisely this role.

While it may be quite possible to argue for evolution without relying on theological propositions, much work remains to be done to explore the plausibility and implications of the many arguments that do rely on God-talk.

Stephen Dilley

REFERENCES AND RECOMMENDED READING

Ayala, Francisco. 1988. "Evolution, The Theory of." In *Encyclopedia Britannica*, 987. 15th ed. Chicago: Encyclopedia Britannica. https://www.britannica.com/science/evolution-scientific-theory.

———. 2007. *Darwin's Gift to Science and Religion*. Washington, DC: Joseph Henry.

Belk, Colleen, and Virginia Borden Maier. 2010. *Biology: Science for Life*. 3rd ed. San Francisco: Pearson/Benjamin Cummings.

Carroll, Sean. 2009. "The Making of the Fittest." Darwin College Lecture Series. January 20. http://sms.cam.ac.uk/media/520976.

Collins, Francis. 2006. *The Language of God*. New York: Free Press.

Coyne, Jerry A. 2009. *Why Evolution Is True*. New York: Penguin.

Darwin, Charles. 1859. *On the Origin of Species*. London: John Murray.

Dawkins, Richard. 2009. *The Greatest Show on Earth: The Evidence for Evolution*. New York: Free Press.

de Beer, Sir Gavin. 1964. *Atlas of Evolution*. London: Thomas Nelson.

Dilley, Stephen. 2012. "Charles Darwin's Use of Theology in the *Origin of Species*." *British Journal for the History of Science* 44 (1): 29–56.

———. 2013. "Nothing in Biology Makes Sense Except in Light of Theology?" *Studies in History and Philosophy of Biological and Biomedical Sciences* 44:774–86.

Dobzhansky, Theodosius. 1973. "Nothing in Biology Makes Sense Except in the Light of Evolution." *American Biology Teacher* 35 (March): 125–29.

Eldredge, Niles. 2000. *The Triumph of Evolution . . . and the Failure of Creationism*. New York: Freeman.

Futuyma, Douglas. 1995. *Science on Trial: The Case for Evolution*. Sunderland, MA: Sinauer.

———. 2013. *Evolution*. 3rd ed. Sunderland, MA: Sinauer.

Gould, Stephen Jay. 1980. *The Panda's Thumb*. New York: W. W. Norton.

———. 2002. *The Structure of Evolutionary Theory*. Cambridge, MA: Harvard University Press.

Herron, Jon C., and Scott Freeman. 2014. *Evolutionary Analysis.* 5th ed. New York: Pearson.

Hunter, Cornelius. 2001. *Darwin's God.* Grand Rapids: Brazos.

———. 2007. *Science's Blind Spot.* Grand Rapids: Brazos.

———. 2014. "Darwin's Principle: The Use of Contrastive Reasoning in the Confirmation of Evolution." *HOPOS: Journal of the International Society for the History of Philosophy of Science* 4 (Spring): 106–49.

Lustig, Abigail. 2004. "Natural Atheology." In *Darwinian Heresies*, ed. Abigail Lustig et al., 69–83. Cambridge: Cambridge University Press.

Miller, Kenneth. 1999. *Finding Darwin's God.* New York: HarperCollins.

Nelson, Paul. 1996. "The Role of Theology in Current Evolutionary Reasoning." *Biology and Philosophy* 11:493–517.

Reece, Jane, Lisa A. Urry, Michael L. Cain, et al. 2011. *Campbell Biology.* 9th ed. San Francisco: Pearson.

Sober, Elliott. 2008. *Evidence and Evolution.* Cambridge: Cambridge University Press.

Williams, George C. 1997. *The Pony Fish's Glow.* New York: Basic Books.

EVOLUTIONARY ARGUMENT AGAINST NATURALISM

Brief Summary of the Argument

Throughout his academic career, **Alvin Plantinga** has defended the intellectual credibility of Christian **theism**. Recently this defense has been expanded to include a bold and controversial claim. Plantinga has argued that not only is theistic belief rational, but the conjunction of metaphysical naturalism (N)—the view that there is no such thing as God or anything like God—and contemporary evolutionary theory (E) is self-defeating. One who accepts both N and E has a "defeater" for her or his belief that human belief-producing mechanisms, so evolved, are reliable. This defeater, furthermore, constitutes a defeater for any belief produced by those mechanisms, including the beliefs that comprise N and E. Therefore, despite the fact that metaphysical naturalism and evolution are typically thought of as very closely and comfortably connected, taken together, their conjunction cannot rationally be held.

Bibliographic History

Plantinga is not the first to notice this line of argument. **C. S. Lewis** in *Miracles* (esp. chaps. 3 and 13) and Richard Taylor in *Metaphysics* (chap. 10) both develop similar lines of argument, although neither develops his arguments nearly as fully as does Plantinga. For Plantinga's part, the argument was initially presented in a 1991 *Logos* article and in chapter 12 of *Warrant and Proper Function* (1993). In *Warranted Christian Belief* (2000), Plantinga revises and expands his argument in subtle respects—in particular, he backs away from what he called "The Preliminary Argument" in his

earlier works. In 2002 the first book-length treatment of the evolutionary argument against naturalism appeared. *Naturalism Defeated?* is a conversation between Plantinga and 11 scholars who each address aspects of Plantinga's argument (Beilby 2002). In his response, Plantinga opines that his argument had "emerged unscathed—or if a bit scathed, then at least bloody but unbowed" (2002, 204–5).

The final evolution of Plantinga's argument involved a substantial streamlining of the initial premises. The new version first appeared in *Knowledge of God* (2008), a dialogue between Plantinga and Michael Tooley, and subsequently in *Science and Religion: Are They Compatible?* (Dennett and Plantinga 2010), a conversation between Plantinga and **Daniel Dennett**. He added some more detail in "Content and Natural Selection" (2011a), and finally, in *Where the Conflict Really Lies* (2011b), Plantinga includes his evolutionary argument against naturalism as part of a broad-based critique of naturalism and discussion of the relationship between science and theistic belief.

A Closer Look at the Argument

Plantinga's "Evolutionary Argument against Naturalism" calls attention to the fact that the mechanisms of evolution select for adaptive behavior, not necessarily true belief. This fact, evidently, was not lost on **Charles Darwin**, who at the end of his life voiced what Plantinga calls "Darwin's Doubt": "With me the horrid doubt always arises whether the convictions of man's mind, which has been developed from the mind of the lower animals, are of any value or at all trustworthy. Would anyone trust the convictions of a monkey's mind, if there are any convictions in such a mind?" (Darwin 1887, 315–16).

The same thought has been put even more explicitly by Patricia Churchland:

> A nervous system enables the organism to succeed in the four F's: feeding, fleeing, fighting, and reproducing. The principal chore of the nervous system is to get the body parts where they should be in order that the organism may survive.... A fancier style of representing [the external world] is advantageous *so long as it is geared to the organism's way of life and enhances the organism's chances of survival.* Truth, whatever that is, definitely takes the hindmost. (Churchland 1987, 548–49, italics in original)

The essence of the problem for naturalism is that it is difficult to see "how it *could* be that the content of a belief, the proposition that is associated with that belief as its content, plays a role in the **causation** of the behavior. Insofar as a belief enters the causal chain leading to behavior, it is by virtue of its neurophysiological properties, not its content" (Plantinga 2002, 253). But if the content of a belief is not causally efficacious with regard to behavior, "then [beliefs] would be, so to speak, *invisible* to evolution; and the fact that they arose during the evolutionary history of these beings would confer no probability on the idea that they are mostly true, or most nearly true, rather than wildly false" (Plantinga 1993, 223, italics in original).

The first premise of Plantinga's argument is that the conditional probability that humans would have developed truth-aimed, reliable, belief-producing mechanisms, given naturalism and contemporary evolutionary theory, is low. This claim can be abbreviated as follows:

(1) P(R/N&E) is low.

P should be read as "the probability of"; R is short for "reliable, truth-aimed belief-forming mechanisms"; the slash [/] should be read as "given the assumption of"; N is short for "naturalism"; and E is short for "current evolutionary theory."

It is this claim that has undergone the greatest evolution in the years since Plantinga first formulated his argument. The earliest versions of his argument involved the claim that P(R/N&E) is either low or, since it is difficult to even start to specify the relevant probabilities, inscrutable to us. Plantinga claimed that the inscrutability of the conditional **probability** of R given N&E was sufficient to create problems for the naturalist. In later versions (Plantinga 2011b; Plantinga and Tooley 2008), he simply argues that P(R/N&E) is low. Moreover, in the early versions of Plantinga's argument, he discusses five mutually exclusive and jointly exhaustive accounts of the relationship between belief and behavior and argues that reasonable estimates of the probabilities are not encouraging for the naturalist. In later versions, Plantinga highlights the fact that naturalists will be materialists with respect to mental phenomena and therefore beliefs would have to be "something like a long-standing event or structure in your brain or nervous system" (Plantinga 2011b, 320–21).

The problem, however, is that it is difficult to see how the content (and truth status) of *beliefs* would play a role in creating adaptive behavior. Organisms must have the ability to track their prey and identify predators, but there is nothing in having those abilities that requires belief formation.

Consequently, while **natural selection** requires accurate indication of an organism's surroundings, nothing follows from that about the reliability of belief formation.

The second premise of Plantinga's argument is:

(2) Anyone who accepts (believes) N&E and sees that P(R/N&E) is low has a defeater for R.

A *defeater* is a reason to reject or withhold belief. There are different kinds of defeaters, but the defeater that Plantinga claims one who accepts N&E has for R is a *rationality* defeater. A rationality defeater of a particular belief *b* "is another belief *d* such that, given my noetic structure, I cannot rationally hold *b*, given that I believe *d*" (Plantinga 2000, 361). Even more specifically, this rationality defeater is an *undercutting* defeater. Plantinga explains this using the following example. Imagine a person enters a factory and sees an assembly line carrying ostensibly red widgets and is informed that these widgets are being irradiated with red light. Armed with such **information**, it would be eminently reasonable for the person to conclude that the probability that the widgets actually are red is inscrutable to her. Therefore, despite the fact that the widgets appear red, she has a good reason to withhold belief about the color of the widgets. It is not the case that she "acquired some evidence for that widget's being nonred, thus rebutting the belief that it is red; it is rather that her grounds for thinking it red have been undercut" (Plantinga 1993, 230). The idea, therefore, is that a naturalist who accepts the first premise of Plantinga's argument acquires an undercutting defeater for his belief that his cognitive faculties, produced by unguided evolution, are reliable.

The third premise is:

(3) Anyone who has a defeater for R has a defeater for any other belief he thinks he has, including N&E itself.

Of course, defeaters can themselves be defeated. But this provides no recourse for the naturalist, for once one accepts that he has a defeater for R, any proposed defeater defeater will be correlated with beliefs that will themselves be subject to defeat.

From the third premise, the fourth follows straightforwardly:

(4) If one who accepts N&E thereby acquires a defeater for N&E, N&E is self-defeating and can't rationally be accepted.

Clarifications

First, Plantinga's argument should not be mistaken for an argument against evolutionary theory in general or, more specifically, the claim that humans might have evolved from more primitive life-forms. Rather, the purpose of his argument is to show that the denial of the existence of a creative deity is problematic. It is the *conjunction* of naturalism *and* evolution that suffers from the crippling deficiency of self-defeat, a deficiency not shared by the conjunction of *theism* and current evolutionary doctrine.

Second, Plantinga's argument does not, of course, suggest that human belief-forming mechanisms are actually unreliable. Rather, he claims that the naturalist is not justified in believing that R is true given his particular cosmological and metaphysical assumptions. In fact, according to Plantinga and other theists, the naturalist's belief-forming mechanisms are in fact reliable, but they are so because they are the product of an intelligent designer.

Finally, Plantinga's undercutting rationality defeater is a *purely alethic* defeater (from the Greek word for truth, *alêtheia*). A purely alethic rationality defeater specifies that the reasons a person might have for sustaining R (and dismissing defeaters for R) must be "successfully aimed at truth (i.e., at the maximization of true belief and the minimization of false belief) and nothing more" (2000, 363; see also Plantinga 2002, 209). For example, it might be completely rational (in one sense of that word) for you to believe that your best friend is not guilty of the heinous crime she is charged with committing. In such a case, the overwhelming evidence will not function to defeat your belief that your friend is innocent as long as defeat is conceived generally. You would, however, have a purely alethic rationality defeater, because that which neutralizes the defeating potential of the evidence is not "alethically aimed." Similarly, Plantinga's claim is that even if his evolutionary argument against naturalism does not give the naturalist a rationality defeater of the general sort, it does give her a purely alethic rationality defeater. Moreover, this defeater cannot itself be defeated, since any prospective defeater defeater would involve beliefs that would be subject to defeat as well.

Avenues of Response

There are four broad avenues of response to Plantinga's bold and intriguing argument. First, one might deny the first premise and argue for an *unguided* evolutionary explanation for truth-aimed, reliable belief-producing mechanisms.

Second, one could accept that the P(R/N&E) is low but argue that this admission does not give the naturalist a purely alethic rationality defeater for R. Third, one could argue that Plantinga's argument indicts theism every bit as much as naturalism. Fourth, one could object to philosophical concepts that Plantinga employs in his argument. For example, one might object to Plantinga's accounts of belief, rationality, or defeat.

James Beilby

REFERENCES AND RECOMMENDED READING

Beilby, James, ed. 2002. *Naturalism Defeated? Essays on Plantinga's Evolutionary Argument against Naturalism.* Ithaca, NY: Cornell University Press.
Churchland, Patricia Smith. 1987. "Epistemology in the Age of Neuroscience." *Journal of Philosophy* 84 (October): 548–49.
Darwin, Charles. 1887. "Letter to William Graham, July 3, 1881." In *The Life and Letters of Charles Darwin Including an Autobiographical Chapter*, ed. Francis Darwin, 1:315–16. London: John Murray.
Dennett, Daniel C., and Alvin Plantinga. 2010. *Science and Religion: Are They Compatible?* Point/Counterpoint Series. New York: Oxford University Press.
Plantinga, Alvin. 1991. "An Evolutionary Argument against Naturalism." *Logos* 12:27–48.
———. 1993. *Warrant and Proper Function.* New York: Oxford University Press.
———. 2000. *Warranted Christian Belief.* New York: Oxford University Press.
———. 2002. "Reply to Beilby's Cohorts." In *Naturalism Defeated? Essays on Plantinga's Evolutionary Argument against Naturalism*, ed. James Beilby, 204–75. Ithaca, NY: Cornell University Press.
———. 2011a. "Content and Natural Selection." *Philosophy and Phenomenological Research* 83, no. 2 (September): 435–58.
———. 2011b. *Where the Conflict Really Lies: Science, Religion, and Naturalism.* New York: Oxford University Press.
Plantinga, Alvin, and Michael Tooley. 2008. *Knowledge of God.* Great Debates in Philosophy Series. Malden, MA: Blackwell.

⚏ EVOLUTIONARY CREATIONISM (Critical View).

What is theistic evolution (TE) — or evolutionary creationism, as it is sometimes now called — and what exactly does it assert? Is it a logically coherent position? Is it a theologically orthodox position? Is it supported by, or consistent with, the relevant scientific evidence? The answer to each of these questions depends crucially on the definition or sense of *evolution* in play. *Theistic evolution* can mean different things to different people, largely because the term *evolution* itself has several distinct meanings.

This entry will describe and evaluate these different concepts of theistic evolution. It will also critique one formulation of the concept of theistic evolution, in particular, the one that affirms the most scientifically controversial, and also metaphysically or religiously charged, meaning of evolution.

Nevertheless, since the term *evolution* has several distinct meanings, it is first necessary to describe the different meanings that are commonly associated with the term in order to evaluate the different possible concepts of theistic evolution that proponents of the idea may have in mind. It will be shown that three distinct meanings of the term *evolution* are especially relevant for understanding three different possible concepts of theistic evolution. Yale biologist Keith Stewart Thomson, for example, has noted that in contemporary biology the term *evolution* can refer to (1) change over time, (2) universal **common ancestry**, and (3) the natural mechanisms that produce change in organisms (Thomson 1982, 521–39). Following Thomson, this entry will describe and distinguish these three distinct meanings of *evolution* in order to foster clarity in the analysis and assessment of three distinct concepts of *theistic evolution*.

Evolution #1: Change over Time

Evolution in its most rudimentary sense simply affirms the idea of "change over time." Many natural scientists use *evolution* in this first sense as they seek to reconstruct a series of past events to tell the story of nature's history (Bowler 1975, 99). Astronomers study the life cycles of stars and the *evolution* (change over time) of the universe or specific galaxies; geologists describe changes (*evolution*) in the earth's surface; biologists note ecological changes within recorded human history, which may have, for example, transformed a barren island into a mature, forested island community. These examples, however, have little or nothing to do with the modern neo-Darwinian theory of evolution.

In evolutionary biology, evolution defined as change over time can also refer specifically to the idea that the life-forms we see today are different from the life-forms that existed in the distant past. The **fossil record** provides strong support for this idea. Paleontologists observe changes in the types of life that have existed over time as represented by different fossilized forms in the sedimentary rock record (a phenomenon known as "fossil succession"). Many of the plants and animals that are fossilized in recent rock layers are different from the plants and animals fossilized in older rocks. The composition of flora and fauna on the surface of the earth today is likewise different from the forms of life that lived long ago, as attested by the fossil record.

Evolution defined as "change over time" can also refer to observed minor changes in features of individual species — small-scale changes that take place over a relatively short period of time. Most biologists think this kind of evolution (sometimes called *microevolution*) results from a change in the proportion of different variants of a **gene** (called *alleles*)

within a population over time. Thus population geneticists study changes in the frequencies of alleles in gene pools. A large number of precise observations have established the occurrence of this type of evolution. Studies of melanism in peppered moths, though currently contested (Coyne 1998, 35–36; Wells 1999, 13), are among the most celebrated examples of microevolution. The observed changes in the size and shape of Galápagos finch beaks in response to changing climate patterns provide another good example of small-scale change over time within a species.

Evolution #2: Common Descent, or Universal Common Descent

Many biologists today also commonly use the term *evolution* to refer to the idea that all organisms are related by common ancestry. This idea is also known as the theory of universal common descent. This theory affirms that all known living organisms are descended from a single common ancestor somewhere in the distant past. In *The Origin of Species*, **Darwin** made a case for the truth of evolution in this second sense. In a famous passage at the end of the *Origin*, he argued that "probably all the organic beings which have ever lived on this earth have descended from some one primordial form" (Darwin 1859, 484). Darwin thought that this primordial form gradually developed into new forms of life, which in turn gradually developed into other forms of life, eventually producing, after many millions of generations, all the complex life we see in the present.

Biology textbooks today often depict this idea just as Darwin did, with a great branching tree. The bottom of the trunk of Darwin's tree of life represents the first primordial organism. The limbs and branches of the tree represent the many new forms of life that developed from it. The vertical axis on which the tree is plotted represents the arrow of time. The horizontal axis represents changes in biological form, or what biologists call "morphological distance."

Darwin's theory of biological history is often referred to as a "monophyletic" view of the history of life because it portrays all organisms as ultimately related as a single connected family. Darwin argued that this idea best explained a variety of lines of biological evidence: the succession of fossil forms, the geographical distribution of various **species** (such as the plants and animals of the Galápagos Islands), and the anatomical and embryological similarities among otherwise different types of organisms.

Evolution in this second sense not only specifies that all life shares a common ancestry, it also implies that virtually no limits exist to the amount of morphological change that can occur in organisms. It assumes that relatively simple organisms can, given adequate time, change into much more complex organisms. Thus evolution in this second sense entails not only change, but also gradual, continuous—and even unbounded—biological change.

Evolution #3: The Creative Power of the Natural Selection/Random Variation (or Mutation) Mechanism

The term *evolution* is also commonly used to refer to the cause, or mechanism, that produces the biological change depicted by Darwin's tree of life. When evolution is used in this way, it usually refers to the mechanism of natural selection acting on random variations or mutations. (Modern neo-Darwinists propose that natural selection acts on a special kind of variation called *genetic mutations*. Mutations are random changes in the chemical subunits that convey **information** in **DNA**. Modern neo-Darwinists would also affirm the role of other apparently undirected evolutionary mechanisms such as genetic drift, although such mechanisms are typically thought to be of minor importance in comparison with mutation/selection in generating the adaptive **complexity** of life.)

This third use of *evolution* entails the idea that the natural selection/mutation mechanism has the creative power to produce fundamental innovations in the history of life. Whereas the theory of universal common descent postulated a pattern (the branching tree) to represent the history of life, the mechanism of natural selection and random variation/mutation represents a causal process that can allegedly generate the large-scale macroevolutionary change implied by the second meaning of evolution (see above). Since proponents of the creative power of the mutation/natural selection mechanism see it (and other similarly materialistic evolutionary mechanisms) as explaining the origin of all the forms and features of life, this definition of evolution is closely associated with, or encompasses, another definition of evolution.

Evolution #3a: The Natural Selection/Random Variation (or Mutation) Mechanism Can Explain the Appearance of Design in Living Systems Apart from the Activity of an Actual Designing Intelligence

Evolutionary biologists since Darwin have affirmed that the natural selection/variation mechanism not only explains the origin of all new biological forms and features, but they have also affirmed a closely related idea, namely, that this

mechanism can explain one particularly striking feature of biological systems: the appearance of design. Biologists have long recognized that many organized structures in living organisms—the elegant form and protective covering of the coiled nautilus, the interdependent parts of the vertebrate eye, the interlocking bones, muscles, and feathers of a bird wing—give the appearance of having been designed for a purpose (Dawkins 1986, 1). During the nineteenth century, before Darwin, biologists were particularly struck by the way in which living organisms seemed well adapted to their environments. They attributed this adaptation of organisms to their environments to the planning and ingenuity of a powerful designing intelligence.

Yet Darwin (and modern neo-Darwinists) have argued that the appearance of design in living organisms could be more simply explained as the product of a purely undirected mechanism, in particular the variation/natural selection mechanism. Darwin attempted to show that the natural selection mechanism could account for the appearance of design by drawing an analogy to the well-known process of "artificial selection" or "selective breeding." Anyone in the nineteenth century familiar with the breeding of domestic animals—dogs, horses, sheep, or pigeons, for example—knew that human breeders could alter the features of domestic stock by allowing only animals with certain traits to breed. A Scottish sheepherder might breed for a woollier sheep to enhance its chances of survival in a cold northern climate (or to harvest more wool). To do so, he would choose only the woolliest males and woolliest ewes to breed. If generation after generation he continued to select and breed only the woolliest sheep among the resulting offspring, he would eventually produce a woollier breed of sheep—a breed better adapted to its environment. In such cases, "the key is man's power of accumulative selection," wrote Darwin. "Nature gives successive variations; man adds them up in certain directions useful to him" (Darwin 1859, 30).

But, as Darwin pointed out, nature also has a means of sifting: defective creatures are less likely to survive and reproduce, while those offspring with beneficial variations are more likely to survive, reproduce, and pass on their advantages to future generations. In the *Origin*, Darwin argued that this process—natural selection acting on random variations—could alter the features of organisms just as intelligent selection by human breeders can. Nature itself could play the role of the breeder and thus eliminates the need for an actual designing intelligence to produce the complex adaptations that living organisms manifest.

Consider once more our flock of sheep. Imagine that instead of a human selecting the woolliest males and ewes to breed, a series of very cold winters ensures that all but the woolliest sheep in a population die off. Now, again, only very woolly sheep will remain to breed. If the cold winters continue over several generations, will the result not be the same as before? Won't the population of sheep eventually become discernibly woollier?

This was Darwin's great insight. Nature—in the form of environmental changes or other factors—could have the same effect on a population of organisms as the intentional decisions of an intelligent agent. Nature would favor the preservation of certain features over others—those that conferred a functional or survival advantage on the organisms possessing them—causing the features of the population to change. The resulting change or increase in fitness (adaptation) will have been produced not by an intelligent breeder choosing a desirable trait or variation—not by "artificial selection"—but by a wholly natural process. As Darwin himself insisted, "There seems to be no more design in the variability of organic beings and in the action of natural selection, than in the course in which the wind blows" (Darwin 1887, 278–79).

Or as the eminent evolutionary biologist Francisco Ayala has argued, Darwin accounted for "design without a designer" since "it was Darwin's greatest accomplishment to show that the directive organization of living beings can be explained as the result of a natural process, natural selection, without any need to resort to a Creator or other external agent" (Ayala 2007, 8567–73).

Indeed, since 1859 most evolutionary biologists have understood the appearance of design in living things as an illusion—a powerfully suggestive one, but an illusion nonetheless. For this reason, **Richard Dawkins** insists in *The Blind Watchmaker* that "biology is the study of complicated things that give the appearance of having been designed for a purpose" (Dawkins 1986, 1). Or as Ernst Mayr explained, "The real core of Darwinism ... is the theory of natural selection. This theory is so important for the Darwinian because it permits the explanation of adaptation, the 'design' of the natural theologian, by natural means, instead of by divine intervention" (Mayr 1982, xi–xii). Or as Francis Crick mused, biologists must "constantly keep in mind that what they see was not designed, but rather evolved" (Crick 1988, 138). Likewise, George Gaylord Simpson, one of the architects of neo-Darwinism, in *The Meaning of Evolution* wrote that neo-Darwinism implies that "man is the result of a purposeless and natural process that did not have him in mind" (Simpson 1967, 345).

But if apparent design is an illusion—if it is just an appearance—as both Darwinists and modern neo-Darwinists have argued, then it follows that whatever mechanism produced that appearance must be wholly unguided and undirected. For this reason, the third meaning of *evolution*—the definition that affirms the creative power of the natural selection/**random mutation** mechanism and denies evidence of actual design in living systems—raises a significant issue for any proponent of theistic evolution who affirms this meaning of evolution.

Assessing Different Concepts of Theistic Evolution (or Evolutionary Creation)

The three different meanings of evolution discussed above correspond to three possible and distinct concepts of theistic evolution, one of which is trivial, one of which is contestable but not incoherent, and one of which appears deeply problematic. In the last case, special attention is due to the important issue of whether theistic evolutionists regard the evolutionary process as guided or unguided.

If by "evolution" the theistic evolutionist means to affirm evolution in the first sense—change over time—and if, further, the theistic evolutionist affirms that God has caused that "change over time," then certainly no theist would contest the theological orthodoxy or logical coherence of such a statement. If a personal God of the kind affirmed by biblical Judaism or Christianity exists, then there is nothing logically contradictory in such a statement, nor does it contradict any specific theological tenets. The Jewish and Christian Scriptures clearly affirm that God has caused change over time, not only in human history but in the process of creating the world and different forms of life.

Given the extensive scientific evidence showing that the representation of life-forms on the earth has changed over time, there does not seem to be any significant theological or scientific basis for questioning evolution, or theistic evolution, where evolution is defined in this minimal sense. Similarly, since God could create different organisms with a built-in capacity to change or "evolve" within limits without denying his design of different living systems as distinct forms of life, and since there is extensive scientific evidence for change of this kind occurring, there does not seem to be any significant scientific or theological basis for questioning evolution in this sense. Understanding theistic evolution this way seems unobjectionable, perhaps even trivial.

Another conception of theistic evolution affirms the second meaning of evolution. It affirms the view that God has caused continuous and gradual biological change such that the history of life is best represented by a great branching tree pattern as Darwin argued. Theistic evolution thus conceived is, again, not obviously logically incoherent since God as conceived by theists, including biblical theists, is certainly capable of producing continuous and gradual change.

Nevertheless, some biblical theists question universal common descent based on their interpretation of the biblical teaching in Genesis about God creating distinct "kinds" of plants and animals, all of which "reproduce after their own kind." Those who think a natural reading of the Genesis account suggests that different kinds of plants and animals only reproduce after their own kind and do not vary beyond some fixed limit in their morphology, question the theory of universal common descent on biblical grounds. Some biblical theists likewise question that humans and lower animals share a common ancestry, believing instead that the biblical account affirms that humans arose from a special creative act, thus excluding the idea that humans originated from nonhuman ancestors.

In addition to these theological objections, there is a growing body of scientific evidence challenging such a "monophyletic" picture of the history of life. These scientific challenges to the theory of universal common descent are reviewed in the biology textbook *Explore Evolution: The Arguments for and against Neo-Darwinism* (Meyer et al., 2007) and discussed in various scientific articles. (See, e.g., Doolittle 2009, 2221–28; Gordon 1999, 331–48; Koonin 2007, 21; Lawton 2009, 34–39; Merhej and Raoult 2012, 113; Raoult 2010, 104–5; Syvanen 2012, 339–56; Woese 2002, 8742–47.) On the specific question of human origins and scientific challenges to the idea that humans and chimps (for example) share a common ancestor, see the book *Science and Human Origins* (Gauger et al. 2012).

An even more foundational issue arises when considering the cause of biological change and the question of whether theistic evolutionists conceive of evolutionary mechanisms as directed or undirected processes.

Some proponents of theistic evolution openly affirm that the evolutionary process is an unguided, undirected process. **Kenneth Miller**, a leading theistic evolutionist and author of *Finding Darwin's God*, has repeatedly stated in editions of his popular textbook that "evolution works without either plan or purpose.... Evolution is random and undirected" (Miller and Levine 1991; 1993; 1995; 1998, 658).

Nevertheless, most theistic evolutionists, including Francis Collins, perhaps the world's best-known proponent of the position, have been reluctant to clarify what they think about this important issue. In his book *The Language of God*, Collins makes clear his support for universal common descent. He also seems to assume the adequacy of standard evolutionary mechanisms but does not clearly say whether he thinks those mechanisms are directed or undirected—only that they "could be" directed.

In any case, where theistic evolution is understood to affirm the third meaning of evolution—the creative power and adequacy of the neo-Darwinian mechanism and its consequent denial of actual design—the concept becomes deeply problematic. Indeed, depending on how this particular understanding of theistic evolution is articulated, it generates either (1) logical contradictions, or (2) a theologically heterodox view of **divine action**, or (3) a convoluted and scientifically vacuous explanation. In addition to this dilemma (or rather "tri-lemma"), a huge body of scientific evidence now challenges the creative power of the mutation/selection mechanism, especially with respect to some of the most striking appearances of design in biological systems. Let's examine each of these difficulties in more detail.

A Logical Contradictory View

In the first place, some formulations of theistic evolution that affirm the third meaning of evolution result in logical contradictions. For example, if the theistic evolutionist means to affirm the standard neo-Darwinian view of the natural selection/mutation mechanism as an undirected process while simultaneously affirming that God is still causally responsible for the origin of new forms of life, then the theistic evolutionist implies that God somehow guided or directed an unguided and undirected process. Logically, no intelligent being—not even God—can direct an undirected process. As soon as he directs it, the "undirected" process would no longer be undirected.

On the other hand, a proponent of theistic evolution may conceive of the natural selection/mutation mechanism as a directed process (with God perhaps directing specific mutations). This view represents a decidedly non-Darwinian conception of the evolutionary mechanism. It also constitutes a version of the theory of **intelligent design**—one that affirms that God intelligently designed organisms by actively directing mutations (or other processes) toward functional endpoints during the history of life. Yet if living organisms are the result of a directed process, then it follows that the appearance of design in living organisms is real, not merely apparent or illusory. Nevertheless, chief proponents of theistic evolution reject the theory of intelligent design with its claim that the appearance of design in living organisms is real. Thus any proponent of theistic evolution who affirms that God is directing the evolutionary mechanism, and who also rejects intelligent design, implicitly contradicts himself or herself. (Of course, there is no contradiction in affirming both a God-guided mechanism of evolution and intelligent design, though few theistic evolutionists have publicly taken this view—see Ratzsch 2001 for a notable exception.)

Theologically Problematic Views

Other formulations of theistic evolution explicitly deny that God is directing or guiding the mutation/selection mechanism, and instead see a much more limited divine role in the process of life's creation. One formulation affirms that God designed the **laws of nature** at the beginning of the universe to make the origin and development of life possible (or inevitable). This view is scientifically problematic, however, since it can be demonstrated that the information necessary to build even a single functional gene (or section of DNA) cannot have been contained in the elementary particles and energy present at the beginning of the universe (Meyer 2010, 147–64). Another formulation holds that God created the laws of nature at the beginning of the universe and also affirms that he constantly upholds those laws on a moment-by-moment basis. Nevertheless, both these understandings of theistic evolution deny that God in any way actively directed the mutation/selection (or other evolutionary) mechanisms. Both formulations conceive of God's role in the creation of life (as opposed to the maintenance of physical law) as mainly passive rather than active or directive. In both views, the mechanisms of natural selection and random mutation (and/or other similarly undirected evolutionary mechanisms) are seen as the main causal actor(s) in producing new forms of life. Thus God does not act directly or "intervene" within the orderly concourse of nature.

Yet this view is theologically problematic, at least for orthodox Jews and Christians who derive their understanding of divine action from the biblical text. This is easy to see in the first of these two formulations, where God's activity is confined to an act of creation or design at the very beginning of the universe. Such a front-end-loaded view of design is, of course, a logically possible view, but it is indistinguishable from **deism**. It therefore contradicts the plainly theistic view of divine action articulated in the Bible where God acts in

his creation after the beginning of the universe. Indeed, the Bible describes God as not only acting to create the universe in the beginning, it also describes him as presently uphold-ing the universe in its orderly concourse and also describes him as acting discretely as an agent within the natural order. (See, e.g., Gen. 1:27: "God created (*bara*) mankind"; Exod. 10:13: "The LORD made an east wind blow.")

The version of theistic evolution that affirms that God created and upholds the laws of nature but does not actively direct the creation of life is also theologically problematic—at least for those who profess a biblical understanding of God's nature and powers. If God is not at least directing the evolutionary process, then the origin of biological systems must be attributed, in some part, to nature acting indepen-dently of God's direction. This entails a diminished view of God's involvement in creation and divine sovereignty at odds with most traditional readings of the Bible (whether Jewish or Christian).

Traditionally, theologians have understood the Bible to affirm the sovereignty of God and the absolute dependence of his creation upon him, not only for its ongoing existence (as in "in him all things hold together," Col. 1:17) but also for its origin in the first place (as in "without him nothing was made that has been made," John 1:3). Logically speak-ing, that means that God's action is both a necessary and sufficient condition for the origin of the universe and created order. By making a natural process causally responsible (i.e., sufficient) to produce various novel biological structures, systems, and their appearance of design, this version of the-istic evolution renders God's action and causal powers at best a merely necessary (but not sufficient) condition for the origin and existence of living things. This arguably entails a diminished and unbiblical view of divine sovereignty.

Indeed, if God did not at least direct the process of mutation and selection (and/or other relevant evolutionary mechanisms), but instead merely sustained the laws of nature that made them possible, then it follows that he did not know, and does not know, what those mechanisms would (or will) produce, including whether they would have produced human beings. Accordingly, many theistic evolutionists who embrace this view have insisted that the evolutionary process might just as well have produced "a big-brained dinosaur" as opposed to a big-brained bipedal hominid—that is, a human being (Miller 1999, 2007; West 2010, 40–45). Since God does not direct or control the evolutionary process, he cannot know what it will produce—a conclusion at odds with God's omniscience and **providence**. Similarly, since

God does not direct the evolutionary process, what it produces cannot be said to express his specific intentions in creation—a conclusion that also stands at odds with the biblical claim that God made man expressly in his own image and "foreknew" him.

A Convoluted (and Scientifically Vacuous) Explanation

Perhaps because evangelical Christian advocates of theistic evolution have not wanted to embrace either the logical or the theological problems associated with affirming the third meaning of evolution, they have typically declined to specify whether they think the natural selection/random mutation mechanism is a directed or an undirected process. Instead, many affirm a scientifically convoluted and vacuous formulation of theistic evolution—at least, insofar as it stands as an explanation for the appearance of design in living organisms.

Recall that from Darwin to the present, leading evolutionary biologists have acknowledged the appearance of design in living organisms and sought to explain its origin. Darwinists and neo-Darwinists have sought to explain this appearance as the result of an undirected and unguided mechanism (natural selection acting on random variations or mutations) that can mimic the powers of a designing intelligence. Theistic evolutionists who affirm the creative power of this (and perhaps other related) evolutionary mechanism(s) have been loath to argue that God actively directed the evolutionary process in any discernible way. That, of course, would constitute a form of intelligent design, and most theistic evolutionists reject this idea outright.

Francis Collins, for example, has explicitly rejected the theory of intelligent design. Yet the theory of intelligent design does not necessarily reject evolution in either of the first two senses above, but instead argues that key appearances of design in living organisms are real, not illusory. In rejecting the theory of intelligent design, Collins would, therefore, seem to be affirming the contrary, namely, that the appearance of design is not real, but just an appearance.

He thus seems to commit himself to the position that the process that produced the appearance of design in living organisms is undirected. That would follow because, again, if it were otherwise—if the process were directed or guided—then the appearance of design in living organisms would be real and not just apparent.

Yet in *The Language of God*, Collins does not specify whether the evolutionary process is directed or not, only that it "could be" (Collins 2006, 205). As he explains, "Evolution

could appear to us to be driven by **chance**, but from God's perspective the outcome would be entirely specified. Thus, God could be completely and intimately involved in the creation of all species, while from our perspective ... this would appear a random and undirected process" (emphasis added).

That God could have acted in such a concealed way is, of course, a logical possibility, but positing such a view, nevertheless, entails difficulties that proponents of theistic evolution rarely address.

First, this version of theistic evolution suggests a logically convoluted explanation for the appearance of design in living systems. Like classical **Darwinism** and neo-Darwinism, this version of theistic evolution denies that anything about living systems indicates that an actual designing intelligence played a role in their origin. Why? Theistic evolutionists, like mainstream neo-Darwinists, affirm the third meaning of evolution—i.e., the sufficiency of the natural selection/mutation mechanism (possibly in conjunction with other similarly naturalistic evolutionary mechanisms) as an explanation for the origin of new forms and features of life. Since natural selection and random mutations can account for the origin of biological systems (and their appearances of design), theistic evolutionists steadfastly deny the need to propose an actual designing intelligence.

Yet having affirmed what classical Darwinists and neo-Darwinists affirm—namely, the sufficiency of standard evolutionary mechanisms—they then suggest that such mechanisms may only appear undirected and unguided. Thus Francis Collins suggests that "from our perspective" mutation and selection "would appear a random and undirected process." Therefore his formulation implies that the appearance or illusion of design in living systems results from the activity of an apparently undirected material process (i.e., classical and neo-Darwinism) except that this apparently undirected process is itself being used by a designing intelligence—or at least it could be, though no one can tell for sure. Or, to put it another way, we have moved from Richard Dawkins's famous statement "Biology is the study of complicated things that give the appearance of having been designed for a purpose" (Dawkins 1986, 1) to the proposition that "biology is the study of complicated things that give the appearance of having been designed for a purpose, though that appearance of design is an illusion (classical Darwinism), even though there may be an intelligent designer behind it all—in which case that appearance wouldn't be an illusion after all."

This tangled—indeed convoluted—view of the origin of living systems adds nothing to our scientific understanding of what caused living organisms to arise. As such, it also represents an entirely vacuous explanation. Indeed, it has no empirical or scientific content beyond that offered by strictly materialistic evolutionary theories. It tells nothing about God's role in the evolutionary process or even whether he had a role at all. It thus renders the modifier *theistic* in the term *theistic evolution* superfluous. It does not represent an alternative theory of biological origins, but a reaffirmation of some materialistic version of evolutionary theory restated using theological terminology.

Of course, theistic evolutionists who hold this view do not typically spell out its implications so as to reveal the convoluted nature of the explanation for the appearance of design that their view entails. Instead, they typically avoid discussing, or offering explanations for, the appearance of design in living systems altogether—though this appearance is so striking that even secular evolutionary biologists have long and consistently acknowledged it (Crick 1988, 138; Dawkins 1986, 1).

Theistic evolutionists such as Collins also deny what advocates of intelligent design affirm, namely, that the past activity of a designing intelligence, including God's intelligence, is detectable or discernible in living systems. Yet denying the detectability of design in nature generates another theological difficulty. In particular, this view seems to contradict what the Bible affirms about the natural world (or "the things that are made") revealing the reality of God and his "invisible qualities," such as his power, glory, divine nature, and wisdom. As John West has explained:

> [Francis Collins's version of theistic evolution] still seriously conflicts with the Biblical understanding of God and His general revelation. Both the Old and New Testaments clearly teach that human beings can recognize God's handiwork in nature through their own observations rather than special divine revelation. From the psalmist who proclaimed that the "heavens declare the glory of God" (Ps. 19:1) to the apostle Paul who argued in Romans 1:20 that "since the creation of the world God's invisible qualities ... have been clearly seen, being understood from what has been made," the idea that we can see design in nature was clearly taught. Jesus himself pointed to the feeding of birds, the rain and the sun, and the exquisite design of the lilies of the field as observable evidence of God's active care toward the world and its inhabitants (Matt. 5:44–45, 48; 6:26–30) ... to head off a direct collision between undirected Darwinism and the doctrine

of God's sovereignty, Collins seems to depict God as a cosmic trickster who misleads people into thinking that the process by which they were produced was blind and purposeless, even when it wasn't. (West 2010, 46–47)

Scientific Difficulties

In addition to these difficulties, the versions of theistic evolution that affirm the creative power of the natural selection/random mutation mechanism are now contradicted by a wealth of scientific evidence from a diverse array of biological subdisciplines, including molecular biology, population genetics, **paleontology**, and developmental biology. Reciting the many empirical studies and mathematical arguments that challenge the creative power of the neo-Darwinian and other materialistic evolutionary mechanisms lies beyond the scope of this entry. Nevertheless, one can find extensive discussion of this evidence in the book *Darwin's Doubt* (Meyer 2013).

Darwin's Doubt also shows that many mainstream evolutionary biologists have rejected orthodox neo-Darwinian evolutionary theory precisely because they recognize that the mutation/natural selection mechanism lacks the creative power to generate novel biological form. In support of this claim, the book also describes the many new theories of evolution (and evolutionary mechanisms) that mainstream evolutionary biologists are now proposing as alternatives. None of these theories, however, has proposed mechanisms with the demonstrated efficacy necessary to explain the origin of morphological novelty or key appearances of design in living systems such as the genetic and epigenetic information they possess (which are necessary to produce new forms of life).

For advocates of theistic evolution (where evolution is understood to affirm the third meaning of evolution), the current state of scientific opinion presents an acute problem, quite apart from the logical and theological considerations outlined above. If evolutionary biologists themselves no longer agree that the mutation/selection mechanism has the creative power to explain novel biological forms, and if no alternative evolutionary mechanism has yet demonstrated that power either, then the claim that apparently unguided evolutionary processes are God's way of creating new forms of life is, increasingly, a relic of an obsolete scientific viewpoint. This raises a question: If the evidence doesn't support the creative power of materialistic evolutionary mechanisms, why attempt to synthesize evolutionary theory with a theistic understanding of creation?

Stephen C. Meyer

REFERENCES AND RECOMMENDED READING

Axe, Douglas, Ann Gauger, and Casey Luskin. 2012. *Science and Human Origins.* Seattle: Discovery Institute Press.

Ayala, Francisco J. 2007. "Darwin's Greatest Discovery: Design without Designer." *Proceedings of the National Academy of Sciences USA* 104 (May 15): 8567–73.

Bowler, Peter J. 1975. "The Changing Meaning of 'Evolution.'" *Journal of the History of Ideas* 36 (1975): 99.

Collins, Francis. 2006. *The Language of God: A Scientist Presents Evidence for Belief.* New York: Free Press.

Coyne, Jerry. 1998. "Not Black and White." Review of Michael Majerus's 1998 book *Melanism: Evolution in Action. Nature* 396:35–36.

Crick, Francis. 1988. *What Mad Pursuit: A Personal View of Scientific Discovery.* New York: Basic Books.

Darwin, Charles. 1859. *On the Origin of Species by Means of Natural Selection.* A facsimile of the first edition, published by John Murray, London, 1859. Repr., Cambridge, MA: Harvard University Press, 1964.

———. 1887. *The Life and Letters of Charles Darwin,* ed. Francis Darwin.

Dawkins, Richard. 1986. *The Blind Watchmaker.* New York: W. W. Norton.

Doolittle, W. Ford. 2009. "The Practice of Classification and the Theory of Evolution, and What the Demise of Charles Darwin's Tree of Life Hypothesis Means for Both of Them." *Philosophical Transactions of the Royal Society, B* 364:2221–28.

Futuyma, Douglas J. 1998. *Evolutionary Biology.* Sunderland, MA: Sinauer.

Gauger, Ann, Douglas Axe, and Casey Luskin. 2012. *Science and Human Origins.* Seattle: Discovery Institute Press.

Gordon, Malcolm S. 1999. "The Concept of Monophyly: A Speculative Essay." *Biology and Philosophy* 14:331–48.

Koonin, Eugene V. 2007. "The Biological Big Bang Model for the Major Transitions in Evolution." *Biology Direct* 2:21.

Lawton, Graham. 2009. "Why Darwin Was Wrong about the Tree of Life." *New Scientist* (January 21): 34–39.

Mayr, Ernst. 1982. Foreword to Michael Ruse, *Darwinism Defended: A Guide to the Evolution Controversies,* xi–xii. Reading, MA: Addison-Wesley.

Merhej, Vicky, and Didier Raoult. 2012. "Rhizome of Life, Catastrophes, Sequence Exchanges, Gene Creations, and Giant Viruses: How Microbial Genomics Challenges Darwin." *Frontiers in Cellular and Infection Microbiology* 2 (August 28): 113.

Meyer, Stephen C. 2010. "The Difference It Doesn't Make." In *God and Evolution: Protestants, Catholics, and Jews Explore Darwin's Challenge to Faith,* ed. Jay Wesley Richards, 147–64. Seattle: Discovery Institute Press.

———. 2013. *Darwin's Doubt: The Explosive Origin of Animal Life and the Case for Intelligent Design.* New York: HarperOne.

Meyer, Stephen C., Paul A. Nelson, Jonathan Moneymaker, Ralph Seelke, and Scott Minnich. 2007. *Explore Evolution: The Arguments for and against Neo-Darwinism.* London: Hill House.

Miller, Kenneth. 1999. *Finding Darwin's God: A Scientist's Search for Common Ground between God and Evolution.* New York: HarperCollins.

———. 2007. Comments during "Evolution and Intelligent Design: An Exchange." At "Shifting Ground: Religion and Civic Life in America" conference, Bedford, NH, sponsored by New Hampshire Humanities Council. March 24.

Miller Kenneth R., and Joseph S. Levine. 1991. *Biology,* 658. Englewood Cliffs, NJ: Prentice Hall.

———. 1993. *Biology,* 658. 2nd ed. Englewood Cliffs, NJ: Prentice Hall.

———. 1995. *Biology,* 658. 3rd ed. Englewood Cliffs, NJ: Prentice Hall.

———. 1998. *Biology,* 658. 4th ed. Upper Saddle River, NJ: Prentice Hall.

Raoult, Didier. 2010. "The Post-Darwinist Rhizome of Life." *Lancet* 375:104–5.

Ratzsch, Del. 2001. *Nature, Design, and Science: The Status of Design in Natural Science.* Albany: State University of New York Press.

Simpson, George Gaylord. 1967. *The Meaning of Evolution.* Rev. ed. New Haven, CT: Yale University Press.

Syvanen, Michael. 2012. "Evolutionary Implications of Horizontal Gene Transfer." *Annual Review of Genetics* 46:339–56.

Thomson, Keith S. 1982. "The Meanings of Evolution." *American Scientist* 70:529–31.

Wells, Jonathan. 1999. "Second Thoughts about Peppered Moths." *Scientist* 13:13.

West, John G. 2010. "Nothing New under the Sun." In *God and Evolution: Protestants, Catholics, and Jews Explore Darwin's Challenge to Faith,* ed. Jay Wesley Richards, 40–45. Seattle: Discovery Institute Press.

Woese, Carl R. 2002. "On the Evolution of Cells." *Proceedings of the National Academy of Sciences USA* 99 (June 25): 8742–47.

↬ EVOLUTIONARY CREATIONISM (Supportive View).

Evolutionary creationism (EC) is the Christian view that God, as creator and sustainer of the cosmos, was pleased to use evolution (see **Evolution, Biological**) as the means for creating biodiversity on earth (Lamoureux 2008, 2009). This view, also known as theistic evolution, has existed since Darwin's time (Livingstone 1984), but in recent years has become increasingly prevalent among evangelical Christians, primarily through the writings of **Francis Collins** and the work of the **BioLogos Foundation** (BioLogos 2016; Collins 2006).

While the primary reason for holding to EC is the abundant evidence supporting evolutionary biology, other factors contribute. Advances in understanding the ancient Near East (ANE) setting of the Genesis narratives makes a strong case that Genesis is not speaking to modern scientific concerns but rather the concerns of its intended audience at that time in history (Walton 2009). Additionally, Christian attempts to undermine evolutionary theory have increasingly been shown to be founded on weak arguments (Venema 2010a, 2014).

Evolution is a theory in the scientific sense, meaning that it is an explanatory framework supported by a large body of experimental evidence that makes accurate predictions about the natural world (Futuyma 2013). In this way, evolution is no different than other scientific theories that Christians readily accept: the heliocentric theory of how our solar system functions (with the sun at its center, rather than the earth), or the chromosomal theory of inheritance. In this sense, Christians are "theistic gravitationists" and "theistic geneticists" in that they view these natural processes as the means by which God orders the solar system and the passage of chromosomes from one generation to the next.

This view sits squarely within the long-held Judeo-Christian view that what we perceive as "natural" is equally the result of the divine **providence** as is what we consider "supernatural." Indeed, the categories of "natural" and "supernatural" are in fact foreign to the biblical **worldview** (Walton

2009). As such, there is no a priori reason for a Christian to reject a scientific theory merely because it offers a non-supernatural explanation for a feature of the created order. Rather, a decision on the validity of evolution should come from a careful examination of the evidence for it.

Evidence for Evolution

Since evolution has been a productive scientific theory for more than 150 years, there is far too much evidence for its validity than can be presented in a brief article. A few examples, however, will illustrate how evolution, as a scientific theory, continues to make accurate predictions and withstand technological developments that allow for observations Darwin could not foresee.

One interesting feature of evolutionary theory is that it can "force" one, in a sense, to make rather counterintuitive predictions. One such example is the origins of modern cetaceans (whales, dolphins, and porpoises). Cetaceans are mammals, and it is highly unlikely that the defining mammalian characteristics arose more than once through an evolutionary process. As such, evolution predicts that cetaceans, like all other mammals, descend from terrestrial, four-limbed (i.e., *tetrapod*) ancestors, even though they are fully aquatic and lack hind limbs. In his *Origin of Species*, Darwin himself speculated on the origins of whalelike creatures through **natural selection** (Darwin 1859, 184):

> In North America the black bear was seen by Hearne swimming for hours with widely open mouth, thus catching, like a whale, insects in the water. Even in so extreme a case as this, if the supply of insects were constant, and if better adapted competitors did not already exist in the country, I can see no difficulty in a race of bears being rendered, by natural selection, more and more aquatic in their structure and habits, with larger and larger mouths, till a creature was produced as monstrous as a whale.

Though Darwin lacked the ability to test his hypothesis, later work would do so.

One obvious prediction of this hypothesis is that the **fossil record**s should preserve forms intermediate between present-day cetaceans and their terrestrial, tetrapod ancestors. While one can never be sure that a fossil **species** is in fact a direct ancestor of any living species, one would expect at least to find species *related* to the direct ancestral lineage, and finding enough such species can provide an overall picture of what sorts of forms were present and when they lived. In Darwin's time, putative "transitional forms" blurring

the distinction between terrestrial mammals and cetaceans were unknown, a fact that antievolutionary apologists were quick to capitalize on (Seeley 1870, 231):

> Thus Mr. Darwin, while he finds it impossible to believe the plain words of Moses ... "sees no difficulty" in believing that a race of bears, by contracting a habit of swimming, gradually lost their legs, and were "developed" into whales of a hundred times their own bulk! And this sort of trash is called "science"!... Let us look, for a moment, at this whale, or bear, or bear-whale. What says Geological Science to it? Geology replies that she finds bears in the crust of the earth, and many of them; and that she also finds whales. But that the whale-bear, or creature which was developing from a bear into a whale, she never met with. And, not finding it, she no more believes in it than in a phoenix or a roc.

Since Darwin's time, however, a number of fossil species have been discovered that might have given Mr. Seeley pause (McGowen et al. 2014; Uhen 2010). For example, basilosaurids are fully aquatic mammals very similar to modern cetaceans that nonetheless have tiny hind limbs. These hind limbs are unable to support their body weight out of water because their bones are not connected to their pelvis or any other bones in the skeleton. The protocetids, again with striking similarities to both present-day cetaceans and basilosaurids, do have hind limbs attached to their pelvis (and large, paddlelike hind limbs that match their forelimbs); however, the pelvis is not an integral part of the backbone as one would expect for a tetrapod mammal. The ambulocetids, however, do have both paddlelike limbs and an integral pelvis. These fossil species support the hypothesis that modern-day cetaceans descend from four-limbed ancestors through forms similar to these, though these are likely close relatives of the lineage leading to modern cetaceans rather than their direct ancestors (McGowen et al. 2014; Thewissen et al. 2009).

Interestingly, it turns out that present-day cetaceans do have four limbs, but only early in development. Modern cetacean embryos develop forelimb and hind-limb buds at precisely the correct developmental stage that all mammals do (Thewissen et al. 2009). In modern cetaceans, however, hind-limb development is actively halted later in development by a regulatory program that overrides the earlier program for making a hind limb (Thewissen et al. 2006). So, cetaceans are tetrapods, but only for a brief period of their embryonic development. This observation also strongly supports the hypothesis that cetaceans descend from tetrapod ancestors.

Of course, with the advent of molecular biology and **DNA** sequencing, we now have additional ways to test this hypothesis. Indeed, genome sequencing had the potential to completely overthrow evolutionary biology, since this new **technology** could have revealed that species are not genetically related to one another, as evolution predicts. For cetaceans, genome sequencing has revealed that they carry **gene**s devoted to terrestrial manners of life—but that they carry them as only remnants that cannot perform their original function. For example, mammals have a large number of genes that assist in hunting and consuming prey: visual pigments that allow us to see using wavelengths of light that readily transmit through air; protein receptors on our nasal surfaces that bind airborne molecules and transmit impulses perceived as smells; and similar protein receptors expressed on the tongue that sense tastes.

Interestingly, all three classes of these genes in whales are reduced: whales do not have nearly the number of genes for these functions that terrestrial mammals do (Feng et al. 2014; McGowen et al. 2008, 2014). Despite this, whales retain many of the sequences for these genes, except that they are riddled with mutations that remove their function: they cannot be used to see, smell, or taste. The reason for this is relatively straightforward: the enzymes that copy chromosomes do not know the function of the sequences they are copying. They merely attempt to copy all sequences as faithfully as possible.

When errors do occur, as they do (if rarely), the enzymes continue to copy the mutated sequence as faithfully as possible. In this way, the remains of genes (**pseudogenes**) can persist in a lineage for hundreds of thousands of generations before they become unrecognizable. Present-day cetaceans thus retain the remains of genes that make sense for a terrestrial mammal: cetaceans do not rely greatly on vision for hunting (rather, they employ sonar); nor do they greatly rely on air-based odorants to find their prey as terrestrial mammals do, since they hunt in water, not air; and their sense of taste is diminished since they live in a high-salt environment and typically swallow their prey whole rather than chewing it (McGowen et al. 2014). Once again, these observations support the hypothesis that cetaceans descend from tetrapod ancestors and are difficult to explain from a nonevolutionary framework.

Evolution, as a theory, has accurately predicted that we should find evidence that cetaceans descend from terrestrial mammals, and observations from fields as disparate as **paleontology**, embryology, and genetics continue to support this idea.

Evidence for Human Evolution

While there is no evidence that modern cetaceans find their terrestrial origins troubling, Christians commonly find the notion of human evolution unsettling. Nonetheless, there is abundant evidence that our lineage is also the result of an evolutionary process. Just as we have seen with species intermediate between modern whales and terrestrial tetrapods, there are a number of fossil species with features that suggest humans share common ancestors with present-day great apes. While we cannot be certain if any fossil species is a direct ancestor to humans, species such as the various *Ardipithecines*, *Australopithecines*, and non-human *Homo* (*habilis*, *erectus*) are at least close relatives of our lineage (Wood and Lonergan 2008). Interestingly, while Christian antievolution groups agree that some of these species are merely "apes" and others "fully human," they disagree on where to draw the line (Wood 2010): such disagreements, however, are expected if the line is being drawn on what is in fact a gradient (see **Evolution, Biological**).

Even more striking than the evidence from paleontology is recent genomic (i.e., DNA) evidence now that the human genome and several great ape genomes have been sequenced. For example, the initial draft of the chimpanzee genome, when compared to the human genome, showed that 2.7 billion DNA letters (out of a total of about 3–3.1 billion) match with only a 5 percent difference between them (Chimpanzee Sequencing and Analysis Consortium 2005). The identity of genes between our two species is even higher, with more than 99 percent identical at the DNA level; moreover, we have our genes arranged in the same order along our chromosomes, with only a few exceptions caused by chromosome breakage and rejoining (Venema 2010a).

At the gene level, humans and chimpanzees overwhelmingly use the same code for the same genes, even though billions of possible codes exist. For example, the gene that codes for insulin (a small protein hormone used to regulate blood sugar levels) in humans starts with the following 36 DNA "letters," that are translated in sets of three letters, called *codons* into 12 amino acids (represented with abbreviations beneath each codon):

Human: atg gcc ctg tgg atg cgc ctc ctg ccc ctg ctg gcg
Met Ala Leu Trp Met Arg Leu Leu Pro Leu Leu Ala

The chimpanzee gene for insulin differs by just one DNA letter for these 12 codons, and has one amino acid that is different as a result:

Chimpanzee: atg gcc ctg tgg atg cgc ctc ctg ccc ctg
ctg g*tg*

Met Ala Leu Trp Met Arg Leu Leu Pro Leu Leu Val

What is of interest here is that for many amino acids, there are multiple ways for the DNA letter code to specify them. For example, there are four ways to code for alanine (the second amino acid in insulin): GCC, GCA, GCT, and GCG will all work. For leucine, the third amino acid, there are six possible codons: CTA, CTC, CTG, CTT, TTA, and TTG. Yet what we see, time and again, is that humans and chimpanzees use the same codons for the same amino acids. Consider this tiny snippet of the insulin gene: there are many possible codon combinations that would code for these exact same amino acids (with the alternatives shown below the two sequences we observe):

Human: atg gcc ctg tgg atg cgc ctc ctg ccc ctg ctg gcg

Chimpanzee: atg gcc ctg tgg atg cgc ctc ctg ccc ctg
ctg g*tg*

Possible options: atg gcc ctg tgg atg cgc ctc ctg ccc
ctg ctg gcg
a a a a a a a a
g c g g c g c c
t t t t t t t t
tta aga tta tta tta tta
ttg agg ttg ttg ttg ttg

In fact, for this short stretch alone, there are (4^2 x 6^6) = 746,496 possible combinations that would work equally well, yet the one we observe is the most consistent with the hypothesis of shared ancestry (Venema 2014). Recall that human genes and chimpanzee genes are more than 99 percent identical for the entire set: this example, though only a short segment, is representative of the whole. Even if chimpanzee and human genes required their amino acid sequences to match, they need not be so nearly identical at the DNA level (Venema 2010a). This level of correspondence, which goes far beyond what is needed for functionality, is exactly what one would predict if the human and chimpanzee genomes are the slightly modified descendants of what was once a common ancestral genome, just as related languages can be identified due to their shared features (see **Evolution, Biological**).

One interesting feature of genomes is that genes that lose their function due to mutation will still be copied as faithfully as possible. The enzymes that copy DNA do not "know" the function (or lack of function) of the sequences they copy. As such, a gene that loses function due to mutation may remain recognizable for thousands of generations after the mutation event. Mutations that render a gene functionless may be as small as a single DNA letter change: for example, some amino acid codons are only one DNA letter different than a "stop" codon, which tells the cellular machinery to stop adding amino acids to the protein chain as it is translated. A premature stop codon early in a gene's coding sequence will very likely destroy the function of the gene. The DNA sequence for that gene, however, remains virtually identical to the functional version of the gene, and it remains in the same chromosome location, with the same genes as neighbors on either side.

When geneticists began sequencing genomes, they found many examples of such genes in the human genome. For example, many of our olfactory receptor genes (genes expressed on the nasal surface that bind to chemicals in the air and transmit signals to our brains that we sense as smell) have mutations in them that prevent them from being translated into functional proteins (Gilad et al. 2003). This in and of itself is not too surprising, since we know that humans (and primates in general) have a less keen sense of smell than other mammals.

When geneticists began sequencing genomes of other primates, they noticed that many of the genes that are mutated in humans are also mutated in chimpanzees. Not only are the same genes mutated, but they are mutated in exactly the same way, at the exact same location in the gene. There are two possible explanations for this. One is that for some unknown reason, the exact same location in many genes independently mutated in exactly the same way in separate species. The other possibility is that the mutations happened once, in a common ancestral population, and were inherited by humans and chimpanzees because these species descend from that common ancestral population. This explanation is a far more likely one and fits with the observed high identity between the two genomes.

Sequencing the gorilla and orangutan genomes has provided further evidence that humans share common ancestral populations with other apes. We share identical mutations with these species as well (Gilad et al. 2003). Moreover, we observe a particular pattern for these shared mutations. Some mutations we share only with chimpanzees; others we share with chimpanzees and gorillas; and still others we share with all three apes. Those that we share with orangutans we share with gorillas and chimpanzees, and those that we share with gorillas we share with chimpanzees.

What we don't observe is also important—for example, mutations shared with orangutans but not with chimpanzees or gorillas. This pattern is what we would expect if some mutations occurred in the common ancestral population of all four species (and were subsequently inherited by all four); if some mutations occurred in the common ancestral population of humans, chimpanzees, and gorillas after the orangutan lineage split off; and if some mutations occurred in the common ancestral population of humans and chimpanzees after the gorilla lineage split off. We would also expect that, given this pattern of speciation (see **Evolution, Biological**), the human genome would be the most identical to the chimpanzee genome, match the gorilla genome as the second most identical, and match the orangutan genome as the third most identical—and this is precisely what we observe. These two lines of genomic evidence match each other; both the pattern of inactivated genes and overall DNA identity tell the same story: we share common ancestors most recently with chimpanzees, then gorillas, and then orangutans (Locke et al. 2011; Venema 2010a).

Many other examples could be given. Humans lack the ability to synthesize vitamin C, though we have the remains of the gene necessary for making it. Other primates also lack a functional version of this gene, and the mutations removing its function are the same in humans as in other primates (Lachappelle and Drouin 2011). Even more striking, humans have the remains of a gene, vitellogenin, that is used for egg yolk formation in egg-laying organisms even though humans are placental mammals and thus do not require functional vitellogenins at all (Brawand et al. 2008). The remains of this gene in the human genome are located next door to a functional gene, and this same functional gene is also next door to the functional vitellogenin in the chicken genome (Brawand et al. 2008). Explaining these observations apart from evolution is challenging, to say the least (Venema 2010a).

Scientific Objections to Evolutionary Creationism

Though evolution is strongly supported by scientific evidence, EC as a Christian position on origins has been criticized on scientific grounds. For example, scholars associated with the **intelligent design** (ID) movement have put forward two main arguments against evolution: that evolution cannot explain the origin of **information** such as we observe in DNA and that certain biological features are best explained as the products of design because they are inaccessible to

evolutionary mechanisms. We will address these arguments in turn.

The ID information argument against evolution has been advanced primarily by **Stephen Meyer** (Meyer 2009). Meyer argues that our uniform experience is that information is the product of a designing intelligence; therefore, if we observe information, we can conclude that it was designed and not the result of natural processes. Meyer has at times claimed that evolution in general is incapable of generating new information (Meyer 1999; Venema 2010b), and at other times has restricted his argument solely to the origin of biological information, that is, the origin of the DNA codon system at the **origin of life** (Meyer 2009; Venema 2011).

The former argument is easily shown to be inaccurate: processes such as gene duplication and subsequent divergence to new functions (Venema 2010b) or even the direct conversion of noncoding DNA into new protein genes (Kaessmann 2010) are well known. The latter argument, however, is more resistant to critique since it concerns an area of science that is not well characterized (Venema 2011). There are, however, known features about how information is stored in DNA that challenge Meyer's assertion that the DNA codon system is in fact a real code—an arbitrary cypher designed by an intelligent designer apart from an evolutionary process. In the present day, codons are matched with their appropriate amino acids through a linking molecule called a *transfer RNA*. A transfer RNA has three "letters" (called an *anticodon*) that matches and binds to the three DNA letters of each codon. Once an amino acid is attached to a specific transfer RNA, the anticodon specifies that the transfer RNA will bind to the appropriate codon, delivering the correct amino acid when a gene is translated into protein (see **Gene**).

What is interesting is that several amino acids directly bind to their codon (or in some cases, their anticodon). This is strong evidence that the transfer RNA system is a later addition, and that at least a portion of the codon "code" was determined by direct chemical interactions without transfer RNA (Fontecilla-Camps 2014; Yarus et al. 2009). If in fact the codon code is a cypher designed apart from an evolutionary process, there is no reason to expect such chemical affinities to be present, yet Meyer offers no explanation for why the genetic code contains these features (Venema 2011). The origin of the DNA code is an event that occurred more than 3 billion years ago and therefore is difficult to study. Nonetheless, progress continues to be made, and basing apologetics arguments on the confidence that the origin of the DNA code will never be solved is a particular example of a general strategy that has not served the church, nor intelligent design, well in the past (Venema 2011).

A second ID argument against evolutionary mechanisms is the argument from irreducible **complexity** (IC) championed by biochemist Michael Behe (Behe 1996, 39).

> Darwin knew that his theory of gradual evolution by natural selection carried a heavy burden: "If it could be demonstrated that any complex organ existed which could not possibly have been formed by numerous, successive, slight modifications, my theory would absolutely break down."
>
> It is safe to say that most of the scientific skepticism about **Darwinism** in the past century has centered on this requirement … critics of Darwin have suspected that his criterion of failure had been met. But how can we be confident? What type of biological system could not be formed by "numerous, successive, slight modifications"?
>
> Well, for starters, a system that is irreducibly complex. By irreducibly complex I mean a single system composed of several well-matched, interacting parts that contribute to the basic function, wherein the removal of any one of the parts causes the system to effectively cease functioning. An irreducibly complex system cannot be produced directly (that is, by continuously improving the initial function, which continues to work by the same mechanism) by slight, successive modifications of a precursor system, because any precursor to an irreducibly complex system that is missing a part is by definition nonfunctional. An irreducibly complex biological system, if there is such a thing, would be a powerful challenge to Darwinian evolution.

One analogy for an IC system is a stone archway: without each stone present, there is no functional arch; each stone in the arch is needed for the structure to stand; and removing any stone will cause the arch to fall. It is, of course, impossible for an archway to be built directly—there is no way for each stone to be placed into the correct position simultaneously in the absence of other components. As such, we can consider a stone archway to be IC. This analogy, however, also reveals a potential flaw in Behe's argument: archways are constructed using scaffolds that support the stones until all the stones are in place. Behe considers this possibility for biological systems but rejects it (Behe 1996, 40):

> Even if a system is irreducibly complex (and thus cannot have been produced directly), however, one can not

definitively rule out the possibility of an indirect, circuitous route. As the complexity of an interacting system increases, though, the likelihood of such an indirect route drops precipitously. And as the number of unexplained, irreducibly complex biological systems increases, our confidence that Darwin's criterion of failure has been met skyrockets toward the maximum that science allows.

Like Meyer's argument from information, Behe's argument from IC depends on a lack of scientific understanding: Meyer's argument depends on science not understanding how the DNA code arose, and Behe's argument depends on science not understanding the process by which every biologically IC system arose. Behe's argument, then, is similarly vulnerable to advances in scientific knowledge.

While science is far from determining the evolutionary history of every IC system (and will remain so for the foreseeable future), scientists have watched IC systems form. As expected, they employ the biological equivalent of scaffolding. One example is a study of how a virus binds to and then infects its host (Meyer et al. 2012). Originally, this biological system was comprised of a virus protein binding to a host cell protein and a subsequent cascade of protein-protein interactions that allowed the virus to enter the cell and replicate. Removing any of these proteins renders the virus unable to function, confirming that this system of multiple, well-matched parts is in fact IC. In the course of an experiment, however, the virus repeatedly evolved the ability to use a second host cell protein for entry, while maintaining its original abilities. This required four mutations to occur within one of the virus's genes, mutations that happened one after the other and not simultaneously (Meyer et al. 2012).

Interestingly, Behe has argued that this number of mutations is inaccessible to evolutionary mechanisms (Behe 2007), something he fails to mention in his attempt to rebut this study (Behe 2012). Once these mutations were in place, the virus could dispense with the original host protein and use the second one. Thus one IC system (using the first host protein) transitioned through a "scaffolded" intermediate (able to use either host protein) to a new state that was also IC (able to use the new host protein even when the original protein was removed) (Meyer et al. 2012). While this one experiment does not, obviously, provide a detailed account of all IC systems, it demonstrates that Behe's argument can easily be overturned with additional evidence.

In contrast to ID, EC is not threatened by advances in

scientific understanding, since EC views science as a means to understand the mechanisms by which God chose (and chooses) to bring about creation. Therefore EC will likely continue to gain adherents among Christians as evidence for evolution continues to accumulate, the arguments of antievolutionary groups are weighed and found wanting, and advances in exegesis reveal that the setting and context of the biblical creation accounts do not place them in conflict with the findings of modern science.

Dennis R. Venema

REFERENCES AND RECOMMENDED READING

Behe, Michael J. 1996. *Darwin's Black Box: The Biochemical Challenge to Evolution.* New York: Free Press.

———. 2007. *The Edge of Evolution: The Search for the Limits of Darwinism.* New York: Free Press.

———. 2012. "More from Lenski's Lab; Still Spinning Furiously." *Evolution News.* January 30. www.evolutionnews.org/2012/01/more_from_lensk055751.html.

BioLogos. 2016. www.biologos.org/. The BioLogos Foundation is the primary evangelical organization that promotes an Evolutionary Creation view.

Brawand, D., W. Wali, and H. Kaessmann. 2008. "Loss of Egg Yolk Genes in Mammals and the Origin of Lactation and Placentation." *PLOS Biology* 6:507–17.

Chimpanzee Sequencing and Analysis Consortium. 2005. "Initial Sequence of the Chimpanzee Genome and Comparison with the Human Genome." *Nature* 437:69–87.

Collins, Francis. 2006. *The Language of God: A Scientist Presents Evidence for Belief.* New York: Free Press.

Darwin, Charles. 1859. *On the Origin of Species by Means of Natural Selection.* London: John Murray.

Feng, P., J. Zheng, S. Rossiter, D. Wang, and H. Zhao. 2014. "Massive Losses of Taste Receptor Genes in Toothed and Baleen Whales." *Genome Biology and Evolution* 6:1254–65.

Fontecilla-Camps, J. 2014. "The Stereochemical Basis of the Genetic Code and the (Mostly) Autotrophic Origin of Life." *Life* 4:1013–25.

Futuyma, D. J. 2013. *Evolution.* 3rd ed. Sunderland, MA: Sinauer.

Gilad, Y., O. Man, S. Pääbo, and D. Lancet. 2003. "Human Specific Loss of Olfactory Receptor Genes." *Proceedings of the National Academy of Sciences USA* 100:3324–27.

Kaessmann, H. 2010. "Origins, Evolution, and Phenotypic Impact of New Genes." *Genome Research* 20:1313–26.

Lachapelle, M., and G. Drouin. 2011. "Inactivation Dates of the Human and Guinea Pig Vitamin C Genes." *Genetica* 139:199–207.

Lamoureux, D. 2008. *Evolutionary Creation: A Christian Approach to Evolution.* Eugene, OR: Wipf and Stock.

———. 2009. *I Love Jesus and I Accept Evolution.* Eugene, OR: Wipf and Stock.

Livinstone, D. 1984. *Darwin's Forgotten Defenders.* Vancouver: Regent College Publishing.

Locke, D., L. W. Hillier, W. C. Warren, et al. 2011. "Comparative and Demographic Analysis of Orang-utan Genomes." *Nature* 469:529–33.

McGowen, M., C. Clark, and J. Gatesy. 2008. "The Vestigial Olfactory Receptor Subgenome of Odontocete Whales: Phylogenetic Congruence between Gene-Tree Reconciliation and Supermatrix Methods." *Systematic Biology* 57:574–90.

McGowen M., J. Gatesy, and D. Wildman. 2014. "Molecular Evolution Tracks Macroevolutionary Transitions in Cetacea." *Trends in Ecology and Evolution* 29:336–46.

Meyer, J., D. Dobias, J. Weitz, J. Barrick, R. Quick, and R. Lenski. 2012. "Repeatability and Contingency in the Evolution of a Key Innovation in Phage Lambda." *Science* 335:428–32.

Meyer, S. 1999. "Teleological Evolution: The Difference It Doesn't Make." In *Darwinism Defeated? The Johnson-Lamoureux Debate over Biological Origins,* ed. P. Johnson and D. Lamoureux. Vancouver: Regent College Publishing.

———. 2009. *Signature in the Cell: DNA and the Evidence for Intelligent Design.* New York: HarperCollins.

Seeley, R. 1870. *Essays on the Bible.* London: n.p.

Thewissen, J., M. Cohn, L. Stevens, S. Bajpai, J. Heyning, and W. Horton Jr. 2006. "Developmental Basis for Hind Limb Loss in Dolphins and the Origin of the Cetacean Body Plan." *Proceedings of the National Academy of Sciences USA* 103:8414–18.

Thewissen, J., N. Cooper, J. George, and S. Bajpai. 2009. "From Land to Water: The Origin of Whales, Dolphins, and Porpoises." *Evolution Education Outreach* 2:272–88.

Uhen, M. 2010. "The Origin(s) of Whales." *Annual Review of Earth and Planetary Sciences* 38:189–219.

Venema, D. 2010a. "Genesis and the Genome: Genomics Evidence for Human-Ape Common Ancestry and Ancestral Hominid Population Sizes." *Perspectives on Science and Christian Faith* 62:166–78.

———. 2010b. "Seeking a Signature: Essay Book Review of *Signature in the Cell: DNA and the Evidence for Intelligent Design* by Stephen C. Meyer." *Perspectives on Science and Christian Faith* 62:276–83.

———. 2011. "Intelligent Design, Abiogenesis, and Learning from History: A Reply to Meyer." *Perspectives on Science and Christian Faith* 63:183–92.

———. 2014. "Intelligent Design and Common Ancestry." Biologos Foundation. March 27. http://biologos.org/blogs/dennis-venema-letters-to-the-duchess/series/intelligent-design-and-common-ancestry=part=1.

Walton, John. 2009. *The Lost World of Genesis One: Ancient Cosmology and the Origins Debate.* Downers Grove, IL: InterVarsity.

Wood, B., and N. Lonergan. 2008. "The Hominin Fossil Record: Taxa, Grades and Clades." *Journal of Anatomy* 212:354–76.

Wood, T. 2010. "Baraminological Analysis Places *Homo habilis, Homo rudolfensis,* and *Australopithecus sediba* in the Human Holobaramin." *Answers Research Journal* 3:71–90.

Yarus, M., J. Widmann, and R. Knight. 2009. "RNA–Amino Acid Binding: A Stereochemical Era for the Genetic Code." *Journal of Molecular Evolution* 69:406–29.

EXISTENCE OF GOD. The belief that God exists continues to be widely held among both academics and nonacademics, among scientists and laypersons. Many reasons and evidences for the existence of God have been propounded, including advanced scientific ones. The focus of this entry will be on arguments for the existence of God in which science has played a role.

One argument type that has a long and rich history is the **cosmological argument**. Utilizing a general structure of reasoning (*logos*), this argument makes an inference from certain facts about the universe (*cosmos*) to the existence of a reality beyond the universe, which is generally understood to be God. One kind of fact utilized is that there are things (events or entities) in the universe whose existence is contingent, which means that such things do not contain within themselves the reason for their existence. Instead, they receive their existence from something external to them.

Furthermore, it is argued that all of the constituents that make up the universe are contingent; all of them could have been different, or all of them could have not existed at all. From these facts, the argument goes, it can be inferred that a noncontingent or necessary cause exists that brought the universe into existence. The argument can be expressed propositionally this way:

1. Everything that exists has a cause of its existence, either within itself or by something external to itself.
2. If the universe has a cause of its existence, that cause is God.
3. The universe exists.
4. Therefore, the cause of the existence of the universe is God.

Both of the first two premises have been challenged, although the first one is widely affirmed. In fact, the **scientific method** and the very practice of science seem to depend on it being true. A well-known response to the second premise was offered by **David Hume** who argued that if each of the parts of a thing has an explanation for its existence, then the existence of the whole is also explained. In one sense this is true, such that the existence of a city can be explained by the existence of each of the constituents of the city (the city exists because there exists in a certain location at a certain time a school, a mayor, a town board, a police force, a population, and so on).

Yet, in another sense this point can be challenged. For when the existence of a constituent of a whole is explained by reference to other constituents of that whole (a police force exists because a part of the population consists of police officers), it does not follow that the whole has been fully explained, since the existence of the contingent constituents that make up the whole are not themselves explained. With respect to the universe, the argument goes, a series of contingent things, no matter how vast, is itself still contingent, and thus dependent on something else (i.e., a noncontingent, necessary cause—namely, God).

Another version of the cosmological argument is the kalam argument, which has roots in medieval Arabic philosophy and theology (the term *kalam* is Arabic for "word" but commonly refers to Islamic medieval **natural theology**). According to this argument, there must be a beginning cause of the universe that is itself external to the universe. Unlike the previous version of the cosmological argument, the kalam does not contend that *everything* that exists must have a cause. Rather, it argues that whatever *begins* to exist

must have a cause. Since the universe itself began to exist, it must have a cause external to it. Furthermore, the argument goes, that cause must be personal. The argument can be expressed propositionally this way:

1. Everything that begins to exist has a cause of its existence.
2. The universe began to exist.
3. Therefore the universe has a cause of its existence.
4. Since no scientific explanation (in terms of natural laws) can provide a causal account of the origin of the universe, the cause must be a personal agent, which we call God.

The first premise is widely held, although objections have been raised to it, including those based on **quantum physics**. At the quantum level, some argue, cause and effect operate differently than at higher levels. The nature of quantum events, and whether they are completely devoid of causal conditions, is a matter of current scientific and philosophical debate (see **Quantum Theory, Interpretations of**). Regarding the second premise, philosophical arguments and scientific evidences have been marshaled in support of it. Philosophically, for example, it is argued that an infinite past is impossible, for if an infinite number of prior events had to occur before the present one, the present one would never arrive. But if the universe were eternal, then it would have an infinite past. So the universe must not be eternal. Furthermore, two widely held scientific theories, the **big bang theory** and the **second law of thermodynamics**, tend to support the origin of the universe in the finite past.

One recent challenge to the origin of the universe in the finite past is that, given the theory of relativity, the **big bang** is not an event after all, for there is neither time prior to the big bang nor a space in which the big bang occurs. How to understand the big bang with respect to the theory of relativity is a matter of ongoing debate among scientists and philosophers of science.

A second type of argument for the existence of God is the design, or teleological, argument (see **Teleological Argument**). There are many versions of it, all of which utilize a general structure of reasoning (*logos*) to make an inference from certain features of the natural world that reflect design, purpose, and goal-oriented intelligence (*telos*) to the existence of a grand designer, God. One version of the argument focuses on the apparent fine-tuning of the universe and can be expressed propositionally this way:

1. The fine-tuning of the universe is due either to physical necessity, **chance**, or design.
2. It is not due to physical necessity or chance.
3. Therefore it is due to design.

In support of the argument, it has been claimed that a number of physical constants of the universe appear to be finely tuned for a life-permitting universe. One of the dozens of examples of these seemingly finely tuned constants is the strong nuclear force that binds together the subatomic particles (protons and neutrons) of the nucleus. If this constant were different by 0.4 percent, there would not be enough of one or the other for life to exist, for variability either way would destroy most of the carbon or oxygen in the stars.

One response to the fine-tuning argument is the **anthropic principle** according to which, if the physical constants were varied to any significant degree, there would be no conscious observers to notice. Given that observers (like us) do exist, it is not surprising that the constants are the way they are. One way of accounting for such observers is the many worlds hypothesis, according to which there exist a large number of universes, perhaps an infinite number of them. While most of these universes likely include life-prohibiting parameters, at least a minimal number of them would probably include life-permitting ones. So it should not be surprising that one of them, ours in this case, is life permitting. Much of the current discussion about the fine-tuning argument turns on the plausibility of the anthropic principle and the many worlds hypothesis.

Other important arguments for the existence of God include the ontological argument, the moral argument (see **Morality**), and the **argument from reason**.

Chad Meister

REFERENCES AND RECOMMENDED READING

Craig, William Lane, and Quentin Smith. 1993. *Theism, Atheism, and Big Bang Cosmology*. New York: Oxford University Press.
Hume, David. (1779) 1998. *Dialogues concerning Natural Religion*, ed. Richard Popkin. Indianapolis: Hackett.
Oppy, Graham. 2006. *Arguing about Gods*. Cambridge: Cambridge University Press.
Swinburne, Richard. 2004. *The Existence of God*. 2nd ed. Oxford: Clarendon.

Recent versions of the cosmological (David Oderberg), teleological (Robin Collins), ontological (E. J. Lowe), and moral (Paul Copan) arguments can be found in *The Routledge Companion to Philosophy of Religion*, 2nd ed., ed. Chad Meister and Paul Copan. London: Routledge, 2012. Recent versions of arguments against the existence of God are also included.

EXPLANATION. Central to the appeal of science is its ability to offer convincing explanations of natural phenomena. For **Aristotle**, the explanation of particular events was committed to realism: it depended on the identification of the real causes in the essential properties of substances. In the twentieth century, when Carl Hempel made explanation a recognized subdivision in the **philosophy of science** (Hempel 1965; Hempel and Oppenheim 1948), many philosophers held antirealist views and sought to analyze explanation as a formal relation between sentences, thus sidestepping metaphysical commitments.

Inspired by the **paradigm** of logical **empiricism**, Hempel saw explanation as a kind of logical argument that related a set of explanatory sentences (the *explanans*) to a sentence to be explained (the *explanandum*). He claimed that the *explanans* must be true and contain at least one law as well as descriptions of relevant particular facts. He distinguished explanation by strict laws (the deductive-nomological [D-N] model, in which the *explanandum* is entailed by the *explanans*) from explanation by statistical laws—the inductive-statistical (I-S) model, in which the *explanans* makes the *explanandum* probable. Hempel's view entails that explanation and prediction are symmetrical: a correct explanation of an event also allows us to predict it.

Unfortunately, philosophers of science soon showed that Hempel's requirements are not sufficient for explanation (Salmon 2006). Given geometrical laws and the length of its shadow, we can deduce the height of a flagpole, but the shadow does not explain the flagpole's height. It might be a law (strict or statistical) that whenever air pressure drops, Joe's arthritis flares up and then a storm comes, so we can deduce that a storm will come from an *explanans* including the law plus the fact that Joe's arthritis flared up. But Joe's arthritis pain does not contribute to explaining the storm. And it is a law that men who take birth-control pills do not get pregnant, but their taking the pills does not explain their not getting pregnant.

Arguably, Hempel's conditions are also not necessary to be an explanation. One can surely explain a puddle of coffee by citing a person accidentally knocking over a cup without specifying the relevant laws. Hempel thought such an "explanation" was an elliptical sketch, but in cases where we do not yet know the laws, it would be odd to say we could give no explanation. A further problem is that not all explanations are predictive. Smoking does not predict cancer (it does not make it probable): it only *raises* the **probability** of cancer. Yet, in a particular case, smoking may contribute to an explanation of a person's cancer.

The common weakness all of these counterexamples expose is that Hempel does not require a substantive (non-logical) relation between the *explanans* and the *explanandum*. Salmon concluded that explanations are not merely formal arguments but depend on objective connections between events; for example, one event may increase the probability of another. Initially, Salmon proposed statistical-relevance (S-R) as the appropriate relation (Salmon 1970). An *explanans* can be statistically relevant to an *explanandum* without making it probable (as in the smoking case).

Developing the idea of *screening off*, Salmon showed that the counterexamples to Hempel could be avoided by showing that they cited statistically irrelevant factors. For example, the probability that a storm is coming given a drop in air pressure is unchanged whether or not Joe's arthritis flares up, but the probability that a storm is coming given that Joe's arthritis flares up does depend on whether there is a drop in air pressure (after all, Joe's arthritis might flare up for a different reason, but a storm isn't likely without the atmospheric change). So Joe's arthritis pain is screened off. Likewise, the true explanation of the height of a flagpole (its purchaser wanted one that high) will screen off the shadow as a possible explanation, since the flagpole would have that height even if it cast no shadow.

However, critics pointed out that explanation does not always track statistical relevance. Suppose we develop birth-control pills that are perfectly effective: then there is no statistical difference in the tendency to become pregnant between women who take the pill and men. Yet the explanation of nonpregnancy is certainly different in the two cases (McGrew et al. 2009, 523). Examples like these led Salmon to conclude that nothing less than a causal relation sufficed for explanation (Salmon 1978). In his causal-mechanical (C-M) model, explanations depend on the interactions of causal processes, and this approach seems to easily dispose of the standard counterexamples to Hempel. A flagpole's shadow clearly does not cause the flagpole to have the height that it does; Joe's arthritis flare-up does not cause a storm to come, and a man's taking birth-control pills does not cause him not to become pregnant.

Though plausible, Salmon's account also has problems. It does not tell us *which* factors in a causal network are salient. For example, Kant's waking up is part of the causal network leading to his writing *The Critique of Pure Reason* but hardly

an illuminating explanation. Also, within science, not all explanations are causal: we sometimes explain one law as a special case of another via a purely logical-mathematical derivation. But more profoundly, antirealists reject Salmon's account because it requires a metaphysical commitment to causes and because it ignores important pragmatic questions, such as "Why do we ask for explanations?" and "What counts as a good explanation for a particular enquirer?"

Philip Kitcher (1981, 1989) argued that the pragmatic purpose of explanation is to find an account that unifies as many phenomena as possible. **Newton**'s theory is a good explanation because a few simple principles reveal a hidden unity behind such apparently diverse phenomena as planetary orbits, the tides, and the path of projectiles. In general, Kitcher suggests a good explanation is an argument pattern with many similar arguments as instances. In this way, he can easily show that shadows, arthritis flare-ups, and birth-control pills for men do not provide simple, unifying explanations.

But like Hempel's theory, Kitcher's antirealist theory does not require a causal connection or clearly distinguish explanation and prediction. Realists like Ian Hacking (1983) maintain that **inference to the best explanation** (see Lipton 2004) helps us to approximate the real structure of **nature**, but antirealists like van Fraassen (1980) note that the best explanation can still be false and suggest that empirical adequacy is enough. He suggests we understand explanation pragmatically—as an answer to a "why" question. An enquirer wants to know why X rather than some alternative to X in a contrast class. A good answer depends on what the enquirer already knows and in that sense is subjective. Thus "Water is wet" might be a good explanation for Joe's being wet to someone from an ice world, but it is not helpful to us. In a similar vein, Achinstein analyzes the ordinary-language use of explanation, suggesting it is an illocutionary act in which the explainer's intention causes an utterance that produces knowledge in the recipient (Achinstein 1983, 2010). However, this view is unacceptable to antirealists because it assumes objective causes.

At present the only consensus is that Hempel's original account of explanation was inadequate. The ongoing debate between proponents of rival accounts largely reflects the underlying, perennial opposition between realism and antirealism.

Angus J. L. Menuge

REFERENCES AND RECOMMENDED READING

Achinstein, Peter. 1983. *The Nature of Explanation*. New York: Oxford University Press.

———. 2010. *Evidence, Explanation and Realism.* New York: Oxford University Press.

Hacking, Ian. 1983. *Representing and Intervening.* New York: Cambridge University Press.

Hempel, Carl C. 1965. *Aspects of Scientific Explanation and Other Essays in the Philosophy of Science.* New York: Free Press.

Hempel, Carl C., and P. Oppenheim. 1948. "Studies in the Logic of Explanation." *Philosophy of Science* 15:135–75.

Kitcher, P. 1981. "Explanatory Unification." *Philosophy of Science* 48:507–31.

———. 1989. "Explanatory Unification and the Causal Structure of the World." In *Scientific Explanation*, ed. P. Kitcher and W. C. Salmon, 410–505. Minneapolis: University of Minnesota Press.

Lipton, P. 2004. *Inference to the Best Explanation.* 2nd ed. New York: Routledge.

McGrew, Timothy, Marc Alspector Kelly, and Fritz Allhoff, eds. 2009. *Philosophy of Science: An Historical Anthology.* Malden, MA: Wiley-Blackwell.

Pitt, Joseph C., ed. 1988. *Theories of Explanation.* New York: Oxford University Press.

Rubin, David-Hillel, ed. 1993. *Explanation.* New York: Oxford University Press.

———. 2012. *Explaining Explanation.* 2nd updated and exp. ed. Boulder, CO: Paradigm.

Salmon, Wesley C. 1970. "Statistical Explanation and Statistical Relevance." In *The Nature and Function of Scientific Theories*, ed. Robert G. Colodny, 171–231. Pittsburgh: University of Pittsburgh Press.

———. 1978. "Why Ask, 'Why?' An Inquiry Concerning Scientific Explanation." *Proceeding and Addresses of the American Philosophical Association* 51 (6): 683–705.

———. 2006. *Four Decades of Scientific Explanation.* Pittsburgh: University of Pittsburgh Press.

Strevens, Michael. 2011. *Depth: An Account of Scientific Explanation.* Cambridge, MA: Harvard University Press.

van Fraassen, Bas C. 1980. *The Scientific Image.* Oxford: Clarendon.

———. 1989. *Laws and Symmetry.* Oxford: Clarendon.

EXTINCTION. Extinction refers to the termination of a biological species' existence. Fossils, prior to the seventeenth century, were regarded as natural or supernatural curiosities. Robert Hooke (1635–1703) demonstrated that fossils were the remains of ancient life on earth, and he suspected that some fossils had no living counterparts. Anatomist Georges Cuvier (1769–1832) determined that mammoths and mastodons were varieties of extinct fossil elephants. As geologists established the relative order of strata across Britain and Western Europe, they recognized a *fossil succession* in which different sets of fossils occupied the various formations (see **Fossil Record**).

Great numbers of **species** disappear from the fossil record during mass extinctions. Based on precision **radiometric dating** of the rock record, typical individual species appear to survive from between 2 to 4 million years and genera to survive from 5 to 20 million years. By the 1980s, a global database of fossil ranges allowed paleontologists to track the number of taxonomic families and genera known in the fossil record over the past 600 million years. Those data reveal the statistical background rate for animal extinctions of about two to five families per million years and identify five major mass extinctions resulting in sudden disappearances of between 50 and 85 percent of known genera (Raup and Sepkoski 1982; Sepkoski 1981).

The end Permian Period event (252 million years ago) involved the extinction of 96 percent of all marine species and 70 percent of terrestrial vertebrate species. Victims of the end Cretaceous event (66 million years ago) included the **dinosaurs**, flying and swimming reptiles, many groups of marine mollusks and plankton, and many terrestrial plant and insect species (note: many paleontologists consider birds surviving dinosaurs). Evidence for causes of the major mass extinctions point to global disruptions of climate and ecosystems resulting from extraordinary volcanic activity, sea level change, or cosmic impacts. About 12,000 years ago, large ice age mammals, including mammoths, mastodons, short-faced bear, and giant beaver vanished. Estimates of modern extinction rates, apparently accelerated by human activity, range from 30,000 to 140,000 species per year.

The concept of species extinction was controversial when proposed because of prevailing philosophical and religious ideas about the continuity of life. The Neoplatonist concept of a Great Chain of Being described the continuum of life-forms from highest to lowest, coexisting in plentitude. This outlook informed the pre-Darwin, evolutionary view of Jean-Baptiste de Lamarck (1744–1829), in which extinctions are inconsistent with gradual and continuous change from species to species (Rudwick 1972). Cuvier believed that extinctions were consistent with the idea of global revolutions in earth history reflected in biblical and other ancient records of catastrophes.

Charles Darwin (1809–82) accepted extinction in evolutionary species succession, but he rejected the concept of mass extinctions. Extinctions appeared to challenge the idea of a "good" creation with creatures made to be fruitful and multiply (specifically referring to marine life and birds in Gen. 1:20–22). **The flood** narrative in Genesis tells of how the ark would preserve "two of all living creatures, male and female" (Gen. 6:19) and how the survivors would "multiply on the earth and be fruitful and increase in number on it" (Gen. 8:17). Modern young-earth creationists hold that extinctions are simply the record of species being destroyed during the Genesis flood (despite the promise of Gen. 8:17) and that extinctions over millions of years are inconsistent with a recent creation and the introduction of physical death only after the fall (Gen. 2:17; 3:19; see **Death; Fall, The**).

Stephen O. Moshier

REFERENCES AND RECOMMENDED READING

Raup, D. M. 1994. "The Role of Extinction in Evolution." *Proceedings of the National Academy of Sciences USA* 91:6758–63.

Raup, D. M, and J. J. Sepkoski Jr. 1982. "Mass Extinctions in the Marine Fossil Record." *Science* 215 (4539): 1501–3.

Rudwick, M. J. S. 1972. *The Meaning of Fossils: Episodes in the History of Palaeontology.* 2nd ed. Chicago: University of Chicago Press.

Sepkoski, J. J., Jr. 1981. "A Factor Analytic Description of the Phanerozoic Marine Fossil Record." *Paleobiology* 7:36–53.

EXTRATERRESTRIAL LIFE. The subject of much popular interest, the question of extraterrestrial life is also a source of serious scientific and theological debate. The general issue may be broken down to three main questions: Do extraterrestrial life-forms (ETs) exist? If so, are there intelligent ETs? And, if so, can we make contact with them?

When addressing these questions, scholars typically employ the Drake equation, developed in the early 1960s by astronomer Frank Drake. The formula is as follows: $N = R^* \cdot f_p \cdot n_e \cdot f_l \cdot f_i \cdot f_c \cdot L$, where N = the number of communicative civilizations, R^* = the rate of formation of suitable stars, f_p = the fraction of those stars with planets, n_e = the number of earthlike (habitable) planets per planetary system, f_l = the fraction of those planets where life develops, f_i = the fraction of life sites where intelligence develops, f_c = the fraction of intelligent life sites where **technology** develops, and L = the lifetime of communicative civilizations.

Scholarly opinions vary, but some are confident that ETs exist in high numbers. For example, philosopher Paul Churchland estimates that intelligent life-forms have emerged in as many as 10^6 planets in our galaxy alone. However, even if this figure is accepted, that does not mean we should expect ET contact, for several reasons. The likelihood of such contact is considerably diminished by spatial scatter, temporal scatter, and potential life-form variation.

With regard to the first of these factors, the planets in our galaxy are spread out over 10^{14} cubic light-years, making the average distance between the planets approximately 500 light-years. Even more important is temporal scatter. Presumably, intelligent life-forms do not all emerge simultaneously. And among our intelligent ET contemporaries, many of these will not be as technologically advanced as we are. Lastly, the physical characteristics of some alien intelligences might make contact impossible or less likely. Still, many scientists believe it is reasonable to expect contact with intelligent ETs. In view of this, the **SETI** (Search for Extraterrestrial Intelligence) Research Center was launched in 1985. SETI employs dozens of research scientists and is devoted not only to making contact with ETs but also to understanding the **origin of life** in the universe.

Proponents of the rare earth hypothesis demur at the notion that ETs are common throughout the cosmos. For instance, Peter Ward and Donald Brownlee have argued that given the biological requirements and the hostility of the cosmos to complex life-forms, we should expect highly developed life-forms to be very rare, if they exist elsewhere in the universe at all (Ward and Brownlee 2000).

These issues beg theological questions. Christian theologians are divided on the issue of ETs for various reasons. Some are skeptical because the Scriptures are anthropocentric. However, this is to be expected regardless of whether ETs exist. For the thesis that humans have a central place in God's plan for earth history does not imply that humans have a central place in God's plan for *cosmic* history. Some major Christian scholars, including Paul Tillich and **C. S. Lewis**, have entertained the possibility of ETs precisely because of their belief in divine creativity. Thus some argue that given the immense diversity of life-forms on our planet, we should likewise expect diversity of life-forms throughout our universe. Such are some of the questions explored in the new field known as astrotheology.

James S. Spiegel

REFERENCES AND RECOMMENDED READING

Lewis, C. S. 2013. *The Space Trilogy.* New York: HarperCollins.

Sagan, Carl. 1980. *Cosmos.* New York: Random House.

Shostak, Seth. 1998. *Sharing the Universe: Perspectives on Extraterrestrial Life.* Landsdowne, PA: Lansdowne.

Tillich, Paul. 1963. *Systematic Theology.* Vol. 3. Chicago: University of Chicago Press.

Vakoch, Douglas A., ed. 2013. *Extraterrestrial Altruism: Evolution and Ethics in the Cosmos.* New York: Springer.

Ward, Peter D., and Donald Brownlee. 2000. *Rare Earth: Why Complex Life Is Uncommon in the Universe.* New York: Copernicus.

Wilkinson, David. 2013. *Science, Religion, and the Search for Extraterrestrial Intelligence.* Oxford: Oxford University Press.

F

⚓ FALL, THE (Evolutionary View). The fall, as used in Christian theology, refers to humanity's transition from the enjoyment of God's blessing to a state of sin in which men and women are alienated from intimate relationship with their Creator. This fall has been understood as a fall from grace or innocence, and the story of this transition is given in Genesis 3. The Bible itself never refers to this story as "the fall"; Galatians 5:4, which does refer to a "fall from grace," applies the phrase to those who try to find relationship with God in keeping the law and is not a reference back to the event in Genesis 3.

Though not a biblical phrase, the fall is still a convenient shorthand to refer to the Genesis 3 happenings, though we will also use other terms (e.g., "the rebellion") to refer to it. The story of the fall has entered the discussion concerning the relationship between the Bible and science particularly as concerns the issues of evolution and the historical Adam. Does the scientific theory of evolution, which today entails the understanding that humanity finds its origin, not in a single pair of *Homo sapiens* but in an original population numbered in the thousands (Venema 2010), undermine the biblical account of the fall? I will argue that there is no necessary contradiction between the account of the fall and science if one properly recognizes the intended claims of the biblical story.

The Biblical Story of the Fall

We begin with an account of the fall as we find it in Genesis 3. The two creation accounts of Genesis 1 and 2 (technically 1:1–2:4a and 2:4b–25) provide the background to the fall, particularly the second account, which focuses on the creation of the first two humans who may not be named in the account (*adam* can simply mean "human" and is clearly not used as a personal name until Genesis 4:25; the woman is first called "Eve" in 3:20). The first man is created from the dust of the ground and the breath of God (2:7), while the first woman is created from the man's side or rib (2:21–23).

I have elsewhere argued that many elements of the story of the creation of the first two humans (dust, breath of God, rib) are best understood as figurative descriptions that have theological significance (see **Adam and Eve**; **Genesis, Book of**). The important point for this essay is that Genesis 2

intends to teach that human beings when first created were innocent creatures who lived in a harmonious relationship with God and thus with each other and with creation. In a word, they lived in a blessed condition. This condition changed radically according to the story found in Genesis 3.

The chapter opens with the abrupt appearance of the **serpent**, who asks the woman, "Did God really say, 'You must not eat from any tree in the garden'?" (3:1). The serpent's appearance in the garden is a surprise to the reader because the narrator does not describe him or explain his appearance. The original readers likely would have immediately recognized the serpent as a representation of evil since walking serpents were well-known symbols of evil in the ancient Near East (see **Serpent**). The serpent's appearance is also a surprise since God had charged Adam and Eve to "work" and "take care" of the garden (2:15). The second verb (*shamar*) certainly implies "guarding" the garden since that is one of the primary meanings of the Hebrew word.

But neither Adam nor Eve guards the garden. The serpent not only finds entry, but Eve engages him in a discussion and Adam sadly remains silent through the whole interchange ("her husband, who was with her," 3:6).

The serpent's opening question is ridiculous on the surface of it since, if the answer to his question was affirmative, then Adam and Eve would starve. But rather than simply ignore the serpent and shoo him out of the garden, Eve dignifies him with an answer and thus opens herself up to persuasion. She explains to the serpent that God has permitted them to eat of the fruit of all the trees with the exception of the fruit of the tree of the knowledge of good and evil. She says that God told them to refrain from eating and touching the fruit of that particular tree.

The prohibition was given to Adam before Eve was created and did not forbid touching the tree, thus Eve adds to God's command, making her the first legalist who tries to guard God's law by adding additional provisions. In the original command, God warned Adam that if he broke the command, "you will certainly die" (Gen. 2:17), and Eve, in her response to the serpent, makes it clear that she understood the consequences of disobedience.

The serpent, however, ridicules God's command and entices Eve with the promise that eating the fruit would open their eyes and make them wise. She allows herself to be persuaded, and she eats the fruit and gives some to Adam, who eats the fruit without argument, and their eyes are indeed opened. However, their newfound "wisdom" does not have a happy, but rather a sad, consequence as they both hurriedly cover their nakedness from each other.

At the end of Genesis 2, the man and the woman stand naked before each other and feel no shame. This attitude of physical openness and vulnerability to each other represents also a psychological, spiritual, and emotional wholeness. Their act of rebellion against God's command severs their relationship with God, which then immediately leads to alienation from each other.

But before proceeding with the story, we must pause here to consider what was at stake when God forbade Adam and Eve from eating the fruit from the tree of the knowledge of good and evil. In what way would eating the tree impart knowledge of good and evil? In an important sense, they already had knowledge of what was good and what was evil. They knew it was evil to eat from the tree. However, in the Hebrew Bible, knowledge is more than intellectual comprehension; it implies experience. In the decision to eat the forbidden fruit, Adam and Eve relegated to themselves and not to God the right to define what was good and what was evil. In other words, they rejected God's authority to define moral categories, and they asserted their own moral autonomy.

The consequences were disastrous. We have already seen that Adam and Eve could no longer stand naked in front of each other, but then God levies other specific punishments on each of the evil actors in the story. When God confronts the man and then the woman, they each point the finger of blame at another, but God understands that they are all guilty and thus punishes them all.

God turns the walking serpent into a slithering one and declares that there will be perpetual war between him and his offspring and the woman and hers. The New Testament sees the fulfillment of this punishment in the struggle between those who follow evil and those who follow God. God also informs the serpent that he will ultimately be vanquished, and the New Testament understands this victory to take place when Christ defeats the serpent on the cross (Gen. 3:15; Rom. 16:20; Rev. 12:9). God punishes the woman by troubling her relationships with those dearest to her. He will increase her pain in childbearing (notice that this phrase implies that there was pain before the fall), she will desire her husband, but he will rule over her. Her desire for her husband has rightly been identified as a desire to control, not a romantic desire (Foh 1974–75), and thus we have here an explanation of the struggle between men and women that has persisted through the millennia. God then punishes Adam in the area of work. There was, of course, work before the fall (the garden was not going to "take care" of itself, and the world outside the garden required "subduing"), but now work would be frustrating (3:17–19). Finally, they are ejected from the garden, separated from eating from the tree of life, and thus **death** is introduced into the world. While physical death does not come as an immediate consequence of eating the forbidden fruit, spiritual death comes since their relationship with God is severed and physical death now becomes inevitable.

The Fall in Later Scripture

Old Testament

Considering the important place of Genesis 3 in the thought of Paul in the New Testament and its consequent role in the development of Christian doctrine, it is surprising to see how rarely later Old Testament books refer back to this story, for that matter, to the creation story. It is clear that humans continue to sin and suffer God's displeasure, but no later Old Testament author looks back to Adam and Eve to explain the presence of sin, or of guilt and death, in the world. Indeed, outside of Genesis 1–5, Adam is named only once in the Old Testament, and there at the head of a genealogy (Hos. 6:7 is a reference to a town named Adam). The absence of reference to the story of the first rebellion in the Old Testament is the reason why a doctrine of **original sin** is missing from Jewish thought (with extremely rare exception; Zevit 2013, 3–27). While certain Jewish books in the immediate pre-Christian era, probably under the influence of Hellenistic ideas, did speak of the effect of Adam (and especially Eve's) sin on later humanity (2 Bar. 48:42–43; Ben Sirah 25:24–26), this line of thinking fell out of favor with the rise of rabbinic Judaism in the early centuries AD (Zevit 2013, 9–10). Thus we move on to the New Testament's appropriation of the story of Genesis 3.

New Testament

Far from the only allusion to the fall (see, e.g., Rom. 8:18–25, which speaks of the creation that had been subjected to frustration), the most significant passage for the subject of the fall is found in Romans 5:12–21. Not surprisingly, the interpretation of this profound and complex passage is contested. At the heart of Paul's argument is an analogy between

Adam and Christ. Through Adam, sin and death have been introduced into the world through his trespass, while through the gracious act of Jesus came the gift of justification. So whereas through Adam came condemnation, through Jesus came "justification and life" (5:18). Later we will consider whether or not the analogy between Adam and Jesus here depends on Adam being a historical individual who is the first human; now we are interested in Adam's significance as the one who introduced sin and death into the world.

Our first observation is that Paul teaches that Adam introduced sin and death into the world. He does not say that Adam introduced guilt into the world; in other words, the point is not that Adam's sin makes people guilty. The story of Adam is the account of innocent humanity's rebellion against God (and thus the first sin) and also the introduction of death into the human experience for the first time. But nowhere does Paul claim that Adam's sin makes anyone other than Adam guilty before God. As a matter of fact, Paul is quite clear that "death came to all people, because all sinned" (5:12), not because Adam sinned. The misconception that we are guilty because of Adam's sin arose due to Augustine, who misunderstood and mistranslated Romans 5:12 as saying that death came to all Adam's later descendants because it is he, "in whom all sinned" (Hays and Herring 2013). Augustine introduced an understanding of original sin that required what today we would call a genetic connection to Adam that spread to his later descendants like a disease.

That said, there is a sense in which "the many died by the trespass of the one man" (5:15) and "the judgment followed one sin and brought condemnation" (5:16; see also vv. 18–19). What is clear from reading Paul is that all humans without exception are sinners, but Paul does not specify how that works, so we are left to speculate. Why is it, as the doctrine of original sin rightly asserts, that the Bible teaches that humans are sinful from birth (the idea of innocent children is not biblical) and that it is impossible for humans not to sin?

As we said, a genetic or inheritance model of original sin is not necessary to preserve the doctrine of original sin and indeed introduces a concept of "alien guilt." The idea of guilt inherited from Adam means a person is condemned because of the act of another, which seems patently unfair. No, each person is guilty for her or his own sin.

So what is the relationship between Adam and Eve's story and my own sin, guilt, and death? In the first place, we can say that Adam and Eve did what we all would do

in the same situation. Apart from Christ's grace, each of us asserts his or her own moral autonomy. In addition, the first sin that introduced death into the world so affected the social, indeed, the cosmic order (Rom. 8:18–25), that it is forever impossible not to sin. Our natural propensity to rebel and the disordered nature of humanity and the creation mean that "all have sinned and fall short of the glory of God" (Rom. 3:23).

Evolution and the Fall

Can one hold to the traditional doctrine of the fall and also affirm evolutionary theory? Some theologians say no, and they fall roughly into two groups. On the one hand, certain theologians argue that if the Bible is true, then evolution is wrong, no matter how strong the evidence. They believe that the doctrines of the fall and original sin depend on God's special act of creating an original historical couple. This describes the view of all young-earth creationists and many old-earth creationists (see **Creationism, Old-Earth**; **Creationism, Young-Earth**). Others say that since evolution is true, then the Bible must be wrong at least in part. There is quite a disparity in this second opinion. On the one hand, there are scholars who affirm the theology of the text but not the history (Enns 2012; Schneider 2010, 2012) and others who believe the evidence leads to atheism (Dawkins 2008).

My view is that there is no necessary contradiction between the traditional doctrine and evolution. Genesis 1–3 is compatible with science as are the New Testament author's reflections on this story. In terms of the latter, we will return our focus to Romans 5:12–21, since this text is widely regarded as the most problematic for those who reject the view of **Evolutionary Creationism** and accept the possibility that there may not have been a historical Adam.

If we read Genesis closely in its ancient context, we recognize textual signals that, while Genesis 1–3 does make broad historical claims, it does not intend to give us historical detail in a precise literal way (for details, see **Genesis, Book of**). The broad historical claims include that God created everything and everyone. However, Genesis 1–3 does not intend to tell us how God created the cosmos and humanity, since the process focuses not on material creation but on how God brings functionality into the cosmos. In addition, we note the pervasive use of figurative language, interplay with ancient Near Eastern creation stories, and a lack of sequence concord. Since the biblical authors are not interested in telling us how God created creation, we can turn to science to answer that question.

But what are the historical claims of the story of the fall in Genesis 3? Genesis 2 makes it clear that God created humans morally innocent and capable of moral choice. Perhaps here we are to think that God used and guided the evolutionary process to produced *homo sapiens*, and when *homo sapiens* emerged from their primate past, God conferred the status of image bearer on them (see **Image of God**). They now represented God on earth and reflected his glory. They were then charged to rule and subdue the earth.

However, rather than obeying their Creator, they rebelled against him. In order to take Genesis 3 seriously, one must insist on a historical fall. An additional complication arises from the scientific community because biologists are convinced that human beings do not descend from a primeval couple, but rather from an original group that numbered some few thousand individuals. How can one think of Adam and Eve if this scientific consensus is true?

Some respond by saying that Adam and Eve are a representative couple within this population of humans, perhaps something akin to royal or priestly figures (Wright 2015), while others allow for the possibility that Adam and Eve are symbolic of the entire population (Longman 2016). If the latter is true, then the original rebellion is not the act of a single couple, but rather of original humanity as a whole.

But what about Romans 5:12–21? Doesn't the analogy between Adam and Jesus depend on Adam being a historical individual? We have already dealt with some of the relevant issues above. We need, however, to add a few more comments.

First, the analogy between Adam and Jesus does not require that both be historical figures. It is crucial that Jesus is historical as Paul argues (1 Cor. 15:13–17). Some worry on the basis of the analogy that if Adam is not historical, then Jesus may not be historical. Or to put it another way, they argue that since Jesus is historical, then Adam must be historical. But these assertions are not at all definitive. To put it quite simply, the analogy holds if Adam is a literary figure since it is possible to draw analogies between a historical figure and a literary one and still make sense.

Such analogies are known in first-century literature (Dunn 1988, 289–90), and we make them all the time even when we speak today. If a man comes home and reports to his spouse, "I have been tilting at windmills all day," his point does not require that Don Quixote (the fictional character alluded to) be historical nor the speaker fictional. Likewise, Paul could have been aware that Adam was not historical in a literal sense but could still appeal to the story since he knew that the fall was a historical event.

Second, whether historical or literary, the analogy between Adam and Jesus is not perfect or equivalent in other senses as well, and this includes how Adam's (original humanity's) introduction of sin and death into the world and Jesus's introduction of grace into the world relates to others. If they were strictly equivalent, just as Adam's sin affects all who come after him, then Jesus's act would justify everyone (universalism), but this is not true. This lack of equivalence, we would argue, extends to how Adam's sin affects his descendants and how Jesus's righteousness comes to those who follow him. This point is important because those who believe that Jesus's righteousness is imputed to those who follow him then insist that Adam's sin is imputed to all of his descendants (Murray 1977), and I have offered a different understanding of original sin above.

Summary

The fall is a pivotal moment, the second act after Creation, in the biblical drama of redemption. Genesis 3 tells the story of humanity's rebellion as they reject God's authority and assert their own moral autonomy. As a result, death enters the human experience. While the Old Testament never explores the ramifications of the account of the fall in an explicit way (though it certainly knows that all humans are sinners), the New Testament writers, especially Paul, make important theological use of the story of Adam, particularly in Romans 5:12–21.

Evolutionary theory presents significant challenges to the traditional understanding of the fall, predominantly with its powerful evidence that favors the evolutionary origins of humanity in a population of some few thousand individuals rather than a single pair. I have argued that on reflection, once the genre and nature of the biblical text is taken into account, there is no necessary contradiction between the Bible and science in these matters. We have here yet another example of how, in Pope John Paul II's words, "science can purify religion" (quoted in Cunningham 2010, 284). Adam as a literary (representing original humanity) rather than a historical figure does not undermine the historicity of the fall (contra Schneider 2010, 2012) or the truth taught by the doctrine of original sin (as presumed by Madueme and Reeves 2014, 209–24), though it does preclude certain theological models (particularly those that necessitate a genetic connection to a primal couple) of how this original sin and the introduction of death affect later generations of human beings.

Tremper Longman III

REFERENCES AND RECOMMENDED READING

Cunningham, C. 2010. *Darwin's Pious Idea: Why the Ultra-Darwinists and Creationists Both Get It Wrong*. Grand Rapids: Eerdmans.

Dawkins, R. 2008. *The God Delusion*. New York: Mariner.

Dunn, J. D. G. 1988. *Romans 1–8*. Word Biblical Commentary. Nashville: Word.

Enns, P. 2012. *The Evolution of Adam: What the Bible Does and Doesn't Say about Human Origins*. Grand Rapids: Brazos.

Foh, S. 1974–75. "What Is the Woman's Desire?" *Westminster Theological Journal* 37:376–83.

Hays, C. M., and S. L. Herring. 2013. "Adam and the Fall." In *Evangelical Faith and the Challenge of Historical Criticism*, ed. Christopher M. Hays and Christopher B. Ansberry. Grand Rapids: Baker.

Longman III, T. 2016. *Genesis*. Story of God Bible Commentary. Grand Rapids: Zondervan.

Madueme, H., and M. Reeves, eds. 2014. *Adam, the Fall, and Original Sin*. Grand Rapids: Baker.

Murray, J. 1977. *The Imputation of Adam's Sin*. Phillipsburg, NJ: P&R.

Schneider, J. 2010. "Recent Genetic Science and Christian Theology on Human Origins: An Aesthetic Supralapsarianism." *Perspectives on Science and Christian Faith* 62:208.

———. 2012. "The Fall of the 'Augustinian Adam': Original Fragility and Supralapsarian Purpose." *Zygon* 47:949–69.

Venema, D. R. 2010. "Genesis and the Genome: Genomics Evidence for Human-Ape Common Ancestry and Ancestral Hominid Population Sizes." *Journal of the American Scientific Affiliation* 62:166–78.

Wright, N. T. 2015. *Surprised by Scripture: Engaging the Contemporary Issues*. New York: HarperOne.

Zevit, Z. 2013. *What Really Happened in the Garden of Eden?* New Haven, CT: Yale University Press.

✛ FALL, THE (Literal View).

God the Son came down to us from heaven, in the **Incarnation**, as the long-promised Redeemer. That the God-man lived for a while among us is not only astonishing but necessary for our salvation; for **Adam and Eve** disobeyed God's explicit commandment, plunging the entire **creation** into moral ruin.

Traditional Christianity has always understood this fall as indispensable to the very **logic** of the gospel. But even if this doctrine is contested today, skepticism about the fall account is no recent development; those events were under scrutiny long before anyone knew the name "Charles Darwin" (e.g., see the firestorm surrounding Isaac La Peyrère in the seventeenth century [Popkin 1987]). Indeed, the debate over the status of Adam's fall opens a window into deeper questions over the meaning of doctrine in a world shaped by scientific ways of knowing.

Rejecting the Fall

The controversy among evangelicals results from scholars grappling seriously, if somewhat belatedly, with difficult questions arising from fields like evolutionary biology, human genetic science, and paleoanthropology (e.g., see Enns 2012;

Giberson 2015; Venema 2010; Walton 2015). That ship has already sailed for nonevangelical scholars, especially those affiliated with the academic discipline of science and religion (e.g., see Harrison 2010; Southgate 2005), who for decades have been doing theology without Adam. Six key moves or assumptions characterize this literature.

First, usually triggered by clues within the text itself, the early chapters of Genesis are interpreted as nonhistorical or mythic (typically Gen. 1–11). Genesis 3 on this reading is neither a narrative about historical events nor an account of evil's origin; as one scholar puts it, "The rise of historical-critical biblical studies accounts for much of the relief from the heavy hand of dogma about the Fall" (Towner 1984).

Second, **Ian Barbour**'s pioneering work identified four key models for relating science and religion—namely, conflict, independence, dialogue, and integration (e.g., Barbour 1990). He commended dialogue and integration partly because they minimize conflict between science and religion (see **Models of Relating Science and Religion**). The conflict model was branded the new "heresy" for interpreting Scripture literally and contravening scientific consensus. The discipline of science and theology has adopted Barbour's methodological parameters and usually dismisses the fall account because it conflicts with mainstream evolutionary interpretations of human origins.

Third, Irenaeus's reading of Genesis 3 is taken to emphasize the *immaturity* and not, as Augustine taught, the *sinlessness* of Adam and Eve. This distinction creates the possibility of consonance between biblical and evolutionary pictures of humanity and seals Irenaeus as the patron saint of theistic evolutionists.

Fourth, there is a strategic shift in emphasis from protology (i.e., origins) to **eschatology**, for if "there is no past golden age," then we must look to the future when God will make all things new (Messer 2007).

Fifth, having barred any access to the first Adam, greater prominence is given to the last Adam, i.e., Jesus. Christology and soteriology are inflated, compensating for the absence of the fall—as one theologian writes, "The paradise story and the concept of inherited sin are the dressing for the otherwise naked proposition that God and God alone is responsible for establishing a divine-human relationship that is *salvific*" (Peters 2003). Jesus must increase, but Adam must decrease (see **Adam and Eve**).

Finally, whence then the *origin* of human sin? The evolutionary demythologizing of Adam generates new answers to that question. Some argue that sinfulness arises from the tension between "nature" and "nurture," sin originating at the interface between genetic constitution and social environment (Hefner 1993). Others point to the concept of entropy as the ultimate origin of sin and evil. Human sinfulness is inherited from evolutionary ancestors who, in turn, derived those predispositions from physical processes in the world (Russell 2008).

Despite this dynamic research program, attempts to develop Christian theology without a historical fall are fraught with problems and must be judged a failure. Genesis 3 cannot be dehistoricized without eviscerating the integrity of the whole Bible (Blocher 1997; Collins 2011). The **genealogies** of Scripture assume the Adamic events as historical (e.g., Gen. 1–11; Luke 3:38), as do the inspired New Testament authors (e.g., Matt. 19:1–11; Mark 10:1–9; Rom. 5:12–21; 1 Cor. 6:16; 15:21–22; Eph. 5:31). The cumulative force of such passages can only be ignored by making speculative historical-critical assumptions that functionally muzzle the voice of God, their primary author. While it is true that "literalism" often promotes bad readings of the Bible and should be avoided, not all fears of literalism are justified. Since New Testament authors readily assume the historicity of Adam and the fall as part of the Old Testament witness, contemporary hermeneutical hand-wringing should not be taken overseriously.

Nineteenth-century narratives of an eternal warfare between science and religion have come to be routinely, and rightly, lambasted in the scholarly literature (contra Draper 1874; White 1876). But it doesn't follow that we should ignore all *temporary* conflicts in the relationship between current scientific perspectives and particular doctrines (cf. Cantor 2010). The nub of the issue is that some scholars are allergic to the idea of conflict and adopt hermeneutical strategies to avoid *any* conflicts between the Bible and science (see **Conflict Thesis**). Traditionalists, however, accept that conflicts sometimes arise; as one historian noted, "To prefer to err with scripture than be right with the innovators: that is the pathos of orthodoxy" (Scholder 1990).

Seeking to protect the faith from ridicule, those who deny a historical fall sometimes look to the doctrine of general **revelation** as a mediating doctrine, for then the relevant scientific theories can be received as divine revelation. But at least two questions must be asked here. First, "general revelation" properly describes how creation reveals God and his attributes (cf. Rom 1; see **Natural Theology**); only recently has it been taken to mean revelation of scientific data—but is that inference legitimate (Gootjes 1995)? Second,

even if we set aside that point, science would only be the human, fallible interpretation of general revelation, a human construct, not the thing itself. Theology is also a human, fallible interpretation of inerrant Scripture; however, as I argue below, this insight should not imply an epistemological parity between Scripture and general revelation.

As to Irenaeus, too much is made of his genuine differences with **Augustine**. Yes, Irenaeus emphasized Adam's imperfection, his childlike, innocent disposition, a creature destined to progress from creation to new creation (Irenaeus 1920). But Irenaeus's theology was always aimed against gnostic heretics, those who located sin and evil within God's creation, an absurdity Irenaeus was at pains to deny. Original creation may have been imperfect, but it was always good, never sinful (Irenaeus 1987). To pit Irenaeus and Augustine against each other on the question of Adam's fall is historically unfounded.

In the end, this problem of the origin of sin leaves denials of a historical fall teetering on the horns of a fateful dilemma (Williams 1927). Either God is morally ambiguous, a comingling of good and evil, perhaps even transcending those very categories (i.e., **monism**), or evil is a coeternal principle alongside a good God (i.e., **dualism**). The only alternative is a **theodicy** wherein evil appears after God created his good world (see **Problem of Evil**).

Retaining the Fall

Recent discussion among theologically conservative evangelicals attempts to preserve space for a historical fall within current paleoanthropological scenarios. Three main approaches are worthy of note (see Madueme 2014). Some defend an old-earth creationism that embraces standard **geology** and cosmology but rejects any evolutionary process within the human **species**; Adam is the first human being, created by God, fallen in **Eden** (e.g., Erickson 2013; Rana and Ross 2005). Others go a step further by including humanity within evolutionary development (e.g., Blocher 2009; Davis 1980). On this view, Adam evolved from an ancestral hominin to become the progenitor of all humanity (opinions vary on the significance of Genesis 2:21–22 and whether Eve also emerged from evolution or was directly created by God).

A third scenario achieves an even higher degree of consonance with human evolutionary science; Adam, freshly evolved from a hominin, was already surrounded by a multitude of hominins, thousands perhaps, just prior to the fall. When he disobeyed God, he acted as a federal head, diachronically *and* synchronically, so that his fall not only affected all his descendants but all his hominin contemporaries as well (e.g., Alexander 2014; Stott 1994). On this view, many human beings alive today are not biological descendants of Adam and Eve (cf. Reeves 2009).

Ironically, Isaac La Peyrère's "pre-adamite" thesis, the pre-Darwinian idea that other human beings were roaming the earth before Adam, judged in his day the greatest heresy under the sun, has become—with suitable adjustments—a key strategy of conservative Christians to preserve a historical Adam in a post-Darwinian world (cf. Livingstone 2008). At any rate, it is clear that one can embrace different strands of the evolutionary story within a theistic framework and still remain committed to a historical fall. The Old Princetonians embraced precisely this strategy a century ago (cf. Gundlach 2013).

These scenarios are all grappling with the biblical material in the early chapters of Genesis. Those that enjoy greater traction with mainstream scientific perspectives invariably display greater tension with the biblical witness, and vice versa. This unavoidable dynamic arises from concordist attempts to display harmony between the tenets of Scripture and the theories of science (see **Concordism**). What tends to happen in the case of the fall is that the main lines of paleoanthropology and related disciplines are taken as epistemologically secure, with theology then obliged to identify the Adamic events within the received scientific story. The fate of Adam is held hostage to the fortunes of science. But science is never settled; as new theories gain ascendancy, scenarios married to old scientific models are left widowed and forlorn.

Scriptural Realism

The heart of this debate, the hinge on which it turns, is the epistemological status of Scripture relative to that of current scientific theory. On the one hand, the **Galileo** affair's enduring lesson to the church is that scientific findings can legitimately compel us to fresh exegesis of Scripture. Modifying or radically shifting our interpretations of the Bible as a direct result of new scientific thinking shouldn't be dismissed preemptively. Our interpretations, and the theology arising from them, are errant; only Scripture is inerrant. On the other hand, this insight on theology's fallibility, handled indiscriminately, can cover over a multitude of sins. The problem is that if the Bible enjoys absolute or final epistemic authority, over against the deliverances of science, then some interpretations of the Bible should never be revised—even when they conflict with widely held scientific

positions—insofar as God has spoken clearly (perspicuity) and definitively (special revelation). Every generation of Christians will therefore cheerfully submit itself, come what may, to those parts of the tradition that faithfully represent what God has clearly (and infallibly) communicated to us (see **Two Books Metaphor**).

Scripture reconciles fallen sinners to the Father (e.g., Rom. 15:4; 2 Tim. 3:15–17). Its main aim is the saving knowledge of God (Bavinck 2003). At the same time, God's redemptive works, such as Christ's incarnation and **resurrection**, take place within human history, so that Holy Writ is inescapably, inextricably, bound up with people, actions, and events in our space-time world. The authority of Scripture, then, is largely but not only relevant to moral and spiritual concerns (contra Rogers and McKim 1979; cf. Woodbridge 1982). More precisely, there are other legitimate windows into the nature of reality (e.g., historical study, natural science, archaeology, etc.), but to the extent that the inerrant Word of God addresses specific areas of this reality, its epistemological reliability in those areas is unqualified—though not exhaustive or encyclopedic.

The internal testimony of the Holy Spirit enables believers to know with confidence, supernaturally, that Scripture's claims have divine authority (e.g., Rom 8:16; 1 Cor. 2:10–16; 1 John 4:6). The assurance that Scripture is divine, **Calvin** wrote, comes from "a higher place than human reasons, judgments, or conjectures, that is, in the secret testimony of the Spirit" (Calvin 1960). It follows from this Spirit-induced confidence—a "pneumatic" confidence—that the entire canon has final epistemic authority; furthermore, some doctrines, particularly those clearly attested and central to the biblical narrative, share derivatively in the authority of Scripture.

This construal of biblical authority and pneumatic confidence, however, cannot predetermine how the disciplines of science and theology relate. Theology should interact eclectically with theories in the natural sciences; Christians should assess scientific theories on a case-by-case basis. Since the natural sciences are complex and multifaceted, different theories will invite a wide range of attitudes and responses—sometimes dialogue, sometimes integration, at times conflict, at times independence. No one size fits all. This eclectic approach assumes a "soft"—not "hard"—concordism.

Harmony between science and theology is the ideal case, but until Christ returns, their relationship will sometimes be strained, confusing, even oppositional. Detailed attempts to harmonize the two disciplines are often premature because

Scripture typically does not answer our scientific questions, and scientific conclusions are always open to revision (not least from the noetic effects of the fall on scientific theorizing). The upshot is that genuine instances of conflict between science and theology will sometimes compel Christians to reject the scientific consensus.

Inerrancy, pneumatic confidence, and an eclectic approach to science are a three-stranded cord—call it scriptural **realism**. From that framework, Adam's historicity and the doctrine of the fall are seen to be nonnegotiable theological touchstones. Adam's fall is clearly taught in Scripture (see above); it is a catholic doctrine (both Augustine and Irenaeus affirm it, as have countless other theologians down through the ages, whether Roman Catholic, Eastern Orthodox, or Protestant); and it is central—not merely peripheral—to the redemptive-historical narrative.

In the garment of systematic theology, the fall is a master thread that ties together other central doctrines of our faith (e.g., our justification secured in Christ's **death** and resurrection presupposes Adam's fall [Rom 5:12–21; 1 Cor. 15:21–22]). Pulling it loose unravels the whole thing—"there is very little of importance in Christian theology, hence also in doxology and practice, that is *not* at stake in the question of whether or not we allow a historical dimension to the Fall" (Farrow 2000, emphasis in original).

Taking these factors together, the risk that we have fundamentally misread Scripture reduces to the point of vanishing. All doctrines depend on fallible human interpretative activity, but when a doctrine is central (e.g., clearly attested in Scripture, catholic, and core to the redemptive-historical narrative), then precisely because the Bible is authoritative, that doctrine will likely never be invalidated. The doctrine of the fall is warranted on the authority of God's word to us in Scripture, needing no evidential support from modern science.

But can a central doctrine like the fall ever be overturned? Yes, under two conditions: First, it is logically possible that new exegesis could warrant a complete overhaul of the traditional understanding of Genesis 3 and related passages. Such a scenario seems highly unlikely, however, given the doctrine's clear biblical basis and the unanimous judgment of the church for almost 1,800 years. Second, it is also possible that a scientific finding may be compelling enough to overturn the doctrine. Christians disagree on the epistemic status of the relevant theories (cf. Caneday and Barrett 2013). Any decision to retire the fall as a church doctrine would have to involve a global spectrum of church leaders, not merely individuals in the academy. In my judgment, however, the biblical testimony to the fall has an intrinsic warrant far greater than any of the conflicting interpretations from evolutionary biology and its related disciplines.

Conclusion

Adam's fall is a classic case study in the relationship between science and theology. The points of tension reflect important questions that have emerged, and are only heightening, since the rise of the modern world. On the one hand, late modern, post-Darwinian plausibility structures suggest that if we lose our nerve here, if we fail to integrate mainstream scientific perspectives into a suitably revised understanding of sin and salvation, then the intellectual credibility of the faith will evaporate in the wind. On the other hand, the contested issues surrounding Adam's fall reveal a law of diminishing returns.

Under pressure from certain scientific accounts, modern approaches to these questions move increasingly from maximalist to minimalist views of biblical authority. Scripture is considered trustworthy on questions of "spiritual" or "religious" significance but cannot be trusted, or is simply irrelevant, on anything else. The challenge is "Gnosticism creep"—as the scientific disciplines extend their explanatory range and power, Scripture speaks less and less meaningfully, or authoritatively, to the actual material world we live in.

The pastoral implications are equally sobering. For revisionists: many who deny Adam's fall still embrace the main lines of orthodox confession and worship, for which we may thank God. It is unclear, however, whether the second and third generations will be able, or will even desire, to sustain such heights of theological dexterity. Will the plausibility of the whole Christian story eventually collapse (cf. Luke 18:8)? For traditionalists: many of their youth see only two options: affirm inerrancy and reject science, or deny the historicity of Adam (and thus inerrancy) and abandon the whole faith. So the unhappy logic goes. But Christians, we must recall, are often not logically consistent. An errantist who denies the fall yet clings by faith to Jesus is infinitely better off than an atheist. Whatever faults belie the dogmatic integrity of that position, surely here we must raise three cheers for inconsistency.

Hans Madueme

REFERENCES AND RECOMMENDED READING

Alexander, Denis. 2014. *Creation or Evolution: Do We Have to Choose?* Rev. and enl. ed. Oxford: Monarch.

Barbour, Ian. 1990. *Religion in an Age of Science*. San Francisco: Harper & Row.

Barrett, Matthew, and Ardel B. Caneday, eds. 2013. *Four Views on the Historical Adam*. Grand Rapids: Zondervan.

Bavinck, Herman. 2003. *Reformed Dogmatics*. Vol. 1, *Prolegomena*. Ed. John Bolt. Trans. John Vriend. Grand Rapids: Baker Academic.

Blocher, Henri. 1997. *Original Sin: Illuminating the Riddle*. Grand Rapids: Eerdmans.

———. 2009. "The Theology of the Fall and the Origins of Evil." In *Darwin, Creation and the Fall: Theological Challenges*, ed. R. J. Berry and T. A. Noble, 149–72. Nottingham, UK: Apollos.

Calvin, John. 1960. *Institutes of the Christian Religion*, ed. John T. McNeill. Trans. Ford Lewis Battles. Philadelphia: Westminster.

Caneday, Ardel, and Matthew Barrett, eds. 2013. *Four Views on the Historical Adam*. Grand Rapids: Zondervan.

Cantor, Geoffrey. 2010. "What Shall We Do with the 'Conflict Thesis'?" In *Science and Religion: New Historical Perspectives*, ed. Thomas Dixon, Geoffrey Cantor, and Stephen Pumfrey, 283–98. Cambridge: Cambridge University Press.

Collins, C. John. 2011. *Did Adam and Eve Really Exist? Who They Were and Why You Should Care*. Wheaton, IL: Crossway.

Davis, John Jefferson. 1980. "Genesis, Inerrancy, and the Antiquity of Man." In *Inerrancy and Common Sense*, ed. Roger Nicole and J. Ramsey Michaels, 137–59. Grand Rapids: Baker.

Domning, Daryl, and Monika Hellwig. 2006. *Original Selfishness: Original Sin and Evil in Light of Evolution*. Burlington, VT: Ashgate.

Draper, John William. 1874. *History of the Conflict between Religion and Science*. New York: D. Appleton.

Enns, Peter. 2012. *The Evolution of Adam: What the Bible Does and Doesn't Say about Human Origins*. Grand Rapids: Baker Academic.

Erickson, Millard. 2013. *Christian Theology*. 3rd ed. Grand Rapids: Baker Academic.

Farrow, Douglas. 2000. "Fall." In *Oxford Companion to Christian Thought*, ed. Adrian Hastings, Alistair Mason, and Hugh Pyper, 233–35. Oxford: Oxford University Press.

Giberson, Karl. 2015. *Saving the Original Sinner: How Christians Have Used the Bible's First Man to Oppress, Inspire, and Make Sense of the World*. Boston: Beacon.

Gootjes, Nicolaas H. 1995. "General Revelation and Science: Reflections on a Remark in Report 28." *Calvin Theological Journal* 30: 94–107.

Gundlach, Bradley J. 2013. *Process and Providence: The Evolution Question at Princeton, 1845–1929*. Grand Rapids: Eerdmans.

Harrison, Peter, ed. 2010. *The Cambridge Companion to Science and Religion*. Cambridge: Cambridge University Press.

Hefner, Philip. 1993. *The Human Factor: Evolution, Culture, and Religion*. Minneapolis: Fortress.

Irenaeus. 1920. *The Demonstration of the Apostolic Preaching*. Trans. Armitage Robinson. London: SPCK.

———. 1987. *Against Heresies*. The Ante-Nicene Fathers. Vol. 1. Comp. A. Cleveland Coxe. Ed. Alexander Roberts, James Donaldson, and Henry Wace. Grand Rapids: Eerdmans.

Livingstone, David N. 2008. *Adam's Ancestors: Race, Religion, and the Politics of Human Origins*. Baltimore: Johns Hopkins University Press.

Madueme, Hans. 2014. "'The Most Vulnerable Part of the Whole Christian Account': Original Sin and Modern Science." In *Adam, the Fall, and Original Sin: Theological, Biblical, and Scientific Perspectives*, ed. Hans Madueme and Michael Reeves, 225–49. Grand Rapids: Baker Academic.

Messer, Neil. 2007. *Selfish Genes and Christian Ethics: Theological and Ethical Reflections on Evolutionary Biology*. London: SCM.

Peters, Ted. 2003. *Playing God? Genetic Determinism and Human Freedom*. 2nd ed. New York: Routledge.

Popkin, Richard H. 1987. *Isaac La Peyrère (1596–1676): His Life, Work and Influence*. New York: Brill.

Rana, Fazale, and Hugh Ross. 2005. *Who Was Adam? A Creation Model Approach to the Origin of Man*. Colorado Springs: NavPress.

Reeves, Michael. 2009. "Adam and Eve." In *Should Christians Embrace Evolution? Biblical and Scientific Responses*, ed. Norman C. Nevin, 43–56. Nottingham, UK: InterVarsity.

Rogers, Jack, and Donald McKim. 1979. *The Authority and Interpretation of the Bible*. San Francisco: Harper & Row.

Russell, Robert J. 2008. *Cosmology: From Alpha to Omega*. Minneapolis: Fortress.

Scholder, Klaus. 1990. *The Birth of Modern Critical Theology: Origins and Problems of Biblical Criticism in the Seventeenth Century*. Trans. John Bowden. London: SCM.

Southgate, Christopher, ed. 2005. *God, Humanity and the Cosmos*. Rev. and enl. ed. New York: T&T Clark.

Stott, John. 1994. *The Message of Romans: God's Good News for the World*. Leicester, UK: InterVarsity.

Towner, W. Sibley. 1984. "Interpretations and Reinterpretations of the Fall." In *Modern Biblical Scholarship: Its Impact on Theology and Proclamation*, ed. Francis A. Eigo, 53–85. Villanova: Villanova University Press.

Venema, Dennis R. 2010. "Genesis and the Genome: Genomics Evidence for Human-Ape Common Ancestry and Ancestral Hominid Population Sizes." *Perspectives on Science and Christian Faith* 62 (2010): 166–78.

Walton, John. 2015. *The Lost World of Adam and Eve: Genesis 2–3 and the Human Origins Debate*. Downers Grove, IL: InterVarsity.

White, Andrew Dickson. 1876. *A History of Warfare of Science with Theology in Christendom*. 2 vols. New York: Dover.

Williams, N. P. 1927. *The Ideas of the Fall and of Original Sin: A Historical and Critical Study*. London: Longman, Green & Co.

Woodbridge, John D. 1982. *Biblical Authority: A Critique of the Rogers/McKim Proposal*. Grand Rapids: Zondervan.

FALSIFIABILITY. The concept of falsifiability, as championed by the twentieth-century philosopher Karl Popper (Keuth 2004, 384), is what sets science apart from all other disciplines. In principle it means that for a theory to be considered scientific, it must be possible to construct tests in which the results could potentially prove the theory to be false. The hypothesis that "two unequal weights dropped in a vacuum will fall at equal rates" is testable and can be proven false if one weight is observed to fall faster than the other. The hypothesis that "God superintends the falling of two weights in a vacuum" cannot be so tested and thus falls outside the realm of scientific investigation. Though not universally accepted as a fundamental demarcation of science (see, e.g., **intelligent design argument**s; Meyer 2002, 151–211), testing for falsifiability is the common practice of science today.

According to young-earth literature, hypotheses about the unobserved past cannot be tested nor falsified and thus fall outside of the bounds of genuine science. This is the basis for distinctions claimed between so-called observational (or experimental) science and historical (or origins) science, where it is argued that only what can be observed happening in the present is testable, repeatable, and falsifiable, and can be rightly qualified as science (Thaxton et al. 1984, 202–6).

The effort to reconstruct past events from evidence left behind is technically referred to as forensic science. Forensic scientists routinely apply the principle of falsifiability, as exemplified by modern crime scene investigations (CSI). Crime-scene detectives regularly piece together evidence, even with no eyewitnesses, to determine what happened in the unobserved past. In a murder case, hypotheses favoring a particular suspect and mode of attack may by proven false if fingerprints on the murder weapon or **DNA** samples from beneath the victim's fingernails fail to match those of the suspected assailant.

The study of the earth's geological and biological history is also forensic science, with tests for falsifiability routinely applied. Considering an example from geologic history, the hypothesis that the earth's early atmosphere lacked oxygen can be tested by examining ancient sedimentary layers around the world for iron oxide minerals that readily form in the presence of oxygen. If iron oxides are found to be common in the oldest deposits, the hypothesis will be proven false. **Paleontology**, the study of past life, works in the same way. The hypothesis that flowering plants did not appear until late in the earth's history (the early Cretaceous) can be tested by examining the myriad sedimentary layers older than the Cretaceous. If fossils of flowering plants or pollen are found in a rock older than the Cretaceous, the hypothesis can be shown to be false. (This test is especially powerful knowing how easily pollen is carried and distributed by wind or water.) Thus study of the earth's past does meet scientific criteria of falsifiability.

Gregg Davidson

REFERENCES AND RECOMMENDED READING

Keuth, Herbert. 2004. *The Philosophy of Karl Hopper.* Cambridge: Cambridge University Press.
Meyer, Stephen C. 2002. "The Scientific Status of Intelligent Design: The Methodological Equivalence of Naturalistic and Non-naturalistic Origins Theories." In *Science and Evidence for Design in the Universe*, 151–211. Proceedings of the Wethersfield Institute. San Francisco: St. Ignatius. www.discovery.org/a/1780.
Thaxton, Charles B., Walter L. Bradley, and Roger L. Olson. 1984. *The Mystery of Life's Origin: Reassessing Current Theories.* Dallas: Lewis and Stanley.

FARADAY, MICHAEL. Michael Faraday (1791–1867) was an English scientist who made notable advances in electricity, magnetism, electrochemistry, and organic chemistry. The son of an ironsmith, Faraday received little schooling and began work as a bookbinder's apprentice under George Ribeau, where he was exposed to writings that stoked his interest in electricity, as well as to Isaac Watts's *Improvement of the Mind*. Following Watts's advice, Faraday cultivated his intellect, ability as a speaker, and scientific knowledge. Through diligence, persistence, and the help from one of Ribeau's customers, he eventually secured appointment as assistant to Humphrey Davy, then England's premier chemist.

Faraday's work with Davy at England's Royal Institution served as a scientific apprenticeship and, when he accompanied Davy on a European tour, allowed him to develop working relationships with leading European researchers. Soon Faraday became renowned as an analytical chemist and independent investigator. His discoveries include benzene and the liquefaction of gases under pressure while his work in electrochemistry helped establish concepts like ions, cathodes, anodes, and oxidation states. Faraday did much to develop the science and **technology** of electricity and magnetism; he discovered electromagnetic induction and electrical capacitance, described diamagnetism and paramagnetism, developed the field concept, and was the first to recognize that electricity and magnetism are the same. His inventions include the first electric motors and "Faraday cages" for electric shielding.

A significant portion of Faraday's time was spent engaged in public service. Notably, he helped Davy develop a miner's safety lamp, engaged in art restoration and preservation projects, and investigated environmental pollution in the Thames. He also sought to make science accessible to the public through the Royal Institution's Friday Evening Discourses and annual Christmas lectures.

Throughout his life, Faraday was associated with the Sandemanians, a small, primitivist, nonconformist Protestant sect formed during the First Great Awakening that emphasized the primacy of biblical authority and was averse to evangelism. Since Faraday was scrupulous about keeping theology out of his scientific publications and rarely spoke about religion to non-Sandemanians, it is sometimes assumed that Faraday kept his faith and science separate. Indeed, he wrote to Ada Loveace that he did "not think it necessary to tie the study of the natural sciences and religion together" (Jones 1870, 197). However, Faraday was responding to Loveace's own "religious" views, which she had described in philosophical terms anathema to Sandemanian sentiments (Cantor 2005). Furthermore, Faraday's comments reflected his aversion to natural theologies that start from **logic** and evidence from the natural world, an aversion in keeping with Sandemanian teachings, which held the Scriptures alone are sufficient for faith.

In fact, Faraday's faith and science were deeply intertwined. He found it relatively easy to live out Sandemanian social ethics as a scientist (Cantor 1991), and his private writings (Levere 1968) and public lectures (Cantor 2005; Faraday 1846) show Faraday's propensity for recognizing God's **providence** in nature. Faraday's faith also helped shape his science (Cantor 1991, 2005; Russell 2000). His view of God as actively working in nature helped shape his thinking about charges as centers of force and electric fields as lines of force, while his search for unity in science, seen in his electric charge theory of chemistry and the unifying of electricity and magnetism, is consistent with his belief in a rational and orderly Creator.

Faraday's faith was also seen in his straightforward and unpretentious demeanor, refusal to patent inventions, and disclaiming of honors. Thus, on his death, he was buried in Highgate Cemetery rather than Westminster Abbey.

Stephen A. Contakes

REFERENCES AND RECOMMENDED READING

Cantor, G. N. 1991. *Michael Faraday: Sandemanian and Scientist: A Study of Science and Religion in the Nineteenth Century.* New York: St. Martin's.

———. 2005. "Michael Faraday Meets the 'High Priestess of God's-Works': A Romance on the Theme of Science and Religion." 2005. In *Science and Beliefs: From Natural Philosophy to Natural Science, 1700–1900*, ed. David M. Knight and Matthew D. Eddy, 157–70. Science, Technology and Culture, 1700–1945. Aldershot, UK: Ashgate.

Eichman, Phillip. 1988. "Michael Faraday: Man of God—Man of Science." *Perspectives on Science and Christian Faith* (June): 40, 91–97.

Faraday, Michael. 1846. "*A Course of Lectures on Electricity and Magnetism.*" *London Medical Gazette* 2 (April 25): 977–82.

Hamilton, James. 2002. *A Life of Discovery: Michael Faraday, Giant of the Scientific Revolution.* 1st US ed. New York: Random House.

Hirshfeld, Alan. 2006. *The Electric Life of Michael Faraday.* New York: Walker.

James, Frank A. J. L. 2010. *Michael Faraday: A Very Short Introduction.* Oxford and New York: Oxford University Press.

Jones, Bence. 1870. *The Life and Letters of Faraday.* 2 vols. London: Longmans, Green.

Kaiser, Christopher B. 1997. *Creational Theology and the History of Physical Science: The Creationist Tradition from Basil to Bohr.* Studies in the History of Christian Thought. Leiden and New York: Brill.

Levere, Trevor Harvey. 1968. "Faraday, Matter, and Natural Theology—Reflections of an Unpublished Manuscript." *British Journal for the History of Science* 4 (14): 95–107.

Russell, Colin A. 2000. *Michael Faraday: Physics and Faith.* Oxford Portraits in Science. Oxford and New York: Oxford University Press.

———. 2007. "Faraday Paper No. 13: Science and Faith in the Life of Michael Faraday." Cambridge, UK: Faraday Institute for Science and Religion, St. Edmund's College. www.faraday.st-edmunds.cam.ac.uk./Papers.php.

FARADAY INSTITUTE FOR SCIENCE AND RELIGION.

The Faraday Institute for Science and Religion is an interdisciplinary research enterprise based at St. Edmund's College, Cambridge. It was established under the leadership of Denis R. Alexander with a $2 million grant from the **John Templeton Foundation** (Faraday Institute 2015). The Templeton Foundation grant was used to launch the Faraday Institute with the objective of conducting research, holding seminars and lectures, and disseminating publications on various topics at the intersection of science and religion; the institute aims to engage academic, religious, and nonreligious communities on matters of science, faith, and culture (John Templeton Foundation 2015).

The Faraday Institute was dedicated to **Michael Faraday**, a renowned physicist and chemist as well as a devout Christian. He was an active leader in the scientific community, having discovered electromagnetic induction and diamagnetism, invented electric motors, and demonstrated the relationship between electricity and chemical bonds—all while being an active deacon, elder, and church member. Biographies of Faraday note that his life and work were influenced by his understanding of the unity of God and nature (Baggott 1991).

The Institutes' stated objectives are to execute the following activities (Faraday Institute 2015):

Support scholarly research and publication on science and religion, including the organization of invited groups of experts to write joint publications.

Provide short-term courses in science and religion.

Organize seminars and lectures on science and religion.

Provide accurate information on science and religion for the international media and wider public.

The institute operates with a staff, advisory board, speakers, and Faraday associates—including notable scientists such as **Alister McGrath** and **John Polkinghorne**—and receives financial support from Cambridge University, Tyndale House, and many other institutions. It provides and promotes course material, conferences, lectures, debates, and seminars with the aim of providing accurate information on science and Scripture to promote discussion, debate, and outreach. The institute has established "Faraday Schools," part of the Learning about Science and Religion (LASAR) project, to support research and education along with providing resources, educational games and apps, and free one-day events for primary and secondary schools. The institute has produced more than 500 multimedia presentations, numerous books, "Faraday Papers," and introductory material for young adults and adults on science and Christianity.

The Faraday Institute has a strong working relationship with BioLogos, founded by Dr. **Francis Collins**, and a number of advocates including the **American Scientific Affiliation**, the John Templeton Foundation, the International Society for Science and Religion, and others. The institute also has a number of detractors, including **Answers in Genesis** led by **Ken Ham**.

Jonathan Howard Fisher

REFERENCES AND RECOMMENDED READING

Baggott, Jim. 1991. "The Myth of Michael Faraday: Michael Faraday Was Not Just One of Britain's Greatest Experimenters. A Closer Look at the Man and His Work Reveals That He Was Also a Clever Theoretician." *New Scientist* (September 21): 1787.
Faraday Institute for Science and Religion website. Accessed May 2015. www.faraday.st-edmunds.cam.ac.uk.
Faraday Schools. Accessed May 2015. www.faradayschools.com.
John Templeton Foundation Grant Summary with the Faraday Institute for Science and Religion. Accessed May 2015. https://www.templeton.org/what-we-fund/grants/faraday-institute-for-science-and-religion-interdisciplinary-research-and-projec.
Test of Faith: Introductory Resources from the Faraday Institute for Science and Religion. Accessed September 28, 2016. www.testoffaith.com.

FEYERABEND, PAUL K. Paul Feyerabend (1924–94) spent the bulk of his career at the University of California, Berkeley, during the heyday of student activism and Anglo-analytic **philosophy of science**. Feyerabend's interlocutors include **Rudolph Carnap**, **Karl Popper**, **Thomas Kuhn**, and **Imre Lakatos**, the best friend to whom his *After Method* is dedicated. The publication of *After Method* has been aptly described as "an event … the Woodstock of philosophy" (Hacking 2010). Feyerabend's notoriety peaked in 1987 when the journal *Nature* named him "the worst enemy of science" (Feyerabend 1995).

After Method's infamous thesis is that the history of modern Western science shows it to be an "anarchic" cognitive enterprise, where the only principle explaining its success is "anything goes" (Feyerabend 2010). Despite its provocative appearance, Feyerabend's thesis is a well-targeted attack on the efforts of Carnap, Popper, and others seeking to identify the principles governing scientific practice that could explain and justify its epistemic authority. Feyerabend argues that the history of science includes transitions from one comprehensive theory to another—from Aristotelian **physics** to Newtonian mechanics, from Newtonian mechanics to Einstein's relativity and Bohr's quantum theories.

Given the comprehensive nature of these theories and what it takes to shift from one to the wholesale acceptance of another, we must conclude that a predecessor and its successor are incommensurable. For Feyerabend, to say that two theories are incommensurable is to say that two theories of worldview-type proportions, where one is the genuine competitor of the other, come with distinct ontologies, differing standards of confirmation, and mutually incompatible truth conditions. Therefore the kind of principles that the Carnapian or Popperian philosopher seeks, principles of rationality that span historic scientific developments, are neither possible nor desirable—impossible because they cannot make sense of actual scientific practice and undesirable because, if imposed, they would prohibit consideration of competitors on the grounds that they are "irrational" as testified by the well-confirmed experiences and discursive resources of the prevailing theory.

Rather than seeing incommensurability as a threat to scientific progress, Feyerabend views the proliferation of incompatible theories as a means of ensuring it. He repeatedly denies advocating an "anything goes" sophomoric relativism. He does, however, consistently call for the tolerance and pluralism defended in John Stuart Mill's *On Liberty*, the benefits of which are threefold: (1) allowing time for potential successors to amass the resources necessary to bridge the communicative gap between them and their predecessor; (2) encouraging us to see the rationality in dethroned theories or **worldview**s; and (3) enabling us to see the epistemic worth of religious or non-Western practices that fail to conform to Euro-American scientific practice and acknowledging their contributions in addressing human need.

Fifteen years after its publication, *After Method* once again made headlines. In a speech challenging the standard Enlightenment story of the Roman Catholic Church's response to Galileo, then-Cardinal Ratzinger cited Feyerabend: "He writes: 'The church at the time of **Galileo** was much more faithful to reason than Galileo himself'" (Ratzinger 1990). In truth, Feyerabend's analysis of the Galileo affair has undergone substantial criticism. Yet three current trends in Christian scholarship reflect a Feyerabendian spirit: (1) recognizing science and religion as distinct but equally valid cognitive endeavors; (2) attending to feminist and postcolonial critiques concerning the epistemic supremacy accorded to Euro-American science; and (3) exploring the prospect of pluralism in ecclesial practices and biblical hermeneutics.

Teri R. Merrick

REFERENCES AND RECOMMENDED READING

Feyerabend, Paul K. 1978. *Science in a Free Society.* London: Verso.
———. 1981a. *Philosophical Papers.* Vol. 1. *Realism, Rationalism and the Scientific Method.* Cambridge: Cambridge University Press.

———. 1981b. *Philosophical Papers*. Vol. 2. *Problems of Empiricism*. Cambridge: Cambridge University Press.

———. 1987. *Farewell to Reason*. London: Verso.

———. 1995. *Killing Time: The Autobiography of Paul Feyerabend*. Chicago: University of Chicago Press.

———. 1999a. *Conquest of Abundance: A Tale of Abstraction versus the Richness of Being*. Chicago: University of Chicago Press.

———. 1999b. *Philosophical Papers*. Vol. 3. *Knowledge, Science and Relativism*. Cambridge: Cambridge University Press.

———. 2010. *Against Method*. 4th ed. London: Verso.

———. 2011. *The Tyranny of Science*. Malden, MA: Polity.

Finocchiaro, Maurice A. 2005. *Retrying Galileo, 1633–1992*. Berkeley: University of California Press.

Hacking, Ian. 2010. "Introduction to the Fourth Edition" in *Against Method*. London: Verso.

Preston, John, Gonzalo Munévar, and David Lamb, eds. 2010. *The Worst Enemy of Science? Essays in Memory of Paul Feyerabend*. New York: Oxford University Press.

Ratzinger, Joseph. 1990. "The Crisis of Faith in Science." *National Catholic Reporter*. March 15. http://ncronline.org/news/ratzingers-1990-remarks-galileo.

van Fraassen, Bas C. 2004. *The Empirical Stance*. New Haven, CT: Yale University Press.

Westphal, Merold. 2009. *Whose Community? Which Interpretation? Philosophical Hermeneutics for the Church*. Grand Rapids: Baker Academic.

FIDEISM. Fideism is often defined as the view that one can believe in God "on faith alone," and so it seems to imply that one does not need reason or evidence to justify one's belief. Influential Christian thinkers thought to have proposed fideistic views include **Blaise Pascal**, William James, Søren Kierkegaard, Karl Barth, and D. Z. Phillips. Fideism is sometimes understood to mean that one can commit to belief in God and various religious creeds and doctrines because faith is above reason, and while open to rational investigation aimed at increasing understanding, faith is not subject to rational interrogation aimed at refutation.

Some fideists regard reason itself as a worldly enterprise, and so it is a form of idolatry to subject religious truth to it (this view is also popular in Eastern religions). Kierkegaard proposed a strong version of fideism with his argument that the very essence of religious belief consists in making "a leap of faith," a somewhat "blind" commitment, even though this commitment creates a tension because of the failure of reason not only to establish the truth of religious beliefs but to capture the essence of the religious way of living. A similar view can be found in Wittgenstein's influential reflections on religion as a language game and form of life.

Fideism has been frequently criticized as an irrational approach to religious belief on the straightforward logical ground that one must first present evidence for and consider the rationality of what one believes before one commits to

and lives by these beliefs. Many religious thinkers support this criticism, especially those who are strong supporters of various arguments of **natural theology** for the **existence of God** and of the rational superiority of a theistic **worldview** over secularist alternatives. Fideists respond by arguing that from God's point of view, the fideist approach is not inappropriate, because what is important in religion are one's beliefs and how one lives, not whether one can discuss one's beliefs rationally or provide evidence. Indeed, some fideists suggest that believing in God on faith alone allows one to live very successfully in terms of spiritual and moral fulfillment, and this success can be taken as a kind of indirect argument for the truth of fideism. Some thinkers have developed such a view to argue for a "rational fideism."

The movement known as Wittgensteinian fideism, represented by Welsh philosopher D. Z. Phillips, has moved to an almost totally metaphorical view of Christianity where one's commitment (sometimes called the expressive side of religious belief) is the only feature that counts, because there is no propositional content to religion. Some would also classify the movement of Reformed **epistemology** led by Alvin Plantinga as a form of fideism because its proponents argue that one can believe in God on the basis of (common, but private) **religious experience**s and that one does not need any further evidence. However, this is not quite fideism as it has been traditionally understood, because the experience would be a kind of evidence for the person involved, and so the belief in God would not be based on a blind commitment, though it might seem that way to outsiders, and very importantly, there would appear to be no communal reassurance of the veridicality of such experiences.

A main criticism of all forms of fideism is that since we cannot know in advance or for certain whether God exists from our limited human vantage point, it is irrational, at least for the philosophers and theologians within a religion, to believe without considering the question of the evidence for and the rationality of what one believes.

Brendan Sweetman

REFERENCES AND RECOMMENDED READING

Bishop, John. 2007. *Believing by Faith*. New York: Oxford University Press.

James, William. 1960. *The Will to Believe, Human Immortality, and Other Essays in Popular Philosophy*. New York: Dover.

Kierkegaard, Søren. 1968. *Concluding Unscientific Postscript*. Princeton, NJ: Princeton University Press.

Pascal, Blaise. 1995. *Pensées*. London: Penguin.

Phillips, D. Z. 2013. *Faith and Philosophical Enquiry*. London: Routledge.

Wittgenstein, Ludwig. 2007. *Lectures and Conversations on Aesthetics, Psychology, and Religious Belief*. 2007. Berkeley: University of California Press.

FINE-TUNING OF THE UNIVERSE AND SOLAR SYSTEM.

Fine-tuning refers to the idea that certain parameters of our universe must occur within stringent limits for the universe to be able to support any conceivable form of life. Fine-tuning is closely related to and commonly involved in any discussion of the **anthropic principle**.

One example of fine-tuning is the strength of one of the fundamental forces in the universe, the strong nuclear force. If the strong force coupling was 2 percent stronger while all other constants stayed the same, hydrogen would be very rare in our universe because most hydrogen nuclei would fuse into stable di-proton nuclei. Without stable hydrogen, we would have no long-lived stars or hydrogen-containing compounds, including water.

Another example of fine-tuning is the mass density of the universe. Within the first second after the **big bang**, the amount of matter in the universe was fine-tuned to 1 part in 10^{60}. If there had been any less matter in the universe, stars and galaxies could not have formed. If there had been more matter in the universe, gravitational attraction would have caused the whole universe to collapse in on itself before there was enough time for stars and galaxies to form. Scientists believe that the matter density was precisely tuned to what it must be through a process called *cosmic inflation*, which is a rapid expansion of the universe sometime within the first 10^{-34} seconds after the big bang.

Cosmic inflation forces the matter density to be the necessary value for a viable universe. Some scientists assert that cosmic inflation, therefore, explains the fine-tuning of the matter density in the universe. But finding a mechanism does not really give a fundamental explanation for the fine-tuning itself. For example, suppose you want to pour gasoline into a small hole in your lawn mower and you decide to use a funnel to do so. You have not really explained the "fine-tuning" needed to get the gasoline into the small hole simply because you now have a tool that forces it to do so. The mechanism of the funnel itself must still be explained. There are many variations of cosmic inflation, and the correct version must occur and be correctly tuned in order to produce the proper matter density.

Although some of the fine-tuned parameters must be related to others, a minimum number of parameters are still required for any universe that could develop and sustain an infrastructure to support life. In his book *Just Six Numbers*, Martin Rees lists six fundamental dimensionless numbers that are crucial for the development of the structure of the universe (Rees 2000). For example, these numbers include the ratio of the strength of the electromagnetic force to the gravitational force, the fraction of the mass of four protons that is released as energy when fused into helium, and the density of matter in proportion to a "critical" density.

One of the first books to discuss fine-tuning was *The Fitness of the Environment*, written in 1913 by chemist Lawrence Henderson, which discussed properties of water that are required for living organisms and the conditions on the earth that make it possible for liquid water to exist. Many other books were written in the latter half of the twentieth century that developed this concept, including *The Accidental Universe* (Davies 1982), *The Intelligent Universe* (Hoyle 1983), and *Cosmic Coincidences* (Gribbin and Rees 1989). One of the most influential and referenced books on this subject is *The Anthropic Cosmological Principle* by **John Barrow** and **Frank Tipler** (Barrow and Tipler 1988).

Although most discussions of fine-tuning deal with fundamental parameters that are necessary if the universe is to develop the structure to support life in general, there are also a large number of factors that must be finely tuned in order to have a specific planet like the earth that can support higher life-forms, defined as any life-form more complicated than bacteria.

When scientists speak of "earthlike" planets, they usually do not mean a planet like the earth, which can support higher life-forms. Instead, they usually mean one of three things: either the planet is the right distance from its central star so that liquid water might exist on the planet's surface, the planet is about the same size as Earth, or the planet is a rocky planet rather than a gaseous planet. Of course, none of these criteria is sufficient to have a true earthlike planet that can support higher life-forms. A more realistic estimate of the fine-tuning necessary for a planet that is to support higher life-forms, compiled by astrophysicist Hugh Ross, includes 322 required characteristics (Ross 2004).

Theists point to the precise tuning of the universe as evidence that an intelligent designer is responsible for its existence. Nontheists propose other solutions to the fine-tuning problem. A popular naturalistic solution is that there are a vast number of universes (a **multiverse**) with different fundamental constants in the different universes, and that we happen to live in the universe with parameters amenable to life. The argument is that if there are enough universes, there is a high **probability** that one of them has the necessary components to support life. **String theory** and inflationary cosmology (see **Inflationary Universe Theory**) are among the theories that either allow for or predict the possibility of a multiverse. It is possible that there will never be any evidence of other universes, so any belief in them may continue to be based on theoretical ideas and naturalistic philosophy rather than scientific observation. Even if we do live in a multiverse, the theistic answer to fine-tuning will remain, since it is possible that God's mechanism for creating this universe includes the creation of other universes as well.

Another criticism directed toward theists who use fine-tuning arguments is related to the weak anthropic principle, which basically states that we can only be observers in a universe that is compatible with our existence. Thus we should not be surprised that the universe looks finely tuned for us. This still leaves open the question of how finely tuned the universe actually is, for it may be possible that we could exist in a universe that is compatible with our existence in which the parameters of the universe could still take on vastly different values.

Underlying all of the debates about the fine-tuning of the universe is the fact that we only have an observable sample of one universe, and it is challenging to make definitive probabilistic statements based on a sample size of one. However, the overwhelming conclusion of scientists who study the subject is that the fine-tuning of this universe for life is real and that some explanation is required. Any appeal to a multiverse may be untestable, while the theistic proposal is certainly compatible with all the observations and is, arguably, the best explanation of the evidence.

Michael G. Strauss

REFERENCES AND RECOMMENDED READING

Barrow, John D., and Frank J. Tipler. 1988. *The Anthropic Cosmological Principle.* Oxford: Oxford University Press.

Davies, Paul. 1982. *The Accidental Universe.* Cambridge: Cambridge University Press.

Gribbin, John, and Martin Rees. 1989. *Cosmic Coincidences: Dark Matter, Mankind, and Anthropic Cosmology.* New York: Bantam New Age.

Hoyle, Fred. 1983. *The Intelligent Universe.* New York: Holt, Rinehart, and Winston.

Rees, Martin. 2000. *Just Six Numbers: The Deep Forces That Shape the Universe.* London: Weidenfeld & Nicolson.

Ross, Hugh. 2004. "Probability for Life on Earth." Reasons to Believe. April 1. www.reasons.org/articles/probability-for-life-on-earth.

FIRMAMENT. In Genesis 1 creation is described as taking place in six days, and on the seventh day God rested. Debate continues over whether verses 1–2 describe the creation of the primordial waters (implied by NIV and NLT) or whether the waters are there at the beginning of the account (NRSV). On the first day, God created light and separated it from the darkness, while on the second day of creation, God separated the waters above from the waters below. God placed the firmament (KJV; NKJV; or "vault" [NIV; NJB] or "dome" [NRSV]; Heb., *raqia'*) between the two bodies of waters to create the separation (1:6–8). The identification of the firmament and its relationship to ancient and modern cosmology are subjects of disagreement today.

The noun is constructed from the verb *raqa'*, which in the basic stem (qal) means "to stamp one's feet" (2 Sam. 22:43; Ezek. 6:11; 25:6) or in a cosmological setting (qal and hiphil) "to spread out" the earth on the sea (Ps. 136:6; Isa. 42:5; 44:24) or the spreading out of the skies (Job 37:18). In another stem (piel), it refers to the process of hammering metal into sheets (Ex. 39:3; Num. 16:39).

Taking their cue from the meaning of the verb (particularly as describing the process of hammering metal into sheets) and the context that describes the *raqia'* as separating the waters above and below, some scholars believe that the *raqia'* was thought to be a hard dome. In addition, the author of Genesis states that on day 4 God placed the celestial bodies in the *raqia'*. On the fifth day of creation, God made the birds, which fly across the *raqia'* (1:20). According to this understanding, the ancient Hebrews' cosmology included the idea that there was a solid dome above the earth into which God placed the sun, moon, and stars.

Other scholars (Walton 2011) suggest that the *raqia'* refers instead to the atmosphere, which would separate the waters below (the oceans, etc.) from the waters above (from which the rains come). **John Walton** points to Job 37:18, where the verb *raqa'* refers to the spreading out of the skies, as a reference to the clouds ("Can you join him in spreading out the skies...?"). However, the second colon of the same verse could take us back to the interpretation that the *raqia'* is a solid dome ("... hard as a mirror of cast bronze?").

Tremper Longman III

REFERENCES AND RECOMMENDED READING

Seely, P. 1991. "The Firmament and the Water Above." *Westminster Theological Journal* 53:227–40.

Walton, J. H. 2011. *Genesis 1 as Ancient Cosmology.* Winona Lake, IN: Eisenbrauns.

FLAT EARTH. The Egyptians, Babylonians, and first Greek philosophers all assumed the earth was flat. However, by the fifth century BC, Greek astronomers had established that the earth was spherical, and the question ceased to be controversial among educated people shortly thereafter. This knowledge of a spherical earth has not been lost at any point since. In particular, throughout the medieval period it was universally believed, both inside and outside the church, that the earth is a sphere. The view that the Christian church encouraged belief in a flat earth during the Middle Ages is a modern myth.

Biblical Cosmology

The Bible contains some passages, in both the Old and New Testaments, for which an overly literalistic reading would imply a flat earth. However, the purpose of these passages is not to impart a geography lesson. The language used is similar to figurative phrases still in use today, such as "the four corners of the earth" in Isaiah 11:12 and Revelation 7:1.

Nonetheless, some early Christian expositors did misinterpret passages in the Bible as presenting a literal flat earth cosmology. This error was most common around Antioch and can even be found in the works of some bishops, including a follower of John Chrysostom, Severian of Gabala. The most famous example is Lactantius, a fourth-century writer and Christian convert who is the only known author in Latin to expound a flat earth. In sixth-century Alexandria, a retired merchant named Cosmas Indicopleustes produced a full-scale flat-earth cosmology. He was roundly mocked for doing so by Christian philosophers such as John Philoponus (Russell 1997, 34).

The Myth of the Flat Earth

Cosmas was the last of those we know of who truly believed that the earth is flat. However, in the sixteenth century, Francis Bacon started the myth that the church had supported a flat earth in the medieval period and even persecuted those who disagreed. Bacon had apparently misread accounts of a dispute in the eighth century between the missionary saints Virgil of Salzburg and Boniface over whether the southern hemisphere was inhabited (Hannam 2010, 29); however, this dispute was not about whether the earth was flat. Stylized medieval maps (known as T-O maps) have similarly led some modern authors to see references to a flat earth where none exist.

Christopher Columbus

The most egregious example of the flat earth myth is the widely held belief that it was Christopher Columbus who

proved that the planet is a sphere. This story dates from a fictionalized biography of Columbus by Washington Irving published in 1828 (Irving 2008). In fact, although the shape of the earth was not a matter of debate in the fifteenth century, its size was. Columbus believed the distance to the East Indies, traveling west, was a great deal shorter than it is. He was wrong about the distance but fortunate enough to chance upon the Americas before running out of food and water.

Today various flat-earth societies exist. Whether these groups actually believe the earth is flat is a matter of some controversy, but their beliefs are, in any case, of no great consequence.

James Hannam

REFERENCES AND RECOMMENDED READING

Cosmas Indicopleustes. 2010. *The Christian Topography of Cosmas, an Egyptian Monk*, trans. J. W. McCrindle. Cambridge: Cambridge University Press.
Hannam, James. 2010. *The Genesis of Science: How the Christian Middle Ages Launched the Scientific Revolution*. New York: Regnery.
Irving, Washington. 2008. *Christopher Columbus*. London: Wordsworth Classics.
Russell, Jeffrey Burton. 1997. *Inventing the Flat Earth: Columbus and Modern Historians*. Westport, CT: Praeger.

FLEW, ANTONY G. N. Arguably the skeptical philosopher who wrote more serious works defending atheism than any other scholar in history, Antony Flew (1923–2010) was born in London in 1923. Though he was the son of a conservative Methodist minister, Flew became an atheist during his midteen years.

Flew's education included an MA from St John's College, Oxford University, where he studied under the well-known philosopher **Gilbert Ryle**, and a DLit from the University of Keele. Flew frequently attended the famous Socratic Club founded in Oxford by **C. S. Lewis**, a scholar who was always willing to dialogue publicly. In fact, Flew was in attendance in February 1948 when Lewis and philosopher Elizabeth Anscombe participated in their celebrated debate.

Not long after completing his MA, Flew read before the Socratic Club what was to become one of his best-known and often-reprinted philosophical works, "Theology and Falsification" (1950). Among his some 30 volumes, other influential publications included *Hume's Philosophy of Belief* (1961), *God and Philosophy* (1966), and *The Presumption of Atheism* (1976).

During his career, Flew taught at Christ Church (Oxford University), as well as the universities of Aberdeen, Keele, and Reading in the United Kingdom, plus York in Toronto, and elsewhere. Ever the philosopher, Flew's interests migrated somewhat later in his career due to current events to political and moral philosophy, of which he seemed never to grow weary of addressing.

In 2004 Flew made the blockbuster announcement that he had come to believe in the **existence of God**, reporting that he made the decision after being inclined during his entire career to follow the evidence wherever it led. Among his reasons for doing so, he listed in order the force of **Aristotle**'s **metaphysics** (see **Aristotle**) and some recent tenets of **Intelligent Design** (Flew and Habermas 2004).

The news shocked much of the philosophical community, but especially skeptics, among whom Flew had understandably been a hero. He also surprised those who thought that he had long employed an a priori rejection of **theism**. Then in 2007 he coauthored the volume *There Is a God: How the World's Most Notorious Atheist Changed His Mind* (Flew and Varghese 2007), which included many details set within the story of his career.

Flew never embraced any revelatory views, at least publicly, and identified his view variously as that of theism or **deism**. Yet he fascinatingly reported that he was open to divine contact (see Flew 2007, 158, 213; Flew also affirmed to me that he was fully open to this possibility). Flew died in 2010.

Gary R. Habermas

REFERENCES AND RECOMMENDED READING

Flew, Antony, and Gary R. Habermas. 2004. "My Pilgrimage from Atheism to Theism: A Discussion between Antony Flew and Gary Habermas." *Philosophia Christi* 6 (2): 197–211.

Flew, Antony, with Roy Abraham Varghese. 2007. *There Is a God: How the World's Most Notorious Atheist Changed His Mind*. New York: Harper.

FLOOD, THE. One of the most widely known, and most often criticized, stories in the Bible is the story of the flood and Noah's ark. All secular geologists and almost all Christian geologists agree that there is no evidence of a worldwide flood that destroyed all of humanity. Christians, in general, disagree on the extent of the flood.

There are a few reasons for believing that the flood story has its basis in an actual event. For instance, more than 200 different cultures on all continents (and possibly as many as 500 cultures) have stories about some kind of flood. It is certainly possible that these various accounts of the flood come from a common origin. Additionally, as Christians we believe that the Bible is God's inspired word (2 Tim. 3:16)

and that any stories in the Bible that are meant to describe actual historical events are, indeed, based in actual history. For many Christians, it is perfectly reasonable to believe that the story of Noah and the flood is based on an actual event. In addition, Jesus's affirmation of the flood story may refer to its historicity (see Matt. 24:37–39).

The major area of disagreement among Christians has to do with the extent of the flood. Was it a global or local flood? Did it destroy all of humanity or only some fraction of humanity? It may seem clear that the English translation of the original Hebrew story of the flood describes a universal event. However, there is disagreement on how best to translate the text and on the origin and purpose of the text's universal language, and it is possible that a proper translation does not refer to a universal event.

Christians hold basically four views about the flood.

1. The flood was a global flood that destroyed all of humanity except Noah and his immediate family.
2. The flood was a large local flood. The water covered everything the survivors on the ark could see and all they knew. To them it was a universal flood, and their story was passed down to the author of Genesis. Consequently, the story written from their point of view is of a universal flood.
3. The flood was a large local flood. The author of Genesis uses superlative language simply to emphasize the theology of God's judgments, not to make a statement about the extent of the flood. (See the article on the **Genesis Flood** by Tremper Longman.)
4. The flood story has a theological purpose regarding God's judgment of sin and is not meant to be based on any actual event.

All of the views would affirm that a key purpose of the story is to present a theological lesson.

In scenarios 2 and 3 above, the scope of human destruction depends on when the flood occurred and the extent of human migration. Some Christians advocate view 2 and believe that humanity had not migrated very far at the time of the flood so that all humans on the earth who were not in the ark were destroyed. **Hugh Ross** refers to this scenario as a "local" and "universal" flood (Ross 2009). Others would maintain that those humans who lived in the flood plain were destroyed, and that fulfilled God's purpose of judgment.

One of the points of contention has to do with how best to translate the Hebrew text into English. The Hebrew phrase that is translated in most flood accounts as "the whole earth" or "all the earth" is *kol haerets* (Gen. 8:9). The word *kol* means "all," but the word *erets* has many meanings, including land, ground, earth, territory, and even inhabitants or people of the land. Most of the uses of the word *erets* in the flood account do not include the word *kol*. While *erets* is used over 2,500 times in the Old Testament and translated "land" about 1,500 times, it is only translated "earth" about one-fourth of the time.

The phrase *kol (ha)erets* is used about 207 times, and it might refer to the planet Earth in about 40 of those. In all of the other occurrences, it is used to refer to something else. For instance, the first two times the phrase is used in the Bible is in Genesis 2:11 and 2:13: "The name of the first [river] is the Pishon; it winds through the entire land [*kol erets*] of Havilah, where there is gold.... The name of the second river is the Gihon; it winds through the entire land [*kol erets*] of Cush." Clearly, the meaning of *kol erets* here is simply the land around the garden of **Eden**, not the whole earth. Another example of the use of *kol haerets* is in Genesis 11:1, where the text says that "the whole world [*kol haerets*] had one language and a common speech." In this context, the phrase means the population of the earth, or possibly the population of a region of the earth, not a geographic location. At times in the Bible, *kol erets* actually means "people" and not land, territory, or earth. In any case, most of the time *erets* is used in the flood account, it is not accompanied by the word *kol*. Consequently, some scholars believe that a proper translation of the flood story should not refer to the whole globe, but simply "the land" or even "the people."

Another factor to consider when trying to determine the extent of the flood is that people in biblical cultures often used universal language for emphasis in a way we would most likely not use in the twenty-first century. For instance, in Daniel 4:1 King Nebuchadnezzar sends out a proclamation to "the nations and peoples of every language, who live in all the earth." In this passage, the great extent "all the earth" does not refer to the earth as we now know it, but to a large fraction of the known earth of Daniel's day. In Colossians 1:6 Paul proclaims that the gospel "is bearing fruit and growing throughout the whole world." Again we see that Paul's use of the phrase "the whole world" is different than how we would use that term. Paul doesn't mean every corner of the seven continents of the world, but rather a large fraction of the known world of his day.

In ancient times, inclusive phrases like "all the world" could mean "a large fraction of the known world" and was used that way to make a point. Consequently, it is possible that the inclusive language about the flood has a similar meaning. This would give credence to view 3 above, that the author is using universal language primarily to make a theological point.

Michael G. Strauss

REFERENCES AND RECOMMENDED READING

Morris, Henry, and John C. Whitcomb. 2011. *The Genesis Flood, 50th Anniversary Edition*. Phillipsburg, NJ: P&R.

Ross, Hugh. 1998. *The Genesis Question*. Colorado Springs: NavPress.

———. 2009. "Exploring the Extent of the Flood." Reasons to Believe. January 1. www.reasons.org/articles/exploring-the-extent-of-the-flood-part-one.

Young, Davis A. 1977. *Creation and the Flood: An Alternative to Flood Geology and Theistic Evolution*. Grand Rapids: Baker.

———. 1982. *Christianity and the Age of the Earth*. Grand Rapids: Zondervan.

———. 1995. *The Biblical Flood: A Case Study of the Church's Response to Extra-biblical Evidence*. Grand Rapids: Eerdmans; Carlisle, UK: Paternoster.

Young, Davis A., with Ralph Stearley. 2008. *The Bible, Rocks and Time*. Downers Grove, IL: InterVarsity.

⚓ FOSSIL RECORD (Evolutionary-Creation View).

The fossil record refers collectively to all evidence of past life currently known and yet to be discovered that is contained within the earth's rock and sediment layers. The scientific study of this record is the purview of **paleontology**, but it is also of theological significance for at least two reasons. First, fossils represent not just past life but also death. The prevailing scientific understanding insists that **death** extends back in time billions of years before humans, which conflicts with interpretations of the Bible that hold that no death existed prior to Adam's sin. Second, the sequence and organization of fossils is of critical importance for arguments supporting **biological evolution**, which conflicts with interpretations of Genesis that insist that each plant and animal "kind" was created *de novo*.

The utility of the fossil record for understanding the geologic and biologic history of the earth is a relatively recent discovery, dating back to the work of William Smith in the late 1700s. Smith, tasked with surveying canal construction through Great Britain, observed that sequential layers contained unique collections of fossil organisms. More important, these layers could be traced with the same fossil groupings in the same sequential order from one side of the country to the other. Others, such as Georges Cuvier and Alexandre Brongniart, found the same sequence in rock layers in France on the opposite side of the English Channel (their study was later but beat Smith to publication; Young and Stearley 2008, 75–94).

Additional researchers soon found matching patterns of fossils throughout Europe and on other continents. The implication was that the earth had a history of repeated appearance and replacement of unique life-forms, such that the presence of a particular collection of fossil organisms (now referred to as index fossils) in a layer could be linked to a specific period of the earth's history.

These discoveries made it possible to determine the relative age of layers separated by great distances. More important, a composite history of the earth as a whole could be pieced together from the partial histories revealed by individual exposures. In simplistic terms, if fossil grouping A was found above fossil grouping B in one location, and fossil grouping C was found below group B fossils in another place, one could argue that rocks with group A fossils were younger than rocks with group C fossils, even though A, B, and C were not found in a continuous sequence at a single location. In similar fashion, if fossil group C was found in one place to sit in a layer directly on top of group B fossils, one could argue that the contact between the two layers represents a gap in time (an *unconformity*), where layers once present were removed during a time of uplift and erosion, or where no deposition was occurring.

Researchers applying this understanding across Europe developed what is now referred to as the geologic column or the geologic timescale (see **Geology**), where the history of the earth is divided into discrete intervals. Names assigned to each geologic period, such as Cambrian, Silurian, or Jurassic, were often derived from the region or the type of rocks where the original studies were performed. As an example, the Jurassic period derives its name from studies of fossil-rich limestone strata found in the Jura Mountains in France.

While relative dating methods using fossils allowed the sequential order of layers to be determined, the absolute age and duration (in years) of each interval of the earth's history was unknown. Significantly, when **radiometric dating** methods were later developed and applied to rock layers, the successive absolute ages were found to be in agreement with the order originally determined based on the observed sequence of fossils.

Index fossils are commonly used for determining the age of newly explored fossil-bearing rocks. To qualify as an index fossil, the organism has to have a widespread geographic distribution (making it more likely to be fossilized and found at a new unstudied site), and have a well-defined first and last appearance in the fossil record. Multiple index fossils are often employed, since many have overlapping ranges (e.g., if two index fossils are found in the same layer, the age is constrained to within the time range of overlap).

Today index fossils include a wide variety of marine microorganisms, such as foraminifera, diatoms, and radiolarians. The consistent ordering of these microfossils all over the world has proven invaluable to the oil industry, where there is a need to match layers in one well with layers of the same age in other wells. Rock cores or cuttings extracted from exploration wells are sent to specialized labs employing paleontologists to identify the microfossils and their placement in the geologic column. As a result of global oil exploration, with many boreholes drilled deeper than any rock exposure on the earth's surface, there are now at least two dozen locations identified around the world where every period of the geologic column is represented, in the expected order, in one stack of rock layers (Robertson Group 1989).

The use of index fossils in dating has led to a common misconception that circular reasoning is employed, where the fossils are used to date the rocks and the rocks are used to date the fossils (Morris 1977). This claim is based on the belief that the geologic column and vast ages were developed on the assumption of evolution (fossil-bearing layers arbitrarily ordered from simple to complex), followed by the use of those same fossils to "date" the rocks in which they are found (Huse 1997, 55–60). The geologic column, however, was already roughed out nearly 20 years before Darwin published *Origin of Species* in 1859.

Although the notion of biologic evolution existed before Darwin's seminal work, it bore little influence on the development of the geologic column. Most of the fossils studied to place the earth's layers into a composite sequence were bottom-dwelling marine invertebrates. Though the shapes and types clearly changed from one sequence to the next, there was not an initial recognition of increasing **complexity** or diversification over time. Several of the early developers or champions of the geologic column, such as Adam Sedgwick and Louis Agassiz, were opposed to evolutionary explanations for the history of life (Young and Stearley 2008, 109–10).

As more and more fossil-bearing layers were discovered and integrated into the geologic column, it became increasingly apparent that there was a pattern in the sequence of fossils. The oldest layers contained evidence of only single-cellular life, followed much later by multicellular marine plant and animal life. Younger layers contained a sequential appearance of fish, nonvascular land plants, amphibians, vascular plants, reptiles, dinosaurs, mammals, birds, and flowering plants. Within any category, such as mammals or flowering plants, a similar pattern is present with fossils in older layers exhibiting minimal variability, followed by increasing diversification in younger layers. Diversification within one group of life-forms often follows the disappearance of another group from all younger layers. The fossil record contains five major breaks where massive numbers of fossil **species**, genera, orders, and even classes abruptly disappeared (see **Extinction**).

The observed order and structure of the fossil record is repeated in rock and sediment layers around the world with enough consistency that the general order represented in the geologic column is widely acknowledged even by young-earth creationists (Morris 1985, 116). Disagreement lies in the explanation for the observed order and the ages.

The reigning scientific **paradigm** is biologic evolution, with life starting as simple single-celled organisms, followed by genetic adaptations over myriad generations, producing all the varied fossil and modern life-forms. Disappearance of a species from the fossil record (extinction) could result either from the death of all representative organisms or from successive adaptations within a population that led to the disappearance of particular identifying features. A classic example of the latter is the purported dinosaur-to-bird transition, of which it is currently thought that the theropod dinosaur lineage never completely died out, but over a large number of generations in select populations, offspring acquired increasingly avian characteristics leading to modern birds.

In the years following Darwin's *Origin of Species*, the paucity of transitional fossils between earlier and later life-forms (so-called missing links) was attributed to the incomplete nature of the fossil record. The **probability** that an organism will be buried intact and fossilized is very low. The fact that most of the organisms that did become fossils lie forever buried beyond our reach makes the known record still more incomplete. Subsequent fossil discoveries did include some spectacular examples of ancient organisms with intermediate characteristics, such as the famous **archaeopteryx** (having both reptile and bird features), but large gaps remained the norm. The rarity of transitional forms gave rise in the 1970s to the theory of **punctuated equilibrium**, which proposed that species remained largely unchanged for long stretches of time, followed by relatively fast adaptations in response to climatic or ecological pressures. In this scenario, the fossil record would be heavily biased toward fossils exhibiting minimal transitional changes (Eldredge and Gould 1972).

The situation today is changed considerably. A wealth of discoveries since the 1990s, as countries like China have become open to exploration, have produced a large number of fossils that exhibit features intermediate between major types of organisms. Some of the best-known transitions include fossils with traits intermediate between reptiles and mammals, between **dinosaurs** and birds, and between diverse Tertiary mammalian forms (including purported transitional series from land mammals to marine mammals and from early primates to hominids). Significantly, the age of the first appearance of many intermediate forms is also broadly consistent with evolutionary expectations (e.g. mammal-like reptiles first appear in the fossil record after the first appearance of reptiles and before the first appearance of true mammals; Martin 2004, 165–73; Prothero 2007, 270–80).

Paleontologists argue that transitions between organisms such as reptiles to mammals are clearly evident in fossils at the class level, with successive changes in jaw and inner ear configuration, dentition, palate construction, and position of the legs, yet also note that it is not possible to confidently trace modern mammals directly through any of the specific mammal-like reptile fossil species. The explanation is that similar adaptations occur in multiple populations in the same time frame in response to newly opened niches, with some populations producing offspring surviving to the present and others dying out. If small adaptations in the jaw of some reptile populations led to improved translation of sound vibrations to the ear, those adaptations could be favored in more than one variety of reptile, leading to several "cousin" species with similar intermediate traits. It is thus easy to identify transitional *features* that exemplify the likely evolutionary pathway, but difficult to identify which individual species are the direct ancestors of modern creatures.

Alternate Interpretations

Progressive creationists do not question the validity of deep time, nor physical death before sin for nonhumans, but they reject so-called macroevolution in favor of a series of miraculous creation events over time consistent with the order described in Genesis 1. This position faces two difficulties. First, the appearance of new fossil species is spread throughout geologic time with no discrete sets of creation events. Though mass extinctions are followed by accelerated appearances of new biologic forms, new species continue to appear in the intervals between the **extinction** events. Second, the order of creatures created in Genesis of flowering plants, fish and birds, and then terrestrial animals, does not fit the observed fossil sequence.

Young-earth creationists start with the assumption that there was no death of any kind before sin. From this perspective, all the earth's fossil-bearing layers, including those lying within and beneath miles of accumulated sedimentary rock, must postdate **Adam and Eve**'s transgression. The enormity of death and displaced sediment over a short span of time requires a global cataclysmic event, giving rise to the associated claim that most of the fossil-bearing layers on earth were deposited during or shortly after the year of Noah's flood. Studies of the earth's layers or natural processes with the intent of finding evidence for a global flood of immense violence is termed flood geology. The general form of the geologic column is accepted, but with most of the periods assigned to "early flood" and "late flood" (e.g., Vail 2003, 36).

Alternate explanations offered by various flood-geology advocates for the observed ordering of the fossil record include (1) ability of more complex organisms to flee to higher ground (Morris 1985, 118–20), (2) sequential burial of distinct ecosystems containing unique types of organisms (Wise 2002, 170–76), (3) hydraulic sorting of organisms during the flood based on size, shape, and density (Huse 1997, 58–59), and (4) postdepositional sorting based on size and density due to vibrations caused by violent and sustained earthquake activity (Brown 2001, 168–81).

Though disavowing classical evolution, many leading young-earth creationists now embrace a form of punctuated equilibrium, where God created *kinds* of creatures (such as a single "cat-kind") *de novo*, with minimal subsequent change prior to the flood and ultrafast evolution after the flood to produce all the variations found in "postflood" layers and observed living today (Lightner 2008; Morris 2001). Advocates of this position coined the term *baraminology* as the study of initial "created kinds" (baramins [Heb. *bara*, "create"]) and their subsequent evolution (Frair 2000).

The primary difficulty for all flood explanations is the nearly complete absence of mixing of organisms that should be expected. Fleeing organisms should bring hyenas together with velociraptors, and eagles together with pterodactyls. Giant tsunamis sweeping across continents should produce layers of jumbled marine and terrestrial organisms as the norm. Hydraulic or vibrational sorting should mix creatures of similar size, like woolly mammoths and triceratops dinosaurs. Air-breathing marine reptiles like mosasaurs should be mixed with air-breathing marine mammals like dolphins. Bloated and floating carcasses should result in some layers with all manner of animal life-forms. And microscopic fossils like pollen from flowering plants that are easily transported great distances should be distributed in layers everywhere. In contrast, the observed fossil record is highly ordered, with examples of mixing limited only to what one might expect from an occasional terrestrial creature falling into a river and being swept out to sea.

Gregg Davidson

REFERENCES AND RECOMMENDED READING

Brown, Walt. 2001. *In the Beginning: Compelling Evidence for Creation and the Flood.* 7th ed. Phoenix: Center for Scientific Creation.

Eldredge, N., and S. J. Gould. 1972. "Punctuated Equilibria: An Alternative to Phyletic Gradualism." In *Models in Palaeobiology*, ed. T. J. M. Schopf. San Francisco: Freeman, Cooper.

Frair, Wayne. 2000. "Baraminology—Classification of Created Organisms." *Creation Research Science Quarterly* 37 (2): 82–91.

Huse, Scott M. 1997. *The Collapse of Evolution.* 3rd ed. Grand Rapids: Baker.

Lightner, Jean. 2008. "Life: Designed by God to Adapt." *Answers in Depth* 3 (June 4). www.answersingenesis.org/articles/aid/v3/n1/life-designed-to-adapt.

Martin, Robert A. 2004. *Missing Links: Evolutionary Concepts and Transitions through Time.* Boston: Jones and Bartlett.

Morris, Henry. 1977. "Circular Reasoning in Evolutionary Biology." *Acts & Facts* 6 (6).

———, ed. 1985. *Scientific Creationism.* 2nd ed. Green Forest, AR: Master.

———. 2001. "The Microwave of Evolution." *Back to Genesis* 152 (August): a–d. www.icr.org/i/pdf/btg/btg-152.pdf.

Prothero, Donald R. 2007. *Evolution: What the Fossils Say and Why It Matters.* New York: Columbia University Press.

Robertson Group. 1989. *Stratigraphic Database of Major Sedimentary Basins of the World.* Llandudno Gwynedd, Wales: Robertson Group.

Vail, Tom, ed. 2003. *Grand Canyon: A Different View.* Green Forest, AR: Master.

Wise, Kurt P. 2002. *Faith, Form, and Time: What the Bible Teaches and Science Confirms about Creation and the Age of the Universe.* Nashville: B&H.

Young, Davis A., and Ralph F. Stearley. 2008. *The Bible, Rocks and Time.* Downers Grove, IL: InterVarsity.

↪ FOSSIL RECORD (Young-Earth Creation View).

When were fossils formed, and under what conditions? A young-earth view, at its core, affirms that (1) creation spanned six 24-hour days in which all things were made (cf. Ex. 20:11; 31:17); (2) the **genealogies** connecting Adam to Abram in Genesis 5 and 11 record a lineage of historical individuals that spans only thousands of years; and (3) sin brings forth profound changes to the natural economy, including both spiritual and physical **death** to humans and physical death to "living" (*nephesh*) creatures.

A resulting corollary is that the bulk of the fossil record is a product of a global destruction by Noah's flood. This contrasts sharply with old-earth and evolutionary views that consider the fossil record as a series of snapshots over a 3.8-billion-year history of life on earth. Here I briefly address some biblical issues that should govern our approach to the fossil record and then survey several notable scientific observations that point toward a rapid, catastrophic, and recent formation of the fossil record.

Biblical Issues

Concerning the core affirmations of young-earth creationism, there is little disagreement that in Genesis 1 *yôm* is intended to mean a normal day rather than some unspecified long period of time (Hamilton 1990; Waltke and Fredricks 2001; Westermann 1984). The larger debate at present concerns the structure, genre, and purpose of Genesis 1 and how the "days" function (e.g., literal versus symbolic; see Charles 2014 for a recent exchange). The arguments for a literal 24-hour day are well supported (see Fretheim 1999 for a brief but substantive defense, and Mortenson and Ury 2008 for more detailed treatments on a number of Gen. 1–11 issues). Regarding the genealogies, the individuals listed in Genesis 5 and 11 are attested as historical in both testaments (e.g., 1 Chron. 1:1–24; Luke 3:34–38; Jude 14). The genealogies need not list *only* father-son relationships to support a young earth; what matters most is that the genealogies record *actual* people with real ancestor-descendant relationships. But the genealogies can only be stretched so far and still retain their accuracy, coherence, and function. Only generations of people, not the named periods or eras of geologic time, can be placed in genealogical gaps.

The timing of animal death and carnivory is more directly related to the fossil record. On day 6 of the creation week, God states, "'I give you every seed-bearing plant on the face of the whole earth and every tree that has fruit with seed in it. They will be yours for food. And to all the beasts of the earth and all the birds in the sky and all the creatures that move along the ground—everything that has the breath of life in it—I give every green plant for food.' And it was so" (Gen. 1:29–30). There appears to be no death among man or animals initially (see Westermann 1984, 164–65), and this places animal carnivory (including that seen in the fossil record) *after* **the fall** (cf. Gen. 3:14, which appears to extend to all animals). Yet old-earth perspectives requires that carnivory, cancer, infection, disease, and suffering have been integral (even necessary) parts of God's "very good" creation for hundreds of millions of years.

The provision of food for animals in Genesis 1:30 mirrors the plants and fruit given to mankind in the previous verse. Averbeck (2014) argues that Genesis 1:30 allows for animal carnivory because plants are the ultimate source of food for all creatures. This logic would likewise permit humans to eat meat at creation. This is difficult to reconcile with Genesis 9:3, where God says to Noah, "Everything that lives and moves about will be food for you. Just as I gave you the green plants, I now give you everything." A vegetarian animal realm also finds parallels in the new creation, for in the new heavens and earth "the lion will eat straw like the oxen" (Isa. 65:25; cf. Isa 11:7; see Hamilton 1990, 140). Poetic passages that find no problem with carnivory have little application to conditions during the creation week, since these passages describe the creation as it operates *today* (e.g., Psalm 104; note esp. the presence of wine and ships).

The scope of Scripture is clear: in the beginning, land animals and birds were given plants just as their human rulers were. Leading up to the flood, God's warning to Noah that he will destroy "all people" (*basar*) because "the earth is filled with violence" (Gen. 6:13) attests to pervasive animal violence (likely including carnivory), and the fossil record is a testimony to this postfall departure from the animals' "very good" initial state.

Scientific Issues

When paleontologists speak of the fossil record, they refer to both the preservation of organisms in general and the overall ordering and sequence of those fossils. The many geochronologic names (e.g., Devonian, Jurassic, and Eocene) reflect the pattern of different types of fossils found in vertical relationships to each other around the world (e.g., armored fish, dinosaurs, and mammals). This pattern is real and must be the basis for discussion among both young-earth creationists and old-earth advocates. In arguing for a global flood as the cause for the majority of the fossil record, I briefly address five scientific issues: the sudden appearance of complex ecosystems, fossil tracks and trails, sediment mixing by organisms, exceptional and unexpected fossil preservation, and transitional forms.

Sudden Appearance of Complex Ecosystems

Paleontologists read the fossil record from the bottom (oldest) toward the top (youngest). One striking feature is the first appearance of a multitude of complex animals, referred to as the Cambrian "explosion" (including marine arthropods, mollusks, echinoderms, brachiopods, numerous worm groups, and even jawless fish). The abrupt appearance of this rich and complex ecosystem stands in stark contrast with the gradualist expectations of evolutionary theory. Old-earth creationists and some **intelligent design** advocates argue that the sudden appearance of the **Cambrian explosion** reflects a design event (e.g., Meyer 2013), while young-earth creationists identify it as among the first marine ecosystems destroyed by Noah's flood (Garner 2009; Snelling 2009; Wise 2002).

Tracks and Trails

As animals move about on fresh, wet sediment, they leave tracks and trails. These imprints are more delicate than bones, shells, and exoskeletons; therefore their preservation as *ichnofossils* ("trace fossils") is uncommon because erosion frequently destroys them soon after their formation. For any chance of preservation, a layer of new sediment must be quickly deposited on top of the tracks. More curious, though, is the propensity for a group (amphibians, dinosaurs, etc.) to have a high diversity of track types found well *below* the peak diversity of the body-part remains of that group (Brand and Florence 1982). It seems that many organisms ran over moist sediment only to be destroyed and deposited in the geological layers situated somewhere above the tracks. This comports well with closely spaced events during a global flood, but is difficult to reconcile with old-earth views where long spans of time would separate the tracks from their track makers.

Bioturbation

Sedimentary rocks are divided into units called *beds*, and these beds frequently display internal, fine-scale layers called *lamina*. Many animals spend their lives burrowing through sediment looking for food. In the ocean floor today, clams, worms, and other organisms are constantly churning up sediments and disrupting the fine lamina (a process called *bioturbation*). The rate at which this happens depends on several factors (sediment type, the organisms involved, etc.), but in many cases the process is very rapid. Replicating the conditions in estuary sediments, one study (Gingras et al. 2008) showed that just 10 burrowing organisms could completely bioturbate a one-meter square unit of sediment in 42 days, and high organism densities could completely bioturbate the same square-meter unit in as little as 61 minutes!

The question, then, is this: If the earth is ancient and past biological/geological processes were similar to today's, why are there *any* lamina preserved in sedimentary rocks at all? The answer lies with catastrophic sediment deposition during Noah's flood, which accounts for ubiquitous lamination and simultaneously disallows normal bioturbation to be accomplished. A unit-by-unit survey over one mile's thickness

of sedimentary rock revealed little evidence of bioturbation: only about 10 percent displayed minor bioturbation, and only about 1 percent full bioturbation (Leonard Brand and Art Chadwick, pers. comm. 2014). The sedimentary record is full of rapidly deposited, finely laminated sediments that display no evidence of being worked over time by animals, features that are unexpected given modern bioturbation rates and old-earth expectations but are in full harmony with a recent global flood.

Fossil Preservation

The fossil record is one of preservation, including patterns of preservation consistent with a recent origin of the entire fossil record but quite inconsistent with old-earth expectations. A wide variety of cases may be explored, and here I focus on three: equivalent preservation among different shell thicknesses, the preservation of unfossilized soft tissues, and the presence of radioactive carbon in fossil remains.

Thick vs. thin shells. An extensive study of marine invertebrate fossils (Behrensmeyer et al. 2005) revealed no preference toward the preservation of thick-shelled marine invertebrates over thin-shelled ones. This is surprising because modern observations confirm that thin-shelled invertebrate remains are degraded more quickly by the actions of waves and other organisms than the more durable thick-shelled forms. Yet the fossil record of marine invertebrates shows no such preservational bias. This is expected in global flood models because the sediments containing the fossils were buried in quick succession by catastrophic processes, leaving little time for degradation. Once again, the modern-day processes used as guides by old-earth proponents do not comport with the geological evidence.

Soft tissue preservation. In 2005 the scientific community was shocked by the discovery of original, unfossilized soft tissue preserved in the femur (upper leg bone) of a *Tyrannosaurus rex* (Schweitzer et al. 2005). Despite an age assignment of 68 million years old, the interior of the femur contained original blood vessels and other tissues (the blood vessels could even be stretched and snapped back into shape), and various proteins were later isolated and identified. In 2009 Schweitzer and her colleagues described another fossil (an 80-million-year-old duck-billed dinosaur) that also retained these and other original soft tissues. Osteocytes (bone-forming cells) and additional proteins were identified, and subsequently fragments of **DNA** were recovered.

A major issue is that the unfossilized proteins and DNA have persisted far beyond all empirically derived preservation time frames. Given realistic burial conditions, even the most durable proteins (such as collagen) would degrade completely over a span of hundreds of thousands of years, not millions. DNA experiences complete degradation within the same time frame only under the best possible conditions (Allentoft et al. 2012). Yet these materials were positively identified in fossils ostensibly tens of millions of years old. Their persistence over this time is beyond unlikely. Instead, recent burial during the flood can explain the recovery of these materials within their empirically determined preservation horizons.

These and dozens of other similar discoveries have been summarized by Thomas (2013), which indicates that original, unfossilized organic material is far more widespread than realized. Schweitzer and her colleagues have proposed that particular chemical reactions involving the iron within these bones could stabilize the original tissues, though these proposals face significant challenges from other empirical studies.

Carbon, carbon everywhere. Scientists refer to organisms as carbon-based life-forms because carbon is the core component of the proteins, carbohydrates, and fats found in all cells. While an organism lives, a small portion of the carbon in its body is radioactive carbon-14 (^{14}C). This carbon is formed in the atmosphere by solar radiation, absorbed during photosynthesis, then passed through the food chain via consumption. As a result, all organisms have a small constituent of ^{14}C in their body tissues. ^{14}C is unstable and decays over time into nitrogen, with a measured half-life of 5,370 years. While an organism is alive, the loss from decay is balanced by gains via consumption. After death the ratio of ^{14}C to nonradioactive carbon (^{12}C) changes as the ^{14}C decays and the organism no longer eats. Thus by comparing the ratios of ^{14}C to ^{12}C, scientists estimate ages of organic materials.

If the earth is young and a recent flood produced the majority of the fossil record, then it is possible that original ^{14}C may still be preserved among fossils. Indeed, measurable amounts of ^{14}C have been discovered with hundreds of examples known from petrified wood, fossil shells, bone, coal, oil, and natural gas, indicating that ^{14}C is ubiquitous in the fossil record (see Snelling 2009 for a review). Each of these instances from fossils and fuels are purportedly tens to hundreds of millions of years old, yet at the fast rate that ^{14}C decays, no measurable ^{14}C should be found in fossils older than 100,000 years. Contamination of *all* of these materials with modern ^{14}C is unlikely, particularly when the chemical compositions are so varied (calcium carbonate

for shells, hydroxyapatite in bone, woody tissues, etc.), as are their depositional and fossilization settings.

More surprising was the discovery of ^{14}C in diamonds conventionally thought to be nearly 2 billion years old (Baumgardner 2005). Contamination is virtually impossible, due to the four strong covalent bonds each carbon atom maintains among its neighboring atoms (these bonds account for why diamond is the hardest naturally occurring substance on earth). No old-earth geologist had previously examined diamonds for ^{14}C due to their presumed ancient age and impregnable nature. But beginning with a young-earth framework, an analysis revealed measurable levels of ^{14}C in all 12 samples submitted for testing, confirming explicitly young-earth predictions.

Some old-earth proponents (e.g., Davidson 2009) argue that all these occurrences reflect contamination or in situ production of new ^{14}C from nearby radioactive activity, rather than original ^{14}C. However, the ^{14}C dates provided by the laboratories are already adjusted in case low levels of contamination occurred during processing, and the concentration of nearby radioactive sources in coal is orders of magnitude lower than needed to produce the ^{14}C observed. Moreover, the ^{14}C in other fossil materials (noted above) from sedimentary host rocks with near-zero radiation sources points away from in situ sources of radiation-produced ^{14}C. Like the discovery of unfossilized proteins and DNA, the widespread presence of original ^{14}C in fossils and diamonds points strongly to a recent creation and a global flood.

Transitional Forms

An important evidence for evolution is the existence of transitional forms, or fossils that appear to bridge morphological gaps between two distinct groups. Transitional forms fall into two categories. The first are transitions that exist *within* a created kind. For example, if the several living horse **species** descended from an original ark-borne pair, then there must be transitions that connect the ark pair to the several modern species. Many young-earth creationists view the Cenozoic fossil record (the "age of mammals") as reflecting the postflood recolonization of earth (Austin et al. 1994; Wise 2002; Snelling 2009). Transitions among the many fossil species of horses, rhinos, camels, and other groups are allowed for, and expected by, these young-earth models.

The second and more difficult category is what Wise (2002) terms "stratomorphic intermediates": fossils that appear to cross between created kinds and that are found in sediments of the right age for the transition, such as

archaeopteryx and various mammal-like reptiles. There are numerous examples of possible stratomorphic intermediates (more than most creationists realize), and their existence can be counted as fulfilled predictions of evolution. Space prevents a detailed treatment of several candidate strato-morphic intermediates, so here the focus briefly will be on one of the most important recent discoveries: the "fishapod" named *Tiktaalik* (Daeschler et al. 2006).

Tiktaalik is a sarcopterygian ("lobe-finned") fish, somewhat similar to living lungfishes and coelocanths. Its physical form includes the expected fish structures of gills and fins, but the fin bones show similarities to the limbs of land-dwelling vertebrates. Its teeth, skull bones, and vertebrae share commonalities not only with other sarcopterygians but also with early amphibians. Given this mix of features and the fact that *Tiktalik* is found in sediments dated prior to the body fossils of amphibians, it appears to be a robust case. But an interesting wrinkle arrived in 2010 when a trackway made by an amphibian was found in sedimentary rocks that predate not only the oldest known amphibian body fossils by 18 million years but also *Tiktaalik* and other likely sarcopterygian transitional candidates by 10 million years (Niedźwiedzki et al. 2010). Following the pattern of tracks and body fossils discussed above, the difficult-to-fossilize amphibian tracks are found far below the easy-to-fossilize bones of *both* their track makers *and* their presumed ancestors.

Conclusions

The fossil record displays numerous features fully consistent with a young earth ravaged by a global flood, and this position finds support throughout church history precisely because it is a robust, consistent, and natural reading of the whole of Scripture. Old-earth and evolutionary conceptions of the fossil record, though often well-argued on scientific grounds, are extraordinarily difficult to reconcile with the biblical text and face significant scientific challenges. What is clear now is that a young-earth and global-flood model can guide scientific research, asking (and answering!) questions that old-earth and evolutionary proponents cannot. Such is the hallmark of good science. Over the past few centuries, numerous old-earth scriptural interpretations have come and gone, having failed to rationally synthesize presumed long ages with Scripture. Though more nuanced and sophisticated than their predecessors, modern attempts to avoid a young earth and global flood will likewise founder, both in the pages of Scripture and on the shoals of the fossil record.

Marcus R. Ross

REFERENCES AND RECOMMENDED READING

Allentoft, Morten E., Matthew J. Collins, David Harker, et al. 2012. "The Half-Life of DNA in Bone: Measuring Decay Kinetics in 158 Dated Fossils." *Proceedings of the Royal Society of London, B* 279 (1748): 4724–33.

Austin, Steven A., John R. Baumgardner, D. Russell Humphreys, et al. 1994. "Catastrophic Plate Tectonics: A Global Flood Model of Earth History." In *Proceedings of the Third International Conference on Creationism*, ed. R. E. Walsh, 609–62. Pittsburgh: Creation Science Fellowship.

Averbeck, Richard. 2014. "A Literary Day, Inter-textual, and Contextual Reading of Genesis 1–2. In *Reading Genesis 1–2: An Evangelical Conversation*, ed. J. Daryl Charles, 7–34. Peabody, MA: Hendrickson.

Baumgardner, John R. 2005. "14C Evidence for a Recent Global Flood and a Young Earth." In *Radioisotopes and the Age of the Earth*, ed. L. Vardiman, A. A. Snelling, and E. F. Chafin, 2:587–630. El Cajon, CA: Institute for Creation Research.

Behrensmeyer, A. K., Franz T. Fursich, Robert A. Gastaldo, et al. 2005. "Are the Most Durable Shelly Taxa Also the Most Common in the Marine Fossil Record?" *Paleobiology* 31 (4): 607–23.

Brand, Leonard, and Art Chadwick. 2014. Personal communication.

Brand, Leonard, and James Florence. 1982. "Stratigraphic Distribution of Vertebrate Fossil Footprints Compared with Body Fossils." *Origins* 9 (2): 67–74.

Charles, J. Daryl, ed. 2014. *Reading Genesis 1–2: An Evangelical Conversation*. Peabody, MA: Hendrickson.

Daeschler, Edward B., Neil H. Shubin, Farish A. Jenkins, et al. 2006. "A Devonian Tetrapod-like Fish and the Evolution of the Tetrapod Body Plan." *Nature* 440:757–63.

Davidson, G. R. 2009. *When Faith and Science Collide*. Oxford, MS: Malius.

Fretheim, Terence E. 1999. "Were the Days of Creation Twenty-Four Hours Long? Yes." In *The Genesis Debate*, ed. Ronald Youngblood, 12–35. Eugene, OR: Wipf and Stock.

Garner, Paul. 2009. *The New Creationism*. Faverdale North, UK: EP Books.

Gingras, Murray K., S. George Pemberton, Shahim E. Dashtgard, et al. 2008. "How Fast Do Marine Invertebrates Burrow?" *Palaeogeography, Palaeoclimatology, Palaeoecology* 270:280–86.

Hamilton, Victor P. 1990. *The Book of Genesis: Chapters 1–17*. Grand Rapids: Eerdmans.

Meyer, Steven. 2013. *Darwin's Doubt*. New York: HarperOne.

Mortenson, Terry, and Thane Ury. 2008. *Coming to Grips with Genesis*. Green Forest, AR: Master.

Niedźwiedzki, Grzegorz, Piotr Szrek, Katarzyna Narkiewicz, et al. 2010. "Tetrapod Trackways from the Early Middle Devonian Period of Poland." *Nature* 463 (7277): 43–48.

Schweitzer, Mary H., Jennifer L. Wittmeyer, John R. Horner, et al. 2005. "Soft-Tissue Vessels and Cellular Preservation in *Tyrannosaurus rex*." *Science* 307:1952–55.

Scheweitzer, Mary H., Wenxia Zheng, Chris L. Organ, et al. 2009. "Biomolecular Characterization and Protein Sequences of the Campanian Hadrosaur *B. canadensis*." *Science* 234:626–31.

Snelling, Andrew. 2009. *Earth's Catastrophic Past*. 2 vols. Dallas: Institute for Creation Research.

Thomas, Brian. 2013. "A Review of Original Tissue Fossils and Their Age Implications." In *Proceedings of the Seventh International Conference on Creationism*, ed. R. E. Walsh. Pittsburgh: Creation Science Fellowship.

VanDoodewaard, William. 2015. *The Quest for the Historical Adam*. Grand Rapids: Reformation Heritage.

Waltke, Bruce K., and Cathi J. Fredricks. 2001. *Genesis: A Commentary*. Grand Rapids: Zondervan.

Westermann, Claus. 1984. *Genesis 1–11: A Commentary*. Minneapolis: Augsburg and London: SPCK.

Wise, Kurt P. 2002. *Faith, Form, and Time*. Nashville: B&H.

FREUD, SIGMUND. Sigmund Freud (1856–1939) was an Austrian physician, neurologist, and writer who is best known for being the founder of **psychoanalysis**. He is widely recognized as one of the greatest scientists and thinkers of the modern era (Gay 1999). His theories not only revolutionized the allied mental health professions but have had a vast, ongoing impact on Western thought, science, and culture. In particular, his theories on personality, the unconscious mind, defense mechanisms, sexuality, and aggression were among the most influential ideas of the twentieth century (Gay 1988).

Life. Freud was born into a poor Jewish family in Freiburg, Moravia (present-day Pøíbor, Czech Republic) in 1856. In 1860 his family moved to Vienna, Austria, where Freud lived and worked for most of his life. He graduated as a doctor of medicine in 1881, subsequently specializing in treating "nervous disorders" and eventually opening a private practice in 1886. The same year he married Martha Bernays, with whom he had six children and remained married his entire life. Near the end of his influential yet controversial career, Freud fled Nazi-occupied Vienna for London, England, where he died in 1939, following a long battle with jaw cancer (Gay 1988).

Key contributions. From the 1890s until 1938, Freud wrote prolifically. His first major work was *Studies on Hysteria* (1895), in which he and Josef Breuer argued that neurosis is caused by repressed sexuality and cured through talk therapy involving free association (i.e., unreservedly saying whatever comes to mind), catharsis (i.e., relieving tension by expressing repressed thoughts and feelings), interpretation (i.e., statements or questions designed to promote insight into unconscious psychodynamics), and dream analysis (i.e., exploring the manifest content and latent meaning of one's dreams).

In *The Interpretation of Dreams* (1900), Freud described his topographic theory (i.e., mind is comprised of the conscious, preconscious, and unconscious), the notion of primary- and secondary-process thought (i.e., irrational, pleasure-seeking vs. rational, reality-constrained thinking), and the idea that dreams represent unfulfilled unconscious wishes.

In *Three Essays on the Theory of Sexuality* (1905) and its subsequent editions, Freud explained his controversial ideas about human sexuality, including his psychosexual-development theory and notions of infantile sexuality. Also, in his *Group Psychology and the Analysis of the Ego* (1921) and *The Ego and the Id* (1923), Freud introduced his structural

theory, arguing that the mind is comprised of the id (i.e., instinctual impulses toward sex/pleasure and rage/aggression), ego (i.e., mediator among instinctual impulses, reality constraints, and internalized moral standards), and superego (i.e., internalized moral arbiter; Gay, 1988).

Freud's bestselling books were *The Psychopathology of Everyday Life* (1901) and *Introductory Lectures on Psychoanalysis* (1916–17). These works popularized psychoanalytic ideas such as repression (i.e., unconsciously motivated forgetting), slips of the tongue ("Freudian slips"), transference (i.e., redirecting unconscious feelings or desires toward a substitutionary person), and making the unconscious conscious (e.g., developing insight; Gay 1988).

Ideas about religion. Freud was a vehement atheist who espoused controversial ideas about religion. Notably, in his books *Totem and Taboo* (1913), *The Future of an Illusion* (1927), *Civilization and Its Discontents* (1930), and *Moses and Monotheism* (1938), Freud argued that religion is a culturally transmitted "obsessional neurosis," God is an "exalted father figure," and **religious experience** is merely illusory wish fulfillment. He viewed science and religion as incompatible enemies, and he yearned for a day when science rendered religion obsolete (Gay 1988).

Edward B. Davis and Andrew D. Cuthbert

REFERENCES AND RECOMMENDED READING

Bland, Earl D., and Brad D. Strawn, eds. 2014. *Christianity and Psychoanalysis: A New Conversation.* Downers Grove, IL: InterVarsity.
Freud, Sigmund. 1953–74. *The Standard Edition of the Complete Psychological Works of Sigmund Freud.* 24 vols. Ed. J. Strachey, A. Strachey, and A. Tyson. London: Hogarth. See www.instituteofcfs.org/informationresources/the-freud-abstracts for abstracts of each volume. See www.freud.org.uk/education for educational resources on Freud.
Gay, Peter. 1988. *Freud: A Life for Our Time.* New York: Doubleday.
———. 1999. "Sigmund Freud." *Time* 153 (12): 66–69.
Hoffman, Marie T. 2011. *Toward Mutual Recognition: Relational Psychoanalysis and the Christian Narrative.* New York: Routledge.
Jones, James W. 1991. *Contemporary Psychoanalysis and Religion: Transference and Transcendence.* New Haven, CT: Yale University Press.
Mitchell, Stephen A., and Margaret J. Black. 1996. *Freud and Beyond: A History of Modern Psychoanalytic Thought.* New York: Basic Books.
Rizzuto, Ana-María. 1998. *Why Did Freud Reject God? A Psychodynamic Interpretation.* New Haven, CT: Yale University Press.

FUNCTIONALISM. Functionalism is the view that mental states are defined by their causes and effects, that is, by their roles within suitably organized systems. In order to be possessed of a mind a system need not include a particular substance or be composed of a certain type of thing but should have a particular type of organization.

The move toward functionalism was brought about by the failure of certain alternatives to unpopular immaterialist views of mind. While **behaviorism** proved incapable of accounting for mental life in the absence of internal mental states, mind-brain identity theory proved incapable of accommodating the different physiological bases for the same mental state within different types of organisms. A family of functionalist views arose in response both to these difficulties and to developments in computer science suggesting that inner states might be systematically describable in computational terms (Putnam 1960, 148–79).

Functionalism holds that inner states are mental not because they possess particular intrinsic properties but because they stand in particular causal relations to environmental stimuli (inputs), behavioral responses (outputs), and—crucially—to other mental states (internal states). For example, according to the functionalist, the belief that "it is icy outside" can be possessed by *any* system capable of being in a state characterized by the relevant relations. These relations might include being caused by the observation (inputs) that the temperature is below zero, being connected to the further belief (internal state) that it has been wet outside, and being a cause of behaviors (outputs) such as careful walking.

Functionalism has bizarre consequences. It is unable to accommodate the intrinsic, qualitative character or "feel" of conscious mental states (*qualia*) that seem from a first person point of view to be essential to them. For example, there is a distinctive experiential quality (as Nagel 1974 expressed it, "something that it is like") to be in pain, and intuitively it is this qualitative aspect that seems essential to the pain itself.

A number of well-known thought experiments illustrate the problem. Consider the issue of "inverted qualia" raised by Block and others (Block 1990, 53–79). Given functionalism, two individuals could be functionally organized in precisely the same way but nevertheless possess totally different qualia. For example, looking at a ripe tomato, both individuals could be in the same functionally defined mental state, describing the tomato as "red," while the quale experienced by one individual is that which the other would experience when looking at a healthy grass lawn. In fact, the experience of the entire color spectrum could be inverted in a way that is functionally irrelevant and hence empirically undetectable.

Chalmers discusses the related problem of "absent qualia." Functionalism seems to imply the possibility of creatures physically indistinguishable from us in all respects other than a complete lack of phenomenal conscious experience. Chalmers argues that the idea of such "philosophical zombies" (Chalmers 1996) is coherent, and this suggests that functionalism is incapable of providing any account of the experiential nature of **consciousness**. This highlights the hopelessness of functionalism to address the features of mental life that are most fundamental to it.

Jonathan Loose

REFERENCES AND RECOMMENDED READING

Block, Ned. 1990. "Inverted Earth." *Philosophical Perspectives* 4:53–79.
Chalmers, David. 1996. *The Conscious Mind: In Search of a Fundamental Theory.* Oxford: Oxford University Press.
Dennett, Daniel C. 1991. *Consciousness Explained.* London: Penguin.
Lewis, David. 1980. "Mad Pain and Martian Pain." In *Readings in the Philosophy of Psychology*, ed. Ned Block. 2 vols. Cambridge, MA: Harvard University Press.
Nagel, Thomas. 1974. "What Is It Like to Be a Bat?" *Philosophical Review* 4:435–50.
Putnam, H. 1960. "Minds and Machines." In *Dimensions of Mind*, ed. Sidney Hook, 148–79. New York: New York University Press.

G

GAIA HYPOTHESIS. As a consultant to NASA, British scientist James Lovelock was tasked to devise an experiment to determine whether there was life on Mars. He argued that a planet with life would have a very different atmosphere from one without life. Thus the earth's atmospheric composition, comprising 0.03 percent carbon dioxide, 78 percent nitrogen, and 21 percent oxygen, must be biologically determined since, in the absence of life, it should have come into chemical equilibrium and comprised 99 percent carbon dioxide. Infrared observations of Mars in the 1960s showed that its atmosphere was 95 percent carbon dioxide, close to the equilibrium value, and therefore incapable of supporting life.

It is considerations such as this that led Lovelock to the Gaia hypothesis, named after the Greek earth goddess, and postulating that the earth can be regarded as a single living organism (Lovelock 1979). More precisely, the biosphere is a self-regulating system that controls and maintains the conditions for life. This is in contrast to the traditional view whereby the planet provides the conditions for life: according to the Gaia hypothesis, life gives rise to the planetary conditions we observe and controls them.

Lovelock thinks that the earth regulates its temperature and composition like a cybernetic control system, using negative feedback loops. For example, "The biosphere actively maintains and controls the composition of the air around us so as to provide an optimum environment for terrestrial life" (Lovelock 1979, 69). Thus, if the oxygen concentration rises, and a rise by as little as 4 percent would spell disaster, it is reduced by combination with methane produced by bacterial fermentation in seabed muds and other wet areas where carbon is buried.

Richard Dawkins, for whom **natural selection** operates at the level of the individual gene, has attacked the Gaia hypothesis because he does not see how life can cooperate to regulate the environment (Dawkins 1982, 234–37). In response, Lovelock has illustrated how the hypothesis is compatible with Darwinian evolution by producing a model, "Daisyworld," of a planet containing dark and light colored daisies. Color determines the proportion of incident light reflected. As the planet's illuminating star grows brighter, the proportion of dark and light daisies alters, but the temperature

remains almost constant over a long period. In contrast, in a traditional model, life has no influence on the environment but merely adapts to it: then the temperature of the planet rises proportionately to the star's luminosity, and daisies die out far sooner (Lovelock 1988, 36–39).

Lovelock is regarded as something of a maverick in the orthodox scientific community, yet his theory cannot be dismissed lightly. What is its relevance for the science-faith discourse?

First, Gaia is a holistic theory and therefore antireductionist. As Lovelock says, the "properties of the planet could not be predicted from the sum of its parts." Second, whether the theory is right or wrong, Lovelock has highlighted some significant facts pertinent to mankind's existence on earth. Thus many of the parameters of the environment are apparently "finely tuned" for us to be here. Oxygen concentration is one; the salinity of the sea maintained at 3.4 percent is another — a rise to 6 percent would destroy life on earth. As Bishop Hugh Montefiore has observed (Montefiore 1985, 43–58), these properties seem contrived for human existence, just like the more familiar anthropic coincidences in cosmology.

Gaian thought may also lead in a more overtly spiritual, albeit pantheist or pagan, direction. Lovelock rejects any creedal form of religion, though he "respects the intuition of those who believe" and is moved by the beauty of the prayer book liturgy (Lovelock 1988, 205). Nevertheless, he has great reverence, of a religious kind, for Gaia, and speaks of "the whole planet celebrating a sacred ceremony." He likens Gaia to the Virgin Mary, close and manageable compared with the more distant Yahweh, and writes, "She is of this Universe and, conceivably, a part of God. On Earth she is the source of life everlasting and is alive now; she gave birth to humankind and we are a part of her" (Lovelock 1988, 206).

Some theologians conceive the world as "God's body" (Jantzen 1984; McFague 1987), and a similar idea underlies the **panentheism** of **Arthur Peacocke** and others (e.g., Peacocke 2001), whether with conscious reference to Gaia or not. As the human body is a complex organization of matter with a mind that interacts with and works through that body, so the world is a highly organized complex system through which God might express his will. However, from the point of view of Christian orthodoxy, this idea is surely best treated as a helpful analogy for **divine action**, via top-down **causation**, rather than a literal account of God's relation to the world.

The name Gaia, and anthropomorphic talk of the earth as a living organism, lend misleading credence to a redeification of nature. But talk of geophysiology and a cybernetic control system would perhaps not have the same ring to it. As Lawrence Osborn has pointed out (Osborn 1992), we need to distinguish carefully between the scientific hypothesis and the myth attached to it.

More recently Lovelock has entered the **climate change** debate. He thinks climate change is irreversible because he sees positive, rather than negative, feedback in, for example, the depletion of Arctic ice (Lovelock 2006, 2009). Moreover, the rate of change due to human activity is much too fast for the planet to autocorrect and maintain stability, as when the much slower Darwinian evolution dominated. His solution is that we should switch to nuclear energy and move to large cities (Lovelock 2009, 2014).

Rodney Holder

REFERENCES AND RECOMMENDED READING

Dawkins, Richard. 1982. *The Extended Phenotype.* Oxford: Oxford University Press.

Holder, Rodney D. 2008. *Nothing but Atoms and Molecules? Probing the Limits of Science.* Cambridge, UK: Faraday Institute for Science and Religion.

Jantzen, Grace M. 1984. *God's World, God's Body.* London: Darton, Longman and Todd.

Lovelock, James. 1979. *Gaia: A New Look at Life on Earth.* Oxford: Oxford University Press.

———. 1988. *The Ages of Gaia: A Biography of Our Living Earth.* Oxford: Oxford University Press.

———. 2006. *The Revenge of Gaia: Why the Earth Is Fighting Back—and How We Can Still Save Humanity.* London: Allen Lane.

———. 2009. *The Vanishing Face of Gaia: A Final Warning.* London: Allen Lane.

———. 2014. *A Rough Ride to the Future.* London: Allen Lane.

McFague, Sallie. 1987. *Models of God.* London: SCM.

Montefiore, Hugh. 1985. *The Probability of God.* London: SCM.

Osborn, Lawrence. 1992. "The Machine and the Mother Goddess: The Gaia Hypothesis in Contemporary Scientific and Religious Thought." *Science and Christian Belief* 4 (1): 27–41.

Peacocke, Arthur. 2001. *Paths from Science towards God: The End of All Our Exploring.* Oxford: Oneworld.

GALILEI, GALILEO. The contributions of Galileo Galilei (1564–1642) to **astronomy**, mathematical **physics**, and experimental methodology make him a founder of modern science. His trial is often regarded as a paradigm instance of conflict between science and religion. When approached on a more human level, Galileo emerges as a cultured Florentine polymath whose efforts to support his family involved him in constant financial struggles throughout his career yet who remained a faithful Catholic by the standards of the time (Drake 1980; Fantoli 2003; Sobel 1999).

In the *Starry Messenger* (1610), Galileo printed the first published observations made with a telescope. He reported mountains on the moon at a time when physicists argued that the lunar surface was smooth. His discovery of the four largest satellites of Jupiter demonstrated that multiple centers of revolution exist in the solar system and proved that a moving planet need not outrun a moon. Unsuspected stars in the lighter regions of the Milky Way suggested the vastness of the universe, which made implausible the ancient notion of a celestial sphere carrying the fixed stars and rotating around the earth every 24 hours.

These sensational discoveries catapulted Galileo onto the world stage, making him a celebrity almost overnight. Galileo's *Letters on Sunspots* (1613) showed that the Sun is not changeless, which suggested that the heavens are corruptible, contrary to Aristotelian cosmology. Galileo reported that, through the telescope, Venus shows a complete set of phases, which implies that it revolves around the sun instead of around the earth. Although the phases of Venus were compatible with the earth-centered cosmologies of Martianus Capella and **Tycho Brahe**, among others, Galileo interpreted all of these discoveries as supporting the sun-centered cosmology that **Nicolaus Copernicus** published the previous century in *On the Revolutions of the Celestial Spheres* (1543).

Galileo published his masterwork in mathematical and experimental physics, the *Discourse on Two New Sciences*, in 1638. In the first section, he laid a foundation for a new science concerning tensile strength and the cohesion of materials. In the second part, drawing on the impetus tradition of **Jean Buridan**, Galileo proved that projectiles follow a parabolic trajectory. In this section, Galileo also demonstrated that falling bodies accelerate so that the distance they traverse is proportional to the squares of their times, regardless of weight. John Philoponos, working in Athens in the sixth century, dropped objects from a tall height to show that they do not fall at speeds proportional to their weight.

Galileo never claimed to drop objects from the Leaning Tower of Pisa, nor did any eyewitnesses claim that he did so. Rather, his insight was to use an inclined plane to slow the rate of freely falling bodies to a measurable speed. The inclined plane experiment, rather than the Tower of Pisa, best represents Galileo's new physics. In an era when physicists were not trained in **mathematics** but sought logical demonstrations based on qualitative principles, he pioneered an approach that combined mathematics and experimentation.

His activities as an engineer in the Republic of Venice provided an important context for his work, encouraging his quantitative and experimental approach to physics, his special interest in the physics of motion and a theoretical understanding of machines, and his development of scientific instruments (Valleriani 2010). For example, his first printed book (*Compasso*, 1606) was a manual for an engineering instrument, a sector compass, containing innovative scales of his own design. He provided the instrument and the book to students who boarded with him for tutorials in military engineering.

Galileo's involvement in medicine and natural history is illustrated by his development of the microscope and thermoscope and his connection to the publication of the most important early natural history of the Americas. Like many astronomers, he was trained in medicine and moved in medical circles in Venice, where he and several friends carried out experiments with the thermoscope, in the course of which they added numerical scales to create the thermometer.

Galileo joined many of the leading naturalists of the day in an early scientific society, the Academy of the Lynx, founded by Prince Federigo Cesi. When Cesi showed him a manuscript of Aztec natural history compiled by Francisco Hernandez in the previous century, Galileo confessed bewilderment at the array of medicines from the Americas. Francesco Stelluti, a founding member of the Lynx, eventually published a definitive edition in 1651. Cesi and Stelluti included notes from the manuscript about American bees in the *Apiarium* (1625). They published this digest of knowledge of the bee to honor the accession to the papacy of their ally, Cardinal Maffeo Barbarini, who became Pope Urban VIII in 1623.

The *Apiarium* reports their observations with an instrument Galileo provided them, which he described as a "telescope accommodated for viewing the very small." Another member of the Lynx named it a "microscope." Thus Galileo was associated with the first publication of observations made through the telescope and the microscope—that is, the *Starry Messenger* and *Apiarium*, respectively.

The polymathic character of Galileo's work illustrates the capacity of mathematics to contribute to subject areas beyond astronomy and physics, including engineering, art, music, and even literary criticism. As a young man, he appears to have studied in the artisanal workshop of Bernardo Buontalenti in Florence where the curriculum emphasized geometry (Valleriani 2010, 13). Fellow students became painters, sculptors, architects, or engineers, depending on their capstone projects. In this connection, perhaps it is not surprising that Galileo's friend, the painter Cigoli, who also studied in Buontalenti's workshop, regarded Galileo as his master in perspective drawing. Historians of art suggest that Galileo's discovery of mountains on the surface of the moon depended as much on his artistic training as on the primitive optics of his early telescope (Edgerton 2009).

Galileo's scientific discoveries were also facilitated by his skill in music. His father, Vincenzo Galilei, a well-known composer for the lute, was an influential music theorist who contributed to the birth of Italian opera. Galileo gave lectures on the acoustics of the lute and recorded the times of balls rolling down the inclined plane to a tenth of a pulse beat. Others with little experience in music were not able to replicate the inclined plane experiment. Like his father, Galileo wrote in dialogue form and recited contemporary poetry by heart. In lectures on Dante, Galileo added Archimedean mathematical techniques to his arsenal as a literary critic in order to defend Dante's geography of hell. Thus, in a multitude of endeavors, Galileo exemplifies the unexpected reach of mathematical perspectives that is perhaps one of the most significant cultural legacies of Renaissance Florence.

Galileo's unfortunate encounter with the church occurred in two main phases: first, events associated with a decree of the Inquisition in 1616 and, second, his later trial, which resulted in a humiliating recantation in 1633. The 1616 decree added Copernicus's *On the Revolutions* (1543) to the Index of Prohibited Books until it could be corrected. The decree did not implicate Galileo directly, although he was instructed by Cardinal Robert Bellarmine not to teach Copernicanism as a demonstrated truth in physics, but to discuss it only hypothetically in the manner appropriate to a mathematician. Corrections to *On the Revolutions* were issued in 1620, which made it permissible to read and discuss again so long as one interpreted it hypothetically.

Prior to the decree, in a vain effort to forestall opposition to Copernicus, Galileo composed a letter to the grand duchess Christina, which circulated in manuscript and was not printed until 1636. In this letter, Galileo quoted **Augustine** to show that traditional methods of interpreting Scripture were able to resolve alleged conflicts between the Bible and Copernicanism. Pope John Paul II used Galilean language to affirm similar hermeneutical principles in 1992.

After receiving permission from Pope Urban VIII to publish an evenhanded account of Copernicanism so that

Protestants would have no basis for mocking the ignorance of Catholics in cosmology, Galileo wrote the *Dialogue on the Two Chief Systems of the World* (1632). The book, replete with sarcastic and entertaining wit, became an immediate bestseller. Despite Urban's caution that Galileo must write hypothetically, Galileo devoted the longest section of the work to a defense of Copernicanism based on a causal argument from the motion of the tides. This was an argument not from mathematics, which was widely perceived as hypothetical, but from physics, and purported to be a demonstrative proof.

Galileo's implausible defense was that the fictional form of the work rendered its arguments hypothetical. The book was swiftly censured, and Galileo was summoned to Rome for trial. The legal grounds for prosecution were undermined, however, when Galileo presented a letter Bellarmine wrote for him in 1616. Accounts of Galileo's trial hinge on different interpretations of the circumstances surrounding Bellarmine's letter, but contemporary observers expected a compromise to be worked out for the Medici's celebrated mathematician. Documentary evidence is not sufficient at present to explain the reasons for Galileo's conviction, but on June 22, 1633, Galileo was led before the College of Cardinals in a penitent's robe and confessed that he had been carried away by vainglorious ambition. The charge was vehement suspicion of heresy, one step shy of heresy itself.

Contrary to widespread belief, there is no evidence that Galileo was tortured by the Inquisition, nor that after his recantation, under his breath, he muttered the defiant claim "And yet it moves." The trial of Galileo is often invoked to justify the idea of an inevitable conflict between science and religion, yet the historical record is far more complex. Some of Galileo's strongest supporters were in the Catholic Church, while many of Galileo's strongest opponents were powerful physicists in the universities. For example, many Jesuits were proficient in the mathematical sciences and were sympathetic to Copernicanism. (One friend of Galileo's, Johann Schreck, who accompanied him during his early telescopic discoveries, then joined the Jesuits and went to China, where he presented a telescope to the Chinese emperor.)

It is appropriate to regard Galileo as a committed Catholic who believed himself called to prevent his church from tragically erring on the matter of Copernicanism, which he regarded as the most important scientific question of the day (Drake 1980; Fantoli 2003). Unfortunately, theologians in the church were no more prepared than physicists in the universities to recognize the unexpected competence of the new mathematical methodologies and the surprising efficacy of Galileo's new science.

Kerry Magruder

REFERENCES AND RECOMMENDED READING

Drake, Stillman. 1980. *Galileo: A Very Short Introduction.* Oxford: Oxford University Press.

Edgerton, Samuel Y. 2009. *The Mirror, the Window, and the Telescope: How Renaissance Linear Perspective Changed Our Vision of the Universe.* Ithaca, NY: Cornell University Press.

Fantoli, Annibale. 2003. *Galileo: For Copernicanism and for the Church.* Studi Galileiani. Vol. 6. 3rd ed. Rome: Vatican Observatory Publications.

Finocchiaro, Maurice, trans. and ed. 2008. *The Essential Galileo.* Indianapolis: Hackett.

Heilbron, John L. 2012. *Galileo.* Oxford: Oxford University Press.

Magruder, Kerry. 2015. *Galileo's World Exhibit Guide.* Norman: University of Oklahoma Libraries.

Numbers, Ronald, ed. 2009. *Galileo Goes to Jail and Other Myths about Science and Religion.* Cambridge, MA: Harvard University Press.

Sobel, Dava. 1999. *Galileo's Daughter: A Historical Memoir of Science, Faith, and Love.* New York: Walker.

Valleriani, Matteo. 2010. *Galileo: Engineer.* Boston Studies in the Philosophy of Science 269. Dordrecht: Springer.

GENE. A gene is a region of a chromosome that codes for either a protein or ribonucleic acid (RNA) product that has a functional role within cells. Chromosomes are long molecules of double-stranded **DNA**, a molecule well suited to **information** storage and transmission because one strand can be used as a template to form a complementary strand. One chromosome may contain thousands of individual genes, with nongene regions between them.

Though DNA is suited for its hereditary role, it is unable to perform enzymatic or structural roles within the cell. These functions are carried out by the products of genes: RNA and proteins. All genes are copied from DNA into a single-stranded RNA molecule through a process known as transcription, since the RNA copy is in the same "language" — nucleotide bases — as the DNA it is copied from. For some genes, the RNA product is the functional entity: for example, transfer RNA (tRNA) and ribosomal RNA (rRNA), both of which are required for translation of protein genes.

Translation, as the name implies, is a transfer of information from one language to another — in this case, from the RNA of protein-coding genes (known as messenger RNA, or mRNA) into the "language" of proteins — a sequence of amino acids. Genes specify a sequence of amino acids through groups of nucleotide bases in mRNA that are read off in groups of three. These groupings are called *codons*, and the four nucleotide bases make 64 possible codons, which in turn specify only 20 amino acids found in proteins. This means that the codon code is partially redundant, and that many amino acids can be coded for by several codons (see **Evolutionary Creationism**). During translation, an rRNA complex called the *ribosome* binds mRNA and recruits tRNA molecules, which recognize codons through a complementary "anticodon" and bring in the prescribed amino acid to add to the growing protein chain (Alberts et al. 2014). The enzymatic process of translation is thus performed solely by the ribosome and tRNA molecules. The observation that this fundamental biological activity of all life is based on RNA enzymes is one line of evidence for the "RNA world" hypothesis that suggests RNA preceded DNA as the hereditary material, since RNA can both store information and act as an enzyme (Cech 2000).

Though DNA replication is highly accurate, errors in chromosome replication can mutate genes (see **Random Mutation**). Such errors produce genes with an altered sequence relative to the template they were copied from. Such alternate versions of genes are called *alleles*. Alleles may have a reduction or loss of gene function, no change in gene function, or a gain (or modification) of function. Larger-scale mutations such as duplication of a section of a chromosome can produce duplicate genes side by side, which then may either be lost (due to mutation), or diverge from each other in function as they acquire further mutations. Examples of mutations that produce new genes from DNA that did not previously produce an RNA or protein product are also known (Kaessmann 2010). Genes are thus in flux over evolutionary timescales (see **Evolution, Biological**).

Dennis R. Venema

REFERENCES AND RECOMMENDED READING

Alberts, B., D. Bray, K. Hopkin, et al. 2014. *Essential Cell Biology.* 4th ed. New York: Garland Science.
Cech, T. 2000. "The Ribosome Is a Ribozyme." *Science* 289:878–79.
Kaessmann, H. 2010. "Origins, Evolution, and Phenotypic Impact of New Genes." *Genome Research* 20:1313–26.

GENEALOGY. A genealogy is a record of ancestors showing a line of descent of a person, family, or group. The Old and New Testaments of the Bible contain many genealogies of different sizes and purposes. Some genealogies are only two or three generations deep, while others show a lengthy line of descent.

While tempting to understand and evaluate biblical genealogies according to modern standards (showing only genetic relationships that are exhaustive and objective), we must define and judge ancient genealogies in their own cognitive environment rather than imposing modern expectations on them. To do so is especially important in the light of those who would use biblical genealogies to date the creation of the first humans to the relatively recent past and also those who would use them to argue that Adam must be a historical individual.

Genesis 4:17–5:32 presents the first two of a number of genealogies in the book of Genesis (see also Gen. 10; 11:10–26; 25:12–18; 36; et al.). Not all these genealogies are of the same type or purpose, but no matter what precise type of genealogy we encounter in Genesis, we must remember that these are ancient Near Eastern, not modern Western, genealogies.

The two main types of genealogies that we find in the Bible are linear and segmented. The former, as illustrated in the present passage, goes from father to one son, while the latter will name a number of sons of one father (see Gen. 10). Ancient genealogies are fluid; that is, they can change to reflect contemporary social and political realities. They can also skip generations, rendering them useless for trying to compute how much actual time is covered by the genealogy (see Numbers 2000; he points to the work of the mid-nineteenth-century Old Testament scholar W. H. Green's demonstrating that genealogies are not consecutive by comparing synoptic genealogies; see below).

According to Wilson, "genealogies are not normally created for historical purposes. They are not intended to be historical records. Rather, in the Bible, as well as in the ancient Near Eastern literature and in the anthropological material, genealogies seem to have been created for domestic, political-jural, and religious purposes, and historical information is preserved in the genealogies only incidentally" (Wilson 1977, 199).

Special mention should be made of the Sumerian King List (SKL), since at least in broad stroke, it seems to share the scope and function of Genesis 4:17–11:26. In terms of scope, both texts list prediluvians (in the case of the SKL, they are kings), followed by an account of **the flood** (much more developed in the biblical text than in the SKL), and then a list of postdiluvians. The purpose of the SKL is to rehearse the emergence of kingship as a gift from heaven to the city of Eridu and then follow the succession of kings down to the last king of Isin (c. 1816–1794 BC; at least in the latest copy of the SKL that we have).

Another striking similarity between the biblical text and SKL has to do with the length of lives/reigns of those listed, which are spectacularly long, particularly for the prediluvians. While the biblical characters live long (Methuselah being the oldest at 969 years), they pale in the light of the length of the reigns of the prediluvian SKL kings (the longest ruling being Alagar of Eridu at 36,000 years). Life spans/reigns are considerably shorter after the flood. Sparks points out that "the lengths of reigns are absurdly long and seem to have been derived using astronomical figures (for the antediluvian chronology) and operations from the sexagesimal **mathematics** (for the postdiluvian chronology)" (Sparks 2005, 346). Our awareness of the similarity between the SKL and Genesis 5 makes us open to the possibility that we should not press the ages of the prediluvians too literally.

Biblical genealogies enter the discussion of the relationship between the Bible and science concerning the issue of the date of creation. According to science, the age of the universe is approximately 14 billion years old and the earth is about 4.5 billion years old (see **Age of the Universe and the Earth**). Young-earth creationists, however, insist that science must be wrong because the genealogies of the Bible, taken literally and as an exhaustive record, indicate that the earth and, since the earth was created during the six literal-day creation period, the universe are only a few thousand years old. Indeed, in the sixteenth century, Bishop **James Ussher** famously dated creation to 4004 BC based on biblical genealogies, a date reiterated by the first edition of the *Scofield Reference Bible*.

Ussher's use of the genealogies to date creation, reiterated by modern advocates of young-earth creationism, commits the error of treating ancient genealogies like modern ones, including believing that they are exhaustive. His view also does not reckon with the fact that the "figures given for the ages of many of the individuals mentioned in the Masoretic text do not agree with the corresponding records in other versions such as the LXX (Greek translation) and the Samaritan Pentateuch" (Harrison 1969, 148).

However, at least since the end of the nineteenth century, theologically orthodox biblical scholars such as W. H. Green and B. B. Warfield, considered the architect of the modern doctrine of biblical inerrancy, have shown that the genealogies do not intend to give a literal, exhaustive accounting of generations. Green demonstrated this by comparing synoptic genealogies, for instance, the line of high priests in 1 Chronicles 6:1 – 14 and Ezra 2:36 – 40. We can also see the skipping of generations in the genealogy of Jesus in Matthew 1 when we compare it with the history of the monarchy in the books of Kings (the former skips Ahaziah [2 Kings 8:25]; Joash [2 Kings 12:1], and Amaziah [2 Kings 14:1]).

The purposes of the genealogies of the Bible are primarily theological and not historical, though they are not ahistorical. They are demonstrably not exhaustive and thus do not allow us to date the creation of the universe or the age of the earth.

That biblical genealogies are primarily theological and only secondarily historical is dramatically illustrated by Luke's genealogy of Jesus that ends "the son of Adam, the son of God." As Nolland states, Luke concludes his genealogy of Jesus not with Adam but with God for theological not historical/genetic reasons: "Luke would have us see that Jesus takes his place in the human family and thus in its (since Adam's disobedience) flawed sonship; however, in his own person, in virtue of his unique origin (Luke 1:35) but also as worked out in his active obedience (4:1 – 13), he marks a new beginning to sonship and sets it on an entirely new footing. In this human situation Jesus is the one who is really the Son of God" (Nolland 1989, 173).

Tremper Longman III

REFERENCES AND RECOMMENDED READING

Green, W. H. 1890. "Primeval Chronology." *Bibliotheca Sacra* 47:285 – 303.

Harrison, R. K. 1969. *Introduction to the Old Testament*. Grand Rapids: Eerdmans.

Johnson, M. D. 2002. *The Purpose of Biblical Genealogies*. 2nd ed. Eugene, OR: Wipf and Stock.

Nolland, J. 1989. *Luke 1 – 9:20*. Word Biblical Commentary. Dallas: Word.

Numbers, R. 2000. "The Most Important Biblical Discovery of Our Time: William Henry Green and the Demise of Ussher's Chronology." *Church History* 69:257 – 76.

Sparks, K. L. 2005. *Ancient Texts for the Study of the Hebrew Bible: A Guide to the Background Literature*. Peabody, MA: Hendrickson.

Ussher, J. 1650 – 1654. *Annales Veteris et Novi Testamenti*.

Warfield, B. B. 1911. "On the Antiquity and Unity of the Human Race." *Princeton Theological Review*, 1 – 25.

Wilson, R. R. 1977. *Genealogy and History in the Biblical World*. New Haven, CT: Yale University Press.

GENESIS, BOOK OF. The book of Genesis is the first book of the Torah, which is the first section of the Hebrew Bible (Christian Old Testament). The Torah, also referred to as the Pentateuch (or "five scrolls"; Genesis, Exodus, Leviticus, Numbers, and Deuteronomy), is really one literary composition divided into five books because an ancient scroll could not contain the whole. Exodus through Deuteronomy tells the story of the exodus from Egypt through the wilderness wandering, culminating in Moses's final sermon

(Deuteronomy) delivered on the plains of Moab across the Jordan River from Jericho, the first target of the conquest narrated in the book of Joshua. Genesis is a prequel to the story of the exodus, and there is a time gap between the end of Genesis and the beginning of Exodus of some few, but indeterminate, centuries.

Authorship, Date, and Composition

Since Genesis is part 1 of the Pentateuch, the question of its authorship, date, and composition is connected to the five books that constitute the literary whole.

Our first observation is that the Pentateuch itself nowhere names an author. Thus the Pentateuch, and Genesis in particular, is anonymous. Even so, the Pentateuch does describe Moses as writing things down, such as law, a travel itinerary, and a song (see Ex. 24:4; 34:27; Num. 33:2; Deut. 31:22). In addition, later Scripture from the Old Testament (Josh. 1:7–8; 2 Chron. 25:4; Ezra 6:18; Neh. 13:1) through the New Testament (Matt. 19:7; 22:24; Mark 7:10; 12:26; John 1:17; 5:46; 7:23), associates the Torah with Moses.

That acknowledged, the book of Genesis, as well as the Torah as a whole, contains material that originates from a post-Mosaic period; there are references to people, places, and events that took place after Moses was gone. The most obvious of these passages is the account of Moses's death in Deuteronomy 34. In Genesis, we might point to the reference to Ur of the Chaldeans, the Chaldeans being the Aramaic-speaking inhabitants of the ancient city of Ur who lived centuries after Moses (Gen. 11:31), as well as a reference to the city of Dan, only named that at the time of the later period of the Judges (Gen. 14:14; see Judg. 18:29).

In addition, there are indications that the author used previous sources in his writing of the Pentateuch, particularly of the book of Genesis. For instance, 11 times Genesis uses a formula to introduce a new section of the book ("This is the account [*toledot*] of X"; see 2:4; 5:1; 6:9; 10:1; 11:10, 27; 25:12, 19; 36:1, 9; 37:2). These likely indicate oral and/or written (see "written account" in 5:1) sources used in the composition of the book of Genesis.

Thus one theory of the composition of the book of Genesis and the Pentateuch as a whole, implied by the biblical text itself, names Moses as the author but acknowledges that he used sources and that there are also editorial additions perhaps up to the postexilic period. Challenges to the idea that Moses had anything to do with the writing of the Pentateuch abound (see description and critique in Longman and Dillard 2006, 4–51).

Structure and Contents

There is more than one way to describe the structure and contents of the book of Genesis. We have already mentioned that the book is composed of 12 sections introduced by the formula "This is the account (*toledot*) of X." With the exception of the first occurrence (2:4), X is a personal name and the section that the *toledot* formula introduces is an account of the descendants of X. So, for example, the final section of the book introduced by "the account of Jacob's family line" (37:2) tells the story of Jacob's 12 sons with a primary emphasis on Joseph.

Yet another way to outline the book recognizes three main parts. The first part narrates events from the creation of the world up to the time of Abraham (1:1–11:26). Here the narrative follows the story of all humanity in the deep past. We learn that though God created the cosmos good and humanity morally innocent, humans chose to rebel against God (Gen. 3). God judges sin but stays involved with his human creatures even though they repeatedly sin (Cain and Abel; **the flood**; the **Tower of Babel**). The second part of the book narrows the focus to one family, Abraham's, for three generations—that of Abraham, his son Isaac, and his grandson Jacob, the so-called patriarchs (11:27–37:1). The third and final section of the book follows the story of Jacob's 12 sons with an emphasis on Joseph (37:2–50:26).

Genesis and Science

The book of Genesis has played a key role in the modern discussions concerning Christianity and science. Most of the book has little to say that impacts the debate, but the primeval history, Genesis 1–11, in particular has been at the center of perhaps the most heated interchanges on the subject, because in this section we find a description of the creation of the cosmos as well as humanity that has often been taken as at odds with the account given by modern science. In addition, the narrative of the flood also has entered the debate. Finally, the **genealogies** of these early chapters of Genesis lead some to believe that the Bible teaches that the creation of the cosmos and humanity are only a few thousand years old as opposed to the scientific consensus that the cosmos is nearly 14 billion years old and that humans emerged about 100,000 years ago.

The details of these issues and different interpretations are discussed in more detail in other articles (**Cosmology, Ancient**; **Creation**; **Eden**; **Fall, The**; **Genealogies**; **Genesis Flood**; **The Genesis Flood and Geology**; **Serpent, The**). In this essay, our focus will be on the question of the genre of the book. Authors adopt specific generic conventions to help readers understand the nature of the truth claims of their writing.

Many conservative Christians, not to speak of Jews and Muslims, read the Genesis narratives and genealogies as if they are giving a detailed, literal account of the process of creation. Not surprisingly, however, there are differences even among those who turn to Genesis for a literal account of the manner in which God created the universe.

For instance, young-earth creationists (YEC) interpret the genealogies of Genesis as giving a nearly exhaustive listing of generations and exact length of life spans. Thus they believe Genesis teaches that the earth is perhaps 6,000 to 10,000 years old. Others compare overlapping genealogies (e.g., 1 Chron. 6:1–14 and Ezra 2:36–40) to demonstrate that Genesis genealogies are constructed and may skip generations (we can also compare Matthew 1 with the history of the monarchy in Kings), while still others point to comparable ancient Near Eastern genealogies like the Sumerian King List, which attributes reigns on the order of tens of thousands of years to suggest that ancient genealogies functioned for ideological/theological reasons rather than strictly historical ones, and thus conclude that we cannot use them to construct a chronology. They accordingly conclude that there is no conflict with scientific accounts of the age of the universe or of the emergence of humanity.

Differences also exists among those who believe that the **days of creation** are literal days, describing a 24-hour-per-day, six-day creation, and those who say that the days are figurative. The latter argue either that the days denote long periods of time, though still describing the sequence of creation (day-age theory), or that the creation week is totally figurative and thus the days are not necessarily sequential.

The figurative view is best known as the framework hypothesis, in which the first three days describe the creation of realms that are filled by the creative acts of the second three days. For instance, on day 1 God creates light and darkness, and on day 4 the sun, moon, and stars that inhabit the realm of light and darkness.

Those who adopt a more literal interpretation point to the fact that each day has an "evening" and "morning," while those who take a more figurative approach to the days argue that they cannot be literal days with literal evenings and mornings because the sun, moon, and stars are not created until the fourth day. Others argue that the evening and morning refer simply to the beginning and ending of an indefinite period of time.

The issues surrounding the significance of the flood (Gen. 6–9) are similar to those surrounding the creation narratives. A literal reading of the flood story leads many to posit a global flood that annihilated all humanity and most animals except those preserved on a large boat. Science does not support a literal reading of the flood story since there is no evidence for a global flood (see **The Genesis Flood and Geology**).

This tension leads some to read the flood narrative as not indicating a global flood but rather a (large) local flood. This interpretation is achieved by translating the Hebrew word ʿeretz not as "earth," but rather as "land." Thus the floodwaters don't cover the earth, but rather a specific, perhaps large, portion of land. Such a translation is possible, but other details of the narrative, such as the fact that "the waters rose and covered the mountains to a depth of more than fifteen cubits" (Gen. 7:20), may suggest that the passage does describe a global flood. Thus others believe, the text is based on a historical event, perhaps a significant local flood, that for theological reasons is described as a global flood, encouraged by similar stories in the ancient Near East, such as the **Gilgamesh Epic** (Longman 2016).

Again, these issues are deeply rooted in one's understanding of the genre of Genesis 1–11, which indicates the intentions of the author. Is the author writing literal history where even the details are meant to be taken at face value? Or is the narrative allegory or myth? A third approach understands that there are historical intentions in the narrative (God created creation; human evil is the result of human rebellion; God brought judgment on sinful humanity), but that these historical events of the deep past are told using figurative language and in dialogue with other ancient Near Eastern texts. In this view, it is a misunderstanding of the intention of the author of Genesis to believe we are getting a literal and precise account of the historical events. Another way to frame disagreements over Genesis is to ask whether we should expect to find modern scientific descriptions of cosmogony and the creation process in Genesis or whether the story is told in the context of its contemporary "cognitive environment" (Longman 2016; Walton 2011).

Tremper Longman III

REFERENCES AND RECOMMENDED READING

Charles, J. D., ed. 2013. *Reading Genesis 1–2: An Evangelical Conversation*. Peabody, MA: Hendrickson.

Longman III, T. 2016. *Genesis*. Story of God Bible Commentary. Grand Rapids: Zondervan.

Longman III, T., and R. B. Dillard. 2006. *An Introduction to the Old Testament.* 2nd ed. Grand Rapids: Zondervan.

Walton, J. 2011. *Genesis 1 as Ancient Cosmology.* Winona Lake, IN: Eisenbrauns.

☙ GENESIS FLOOD (Global View).

A global flood is attested throughout church history, including by more early church fathers, Reformers, and moderns than can be mentioned (see VanDoodewaard 2015 for a comprehensive review). But it is not simply because this view is historically pedigreed that it is preferable; it is because it is robust in its approach to the issues. Can a global flood view provide a synthesis of the modern biblical and scientific issues and evidences? I believe it can. Here I focus on four themes: the pitfalls of local and mythological perceptions of the flood, the biblical affirmation of a global flood in Genesis 6–9, the use of the flood narrative in the New Testament, and geological evidences for a global flood.

Pitfalls of Local Flood and Mythological Perceptions

The flood account, like the rest of Genesis 1–11, has a thematically universal view of the world, its inhabitants, and its history. God's purpose for sending the flood, given in Genesis 6:17, is to destroy all flesh (*basar*), yet God also preserves life through righteous Noah and his ark. Various old-earth proponents (e.g., Ross 2014) have claimed that the flood was universal with respect to humanity but geographically limited to Mesopotamia. The biblical text does not immediately lend itself to such views (see below), and neither does extrabiblical evidence when viewed from *within* an old-earth perspective. For example, if one affirms old-earth chronology, then the oldest fossils of *Homo sapiens* are from Africa about 200,000 years ago. Subsequent migrations from Africa to Europe, Asia, and Australia were variously undertaken from 125,000 through 40,000 years ago, and by 13,000 years ago the Americas were inhabited.

When one adopts an old-earth view, there appears to be no temporal placement for a local flood in and/or near Mesopotamia that permits the destruction of all humanity, since humans are spread far beyond this area at all points of history.

If historical and universal for humanity, the flood *must* be global in scope in order to accomplish God's divine judgment. Yet when assuming an old-earth chronology, there is no evidence for such a flood in the earth's uppermost soils and sediments (a young-earth position, discussed below, alleviates this problem). Some evangelicals have abandoned a universal flood altogether, arguing instead that the flood narrative is a **mythology** that may or may not be rooted in some local event (e.g., Enns 2012; Lamoureux 2009). Similarities with the ANE mythologies of *Eridu*, **Atrahasis**, and *Gilgamesh* provide advocates with arguments that the flood narrative may have functioned like (or been derived from) these and other ANE texts and flood traditions since they center on a hero who, using a boat, saves himself, others, and animals from the wrath of the gods' watery judgment.

These ANE stories share many similarities (e.g., warnings, birds [at least in the later texts], sacrifices, mountains), but differ significantly in both structure and details. Westermann (1984) notes differences in the structures of polytheism/monotheism, components of an epic/standalone narrative, epic verse/simple prose, and others. Kitchen (1977) lists numerous and important differences in account details, as do Millard (1967) and Tsumura (1994), which indicates that a heavy reliance on comparative studies to understand the flood narrative may be unwarranted. Several of these are summarized in table 1.

Table 1. Notable differences in ANE flood mythologies and the Genesis flood narrative

ANE Mythologies	Genesis Flood Narrative
A flood is brought about because the gods are angered by human noise/overpopulation, or no specified reason.	God is grieved by sin.
The hero cheats death and becomes immortal.	Noah is righteous but dies as all men do.
Riches are taken aboard the ark.	There is no need to store up wealth, for all humanity dies.
Family, guild members and/or boatmen (to navigate) are taken aboard.	Only Noah and his family enter, and God alone preserves and oversees the ark.
The floodwaters rise and fall quickly (six to seven days), as in a local flood.	The flood lasts over a year with globe-covering waters.
The hero exits the boat on his own volition, and a sacrifice is offered to appease the gods.	Noah stays in the boat until instructed, and his sacrifice is for thanksgiving.
Hungry gods descend on the sacrifice "like flies."	Noah's sacrifice is pleasing to God but is not consumed.

Biblical Affirmation of a Global Flood in Genesis 6–9

From within the text itself, a global perspective of the flood is everywhere affirmed, and the use of *mabbul* for only this event in the Old Testament and *kataklysmos* in the Septuagint (LXX) and New Testament both argue for its uniqueness. Many points can be made in support of a global flood. These include but are not limited to the following: the ark's dimensions and cargo, the duration of the flood, the use of universal language, the landing of the ark, Noah as a type of Adam, and the bow covenant.

The ark's dimensions and cargo

Unlike the stylized cube/ziggurat of Utnapishtim and circular coracle of *Atrahasis*, Noah's barge-shaped vessel is properly proportioned for a massive flood. Noah is instructed to load "kinds" of land animals and birds on board the ark (not species, as frequently claimed by critics; see below). The dimensions and cargo comport with global catastrophe and make little sense if the flood is local or ahistorical. Aside from the ability to move/migrate away from a local flood (particularly given ample time to prepare), consider that *birds* are frequently specified for preservation on the ark (Gen. 6:20; 7:3, 8; 8:17, 19). Their inclusion is absurd if the flood is local, since birds do not die en masse during local floods.

The duration of the flood

From Noah's entrance into the ark to exit, the flood lasts over a year (cf. Gen. 7:11; 8:14), with the earth inundated by water for the majority of this time. Local storms do not last for 40 days, and even the worst local floods do not last for a year.

Universal language

"All" and "every/everything" are used extensively (30 and 32 times, respectively) throughout Genesis 6–9 in reference to mankind, animals, birds, the extent of the flood, and promises made to the survivors. This is not mere hyperbole. Constant and repetitive, their emphasis impresses on the reader that indeed *all* flesh was destroyed and *all* the high mountains under the *entire* heavens were covered, with no relief anywhere on earth (contra Walton 2001 and H. Ross 2014; see Cassuto 1964; Leupold 1942; Waltke and Fredricks 2001; Wenham 1987; Westermann 1984). This destruction must be global, since it affects not only all humans (whose wickedness brought judgment on themselves) but also all

animals, birds, and creatures that move along the ground. Every living thing was "wiped out," fulfilling the purpose of the flood stated in Genesis 6:17. This universal destruction is then climactically contrasted with "Only Noah was left, and those with him in the ark" (Gen. 7:23).

Likewise, the phrases the "waters rose," "increased," and "flooded" are seen six times in Genesis 7:17–24 as a continuous reminder that the waters of the flood (*mabbul*) are drowning the entire world, not just a localized region. By completely covering (*submerging*; Cassuto 1964; Hamilton 1990; Wenham 1987) all the mountains by 15 cubits (Gen. 7:20), the flood left no place for animals or humans to escape, and indeed all perished (cf. 1 Peter 3:20).

The ark lands on the mountains of Ararat; tops of mountains become visible

The text states that "the ark came to rest on (*al*) the mountains of Ararat" (Gen. 8:4), rather than "near," "beside," or "next to." Ten weeks later, the tops of the mountains finally appear (Gen. 8:4–5) as the waters recede. Walton (2001) notes that the latter description argues strongly for a global flood.

Noah as a type of Adam

With the flood ended, Noah and the animals exit the ark, and the narrative draws heavily on creation motifs. The description of Noah and his family, the animals, and the earth recounts the events of Genesis 1–4 in ways that are clearly intended to emphasize the completely new beginning to the world, including both humans and animals. Consider the postflood parallels between Adam and Noah in table 2.

Table 2. Postflood parallels between Adam and Noah

Adam	Noah
Ground is cursed because of man's sin (3:17–18).	Ground will never again be cursed because of man (8:21).
"Be fruitful and increase in number; fill the earth" (1:28).	"Be fruitful and increase in number and fill the earth" (9:1, 7).
Man is to have dominion and rule over animals (1:28).	Animals will have fear and dread of man (9:2).
Man is commanded to eat plants only (1:29).	Man is given permission to eat animals along with plants (9:2–4).

Adam	Noah
Poetic interlude includes "God created mankind in his own image" (1:27).	Poetic interlude includes "In the image of God has God made mankind" (9:6).
Three sons of Adam are named (4:1–2, 25).	Three sons of Noah are named (5:32; 9:18).
One son (Cain) perpetrates grievous sin and is cursed (4:8, 11–16).	One son (Ham) perpetrates grievous sin, and his son Canaan is cursed (9:22–27).

These parallels and others (see Waltke and Fredricks 2001) emphasize the importance of Noah as a type of Adam. Noah and his family must begin humanity afresh and fulfill the dominion role over the animals and the earth precisely *because* all life outside the ark has been destroyed. Nonglobal flood perspectives run aground here, since they logically require humans and animals to exist outside of, and oblivious to, the flood's influence.

Never again rainbow covenant

The covenant of God with Noah to never again destroy the world with the *mabbul* can only be taken as a legitimate and continuing promise with a global flood. If the flood were local, the bow in the clouds would be empty of meaning both historically and presently. Since not all human and animal life would have been killed, the bow would provide no real reminder of protection from judgment. Moreover, the promise never again to destroy the world with a *mabbul* is given not only to Noah but also to *all* the creatures of the earth (eight references to "all life" and "every living creature" in Gen. 9:8–17). Why would the animals need a promise of no future judgment if the vast majority of them were unaffected by a local flood? Only a global flood makes sense of the bow covenant in which God continues to "remember the *everlasting* covenant between God and all living creatures of every kind on the earth" (Gen. 9:16, emphasis added).

The Use of the Flood Narrative in the New Testament

While Noah and the flood narrative are infrequently referenced in the Old Testament outside of the primeval history (e.g., 1 Chron. 1:4; Pss. 29:10; 104:6–9; Isa. 54:9; Ezek. 14:14, 20), their historicity is affirmed (esp. 1 Chron. 1:4). Their presence in the New Testament is more integrated within Christian theology. The genealogy of Jesus (Luke 3:36) includes Noah among other primeval historical figures (e.g., Adam). Jesus speaks of Noah and the flood as historical (Matt. 24:37–39; Luke 3:36; 17:26–27), as do the writer of Hebrews (11:7) and Peter (1 Peter 3:20; 2 Peter 2:5–6; 3:1–7). Matthews's observation that "for the author of Genesis the flood event is as real as the birth of Abraham" (Matthews 1996, 376) rings just as true for all other Old Testament and New Testament authors.

We must remember that what may appear to be a permissible reading of Genesis 6–9 in isolation may not be permissible in the light of the New Testament. For example, Walton's (2001) arguments for a nonglobal flood are largely anchored in assuming that the Israelites had an ancient Near Eastern conception of world geography. They may have, but the geography known to Jesus and Peter was far broader, and both affirm that *all* people outside the ark were destroyed, just as *all* will be impacted at Christ's return. Second Peter 3:1–7 is especially notable because it presents a threefold parallel among the universal events of creation, flood, and second coming/*parousia* (Bauckham 1983, who also notes this in 2 Peter 2:5). If the flood account is historical, a local flood is insufficient to destroy the entire "world of that time" (2 Peter 3:6; see Donelson 2010; Schaeffer 1973). If ahistorical, then these New Testament statements become unmoored.

Geological Evidences for a Global Flood

With regard to scientific issues, a global flood has historically faced difficulties from **geology**, where most scientists affirm an ancient age of the earth and evidence for a flood in the highest (most recent) soils and sediments is absent. I submit that these geologists are looking in the wrong place: the evidence for the flood is found not in the topmost deposits, but in the bulk of the rock and **fossil record** itself. This idea has roots in antiquity, as many church fathers and reformers affirmed that fossils in rocks were evidence of the flood (including Tertullian, Aquinas, and Luther; VanDoodewaard 2015). *The Genesis Flood* (Whitcomb and Morris 1961) was the first scientifically modern model for the flood as a geological agent. Much has developed since then, and the reader is referred to Garner (2009), Snelling (2009), and Wise (2002) for current perspectives.

A number of features argue for rapid, catastrophic deposition of the majority of the rock record. While old-earth and evolutionary advocates recognize these features and provide alternate interpretations, the following comport well with a recent and global flood (see Snelling 2009 for details and documentation):

- The vast majority of sedimentary rocks and fossils found on the continents have *marine* origins, not terrestrial. Overall, the geological record preserves abundant marine rocks in the lower fossiliferous units, with increasing terrestrial components higher up. This pattern may reflect the sequential destruction of various ecosystems as the flood brought marine materials onto the preflood continents.
- Thin but broad sedimentary units, often extending across much of a continent, are inconsistent with modern-day sedimentary systems but explicable by large-scale flood conditions.
- Indicators of water flow direction in sedimentary rocks (such as preserved ripples and cross-beds) indicate nearly unidirectional currents flowing over the North American continent throughout much of its geological history. Modern settings, in contrast, show a multitude of current directions based on regional drainage basins and shoreline processes.
- The weathered rock fragments and minerals that comprise sedimentary rock have often been transported immense distances before deposition. For example, some sand grains in Grand Canyon rocks appear to have been derived from rocks in the Appalachians.
- A near-universal erosional scour exists near the base of the world's fossiliferous rock units. This scour, called the "Great Unconformity," likely represents the destructive advance of the floodwaters. Below it, complex fossils are rare, while immediately above it complex marine fossils (such as diverse arthropods, mollusks, worms, and many others) are abundant.
- Also above the Great Unconformity are a series of *megasequences*. These are continental-scale, recurring patterns of coarse-to-fine sedimentary units, such as sandstones covered by shales covered by limestones. Erosional scours (unconformities) frequently separate the megasequences, which likely reflect pulses of the floodwaters that affected the types and sources of sediment deposited.
- Fossilization is a very rare occurrence today, yet the rock record not only preserves a multitude of fossils but numerous instances of "fossil graveyards," where entire ecosystems have been destroyed and preserved. A global flood provides the mechanisms both to produce and preserve large quantities of fossils, particularly over widespread areas. This is

quite different from the few modern environments conducive to fossilization, which have a highly localized nature.

Young-earth geologists have also worked to develop more robust geological models to understand how the flood reshaped the face of the earth and to make predictions based on those models. Catastrophic Plate Tectonics (CPT; Austin et al. 1994; see also Wise 2002 for a readable discussion) combines biblically based temporal constraints, field observations, and computer modeling to propose a rapid movement of the continental and ocean crust during the flood (a "continental sprint" rather than "continental drift"). CPT also explains the source of the water for the flood as primarily from the oceans, not a water canopy (as in earlier young-earth writings), and accounts for many of the earth's surface features (e.g., timing and formation of mountain belts, locations of major volcanoes and earthquakes, distribution of sedimentary rocks and their fossils). CPT marks an important advance in the development of young-earth creationism and flood geology because, rather than mere antievolution rhetoric, it puts forth a testable model that can guide research and be evaluated by future discoveries, illustrative of the increasing sophistication of young-earth creationism.

One final note: the many logistical issues concerning the ark frequently raised by critics (e.g., numbers of animals, care, provisions, oceangoing stability) have been thoroughly addressed within young-earth literature (Snelling 2009; Woodmorappe 1996). Suffice it to say that claiming Noah must take 6 million species aboard the ark (Lamoureux 2009) fails to recognize that (a) the vast majority of species are microbes, aquatic invertebrates, and fish (Noah built an ark, not an aquarium); and (b) equating the Hebrew term "kind" (*min*) to biological species improperly imports modern concepts into the text. We can rest assured that the ark was sufficient to accomplish the task of preserving life through the flood, particularly since its materials and dimensions were designated by God himself.

Marcus R. Ross

REFERENCES AND RECOMMENDED READING

Austin, Steven A., John R. Baumgardner, D. Russell Humphreys, et al. 1994. "Catastrophic Plate Tectonics: A Global Flood Model of Earth History." In *Proceedings of the Third International Conference on Creationism*, ed. R. E. Walsh, 609–62. Pittsburgh: Creation Science Fellowship.
Bauckham, Richard. 1983. *Jude, 2 Peter.* Word Biblical Commentary. Waco, TX: Word.

Boyd, Steven A., and Andrew A. Snelling. 2014. *Grappling with the Chronology of the Genesis Flood*. Green Forest, AR: Master.

Cassuto, Umberto. 1964. *Commentary on the Book of Genesis*. Jerusalem: Hebrew University, Magnes.

Donelson, Lewis R. 2010. *I and II Peter and Jude: A Commentary*. New Testament Library. Louisville, KY: Westminster John Knox.

Enns, Peter. 2012. *The Evolution of Adam: What the Bible Does and Doesn't Say about Human Origins*. Grand Rapids: Brazos.

Garner, Paul. 2009. *The New Creationism*. Faverdale North, UK: EP Books.

Hamilton, Victor P. 1990. *The Book of Genesis: Chapters 1–17*. Grand Rapids: Eerdmans.

Kitchen, Kenneth A. 1977. *The Bible in Its World: The Bible and Archaeology Today*. Downers Grove, IL: InterVarsity.

Lamoureux, Denis O. 2009. *Evolutionary Creation*. Eugene, OR: Wipf and Stock.

Leupold, H. C. 1942. *Exposition of Genesis*. Vol. 1. Grand Rapids: Baker.

Matthews, Kenneth A. 1996. *Genesis 1–11:26*. Nashville: Broadman and Holman.

Millard, A. R. 1967. "A New Babylonian 'Genesis' Story." *Tyndale Bulletin* 18:3–18.

Ross, Hugh. 2014. *Navigating Genesis*. Covina, CA: RTB Press.

Schaeffer, Francis A. 1973. *Genesis in Space and Time: The Flow of Biblical History*. London: Hodder & Stoughton.

Snelling, Andrew. 2009. *Earth's Catastrophic Past*. 2 vols. Dallas: Institute for Creation Research.

Tsumura, David Toshio. 1994. "Genesis and Ancient Near Eastern Stories of Creation and Flood: An Introduction." In Richard S. Hess and David Toshio Tsumura, *I Studied Inscriptions from before the Flood: Ancient Near Eastern, Literary and Linguistic Approaches to Genesis 1–11*, 27–57. Winona Lake, IN: Eisenbrauns.

VanDoodewaard, William. 2015. *The Quest for the Historical Adam*. Grand Rapids: Reformation Heritage.

Waltke, Bruce K., and Cathi J. Fredricks. 2001. *Genesis: A Commentary*. Grand Rapids: Zondervan.

Walton, John H. 2001. *The NIV Application Commentary: Genesis*. Grand Rapids: Zondervan.

Wenham, Gordon J. 1987. *Genesis 1–15*. Word Biblical Commentary, volume 1. Waco: Word Books.

Westermann, Claus. 1984. *Genesis 1–11: A Commentary*. Minneapolis: Augsburg; London: SPCK.

Whitcomb, John C., and Henry M. Morris. 1961. *The Genesis Flood*. Philadelphia: P&R.

Wise, Kurt P. 2002. *Faith, Form, and Time*. Nashville: B&H.

Woodmorappe, John. 1996. *Noah's Ark: A Feasibility Study*. Dallas: Institute for Creation Research.

GENESIS FLOOD (Theological View)

The Context of the Flood Story

The flood story (Gen. 6–9) plays a central role in the primeval narrative (Gen. 1–11) that opens the book of Genesis. The primeval narrative begins with two accounts of the creation of the cosmos and humanity (1:1–2:4a; 2:4b–25). Humanity is created in the **image of God**, thus reflecting God's glory. Men and women are morally innocent when created by God, but Genesis 3 recounts their rebellion against divine authority, an event referred to as **the fall** by Christian theologians.

Three additional stories connected by **genealogies** complete the opening section of Genesis before turning to the story of the patriarchs (chaps. 12–50). These three stories—Cain and Abel (4:1–16), the flood (chaps. 6–9), and the **Tower of Babel** (11:1–9)—all follow a narrative pattern similar to the story of the fall (Clines 1997; Longman 2016). Each one tells of egregious sin (Cain murders Abel; all humanity with the exception of Noah becomes evil; arrogant people build a city and a tower to make a name for themselves) that brings on God's judgment. The execution of the judgment is preceded by a speech that announces God's intentions. But with the possible exception of the tower story, there is always a token of grace that indicates God's intention to stay involved with his sinful people.

The Biblical Account of the Flood

With this pattern (sin/judgment speech/token of grace/judgment) in mind, let's take a closer look at the flood story. Human sin has reached unprecedented proportions, as indicated by the narrator's report that "the LORD saw how great the wickedness of the human race had become on the earth, and that every inclination of the thoughts of the human heart was only evil all the time" (6:5), as well as "The earth was corrupt in God's sight and was full of violence. God saw how corrupt the earth had become, for all the people on earth had corrupted their ways" (6:11–12). The enigmatic story that begins Genesis 6 (vv. 1–4), in which the "sons of God" marry the "daughters of humans" and produce the Nephilim, is an example of such wickedness. There are debates about the precise identity of the players (angels having intercourse with humans; sons of the godly line marrying daughters of the ungodly line, etc.) in this opening tragic drama, but there is no doubt about the fact that a serious sexual transgression of some sort has taken place (Longman 2016).

As a result of the egregious sin of humanity, God determines to destroy his creatures and announces that he will "wipe from the face of the earth the human race I have created—and with them the animals, the birds and the creatures that move along the ground—for I regret that I have made them" (6:7).

However, God first extends a token of grace anticipated by the narrator's comment that "Noah found favor in the eyes of the LORD" (6:8). Before executing his judgment by means of a flood, he warns Noah of the impending disaster. He will destroy humanity and the animals by means of a flood. Thus he tells Noah to build an ark that will preserve him, his immediate family, and representatives of animals.

God gives Noah instructions on the construction of the ark, and it is huge. The ark is to be 300 cubits (450 feet) long, 50 cubits (75 feet) wide, and 30 cubits (45 feet) high. He is then to gather seven pairs of ritually clean animals and one pair of all other animals on board.

Once the ark was loaded, God then sent the waters from the heavens and also from the "springs of the great deep" (7:11). The rains came for 40 days and nights. The waters rose on the earth so that "all the high mountains under the entire heavens were covered" (7:19) and "every living thing on the face of the earth was wiped out; people and animals and the creatures that move along the ground and the birds were wiped from the earth. Only Noah was left, and those with him in the ark" (7:23).

After God's purposes were accomplished, the floodwaters receded. After a while the tops of the mountains could be seen, and Noah let out three birds one after another (raven, dove, dove) until the last returned with a plucked olive leaf, which indicated to Noah that he and his family could disembark.

When they disembarked, Noah immediately built an altar and offered a sacrifice to God. God instructs Noah to "be fruitful and increase in number; multiply on the earth" (9:7) — words reminiscent of those originally delivered to the first man and woman (1:28). Noah is the new Adam, from whom will descend humanity.

God enters into a covenant with Noah in which he promises that he will not destroy humanity again by flood. He confirms that the earth will be stable, and he points to the rainbow as a sign of his commitment.

The Noah narrative ends with a final story about Noah's getting drunk and his son Ham dishonoring him (9:18–22). The purpose of this short narrative seems to be that in spite of new beginnings, humanity remains sinful, though God maintains his relationship with them and continues to work toward their redemption and restoration.

The above summary gives an overview of the flood story and an indication of its function in the overall narrative of Genesis 1–11. Humanity was created innocent but rebelled against God. God judges sinful humans, but also through tokens of grace (beginning with the clothes he provided for **Adam and Eve**), shows his intention to work toward their redemption. The flood story is another episode that speaks of human sinfulness, God's judgment, but also redemption.

A second way to understand the flood story's place in the primeval narrative is explained by Westermann. He saw a movement from creation to uncreation to re-creation. After all, at the beginning of the creation process, the earth is depicted as a watery mass (1:1–2) that God shaped into something habitable over the six **days of creation**. The floodwater returns the earth to its original "formless and empty" state, but as the floodwaters recede and God gives his instructions to Noah, the world is re-created.

Genesis 1–11 functions as a preamble to the story of Abraham. The cycle of sin, judgment, and grace gives way to the call to Abraham (12:1–3). God will pursue the redemption of humanity through his election of the patriarch, and through him he will reach "all peoples on earth" (12:3).

The Flood and Modern Science

Now that we have reviewed the main contours of the flood story and its place in the narrative of Genesis, we move on to the question of the relationship between the flood story and science, because there is no geological evidence for the flood and there should be if there was a global inundation of the earth. Efforts to find such evidence over the years have failed. Evidence put forward today by some outlier thinkers is based on **pseudoscience** and is not accepted by the scientific community (for details, see **The Genesis Flood and Geology**).

One response to the lack of evidence of a global flood is to argue that the Bible describes a local flood. Rather than a flood that covers the entire surface of the earth, advocates of the local flood interpretation suggest that the Bible really describes a flood that is more restricted than the flood of the traditional view. This interpretation is accomplished by translating the Hebrew word 'eretz as "land" rather than "earth," thus yielding translations like "For forty days the flood kept coming on the land, and as the waters increased they lifted the ark high above the land. The waters rose and increased greatly on the land" (7:17–18a).

In my opinion, this is a move of desperation to account for the lack of geological evidence for a global flood. Certainly, 'eretz can be translated "land" in some contexts, but the context of the flood story suggests that the narrator pictures the floodwaters as covering the "earth," at least how he understood the earth. We should remember that the original author and audience would not have understood the earth as a globe, so the nomenclature "global flood" is an anachronism, though we will still use it as a convenient shorthand expression.

That the original author pictures a flood that covers the earth can be seen in:

1. God's judgment being brought on humanity as a whole (6:5, 11–12; see esp. 6:13, "I am going to put an end to all people")
2. The need to bring all the animals on board (if not covering the entire earth, then animals would survive; only ones in the flood zone would die)
3. The waters covering the "high mountains" (7:19) to "a depth of more than fifteen cubits" (22.5 feet; 7:20)

These are just several indications within the story that point toward a flood that covers the earth and not just a local land.

Thus we are left with a biblical text that describes a flood that covers the earth and an absence of any geological or archaeological evidence of such a flood. Here we have a case where the dictum that "the absence of evidence is not evidence of absence" is not relevant. If there was a global flood, then we should certainly find evidence of it.

Some advocates of a global inundation refer to flood traditions that are found around the world (a rather full listing can be found at www.talkorigins.org/faqs/flood-myths.html). These flood legends (with some exceptions, see below on Mesopotamian traditions of the flood) bear no significant connection to the biblical story, most often describing local floods. It's not surprising to find independent flood stories around the world. In some cases, they are influenced by biblical or other ancient Near Eastern flood stories, and in other cases, they arise out of the rather common experience of destruction by water.

What then are we to conclude? Is the biblical flood story misleading or wrong? To answer this question, we have to ask what the biblical author is intending to teach us by relating the flood story. The modern concept of the inerrancy of Scripture asserts that it is true in all it intends to teach; and to discover what a passage intends to teach, we must consider its genre.

In my opinion, the book of Genesis may be described as a work of theological history. Genesis makes historical claims (it is not fiction, myth, legend, or parable), but it recounts the past for theological purposes; that is, the book speaks of the past in order to reveal God and his relationship to his people. God has revealed himself by acting in space and time, and the author of the book of Genesis interprets (under divine inspiration) that history for his audience.

While some attribute a different genre to Genesis 1–11 from the rest of the book, there are strong textual indicators

that prevent us from doing so. In the first place, there is no break between Genesis 1–11 and 12–50 in terms of narrative style (*waw* consecutive verbal form). In addition, both Genesis 1–11 (see 2:4; 5:1; 6:9; 10:1; 11:10, 27) and 12–50 (25:12, 19; 36:1, 9; 37:2) use the *toledoth* formula that structures the book (see **Genesis, Book of**).

Though the entirety of Genesis is theological history, there is a decided difference between Genesis 1–11 and 12–50 in terms of interest in historical detail. Genesis 1–11 covers what we might call the deep past, an incredibly long period of time from creation to Abraham, in a mere 11 chapters, whereas Genesis 12–50 concerns only four generations (Abraham through Joseph). Genesis 1–11 has as its subject the whole world, while Genesis 12–50 gives an account of a single family with a focus on one person at a time.

Another factor for our consideration as we read the flood story as theological history is the intense interaction between the stories of Genesis 1–11 and ancient Near Eastern literature. This interaction is well known for the creation story (***Atrahasis; Enuma Elish***) as well as the flood account.

Earlier I noted that the commonly cited idea of the flood story being found often in literature and thought around the world is based on weak parallels and is unlikely to be the result of shared experience or literary influence. However, this is not the case with the Mesopotamian flood tradition, in which the flood legend is known from the earliest phases of Mesopotamian literature (Sumerian King List; the Eridu Genesis). The similarities and differences between the biblical account and the Mesopotamian tradition are seen most dramatically in *Atrahasis* and especially the eleventh tablet of the ***Gilgamesh Epic*** (details may be found in those articles in the present volume).

We also observe a propensity in Genesis 1–11 to use figurative language to describe historical events. In the creation account, the days are figurative (no sun, moon, and stars until the fourth day), God makes Adam from dust and his breath (but God, a spirit, does not have lungs), and so on. In Genesis 3 a walking **serpent** (a well-known symbol of evil in the ancient Near East) persuades Eve and Adam to eat the forbidden fruit.

One who pays attention to the generic signals of Genesis 1–11 and reads the text in the context of its ancient cognitive environment will not expect to find a detailed or precise prosaic account of the past, but rather a figurative depiction of a historic event.

What implications does this have for our understanding

of the flood story? To honor the historical intention of the author, we are right to see a historical event behind the flood story; it presumes a catastrophic flood. But in order to forward its theological message (about sin and judgment), the author, perhaps influenced by the Mesopotamian flood story, recounts it as a flood that covers all the earth, whereas the event behind the story is more likely a particularly devastating local flood. Even so, we are certainly not to understand the biblical account as a parroting of the Mesopotamian story. Indeed, the differences are highlighted by the similarities as explained in the article on the *Gilgamesh Epic.* The differences have to do primarily with the different conception of deity. Whereas the Mesopotamian gods and goddesses are petulant and petty, fighting not only against humanity but also with each other, the God of the biblical flood story is sovereign and moral in his judgments and redemption.

For centuries, the problems with reading the flood story literally have been much discussed. The size of the ark, its seaworthiness, the hydraulics of the flood, and in (modern times) the lack of the slightest geologic evidence for the flood have led to some preposterous theories or appeals to miracle (how could Noah and his family build a boat the size of one and a half football fields?) that is not even hinted at in the biblical text.

Conclusion

If read according to its genre (theological history) and within its cognitive environment, that is, according to the intention of its author, we will understand that Genesis 6–9 does not intend to give us a precise and literal description of the event that lies behind the story. The author, perhaps in response to the Mesopotamian account as we know it particularly in the *Gilgamesh Epic,* has told the story of a devastating flood in order to teach his contemporaries about the dangers of sin in the light of God's judgment. The author also has a message of hope for his readers. God will not abandon his sinful people but will continue to work toward their redemption and restoration.

Tremper Longman III

REFERENCES AND RECOMMENDED READING

Clines, D. J. A. 1997. *The Theme of the Pentateuch.* 2nd ed. London: T&T Clark.
Kaminski, C. M. 2014. *Was Noah Good? Finding Favour in the Flood Narrative.* London: T&T Clark.
Longman III, T. 2016. *Genesis.* Story of God Bible Commentary. Grand Rapids: Zondervan.
Westermann, C. 1984. *Genesis 1–11: A Commentary.* Minneapolis: Fortress.

GENESIS FLOOD AND GEOLOGY, THE

The Prescientific Era

For centuries the story of Noah and the great flood in Genesis 6–9 has stimulated speculation about the possible physical effects of the devastating inundation. In the second century, Theophilus of Antioch asserted that remnants of the ark were visible in the "Arabian" mountains. In the sixth century, Procopius of Gaza maintained that marine remains discovered in "lofty mountains" had been deposited by the deluge. A millennium later Martin Luther wrote that pieces of petrified wood and fossils of fish recovered from mines were relics left behind by a watery cataclysm so extensive that it covered the Himalaya range.

Sedimentary Rocks as Evidence for the Deluge

During the next couple of centuries, scholars began formulating creative theories about the flood's effects on the landscape. John Woodward (1665–1722), for example, claimed that widespread terrestrial strata of now consolidated sand and gravel had been deposited from the floodwaters with dense, coarse-grained layers accumulating first and less-dense, finer-grained material settling on top. Woodward's opponents pointed out that his hypothesis failed spectacularly; thick stacks of sedimentary strata in fact demonstrate no regular systematic change in rock density from bottom to top. Dense limestone layers commonly lie above less-dense sandstones, and low-density salt deposits occur beneath denser shales.

Another seventeenth-century scholar, Nicolaus Steno (1638–86), also believed that stratified rocks resulted from the deluge. Steno, however, worked out basic principles for reconstructing the temporal sequence of events that formed stacks of strata, and later application of Steno's principles served to undercut the deluge hypothesis. Throughout the eighteenth century, numerous natural philosophers, among them Giovanni Arduino, Johann Gottlieb Lehmann, Georg Christian Füchsel, and Abraham Gottlob Werner, carefully traced the individual strata within stratigraphic successions across the countryside and measured their thicknesses. They recognized consistent continuity and orderliness in successions of strata of great extent, and they found no indications of chaotic disorder that a turbulent deluge might generate.

In the early nineteenth century, William Smith (1769–1839) demonstrated that packages of sedimentary rock layers throughout England were also characterized by distinctive fossil remains and that the types of preserved organisms changed upward through thick successions of rock strata.

Further studies in the early nineteenth century indicated that some sedimentary layers contained shelly marine organisms such as trilobites and brachiopods, whereas other layers contained remains of land-dwelling tetrapods (quadrupeds), a feature suggesting that many sedimentary rock successions resulted from repeated interchanges of land and sea.

The recognition of the great thicknesses of sedimentary rock accumulations in many localities, the regularity in the order of succession of the strata, the orderly distribution of fossil remains in the sedimentary layers, and the alternation between marine and terrestrial deposits made it clear that the great bulk of layered rocks had not been deposited as sediments during a single year-long global deluge. Early nineteenth-century geologists, many of whom were Christians, became aware that the sedimentary rock record told the story of a long and complex terrestrial history.

Unconsolidated Surface Deposits as Evidence for the Deluge

Where then was evidence for the great flood to be found? Several geologists, among them William Conybeare, Georges Cuvier, William Buckland, Jean-Andre de Luc, Adam Sedgwick, and George Bellas Greenough, posited that vast accumulations of unconsolidated gravel and sand spread over large regions of the globe, particularly in northern North America and northern Europe, provided the answer. The fact that such gravel accumulations were commonly accompanied by large erratic boulders that had been transported from distant outcrops in regions such as Canada or Scandinavia provided further support for the concept of a catastrophic flood of continental, if not global, dimensions. For example, Cuvier (1768–1832), illustrious founder of vertebrate anatomy, envisioned that surface deposits represented the most recent catastrophe about 6,000 years old, although he did not specifically identify it with the biblical flood.

In an English cave, Buckland (1784–1856) discovered remains of numerous extinct vertebrate **species** accompanying abundant hyena bones embedded in crystalline cave deposits. These fossil-bearing gravel deposits were covered by a layer of red mud on which lay more crystalline cave material that was generally devoid of fossils. Buckland suggested that hyenas had feasted on carcasses that they had dragged into the cave and that a great inundation had deposited the red mud and eradicated the now extinct animals.

New England geologist Edward Hitchcock (1793–1864)

attributed the extensive gravel deposits of the northeastern United States to a large-scale deluge accompanied by icebergs containing rocks of various sizes. After floating long distances, the icebergs finally melted, and the large rocks were released from the ice to be deposited as the erratic boulders associated with gravel deposits.

Recognition of the Ice Age

Scottish naturalist and Church of Scotland minister John Fleming (1785–1857) argued that British gravel deposits had been formed during separate flooding events rather than a single large flood. More devastating to the catastrophic flood idea, however, was the demonstration by Ignatz Venetz, Jean de Charpentier, and especially Louis Agassiz (1807–73) that many of the extensive surface gravels were better explained as products of glacial action. By studying modern glaciers in central Europe, Agassiz became familiar with the effects of glaciation, including striation, smoothing and polishing of rock outcrops, and rounding of individual boulders transported by glacial ice. By applying his observations on modern glaciers to localities in northern Europe where erratic boulders and striated bedrock occurred far from active glaciers, Agassiz concluded that ice sheets must have formerly covered vast portions of Europe. Ultimately he postulated the concept of an ice age when vast glacial ice sheets prevailed in northern latitudes.

American geologists, too, came to realize that striated bedrock, common throughout the northeastern United States and Canada, provided evidence that a widespread ice sheet had once covered that area. With the triumph of the glacial theory, geologists no longer considered widespread gravel deposits as evidence for a global deluge.

In response to these developments, some geologists began to link the biblical flood to the end of the ice age. For example, George Frederick Wright referred the flood to melting of the continental ice sheets coupled with postglacial vertical land movements to create basins, such as the Caspian Sea, a site that was also favored by Hugh Miller.

A much more recent variant of this last hypothesis was published in 1998 by Walter Pitman and William Ryan of Columbia University's Lamont-Doherty Earth Observatory. They postulated that the Black Sea was a remnant of Noah's flood. In their view, thanks to an abundance of glacial melt water at the close of the ice age, the level of the Mediterranean Sea rose so dramatically that water flowed rapidly over a previously exposed barrier of rock that separated the Mediterranean from a great basin now occupied by the Black

Sea. Inhabitants of the largely dry basin, which allegedly had been settled during the ice age, were thought to be decimated by the catastrophic influx of water.

The Discovery of Ancient Near Eastern Flood Legends

In the mid- to late nineteenth and early twentieth centuries, a new line of nongeological evidence with profound implications for the interpretation of the biblical flood narrative emerged from the field of archaeology. Fragments of ancient cuneiform documents inscribed on clay tablets were discovered at several excavation sites in the Middle East. Some of the reconstructed documents told the story of a great flood, preeminently the *Gilgamesh Epic*, which contains a flood narrative closely resembling that of Genesis. Gilgamesh, a Sumerian king, in searching for the secret of immortality, sought out Utnapishtim, the long-lived survivor of the great flood. Utnapishtim had constructed a giant vessel in the form of a cube, loaded all manner of animals on board, and rode out the deluge. When the flood began to recede, he sent out a dove, a swallow, and a raven in succession to determine whether the land had yet dried. The *Atrahasis* epic contained a similar flood story.

Given the Mesopotamian setting of these epics, scholars began to suspect that the Genesis flood might also have been a major flood confined to the Mesopotamian basin. Moreover, twentieth-century excavations in Iraq uncovered flood strata at Ur, Kish, Fara, and Nineveh. Some overly optimistic excavators identified specific flood layers with the Genesis flood, but careful dating of flood deposits at different sites confirmed that they were products of temporally distinct flood events. Nonetheless, it became clear that large-scale flooding had characterized Mesopotamia throughout its history to a degree sufficient to generate legends of exceptionally memorable deluges.

Despite centuries of accumulating evidence that the biblical flood could not account for the earth's sedimentary strata or even its surficial unconsolidated gravel deposits, the mid-twentieth century witnessed a revival of global flood geology, triggered by *The Genesis Flood* by **John C. Whitcomb** and **Henry M. Morris**, who, in effect, sought to give the speculations of the early twentieth-century Seventh-day Adventist writer, **George McCready Price**, greater scientific credibility. To this day the young-earth creationist movement wields pervasive influence in theologically conservative circles in espousing the idea that much of the sedimentary rock record owes its origin to the Noahic deluge.

The Current State of Geological Evidence
Sedimentary rocks

Despite widespread influence among rank-and-file believers, young-earth creationists have failed to persuade the mainstream geological community, which includes the vast majority of Christian geologists with advanced degrees in geology, of their position for one simple reason—the geological evidence is overwhelmingly incompatible with a global flood theory. For those who hold to the belief that the geological record supports the theory of a recent global deluge, an all-too-brief synopsis of relevant **information** extracted from sedimentary, igneous, and metamorphic rocks must suffice to support my contention.

Sedimentary rocks consist primarily of conglomerate, sandstone, shale and mudstone, limestone, coal, and evaporites such as gypsum. These rocks were formed from accumulations of gravel, sand, mud, lime and/or plants deposited from water, air, or glacial ice, or, in the case of gypsum, by crystallization from evaporating bodies of water. Accumulations of sediment commonly attain thicknesses in excess of 20 kilometers (65,000+ feet).

Flood geologists argue that a significant proportion of these successions of stratified sedimentary rocks were deposited as unconsolidated sediment during the yearlong biblical cataclysm. But the sedimentary rocks do not reflect such an origin. For example, the surfaces of successive layers of mudstones commonly contain fossil mud cracks identical to those that form on present-day dried-out lake bottoms or tidal flats. The existence of successive layers containing fossil mud cracks implies repeated alternation of saturation and desiccation of sediment during deposition of the mud layers. A world drowned by a global deluge, however, does not undergo a drying phase until the water is gone.

Both layered sedimentary rock stacks, as well as piles of volcanic lava flows, commonly include fossil soil horizons, indicating that a sedimentary rock layer or lava flow directly beneath the soil was exposed to the atmosphere for an extended period of time in order to weather the rock and form soil, before the soil itself was buried beneath a new layer of sediment or lava. Besides, soils would likely be swept away by the giant flood envisioned by flood geologists. As examples, the basaltic lavas of the Hawaiian Islands, the Columbia River Plateau (beautifully exposed along the Snake and Columbia River valleys in Idaho and Washington), and the Isle of Skye off the northwest coast of Scotland are interlayered with numerous soil horizons of varying thicknesses. In some instances plant or animal fossils occur in the soil horizons.

Some flood geologists claim that the folding commonly displayed by thick successions of sedimentary rocks in the Appalachians, Alps, Canadian Rockies, and other mountain systems must have occurred shortly after or during deposition of still waterlogged sediments. However, sedimentary rock piles contain abundant evidence that layers of sediment were cemented and consolidated into rock before folding and in many cases before deposition of succeeding layers. For example, folded sedimentary rocks of the Valley and Ridge Province of central Pennsylvania, western Virginia, and eastern Tennessee contain fossils that have been distorted from the original shapes of the living organisms. If the sediment had been unconsolidated during folding, the fossils would have retained their original shapes. There would also be more compelling evidence of large-scale slumping and contortion of soft sediment layers due to gravity, but such features are typically encountered only on a local scale.

In the Grand Canyon of the Colorado River, the lowermost layers of the Redwall Limestone contain angular rock fragments that were eroded from the underlying Muav Limestone. An erosional boundary known as an unconformity also separates the Redwall from the Muav.

The fragments from the Muav Limestone could not have been composed of soft sediment at the time they were eroded and incorporated into the new Redwall deposits; otherwise they would have easily been torn apart. The same situation applies to untold numbers of cases in which rounded pebbles or angular fragments were embedded in conglomerate layers after being eroded from the already solid layers beneath. In addition, the Redwall Limestone contains indications that karst topography, characterized by sinkholes partially filled by blocks of Redwall rubble, developed prior to deposition of the overlying Supai Group rocks. These observations refute the false notion that entire thick stacks of sediment layers remained unconsolidated until the entire pile of pliable sediment had accumulated during the flood, as would be expected in a gigantic global deluge that was depositing mud, sand, silt and pebbles at an incredibly high rate.

Finally, stacks of sedimentary layers commonly rest on eroded "basement" consisting of older metamorphic and igneous rocks. Flood geologists have often suggested that the top of the basement was at the surface of the earth prior to the onset of the deluge. If true, plants would have been growing on that eroded basement surface, and a variety of animals would have been wandering over, or burrowing into, that

surface. If a global deluge occurred only a few thousands of years ago, numerous modern forms would have been among these organisms. Thus sedimentary rock layers at the base of thick piles that rest directly on basement rocks—for example, the Tapeats Sandstone near the bottom of the Grand Canyon, the Flathead Quartzite in Montana, the Hardyston Quartzite in northern New Jersey, the Potsdam Sandstone on the outskirts of the Adirondack Mountains in New York, or the Sawatch Quartzite in Colorado—should contain some fossils of familiar organisms, such as leaves, seeds, and stems of coniferous and deciduous shrubs and trees, as well as skeletal remains and even trackways of small land animals that could not quickly escape to high ground, such as mice, snakes, toads, lizards, and squirrels. But we find no remains of mammals, reptiles, or trees in such formations.

Fossils that have been discovered in these rocks invariably represent extinct, ancient types of organisms, not the kinds of familiar organisms living in the present. If the earth had been suddenly drowned in a cataclysmic flood, some of these creatures should have been quickly embedded in a slurry of thick sediment, but after centuries of searching, no one has discovered modern fossils in the formations listed above.

Igneous rocks

Igneous rocks form when intensely hot (as much as 1150°C, or 2100°F) molten rock termed magma solidifies to crystals and/or glass. Coarsely crystallized igneous rocks, such as granite, syenite, diorite and gabbro, crystallize beneath the surface (in many cases tens of kilometers) where magma is intruded into preexisting rocks. Such intrusive bodies encompass a wide range of sizes and shapes. The largest of these bodies (tens to hundreds of kilometers in width and length), typically consist of granitelike rocks and are termed batholiths. Examples include the batholiths in the Sierra Nevada and Peninsular ranges of California, the Coast Ranges of British Columbia, the Andes, and Japan.

Many batholiths comprise dozens of igneous rock masses representing successive individual injections of magma that cut through previously crystallized masses. Calculations based on the shape, dimensions, and thermal properties of magmas, igneous rocks, and the deep-seated rocks into which the magmas were intruded, strongly suggest that batholithic intrusions required very large drafts of time (hundreds of thousands of years in several instances) to cool, crystallize, and be elevated to the surface. These batholiths cannot have been intruded during or even after a year-long deluge.

Moreover, piles of volcanic lava that are thousands of feet thick, such as at Mauna Loa and Mauna Kea on the Island of Hawaii, also required thousands of years to accumulate given the total thickness of the lava pile, the number of individual lava flows, and the rate of eruption.

Metamorphic rocks

Huge tracts of metamorphic rock include the gneisses of eastern Ontario and Quebec, the schists in the Piedmont region east of the Appalachian Mountains in the eastern United States, and the chert, schists, and greenstones of the Franciscan Formation exposed in the Coast Ranges of California. Such rocks represent material that previously consisted of sedimentary rocks formed at the earth's surface. In rare instances, fossils have been preserved in the metamorphosed rocks. If it is suggested that the biblical flood deposited the original sediments, how do we account for the metamorphism, which must have occurred during or after the flood? Some of the alleged flood deposits were deeply buried as much as 150 kilometers in order to experience the extremely high temperatures (as much as 1000°C) and pressures required for metamorphism, a complex process involving chemical reactions that produce minerals, such as garnet, sillimanite, staurolite, chlorite, kyanite, cordierite, actinolite, glaucophane, and muscovite, which are characteristic of metamorphic rocks, not to mention, in rare cases, diamond! Under the high pressures at depth, banded rocks become ductile and are intensely deformed into spectacular folds.

Any metamorphic rock that now occurs at the surface must have been uplifted and ultimately exposed by erosion of the overlying rocks. Such processes are inexplicable on the basis of a yearlong flood; in short, metamorphism is an extremely time-consuming process.

Concluding Thoughts

Geological evidence has demonstrated that thick accumulations of sedimentary rock, whether in the Grand Canyon, the Canadian Rockies, the Andes, the Drakensberg Mountains of South Africa, the Alps, or the Himalaya, are not the product of a yearlong global flood. Nor are the vast gravel and sand deposits that mantle the north-central and northeastern United States, southeastern Canada, Scandinavia, or northern Europe the result of continent-wide inundations of water. Although sufficient geological evidence exists to document the former existence of a couple of large-scale floods in the western United States associated with ancient

lakes in Missoula (Montana) and Bonneville (Utah), geological evidence for a large-scale biblical deluge is lacking.

Davis A. Young

REFERENCES AND RECOMMENDED READING

Montgomery, David R. 2011. *The Rocks Don't Lie: A Geologist Investigates Noah's Flood.* New York: W. W. Norton.

Young, Davis A. 1995. *The Biblical Flood: A Case Study of the Church's Response to Extrabiblical Evidence.* Grand Rapids: Eerdmans.

Young, Davis A., and Ralph F. Stearley. 2008. *The Bible, Rocks and Time: Geological Evidence for the Age of the Earth.* Downers Grove, IL: InterVarsity.

⚡ GENESIS, INTERPRETATION OF CHAPTERS 1 AND 2 (Canonical View).

Hermeneutics is the science of interpretation—asking questions about the nature of interpretation and developing principles of interpretation. In a broad sense, all human mental activity involves interpretation, from stopping at a stop sign to responding to another person's wave of a hand, diagnosing a disease, engaging in conversation with one's children, applying a law, or reading the morning newspaper. The list could be endless; we are interpreting animals.

In this article, we are interested in the interpretation of Genesis 1–2. While discussing the nature of biblical hermeneutics, we will consider the implications of hermeneutics for the question of the relationship between the Bible and science, the latter also being, of course, an interpretive enterprise (see **Hermeneutics, Biblical and Scientific**). Many of the issues that I will discuss are contested, though the nature and scope of this article will not allow a full description or refutation of alternate approaches (but see Fee and Stuart 2014; Klein et al. 2004; Longman 1997; and Osborne 2007 for hermeneutics in general; and Longman 2016 specifically for Genesis). Hermeneutics is a rich and extensive discipline, and we will have to be selective in our treatment, choosing those topics we consider most relevant for the interaction between the study of the Bible, particularly Genesis 1–2, and science.

The Text

We are interested in the interpretation of the biblical text, Old and New Testaments, considered canonical (the standard of faith and practice) by the Christian church. Traditionally, and still by many across the world today (including me), the Bible is understood to be the Word of God and therefore true in all it intends to teach. God speaks to us through the written words of his human spokespeople, and as with any act of communication, the hearer/reader must interpret the words of the speaker/writer in order to hear the message of the text.

One of the most fundamental questions of hermeneutics is where the message is to be found. Or to put it another way, where is the meaning of the text located?

Any act of written communication, including the Bible, involves three basic parts: author, text, and reader. An author writes a text in order to communicate with a reader.

It seems straightforward enough on the surface that the meaning of the written text would be found in the author's intention. Thus when we read/interpret a text, we do so to discover the author's intended message. Thus, in answer to the question "Where is meaning located?" we would answer, "In the author's intention." Even so, as many since the New Critics of the mid-twentieth century have pointed out, even with a text where the author still is alive and able to be interviewed, she is not inevitably a reliable interpreter of her work. She may forget what she meant or over time change her interpretation, or not even be fully aware of the full implications of what she wrote (as those who study intertextuality point out). In the case of the Bible, there is no independent access to the author. In the first place, the question of authorship is complex, particularly for those of us who believe that God is the ultimate author of the Bible. Does the human author fully understand the intentions of God? And in any case, the human authors are dead and God has not chosen to give us an inerrant guide to interpretation.

Understanding this, however, should not lead us to give up, as some do, on the idea of identifying the message of the text with the intention of the author, but the issues surrounding authorial intention do remind us that we gain access to that intention only through the text (*sola scriptura*). We should also be aware of the role of the reader as we interpret. We all approach the Bible from our limited and fallen human perspective. This awareness should not lead us to despair, but it should humble us as interpreters and also encourage us to listen to other interpreters who may help us see dimensions of the text that we have missed.

We should also rest assured that the most important message of the Bible is absolutely clear since it is taught in so many ways and pervasively throughout Scripture. I am speaking here of the gospel message, and the church has affirmed rightly through what is often called the *doctrine of the perspicuity of Scripture* that the Bible clearly teaches that all of us are sinners in need of a Savior, and that Savior is Jesus Christ. Of course, these are not the only teachings that are clear in the Bible, but my point is that not everything in the Bible is interpreted with equal certitude, and a number of biblical texts give rise to many of the debates among Christians, including those that have to do with the relationship between Christianity and modern science (e.g., What are the nature of the days in Genesis? Was **the flood** local or universal? Is the **soul** nonmaterial?).

In summary, where is the meaning of the text to be found? What are we doing when we are reading the Bible? We, as readers, study the text (Bible) to hear the message of the author, the human author in the first place but ultimately the divine author.

Scripture as an Act of Incarnation: Studying Scripture in Its "Cognitive Environment"

As I intimated above, God is the ultimate author of Scripture, but he used human authors (Moses, David, Paul, and a host of others, some of whose names we may not even know) over many centuries to produce the Bible that we hold in our hands in the twenty-first century AD. Theologians have often thought of the Bible on analogy with the **incarnation** of Jesus Christ. The doctrine of the incarnation asserts that Jesus is fully divine and fully human. In a similar sense, the Bible is fully divine and fully human. While the Bible teaches that humanity is sinful, Jesus is fully human without sin. In the same way, we can argue that the Bible, though written by human beings (under the inspiration of God; 2 Tim. 3:16–17), is without error (in the original manuscripts) in all that it teaches (contra Sparks 2008).

However, the humanity of Scripture reminds us that the Bible did not descend out of the sky, nor was it unmediated by human agency (something like the alleged story of the golden tablets of Joseph Smith). The human authors of Scripture wrote in the language of their day (Hebrew, Aramaic, Greek), and they utilized the literary conventions and styles of their time. To put it bluntly, the Bible was written for us but not to us. For example, the books of Samuel and Kings were written to Judeans during the exile in Babylon; the book of Romans is so called because it was written to the Romans. The book of Genesis was written to an ancient Israelite audience.

We must not read the Bible as if it is the morning newspaper, but rather in its "cognitive environment" (Walton 2011, 6–15). Again, a reminder, we can still get the big picture without reading it in its original environment, but to truly understand the depths of Scripture and to place our interpretation on firm ground, we must study it in its original context. And here is where the study of the ancient context, the ancient Near Eastern context for the Old Testament and the Greco-Roman culture of the New Testament, becomes so important for modern readers.

If one objects to the need for the study of the ancient context to fully understand the Bible based on a feeling that "all I need is the Bible," let us remember that no one today can read even one word of the Bible without the help of someone who has studied ancient Hebrew, Aramaic, and Greek. And anyone who has studied the ancient languages realizes that even the translation of Hebrew words involves study of cognate languages like Ugaritic, Akkadian, Arabic, and so on.

And that is how we enhance our understanding of the cognitive environment of the Bible: we study the languages and literatures of the contemporary world of the Old and New Testaments. This is critical in the study of Genesis 1 and 2.

Like the entirety of the Bible, Genesis 1–2 was written *for us*, but not *to us*. Scholars debate precisely when Genesis 1 and 2 were written (see **Genesis, Book of**), but no one doubts it was composed in the context of the ancient Near East. It was written to address the questions of an ancient Hebrew audience, using language and concepts that they understood. The primary question they were interested in was "Who created the world?" not "How was the world created?" They asked this question in the light of the claims of rival creation stories (e.g., *Atrahasis* and *Enuma Elish*) and proclaimed that Yahweh, the God they worshiped, was the creator of everything and everyone. The teaching about creation in Genesis 1–2 does not directly interact with **Charles Darwin** but with these rival ancient Near Eastern accounts of creation.

Remember that the evangelical doctrine of inerrancy claims that the Bible is true in everything that it intends to teach, and reading Genesis 1 and 2 in its cognitive environment informs us of what it does teach and what it doesn't teach. One would not necessarily expect to find anything like a modern scientific understanding of cosmogony or the process of creation (contra **Hugh Ross** and **Reasons to Believe**).

The Importance of Genre

Among the most important principles of hermeneutics is the significance of genre to the interpretive task. To put it pointedly, genre triggers reading strategy.

In literary studies, genre refers to a category of texts that are closely related in form, content, tone, or some combination of elements. Genres are not rigid categories or discrete sets, but rather fluid and overlapping. They do not fall from heaven or arise from some kind of authoritarian literary dictate, but they arise because authors write in literary traditions, sending signals to their readers as to how to take their words. Genre has helpfully been described as a kind of code or convention or a contract that exists between author and reader.

A common (nonbiblical) example of such a generic signal would be an opening line like "Once upon a time," which would tell a competent modern reader that what follows is a fairy tale, not a scientific or historical treatise. Anyone who has walked into a modern bookstore or library is familiar with genre in that there are separate sections where one might find novels, biographies, how-to books, and so on. We expect different things and know that their authors make different truth claims based on our recognition of their genre. Works of fiction make different truth claims than nonfiction works. We learn much about life and the human condition, for instance, from J. R. R. Tolkein's *The Hobbit*, even if such short creatures with furry feet don't actually exist.

I can illustrate the above premise that genre triggers reading strategy with a biblical example that has been the subject of interpretational dispute over the centuries. The Song of Songs opens with:

> Let him kiss me with the kisses of his mouth —
> for your love is more delightful than wine.
> Pleasing is the fragrance of your perfumes;
> your name is like perfume poured out.
> No wonder the young women love you!
> Take me away with you — let us hurry!
> Let the king bring me into his chambers. (1:2–4)

How are we to interpret these words? For many years (we have evidence of interpretation beginning around AD 100), the Song was identified as an allegory. Thus in Jewish tradition, for instance, the woman, who here speaks, was thought to be Israel and the man, to whom she speaks, was thought to be God. Thus the Targum to the Song interprets this passage as a reference to Israel. The woman, Israel, asks the man, God, to bring her into his bedroom (the Promised Land).

Today very few, if any, scholars of any stripe believe that the Song is an allegory since there are no generic signals that a reader should take it as an allegory (read *Pilgrim's Progress* to learn how obvious such signals are). Thanks in part to the rediscovery of ancient Near Eastern love poems (see above for the importance of reading in an ancient "cognitive environment"), interpreters of the Song would take the above verses as part of a love poem in which a woman expresses her desire for physical intimacy with the man.

The Bible is not a monolithic book; it contains examples of many different genres: history, law, wisdom, poetry of all sorts, prophecy, apocalyptic, gospel, epistle, to name but a few. Each of these trigger different reading strategies (see Longman 1997).

One of the reasons why there are radical differences concerning the proper interpretation of Genesis 1–2 among Christian interpreters has to do with genre identification. On the extremes are those who argue that the creation accounts of Genesis 1–2 are literal (or plain) history, not only telling us that God created everything but giving us a precise account of how he did it. Thus we turn to the Bible rather than to science to learn that God created Adam, the first man, from the dust and breathed into him. On the other extreme are those who argue that Genesis 1 and 2 are closer to poetry or myth or a parable.

In my estimation, both these extremes point to something true but are ultimately mistaken. In terms of genre signals, I would highlight four points.

First, the text reflects on the past, the deep past to be sure. It is making historical claims at least in the broad sense. It is saying that Yahweh, and none other, created the cosmos and its inhabitants. We see this partly in the narrative style of the text (technically in the use of the *waw* consecutive [a Hebrew syntactical form], which is often, but not exclusively, used to recount the past) as well as the fact that Genesis 1–2 is a part of the so-called primeval history of Genesis 1–11. It shares similarities with the rest of Genesis 12–50, which is clearly historical in intent (technically seen in the shared *toledot* structure of the entire book, for which see **Genesis, Book of**). However, we should note how Genesis 12–50 slows down the narrative pace and narrows the scope (focusing on individuals like Abraham), thus showing a greater concern for what we might roughly call the details of history.

Second, Genesis 1 and 2 contain much figurative language, rendering dubious attempts to treat the text as a literal description of how God created the cosmos. Since the early church, the fact that the sun, moon, and stars aren't created until the fourth day has indicated that the first three days are not literal 24-hour periods of an evening and a morning. The description of God creating Adam from the dust and his breath (2:7) must also be figurative since God is a pure spirit and does not have lungs.

Third, the intense interplay between Genesis 1 and 2 and ancient Near Eastern creation accounts also raise doubts about whether the author of the former intends us to take his description literally. After all, *Atrahasis* and *Enuma Elish* also describe the creation of the first humans from an earthly component (clay) and a divine one (blood of a demon god and the spit of the gods). The best understanding of this particular interplay is that the biblical author is not giving us a literal description of how God created as much as making a polemical statement disputing the ancient Near East claim and its rather contemptible view of humanity.

Fourth, the long-recognized lack of sequence between the two creation accounts in Genesis 1 and 2 also makes suspect any attempt to impose a literal reading on the text. One example of the lack of concord is the observation that, while in the first account (1:1–2:4b) vegetation is created before humanity, in the second (2:4b–25) it is created after Adam.

Whether or not one agrees with this understanding of the genre of Genesis 1 and 2, there is no denying the importance of the issue of genre on the question of what God wants to teach us in these chapters.

Canonical Interpretation

A final topic in this selective treatment of hermeneutics is canonical interpretation. One of the most basic principles of interpretation insists that we read any text in its context. To lift a passage out of its context results in what has been called *proof texting*, which runs the high risk of distorting the meaning of the passage since words find their meaning in the context of sentences, sentences find their meaning in the context of paragraphs, paragraphs in the context of the broader discourse, and so one.

Canonical interpretation acknowledges that all biblical texts exist today in the context of the Bible as a whole. That means any single passage must be read today in the context of the whole canon, which for the Christian includes both Old and New Testaments.

The example that I have been using in this essay, the two creation accounts found in Genesis 1 and 2, stand today at the beginning of the canon. Interpreting them canonically would take much more space than allowed for in this article, so I will make just a couple of observations.

First, Genesis 1–2 is not the only creation account in the Bible; we can find descriptions of God's creation of the cosmos and humans also in the Psalms (8; 19; 24; 33; 74; 104; 136), the book of Proverbs (3:19–20; 8:22–31), and Job (38:4–11), as well as texts in the New Testament (John 1:1–5; Rom. 1:18–20; Col. 1:15–20). When we compare these accounts, we are struck by the high incidence of figurative language.

God creates by defeating a multiheaded monster named Leviathan (Ps. 74:14); he commands the personified Sea not to go beyond the borders he has set (Job 38:11; Prov. 8:29); a woman named Wisdom observes his creative actions and even helps him (Prov. 8:22–31); and on and on. Close analysis of these poems is not possible here, but even a quick look supports our understanding of Genesis 1–2 as not interested in a literal, precise description of creation (Carlson and Longman 2010).

Second, Genesis 1–2 plays a crucial foundational role in the overall story of Scripture, which is often described as a drama having four acts. Genesis 1–2 is the first act (creation), followed by Genesis 3 (**the fall**), then Genesis 4–Revelation 20 (redemption), followed by Revelation 21–22 (consummation). Interestingly, the final scene, like the first, is described using highly figurative language that repeats some of the opening scene's images (the garden leads to a city [the New Jerusalem], but there is a garden with two trees of life in the city). Thus we might say that the Bible employs figurative language when describing both the deep past (creation) and the far-distant future (consummation).

Third, it is important to point out, though not necessarily directly relevant to the issue of the relationship between science and religion, that when read canonically, all Scripture points ultimately to Jesus Christ (Luke 24:25–27, 44–45). While it is crucial to first interpret an Old Testament text like Genesis 1–2 in its original context, the Christian interpreter heeds Jesus's insistence that the entire Old Testament ultimately points to him. When interpreting Genesis 1–2 in the light of the full canon, we are thus drawn to those passages that describe Jesus as a participant in the creation process.

Conclusion

All readers of the Bible must interpret it. The field of hermeneutics studies the interpretive process and reflects on the principles that guide the reader to the proper interpretation defined here as that which leads us to the ultimate Author's message in the text. My contention in regard to the question of the relationship of **science and the Bible** is that proper interpretive practice will steer clear of improper readings (like those that expect to find modern science in the text) and toward the proper ones. And when the original setting and its "cognitive environment," the genre of the text, and the canonical context are taken into consideration, we will see that there is no clash between the book of God's special **revelation**, the Bible, and the book of God's general revelation, nature, the realm studied by science.

Tremper Longman III

REFERENCES AND RECOMMENDED READING

Carlson, R. F., and T. Longman III. 2010. *Science, Creation, and the Bible.* Downers Grove, IL: InterVarsity.
Fee, G. D., and D. Stuart. 2014. *Reading the Bible for All Its Worth.* 4th ed. Grand Rapids: Zondervan.
Klein, W. W., C. L. Blomberg, and R. I. Hubbard Jr. 2004. *Introduction to Biblical Interpretation.* Nashville: Thomas Nelson.
Longman III, T. 1997. *Reading the Bible with Heart and Mind.* Colorado Springs: NavPress.
———. 2016. *Genesis.* Story of God Bible Commentary. Grand Rapids: Zondervan.
Osborne, G. 2007. *The Hermeneutical Spiral: A Comprehensive Introduction to Biblical Interpretation.* Grand Rapids: Zondervan.
Sparks, K. L. 2008. *God's Word in Human Words: An Evangelical Appropriation of Critical Biblical Scholarship.* Grand Rapids: Baker.
Walton, J. 2011. *Genesis 1 as Ancient Cosmology.* Winona Lake, IN: Eisenbrauns.

GENESIS, INTERPRETATION OF CHAPTERS 1 AND 2 (Factual View)

Governing Philosophical Presuppositions

Platonism and ancient interpreters. Contemporary disagreements about whether Genesis 1–2 should be interpreted literally or figuratively have ancient antecedents. Because they all were influenced by Platonism and Philo, ancient Christians, such as Clement of Alexandria, Origen, and **Augustine**, could not conceive that God's act of creating all things spanned six days. They embraced Philo's notion that God instantaneously created everything at once (Philo 1993, III). Additionally, Augustine supported this belief by appealing to the Vulgate's mistranslation of Sirach 18.1, *omnia simul,* "all together." Reflecting Platonism's influence, Origen wonders, "Now who is there, pray, possessed of understanding, that will regard the statement as appropriate, that the first day, and the second, and the third, in which also both evening and morning are mentioned, existed without sun, and moon, and stars—the first day even without a sky?" (Origen 1982, 4.1.16).

Though Genesis presents God's creative acts as occurring on six sequential days, these early Christians interpreted the succession not as temporal but as an allegorical device to prioritize creation's increasing worth, with humans ranked highest, showing the influence of Philo's numerological explanation of creation's days (Clement 1982, 6.16; Augustine 1982, 1.135–36).

Again, Origen derisively inquires, who could be "so ignorant as to suppose that" God took on the role of a farmer who planted trees in a garden, the fruit of which when bitten would yield life or the knowledge of good and evil, and that

God walked in the garden and found Adam hiding under a tree? He doubts that no one could fail to recognize that God took no such role but that these are "related figuratively in Scripture, that some mystical meaning may be indicated by it" (Origen 1982, 4.1.16).

Evolution and modern interpreters. Since modern **geology**, archaeology, and biology have secured **worldview** hegemony, many Christians find it difficult to resist looking for harmony between the Bible's claims concerning origins and those of science. Thus Christians tend to interpret Genesis 1–3 in accord with whatever age of the earth they presuppose, wittingly or not. The result is a renewal of conflicts among Christians over origins of the universe and of life. Perhaps the greatest impetus for this renewal came when recent interpretation of human genome research prompted the launch of **BioLogos** in 2007 to call Christians to embrace harmoniously biblical faith and evolutionary creation as the explanation of how God created all earthly life. BioLogos advocates believe, "If scientific results seem to conflict with a given reading of the Bible, careful consideration should be given to the possibility that a somewhat different way of understanding the Bible might be more appropriate" (Carlson and Longman 2010, 125–26).

Because Genesis does not reveal "how God created the world and humanity," it is permissible and proper to turn to human scientific inquiry to seek the answer (Longman 2013, 103). Many advocates of evolutionary creation are confident that knowledge derived from both modern sciences and from archaeological discoveries made in the nineteenth century enable us to set aside the notion that the creation accounts of Genesis 1–2 portray reality with God creating all things successively over a six-day period (Carlson and Longman 2010, 112–14; Lamoureux 2013, 46–55). They contend that given evolution's veracity, correlations between the cosmologies of Genesis 1 and of ancient Near Eastern creation stories correct mistaken readings of Genesis 1–2 held by previous generations of Christians. Thus one advocate starkly states, *"Holy Scripture makes statements about how God created the heavens that in fact never happened."* He reiterates, *"Holy Scripture makes statements about how God created living organisms that in fact never happened"* (Lamoureux 2013, 54, 56, emphasis in original). He asks, "Did God lie in the Bible?" and answers, "No!" He explains that God accommodated errant ancient science "as an incidental vessel to reveal" that he created life, albeit not actually the way that his sacred Word tells it (Lamoureux 2013, 54, 57). Accordingly, evolutionary science, not Genesis, discloses how God

created life. Others have ably identified problems with claiming that the biblical story of creation reflects those ancient pagan cosmologies (Weeks 2010, 219–36). So, what follows focuses on the text of Genesis 1–2.

Interpretation Is Neither Literal nor Figurative

As in the ancient church, to dispute whether *interpretation* is literal or symbolic polarizes advocates on both sides because of a shared mistake embraced to varying degrees. At a popular, even semi-scholarly, level many falsely suppose that if literal is *actual*, then figurative is *imaginary, unreal*. The result is "interpretive woodenness" (literalism) that suppresses biblical imagery and incites ridicule and dissociation. Scholars are not inoculated against falling prey to this error. It routinely impairs conversation by distancing participants on either side to extremes and by reducing debate to a stalemate between literal interpretation and figurative interpretation of the creation accounts, a problem that seems apparent in J. Daryl Charles's *Reading Genesis 1–2: An Evangelical Conversation.*

The error is to shift the literal sense (*sensus literalis*) from the act of writing to the act of interpreting a text. To break the standoff, it is necessary to abandon the notion that interpretation is either literal or figurative. It is neither, for literal and figurative are not proper descriptions of how we are to interpret any text or speech. Rather, literal or figurative are ways speakers and writers portray reality. This is true because both literal and symbolic concern how speakers and writers refer to things. If we were to interpret literally or figuratively our ordinary conversations with one another, we would render communication silly, even impossible. For often we figuratively refer to concrete things, such as, "I ride in my rust bucket to work." This is a figurative portrayal of something real; this is not figurative interpretation.

The sun's absence on the first three days: a problem? Admittedly, that the sun is not mentioned within creation week's first three days is a point of stumbling that prompts advocates of literal and figurative interpretations to pose the question whether the days of Genesis 1 are literal, allegorical, or figurative. The question is mistaken and misguided, for the days themselves are neither literal nor figurative. The query needs reframing: Does Genesis present the days literally or figuratively? This is not a distinction without a difference. The distinction and difference are lost on us because we have become so mired in quibbling over literal interpretation versus figurative interpretation.

The proper question is: How does Genesis 1 portray the successive days filled with God's creative acts? Does the text present the days of the Creator's work literally or figuratively or both? If Genesis literally presents the days, we are mistaken to call the days *literal*; instead, the days are *actual*. Again, if the text literally presents the days, this hardly implies that the text does not invest symbolic function in God's acts and the events of the sequential days. Likewise, if Genesis presents "day" with figurative significance, this does not mean that "day" is not real but illusory or simply accommodating erroneous ancient science.

Genesis 1–2 uses "day" (*yôm*) literally and figuratively. After God creates light, he calls the light "day" and the darkness "night" (1:5). The text reiterated this use when God creates the heavenly lights on the fourth day, "the greater light to govern the day" (1:14–16). Also, 1:5 uses "day" in a second literal way for the cycle of darkness and light, "and there was evening, and there was morning—the first day," the first of six successive days of God's creative work. Though the text uses the cardinal number, "day 1," in a Hebrew clause of this type the cardinal functions as an ordinal number, "first day" (Waltke and O'Connor 1990, 274). The next five designations of "day," defined by the preceding temporal phrase, "and there was evening, and there was morning," are all ordinal numbers indicating sequence.

Thus Genesis 1 literally portrays God's creative deeds as spanning six days, as reckoned by humans. The seventh day is unique, for the temporal phrase that precedes the first six is not repeated because its presence would signify its transition to the next day (Cassuto 1961, 28). For "evening" and "morning" signify, respectively, the ending of daylight, when God suspends his creative work, and the renewal of light, when he resumes creating (Sarna 1989, 8). Thus absence of the evening and morning emphasizes that when God ceases his creating at the close of the sixth day, his creative work is complete and he does not resume creating after the seventh day comes to an end. A fourth use of "day" occurs in a prepositional phrase (*beyôm*), which bears the idiomatic sense of "on the day when" or "at the time when" (2:4).

For many contemporaries, as with Origen, they think the sun's absence on the first three days requires that the days of Genesis 1 cannot be actual days. That the True Light (John 1:9), by whom all things were made (John 1:3) and by whom all things consist (Col. 1:17), created light and called it "day" is explicit in Genesis 1:3–5. That the sun is not introduced until the fourth day does not necessarily mean that it was absent, for the Hebrew of 1:14 states, "God said, 'Let the lights in the expanse be for separating the day from the night'" (Sailhamer 1996, 93). As such, the text assumes

that the lights were already in the heavens from day 1 but that on the fourth day, as with all creatures, the heavenly bodies are subject to the Creator's will. So God commands them and they obey by serving their respective purposes, "to govern the day and the night" (1:18) and to "serve as signs to mark sacred times, and days and years" (1:14).

Anthropomorphic portrayal of God: a problem? Again, contemporaries follow the lead of Origen by appealing to the portrayal of God "as a human being who has a body with lungs so he can breathe into dust" as proof that "the account of Adam's creation must be figurative" so that it does "not inform the reader how God made the first human being" (Longman 2013, 106).

Indeed, the portrayal of God is anthropomorphic. The same is true of every depiction of God throughout Genesis 1–2 and all of Scripture.

How could God truly reveal himself and his acts to humans other than analogically, which is to say, anthropomorphically? For example, every verse throughout Genesis 1 is filled with anthropomorphic representation of God as speaking, naming, seeing, making, separating, self-consulting, blessing, resting, and so on. That Scripture figuratively represents the Creator this way does not render God's portrayed actions as unreal, mythical, or accommodating errant ancient pagan science as claimed by BioLogos advocates and others (e.g., Walton 2013, 147–62). Because the Creator formed Adam from the ground and breathed into him the breath of life, making him after his own likeness (his earthly analogue), God reveals himself to his creatures in their likeness as if he wears their form and qualities, when in truth his creatures wear their Creator's likeness (Caneday 2003, 161).

Following the church fathers, both Martin Luther and **John Calvin** insist that because God in his essence is unknowable to humans, he condescends to our creatureliness to reveal himself after our likeness, even adapting himself to the simplicity of a child that he might make himself known to us (Luther 1960, 2.46). Because they believe that God always reveals himself this way, both Reformers believed that God created all things within six actual days (Calvin 1960, 1.14.1; Calvin 1979, 1.78, 1.105; Luther 1960, 1.3, 5–6). Contemporary scholars misconstrue the Reformers' understanding of divine accommodation when they marshal them to support their claims that uses of "day" in the creation accounts of Genesis allows for millions of years (Caneday 2011, 31–35).

Throughout church history, numerous brilliant Christians have acknowledged "that Scripture does not just contain a few scattered anthropomorphisms but is anthropomorphic through and through" (Bavinck 2004, 2.99). Thus God's **revelation** "is in every respect finite and limited, but not for that reason impure or untrue" (Bavinck 2004, 2.106; against Enns 2011, 144). Because all of God's revelation, whether in nature or in Scripture, is directed to humans, he speaks as a human who is earthbound and takes on human forms. Thus Scripture's initial statement — "In the beginning God created the heavens and the earth" — reveals God *analogically*, neither as he is in himself (*univocally*) nor entirely unlike his human creatures (*equivocally*) (cf. Van Til 1976, 212). God spans the Creator-creature chasm by anthropomorphically revealing himself and his deeds to humans. The Creator enters his own creation as a potter who forms Adam "from the dust of the ground and breathe[s] into his nostrils the breath of life" (Gen. 2:7).

This analogy is rich, for God, who has no hands, forms Adam, and he who has no lungs "breathed into his nostrils the breath of life, and man became a living being" (Mickelsen 1963, 314 – 15; cf. Silva 1990, 22). He took on the form of the human he was fashioning from the ground to reveal the vast distinction between himself as Creator and Adam as creature, who is like and unlike his Creator, which is what "in our likeness" (Gen. 1:26) implies. Throughout the Old Testament, the Creator, who never reveals himself to humans as he is in himself lest they perish (Ex. 33:15 – 23), reveals himself to humanity as though he were human, veiling his full glory as he foreshadows the incarnation of the Word (John 1:14).

Conclusion

Debates over literal interpretation versus figurative interpretation misdirect our reading of both the first and last books of the Bible. Thus it is not surprising that the church has so many disagreements and divergent views concerning the origins and consummation of all things.

To inquire whether we should interpret the apocalypse literally or figuratively is to pose the question wrongly, thus prejudicing the response. Interpretation is neither literal nor figurative, for with vivid imagery John *nonliterally rehearses* each of his visions of heavenly realities. After he sees the new heavens and new earth, he *figuratively portrays* his vision of coming reality by using exaggerated and extravagant analogies of familiar earthly things. Each city gate carved from enormous singular pearls and a main street paved with pure gold, transparent as glass (Rev. 21:21), entail a *figurative portrayal* of the reality he saw. John presents the city as real, not unreal or illusory, so superlative that the most

exquisite metropolis imaginable, constructed from the most expensive gems and metals known on earth, is a lackluster earthly analogue.

Similarly, to inquire whether we should interpret the early chapters of Genesis literally or figuratively is to ask the question incorrectly, which renders the discussion tendentious. We are not to interpret Genesis 1 – 2 either literally or nonliterally. The proper question is, how does the text represent God's creation of all things? Does Genesis portray these things nonfiguratively or figuratively? Genesis portrays the reality of God's creative acts with literalness — "God created the heavens and the earth."

This is not literal interpretation versus nonliteral exegesis. The literalness of God's creative acts is not the property of our reading but of the writing of the text of Genesis, in how the narrative portrays these things. This is so because the narrative factually presents the Creator's acts without exaggeration or embellishment, albeit anthropomorphically. Thus the factual portrayal of Genesis 1 – 2 does not mean that the creation accounts are void of figurative language. Indeed, everything God does — speaking, creating, seeing, naming, separating, self-consulting, creating humans after his likeness, appointing humans over creation, blessing, resting, forming Adam from the ground, breathing life into Adam, and placing humans in Eden — entails anthropomorphism.

That these are all anthropomorphic portraits of God does not render them nonfactual. Rather, the narrator presents all of God's creative acts in full continuity with the way the remainder of the Bible everywhere employs anthropomorphism to portray God as acting and speaking. Because Genesis portrays these things as factual, Scripture's writers in both the Old and New Testaments accept their historicity (e.g., Matt. 19:4 – 6) while at the same time recognizing their suffused symbolic significances as they prefigure the coming new creation in the promised Messiah (e.g., 2 Cor. 4:6). Expressed differently, for Scripture's writers, theological continuity between creation's portrayal in Genesis 1 – 2 and new creation's coming in Christ Jesus is embedded indivisibly in both the factuality and the symbolic significances of what the creation accounts portray.

Ardel B. Caneday

REFERENCES AND RECOMMENDED READING

Augustine. 1982. *The Literal Meaning of Genesis*, trans. and ann. John Hammond Taylor. Vol. 1. New York: Paulist.
Bavinck, Herman. 2004. *Reformed Dogmatics*. Vol. 2, *God and Creation*. Ed. John Bolt. Trans. John Vriend. Grand Rapids: Baker Academic.
Beall, Todd. 2013. "Reading Genesis 1 – 2: A Literal Approach." In *Reading*

Genesis 1–2: An Evangelical Conversation, ed. J. Daryl Charles, 45–59. Peabody, MA: Hendrickson.

Calvin, John. 1960. *Institutes of the Christian Religion.* Philadelphia: Westminster.

———. 1979. *Commentary on the First Book of Moses Called Genesis.* Vol. 1. Trans. John King. Edinburgh: Calvin Translation Society; Grand Rapids: Baker.

Caneday, A. B. 2003. "Veiled Glory: God's Self-Revelation in Human Likeness—A Biblical Theology of God's Anthropomorphic Self-Disclosure." In *Beyond the Bounds: Open Theism and the Undermining of Biblical Christianity*, ed. John Piper, Justin Taylor, and Paul Kjoss Helseth, 149–99. Wheaton, IL: Crossway.

———. 2011. "The Language of God and Adam's Genesis and Historicity in Paul's Gospel." *Southern Baptist Journal of Theology* 15:26–59.

Carlson, Richard, and Tremper Longman III. 2010. *Science, Creation, and the Bible: Reconciling Rival Theories of Origins.* Downers Grove, IL: IVP Academic.

Cassuto, U. 1961. *A Commentary on the Book of Genesis: Part One—From Adam to Noah.* Trans. Israel Abraham. Jerusalem: Magnes.

Clement of Alexandria. 1982. *The Stromata.* Vol. 2. The Ante-Nicene Fathers. Comp. A. Cleveland Coxe. Ed. Alexander Roberts, James Donaldson, and Henry Wace. Grand Rapids: Eerdmans.

Enns, Peter. 2011. *The Evolution of Adam: What the Bible Does and Doesn't Say about Human Origins.* Grand Rapids: Brazos.

Lamoureux, Denis. 2013. "No Historical Adam: Evolutionary Creation View." In *Four Views on the Historical Adam*, ed. Matthew Barrett and Ardel B. Caneday. Grand Rapids: Zondervan.

Longman, Tremper, III. 2013. "What Genesis 1–2 Teaches (and What It Doesn't)." In *Reading Genesis 1–2: An Evangelical Conversation*, ed. J. Daryl Charles, 103–28. Peabody, MA: Hendrickson.

Luther, Martin. 1960. *Lectures in Genesis.* Luther's Works. Vols. 1–2. Trans. George Schick. St. Louis: Concordia.

Mickelsen, A. Berkeley. 1963. *Interpreting the Bible.* Grand Rapids: Eerdmans.

Origen. 1982. "De Principiis." The Ante-Nicene Fathers. Vol. 4. Comp. A. Cleveland Coxe. Ed. Alexander Roberts, James Donaldson, and Henry Wace. Grand Rapids: Eerdmans.

Philo. 1993. "On the Creation." Vol. 3 of *The Works of Philo: Complete and Unabridged.* Trans. C. D. Yonge. Peabody, MA: Hendrickson.

Sailhamer, John. 1996. *Genesis Unbound: A Provocative New Look at the Creation Account.* Sisters, OR: Multnomah.

Sarna, Nahum J. 1989. *Genesis.* JPS Torah Commentary. Philadelphia: Jewish Publication Society.

Silva, Moisés. 1990. *God, Language, and Scripture: Reading the Bible in the Light of General Linguistics.* Foundations of Contemporary Interpretation. Vol. 4. Grand Rapids: Zondervan.

Van Til, Cornelius. 1976. *An Introduction to Systematic Theology.* Nutley, NJ: Presbyterian & Reformed.

Waltke, Bruce, and M. O'Connor. 1990. *An Introduction to Biblical Hebrew Syntax.* Winona Lake, IN: Eisenbrauns.

Walton, John H. 2013. "Reading Genesis 1 as Ancient Cosmology." In *Reading Genesis 1–2: An Evangelical Conversation*, ed. J. Daryl Charles, 114–69. Peabody, MA: Hendrickson.

Weeks, Noel. 2010. "The Ambiguity of Biblical 'Backgrounds.'" *Westminster Theological Journal* 72:219–36.

GENETIC ENHANCEMENT. Part of the larger project of human enhancement, genetic enhancement is a means of augmenting the human genome or genetic blueprint to create "better humans." The idea of manipulating the genetic structure, or **DNA**, of living entities dates back at least to Gregor Mendel's experiments with pea plants. The **Human Genome Project**—the effort to map the entire human genetic blueprint—recently has spawned new hopes for the genetic manipulation of humans, not only to eradicate diseases, but to extend human life span and enhance traits like IQ, eyesight, memory, athletic ability, musical abilities, etc.

Having once been the subject of science fiction, proponents of genetic enhancement hope it will soon become science fact. Philosopher John Harris sees the project of enhancement as a way of directing human evolution (see Harris 2010). The aim according to thinkers like Nick Bostrom is to create a new **species** of posthumans, transitional humans (or transhumans) who are ultimately engineered to develop enhanced traits such that they can no longer be considered mere humans (see **Robert Jastrow**).

There are essentially three **scientific method**s of manipulating human genetics. First, researchers may manipulate the genetic material in sperm or eggs, the so-called germ cells. A cleft chin, for instance, is a single-gene dominant trait passed from one generation to the next through normal human procreation. If it were determined that "enhanced" human beings would not have a cleft chin, it might be possible to "turn off" that **gene** in the germ cell so that it is not expressed in future generations.

Next, the genetic material of a human embryo might be manipulated in vitro. The genetic material from the sperm and egg combine in in vitro fertilization to generate a genetically unique member of the human species, namely, an individual person. This person has two types of cells in his or her body, germ cells and somatic cells. The germ cells, or reproductive cells, are passed to future generations. The somatic, or body cells, are unique to that individual. Currently, specialists are able, through pre-implantation genetic diagnosis (PGD), to identify genetic anomalies in vitro, like the gene for Tay-Sachs disease, Duchenne muscular dystrophy, or Down syndrome, but are unable to eradicate those genes without destroying the embryo. Consequently, PGD is used most often to select embryos for transfer to a woman's uterus. Those not selected are either frozen, destroyed in the process of research, or discarded.

The successful manipulation of the genetics of the embryo—in either germ cells or somatic cells—appears to be especially difficult. There is little reason to expect this to change very soon. Germline modification is currently not supported by government funding in the United States and many other countries, but some jurisdictions, including the United Kingdom, are beginning to experiment with modification of mitochondrial DNA.

Finally, researchers hope to be able to modify the DNA of adults in the not-too-distant future. Gene therapy might be a means of treating a disorder by inserting or deleting certain genes. Once this is possible, some hope that the same techniques might be used to enhance the genetic traits of an individual, either in the germ cells or somatic cells. Gene therapy has been attempted for a limited number of different conditions, but without much success. Whether or not these techniques will enable scientists to enhance human genetics depends on the answers to a number of questions.

First, genetic enhancement depends on the development of genetic science. Experts predict that the current gap between the ability to diagnose genetic conditions and treat genetic conditions will exist for quite a while. Closing this so-called diagnosis-therapy gap will not be easy, but there is little reason to doubt that the gap will be narrowed over time. And even if single gene manipulations become available, traits like IQ are multifactorial and notoriously complex. Increasing IQ by 10 points will be demanding to say the least. Likewise, just because a modification of a person's fast twitch muscles becomes possible, this does not mean that person will be a better baseball or cricket player. Some rightly worry that an incredibly smart person who is also incredibly mean would create havoc. So moral enhancement could be considered necessary also. Even if they exist, the genes for moral traits would likely be quite elusive.

Second, and even more problematically, society will have to reach consensus about the nature and goals of human enhancement. Who determines what is an enhancement? By definition an enhancement is an improvement. Philosophers like Gregory Pence consider adding vitamins to cereal or giving people smart phones a form of human enhancement (see Pence 2015). Although the therapy-versus-enhancement distinction is somewhat fuzzy, there seems to be a categorical difference between correcting someone's vision with contact lenses and, say, manipulating a soldier's genome so that he can see long distances at night. Similarly, there seems to be a difference between the attention-enhancing qualities of a cup of coffee and altering one's genetic structure so that one could stay awake and alert a week at a time.

Given normative human functioning, it is not clear to everyone that nonsomnolence is an enhancement. Furthermore, some genetic conditions have positive side effects that might be lost by manipulation. For example, the same gene associated with sickle cell trait also protects against malaria.

Knocking out the sickle cell gene would at the same time make a person more susceptible to malaria.

Third, not every means is justified by the ends. That is, even if we could agree that certain genetic enhancements were desirable, that does not entail that the means to attain them are ethically acceptable. Because of the difficulty, **complexity**, and problem of unintended side effects, experimenting on human embryos for the sake of enhancements is extraordinarily difficult to justify. We might put a child at risk to save her life, but do we really want to put a child at risk in an effort to increase her IQ or give her a boost in memory? It is hard to imagine which so-called genetic enhancements might warrant clinical trials on human beings.

Finally, Christian theology teaches that every human being, regardless of genetic traits, abilities, disabilities, age, or capacities is made in the image and likeness of God (Gen. 1:27–28). As such, we are contingent beings whose existence depends on Jesus, the risen Messiah, who "upholds the universe by the word of his power" (Heb. 1:3 ESV). The pursuit of genetic enhancements might tempt us to trust in **technology** for shalom (completeness, a proper ordering of things) rather than God. Moreover, because of the fallenness of the created order, we can be certain that, short of the consummation, human frailty of one sort or another will persist, whether genetic or from some other source.

C. Ben Mitchell

REFERENCES AND RECOMMENDED READING

Agar, Nicholas. 2013. *Truly Human Enhancement: A Philosophical Defense of Limits.* Cambridge, MA: MIT Press.

Harris, John. 2010. *Enhancing Evolution: The Ethical Case for Making Better People.* Princeton, NJ: Princeton University Press.

Maxwell J. Mehlman, 2003. *Wondergenes: Genetic Enhancement and the Future of Society.* Bloomington: Indiana University Press.

Meilaender, Gilbert. 2013. *Bioethics: A Primer for Christians.* 2nd ed. Grand Rapids: Eerdmans.

Pence, Gregory. 2015. *Medical Ethics: Accounts of Ground-Breaking Cases.* 7th ed. New York: McGraw-Hill Higher Education.

President's Council on Bioethics and Leon Kass. 2003. *Beyond Therapy: Biotechnology and the Pursuit of Happiness.* New York: Harper Perennial.

Ramsey, Paul. 1970. *Fabricated Man: The Ethics of Genetic Control.* New Haven, CT: Yale University Press.

Sandel, Michael J. 2009. *The Case against Perfection.* Cambridge, MA: Belknap.

Waters, Brent. 2006. *From Human to Posthuman: Christian Theology and Technology in a Postmodern World.* Burlington, VT: Ashgate.

———. 2009. *This Mortal Flesh: Incarnation and Bioethics.* Grand Rapids: Brazos.

GENETIC TESTING. Since the completion of the **Human Genome Project** in 2000, and the resultant explosion of genetic **information**, numerous diagnostic tests are now available that can test for a variety of genetic links and predispositions, both in adults and in fetuses in the womb. In fact, prenatal genetic testing has become a part of routine prenatal care for pregnant women. With adults, genetic information can at times be very useful in both treatment and prevention. But at other times, when medicine can do very little for the patient, these patients are often ambivalent about knowing their genetic information.

Prenatal genetic testing has become common and can be done in a variety of ways—through blood testing, through ultrasound imaging, which can eliminate many genetic abnormalities simply by looking at the fetus, and through more sophisticated testing such as amniocentesis, in which amniotic fluid is drawn out from the woman's abdomen with a needle and the baby's cells in the fluid are analyzed. Usually, if blood tests and ultrasound give cause for concern, amniocentesis is performed. If the expectant couple receives bad news back from amniocentesis, they are faced with difficult decisions about continuing or ending the pregnancy.

Genetic testing in adults can be useful for prevention, in that a person who is at high risk for acquiring a disease can take a variety of measures to minimize the chances of actually getting the disease. At times, however, there is more certainty of a genetic link as opposed to a predisposition, which only indicates an increased risk. For example, individuals with the genetic link to Huntington's disease (a degenerative neurological disease) will almost certainly get the disease, whereas those with a genetic link for breast cancer have an increased likelihood of contracting breast cancer, but it is not certain that they will.

Genetic testing is often very relevant for adults when it comes time to consider starting a family. If they have a history of genetic abnormality in their extended family, they might want to consider being tested for that abnormality prior to the decision to start a family naturally. If such a test comes back positive, there is generally a 50 percent chance of passing along the defective gene, or at times a significantly lesser chance if it is a recessive gene. Families with this kind of genetic risk may want to consider other alternatives to procreating naturally, including adoption. Or they might consider a form of genetic testing known as pre-implantation genetic diagnosis (PGD), in which a cell is taken from the embryo and screened (some call this an "embryo biopsy"). This requires that multiple embryos are created through in vitro fertilization (IVF), and the embryos that have the genetic abnormality are discarded while the ones that are clear are implanted.

This raises ethical issues in the discard of the defective embryos since there is no morally relevant distinction between discarding defective embryos and aborting fetuses with genetic abnormalities. However, other families are comfortable taking the risk of passing along genetic problems and attempt to have a child naturally. These families often have prenatal genetic testing done on their fetus in the womb to aid them in deciding whether to continue the pregnancy and, if they decide to do so, to prepare them for the special needs of the child who is coming. Families should be aware that they may receive pressure to end such pregnancies from their physicians or genetic counselors (see also **Bioethics**; **Cloning**; **Genetic Enhancement**).

For families who view the fetus as a full person from conception forward, getting bad news on the genetic test will not likely affect the decision to continue the pregnancy. Christian ethics suggests that ending the pregnancy due to such bad news is problematic, for several reasons. First, it may be that the test is mistaken, not a common result, but not unheard of either. Second, many prenatal genetic tests cannot predict the degree of deformity, as it may vary from patient to patient. But even if those two items could be predicted with certainty, the reality is that the child in the womb is still a person with the right to life—that is, assuming that the genetic abnormality is a causal link to getting the disease, as opposed to a predisposition that only increases the risk.

Even in the cases of causal links, it is presumptuous to assume that disability necessarily leads to unhappiness in life, a presumption that is insulting to people who live with disabilities and to their loved ones. It is further a question-begging argument to suggest that genetic abnormality is a justifiable basis for ending a pregnancy, because it is only with the assumption that the fetus is not a person that such a justification makes sense. For if the fetus is not a person, then justifying ending the pregnancy on the basis of genetic abnormality would also justify ending the lives of adults with similar genetic abnormalities, which society clearly does not allow.

The availability of genetic testing in the developing world presents acute ethical dilemmas for physicians who want to provide the best prenatal care for their pregnant patients. Some families make decisions to end pregnancies based on test results that reveal the sex of their child. This is especially a problem in parts of the world where there is a strong cultural preference for male children. It also occurs in the West, with **abortion** decisions that don't require reasons being given to physicians prior to ending pregnancies. Christians see such a practice as deeply problematic given that Christian ethics upholds the equal value of men and women—born and unborn—before God.

Some couples use genetic testing (and reproductive **technology**) to do the opposite of what is normally done. Rather than use these technologies to ensure that genetic abnormalities are eliminated, some use this technology to ensure that a genetic abnormality is not precluded. That is, they use these technologies intentionally to produce a child that has a specific genetic anomaly. Take the well-publicized case of the British couple who were both hearing impaired using technology to ensure that their child also was deaf (see Glover 2006). Many see such use of technology as misuse to inflict harm on a child. Yet in a culture that is based on autonomy, or the right to make one's own choices, making a case for why such use of technology is problematic is challenging. Nevertheless, from the perspective of Christian ethics, it is clear that such use of technology is interfering with God's design for the child.

Scott B. Rae

REFERENCES AND RECOMMENDED READING

Glover, Jonathan. 2006. *Choosing Children: Genes, Disability and Design.* New York: Oxford University Press.

Mitchell, C. Ben, Edmund D. Pellegrino, Jean Bethke Elshtain, John F. Kilner, Scott B. Rae. 2007. *Biotechnology and the Human Good.* Washington, DC: Georgetown University Press.

Peterson, James. 2001a. *Changing Human Nature: Ecology, Ethics, Genes, and God.* Grand Rapids: Eerdmans.

———. 2001b. *Genetic Turning Points: The Ethics of Human Genetic Intervention.* Grand Rapids: Eerdmans.

GEOCENTRISM/HELIOCENTRISM.

Few educated people today who observe the motion of the sun across the daytime sky or the motion of the stars in great circles overhead at night are likely to think that the earth is stationary while the sky moves around us. Yet, the notion of a moving earth we all learn in school is counter-intuitive. As early as the fourth century BC, **Aristotle** knew that the earth is spherical, and its approximate size was calculated correctly in Alexandria around 250 BC. That knowledge was never lost, and only rarely questioned, in subsequent centuries. Anyone familiar with these facts knows that if the earth is really spinning on its axis once a day, we are all moving at several hundred miles an hour, a proposition so contrary to ordinary observation and common sense that it beggars belief.

Thus, when **Copernicus** challenged the traditional geocentric view that the earth lies at rest in the center of the universe, with all other celestial objects circling around it, the burden of proof was entirely on him. His arguments persuaded hardly anyone, until **Galileo Galilei** turned his telescope on the heavens and found new observational evidence favoring Copernicus's heliocentric theory.

Although Copernicus had actually received unambiguous encouragement from Roman Catholic officials to publish his ideas, as his ideas trickled down, biblical objections were raised by both Catholic and Protestant authorities. Martin Luther famously invoked Joshua 10:12–13, a passage that Galileo dealt with cleverly; other texts include Ecclesiastes 1:5 and Psalms 19:6–7, 93:1, and 104:5. In each case, the Bible was understood to be teaching geocentrism, according to the plain meaning of the words, rather than merely speaking phenomenally from the point of view of the ordinary person (which is how most Christians approach these texts now).

Matters came to a head in 1616 when the Vatican issued a decree against heliocentrism, resulting in a ban on reading uncensored copies of Copernicus's book that was not officially reversed until the early nineteenth century (Gingerich 2002, 103). By then it was a moot point: the scientific controversy had been settled long before, and almost all exegetes had accepted Galileo's appeal to **Augustine**'s principle of accommodation to argue that the Bible was not meant to teach scientific facts or theories (Langford 1992).

Nevertheless, the hermeneutical questions raised by heliocentrism have not entirely faded into oblivion. Although nearly all contemporary creationists accept heliocentrism, most have major reservations about Galileo's use of accommodation; a tiny handful, including Gerardus Bouw, Robert Sungenis, and the late Walter Lang, have also rejected the motion of the earth (Davis and Chmielewski 2008). Bouw and Sungenis defend a sophisticated type of geocentrism, updated with ideas from Einstein's theory of relativity, in order to affirm the literal accuracy of Joshua 10 and other biblical passages.

Edward B. Davis

REFERENCES AND RECOMMENDED READING

Davis, Edward B., and Elizabeth Chmielewski. 2008. "Galileo and the Garden of Eden: Historical Reflections on Creationist Hermeneutics." In *Nature and Scripture in the Abrahamic Religions: 1700–Present,* ed. Jitse M. van der Meer and Scott H. Mandelbrote, 2:437–64. Leiden: Brill Academic.

Gingerich, Owen. 2002. "The Copernican Revolution." In *Science and Religion: A Historical Introduction,* ed. Gary B. Ferngren, 95–104. Baltimore: Johns Hopkins University Press.

Langford, Jerome J. 1992. *Galileo, Science and the Church.* 3rd ed. Ann Arbor: University of Michigan Press.

GEOLOGY. Geology is the study of the minerals and rocks that comprise the earth, including the physical and chemical processes that form the earth's crust with continents and ocean basins, the mantle below the crust, and the core of the earth.

The following are some of the major specialties relevant to our daily lives and to the discussion about Christianity and geology: (1) mineralogy and economic geology—study of minerals in ore deposits and of precious gems for jewelry; (2) stratigraphy—study of the layered strata, including those of the Grand Canyon and the Gulf of Mexico, with its huge oil and gas reserves; (3) structural geology—study of rocks under high pressure and stress, how rocks bend and fracture, and how mountains form; (4) **paleontology**—study of fossils; (5) petroleum geology—study of how oil and gas are formed and get trapped in reservoirs; (6) geochemistry—study of the chemical cycles in the earth and oceans and the application of **radiometric dating** methods to learn about earth history; and (7) geophysics—study of the internal structure of the earth to understand the magnetic field and plate tectonics, both absolutely critical for life to exist here on earth. God has fine-tuned this universe and prepared a planet where we can live.

Geology as an investigation of natural science has its roots in the seventeenth century. Concepts of earth history centered on the **genealogies** in the Bible, and this guided Archbishop **James Ussher** of Ireland in 1650 to determine that the creation occurred in 4004 BC. With the dominant influence of the Bible on understanding creation, significant effort was put forth to demonstrate the evidence of Noah's flood. *A New Theory of the Earth* by William Whiston was published in 1696 and widely accepted, reasoning that the great flood had formed the rock strata of the earth. The seventeenth century also included debate between religion and science that triggered the systematic study of the earth's strata, with Nicolas Steno as an important pioneer in the study of geology (see **The Genesis Flood and Geology**).

During the eighteenth century, the term *geology* was first used technically and became a distinct field of study at educational institutions. With the increasing influence of chemistry, Abraham Gottlob Werner of Germany argued that the earth's rocks such as basalts and granites precipitated from ocean waters, and those believing in this theory became known as Neptunists. In contrast, Scottish naturalist James Hutton argued that these rocks formed from a molten lava, and this theory became known as Plutonism. He observed unconformities where ancient rock had been upturned and eroded, and then horizontal sediments were deposited on top, giving evidence of an exceedingly long and complex history. In 1785 he proposed the theory of **uniformitarianism**, which states that the present is the key to the past and that the type of geologic processes observed today are those that formed the evidence left behind from the past. He recognized that this **complexity** could not possibly be explained within the commonly accepted biblical chronology of his day. Based on his observations and influence, James Hutton is considered the father of modern geology.

Early in the nineteenth century, the Industrial Revolution stimulated a rapid understanding of the geologic column with the identification of fossils and distinguishing layers of sediments by their unique fossils. In England a mining surveyor named William Smith produced the first geological map of Great Britain, which was published in 1815.

Paleontology and the fossil record were applied to establish "relative age dating" for the geologic column. The fossil record and thick sedimentary sequences had convinced geologists that the earth was exceedingly old, but no methods were available to offer a credible quantitative measurement. Several attempts were made but left large uncertainties. Irish geologist John Joly collected data on the amount of sodium in the oceans and the rate at which rivers carried sodium into the oceans, and in 1899 calculated it would take 80–90 million years for the oceans to reach the present sodium concentration. William Thompson (later Lord Kelvin) considered the cooling of the earth from an initial hot, molten state, and the time necessary for this to occur by the flow of heat to the surface. This resulted in estimates of the earth's age of 20 to 40 million years, reported in 1899. Both of these methods included assumptions that later proved invalid.

Radioactivity was discovered in 1896, and scientists learned that the decay of radioactive atoms added heat to the interior of the earth, making Lord Kevin's calculation invalid. But ultimately radioactivity provided a credible quantitative measurement for the age of igneous rocks. In 1905 a leading British physicist, John William Strutt, made the first radioactive dating estimate by measuring helium in radium-containing rocks to determine an age of 2 billion years. During the next two to four decades, geologists developed radioactive decay into "robust dating methods" of igneous rocks, commonly applied today (see **Radiometric Dating**).

Geologic Time Scale

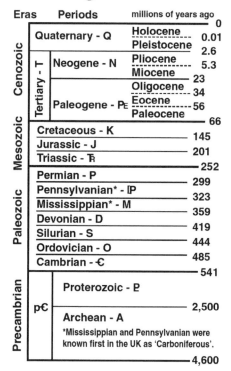

The Geologic Time Scale integrates the rock and fossil records with radiometric dating. The relative order and names of the geologic periods were largely established in Europe in the 19th century. When the radiometric dating methods were developed during the early 20th century, resulting absolute ages confirmed the relative age succession established with the fossil records.

Twentieth-Century Views of the Age of the Earth

By the late nineteenth and twentieth century, many conservative theologians had accepted the abundant evidence for the antiquity of the earth, as accumulated by Christian and secular geologists. These theologians included some authors of *The Fundamentals* and notables such as **Charles Hodge**, A. A. Hodge, J. Gresham Machen, William G. T. Shedd, Benjamin B. Warfield, R. A. Torrey, and Edward J. Young. Well-known evangelists Billy Graham and Oral Roberts accepted the scientific understanding of the age of the earth and made no issue about it in their evangelistic ministries.

The **American Scientific Affiliation** was founded in 1941 at Moody Bible Institute as an organization of Christian professional scientists, and its members largely accepted the antiquity of the earth as well.

All this changed with the publication in 1961 of *The Genesis Flood* by **John Whitcomb** and **Henry M. Morris** Jr. This book launched the modern young-earth creationist movement, which claims that the earth is young—less than 10,000 years—and that Noah's flood formed the Grand Canyon, deposited most sedimentary rocks, and formed the mountain ranges around the world. Based on a poll by Lifeway Research, this movement has captured the ear of almost half the pastors in the United States. The concept for *The Genesis Flood* has its roots in teachings of the late nineteenth century of Ellen G. White and the Seventh-day Adventist Church.

Conventional Geology vs. Flood Geology

Conventional, or modern, geology allows the evidence in the earth to tell its own story. It is based on the regularity of nature, making observations of rocks, conducting laboratory measurements, and developing the most logical, commonsense interpretations of how God's natural laws formed these rocks in the past—like forensic police work. The objective is to follow the data, just as researchers do in medicine. Radiometric dating methods developed and applied to all types of igneous rocks have calculated the age of the earth to be 4.56 billion years.

Conventional geology recognizes that the Grand Canyon sediments are of the Paleozoic era, with fossils of the Cambrian, Devonian, Mississippian, Pennsylvanian, and Permian periods. The Ordovician and Silurian age rocks are missing. The Redwall Limestone is the type of rock that is most commonly formed slowly, and usually on a coral reef like the Great Barrier Reef. The top of the Redwall Limestone is riddled with caves showing evidence that this limestone was exposed to weathering with enough time for caves to form. The tight folded rocks in the Carbon Canyon are also riddled with fractures, demonstrating that these rocks were hard before they were folded and moved by earth stresses.

Ken Wolgemuth

REFERENCES AND RECOMMENDED READING

Davidson, G. R. 2009. *When Faith and Science Collide: A Biblical Approach to Evaluating Evolution and the Age of the Earth.* Oxford, MS: Malius.

Greene, Jon W. 2012. "A Biblical Case for Old-Earth Creationism." Evidence for God. August 2. http://godandscience.org/youngearth/old_earth_creationism.html.

Hill, C., G. Davidson, T. Helble, and W. Ranney, eds. 2016. *Grand Canyon, Monument to an Ancient Earth: Can Noah's Flood Explain the Grand Canyon?* Grand Rapids: Kregel.

Roach, David. 2012. "Poll: Pastors Oppose Evolution, Split on Earth's Age." Lifeway Reasearch. January 9. http://www.lifeway.com/Article/Research-Poll-Pastors-oppose-evolution-split-on-earths-age#Image-Gallery.

Young, Davis A., and Ralph F. Stearley. 2008. *The Bible, Rocks and Time: Geological Evidence for the Age of the Earth.* Downers Grove, IL: InterVarsity.

Werner, Abraham Gottlob. 1787. *Short Classification and Description of Rocks.* See Google, accessed August 9, 2015.

GIFFORD LECTURES.

GIFFORD LECTURES. The Gifford Lectures have become the most prestigious lecture series in the world dealing with religion, science, and philosophy. They are given annually at the four Scottish universities: Edinburgh, Glasgow, Aberdeen, and St. Andrews.

In 1885, the Scottish judge Lord Adam Gifford bequeathed £80,000 to these universities for the purpose of: "Promoting, Advancing, Teaching, and Diffusing the Study of Natural Theology," in the widest sense of that term, in other words, "The Knowledge of God, the Infinite, the All, the First and Only Cause, the One and the Sole Substance, the Sole Being, the Sole Reality, and the Sole Existence, the Knowledge of His Nature and Attributes, the Knowledge of the Relations which men and the whole universe bear to Him, the Knowledge of the Nature and Foundation of Ethics or Morals, and of all Obligations and Duties thence arising." (Lord Adam Gifford's Will)

Gifford was an advocate of **natural theology**, which in his day meant the attempt to find God through reason and empirical science. But he did not place any restrictions on the lecturers in terms of the viewpoints they would present, so long as they would take up the question of God apart from supernatural considerations. Some lecturers have stretched the clause "in the widest possible sense" to lengths such that Gifford would have had trouble recognizing their work as natural theology. But the lecturers reflect the changing times throughout the twentieth century, and this makes the Gifford Lectures one of the best repositories of thinking about God in the context of what we know about the world through natural science.

Some of the most renowned scientists, theologians, and philosophers have been invited to give the lectures, and their resulting books have become classics in their fields. These include the following:

William James (1901–2 at Edinburgh), *The Varieties of Religious Experience*

Alfred North Whitehead (1928 at Edinburgh), *Process and Reality*

Reinhold Niebuhr (1939 at Edinburgh), *The Nature and Destiny of Man*

Michael Polanyi (1951–52 at Aberdeen), *Personal Knowledge*

Werner Heisenberg (1955 at St. Andrews), *Physics and Philosophy*

Richard Swinburne (1982–84 at Aberdeen), *The Evolution of the Soul*

Iris Murdoch (1982 at Edinburgh), *Metaphysics as a Guide to Morals*

Freeman Dyson (1983–85 at Aberdeen), *Infinite in All Directions*

John Hick (1986–87 at Edinburgh), *An Interpretation of Religion*

Ian Barbour (1989–90 at Aberdeen), *Religion in an Age of Science*

Mary Midgley (1989–90 at Edinburgh), *Science as Salvation*

John Polkinghorne (1993–94 at Edinburgh), *The Faith of a Physicist*

Charles Taylor (1998–99 at Edinburgh), *A Secular Age*

J. B. Stump

REFERENCES AND RECOMMENDED READING

Jaki, Stanley. 1987. *Lord Gifford and His Lectures.* Macon, GA: Mercer University Press.

"Lord Adam Gifford's Will." Accessed May 26, 2014. www.giffordlectures.org/will.asp.

Witham, Larry. 2005. *The Measure of God: History's Greatest Minds Wrestle with Reconciling Science and Religion.* San Francisco: HarperSanFrancisco.

GILGAMESH EPIC.

GILGAMESH EPIC. The *Gilgamesh Epic* is perhaps the best-known Mesopotamian literary composition today, and it has important connections to the biblical story of the flood, though the account of **the flood** in *Gilgamesh* is only an episode within the larger narrative.

The *Gilgamesh Epic* is best known from its neo-Assyrian recension, which is the fullest telling of the story. Tigay (1982) has described its tradition history and redaction from earlier Sumerian legends (second half of the third millennium BC) and an Old Babylonian version (eighteenth century BC).

The plot of the *Gilgamesh Epic* begins in the city of Uruk

in southern Mesopotamia, where Gilgamesh is a young king. Though the epic presents an obviously legendary picture of Gilgamesh, we know from contemporary royal inscriptions that he was a king who ruled this Sumerian city in the twenty-fifth century BC. The story does not present Gilgamesh as an evil man, but rather as an immature king. His subjects detest him because he injured young men of the city on the sports field and also took advantage of his position to sleep with new brides on their wedding nights. For these reasons, the citizens of Uruk pray to the gods to help them with their young impetuous king.

The gods answer their prayers in a strange way, by creating a primal man, named Enkidu, placing him in the countryside outside the city of Uruk. Enkidu, described almost like an animal, runs with the wild animals and pays no attention to civilization. The people of Uruk lure him into the city by sending out a prostitute named Shamhat. She seduces him, and afterward the animals will have nothing to do with him.

He reluctantly goes with Shamhat to Uruk, but as he hears reports of Gilgamesh's activities, he grows increasingly angry; so when he encounters the king, he engages him in combat. The fight is fierce, but eventually Gilgamesh prevails. Even though Enkidu loses, Gilgamesh and Enkidu forge a deep bond of friendship as a result, and thus the two leave Uruk in search of adventure and glory. And so the gods answer the prayers of the people of Uruk.

And indeed, Gilgamesh and Enkidu experience many adventures. One of the most notable is the defeat of the demon creature that guards the cedar forests of Lebanon. After this battle, Gilgamesh is washing the blood off his naked body when he is observed by Ishtar, the goddess of love and war.

His blood-soaked, naked body overwhelms Ishtar, who then propositions him. Gilgamesh, however, rejects her advances, knowing well the sorry fates that her previous lovers have experienced. The spurned Ishtar goes to her father, Anu, the god of heaven, to complain. Though he seems to understand Gilgamesh's reluctance, he responds to Ishtar's nagging by sending the bull of heaven against Gilgamesh. Nevertheless, Gilgamesh easily defeats the bull, tears off its forelock, and throws it in the face of Ishtar. Now Anu must act against this outrage toward Ishtar, but rather than harming Gilgamesh directly, he kills his dear friend Enkidu.

As Enkidu is dying in Gilgamesh's arms, the king realizes that he too will one day die. This realization creates in him a desire to escape that ultimate fate, so he sets out in search of everlasting life. This intention is what brings him ultimately to Utnapishtim, the only mortal who was ever given the gift of eternal life. On the way to his encounter with Utnapishtim, whose name means "long lived," he stops at an ale house where the "ale wife" tells him that everlasting life is not possible for humans. In words reminiscent of the thinking of the Teacher in the book of Ecclesiastes, she tells him: "When the gods created mankind, death for mankind they set aside. Life in their own hands retaining. Thou, Gilgamesh, let full be thy belly, Make thou merry by day and by night" (from the Old Babylonian version; translation by Speiser 1958, 90).

Even so, he still seeks out Utnapishtim, the only human known to have achieved eternal life. Transported to him by the ferryman, Urshanabi, Gilgamesh meets with Utnapishtim to ask how he achieved immortality.

In answer to Gilgamesh's question, Utnapishtim relates the story of the flood. He tells Gilgamesh about Enlil's decision to send a flood because he is disturbed by the noise that the increasing population of humans make. Though bound by oath not to tell any human, the god of wisdom, Ea, goes to the city of Shuruppak, where his devotee Utnapishtim lives, and tells his reed hut that a flood is coming and to "build an ark and save life. Take aboard ship seed of all living things" (Foster 1997, 458).

Utnapishtim follows his instructions and builds an ark that has the form of a cube. Before the onset of the deluge Utnapishtim brings on board his family, the animals, and the skilled craftsmen who helped him build the ark.

Once on board, the rains start. The storm is so powerful that even the gods themselves are frightened. They are described as cowering like dogs. And Ishtar "screamed like a woman in childbirth."

After seven days of storm, the rains stop, and "all of mankind had turned to clay." After a while, the ark comes to rest on the top of Mount Nimush. After seven days, Utnapishtim releases a series of three birds—first a dove, then a swallow, and finally a raven. The last one does not come back to the ark, indicating that the waters have receded to the point that there is sufficient exposed land.

Accordingly, Utnapishtim and the others disembark from the ark. His first action is to offer a sacrifice. The gods respond like those who have not eaten in a long time: "The gods smelled the savor, the gods smelled the sweet savor, the gods crowded around the sacrifice like flies."

When Enlil discovers that there are survivors of the flood, he is extremely angry. When he finds out that Ea had warned his devotee, he confronts him. Ea defends himself by challenging the wisdom of the flood. He calls Enlil's plan "unreasoning." After all, if there are no humans, who will offer the sacrifices that provide the gods with their food? He then advises Enlil to take less extreme measures in the future. Rather than a total extermination, Enlil should use disease, wild animals, and other less extreme measures to diminish the population.

Ea then asks Enlil to consider Utnapishtim (also called **Atrahasis**), and Enlil then grants him status like that of the gods. Thus, in answer to Gilgamesh's question, Utnapishtim tells him that it is a one-off event; thus Gilgamesh cannot himself achieve eternal life in this way.

However, Utnapishtim does advise Gilgamesh that there is a plant at the bottom of the sea that can give him life. At great effort, Gilgamesh gets the plant, but before he can eat it, a snake comes and takes it away (explaining how snakes rejuvenate themselves by sloughing off their skin).

Now at the end of possibilities, Gilgamesh finally returns home to his native Uruk. As he sees its walls from afar, he has an epiphany. He may not gain eternal life, but if he is a wise and responsible king, he will gain an everlasting legacy. Thus we come full circle to the beginning of the story. In a roundabout way, the gods do answer the concerns of the citizens of the city of Uruk, for as he returns from his adventures, Gilgamesh has matured to the point where he can be an effective king.

Scholars have recognized the importance of the *Gilgamesh Epic* since its discovery and first translation, most importantly in relationship to the flood story in Genesis 6–9. There certainly are similarities. Enlil, like Yahweh, uses a flood to destroy humanity. Ea, also like Yahweh, warns a devotee (Noah/Utnapishtim) to build an ark and gather family and animals on board to survive the storm. There are also similarities of detail. To find out whether the waters had receded enough to disembark, both the Babylonian and the biblical flood hero sends out three birds in succession, the last one returning with a leaf from a tree. After disembarking from the ark, Utnapishtim, like Noah, offers a sacrifice.

These similarities make it highly likely that there is some connection between these flood traditions, but exactly what relationship is a matter of speculation. We do not know precisely when the *Gilgamesh Epic* or, for that matter, the biblical account was first composed. Those who take the biblical account literally might argue that they both go back to the flood event and eventually were passed down independently. Those who take the story as fictional, or perhaps as an account of an event elaborated for theological purposes,

might argue that the biblical account was developed with the Mesopotamian account in the background in order to provide a different theological interpretation of the event.

The latter interpretation is supported by the differences between the two accounts. There are differences of detail (the size of the ark, the duration of the storm), but these are relatively trivial. The significant differences are theologically telling, indicating a completely different understanding of the divine realm. In the Mesopotamian story, the multiple gods are at cross-purposes with each other (Enki orders the flood, and Ea warns Utnapishtim), while in the biblical text, Yahweh, the one God, both orders and warns. The motivation for the flood in the *Gilgamesh Epic* is overpopulation and human noise disturbing Enlil, while in the biblical text God brings about a flood because of humanity's sin. The response of the gods to Utnapishtim's sacrifice is to crowd around it like flies since they depend on sacrifices of their devotees for their food. Yahweh receives Noah's sacrifice as an act of worship and enters into a covenant with him.

Tremper Longman III

REFERENCES AND RECOMMENDED READING

Foster, B. R. 1997. "Gilgamesh." In *The Context of Scripture: Canonical Compositions from the Biblical World*, ed. William W. Hallo and K. Lawson Younger, 1:458–60. Leiden: Brill.
Speiser, E. A. 1958. "Gilgamesh." In *Ancient Near Eastern Texts*, ed. J. Pritchard, 77–92. Princeton, NJ: Princeton University Press.
Tigay, J. 1982. *The Evolution of the Gilgamesh Epic*. Philadelphia: University of Pennsylvania Press.

GISH, DUANE. Duane Tolbert Gish (1921–2013) was a professional biochemist by training, a former leader of the **Institute for Creation Research** (ICR), an author, and a prominent debater for scientific creationism and biblical creationism. Gish was known for his leadership, creationist writings, and the more than 300 debates in which he participated. Some people called Gish "creationism's T. H. Huxley" or "bulldog" for the way he "relished the confrontations" during his formal debates with prominent scientists, including George Bakken, Kenneth R. Miller, Massimo Pigliucci, Kenneth Saladin, Michael Shermer, and William Thwaites (NCSE 2013). YouTube provides some 950 full or partial videos of Duane Gish debates. Gish may be best known for having once debated media personality and author Phil Donahue (Numbers 1993).

Gish, a twin, was born on February 17, 1921, in White City, Kansas, the youngest of nine children. He served in the US Army from 1940 to 1946 in the Pacific Theater, attaining the rank of captain and being awarded a bronze star (Legacy 2013). He earned a BS in chemistry from the University of California, Los Angeles, in 1949, and then a PhD in Biochemistry from the University of California, Berkeley, in 1953. Gish continued his professional development and research as a postdoctoral fellow and then assistant professor of biochemistry at Cornell University Medical College before returning to research at the University of California–Berkeley, until 1960. Gish was a senior research associate in biochemistry at the Upjohn Company between 1960 and 1971.

Gish grew up as a confessing Christian in the Methodist church but later became a member of the Regular Baptist Church. Numbers (2006, 225) notes that Gish always considered the Genesis creation account to be a factual historical event. In the late 1950s, Gish became persuaded upon reading John R. Howitt's anonymously published booklet *Evolution: Science Falsely So-Called* that science had produced falsifying evidence against biological evolutionary theory, leading him to join the American Scientific Affiliation (ASA). He soon realized that the ASA did not promote the view of biblical creationism that he supported. Walter Lammerts and William Tinkle recruited Gish, **Henry M. Morris**, and others to organize a Creation Research Advisory Committee in response to disillusionment over the direction of the American Scientific Affiliation.

The Creation Research Advisory Committee quickly transitioned into the Creation Research Society during June 1963 and began to organize its first conferences (Numbers 1993). Gish was active with the Creation Research Society until 1971 when he became a faculty member at Christian Heritage College (now San Diego Christian College), working with Morris in the research division that ultimately became the Institute for Creation Research. He was promoted to the position of vice president and later retired as emeritus vice president.

Gish's first major creationist publication was *Evidence against Evolution* (Gish 1972), while his most popular book, *Evolution? The Fossils Say No!* (Gish 1979), went through multiple printings and editions. He authored 10 books and coauthored 11 others, primarily through the Creation-Life and Master publishing houses. Gish's book *Creation Scientists Answer Their Critics* (1993) was critically reviewed and responded to by the ASA. His most recent book was *Letter to a Theistic Evolutionist* (Gish 2012).

Gish died on March 6, 2013, and was survived by his wife, Lolly, four children by his deceased first wife (also named

Lolly), nine grandchildren, and three great-grandchildren (Legacy 2013).

Jonathan Howard Fisher

REFERENCES AND RECOMMENDED READING

Gish, Duane T. 1972. *Evidence against Evolution*. Wheaton, IL: Tyndale.
———. 1979. *Evolution? The Fossils Say No!* San Diego: Creation-Life.
———. 1993. *Creation Scientists Answer Their Critics*. El Cajon, CA: Institute for Creation Research.
———. 2012. *Letter to a Theistic Evolutionist*. London: ICON.
ICR. 1970. *Evolution: Science Falsely So-Called*. Toronto: International Christian Crusade.
Legacy. 2013. "Duane T. Gish Obituary/Condolences." 2013. Legacy.Com, Inc. www.legacy.com/obituaries/utsandiego/obituary.aspx?n=duane-t-gish&pid=163795335#fbLoggedOut.
NCSE. 2013. "Duane T. Gish Dies." National Center for Science Education. March 6. http://ncse.com/news/2013/03/duane-t-gish-dies–0014753.
Numbers, Ronald. 1993. *The Creationists: The Evolution of Scientific Creationism*. Berkeley: University of California Press.
"Remembering Dr. Duane T. Gish, Creation's 'Bulldog.'" 2013. Institute for Creation Research. March 6. www.icr.org/article/remembering-dr-duane-t-gish-creations/.

GOD OF THE GAPS. "God of the gaps" refers to a fallacious inference based on a deficient understanding of **natural theology** and scientific methodology. The classic form of a God-of-the-gaps argument is: "There is no known natural scientific explanation of X; therefore we know that a supernatural action of God explains X." This is an argument from ignorance (a logical fallacy), since it erroneously claims that our *not* knowing something (a natural scientific explanation of X) entails that we *do* know something else (a supernatural explanation of X).

A frequent claim is that God-of-the-gaps arguments are harmful to theology and science. Thus **Henry Drummond** complained, "There are reverent minds who ceaselessly scan the fields of Nature and the books of Science in search of gaps—gaps which they fill up with God. As if God lived in gaps? What view of Nature or of Truth is theirs whose interest in Science is not in what it can explain but in what it cannot, whose quest is ignorance not knowledge?" (Drummond 1908, 333).

Theologically, confining God to gaps in our knowledge is troubling. Doing so suggests that as science advances and those gaps shrink, there is less room for God in the world. This denies God's omnipresence and encourages **deism**. Dietrich Bonhoeffer emphasized that God is at work everywhere: "We are to find God in what we know, not in what we don't know; God wants us to realize his presence, not in unsolved problems but in those that are solved" (Bonhoeffer 2002, 276).

Scientifically, a major concern is that if science prematurely infers supernatural causes, it may retard the discovery of natural causes. And if natural causes are found, this may damage the faith of scientifically informed believers (BioLogos, "Gaps").

Francis Collins, who established the **BioLogos Foundation** in 2007 to promote the view that evolution is compatible with Christian faith (BioLogos, "History"), charges that **intelligent design** is guilty of God-of-the-gaps reasoning (Collins 2006). In Collins's view, the **design argument** is that because naturalistic evolution fails to explain something (e.g., the complex specified **information** in **DNA**), it is best explained by an intelligent designer. However, defenders of design deny this allegation, claiming that their argument appeals not to ignorance but to knowledge: knowledge of the limits of undirected processes and of the causal powers of intelligent agents, such as engineers (Meyer 2009, chap. 18; 2013, 360). They also argue that excluding intelligent design as a possible explanation allows a symmetrical materialism-of-the-gaps fallacy to proliferate unopposed.

Angus J. L. Menuge

REFERENCES AND RECOMMENDED READING

BioLogos. "Are Gaps in Scientific Knowledge Evidence for God?" BioLogos. Accessed September 30, 2016. http://biologos.org/questions/god-of-the-gaps.
Biologos. "Our History." BioLogos. Accessed September 30, 2016. https://biologos.org/about/history.
Bonhoeffer, Dietrich. 2002. Letter to Eberhard Bethge, May 29, 1944. In *Letters and Papers from Prison*, ed. Eberhard Bethge. Enl. ed. London: Folio Society.
Collins, Francis. 2006. *The Language of God: A Scientist Presents Evidence for Belief.* New York: Free Press.
Drummond, Henry. 1908. *The Ascent of Man.* New York: James Pott. https://archive.org/details/lowelllectureso01drumgoog.
Meyer, Stephen C. 2009. *Signature in the Cell.* New York: HarperCollins.
———. 2013. *Darwin's Doubt.* New York: HarperCollins.

GOD PARTICLE. The "God particle" is a nickname given to the subatomic particle known to physicists as the "Higgs boson" or "Higgs particle." Nobel Prize–winning physicist Leon Lederman wrote a popular book in 1993 about the history of particle **physics** and the construction of the Superconducting Super Collider (SSC), which was being built at the time as a tool for discovering the proposed Higgs boson. Construction on the SSC was canceled that same year. In the book, Lederman explains the title by saying, "This boson is so central to the state of physics today, so crucial to our final understanding of the structure of matter, yet so elusive, that I have given it a nickname: the God Particle" (Lederman 1993). Rumors persist that, in reality,

Lederman simply agreed to "go ahead with this moniker at the advice of his publishing agents to sell more books," as reiterated by physicist Vivek Sharma. The name does not give any insight into the properties of the particle, nor does it have any more, or less, connection to God than the many other fundamental subatomic particles.

The Higgs boson is named after British theoretical physicist Peter Higgs. In the basic scientific theory of the fundamental particles and interactions in the universe, truly elementary particles have no intrinsic mass. In 1964 three papers were independently published, which together proposed a relativistic mechanism to give mass to fundamental particles (Englert and Brout 1964; Guralnik et al. 1964, Higgs 1964). In their proposal, the elementary particles acquire mass by interacting with a field that permeates all of space and can be detected through quantum interactions with individual field particles, or Higgs particles. The Higgs particle is a boson, meaning that it has an intrinsic spin that is an integer multiple of Planck's constant divided by 2 times pi. The Higgs particle is the only known fundamental particle with a spin of zero.

In 2012 two independent experiments at Europe's particle physics lab (CERN) located on the Large Hadron Collider (LHC) independently discovered the proposed Higgs particle. In 2013 Peter Higgs and Francois Englert shared the physics Nobel Prize for their proposal of a mechanism that gives mass to fundamental particles and which was confirmed with the discovery of the Higgs boson. The Nobel Prize citation (see http://www.ph.ed.ac.uk/higgs) reads, in part, "for the theoretical discovery of a mechanism that contributes to our understanding of the origin of mass of subatomic particles, and which recently was confirmed through the discovery of the predicted fundamental particle, by the ATLAS and CMS experiments at CERN's Large Hadron Collider."

Michael G. Strauss

REFERENCES AND RECOMMENDED READING

Englert, F., and R. Brout. 1964. "Broken Symmetry and the Mass of Gauge Vector Mesons." *Physical Review Letters* 13:321.
Guralnik, G., C. Hagen, and T. Kibble. 1964. "Global Conservation Laws and Massless Particles." *Physical Review Letters* 13:585.
Higgs, P. 1964. "Broken Symmetries and the Masses of Gauge Bosons." *Physical Review Letters* 13:508.
Lederman, Leon. 1993. *The God Particle: If the Universe Is the Answer, What Is the Question?* New York: Dell.
Moscowitz, Clara. 2011. "What Should 'God Particle' Be Renamed? Physicists Weigh In." Live Science. December 14. www.livescience.com/17489-god-particle-higgs-boson.html.
Sharma, Vivek. See http://vsharma.ucsd.edu/papers.php.

GÖDEL'S THEOREM. Born April 28, 1906, and baptized in Brno (Bruno), Austria, to a German Austrian *Evangelisch* family, Kurt Gödel was a precocious child. After his arrival at the University of Vienna, he studied **physics**, shortly thereafter shifting his interests to **mathematics** (number theory) and thence to the logical foundations of mathematics. In contrast to the regnant logical positivist Wiener Kreis and the constructivism of L. E. J. Brouwer, Gödel was to remain throughout his life an intellectual Platonist.

Conceived as a mathematical expedient to set forth a logically rigorous mathematical proof of the self-consistency and aseity of the massive body of mathematical knowledge, Gödel's incompleteness theorem is, in many ways, a response to the logicism of **Alfred North Whitehead** and **Bertrand Russell** of the preceding generation of mathematicians and logical positivist philosophers. In their *Principia Mathematica*, Russell and Whitehead, inspired by groundbreaking efforts on the part of Gustav Peano, attempted to demonstrate that all mathematics is ultimately reducible to logic; that is, mathematics is a species of logic.

Under the influence of Ernst Zermelo, the progenitor of the Zermelo-Frankel (ZF) axiom, Gödel published his "Completeness" theorem in 1930. According to Douglas Hofstadter (1979, 101), completeness means that "every true statement which can be expressed in the notation of a system is a theorem." He was to follow this logical insight in 1931 with his first incompleteness theorem, published in *Monatshefte für Mathematik und Physik* (38:173–98) and shortly thereafter translated into English as "On Formally Undecidable Propositions of *Principia Mathematica* and Related Systems." Hofstadter (via Gödel 1962) states that "there are truths belonging to number theory which are not provable within the system," or there are true statements that are not theorems. Goldstein (2005) states this formally:

1. ~Pr(GN [*p*] if and only if *p* is not provable).
2. g = GN(~Pr [g])
3. G = ~Pr(g)
4. ~Pr(g) if and only if G is not provable.

The second incompleteness theorem follows upon the first with the following spectacular *differentia* from the earlier quest of Russell and Whitehead. Taussky-Todd (1988) describes it in this manner: "For Gödel's results show that **logic** is not a subject that stands alone and is a *basis* for mathematical thinking; it is in fact *part* of mathematics."

Thus, for the theological enterprise, Gödel's incompleteness theorem exerts a far-reaching influence, the distillate of which is that theological truths can be incomplete; that is, a theological proposition can be true without formal logical provability.

Gödel's later years at the Institute for Advanced Study, to which he and his wife, Adele, had moved permanently in 1940, were to be marked by renewed labor on a mathematized (formalized) version of St. Anselm's proof for the **existence of God** that Gödel revealed to no one until 1970, and by extensive collaboration with **Albert Einstein** and John von Neumann. Gödel was to remain at the institute until his death on January 14, 1978.

Van Herd

REFERENCES AND RECOMMENDED READING

Casti, John L., and Werner DePauli. 2000. *Gödel: A Life of Logic.* New York: Basic Books.

Dawson, John W., Jr. 1996. *Logical Dilemmas: The Life and Work of Kurt Gödel.* Wellesley, MA: A. K. Peters.

———. 1999. "Gödel and the Limits of Logic." *Scientific American* 280:76–81.

Franzén, Torkel. 2005. *Gödel's Theorem: An Incomplete Guide to Its Use and Abuse.* Wellesley, MA: A. K. Peters.

Gödel, Kurt. 1930. "Über formal unentscheidbare Sätze der Principia Mathematica und verwandter Systeme." In *Monatshefte für Mathematik und Physik* 38:173–98.

———. 1950. "Rotating Universes in General Relativity Theory." *Proceedings of the International Congress of Mathematicians in Cambridge* 1:175–81.

———. 1962. *On Formally Undecidable Propositions of* Principia Mathematica *and Related Systems.* Trans. B. Meltzer, with a comprehensive introduction by Richard Braithwaite. New York: Basic Books.

Goldstein, Rebecca. 2005. *Incompleteness: The Proof and Paradox of Kurt Gödel.* New York: W. W. Norton.

Grattan-Guinness, Ivor. 2000. *The Search for Mathematical Roots 1870–1940.* Princeton, NJ: Princeton University Press.

Hawking, Stephen, ed. 2005. *God Created the Integers: The Mathematical Breakthroughs That Changed History.* Philadelphia: Running Press. Gödel's paper starts on p. 1089, with Hawking's commentary starting on p. 1097.

Hintikka, Jaakko. 2000. *On Gödel.* New York: Wadsworth.

Hofstadter, Douglas R. 1979. *Gödel, Escher, Bach: An Eternal Golden Braid.* Brighton, NJ: Harvester Press.

Nagel, Ernest, and James R. Newman. 1958, *Gödel's Proof.* New York: New York University Press.

Oppy, G. 1996. "Gödelian Ontological Arguments." *Analysis* 56:226–30.

———. 2000. "Response to Gettings." *Analysis* 60:363–67.

Procházka, Jiœí. 2006–10. *Kurt Gödel: 1906–1978: Genealogie.* Brno, Czech Republic: ITEM. Translation: Princeton University Press.

———. 2012. *Kurt Gödel: 1906–1978: Historie.* Vol. 1. Brno, Czech Republic: ITEM. Translation: Princeton University Press.

Smullyan, Raymond. 1992. *Gödel's Incompleteness Theorems.* Oxford: Oxford University Press.

Taussky-Todd, Olga. 1988. "Remembrances of Kurt Gödel (1983)." *Engineering and Science* 51 (2): 24–28.

Wang, Hao. 1987. *Reflections on Kurt Gödel.* Cambridge, MA: MIT Press.

———. 1996. *A Logical Journey: From Gödel to Philosophy.* Cambridge, MA: MIT Press.

Yourgrau, Palle. 1999. *Gödel Meets Einstein: Time Travel in the Gödel Universe.* Chicago: Open Court.

———. 2005. *A World without Time: The Forgotten Legacy of Gödel and Einstein.* New York: Basic Books.

GOODENOUGH, URSULA.

Ursula Goodenough (1943–) is a Harvard- and Columbia-trained professor of biology at Washington University in St. Louis, Missouri. A renowned cell and molecular biologist, she does laboratory research focused on the molecular control and evolution of the transition of sexual life-cycle stages, from vegetative growth to gametic differentiation to zygote development. Her research uses the model organism *C. reinhardtii*, a green alga found in soil. Her laboratory is responsible for **cloning** many of the **gene**s responsible for these life-cycle stage changes. Recently the lab has focused on two of these genes: Gsm1 and Gsp1. Both are homeodomain-containing proteins that dimerize when gametes fuse and regulate the transcription of genes important in progression through the life-cycle of *C. reinhardtii*. More recently, her work has included studies of the production of triglycerides, which may contribute to the use of algae as a biodiesel source. She has published extensively in peer-reviewed journals. Goodenough has also served as the president of the American Society of Cell Biology and is a fellow of the American Academy of Arts and Sciences.

Goodenough is a proponent of religious **naturalism**, which she introduces and explores in her bestselling book *The Sacred Depths of Nature*, published in 2000. The book consists of 12 parts in which a scientific story is followed by a spiritual reflection based on the story. Since publication of this book, she has become one of the primary proponents of the religious naturalism movement, a movement that seeks religious orientation through interaction with the natural world. She asserts that religious orientation includes reconciliation, or finding self and a focus for worship; spirituality, or the experience of awe, wonder, gratitude, and communion or empathy; concern for suffering; and reaching out. She argues that a scientific **worldview** has religious potential without invoking the supernatural and that, unlike traditional religions, the fact that this worldview is not organized around a purpose maker gives it the potential for global agreement.

Calling herself a nontheist, Goodenough concludes that while there is sacredness in the natural world, there is no God, no unmoved mover, no purpose. She is content to experience gratitude simply for "what is" rather than needing a being to whom gratitude is given. She argues that meaning comes from "what is," and that through a religious orientation derived from a purely scientific **worldview**, we find a doctrine that compels us to care for the natural world in general and humans specifically.

Goodenough is active in public forums that seek to better understand the relationship between science and religion. She joined the Institute on Religion in an Age of Science in 1989, serving as its president from 1992 to 1996, and is a regular speaker at its annual conference. She was a contributor to NPR's blog *13.7: Cosmos and Culture*, until 2011.

Sara Sybesma Tolsma

REFERENCES AND RECOMMENDED READING

Cosby, Donald A. 2014. *The Thou of Nature: Religious Naturalism and Reverence for Sentient Life*. New York: State University of New York Press.

Goodenough, Ursula. 2000. *The Sacred Depths of Nature*. Oxford: Oxford University Press.

Raymo, Chet. 2008. *When God Is Gone, Everything Is Holy: The Making of a Religious Naturalist*. Notre Dame, IN: Sorin.

Rue, Loyal. 2012. *Nature Is Enough: Religious Naturalism and the Meaning of Life*. Albany, NY: SUNY Press.

GOULD, STEPHEN JAY.

Stephen Jay Gould (1941–2002) was raised by secular Jewish parents in Queens, New York City. As a child he was inspired by the popular evolutionary writings of George Gaylord Simpson. Following undergraduate education at Antioch College, Ohio, Gould went to Columbia University as a graduate student in **paleontology** (1963–67). There he undertook quantitative studies of diverse organisms and completed a dissertation on the fossil (Pleistocene) land snails of Bermuda. His mentors at Columbia included Norman Newell, who during that interval was investigating the phenomenon of large-scale biological extinctions during geologic history. After completing his PhD degree, Gould was appointed professor of **geology** and biology at Harvard University, where he taught until his death.

Early on, Gould steeped himself in the historical literature on the measure and analysis of organismal form. He later acknowledged intellectual indebtedness to D'Arcy Thomson, Étienne Geoffroy Saint-Hilaire, and many others. Between 1965 and 1975, he undertook, by himself or in collaboration, studies on allometric change and organismal function in snails, scallops, Jurassic oysters, Permian pelycosaurs, primates, and the Pleistocene "Irish elk." During this time, he published significant review papers on allometric variation and its role in the evolution of lineages through time. His book *Ontogeny and Phylogeny* (1977) remains a masterful study of the history of ideas and biological bases for the connections between the factors governing organismal development, and its outworking during lineage history.

During the early 1970s, Gould partnered with Niles Eldredge to introduce the theory of **punctuated equilibrium**, or "punk eek" as it became known; and with David Raup, Daniel Simberloff, and Thomas Schopf to mathematically model the shape of life's diversification. Through both efforts, Gould prodded and stimulated mainstream paleontologists. Gould and Eldredge suggested that the phenomenon of **species** stasis over significant geological time was real and often followed fairly rapid speciation events. This claim could be and was interpreted as a challenge to operational Neo-Darwinian gradualism or, alternatively, as a valued contribution to an enhanced **Darwinism**.

In 1974 Gould began to write a regular essay for each issue of *Natural History* magazine, a series titled "This View of Life" (the title taken from a phrase in Darwin's *Origin of Species*). This continued over the next 26 years, resulting in 300 essays. Most of these were periodically collected into volumes, the first being *Ever Since Darwin* (1977) and the last, *I Have Landed* (2002). While written for a general audience, the language of the essays was elaborate. Gould often employed a historical personage or personages, scientist or otherwise, as a springboard to a discussion about common misunderstandings of evolutionary theory. These essays also provide a sidelong view into Gould's changing views on the nature of the evolutionary process.

The earliest essays in the series are much more "doctrinally Darwinian." Several of these depict the evolutionary process as "tinkering," in contrast to an intentional elaboration. An example of such tinkering is the Panda's thumb, in reality a modified sesamoid bone with accompanying musculature, which assists the creature to strip leaves from bamboo. "Odd arrangements and funny solutions are the proof of evolution—paths that a sensible God would never tread but that a natural process, constrained by history, follows perforce" (Gould 1978).

Gould evolved as an evolutionist. His studies of organismal form and his engagement with the European continental literature on morphological integration and the limits of form—what would be characterized as "evolutionary constraints"—led him to realize that **natural selection** was not necessarily the final arbiter of lineage success. In addition, during the 1980s, the recognition among paleontologists that mass extinctions were a real phenomenon and not some artifact of an imperfect fossil record, established the fact that well-adapted species could be removed from the organic world by large-scale accidents. David Raup, one of Gould's collaborators, would write a book titled *Extinction: Bad Genes or Bad Luck?* for which Gould contributed the preface. Thus the shape of life was simultaneously more determined (internally) and more contingent (externally) than portrayed by the architects of the classic **Neo-Darwinian synthesis**.

Gould's *Wonderful Life* elaborated his strong stance on the contingency of organic life's history through his metaphor of "replaying life's tape" (1989). If started anew, life would diversify much differently than it has in our world. From his perspective, this radical contingency must undermine any attempt to see progress expressed in the history of life. He was particularly abrasive with regard to orthogenetic ideas popular in the decades around 1900, and the metaphoric employment of ladders to depict evolutionary histories, rather than branching bushes as **Darwin** originally illustrated in *On the Origin of Species*.

In several of his popular essays, as well as the volume *Rocks of Ages: Science and Religion in the Fullness of Life*, Gould attempted to site religion and science as two completely disparate realms of thought and action. He designated his approach "nonoverlapping magisteria," or NOMA. He was critical of sociobiological explanations for human behavior. Yet he repeatedly insisted that the evolutionary process could not possibly be guided and that adaptation represented a tinkering process—statements about what a God could or could not accomplish.

Gould received numerous awards during his life, including the Charles Schuchert Award of the Paleontological Society, the Linnean Society's Darwin-Wallace medal, and a McArthur Fellowship. He married Deborah Lee in 1965; they had two children, Jesse and Ethan. Gould and Lee divorced in 1995. That same year Gould was remarried to Rhonda Roland Shearer, who survived him.

Ralph Stearley

REFERENCES AND RECOMMENDED READING

Selected Publications of S. J. Gould (Allmon lists 814 titles, of which at least 154 were peer-reviewed)

1966. "Allometry and Size in Ontogeny and Phylogeny." *Biological Reviews* 41:587–640.

1972. With Niles Eldredge. "Punctuated Equilibria: An Alternative to Phyletic Gradualism." In *Models in Paleobiology*, ed. T. J. M. Schopf, 82–115. San Francisco: Freeman, Cooper.

1973. Raup, D. M., S. J. Gould, T. J. M. Schopf, and D. S. Simberloff. "Stochastic Models of Phylogeny and the Evolution of Diversity." *Journal of Geology* 81 (5): 525–42.

1977a. *Ever Since Darwin*. New York: W. W. Norton.

1977b. *Ontogeny and Phylogeny*. Cambridge, MA: Harvard University Press.

1977c. With R. C. Lewontin. "The Spandrels of San Marco and the Panglossian Paradigm: A Critique of the Adaptationist Programme." *Proceedings of the Royal Society of London*, B 205:581–98.

1977d. Gould, S. J., D. M. Raup, J. J. Sepkoski Jr., T. J. M. Schopf, and D. S. Simberloff. "The Shape of Evolution: A Comparison of Real and Random Clades." *Paleobiology* 3 (1): 23–40.

1978. "The Panda's Peculiar Thumb." *Natural History* 87 (9): 20–30. Repr. and rev. in *The Panda's Thumb*. New York: W. W. Norton, 1980.

1980a. "The Promise of Paleobiology as a Nomothetic Evolutionary Discipline." *Paleobiology* 6 (1): 96–118.

1980b. "Is a New and General Theory of Evolution Emerging?" *Paleobiology* 6 (1): 119–30.

1983. "The Hardening of the Modern Synthesis." In *Dimensions of Darwinism: Themes and Countertbemes in Twentieth-Century Evolutionary Theory*, ed. Marjorie Grene, 71–96. Cambridge: Cambridge University Press.

1985. "The Paradox of the First Tier: An Agenda for Paleobiology." *Paleobiology* 11 (1): 2–12.

1987. *Time's Arrow, Time's Cycle: Myth and Metaphor in the Discovery of Geological Time*. Cambridge, MA: Harvard University Press.

1988. "Trends as Changes in Variance: A New Slant on Progress and Directionality in Evolution." *Journal of Paleontology* 62 (3): 319–29.

1989. *Wonderful Life: The Burgess Shale and the Nature of History*. New York: W. W. Norton.

1993. *The Book of Life: An Illustrated History of the Evolution of Life on Earth*, ed. Stephen Jay Gould. New York: W. W. Norton.

1996. *Full House: The Spread of Excellence from Plato to Darwin*. New York: Harmony.

1999. *Rocks of Ages: Science and Religion in the Fullness of Life*. New York: Ballantine.

2002. *I Have Landed: The End of a Beginning in Natural History*. New York: Harmony.

2002. *The Structure of Evolutionary Theory*. Cambridge, MA: Harvard University Press.

Secondary Sources

Allmon, W. D., P. H. Kelley, and R. M. Ross, eds. 2009. *Stephen Jay Gould: Reflections on His View of Life*. Oxford: Oxford University Press. Includes many thoughtful chapters by students or colleagues of Stephen Jay Gould.

Cain, J. 2009. "Ritual Patricide: Why Stephen Jay Gould Assassinated George Gaylord Simpson." In *The Paleobiological Revolution: Essays on the Growth of Modern Paleontology*, ed. D. Sepkoski and M. Ruse, 346–63. Chicago: University of Chicago Press.

Sepkoski, D. 2012. *Rereading the Fossil Record: The Growth of Paleobiology as an Evolutionary Discipline*. Chicago: University of Chicago Press.

Vrba, E. S., and N. Eldredge, eds. 2005. *Macroevolution: Diversity, Disparity, Contingency: Essays in Honor of Stephen Jay Gould*. Supplement to *Paleobiology* 31 (2). Lawrence, KS: Paleontological Society.

GRAND UNIFIED THEORY.

GRAND UNIFIED THEORY. There are four known fundamental forces in nature: gravity, electromagnetism, weak force, and strong force. In particle **physics**, a grand unified theory (GUT) that correctly describes nature is a mathematically and experimentally verified theory that combines the three forces of **the standard model** of particle physics—electromagneticsm, weak force, and strong force—into a single unified force. A theory that combines all four forces into a single force is called a "theory of everything" (TOE).

There are many reasons for expecting that at very high energies the forces of nature should be manifest as a single force. Historically, forces that were once thought to be separate have been combined. For instance, in the early nineteenth century no known connection existed between electric and magnetic forces. But experiments by Hans Christian Orsted, **Michael Faraday**, and others seemed to show a connection between these forces. For instance, an electric current produces a magnetic field, and a changing magnetic field can produce an electric current. Eventually, these ideas were formulated by **James Clerk Maxwell** into a consistent theory that explicitly described the unified nature of electromagnetism.

In the 1960s Abdus Salam, Sheldon Glashow, and **Steven Weinberg** developed a mathematical theory that combined the electromagnetic force with the weak force. Predictions of this electroweak theory were shown to be true by experiments in the 1970s and 1980s, including the discovery of so-called neutral current interactions in particle scattering experiments, and the discovery of the predicted carriers of the weak force, the W and Z particles, collectively known as intermediate vector bosons. The formalism of the electromagnetic unification is quite different from that of the electroweak unification, and the exact nature of further GUT unification is unknown.

Another motivation for a GUT involves the precise equal-but-opposite balance of the elementary charge of an electron and a proton. There is no fundamental reason for this balance within the standard model, yet such a balance is mandatory for the existence of the macroscopic universe as we know it. This balance can be achieved by appropriate charge quantization, which is a natural consequence of a GUT.

The gravitational force is 38 orders of magnitude weaker than the strong force, 36 orders of magnitude smaller than the electromagnetic force, and about 29 orders of magnitude weaker than the weak force. Thus it plays basically no role in the interactions of subatomic particles. It is expected that there must be a fundamental reason for the extreme imbalance between the force of gravity and the other forces of nature, though none is currently known. (The extra dimensions inherent in **string theory** provide one possible explanation if the gravitational force extends to dimensions not accessible by the other three forces.) In any case, this imbalance, coupled with the inherent problems of developing a quantum theory of gravity, presents extreme challenges in trying to develop a TOE.

Michael G. Strauss

REFERENCES AND RECOMMENDED READING

Greene, Brian. 1999. *The Elegant Universe*. New York: W. W. Norton
Hawking, Stephen. 1988. *A Brief History of Time*. New York: Bantam.

H

HABITABLE ZONE. The habitability of a region of the universe is a measure of its capacity to host simple or complex life for some extended period of time. Even if a region is considered habitable, it might not actually host life. Thus habitability is a set of necessary but insufficient conditions for life. Astrobiologists denote a habitable region as a habitable zone. In the mid-nineteenth century, **William Whewell** defined the first habitable zone concept, one restricted in its application to the solar system. It is now called the *circumstellar habitable zone* (CHZ), and, as the name implies, it is the zone around the sun within which the earth must be located for it to be habitable.

A few decades ago, the CHZ concept was generalized and extended in its application to include any earthlike planet around a sunlike star that can maintain liquid water on its surface. Today, while this is still the main part of the definition of the CHZ concept, it has become obvious that additional factors are relevant to the habitability of a terrestrial planet. These include planetary dynamics, impact risks, stellar variability, and the details of planet formation. For example, Mars's proximity to the asteroid belt causes it to suffer more frequent impacts than does the earth.

In recent years, two additional types of habitable zones have been introduced. One, the Galactic Habitable Zone (GHZ), applies to the Milky Way galaxy, a flattened self-gravitating system containing some 200 billion stars and spanning 100,000 light-years. The boundaries of the GHZ are set by threats to life and the required planetary "building blocks" for habitable planetary systems. Galactic-scale threats to life include supernovae, gamma ray bursts, radiation outbursts from the Galactic nucleus, and perturbations of Oort cloud comets leading to comet showers. All these threats increase toward the Galactic center. On the other hand, the chemical elements that go into making planets decrease in abundance as one moves away from the Galactic center. Therefore, in order to be habitable, a planetary system must be close enough to the Galactic center to have available sufficient elemental building blocks but not so close that it suffers too frequent life-threatening events. The GHZ concept has also been applied to the nearby large spiral galaxy in Andromeda.

The third type of habitable zone, the Cosmic Habitable Age (CHA), applies to the cosmos as a whole. Within the context of big bang cosmology, the space between the galaxies in the universe has been expanding since its creation. During this time, the galaxies have changed in several important ways that are relevant to their habitability. As the universe aged, the overall supernova rate eventually declined to a level that was not overly threatening to life in a typical galaxy, and the abundances of the essential elements have risen to a level that permits habitable planetary systems to form. The universe has thus entered its CHA. In the future, habitability will be limited by the availability of sunlike stars and long-lived radioisotopes.

Guillermo Gonzalez

REFERENCES AND RECOMMENDED READING

Gonzalez, Guillermo. 2005. "Habitable Zones in the Universe." *Origins of Life and Evolution of Biospheres* 35:555–606.
———. 2014. "Setting the Stage for Habitable Planets." *Life* 4:35–65.

HAM, KEN. Ken Ham (1951–) is an Australian immigrant to the United States, a well-known young-earth creationist, and CEO of the apologetics ministry **Answers in Genesis**.

Ken Ham earned a bachelor's degree in applied science at Queensland Institute of **Technology** and a diploma of education from the University of Queensland, after which he taught science in the Australian public school system. Along with John Mackay, Ham cofounded Creation Science Foundation (CSF) in 1977 as an evangelistic outreach with a message of the relevance of Genesis to Christianity. He left the classroom to pursue full-time creation ministries with CSF in 1979. Following a series of US speaking tours, Ham was invited to join the **Institute for Creation Research** (ICR) in 1986. Ham frequently toured with ICR scientists, presenting "Back to Genesis" seminars at churches and other venues. Ham's dynamic presentation style and emphasis on biblical and relevance issues proved popular and further increased ICR's visibility among conservative Christians.

Ham left ICR in December of 1993 and moved to Kentucky, where he and others founded Creation Science Ministries (now Answers in Genesis [AiG]). As before, Ham frequently presented seminars, and AiG quickly rose in prominence in the United States in the late 1990s and early 2000s. During this time, Ham remained on the board of CSF, and the two ministries eventually united under the AiG name. Though legally separate, the organizations operated closely, sharing resources and content. The combined AiG ministries grew beyond Australia and the United States, forming satellite branches in New Zealand, South Africa, Canada, and the United Kingdom. Internal tensions between the US and Australian leadership resulted in a split in 2006. The US and UK offices retained the AiG name, while the remaining groups rebranded as Creation Ministries International. AiG is the largest apologetics ministry in the world and among the most influential young-earth creation organizations.

In 2007 AiG opened the Creation Museum, a multi-million-dollar facility in northern Kentucky dedicated to presenting a young-earth view of Scripture and science. The museum averages 300,000 visitors per year. In 2016 AiG opened a full-scale reproduction of **Noah's ark**, called the Ark Encounter, located in Kentucky, 45 miles from the Creation Museum.

In February 2014 Ham engaged in a high-profile debate with Bill Nye ("The Science Guy"; famous for his children's science program on PBS) over the topic "Is creation a viable model of origins in today's modern scientific era?" The debate was live-streamed over the Internet and drew more than 3 million viewers. Millions more have since watched the debate via YouTube.

Two of Ham's books have been highly influential in the creation-evolution debate. *The Lie* is an extended presentation of Ham's relevance message. Since its publication in 1987, *The Lie* has sold more than 1 million copies and has been translated into numerous languages. *The Answers Book* grew from recurring questions encountered at seminars. The multiauthored *Answers Book* and its three follow-up volumes (each edited by Ham) are the most widely read creation apologetics books in the world. AiG produces numerous other books and videos, *Answers Magazine*, and *Answers Research Journal*.

Marcus R. Ross

REFERENCES AND RECOMMENDED READING

Ham, Ken, ed. 2007. *The New Answers Book 1*. Green Forest, AR: Master.
———. 2012. *The Lie*. 25th ann. ed. Green Forest, AR: Master.

Websites
Answers in Genesis homepage: www.answersingenesis.org
Ark Encounter homepage: www.arkencounter.org
Creation Museum homepage: www.creationmuseum.org

HANDMAIDEN METAPHOR. Christians since the church fathers have often thought of science as a "handmaiden" to theology, and theology in turn as "queen" of the sciences (see **Science and the Church Fathers**). This concept was expressed in similar but not identical words by a Hellenistic Jewish philosopher, Philo of Alexandria. Seeking to integrate Greek and Jewish thought, Philo taught that "philosophy is the practice or study of wisdom, and wisdom is the knowledge of things divine and human and their causes. And therefore just as the culture of the schools is the bond-servant (*doulē*) of philosophy, so must philosophy be the servant of wisdom" (Philo 1932, 497). Elsewhere in the same passage, he used the term *handmaid* (*therapainis*). His overall point was that all forms of knowledge—the original meaning of the English word *science*—should serve Scripture, and ultimately that reason should serve faith (Wolfson 1947, 1:149–51).

Many of the greatest Christian thinkers down through the High Middle Ages used the handmaiden metaphor in just this way: Clement of Alexandria, Origen, Basil of Caesarea, **Augustine**, Bede, Roger Bacon, Bonaventure, and **Thomas Aquinas** (Grant 2001, 33–34; Lindberg 2013, 274–77). An entire literary genre, the hexameral treatise—commentaries on the six **days of creation**—conformed to this scheme; authors such as Basil used Greek **natural philosophy** to help understand biblical references to nature, such as the "waters above the **firmament**."

During the Renaissance, however, natural philosophers began to elevate the status of their "science" from wholly subservient handmaiden to equal partner in the search for truth (see **Science and the Renaissance, Early Modern Christianity**). Holding up "the book of God's word" alongside "the book of God's works," **Francis Bacon** advocated "an endless progress or proficience in both," provided that we "do not unwisely mingle or confound these learnings together" (Bacon 1973, 8).

Galileo Galilei went even further. Concerned that theologians might invoke Scripture against Copernican **astronomy**, Galileo rejected the idea "that since theology is queen of all the sciences, she need not bend in any way to accommodate herself to the teachings of less worthy sciences which are subordinate to her." Allowing that "theology might be queen" because her subject "excels in dignity all [other] subjects" and "because her teachings are divulged in more sublime ways," he nevertheless denied her the competence simply to veto scientific conclusions (Drake 1957, 191–92).

Although most modern Christian writers probably agree with Galileo, many young-earth creationists keep science in a fully subordinate role.

Edward B. Davis

REFERENCES AND RECOMMENDED READING

Bacon, Francis. 1973. *The Advancement of Learning*, ed. G. W. Kitchen. London: J. M. Dent & Sons.
Drake, Stillman. 1957. *Discoveries and Opinions of Galileo*. Garden City, NY: Doubleday.
Grant, Edward. 2001. *God and Reason in the Middle Ages*. Cambridge: Cambridge University Press.
Lindberg, David C. 2013. "Science and the Medieval Church." In *The Cambridge History of Science*, ed. David C. Lindberg and Michael H. Shank, 2:268–85. Cambridge: Cambridge University Press.
Philo. 1932. *De congressu quaerendae eruditionis gratia*. In *Philo: Volume IV*, Loeb Classical Library, 449–51. Trans. F. H. Colson and G. H. Whitaker. Cambridge, MA: Harvard University Press.
Wolfson, Harry Austryn. 1947. *Philo: Foundations of Religious Philosophy in Judaism, Christianity, and Islam*. 2 vols. Cambridge, MA: Harvard University Press.

HARRIS, SAM. Sam Harris (1967–) is an American philosopher and atheist who gained prominence through his book *The End of Faith* (2004), which marked the beginning of "the **new atheism**" movement, which advocated a strident renunciation of religion in toto. Biologist Richard Dawkins's book *The God Delusion* (2006) gave the movement more momentum. Spurred by the Muslim terrorist attacks of September 11, 2001, Harris, while still a graduate student in **neuroscience**, issued a broadside not merely against Islam, but against all religion. Taking the worst possible examples from various religions, Harris claimed that "faith" is the antithesis of reason and the cause of most of the ills in the world. He made similar claims in his short book *Letter to a Christian Nation* (2006).

Harris's website identifies him as a cofounder and the CEO of Project Reason, a nonprofit foundation devoted to spreading scientific knowledge and secular values in society. He received a degree in philosophy from Stanford University and a PhD in neuroscience from UCLA. Project Reason is his platform for writing and speaking.

In Harris's pro-atheist, antireligion writings, he consistently fails to address the best philosophical proponents of Christianity, such as **William Lane Craig**, **J. P. Moreland**, and **Alvin Plantinga**. However, he did debate Craig on whether or not **morality** depends on God. He defines faith as credulity, something for which there can be no evidence, and he warns of the dangers of its perils, such as Muslim fanaticism.

Since his overtly pro-atheist and anti-theist writings, Harris has written two very short books: *Lying* and *Free Will*. *Lying* argues for the benefits of veracity in human conduct but without basing this duty on the inherent dignity of human nature or on any divine command. In *Free Will*, Harris claims that the science of the brain has eliminated any agent autonomous of the giant machine of nature.

Harris defends a morality without God in *The Moral Landscape* (2011), claiming that science alone can determine what human well-being is and how to attain it. Harris has also contributed to the spiritual atheist movement, which seeks to carve out a naturalistic spirituality for those who believe in neither God nor the **soul** nor the afterlife. *Wake Up* (2014) defends and articulates a way of being spiritual in an atheistic world.

Douglas Groothuis

REFERENCES AND RECOMMENDED READING

Harris, Sam. 2005. *The End of Faith*. Repr. ed. New York: W. W. Norton.
———. 2014. *Wake Up: A Guide to Spirituality without Religion*. New York: Simon & Schuster.

HARRISON, PETER. Peter Harrison (1955–) of Queensland, Australia, is a distinguished scholar specializing in the intellectual history of the early modern period and in the connections between Christian thought and the rise of natural science.

After receiving advanced degrees from Yale University and University of Queensland, Harrison spent 17 years as a professor of history and philosophy at Bond University. In 2007 he was named the Andreas Idreos Professor of Science and Religion at University of Oxford, where he served for four years as director of the Ian Ramsey Centre and fellow of Harris Manchester College. In 2011 he returned to the University of Queensland to take the role of research professor and director of the Centre for the History of European Discourses at the University of Queensland. He has received numerous honors and awards, including a Gifford Lectureship, a DLitt degree from the University of Oxford, and the Australian Research Council's Australian Laureate Fellowship.

Harrison's publications include four major monographs, two edited volumes (plus three forthcoming), and more than a hundred articles, book chapters, and book reviews. While focusing most frequently on seventeenth-century England, these works also display wide-ranging knowledge of ancient Greek philosophy, early Christianity, medieval Catholicism,

Protestant theology, and various modern intellectual movements. His monographs establish central theses that expand on or support many of the arguments made in shorter essays. Three of his most important theses will be summarized briefly here.

Thesis 1: "Religion" is a historically unstable concept. The early modern period downplayed the idea of religion as individual piety and emphasized the importance of correct belief. Consequently, the validation of religion came into alignment with the belief-testing empirical methods that emerged during the seventeenth century (Harrison 1990, 2015).

Thesis 2: Protestant understandings of Scripture and sin created motivation for the empirical validation of religious beliefs. By rejecting the emblematic hermeneutic tradition that found spiritual meanings in natural things and creatures, the Reformation left Christians with little understanding of what God's book of nature meant. Empirical methods were adopted as a way of searching for this meaning. Some even hoped that the new methods would allow them to recover the untainted knowledge of **Eden**. For those who doubted that the noetic effects of sin could ever be overcome methodologically, the promise of technological development and societal goods provided an alternative set of reasons for supporting the empirical project (Harrison 1998, 2007).

Thesis 3: "Science" is a historically unstable concept. In medieval Christian philosophy, *scientia* meant habitual attentiveness to natural things and creatures and was intended to lead an individual to the contemplation of God and theological truth. Only through the development of modern technologies and complex bodies of knowledge did the modern concept of science become disembodied, institutionalized, and potentially separable from a broader theological framework (Harrison 2015).

Harrison's work has introduced both a new level of historiographic caution and a new framework for historical explanation into mainstream science-and-religion discussions. His reading of history offers powerful correctives to both the "conflict" and the "harmony" narratives of science and religion that became popular during the twentieth century.

Matthew Walhout

REFERENCES AND RECOMMENDED READING

Harrison, Peter, 1990. *"Religion" and the Religions in the English Enlightenment.* Cambridge: Cambridge University Press.

———. 1998. *The Bible, Protestantism, and the Rise of Natural Science.* Cambridge: Cambridge University Press.

———. 2007. *The Fall of Man and the Foundations of Science.* Cambridge: Cambridge University Press.

———. 2015. *The Territories of Science and Religion.* Chicago: University of Chicago Press.

HARTSHORNE, CHARLES. Charles Hartshorne (pronounced "Harts-horn") (1897–2000) was an American philosopher and theologian most noted for his work on the ontological argument for the **existence of God** and for advancing **Alfred North Whitehead**'s **process philosophy** into an elaborate process theology. Professor Hartshorne studied at Harvard University, where he earned a BA, MA, and PhD. He then pursued postdoctoral studies in Germany at the University of Freiburg, studying under Edmund Husserl, and also at the University of Marburg, studying under Martin Heidegger, though neither of these philosophers influenced his thinking as much as C. S. Peirce, whose collected papers he coedited. He later returned to Harvard University as a research fellow, assisting Whitehead.

Upon completing his postgraduate work at Harvard, Hartshorne taught philosophy at the University of Chicago from 1928 to 1955, at Emory University from 1955 to 1962, and then at the University of Texas at Austin from 1962 until his retirement in 1978. He was elected a fellow of the American Academy of Arts and Sciences. After his retirement, he remained academically engaged, publishing well into his nineties and delivering his final lecture at the ripe age of 98. Perhaps somewhat of an eccentric, he never owned an automobile and always abstained from caffeine and alcohol.

Hartshorne is remembered for his thoroughgoing defense of the rationality of **theism**, which he championed for most of his career at a time when it was not philosophically fashionable to do so. One significant example is his rediscovery and development of Anselm's ontological argument. Even more consequentially, however, are his views on the nature of God and the God-world relation. Hartshorne argued that classical theism was bereft of coherence, filled with logical and metaphysical inconsistencies, and religiously unsatisfying. Rejecting Aristotelian **metaphysics**, and affirming contemporary evolutionary biology and cosmology, he formulated a process-based conception of God and the world that he dubbed "neoclassical theism" in which God is a participant in cosmic evolution—a supreme becoming rather than a static, unchanging being.

For Hartshorne, God is not impassible nor omnipotent nor omniscient in the classical senses of those terms. Rather than being unmoved by human suffering, for example, God experiences both joy and pain. And rather than determining events, God lures the evolving and free creation ever forward toward ultimate goodness and perfection.

Deeply entrenched in both metaphysical and scientific inquiry, Hartshorne affirmed panpsychism, the view that each active entity in the natural world—even such things as photons and individual cells that do not exhibit a mental life—has a mental life and, as such, has intrinsic value. This furnished a fundamental grounding for value in nature, and it also afforded an environmental ethics where both intrinsic and instrumental values in the natural world could be assessed. His concern for nature was especially manifest in his passion for ornithology, particularly birdsong, and he taught that birds have a subjective life and are motivated by the enjoyment of singing. He did extensive research in support of this theory and became an internationally recognized expert in the field, publishing *Born to Sing: An Interpretation and World Survey of Bird Song*.

Hartshorne's conception of the divine has had a wide influence on philosophers and theologians, particularly process thinkers and open theists. His important publications include the recommended resources below.

Chad Meister

REFERENCES AND RECOMMENDED READING

Hartshorne, Charles. 1948. *The Divine Relativity*. New Haven, CT: Yale University Press.
———. 1953. *Philosophers Speak of God*. Chicago: University of Chicago Press; repr., Amherst, NY: Humanity, 2000.
———. 1984. *Omnipotence and Other Theological Mistakes*. Albany, NY: SUNY Press.
———. 2011. *Creative Experiencing*. Albany, NY: SUNY Press.

HAWKING, STEPHEN W. Stephen W. Hawking (1942–) is one of the most famous theoretical physicists of the twentieth century, a circumstance both illustrated and extended by the Academy Award–winning film based on his life, *The Theory of Everything* (2014). Born in Oxford 300 years after the **death** of **Galileo** and the birth of Sir **Isaac Newton**, Hawking showed extraordinary talent in **physics** and **mathematics** from an early age. His interests in thermodynamics, relativity theory, and quantum theory had their genesis while he was an undergraduate at Oxford and have remained with him throughout his career. He completed a first-class honors degree in physics at Oxford in 1962 and entered Cambridge University as a research student in general relativity that same year.

At the age of 21, early in his graduate studies, he was diagnosed with amyotrophic lateral sclerosis (ALS, more commonly known as "Lou Gehrig's disease") and given

two years to live. While the disease progressively eliminated his movement and speech, Hawking heroically defied his terminal diagnosis, and with the sacrificial help of Jane Wilde, the woman who became his first wife, he continued his studies, completed his doctoral work in relativity under Dennis Sciama, and went on to a distinguished and productive scientific career. He was elected a Fellow of the Royal Society in 1974. In 1979 he became Lucasian Professor of Mathematics at Cambridge, a post once held by Sir Isaac Newton. He retired from this position in 2009 and now holds an endowed chair as the director of research at the Department of Applied Mathematics and Theoretical Physics (DaMTP) at Cambridge. He was awarded CBE (Commander of the Order of the British Empire) in 1982.

From its start, Hawking's research has focused on singularities—locations in the space-time continuum where the laws of physics break down—the primary example of which is a black hole. Working with Roger Penrose in the late 1960s, Hawking succeeded in showing that if general relativity is correct, then regardless of which solution of Einstein's equations is in view, there must have been a singularity from which universal space-time and everything in it began (see **Big Bang Theory**). In 1970 Hawking's research turned to the properties of black holes. Black holes are objects so massive and dense that not even light can escape their gravity. The boundary around them, from inside which nothing can escape, is called the *event horizon*. Hawking realized that the surface area of this boundary could never decrease over time, only increase or remain constant—a property also shared by the entropy (randomness) of a physical system (see **Second Law of Thermodynamics**)—so the surface area of the event horizon could be understood as a measure of the entropy of a black hole.

Over the next four years, working with other physicists, Hawking was able to prove John Wheeler's conjecture, known as the "no hair theorem." This theorem states that the only properties of matter preserved after entering a black hole are mass, angular momentum, and charge—everything else about its history and identity gets lost. In the late 1970s, Hawking turned his attention to the behavior of matter in the vicinity of a black hole and, applying quantum theory to its description, paradoxically discovered that black holes could emit thermal radiation (subsequently dubbed "Hawking radiation") with the ultimate consequence that their surface area *decreases*, their temperature rises, their rate of radiation emission increases, and in the long term, they "evaporate." When they disappear, Hawking claimed, all of the information associated with the matter that had fallen into them is lost.

This claim was called the *black hole information **paradox*** since—according to quantum theory—such information is conserved as part of the wave function describing how these particles develop through time. The paradox was resolved in the 1990s, contrary to Hawking's contention, through proofs of black hole complementarity and the holographic principle (see **Holographic Universe**).

Since the end of the 1970s, much of Hawking's work has been directed toward finding a synthesis of quantum theory and general relativity that would lead to a quantum theory of gravity. His best-known efforts have focused on the construction of quantum cosmological models in which the quantum-gravitational wave function of the universe—cast as a sum over all paths describing four-dimensional space-times with associated matter configurations—"tunnels into existence" from a background mathematical space in a manner constrained to yield our universe as one of the most probable results.

In making the equations solvable, Hawking and his collaborator, James Hartle, subjected the space-time of general relativity to a mathematical transformation that rendered time directionless and beginningless. Because time lacks an initial boundary (starting point) in their model, they named this approach the "no boundary proposal," and Hawking has asserted in his popular work that this relieves us of any need to appeal to transcendent explanations for the existence of the universe. "If the universe is really completely self-contained, having no boundary or edge, it would have neither beginning nor end: it would simply be. What place, then, for a creator?" (Hawking 1988, 141).

As his popular works indicate, Hawking is a much better theoretical physicist and mathematician than he is a philosopher or theologian. I conclude with a few illustrations of the inconsistencies and oversights in his philosophical pronouncements and his shortsightedness with respect to the limitations of his theoretical work. Hawking has repeatedly claimed to be a positivist and instrumentalist (see **Instrumentalism**; **Logical Positivism**) regarding the significance of his work, asserting "I take the positivist viewpoint that a physical theory is just a mathematical model and that it is meaningless to ask whether it corresponds to reality. All that one can ask is that its predictions should be in agreement with observation" (Hawking and Penrose 1996, 3–4). Of course, if it is meaningless to ask whether a theory corresponds to reality, it is nonsensical to assert

that it *explains* anything about the world. But if it fails to explain anything about the world, it certainly does not explain how it could exist without a Creator. Interpreted instrumentally, mathematical models license no metaphysical conclusions whatsoever.

Hawking has nonetheless recently claimed that "because there is a law like gravity, the universe can and will create itself from nothing.... Spontaneous creation is the reason there is something rather than nothing, why the universe exists, why we exist. It is not necessary to invoke God to light the blue touch paper and set the universe going" (Hawking and Mlodinow 2010, 180). Now, even *if* it were true that quantum gravitational laws—which, incidentally, we still do not have—permitted the "spontaneous" generation of universes, we would still be thrown back on the question that Hawking himself once asked, namely, "What is it that breathes fire into the equations and makes a universe for them to describe?" (Hawking 1988, 174).

Even more fundamentally, what explains the fact that we have these equations and not others? This question is not answered by appealing to **multiverse** theories—most notably the inflationary string multiverse that Hawking references—in which the laws of physics can vary from universe to universe, and then invoking "observer selection" because we could only find ourselves in those regions of the multiverse that are compatible with our existence (see **Cosmology, Contemporary**; **Multiverse**; **String Theory**).

All such multiverse "explanations" must instantiate a variety of stable mechanisms in order to function (Collins 2009; Gordon 2011): (1) a *mechanism supplying energy* driving the expansion of space: the hypothesized inflaton field; (2) a *mechanism to form bubble universes*: Einstein's equations of general relativity; (3) a *mechanism of energy conversion* that transforms inflaton energy into the normal mass-energy constitutive of our universe: Einstein's mass-energy equivalence and a hypothesized coupling constant between inflaton fields and the matter and radiation fields of our experience; (4) a *mechanism of variation* that allows different bubble universes to exhibit different laws and constants: random quantum jumps in the topology of the compactified extra dimensions of space; and (5) the *right meta-laws* governing the behavior of the multiverse generator—(a) the *trans-universal laws* instantiated in the universe-creating machine itself, (b) a *principle of quantization* that governs all fields and permits the stability of matter, and (c) an *exclusion principle* akin to Pauli's that allows the formation of complex structures. If any of these law-like features of the multiverse is unstable, the universe-generating mechanism will break down. In short, the universe generators that multiverse explanations require have finely tuned design parameters that themselves require explanation. Therefore appealing to a multiverse to explain why our universe has *these* law-like regularities and not others does not obviate the need for an explanation; it merely bumps it up to the next level. Avoiding an infinite regress of explanatory demands requires that explanation terminate upon a necessarily existent transcendent cause that is capable of action and, since it exists *timelessly* logically prior to any universe or multiverse, requires no explanation of its own existence.

So the bottom line is that states of affairs that are contingent, that could have been otherwise than what they are, *require* an explanation (see **Sufficient Reason, Principle of**). If the no-boundary proposal were correct, therefore, and the universe did not have a beginning in time, it would *still* be a contingent entity and thus *still* require an explanation that could only be provided by a necessarily existent transcendent cause (see **Cosmological Argument**).

But such philosophical inconsistencies and oversights are compounded by an overreach that hides the limitations in his models. As Hawking recognizes, the mathematical transformation that makes his equations solvable and renders time beginningless must be reversed after the computation is complete if the model has any hope of describing the universe as we know it (Hawking 1988, 139). After the reversal, **the singularity** at the beginning of time reappears, however, so we cannot maintain that the universe did not have a beginning. Furthermore, a realistic interpretation of the model, which is required if it is to have any explanatory force, entails accepting the technically deficient and metaphysically problematic many-worlds interpretation of quantum theory (see **Quantum Theory, Interpretations of**), a condition that hardly counts in its favor. Lastly, as Alexander Vilenkin, one of Hawking's colaborers in quantum-cosmological research has admitted, "An observational test of quantum cosmology does not seem possible … [it] is not likely to become an observational science" (Vilenkin 2002, 12–13).

In the final analysis, then, despite Hawking's amusing proclamation that "philosophy is dead" (Hawking and Mlodinow 2010, 5), his own excursions in quantum cosmology amount to little more than speculative forays into highly mathematicized **metaphysics**. (For further discussion of these matters, see Copan and Craig 2004; Craig and Smith 1993; Gordon 2011, 563–69; Lennox 2011.)

Bruce L. Gordon

REFERENCES AND RECOMMENDED READING

Bardeen, James B., Brandon Carter, and Stephen W. Hawking. 1973. "The Four Laws of Black Hole Mechanics." *Communications in Mathematical Physics* 31:161–70.

Collins, Robin. 2009. "The Teleological Argument: An Exploration of the Fine-Tuning of the Universe." In *The Blackwell Companion to Natural Theology*, ed. William L. Craig and J. P. Moreland, 202–81. Oxford: Blackwell.

Copan, Paul, and William Lane Craig. 2004. *Creation Out of Nothing: A Biblical, Philosophical and Scientific Exploration.* Grand Rapids: Baker Academic.

Craig, William Lane, and Quentin Smith. 1993. *Theism, Atheism, and Big Bang Cosmology.* Oxford: Clarendon.

Gordon, Bruce L. 2011. "Balloons on a String: A Critique of Multiverse Cosmology." In *The Nature of Nature: Examining the Role of Naturalism in Science*, ed. Bruce L. Gordon and William A. Dembski, 558–601. Wilmington, DE: ISI Books.

———. Forthcoming. "The Necessity of Sufficiency: The Argument from the Incompleteness of Nature." In *Two Dozen (or So) Arguments for God: The Plantinga Project*, ed. Trent Dougherty and Jerry Walls. Oxford: Oxford University Press.

Hartle, James, and Stephen W. Hawking. 1976. "Path Integral Derivation of Black Hole Radiance." *Physical Review* D13:2188–2203.

———. 1983. "Wave Function of the Universe." *Physical Review* D28:2960–75.

Hawking, Stephen W. 1965. "Occurrence of Singularities in Open Universes." *Physical Review Letters* 15:689–90.

———. 1972. "Black Holes in General Relativity." *Communications in Mathematical Physics* 25:152–66.

———. 1974. Black Hole Explosions." *Nature* 248:30–31.

———. 1975. "Particle Creation by Black Holes." *Communications in Mathematical Physics* 43:199–220.

———. 1977. "The Quantum Mechanics of Black Holes." *Scientific American* 236:34–49.

———. 1987. "Quantum Cosmology." In *300 Years of Gravitation*, ed. Stephen W. Hawking and Werner Israel, 631–51. Cambridge: Cambridge University Press.

———. 1988. *A Brief History of Time from the Big Bang to Black Holes.* New York: Bantam.

———. 1998. "Is Information Lost in Black Holes?" In *Black Holes and Relativistic Stars*, ed. Robert Wald, 221–40. Chicago: University of Chicago Press.

———. 2001. *The Universe in a Nutshell.* New York: Bantam.

Hawking, Stephen W., and George F. R. Ellis. 1973. *The Large-Scale Structure of Space-Time.* Cambridge: Cambridge University Press.

Hawking, Stephen W., and Leonard Mlodinow. 2010. *The Grand Design.* New York: Bantam Books.

Hawking, Stephen W., and Roger Penrose. 1970. "The Singularities of Gravitational Collapse and Cosmology." *Proceedings of the Royal Society of London*, A 314:529–48.

———. 1996. *The Nature of Space and Time.* Princeton, NJ: Princeton University Press.

Lennox, John. 2011. *God and Stephen Hawking: Whose Design Is It Anyway?* Oxford: Lion Hudson.

Susskind, Leonard. 2008. *The Black Hole War: My Battle with Stephen Hawking to Make the World Safe for Quantum Mechanics.* New York: Little, Brown.

Unruh, William. 2014. "Has Hawking Radiation Been Measured?" January 26. http://arxiv.org/pdf/1401.6612v1.

Vilenkin, Alexander. 2002. "Quantum Cosmology and Eternal Inflation." April 18. http://arxiv.org/pdf/gr-qc/0204061v1.pdf.

HEISENBERG'S UNCERTAINTY PRINCIPLE.

German theoretical physicist Werner Heisenberg (1901–76)

was the first to demonstrate the existence of a fundamental limit to the precision with which certain characteristics (called *complementary pairs*) of physical particles can be known and measured. For example, he noted that the more accurate a researcher's determination of a particle's position, the less accurately that researcher can determine its momentum, and vice versa. Thus the principle bears his name.

While Heisenberg was the first to show that this measuring limit exists, theoretical physicists Hermann Weyl and Earle Kennard were the ones to determine how large the uncertainty actually is. It is far from trivial. If a physicist determines the momentum of a typical subatomic particle with the best precision available using modern equipment, she or he would only be able to pin its location to within about plus or minus one-third of a mile. However, the greater the number of particles included in the measurement, the lesser the uncertainty for that aggregate. For any chunk of matter large enough to be visible to the naked eye, for example, the uncertainty drops to near zero.

Heisenberg's uncertainty principle also means that within an ensemble of particles, a few will climb over a barrier that in classical **physics** would be considered unassailable (see **Isaac Newton**). Consider this analogy: According to classical physics, a marble released from the rim of a bowl will roll down to the bottom of the bowl and up the other side (depending on the level of friction) to a height no greater than the height at which it was released. That is its barrier height. For individual particles, however, the uncertainty principle means that some of the particles (in an ensemble of particles) will have insufficient momentum to carry them to the height barrier while others' momentum will carry them over that barrier.

This barrier-surpassing phenomenon is called *quantum tunneling*. Quantum tunneling shows that the uncertainty principle is not just about how well we can measure but about how well nature can constrain things, in some sense. Theoreticians have demonstrated that quantum tunneling plays an essential role in the nuclear fusion reactions that make stable burning stars possible. Without these stars, life's elemental building blocks would not exist. Quantum tunneling is also crucial to the operation of a type of transistor—a tunnel diode—that has made the modern electronics revolution possible. Such diodes are now known to operate within the bodies of all vertebrate and most invertebrate animals. Quantum tunneling, then, plays a critical role in living systems, for example, in allowing hemoglobin to transport the right amount of oxygen to cells.

For advanced life to be possible, quantum tunneling must be possible, and for quantum tunneling to be possible, the degree of uncertainty in the Heisenberg uncertainty principle must be precisely as it is, neither greater nor lesser. In the early days of quantum theory, **Albert Einstein** reacted negatively. In a letter to his quantum physicist friend Max Born, he wrote, "I, at any rate, am convinced that He ("the Old One," as he referred to the deity) does not throw dice." Today a scientist might say that God does, in a sense, "play dice," but he very carefully designs the dice to produce the outcome essential for life.

Hugh Ross

REFERENCES AND RECOMMENDED READING

Heisenberg, Werner. 1929. *The Physical Principles of Quantum Theory.* Chicago: University of Chicago Press.
Messiah, Albert. 1966. *Quantum Mechanics.* Vol. 1. New York: Wiley.
Wick, David. 1995. *The Infamous Boundary: Seven Decades of Controversy in Quantum Mechanics.* Boston: Berkhäuser.

HEMPEL, CARL G. Carl Gustav Hempel (1905–97) was a highly influential philosopher of science who was associated with the logical empiricists of the Vienna Circle (see **Logical Positivism**). He studied with **Rudolf Carnap** (1891–1970) in Vienna in 1929–30, participating in the Vienna Circle debates about observation sentences, and he completed his doctorate, which focused on the **logic** of **probability**, under **Hans Reichenbach** (1891–1953) at the University of Berlin in 1934. He moved to the United States to continue working with Carnap at the University of Chicago in 1937–38 and then taught at Queen's College in New York and Yale University before moving to Princeton University, where he taught from 1955 to 1975. His work on the logic of **confirmation** and the nature of scientific explanation broke new ground and remains central to examinations of these subjects today.

Hempel was influenced by the physicalist school of positivists (see **Physicalism**), particularly Otto Neurath (1882–1945) and Rudolf Carnap, and his early work focused on the analytical development of this perspective. In the late 1940s, he collaborated with Paul Oppenheim on a series of papers dealing with the logic of confirmation and explanation (Hempel 1945; Hempel and Oppenheim 1945, 1948) and retained an interest in these subjects throughout his career (Hempel 1952, 1962a, 1962b, 1965b, 1966b, 1981). Some of his most influential papers on these subjects—and related concerns of scientific concept formation, the nature of scientific theories, and criteria of meaningfulness—were collected into a volume titled *Aspects of Scientific Explanation* (1965b). He also authored a highly influential introductory text, *Philosophy of Natural Science* (1966a), which was widely used for many years.

Later in his career, **Thomas Kuhn** (1922–96) became one of his colleagues at Princeton, and their interaction shifted Hempel's attention from positivistic analyses into engagement with historical and pragmatic issues in the **philosophy of science** (George 2012; Hempel 1970, 1979, 1983; Kuhn 1970, 1977, 2000).

One of the most famous parts of Hempel's discussion of the logic of confirmation (1945) is the "raven **paradox**." Hempel observed that many scientific hypotheses or laws take the form of universal generalizations, such as "All *F*s are *G*s," or more specifically, statements like "All ravens are black things." The observation of a black raven would obviously support this hypothesis. But Hempel then noted that if a very intuitive principle is affirmed, namely, that anything confirming a statement also confirms any other statement that is logically equivalent to it, we get counterintuitive consequences. For instance, "All non-black things are non-ravens" is logically equivalent to "All ravens are black things"; so the existence of yellow bananas, which confirms the non-blackness of non-ravens, also confirms that all ravens are black. This and other "paradoxes of confirmation" were obstacles to constructing a purely formal logic of confirmation and the focus of much discussion.

Hempel's work on the logic of scientific explanation (Hempel 1965b et al.; Hempel and Oppenheim 1948) was also of key importance. Most notably, he articulated the so-called deductive-nomological or covering-law model of scientific explanation, which maintains that genuine scientific explanation of a phenomenon has the form of a valid deductive argument proceeding from premises that are statements of the general laws and initial conditions governing that phenomenon to observed behavior as the conclusion of the argument. The "D-N model" has served as a starting point for all subsequent discussions of the nature of scientific explanation (Fetzer 2000; Lambert and Brittan 1992, 9–50).

Finally, Hempel's critical analyses of the verifiability criterion of meaning (**Verification Principle**; Hempel 1950, 1965a) were helpful in mitigating the noncognitivist accounts of ethics and religion characteristic of positivism. As Hempel concluded regarding the work of Ayer (1970) and others (Hempel 1950, 63), "the idea of cognitive significance, with its suggestion of a sharp distinction between significant and non-significant sentences or systems of such, has lost its promise and fertility as an explicandum … it had better be replaced by certain concepts that admit of differences in degree … to offer the most promising way of advancing further the clarification of the issues implicit in the idea of cognitive significance." As Charles Taliaferro (2005, 348–61) notes, debates over positivism and its demise reinvigorated discussions of the meaning of religious language and its explanatory functions, helping to open the door to the renaissance in Christian **philosophy of religion** in the late twentieth century.

Bruce L. Gordon

REFERENCES AND RECOMMENDED READING

Ayer, Alfred J. (1936) 1970. *Language, Truth, and Logic.* New York: Penguin.
Fetzer, James H., ed. 2000. *Science, Explanation, and Rationality: Aspects of the Philosophy of Carl G. Hempel.* Oxford: Oxford University Press.
———. 2014. "Carl Hempel." In *Stanford Encyclopedia of Philosophy.* ed. Edward N. Zalta. August 4. http://plato.stanford.edu/entries/hempel/.
George, Alexander. 2012. "Opening the Door to Cloud-Cuckoo Land: Hempel and Kuhn on Rationality." *Journal for the History of Analytical Philosophy* 1 (4): 1–17.
Hempel, Carl G. 1945. "Studies in the Logic of Confirmation, I and II." *Mind* 54:1–26, 97–121.
———. 1950. "Problems and Changes in the Empiricist Criterion of Meaning." *Revue Internationale de Philosophie* 41 (11): 41–63.
———. 1952. *Fundamentals of Concept Formation in Empirical Science.* Chicago: University of Chicago Press.
———. 1962a. "Deductive-Nomological vs. Statistical Explanation." In *Minnesota Studies in the Philosophy of Science*, ed. H. Feigl and G. Maxwell, 3:98–169. Minneapolis: University of Minnesota Press.
———. 1962b. "Explanation in Science and in History." In *Frontiers of Science and Philosophy*, ed. R. G. Colodny, 9–33. Pittsburgh: University of Pittsburgh Press.
———. 1965a. "Empiricist Criteria of Cognitive Significance: Problems and Changes." In C. G. Hempel, *Aspects of Scientific Explanation*, 101–19. New York: Free Press.
———. 1965b. "Aspects of Scientific Explanation." In C. G. Hempel, *Aspects of Scientific Explanation*, 331–496. New York: Free Press.
———. 1966a. *Philosophy of Natural Science.* Englewood Cliffs, NJ: Prentice-Hall.
———. 1966b. "Recent Problems of Induction." In *Mind and Cosmos*, ed. R. G. Colodny, 112–34. Pittsburgh: University of Pittsburgh Press.
———. 1970. "On the 'Standard Conception' of Scientific Theories." In *Minnesota Studies in the Philosophy of Science*, ed. M. Radner and S. Winokur, 4:142–63. Minneapolis: University of Minnesota Press.
———. 1979. "Scientific Rationality: Analytic vs. Pragmatic Perspectives." In *Rationality To-Day*, ed. T. S. Geraets, 46–58. Ottawa: University of Ottawa Press.
———. 1981. "Turns in the Evolution of the Problem of Induction." *Synthese* 46:193–404.
———. 1983. "Valuation and Objectivity in Science." In *Physics, Philosophy, and Psychoanalysis: Essays in Honor of Adolf Grunbaum*, ed. Robert S. Cohen and Larry Laudan, 73–100. Dordrecht: Kluwer.
Hempel, C. G., and P. Oppenheim. 1945. "A Definition of 'Degree of Confirmation.'" *Philosophy of Science* 12:98–115.
———. 1948. "Studies in the Logic of Explanation." *Philosophy of Science* 15:135–75.

Kuhn, Thomas S. 1970. *The Structure of Scientific Revolutions*. 2nd ed. Chicago: University of Chicago Press.

———. 1977. *The Essential Tension: Studies in Scientific Tradition and Change*. Chicago: University of Chicago Press.

———. 2000. *The Road since Structure: Philosophical Essays 1970–1993*. Ed. J. Conant and J. Haugeland. Chicago: University of Chicago Press.

Lambert, Karel, and Brittan, Gordon G. 1992. *An Introduction to the Philosophy of Science*. 4th ed. Atascadero, CA: Ridgeview.

Taliaferro, Charles. 2005. *Evidence and Faith: Religion and Philosophy since the Seventeenth Century*. Cambridge: Cambridge University Press.

HERMENEUTICS, BIBLICAL AND SCIENTIFIC.

The word *hermeneutics* is a derivation from the Greek word *hermēnuetēs*, meaning "interpreter." Since the Middle Ages, the term *hermeneutics* has been closely tied to the formulation of principles intended to produce a valid interpretation of the Bible. More recently its meaning has expanded to denote the study of the theories and methods involved in the study of texts more generally. It has become a method of interpretation whose goal is to understand the author's mind, and hence to identify his or her intention—the specific meaning that the author has imparted to the text in question. Recently the concept of text has been extended beyond written or oral texts to include objects such as film, art, and other things that can be treated as texts and hence that are subject to interpretation.

In this essay the traditional topic of biblical hermeneutics is addressed along with the extension of the idea of hermeneutics to the natural sciences, a topic of some concern to biblical understanding and Christian theology. Natural science hermeneutics are of interest to Christians because of the recognition that God has written two books—the book of our Scriptures and the book of nature, the study and understanding of the latter comprising the natural sciences.

Biblical Hermeneutics

A number of difficulties face the reader in understanding and applying the Bible, a book of the distant past. The Bible addresses cultures and historical situations far different from our own. Furthermore, the interpreter must pick from a number of different hermeneutical methods. In reading the Bible, a person always applies an interpretive principle, for one cannot read any piece of literature in the absence of one.

All contemporary approaches to biblical hermeneutics involve three main components—the author, the text, and the reader. Each hermeneutical method shares two main goals—to get to what the text meant to its first recipients and to aid the contemporary reader in formulating an

appropriate current understanding. All methods begin with content and context.

Content (exegesis)

A number of steps are involved in determining the content of the text of interest, a process called *exegesis*.

1. The text in its original language is the ideal starting place. However, this requires knowledge of that ancient language. Scholars have compared the many extant manuscripts of the New Testament in creating a trustworthy critical Greek text, the Nestle-Aland version. The Hebrew Old Testament, *Biblia Hebraica Stuttgartensia*, is widely used by scholars for Old Testament study.

2. Many times the words chosen by the biblical writer present problems, for the meaning of biblical words in Hebrew and Greek have undergone change since their original biblical use. Fortunately, lexicons exist that trace these meanings over time.

3. The nuances of a particular grammatical construction may hold the key to the understanding of a passage, implying that a thorough knowledge of the ancient grammar aids in understanding.

4. Awareness of the syntax is an additional factor in determining the meaning of a unit as a whole. This refers to all the interrelationships within a sentence, including those between words, phrases, clauses, and even between sentences.

In summary, the goal in determining the content is to produce an accurate translation of the biblical text into the language of the reader. Many readers of the Bible will not have the tools to do this and hence must depend on an available translation. A plethora of modern translations that attempt to competently carry out the exegetical steps outlined here are available to English language readers, who may choose one or more for study.

Context

The accurate determination of the content of a text is a necessary but not a sufficient step for complete biblical interpretation. Awareness of the context of the passage of interest constitutes another important component in understanding the author's motivation. The following steps aid in doing so.

1. Biblical authors write in particular literary genres. The identification of the genre of a passage plays a crucial role in the understanding of the author's intent.

2. The historical and cultural context is another step in determining the purpose of a given passage. The historical setting in which the original recipients found themselves

possibly provided motivation and context for the biblical author as he spoke to their situation. The culture of the recipients or the culture of their setting may have influenced the writing of a particular passage.

3. The social or religious context addresses the use of a passage by its recipients. The form of communication (writing) was generally appropriate for the social or religious setting, and that form should be identified by the reader. For example, psalms were used by the people of Israel in worship.

4. Understanding the style, literary forms, or tone of a passage gives a clue to understanding what the author was trying to accomplish in that passage. The intent may be revealed by his attitude and emotions through the passage's tone. Compare the apostle Paul's gentle attitude of approval toward the Philippian church with his harsh comments of criticism to the Galatians ("I am astonished.... You foolish Galatians!" [Gal 1:6; 3:1]).

5. A biblical writer sometimes acted as an editor, incorporating sources in a passage or a book. The choice of sources may give a clue to understanding the editor's intended message.

6. An additional principle of interpretation that applies especially to Bible study involves determining how a given passage compares with other biblical passages. The principle of comparing Scripture with Scripture assists in trying to get a full understanding of a passage. Considerations include how a given passage fits into the biblical book in which it is found, into the section of its testament, and into the whole of Scripture.

7. The final step is that the hearer or the reader must understand the point of the passage and the author's motivation and message to his intended audience.

Together these steps of interpretation constitute careful Bible study.

Reader response (uptake)

Thorough Bible study will take time and effort, for the study of the Bible deserves such. One should not casually flip to a passage, read it, especially in isolation from other passages, and thereby always expect to understand the author's purpose and message to the original audience. Such an understanding and application would be open to question when a person uses a casual and short-cut approach, especially in reference to complex issues. This does not refer to truths that simply leap out of the Bible, but pertains especially to issues over which interpretive questions have arisen within the church, issues such as the creation-evolution conflict.

Scientific Hermeneutics

At first glance it would seem that scientific hermeneutics should be somewhat easier to deal with than biblical hermeneutics. After all, modern Western scientific strategy has been successfully in place for some 300–400 years now. In the form of the hypothetical-deductive method, science has proven to be fruitful, as there is general understanding and agreement among practicing (active) scientists for the majority of phenomena that have been investigated. With the development of the **technology** of the twentieth and twenty-first centuries, the past 100-plus years have been a very fruitful time for science, as the spheres of size, mass, time, and distance open to investigation have increased beyond the imaginations of people at the opening of the twentieth century. This **scientific method** has been used to study the universe and the earth from the submicroscopic regimen of particle **physics** (e.g., the Higgs boson; see **God Particle**) to the cosmological; and the study of **dark matter**, involving times as short as the Planck time, 10^{-43} seconds, to beyond the age of the universe of 13.8 billion years; and masses as small as the electron to cosmological masses. But one result is that contemporary science and its understanding are not so easily investigated. What is the meaning of quantum theory, black holes, **string theory**, fractals, and **chaos theory**? The following is a discussion of three factors that result in challenges to the clear interpretation of scientific research and concepts.

Phenomena not directly observable (too small and too big)

A significant component of scientific work relates to phenomena that cannot be observed directly with our unaided senses. The microworld of molecular sizes and smaller cannot be observed directly with our eyes. Various kinds of microscopes—optical, ultraviolet, and scanning electron microscopes—come to our aid here. The scanning electron microscope is a complicated and subtle microscope, with its operation and understanding depending on a knowledge of electromagnetic and atomic theory. We depend on the theories of instrumentation to be correct, and this is crucial in doing scientific hermeneutics—interpreting the optical and electrical signals that result from the profiling of a microscopic object on the order of 0.0000000001 meters or so in size.

The process of investigation becomes even more indirect when we seek details of the structure of the nuclei of atoms. Specialized nuclear detectors are used to measure the presence and energies of the nuclear particles involved in such investigations. These particles are not directly observed, but they produce tiny flashes of light in the detector material that is converted to an electrical pulse by a photosensitive device. These electrical pulses are transmitted from the (radioactive) experimental room to a data-processing location, where banks of electronic modules perform logical operations on the electrical pulses, eventually yielding the kind of useful information that is stored in a computer as bits of information representing the numerical data. Physicists then take this computer information and interpret it in terms of the nuclear information that is being sought in the research program. The result is that flashes of light eventually are interpreted in terms of nuclear reactions.

Those who investigate nuclear physics must realize they will never directly observe a nucleus or a nuclear reaction. They must be satisfied that they understand every aspect of the operation of the experimental equipment and data-processing devices, including the computer analysis. They must account for each puzzling (or not puzzling) outcome when expected (or unexpected) incidents occur during the course of the experiment and subsequent data analysis. Understanding within the confines of physical theory, the operation of all sorts of experimental equipment, and self-consistency are the minimum goals of the entire procedure. One can never be 100 percent sure that the outcome is valid. The investigational team for a given study must be the hardest critics of the project, and incompetent or dishonest work among scientists is penalized by exclusion from the scientific research community. The stakes are high.

The cosmological is another regimen that provides challenges to the research scientist. The study of the cosmos requires sophisticated and complicated equipment and understanding, all of which depends on the correctness of understanding in many fields of physics, **astronomy**, cosmology, chemistry, earth science, etc. Once again, understanding the correct operation of instrumentation, and competent and sufficient data collecting and data processing are crucial in interpreting the optical and electrical bits of information in cosmological studies, just as in the case of microscopic science.

The historical sciences

Laboratory and field scientists have the advantage of repeating investigations until they are satisfied they have finally gotten it right. Historical scientists do not have that privilege. There never will be another **big bang**. And yet applying scientific knowledge to phenomena observed in the cosmos

and on our earth have allowed, for instance, investigations into the age of the universe and of the earth. In each case, independent methods have been used to determine these ages, and results for both the earth and the universe are surprisingly consistent.

Scientists doing these types of investigations are confident that the age of the universe is 13.8 billion years and the earth is 4.54 billion years, with each age determination accurate to within 1 percent. For example, radioactive dating can be used for determining the age of the earth by studying long-lived isotopes of heavy atoms embedded in rocks. For shorter time spans, carbon-14, with a half-life of 5,730 years, can be used to date formerly living objects (e.g., animals and trees) with ages of a few and up to several carbon-14 half-lives, to 50,000 or so years. The consistency in the consequent age determinations give scientists confidence that certain important events of the past can be dated with surprising precision.

This kind of scientific success might be evidence that other historical questions could possibly be successfully investigated using scientific methods. The development of life on our earth is one of these issues on which biological scientists believe significant progress has been made, as the consensus among active researchers is that the current version of evolutionary understanding successfully interprets a vast amount of relevant existing data. It is true that the question of how the first life — the first self-replicating cells — came into being remains open. But researchers believe this is a question that can be successfully addressed, and work continues. Apart from this question of the beginning of the first life on earth, the majority of biological scientists are convinced they have a good handle on subsequent development of life and its many forms from the first life to the present time.

In many senses, the interpretation of data related to the historical is much the same as for laboratory and field sciences. Many of the techniques are the same. And the question is always, how much data is sufficient? When does the investigation stop?

Quantum theory

There is general agreement that quantum theoretical equations, developed early in the twentieth century, account well for microscopic phenomena. Measurable predictions (results) from quantum theory account for all sorts of microscopic phenomena. One formulation of the theory involves the Schrödinger equation, a sort of reformulation of the principle of **conservation of energy** but applied to microscopic processes.

The Schrödinger equation is an equation of motion and produces a "wave function" that can lead to a description of the behavior of the system in question, whether it is an atomic process, nuclear process, or some other. But the meaning of the wave function itself remains open for question. There are two main interpretations of the implications of quantum results, with famous physicists on either side of the argument. For example, **Niels Bohr** took an opposing position to that of **Einstein**'s. But there is also a version of quantum theory initiated by David Bohm that, though quite different, gives identical measurable results.

So although successful accounts and predictions of microscopic processes and entities can be made by quantum theorists, the underlying meaning of quantum theory has not been settled.

Summary

The contemporary scientific enterprise results in some challenges to Christian theology. One key question is, are scientific results—results that are derived from the modern scientific method that employs naturalistic methodology—consistent with Christian theological understanding? God has written two books—the revealed book of Scripture, but also the book of nature (the purview of science.) Shouldn't there at least be no conflict between the two books? And yet for the past 200 or so years there has been conflict. Why? Can there be reconciliation? And if so, will biblical and/or scientific hermeneutics play a role, perhaps a key role?

Richard F. Carlson

REFERENCES AND RECOMMENDED READING

Carlson, Richard F., and Tremper Longman III. 2010. *Science, Creation and the Bible-Reconciling Rival Theories of Origins.* Downers Grove, IL: InterVarsity.
Murphy, Nancey. 1990. *Theology in the Age of Scientific Reasoning.* Ithaca, NY: Cornell University Press.
Osborne, Grant R. 1991. *The Hermeneutical Spiral—A Comprehensive Introduction to Biblical Interpretation.* Downers Grove, IL: InterVarsity.
Polkinghorne, John. 1995. *Serious Talk—Science and Religion in Dialogue.* Valley Forge, PA: Trinity Press International, 1995.
———. 2002. *Quantum Theory—A Very Short Introduction.* Oxford: Oxford University Press.

HIDDENNESS OF GOD. According to various skeptics about God's existence, including **Richard Dawkins** in *The God Delusion*, the claim that God exists must be evaluated along the lines of a typical scientific hypothesis. If, however, God is a personal agent who has redemptive purposes in hiding from people at times, we are not dealing with a typical scientific hypothesis in the claim that God exists. Instead, we are dealing with a claim about a unique personal agent who is no scientific object but is intentionally elusive at times and nonetheless worthy of worship.

The Jewish-Christian God does not appear constantly in the awareness of people, because this God avowedly hides from people at times. The book of Isaiah announces, "Truly you are a God who has been hiding himself, the God and Savior of Israel" (Isa. 45:15). A similar theme recurs in the Psalms; for instance, the psalmist asks God: "Why do you hide your face and forget our misery and oppression?" (Ps. 44:24). Jesus himself picks up the theme of divine hiding regarding the things of his own ministry, and gives thanks to God for this hiding: "Jesus said, 'I praise you, Father, Lord of heaven and earth, because you have hidden these things from the wise and learned, and revealed them to little children'" (Matt. 11:25; Luke 10:21). In a similar vein, the apostle Paul speaks of God's "hidden wisdom," specifically the treasures of God's wisdom "hidden" in Christ (see 1 Cor. 2:7; Col. 2:3). We should hesitate, then, to suggest that God is constantly obvious to all people.

Some philosophers of religion have identified a "problem" of divine hiddenness; they ask whether a perfectly loving God could fail to be self-revealed in a manner that removes all reasonable human doubt about God's reality. Some of these philosophers hold that perfect love would preclude God's hiding from humans in a way that leaves reasonable human doubt about God's existence. If they are right, one must face the consideration that God's existence is not beyond reasonable doubt according to many normal adult humans. According to these humans, we may reasonably deny that God exists or at least refrain from believing that God exists.

A consideration about divine hiddenness, then, can figure in a case for atheism or at least agnosticism. It seems, however, that God's hiding from some people does not entail either God's hiding from *everyone* always or *everyone's* lacking adequate evidence for God's existence; nor does God's hiding entail anyone's lacking *available* evidence for God's existence, beyond the evidence one actually has. Evidence of God's existence can be variable among persons in a way that the truth about God's existence is not. One reason for this variability is straightforward: people can have different experiences regarding God, including with different degrees of salience.

Some philosophers offer the *freedom response* to the problem of divine hiddenness. This response, suggested by John

Hick (2010) and others, implies that God would hide at least to some extent to enable people *freely* to love, trust, and obey God, that is, to avoid the divine coercion of humans. The key idea is that if God self-revealed without any hiding, humans would be overwhelmed in a way that extinguishes their free response to God. This response, however, raises a question: could not God supply a less elusive or less obscure self-**revelation** without extinguishing human freedom in responding to that revelation? It seems so, according to many people. A self-revelation of God with a bit more clarity or salience would seem not to overwhelm people by removing freedom from their response. If this is so, and it does seem plausible, the freedom response will not serve as a full response to the problem of divine hiddenness.

Some philosophers offer the *proper-motivation response* to the problem of divine hiddenness. This response, suggested by **Blaise Pascal** (2008) and others, implies that God would hide to avoid, or at least to reduce the likelihood of, a human reply to God from improper motives, such as selfish fear or pride. According to this response, God's self-revelation without hiding would prompt humans to have selfish fear or pride in their response. God would hide, however, to discourage such fear and pride, because such fear and pride do not fit with the kind of human moral character sought by God. But this response prompts a simple question: could not God supply a less elusive or less obscure self-revelation without eliciting improper motives in a human response to that revelation? It seems so, in the view of many people. A bit more clarity in God's self-revelation would seem not to require human fear and pride; or, at least, one would need to make a good case for a contrary position. If this is so, we cannot offer the proper-motivation response as a full response to the problem of divine hiddenness.

The *divine-purposes response* implies that God would restrain divine self-revelation, at least for a time, to at least some humans to enhance the satisfaction of *various* perfectly loving purposes which God has for humans. This response, suggested in some of my own writings (Moser 2008, 2010), allows that the amount and the kind of God's self-revelation can vary among people, and the variation can result from God's perfectly loving purposes for recipients of the revelation. If these purposes are perfectly loving, God can be perfectly loving in giving varied and elusive self-revelation to humans. The exact details of God's purposes could sometimes be unclear to us, as we should expect given God's transcendent cognitive superiority relative to us. Even when unclear on the details of divine purposes, however, one could know

and reasonably trust the God who hides for a time, if God has lovingly intervened elsewhere in one's experience with adequate evidence. So, a general argument for atheism or agnosticism will not find a foothold here, contrary to Schellenberg (2006) and some others.

If God is truly redemptive toward humans, in seeking their well-being (all things considered), then we should expect God's self-revelation to come with redemptive purposes for humans. We should not expect this self-revelation to be just an intellectual matter, as if God aimed merely to prompt humans to believe that God exists. Instead, we should expect God's self-revelation to encourage people to cooperate with God, in loving God fully, above all else, and in loving others as God loves them, even one's enemies. Such cooperation from humans would be a fitting response to a God who is worthy of worship and hence self-sufficiently morally perfect. It would also enable human fellowship with God, in reconciliation to God, and thereby restore humans from their alienation from God. In that regard, human cooperation with God would be curative for humans, relative to human spiritual sickness (see Mark 2:17).

A problem faced by a redemptive God is that many people are not ready or willing to enter into cooperation with God. Their own commitments and plans interfere with such cooperation, and they are aware of this, sometimes painfully (cf. Mark 10:17–27). As a result, God may decide to hide from them for a time, so as not to deepen their antipathy to God or the purposes of God. The problem concerns a refusal to follow Jesus in Gethsemane, where he yielded his will to God, even when **death** was the result. This is more than an intellectual problem; it goes to who one is as a volitional agent before God. As redemptive, God chooses to bob and weave toward humans, looking for a curative opportunity. Accordingly, God is not like the nonpersonal objects of the sciences. God has profound redemptive purposes, and they account for divine hiding, even when humans, like Job, are unable to comprehend those purposes. Cognitive modesty, then, is the order of the day in the area of divine hiddenness.

Paul K. Moser

REFERENCES AND RECOMMENDED READING

Hick, John. 2010. *Evil and the God of Love*. London: Macmillan.
Moser, Paul. 2008. *The Elusive God*. Cambridge: Cambridge University Press.
———. 2010. *The Evidence for God*. Cambridge: Cambridge University Press.
Pascal, Blaise. 2008. *Pensées*. Oxford: Oxford University Press.
Schellenberg, J. L. 2006. *Divine Hiddenness and Human Reason*. Ithaca, NY: Cornell University Press.

HODGE, CHARLES.

HODGE, CHARLES. Historians of science today increasingly recognize the warfare description of the relationship between science and religion during the rise of modernity to be largely a-historical (see **Conflict Thesis**). Nevertheless, few would deny that nineteenth-century tensions surfaced over how best to evaluate and engage with the emergence of **Charles Darwin**'s landmark publication *On the Origin of Species* (1859). Prominent pastor-scholars such as the renowned American theologian and Princeton Seminary professor Charles Hodge (1797–1878) grappled with the complexity of Darwin's observations but not with the opposition that has so often been reported.

Hodge's three-volume *Systematic Theology* (pub. 1872–73) reveals how key aspects of his theology opened the door for conversation with scientific advancement. For example, his defense of the plenary inspiration of Scripture as the work of the Holy Spirit included the denial of dictation theory and the affirmation of human authorship. Consequently, the writers were not infallible in *every* regard and endowed with plenary knowledge of *all* matters, according to Hodge. As God's mouthpiece, Scripture's infallible truth was limited to the purposes of God, a point long held in the Reformed tradition.

With apologetic fervor, Hodge claimed that biblical writers did not rise above their context in unreasonable ways: "Their inspiration no more made them astronomers than it made them agriculturists" (Hodge 1872, 165). In this way, biblical hermeneutics and scientific advancement were both maintained without conflict. Scripture could never contradict the facts of God, only the theories of humanity. For example, Hodge noted that previous generations had once interpreted Scripture according to the Ptolemaic **worldview** until the Copernican system took hold without threat to Scripture.

Although Christians of Hodge's time maintained that the earth originated a mere few thousand years before, Hodge showed no concern if geologists were able to prove that the earth existed much longer than that. He wrote, "It will be found that the first chapter of Genesis is in full accord with the facts, and that the last results of science are embodied on the first page of the Bible. It may cost the Church a severe struggle to give up one interpretation and adopt another, as it did in the seventeenth century, but no real evil need be apprehended. The Bible has stood, and still stands in the presence of the whole scientific world with its claims unshaken" (Hodge 1872, 171).

Soon after, Hodge engaged directly with the theological implications of evolutionary theory in his essay *What Is Darwinianism?* (1874). After summarizing Darwin's laws of heredity, variation, overproduction, and **natural selection**, Hodge granted that Darwin's account of the universe provided a satisfactory explanation of the adaptations of organisms. Instead, Hodge's primary concern was over the claim that purposeful design or telos was absent from biological change (see **Teleology**). For Hodge, a process that functioned blindly according to natural laws and without intention rendered Darwinianism equivalent to atheism. In opposition, Hodge defended the agency of God as Creator of the world and as the governor of all physical **causation** without denying the efficiency of secondary causes in cooperation with God's will (see **Divine Action**). For Hodge, Darwinianism overstepped its disciplinary bounds and evidential support by seeking to answer the question of the origins of the universe.

Overwhelmingly, Hodge's theology was marked by the desire to harmonize science and religion while at the same time maintaining historic Protestant commitments and convictions. Consequently, although Hodge defined theology as an "inductive science" that gathered data from Scripture, he did not turn his back on the Reformed understanding of the Holy Spirit's internal revelation of Scripture's truths. In no uncertain terms, Hodge denounced the growing alienation between the clergy and scientists of his time (Hodge 1874, 126).

Jennifer Powell McNutt

REFERENCES AND RECOMMENDED READING

Battle, John A. 1997. "Charles Hodge, Inspiration, Textual Criticism, and the Princeton Doctrine of Scripture." *WRS Journal* 4 (2): 28–41.
Gundlach, Bradley J. 1997. "McCosh and Hodge on Evolution: A Combined Legacy." *Journal of Presbyterian History* 75 (2): 85–102.
Gutjahr, Paul C. 2011. *Charles Hodge: Guardian of American Orthodoxy.* New York: Oxford University Press.
Hodge, Charles. 1872. *Systematic Theology.* New York: Scribner.
———. 1874. *What Is Darwinianism?* New York: Scribner.
Moore, James. 1979. *The Post-Darwinian Controversies: A Study of the Protestant Struggle to Come to Terms with Darwin in Great Britain and America 1870–1900.* Cambridge: Cambridge University Press.
Stewart, John, and James Moorehead, eds. 2002. *Charles Hodge Revisited: A Critical Appraisal of His Life and Work.* Grand Rapids: Eerdmans.

HOLOGRAPHIC UNIVERSE.

HOLOGRAPHIC UNIVERSE. A *hologram*, as we commonly experience it, is a two-dimensional representation of three-dimensional information in the form of a photograph from which a three-dimensional image can be reconstructed. The principles underlying ordinary holograms were discovered by the Hungarian physicist Dennis Gabor in 1947. The *holographic principle*, in modern **physics**, states that the information contained in any bounded region of space is mathematically equivalent to the information content held on the boundary of that space. More technically, we could say that the information contained in an *n*-dimensional space is isomorphic (can be brought into a structure-preserving one-to-one correspondence) to the information contained on its (*n* − 1)-dimensional bounding surface (for purposes of visualization, think of this as a relationship between the informational content contained in the three-dimensional interior of a sphere and that on the two-dimensional curved surface that constitutes its boundary).

This principle emerged from discussions among theoretical physicists about the fate of the information associated with quantum particles that fall into a black hole, where "black holes" are understood to be objects so massive and dense that nothing, not even light, can escape their gravity. As applied to a black hole, the holographic principle shows that the information associated with quantum particles falling into it is stored on its *event horizon*, namely, the mathematical boundary from inside which nothing can escape the black hole's gravity. This principle was a key to resolving the *black hole information* **paradox**.

In the early 1970s, **Stephen Hawking** showed that because of **Heisenberg's uncertainty principle** in quantum theory (see **Quantum Mechanics, Interpretations of**; **Quantum Physics**), when virtual particle-antiparticle pairs with zero net energy are produced near the event horizon of a black hole, rather than annihilating each other, one can fall in and the other escape, appearing for all practical purposes to have been emitted by the black hole.

This phenomenon is known as "Hawking radiation," and arguably, it has been observed (Unruh 2014). Hawking also showed that, as a black hole emits radiation, its surface area decreases, its temperature rises, and its rate of emission increases. Eventually the black hole "evaporates" as a consequence of this process, and Hawking claimed that when it does, the trapped bits of information from all the particles that have fallen into it are irretrievably lost. This created a problem for quantum theory, which conserves this information as part of the wave function describing how the physical state of these particles develops through time. This tension between black hole evaporation and quantum theory is called the *black hole information paradox*.

Elementary particle and string theorist Leonard Susskind took up Hawking's challenge, arguing that information falling into a black hole is preserved on its surface and eventually emitted as Hawking radiation: it is *not* ultimately lost when a black hole evaporates. With the help of quantum cosmologist and gravitational theorist Don Page, he was able to show that the two perspectives on quantum information were mutually exclusive: *either* the information was lost inside the black hole *or* it could be recovered from Hawking radiation, but these two things could not be true simultaneously.

This theoretical result is called *black hole complementarity* in analogy with **Niels Bohr**'s principle of complementarity in ordinary quantum mechanics, which interprets wave-particle duality in a similar way: quantum behavior manifests itself as waves in certain experimental contexts and as particles in others, but never as both at once. With black hole complementarity in place, what remained to be shown was that information falling into a black hole was preserved on its surface for later release. This was achieved when Susskind, with inspiration from the Dutch physicist Gerard t'Hooft, proved the holographic principle.

But Susskind did not stop here. He went on to speculate that *everything* in the observable universe, including you and me, is a low-energy holographic projection of information encoded on our universe's cosmic horizon (Baggott 2013, 234–60; Susskind 1994; 2008, 290–432). This idea of a *holographic universe* got further attention from subsequent developments in string theory, a branch of theoretical physics that postulates the fundamental constituents of nature are one-dimensional filaments instead of particles (see **String Theory**).

To describe these developments as simply as possible, in the late 1990s, the Argentinian theoretical physicist Juan Maldacena (1998) discovered that one of the five viable classes of string theory (Type IIB) in *n*-dimensional spacetime is mathematically equivalent to a low-energy quantum field theory on its (*n* − 1)-dimensional boundary (technically, this is known as the AdS/CFT duality). What is surprising about this equivalence is that string theory *includes* gravity while quantum field theory does not. Edward Witten, the well-known mathematical physicist at the Institute for Advanced Study in Princeton, then used Maldacena's result to show that a black hole in bulk space-time is equivalent to a "hot soup" of elementary particles on its surface boundary (Witten 1998). This equivalence further solidified Susskind's holographic solution to the black hole information paradox.

The question arises, of course, whether the holographic universe captures the nature of physical reality. Is the universe of our experience an illusion holographically projected from information stored on its boundary surface? There is little reason to think so. Since mathematical symmetry does not mandate causal symmetry, the mathematical equivalence of two representations of the universe allows one to be causally basic and the other a secondary consequence.

While the holographic universe hypothesis takes the boundary information as the fundamental reality, nothing prevents flipping this around so the boundary information is parasitic on the spatial reality of our three-dimensional universe. Nonetheless, if the suggestion that the world of our experience is not physically substantial but rather a holographic projection is taken seriously, it might lend credence to a theistic form of idealism in which the "physical" world of our experience is merely phenomenological and we exist fundamentally as immaterial mental substances whose perceptions of "physical" reality are provided by God. Such a picture of reality would also shed light on the nature of divine omnipresence, omniscience, and omnipotence. While grounding the **metaphysics** of theistic idealism on the holographic principle might be dubious, a stronger basis for it may, in fact, be found in quantum theory itself (see **Idealism**; **Occasionalism**; **Quantum Mechanics, Interpretations of**; see also Gordon 2011, 2013, forthcoming).

Bruce L. Gordon

REFERENCES AND RECOMMENDED READING

Baggott, Jim. 2013. *Farewell to Reality: How Modern Physics Has Betrayed the Search for Scientific Truth.* New York: Pegasus.

Gordon, Bruce. 2011. "A Quantum-Theoretic Argument against Naturalism." In *The Nature of Nature: Examining the Role of Naturalism in Science*, ed. Bruce L. Gordon and William A. Dembski, 179–214. Wilmington, DE: ISI Books.

———. 2013. "In Defense of Uniformitarianism." *Perspectives on Science and Christian Faith* 65 (2): 79–86.

———. Forthcoming. "The Necessity of Sufficiency: The Argument from the Incompleteness of Nature." In *Two Dozen (or So) Arguments for God: The Plantinga Project*, ed. Trent Dougherty and Jerry Walls. Oxford: Oxford University Press.

Maldacena, Juan. 1998. "The Large *N* Limit of Superconformal Field Theories and Supergravity." *Advances in Theoretical and Mathematical Physics* 2:231–52. http://arxiv.org/pdf/hep-th/9711200v3.pdf.

Susskind, Leonard. 1994. "The World as a Hologram." September 28. http://arxiv.org/pdf/hep-th/9409089v2.pdf.

———. 2008. *The Black Hole War: My Battle with Stephen Hawking to Make the World Safe for Quantum Mechanics.* New York: Little, Brown.

Unruh, W. G. 2014. "Has Hawking Radiation Been Measured?" January 26. http://arxiv.org/pdf/1401.6612v1.

Witten, Edward. 1998. "Anti–de Sitter Space and Holography." *Advances in Theoretical and Mathematical Physics* 2:253–91. http://arxiv.org/pdf/hep-th/9802150v2.pdf.

⚓ HOMINID FOSSILS (Evolutionary View). The **fossil record** of our emergence from the great ape lineage is

found in Africa. Here a variety of fossilized skeletal remains from many transitional **species** have been found that illustrate features of the change from walking on four legs to two, from using forelimbs for swinging through trees to using them for the finely tuned manipulation of objects, from small brains to large, and from the face of an ape to the facial features of a human being.

It is one thing, however, to identify transitional features in the fossil record, but it is another to show that their existence was timed in a manner consistent with a progressive sequence from ape to human. Nowhere is the progressive timing of the transitions better documented than in the Great Rift Valley of northeastern Africa where Ethiopia, Kenya, and Tanzania exist today. This valley has come into existence through the geological splitting action caused by two continental plates that have been sliding apart from one another for millions of years. The resulting valley is still subject to flooding just as it has been throughout this span, and animals still get stuck in the muddy flood sediment just as they have for millions of years. After their bodies decay within that mud, the resulting skeletal remains—if undisturbed—are cemented in place. As the sediment continues to harden over future millennia, they will become tomorrow's fossils.

The age of fossils can be readily determined because of another unique geological feature of the region. The geological instability caused by the sliding continental plates results in frequent volcanic eruptions, and this sporadic activity produces precise layers of ash embedded in the sediment just like the fossils. So although the fossils can't be dated, the ash can.

The oldest fairly complete hominin skeleton representing the species, *Ardipithicus ramidus,* nicknamed Ardi, was identified in this region and dated to 4.4 million years ago (MYA). (The term *hominin* refers to members of any species in that lineage, which includes *Homo sapiens* but not the great apes. Some authors use the older term *hominid*.)

The story of Ardi's existence began in November 1994, when a single hand bone was found peeking out of some sedimentary rock. Careful excavation of the site resulted in the recovery of 45 percent of the skeletal remains from one individual, a female. It is likely that Ardi was bipedal like us. She certainly didn't have the skeletal features that would have enabled her to be a knuckle-walker like chimpanzees and gorillas. Instead, she had features that pointed to a lifestyle adapted to both trees and ground (Lovejoy 2009, 72). Like today's great apes, she had a splayed big toe that would have served well in tree climbing. She had hands and arms that were well suited for life in the trees as well. There is no sign of stone tools at any of the many archaeological sites of this age or even up to a million years later (Harmand et al. 2015, 310–15), so it is unlikely that members of her species were using tools.

Although *Ardipithicus* is the most complete early hominin fossil found to date, there are several other specimens less complete and not discussed here that are a million or so years older. What is especially important to note is that the first sign of hominin fossils takes place beginning about 5 to 6 million years ago. This represents only the last 0.1 percent of earth's history. The rocks of the entire 99.9 percent of earlier history, despite widespread geological analysis, have never yielded any hominin bones or stone tools. Furthermore, despite geological surveys the world over, no hominin fossil other than those representing our own genus, *Homo,* has ever been found on any other continent than Africa and, more specifically, the eastern and southern part of Africa. Thus paleontologists conclude that there was a highly specific period of time when, and a single area of the world where, hominins originated.

Although the record is sparse prior to 3.8 MYA, the situation changes dramatically after that. In studies covering the next 2 million years, thousands of fossils from hundreds of individuals representing almost a dozen species have been found. The genus *Australopithicus* predominates throughout this period, and *Australopithicus afarensis,* one of five species, is the most thoroughly represented and studied. Investigators have found several fairly complete specimens of *A. afarensis* (the well-known Lucy is one) spanning the interval of 3.8 to 2.9 MYA, after which the species is never found again.

The shinbone of *A. afarensis* was structured such that it would have attached to the ankle in a manner that resembled how ours is attached rather than in the way it is joined in the chimpanzee. Moreover, the structure of the ankle is humanlike. On the other hand, the face was apelike with a flattened nose and strongly protruding lower jaw. The brain was about one third the size of ours. The shoulder blade was not humanlike; rather, it resembled that of a gorilla. In short, *A. afarensis* had a body that would have been well adapted for an existence in trees as well as on the ground. Interestingly, the hyoid bone, a part of the voice box, was structured in a manner that is much closer to that of a gorilla than a human, and this suggests that Lucy and her kin had apelike vocal abilities (Tattersall 2015).

Beginning at 2.5-million-year-old sites, fossils from a set of species representing a genus closely related to *Australopithecus*

appear at certain sites. Their genus, *Paranthropis,* (represented by three species) is noted for its robust characteristics. Individuals had larger, tougher teeth, a bigger area for attachment of its presumptively huge chewing muscles, and a large face. They also shared many characteristics in common with the Australopiths and indeed were earlier placed within that genus. Since the *Paranthropis* species have a number of new anatomical features not found in our lineage, most investigators believe they are a group of cousin species—a side branch—not on the direct lineage to *Homo.* The fossil record for members of this genus ceases at 1.2 MYA.

Although the anatomical features of *Ardipithicus* strongly suggest that bipedality arose early in hominin history—at least 4.4 MYA—the most poignant demonstration of bipedality comes from a set of 3.6-million-year-old footprints of two individuals extending over a distance of about 80 feet in what would have been wet volcanic ash. The big toe was almost parallel to the other toes; it was not splayed outward as with Ardi. Detailed analysis of the gait of the pair indicates that they walked in a manner almost indistinguishable from us. The footprints likely belonged to Lucy's species, especially given that *A. afarensis* fossils were found nearby in the same layer of volcanic ash.

Our genus, *Homo,* enters the fossil record with a whimper, not a bang. All we have so far from 2.8 MYA to 1.9 MYA are two independent finds from Ethiopia—portions of the *Homo* jaw—one from a 2.8 MYA site (Callaway 2015; Gibbons 2015) and the other dated at 2.3 MYA (Kimbel et al. 1997, 235–62). The whimper changes dramatically at 1.9 MYA, when *Homo* begins to predominate the hominin fossil record. As Homo emerges, *Australopithicus* fades from the fossil scene (the last find is at a site precisely dated at 1.98 MYA). *Paranthropis* persists as a side branch up to 1.2 MYA.

Homo is generally defined by a larger brain, a narrower, less stocky body shape, shorter arms, and longer legs. It is not currently possible to define a specific trajectory to the various *Homo* species, in part because it seems likely that the genus originated well before the fossils became abundant. If further fossil finds confirm and extend the finding of a *Homo* jaw at 2.8 MYA, then that would mean we currently have a 900,000-year period where *Homo* existed but almost no fossils have been found.

As *Homo* becomes well established in the fossil record beginning 1.9 MYA, two species, *Homo habilis* and *Homo rudolfensis,* stand out as being the most primitive (i.e., Australopithicus-like). The somewhat more "derived" (less primitive) *Homo erectus* appears at other locations at just about the same time. It seems likely that there were as many as three lineages of *Homo* present in Africa during this period, along with certain species of *Australopithicus* and *Paranthropis* that had not yet gone extinct.

Almost simultaneous with the appearance of *Homo erectus* in Africa's fossil beds, the same species (or a closely related variety of it) emerges onto the fossil scene in Asia. Initially represented by five skulls—the oldest of which is dated at 1.85 MYA—at a cave in Dmanisi, Republic of Georgia (Lordkipandze et al. 2013, 326–31), its fossils are also represented at 1.6-million-year-old sites near Beijing in China and in Indonesia. Indeed, *H. erectus* (or closely related varieties) persisted in parts of Asia until at least a few hundred thousand years ago and possibly even longer. (Some recent finds in an isolated region of southwest China suggest the species may have persisted until 14,000 years ago [Cumoe et al. 2015].) So the geographic distribution of *Homo erectus*—from various locations in Africa to many parts of Asia—was widespread. Throughout the first million years of the existence of this species, the brain size was gradually increasing. Most of the earliest recovered skulls indicate a brain size only slightly larger than that of apes. However, over time there was a gradual increase in brain volume until it eventually reached a volume close to that of our own (Schoenemann 2013, 136–64).

In September 2015 the largest and most complete find ever for any hominin species, *Homo naledi* was announced (Berger et al. 2015). This species, found in a South African cave, bears considerable resemblance to *Australopithicus* with its small brain, archaic pelvis, shoulder, and rib cage. However, its hand, wrist, foot, and ankle are quite similar to our own. At this writing, the specimens remain undated, but given the primitive, australopithecine-like sections of the anatomy, it seems likely that they lived near the time of the transition from *Australopithicus* to *Homo*—perhaps 2.5 to 2 MYA. Anatomical features alone, however, are insufficient to give anything more than a fairly speculative estimate of their age.

Our own species, *Homo sapiens*, first appears in the Rift Valley fossil record at a site dated at 195,000 years ago (YA). Preceding this, another species, *Homo heidelbergensis*, lived from about 700,000 to 200,000 YA, and many investigators consider it to have been an ancestral species of our own. *H. heidelbergensis* is represented in the fossil record as far south as South Africa, as far north as England and Germany, and as far east as China. Indeed, as a result of work just reported in 2015, we now have a significant amount of the **DNA** coding **information** from one set of 300,000-year-old *H. heidelbergensis* bones (Gibbons 2015, 1270).

Beginning about the same time as modern humans (*H. sapiens*) appear in the fossil record in the Great Rift Valley region of Africa, the Neanderthals (*Homo neanderthalensis*) emerge in the fossil record at various locations in Europe and western Asia. Unlike as with our species, however, the Neanderthal fossil record ceases abruptly 39,000 YA. The DNA of this species has recently been isolated from fossils and fully sequenced. Amazingly, we now know that, depending on our ethnic heritage, many of us have genetic traits not derived from the original *H. sapiens*, but from *H. neanderthalensis*. On average those whose lineage traces back to outside of Africa contain about 2 percent Neanderthal DNA as a result of interspecies mating that took place about 50,000 years ago as our species moved into Neanderthal territory. Indeed, investigators have a fossil from an *H. sapiens* individual who, based on DNA sequence, had a Neanderthal great-grandparent four to six generations back (Fu 2015, 216–19).

Based on the many artifacts found at Neanderthal archaeological sites, it is clear that they were skilled and intelligent hunters, equipped to survive the arctic conditions of the ice age. However, they showed little sign of creative activity. Based on analysis of the extensive artifacts at Neanderthal sites, their cognition was much different than ours, and they likely lacked the ability to use symbols for even relatively simple logic-based activity.

One of the most important finds of the past 15 years was the discovery of a diminutive hominin species that lived on an island called Flores in the Indonesian archipelago up to about 12,000 YA (Brown et al. 2004, 1055–61). Fossils of the species, *Homo florisiensis*, date back 100,000 years, and stone tools date to 800,000 YA. This ancient presence, together with the highly primitive anatomical characteristics of the fossils, has led to the conclusion that an early *Homo* species colonized the island over 1 MYA and then, being isolated, underwent substantial change to become its own unique species. Diminished size is frequently a manifestation of that which happens on an isolated island where predators are no longer present and large size is no longer an advantage. An extinct tiny species of the elephant family was also found in the fossil record there.

Although the 2004 discovery of *H. florisiensis* was remarkable, equally stunning was the discovery of yet another heretofore-unknown species, *Homo denisova*, which lived in Asia until at least 50,000 YA (Sawyer et al. 2015). This species is known not through its anatomical characteristics (all that we have are two molar teeth and a portion of a finger bone) but through its DNA. We never would have known about the existence of this species had it not been for the fact that its genetic information was extracted from those three tiny fossils. When analyzed, the genome proved to be much different than that of Neanderthals and our own species. The analysis showed that all three hominin species have descended from a single ancestral species that existed about 700,000 years ago.

All of this illustrates one of the most important points to emerge from paleoanthropology. Although we have thousands of fossils from a time period spanning 6 million years, it is clear that our understanding of hominin history is fragmentary. Our own history is by far the best studied and is the most complete paleontological record of any other species on earth—but still, all we have is a set of isolated snapshots. Fossilization is a very rare event, and all we can expect from those snapshots are little glimpses into the album of hominin history. This is something that we have known for a long time—many highly specific conditions have to be met for the bones of an animal to be preserved and subsequently discovered. This is why we essentially do not even have snapshots of the lineage leading to today's great apes, for example. Their ancestors lived in jungles, a habitat that is notoriously fruitless in fossil preservation.

So the remarkable thing about the hominin lineage is not the many gaps—they are to be expected—rather, it is the many snapshots and just how far those glimpses have enabled our knowledge to move forward despite the expected incompleteness of the fossil record. For at least the first 800,000 years of *Homo* existence (beginning at 2.8 MYA) all we have to show for it so far are two jaw fragments. Similarly, our own cousin species, the Denisovans, coexisted with our species in Asia for tens of thousands of years, but all the fossils we have are two teeth and one part of a tiny finger bone. Given this sparseness, we know for certain that there was much going on that we don't know about. But the most amazing thing of all is how much we do know, and the number conclusions so solid they verge on certainty.

Given the gaps in the fossil record, some Christians propose that the many hominin species are independent *ex nihilo* creation events. However, it is not just bones that provide evidence for **common ancestry** anymore. DNA allows investigators to trace the ancestry of the species from whom the bones were derived. By tracing both DNA and anatomical changes back over 300,000 years so far, the case for common ancestry is considered to be essentially certain by virtually all paleoanthropologists and paleogeneticists. This does not in any way imply that the activity of our Creator is somehow removed as the ultimate and ever-present causal agent. What it demonstrates is that creation is a gradual process.

The God of the Bible—of Christian theology—frequently takes much time to carry out his purposes. Events are not less a response to divine purpose and direction when they take place gradually rather than instantaneously.

As we examine the creation pathway that led to humankind, we are drawn to worship. Like David as he reflected on the natural world, we share his awe: "When I look at your heavens, the work of your fingers, the moon and the stars that you have established; what are human beings that you are mindful of them, mortals that you care for them? Yet you have made them a little lower than God, and crowned them with glory and honor" (Ps. 8:3–5 NRSV).

Nothing has been discovered to change that. Indeed, the discoveries ought only to enhance and enrich our sense of awe as we observe nature with the same reverent attitude as David. As biological knowledge advances every day, we see more clearly now than ever before just how "fearfully and wonderfully made" we really are.

Darrel R. Falk

REFERENCES AND RECOMMENDED READING

Berger, L., et al. 2015. "*Homo Naledi*: A New Species of the Genus *Homo* from the Dinaledi Chamber, South Africa." *eLife* 4:e09560.

Brown, P., T. Sutikna, M. J. Morwood, et al. 2004. "A New Small-Bodied Hominin from the Late Pleistocene of Flores, Indonesia." *Nature* 431:1055–61.

Callaway, Ewen. 2015. "Ethiopian Jawbone May Mark Dawn of Humankind." *Nature* (March 4). doi:10.1038/nature.2015.17039.

Curnoe, Darren, Ji Xueping, Wu Liu, et al. 2015. "A Hominin Femur with Archaic Affinities from the Late Pleistocene of Southwest China." *PLOS ONE* (December 17). doi:10.1371/journal.pone.0143332.

Falk, Dean. 2011. *The Fossil Chronicles: How Two Controversial Discoveries Changed Our View of Human Evolution.* Berkeley: University of California Press.

Fu, Qiaomai, Mateja Hajdinjak, et al. 2015. "An Early Modern Human from Romania with a Recent Neanderthal Ancestor." *Nature* 524:216–19.

Gibbons, Ann. 2015. "Deep Roots for the Genus *Homo*." *Science* 349:1056–57.

———. 2015. "Humanity's Long, Lonely Road." *Science* 349:1270.

Harmand, Sonia, Jason E. Lewis, Craig S. Feibel, et al. 2015. "3.3-Million-Year-Old Stone Tools from Lomekwi 3, West Turkana, Kenya." *Nature* 310:310–15.

Kimbel, W. H., Donald C. Johansen, and Yoel Rak. 1997. "Systematic Assessment of a Maxilla of *Homo* from Hadar, Ethiopia." *American Journal of Physical Anthropology* 103:235–62.

Lordkipanidze, David, Marcia S. Ponce de León, Ann Margvelashvili, et al. 2013. "A Complete Skull from Dmanisi, Georgia, and the Evolutionary Biology of Early *Homo*." *Science* 342:326–31.

Lovejoy, C. Owen, Bruce Latimer, Gen Suwa, et al. 2009. "Combining Prehension and Propulsion: The Foot of *Ardipithecus ramidu*." *Science* 326:72.

Sawyer, Susanna, Gabriel Renaud, Bence Viola, et al. 2015. "Nuclear and Mitochondrial DNA Sequences from Two Denisovan Individuals." *Proceedings of the National Academy of Sciences* 112, no. 51 (December 22). doi:10.1073/pnas.1519905112.

Schoenemann, P. Thomas. 2013. "Hominid Brain Evolution." In *A Companion to Paleoanthropology*, ed. D. R. Begun, 136–64. Chichester, UK: Wiley-Blackwell.

Smithsonian Human Origins website. http://humanorigins.si.edu/evidence/human-fossils.

Tattersall, Ian. 2015. *The Strange Case of the Rickety Cossack*. New York: Palgrave, Macmillan.

Wood, Bernard, and Nicholas Lonergan. 2008. "The Hominin Fossil Record: Taxa, Grades and Clades." *Journal of Anatomy* 212:354–76. www.ncbi.nlm.nih.gov/pmc/articles/PMC2409102/pdf/joa0212–0354.pdf.

☙ HOMINID FOSSILS (Unique-Origin View).

Paleoanthropologists have discovered an impressive diversity of hominid fossils over the past century, leading to numerous assertions that our own **species**, *Homo sapiens*, is descended from ape-like ancestors. Yet hominid fossils generally fall into one of two groups: apelike species and humanlike species, with a large, unbridged gap between them. There are arguably no fossils documenting a transition from apelike hominids to the humanlike members of the genus *Homo*.

The Fragmented Hominid Fossil Record

Terminology in paleoanthropology is sometimes used inconsistently, which can lead to confusion. Strictly speaking, hominids are members of the family *Hominidae*, which includes the great apes, humans, and any organisms tracing back to their most recent supposed common ancestor. However, "hominid" is also often used as a synonym for "hominin," which means any organisms on the branch that includes humans, tracing back to our most recent supposed common ancestor with chimpanzees (*Pan*), and excluding the branch that led to chimps. Following White et al. 2009, this essay will define "hominid" in the latter sense.

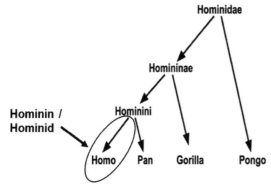

Figure 1. Definition of hominid

The hominid fossil record is fragmented in multiple senses, making it difficult to bolster any evolutionary account of human origins.

First, the record itself is fragmented. Hominid fossils are rare, and long periods of time often exist for which there are few fossils (Gibbons 2002, 2011a; Kimbel 2013). So sparse is the data that according to **Richard Lewontin** (1995), "When we consider the remote past, before the origin of the actual species *Homo sapiens*, we are faced with a fragmentary and disconnected fossil record. Despite the excited and optimistic claims that have been made by some paleontologists, no fossil hominid species can be established as our direct ancestor."

Similarly, a major 2015 review of hominin evolution laments "the dearth of unambiguous evidence for ancestor-descendant lineages," and concedes, "The evolutionary sequence for the majority of hominin lineages is unknown. Most hominin taxa, particularly early hominins, have no obvious ancestors, and in most cases ancestor-descendant sequences (fossil time series) cannot be reliably constructed" (Wood and Grabowski 2015).

A second challenge is the fragmented nature of the specimens themselves. The vast majority of hominid specimens consist of a few bone fragments, making it difficult to make definitive conclusions about their morphology, behavior, and relationships. As Stephen Jay Gould noted, "Most hominid fossils, even though they serve as a basis for endless speculation and elaborate storytelling, are fragments of jaws and scraps of skulls" (Gould 1980).

A third difficulty is accurately reconstructing the behavior, intelligence, or internal morphology of extinct organisms (De Waal 2001). The famed Harvard physical anthropologist Earnest Hooton presciently warned, "Alleged restorations of ancient types of man have very little, if any, scientific value and are likely only to mislead the public" (Hooton 1946).

Because of the fragmented data and the emotional nature of the topic of human origins, the field of evolutionary paleoanthropology itself is fragmented. An article in *Science* titled "The Politics of Paleoanthropology" acknowledges that "the primary scientific evidence" used "to construct man's evolutionary history" is "extremely paltry" and "a pitifully small array of bones," making it "difficult to separate the personal from the scientific disputes raging in the field" (Holden 1981). Henry Gee describes the situation thusly: "Fossil evidence of human evolutionary history is fragmentary and open to various interpretations" (Gee 2001).

The Standard Story of Human Evolutionary Origins

Despite the widespread disagreements and controversies, a standard account of human origins is retold in countless textbooks, museum displays, and news media articles. A typical hominid phylogeny is portrayed below.

Starting with the early hominins at the bottom left of figure 2, and moving upward through the australopithecines, and then into members of the genus *Homo*, this essay will review key fossil evidence and find that it does not support the claim that humans evolved from apelike precursors. Many if not most of the scientists cited in this essay accept some evolutionary account of human origins, but their opinions on crucial portions of that story show that this standard story has many scientific problems. This is not merely criticism for the sake of criticism. As will be demonstrated, in a crucial part of the standard evolutionary tree—precisely where humanlike members of *Homo* arise—we see a distinct break in the fossil evidence that fails to show that humans evolved from apelike creatures.

Early Hominids

Sahelanthropus tchadensis (the "Toumai skull") is known only from one skull and some jaw fragments from 6 to 7 million years ago (MYA), but it has been called the oldest known hominid that lies on the human line. Not everyone agrees. When the fossil was first reported, some researchers suggested it was a gorilla skull (BBC News 2002). One *Nature* article links the specimen with chimpanzees and gorillas, calling *Sahelanthropus* "an ape" (Wolpoff et al. 2002).

Orrorin tugensis was a chimpanzee-sized primate known from "an assortment of bone fragments," including pieces of the arm, thigh, and lower jaw, as well as some teeth (Potts and Sloan 2010). Despite initial reports calling it "the earliest known ancestor of the human family" capable of bipedal (upright walking) locomotion (Wilford 2001), a later commentary admitted, "There is currently precious little evidence bearing on how *Orrorin* moved" (Sarmiento et al. 2007).

Unveiled in 2009, *Ardipithecus ramidus*, or "Ardi," was named "breakthough of the year" by *Science* because it

Figure 2. A standard phylogeny of hominids/hominins. (Gibbons 2009b; Leakey and Walker 2003; Potts and Sloan 2010; Zimmer 2005)

Illustration: Jonathan Jones

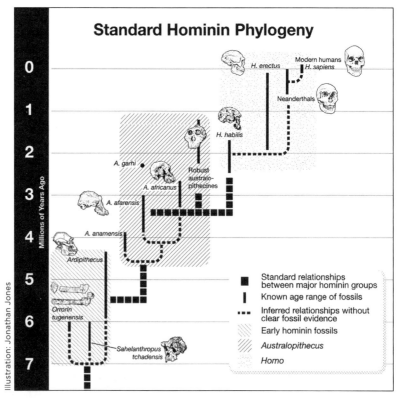

apparently represented an upright-walking human ancestor—the "Rosetta stone for understanding bipedalism" (Gibbons 2002, 2009a, 2009b). Claims about bipedal locomotion require precise measurements of key bones like the pelvis, but various articles reported Ardi's bones were "chalky," "distorted," "crushed nearly to smithereens," "so fragile they would turn to dust at a touch," and needed "extensive digital reconstruction" (Gibbons 2002; Lemonick and Dorfman 2009; Shreeve 2009). In particular, Ardi's pelvis initially "looked like an Irish stew" (Lemonick and Dorfman 2009). After morphological and cladistics reanalyses, paleoanthropologists have challenged claims of Ardi's bipedality, and there is no consensus that she was a human ancestor (Gibbons 2009b; Harrell 2010; New York University 2011; Sarmiento 2010; Sarmiento and Meldrum 2011; Wilford 2010; Wood and Harrison 2011). One paleoanthropologist "regards the hype around Ardi to have been overblown" (Harrell 2010).

The Australopithecines

Australopithecus (literally "southern ape") is a genus of extinct hominids that lived in Africa from about 1–4 MYA. While a majority of evolutionary paleoanthropologists believe the australopithecines were ancestral to humans, controversy remains over whether they were upright-walking ancestors of *Homo*.

The four most commonly accepted australopithecine species are *afarensis*, *africanus*, *robustus*, and *boisei*. *Robustus* and *boisei* are larger boned and thought to belong to an extinct lineage. The smaller "gracile" forms, *africanus* and *afarensis* (which includes the famous fossil "Lucy"), lived earlier and are often said to be ancestral to humans.

Lucy is one of the most complete known pre-*Homo* hominid fossils, although only 40 percent of her skeleton was found. She is often claimed to have been a bipedal hominid with a chimp-like head—an ideal precursor to humans. But there are good reasons for skepticism.

Many have claimed Lucy's pelvis supports bipedal locomotion, but her discoverers reported it was "badly crushed" with "distortion" and "cracking" (Johanson et al. 1982), and one paper argues her pelvis appears humanlike because of "error in the reconstruction" (Marchal 2000). A lack of fossil data prevents firm conclusions about Lucy's mode of locomotion (Abitbol 1995). One *Nature* paper found that much of her body was "quite apelike," with hand bones indicating she "'knuckle-walked, as chimps and gorillas do today'" (Collard and Aiello 2000).

Another *Nature* paper found that the australopithecine

skeleton is most like that of an orangutan, and questioned whether "any of the australopithecines is a direct part of human ancestry" (Oxnard 1975). All told, various studies have found that the arms, hand bones, abdomen, fingers, shoulders, striding gait, brain size, toes, chest, teeth, inner-ear canals, developmental patterns, and tree-dwelling ecological habits of australopithecines are unlike humans and more like apes (Collard and Aiello 2000; Leakey and Lewin 1993; Spoor et al. 1994).

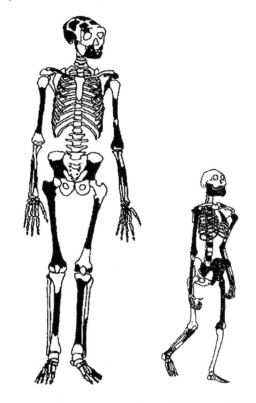

Figure 3. A comparison of *Australopithecus* (right) to early *Homo* (left). Shaded bones are those that have been found.

Illustration from figure 1, John Hawks et al., "Population Bottlenecks and Pleistocene Human Evolution," *Molecular Biology and Evolution*, copyright 2000, 17 (1): 2–22, by permission of the Society for Molecular Biology and Evolution.

Some maintain that a recently discovered species, *Australopithecus sediba*, was ancestral to *Homo* (Pickering et al. 2011). Critics respond that it postdates the appearance of *Homo*, and leading paleoanthropologists doubt it was a human ancestor (Gibbons 2011a; White 2013). A *Nature* study of *sediba*'s anatomy found it was not ancestral to humans, concluding, "The evolutionary events that led to the origin of the *Homo* lineage are an enduring puzzle in paleoanthropology" (Kimbel 2013). Another paleoanthropologist called it "way too primitive to be the ancestor of the human genus *Homo*" and warned the fossil's "discovery is surrounded by hype and over-interpretation" (Macknight 2010). Commenting on *sediba*, Harvard paleoanthropologist Daniel Lieberman stated, "The origins of the genus *Homo* remain as murky as ever" (Zimmer 2010), and Donald Johanson (Lucy's discoverer) lamented, "The transition to *Homo* continues to be almost totally confusing" (Balter 2010).

Evolutionary anthropologist Leslie Aiello observed, "Australopithecines are like apes, and the *Homo* group are like humans. Something major occurred when *Homo* evolved, and it wasn't just in the brain" (Leakey and Lewin 1993). The something major was the abrupt appearance of the human body plan — without direct evolutionary precursors — in the fossil record.

A Big Bang Theory of *Homo*

If humans evolved from apelike creatures, what were the transitional species between the apelike hominids just discussed and the truly humanlike members of the genus *Homo*? There are no good fossil candidates.

Many have cited *Homo habilis*, dated at about 1.9 MYA as a transitional species between the australopithecines and our genus *Homo*, but chronologically, *habilis* cannot be a "link" because it postdates the earliest fossil evidence of true *Homo*, from about 2 MYA (Spoor et al. 2007).

Morphological analyses further confirm that *habilis* is an unlikely candidate for an "intermediate" between *Australopithecus* and *Homo*. An authoritative review in *Science* found that *habilis* is different from *Homo* in terms of body size, body shape, locomotion, jaws, teeth, developmental patterns, and brain size, and should be reclassified within *Australopithecus* (Wood and Collard 1999). Another paper noted that *habilis* "matured and moved less like a human and more like an australopithecine," with a dietary range "more like Lucy's" (Gibbons 2011b). An analysis of habiline ear canals found that its skull is most similar to baboons and suggested it "relied less on bipedal behaviour than the australopithecines," making it "an unlikely intermediate" (Spoor et al. 1994). Another study found *habilis* was *more* similar to living apes than were australopithecines like Lucy, and concluded, "It is difficult

to accept an evolutionary sequence in which *Homo habilis*, with less human-like locomotor adaptations, is intermediate between *Australopithecus afaren[s]is* ... and fully bipedal *Homo erectus*" (Hartwig-Scherer and Martin 1991).

One coauthor called those results "unexpected in view of previous accounts of *Homo habilis* as a link between australopithecines and humans" (Hartwig-Scherer 1998).

Without *habilis* as an intermediate, it is difficult to find fossil hominids to serve as direct transitional forms between the australopithecines and *Homo*. Rather, the fossil record shows dramatic and abrupt changes that correspond to the appearance of *Homo*.

A study of pelvic bones proposed "a period of very rapid evolution corresponding to the **emergence** of the genus *Homo*" (Marchal 2000). Likewise, about 2 MYA, "cranial capacity in *Homo* began a dramatic trajectory" that resulted in an "approximate doubling in brain size." (Falk 1998). Wood and Collard (1999) found that only one single trait of one hominid species qualified as "intermediate" between *Australopithecus* and *Homo*: the brain size of *Homo erectus*. Yet brain size is a complex trait, often unrelated to intelligence, and of unclear evolutionary significance (Deacon 1997; Molnar 2002; Wood and Collard 1999). A few skulls of intermediate size do little to bolster the case for **human evolution**.

A paper in the *Journal of Molecular Biology and Evolution* found that *Homo* and *Australopithecus* differ significantly in brain size, dental function, increased cranial buttressing, expanded body height, visual, and respiratory changes and stated: "We, like many others, interpret the anatomical evidence to show that early *H. sapiens* was significantly and dramatically different from ... australopithecines in virtually every element of its skeleton and every remnant of its behavior" (Hawks et al. 2000).

Noting these many changes, the study called the origin of humans "a real acceleration of evolutionary change from the more slowly changing pace of australopithecine evolution" and stated that such a transformation would have included radical changes: "The anatomy of the earliest *H. sapiens* sample indicates significant modifications of the ancestral genome and is not simply an extension of evolutionary trends in an earlier australopithecine lineage." These rapid changes are termed "a genetic revolution" where "no australopithecine species is obviously transitional" (Hawks et al. 2000).

Three Harvard paleoanthropologists confirm the lack of evidence for a transition from *Australopithecus* to *Homo*: "The transition from *Australopithecus* to *Homo* was undoubtedly one of the most critical in its magnitude and consequences.

As with many key evolutionary events, there is both good and bad news. First, the bad news is that many details of this transition are obscure because of the paucity of the fossil and archaeological records" (Lieberman et al. 2009).

As for the good news, the authors admit: "Although we lack many details about exactly how, when, and where the transition occurred from *Australopithecus* to *Homo*, we have sufficient data from before and after the transition to make some inferences about the overall nature of key changes that did occur" (Lieberman et al. 2009). Essentially, the fossil record shows apelike australopithecines ("before"), and humanlike *Homo* ("after"), but not fossils documenting a transition between them. In the absence of intermediates, we are left with inferences of a transition based strictly on the assumption of evolution—that an undocumented transition must have occurred somehow, sometime, and someplace.

Likewise, evolutionary biologist Ernst Mayr recognized our abrupt appearance: "The earliest fossils of *Homo, Homo rudolfensis* and *Homo erectus*, are separated from *Australopithecus* by a large, unbridged gap. How can we explain this seeming saltation? Not having any fossils that can serve as missing links, we have to fall back on the time-honored method of historical science, the construction of a historical narrative" (Mayr 2004).

The evidence shows a "big bang" appearance of our genus *Homo* in the hominid fossil record (University of Michigan News Service 2000).

All in the Family

In contrast to the australopithecines, the major members of *Homo*—such as *erectus* and the Neanderthals (*Homo neanderthalensis*)—are very similar to modern humans. Several paleoanthropologists have classified them as members of our own species, *Homo sapiens* (Hawks et al. 2000; Luskin 2012).

Homo erectus means "upright man," and below the neck they were extremely similar to modern humans (Hartwig-Scherer and Martin 1991). While the average brain size of *Homo erectus* is smaller than modern humans, it is well within the range of normal human variation (Luskin 2012; Molnar 1998; Wood and Collard 1999). Donald Johanson suggests that if *erectus* were alive today, it could reproduce with modern humans, and we would be members of the same species (Johanson and Edey 1981).

Though Neanderthals have been stereotyped as bungling, primitive precursors to modern humans, they were so similar to us that if a Neanderthal walked down the street, you probably wouldn't notice the differences. Neanderthal body shape was "within the range of variation seen in modern humans" (Wood and Collard 1999), and their mean brain size was actually slightly larger than modern humans (Molnar 2002). Paleoanthropologist Erik Trinkaus argues, "They may have had heavier brows or broader noses or stockier builds, but behaviorally, socially and reproductively they were all just people" (Lemonick 1999). Archaeologist Francesco d'Errico concurs: "Neanderthals were using **technology** as advanced as that of contemporary anatomically modern humans and were using symbolism in much the same way" (Alper 2003). While some paleoanthropologists disagree, the presence of "morphological mosaic" skeletons suggest that Neanderthals and modern humans "are members of the same species who interbred freely" (Trinkaus and Duarte 2003). Contrary to popular perceptions, Neanderthals do not show we are related to some nonhumanlike species.

According to Siegrid Hartwig-Scherer, differences between these humanlike members of the genus *Homo* can be explained as microevolutionary effects of "size variation, climatic stress, genetic drift and differential expression of [common] genes" (Hartwig-Scherer 1998). These small-scale differences do not demonstrate humans evolving from more primitive apelike creatures.

Conclusion

While the hominid fossil record is marked by incomplete and fragmented fossils, the evidence shows that our genus *Homo* appears abruptly, without transitional forms from apelike species. Unambiguous members of the genus *Homo* are very similar to modern humans, and their differences entail small-scale microevolutionary changes. The standard neo-Darwinian evolutionary view that humans evolved from apelike ancestors requires inferences that go beyond the evidence and is not supported by the hominid fossil record.

Of course there is room for healthy disagreement among Christians on these questions. But evolutionary creationists and theistic evolutionists who believe humans evolved from apelike species should temper their rhetoric in light of the evidence and use caution and humility rather than simply adopting the standard evolutionary view and then adamantly asserting that the church should accept it.

Casey Luskin

REFERENCES AND RECOMMENDED READING

Abitbol, M. Maurice. 1995. "Lateral View of *Australopithecus Afarensis*: Primitive Aspects of Bipedal Positional Behavior in the Earliest Hominids." *Journal of Human Evolution* 28:211–29.

Aguirre, Emilio. 1994. "*Homo Erectus* and *Homo Sapiens*: One or More Species?" In *100 Years of Pithecanthropus: The Homo Erectus Problem 171 Courier Forschungsinstitut Senckenberg*, ed. Jens Lorenz, 333–39. Frankfurt: Courier Forschungsinstitut Senckenberg.

Alper, Joe. 2003. "Rethinking Neanderthals." *Smithsonian*. June. www.smithsonianmag.com/science-nature/rethinking-neanderthals–83341003/.

Balter, Michael. 2010. "Candidate Human Ancestor from South Africa Sparks Praise and Debate." *Science* 328:154–55.

BBC News. 2002. "Skull Find Sparks Controversy." *BBC News*, July 12. http://news.bbc.co.uk/2/hi/science/nature/2125244.stm.

Clarke, Ronald J., and Phillip V. Tobias. 1995. "Sterkfontein Member 2 Foot Bones of the Oldest South African Hominid." *Science* 269:521–24.

Collard, Mark, and Leslie C. Aiello. 2000. "From Forelimbs to Two Legs." *Nature* 404:339–40.

Deacon, Terrence W. 1997. "What Makes the Human Brain Different?" *Annual Review of Anthropology* 26:337–57.

De Waal, Frans B. M. 2001. "Apes from Venus: Bonobos and Human Social Evolution." In *Tree of Origin: What Primate Behavior Can Tell Us about Human Social Evolution*, ed. Frans B. M. de Waal, 39–69. Cambridge, MA: Harvard University Press.

Falk, Dean. 1998. "Hominid Brain Evolution: Looks Can Be Deceiving." *Science* 280:1714.

Gee, Henry. 2001. "Return to the Planet of the Apes." *Nature* 412:131–32.

Gibbons, Ann. 2002. "In Search of the First Hominids." *Science* 295:1214–19.

———. 2009a. "Breakthrough of the Year: *Ardipithecus ramidus*." *Science* 326:1598–99.

———. 2009b. "A New Kind of Ancestor: *Ardipithecus* Unveiled." *Science* 326:36–40.

———. 2011a. "Skeletons Present an Exquisite Paleo-Puzzle." *Science* 333:1370–72.

———. 2011b. "Who Was *Homo Habilis*—and Was It Really *Homo*?" *Science* 332:1370–71.

Gould, Stephen Jay. 1980. *The Panda's Thumb: More Reflections in Natural History*. New York: W. W. Norton.

Harrell, Eben. 2010. "Ardi: The Human Ancestor Who Wasn't?" *Time*. May 27. http://content.time.com/time/health/article/0,8599,1992115,00.html.

Hartwig-Scherer, Sigrid. 1998. "Apes or Ancestors?" In *Mere Creation: Science, Faith and Intelligent Design*, ed. William Dembski, 212–35. Downers Grove, IL: InterVarsity.

Hartwig-Scherer, Sigrid, and Robert D. Martin. 1991. "Was 'Lucy' More Human Than Her 'Child'? Observations on Early Hominid Postcranial Skeletons." *Journal of Human Evolution* 21:439–49.

Hawks, John, Keith Hunley, Sang-Hee Lee, and Milford Wolpoff. 2000. "Population Bottlenecks and Pleistocene Human Evolution." *Journal of Molecular Biology and Evolution* 17 (1): 2–22.

Holden, Constance. 1981. "The Politics of Paleoanthropology." *Science* 213:737–40.

Hooton, Earnest Albert. 1946. *Up from the Ape*. Rev. ed. New York: Macmillan.

Johanson, Donald C., and Maitland Edey. 1981. *Lucy: The Beginnings of Humankind*. New York: Simon & Schuster.

Johanson, Donald C., C. Owen Lovejoy, William H. Kimbel, Tim D. White, Steven C. Ward, Michael E. Bush, Bruce M. Latimer, and Yves Coppens. 1982. "Morphology of the Pliocene Partial Hominid Skeleton (A.L. 288–1) from the Hadar Formation, Ethiopia." *American Journal of Physical Anthropology* 57:403–51.

Kimbel, William H. 2013. "Hesitation on Hominin History." *Nature* 497:573–74.

Leakey, Meave, and Alan Walker. 2003. "Early Hominid Fossils from Africa." *Scientific American* 13 (2): 14–19.

Leakey, Richard, and Roger Lewin. 1993. *Origins Reconsidered: In Search of What Makes Us Human*. New York: Anchor.

Lemonick, Michael D. 1999. "A Bit of Neanderthal in Us All?" *Time*. April 25. http://content.time.com/time/magazine/article/0,9171,23543,00.html.

Lemonick, Michael D., and Andrea Dorfman. 2009. "Ardi Is a New Piece for the Evolution Puzzle." *Time*. October 1. http://content.time.com/time/printout/0,8816,1927289,00.html.

Lewontin, Richard. 1995. *Human Diversity*. New York: Scientific American Library.

Lieberman, Daniel E., David R. Pilbeam, and Richard W. Wrangham. 2009. "The Transition from *Australopithecus* to *Homo*." In *Transitions in Prehistory: Essays in Honor of Ofer Bar-Yosef*, ed. John J. Shea and Daniel E. Lieberman, 1–22. Cambridge: Oxbow Books.

Luskin, Casey. 2012. "Human Origins and the Fossil Record." In Douglas Axe, Ann Gauger, and Casey Luskin, *Science and Human Origins*. Seattle: Discovery Institute Press.

Macknight, Hugh. 2010. "Experts Reject New Human Species Theory." *The Independent*. April 8. www.independent.co.uk/news/science/experts-reject-new-human-species-theory–1939512.html.

Marchal, François. 2000. "A New Morphometric Analysis of the Hominid Pelvic Bone." *Journal of Human Evolution* 38:347–65.

Mayr, Ernst. 2004. *What Makes Biology Unique? Considerations on the Autonomy of a Scientific Discipline*. Cambridge: Cambridge University Press.

Molnar, Stephen. 1998. *Human Variation: Races, Types, and Ethnic Groups*. 4th ed. Upper Saddle River, NJ: Prentice Hall.

———. 2002. *Human Variation: Races, Types, and Ethnic Groups*. 5th ed. Upper Saddle River, NJ: Prentice Hall.

New York University. 2011. "Fossils May Look Like Human Bones: Biological Anthropologists Question Claims for Human Ancestry." *ScienceDaily*. February 16. www.sciencedaily.com/releases/2011/02/110216132034.htm.

Oxnard, C. E. 1975. "The Place of the Australopithecines in Human Evolution: Grounds for Doubt?" *Nature* (December 4): 389–95.

Pickering, Robyn, Paul H. G. M. Dirks, Zubair Jinnah, et al. 2011. "*Australopithecus sediba* at 1.977 Ma and Implications for the Origins of the Genus *Homo*." *Science* 333:1421–23.

Potts, Richard, and Christopher Sloan. 2010. *What Does It Mean to Be Human?* Washington, DC: National Geographic.

Richmond, Brian G., and David S. Strait. 2000. "Evidence That Humans Evolved from a Knuckle-Walking Ancestor." *Nature* 404:382–85.

Sarmiento, Esteban E. 2010. "Comment on the Paleobiology and Classification of *Ardipithecus ramidus*." *Science* 328:1105b.

Sarmiento, E. E., and D. J. Meldrum. 2011. "Behavioral and Phylogenetic Implications of a Narrow Allometric Study of *Ardipithecus Ramidus*." *HOMO: Journal of Comparative Human Biology* 62:75–108

Sarmiento, Esteban E., Gary J. Sawyer, and Richard Milner. 2007. *The Last Human: A Guide to Twenty-Two Species of Extinct Humans*. New Haven, CT: Yale University Press.

Shreeve, Jamie. 2009. "Oldest Skeleton of Human Ancestor Found." *National Geographic*. October 1. http://news.nationalgeographic.com/news/2009/10/091001-oldest-human-skeleton-ardi-missing-link-chimps-ardipithecus-ramidus.html.

Spoor, F., M. G. Leakey, P. N. Gathogo, et al. 2007. "Implications of New Early *Homo* Fossils from Ileret, East of Lake Turkana, Kenya." *Nature* 448:688–91.

Spoor, Fred, Bernard Wood, and Frans Zonneveld. 1994. "Implications of Early Hominid Labyrinthine Morphology for Evolution of Human Bipedal Locomotion." *Nature* 369:645–48.

Tattersall, Ian. 1992. "The Many Faces of *Homo Habilis*." *Evolutionary Anthropology* 1:33–37.

———. 2000. "Once We Were Not Alone." *Scientific American* (January 1): 55–62.

Tattersall, Ian, and Jeffrey H. Schwartz. 2009. "Evolution of the Genus *Homo*." *Annual Review of Earth and Planetary Sciences* 37:67–92.

Trinkaus, Erik, and Cidália Duarte. 2003. "The Hybrid Child from Portugal." *Scientific American* (August): 32.

University of Michigan News Service. 2000. "New Study Suggests Big Bang Theory of Human Evolution." University of Michigan News Service. January 10. http://ns.umich.edu/Releases/2000/Jan00/r011000b.html.

Walker, Alan. 1993. "The Origin of the Genus *Homo*." In *The Origin and Evolution of Humans and Humanness*, ed. D. Tab Rasmussen, 29–48. Boston: Jones and Bartlett.

White, Tim. 2013. "Five's a Crowd in Our Family Tree." *Current Biology* 23:R112–15.

White, Tim D., Berhane Asfaw, Yonas Beyene, et al. 2009. "*Ardipithecus ramidus* and the Paleobiology of Early Hominids." *Science* 326:75–86.

Wilford, John Noble. 2001. "On the Trail of a Few More Ancestors." *New York Times*. April 8. www.nytimes.com/2001/04/08/world/on-the-trail-of-a-few-more-ancestors.html.

———. 2010. "Scientists Challenge 'Breakthrough' on Fossil Skeleton." *New York Times*. May 27. www.nytimes.com/2010/05/28/science/28fossil.html.

Wolpoff, Milford H., Brigitte Senut, Martin Pickford, and John Hawks. 2002. "*Sahelanthropus* or '*Sahelpithecus*'?" *Nature* 419:581–82.

Wood, Bernard. 2002. "Hominid Revelations from Chad." *Nature* 418:133–35.

Wood, Bernard, and Mark Collard. 1999. "The Human Genus." 1999. *Science* 284:65–71.

Wood, Bernard, and Mark Grabowski. 2015. "Macroevolution in and around the Hominin Clade." *Macroevolution: Explanation, Interpretation and Evidence*, ed. Serrelli Emanuele and Nathalie Gontier, 347–76. Heidelberg: Springer-Verlag.

Wood, Bernard, and Terry Harrison. 2011. "The Evolutionary Context of the First Hominins." *Nature* 470:347–52.

Zimmer, Carl. 2005. *Smithsonian Intimate Guide to Human Origins*. Toronto: Madison Books.

———. 2010. "Yet Another 'Missing Link.'" *Slate*. April 8. www.slate.com/articles/health_and_science/science/2010/04/yet_another_missing_link.2.html.

HOYLE, FRED. Fred Hoyle (1915–2001) was a bluff Yorkshireman who was a truly great scientist with a maverick temperament. Most of his career was spent at Cambridge University, where he founded the Institute of Theoretical **Astronomy**, though he later resigned over internal politics. He is most famous as a founder of the "steady state" theory in cosmology, which explained the observed expansion of the universe by postulating the continuous creation of matter in the space between receding galaxies at just the right rate to yield an eternal, unchanging universe (Hoyle 1948). Hoyle coined the term "big bang" for the rival theory, which he hated, in a BBC radio broadcast in 1949 (Mitton 2003, 129).

Hoyle disliked the **big bang theory** because, he wrote, "it is against the spirit of scientific enquiry to regard observable effects as arising from 'causes unknown to science,' and this is in principle what creation-in-the-past implies" (Hoyle 1948, 372). More especially, the big bang requires starting conditions "which we are obliged to accept as conditions arbitrarily imposed for no reasons that we understand" and this is a procedure "characteristic of the outlook of primitive peoples" who postulated the existence of gods to explain the starting conditions (Hoyle 1970, 351). As a militant atheist, Hoyle clearly had ideological reasons for preferring the steady state. What he failed to appreciate, like **Stephen Hawking** and others today, is that the Christian doctrine of creation is much more about answering the question of why there is a universe than about "lighting the blue touch paper" at the beginning, and also that Christian doctrine is compatible with either the steady state theory or the big bang theory—as theologians such as E. L. Mascall said at the time.

Hoyle strongly defended the steady state against his rival in Cambridge, the radio astronomer Martin Ryle, whose observations of radio source counts during the 1950s and early 1960s were increasingly incompatible with the steady state. He only came to terms with the big bang when microwave background radiation, which confirmed the theory once and for all and which could not be explained on the basis of the steady state, was observed in 1965 (Hoyle 1965).

Hoyle's atheism was manifested in his broadcasts on the BBC, where he described religion as illusory, and his writings often contained antireligious polemics, though his picture of religion was a caricature of the reality (Holder 2012, 42–49).

In addition to the steady state theory, Hoyle is also well known for his maverick anti-Darwinian stance and for proposing, with Chandra Wickramasinghe, that life on earth is seeded from outer space (*panspermia*), a stance that put him on the fringe of scientific respectability (Hoyle and Wickramasinghe 1978). What is less well known in the popular mind is his truly great and enduring contribution to astrophysics, namely, his work on the manufacture of the chemical elements in stars. The magisterial paper produced with Geoffrey and Margaret Burbidge and William Fowler, invariably abbreviated as B²FH, likely should have earned him a share of the Nobel Prize in 1983 (Burbidge et al. 1957). In St John's College Library in Cambridge there is a letter from Fowler to Hoyle regretting the injustice that Hoyle was not included in the award (Fowler 1983).

Hoyle's work on stellar nucleosynthesis led him to make startling remarks rather at variance with what he had said earlier about religion. He famously predicted a "resonance," an enhanced effect in the carbon atom at just the right level to ensure that carbon could be manufactured by crashing three helium nuclei together, despite the intermediate element beryllium being unstable. It further transpired that there was an energy level in the oxygen atom below which the production of oxygen would have been resonant and would have destroyed all carbon. These "coincidences" are necessary for carbon-based life to exist in the universe—without them we could not be here. Hoyle said about his discovery,

If this were a purely scientific question and not one that touched on the religious problem, I do not believe that any scientist who examined the evidence would fail to draw the inference that the laws of nuclear **physics** have been deliberately designed with regard to the consequences they produce inside the stars. (Hoyle 1959, 64)

And again:

A common sense interpretation of the facts suggests that a superintellect has monkeyed with physics, as well as with chemistry and biology, and that there are no blind forces worth speaking about in nature. The numbers one calculates from the facts seem to me so overwhelming as to put this conclusion almost beyond question. (Hoyle 1981, 12)

Hoyle was prepared to follow where his science led him, even if that meant talking about a "superintellect" behind the universe.

Rodney Holder

REFERENCES AND RECOMMENDED READING

Burbidge, E. M., G. R. Burbidge, W. A. Fowler, and F. Hoyle. 1957. "Synthesis of the Elements in Stars." *Review of Modern Physics* 29:547–650.

Fowler, William F. 1983. Letter to Fred Hoyle in St John's College Library, Cambridge. www.joh.cam.ac.uk/sites/default/files/images/article_images/hoyle-object03_big_0.jpg.

Holder, Rodney D. 2012. "Georges Lemaître and Fred Hoyle: Contrasting Characters in Science and Religion." In *Georges Lemaître: Life, Science and Legacy*, ed. Rodney D. Holder and Simon Mitton, 39–53. Heidelberg: Springer.

Hoyle, Fred. 1948. "A New Model for the Expanding Universe." *Monthly Notices of the Royal Astronomical Society* 108 (5): 372–82.

———. (1955) 1970. *Frontiers of Astronomy*. London: Heinemann.

———. 1959. *Religion and the Scientists*, ed. Mervyn Stockwood. London: SCM.

———. 1965. "Recent Developments in Cosmology." *Nature* 208 (5006): 111–14.

———. 1981. "The Universe: Some Past and Present Reflections." *Engineering & Science.* November 8–12. http://calteches.library.caltech.edu/527/2/Hoyle.pdf.

Hoyle, Fred, and N. C. Wickramasinghe. 1978. *Lifecloud: The Origin of Life in the Universe*. London: J. M. Dent.

Mitton, Simon. 2003. *Fred Hoyle: A Life in Science*. London: Aurum.

HUMAN GENOME PROJECT. The Human Genome Project (HGP) was an international, collaborative research program whose goal was the complete mapping and understanding of all the genes of human beings. The entire collection of human genes together is known as the "genome." The genome of all living organisms is made up of two long strands of **DNA** wound around each other into the famous double helix. Each of the 46 human chromosomes consist of one long DNA molecule, typically about two inches long and with a width that corresponds to one thousandth of that of a human hair. Given that there are 46 DNA molecules in a cell, the total length of DNA in each cell is about nine feet.

DNA consists of coding units called *bases*, and our genome as a whole consists of about 3 billion bases present in two copies, one set of 23 DNA molecules from each parent. The bases are arranged along the thread in a distinct order known as a *sequence*. The goal of the human genome project was to determine the sequence of all 3 billion coding units.

Genes correspond to segments of code along the DNA molecule. Generally each **gene** specifies the **information** on how to make a particular protein molecule, and we have about 20,500 genes in all. The genome also consists of portions of the DNA molecule that regulates which genes are read by the cell at any given time and any given tissue. Significant portions of the DNA act as switches; they turn the expression of particular genes on and off. Although there is still much work to be done to fully understand details of how the code works, in essence, with the complete sequence of the human genome, scientists have the instruction book on how to build a human body.

The project was massive—by far the biggest coordinated effort ever attempted in the history of biology. It began in 1990 under the leadership of James Watson, with **Francis Collins** becoming the director in 1993. Initially projected to be completed in 2005, it was completed two years early at a cost of $400 million under its $3 billion budget. Throughout the process the costs continued to decrease significantly, so although the reading of the first genome cost about $2.6 million, today a whole genome can be sequenced for about $1,000.

Over 6,000 identified inheritable diseases are caused by defects in the DNA coding information. Now that genomes can readily be sequenced and compared to the reference genome, it is often possible to diagnose specific illnesses more rapidly than previously dreamed possible. Other illnesses like cancer are frequently caused by a set of genetic abnormalities (changes in the DNA sequence) that are not necessarily a result of inheritance from parents, but rather changes in the sequence that have taken place within the body during the lifetime of the individual. Those changes may result in uncontrolled multiplication of cells into tumors, which, depending on the specific genetic changes, may be metastatic. Other diseases are caused by multiple inherited genetic changes that create disease through an additive effect. In all cases, knowing the DNA sequence of cells within the body often will lead to more effective treatment.

This is the foundational basis for personalized medicine that is bound to revolutionize the face of medicine in the twenty-first century. And all this progress stems from the success of the human genome project.

Darrel R. Falk

REFERENCES AND RECOMMENDED READING

Collins, Francis. 2006. *The Language of God.* New York: Free Press.
National Institutes of Health. 2016. *An Overview of the Human Genome Project.* May 11. www.genome.gov/12011238.
Topol, Eric. 2015. *The Patient Will See You Now.* New York: Basic Books.

HUME, DAVID. David Hume (1711–76) was a Scottish philosopher, economist, historian, diplomat, and essayist who distinguished himself as the foremost proponent of radical **empiricism**. The consistency of Hume's empiricism elicited an all-consuming skepticism that left a path of intellectual bankruptcy in its wake.

Wielding his quill skillfully in the service of a comprehensive critique of deductive reasoning, Hume leveled his unrelenting intellectual blows—much more thoroughly than Locke and Berkeley had ever done—on the weakened edifice of Continental rationalism (see **John Locke**). Hume assumed that all knowledge originates in sense perception. He also believed that by eliciting the use of the imagination, the human mind could identify and differentiate ideas conceived at different times and subsequently lodged in the memory. The ability to compare ideas could then be used to formulate a theory of spatial and temporal continuity. It would even be possible to recognize the different properties of numbers. Contrary to what could be expected as the logical outcome of skepticism if followed to the end, Hume made allowance in his philosophical system for the human ability to compute mathematically.

The most momentous contribution to the decline of empiricism was Hume's acerbic criticism of the traditional theory of **causation**. He attempted to hammer the last nail in the coffin of Locke's philosophy by exposing its inner contradictions. In his analysis of the problem of causation, the Scottish philosopher divided all objects of knowledge into two categories—"relations of ideas" and "matters of fact." He maintained that all truth-claims of facts in this first category of knowledge—"relations of ideas"—could be examined by taking into account the interaction of ideational aspects, in particular their clearness and distinctness. The attempt to falsify a true proposition in this category would end up as a logical contradiction. As an aside, one could ask whether this twofold division itself is a relation of ideas or a matter of fact.

Hume called the second category of knowledge "matters of fact"; these contained details, among others, of geography, chemistry, and history. The opposite of any proposition in this category would not lead to a logical contradiction. For example, a statement such as "the American Declaration of Independence was issued in 1776" does not constitute a logical contradiction, nor does the formula of NaCl denoting the chemical composition of salt. In seeming contradiction to what he set out to prove, Hume maintained that these principles are derived from the concept of cause and effect.

To prevent his detractors from concluding that skepticism is nothing more than a mental confusion, Hume opined that ideas could neither be objects nor the content of the mind (i.e., innate ideas), and thus knowledge concerned itself merely with essences that emerge once ideas are being compared by the human mind. The inevitable inference of this line of reasoning was that knowledge did not consist of absolutely true propositions but could claim for itself only a more or less probable certainty. Hence it was a short step from postulating varying degrees of **probability** to the denial of the traditional concept of causation (Coventry 2006, 91–92). The upshot of this theory was that the door to the inner chambers of what he identified as the interplay between cause and effect—namely, random **chance** rather than mathematical proof—was utterly inaccessible to any human being.

In concluding his argument, Hume admitted that a certain cause may bring forth a predetermined effect in a number of cases, while not doing so in still others (Hume 1777, 110–11). In the end, all would depend on a ratio of probability that could be calculated. It would preclude, however, the empirical demonstration of a uniform procession of natural phenomena. Nonetheless, Hume conceded that the hypotheses of causation and the uniformity of nature could, at times, be extremely useful.

Analyzing the problem of causation from a psychological perspective, Hume took note of the three fundamental aspects of this concept as he defined them: contiguity, succession, and necessity (Hume 1739–40, 167). Admitting freely that contiguity and succession were sensations that could be perceived by the senses, he adamantly objected to the notion that necessity would also affect the mind as a sense-mediated impression (Hume 1739–40, 78). Thus necessity is not a quality or a relationship inherent in the impressions themselves. The apparent impression of fire producing heat is merely a conventional mode of thinking ("constant conjunction"), a habit of the mind that helps human beings to connect conceptually two distinct impressions, although, in reality, there is no such causal relationship (Hume 1739–40, 79).

Consequently, it is hardly surprising that, at the core of Hume's skepticism, irrationalism reared its head out from under an eclectic heap of metaphysical presuppositions. The Scottish philosopher believed that every abstract idea, including even the notion of the existence of material substances, was devoid of meaning. Declaring in his customary apodictic fashion that no single object, animated or not, can be known for what it truly is in itself, Hume asserted that each human being succumbs to the deceptive habit of identifying what is being perceived with what is thought to be real. If this chimerical thought process was exposed for what it is, the belief in the continuity of human nature would be shattered once and for all.

Hume would not allow any certainty of knowledge to stand in his way of ascertaining the truth, as he saw it, of the absolute validity of skepticism. While the philosophical idealist George Berkeley, due to his religious inclination, had still insisted on the existence of spiritual substances, Hume went so far as to deny both the concept of spiritual substances and the concept of self. Vigorously brandishing the hatchet of skepticism, he set out to demolish the notion that humans could actually know who they are.

The only answer he gave to the central question of what constitutes personhood was the injunction to each human being to define it for himself (Ayer 1946, 135–36). And yet in reality he had no answer to give, because even despite his blatant skepticism, Hume would not question his own existence or, for that matter, the existence of everyone else. In the development of his philosophical position, he simultaneously affirmed and denied what he, based on his skeptical presuppositions, could neither prove nor negate to exist.

Hume's radical aversion to allowing for the law of causation, being neither necessary nor sure, did not keep him from averring the seemingly contradictory notion of some kind of natural law. In a certain respect, Hume's view of science shows a similarity with that of Berkeley. Despite Hume's postulate that ideas are passive and devoid of all force, they still exhibit a sequential regularity, and thus science sets out simply to describe this regularity. While Berkeley pointed to the Spirit of God as the controlling agent in causing the regularity of ideas, Hume, being a skeptical deist, could only state that the successive occurrence of impressions is a brute, inexplicable fact. His definition of **miracles** was, therefore, nothing else but "a transgression of a law of nature."

Hume's skepticism threatened to destroy entirely the Newtonian view of nature that relied fully on the reality of causal relations between events and objects. If Hume were right in his assumption that causation and the uniformity of nature were at best merely useful hypotheses, these would simply be figments of the mind without any grounding in reality. Granted, this logical application of Lockean empiricism was far removed from what Locke had in mind when he contemplated the actual outworking of the principles of his philosophy. He never would have conceded to Hume the satisfaction of having advanced the better argument. And yet Hume succeeded to tear down, in the eyes of many, the once lofty edifice of Lockean empiricism.

Martin Erdmann

REFERENCES AND RECOMMENDED READING

Allison, H. E. 2008. *Custom and Reason in Hume*. Oxford: Oxford University Press.

Ayer, Alfred Jules. 1946. *Language, Truth and Logic*. Repr. ed. New York: Penguin.

Bailey, Alan, and Dan O'Brien. 2006. *Hume's "Enquiry concerning Human Understanding": A Reader's Guide*. New York: A&C Black.

Baxter, D. L. M. 2008. *Hume's Difficulty*. London: Routledge.

Coventry, Angela M. 2006. *Hume's Theory of Causation*. Continuum Studies in British Philosophy. New York: A&C Black.

Dicker, Georges. 2002. *Hume's Epistemology and Metaphysics: An Introduction*. London: Routledge.

Earman, J. 2000. *Hume's Abject Failure: The Argument against Miracles*. Oxford: Oxford University Press.

Fieser, James. 2003. *A Bibliography of Hume's Writings and Early Responses*. Bristol, UK: Thoemmes.

Hume, David. 1739–40. *A Treatise of Human Nature: Being an Attempt to Introduce the Experimental Method of Reasoning into Moral Subjects*. London: John Noon.

———. 1740. *An Abstract of a Book Lately Published; Entitled, "A Treatise of Human Nature," &c. Wherein the Chief Argument of That Book Is Farther Illustrated and Explained*. London: C. Borbett.

———. 1741–42. *Essays: Moral, Political, and Literary*. Edinburgh: A. Kincaid.

———. 1745. *A Letter from a Gentleman to His Friend in Edinburgh: Containing Some Observations on a Specimen of the Principles concerning Religion and Morality, Said to be Maintain'd in a Book Lately Publish'd, Intituled a Treatise of Human Nature Etc.* Edinburgh: n.p.

———. (1748) 1777. *An Enquiry concerning Human Understanding*. London: A. Millar.

———. (1751) 1907. *An Enquiry concerning the Principles of Morals. David Hume, Essays Moral, Political, and Literary*, ed. with preliminary dissertations and notes by T. H. Green and T. H. Grose, 1:1–8. London: Longmans, Green.

———. (1752–58) 1993. *Political Discourses/Discours politiques*. English-French ed. Trans. Fabien Grandjean. Mauvezin, France: Trans-Europ-Repress.

———. 1757. *Four Dissertations*. London: A. Millar.

———. 2011. *The Letters of David Hume: 1727–1765*. The Letters of David Hume. Vol. 1. Ed. J. Y. T. Greig. Oxford: Oxford University Press.

Huxley, Thomas Henry. 2011. *Hume*. English Men of Letters 39. Cambridge: Cambridge University Press.

Kail, P. J. E. 2007. *Projection and Realism in Hume's Philosophy*. Oxford: Oxford University Press.

Mossner, Ernest Campbell. 1980. *The Life of David Hume*. Oxford: Oxford University Press.

Mounce, H. O. 2002. *Hume's Naturalism*. London: Routledge.

Norton, David Fate. 1982. *David Hume: Common-Sense Moralist, Sceptical Metaphysician.* Princeton, NJ: Princeton University Press.

Norton, David Fate, and Jacqueline Taylor, eds. 2009. *The Cambridge Companion to Hume.* Cambridge: Cambridge University Press.

Passmore, John A. 2013. *Hume's Intentions.* Cambridge: Cambridge University Press.

Read, Rupert, and Kenneth Richman, eds. 2002. *The New Hume Debate.* London: Routledge.

Spencer, Mark G., ed. 2013. *David Hume: Historical Thinker, Historical Writer.* Philadelphia: Penn State University Press.

Strawson, Galen. 2014. *The Secret Connexion: Causation, Realism, and David Hume.* Chicago Studies in Ethnomusicology. Oxford: Oxford University Press.

HUXLEY, THOMAS HENRY. T. H. Huxley (1825–95) was born into a lower-middle-class family on the outskirts of London. Between the ages of 13 and 16, Huxley endured apprenticeships to two surgeons, ministering to London slum residents in appalling conditions. During 1841–42, funding from family members enabled Thomas to attend Sydenham College, where he attained prizes in botany and medicinal chemistry. His abilities won him a free scholarship to the medical school at Charing Cross (1842–46). Studying to become a physician, he passed his first medical examination but did not undertake the second. Early on he developed a fine talent for anatomical drawing, a skill that he would deploy with great effect throughout his career.

Desperate to repay debts, in May 1846 Huxley enlisted as a Royal Navy surgeon's assistant. He served as surgeon's mate and ship's naturalist on the voyage (1847–50) of the H.M.S. *Rattlesnake*, under Captain Owen Stanley. This voyage was directed to survey the coastline and inshore waters of northern and eastern Australia and southeastern New Guinea. Here Huxley undertook pioneering studies of the structure and systematics of siphonophores and ascidians, which afterward resulted in recognition of his abilities as an invertebrate zoologist. While ashore in Sydney in 1847, Huxley met and later became engaged to Henrietta (Nettie) Heathorn, whom he married in 1855.

Upon Huxley's return to England, he was nominated for membership in the Royal Society by the marine biologist Edward Forbes. He won the Royal Society's medal in 1859 for his work on siphonophores. Huxley's competence as a marine biologist was widely recognized: from 1881 to 1885, he served as Inspector of Fisheries; and from 1884 to 1890 he served as president of the Marine Biological Association. Late in life he published a thorough anatomical study of the crayfish.

In 1851 the British government established the Royal School of Mines, later a part of Imperial College London. In 1854 Huxley was appointed professor of natural history, serving until 1885. Over this span, he turned his attention to diverse groups of fossils, chiefly those of vertebrate animals. Significant organisms that Huxley analyzed include the lobe-finned fishes, for which he generated the term *crossopterygii*, crocodiles, dinosaurs, and mammals. Huxley famously argued the dinosaurian affinities of birds, addressing the anatomy of the Jurassic bird *Archaeopteryx lithographica*. His proficiency in anatomy led to his election to the Hunterian Professorship of the Royal College of Surgeons (1863–69). Huxley's laboratory teaching assistants went on to become a generation of significant evolutionary morphologists.

Early in his career, Huxley realized the value of embryological studies for ascertaining what Richard Owen would term *homologies*. Huxley's view on the application of embryological evidence, derived from the German school represented by Von Baer, differed from Owen's fundamental concept of the vertebrate archetype and contributed to a degenerating antagonism between the two. Huxley's original conception of the permanence of type initially led him to question **Darwin**'s gradualistic view of evolution, but he later reversed this stance. And though a close friend to Darwin, Huxley felt free to challenge him on particulars of evolutionary process.

At an early age, Huxley felt compelled to question all received religious concepts and developed a personal stance that he termed *agnosticism*. (His employment of the term began its broader cultural usage.) He convened a group of like-minded scientists, including the botanist Joseph Hooker, the physicist William Tyndall, and the anthropologist John Lubbock, who met regularly and termed themselves the X Club. Yet Huxley dissociated himself from more rabid forms of positivism and favored the reading of the Bible in public schools.

Beginning in 1855, Huxley provided lectures on the natural sciences for working men, which he termed his "lay sermons." Many of these were pirated and published in street editions; Huxley would eventually (1870) publish a collection. These lectures also provided opportunities to critique the established social order, including the role of the Anglican Church, and promote the sciences as the primary source of authority, rather than tradition or Christian doctrine. After becoming convinced that Darwin's theory of descent was valid, he spoke often at various venues on the evidences for organic evolution, earning him the nickname

"Darwin's Bulldog." In June 1860 the British Association for the Advancement of Science met in Oxford; Huxley provided a caustic reply to a long speech delivered by Bishop Wilberforce critical of Darwinian evolution. This event has been enshrined in popular histories of science as the "Oxford debate" but represents only one instantiation of Huxley's public argument in print and in lecture in support of Darwin's proposal.

While Darwin was initially circumspect regarding implications of a genealogical approach to the organization of life for human beings, Huxley took on the task of providing a résumé of the evidences—at that time chiefly anatomical—for human ancestry within the apes. These were published as *Man's Place in Nature* (1863).

Thomas and Henrietta Huxley had eight children. Their first child, Noel, died at the age of four, causing the couple great sorrow. The novelist Aldous Huxley and the biologists Sir Julian Huxley and Sir Andrew Huxley were all sons of Thomas's son Leonard.

Ralph Stearley

REFERENCES AND RECOMMENDED READING

Bowler, P. J. 1996. *Life's Splendid Drama: Evolutionary Biology and the Reconstruction of Life's Ancestry, 1860–1940.* Chicago: University of Chicago Press.

Cosans, C. 2009. *Owen's Ape and Darwin's Bulldog.* Bloomington: Indiana University Press.

Desmond, Adrian. 1994. *Huxley: From Devil's Disciple to Evolution's High Priest.* Reading, MA: Addison-Wesley.

DiGregorio, M. A. 1984. *T. H. Huxley's Place in Natural Science.* New Haven, CT: Yale University Press.

Hesketh, I. 2009. *Of Apes and Ancestors: Evolution, Christianity and the Oxford Debate.* Toronto: University of Toronto Press.

Huxley, Thomas Henry. 1859a. *The Oceanic Hydrozoa.* London: Ray Society.

———. 1859b. "On the Theory of the Vertebrate Skull." *Proceedings of the Royal Society, Scientific Memoirs,* 1:538–606.

———. (1863) 1971. *Man's Place in Nature.* Ann Arbor, University of Michigan.

———. 1865. "On a Piece of Chalk." *MacMillan's Magazine* 18:396–408.

———. 1868. "A Liberal Education and Where to Find It." *MacMillan's Magazine* 17:367–78.

———. 1870a. "Further Evidence of the Affinity between the Dinosaurian Reptiles and Birds." *Quarterly Journal of the Geological Society* 26:12–31.

———. 1870b. *Lay Sermons, Addresses and Reviews.* London.

———. 1876. "Three Lectures on Evolution." In *Collected Essays,* 4:46–138. New York: Appleton.

———. 1878. *A Manual of Anatomy of Invertebrated Animals.* New York: Appleton.

———. 1880a. *The Crayfish: An Introduction to the Study of Zoology.* London: C. Kegan Paul.

———. 1880b. "On the Application of the Laws of Evolution to the Arrangement of the Vertebrata and More Particularly of the Mammalia." *Proceedings of the Zoological Society* 1880:649–61.

McCalman, I. 2009. *Darwin's Armada: Four Voyages and the Battle for the Theory of Evolution.* New York: W. W. Norton.

Rupke, N. 1994. *Richard Owen: Biology without Darwin.* Chicago: University of Chicago Press.

HYPATIA. Hypatia (d. 415) was a highly respected Neo-platonic teacher who lived and worked in Alexandria, Egypt. She was murdered by a mob who were allegedly supporters of Cyril, patriarch of the city.

Life

Hypatia's father, Theon, was attached to the museum in Alexandria and a mathematician of some repute. He prepared the standard edition of Euclid's geometry textbook, *The Elements,* arranging the material with an eye to clarity rather than philological accuracy.

Hypatia counted both Christians and pagans among her friends and admirers. Synesius, the bishop of Ptolemais in Libya, was a former pupil who continued to write admiring letters to her after they parted. Her teaching appears to have been based on mystical Neoplatonism of the kind popular among pagan thinkers of the time. She saw **mathematics** as a way of training the mind for the contemplation of higher things. Her most lasting achievement was her edition of the Greek text of the *Almagest* by Ptolemy, which mathematically described a geocentric universe. Although her philosophy was typical of its time, she stood out as being a woman in a man's world. She maintained her professional status by remaining aloof and unobtainable to any male suitors (Dzielska 1996).

Death

Because Hypatia was a respected member of Alexandrian society, it was impossible for her not to be drawn into city politics. A dispute arose between the bishop, a distinguished, if militant, theologian by the name of Cyril and the Alexandrian governor Orestes. Their fierce rivalry spilled over into the streets. Both leaders were Christians, and the mob violence that had plagued Alexandria for centuries gained new impetus from their rivalry. Hypatia, who was in the camp of the governor, was murdered in AD 415 by a posse of Cyril's partisans who surrounded her chariot and dragged her away. Her death was most likely a spontaneous act of violence rather than a conspiracy arranged by Cyril.

There is no evidence that she was a victim particularly because of her pagan religion, although her status as a prominent female philosophy teacher could have made her a high-profile target. The contemporary Christian chronicler Socrates Scholasticus reported that her murder "could not fail to bring the greatest opprobrium, not only upon Cyril, but also upon the whole Alexandrian church. And surely nothing can be further from the spirit of Christianity than the allowance of massacres, fights and transactions of that sort" (Socrates Scholasticus 1853, 349, 7:15). Later Christian writers were less charitable about her.

Legacy

If Hypatia was the editor of Ptolemy's *Almagest*, her mathematical legacy was pervasive and long-lasting. However, she is better known as a romantic heroine. In 1853 Charles Kingsley, an Anglican vicar, published *Hypatia or New Foes with an Old Face*, which fictionalized her as a convert to Christianity. More recently a heavily romanticized account of her life was made into the movie *Agora* (2009), with the British actress Rachel Weisz in the title role. Although she is almost always portrayed as a young and attractive woman, we have no record of Hypatia's appearance. She was probably in her 50s, a ripe old age at the time, when she was murdered.

James Hannam

REFERENCES AND RECOMMENDED READING

Dzielska, Maria. 1996. *Hypatia of Alexandria*, trans. F. Lyra. Cambridge, MA: Harvard University Press.

Kingsley, Charles. 1915. *Hypatia or New Foes with an Old Face*. Oxford: Oxford University Press.

Socrates Scholasticus. 1853. *The Ecclesiastical History*, trans. Henry Bohn. London: Henry G. Bohn.

IDEALISM. Idealism is a philosophical view that claims reality is, in some sense, mental. The different senses in which the mental character of reality is affirmed lead to different versions of idealism. We discuss them briefly in historical order. **Plato**'s (428–348 BC) theory of ideas (or forms) maintains that the material world is a pale shadow of the absolute reality constituted by eternal, unchanging, ideal forms that are grasped by the mind.

Participation in these forms gives identity to everything in the world of our experience and understanding these forms is the objective of all knowledge. While Platonic forms can only be apprehended by minds, the Platonic theory is not often called idealism today because the forms, while not material, are also not mind dependent. The Neoplatonism of Gregory of Nyssa (c. 335–c. 395) and **Augustine** (354–430), which turned Platonic forms into ideas in the mind of God that differentiate and give intelligibility to the world of our experience—an interpretation of the *logos* doctrine (John 1:1–3; Col. 1:16–17) as the divine reason infusing reality—is accurately classified as a form of idealism and strongly influenced later Christian forms of idealism, including those of John Scotus Eriugena (815–877) and George Berkeley (1685–1753).

Arguably, variations of this metaphysic also undergird the primary role accorded to **information** among theistically oriented philosophers, scientists, and mathematicians pursuing **intelligent design** research in **physics**, cosmology, and biology (Dembski 1999, 2014; Gordon 2011, 2013, 2017; Meyer 2009; Sternberg 2008a, 2008b, 2017).

In the context of modern philosophy, idealism is most often associated with either Berkeleyan immaterialism or German idealism and its ideological descendants (Adams 1973, 2007; Boyle et al. 2013; Cowan and Spiegel 2016; Daniel 2001; Downing 2004; Farris, et al. 2016; Foster 1982, 2000, 2008; Gersh and Moran 2006; Hill 2009; Kim and Hoeltzel 2014; Redding 2010; Robinson 1994; Rohlf 2010; Wainwright 2012). Berkeley held that what we regard as physical things (tables, chairs, trees, mountains, our own bodies) are really orderly collections of mind-dependent ideas that are ultimately produced by and reliant on the mind of God. In Berkeley's view, there is no materially substantial reality that exists and causes our perceptions, nor

any substantial physical body we possess that mediates our experience of the world. Rather, physical things exist solely as ideas in the mind of God, who is the ultimate cause of the sensations and ideas that we, as finite spiritual (immaterial) beings, experience objectively and intersubjectively as the physical universe. In this manner, the universe functions (as its order, pattern, and regularity would indicate) as one mode of God's speech and communication with us.

The German strain of idealism begins with **Immanuel Kant** (1724–1804). Kant held that there is a reality that exists independently of us, but how it appears to us is determined by the structure of the human mind. Our perceptions of the world are organized by space and time as modes of human cognition and by innate categories of the understanding (quantity, quality, relation, modality) that structure our perception and conception of what is given to us in experience. The self as a transcendental unity of **consciousness** preceding and grounding experience—what Kant called the "transcendental unity of apperception"—is the source of these modes of cognition and categories of understanding, and it applies them to our "raw" experience of the world. Thus we never experience reality-in-itself (noumenal reality) but only reality as it *appears* to us (phenomenal reality) through the innate structuring of the human mind.

G. W. F. Hegel (1770–1831) rejected Kant's transcendental idealism, denying a difference between what is given in experience and the categories that structure it—in short, denying any real distinction between subject and object—and asserting instead that everything (including all finite consciousness) exists in interrelationship with everything else as part of one evolving conscious substance conceived as Absolute Spirit. This Absolute Spirit is a perfectly interrelated, all-inclusive thinking whole that is in the process of actualizing and fulfilling the transient existence of all finite things. Thus, in contrast to Berkeleyan and Kantian idealism, which recognize a plurality of mental subjects, Hegelian idealism is monistic, even pantheistic, maintaining that everything that exists is a form of self-actualizing Absolute Spirit. While this absolute idealism subsequently took many forms, especially among the British idealists T. H. Green (1836–82), F. H. Bradley (1846–1924), and Bernard Bosanquet (1848–1923), all of them were broadly monistic and emphasized the interrelatedness and funda-mentally mental character of reality.

As a final note, elements of idealism¯understood as affirm-ing that reality is, in *some* irreducible sense, mental¯are present in various strands of personalist philosophy reacting to the post-Enlightenment depersonalization of nature (Williams 2013), as well as in process thought and panpsychist phi-losophy. **Alfred North Whitehead**'s (1861–1947) **process philosophy** and its theological outworking (Cobb and Griffin 1976; Haught 2001; Jungerman 2000; **Teilhard de Chardin** [1959] 2004; Whitehead [1929] 1979) offer an essentially neo-Hegelian conception of nature's historical progression in which all things have an irreducibly mental aspect and are being drawn by a divine "lure" toward actualization and fulfillment. An irreducible mental aspect as part of even the most physical components of the universe is also affirmed by panpsychist theories on the nature of reality, the most notable recent example being the views of **Thomas Nagel** (Nagel 2012; see also Seager 2010).

Bruce L. Gordon

REFERENCES AND RECOMMENDED READING

Adams, Robert. 1973. "Berkeley's 'Notion' of Spiritual Substance." *Archiv für Geschichte der Philosophie* 55:47–69.

———. 2007. "Idealism Vindicated." In *Persons: Human and Divine*, ed. Peter van Inwagen and Dean Zimmerman, 35–54. New York: Oxford University Press.

Boyle, N., L. Disley, and K. Ameriks, eds. 2013. *The Impact of Idealism: The Legacy of Post-Kantian German Thought.* Philosophy and Natural Sciences. Vol. 1. Cambridge: Cambridge University Press.

Cobb, John, and David Ray Griffin. 1976. *Process Theology: An Introductory Exposition.* Philadelphia: Westminster.

Cowan, Steven, and James S. Spiegel, eds. 2016. *Idealism and Christian Philoso-phy.* Idealism and Christianity. Vol. 2. New York: Bloomsbury Academic.

Daniel, Stephen H. 2001. "Berkeley's Christian Neoplatonism, Archetypes, and Divine Ideas." *Journal of the History of Philosophy* 39 (2): 239–58.

Dembski, William A. 1999. *Intelligent Design: The Bridge between Science and Theology.* Downers Grove, IL: InterVarsity.

———. 2014. *Being as Communion: A Metaphysics of Information.* Burlington, VT: Ashgate.

Downing, Lisa. 2004. "Berkeley." In *Stanford Encyclopedia of Philosophy*, ed. Edward N. Zalta. http://plato.stanford.edu/archives/win2004/entries/berkeley/.

Dunham, J., I. H. Grant, and S. Watson. 2011. *Idealism: The History of a Philosophy.* Montreal: McGill-Queen's University Press.

Farris, Joshua, Mark Hamilton, and James S. Spiegel, eds. 2016. *Idealism and Christian Theology.* Idealism and Christianity. Vol. 1. New York: Blooms-bury Academic.

Foster, John. 1982. *The Case for Idealism.* London: Routledge and Kegan Paul.

———. 2000. *The Nature of Perception.* Oxford: Oxford University Press.

———. 2008. *A World for Us: The Case for Phenomenalistic Idealism.* Oxford: Oxford University Press.

Gersh, Stephen, and Dermot Moran, eds. 2006. *Eriugena, Berkeley, and the Idealist Tradition.* Notre Dame, IN: University of Notre Dame Press.

Gordon, Bruce L. 2011. "A Quantum-Theoretic Argument against Natural-ism." In *The Nature of Nature: Examining the Role of Naturalism in Science*,

ed. Bruce L. Gordon and William A. Dembski, 79–114. Wilmington, DE: ISI Books.

———. 2013. "In Defense of Uniformitarianism." *Perspectives on Science and Christian Faith* 65 (2): 79–86.

———. 2017. "The Necessity of Sufficiency: The Argument from the Incomplete-ness of Nature," in Trent Dougherty and Jerry Walls, eds., *Two Dozen (or So) Arguments for God: The Plantinga Project.* Oxford: Oxford University Press.

Gould, Paul, ed. 2014. *Beyond the Control of God? Six Views on the Problem of God and Abstract Objects.* New York: Bloomsbury Academic.

Haught, John F. 2001. *God after Darwin: A Theology of Evolution.* Boulder, CO: Westview.

Hill, Jonathan. 2009. "Gregory of Nyssa, Material Substance and Berkeleyan Idealism." *British Journal for the History of Philosophy* 17 (4): 653–83.

Jungerman, John A. 2000. *World in Process: Creativity and Interconnection in the New Physics.* Albany, NY: SUNY Press.

Kim, H., and S. Hoeltzel, eds. 2014. *Kant, Fichte, and the Legacy of Transcendental Idealism.* Lanham, MD: Lexington.

Meyer, Stephen C. 2009. *Signature in the Cell: DNA and the Evidence for Intel-ligent Design.* San Francisco: HarperOne.

Moran, Dermot. 1989. *The Philosophy of John Scottus Eriugena: A Study of Idealism in the Middle Ages.* Cambridge: Cambridge University Press.

Nagel, Thomas. 2012. *Mind and Cosmos: Why the Materialist Neo-Darwinian Conception of Nature Is Almost Certainly False.* New York: Oxford Uni-versity Press.

Redding, Paul. 2010. "Georg Wilhelm Friedrich Hegel." In *Stanford Encyclope-dia of Philosophy*, ed. Edward N. Zalta. http://plato.stanford.edu/entries/hegel/#NatIdeGerTra.

Robinson, Howard. 1994. *Perception.* New York: Routledge.

Rohlf, Michael. 2010. "Immanuel Kant." In *Stanford Encyclopedia of Philosophy*, ed. Edward N. Zalta. http://plato.stanford.edu/entries/kant/.

Seager, William. 2010. "Panpsychism." In *Stanford Encyclopedia of Philosophy*, ed. Edward N. Zalta. http://plato.stanford.edu/entries/panpsychism/.

Sternberg, Richard. 2008a. "DNA Codes and Information: Formal Structures and Relational Causes." *Acta Biotheoretica* 56 (3): 205–32.

———. 2008b. "How My Views on Evolution Evolved." Available at www.richardsternberg.com/pdf/sternintellbio08research.pdf (accessed Novem-ber 7, 2016).

———. 2017. *The Immaterial Genome.* Forthcoming. Publisher TBA.

Teilhard de Chardin, Pierre. (1959) 2004. *The Future of Man.* New York: Image.

Wainwright, William 2012. "Jonathan Edwards." In *Stanford Encyclopedia of Phi-losophy*, ed. Edward N. Zalta. http://plato.stanford.edu/entries/edwards/#2.2.

Whitehead, Alfred N. (1929) 1979. *Process and Reality.* New York: Free Press.

Williams, Thomas D. 2013. "Personalism." In *Stanford Encyclopedia of Philoso-phy*, ed. Edward N. Zalta. http://plato.stanford.edu/entries/personalism/.

IMAGE OF GOD.

IMAGE OF GOD. After announcing his intentions ("Let us make mankind in our image, in our likeness," Gen. 1:26), God created human beings in his image ("So God created mankind in his own image, in the image of God he created them; male and female he created them," v. 27). Genesis 5:1 looks back on the creation of humanity in God's "likeness," and God tells Noah that he will "demand an accounting for the life of another human being" based on the fact that humans are made "in the image of God" (9:6).

Surprisingly, this obviously profound proclamation that humans are created in the image of God is not found elsewhere in the Old Testament, nor is it explained. Thus interpreters over the centuries have struggled to describe exactly what it means to be created in the image of God. Also, since humans are said to be uniquely created in the image of God, questions arise about whether such a dignified view of humanity is compatible with evolutionary theory that suggests that humans share a **common ancestry** with primates and other creatures.

Early church fathers tended to identify the image of God in humans with some aspect of humanity that makes humans different from other creatures, such as their reason (Clement of Alexandria, so Louth 2001, 29) or their "inner man, invisible, incorruptible and immortal" (Origen, also John Cassian, so Louth 2001, 31).

A better strategy toward understanding is to see how the words "image" and "likeness" are used elsewhere in Scripture even when not in connection with the idea of God's image. When we do, we see that "image" often refers to statues of kings that they set up around their kingdoms to represent their presence and royal authority (notably, e.g., in Dan. 3). This view of image and likeness is supported by an extrabiblical reference to this pair of words in an Aramaic-Akkadian inscription on a statue from Tell Fakhariyeh in the Upper Habur region of Syria, which refers to the statue as providing the "image" and "likeness" of King Hadad-yis'i (Garr 2000, 2003). Also relevant are passages in which the false gods of the nations are represented by "images" or "idols." These images are intended to represent the presence and authority of deities in the world.

Thus the best understanding of the "image of God" is that it points to humanity's status as representatives of God in the world. Humans reflect God's glory and authority in the world. In this regard, it is notable that the image of God is connected to God's commission to his human creatures that they "be fruitful and increase in number; fill the earth and subdue it. Rule over the fish in the sea and the birds in the sky and over every living creature that moves on the ground" (Gen. 1:28). In other words, humans represent God's royal authority in the earth (recognized by Gregory of Nyssa, so Louth 2001, 34). According to Brueggemann, "it is now generally agreed that the image of God reflected in human persons is after the manner of a king who establishes himself to assert his sovereign rule where the king himself cannot be present" (Brueggemann 1982, 32; also Longman 2016; McDowell 2015; Middleton 2005, 27).

Recent research has also seen linguistic and conceptual connections between the description of humans as image bearers and the forbidden use of images to represent false deities or in some cases even God himself (as forbidden by the second commandment, Ex. 20:4–6). Indeed, the creation of images of God not only errs by violating God's status as Creator, but also by violating the status of humans as the only divinely authorized image of God.

Accordingly, contra many of the theologians of the early church, the image is not a property of human beings, but rather a status. Humans, male and female, reflect God's glory and authority and serve as benevolent rulers over the rest of God's creation. This status was tarnished by **the fall** (Gen. 3) but not eviscerated (Gen. 9:6).

As we turn to the New Testament, we learn that Jesus is "the image of the invisible God" (Col. 1:15). He reflects the divine glory (2 Cor. 4:4), and Paul writes that human beings are called to become new creatures in Christ and thus "to be like God in true righteousness and holiness" (Eph. 4:24).

Understanding that the image of God is a status means that it does not provide a theological objection to evolutionary theory that asserts that humans share a common ancestry with other creatures. If one thinks that God, in his wisdom and for his own purposes, chose to use evolution as the means of creating humans, then at the point where some of his creatures attain the possibility of moral choice and are morally innocent, he could have conferred on them the status of image bearers. Humans (*Homo sapiens*) are those whom he made "a little lower than the angels and crowned … with glory and honor" (Ps. 8:5).

Tremper Longman III

REFERENCES AND RECOMMENDED READING

Brueggemann, W. 1982. *Genesis*. Louisville, KY: Westminster John Knox.
Garr, W. R. 2000. "'Image' and 'Likeness' in the Inscription from Tell Fakhariyeh." *Israel Exploration Journal* 50:227–34.
———. 2003. *In His Own Image: Humanity, Divinity, and Monotheism*. Leiden: Brill.
Longman III, T. 2016. *Genesis*. Story of God Bible Commentary. Grand Rapids: Zondervan.
Louth, A., ed. 2001. *Genesis 1–11*. Ancient Christian Commentary on Scripture: Old Testament. Vol. 1. Downers Grove, IL: InterVarsity.
McDowell, C. 2015. *The "Image of God" in Eden: The Creation of Mankind in Genesis 2:5–3:24 in Light of the mis pi pit pi and wpt-r Rituals of Mesopotamia and Ancient Egypt*. Winona Lake, IN: Eisenbrauns.
Middleton, J. R. 2005. *The Liberating Image: The Imago Dei in Genesis 1*. Grand Rapids: Brazos.

IMMANENCE AND TRANSCENDENCE. In Christian contexts, transcendence usually refers to some reality's— especially God's—insurmountable epistemological and/or metaphysical *distance* or *difference* from the empirical or everyday, such that the transcendent cannot be known, studied, or encountered in the ways that worldly realities are, since it cannot be categorized with or assimilated to—is not "at the same level" as—any of them. Correspondingly, immanence refers to some reality's *closeness* to or *intimacy* with this world at its deepest levels—although, as with transcendence, that closeness, not being a result of similarity or integration, does not by itself mean that the reality in question can be understood empirically.

Affirmation of the transcendence of God—God's radical nonidentity with this world in any aspect—is a staple of biblical theology, as well as of mystical experience. Yet this is regularly paired with the affirmation of God's immanence—God's radical "direct" contact with even the innermost particulars of this world, as, paradigmatically, in Psalm 139's celebration of God's pervasive presence and unsurpassable knowledge, or in Isaiah 40's insistence on the unidirectional dependence of the world and all nations on the creative power of God.

Augustine speaks for much of Christian theological tradition in his evocative characterization of God as—despite Augustine's attempts at evasion—"closer than my inmost, higher than my highest" (*Confessions* 3.6.11). The Trinitarian identification of God has been used to interpret the conjunction of divine transcendence and immanence: "Only the persons of the Son and Spirit act directly in creation. The Father acts in the world only through the Son and Spirit. He himself remains transcendent" (Pannenberg 1991, 328).

The notions of transcendence and immanence are near the heart of what makes dialogue between Christianity and the natural sciences complicated. That which is transcendent and/or immanent is not subject to empirical analysis, cannot be included in a "catalog" either of the contents of the universe or of the regularities governing its structure and dynamics. But then, what is the relationship, if any, between God, who is both transcendent and immanent, and the natural world? How is that relationship to be recognized and understood?

The thesis of **panentheism** (Clayton and Peacocke 2004; Moltmann 1993), in which the world is construed as being *in* but not (as in **pantheism**) identical to God, is one attempt to do justice both to God's transcendence and to God's immanence, as well as to the universe's radical dependence on God as its creative origin, although it is not entirely clear how much added insight panentheism actually offers.

The traditional Christian affirmation of God's transcendence and/or immanence also raises questions about **divine action**. Does God, who is not part of this world, cause events and results in it, as required by **providence**, **revelation**, **miracles**, and so forth, in a way or ways at all analogous to the connection between causes and effects apparent in our daily experience? How does God act on and within the created order? Are **information**, matter, or energy created *ex nihilo*, inserted from the "outside," or annihilated without remainder? Would not such a possibility have consequences for the principles of conservation that undergird our comprehension and manipulation of natural events? Or is divine causality a different sort of thing, on a different "level" entirely from creaturely causality (Thomas Aquinas, *Summa theologiae*; Tanner 2001)? Questions such as these remain under discussion.

Maurice Lee

REFERENCES AND RECOMMENDED READING

Augustine. (397–401) 2014–2016. *Confessions*. Tr. Carolyn J.-B. Hammond. Loeb Classical Library 26–27. Cambridge: Harvard University Press.

Clayton, Philip, and Arthur Peacocke, eds. 2004. *In Whom We Live and Move and Have Our Being: Panentheistic Reflections on God's Presence in a Scientific World*. Grand Rapids: Eerdmans.

Moltmann, Jürgen. 1993. *God in Creation: A New Theology of Creation and the Spirit of God*. Minneapolis: Fortress.

Pannenberg, Wolfhart. 1991. *Systematic Theology*. Vol. 1. Grand Rapids: Eerdmans.

Tanner, Kathryn. 2001. *Jesus, Humanity and the Trinity: A Brief Systematic Theology*. Minneapolis: Fortress.

INCARNATION. The doctrine of the incarnation, meaning "enfleshment," is derived from clear biblical texts affirming both the full deity and humanity of Jesus of Nazareth, two natures in one person: John 1:1 ("The Word was God"); 1:14 ("The Word became flesh and made his dwelling among us. We have seen his glory …"); Matt. 1:23 ("God with us"); and so on.

This doctrine was affirmed by the Nicaean (AD 325) and Chalcedonian (AD 451) councils. Nicaea affirmed the Son of God as *homoousios*—of the same substance or being as the Father, that he "came down from heaven" and became "incarnate by the Holy Spirit of the Virgin Mary." Chalcedon stated that the distinct divine and human natures are preserved without confusion, change, division, or separation in the person of Jesus of Nazareth; he is "truly God and truly man, of a [rational] **soul** and body; consubstantial with the Father according to the Godhead, and consubstantial with us according to the Manhood; in all things like unto us, without sin."

Although considered metaphysically impossible and

logically contradictory by critics (e.g., Martin 1991), various philosophers and theologians have defended the doctrine as rationally coherent, without denying the "**mystery** of godliness" (1 Tim. 3:16 ESV). The incarnation was possible precisely because human beings have been made in God's image (Gen. 1:26–27; Ps. 8, esp. v. 5: "a little lower than the angels"). What is essential to humanness is derived from God's nature; thus the incarnate Christ is the truest or archetypal human—"*the* **image of God**" (see 2 Cor. 3:18; Col. 1:15; Heb. 1:3): "It is because man in the creative order bears the image of his Creator that it was possible for the Son of God to become incarnate as man and in His humanity to display the glory of the invisible God" (Bruce 1957, 194).

To understand the incarnation's logic, some have proposed a *kenosis* theory (cf. Phil. 2:7 ESV, where the Son, equal with God, "emptied himself"); thus God's Son sheds divine properties such as omniscience and omnipotence in assuming humanity. If such great-making properties can be surrendered, they must not be necessary properties of God. Or perhaps, it is argued, this "loss" of divine properties was simulated: the Son only appeared to lack them. The problem here is that of a divinely created false impression, similar to the gnostic heresy of Docetism. A view of *kenosis* that affirms Jesus's limited exercise of undiminished, divinely necessary powers, however, poses no theological problem (see Davis et al. 2004; Evans 2006).

Philosopher Thomas Morris's "two-minds" proposal also shows promise (Morris 1986, 1990; also DeWeese 2007). He makes three crucial distinctions.

1. *Nature and person.* A thing's nature or essence makes it what it is; without essential properties, necessarily that thing would not exist. A person—that is, a center of (self-) **consciousness**, will, action, and responsibility—has a nature. Those qualifying as persons include humans, angels, and members of the triune Godhead. Jesus is one person who shares our human nature while still possessing the divine nature.

2. *Fully versus merely human.* Although humans commonly sin, have four limbs, and die, these are merely—not essentially—human characteristics. For example, redeemed humans will be sinless in the afterlife, and Enoch and Elijah didn't die. Thus, being essentially or fully human does not exclude the possibility of being fully divine. We are essentially—not merely—God's image bearers, with rational, relational, creative, spiritual, and moral capacities to carry out our function as God's representative king-priests on earth. These qualities derive from God as a finite subset of infinite divine qualities.

3. *Divine awareness and human awareness.* These are comparable to our two levels of "consciousness"—conscious and subconscious—working in tandem. The Son of God came to fully identify with human beings, becoming a first-century, Aramaic-speaking Nazarene who grew in virtue (Luke 2:52; Heb. 2:18; 5:8) and in the understanding of his mission as he read the Hebrew Scriptures. All the while he possessed the eternal, divine "subconsciousness," drawing on this as necessary to accomplish his triunely predetermined task on earth (cf. John 17:5, 22–26; Phil. 2:6–11). These two levels of awareness do not require positing two wills.

Jesus's mission included human weakness and self-restricted access to knowing it was impossible to sin (cf. James 1:13) and to the timing of his return (Matt. 24:36). The "divine reality was not fully and comprehensively present to the [human] mind of Jesus" (O'Collins 1983, 186). While Jesus could have had access to knowing these matters, he voluntarily gave up access in order to faithfully live out Adam's (humanity's) and Israel's story and calling. As Jesus was "led by the Spirit" (Luke 4:1) in the face of temptation, we are to be likewise led (Rom. 8:14).

To share in our struggle with temptation, Jesus did not engage in playacting but rather gave up having access to the knowledge that sinning for him as God was impossible (cf. James. 1:13), just as he gave up other items of knowledge (O'Collins 1995, 271). We can furthermore argue that temptation does not have to involve the possibility of sin.

Admittedly, God's identification with humanity is a unique situation. However, temptation without the possibility of sinning is conceivable. Imagine entering a room and, unbeknownst to you, the door has an automatic two-hour time lock. You consider leaving once or twice, but you freely decide to read for the full two hours, after which you leave the room. While you would not have been able to leave the room during that time, you did not bother to move toward the door to try getting out because you freely decided to stay put. Or consider a spy who goes on a dangerous mission and takes along with him—in case he is tortured to give top-secret **information**—a limited-amnesia-producing pill with an antidote for later use. He would be under the effects of the amnesia pill if captured but would still possess the information in his mind even though he had chosen a self-limitation (Morris 1986, 149–50, 91).

Some have charged that this view smacks of a heretical Nestorianism—two persons in Christ (Moreland and Craig 2003, 612). This criticism is not worrisome, as we can readily recognize the integration of conscious and subconscious minds within one person without suspicion of schizophrenia. Why could this not be true of human and divine awarenesses in Jesus of Nazareth? One modification of this two-levels-of-awareness view is that, instead of using the analogy of the "subconscious," one can appropriate the notion of a "preconscious" awareness. This could be compared to a person's ready access to familiar calculus formulas in his mind—even though he is not consciously thinking about them. Likewise, the voluntarily restrained powers of, say, divine omniscience and omnipotence in Jesus of Nazareth would be located and readily accessible in this preconscious awareness of his mind (Loke 2014).

The doctrine of the incarnation has wide-ranging implications. It reaffirms the goodness of the physical world (Gen. 1:31) and the worthy enterprise of studying it (Ps. 111:2)—in stark opposition to gnosticism's denigration of matter. Furthermore, the incarnation was not temporary but permanent, sealed in immortality through Jesus's bodily **resurrection** unto imperishability (1 Cor. 15; Phil. 3:21). This "eighth day of creation," as Irenaeus called it, sets in motion the new creation (cf. 2 Cor. 5:17) that leads to a final, incorruptible "transformed physicality" of all the redeemed and of heaven and earth (see Wright 2006). The doctrines of creation and incarnation stand in opposition to Eastern philosophical views like **monism**, which regards the physical world as illusory and thus negates the scientific enterprise, and **pantheism**, which divinizes all things and diminishes both humans as God's unique image bearers and the worthiness of scientific study. These doctrines also oppose the dominant view of **scientism** that assumes only matter exists.

Indeed, the history of science demonstrates that the doctrines of creation and incarnation have made modern science possible. They emphasize a rational God who designs an orderly, predictable universe that can be studied and delighted in by rational humans made in God's image, with Jesus of Nazareth as the archetypal human. Nature can be studied without denying its reality, without idolizing it, and without reducing it to a mass of unguided material processes. **Stanley Jaki** rightly argues that the incarnate Christ is "the Savior of science" (Jaki 1988; cf. Stark 2005).

Paul Copan

REFERENCES AND RECOMMENDED READING

Bruce, F. F. 1957. *The Epistles of Paul to the Ephesians and to the Colossians.* New International Commentary on the New Testament. Eds. E. K. Simpson and F. F. Bruce. Grand Rapids: Eerdmans.

Davis, Stephen T., David Kendall, and Gerald O'Collins, eds. 2004. *The Incarnation: An Interdisciplinary Symposium on the Incarnation of the Son of God.* Oxford: Oxford University Press.

DeWeese, Garrett. 2007. "One Person, Two Natures: Two Metaphysical Models of the Incarnation." In *Jesus in Trinitarian Perspective,* ed. Fred Sanders and Klaus Issler, 114–53. Nashville: B&H Academic.

Evans, C. Stephen, ed. 2006. *Exploring Kenotic Christology: The Self-Emptying of God.* Oxford: Oxford University Press.

Jaki, Stanley. 1988. *The Savior of Science.* Washington, DC: Regnery.

Loke, Andrew Ter Ern. 2014. *A Kryptic Model of the Incarnation.* Burlington, VT: Ashgate.

Martin, Michael. 1991. *The Case against Christianity.* Philadelphia: Temple University Press.

Moreland, J. P., and William Lane Craig. 2003. *Philosophical Foundations for a Christian Worldview.* Downers Grove, IL: IVP Academic.

Morris, Thomas. 1986. *The Logic of God Incarnate.* Ithaca, NY: Cornell University Press.

———. 1988. "The Metaphysics of God Incarnate." In *Trinity, Incarnation, and Atonement,* ed. Ronald Feenstra. Notre Dame, IN: University of Notre Dame Press.

———. 1990. *Our Idea of God.* Downers Grove, IL: InterVarsity.

O'Collins, Gerald. 1983. *Interpreting Jesus.* Ramsey, NJ: Paulist.

———. 1995. *Christology.* Oxford: Oxford University Press.

Stark, Rodney. 2005. *The Victory of Reason: How Christianity Led to Freedom, Capitalism and Western Success.* New York: Random House.

Wright, N. T. 2006. *Evil and the Justice of God.* Downers Grove, IL: InterVarsity.

INDETERMINISM. Simply stated, **determinism** is the idea that any event that happens does so necessarily. Deterministic events have a cause, but according to determinism, these events could not have been otherwise; so in another possible world, given the identical conditions, the identical effects would follow. Technically, while indeterminism is simply the contrary of determinism, indeterminism often refers to randomness or even, according to some, uncausedness. However, in discussions of personal agency, **libertarian free will** would not fit into either category. This is the view that it is up to the agent or self to bring about an event because of a certain goal in mind—what **Aristotle** called *final* causality.

Discussions of determinism and indeterminism are chiefly concerned with a productive or *efficient* causality (see **Aristotle's Four Causes**). According to the libertarian free will view, even if certain factors (e.g., the external environment or even various internal dispositions or inclinations) can influence the will, the "buck stops" with the self or agent as the fundamental or initiating cause of an action (see **Libertarian Free Will**).

However, concepts of determinism and indeterminism are simpler and clearer when applied to physical science. An indeterministic event has nothing that causes it to occur; it is a pure **chance** or random event. A scientific theory is deterministic in the case that its laws are deterministic. Additionally, a notion accepted by many in the sciences is that all events in nature are deterministic. But evidence suggests to some that there are fuzzy complications in the physical world.

At first glance it appears that classical **physics** is deterministic and quantum mechanics is indeterministic. Consider classical physics first. The laws of physics formulated before the end of the nineteenth century have a deterministic character. For example, expressing the time development of a system involving mechanical interactions through Newton's laws involves the solution of second-order differential equations, including specifying the initial conditions (positions and velocities) for the components of the system.

This is deterministic. But **chaos theory** was developed in the twentieth century when it was realized that, for many physical systems, the initial conditions cannot inherently be specified accurately enough to allow the unambiguous determination of the evolution of these systems in time. The result is that even though a system can be represented by deterministic equations, there can be no satisfactory determination of the behavior of the system in the absence of sufficiently precise specified initial conditions. And hence any system is indeterministic in the sense that the precise determination of its time evolution is limited if the precise initial condition requirement is not met.

The Schrödinger version of **quantum theory** gives a good accounting for many microscopic phenomena (see **Schrödinger's Cat**). For example, the half-life of a radioactive nucleus can be successfully calculated using the Schrödinger quantum mechanical equation of motion and knowledge of the relevant nuclear forces. This result applies only to the average behavior of the radioactive nuclei of interest, for the decay time of an individual nucleus cannot be determined completely. All that can be known is that there is a 50 percent **probability** that an individual nucleus will decay sometime within a half-life time interval. If and when the decay takes place cannot be determined with any more precision than that. However, the measured mean half-life of a statistically large enough sample will be found to be the predicted half-life resulting from the quantum calculation.

And so the Schrödinger version of quantum mechanics is inherently indeterministic. But an alternative version, developed by Louis de Broglie and David Bohm, uses what are called *pilot waves*, which evolve in a deterministic way. Thus we have deterministic quantum interpretations, not merely indeterministic ones.

The conclusion, though, is that the deterministic classical physics of Newton is a version of physics that can be used to put a person on our moon and that can calculate the next solar eclipse but which also has some indeterministic aspects. And there is still debate among physicists regarding the status of quantum theory, a theory that can successfully predict the existence of such exotic elementary particles as the Higgs boson but cannot precisely tell us when a ^{137}Cesium nucleus will decay. Although a quantum mechanical calculation can give a definite prediction for the half-life for a ^{137}Cs nucleus, and hence a precise number of such decays over a given period can be determined for a statistically significant sample, for a single ^{137}Cs nucleus we only can know that it has a 50 percent chance of surviving for the time span on one half-life, which is 30 years.

Indeterminism and Theology

Indeterminism also falls under the category of divine foreknowledge and the doctrine of God. There are several positions that theologians take on this issue, from the classical position known as the Augustinian-Calvinist view at one end of this spectrum to the opposite view of **open theism**, with at least two intermediate views of a modified Calvinistic perspective — simple foreknowledge and the Arminian/Molinist position of middle knowledge.

Briefly, in the Augustinian-Calvinist (Reformed) view, God knows all that will come to pass since God foreordains all. The middle knowledge position holds that God knows all that will come to pass — the actual world God chooses to create, which includes creaturely free choices — in addition to what would have come to pass (i.e., possible worlds) had he created a universe different from our universe. The simple foreknowledge view is that God simply knows what will come to pass. Lastly, the open-theistic position is that the future is partly open to God's knowledge, for God cannot know what decisions free agents will make, and even certain features of natural processes are unknown to God. Much of this discussion centers on God's knowledge of human actions, but there has also been some scientific discussion, mainly by scientists-theologians who are interested in God's foreknowledge of the unfolding of scientific processes.

There is agreement that God is omniscient, in that he knows all reality perfectly. The key question is, what is the content of that reality? And how is it related to the doctrine of creation? The content of God's infallible knowledge is exhaustively settled from all eternity. But some would say that reality is composed of both settled and open aspects, whereas others would say that all of reality is settled. To put it another way, reality is composed of both settled and open aspects, according to open theism. God settles whatever he wants to settle and hence perfectly foreknows whatever he wants to. But God leaves open whatever he chooses to leave open and hence knows as much of the future as possible under this kenotic position. The result is that there is a certain amount of openness, both for humanity and for creation processes. A key question in this discussion is "Is this position of theistic openness credible?" The answer has ramifications resulting in people making their own free decisions, to the universe/earth developing in a free way, to God altering physical processes in response to humans' **prayer**s, to God responding as he observes the outworking of this freedom in the universe and on earth.

Many theologians who are interested in maintaining that God actively responds to prayer almost of necessity support the conclusion that there is true openness in physical process and thereby tend to support the open theistic position. For example, **John Polkinghorne** holds to the idea of a component of free will for humans and free process for the physical and biological developing worlds. But this is a limited freedom, for the combination of chance and necessity—or put another way, the idea of lawful randomness—characterizes God's relationship to humanity and to creation. But this randomness/indeterminacy is fenced in by the physical laws of the universe. This gives the universe, the earth, and life on earth the ability to explore/develop, not in a haphazard way, but in a way that is truly explorative yet bounded by the characteristics and laws of the universe.

These fine-tuned characteristics and laws of the universe have resulted in sentient life on our earth developing some 13.8 billion years post–big bang. Additionally, God (often) answers prayer in a manner hidden to scientific investigation but in a way that followers of Jesus can observe. And with God's goal for the universe clearly in his sight, God is able to respond to prayer and the actions of humanity and creation as only a master improviser can do to eventually produce the eschatological result of his choice.

Richard F. Carlson

REFERENCES AND RECOMMENDED READING

Beilby, James K., and Paul R. Eddy, eds. 2001. *Divine Foreknowledge: Four Views.* Downers Grove, IL: InterVarsity.
Bishop, Robert C. 2006. "Determinism and Indeterminism." In *Encyclopedia of Philosophy*, 3:29–35. 2nd ed. Farmington Hills, MI: Thomson Gale.
D'Espagnat, Bernard. 1989. *Reality and the Physicist.* Cambridge: Cambridge University Press.
Polkinghorne, John. 1989. *Science and Providence.* London: SPCK.
———. 1994. *The Faith of a Physicist.* Princeton, NJ: Princeton University Press.
———. 1998. *Science and Theology: An Introduction.* London: SPCK.

Ware, Bruce A., ed. 2008. *Perspectives on the Doctrine of God: Four Views.* Nashville: B&H Academic.

INDUCTION, PROBLEM OF. When you infer that it will rain based on observation of dark clouds and your previous experience that such clouds lead to rain, you are making an inductive argument. Induction can be contrasted with deduction. In a valid deductive argument, the conclusion of the argument is guaranteed to be true if the premises are true. There are various types of inductive arguments, but one thing they share in common is that they do not guarantee their conclusions. Your inference that it will rain may be a good one, but the outcome is not guaranteed. Or to take another example, the fact that all *observed* emeralds are green does not guarantee that *all* emeralds are green. Perhaps it is reasonable to believe the conclusion or to say that the conclusion is probably true, but it could in fact turn out to be false. Induction is therefore closely related to scientific reasoning and evidential reasoning more generally. Evidence is taken to support or confirm a hypothesis, but it does not guarantee that the hypothesis is true; new evidence could undermine the hypothesis.

David Hume raised a serious question about inductive reasoning, which is known as the problem of induction. Hume argued that there is no justification for accepting the conclusions of inductive arguments. Essentially, he claimed that there can be no deductive argument in support of induction because deductive reasoning cannot take us from observed cases to unobserved cases, and any attempt to provide an inductive argument in support of induction would beg the question. It is important to emphasize the radical nature of his argument. Consider again the example of inferring rain from dark clouds. It might be thought that we are justified in believing that it will probably rain even if we are not justified in believing that it will actually rain, but Hume denied this. For Hume, we are not justified *at all* in believing the conclusion of an inductive argument. Furthermore, any satisfactory account of induction must deal not only with Hume's problem, but also with Nelson Goodman's "new riddle of induction" (Goodman 1983).

Various responses to the problem of induction have been given. **Karl Popper** agreed with Hume that induction could not be justified, but he tried to give an account of the rationality of science without it. However, significant objections to Popper's approach have been raised, and it is far from clear that he was really able to avoid induction anyway.

Some have argued that induction is justified because what we *mean* by being justified in believing a hypothesis on the basis of evidence is that we are applying inductive standards. Others have argued that the past success of inductive reasoning provides justification of induction. Of course, this is an inductive argument itself, but its defenders have claimed that the circular reasoning involved here is not fatal to their argument. Still others have proposed a pragmatic justification of induction that does not claim that induction leads to the truth, but that if there is a truth to be found, induction is the best way to find it.

Finally, given the success of Bayesian reasoning as an approach to scientific inference, it could be seen as providing an answer to the problem of induction (see **Bayes' Theorem**). Bayesianism provides a justification for how to update beliefs on the basis of evidence, and some formal results show how it can converge to the truth. However, there is no consensus that this approach, or any of the others mentioned, provides a completely satisfactory resolution to the problem of induction.

David Glass

REFERENCES AND RECOMMENDED READING

Goodman, Nelson. 1983. *Fact, Fiction, and Forecast.* 4th ed. Cambridge, MA: Harvard University Press.

Huber, Franz. 2007. "Confirmation and Induction." In *The Internet Encyclopedia of Philosophy*, ISSN 2161–0002. (Accessed 3 July 2015) www.iep.utm.edu/conf-ind/.

Swinburne, Richard, ed. 1974. *The Justification of Induction.* Oxford: Oxford University Press.

INFERENCE TO THE BEST EXPLANATION.

Differing from both **deduction** and **induction**, inference to the best explanation (IBE), or abduction as it is also known, is a mode of reasoning that gives priority to explanatory considerations. When a detective infers that Jones committed the crime because this hypothesis explains all the evidence better than any other hypothesis, an IBE has been made. So Sherlock Holmes is incorrect when he describes his reasoning as *deductive* since it is more accurately characterized as *abductive*. This kind of reasoning is commonplace in everyday life, in medical diagnosis, and in science more generally. It is often claimed, for example, that scientists decide between competing hypotheses on the grounds of how well they explain the relevant evidence.

Despite its intuitive appeal, IBE has been the subject of considerable discussion and debate. The question of how hypotheses are to be compared in terms of explanatory cogency is of central importance. Various explanatory virtues are usually appealed to, such as simplicity, scope, coherence, fit with other theories, explanatory (or predictive) power, etc. The idea is that the best explanation is the one that ranks best overall. In a given case, one explanation might do better on some virtues and another explanation on other virtues, which means that making a comparison might be difficult. In other cases, one explanation might do much better across a wide range of virtues and so make the comparison much easier.

As a nondeductive form of inference, IBE does not guarantee the truth of what is inferred. In light of this, it seems more reasonable to infer not that the best explanation is true, but that it is probably or approximately true. A further issue, which has been raised by the philosopher **Bas van Fraassen**, is that the inference made when using IBE depends on what explanations are considered in the first place. If the list of potential explanations being considered in a given case does not contain the true explanation, then the truth cannot be found and an inference will be made to the "best of a bad lot." For this reason, a more plausible version of IBE will claim only that the best explanation is *more likely* to be true (or closer to the truth) than the alternatives that have been considered. However, if there are good reasons for thinking that the list of potential explanations exhausts all the options, then a stronger conclusion may be warranted.

Another objection to IBE raised by van Fraassen concerns its relationship to Bayesian reasoning (see **Bayes' Theorem**). Essentially, his argument is that if IBE is formulated in terms of **probability**, then it will involve updating beliefs in a way that is either the same as Bayesianism, in which case IBE is redundant, or in conflict with Bayesianism, in which case it is irrational. Many advocates of IBE argue that it is compatible with Bayesianism, but that this does not mean IBE is redundant. They argue that explanatory considerations can play a key role in implementing Bayesianism. Others have argued that IBE can be rational even if it contradicts Bayesianism in certain ways.

Finally, IBE is often used in debates about the existence of God, particularly in the context of design arguments, but it is also used in arguments for specifically Christian beliefs. For example, the **resurrection of Jesus** is often proposed as the best explanation of a range of evidence relating to the events after the crucifixion.

David Glass

REFERENCES AND RECOMMENDED READING

Douven, Igor. 2011. "Abduction." In *Stanford Encyclopedia of Philosophy*, ed. Edward N. Zalta. http://plato.stanford.edu/archives/spr2011/entries/abduction/.

Lipton, Peter. 2004. *Inference to the Best Explanation*. 2nd ed. London: Routledge.

van Fraassen, Bas. 1989. *Laws and Symmetry*. Oxford: Clarendon.

INFINITY. The term *infinite* describes something without limits—beginningless, endless, or both. Strictly speaking, the infinite quantity can comprise events, points, causes, space, time, and more.

Dating back to Aristotle, philosophers have distinguished between two types of infinities: *potential infinities* and *actual infinities*. A potential infinity arises by continually adding a new member to a series in a process that continues without end. At any given point, the number of members in the series is finite, but the number grows without bound. For example, assuming nothing causes the universe to cease, the passage of time represents a potential infinity. In contrast, an actual infinity occurs when a completed set contains an unlimited number of members. Scientists, theologians, philosophers, and mathematicians debate whether an actual infinity can truly exist.

Various philosophical, theological, and scientific discussions involve the concept of infinity. Zeno's paradox of motion uses the infinite divisibility of distance to argue for the impossibility of motion. Olbers's paradox notes that an infinitely large, eternal universe (the prevailing scientific view of the universe in the early nineteenth century) results in a sky as bright as the sun at every point. In mathematics, Torricelli's trumpet (or Gabriel's horn), when extended to an infinite length, can hold only a finite amount of paint yet requires an infinite amount of paint to cover its surface. Various Christian and Islamic philosophers argued for a beginning to the universe since an eternal universe would require traversing an infinite temporal regress (see Craig 2000). More recently, particle physicists have appealed to infinities in calculations of measurable quantities confirmed by results from accelerator experiments.

Mathematicians, scientists, and philosophers approach infinities with different concerns (see **Mathematics**). Mathematicians start from a few postulates and use well-established mathematical rules to derive other true statements. Scientists seek to determine the proper way to understand how the universe operates, and they utilize extensive tests that compare different mathematically based models against observations of the universe to assess which model works best. Philosophers evaluate different propositions according to principles built from foundational logical concepts such as the law of cause and effect or the law of noncontradiction. The key question then is how infinities interact with these mathematical, scientific, and philosophical endeavors and whether actual infinities can exist in the real world.

During the late nineteenth and early twentieth centuries, mathematician Georg Cantor formalized a mathematically consistent system for describing and ordering infinite series within the context of set theory (a fundamental theory in mathematics). His work brought infinities comfortably into the mathematical world.

However, one main philosophical concern relates to how infinities affect foundational concepts such as the law of noncontradiction (two contradictory statements cannot both be true in the same sense at the same time). The existence of an actual infinite appears to violate (or at least modify) this principle.

Consider a hypothetical hotel, first articulated by mathematician David Hilbert, which contains an infinite number of rooms. When an infinite number of football players arrive, they "fill" the hotel (more precisely, the players can be put into a one-to-one correspondence with the rooms in the hotel). When a second infinite number of baseball players arrive, they also fit into the "full" hotel. The hotel owner simply moves each of the football players to the room twice their current number (1 moves to 2, 2 moves to 4, 3 moves to 6 and so on). This leaves the infinite number of odd rooms unoccupied. In arithmetic form, infinity + infinity = infinity, or 2 x infinity = infinity.

Hilbert originally proposed the hotel example to demonstrate the counterintuitive nature of infinite quantities compared to finite quantities. Hilbert's illustration does not even deal with the different levels of infinity delineated by Cantor. For example, the set of counting numbers is a smaller infinity than the set of real numbers. However, many philosophers claim that Hilbert's hotel leads to absurd conclusions and, therefore, actual infinities must not exist.

Physicists invoke infinities when trying to understand how the universe behaves on both large and small scales. In quantum field theory (QFT), the calculations required to determine measurable characteristics and behavior of subatomic particles results in infinite values. However, the well-defined method called *renormalization* subtracts other infinite quantities to arrive at finite numbers that physicists compare with data collected from sensitive instruments surrounding powerful particle accelerators. Reminiscent of Hilbert's hotel, infinite quantities subtracted from other infinite quantities result in well-defined finite quantities that correspond to measurements in the real world. One point to note: the infinities in QFT usually result from treating fundamental particles as point-like; that is, with no discernible size. For example, any density-related calculation for the particle leads to an infinite value. Many physicists consider this value to be an artifact of an incomplete theory, resulting in a growing level of interest in and support for models like string theory. In string theory, the finite size of particles eliminates many, if not all, of the infinities that arise in QFT.

Infinities also come to bear on another highly successful theory called *general relativity*. All mass exerts a gravitational pull, described by general relativity, on any other mass in the universe. This pull draws the mass toward a common center, and unless some repulsive force counteracts the gravitational pull, the mass collapses to a point of infinite density called a *black hole*. Again, the infinity appears because the mass ends in a point with zero volume. Scientists view the infinity as an indicator that general relativity breaks down and that a more comprehensive quantum theory of gravity will accurately describe black holes without any infinities. However, an infinite temporal regress associated with a past eternal universe doesn't seem to trouble most scientists.

Cosmologists also encounter infinities as they try to understand the large-scale behavior of the universe. A growing body of evidence shows that the universe underwent an inflationary epoch in the earliest fractions of a second of its origin. As cosmologists build models to explain the mechanism behind this inflation, the models usually lead to the conclusion that the universe is part of a much larger multiverse (multiple universes). The number of universes, all of which experience a beginning like this one, grows without bound, and the spatial dimensions of the universe also grow without bound. Although both of these infinities presumably represent potential infinities, many scientists argue that an infinite number of spatially infinite universes adequately explains, without need for God, the fine-tuning observed for life in the universe (see **Multiverse**; Guth 1997).

Infinity plays a prominent role in apologetic arguments for the beginning of the universe. For example, if the universe had existed forever, an infinite series of temporal events has passed to arrive at this point. This infinite series of events would represent an actual infinity. If actual infinites cannot exist, then one can definitively argue that the universe must have a beginning—a conclusion that directly buttresses the second premise of the kalam **cosmological argument**:

1. Everything that has a beginning of its existence has a cause of its existence;
2. the universe has a beginning of its existence; therefore
3. the universe has a cause of its existence. (Craig 2000)

Consider how philosophers, mathematicians, scientists, and theologians might approach the proposition of an actual infinite such as a spatially infinite universe. A philosopher might argue against such a proposition by noting that actual infinities lead to contradiction. The mathematician might counter that no contradictions exist because everything in this spatially infinite universe behaves properly according to the well-defined rules of infinite set theory. The scientist might add that we must account for the finite nature of the measuring instruments (namely, humans) before declaring something contradictory. The theologian might clarify that a spatially infinite universe need not conflict with a sovereign God because God would be the highest level of infinite. However, actual (quantitative) infinities need not exist to account for God's attributes, such as omniscience (a qualitative infinite).

Scientists, theologians, philosophers, and mathematicians will continue to debate the existence of actual infinities. However, they all agree that something is either finite *or* infinite. A finite universe cannot grow to be infinite in any finite time, nor could an infinite universe be subdivided into only finite sets.

Jeff Zweerink

REFERENCES AND RECOMMENDED READING
Craig, William Lane. 2000. *The Kalam Cosmological Argument*. Repr. ed. Eugene, OR: Wipf and Stock.

Dauben, Joseph Warren. 1990. *Georg Cantor: His Mathematics and Philosophy of the Infinite*. Princeton, NJ: Princeton University Press.

Guth, Alan. 1997. *The Inflationary Universe*. Reading, MA: Addison-Wesley.

INFLATIONARY UNIVERSE THEORY. Cosmic inflation refers to an event in which the universe expanded in volume by a factor of 10^{78} or more, starting when the universe was between 10^{-36} (a trillionth of a trillionth of a trillionth) and 10^{-35} seconds old and ending when it was between 10^{-33} and 10^{-32} seconds old. This extremely brief inflationary episode answers important big bang questions—such as why a universe so young (13.8 billion years) and so large exhibits large-scale uniformity and homogeneity and why its spatial geometry is flat. Inflation also explains why the universe is made up of galaxy clusters and superclusters, with giant voids between them. Quantum mechanical fluctuations during the inflationary era would have been magnified to become the seeds from which galaxy clusters and superclusters sprang.

Inflation is a component of many biblically based cosmic creation models. Millennia before astronomers discovered the universe's big bang features, the Bible stood alone in declaring that the universe arose from a space-time beginning (Gen. 1:1; Heb. 11:3). Some students of Scripture find biblical evidence that the universe was "stretched out," or expanded, from that beginning under constant physical laws, including a pervasive law of decay.

By the 1980s, physical evidence for the big bang and the obvious existence of life persuaded astronomers that an inflation episode must have occurred. Not until 2013, however, did measurements definitively show that a hyperinflationary event took place (Ade et al. 2013). The first data release of the Planck satellite contained measurements of the polarization signals in the radiation remaining from the big bang cosmic creation event (aka the cosmic background radiation) that yielded a value of what is called the *scalar spectral index*.

For a universe in which no inflation occurred, the scalar spectral index would measure to be 1.0 or greater. For a universe that experienced a simple inflationary event, the index would measure exactly 0.95. For a complex inflationary event, the index would measure between 0.96 and 0.97. The Planck satellite measured a value of 0.9603±0.0073. While verifying inflation, this measurement could not distinguish between simple and complex inflation.

In March 2014 the BICEP2 instrument at the South Pole detected the B-modes from the gravitational waves that were emitted as a result of the cosmic inflation event (Overbye 2014). While yielding an independent **confirmation** of the big bang inflation event, it, too, could not distinguish between simple and complex inflation. Researchers anticipate that future data releases from Planck and BICEP2 will pin down what kind of inflation the universe experienced. This knowledge holds potential to reveal more design features, more fine-tuning, essential for the existence of advanced life.

The particle thought to be responsible for the early inflationary event is called, generically, an *inflaton*. Astronomers have seen some evidence—an excess signal in a certain X-ray spectral line emitted from our galaxy's center (Prokorov and Silk 2010) and an excess cooling in white dwarf stars (Isern et al. 2009, 2010)—that may be consistent with existence of such inflatons.

Hugh Ross

REFERENCES AND RECOMMENDED READING

Ade, P. A. R., N. Aghanim, C. Armitagecaplan, et al. 2013. "Cosmological Parameters." *Astronomy and Astrophysics.* March 20. arXiv:1303.5076.

Isern, J., S. Catalán, E. García-Berro, and S. Torres. 2009. "Axions and the White Dwarf Luminosity Function." *Journal of Physics Conference Series* 172, no. 1 (June 3): id. 012005.

Isern, J., E. García-Berro, L. G. Althaus, and A. H. Córsico. 2010. "Axions and the Pulsation Periods of Variable White Dwarfs Revisited." *Astronomy & Astrophysics* 512 (April): A86.

Overbye, Dennis. 2014. "Space Ripples Reveal Big Bang's Smoking Gun." *New York Times.* March 17.

Prokorov, Dimitri, and Joseph Silk. 2010. "Can the Excess in the Fe XXVI Iyǎ Line from the Galactic Center Provide Evidence for 17 keV Sterile Neutrinos?" *Astrophysical Journal Letters* 725 (December 20): L131–34.

INFORMATION. "In the beginning was the word." This opening of John's gospel has served as a rich source for theological reflection. Words are the instruments for conveying intentions, securing meanings, and demonstrating intelligence. The interesting thing is that word, as developed by modern information theory, is not merely of theological or philosophical significance but also a proper object of scientific study.

Modern information theory takes its cue from Claude Shannon (Shannon and Weaver 1949), a mathematician active especially in the 1930s and 40s. During that time, as a student at MIT and then subsequently as a researcher at Bell Labs, he was concerned with "the transmission of intelligence," as he called it. His being an age of telephones and radios, he needed to transmit signals across communication channels and do so reliably in the presence of noise. His theory of information showed how to do this efficiently and how to counteract the effects of noise.

Shannon's theory of information was subsequently generalized and mined for deeper insights into nature. Information, for Shannon, was confined to symbol strings coded and transmitted down communication channels. But the concept of information implicit in Shannon's theory is considerably broader. At its core, information is about the impartation of patterns. For Shannon, the patterns took the form of particular symbol strings transmitted by communication engineers. But wherever there are patterns, there is information.

Patterns, by their very nature, are distinctive, taking one form to the exclusion of others. In fact, we could turn this around: wherever there is an inclusion-exclusion, there is a pattern signifying what was included in place of what was excluded. It follows that information is at the core of every intelligent act, for intelligences act by deciding on one course of action to the exclusion of others.

In his book *Orthodoxy*, G. K. Chesterton underscored this point as follows: "Every act of will is an act of self-limitation. To desire action is to desire limitation. In that sense every act is an act of self-sacrifice. When you choose anything, you reject everything else.... Every act is an irrevocable selection and exclusion" (Chesterton 1986, 243). When we act, we imprint a pattern on reality, a pattern that would have been different had we acted differently.

Information may therefore properly be conceived as a verb rather than a noun, as an active force rather than a passive object. To be sure, we often speak of items of information, as with a book whose text, obviously, contains information. But the information in that book can be represented in many ways. What is crucial about the information in a book is how its textual pattern was conceived and imparted. Information is about giving form to something; it is about transformation, taking something without a given pattern and then giving it that pattern.

Information is how intelligence gets transmitted. For this reason, information is a key concept in **intelligent design**. The type of information most widely used among design theorists is **specified complexity**.

William A. Dembski

REFERENCES AND RECOMMENDED READING

Chesterton, G. K. 1986. *Orthodoxy*. In *Collected Works of G. K. Chesterton*. Vol. 1. San Francisco: Ignatius.
Dembski, William A. 2014. *Being as Communion: A Metaphysics of Information*. Surrey, UK: Ashgate.
Gleick, James. *The Information: A History, a Theory, a Flood*. New York: Vintage.
Shannon, C., and Warren Weaver. 1949. *The Mathematical Theory of Communication*. Urbana: University of Illinois Press.

INSTITUTE FOR CREATION RESEARCH. Dr. **Henry M. Morris** (1918–2006), coauthor of the *Genesis Flood*, father of the modern creationist movement, and former university academic, founded the Institute for Creation Research (ICR) in 1972. ICR is a Christian apologetics institute with the objective to provide research, education, and communications that promote and defend the principles of scientific creationism and biblical creationism.

In short, ICR promotes biblical inerrancy and the understanding that the Bible can be read literally to understand scientific and historical facts about the world in which we live. A more complete statement of its tenets can be found on its website (ICR, "Principles of Scientific Creationism"). The research, educational material, and scientific principles promoted by ICR found acceptance within the evangelical community but were strongly rejected and ridiculed by mainstream academia, the **American Scientific Affiliation**, the **National Center for Science Education** (NCSE), and others (Numbers 1993).

Dr. Henry Morris had an impressive academic career in engineering at a number of universities between 1942 and 1970, holding positions from instructor to department chair on the faculties at Rice, the University of Minnesota, the University of Lafayette, Southern Illinois University, and Virginia Polytechnic Institute and State University. Tensions grew over his views on flood **geology** during the 1960s until he voluntarily left the Virginia Polytechnic Institute and State University (Virginia Tech) in 1970. Upon leaving, Dr. Morris and Dr. Timothy LaHaye, the author of the Left Behind series, first cofounded the Christian Heritage College (now San Diego Christian College) in 1970 with the intent to provide Christian education to train both the heart and the mind, built on a framework of biblical literalism, including scientific creationism based on the young-earth creation interpretation of Genesis.

Morris launched the Creation Science Research Center as an adjunct to the university, but leadership within the organization was in conflict over the goals of the center, leading Morris to reorganize it as the Institute for Creation Research in 1972. ICR maintained its affiliation with Christian Heritage University until the early 1980s. In 2007 the institute relocated from California to Dallas, Texas, after the death of its founder. ICR is presently led by Dr. Henry Morris III (chairman) and Dr. John D. Morris (president). ICR mentored **Ken Ham** between 1987 and 1994 when he left to found **Answers in Genesis**.

Douglas Futuyma (1995) and the NCSE have noted that the research function of ICR has a strong following within the creation science community and homeschooling community, with no success being accommodated by the mainstream scientific community or a large part of the broader evangelical community. Some prominent evangelical leaders like Albert Molher and John MacArthur promote **young-earth creationism** and ICR. ICR has been ridiculed by the scientific community with more than 109 scientific and scholarly organizations denouncing their basic tenets (NSCE 2014). Other Christian organizations, including the American Scientific Affiliation, **Reasons to Believe**, and **BioLogos**, have also criticized their research. Authors like **Bernard Ramm** (1954), Alan Hayward (1995), **Hugh Ross** (1994), Andrew Balian (2011), and David Snoke (2006) have documented errors and logical fallacies within ICR material. Even Answers in Genesis, the young-earth creationist organization founded by Ken Ham, has denounced some of ICR's creation science (AiG 2014).

ICR faced many obstacles establishing graduate level science and science education programs throughout the 1980s and 1990s in California but received accreditation in 1982 from the Transnational Association of Christian Colleges and Schools (TRACS). ICR filed a lawsuit and was later awarded a settlement and granted permission by the State of California to continue their graduate program. Legal issues continued when ICR moved to Texas in 2007, ultimately leading the organization to end their graduate science education program after multiple rounds of rejection by the Texas Higher Education Coordinating Board (THECB) and finally a ruling by the District Court for the Western District of Texas. In 2010 ICR's board of directors voted to close their science education program and open a School of Biblical Apologetics (NCSE 2010; Numbers 1993).

ICR has been very successful in their communications function, having published numerous books, DVDs, Bible commentaries, and related material. ICR representatives regularly engage and debate with mainstream scientists. Dr. **Duane Gish** was probably ICR's best-known debater, having once debated media personality and author Phil Donahue. ICR publishes a monthly magazine, *Acts & Facts*, multimedia programs, mobile apps, and books.

Jonathan Howard Fisher

REFERENCES AND RECOMMENDED READING

AiG. 2014. "Arguments to Avoid." Answers in Genesis. https://answersingenesis.org/creationism/arguments-to-avoid/.
Balian, Andrew S. 2011. *The Unintended Disservice of Young Earth Science.* Charleston, SC: Christian Research.
Flank, Lenny. 2007. *Deception by Design: The Intelligent Design Movement in America.* St. Petersburg, FL: Red and Black.
Futuyma, Douglas J. 1995. *Science on Trial: The Case for Evolution.* Sunderland, MA: Sinauer.
Hayward, Alan. 1995. *Creation and Evolution: Rethinking the Evidence from Science and the Bible.* Bloomington, MN: Bethany House.
ICR. "Principles of Scientific Creationism." Institute for Creation Research. Accessed October 10, 2016. www.icr.org/tenets/.
Morris, Henry, and John C. Whitcomb. 2011. *The Genesis Flood, 50th Anniversary Edition.* Phillipsburg, NJ: P&R.
NCSE. 2010. Glenn Branch. "ICR Concedes Defeat over Its Graduate School." National Center for Science Education. September 1. http://ncse.com/news/2010/09/icr-concedes-defeat-over-its-graduate-school-006160.
———. "Statements from Scientific and Scholarly Organizations." National Center for Science Education. Accessed October 10, 2016. http://ncse.com/media/voices/science.
Numbers, Ronald. 1993. *The Creationists: The Evolution of Scientific Creationism.* Berkeley: University of California Press.
Ramm, Bernard. 1954. *The Christian View of Science and Scripture.* Grand Rapids: Eerdmans.
Ross, Hugh. 1994. *Creation and Time.* Colorado Springs: NavPress.
Snoke, David. 2006. *A Biblical Case for an Old Earth.* Grand Rapids: Baker.

INSTRUMENTALISM. Broadly considered, modern instrumentalist ideas trace their ancestry back to **Francis Bacon** (1561–1626), who advocated an inductive methodology aimed at prediction and control (Bacon [1620] 2000) as the proper pathway to knowledge, itself conceived as power over nature, with the ultimate goal of finding a panacea for the human condition and creating a societal utopia (Bacon [1626] 1996). In this inductivist lineage, mediated by **empiricism** and an evolutionary conception of knowledge influenced by Hegel and Darwin, the American pragmatist John Dewey (1859–1952) explicitly appropriated the term *instrumentalism* as the name for his philosophy (see **Induction, Problem of**).

Dewey held that ideas should be evaluated experimentally and experientially in terms of their adaptive utility for beneficial progress in the management of nature and human society (Dewey [1910] 1997, [1920] 1957, 1922, [1938] 1991). Dewey's account of concepts, scientific and otherwise, treated them functionally as tools for rational action directed toward the integration, prediction, and control of the world of our experience. Eschewing what he called a "spectator theory of knowledge" that would differentiate between knowing and doing, representation and reality, Dewey made knowledge inseparable from the contexts of experimental inquiry, leading him to a view of truth as instrumentally warranted assertability rather than representational correspondence with the world (Dewey 1941). His approach rejected the **dualism** between theory and observation and any notion that scientific theories were representations of an independent metaphysical reality.

Most philosophers would maintain that saying something is true is conceptually different from saying that its assertion is warranted, however, so they would reject Dewey's account of truth—and pragmatist accounts of truth in general—as category mistakes that do not respect the meaning of the truth predicate. In particular, both **Hans Reichenbach** and **Bertrand Russell** roundly criticized Dewey's approach to science and **logic** (Reichenbach [1939] 1989; Russell [1939] 1989; see also **Theories of Truth**).

While Dewey's form of instrumentalism has not been influential in twentieth-century **philosophy of science**, it nonetheless has some similarities to the instrumentalism of the logical positivists (see **Logical Positivism**) arising from their emphasis on the verifiability theory of meaning (see **Verification Principle**). In this context, while the ordinary semantics of the truth predicate is accepted, scientific theories are not candidates for truth or falsity, but rather tools for the prediction, manipulation, and representation of data.

One form of positivist instrumentalism, associated with the work of Percy Bridgman (1927), is called *operationalism*. Operationalists hold that all physical entities, properties, and processes employed in a scientific theory are to be defined instrumentally in terms of the operations and experiments by which they are measured and apprehended. More generally, positivist instrumentalism takes theories as convenient instruments for moving from a given set of observations to another predicted set of observations (Bird 1998, 125–31). Informational input passes through the "black box" of the theory and generates informational output. Since observational input and output is representable in statements that are either true or false, to maintain that the theories themselves are neither true nor false requires distinguishing between observation statements and theoretical statements, the former being truth evaluable and the latter not. But making a clear distinction between observational and theoretical statements has proven intractable, and since logical deduction is necessary for deriving predictions from theories, the contention that the theories themselves lack truth values is now also largely regarded as untenable (as is **logical positivism** itself on the basis of many considerations).

For reasons such as these, modern instrumentalism has been assimilated to generic antirealism (see **Realism and Antirealism**). Philosophers of science appropriating the instrumentalist label today would mostly acknowledge that theories are either true or false, but they would still deny that every aspect of a theory should be construed realistically and would maintain that the reasons for accepting a theory as useful or empirically adequate need not be reasons for regarding it as true.

Recognition that the truth of scientific theories is always underdetermined (see **Underdetermination**) to some extent by the data and that the history of science is a graveyard of discarded theories once regarded as true (Laudan 1981) is central to an instrumentalist (antirealist) view of scientific theories. For example, both **Thomas Kuhn** (1970, 1977), who locates the value of scientific theories in their problem-solving utility, and **Larry Laudan** (1977, 1984), who characterizes scientific progress in terms of *increased* problem-solving ability,

are instrumentalists who allow theories to have truth values but regard truth or falsity as tangential to understanding the nature and progress of science.

Bruce L. Gordon

REFERENCES AND RECOMMENDED READING

Bacon, Francis. (1620) 2000. *The New Organon*. Cambridge Texts in the History of Philosophy. Eds. Lisa Jardine and Michael Silverthorne. Cambridge: Cambridge University Press.
———. (1626) 2017. *New Atlantis and the Great Instauration, Second Edition*. Jerry Weiberg, ed. Malden, MA: John Wiley & Sons. http://oregonstate.edu/instruct/phl302/texts/bacon/atlantis.html.
Bird, Alexander. 1998. *Philosophy of Science*. Montreal: McGill-Queen's University Press.
Bridgman, Percy W. 1927. *The Logic of Modern Physics*. New York: Macmillan.
Dewey, John. (1910) 1997. *The Influence of Darwin on Philosophy and Other Essays*. Amherst, NY: Prometheus.
———. (1920) 1957. *Reconstruction in Philosophy*. Boston: Beacon.
———. 1922. *Human Nature and Conduct: An Introduction to Social Psychology*. New York: Henry Holt.
———. (1938) 1991. *Logic: The Theory of Inquiry*. Carbondale: Southern Illinois University Press.
———. 1941. "Propositions, Warranted Assertability, and Truth." *Journal of Philosophy* 38:169–86.
Kuhn, Thomas S. 1970. *The Structure of Scientific Revolutions*. 2nd ed. Chicago: University of Chicago Press.
———. 1977. *The Essential Tension: Selected Studies in Scientific Tradition and Change*. Chicago: University of Chicago Press.
Laudan, Larry. 1977. *Progress and Its Problems: Toward a Theory of Scientific Growth*. Berkeley: University of California Press.
———. 1981. "A Confutation of Convergent Realism." *Philosophy of Science* 48:19–49.
———. 1984. *Science and Values: The Aims of Science and Their Role in Scientific Debate*. Berkeley: University of California Press.
Reichenbach, Hans. (1939) 1989. "Dewey's Theory of Science." In *The Philosophy of John Dewey*, ed. P. A. Schilpp and L. E. Hahn, 157–92. La Salle, IL: Open Court.
Russell, Bertrand. (1939) 1989. "Dewey's New Logic." In *The Philosophy of John Dewey*, ed. P. A. Schilpp and L. E. Hahn, 135–56. La Salle, IL: Open Court.

INTELLIGENT DESIGN. Is it possible for nature to exhibit patterns that reliably point to the effect of an intelligence? More simply, could design in nature be detectable (such as in the **DNA** of cells)? Christians, in believing that God created the world for a purpose, hold that there is design or intention in nature. Nature is not what it is on account of a random accident but because God, by intention or design, made it that way. Christians do, however, dispute whether such design is detectable in the sense that the methods of science could detect it.

According to intelligent design proponents, **information**, especially **specified complexity**, is the key to detecting design. A large scientific and philosophical literature now alternately defends or attacks the idea that design in nature is detectable by the methods of science. Nevertheless, this central point of intelligent design is also resisted on theological grounds.

Theistic evolutionists, for instance, hold that as far as the science of evolution is concerned, Darwin largely got it right, so that all we see, as scientists, is the activity of natural forces (such as **natural selection** acting on random variations). Such forces give no direct evidence of purposive activity by God. Rather, God sets up that backdrop of nature in which nature essentially does its own creating. According to theistic evolution, design is undetectable scientifically.

Young-earth creationists tend also to resist intelligent design. It is not that they necessarily think that signs of intelligence in nature may not be reliably detected through **scientific method**s. Rather, they tend to regard such an endeavor as pointless. Indeed, if the earth is but a few thousand years old, then there was no time for evolution to produce organisms, so they must instead have been specially created by God (organisms can't just magically materialize). Design detection thus becomes superfluous. Moreover, intelligent design at best shows that an intelligence was behind the world, not that this intelligence is the Judeo-Christian God depicted in Genesis.

Intelligent design is at once too radical for theistic evolutionists and not radical enough for young-earth creationists. Theistic evolutionists, for instance, will agree with atheistic evolutionists about the science of evolution but then dispute with them the theological implications of evolution (as when **Richard Dawkins** claims that Darwin made it possible to be an intellectually fulfilled atheist). To this, intelligent design says that atheistic evolutionists are not just getting the theology wrong but also the science. Young-earth creationists, on the other hand, see intelligent design as not sufficiently close to the Bible and therefore as not going far enough.

The intelligent design community, by contrast, sees itself, like the little bear's porridge in *Goldilocks*, as having settled on just the right solution to the origins problem. In finding clear signs of intelligence in cosmology (as in the fine-tuning of the universe) and in biology (as in the nano-engineered structures in all living cells), it sees itself as going as far in inferring design in nature as the scientific evidence allows.

William A. Dembski

REFERENCES AND RECOMMENDED READING

Dembski, William A. 2004. *The Design Revolution: Answering the Toughest Questions about Intelligent Design.* Downers Grove, IL: InterVarsity.
Dembski, William A., and Jonathan Wells. 2008. *The Design of Life: Discovering Signs of Intelligence in Biological Systems.* Dallas: Foundation for Thought and Ethics.
Gonzalez, Guillermo, and Jay W. Richards. 2004. *The Privileged Planet: How Our Place in the Cosmos Is Designed for Discovery.* Washington, DC: Regnery.
Meyer, Stephen C. 2009. *Signature in the Cell: DNA and the Evidence for Intelligent Design.* San Francisco: HarperOne.
———. 2014. *Darwin's Doubt: The Explosive Origin of Animal Life and the Case for Intelligent Design.* San Francisco: HarperOne.

INTELLIGIBILITY OF THE UNIVERSE. Albert **Einstein** (1879–1955) famously remarked that "the eternal **mystery** of the world is its comprehensibility.... The fact that it is comprehensible is a miracle" (Einstein 1936). And the mathematical physicist Eugene Wigner (1902–95) opined, "The miracle of the appropriateness of the language of **mathematics** for the formulation of the laws of **physics** is a wonderful gift which we neither understand nor deserve" (Wigner 1960; see also Steiner 1998). As these remarks highlight, the intelligibility of the universe to the human mind begs explanation in two respects. The first is ontological: Why is nature ordered in such a way that it can be understood? The second is epistemological: Why is the human mind able to understand the natural order?

For science to be possible, order must be present in nature, and it has to be discoverable by the human mind. But why should either of these conditions be met? Historically, while there were temporary manifestations of systematic research into nature in ancient Greece and early Islam and isolated discoveries elsewhere, the seeds of modern science first came to concentrated and sustained fruition in Western culture before its methodologies and achievements were disseminated throughout the world. This lasting and world-changing development emerged in the context of the Judeo-Christian **worldview** that permeated medieval Europe (Gordon 2011; Hannam 2011; Lindberg 2007; Pearcey and Thaxton 1994; Whitehead 1925). What drove it was a deeply entrenched society-wide conception of the universe as the free and rational creation of God's mind so that human beings, as rational creatures made in God's image, were capable of searching out and understanding a divinely ordered reality (see **Image of God**). The freedom of God's creative will meant this order could not be deduced abstractly—it had to be discovered through observation and experiment—but God's stable and faithful character guaranteed it had a rational structure that diligent study could reveal.

This theological foundation gave solid answers to ontological and epistemological questions concerning the intelligibility of the universe, but as the quotes from Einstein and Wigner make clear, this foundation had been lost by the middle of the twentieth century. Why?

Some see it as the outworking of the seventeenth-century mechanical philosophy that sought to explain all natural phenomena in terms of material contact mechanisms (Ashworth 2003). On this view, the mechanical philosophy conceptually reduced scientific causality to efficient and material causes, purging Aristotelian notions of formal and final causality from science (see **Aristotle's Four Causes**). This is perhaps accurate methodologically but not metaphysically (Gordon 2011). The conception of mechanism in the mechanical philosophy retained formal causes in their *design* and final causes in the *purpose* they were created to serve.

The break with **Aristotle** arose from the fact that in the conception of the theistic and deistic mechanical philosophers, design and purpose were *transcendently* imposed rather than *immanently* active, so the search for scientific explanations turned to the material implementation of efficient mechanisms (see **Deism**). The purge of any sense of design and purpose from the "scientific" conception of nature must be located with the late nineteenth-century rise of (naturalistic) Darwinian philosophy, which sees the mechanisms of nature as brute facts and the course of their development as completely blind and purposeless (Gordon 2011).

It is **Darwinism**, so conceived, that renders the existence of mathematically describable regularities in nature and their intelligibility to the human mind (itself conceived as the accidental result of blind processes) such a surprise, for it assumes **naturalism**—the self-contained character of nature and the denial of supernaturalism—as the context for science. Under the aegis of naturalism, there can be no expectation that nature is regular in a way that allows presently operative causes to be projected into the past to explain the current state of the universe or into the future to predict its development. The absence of any sufficient cause to explain why nature exists at all leaves the naturalist with no reason to think that what does exist should be ordered, or that any order she or he finds should be projectable into the past or the future (Craig and Moreland 2000; Goetz and Taliaferro 2008; Plantinga 2006; Rea 2002).

By denying transcendence and defaulting to a conception of the universe as a closed and ultimately arbitrary system of causes and effects, naturalism makes science the uncanny enterprise on which Einstein and Wigner remarked. On the other hand, the Judeo-Christian worldview recognizes that nature exists and is regular not because it is closed to divine activity but because—and *only* because—divine causality is operative. It is only because nature is a creation and thus *not* a closed system of causes and effects that it exists in the first place and exhibits the regular order that makes science possible. God's existence and action are not obstacles to science; they are the very basis of its possibility (Gordon 2011, 2013; Nash 1997; Plantinga 2011b).

Finally, if naturalism were true, there would be little basis for supposing the human mind capable of doing science at all (Lewis 1960; Nash 1997; Plantinga 1993, 2011a, 2011b). The prospect of human knowledge depends on the reliability and veridicality of our perceptual faculties and reasoning processes. If our perceptions and inferences provide a genuine grasp of how reality *must* be, independent of our minds, then knowledge is possible; but if the certainty we experience is a mere feeling and not a reliable guide to how things are, then we do not have knowledge. Naturalism tells us our cognitive faculties are the end result of mindless causes and historical accidents, taking *no account* of truth or logic. This means that *any* complex of perceptions and desires conducive to survival could be locked in by **natural selection** as the way our minds *just happen* to work. That our beliefs would be *true* under such conditions seems quite unlikely; at the very least, their truth or falsity would not be ascertainable (Beilby 2002; Plantinga 2011a, 2011b). So if naturalism were true, our reasoning processes would be so discredited that neither naturalism itself nor the practice of science would be supportable (see **Evolutionary Argument against Naturalism**).

In short, **theism** not only catalyzed the rise of modern science, but it remains the only worldview on which the origin, order, and intelligibility of nature make any sense.

Bruce L. Gordon

REFERENCES AND RECOMMENDED READING

Ashworth, William B., Jr. 2003. "Christianity and the Mechanistic Universe." In *When Science and Christianity Meet*, eds. David C. Lindberg and Ronald L. Numbers, 61–84. Chicago: University of Chicago Press.

Beilby, James, ed. 2002. *Naturalism Defeated? Essays on Plantinga's Evolutionary Argument against Naturalism*. Ithaca, NY: Cornell University Press.

Craig, William Lane, and J. P. Moreland. 2000. *Naturalism: A Critical Analysis.* New York: Routledge.

Einstein, Albert. 1936. "Physics and Reality." *Journal of the Franklin Institute* 221 (3). Repr. in Albert Einstein, *Ideas and Opinions*, 290–323. New York: Crown, 1954.

Goetz, Stewart, and Charles Taliaferro. 2008. *Naturalism*. Grand Rapids: Eerdmans.

Gordon, Bruce. 2011. "The Rise of Naturalism and Its Problematic Role in Science and Culture." In *The Nature of Nature: Examining the Role of Naturalism in Science*, eds. Bruce L. Gordon and William A. Dembski, 3–61. Wilmington, DE: ISI Books.

———. 2013. "In Defense of Uniformitarianism." *Perspectives on Science and Christian Faith* 65 (2): 79–86.

Hannam, James. 2011. *The Genesis of Science: How the Christian Middle Ages Launched the Scientific Revolution*. Washington, DC: Regnery.

Lewis, C. S. (1947) 1960. *Miracles: A Preliminary Study*. New York: Macmillan.

Lindberg, David C. 2007. *The Beginnings of Western Science: The European Scientific Tradition in Philosophical, Religious, and Institutional Context, Prehistory to A.D. 1450.* 2nd ed. Chicago: University of Chicago Press.

Nash, Ronald. 1997. "Miracles and Conceptual Systems." In *In Defense of Miracles: A Comprehensive Case for God's Action in History*, eds. R. Douglas Geivett and Gary Habermas, 115–31. Downers Grove, IL: IVP Academic.

Pearcey, Nancy, and Charles Thaxton. 1994. *The Soul of Science: Christian Faith and Natural Philosophy.* Wheaton, IL: Crossway.

Plantinga, Alvin. 1993. *Warrant and Proper Function.* New York: Oxford University Press.

———. 2006. "Against Materialism." *Faith and Philosophy* 23 (1): 3–32.

———. 2011a. "Evolution versus Naturalism." In *The Nature of Nature: Examining the Role of Naturalism in Science*, eds. Bruce L. Gordon and William A. Dembski, 137–51. Wilmington, DE: ISI Books.

———. 2011b. *Where the Conflict Really Lies: Science, Religion, and Naturalism.* New York: Oxford University Press.

Rea, Michael. 2002. *World without Design: The Ontological Consequences of Naturalism.* New York: Oxford University Press.

Steiner, Mark. 1998. *The Applicability of Mathematics as a Philosophical Problem.* Cambridge, MA: Harvard University Press.

Whitehead, Alfred North. 1925. *Science and the Modern World.* New York: Macmillan.

Wigner, Eugene. 1960. "The Unreasonable Effectiveness of Mathematics in the Natural Sciences." *Communications on Pure and Applied Mathematics* 13, no. 1. Repr. in Eugene Wigner, *Symmetries and Reflections*, 222–37. Bloomington: Indiana University Press, 1967.

INTUITION. In **epistemology**, beliefs are said to be inferential when they are logically inferred from other beliefs and noninferential when they are not. Many sorts of beliefs, such as those produced by sense perception, testimony, and memory are noninferential in this sense, so the term *intuition* is reserved for noninferential beliefs other than those produced by sense perception, testimony, and memory. Intuitionists hold that some noninferential (sometimes called *prephilosophical*) beliefs are rationally credible, so we may appeal to them in the course of our reasoning. Anti-intuitionists deny this.

All of the following have been thought of as intuitions, according to the above definition:

1. Basic principles of logic, such as the law of noncontradiction or the validity of inference patterns such as *modus ponens*.
2. Metaphysical principles such as the **principle of sufficient reason**.
3. Particular metaphysical judgments in thought experiments concerning, for example, identity, survival, or **causation**.
4. General moral principles such as the claim that promise breaking is wrong.
5. Moral judgments about particular cases (e.g., that it would be wrong to take organs from one healthy person to save the lives of five persons needing transplants).
6. General principles of epistemology, such as the principle of evidentialism, that we should not believe any proposition without sufficient evidence.
7. Epistemological judgments about particular cases (e.g., that in certain circumstances some person does not know some proposition).

This is important because many claims to scientific, theological, and everyday knowledge cannot be sustained unless we are permitted premises beyond the austere minimum afforded by **empiricism**. That is, intuitionism appears necessary if we are to avoid solipsism, skepticism, or **reductionism**.

Some anti-intuitionists argue that we have no reason to think that our intuitions are reliable (i.e., mostly true). They claim that intuitions are by definition unsupported by argument, that their truth cannot be independently checked, and that until we have some reason to think them reliable, we should regard them as no better than hunches. Other anti-intuitionists go further, arguing that we have reason to think intuitions unreliable (i.e., mostly false). They point to experimental findings of neurophysiology that purport to explain how intuitions arise, and that suggest their contingency, malleability, and variability. Much of what has become known as "experimental philosophy" draws on such findings to discredit appeal to intuitions in "armchair philosophy."

Some intuitionists have replied by characterizing intuitive beliefs as expressing relations between concepts, and that our ability to grasp such relations ensures that the resulting beliefs are reliable. Others have replied that the uncheckability of intuitions is just another example of the epistemic circularity that characterizes most basic sorts of belief, including those favored by the anti-intuitionist: for example, the reliability of perceptual beliefs cannot be established without appealing to perceptual beliefs, and the reliability of memory beliefs cannot be established without appealing to other beliefs. Still others have replied that some appeal to intuitions is inescapable even by anti-intuitionists: any normative epistemological principle that excludes intuitions is itself an intuition.

Mark T. Nelson

REFERENCES AND RECOMMENDED READING

Alston, William P. 1993. *The Reliability of Sense Perception.* Ithaca, NY: Cornell University Press.

Appiah, Anthony. 2008. *Experiments in Ethics.* Cambridge: Cambridge University Press.

Bealer, George. 1998. "Intuition and the Autonomy of Philosophy." In *Rethinking Intuition: The Psychology of Intuition and Its Role in Philosophical Inquiry*, ed. Michael R. DePaul and William Ramsey. Lanham, MD: Rowman & Littlefield.

Greene, J. R., R. Sommerville, L. Nystrom, J. Darley, and J. Cohen. 2001. "An fMRI Investigation of Emotional Engagement in Moral Judgment." *Science* 293:2105–8.

IRREDUCIBLE COMPLEXITY. The term *irreducible complexity* refers to a property of a system of separate parts that interact with each other to accomplish a specific function, in which the removal of one or more of the parts eliminates the function of the system. The term first gained widespread use after the publication in 1996 of my book *Darwin's Black Box.*

The term was introduced to focus attention on an apparent difficulty for Darwin's theory of evolution by random variation and **natural selection**, which, as Darwin insisted, was required to build biological systems by "numerous, successive, slight modifications" over long periods of time (see **Natural Selection; Neo-Darwinian Synthesis**). The difficulty is that, if irreducibly complex (IC) systems do not achieve their function until all of the necessary parts are in place, and if one or more IC systems occur in biology, natural selection would not have available the long series of gradually improving functional intermediates it required to construct them, and thus a Darwinian explanation for at least some parts of life would be stymied.

As an illustration of the concept, consider a common mechanical mousetrap. A mousetrap often is composed of multiple parts, such as a wooden platform, metal spring held in place by two staples with one end shaped to press against the platform and the other end to overlap another metal part, the hammer, pressing on it when the trap is set. Another metal part, the holding bar, stabilizes the hammer, and it must have its one end held in place by a staple and its other end inserted into a movable piece called the *catch.* The removal of one or more of the components of the mousetrap renders it incapable of catching mice. Thus the trap is irreducibly complex.

Many molecular biological systems also are irreducibly complex, in that removal of one of their components necessarily causes the loss of the system's function. Examples given in *Darwin's Black Box* include the vertebrate blood clotting system, the bacterial flagellum, and intracellular transport. A common strategy in molecular biology to identify required components of a system is to "knock out" (render inoperative) **gene**s for suspected parts to see if the system fails. Such systems are IC.

I have expanded the basic definition of irreducible **complexity** given above to clarify its relevance to **biological evolution**. *Darwin's Black Box* (Behe 2006) explains that the term should be reserved to a "single" system containing several "well-matched" parts. The reason for "single" is to avoid the confusion that can arise when an entity is an aggregate of many complex systems, some irreducible, some not. For example, a city has many independent components (buildings, streets, sewers, and so forth) that can be removed without bringing it to a halt, but an incandescent electric light within the city fails without a filament. Similarly, a bacterial cell can live without a flagellum, but a flagellum cannot operate without one of its necessary parts. Thus in biology the term *irreducibly complex* should usually be confined to describing molecular systems. The reason for "well-matched" is to focus attention on the function of the system that requires the greatest amount of the system's internal complexity (the shape, placement, or composition of the parts).

Because it has been used to question Darwinian evolution, the concept of irreducible complexity is controversial, and some misconceptions concerning it have spread. One confusion is over whether a system is IC if a gradual, perhaps indirect, route to its evolutionary construction can be found. The definition of IC, however, just states that removal of a part causes it to cease its function; whether the system can be produced gradually is a separate question. A related misconception concerns whether a system is IC if the individual parts can be used for other purposes when removed from the original arrangement. For example, parts of a mousetrap can be used in isolation as paperweights or toothpicks. The term *function* in the definition of irreducible complexity, however, refers to that of the system (e.g., a mousetrap's ability to trap mice), not to uses that may be found for the individual components.

Some complex systems contain parts that are helpful but not absolutely required for function, or they may contain redundant components. As an example of the former, adding bait such as cheese helps attract a mouse toward a trap but is not itself part of the essential mechanism. An example of the latter is a rattrap that contains two springs for extra force. One of the springs may be removed and the trap will still work, but if both are removed, it won't. Thus the occurrence of either nonessential or redundant components in a biological system containing an irreducibly complex core cannot eliminate the conceptual difficulties for its Darwinian evolution.

Molecular biological systems are much more complex than machines such as mousetraps, and face proportionately severe problems for their putative undirected evolutionary construction. Molecular machines are composed of proteins and/or nucleic acids—linear biopolymers of hundreds or thousands of amino acid or nucleotide residues. Thus even one protein of a multiprotein system will have many critical features that can affect the function of the system, much as one named "part" of a mousetrap (such as the holding bar) can have various critical features (such as its length, rigidity, bends, and curls) that affect the function of the system. When considering proposed evolutionary explanations, all such features must be accounted for.

One vitally important difference between man-made and biological machinery is that cellular apparatuses must self-assemble—no intelligent agent directs their construction. Much of the information for assembly of molecular machines is contained in the geometric and chemical complementarity of interacting protein surfaces where, for example, a negative charge, oily patch, and hydrogen-bond donor on one convex surface might sit opposite a positive charge, oily patch, and hydrogen-bond acceptor on the complementary concave surface. Such features that cause the self-assembly of molecular machines are part of the irreducibly complex system, which would fail without them, because the parts would not adhere correctly to each other.

At a finer level of molecular biology, two different proteins can have similar but not identical amino acid sequences and similar but not identical biological activities. It has been widely assumed that Darwinian processes in all instances could convert one into the other over evolutionary time, but recent research has called this into question because, in at least some cases, the necessary, small, individual changes in sequence are either unhelpful (and thus not favored by natural selection) or deleterious (and thus actively disfavored by selection).

Only when several evolutionary changes have occurred is there a net benefit to the organism. It can be useful to apply the concept of irreducible complexity to such cases. The discrete amino acid changes required for transformation would then each be considered individual parts of the protein system, and a degree of irreducible complexity could be assigned to the evolutionary pathway. Thus, if each of several required changes were beneficial, the degree of IC would be zero. If one necessary change were deleterious by itself, the degree of IC would be one. If two were deleterious, the degree would be two, and so forth. In *The Edge of Evolution* (Behe 2007), I argue that, due to the exponentially decreasing likelihood of finding an evolutionary target if a step is not favored by selection, only a few such deleterious changes would place it beyond the reach of Darwinian processes.

Michael J. Behe

REFERENCES AND RECOMMENDED READING

Behe, M. J. 2000. "Self-Organization and Irreducibly Complex Systems: A Reply to Shanks and Joplin." *Philosophy of Science* 67:155–62.

———. 2001. "Darwin's Breakdown: Irreducible Complexity and Design at the Foundation of Life." In *Signs of Intelligence: Understanding Intelligent Design*, ed. W. A. Dembski, chap. 7. Grand Rapids: Brazos.

———. 2002. "The Challenge of Irreducible Complexity." *Natural History* 111:74.

———. 2004. "Irreducible Complexity: Obstacle to Darwinian Evolution." In *Debating Design: From Darwin to DNA*, ed. M. Ruse and W. A. Dembski, 352–70. Cambridge: Cambridge University Press.

———. 2006. *Darwin's Black Box: The Biochemical Challenge to Evolution.* 10th ann. ed. New York: Free Press.

———. 2007. *The Edge of Evolution: The Search for the Limits of Darwinism.* New York: Free Press.

Draper, P. 2002. "Irreducible Complexity and Darwinian Gradualism." *Faith and Philosophy* 19:3–21.

Miller, K. R. 2002. "The Flaw in the Mousetrap." *Natural History* 111:75.

Shanks, N., and K. H. Joplin. 1999. "Redundant Complexity: A Critical Analysis of Intelligent Design in Biochemistry." *Philosophy of Science* 66:268–82.

J

JAKI, STANLEY. The Reverend Dr. Stanley Jaki (1924–2009) was born in Győr, Hungary. Jaki attended the Jedlik Preparatory School and Junior College and in 1942 joined the order of St. Benedict. In 1947 he completed undergraduate work in philosophy, theology, and **mathematics** and moved to Rome for graduate study in theology at the Pontifical Institute of San Elmo. In 1948 he was ordained a priest, and in 1950 he completed a doctorate with his thesis "Les tendances nouvelles de l'ecclésiologie" (New Trends in Ecclesiology).

From 1951 to 1954, Jaki taught systematic theology at the School of Theology of St. Vincent College in Latrobe, Pennsylvania, where he also earned a bachelor of science degree. Jaki then began doctoral work in **physics** at Fordham University under the mentorship of Nobel laureate Victor Hess. In 1958 he completed his degree; the core of his thesis was published in the *Journal of Geophysical Research* as "A Study of the Distribution of Radon, Thoron, and Their Decay Products above and below the Ground."

Postdoctoral study in the history and **philosophy of science** at Stanford and UC Berkeley immediately preceded publication of his seminal work *The Relevance of Physics* (1966).

In 1965 he joined the faculty at Seton Hall, where he remained till his death. While there, Jaki became an internationally recognized scholar, serving as a fellow and guest lecturer at numerous institutions. Perhaps his most notable landmarks were appointments in 1974–75 and 1975–76 as the Gifford lecturer at the University of Edinburgh.

Jaki contributed to a variety of fields as evidenced by his receipt of the Lecomte du Nouy Medal (1970), the Templeton Prize (1987), and nine honorary doctorates spanning literature, systematic theology, science, and law. Jaki's most well-known contributions to the faith-and-science discourse are captured in two of his major works, *The Relevance of Physics* and *Science and Creation* (1974).

The Relevance of Physics is a historical analysis of the methods and limitations of exact science, particularly regarding physics. Jaki describes the implications of the heavy reliance of the natural sciences on "first order logic" and mathematics. He later explores these implications within the interaction of physics with theology, philosophy, other

sciences, and society in general. Significant threads from his later works can be traced back to this work. Most notably, stemming from his analysis of **Duhem**, **Quine**, and others, he elaborates on important aspects of the underdetermination of scientific theory by fact. He also articulates an application of Gödel's incompleteness theorem to physics (see **Gödel's Theorem**) and a "theory of everything."

Jaki's later and more widely read *Science and Creation* explores what he calls "the invariable stillbirths of the scientific enterprise" in a variety of historical cultures. The main thrust of the book elaborates on ideas from **Pierre Duhem**'s "*Système du Monde*" (1914). Jaki's historical/philosophical analysis of the importance of a Christocentric, monotheistic **worldview**, and specifically the doctrine of creation, as the only "viable birth" of the scientific enterprise in medieval Europe has been met with, in his own words, both jubilation and scorn (Jaki 2002).

In later works, Jaki explored the intersections of science and religion, believing that the two were more deeply interdependent than most scientists or theologians would care to admit and that "science naturally opened out toward the affirmation of faith" (Tobin 2009).

Father Jaki died of a heart attack in Madrid, Spain, on April 7, 2009, returning from a lecture at the headquarters of the Pontifical Academy of Sciences.

Jeffrey T. Ploegstra

REFERENCES AND RECOMMENDED READING

Duhem, Pierre. 1914. *Le Système du Monde: Histoire des Doctrines Cosmologiques de Platon à Copernic.* 2:390. English translation: *The System of World: A History of Cosmological Doctrines from Plato to Copernicus.*
"Father Stanley L. Jaki, O.S.B." Seton Hall faculty biographical sketch. Accessed October 2, 2014. www.shu.edu/academics/artsci/physics/jaki.cfm.
Jaki, Stanley. 1966. *The Relevance of Physics.* Chicago: University of Chicago Press.
———. 1974. *Science and Creation: From Eternal Cycles to an Oscillating Universe.* Edinburgh: Scottish Academic Press.
———. 2002. *A Mind's Matter: An Intellectual Autobiography.* Grand Rapids: Eerdmans.
"Stanley Jaki Curriculum Vitae." Accessed October 2, 2014. www.rbsp.info/rbs/RbS/CLONE/jaki00.html.
Tobin, G. Gregory. 2009. "Death of Rev. Stanley L. Jaki, O.S.B." *Seton Hall News and Events.* April 7.
Weber, Bruce. 2009. "The Rev. Stanley L. Jaki, Physicist and Theologian, Dies at 84." *New York Times.* April 12. www.nytimes.com/2009/04/13/nyregion/13jaki.html?_r=0.

JAMES, WILLIAM.

JAMES, WILLIAM. A leading figure in the American philosophical movement known as "pragmatism," William James (1842–1910) made major contributions to several academic fields. Like his siblings, who included the famed novelist Henry James, William received broad academic training in the arts and **science**s. Although he trained to be a physician, he never actually practiced medicine, turning instead to **psychology** and philosophy in the professorate at Harvard. But James retained a strong empirical bent throughout his scholarly career.

Early on, James developed an intense interest in the question of human freedom, becoming a fierce critic of **determinism** and defender of free will. This led him to the study of psychology. This culminated in the publication of *The Principles of Psychology* ([1890] 1950), which subsequently became a standard text in the field for decades. One of James's primary aims in writing the *Principles* was to turn psychology into a bona fide science. His success in this endeavor profoundly impacted the history of psychology in the twentieth century. Ironically, this also led to a predominance of determinism in the field of psychology (most explicitly evident in the behaviorist and Freudian psychoanalytic schools), a fact that James would no doubt have met with chagrin.

James's interests afterward turned primarily to issues in **epistemology**, philosophical **anthropology**, and **philosophy of religion**, but his interest in **moral psychology** never waned. Indeed, he applied his insights in this area to most of the issues he pursued, often with novel results. In such essays as "The Dilemma of Determinism," "The Will to Believe," and "The Sentiment of Rationality" James explored the nature of human freedom and the role of the will in belief formation. He defended the thesis that the passions not only sometimes are but also *ought* to be decisive when it comes to arriving at one's views on matters related to **morality** and religion.

Influenced by C. S. Peirce, James adopted the view known as pragmatism, which is an epistemological orientation that understands truth and theoretical adequacy in terms of practical usefulness. Thus James endorsed a verificationist view of truth, according to which true ideas are those that can somehow be verified or applied in sense experience. Many of his essays related to the subject were eventually published in the book *Pragmatism* ([1907] 1979).

James delivered the **Gifford Lectures** in 1901–2, which were published under the title *The Varieties of Religious Experience* (1982). James's extensive research on religious practice and mystical experience made a profound impact, prompting him toward a more sympathetic view of religious belief than he had held previously in his career. In the work, however, he does not abandon his pragmatist and even strong empiricist approach. Rather, these epistemic standards are broadened in application to include human experiences that defy standard scientific analysis. In many ways, the *Varieties* represents a culmination of a central interest in his philosophical pursuits: how to reconcile the empirical method with the human experience of the transcendent. The work is a classic and, arguably, a model for inquiry into issues at the interface of faith and science.

James S. Spiegel

REFERENCES AND RECOMMENDED READING

Gale, Richard M. 2004. *The Philosophy of William James: An Introduction.* Cambridge: Cambridge University Press.

James, William. (1890) 1950. *The Principles of Psychology.* Vols. 1–2. New York: Dover.

———. 1956. *The Will to Believe and Other Essays in Popular Philosophy.* New York: Dover.

———. (1907) 1979. *Pragmatism.* Cambridge, MA: Harvard University Press.

———. 1982. *The Varieties of Religious Experience.* New York: Penguin.

Myers, Gerald. 1986. *William James: His Life and Thought.* New Haven, CT: Yale University Press.

Proudfoot, Wayne, ed. 2004. *William James and a Science of Religions.* New York: Columbia University Press.

Suckiel, Ellen Kappy. 1982. *The Pragmatic Philosophy of William James.* Notre Dame, IN: University of Notre Dame Press.

JASTROW, ROBERT.

JASTROW, ROBERT. Robert Jastrow (1925–2008) was a highly accomplished research scientist, science popularizer, research administrator, and writer. After receiving a PhD in **physics** at Columbia, he went on to teach and do research at Leiden, Princeton, Berkeley, and Yale.

In the 1950s Jastrow joined Project Vanguard, America's first effort to put an artificial satellite in orbit around the earth, and then he served as head of the theoretical division of the newly formed NASA. He remained involved in various aspects of the US space program through the 1960s and founded the Goddard Institute for Space Studies near Columbia in 1961. During this time Jastrow shifted his interests from theoretical particle physics to **astronomy**, space science, and **geology**, having taught these subjects at Columbia and later at Dartmouth.

Jastrow also began to develop his interest in atmospheric science and climatology while running the Goddard Institute. Between 1962 and 1974, he edited the *Journal of Atmospheric Sciences.* His interest in this field would later find expression in the George C. Marshall Institute, a public science policy nonprofit organization he cofounded in 1984. The institute is best known for its support of the Strategic Defense Initiative and its skeptical stance on global warming alarmism. But his interest in communicating science to the public began years earlier with several popular science books and frequent appearances on TV to discuss space science.

Jastrow is arguably best remembered today for his popular science book *God and the Astronomers*, wherein he recounted the history of modern **cosmology**. In particular, he noted the nearly universally negative reactions of leading scientists to the **big bang theory**. The most widely cited passages include these two:

> Now we see how the astronomical evidence supports the biblical view of the origin of the world. The details differ, but the essential elements in the astronomical and biblical accounts of Genesis are the same: the chain of events leading to man commenced suddenly and sharply at a definite moment in time, in a flash of light and energy. (Jastrow 1978, 3–4)
>
> For the scientist who has lived by his faith in the power of reason the story ends like a bad dream. He has scaled the mountains of ignorance; he is about to conquer the highest peak; as he pulls himself over the final rock, he is greeted by a band of theologians who have been sitting there for centuries. (105–6)

In addition, in Jastrow's earlier book *Until the Sun Dies*, he expressed his anthropocentric interpretation of our place in the cosmos: "Finally, man stands on the earth, more perfect than any other" (Jastrow 1977, 138). Yet in spite of these God-friendly statements, Jastrow consistently described himself as a reductionist and agnostic. He was clearly conflicted on the question of God, and he admitted as much in *The Privileged Planet* film documentary.

Jastrow fully accepted Darwinian evolution and used it as a basis for a "natural religion," uniting biological and cosmic evolution. In *The Enchanted Loom* he adds an eschatological transhumanist element to his religion by proposing a strong form of **artificial intelligence** in which humans download their minds into machines (Jastrow 1981).

Guillermo Gonzalez

REFERENCES AND RECOMMENDED READING

Jastrow, Robert. 1977. *Until the Sun Dies*. New York: W. W. Norton.
———. 1978. *God and the Astronomers*. New York: Warner.
———. 1981. *The Enchanted Loom: Mind in the Universe*. New York: Simon & Schuster.
The Privileged Planet. 2004. DVD. La Mirada, CA: Illustra Media.

JOHN TEMPLETON FOUNDATION. The John Templeton Foundation (JTF) was established in 1987 by Sir John Templeton (1912–2008). Templeton earned his fortune in the mutual fund industry, which he entered in 1954 when he established the Templeton Growth Fund. He sold the Templeton family of funds to the Franklin Group in 1999. The John Templeton Foundation, with an endowment of over $3 billion, oversees the Templeton Prize, awards grants, funds conferences, and publishes under the Templeton Foundation Press.

The John Templeton Foundation was established to fund scholarship at the intersections of both science and religion and religion and society. It encourages research relating to the "big questions" of life. The foundation currently considers grant applications in five core funding areas: science and the big questions, character virtue development, individual freedom and free markets, exceptional cognitive talent and genius, and genetics. Inquiries are accepted and reviewed twice each year. Full proposals are by invitation only after an applicant submits a successful inquiry.

Research relevant to the relationship between science and faith, human purpose and meaning, evolution, cosmology, creativity, and human psychological topics including forgiveness, love, and free will are among the many areas that are supported financially within the five core funding areas. Grants from the John Templeton Foundation encourage and enable respectful, informed dialogue between scientists, theologians, philosophers, and other experts, and are thus often interdisciplinary in nature. Published scholarly work supported by the JTF, in the form of books, essays, conference presentations, and other projects, are also often interdisciplinary.

In addition to supporting research through grant awards, the John Templeton Foundation oversees and awards the annual Templeton Prize, established in 1972, to a living person who is considered an "entrepreneur of the spirit." Scholars, practitioners, journalists, and others who demonstrate creativity and innovation, and whose work impacts and demonstrates progress in understanding spiritual realities are awarded the annual prize of £1.1 million.

The Templeton Foundation Press publishes books, designs websites, provides scholarships, designs apps for smartphones and tablets, and promotes public action campaigns that explore the themes of human virtues, science and the big questions, health and spirituality, and freedom and free enterprise. The Templeton Foundation Press has published more than 200 titles since it was established in 1997.

The JTF blog, *Big Questions Online*, and their Big Questions Essays list of authors reads like a who's who of scientists, philosophers, and theologians engaged in serious scholarly work at the interface of science, religion, and spirituality.

Some questions and concerns about the influence of JTF have surfaced in the past (Waldrop 2011, 323–25), perhaps not surprising for an institution with the financial power of a $3 billion endowment. It appears, however, that the number of outspoken critics is small, and the foundation has worked to make changes to address some concerns.

Jack Templeton, a surgeon and the son of Sir John Templeton, is the current president and chair of the John Templeton Foundation.

Sara Sybesma Tolsma

REFERENCES AND RECOMMENDED READING

Hermann, Robert L. 2008. *Sir John Templeton: Supporting Scientific Research for Spiritual Discoveries.* Philadelphia: Templeton Foundation.
———. 2013. *Looking Forward, Looking Upward: My Life, My Friendship with Sir John, and the Early Years of the Templeton Foundation.* Philadelphia: Templeton Foundation.
John Templeton Foundation. Accessed January 29, 2015. www.templeton.org/.
Templeton, Sir John. 1997. *Golden Nuggets from Sir John Templeton.* Philadelphia: Templeton Foundation.
Waldrop, Mitchell M. 2011. "Religion: Faith in Science." *Nature* 470:323–25. doi:10.1038/470323a.

JUNG, CARL G. Carl Jung (1875–1961) was born in Kesseil, Switzerland. His father was a minister in the Swiss Reformed Church, and his mother was the daughter of a Christian theologian. His family's spiritual life included influences from the occult and spiritualism as well as Christianity. These influences converged on Jung and influenced his later theoretical developments.

As a child, Jung spent many hours focusing on his inner experiences. At the age of three he remembers feeling a sense of abandonment when his mother was hospitalized for several months. This separation deeply troubled him. He recalled associating the figure of "women" with unreliability and "Father" with images of "reliable but powerless" (Jung 1961). This first sense of self-exploration was the beginning of a lifetime of self-exploration for Jung. During his teenage years, Jung sensed a division within his personality. The first personality, which he called "Number 1" was extroverted and helped him take care of his daily routine. The other personality, "Number 2," was introverted and allowed him to explore his

inner experiences. Jung's early occupation with self-exploration and identity greatly influenced his later psychological ideas.

This desire to explore the inner life led Jung to study psychiatry (Singer 1994). He earned his medical degree from the University of Basel in 1900 and studied in Zurich with Eugene Bleuler, a leading expert on schizophrenia. Jung's interests led him to read **Sigmund Freud**'s *The Interpretation of Dreams*. Jung struck up a correspondence with Freud that later led them to meet face-to-face in 1907. It is said that they conversed for 13 continuous hours (Singer 1994). Freud found Jung to be an exceptional intellect and appointed him the first president of the International Psychoanalytic Association. Their friendship lasted until 1913. While on a lecture tour to Clark University, Freud and Jung experienced personal and theoretical differences, causing them to go their separate ways.

After Jung's split with Freud, he entered a dark period of self-exploration from December 1913 until 1917. During these years, Jung suffered what Marvin Goldwert (1992) calls a "creative illness." Through his exploration of fantasy, images, culture, art, and myth, Jung proposed that people share in a "collective unconscious" in which all of humanity shares primordial images called *archetypes*. Jung believed that when a person explores and integrates these archetypes, he or she can experience a psychological rebirth called *individuation* (Jung 1961).

Jung died on June 6, 1961, after a long career as a teacher, private practitioner, and psychological theorist. Jung's school of psychoanalytic exploration called *analytical psychology* has influenced a number of fields. His influence is felt in the disciplines of **psychology**, philosophy, religion, and in pop culture (Brome 1978). While he claimed to be a Christian, he was not a churchgoer and seems to have been strongly influenced by his interest in **alchemy**, archaeology, gnosticism, and Eastern philosophies. His theory, while popular, is often critiqued because of its inability to be scientifically explored, a common critique of most psychoanalytical theorists.

Dominick D. Hankle

REFERENCES AND RECOMMENDED READING

Brome, V. 1978. *Jung: Man and Myth.* New York: Atheneum.
Goldwert, M. 1992. *The Wounded Healers: Creative Illness in the Pioneers of Depth Psychology.* Lanham, MD: University Press of America.
Jung, C. G. 1933. *Modern Man in Search of a Soul.* Orlando: Harcourt.
———. 1958. *The Undiscovered Self.* New York: Signet.
———1961. *Memories, Dreams, Reflections.* Ed. A. Jaffe. New York: Random House.
———. 1964. *Man and His Symbols.* New York: Doubleday.
Singer, J. 1994. *Boundaries of the Soul: The Practice of Jung's Psychology.* 2nd ed. New York: Doubleday.

JUST-SO STORIES.

JUST-SO STORIES. The term *just-so story* is a pejorative label often used by scientists when critiquing a scientific hypothesis as lacking a concrete, testable, evidential basis or strong explanatory power. Rather, "just-so stories" are typically viewed as relying on mere speculation or storytelling, providing only a veneer of explanation.

The term was inspired by Rudyard Kipling's 1902 book *Just So Stories*, which included whimsical tales such as "How the Camel Got His Hump," "How the Rhinoceros Got His Skin," and "How the Leopard Got His Spots." Though offending modern standards of political correctness, the latter story is one of Kipling's most famous, recounting that the leopard got its spots after an Ethiopian hunter smudged the "blackish-brownish colour" off his fingertips onto the leopard's coat to provide camouflage for hunting in the forest (Kipling 1902).

Because Kipling's *Just So Stories* parodied investigations of biological origins, the term has often been employed by those critiquing evolutionary explanations. As one article in the *Chronicle of Higher Education* explains, "Among evolutionary biologists in particular, that can be a scathing criticism: To call something a 'just-so story' is to dismiss it as unscientific moonshine.... It is easy—too easy, in many cases—to come up with 'explanations' of biological reality that reveal more about the writer's creativity than about evolution's" (Barash and Lipton 2010).

For example, when various scientists and mathematicians convened at the Wistar Symposium at the University of Pennsylvania in 1966 to debate the **neo-Darwinian synthesis**, anthropologist Loren Eisley asked, "Have we really answered all the questions; or is there something peculiarly attractive, almost like a Kipling 'Just So' story, about **natural selection**?" (Eisley 1967).

The field of evolutionary **psychology** has long faced accusations of purveying just-so stories. Philosopher **Daniel Dennett** charges that "sociobiologists from Thomas Hobbes to the present have offered Just So Stories about the evolution of **morality**, but, according to some philosophers, any such attempt commits the '**naturalistic fallacy**': the mistake of looking to facts about the way the world *is* in order to ground—or reduce—ethical conclusions about how things *ought* to be" (Dennett 1995). Likewise, in an article titled "How the Human Got Its Spots," psychologist Henry Schlinger writes that "Evolutionary psychology, while different in many respects from its predecessor sociobiology, is still subject to the accusation of telling just so stories" (Schlinger 1996).

Sometimes scientists tolerate just-so stories when they assist in propping up a materialistic **worldview**. Harvard evolutionary biologist **Richard Lewontin** acknowledges, "We take the side of science in spite of the patent absurdity of some of its constructs, in spite of its failure to fulfill many of its extravagant promises of health and life, in spite of the tolerance of the scientific community for unsubstantiated just-so stories, because we have a prior commitment, a commitment to materialism" (Lewontin 1997).

Indeed, evolutionary psychologists David Barash and Judith Eve Lipton recommend embracing just-so stories—even when they entail "mere guessing"—because "the alternative to proposing a just-so story" is the possibility that "God did it" (Barash and Lipton 2010).

Philosopher of science Carol Cleland observes that experimental scientists sometimes charge that the claims of historical scientists are untestable, asserting, "That they can't falsify their hypotheses or that their confirmatory arguments resemble just-so stories (Rudyard Kipling's fanciful stories, e.g., how leopards got their spots). The startling number of physicists and chemists who attack the scientific status of neo-Darwinian evolution provides telling examples of this phenomenon" (Cleland 2001).

Cleland argues that historical scientific claims *can* be tested scientifically (though in a different manner than experimental sciences), but concludes that if a historical scientific hypothesis lacks some positive confirming evidence, which only that hypothesis can uniquely explain, then it may be "a dreaded just-so story" (Cleland, 2001).

Casey Luskin

REFERENCES AND RECOMMENDED READING

Barash, David P., and Judith Eve Lipton. 2010. "How the Scientist Got His Ideas." *Chronicle of Higher Education.* January 3. http://chronicle.com/article/How-the-Scientist-Got-His/63287/.

Cleland, Carol E. 2001. "Historical Science, Experimental Science, and the Scientific Method." *Geology* 29 (November): 987–90.

Dennett, Daniel C. 1995. *Darwin's Dangerous Idea: Evolution and the Meanings of Life.* New York: Simon & Schuster.

Eisley, Loren C. 1967. "Introduction to the Conference." In *Mathematical Challenges to the Neo-Darwinian Interpretation of Evolution: Wistar Institute Symposium Monograph No. 5,* ed. P. S. Moorhead and M. M. Kaplan, 1–4. New York: Liss.

Kipling, Rudyard. 1902. "How the Leopard Got Its Spots." In *Just So Stories* (many editions). boop.org/jan/justso/leopard.htm.

Lewontin, Richard. 1997. "Billions and Billions of Demons." *New York Review of Books* 44 (January 9): 28.

Mazur, Susan. 2010. *The Altenberg 16: An Exposé of the Evolution Industry.* Berkeley, CA: North Atlantic Books.

Schlinger, Henry D., Jr. 1996. "How the Human Got Its Spots: A Critical Analysis of the Just So Stories of Evolutionary Psychology." *Skeptic* 4:68–76.

K

KANT, IMMANUEL. The philosophy of Immanuel Kant (1724–1804) and its aftermath stand between two great philosophical epochs. With the modernists, Kant's philosophy affirms the epistemic preeminence of science; yet in anticipation of **postmodernism**, he presents a radically new approach to the foundations of science. "But though all our knowledge begins with experience," Kant famously writes, "it does not follow that it all arises out of experience." Euclidean geometry, Newtonian **physics**, Keplerian **astronomy**, and Leibnizian calculus frame Kant's thinking. His concern, however, is not with the development of science as such, but rather with its philosophical underpinnings.

For David Hume, **mathematics** and science relied on synthetic a posteriori knowledge and its corollary, the "relations of ideas." Rationalists, such as René **Descartes** and Gottfried Wilhelm von Leibniz, dealt with science similarly, but determined mathematics to be grounded in analytic a priori knowledge. The problem with both was that science was grounded on the shifting sands of inductive inference, and mathematics was incapable of giving it sufficient grounding support. Kant's "Copernican Revolution" in philosophy did something for philosophy that pre-Kantian philosophy could not do on its own—namely, ground mathematics *and* science in the rational recesses of reason.

For Kant, cause and necessity ground natural science. However, they are not inherent in natural objects. They are receptive capabilities of the knowing mind. Kant calls these receptive capabilities "synthetic a priori" knowledge. **Space and time** as "forms of **intuition**" and the 12 categories as "forms of conception" constitute the world as it appears to us. They are neither inductive generalizations (per Hume) nor a priori axioms (per Spinoza), but rather the very constituents of reason that give it an active capacity for constructing and knowing nature.

Building on these insights, Kant's seminal ideas on science are found in the *Critique of Pure Reason* ([1781] 1997) and *Metaphysical Foundations of Science* ([1786] 2004). In these works, Kant defines science quite narrowly. Science contains a body of knowledge ordered systematically on pure rational principles known a priori but with the "**consciousness** of their necessity" (4:468). Only physics, thought Kant, rises to the level of being a proper science in this sense, because it alone provides apodictic certainty regarding its transcendental constituents. Chemistry and **geology**, for example, study the "particular nature" of empirical objects but do not entail transcendental knowledge of a thing in general.

Importantly, Kant grounds the inorganic and the organic "sciences" in different dimensions of the critical philosophy. Biology, though it requires experimental observation, is a matter of teleological judgment. An organism, argues Kant, is both "the cause and effect of itself" (5:370) and therefore has inherent "purposiveness" that allows it to interact with its environment in self-determining ways. This understanding of biology provides Kant with an analogy for understanding the synthetic "purposiveness without a purpose" of aesthetic judgment. It implies a meaningful ontology at the ground of nature but, from reason alone, is inexplicable in terms of its origin and end. Kant's discovery and employment of synthetic reasoning in these natural processes foreshadows Charles Darwin's theory of evolution and is explicitly worked out in the great German Idealists of the nineteenth century.

Studies of Kant's contributions to contemporary science continue to flourish. It seems clear to many that the subjective nature of transcendental knowledge lays the philosophical groundwork for **Einstein**'s theory of relativity and even certain aspects of quantum theory, for example. Still, it is not clear that Kant ever envisioned these revolutionary developments nor that his philosophy is ready-made to support them.

Chris L. Firestone

REFERENCES AND RECOMMENDED READING

Brittan, Gordon, Jr. 1978. *Kant's Theory of Science.* Princeton: Princeton University Press.

Friedman, Michael. 1992. *Kant and the Exact Sciences.* Cambridge, MA: Harvard University Press.

Kant, Immanuel. 1952. *Critique of Judgment.* Trans. James Creed Meredith. Oxford: Clarendon.

———. 1993. *Opus Postumum.* Ed. Eckart Förster. Trans. Eckart Förster and Michael Rosen. Cambridge: Cambridge University Press.

———. (1781) 1997. *Critique of Pure Reason.* Trans. and eds. Paul Guyer and Allen W. Wood. Cambridge: Cambridge University Press.

———. (1786) 2004. *Metaphysical Foundations of Natural Science.* Trans. Michael Friedman. Cambridge: Cambridge University Press.

Quarfood, Marcel. 2004. *Transcendental Idealism and the Organism.* Stockholm: Almquist & Wiksell.

Watkins, Eric, ed. 2001. *Kant and the Sciences.* New York: Oxford University Press.

KAUFFMAN, STUART A. Stuart Kauffman (1939–) is a theoretical biologist and researcher of complex systems (Closer to Truth). He is a leading advocate of self-organization, the broad hypothesis that physical or biological systems that are either simple or complex possess collective properties that enable them to self-organize (Kauffman 1993, 16).

An MD and a graduate of the University of Chicago, the National Institutes of Health, and University of Pennsylvania, Kauffman also was cofounder, faculty, and external professor at the Santa Fe Institute (NPR). Kauffman also held positions at University of Calgary (Edge) and at Tampere University of Technology in Finland. More recently, he became a research professor at the University of Vermont (NPR; University of Vermont). Currently, Kauffman is an affiliate faculty at the Institute of Systems Biology in Seattle (Wikipedia; Institute of Systems Biology).

Kauffman has published approximately 300 articles (NPR) and four major books: *The Origins of Order* (1993), *At Home in the Universe* (1995), *Investigations* (2000), and *Reinventing the Sacred* (2008). He released a fifth book in 2015 called *Humanity in a Creative Universe.*

As a self-organization proponent, Kauffman rejects pure **reductionism** (Kauffman 2003, 903; 2008, 3). By themselves, he asserts, Darwinian processes exhaust nature's available time resources (Kauffman 1993, 16). He hypothesizes an interactive, complementary process between collective self-organizational mechanisms and Darwinian selection mechanisms (Kauffman 1995, 25, 71, 90–91, 185).

Kauffman mentions observed examples that point toward self-organization, including snowflakes (Kauffman 2000, 1) and growing sand piles (20–21), as well as human **technology** and business dynamics (Kauffman 1995, 191–92, 203–6). Kauffman also supplies evidence for self-organization by likening Boolean network simulation models to gene regulatory networks, or by representing biological self-organizational tendencies as searches or interactions of rugged fitness landscapes.

Kauffman hypothesizes that both "the **origin of life** itself and … the origins of order in the ontogeny of each organism" include self-organizing processes (Kauffman 1993, xiv). He asserts that in both domains, spontaneous order emerges in complex collective systems poised at the threshold—or "phase transition"—between order and chaos (26, 223).

He proposes that life—or what he calls "autonomous agents" (Kauffman 2000, 8)—could spontaneously emerge when "sufficiently complex mixes" (Kauffman 1995, 24) of polymers reach the phase transition and become autocatalytic (Kauffman 2000, 16). They then may perform thermodynamic work cycles by being held out of equilibrium "by outside sources of matter or energy" (4, 64).

Regarding organismal development, Kauffman theorizes that properties of certain complex systems could constrain cell types and tissue and organ forms to small, simple, orderly subsets of possibilities (Kauffman 1993, 637; 1995, 111).

In a more recent article, Kauffman proposes that because nature contains *formal cause laws*, and not merely efficient causes (Kauffman 2013, 1), "the evolution of the biosphere is unentailed and often unprestatable" (7; see **Aristotle's Four Causes**). Again repudiating reductionism, Kauffman has also recently proposed a possible quantum source for responsible **consciousness** in a fully natural world (Kauffman 2014).

Kauffman's hypotheses have religious implications. He claims that a creator God is unnecessary to explain life's origins (Kauffman 2008, 4). Instead, he advocates a view of the divine seemingly akin to **pantheism**, asserting that this "fully natural God … is the very creativity in the universe" (6). Additionally, he admits his quantum **mind** hypothesis (Kauffman 2014, 6) could imply panpsychism (19).

James Charles LeMaster

REFERENCES AND RECOMMENDED READING

Barbour, Julian. "Stuart A. Kauffman." Edge. Accessed January 28, 2015. http://edge.org/memberbio/stuart_a_ Kauffman.

"Contributor: Stuart Kauffman." Closer to Truth. Accessed January 28, 2015. www.closertotruth.com/contributor/stuart-kauffman/profile.

Institute for Systems Biology. Affiliate Faculty. Accessed January 28, 2015. www.systemsbiology.org/affiliate-faculty.

Kauffman, Stuart A. 1993. *The Origins of Order: Self-Organization and Selection in Evolution.* New York: Oxford University Press.

———. 1995. *At Home in the Universe: The Search for Laws of Self-Organization and Complexity.* New York: Oxford University Press.

———. 2000. *Investigations.* New York: Oxford University Press.

———. 2003. "Beyond Reductionism: Reinventing the Sacred." Zygon 42, no. 4 (December): 903–14.

———. 2008. *Reinventing the Sacred: A New View of Science, Reason, and Religion.* New York: Basic Books.

———. 2013. "Beyond Reductionism: No Laws Entail Biosphere Evolution; Formal Cause Laws beyond Efficient Cause Laws." Cornell University Library. March 20. Accessed January 29, 2015. http://arxiv.org/abs/1303.5684.

———. 2014. "Beyond the Stalemate: Conscious Mind-Body Quantum Mechanics—Free Will—Possible Panpsychism—Possible Interpretation of Quantum Enigma." Cornell University Library. October 20. http://arxiv.org/abs/1410.2127.

NPR. *About 13.7: Cosmos and Culture.* Accessed January 21, 2015. www.npr.org/blogs/13.7/about.html.

University of Vermont. "Stuart Kauffman." Accessed January 28, 2015. www.uvm.edu/~cems/?Page=employee/profile.php&SM=employee/_employeemenu.html&EmID=1053.

Wikipedia. "Kauffman, Stuart." Wikipedia. Accessed January 28, 2015. http://en.wikipedia.org/wiki/Stuart_Kauffman.

KENYON, DEAN.

Dean Kenyon (1939–) is professor of biology emeritus at San Francisco State University (SFSU) and one of the early cofounders of the **intelligent design** (ID) movement.

While earning his undergraduate degree in **physics** at the University of Chicago, Kenyon attended the Darwin Centennial Celebration in 1959 and became interested in biological origins. He earned his PhD in biophysics from Stanford University in 1965 and then did a postdoctoral fellowship under Nobel Laureate Melvin Calvin at University of California at Berkeley. He began teaching biology at SFSU in 1966.

Kenyon's 1969 book *Biochemical Predestination*, cowritten with biophysicist Gary Steinman, was, according to Calvin, who wrote the foreword, "the first attempt" to produce a "basic textbook for a systematic discussion" of the **origin of life** (Calvin 1969). The book advocates a naturalistic origin of life, arguing for a purely physical and chemical basis for the origin of cellular components. Kenyon also published various technical scientific papers supporting the chemical origin of life, making him a prominent researcher in the field (Kenyon 1974, 1975, 1988; Kenyon and Nissenbaum 1976; Nissenbaum et al. 1975; Smith and Kenyon 1972a, 1972b; Steinman et al. 1966).

At SFSU, Kenyon taught evolution and the origin of life, but in the mid–1970s he began to doubt a naturalistic origin of life, as well as Darwinian evolution. A student challenged him to explain how proteins could assemble without genetic instructions, leading Kenyon to doubt that functional proteins could arise without the information in **DNA** (Illustra 2001; Woodward 2003). Kenyon subsequently became a proponent of intelligent design, stating, "The more … we have learned … about the chemical details of life, from molecular biology and origin-of-life studies … the less likely does a strictly naturalistic explanation of origins become" (Meyer 1994).

In 1989 Kenyon copublished with biologist Percival Davis the textbook *Of Pandas and People*, one of the first books to argue for ID: "If science is based upon experience, then science tells us the message encoded in DNA must have originated from an intelligent cause. But what kind of intelligent agent was it? On its own, science cannot answer this question; it must leave it to religion and philosophy. But that should not prevent science from acknowledging evidences for an intelligent cause origin wherever they may exist" (Davis and Kenyon 1989).

Pandas became the focus of controversy during the *Kitzmiller v. Dover* lawsuit after a federal judge found it unconstitutional to use in public schools because prepublication drafts used creationist terminology (Jones 2005). Kenyon did not write the controversial prepublication drafts of *Pandas*—they were written by his coauthor, Davis. But defenders of *Pandas* note that the substance of the prepublication versions differed from creationist ideas because they stated that **information**-rich sequences in DNA "cannot tell us if the intellect behind them is natural or supernatural" (DeWolf et al. 2007). Charles Thaxton, the academic editor for *Pandas*, explains that early drafts adopted ID terminology over creationist terminology not to hide some religious argument but because creationists "were wanting to bring God into the discussion, and I was wanting to stay within the empirical domain" (Thaxton 2005).

Kenyon also faced controversy over his instruction at SFSU. After becoming an ID proponent, he continued to teach the evidence for evolution but also began to cover scientific challenges to evolution, including ID. In 1992 Kenyon was forced to stop teaching introductory biology after being ordered by his dean and department chair to stop teaching "creationism" and only teach "the dominant scientific view" (Meyer 1993). Kenyon believed he was not teaching creationism and that his instruction was protected by academic freedom. SFSU's Academic Freedom Committee and faculty senate ultimately agreed with Kenyon, and he was reinstated (Johnson 1994).

Casey Luskin

REFERENCES AND RECOMMENDED READING

Calvin, Melvin. 1969. Foreword to Dean H. Kenyon and Gary Steinman, *Biochemical Predestination*. New York: McGraw-Hill.

Davis, Percival, and Dean H. Kenyon. 1989. *Of Pandas and People: The Central Question of Biological Origins*. Dallas: Foundation for Thought and Ethics.

DeWolf, David K., John G. West, and Casey Luskin. 2007. "Intelligent Design Will Survive *Kitzmiller v. Dover*." *Montana Law Review* 68:7–57.

Illustra. *Unlocking the Mystery of Life*. 2001. DVD. La Mirada, CA: Illustra Media.

Johnson, Phillip. 1994. "Is God Unconstitutional?" *University of Colorado Law Review* 66:461–75.

Jones, Judge John E. 2005. *Kitzmiller v. Dover Area School District*, 400 F. Supp. 2d 707 (M.D. Pa. 2005).

Kenyon, Dean H. 1974. "Prefigured Ordering and Protoselection in the Origin of Life." In *The Origin of Life and Evolutionary Biochemistry*, ed. K. Dose, S. W Fox, G. A. Deborin, and T. E. Pavlovskaya, 207–20. New York: Plenum.

———. 1975. "On Terminology in Origin of Life Studies" *Origins of Life* 6 (July): 447–48.

———. 1988. "A Comparison of Proteinoid and Aldocyanoin Microsystems as Models of the Primordial Protocell." In *Molecular Evolution and Protobiology*, eds. K. Matsuno, K. Dose, K. Harada, and D. L. Rohlfing, 163–88. New York: Plenum.

Kenyon, Dean H., and A. Nissenbaum. 1976. "Melanoidin and Aldocyanoin Microspheres: Implications for Chemical Evolution and Early Precambrian Micropaleontology." *Journal of Molecular Evolution* 7:245–51.

Kenyon, Dean H., and Gary Steinman. 1969. *Biochemical Predestination*. New York: McGraw-Hill.

Meyer, Stephen C. 1993. "A Scopes Trial for the '90s." *Wall Street Journal*. December 6.

———. 1994. "The Methodological Equivalence of Design and Descent: Can There Be a Scientific Theory of Creation?" In *The Creation Hypothesis: Scientific Evidence for an Intelligent Designer*, ed. J. P. Moreland, 67–112. Downers Grove, IL: InterVarsity.

Nissenbaum A., Dean H. Kenyon, and J. Oro. 1975. "On the Possible Role of Organic Melanoidin Polymers as Matrices for Prebiotic Activity." *Journal of Molecular Evolution* 6 (December 29): 253–70.

Smith, Adolph E., and Dean H. Kenyon. 1972a. "Is Life Originating De Novo?" *Perspectives in Biology and Medicine* 15 (Summer): 529–42.

———. 1972b. "The Origin of Viruses from Cellular Genetic Material." *Enzymologia* 43 (July 31): 13–18.

Steinman, Gary, Dean H. Kenyon, and Melvin Calvin. 1966. "The Mechanism and Protobiochemical Relevance of Dicyanamide-Mediated Peptide Synthesis." *Biochimica et Biophysica Acta* 124 (August 24): 339–50.

Thaxton, Charles. 2005. Deposition Testimony in *Kitzmiller v. Dover Area School District*, 400 F. Supp. 2d 707 (M.D. Pa.).

Woodward, Thomas. 2003. *Doubts about Darwin: A History of Intelligent Design*. Grand Rapids: Baker.

KEPLER, JOHANNES. Johannes Kepler (1571–1630) was the imperial astronomer to the Holy Roman Emperor. He developed the theory that the planets orbit the sun in ellipses and thereby helped to prove that the earth was not the center of the universe.

Life

Kepler was born near Stuttgart, Germany. He attended the University of Tübingen with the intention of becoming a Lutheran clergyman, but despite his great piety he was unable to subscribe to all aspects of Luther's teaching. Instead, inspired by his professor at Tübingen, he became an astronomer. "For a long time, I wanted to be a theologian," Kepler later wrote, "now however, behold how through my effort God is being celebrated through **astronomy**" (Linton 2004, 170).

In 1597 Kepler published his first book, *The Mystery of the Universe*, in which he followed **Copernicus**'s hypothesis that the planets orbited the sun. The book was well reviewed and Kepler was now sufficiently qualified to become the assistant of the Danish astronomer **Tycho Brahe**, who worked for the Holy Roman Emperor Rudolf II. On Brahe's death, Kepler became imperial astronomer himself. His main role was providing astrological prognostications, but he also prepared Tycho Brahe's astronomical observations for publication.

Kepler's personal life was often unsettled. In 1611 he lost a son to smallpox, and his wife died shortly afterward. Soon after her death, he lost his job as imperial astronomer, following the death of his patron, Rudolf II. Then, in 1615, his mother was falsely accused of witchcraft in a case that dragged out for six years. Although she was eventually acquitted, she never recovered from the ordeal.

Astronomical Theories

Using Brahe's data, Kepler refined his model of the solar system. He devoted particular attention to the orbit of Mars and noticed that his best existing model contained an error of eight minutes of arc. Since he knew the universe was created by a perfect God, he believed that this imperfection had to be in his model and not in nature. He later called the error a "good deed of God" because it led him to the correct answer (Caspar 1959, 128).

By showing that the planets have elliptical rather than circular orbits, Kepler was able to create a model of the heavens of unprecedented accuracy and elegance. When he finally published Brahe's observations as the *Rudulphine Tables*, they contained predictions of the planetary movements better than anything else available. It was the precision of these tables, as much as anything else, which convinced Europe that the earth really was orbiting the sun with the other planets.

Optical Work and Legacy

In addition to his work on astronomy, Kepler also laid out the modern understanding of vision, noting how the lens in our eyes focuses incoming light into a sharp image on the retina. He showed this image is upside down by using the lens from a bull's eye to project an image. He used his insights to invent an improved telescope that also produced an inverted image.

Johannes Kepler stands in the front rank of scientific innovators. He solved two of the major problems that had perplexed philosophers since the ancient Greeks—how vision works and how the planets move. And, in all he did, his Christian faith was his central inspiration.

James Hannam

REFERENCES AND RECOMMENDED READING

Caspar, Max. 1959. *Kepler*. Trans. C. Doris Hellman. New York: Abelard-Schuman.

Lindberg, David. 1981. *Theories of Vision from al-Kindi to Kepler*. Chicago: University of Chicago Press.

Linton, C. M. 2004. *Eudoxus to Einstein: A History of Mathematical Astronomy*. Cambridge: Cambridge University Press.

Stephenson, Bruce. 1994. *The Music of the Heavens: Kepler's Harmonic Astronomy*. Princeton: Princeton University Press.

KRAUSS, LAWRENCE. Physicist Lawrence Krauss (1954–) is a leading public figure who contends in books, articles, and debates, that science and religion are incompatible. He is an outspoken atheist who believes that **physics** offers no evidence for a creator or designer. Krauss is a professor of physics at Arizona State University. Accomplished as both an academic and a popular writer, Krauss poses challenges to Christianity as an intellectually credible **worldview**. Krauss gained a popular audience with books such as *The Physics of Star Trek* (1995) and, more recently, his bestselling *A Universe from Nothing: Why There Is Something Rather Than Nothing* (2012), which features an afterword by biologist and atheist **Richard Dawkins**.

Krauss resides firmly in the camp of the New Atheists (see **New Atheism**), along with Dawkins and **Sam Harris**. Krauss, like **Stephen Hawking**, takes the role of the expert physicist who has disproven God. To that end, he was involved in two informal debates with Christian philosopher **William Lane Craig**. During these events in Australia, Krauss did not address Craig's arguments, but repeatedly interrupted him and engaged in ad hominem attacks—even using a buzzer to disrupt Craig's opening presentation.

Philosophy of science is not Professor Krauss's forte. In *A Universe from Nothing*, he admits that his "intellectual bias" leads him to be dismissive of philosophy. Krauss's limitations are on display in *A Universe from Nothing*, which was written to dispose of the theistic claim that God created the universe ex nihilo. It is significant that many atheist physicists grapple with the claim that nothing is the source of everything. The older atheist approach put nothing in its place by claiming that something must have always existed, as long as that something is not Someone. But Krauss ends up doing much the same, although he uses the word *nothing*, but ambiguously. Krauss's sense of *nothing* is not really nothing, but an esoteric version of *something*, that is something very similar to the **quantum vacuum** of this universe. Thus he commits the fallacy of equivocation.

Krauss dismisses the theistic idea that God created the universe ex nihilo because this claim cannot answer the question of who created God. Yet **theism** claims that, unlike the cosmos, God is not a collection of contingent objects and events, but a self-existent being, so that there can be no creator of God.

Douglas Groothuis

REFERENCES AND RECOMMENDED READING

Halverson, Dean. 2013. "The New Nothingness: A Look at Lawrence Krauss's *A Universe from Nothing*." *The Christian Research Journal* 36 (6).

Krauss, Lawrence. 2012. *A Universe from Nothing: Why There Is Something Rather Than Nothing.* New York: Atria.

KUHN, THOMAS S. Thomas Kuhn (1922–96) was one of the most important philosophers and historians of science of the twentieth century. His book *The Structure of Scientific Revolutions* published in 1962 changed society's view of science and scientific progress. Two of his ideas from the book, *paradigms* and *paradigm shifts,* have taken on a life of their own and become common concepts in contemporary discourse.

Kuhn was born in Cincinnati, Ohio, of nonpracticing Jewish parents. His father was a hydraulic engineer and his mother an educator and professional editor. After attending several private schools in New York, Pennsylvania, and Connecticut, he went on to Harvard, his father's alma mater, to study **physics**. In 1943 he earned his bachelor's degree, and in 1946 his master's.

It was during his doctoral studies in 1947 that a **chance** teaching assignment turned his interest toward the history of science. He was asked by the renowned chemist and president of Harvard, James B. Conant, to assist in teaching a newly conceived history of science class for nonscience majors in the college. In preparation for his lectures, Kuhn began reading ancient texts on mechanics and motion, especially **Aristotle**'s *Physics.* He was initially struck by how "incorrect" by modern standards Aristotle had been. Finally, another perspective dawned on him. "Aristotle was not writing bad physics but good Greek philosophy!" (Gregory 2003). Kuhn realized that taken on his own terms and within his own conceptual framework (his "paradigm"), Aristotle's physics were not illogical or irrational but made perfect sense. Furthermore, he realized it was dangerous and even wrong to study Aristotle's theory of motion from a modern point of view (or "paradigm").

Kuhn decided at this point to switch fields. In his own words, he would become "a physicist turned historian for philosophical purposes" (Kuhn 2000, 320). Nevertheless, he completed his PhD in physics in 1949 and became a junior fellow in the Harvard Society of Fellows until 1951. It was during this time as a postdoctoral fellow that he trained himself in the history of science. He began his formal teaching career as an assistant professor of general education and the history of science at Harvard in 1952. While there he wrote his first book, *The Copernican Revolution* (published in 1957), detailing the seismic shift in **astronomy** from the geocentric **worldview** to heliocentrism, as a case study in paradigmatic change.

In 1956 Kuhn left Harvard to teach at the University of California at Berkeley, where he published his groundbreaking monograph, *The Structure of Scientific Revolutions*, in 1962 (hereafter referred to as *Structure*). Two years later he left for Princeton to become M. Taylor Pyne Professor of Philosophy and History of Science, teaching there until 1979. Kuhn completed his teaching career at MIT as Laurence S. Rockefeller Professor of Philosophy, retiring in 1991. After *Structure*, much of Kuhn's scholarly work concentrated on the historiography of quantum mechanics.

In his book *Structure,* Kuhn argued that the traditional notion of science as a cumulative, linear, and logical progression of advancement is incorrect. The development of science, instead, is characterized by periods of stable progress called "normal science" and punctuated from time to time by "revolutionary" or "extraordinary" science. Normal science is guided and controlled by a "**paradigm**" or a conceptual framework that is commonly accepted by the scientific community and within which the investigator works. Paradigms include shared commitments to theories, concepts, methods, and instrumentation. Paradigms also determine what problems are significant and how to solve them. Kuhn characterized normal science as "puzzle solving." But one problem with normal science is that it does not seek to change or overturn its paradigm. Its goal is to articulate and extend it.

Over time anomalies appear that do not conform and may even contradict the accepted conceptual model. A stage of "crisis" results when these anomalies persist and continue to resist solution under the reigning paradigm. Once at a stage of crisis, alternative paradigms are suggested until a new paradigm is adopted and replaces the old one. Normal science then proceeds under the new paradigm.

Kuhn's primary example of this process is the Copernican Revolution. Astronomy had proceeded quite successfully for 2,000 years under the Aristotelian-Ptolemaic formulation. During this time, it had successfully predicted the positions of the stars and planets. Over time, however, and with more accurate observations in the progress of normal science, discrepancies and anomalies began to appear and loom larger. Now, when calculating the positions of the planets and the precession of the equinoxes, for example, the

system began to break down, and in the sixteenth century, astronomy had reached a crisis point. As **Copernicus** himself famously complained in the preface to his *De Revolutionibus*, "the astronomical tradition he inherited had finally created only a monster" (Kuhn 1962, 69).

It is important to recognize in detail how truly revolutionary Kuhn's history of **scientific revolution**s is. In the first place (by Kuhn's account), revolutions and theory choice are not necessarily logical, rational, or scientific decisions. They are rather historically and socially conditioned. There were many other factors that led Copernicus and those after him to adopt the heliocentric point of view. In fact, at first Copernicus's system was no more accurate than Ptolemy's. Other factors, such as calendar design, aesthetics, and even **astrology**, came into play.

Second, science does not necessarily progress in a cumulative and linear fashion, because new paradigms are "incommensurable" with old ones. That is, they do not build on each other, because a paradigm shift involves such a dramatic change in view that investigators almost "live in two different worlds." Even basic definitions of terms mean different things and bear different relations. This switch is likened to the Gestalt visual experiment where one sees the image as either a "duck" or a "rabbit" but not as both at the same time. For example, where an Aristotelian sees a heavy object swinging on a string as the element Earth struggling to reach its place of rest, **Galileo** sees a "pendulum" struggling to achieve perpetual motion (Kuhn 1962, 119). The incommensurability and changeability of paradigms also imply a certain "relative" (and not objective) quality to science.

Kuhn contributed to the history and **philosophy of science** by refuting the dominant philosophy of science in the 1960s known as **logical positivism**. Represented by such men as **Rudolph Carnap** and **Karl Popper**, logical positivism held that science progressed cumulatively and linearly by means of logical rules toward an objective reality. Kuhn emphasized the importance of the study of the history of science because such study reveals that logical positivism's vision is not the case. Instead, science progresses by means of revolutionary paradigm shifts that are socially and historically conditioned and not determined solely by scientific or philosophical rules. Science and scientific progress therefore is not as straightforward and objective as we might wish it to be.

Kuhn's *Structure of Scientific Revolutions* is considered among the hundred most influential books of the twentieth century and is one of the most cited academic works of all time. Translated into some 20 different languages, it has sold over 1 million copies in four editions. It is a standard text in college philosophy and history of science courses, and its ideas of paradigms and paradigm shifts have been adopted and adapted into numerous other contexts from **sociology** and feminism to business management and economics.

Milton Eng

REFERENCES AND RECOMMENDED READING

Andersen, Hanne. 2001. *On Kuhn*. Belmont, CA: Wadsworth/Thomson Learning.

Bird, Alexander. 2001. *Thomas Kuhn*. Philosophy Now. Princeton, NJ: Princeton University Press.

———. 2013. "Thomas Kuhn." in *Stanford Encyclopedia of Philosophy*, ed. Edward N. Zalta. http://plato.stanford.edu/archives/fall2013/entries/thomas-kuhn.

Gordon, Peter E., et al. 2012. "Forum: Kuhn's *Structure* at Fifty." *Modern Intellectual History* 9 (1): entire issue.

Gregory, Frederick. 2003. "Lecture One: Science in the 18th and 19th Centuries." *The History of Science: 1700–1900*. MP3. Chantilly, VA: The Great Courses.

Hoyningen-Huene, Paul. 1993. *Reconstructing Scientific Revolutions: Thomas S. Kuhn's Philosophy of Science*. Chicago: University of Chicago Press.

———. 1998. "Kuhn, Thomas Samuel." *Routledge Encyclopedia of Philosophy*. Ed. Edward Craig. London: Routledge.

Irzik, Gürol. 2008. "Kuhn, Thomas Samuel." *New Dictionary of Scientific Biography*. Ed. Noretta Koertge. Detroit: Scribner/Thomson Gale.

Kuhn, Thomas S. 1957. *The Copernican Revolution: Planetary Astronomy in the Development of Western Thought*. Cambridge, MA: Harvard University Press.

———. (1962) 2012. *The Structure of Scientific Revolutions*. 50th ann. ed. with introductory essay by Ian Hacking. Chicago: University of Chicago Press. Second ed. (1970) contains Kuhn's important postscript.

———. 1977. *The Essential Tension: Selected Studies in Scientific Tradition and Change*. Chicago: University of Chicago Press.

———. 2000. *The Road since Structure: Philosophical Essays, 1970–1993, with an Autobiographical Interview*. Eds. James Conant and John Haugeland. Chicago: University of Chicago Press. Contains a complete list of all of Kuhn's writings.

Nickles, Thomas, ed. 2002. *Thomas Kuhn*. New York: Cambridge University Press.

L

LAKATOS, IMRE. Imre Lakatos (1922–74) was one of the leading philosophers of science of the twentieth century. Born Imre Lipschitz to a Jewish family in Hungary, Lakatos escaped Nazi persecution during World War II by changing his name to Imre Molnár; he became Imre Lakatos after the war. He came to the United Kingdom following the Soviet invasion of Hungary in 1956. He lectured at the London School of Economics from 1960, while **Karl Popper** was still there, and received a PhD from Cambridge University in 1961. His famous "methodology of scientific research programmes" (Lakatos 1978) is to be contrasted both with Popper's falsificationism and with the relativism of **Thomas Kuhn**.

Popper had recognized that scientific theories cannot be verified in the sense of **logical positivism**, since one cannot observe all instances of a general law. Rather, to be scientific, a theory must be falsifiable. For example, Newton's law of gravity could be falsified by a single counterexample.

Lakatos realized that this does not capture how science works in practice. It was known in the nineteenth century that the orbit of the planet Uranus did not match predictions made utilizing Newton's theory. But that theory was not abandoned. Adams and LeVerrier calculated that Uranus's orbit would fit if there were another planet around, thereby predicting the existence of Neptune.

Lakatos saw theories held within much broader "scientific research programmes," which either grow or shrink, depending on how they adapt to new data. Such research programs have a "hard core" of well-established theories, which are highly resistant to change, and a large "protective belt" of less secure "auxiliary hypotheses" (Lakatos 1978, 4). Research programs are "progressive" if they successfully predict novel facts, or "degenerating" if they keep requiring ad hoc modifications to accommodate the facts (Lakatos 1978, 5). Thus the Ptolemaic model of the universe had to be saved by introducing ever more complex patterns of epicycles (see **Copernicus, Nicolaus**). The new cosmology developed by Copernicus, Galileo, and ultimately Newton explained the facts beautifully and simply and predicted new ones, such as the existence of Neptune (though Lakatos's own take on the story is more complex than this—see Lakatos 1978, 168–92).

Lakatos's methodology is both rational and more closely resembles how science actually proceeds than the methodologies of either Popper or Kuhn, whose "**paradigm** shifts" occur more for sociological than logical reasons (Kuhn 1980).

The relevance of Lakatos to theology comes from philosophers and theologians who see theology as a rational pursuit needing justification, just like science. For example, both Philip Hefner and **Nancey Murphy** argue that theology presents scientific research programs in Lakatos's sense.

Hefner and Murphy see German theologian **Wolfhart Pannenberg** as providing just such a program (Hefner 1988, 281–86; Murphy 1990, 174–211). The "hard core" would be God, the all-determining reality, bestowing meaning to the presently incomplete totality of reality, with the completion coming eschatologically. "Auxiliary hypotheses" relate both to the biblical/theological tradition and to scientific theories which at least "leave open the conjecture that they manifest the effects of God's all-determining totality" (Hefner 1988, 283).

Murphy extends Lakatos's methodology to other theological programs—for example, Catholic modernism, a movement of early twentieth-century Roman Catholics that aimed to reconcile Catholicism with modernist thought, including biblical criticism and empiricist **epistemology**.

The need to predict novel facts is perhaps the greatest difficulty here. Examples offered tend to be rather vague compared with those of science. The problem is avoided in the alternative approach of Bayesian **confirmation** theory (see **Bayes' Theorem**). Thus Richard Swinburne argues that the **probability** of a hypothesis is the same regardless of whether what it explains is known before or only after the hypothesis is framed, a point known to Lakatos himself (Lakatos 1978, 39; Swinburne 2004, 69–70).

Rodney Holder

REFERENCES AND RECOMMENDED READING

Hefner, Philip. 1988. "The Role of Science in Pannenberg's Theological Thinking." In *The Theology of Wolfhart Pannenberg*, ed. Carl E. Braaten and Philip Clayton, 266–86. Minneapolis: Augsburg.

Kuhn, Thomas S. (1962) 1980. *The Structure of Scientific Revolutions.* Chicago: University of Chicago Press.

Lakatos, Imre. 1978. *The Methodology of Scientific Research Programmes: Philosophical Papers.* Vol. 1. Cambridge: Cambridge University Press.

Murphy, Nancey. 1990. *Theology in the Age of Scientific Reasoning.* Ithaca, NY: Cornell University Press.

Swinburne, Richard. 2004. *The Existence of God.* 2nd ed. Oxford: Oxford University Press.

LAMARCK, JEAN-BAPTISTE. Jean-Baptiste Lamarck (1744–1829) began his scientific career as a botanist and taxonomist. Much of his botanical research was published in three volumes of *Flore francaise*, which used dichotomous keys for plant identification, articles in the *Mémoires* of the Academy of Sciences, and three volumes of the *Encyclopédie méthodique*.

Lamarck's career was radically altered when the Jardin du Roi, of which he was a member, became the Muséum National d'Historie Naturelle. Because other colleagues were named professors of botany for the Muséum, Lamarck was made professor of "insects, worms, and microscopic animals." Although it was the least prestigious of the Muséum's professorships, Lamarck used the opportunity to accomplish groundbreaking taxonomy of invertebrates. Much of this work was published in two volumes of *Histoire naturelle des Animaux sans vertébres.* He is even credited with the invention of the word *invertebrate*.

Lamarck's interests were not limited to taxonomy, botany, or invertebrate zoology. As a self-proclaimed "naturalist philosopher," he proposed extensive theories of physics, chemistry, meteorology, and the geologic history of Earth, many of which were published in *Hydrogéologie* in 1802.

One of the first naturalists to develop and propose a comprehensive theory of evolution, Lamarck began to publish his ideas on the origins of life in 1801. In his most famous work, *Philosophie zoologique*, Lamarck proposed that life came to be through a natural process he called the "transmutation of **species**," an outdated term for evolution. While his book hinted at foundational modern understandings like cell theory and **natural selection**, he never fully developed these ideas. Lamarck's theory of evolution differed significantly from the modern Darwinian synthesis, understandably reflecting a lack of consideration of Mendelian principles and Pasteur's *Omne vivum ex vivo,* which were discovered later. Lamarck argued that simple organisms (protists) were continually spontaneously generated and that species disappeared, not because of **extinction**, but because they evolved into a more complex species.

A key mechanism underlying his theory, referred to as Lamarckism or Lamarckianism today, is that heritable traits can be acquired by the interaction of an organism with its physical environment, the organism's effort, or by the use or disuse of body structures by the organism. Although Lamarckism is often seen as irrelevant in light of a modern understanding of evolution, even Darwin saw Lamarck as an important forerunner of evolutionary thought. Darwin (1872) wrote: "[Lamarck] first did the eminent service of arousing attention to the **probability** of all changes in the organic, as well as in the inorganic world, being the result of law, and not of miraculous interposition." And the recent discovery of epigenetic mechanisms of heredity has made Lamarck's theory relevant once again. We now know that acquired characteristics, such as **DNA** methylation, can be heritable.

Many of Lamarck's contemporaries harshly criticized his claim that life came to be through natural processes rather than miraculous intervention. They believed that nature reflected God's direct handiwork and design. Therefore they saw Lamarck's evolutionary ideas as excluding the possibility of God working to create living things.

Unfortunately, in spite of his significant contributions to botany, invertebrate zoology, and evolutionary thought, Lamarck died in poverty and obscurity.

Sara Sybesma Tolsma

REFERENCES AND RECOMMENDED READING

Darwin, Charles. 1872. *On the Origin of Species.* 6th ed. www.gutenberg.org/files/2009/2009-h/2009-h.htm.
Gissis, Snait B., Eva Jablonka, and Anna Zeligowski. 2011. *Transformations of Lamarckism: From Subtle Fluids to Molecular Biology.* Cambridge, MA: MIT Press.
Lamarck, Jean-Baptiste. 1914. *Zoological Philosophy: An Exposition with Regard to the Natural History of Animals.* Trans. Hugh Elliot. London: Macmillan.

LANGUAGE, ORIGIN OF. The **Tower of Babel** account in Genesis 11 presents an etiology of the diversity of human languages, yet the story's purpose is more likely a negative association of Babylon with human hubris and the overstepping of divinely ordained boundaries (Wenham 1987). Furthermore, the origin of human language as such is not narratively explained. Nevertheless, the story's placement in Genesis and its echoes in the Pentecost event in Acts 2 testify to the importance of language within the biblical witness and to its centrality to the divine-human encounter.

The biological and cultural events giving rise to human language have been the subject of intense debate. The study of language, long the monopoly of linguistics and philosophy, is now vigorously pursued by cognitive and evolutionary **psychology**. Within an evolutionary framework, attempts to understand the origin of language raise questions such as, was the human capacity for language an adaptation, giving its possessors advantages in survival and reproduction? Or did language emerge as a "side effect," as it were, of other, more directly selected-for cognitive developments? Productive investigation of these issues requires clarifying the original function of language—a question just as debated. Is language a tool for "the communication of propositional structures over a serial channel" (Pinker and Bloom 1990)? Or is it fundamentally an instrument of power, "an efficient way to change another's behavior" (Catania 1990)? Or is it more about "gossip," keeping track of individuals in and out of the group (Dunbar 1988)?

Given both the sparseness of our knowledge of the neurobiological substrate of language and the lack of physical artifacts left by primal language use, it can be hard for these discussions to escape an air of speculation.

As far as we can tell, other **species** either do not use language or use something analogous to human language but in extremely limited ways. Does this mean that the capacity for language is unique to human beings? And, from a Christian perspective, does this indicate that human language is not of natural origin, that despite the seeming similarities and continuities with other species' forms of communication, no purely natural explanation can rightly say where language came from? Such arguments have been made: "Man speaks, and no brute has ever uttered a word.... No process of **natural selection** will ever distil significant words out of the notes of birds and the cries of beasts" (Müller 1862, 354). This claim, however, entails presuppositions about what natural selection is or is not capable of.

Yet there are features of human language that are, when regarded from a purely natural standpoint, fascinating and problematic. How did language come to signify, for purposes of mutually comprehensible interpersonal communication, anything invisible—abstractions, moral obligations, past history, fantasies, spirits? How is it, in particular, that human language can be used to refer to, call upon, and take positions vis-à-vis the divine, which is not part of the world to which we have empirical access? An obvious materialist explanation is that such language points to things that are imagined, not corresponding to any existing reality. But this still leaves open questions about how and why the linguistic—and thus social—movement from statements about the natural world such as "There are some berries" to supernatural statements such as "A God created us" was made.

Maurice Lee

REFERENCES AND RECOMMENDED READING

Catania, A. Charles. 1990. "What Good Is Five Percent of a Language Competence?" *Behavioral and Brain Sciences* 13:729–31.

Dunbar, Robin. 1988. *Grooming, Gossip, and the Evolution of Language.* Cambridge, MA: Harvard University Press.
Müller, Friedrich Max. 1862. *Lectures on the Science of Language Delivered at the Royal Institution of Great Britain in April, May, and June, 1861.* New York: Scribner.
Pinker, Steven, and Paul Bloom. 1990. "Natural Language and Natural Selection." *Behavioral and Brain Sciences* 13:707–84.
Wenham, Gordon J. 1987. *Genesis 1–15.* Word Biblical Commentary. Vol. 1. Waco, TX: Word.

LAPLACE, PIERRE-SIMON. Pierre-Simon Laplace (1749–1827) may be best known in popular culture today for his reputed response when Napoleon Bonaparte noted the absence of references to God in Laplace's magisterial *Mécanique céleste*. Laplace is said to have replied that he "had no need of that hypothesis." Like the story of Newton and the falling apple, this anecdote is founded in plausibility, not documentary evidence. It is, however, in keeping with perceptions of the work of this most important French natural philosopher and mathematician of the late eighteenth and early nineteenth century.

Laplace's career spanned the tumult of the French Revolution as well as the efflorescence of French mathematical **physics**. From humble origins, Laplace quickly rose to become one of the most important figures of the European mathematical and scientific landscape, making significant contributions to **probability**, analysis, **astronomy**, and physics. He weathered the various political upheavals of the period, including the Terror, the rise and fall of Napoleon, and the restoration of the Bourbons. Indeed, Laplace's opportunistic political maneuvering (voting for the restoration of the monarchy, for instance, after having been decorated by Napoleon and given a post in his government) brought him some criticism.

Like many of his peers, Laplace received his early education at the hands of the church and was matriculated at the University of Caen with the intention of becoming a priest. During this period, the contemporary debates over religion resulted in him abandoning this intention as well as his Christian faith. For the rest of his career, Laplace was functionally agnostic. Though there is at least one account of him expressing unambiguous atheism (Hahn 2005, 67), in his published writings he remained silent on religious topics. In unpublished manuscripts, however, he expressed his denial of **miracles** and other fundamental Christian beliefs, taking these as examples of the credulous nature of mankind.

Laplace established the field of celestial mechanics, a term he coined for the application of universal gravitation to describe completely the complex motions of the solar system. Laplace was able to show that variations in the motions of the planets were not secular—meaning they would not be magnified over time but were periodic within specific boundaries. In other words, the solar system was stable. He popularized his work in his *Exposition du système du monde* (1796), "one of the most successful works of science ever composed" (Gillispie 1997, 169). (The four-volume *Mécanique céleste*, published from 1799 to 1805, provides a much more technical treatment.)

It was a single concluding section of the *Exposition* (the sixth chapter of Book V) that gained notoriety as offering a naturalistic explanation of the evolution of the solar system. Here Laplace outlined what was originally a hypothesis to explain the orderly properties of the solar system. Consider, Laplace said, the fact that all the planets and their satellites orbit the sun and rotate on their axes in the same direction and in the same plane (as believed at the time, though Laplace ignored the counterexample of Uranus's newly discovered moons). Laplace showed mathematically the great unlikelihood of this occurring by **chance**. Instead, he speculated that in the past a younger, hotter sun had a larger atmosphere from which the planets condensed as this atmosphere receded, their orbits thus naturally sharing the sun's rotational direction and axial inclination.

Because **Immanuel Kant** (1724–1804) independently made similar speculations, this theory is sometimes referred to as the Kant-Laplace nebular hypothesis.

Laplace's work in astronomy was linked to his mathematical work in probability. As a determinist, Laplace did not believe in randomness in nature and famously said that if an intelligence knew the exact relations of all entities in the universe, it would be able to predict the future as well as reconstruct the past from physical laws (Gillespie 1997, 26–27). Probability and chance were simply expressions of human ignorance regarding outcomes. Such a view was in keeping with Laplace's physical program, which involved explaining everything from planetary motions to the nature of heat by physical laws describing relations between particles and bodies. Upon his death, Laplace's last words were reported to have been "What we know is insignificant, what we do not know is immense" (Hahn 2005, 204).

Stephen Case

REFERENCES AND RECOMMENDED READING

Gillispie, Charles Coulston. 1997. *Pierre-Simon Laplace 1749–1827: A Life in Exact Science.* Princeton, NJ: Princeton University Press.

Hahn, Roger. 2005. *Pierre-Simon Laplace 1749–1827: A Determined Scientist.* Cambridge, MA: Harvard University Press.
Laplace, Pierre-Simon. 1809. *The System of the World.* Trans. J. Pond. 2 vols. London: Richard Phillips.
———. (1829–39) 1966. *Celestial Mechanics.* Trans. Nathaniel Bowditch. 4 vols. New York: Chelsea.
Suzuki, Jeff. 2007. "De Laplace, Pierre-Simon." In *Biographical Encyclopedia of Astronomers,* ed. Thomas Hockey, 543–45. New York: Springer-Verlag.

LAUDAN, LARRY. Larry Laudan (1941–) is an epistemologist and philosopher of science at the University of Texas–Austin, a leading antirealist in the **philosophy of science**, and a critic of the demarcationist program. Educated at the University of Kansas (BA in **physics**, 1962) and Princeton University (MA and PhD in philosophy, 1964–65), Laudan began his teaching career at the University of London (1965–69), then moved to the University of Pittsburgh, where he helped to establish its history and philosophy of science (HPS) program. In 1972 Laudan became full professor in the departments of philosophy, history, and HPS at Pittsburgh, serving in that capacity until 1983. From 1987 to 1997 Laudan was professor of philosophy at the University of Hawaii, and he now teaches at the University of Texas–Austin.

Throughout his career, Laudan has argued against the realist understanding of scientific knowledge and progress, under which science steadily "converges" on the truth. In his most influential antirealist publication, "A Confutation of Convergent Realism" (1981), Laudan contends that abundant historical evidence contradicts the key tenets of **realism** (e.g., that the central terms of empirically "successful" theories refer to genuinely existing entities). The stable (nonmoving) continents of physical **geology**, for instance, widely held to be the case prior to plate tectonics theory, are not today regarded as real. At bottom, concludes Laudan, we are not warranted in affirming the truth of any theory merely because it "had some true consequences" (1981, 45): this would represent the fallacy of affirming the consequent.

Within the field of science and religion, Laudan is best known as a critic of the demarcationist program, according to which—by some criterion (or criteria)—natural science can be reliably demarcated from all other aspects of human knowledge or practice. On the contrary, argues Laudan (1983), no criterion yet proposed cleanly separates "scientific" propositions or theories from "nonscientific" statements (see **Demarcation, Problem of**). Historically, Laudan observes, demarcation criteria have been deployed as "*machines de* *guerre*" (weapons of war) between rival camps, with the unsurprising consequence that the theory under scrutiny by one of the parties turns out to be "unscientific" in the light of a supposedly dispassionate epistemic standard. In this vein, Laudan turned his critical lens on the 1981 federal trial (*McLean v. Arkansas*) philosophy of science testimony of his colleague **Michael Ruse** (albeit implicitly; Ruse is never named in Laudan 1982, though the criteria employed by Judge William Overton, who is named, were supplied by Ruse).

While expressing no sympathy for creationism, Laudan argues that many of its assertions, contrary to Overton's opinions, are testable, and indeed have failed those tests. "Debating the scientific status of creationism," concludes Laudan, "is a red herring that diverts attention away from the issues that should concern us" (1982, 19).

Paul Nelson

REFERENCES AND RECOMMENDED READING

Laudan, L. 1981. "A Confutation of Convergent Realism." *Philosophy of Science* 48:19–49.
———. 1982. "Science at the Bar: Causes for Concern." *Science, Technology and Human Values* 7:16–19.
———. 1983. "The Demise of the Demarcation Problem." In *Physics, Philosophy and Psychoanalysis*, ed. Robert Cohen and L. Laudan, 111–28. Dordrecht: Reidel.

LAWS OF NATURE. The view that nature is governed by laws, so that events unfold in a regular and predictable manner, is widely held. This basic idea has been helpful in developing simple explanations of a wide variety of complex phenomena (e.g., **Isaac Newton**'s law of gravitation allows a unified explanation of the behavior of projectiles, the tides, and planetary orbits).

The concept of a law of nature appears to derive from several sources. **Plato** contributed the idea that we can make sense of the ever-changing world of appearances by appealing to universals. However, Plato believed that perfect and rational connections obtained only in the ideal realm of the forms, and not in the natural world, which was made in the imperfect likeness of the forms (Plato in Hamilton and Cairnes 1963). By suggesting that the forms were in particular things as essences, **Aristotle** contributed the important idea that objects will behave in predictable ways (according to their nature). But these ingredients do not fully capture the thought that nature is governed by rational principles analogous to the legal system of a state.

Many scholars agree that an essential element that birthed the modern idea of a law of nature is theological (see **Science and the Medieval Church**). **A. N. Whitehead** argued that "the inexpugnable belief that every detailed occurrence can be correlated with its antecedents in a perfectly definite manner, exemplifying general principles" derived from "the medieval insistence on the rationality of God, conceived as with the personal energy of Jehovah and with the rationality of a Greek philosopher" (Whitehead 1997, 13). Likewise, A. R. Hall argued that the medieval idea of a law of nature was "related to the concept of natural law in the social and moral senses familiar to medieval jurists.... The use of the word 'law' in such contexts would have been unintelligible in antiquity, whereas the Hebraic and Christian belief in a deity who was at once Creator and Law-giver rendered it valid" (Hall 1954, 171–72).

Today this transcendent understanding of a law of nature is rejected by most philosophers. Some maintain that a law of nature is simply a regularity that supervenes on local facts (e.g., Earman and Roberts 2005a, 2005b), a view attributed to the eighteenth-century philosopher **David Hume** (Hume [1748] 2008), though some say mistakenly (Strawson 1989). Many reject the regularity theory because it does not distinguish a law (like the **second law of thermodynamics**) from an accidentally true generalization (e.g., suppose everyone in Green Bay is a Packers fan). In the former but not the latter case, there is something about nature that makes the generalization true, and the law supports counterfactuals (statements about what would happen in nonactual cases), but an accidental generalization does not (if Steelers fans moved from Pittsburgh to Green Bay, they would not instantly become Packers fans).

To avoid this difficulty, some philosophers propose that laws of nature are necessary connections between universals (Armstrong 1983; Tooley 1987). However, some regard these connections as mysterious and nonnaturalistic, and a few even deny that laws of nature exist (van Fraassen 1990).

Angus J. L. Menuge

REFERENCES AND RECOMMENDED READING

Armstrong, David. 1983. *What Is a Law of Nature?* New York: Cambridge University Press.
Earman, J., and J. Roberts. 2005a. "Contact with the Nomic: A Challenge for Deniers of Humean Supervenience about Laws of Nature (Part I)." *Philosophy and Phenomenological Research* 71:1–22.
———. 2005b. "Contact with the Nomic: A Challenge for Deniers of Humean Supervenience about Laws of Nature (Part II)." *Philosophy and Phenomenological Research* 71:253–86.
Hall, A. R. 1954. *The Scientific Revolution 1500–1800: The Formation of the Modern Scientific Attitude*. London: Longmans, Green.

Hamilton, Edith, and Huntington Cairnes, eds. 1963. *The Collected Dialogues of Plato: Including the Letters.* "Timaeus." Princeton, NJ: Princeton University Press.

Hume, David. (1748) 2008. *An Enquiry concerning Human Understanding.* New York: Oxford World Classics.

Strawson, Galen. 1989. *The Secret Connexion: Causation, Realism, and David Hume.* Oxford: Oxford University Press.

Tooley, Michael. 1987. *Causation.* Oxford: Clarendon.

Trevena, J., and Miller, J. 2010. "Brain preparation before a voluntary action: Evidence against unconscious movement initiation." *Consciousness and Cognition,* 19(1), 447–56. http://dx.doi.org/10.1016/j.concog.2009.08.006

van Fraassen, B. 1990. *Laws and Symmetry.* Oxford: Clarendon.

Whitehead, A. N. 1997. *Science and the Modern World.* New York: Free Press.

LEIBNIZ, GOTTFRIED WILHELM.

Gottfried Wilhelm Leibniz (1646–1716) was arguably the preeminent German intellectual of his generation. Born in Leipzig and the son of a professor of moral philosophy, Leibniz was inclined toward the academic life early on. A voracious reader from youth (especially of the church fathers), he earned a doctorate in law at the University of Altdorf in 1687.

Rather than accept an invitation to join the faculty at Altdorf, Leibniz opted to enter service in the court of the elector of Mainz. The extensive travels of this service afforded him the opportunity to interact with other leading scholars of his day, including Nicolas Malebranche, Antoine Arnauld, and **Baruch** (Benedict) **Spinoza**.

Despite forgoing a professional academic life, Leibniz's intellectual pursuits ranged from theology, law, and diplomacy to **physics**, calculus, and philosophy. Beyond his own research, Leibniz influenced the founding of numerous learned societies and scholarly journals. Upon his death in 1716 in Hanover, Leibniz had published little in the way of sustained, systematic treatises; the majority of his written work is to be found in private letters and countless (largely unpublished, as yet) papers.

Although steeped in Aristotelian-laden scholasticism, with its affirmation of substantial forms, final causes, and divine design, Leibniz soon became enamored of the "mechanistic philosophy" previously embraced by **Francis Bacon** and **René Descartes**. Whereas the scholasticism dominant throughout the medieval era understood natural phenomena in terms of various "matter" and "form" composites and the causes thereof, the modern mechanistic scheme sought to explain natural phenomena solely in terms of mechanics (i.e., the size, shape, position, and motion of matter). It was largely the writings of Pierre Gassendi that brought this influence to Leibniz, as well as to **Isaac Newton**.

Perhaps the most extreme version of the mechanistic philosophy, **atomism** reduced matter to discrete, indivisible atoms that constitute the basic ontology of the material world. Although he rejected atomism, Leibniz ultimately remained committed to the mechanistic philosophy—yet in an attempt to reconcile this with Aristotelianism, he sought to preserve a place for substantial forms. Indeed, he argued, matter could not exist without such an "incorporeal principle."

Leibniz's mature expression of this reconciling position is his doctrine of *monads* (simple, immaterial—even soul-like—substances that conjoin to form compound bodies). These monads, created by God and held in existence by him, each contain within themselves their own unique principle of action. While acting in causal independence from one another, the behavior of each monad unfolds in accordance with God's preestablished harmony. The idea is that, at **creation**, God providentially ordered a perfect harmony between the "kingdoms" of efficient and final causes (see **Aristotle's Four Causes**); the mechanism of the natural world, unfolding in the monadic activity, is reflective of God's intentions.

Closely tied to his notion of preestablished harmony is Leibniz's belief that the actual world is in fact the best of all possible worlds. In this claim, Leibniz held, is found the key to unlocking intricate theological questions—notably, the **problem of evil**: since this is the *best* possible world, God does not prevent evil because doing so would change the world for the worse.

R. Keith Loftin

REFERENCES AND RECOMMENDED READING

Adams, Robert Merrihew. 1994. *Leibniz: Determinist, Theist, Idealist.* New York: Oxford University Press.

Ariew, Roger, and Daniel Garber, trans. and eds. 1989. *G. W. Leibniz: Philosophical Essays.* Indianapolis: Hackett.

Jolley, Nicholas, ed. 1995. *The Cambridge Companion to Leibniz.* New York: Cambridge University Press.

Leibniz, Gottfried Wilhelm. 1969. *Philosophical Papers and Letters.* Trans. and ed. Leroy E. Loemker. 2nd ed. Dordrecht: Kluwer.

———. 1985. *Theodicy.* Ed. Austin Farrer. La Salle, IL: Open Court.

Woolhouse, R. S., ed. 1994. *Gottfried Wilhelm Leibniz: Critical Assessments.* New York: Routledge.

LEMAÎTRE, GEORGES.

Georges Lemaître (1894–1966) was a Belgian physicist and astronomer as well as a Catholic priest. Along with the Russian mathematician Alexander Friedmann (1888–1925), who independently made a similar finding, Lemaître was the discoverer of the expanding universe solutions to **Einstein**'s **general theory of relativity**.

These solutions were ancestral to the **big bang theory**, which is foundational to **contemporary cosmology** (see Belinkiy 2012; Berger 1984; Dirac 1968; Friedmann 1922, 1924; Godart and Heller 1985; Kragh 1987; 1996, 1–79; Lemaître 1925, 1927, 1929, 1931a, 1931b, 1933a, 1933b, 1934, 1936, 1946, 1949a, 1949b, 1958).

Trained in classical languages, humanities, and theology at a Jesuit school in Louvain, Lemaître entered the Catholic University of Louvain in 1911 as a student in engineering, intent on a career that would help support his family. These plans were disrupted by World War I. Lemaître volunteered for the Belgian army and served as an artillery officer, seeing heavy fighting and, most notably, the first attack with poison gas (chlorine) in the history of warfare. He was later awarded various military honors for his service, including the Croix de Guerre avec Palmes.

Lemaître read up on **physics** during the war and, when it ended, returned to Catholic University to finish a degree in **mathematics** and physics, which he did in short order, and then began graduate studies in theology in 1920. While pursuing these studies, he maintained an interest in complicated mathematics, for which he had considerable ability, and he became fascinated with general relativity. He was ordained to the priesthood on completion of theological studies in 1923 and began a clerical career that paralleled his scientific career. He rose through the Catholic hierarchy to the level of monseigneur, was appointed to the Pontifical Academy of Sciences when it was established in 1936, and served as the president of the academy from 1960 until his death in 1966.

Lemaître spent the 1923–24 academic year at Cambridge studying relativity with **Arthur Eddington**, followed by two years in the United States working toward a PhD in **astronomy** at the Massachusetts Institute of Technology. While in America, he was influenced by the theories of astronomers Edwin Hubble (1889–1953) and Harlow Shapley (1885–1972) regarding an expanding universe. He earned his PhD in 1927 and the same year was appointed professor of astrophysics at the Catholic University of Louvain, a position he held until his retirement in 1964.

While at MIT, Lemaître was increasingly drawn to the study of the universe and, in 1925, proposed a modification of Willem de Sitter's (1872–1934) cosmology that was nonstatic and involved a redshift induced by the Doppler effect (Lemaître 1925). He continued this work after his return to Louvain and soon proposed a new theory (Lemaître 1927) that offered a solution of Einstein's general relativistic field equations in which the universe was expanding and a velocity-distance relation could be calculated.

Lemaître's (1927) basic equation was similar to Friedmann's (1922) but was derived independently. Eddington endorsed Lemaître's work and had it translated into English in 1931. Though his model did not entail an instant of creation or a definite age for the universe, Lemaître moved from relative obscurity to scientific celebrity in 1931 when he published a paper in *Nature* (Lemaître 1931b) proposing that the universe might have originated from a quantum of enormous energy.

Later that year he developed this scenario into his hypothesis of a primeval atom (see Lemaître 1946 for a full account). He published several explanations of his proposal in the 1930s. These articles constituted the first version of what would later be called "big bang cosmology." Lemaître suggested the theory could be tested observationally by examining cosmic rays and the formation of galaxies and clusters of galaxies (Lemaître 1933a, 1933b, 1934, 1936). In the late 1940s, George Gamow (1904–68) and his graduate student Ralph Alpher (1921–2007) improved the theoretical and experimental basis for the theory, which is now the received view in cosmology.

Given the fact that Lemaître was a priest, it is often supposed his primeval atom hypothesis was motivated by belief in creation ex nihilo. While this motivation may have played a role in his cosmological theorizing in the 1920s (Graves 1996, 161), Lemaître resolutely denied it from the 1930s onward. In various interviews and public lectures, he made it clear he thought that neither the Bible nor theology was, in any sense, relevant to scientific cosmology, and that no theological conclusions could be justified on the basis of science (e.g., *Literary Digest* 1933; Farrell 2005; Godart and Heller 1978, 1979; Laracy 2009).

In modern parlance, Lemaître contended that science and theology were strictly complementary, occupying separate domains of discourse. When Pope Pius XII, influenced by the physicist Sir Edmund Whittaker's (1873–1956) overt scientific apologetics (Whittaker 1943, [1946] 2008), argued that the big bang theory was evidence for the Christian doctrine of creation (Berger 1984, 387–88), Lemaître was upset and later, at the eleventh Solvay Conference, stated that his primeval atom theory "remains entirely outside any metaphysical or religious question. It leaves the materialist free to deny any transcendental Being" (Lemaître 1958, 7).

Lemaître's protestations likely were related to perceptions in the scientific community that his theory was theologically motivated, a perception made obvious by the efforts of **Fred Hoyle** (1915–2001) to advance the steady state theory as an alternative lacking theistic implications. Ironically, Hoyle's theory faced no parallel charges of atheistic motivation; it simply failed to account for the evidence and was eventually abandoned. Similar philosophical prejudices afflict the scientific community today, but criticizing a theory on the basis of what motivated it remains an instance of the genetic fallacy. The influence of an individual scientist's **worldview** on any theory he proposes is as unavoidable as it is irrelevant to an assessment of that theory's viability (Plantinga 1996).

Bruce L. Gordon

REFERENCES AND RECOMMENDED READING

Belinkiy, Ari. 2012. "Alexander Friedmann and the Origins of Modern Cosmology." *Physics Today* 65 (10): 38–43. http://hrsbstaff.ednet.ns.ca/jenninj2/Physics%2011/2012–3/Projects/Cosmology/Alan%20Friedmann%20and%20the%20Origins%20of%20Modern%20Cosmology.pdf.

Berger, A., ed. 1984. *The Big Bang and Georges Lemaître: Proceedings of a Symposium in Honour of G. Lemaître Fifty Years after His Initiation of Big-Bang Cosmology.* Dordrecht: Reidel.

Dirac, Paul A. M. 1968. "The Scientific Work of Georges Lemaître." *Pontificia Accademia delle Scienze: Commentarii* 2 (11): 1–20.

Farrell, John. 2005. *The Day without Yesterday: Lemaître, Einstein, and the Birth of Modern Cosmology.* New York: Avalon.

Friedmann, Alexander. 1922. "Über die Krümmung des Raumes." *Zeitschrift für Physik* 10:377–86.

———. 1924. "Über die Möglichkeit einer Welt mit konstanter negativer Krümmung des Raumes." *Zeitschrift für Physik* 21:326–32.

Godart, O., and M. Heller. 1978. "Un travail inconnu de Georges Lemaître." *Revue d'Histoire des Sciences* 31:345–56.

———. 1979. "Les relations entre la science et al foi chez Georges Lemaître." *Pontificia Accademia delle Scienze: Commentarii* 3:1–12.

———. 1985. *Cosmology of Lemaître.* Tucson: Pachart.

Graves, Dan. 1996. *Scientists of Faith.* Grand Rapids: Kregel.

Heller, Michael. 2012. "Light in the Beginning: Georges Lemaître's Cosmological Inspirations." In *Light from Light: Scientists and Theologians in Dialogue*, ed. Gerald O'Collins and Mary Ann Meyers, 28–42. Grand Rapids: Eerdmans.

Holder, Rodney D., and Simon Mitton, eds. 2012. *Georges Lemaître: Life, Science, and Legacy.* Astrophysics and Space Science Library. Vol. 395. New York: Springer.

Kragh, Helge. 1987. "The Beginning of the World: George Lemaître and the Expanding Universe." *Centaurus* 32:114–39.

———. 1996. *Cosmology and Controversy: The Historical Development of Two Theories of the Universe.* Princeton, NJ: Princeton University Press.

Laracy, Joseph R. 2009. "The Faith and Reason of Father George Lemaître." CatholicCulture.org. February. https://www.catholicculture.org/culture/library/view.cfm?recnum=8847.

Lemaître, George. 1925. "Note on de Sitter's Universe." *Journal of Mathematics and Physics* 4:188–92.

———. 1927. "Un univers homogène de masse constant et de rayon croissant rendant compte de la vitesse radiale des nébuleuses extra-galactiques." *Annales de Société Scientifique de Bruxelles* 47:49–56. Translated as "A Homogeneous Universe of Constant Mass and Increasing Radius Accounting for the Radial Velocity of Extra-Galactic Nebulae." *Monthly Notices of the Royal Astronomical Society* 91 (1931): 483–90.

———. 1929. "La grandeur de l'espace." *Revue des Questions Scientifiques* 15:189–216.

———. 1931a. "The Expanding Universe." *Monthly Notices of the Royal Astronomical Society* 91:490–501.

———. 1931b. "The Beginning of the World from the Point of View of Quantum Theory." *Nature* 127:706.

———. 1933a. "L'Universe en expansion." *Annales de Société Scientifique de Bruxelles* 53:51–85.

———. 1933b. "La formation des nébuleuses dans l'univers en expansion." *Comptes Rendu de l'Académie des Sciences* 196:1085–87.

———. 1934. "Evolution of the Expanding Universe." *Proceedings of the National Academy of Sciences USA* 20:12–17.

———. 1936. "On the Geometric Analysis of Cosmic Radiation." *Physical Review*, 2nd ser. 49:719–26.

———. 1946. *L'Hypothèse de l'Atome Primitif: Essai de Cosmogonie.* Neuchatel: Éditions du Griffon. Trans. Betty H. Korff and Serge A. Korff as *The Primeval Atom: An Essay on Cosmogony.* New York: D. Van Nostrand, 1950.

———. 1949a. "Cosmological Applications of Relativity." *Reviews of Modern Physics* 21:357–66.

———. 1949b. "The Cosmological Constant." In *Albert Einstein: Philosopher-Scientist*, ed. Paul A. Schlipp, 437–56. Evanston, IL: Library of Living Philosophers.

———. 1958. "The Primeval Atom Hypothesis and the Problem of the Clusters of Galaxies." In *La Structure et l'Évolution de l'Univers*, ed. R. Stoops, 1–32. Brussels: Coudenberg.

Literary Digest. 1933. "Salvation without Belief in Jonah's Tale." *Literary Digest* 115 (1): 23. www.unz.org/Pub/LiteraryDigest–1933mar11–00023.

Plantinga, Alvin C. 1996. "Science: Augustinian or Duhemian?" *Faith and Philosophy* 13:368–94.

Whittaker, Edmund. 1943. *The Beginning and End of the World.* Riddell Lectures 1941. London: Oxford University Press.

———. (1946) 2008. *Space and Spirit: Theories of the Universe and the Arguments for the Existence of God.* Donnellan Lectures 1946. Whitefish, MT: Kessinger.

LENNOX, JOHN.

John Lennox (1943–) is a professor of **mathematics** emeritus at Oxford University and enjoys a distinguished career in that discipline. In 2004 he coauthored *The Theory of Infinite Soluble Groups* as part of the Oxford Mathematical Monographs. But in recent years, he has written and spoken very publicly on Christianity and science.

Although he has been teaching and writing in the area of theology, philosophy, and science for many years (speaking often in Eastern Europe), Lennox came into prominence in the 2000s as a leading thinker and debater on matters of science in relation to Christianity. This was due primarily to his book *God's Undertaker: Has Science Buried God?* (2009) and because of his debate with atheistic biologist and provocateur **Richard Dawkins** in 2008. He also debated atheist philosopher Michael Tooley. Other books by Lennox include *Seven Days That Divide the World: The Beginning according to Genesis and Science* (2011c), *Gunning for God: Why the New Atheists Are Missing the Target* (2011b), and *God and Stephen Hawking* (2011a), which *Christianity Today* named the best apologetics book of 2011.

Lennox's academic credentials include three doctorates. He combines an avuncular manner with an acute intellect and a polished delivery. This provides a strong platform for his many debates. Unlike many scientists, Lennox is an able philosopher as well as a scientist.

Lennox challenges **methodological naturalism** in scientific investigation. Methodological **naturalism** is an **epistemology** of science that allows only natural and unintelligent causes to explain the material world. For example, the **information** in **DNA** and RNA must be explained without benefit of any designing **mind** to account for their specific and complex messaging system. Thus any **explanation** in chemistry, biology, and **physics** must necessarily avoid anything nonmaterial. This makes Lennox unique as a high-level public Christian intellectual in Britain, given his rejection of methodological naturalism and his orthodox theological stance.

Lennox claims that modern science has revealed aspects of design hitherto unknown, both at the cosmic (fine-tuning or anthropic coincidence) and the cellular level (molecular machines and DNA). Lennox advocates a **philosophy of science** that pursues the evidence wherever it leads, even if it leads to a designer outside the universe itself. He also debunks some legendary accounts—such as the Huxley-Wilberforce debate—of how science always defeats Christian **theism**.

Although Lennox argues against **Darwinism** as a sufficient explanation of biology, he avers in *Seven Days That Divide the World* that the Bible does not teach that the earth is but a few thousand years old. Therefore, Lennox does not argue against the antiquity of the cosmos, but rather against philosophical **materialism** to explain its origin or operation.

Douglas Groothuis

REFERENCES AND RECOMMENDED READING

Lennox, John. 2009. *God's Undertaker.* Oxford: Lion Hudson.
———. 2011a. *God and Stephen Hawking.* Oxford: Lion Hudson.
———. 2011b. *Gunning for God.* Oxford: Lion Hudson.
———. 2011c. *Seven Days That Divide the World.* Grand Rapids: Zondervan.

LEWIS, C. S. Clive Staples Lewis (1898–1963) was a phenomenally popular Anglo-Irish writer and scholar best known for his children's series The Chronicles of Narnia and works of popular theology and adult fiction such as *Mere Christianity* and *The Screwtape Letters*. Lewis was a noted scholar of medieval and Renaissance English literature, serving for many years as a tutor at Magdalen College,

Oxford University, and finishing his career as a professor at Magdalene College, Cambridge University.

Lewis had a keen interest in the impact of science on culture and ultimately wrote nine books, nearly 30 essays, and several poems that explored science and its cultural ramifications (West 2012). Many of Lewis's contributions to the science and culture debate have proved to be remarkably prophetic, and his ideas are frequently cited by proponents of **intelligent design** and other participants in the dialogue between faith and science.

He was also one of the early voices to challenge the idea that the Middle Ages were the "Dark Ages" when it came to science, debunking in particular the myth that thinkers during the Middle Ages believed the earth was flat (Akins 2012) (see **Dark Ages**; **Flat Earth**; **Science and the Medieval Church**). In his final academic work, meanwhile, Lewis offered a sophisticated analysis of the provisional nature of scientific theories and the cultural roots of **scientific revolution**s (Lewis 1964).

Lewis also challenged the rise of **scientism**, the effort to apply science outside its proper sphere. In books such as *The Abolition of Man* and the novel *That Hideous Strength*, Lewis critiqued the rise of what he called "technocracy," government in the name of science by officials who are granted political power because of their presumed scientific expertise. According to Lewis, technocracy was fundamentally misguided because "government involves questions about the good for man, and justice, and what things are worth having at what price; and on these a scientific training gives a man's opinion no added value" (Lewis 1970).

There is disagreement over Lewis's views on one particular flashpoint in science and religion debates: evolution. Philosopher Michael Peterson has stressed Lewis's support for evolution, going so far as to claim that Lewis would have been hostile to recent thinkers who see evidence of intelligent design in nature (Peterson 2010). Others disagree, arguing from both Lewis's published and unpublished writings that he was sharply critical of key tenets of orthodox Darwinian theory (West 2012). Other scholars have pointed out Lewis's growing skepticism of evolutionary theory in the later years of his life (Ferngren and Numbers 1996).

Perhaps Lewis's most influential contribution to the discussion of evolution was his critique of evolutionary accounts of **mind**. In the book *Miracles*, Lewis argued that attributing the development of human reason to a nonrational process like **natural selection** ends up undermining our confidence in reason itself. After all, if reason is merely an unintended by-product of a fundamentally nonrational process, what grounds do we have for trusting its conclusions (see **Reason, Argument from**)? Lewis adapted this argument from *Theism and Humanism* by Arthur Balfour. Post-Lewis, the argument has been further advanced by noted Christian philosopher **Alvin Plantinga** (Plantinga 2011) and atheist philosopher **Thomas Nagel** (Nagel 2012).

John G. West

REFERENCES AND RECOMMENDED READING

Aeschilman, Michael D. 1998. *The Restitution of Man: C. S. Lewis and the Case against Scientism.* 2nd ed. Grand Rapids: Eerdmans.
Akins, Jake. 2012. "C. S. Lewis, Science, and the Medieval Mind." In *The Magician's Twin: C. S. Lewis on Science, Scientism, and Society*, ed. John G. West, 59–67. Seattle: Discovery Institute Press.
Balfour, Arthur J. 2000. *Theism and Humanism.* Ed. Michael W. Perry. Seattle: Inkling.
Ferngren, Gary B., and Ronald L. Numbers. 1996. "C. S. Lewis on Creation and Evolution: The Acworth Letters, 1944–1960." *Perspectives on Science and Christian Faith* 48:28–33.
Lewis, C. S. 1955. *The Abolition of Man.* New York: Macmillan.
———. 1960. *Miracles: A Preliminary Study.* New York: Macmillan.
———. 1964. *The Discarded Image.* Cambridge: Cambridge University Press.
———. 1965. *That Hideous Strength.* New York: Macmillan.
———. 1970. "Is Progress Possible? Willing Slaves of the Welfare State." In *God in the Dock*, ed. Walter Hooper, 311–16. Grand Rapids: Eerdmans.
Nagel, Thomas. 2012. *Mind and Cosmos: Why the Materialist Neo-Darwinian Conception of Nature Is Almost Certainly False.* New York: Oxford University Press.
Peterson, Michael L. 2010. "C. S. Lewis on Evolution and Intelligent Design." *Perspectives on Science and the Christian Faith* 62:253–66.
Plantinga, Alvin. 2011. *Where the Conflict Really Lies: Science, Religion, and Naturalism.* New York: Oxford University Press.
West, John G., ed. 2012. *The Magician's Twin: C. S. Lewis on Science, Scientism, and Society.* Seattle: Discovery Institute Press.

LEWONTIN, RICHARD.

Richard Lewontin (1929–) is a geneticist, evolutionary theorist, and emeritus professor of biology at Harvard University. Born in New York City in 1929, Lewontin was educated at Harvard College (BS in biology, 1951) and Columbia University (PhD in zoology, 1954), where he was mentored by *Drosophila* geneticist and leading neo-Darwinian theoretician Theodosius Dobzhansky.

Following faculty positions at North Carolina State University, the University of Rochester, and the University of Chicago, in 1973 Lewontin was appointed as Alexander Agassiz Professor of Zoology and Biology at Harvard University, a position he held until 1998. While at Chicago, working with fellow Chicago geneticist Jack Hubby, Lewontin pioneered the use of the technique of gel electrophoresis to measure levels of genetic heterozygosity (i.e., allelic variation) in the proteins of the fruit fly genus *Drosophila*, experimental work,

the theoretical implications of which he explored in his influential 1974 book *The Genetic Basis of Evolutionary Change.*

At the same time, Lewontin became increasingly critical of what he and fellow Harvard professor, paleontologist Stephen Jay Gould, called the "adaptationist programme," a view of evolution they challenged in their widely cited 1979 paper "The Spandrels of San Marco and the Panglossian Paradigm." Lewontin doubted that **natural selection** optimized organisms, holding that many evolutionary outcomes owed more to **chance** processes and nonadaptive constraints. Politically left-wing, Lewontin also argued against genetic **determinism** and the application of sociobiology to human affairs, developing his thinking in collaboration with Harvard biologist Richard Levins, work they published jointly in *The Dialectical Biologist* (1985).

In the area of faith and science, Lewontin's most significant contribution stemmed from a 1997 essay in the *New York Review of Books*, "Billions and Billions of Demons," a review of *The Demon-Haunted World* by astronomer **Carl Sagan**. In the essay, Lewontin (an atheist) argued that natural sciences are committed under "an *a priori* adherence" to "**materialism**," and thus necessarily must reject any **divine action** within, or affecting, the physical universe. "Moreover," he concluded, "that materialism is absolute, for we cannot allow a Divine Foot in the door." Lewontin noted, however, that this materialism is historically recent and contingent, and would have been alien to figures such as **Isaac Newton**.

Lewontin's statement about the absolute inadmissibility of divine action (i.e., the "Divine Foot in the door" remark) has achieved the standing of a cultural aphorism within ongoing debates about **methodological naturalism** and **intelligent design**. In 2015 Lewontin was awarded the Crafoord Prize (evolutionary biology's equivalent of the Nobel Prize) for his electrophoresis work and theoretical analyses.

Paul Nelson

REFERENCES AND RECOMMENDED READING

Lewontin, R. 1974. *The Genetic Basis of Evolutionary Change.* Chicago: University of Chicago Press.
———. 1997. "Billions and Billions of Demons." *New York Review of Books.* January 9. www.nybooks.com/articles/1997/01/09/billions-and-billions-of-demons/.
Lewontin, R., and Stephen Jay Gould. 1979. "The Spandrels of San Marco and the Panglossian Paradigm: A Critique of the Adaptationist Programme." *Proceedings of the Royal Society of London, B* 205:581–98.

LIBERTARIAN FREE WILL.

Discussion of free will usually begins by distinguishing the different possibilities.

Suppose first that we are in a deterministic universe. Some philosophers argue that free will is incompatible with **determinism**, whereas others argue that it is compatible.

What is important for compatibilists is that a person does what he or she wants to do. There are no external constraints on the person's action. So, if I decide to throw a brick through my neighbor's window, that is a free action on my part, even if it is determined by the physical processes going on in my brain, which are all themselves determined by prior physical processes, going back as far as the cause and effect sequence will go, to the initial conditions at the **big bang**, if need be. It would not be a free action if someone else grabbed my arm, forcing me to pick up the brick and throw it; apart from such external constraints it would be free.

A third group of philosophers is not satisfied with this account of free will. I may do what I want to do, but what I want to do is determined by events going back to the beginning of time, even predetermined by God from "before the foundation of the world." That does not sound like genuine free will and in addition makes the problem of **theodicy** particularly acute. Supposing the universe to be indeterministic, this third group of philosophers argues that what matters is having genuine alternative choices. I may choose to throw the brick, but I could have done otherwise. It was in my power either to throw the brick or not to throw it. Moreover, only if this is the case can I be held responsible for my actions. This is "libertarian free will."

These different accounts of free will fit more or less comfortably with different accounts of what science says, and with different theological perspectives. Neither is without its problems, making it difficult to navigate a satisfying overall position.

For libertarian freedom **indeterminism** is a necessary but not sufficient condition. Thus it would not be compatible with the rigid **determinism** of a closed Laplacian universe (Laplace [1814] 1902). However, the standard probabilistic, Copenhagen interpretation of quantum mechanics makes libertarian freedom possible but by no means guarantees it. Similarly with regard to **divine action**, God is not simply upholding deterministic laws that he has decreed from the foundation of the world but is able to act within the openness and flexibility of indeterminate, unpredictable processes.

For Robert John Russell "the somatic enactment of incompatibilist human freedom requires lower-level indeterminism" (Russell 2001, 317). This leads Russell to see God acting in all quantum events in the universe until life and **consciousness** arise but then gradually refraining from

determining outcomes so as to allow their determination by humans (318).

In contrast, **Nancey Murphy** proposes that God determines *every* quantum event. However, that still leaves room for "top-down **causation**" to make possible human free will. She rejects the reductionist view that if all quantum events are determined by God, then all events tout court are so determined, as had been thought by earlier thinkers, especially the physicist-turned-theologian William Pollard (Pollard 1958), since that way lies **occasionalism** (Murphy 1995, 343).

A problem with invoking quantum theory is that quantum indeterminacies tend to disappear at the macroscopic level. Peter Clarke, for example, argues that they are irrelevant at the level of brain function (Clarke 2010), and in any case free will requires more than randomness. For both human and divine action, quantum events would need to be agent-controlled and yet must not conflict with the probabilistic laws. **John Polkinghorne** sees the influences that do or might occur, by their "episodic nature," to be inadequate to describe the "flexible actions of agents" (Polkinghorne 2001, 189), and therefore turns to **chaos theory** as a more promising locus for both human and divine action in the world.

Chaotic systems are theoretically deterministic but unpredictable in practice. However, Polkinghorne argues that what we take to be lower-level deterministic laws are in any case best viewed as approximations, since we have obtained them by treating systems as if they were isolated from the whole, a procedure intrinsically impossible. Polkinghorne concludes: "There is an emergent property of flexible process, even within the world of classical **physics**, which encourages us to see Newton's rigidly deterministic account as no more than an approximation to a more supple reality" (Polkinghorne 2005, 35–36).

If we accept libertarian free will, there are further philosophical and theological ramifications. If I have a genuine choice of options, can God know the future? It would seem not, because I have a say in what happens in the future through my choices. If God foreknows now what I am going to eat for breakfast a month from today, a matter that I will not even think about until that day comes, it would seem that my choice is already foreclosed and decided for me; it will be a delusion to think I really have a choice when the day comes. Denying that God knows the future arguably does not compromise his omniscience, since even God can know only what can logically be known, and future contingent decisions of free agents would not be knowable on the libertarian view.

Nelson Pike's argument along these lines (Pike 1965) seems unassailable, but it relates to a picture of God being involved in time. However, the alternative, classical view that God is timeless, and that God sees all moments—past, present, and future—of our flowing time in a single timeless present, is quite problematic. On that view, God does not experience the passing of time (is this the seemingly interactive God of the Bible?), but neither, it seems, can creatures possess libertarian freedom, since it is hard to see what difference it makes whether God knows timelessly my breakfast choice on a particular day or whether he knows it, within time, in advance of that day.

Even if God does not know the future, that does not mean that God cannot bring about his purposes in the world. A chess grand master playing an average club player will not know what moves his opponent will play beforehand but will assuredly be able to bring about checkmate whatever he does: "God, like some grand master of chess, can carry out his plan even if he has announced it beforehand.... No line of play that finite players may think of can force God to improvise: his knowledge of the game already embraces all the possible variant lines of play; theirs does not" (Geach 1977, 58).

Another helpful picture is given by J. R. Lucas: "God's plan for the future must be like that of the Persian rugmakers, who let their children help them. In each family the children work at one end of the rug, the father at the other. The children fail to carry out their father's instructions exactly, but so great is their father's skill, that he adapts his design at his end to take in each error at the children's end, and work it into a new, constantly adapted, pattern. So too, God" (Lucas 1976, 39).

These analogies help us to see how, in responding to the actions of the free agents, human beings, whom he has created, God can nevertheless perfectly well attain his purposes for the world, even if there are many possible routes by which he does so. Even so, libertarian versus compatibilist free will remains a controversial issue in theology and philosophy.

Rodney Holder

REFERENCES AND RECOMMENDED READING

Clarke, P. G. H. 2010. "Determinism, Brain Function and Free Will." *Science and Christian Belief* 22:133–49.
Geach, Peter. 1977. *Providence and Evil*. Cambridge: Cambridge University Press.
Holder, Rodney D. 2012. "Quantum Theory and Theology." In *The Blackwell Companion to Science and Christianity*, eds. James B. Stump and Alan G. Padgett, 220–30. Chichester, UK: Wiley-Blackwell.
Laplace, P. S. (1814) 1902. *A Philosophical Essay on Probabilities*. Trans. F. W. Truscott and F. L. Emory. New York: Wiley; London: Chapman and Hall.
Lucas, J. R. 1976. *Freedom and Grace: Essays*. London: SPCK.
Murphy, N. 1995. "Divine Action in the Natural Order: Buridan's Ass and Schrödinger's Cat." In *Chaos and Complexity: Scientific Perspectives on Divine Action*, ed. R. J. Russell, N. Murphy, and A. R. Peacocke, 325–58. Vatican City: Vatican Observatory; Berkeley, CA: Center for Theology and the Natural Sciences.
Pike, Nelson. 1965. "Divine Omniscience and Voluntary Action." *Philosophical Review* 74:27–46.
Polkinghorne, J. C. 2001. "Physical Process, Quantum Events, and Divine Agency." In *Quantum Mechanics: Scientific Perspectives on Divine Action*, eds. R. J. Russell, P. Clayton, K. Wegter-McNelly, and J. C. Polkinghorne, 5:181–90. Vatican City: Vatican Observatory; Berkeley, CA: Center for Theology and the Natural Sciences.
———. 2005. *Science and Providence: God's Interaction with the World*. 2nd ed. West Conshocken, PA: Templeton Foundation.
Pollard, W. G. 1958. *Chance and Providence: God's Action in a World Governed by Scientific Laws*. London: Faber and Faber.
Russell, R. J. 2001. "Divine Action and Quantum Mechanics: A Fresh Assessment." In *Quantum Mechanics: Scientific Perspectives on Divine Action*, ed. R. J. Russell, P. Clayton, K. Wegter-McNelly, and J. C. Polkinghorne, 5:293–328. Vatican City: Vatican Observatory; Berkeley, CA: Center for Theology and the Natural Sciences.
van Inwagen, Peter. 1983. *An Essay on Free Will*. Oxford: Clarendon.

LIBET, BENJAMIN.

LIBET, BENJAMIN. Benjamin Libet (1916–2007) earned his PhD in physiology from the University of Chicago in 1939. His early work focused on central nervous system functioning, such as synaptic mechanisms and spinal cord functions, and is relatively unknown outside the field of physiology.

In contrast, his later studies on the physiological bases of **consciousness** control is known across numerous disciplines and is most noteworthy for a discussion of Christianity and science. Libet and colleagues conducted a program of research in which participants viewed a light revolving around a circle every 2.5 seconds and were instructed to move their finger anytime they desired, but to note where on the circle the light was when they first became aware of their urge to move their finger. Libet used an electroencephalograph (EEG) to measure the build-up of electrical potential (readiness potential, RP) in the motor cortex of the brain related to the finger movement. As expected, the self-report of the desire to move preceded the movement of the finger. Surprisingly, the RP preceded the desire to move.

These studies have been interpreted by many as showing that the brain initiates voluntary movements before our awareness of deciding to move, meaning a conscious decision to act is not the true cause of the movement. These interpretations lead to the view that conscious control is epiphenomenal or an illusion.

Though the findings have been replicated, the meaning of these findings are as controversial as they are interesting. Critics have posited numerous possible problems with the study and subsequent findings. The design of the study allows for various types of error related to the determining of the findings, such as estimating the onset of the RP and the onset of the conscious desire. Most noted is the fact that the timing of the awareness of the urge to act is self-reported. Criticism has also been directed toward the area of the brain in which the RP was detected, noting that this brain region can cause movements but cannot cause the will to move. Other critiques have focused on the low-level action involved in the study, movement of a finger, and take issue with that being a representative task to test for conscious control.

Beyond the rational arguments against the anticonscious control interpretations are two research-based arguments against those same interpretations. Trevena and Miller (2009) used a methodology similar to Libet's in which participants were to decide whether or not to move their finger after hearing a tone. They found that the RP occurred regardless of whether the participants decided to move their fingers or not, suggesting the RP from Libet's studies were unspecified neural activity and not predictive of action preparation. Aaron Schurger has proposed that the RP is not actually a preparation for action by the brain, but is random noise in the neurological system and therefore not necessary for the decision to act.

Given the original findings, the critiques of the interpretations and the more recent data, it may be most helpful to reframe the discussion within a simple framework of distal and proximal intentions. Many who take the Libet findings as evidence against conscious control ignore the fact that by agreeing to participate in the Libet studies participants have already consciously decided to act. The Libet studies may show that the distal intention, at the beginning of the study, to act in the future leads to an unconscious proximal urge to act of which one then becomes conscious. From this perspective there is no reason to interpret Libet's findings as antagonistic to conscious control.

C. Eric Jones

REFERENCES AND RECOMMENDED READING

Ekstrom, Laura. 2000. *Free Will: A Philosophical Study.* Boulder, CO: Westview.
Libet, Benjamin. 1999. "Do We Have Free Will?" In *The Volitional Brain: Towards a Neuroscience of Free Will*, ed. Benjamin Libet, Anthony Freeman, and Keith Sutherland. Exeter, UK: Imprint Academic.
Mele, Al. 2006. *Free Will and Luck.* New York: Oxford Press.
Menuge, Angus. 2004. *Agents under Fire.* Lanham, MD: Rowman & Littlefield.

LIFE. Life (from Old Frisian for life, body, or person) is the condition or attribute that distinguishes organic from

inorganic and animate from inanimate objects, whether vegetable, animal, human, angelic, or divine.

The earth is made up of four basic systems: the lithosphere, hydrosphere, atmosphere, and the system of living things, the biosphere. All living organisms are composed of six basic elements: carbon, hydrogen, nitrogen, oxygen, phosphorous, and sulfur. Likewise, all living **species** are made of cells that are organized into tissue, organs, and organ systems. At the basic molecular level, all living cells include polysaccharides, polypeptides, and polynucleotides (Poe and Davis 2012).

For the early Greek philosophers, some sort of animating principle gave life to organic things. For instance, for **Aristotle**, sometimes described as the first empirical scientist, life was animation, that is, the ability to be self-moving (see his *De Anima*). All living things are self-animating because they have a **soul**, where soul is just that property of self-motion. The soul is what separates the animate from the inanimate things in the world. All animate things have a nutritive soul and a reproductive soul that sustain their lives. In addition to nutritive and reproductive souls, animals have locomotive and sensitive souls that enable them to perceive and experience the world around them. Humans, alone among animals, also have rational souls.

Origins of Life

Every major **worldview** or religion has an account of the origins of life. Those accounts are either naturalistic or supernaturalistic. Naturalistic evolution is the view that organic life is the result of either a cataclysmic event like a **big bang** or a slow coincidence of events that combined by accident the elements necessary for life. Whatever the first cause, it had no divine origin but is assumed to be the result of purely mechanistic and naturalistic movement within the closed system of the universe. Oxford scientist **Richard Dawkins**, for example, has famously argued that although the universe and the things that live in it appear to be designed, they are not (cf. *The Blind Watchmaker* and *The Selfish Gene*). From the moment of life's origin, some 3 to 4 billion years ago, living things have adapted to their environment through the process of **natural selection**.

Supernaturalist accounts of the **origin of life** fall on a spectrum from evolutionary theories to nonevolutionary theories. What these theories hold in common is the affirmation that, in the words of the Nicene Creed, God is the "Maker of all things, visible and invisible." Or, according to the Hebrew Scriptures, God (Yahweh) himself is a living, eternal, self-sustaining, noncontingent being who made from nothing (ex nihilo) everything that exists. This living God is the source of all other life and all living things, including vegetation, plants, and trees (Gen. 1:11–12); birds, fish, and other sea creatures (Gen. 1:20–22); insects, cattle, and other land animals (Gen. 1:24–25); and human beings, who are uniquely made in the divine image and likeness (Gen. 1:26–28). *How* God made all things and *when* these things came into existence is theory-dependent. That is, various theories offer various accounts of the origins.

Evolutionary creationism, sometimes known as theistic evolution, is the view that once God created **space and time**, he made a "fine-tuned" universe of physical constraints that were hospitable to life, including human life (the **anthropic principle**; see also **Fine-Tuning of the Universe and Solar System**). Constants such as gravity, electromagnetic force, and so-called carbon resonance, which accounts for the efficient production of carbon, are all features of a world that is especially welcoming to organic life forms. Cambridge paleontologist Simon Conway Morris put it this way:

> The history of life on Earth appears impossibly complex and unpredictable, but take a closer look and you'll find a deep structure. Physics and chemistry dictate that many things are simply not possible, and these constraints extend to biology. The solution to a particular biological problem can often be handled in one of a few ways, which is why when you examine the tapestry of evolution you see the same patterns emerging over and over again. (Morris 2002, 26)

Although these constants do not prove the existence of a creator, proponents of evolutionary creationism understand **theism** to be the most plausible **explanation** for the evidence. Similarly, according to proponents of theistic evolution, the evidence points to evolution as the most plausible account of the means God has used to bring creation to its current stage.

Evolutionary creationism creates potential difficulties for a traditional view of human origins. On the traditional view, God created Adam *de novo* and Eve from Adam's rib (Gen. 2:4–25). Current understandings of molecular biology, however, make it difficult to affirm the *de novo* creation of *Homo sapiens*. Some argue that the genetic diversity among humans today could not have come from just two individuals in the past. A population of thousands would be necessary. If, however, Adam and Eve are not the first human parents, theological problems arise. For instance, take Romans 5:18–19: "Therefore, as one trespass led to condemnation for all men, so one act of righteousness lead to justification and life for all men. For the one man's disobedience the many were made sinners, so by the one man's obedience the many will be made righteous." Here the apostle Paul is drawing an important parallel between Adam and Jesus. Christians differ about how to understand this parallelism (see **Adam and Eve**).

At the other end of the spectrum is **young-earth creationism** (YEC). YECs have a more literal interpretation of the Genesis account, holding that God made the heavens and the earth within the span of six 24-hour days. Thus, on some accounts, rather than billions of years old, the earth is 10,000 years old or less. They agree with theistic evolutionists that God has made a fine-tuned universe and that the anthropic principle holds. Yet, though YECs do not deny that microevolution takes place, they repudiate evolution as God's means of creation.

Artificial Life

Recent efforts are under way to synthesize life. Using the tools of synthetic biology, researchers like Harvard's George Church and molecular biologist Craig Venter are attempting to create novel life forms through genetic recombination. There are potentially valuable prospects for biomedicine and bioenergy through synthetic biology, including cleaner energy sources, customized vaccines, targeted medicines, environmental cleansers, and hardier crops.

At the same time, there are troublesome ethical, legal, and social questions about this new arena of experimentation. One of the biggest concerns is the risk of a bioengineered organism being released into the environment. What if the organism multiplies and produces harm to other life forms, including humans? What if the organism mutates and is unable to be contained? These are concerns that call on multinational organizations to exercise vigilant risk assessment and oversight.

C. Ben Mitchell

REFERENCES AND RECOMMENDED READING

Barrett, Matthew, and Ardel B. Caneday, eds. 2013. *Four Views on the Historical Adam*. Grand Rapids: Zondervan.

Church, George, and Ed Regis. 2014. *Regenesis: How Synthetic Biology Will Reinvent Nature and Ourselves*. New York: Basic Books.

Dawkins, R. 1986. *The Blind Watchmaker: Why Evidence of Evolution Reveals a Universe without Design*. New York: W. W. Norton.

———. 2006. *The Selfish Gene: 30th Anniversary Edition*. Oxford: Oxford University Press.

Giberson, Karl. 2012. *The Wonder of the Universe: Hints of God in Our Fine-Tuned World*. Downers Grove, IL: IVP Academic.

Harrison, Peter. 2015. *The Territories of Science and Religion.* Chicago: University of Chicago Press.

McGrath, Alister E. 2009. *A Fine-Tuned Universe: The Quest for God in Science and Theology.* Louisville, KY: Westminster John Knox.

Morris, Simon Conway. 2002. "We Were Meant to Be …" *New Scientist* 176:26–29.

Poe, Harry Lee, and Jimmy H. Davis. 2012. *God and the Cosmos: Divine Activity in Space, Time and History.* Downers Grove, IL: IVP Academic.

Walton, John. 2009. *The Lost World of Genesis One: Ancient Cosmology and the Origins Debate.* Downers Grove, IL: IVP Academic.

Wood, Todd Charles, and Megan J. Murray. 2003. *Understanding the Pattern of Life: Origins and the Organization of the Species.* Nashville: B&H.

LIFE, ORIGIN OF. Although philosophical speculations about life's origin from inanimate matter date from the time of Anaximander, origin of life science, begun after the nineteenth-century demise of vitalism (Farley 1977; Fry 2000), helped spur Darwin to speculate that life arose in a "warm little pond" (Darwin 1887, 18). Alexander Oparin and J. B. S. Haldane advanced the first concrete ideas in the 1920s; their "Oparin-Haldane hypothesis" held that life arose in water under a reducing atmosphere.

Experimental investigation dates from the 1953 Miller-Urey experiment in which Miller produced small amounts of natural amino acids by passing a lightning-simulating electric discharge through a simulated early atmosphere of ammonia, methane, water, and hydrogen (Miller 1953). Subsequent prebiotic syntheses gave nucleobases, sugars, fatty acids, and nucleotides from small molecule precursors (Miller 1998; Powner et al. 2009), while the identification of amino acids and other biochemicals in the Murchinson meteorite supported the validity of some prebiotic syntheses (Pizzarello and Shock 2010; Schmitt-Kopplin et al. 2010).

Origin of life research's main challenge is to explain how biological molecules can be assembled into complex networks of shape selective (stereospecific) carbohydrates, lipids, proteins, and nucleic acid polymers (the latter two of which exhibit specific sequences) organized in a membrane-enclosed cell. Plausible hypotheses have been advanced for shape selectivity (i.e., the homochirality problem; Blackmond 2010), the formation of self-replicating biopolymers, and the construction of semisynthetic minimal cells (Mann 2012; Stano and Luisi 2013), but the development of a credible overarching origin scenario faces significant challenges. Among the numerous proposals, two approaches dominate:

1. *Replicator-first hypotheses* posit that life arose from self-replicating biopolymers or supramolecular structures (like lipid vesicles); selection among these gave ordered metabolic systems. A prominent example is the prebiotic RNA World (Atkins et al. 2011), which holds that life was originally RNA-based and later became RNA-DNA-protein based. However, though self-replicating ribozymes have been demonstrated under laboratory conditions (Cheng 2010; Lincoln and Joyce 2009), it is not clear how self-replicating ribozymes arose naturally, were assembled into a functional metabolism, or replaced.

2. *Metabolism-first approaches* posit that life arose from a series of organized energy-converting reactions that were eventually encapsulated and produced replicators. Prominent proposals include template reactions on clay mineral surfaces (Cairns-Smith and Hartman 1986; Hazen and Sverjensky 2010) and the iron-sulfur world theory (Wächtershäuser 1992), which holds that life arose via a series of metal-sulfur catalyzed reductions in the sulfur-rich environments of hydrothermal vents. Although many iron-sulfur world reactions have been demonstrated (Cody et al. 2000; Novikov and Copley 2013), it is unclear how mineral-based metabolism eventually gave rise to self-replicating biomolecules or became encapsulated.

In summary, despite its significant progress and promise, **origin of life** science still needs a plausible mechanism for forming specific biopolymer sequences and primitive functional cells.

Since origin of life science illuminates both the rich chemical diversity that makes life possible and the challenges associated with its spontaneous formation, it has occasioned considerable metaphysical reflection. Although most workers in the field simply look to the existence of plausible physiochemical ideas about the origin of life and the past success of scientific explanations as a reason to expect that life arose by natural processes, they disagree over the relative importance of deterministic laws and **chance** (Luisi 2006, 4–10). Some workers claim that the conditions that make life possible render it probable or even inevitable while others emphasize the importance of contingent events.

These competing emphases are evident in debates over the theological significance of origin of life science, although both have been employed to argue for and against religion. **Determinism** underlies both natural theologies based on scientific laws as well as claims that naturalistic accounts invalidate the Christian story (de Duve 2002). Believers and atheists have both embraced arguments based on randomness in nature, with atheists claiming that it indicates purposelessness and theists claiming that random processes alone cannot explain the **complexity** of nature.

Indeed, many Christian approaches to the origin of life emphasize the complexity of living things or the seemingly improbable anthropic coincidences that make life possible (Barrow and Tipler 1986; Barrow et al. 2008). Young-earth creationists (Gish 1972; Morris 1996; Wilder-Smith 1970) and **intelligent design** (ID) theorists (Behe 1995; Pullen 2005; Thaxton et. al. 1984) claim that natural mechanisms alone are inadequate; ID advocates even claim that anthropic coincidences and biological complexity are positive evidence for purposeful design, although their proposals have occasioned considerable criticism (Dembski and Ruse 2004; Pennock 2001).

Their early approaches tended to emphasize the significant difficulties facing origin of life proposals (Thaxton et al. 1984, chap. 4) or claim that the **second law of thermodynamics** makes a natural origin of life impossible or unlikely (Gish 1978; Morris 1978; Thaxton et al. 1984, chap. 7). However, in effect the second law is not the real issue; since entropy-lowering processes can occur when coupled to entropy-increasing ones, most creationists and ID theorists focus on the lack of an identifiable mechanism for coupling entropy production to an increase in biological **information** (Bradley 1988, 2004; Thaxton et al. 1984, chap. 9).

In effect these creationist and ID proponents claim that the problem of biopolymer sequences and molecular complexity is insoluble. This issue has been extensively explored by ID writers; however, the specific arguments used to advance this assertion are problematic. For example, **William Dembski**'s claim (2002) that biopolymers exhibit "**specified complexity**" indicative of the working of a designer has been criticized as poorly argued based on an inadequate scholarship (Shallit 2002), while **Michael Behe**'s claims (1995, 2007) that biochemical machinery could not have arisen naturally due to its **irreducible complexity** have been challenged on scientific (Carroll 2007; Miller 1999, 2007), philosophical (Boudry 2010), and theological (Alexander 2012) grounds.

More recently, **Stephen Meyer** (2009) argues that, given the difficulties inherent in explaining the origin of biochemical information, an intelligent designer is simply the "best explanation" for life's origin. Given the current state of the science, his argument is difficult to refute, but critics worry he is invoking a "**God of the gaps**" (Venema 2011), complain that he did not adequately grapple with current origin of life research, or argue that his proposal is a science stopper with "no theory of design, and no vigorous hypotheses to advance [the ID] movement" (Venema 2010, 282).

Old-earth creationists Fazale Rana and **Hugh Ross** (Rana and Ross 2004) offer a concordist model for life's origin with testable predictions they claim can be used to adjudicate between "biblical" and purely naturalistic accounts. In particular they argue that Genesis 1:2 teaches that complex life-bearing evidence of design arose early in the earth's history, persisted through hostile early-earth conditions, and subsequently developed into qualitatively different multicellular forms; naturalistic accounts, they assert, must instead involve the gradual development of simple life forms under relatively mild conditions. However, Ross and Rana's "biblical" model predictions aren't necessarily incompatible with origin of life science; consequently they have been criticized as a mix of repackaged naturalistic predictions and untestable metaphysical assertions (Hurd 2007).

Other Christian thinkers are more accepting of naturalistic accounts of life's origin. **Pierre Teilhard de Chardin** (1959) proposed that life arose from an inherent **teleology** within nature. Although his **natural theology** has been welcomed for his embrace of teleology and connection of natural theology with ethics (Grumett 2007), his views have been criticized as scientifically unwarranted and unhelpful (Thom 2008) and as embedded in an evolution-centric theology of questionable orthodoxy (Ward 1982).

Alister McGrath also accepts the sufficiency of physiochemical mechanisms and teleology in nature; however, he does not attempt to embed teleology in nature as much as see teleology within it. Furthermore, McGrath's approach to natural theology explicitly rejects Paleyan design arguments in favor of demonstrating consonance between science and preexisting faith. Thus he views scientific accounts of life's origin as consistent with **Augustine**'s conception of "embedded causalities" in creation (McGrath 2009, 107; 2011). However, although McGrath's approach has been welcomed as conducive to both science and theology, there are questions over whether it can or should support a distinctly Christian natural theology (Palmer 2012).

Stephen Contakes

REFERENCES AND RECOMMENDED READING

Alexander, Denis. 2012. "A Critique of Intelligent Design." In *Darwinism and Natural Theology: Evolving Perspectives*, ed. Andrew Robinson, 101–25. Cambridge: Cambridge Scholars Press.

Atkins, John F., Raymond F. Gesteland, and Thomas Cech. 2011. *RNA Worlds: From Life's Origins to Diversity in Gene Regulation*. Cold Spring Harbor, NY: Cold Spring Harbor Laboratory Press.

Barrow, John D., Simon Conway Morris, Stephen J. Freeland, and Charles L. Harper Jr., eds. 2008. *Fitness of the Cosmos for Life: Biochemistry and Fine-Tuning*. Cambridge Astrobiology. Vol. 2. Cambridge: Cambridge University Press.

Barrow, John D., and Frank J. Tipler. 1986. *The Anthropic Cosmological Principle.* Oxford: Oxford University Press.

Behe, Michael J. 1996. *Darwin's Black Box: The Biochemical Challenge to Evolution.* New York: Free Press.

———. 2007. *The Edge of Evolution: The Search for the Limits of Darwinism.* New York: Free Press.

Blackmond, Donna G. 2010. "The Origin of Biological Homochirality." *Cold Spring Harbor Perspectives in Biology* 2, no. 5 (May): 1–17. doi:10.1101/cshperspect.a002147. www.ncbi.nlm.nih.gov/pmc/articles/PMC2857173/pdf/cshperspect-ORI-a002147.pdf.

Boudry, Maarten. 2010. "Irreducible Incoherence and Intelligent Design: A Look into the Conceptual Toolbox of a Pseudoscience." *Quarterly Review of Biology* 85 (4): 473–82.

Bradley, Walter L. 1988. "Thermodynamics and the Origin of Life." *Perspectives on Science and Christian Faith* 40 (2): 72–83.

———. 2004. "Information, Entropy, and the Origin of Life." In *Debating Design: From Darwin to DNA*, ed. William A. Dembski and Michael Ruse, 331–51. Cambridge: Cambridge University Press.

Cairns-Smith, A. G., and H. Hartman. 1986. *Clay Minerals and the Origin of Life.* Cambridge and New York: Cambridge University Press.

Carroll, Sean B. 2007. "God as Genetic Engineer." *Science* 316 (5830): 1427–28.

Cheng, Leslie K. L., and Peter J. Unrau. 2010. "Closing the Circle: Replicating RNA with RNA." *Cold Spring Harbor Perspectives in Biology* 2 (10): 16.

Cleaves, H. James, John H. Chalmers, Antonio Lazcano, Stanley L. Miller, and Jeffrey L. Bada. 2008. "A Reassessment of Prebiotic Organic Synthesis in Neutral Planetary Atmospheres." *Origin of Life and Evolution of Biospheres* 38:105–15.

Cody, George D., Nabil Z. Boctor, Timothy R. Filley, Robert M. Hazen, James H. Scott, Anurag Sharma, and Hatten S. Yoder. 2000. "Primordial Carbonylated Iron-Sulfur Compounds and the Synthesis of Pyruvate." *Science* 289, no. 5483 (August 25): 1337–40.

Darwin, Francis 1887. *The Life and Letters of Charles Darwin, Including an Autobiographical Chapter.* 3 vols. London: John Murray.

De Duve, Christian. 2002. *Life Evolving: Molecules, Mind, and Meaning.* Oxford and New York: Oxford University Press.

Dembski, William A. 2002. *No Free Lunch: Why Specified Complexity Cannot Be Purchased without Intelligence.* Lanham, MD: Rowman & Littlefield.

Dembski, William A., and Michael Ruse. 2004. *Debating Design: From Darwin to DNA.* New York: Cambridge University Press.

Farley, John. 1977. *The Spontaneous Generation Controversy from Descartes to Oparin.* Baltimore: Johns Hopkins University Press.

Fry, Iris. 2000. *The Emergence of Life on Earth: A Historical and Scientific Overview.* New Brunswick, NJ: Rutgers University Press.

Gish, Duane T. 1972. *Speculations and Experiments Related to Theories on the Origin of Life: A Critique.* ICR Technical Monograph No. 1. San Diego: Institute for Creation Research.

———. 1978. "Thermodynamics and the Origin of Life (Part 2)." *Acts & Facts* 7 (4). Institute for Creation Research. www.icr.org/article/thermodynamics-origin-life-part-ii/.

Grumett, David. 2007. "Teilhard De Chardin's Evolutionary Natural Theology." *Zygon* 42 (2): 519–34.

Hazen, Robert M., and Dimitri A. Sverjensky. 2010. "Mineral Surfaces, Geochemical Complexities, and the Origins of Life." *Cold Spring Harbor Perspectives in Biology* 2 (5): 21.

Hurd, Gary S. 2007. "Review: Origins of Life." *Reports of the National Center for Science Education* 27 (3–4): 45–47.

Lazcano, A. 2010. "Historical Development of Origins Research." *Cold Spring Harbor Perspectives in Biology* 2, no. 11 (November): a002089.

Lincoln, Tracey A., and Gerald F. Joyce. 2009. "Self-Sustained Replication of an RNA Enzyme." *Science* 323 (5918): 1229–32.

Luisi, P. L. 2006. *The Emergence of Life: From Chemical Origins to Synthetic Biology.* Cambridge: Cambridge University Press.

Mann, Stephen. 2012. "Systems of Creation: The Emergence of Life from Nonliving Matter." *Accounts of Chemical Research* 45, no. 12 (December 18): 2131–41.

McGrath, Alister E. 2009. *A Fine-Tuned Universe: The Quest for God in Science and Theology.* 2009 Gifford Lectures. Louisville, KY: Westminster John Knox.

———. 2011. *Surprised by Meaning: Science, Faith, and How We Make Sense of Things.* Louisville, KY: Westminster John Knox.

Meyer, Stephen C. 2009. *Signature in the Cell: DNA and the Evidence for Intelligent Design.* 1st ed. New York: HarperOne.

———. 2011. "Of Molecules and (Straw) Men: A Reply to Dennis Venema's Review of *Signature in the Cell.*" *Perspectives on Science and Christian Faith* 63, no. 3 (September): 171–82.

Miller, Kenneth R. 1999. *Finding Darwin's God: A Scientist's Search for Common Ground between God and Evolution.* New York: Cliff Street.

———. 2007. "Falling over the Edge." *Nature* 448, no. 28 (June): 1055–56.

Miller, Stanley L. 1953. "A Production of Amino Acids under Possible Primitive Earth Conditions." *Science* 117 (3046): 528–29.

———. 1998. "The Endogenous Synthesis of Organic Compounds." In *The Molecular Origins of Life*, ed. A. Brack, chap. 3. Cambridge: Cambridge University Press.

Morris, Henry. 1978. "Thermodynamics and the Origin of Life (Part 1)." *Acts & Facts* 7 (3). Institute for Creation Research. www.icr.org/article/thermodynamics-origin-life-part-i/.

Morris, John D. 1996. "How Did Life Originate?" *Acts & Facts* 25 (8). Institute for Creation Research.www.icr.org/article/how-did-life-originate/.

Normandin, Sebastian, and Charles T. Wolfe. 2013. *Vitalism and the Scientific Image in Post-Enlightenment Life Science, 1800–2010.* Dordrecht: Springer.

Novikov, Yehor, and Shelley D. Copley. 2013. "Reactivity Landscape of Pyruvate under Simulated Hydrothermal Vent Conditions." *Proceedings of the National Academy of Sciences USA* 110, no. 33 (August 13): 13283–88.

Palmer, Stephen J. 2012. "Review of Alister E. McGrath, *Surprised by Meaning: Science, Faith, and How We Make Sense of Things.*" *Themelios* 37 (1): 131–32.

Pennock, Robert T. 2001. *Intelligent Design Creationism and Its Critics: Philosophical, Theological, and Scientific Perspectives.* Cambridge, MA: MIT Press.

Pizzarello, Sandra, and Everett Shock. 2010. "The Organic Composition of Carbonaceous Meteorites: The Evolutionary Story Ahead of Biochemistry." In *The Origins of Life*, Cold Spring Harbor Perspectives, ed. David Deamer and Jack W. Szostak, 89–108. Cold Spring Harbor, NY: Cold Spring Harbor Laboratory Press.

Powner, Matthew W., Béatrice Gerland, and John D. Sutherland. 2009. "Synthesis of Activated Pyrimidine Ribonucleotides in Prebiotically Plausible Conditions." *Nature* 459 (7244): 239–42.

Pullen, Stuart. 2005. *Intelligent Design or Evolution: Why the Origin of Life and the Evolution of Molecular Knowledge Imply Design.* Raleigh, NC: Intelligent Design.

Rana, Fazale, and Hugh Ross. 2004. *Origins of Life: Biblical and Evolutionary Models Face Off.* Colorado Springs: NavPress.

Rau, Gerald. 2012. *Mapping the Origins Debate: Six Models of the Beginning of Everything.* Downers Grove, IL: IVP Academic.

Schmitt-Kopplin, Philippe, Zelimir Gabelica, Régis D. Gougeon, Agnes Fekete, Basem Kanawati, Mourad Harir, Istvan Gebefuegi, Gerhard Eckel, and Norbert Hertkorn. 2010. "High Molecular Diversity of Extraterrestrial Organic Matter in Murchison Meteorite Revealed 40 Years after Its Fall." *Proceedings of the National Academy of Sciences USA* 107, no. 7 (February 16): 2763–68.

Seckbach, J., ed. 2012. *Genesis—In the Beginning: Precursors of Life, Chemical Models and Early Biological Evolution.* Cellular Origin, Life in Extreme Habitats and Astrobiology. Dordrecht: Springer.

Shallit, Jeffrey. 2002. "Book Review: *No Free Lunch: Why Specified Complexity Cannot Be Purchased without Intelligence*, William Dembski, Rowman & Littlefield, 2002." *BioSystems* 66 (2): 93–99.

Stano, Pasquale, and Pier Luigi Luisi. 2013. "Semi-Synthetic Minimal Cells: Origin and Recent Developments." *Current Opinion in Biotechnology* 24 (4): 633–38.

Teilhard de Chardin, Pierre. 1959. *The Phenomenon of Man*. New York: Harper.

Thaxton, Charles B., Walter L. Bradley, and Roger L. Olsen. 1984. *The Mystery of Life's Origin: Reassessing Current Theories*. New York: Philosophical Library.

Thom, Rene. 2008. "Comments [on *The Basic Ideas of Biology* by C. H. Waddington]." In *The Origin of Life: Toward a Theoretical Biology*, ed. C. H. Waddington, 32–41. New Brunswick, NJ: Aldine Transaction.

Venema, Dennis. 2010. "Seeking a Signature." *Perspectives on Science and Christian Faith* 62 (4): 276–83.

———. 2011. "Intelligent Design, Abiogenesis, and Learning from History: A Reply to Meyer." *Perspectives on Science and the Christian Faith* 63, no. 3 (September): 183–92.

Wächtershäuser, Günter. 1992. "Groundworks for an Evolutionary Biochemistry: The Iron-Sulphur World." *Progress in Biophysics and Molecular Biology* 58 (2): 85–201.

———. 2013. "Origin of Life: RNA World versus Autocatalytic Anabolist." In *The Prokaryotes: Prokaryotic Biology and Symbiotic Associations*, ed. Eugene Rosenberg, Edward F. DeLong, Stephen Lory, Erko Stackebrandt, and Fabiano Thompson, 81–88. Dordrecht: Springer.

Ward, Terry A. 1982. "The Spirituality of Teilhard De Chardin: An Evangelical Critique." *Journal of the American Scientific Association* 34, no. 2 (June): 103–5.

Wilder-Smith, A. E. 1970. *The Creation of Life: A Cybernetic Approach to Evolution*. Wheaton, IL: Harold Shaw.

Zubay, Geoffrey L. 2000. *Origins of Life on the Earth and in the Cosmos*. 2nd ed. San Diego: Academic Press.

LIFE AFTER DEATH. Central to a Christian understanding of life after death is the hope of a general resurrection: a divine gift enabling individuals who have died to live again through bodies related to those they previously possessed (Davis 2010, 108–23). Whether resurrection is a coherent possibility will depend on what human persons *are*. In particular it will depend on whether there is any way in which particular pre- and postmortem human beings could in fact be the very same person (i.e., numerically identical individuals).

The traditional and culturally widespread claim that a human person is an immaterial soul accommodates the possibility of resurrection. The **soul** does not depend for its existence on the continuation of the earthly body, and if a person's soul persists through death to resurrection, then that person does too. In contrast, if that soul does not persist, then even a next-worldly individual perfectly similar in all physical and psychological respects would be a mere duplicate.

Soul-belief continues to be defended and explicated as knowledge of the natural world increases (see Baker and Goetz 2011; Goetz and Taliaferro 2011; Robinson 2012). Nevertheless, some Christian scholars energetically resist dualistic accounts, taking them to be misplaced and unnecessary. For example, Lynne Baker describes souls as *surds* in nature, and N. T. Wright has claimed that "we do not need what has been called '**dualism**' to help us over the awkward gap between bodily death and bodily resurrection" (Baker 2010; Wright 2011). Hence accounts of life after death without dualism have been sought.

One popular physicalist approach is re-creation: an individual survives because God creates a being in the next world who is perfectly similar to the deceased in all physical and psychological respects. However, if this is possible, then there is no reason in principle why only *one* such being could be created. There could therefore be multiple, simultaneous, qualified candidates to continue the life of the premortem individual.

Note that the problem is not merely that an observer would be unable to identify which of the candidates is the premortem individual. Rather, it is that all of the candidates meet in full the criteria to actually *be* that individual. The situation is logically contradictory since it is not possible that multiple distinct persons could also be one person. This impossibility demonstrates that creations of this type can be nothing more than duplicates of the deceased. Another way to express the point is to note that identity is a *necessary* relation, but this re-creation view requires that it be *contingent* instead, since pre- and postmortem individuals are only identical *if* there are no other qualified candidates.

One way to constrain re-creation is to demand that it make use of atoms associated with the premortem body. This is no help, since bodies slough off all their matter more than once during earthly life, and so the same multiple-candidate problem arises. To limit re-creation further to just the matter composing the body at the time of death would render a general resurrection impossible because this matter would no doubt have been caught up in other bodies over time, producing multiple "claimants" for the same matter at that point.

The reassembly of all would be impossible. However, the physicalist could deny the possibility of multiple claimants. For example, Peter van Inwagen suggests that physicalist resurrection is possible as a result of divine body switching. If God instantaneously replaces bodies at the point of death with indistinguishable copies, then the duplicate can be buried while the "real" body is kept for a future resurrection (van Inwagen 1978, 2006). This implausible suggestion is intended only to show that physicalist resurrection is metaphysically possible, leaving one free to assume that God actually achieves it in another, unknown way. However, on this view, resurrection is only possible given God's systematic deception of the bereaved. This motivates Zimmerman's alternative suggestion.

Consider a tornado continually acquiring and throwing off matter. The only stable feature that unites the tornado over time is the fact that its state at each moment is directly caused by its state at the previous moment: there is an *immanent causal connection* through time. Corcoran, Zimmerman, and others explain the ongoing identity of bodies this way (Baker 2000; Corcoran 2006; Loose 2012; Zimmerman 1999).

Zimmerman then uses this idea to offer an alternative account of the possibility of resurrection. At death God could cause the smallest elements that make up a body to *bud* such that there come to be two identically structured bodies—one in this world and one in the next. Since the dying body will be immanent-causally connected to both products of budding, each will have a claim to be identical with it. In this case, the body left in this world is not a duplicate introduced from outside, and so van Inwagen's deception problem might be avoided. However, since this view allows two bodies to have a claim to identity with the premortem body, it also denies the necessity of identity with the attendant likelihood of incoherence or absurdity (Loose 2012).

Finally, the physicalist may seek other ways to articulate the relationship between a wholly physical person and her or his body. Such theories are aligned with wider attempts in the philosophy of **mind** to account for mental life within a physicalist scheme. For example, Lynne Baker suggests that persons are in fact *constituted by* rather than identical to bodies. To illustrate, imagine yourself admiring Michelangelo's *David*. You would be admiring both a statue and a lump of marble, but are these two things or one? If one, then all the properties of the statue must be properties of the marble, and vice versa.

However, imagine further that each of *David*'s molecules was replaced with copper such that the lump of marble is annihilated while the statue remains. The conceivability of this implies to Baker that the marble and statue have distinct properties necessitating that they are in fact two different objects. They are not identical, but one constitutes the other. Baker argues that persons are similarly constituted by bodies and are thus able to persist through a change of body (Baker 2000). The central question for all views of this type is whether they in fact offer coherent and adequate accounts of the nature of human persons that avoid identity with the body on the one hand and dualism on the other. For example, it is uncertain whether constitution and identity can be coherently distinguished and, if they can, whether the

distinctive property that Baker considers essential to persons can be accommodated in a physicalist scheme (Moreland 2009; Wasserman 2004).

Even if these accounts succeed in demonstrating the bare metaphysical possibility of physicalist resurrection, they would be unable to account for a period of conscious disembodiment between bodily death and resurrection. Recent debate about whether the idea of an intermediate state can be read out of the Bible is found in the work of John Cooper and Joel Green (Cooper 2000; Green 2008). Cooper argues that neither immediate resurrection nor extinction–re-creation accounts are possible since the biblical evidence supports a conscious intermediate state followed by a future resurrection. He concludes that a proper Christian account of life after death requires *dualistic holism*, which he believes "is faithful to Scripture, upholds the traditional teaching of the church about the afterlife, and is perfectly consistent with the 'assured results' of contemporary science and philosophy" (Cooper 2000, 4).

Cooper offers five lines of evidence for the intermediate state: First, the Old Testament indicates some **consciousness** among the dead (*rephaim*) in their world (*sheol*); second, the most prominent views within second temple Judaism include it; third, texts in Luke (e.g., Luke 16:19–31; 23:42–44; 24:36–39) and Paul (e.g., 2 Cor. 12:2–4) require dualistic interpretation; and fourth, 2 Corinthians 5:1–10 supports an intermediate state rather than an immediate resurrection. Finally, Luke clearly aligns Paul with the dualistic **anthropology** of the Pharisees (Acts 23:6–8).

Green rejects dualism and challenges this evidence. He argues that the *rephaim* are the dead in the grave without God and lacking personal existence; there is no dominant dualistic strand within second temple Judaism, and the writings of neither Luke nor Paul support an intermediate state. He thus urges that the idea of a human soul "stands in tension" with the Bible's teaching about resurrection (Edgar 2002; Green 2008, 158) and claims that the radical distinction between frail earthly bodies and glorified heavenly ones is something to which the capacities of human persons can make no contribution at all (Green 2008, 175).

Cooper replies that Green misrepresents his view of Old Testament interest in life beyond the grave and provides an insufficient account of intertestamental anthropological belief. He also claims Green's analyses of New Testament texts reject majority positions without adequate argument, ignore crucial passages, and introduce a false dichotomy between **eschatology** and anthropology (Cooper 2007).

Most important, he looks to N. T. Wright's detailed work supporting an intermediate state view as support for his own position (Cooper 2009; Wright 2003, 2007). Wright is open to accusations of confusion since he also eschews dualism (Moreland 2014). The debate emphasizes the need for careful integration of theological and philosophical concerns.

In summary, the physicalist finds a resonance between the Bible's anthropological holism, the present unpopularity of dualism in philosophy and biblical studies, and developments in natural science. This faces him with a significant challenge to establish even the bare possibility of resurrection, which may itself be only a part of the Christian notion of life after death if an intermediate state is also required.

The dualist sees a prephilosophical notion of soul within the Bible's holistic picture and finds this to be in accord with both theological tradition and first-person **intuition** while not being inconsistent with increasing scientific knowledge. Some dualists also find evidence from near-death experiences to be consistent with or even supportive of their position (see **Near-Death Experiences**). The prospects for life after death are much better on dualism than on **physicalism**, but the dualist must seek to articulate soul-belief persuasively within an academic milieu made resistant by a dominant **naturalism**.

Jonathan Loose

REFERENCES AND RECOMMENDED READING

Baker, Lynne Rudder. 2000. *Persons and Bodies: A Constitution View.* Cambridge: Cambridge University Press.

———. 2010. "Persons and the Metaphysics of Resurrection." In *Personal Identity and Resurrection: How Do We Survive Our Death?* 161–76. Surrey, UK: Ashgate.

Baker, Mark C, and Stewart Goetz. 2011. *The Soul Hypothesis: Investigations in the Existence of the Soul.* New York: Continuum.

Cooper, John W. 2000. *Body, Soul and the Life Everlasting: Biblical Anthropology and the Monism-Dualism Debate.* Grand Rapids: Eerdmans.

———. 2007. "The Bible and Dualism Once Again." *Philosophia Christi* 9 (2): 459–69.

———. 2009. "Exaggerated Rumors of Dualism's Demise: A Review Essay on Body, Soul, and Human Life." *Philosophia Christi* 11 (2): 453–64.

Corcoran, Kevin J. 2006. *Rethinking Human Nature.* Grand Rapids: Baker Academic.

Davis, Stephen T. 2010. "Resurrection." In *The Cambridge Companion to Christian Philosophical Theology*, ed. Charles Taliaferro and Chad Meister, 108–23. Cambridge: Cambridge University Press.

Edgar, Brian. 2002. "Biblical Anthropology and the Intermediate State." *Evangelical Quarterly* 74 (1–2): 1–20.

Goetz, Stewart, and Charles Taliaferro. 2011. *A Brief History of the Soul.* Oxford: Wiley Blackwell.

Green, Joel B. 2008. *Body, Soul, and Human Life: The Nature of Humanity in the Bible.* Grand Rapids: Baker Academic.

Loose, Jonathan. 2012. "Constitution and the Falling Elevator." *Philosophia Christi* 14 (2): 439–50.

Moreland, J. P. 2009. *The Recalcitrant Imago Dei: Human Persons and the Failure of Naturalism.* London: SCM.

———. 2014. *The Soul: How We Know It's Real and Why It Matters.* Chicago: Moody.

Robinson, Howard. 2012. "Dualism." In *Stanford Encyclopedia of Philosophy*, ed. Edward N. Zalta. Winter. http://plato.stanford.edu/archives/win2012/entries/dualism/.

van Inwagen, Peter. 1978. "The Possibility of Resurrection." *International Journal for the Philosophy of Religion* 9 (2): 114–21.

———. 2018 forthcoming. "I Look for the Resurrection of the Dead and the Life of the World to Come." In Loose, Jonathan J., Angus J. L. Menuge, and J. P. Moreland, eds. *The Blackwell Companion to Substance Dualism.* Oxford, UK: Wiley Blackwell. Based on a paper with that title, 2006.

Wasserman, Ryan. 2004. "The Constitution Question." *Nous* 38 (4): 693–710.

Wright, N. T. 2003. *The Resurrection of the Son of God.* London: SPCK.

———. 2007. *Surprised by Hope.* London: SPCK.

———. 2011. "Mind, Spirit, Soul and Body: All for One and One for All: Reflections on Paul's Anthropology in His Complex Contexts." NTWrightPage. March. http://ntwrightpage.com/Wright_SCP_MindSpiritSoulBody.htm.

Zimmerman, Dean W. 1999. "Materialism and Survival: The Falling Elevator Model." *Faith and Philosophy* 16:194–212.

LINDBERG, DAVID C. A leading historian of medieval **science**, David C. Lindberg (1935–2015) was born into a family of fundamentalist missionaries. After studying **physics** at Wheaton College and Northwestern University, he earned a doctorate in the history and **philosophy of science** at Indiana University and taught at the University of Wisconsin for 34 years.

At the pinnacle of his career, encouraged by his departmental colleague Ronald L. Numbers, Lindberg joined with Numbers to lead major projects on the history of Christianity and science. They began by organizing a conference for church historians and historians of science, held in Madison, Wisconsin, in April 1981. This led to the publication of a collection of essays (Lindberg and Numbers 1986) that directly challenged the **conflict thesis** of **Andrew Dickson White** and others, which had dominated historiography to that point. As they wrote in a separate article, "The historical relationship between science and Christianity—or, more properly, scientists and theologians—cannot be reduced simply to conflict or warfare." At the same time, "we do not in any way mean to suggest that Christianity and science have been perennial allies. Such an interpretation, though widely held in some circles, particularly among Christian apologists, fails to pass historical muster" (Lindberg and Numbers 1987, 147–48).

Subsequent projects resulted in further, jointly edited volumes advancing a similar view (Lindberg and Numbers 2003, 2009).

Ironically, in parallel with his increasing scholarly interest in Christianity and science, Lindberg's personal religious trajectory was moving him gradually away from Christian faith. Following his retirement, Lindberg told Numbers that he and his wife had been "assailed by theological doubts" even in graduate school (Lindberg 2003). His theology changed rapidly during the 1970s, leading the Lindbergs to help start a local congregation of the Reformed Church in America that would accept dissent and be more liberal in theological attitude. Over the years, however, conservative members gained control. The Lindbergs left in 1986 and "hardly darkened the door of a church" subsequently.

Assessing his own journey, Lindberg claimed that the study of history can have a "corrosive effect" on religious belief. Nevertheless, his scholarly work remains invaluable.

Edward B. Davis

REFERENCES AND RECOMMENDED READING

Lindberg, David C. 2003. *Oral History Program interview with David Lindberg.* University Archives. Madison: University of Wisconsin.

Lindberg, David C., and Ronald L. Numbers., eds. 1986. *God and Nature: Historical Essays on the Encounter between Christianity and Science.* Berkeley: University of California Press.

———. 1987. "Beyond War and Peace: A Reappraisal of the Encounter between Christianity and Science." *Perspectives on Science and Christian Faith* 39:140–49.

———, eds. 2003. *When Science and Christianity Meet.* Chicago: University of Chicago Press.

———, eds. 2009. *Galileo Goes to Jail and Other Myths about Science and Religion.* Cambridge, MA: Harvard University Press.

LINNAEUS, CAROLUS. The Swedish naturalist Carolus Linnaeus (1707–78) is deservedly considered the "father of taxonomy" for establishing the principles of biological classification and taxonomy. His many contributions include the *Systema Naturae* (1735), a volume that organized morphologically similar organisms together into nested hierarchies—similar genera nested within the same order and similar orders included within the same class. This system allowed for the deluge of newly described or discovered organisms to be neatly associated with those most similar to them.

In addition, Linnaeus brought order to the system of assigning names to **species** by giving each a unique binomial (two-word name). This greatly simplified the increasingly cumbersome and variable system of polynomials in which a species name often consisted of 10 or more terms. His volume *Species Plantarum* (1753) attempted to catalog all known plant species using his system of unique binomials. He also associated those names with known synonyms and provided detailed descriptions of each species. This work marks an important milestone in biological nomenclature, and no officially recognized species names predate its publication.

More controversial at the time was Linnaeus's use of plant sexual organs as the primary morphological characteristics utilized in his hierarchical system. Because reproduction is an essential biological activity, he believed his sexual system of classification was more useful than systems based on vegetative features. Linnaeus's tendency to describe male and female flower parts in terms typically applied to humans was considered particularly provocative. Although application of this system was highly practical, it did not sit well with his more prudish peers.

Early in his career, Linnaeus ascribed to the fixity of species, believing that species were essentially unchanged since their initial creation. This belief allowed him the confidence to base his species descriptions on a single (or few) observed "type" specimen(s). He considered species "natural entities" having reality in the scheme of creation. In contrast, he regarded higher levels in the taxonomic hierarchy (e.g., orders and classes) as artificial constructs facilitating organization of species and did not assume any type of natural relatedness among the group members.

Later in life Linnaeus recognized that plants of different species could hybridize, creating new forms and possibly giving rise to new genera. While holding to his belief that God had initially and specially created species, he also acknowledged that nature might play a role in the production of new species as well. He revised later editions of *Systema Naturae* to reflect his changing views.

Like many naturalists of his time, Linnaeus regarded the careful scientific study of creation as an act of worship, and he considered himself uniquely called and equipped to carry out his work. His systematic approach to the naming and classification of organisms was an attempt to describe the God-ordained order of creation. Linnaeus's own motto was *Deus creavit, Linnaeus disposuit*: "God created, Linnaeus arranged."

Although our present understanding of biological species with their richness and relatedness has surpassed that of Linnaeus's time, his binomial system and approach to classification are still largely employed.

Laura Furlong

REFERENCES AND RECOMMENDED READING

Blunt, Wilfrid. 1971. *The Compleat Naturalist: A Life of Linnaeus.* New York: Viking.

Frängsmyr, Tore, ed. 1983. *Linnaeus: The Man and His Work.* Berkeley: University of California Press.

Harrison, Peter. 2009. "Linnaeus as a Second Adam? Taxonomy and the Religious Vocation." *Zygon* 44:879–93.

Morris, Mary J., and Leonie Berwick, eds. 2008. *The Linnaean Legacy: Three Centuries after His Birth.* Linnaean special issue no. 8. Oxford: Wiley-Blackwell. https://ca1-tls.edcdn.com/documents/Special-Issue-8-The-Linneaen-Legacy.pdf?mtime=20160213060737.

Paterlini, Marta. 2007. "There Shall Be Order—The Legacy of Linnaeus in the Age of Molecular Biology." *EMBO Reports* 8:814–16.

Reid, Gordon McGregor. 2009. "Carolus Linnaeus (1707–1778): His Life, Philosophy and Science and Its Relationship to Modern Biology and Medicine." *TAXON* 58:18–31.

LOCKE, JOHN. John Locke (1632–1704) was born in Wrington, Somerset, and died in Oates, Epping Forest, Essex. Of his prodigious literary output, the most important philosophical works are the *Two Treatises on Government* (1690), *An Essay concerning Human Understanding* (1690a), and *A Vindication of the Reasonableness of Christianity* (1695). Locke was an English philosopher and physician who is generally regarded as the "father of classical liberalism," since he championed the cause of limited government (Locke [1689] 2006, 5). His philosophy also influenced contemporary views on theology, religious toleration, and educational theory.

The publication of *An Essay concerning Human Understanding* (1690) marked the beginning of the **Enlightenment** era, an age of unbounded optimism that came to a close nearly 100 years later with **Immanuel Kant**'s *Critique of Pure Reason* (1781). Almost the entire eighteenth century witnessed the appearance of a new intellectual outlook that permeated European thought.

The earlier era of Renaissance humanism (i.e., the humanities [*humanitiatis*]) had been a predominantly Christian movement (Kristellar 1961, 1965). Its proponents had utilized classical themes and images—much like the Puritan poet John Milton would later do—while avant-garde Enlightenment thinking would diminish or even abandon this heritage, favoring humans as the measure of all things in **epistemology**, ethics, and politics. The essence of this new philosophy would eventually turn naturalistic in its perspective. Discarding the intellectual framework of Christian **revelation** as recorded in the Scriptures, Enlightenment thinkers regarded natural law as the infallible guide to truth. Scientific methodology opened up a novel approach to unlock the secrets of the natural world and the human constitution. Despite its secular veneer, it was no less dogmatic than previous attempts to explain the mysteries of human existence.

At the outset of the Enlightenment era, John Locke made his mark as the most influential proponent of the new sentiments. Although he held that humans were God's workmanship, he gave the biblical idea of indwelling human depravity short shrift while confidently asserting the natural goodness of each individual. As the first social theorist, his most ambitious goal was to reformulate the prevalent philosophical, political, and economic ideas on the basis of, and in conformity with, Newton's mechanistic **worldview**. Instead of **Descartes**'s rationalism, he sought to establish a new philosophy that would stand squarely on the foundation of empirical epistemology. His particular interest focused on an analysis of the human mind and its acquisition of knowledge. True knowledge could not be substantiated through innate ideas, as conventional philosophy had postulated (Locke, 1690a, 1.1.3). Rather, he believed all mental concepts originate in the operations of the senses on the mind.

According to one interpretation of Locke's critique of nativism, ideas are mental *objects*, meaning that when a person perceives an external object like a tree, there is some*thing* in the mind that represents that tree. The perception of a tree is simply the *idea* of that tree. An alternative interpretation postulates that ideas are mental *actions*. The human perception of a tree is direct and not mediated in any way.

In recent years most commentators have opted for the first of these two perspectives. Thus it is important to note that Locke's position is more nuanced than is apparent at first glance. He made it clear that the mind has any number of inherent capacities, predispositions, and inclinations prior to receiving any ideas from sensation. His argument was that none of these is exercised until the mind receives ideas from sensation. Consequently, he rejected the proposition of elementary ethical principles being actively engaged in informing an innate conscience.

Equally offensive to Locke was the suggestion of a *sensus divinitatis*, the universal idea of God's existence residing in the spiritual recesses of each human **soul**. However, Locke never doubted in public the reality of God or the immortality of the soul. What he objected to was the argument that these beliefs could ever be verified by an appeal to innate ideas. In *The Reasonableness of Christianity as Delivered in the Scriptures* ([1695] 2012), he even set out to demonstrate the truthfulness of Christian faith. Advocating an ecumenical form of Christianity, this work drew criticism from Anglican Church dignitaries such as Edward Stillingfleet, the bishop of Worcester, because it argued in true deistic fashion that many beliefs traditionally believed to be mandatory for Christians were unnecessary.

According to Locke, the faculties of the human mind

could readily combine elementary ideas to form complex notions such as **beauty** and misery (Locke 1690a, 2.4.18). The mind would even be able to place simple and complex ideas side by side and consider them each individually or simultaneously as a whole. As soon as the senses informed the mind of certain objects being observed, mental processes would be set in motion to obtain real knowledge in the form of three types of elementary ideas, the first of which Locke labeled sensation, the second reflection, and the third experiences such as pleasure, pain, existence, and the succession of events in time. The ability to abstract an idea from associated concepts constituted another function of the mind (2.8.22).

Contrary to the propositions of Platonic and Aristotelian universals as independent realities or particular entities, Locke erected his philosophy on the basis of sense-induced notions that became the mental building blocks of basic presuppositions. He never refuted the objection that these presuppositions lacked the essential quality of verifiability. Insisting on sensation and reflection as being the operative principles to gain real knowledge, the Lockean epistemology had to accommodate different degrees of knowledge.

Intuition would be the highest form of cognitive certainty, such as the instant realization that a circle is not a triangle (4.2.1). Demonstrative knowledge would be a slightly less certain form of knowledge. Intuition would be needed to ascertain its validity. Sense perception would be the least reliable kind of knowledge. It could give assurance of the existence of an external world outside of the human mind but would be incapable of providing any further **information**. Thus Locke's **empiricism** limited human knowledge to the nominal essence of objects (see **Nominalism**) but excluded any possibility of knowing their real essence (4.2.14).

Since any true learning would originate in sense perception, which, according to Locke, is the least certain form of knowledge, absolute certainty is excluded. Testing the reliability of things in existence would be possible, to some extent, on the basis of experience; but perfectly reliable knowledge, except in **mathematics** and ethics, would ever elude the grasp of human cognition. Knowledge can be based only on **probability** and the presumed agreement or disagreement of ideas and not on propositions (4.2.2). Locke further discussed the extent of human knowledge in book 4, chapter 3 of *An Essay concerning Human Understanding*.

Locke never seemed to be aware of the grave deficiencies of his philosophy of empiricism. Rejecting entirely the reality of innate ideas precluded the possibility of a human conscience existing independently from the sense-mediated interaction of the mind with the material world. Thus Lockean empiricism left unexplained the question of how unconscious matter could produce human **consciousness** merely by the mind's contact with the external world through sense experience.

Determinism, in all its varied forms in politics, education, **psychology**, and many other areas, exerted itself in the wake of empiricism's broad acceptance in the Western world. Empiricism may suggest that human beings are products of valueless, deterministic material forces, suggesting that whole societies are a powderless keg in the tossing surge of political forces beyond their control. An empiricism without reference to the divine would imply a denial of human dignity, with humans being caught in the net of a soul-deadening **materialism**. Despite the problems of empiricism, Locke, the Christianized empiricist, nevertheless affirmed that "all mankind" are "all equal and independent" and that "no one ought to harm another in his life, health, liberty, or possessions." The reasoning behind this is that all humans are "the workmanship of one omnipotent, and infinitely wise maker" (Locke [1690a] 1988, 2.6).

Martin Erdmann

REFERENCES AND RECOMMENDED READING

Anstey, Peter R., ed. 2003. *The Philosophy of John Locke: New Perspectives.* London: Routledge.

Ayers, Michael R. 1991. *Locke: Epistemology and Ontology.* London: Routledge.

Dunn, John. 1969. *The Political Thought of John Locke: An Historical Account of the Argument of the "Two Treatises of Government."* Cambridge: Cambridge University Press.

———. 1984. *Locke.* Oxford: Oxford University Press.

Hudson, Nicholas. 1997. "John Locke and the Tradition of Nominalism." In *Nominalism and Literary Discourse: New Perspectives, Critical Studies,* ed. Hugo Keiper, Christoph Bode, and Richard J. Utz, 283–99. Amsterdam: Rodopi.

Kristellar, P. O. 1961. *Renaissance Thought: The Classic, Scholastic, and Humanistic Strains.* New York: Harper & Row.

———. 1965. "The Moral Thought of Renaissance Humanism." In P. O. Kristellar, *Renaissance Thought II: Papers on Humanism and the Arts.* New York: Harper & Row.

Locke, John. (1689) 2006. *Epistola de tolerantia (A Letter concerning Toleration).* Ed. J. R. Milton and P. Milton. Oxford: Oxford University Press.

———. (1690a) 1997. *An Essay concerning Human Understanding.* Ed. Roger Woolhouse. New York: Penguin.

———. (1690b) 1988. *Locke: Two Treatises of Government.* Ed. P. Laslett. Cambridge: Cambridge University Press.

———. (1691) 1824. *Some Considerations of the Consequences of the Lowering of Interest, and the Raising of the Value of Money.* The Works of John Locke in Nine Volumes. Vol. 4. 12th ed. London: Rivington.

———. (1692a) 1983. *A Second Letter concerning Toleration.* Ed. James H. Tully. Indianapolis: Hackett.

———. (1692b) 2010. *A Third Letter for Toleration.* Cambridge: Cambridge University Press.

———. (1693) 1996. *Some Thoughts concerning Education and of the Conduct of the Understanding.* Eds. Ruth W. Grant and Nathan Tarcov. Indianapolis: Hackett.

———. (1695) 1997. *The Reasonableness of Christianity as Delivered in the Scriptures.* Dulles, VA: Thoemmes Press.

———. (1706) 1901. *Of the Conduct of the Understanding.* Oxford: Clarendon.

———. 1954. *Essays on the Law of Nature: The Latin Text with a Translation, Introduction and Notes, Together with Transcripts of Locke's Shorthand in His Journal for 1676.* Ed. W. von Leyden. Oxford: Clarendon.

LoLordo, A. 2012. *Locke's Moral Man.* Oxford: Oxford University Press.

Lowe, E. J. *Locke.* 2005. New York: Routledge.

Moseley, Alexander. 2008. *John Locke.* Continuum Library of Educational Thought. New York: Bloomsbury Academic.

Newman, L. 2007. *The Cambridge Companion to Locke's Essay concerning Human Understanding.* Cambridge: Cambridge University Press.

Pyle, A. J. 2013. *Locke.* London: Polity.

Rickless, S. 2014. *Locke.* Malden, MA: Blackwell.

Stuart, M. 2013. *Locke's Metaphysics.* Oxford: Oxford University Press.

Waldron, Jeremy. 2002. *God, Locke, and Equality: Christian Foundations in Locke's Political Thought.* Cambridge: Cambridge University Press.

Woolhouse, Roger. 2009. *Locke: A Biography.* Cambridge: Cambridge University Press.

Yolton, John W., ed. 1969. *John Locke: Problems and Perspectives.* Cambridge: Cambridge University Press.

———, ed. 1993. *A Locke Dictionary.* Oxford: Blackwell.

Zuckert, Michael P. 2002. *Launching Liberalism: On Lockean Political Philosophy.* Lawrence: University Press of Kansas.

LOGIC. Logic is the study and use of methods for evaluating reasoning. Reasoning is a psychological process involving inference from one or more truth claims to another. An example is inferring that there is an intelligent designer of the universe from observing that the universe appears to be designed.

The truth claims on which an inference is based are premises, and the truth claim inferred from a premise or premises is a conclusion. Any combination of premises and conclusion is an argument. For instance, the premise of the preceding inference is the claim that the universe appears to be designed, and the conclusion is the claim that there is an intelligent designer of the universe. That combination of premise and conclusion is an argument—a version of the design argument for God's existence.

Arguments are deductive or inductive. The conclusion of a deductive argument is intended to be a necessary consequence of the premise(s) of that argument. The conclusion of an inductive argument is intended to be a probable but not necessary consequence of the premise(s) of that argument. If the conclusion of a deductive argument is a necessary consequence of the premise(s) of that argument, then the argument is valid. Otherwise it is invalid. If the conclusion of an inductive argument is a probable (but not necessary) consequence of the premise(s) of that argument, then the argument is strong. If an inductive argument's premises do not make its conclusion probable, the argument is weak. The main purpose of deductive logic is to determine whether deductive arguments are valid or invalid, and the main purpose of inductive logic is to determine whether and to what degree inductive arguments are strong or weak.

The design argument is often intended as an inductive argument. It is generally granted that the appearance of design does not guarantee but at best makes probable the existence of a designer. Some critics of this argument contend that its strength is diminished (i.e., the **probability** of its conclusion given its premise is decreased) because the theory of evolution by **natural selection** provides an alternative, naturalistic explanation of the appearance of design in the universe.

This question concerning the design argument's degree of strength is a question of inductive logic. The inductive design argument can be made deductive by adding the premise that whatever appears to be designed has an intelligent designer. This premise, together with the premise that the universe appears to be designed, necessitates the conclusion that the universe has an intelligent designer. Deductive logic guarantees this argument's validity.

Deductively valid arguments with true premises are sound, and inductively strong arguments with true premises are cogent. Moreover, if a deductive argument is sound, then its conclusion is true. And if an inductive argument is cogent, then its conclusion is probably true. Critics of the inductive design argument will likely grant the truth of its premise but deny the argument's strength on inductive logic grounds. Critics of the deductive design argument will likely grant its validity on deductive logic grounds but deny its soundness on nonlogical grounds that question the truth of one or more of its premises. In both cases, argument evaluation requires employing the methods of logic.

James Taylor

REFERENCES AND RECOMMENDED READING

Hardy, Lee, Del Ratzsch, Rebecca K. De Young, and Gregory Mellema. 2013. *The Little Logic Book.* Grand Rapids: Calvin College Press.

Howard-Snyder, Francis, Daniel Howard-Snyder, and Ryan Wasserman. 2013. *The Power of Logic.* 5th ed. New York: McGraw-Hill.

LOGICAL POSITIVISM. Logical positivism is a philosophical movement that thrived in the 1920s and 1930s in Europe and the 1940s and 1950s in the United States. The most prominent early center of the movement was the

Vienna Circle. This coalition of philosophers, scientists, and mathematicians met under the leadership of Mortiz Schlick (1882–1936) from 1924 until Schlick's murder in 1936.

Notable thinkers associated with logical positivism include **Hans Reichenbach** (1891–1953), Otto Neurath (1882–1945), Philipp Frank (1884–1966), **Rudolf Carnap** (1891–1970), A. J. Ayer (1910–89), and **Ludwig Wittgenstein** (1889–1951). By the 1960s and 1970s, the movement was largely abandoned, but its influence continues whether recognized or not in debates over the nature of science, religion, and philosophy.

By the beginning of the twentieth century, science had achieved near dominance. Domains of enquiry such as **physics**, biology, chemistry, and **psychology**, which had traditionally been philosophical concerns, were now pursued independently from philosophy.

The challenge to philosophy was to state its own subject matter and formal methods of enquiry. With the material world surrendered to science and the mental world surrendered to psychology, philosophy's domain, according to the logical positivists, was the world of meaning as it occurred in linguistic expressions. Its methodology was to be the logical analysis of linguistic expressions in order to clarify their meaning or declare them as nonsense. Taking its cue from empirical science, the positivist sought to locate all knowledge in the sensible world by proposing various verification principles.

The core idea of verificationism is that a nonlogical sentence is meaningful when one knows the method of its empirical verification. The sentence "Smith is blushing" is meaningful because it can be verified as true or false through observation, but the sentence "God is loving," while grammatically similar in form, is unverifiable empirically and therefore not merely false, but meaningless. On these grounds, much of traditional **metaphysics**, including theology, was declared nonsense (see **Verification Principle**).

Understandably, many saw in this radical antimetaphysical stance a real danger to religion in general and Christianity in particular. On this view, there can be no dispute between Christianity and science, not because they both converge on the truth, but because there is nothing to dispute about. Theological statements are not claims to know anything. Rather, they merely express the emotions of the speaker. In partial response, one may simply note that statements such as "God is loving" are clearly meaningful and that theological statements clearly make claims to knowledge, and therefore verificationism is false (Plantinga 1984).

More generally, the main problem with verificationism is that the verification principle itself eludes verification and is thereby self-refuting (although some formulations of the principle manage to avoid self-refutation by giving up the notorious "metaphysics-is-once-and-for-all-meaningless" claim, a central plank of the positivist program). The elimination of metaphysical claims from theory construction is impossible. The salient issue is whether or not there are good epistemic grounds for holding the metaphysical belief in question, not whether the belief is confirmable via some empirical criterion of meaning.

Paul M. Gould

REFERENCES AND RECOMMENDED READING

Ayer, A. J. 1936. *Language, Truth, and Logic.* London: Victor Gollancz.
Blumberg, Albert, and Herbert Feigl. 1931. "Logical Positivism." *Journal of Philosophy* 28 (11): 281–96.
Flew, Antony, and Alasdair MacIntyre. 1955. *New Essays in Philosophical Theology.* London: SCM.
Klocker, Harry. 1968. *God and the Empiricists.* Milwaukee: Bruce.
Plantinga, Alvin. 1984. "Advice to Christian Philosophers." *Faith and Philosophy* 1 (3): 253–71.
Price, H. H. 1935. "Logical Positivism and Theology." *Philosophy* 10 (39): 313–31.

M

MACKAY, DONALD M. Donald MacKay (1922–87), the son of a Free Church of Scotland minister, studied **physics** at the University of St. Andrews and upon graduation in 1943 joined the Admiralty Signal Establishment to assist in the secret development of radar for battleships during World War II. Here, dealing with questions of the rudimentary **artificial intelligence** required by a machine attempting to detect signals in the midst of noise, MacKay began forming the early questions that would characterize his research career in **neuroscience** and **information** theory. He then taught physics at King's College, London, for 14 years and earned a PhD, working on a hardware solution to a mathematical problem. In 1951, as a Rockefeller fellow under the guidance of Warren McCullough, he toured the United States for 12 months, visiting all of the major neuroscience labs, establishing relationships he would maintain throughout his lifetime.

MacKay moved to Keele University, Staffordshire, in 1960 and set up a lab that conducted research in psychophysics, electrophysiology, and electron microscopy, experimenting on the visual and auditory systems of humans and animals. In the human visual experiments, subjects were exposed to a variety of simple still or moving lines or dots on a screen, sometimes in the context of background visual "noise." These images invoked various optical illusions that were useful in revealing how the brain organized, interpreted, and processed visual information. From these and other experiments, he was able to prove that the brain's systems are not merely passive receptors, but actively searching through visual stimuli for patterns. These experiments were important for establishing a larger philosophical and theological point that our brains are not merely passive reflex machines but active agents.

As a Calvinist, MacKay was a compatibilist regarding predestination and free will, in contrast to reductionist philosophers of his time such as **Gilbert Ryle**, and scientists such as Jacques Monod, **Francis Crick**, and B. F. Skinner, whom he debated on William Buckley's television show *Firing Line*. Philosophically, he explained that there is a "logical indeterminacy" or "logical relativity" that results from regarding God as a creator outside of time and free agents acting within time. Statements true from the perspective of the creator might be incompatible with the perspective of the temporal agent. MacKay often described differences of standpoint as "complementary" and thus not contradictory.

This theology also formed the basis of his acceptance of free will within a physical brain. A thermostat is a very basic machine that includes a temperature sensor, an ability to turn on heat and cooling, and a comparator with a set point. One sets the thermostat, and it compares the setting with the ambient temperature and takes the appropriate action. MacKay imagined human agency as such a control system but modified in a special way. The human agent has an additional feature that allows it to change its set point—that is, change its goals. This distinguishes us from mere machines, while at the same time including a concept of free agency entirely within a machine.

McKay was a founding editor of the journal *Experimental Brain Research*, served as a series editor for the *Handbook of Sensory Physiology* (1971–81), and was an editor for the journal *Vision Research*. MacKay participated in numerous international conferences on neuroscience and philosophy, providing a well-informed and subtle Christian perspective on key questions.

Jason M. Rampelt

REFERENCES AND RECOMMENDED READING

MacKay, Donald M. 1951. "Mind-Like Behaviour in Artefacts." *British Journal for the Philosophy of Science* 2 (6): 105–21.
———. 1956. "Towards an Information-Flow Model of Human Behaviour." *British Journal of Psychology* 47, no. 1 (February): 30–43.
———. 1960. "On the Logical Indeterminacy of a Free Choice." *Mind* 69 (273): 31–40.
———. 1961. "Visual Effects of Non-redundant Stimulation." *Nature* 192, no. 4804 (November 25): 739–40.
———. 1967. *Freedom of Action in a Mechanistic Universe.* Arthur Stanley Eddington Memorial Lecture. Cambridge: Cambridge University Press.
———. 1968. "The Sovereignty of God in the Natural World." *Scottish Journal of Theology* 21, no. 1 (March): 13–26.
———. 1969. *Information, Mechanism, and Meaning.* Cambridge, MA: MIT Press.
———. 1974. *The Clockwork Image: A Christian Perspective on Science.* London: IVP.
———. 1977. *Human Science and Human Dignity: London Lectures in Contemporary Christianity.* London: Hodder and Stoughton.
———. 1978. *Science, Chance and Providence.* Riddell Memorial Lecture. Oxford: Oxford University Press.
———. 1980. *Brains, Machines and Persons.* Henry Drummond Lectures. University of Stirling. Grand Rapids: Eerdmans.
———. 1986. *Behind the Eye.* Gifford Lectures. Glasgow University. Ed. Valerie MacKay. Oxford: Basil Blackwell.

MATERIALISM. In its most basic form, materialism is the belief that all existence is either matter or derived from matter or material processes. This raises questions about the nature of matter itself, its properties, and its possible ontological and epistemological implications. As such, **Antony Flew** (1923–2010), writing before his conversion to **theism**, noted that materialism is a "somewhat ill-defined group of doctrines rather than one specific thesis," often pursued as a "policy of research rather than a statement of a result of research" (Flew 1984, 222).

Eschewing all immaterial entities—spirits, angels, deities—for a thoroughgoing physical **monism**, materialism has been haunted by the problem of the mind and immaterial agency (see **Mind**; **Mind-Body Problem**; **Soul**). Indeed, humans' subjective awareness—**qualia** or phenomenal **consciousness**—has vexed materialists. "I myself still want to embrace materialism," admitted one philosopher, "but I don't know what an adequate materialist account of phenomenal consciousness would look like" (Horgan 2006, 179).

While most ordinary mechanistic materialism is associated with **reductionism**, and hence physical monism, an attempt to resolve the mind-body problem has been proposed in nonreductive materialism, whereby the mind is considered as ontologically part of the material world but not reducible to physical entities or properties—the mind simply *is*. A third form, developed by Karl Marx (1818–83) and Friedrich Engels (1820–95), was coined by Joseph Dietzgen (1828–88) as "dialectical materialism." Here materialism is not static but dynamic, interacting with certain tensions and contradictions resulting in progressive change. While ostensibly a description of science and nature, it really constitutes a socioeconomic model for Marxist class struggle.

Materialism has often been an important underpinning of **methodological naturalism** and an overarching **scientism** that had early proponents in Thomas Hobbes (1588–1679), La Mettrie (1709–51), and Baron d'Holbach (1723–89). While not requisite, the materialism implicit in Darwinian evolution—though not necessarily in other evolutionary theorists (e.g., **Alfred Russel Wallace** [1823–1913], St. George Mivart [1827–1900], Henri Bergson [1859–1941])—has found currency among many atheists, such as Will Provine, **Daniel Dennett**, and **Richard Dawkins**.

Despite its long and enduring history, there are reasons for doubting materialism. First, it cannot be proved. Even if all the issues attending materialism could be clarified,

noted Flew, "There are certainly no observational or analytical methods of establishing it as true" (Flew 1984, 222). Second, materialism offers no satisfactory explanation for the origin and nature of life, a deficit that helped convert Flew to belief in a deistic God (Flew with Varghese 2007, 124–26). Finally, there is nature itself: the nonlocality and nonlocalizability of quantum phenomena have led some to confess, "We find the harder we have looked [at **quantum physics**], the more ephemeral material reality has gotten, until it finally looks like nothing is there" (Gordon 2011, 205).

Even with these difficulties, materialism will continue to be maintained and defended, if not as a demonstrable fact then as an article of faith.

Michael A. Flannery

REFERENCES AND RECOMMENDED READING

Flew, Antony. 1984. *A Dictionary of Philosophy.* 2nd rev. ed. New York: St. Martin's.
Flew, Antony, with Roy Abraham Varghese. 2007. *There Is a God: How the World's Most Notorious Atheist Changed His Mind.* New York: HarperCollins.
Gordon, Bruce L. 2011. "A Quantum-Theoretic Argument against Naturalism." In *The Nature of Nature,* ed. Bruce L. Gordon and William A. Dembski, 179–208. Wilmington, DE: ISI Books.
Horgan, Terry. 2006. "Materialism: Matters of Definition, Defense, and Deconstruction." *Philosophical Studies* 131, no. 1 (October): 157–83.

MATHEMATICS. Two principal issues often arise in the interface of Christian theology and the mathematics applied in science: (1) whether the truth of our best scientific theories commits us to the reality of the mathematical entities employed in those theories, and (2) what explanation can best be given for the applicability of mathematics to the physical world.

With respect to the first question, both Platonists and fictionalists tend to agree that the truth of our best scientific theories is ontologically committing to mathematical objects like numbers, functions, matrices, and so forth. Platonists therefore conclude that there are, in addition to the concrete objects posited by our best theories, an **infinity** of abstract, mathematical objects. Fictionalists, on the other hand, conclude that our best scientific theories are not wholly true. The abstract content of those theories is false, since abstract objects do not exist, being merely useful fictions akin to ideal gases, frictionless planes, points at infinity, and so on. It is useful, and perhaps indispensable, to speak as if such entities do exist, but such statements are not really true.

Christian theologians have a vital stake in this debate because mathematical objects, if they exist, are typically regarded as uncreated, necessary, and eternal, in contradiction to the Christian doctrines of divine aseity and creation ex nihilo. In the Judeo-Christian tradition, God is regarded as the sole ultimate reality, the Creator of all things apart from himself. Therefore the mainstream Christian position, from the early Greek apologists through the medieval scholastic theologians, was united in rejecting Platonism in favor of a divine conceptualism. Following the lead of the Middle Platonists and in particular the Jewish philosophical theologian Philo of Alexandria (20 BC–AD 50), Christian thinkers took allegedly abstract objects to be, in fact, ideas in the *Logos* or mind of God.

Conceptualism is still a form of (nonplatonic) **realism** about mathematical objects. Whether divine thoughts can successfully play the roles typically ascribed to abstract objects remains an open question. Fortunately, on the contemporary scene there is a wide variety of antirealisms also available to the Christian theologian for turning back the challenge of Platonism. These views, while sharing fictionalism's antirealism, differ from it in affirming the truth of mathematical sentences. Constructibilism and modal structuralism offer paraphrases of mathematical sentences that are not ontologically committing to mathematical objects. Neutralism, free logic, and neo-Meinongianism reject, in whole or in part, the criterion of ontological commitment assumed by both Platonists and fictionalists, so that true mathematical sentences do not have the ontological commitments that Platonists and fictionalists think they have.

Pretense theorists and figuralists deny that mathematical sentences should or must be taken literally but can be taken either as figuratively true or as statements prescribed to be imagined as true. The contemporary debate is a young one, and Christian theologians have scarcely begun to profit from it.

The second issue raised by the interface of Christian theology and applied mathematics is what physicist Eugene Wigner famously called the "unreasonable effectiveness of mathematics." This problem has baffled both realists and antirealists alike.

For the Platonist, the fact that physical reality conforms to the structure of acausal mathematical entities existing beyond **space and time** is, in the words of philosopher of mathematics Mary Leng, just "a happy coincidence." For the antirealist, there is no abstract realm to which the physical world conforms, but what remains unexplained is why the physical world exhibits so complex and stunning a mathematical structure in the first place, so as to make successful scientific theorizing on the basis of mathematics possible.

Now, whether one is a realist or an antirealist about mathematical objects, it appears that the theist enjoys a considerable advantage over the naturalist in explaining the uncanny success of mathematics in physical science.

The theistic realist can argue that God has fashioned the world on the structure of the mathematical objects. This is essentially the view that **Plato** defended in his dialogue *Timaeus*. God looks to the realm of mathematical objects and models the world on it. The world has a mathematical structure as a result. Thus the realist who is a theist has a considerable advantage over the naturalistic realist in explaining why mathematics is so effective in describing the physical world.

Similarly, the theistic antirealist has a ready explanation of the applicability of mathematics to the physical world: God has created it according to a certain blueprint that he imagined. In theistic antirealism, the world exhibits the mathematical structure it does because God has chosen to create it according to the imaginary model he had in mind. This was the view of Philo of Alexandria, who maintained in his treatise *On the Creation of the World* that God created the physical world based on the mental model in his mind.

The theist—whether he be a realist or an antirealist about mathematical objects—thus has the explanatory resources to account for the mathematical structure of the physical world and hence for the otherwise unreasonable effectiveness of mathematics—resources the naturalist lacks. We have here the makings of a powerful contribution to **natural theology**.

William Lane Craig

REFERENCES AND RECOMMENDED READING

Balaguer, Mark. 1998. *Platonism and Anti-Platonism in Mathematics.* New York: Oxford University Press.

———. 2009. "Platonism in Metaphysics." In *Stanford Encyclopedia of Philosophy.* April 7. http://plato.stanford.edu/entries/platonism/.

Bauckham, Richard. 2008. "God Crucified." In *Jesus and the God of Israel.* Grand Rapids: Eerdmans.

Copan, Paul, and William Lane Craig. 2004. *Creation Out of Nothing: A Biblical, Philosophical, and Scientific Exploration.* Grand Rapids: Baker Academic.

Gould, Paul, ed. 2014. *Beyond the Control of God? Six Views on the Problem of God and Abstract Objects.* With articles, responses, and counterresponses by K. Yandell, R. Davis, P. Gould, G. Welty, W. Craig, S. Shalkowski, and G. Oppy. London: Bloomsbury.

Leng, Mary. 2010. *Mathematics and Reality.* Oxford: Oxford University Press.

Plantinga, Alvin. 2011. *Where the Conflict Really Lies: Science, Religion, and Naturalism.* Oxford: Oxford University Press.

MAXWELL, JAMES CLERK.

Born in Scotland, the son of a wealthy landowner, James Clerk Maxwell (1831–79) had an early education carried out by his mother at the family's remote estate, Glenair. By the age of eight, he could recite, among other things, all 176 verses of Psalm 119. His mother died that same year, and after two unproductive years with a hired tutor, he was sent to live with his aunt in Edinburgh, where he enrolled in Edinburgh Academy at age 10. While there, he was in the habit of writing mathematical "props," or propositions, and by age 14 he had independently discovered a set of bifocal ovals first discussed by **René Descartes**, although Maxwell's derivation was simpler, and extended Descartes's work. This became Maxwell's first scientific publication. It was presented to the Royal Society of Edinburgh by family friend and professor of **natural philosophy** James Forbes of Edinburgh University, since Maxwell was considered too young to address the society himself.

Maxwell's higher education was at the University of Edinburgh, followed by Cambridge University, where he was a member of Trinity College, earning 2nd Wrangler (i.e., second place) on Cambridge's famous Mathematical Tripos examination, and sharing the more prestigious Smith Prize with his friend, 1st Wrangler Edward Routh. Maxwell's commitment to inductive reasoning was influenced by **William Whewell**, Anglican priest and master of Trinity College at Cambridge University while Maxwell was a student there. Whewell's 1840 book *The Philosophy of the Inductive Sciences: Founded upon Their History* lays out a **philosophy of science** guided by the twin epistemologies of inductive and deductive reasoning, wherein leaps of insight coupled with deductions are tested against experiment and observation. In Maxwell's own words, "It is hard work grinding out 'appropriate ideas,' as Whewell calls them. However, I think they are coming out at last, and by dint of knocking them against all the facts and half-digested theories afloat, I hope to bring them to shape" (Hutchinson 2014, 93).

This powerful method of reasoning overarched both Maxwell's scientific pursuits and his examination of his own Christian faith. As he wrote to his friend Lewis Campbell during his second year at Cambridge, "Now my great plan ... is to let nothing be wilfully left unexamined. Nothing is to be holy ground consecrated to Stationary Faith.... Now I am convinced that no one but a Christian can actually purge his land of these holy spots" (Campbell and Garnett 1882, 96). Other letters from Maxwell to Campbell contain expositions of passages in the Pauline epistles and reveal that Maxwell taught a Sunday school class while visiting Campbell. He chose which church to attend in London partly because the pastor "[did] what he [could] to let the statements in the Bible be understood by his hearers" (170).

Maxwell's most famous work lay in creating a unified theory of magnetism and electricity now called *electrodynamics*, or simply *Maxwell's equations*. The key insight was to postulate a symmetry, reasoning that if a changing magnetic field produces an electric field, then a changing electric field should produce a magnetic field. Maxwell's method of reasoning by symmetry continues to be a major driver of discoveries in **physics** today. Maxwell's equations showed that electricity and magnetism are intimately intertwined, like two sides of the same coin, and even showed that light itself is an electromagnetic wave.

Maxwell made many other remarkable discoveries, contributing fundamental ideas to our understanding of optics and color vision, providing a detailed theory of the statistical mechanics and thermodynamics of gases (the Maxwell-Boltzmann distribution), and discovering that Saturn's rings are particulate rather than rigid. The Nobel Prize–winning theoretical physicist Richard Feynman remarked, "From a long view of the history of mankind—seen from, say, 10,000 years from now—there can be little doubt that the most significant event of the nineteenth century will be judged as Maxwell's discovery of the laws of electrodynamics" (Feynman et al. 1964). Surely Maxwell, who spent time lecturing at a workingmen's college because of a Christian conviction to help others, would be pleased to see that the technologies enabled by Maxwell's equations of electrodynamics continue to raise the standard of living of people all over the globe.

Erica W. Carlson

REFERENCES AND RECOMMENDED READING

Campbell, Lewis, and William Garnett. 1882. *The Life of James Clerk Maxwell*. London: Macmillan.

Feynman, Richard P., Robert B. Leighton, and Matthew Sands. 1964. *The Feynman Lectures on Physics*. Chap. 1, sec. 6. Boston: Addison-Wesley. Accessed September 7, 2016. http://feynmanlectures.caltech.edu/.

Hutchinson, Ian H. 2014. "The Genius and Faith of Faraday and Maxwell." *New Atlantis*, no. 41 (Winter): 81–99. See also http://silas.psfc.mit.edu/maxwell/.

Mahon, Basil. 2004. *The Man Who Changed Everything: The Life of James Clerk Maxwell*. New York: Wiley.

MCGRATH, ALISTER. Alister E. McGrath (1953–) was born in Belfast, Ireland, and is one of the central figures in evangelicalism dealing with the relationship between theology and science. Although he has held posts at the University of London, the vast majority of his training and career has been located in Oxford, England. During his high school and early college years, he was a committed atheist with great interest in Marxism and the natural sciences.

But during his first year of study at Oxford, he converted to Christianity after finding it to be far more intellectually robust than he had previously imagined. He earned a PhD in molecular biophysics from Oxford in 1978. During his doctoral work, however, he also began formally studying theology and would later go on to take additional undergraduate (1978), graduate (1983), and doctoral (2001) degrees in theology and historical theology from Oxford.

McGrath's influence in the contemporary discussion about science and theology cannot be overstated. From 2001 to 2003 his seminal work was published as a three-volume series titled *A Scientific Theology*, with each of the three volumes dealing with the issues of nature, reality, and theory respectively. Against modernism and its tendencies toward naive **realism**, and **postmodernism** and its commitment to **antirealism**, McGrath defends a perspective of truth and knowledge that has come to be known as **critical realism**. With modernism this approach continues to hold to realism and the possibility of knowledge. With postmodernism, his approach recognizes and acknowledges the role of context, history, and other such factors that shape our view of the world and cause potential blind spots (see **Realism and Antirealism**; **Critical Realism**).

A Scientific Theology has serious implications for the relationship of science and theology. In it McGrath shows how both theology and science have employed a critical realist perspective throughout their histories in the formation of their most important doctrines and theories. Thus McGrath argues that far from being bitter enemies, science and theology are natural dialogue partners with much to learn from each other. Moreover, throughout *A Scientific Theology*, he seeks to reenvision **natural theology** by allowing it to operate from within and in light of the teachings of Christianity. Here natural theology is not required to strip away its articles of faith and start from a supposed neutral view of nature in an attempt to prove God's existence. Instead, in his approach natural theology assumes a view of creation that is distinctly Christian and sees itself as an enterprise that yields **confirmation** of beliefs that are already held to be true by the church.

Since 2000 much of McGrath's work on science and theology has been focused on responding to the **New Atheism**, with a particular focus on **Richard Dawkins**. In several publications and countless public speeches, McGrath has countered many of Dawkins's claims, showing their weakness, inconsistencies, and overall negative social consequences. In addition to this, McGrath has also written extensively on Christianity and evolution, showing how evolutionary thought can not only be reconciled with Christianity but how in many cases it can be used to confirm the Christian faith.

James K. Dew Jr.

REFERENCES AND RECOMMENDED READING

McGrath, Alister E. 1998. *The Foundations of Dialogue in Science and Religion.* Oxford: Blackwell.
———. 1999. *Science and Religion.* Oxford: Blackwell.
———. 2001–3. *A Scientific Theology.* 3 vols. Grand Rapids: Eerdmans.
———. 2004. *The Science of God.* Grand Rapids: Eerdmans.
———. 2006. *The Order of Things: Explorations in Scientific Theology.* Oxford: Blackwell.
———. 2008. *The Open Secret: A New Vision for Natural Theology.* Oxford: Blackwell.
McGrath, Alister E., and Joanna Collicutt McGrath. 2007. *The Dawkins Delusion?* London: SPCK.

MCMULLIN, ERNAN. Ernan McMullin (1924–2011) was an Irish-born philosopher and Catholic priest who spent his career at the University of Notre Dame. He held many visiting appointments, including at Princeton and Yale, and made significant contributions in the areas of **philosophy of science**, history of science, and **philosophy of religion**. His many publications ranged over the relationship between Catholicism and science, the **Galileo** affair, and the nature of science.

McMullin is probably best known for his dialogue approach to the debate concerning religion and evolution, where he advanced a version of the view known as theistic evolution. He was a critic of **creation science** and **intelligent design** theory, and supported the distinction between methodological and metaphysical **naturalism**. He also defended a realist position in the philosophy of science.

He was convinced by the theory of evolution; on this he disagreed with **Alvin Plantinga**. He argued that the two main lines of evidence from the **fossil record** and **DNA** analysis were convincing, and he was also impressed with the universal support that evolution has among experts in the relevant fields of natural science.

Influenced by **Augustine**'s approach to the relationship between religion and science, McMullin argued that Christianity and evolution are quite compatible. Augustine argued that the creation of the universe is best understood from the point of view that God is outside of time; all things were already present in the first instance of the universe's temporal appearance, and so creation was not sequential. It follows that the book of Genesis need not be read in a literal way. Augustine then argued for the metaphor of the *rationes seminales,* or seed-like principles, that are present from the cosmic beginning and in each of which is contained the potential for the later development of a specific living kind.

McMullin developed this view to argue that these seed-like principles contained in them the potentialities for all the living kinds that would later appear, and so **miracles**, or special interventions in nature, would not be necessary. He suggested that such a view could be developed by appeal to the theory of evolution. Evolution may be a way of explaining how the seed-like principles are supposed to work, and so he held that this approach would support a plausible cosmogony which respects at once the findings of the natural sciences and the deepest insights of the Christian theology of creation.

To the objections that evolution operates by **chance** and that it is usually presented as an unguided process, McMullin invoked in response the traditional distinction between primary and secondary causality. God is the primary cause of the universe and life because he created it out of a set of initial ingredients, together with the laws of science, and built in certain ends at the beginning of the process. Secondary **causation** then refers to the fact that everyday physical events in the universe (including in evolution) proceed naturally, governed by scientific laws. McMullin also agreed with a number of modern theologians that in the process of secondary causality, God could have used chance elements to bring about his teleological goals, that chance events are as much the work of the Creator as are the **laws of nature**.

(See also **Augustine**; **Chance**; **Creationism** articles; **Evolution** articles; **Intelligent Design Theory**; **Methodological and Metaphysical Naturalism**; **Religion and Science**; **Theistic Evolution**.)

Brendan Sweetman

REFERENCES AND RECOMMENDED READING

Allen, Paul. 2013. *Ernan McMullin and Critical Realism in the Science-Theology Dialogue.* Aldershot, UK: Ashgate.

McMullin, Ernan, ed. 1985. *Evolution and Creation.* South Bend, IN: University of Notre Dame Press.

———. 1991. "Plantinga's Defense of Special Creation." *Christian Scholar's Review* 21 (1): 55–79.

———. 2013. "Cosmic Purpose and the Contingency of Human Evolution." *Zygon* 48 (2): 338–63.

Sweetman, Brendan. 2012. "The Dispute between Plantinga and McMullin over Evolution." *American Catholic Philosophical Quarterly* 86 (2): 343–54.

MEMES. *Memes* is a term proposed by **Richard Dawkins** ([1976] 2006) to refer to units of cultural **information**—analogous to **gene**s—that influence human behavior in ways not determined by genes alone. The idea addresses three main issues.

First, human behavior does not appear fully reducible to genetic influence. Strictly speaking, no trait of any **species** is "reducible" to genetics, since gene expression is modified by environment. But the cultural environment is unique in containing information that is created by the organism itself and that is also transmitted to others.

Second, memes seek to explain what some view as a distinctive human capacity for fitness-relinquishing behavior: memes not only are irreducible to but also are able to oppose genetic influence (see **Altruism**). The idea is that memes can "infect the **mind**," overriding genetic influence much like a virus.

Third, unlike many sociological theories of culture, memes are understood to be relatively discrete units of information that differentially replicate themselves by transmission from mind to mind, amenable to a Darwinian account of cultural evolution by **natural selection**.

The notion that ideas and other cultural innovations actually *have consequences for*, rather than merely *being consequences of*, genetic influence is—after a period of dominance by reductive **materialism**—widely accepted as "dual inheritance theory" or "gene culture coevolution" (Richerson and Boyd 2006; see **Reductionism**). But the specific claims of memetics are hotly debated within and outside biology for several reasons (Aunger 2001).

First, there is uncertainty about what actually constitutes a meme. It could be anything that is transmitted from mind to mind: an idiom, a catchy tune, a dance move, some kinds of ideas. But is science itself a complex of memes? And in contrast to genetics, how does memetics quantify memes, and what distinguishes one meme from another? Moreover, if memes "literally parasitize my brain," should they "be regarded as living structures" (Dawkins [1976] 2006, 192)? Even proponents of memetics disagree on these questions.

Second, critics point out that although memetics is non-reductionistic in postulating that culture transcends genes, it is problematically reductionistic in construing culture itself as particulate. And even if one grants cultural particles, not all prevail by transmission. Some are independently arrived at through reason, others by convergent artistic imagination or moral (or religious) "**revelation**."

Finally, what is the actual causal mechanism by which memes "resist" the fitness-enhancing thrust of genes (Dawkins [1976] 2006)? Some criticize these ideas as, at best, tautological—memes have this power because they obviously have this power—or, worse, quasi-magical. Others claim attributing to memes behaviors that ostensibly transcend genetic influence has no more empirical merit than affirming free will, cognitive **emergence** (see **Emergence**), or even a nonmaterial **soul**.

Memetics has several fascinating implications for Christian understanding. One is the account of religion itself. In the view of some, "faith" is a pathological viral meme, alien to our natural dispositions, that subverts human well-being. In the view of others, religion is both an innate cognitive inclination and a cultural innovation that stabilizes cooperation and benefits individual and social flourishing (Schloss and Murray 2010). Another important implication is the unexpected affirmation of human distinctiveness: "Like other animals, we have built-in desires to reproduce and to do pretty much whatever it takes to achieve this goal, but we also have creeds, and the ability to transcend our genetic imperatives. This fact does make us different" (Dennett 2007, 4).

Jeffrey P. Schloss

REFERENCES AND RECOMMENDED READING

Aunger, Robert. 2001. *Darwinizing Culture: The Status of Memetics as a Science.* Oxford: Oxford University Press.

Dawkins, Richard. 2006. *The Selfish Gene: 30th Anniversary Edition.* Oxford: Oxford University Press.

Dennett, Daniel. 2007. *Breaking the Spell: Religion as a Natural Phenomenon.* New York: Penguin.

Richerson, Peter, and Robert Boyd. 2006. *Not by Genes Alone: How Culture Transformed Human Evolution.* Chicago: University of Chicago Press.

Schloss, Jeffrey, and Michael Murray, eds. 2010. *The Believing Primate: Scientific, Philosophical, and Theological Reflections on the Origin of Religion.* Oxford: Oxford University Press.

MENDEL, GREGOR. Gregor Johanne Mendel (1822–84) was an Augustinian friar, botanist, and "father of modern genetics." Gregor Mendel was born Johanne Mendel in July of 1822, to peasant, farming parents Anton and Rosine Mendel, in Heinzendorf (Hynèice), Austrian Silesia (now the Czech Republic). Though his schooling created tremendous financial strain and limited his ability to aid his crippled father in tending the farm, Mendel excelled in academic studies. He began in Leipnik, and attended Troppau and the University of Olmütz, before being admitted into the Abbey of St. Thomas at Brno in 1843 (where he received the name Gregor).

After being ordained as a priest, Mendel taught science and **mathematics** until 1851, when he studied for two years at the University of Vienna, working under the influential scientists Christian Doppler and Franz Ungler, before returning to the monastery in Brno. Among his other accomplishments, Mendel founded the Austrian Meteorological Society.

Mendel began his famous experiments around 1854 and would labor on this work for eight years. He initially used mice in his experiments on heredity, but "animal sex" was frowned upon, and he opted to focus on a number of conspicuous traits observed in the common pea (*Pisum*). At the time, Mendel was unsure which (or how many) **species** he was working with. His principle goal was to discover "what is inherited and why," and he utilized many thousands of replicated experiments in his work. To his great fortune, many of these traits (at least seven) were dichotomous, including wrinkled or smooth texture, green or yellow seed color, white or purple flower color, tall or dwarf growth habits, and several others. *Pisum spp.* are also capable of self-pollination, which enabled Mendel to inbreed pure genetic strains and observe resulting trait states.

Through his experiments, Mendel was able to demonstrate that many traits are the products of interactions between discrete heritable units (now commonly thought of as **gene**s) passed on to progeny by parent plants. Moreover, some heritable units for traits (recessive alleles) appeared to be masked by other heritable units (dominant alleles) for those same traits. A plant that received an allele for wrinkled texture from one parent would still produce smooth peas if it had inherited the smooth texture allele from the second parent. Thus the wrinkled texture trait would only be seen if the plant received the wrinkle texture allele from both parents. Progeny with the same two alleles were termed *homozygous*, while those carrying two different alleles for a trait were called *heterozygous*. Mendel also demonstrated that the alleles responsible for different traits (e.g., color, texture, size, etc.) were not linked, but sorted independently during reproduction.

From this breakthrough, Mendel also made mathematical predictions regarding the expected ratios of expressed traits (phenotypes) among progeny, given the two alleles that each parent could potentially pass on. Thus he was the first to demonstrate and model the expression of discrete heritable units responsible for physical traits in an organism. Mendel reported these findings in a series of publications and oral presentations beginning in 1865. However, the full realization of the importance of his work would not be widely celebrated until 1900. In 1935 the famed geneticist R. A. Fisher showed evidence that Mendel's data were too close to predicted ratios to be authentic. The debate over whether or not Mendel falsified data continues, but the major findings are not in question. In 1868 Mendel assumed the position of abbot, which he retained until his death in 1884.

Wayne Rossiter

REFERENCES AND RECOMMENDED READING

Franklin, A. 2008. "The Mendel-Fisher Controversy." In *Ending the Mendel-Fisher Controversy*, ed. Allan Franklin, A. W. F. Edwards, Daniel J. Fairbanks, Daniel L. Hartl, and Teddy Seidenfeld, 1–77. Pittsburgh: University of Pittsburgh Press.
Henig, R. M. 2001. *The Monk in the Garden: The Lost and Found Genius of Gregor Mendel, the Father of Genetics*. New York: Mariner.
"Mendel, Mendelism." 2012. *New Advent*. www.newadvent.org/cathen/10180b.htm.
Miko, I. 2008. "Gregor Mendel and the Principles of Inheritance." *Nature Education* 1(1):134. www.nature.com/scitable/topicpage/Gregor-Mendel-and-the-Principles-of-Inheritance–593.

MERTON THESIS.

The Merton thesis is the claim of a positive correlation between Protestant religion and scientific productivity during the early modern period (i.e., the sixteenth and seventeenth centuries). Scholars continue to debate the validity of the thesis, which can seem more or less credible depending on how it is formulated.

The claim originated with the sociologist Robert K. Merton (1910–2003) and was first published in 1936 as his doctoral thesis. Merton was inspired by the famous claim of Max Weber (first published in English in 1930) that the "Protestant work ethic" was a driving force in the development of capitalism. Merton focused on the cultural values of the English Puritans and how they may have encouraged the rise of experimental science in England, but his sociological claims were difficult to evaluate because of ambiguities concerning who is and isn't a Puritan and concerning which activities are and aren't "science."

The Merton thesis is often expanded beyond Merton's original focus on English Puritans to encompass a general inequality in the scientific productivity of Protestants and Catholics during the early modern period (or even more recently). Evidence does indeed exist that Protestants made up a higher fraction of the population of productive scientists than did of the population generally. However, this effect is sometimes overstated, perhaps in part because modern English speakers tend to be more familiar with English history. In fact, Italians and French and other Catholics did play important roles in the **Scientific Revolution**.

Furthermore, even for those aspects of inequality that

do clearly exist, it is difficult to ascertain the sociological cause. Some have suggested that the scientific productivity of early modern Catholics was significantly depressed by reactions to the cases of **Giordano Bruno** and **Galileo**, though this view is largely due to a spurious perception of the Bruno case as being about science and of both cases as being part of a trend. Some have suggested that the scientific productivity of early modern Protestants was enhanced by specific Protestant doctrines, such as those concerning nature or work or the accessibility of understanding God and his ways, though this view meets with significant opposition among scholars. Also, other factors such as inequalities in affluence (which, per Weber, themselves may or may not be attributable to differences in religion) may have a greater effect on scientific productivity than directly religious factors.

In any case, any application of the Merton thesis beyond the early modern period is clearly problematic. Too many factors have affected cultural development during the past half millennium for us to be certain that any modern differences between Protestant-majority and Catholic-majority countries can be attributed directly to religion.

Matthew S. Tiscareno

REFERENCES AND RECOMMENDED READING

Fenn, R. K. 1991. *Sociological Analysis* 52 (3): 307–10.
Henry, J. 2010. "Religion and the Scientific Revolution." In *The Cambridge Companion to Science and Religion*, ed. P. Harrison, 39–58. Cambridge: Cambridge University Press.

METAPHYSICS.

Metaphysics (the study of what there is and how it is) is usually contrasted with **epistemology** (the study of knowledge and rational belief), **logic** (the study of truth-preserving inference), and ethics (the study of the good, the right, and the just) as one of the major domains of philosophy. While metaphysics and science are both concerned with what exists, the details of their concerns and their methods typically differ markedly.

Metaphysics is concerned with what is ultimate or most fundamental about existence. In both ancient and modern contexts, metaphysics is "beyond physics," subjecting to scrutiny, analysis, and perhaps revision the nature of the objects, characteristics, and the relations cited in the sciences themselves. Scientists are concerned with the causes of various effects, while metaphysicians are concerned with what it is for one thing, event, or fact to cause another. Scientists are concerned with how the brain works and which areas are associated with various cognitive activities or experiences, while metaphysicians are concerned with what it is to engage in any kind of cognitive activity or to have any kind of conscious experience. Scientific concerns are typically handled with empirical, often quantitative, methods, while philosophical concerns are typically handled with methods that are a priori, purely rational, not requiring empirical investigation.

Metaphysics is the title given by an editor of **Aristotle**'s works to the volume appearing after the collection known as the *Physics*. It concerned "first philosophy" or "being *qua* being," in contrast with *Physics* and some of his other works that concerned specific kinds of things, such as oak trees or horses. Ancient metaphysics included theology by encompassing God/gods, creation, first causes, and what was changeless, thus encompassing eternal matters. With the rise of modern science, philosophy extended the range of metaphysical questions to include questions of what was fundamental to temporal and contingent matters.

These are some common metaphysical questions: What is the nature and the origin/explanation of the universe? Are there many objects or just one? If many, what accounts for the characteristics of and relations among particular, typically concrete, objects? Which things exist "in themselves," not depending on others? Is motion or change possible? If change is possible, how do objects endure through change, if at all? What is the relation between the **mind** and the body? What is the nature of **consciousness**? Do any rational agents have free will? Is free will compatible with determinism? What are the essential characteristics of any particular or any specific kind of thing? What is the nature of possibility? Is there necessity in nature? What is it for one thing or event or fact to cause another? Does space exist in its own right, or is it just the spatial relations among concrete objects that "inhabit" space? What is the nature of time? Does time flow? Does only the present moment exist, or do the past and/or the future also exist? Does the present moment have privileged status among existing times? How much of reality is dependent on the existence and activities of minds?

The practice of science is always and everywhere metaphysically loaded. It is contingent on what scientists take to be real or illusory. Illusions, by their nature, are thought not to represent reality accurately; so their content is not investigated in the process of discovering how things are. Rather, the causes, effects, and perhaps preventions or facilitations of the illusion might be the subject of scientific inquiry. A metaphysics of waves, rather than particles, affects how one would detect the phenomenon in question. A metaphysics of individuals makes it sensible to track an object through time, space, and interactions with other individuals. A metaphysics in which individuality is either nonexistent or breaks down under certain conditions makes such tracking inappropriate.

However, the practice of science does not require that one adopt a naturalist/antisupernaturalist metaphysical framework. Only the much more modest assumption that the subject of investigation is not affected by the unusual activities of the supernatural associated with **miracles** is required.

Whether metaphysical questions are fruitful subjects for philosophical progress is itself an ancient and modern philosophical question. Some have maintained that metaphysical claims arise from confusions about the functions of portions of language. Others have rejected many metaphysical claims because they are thought to arise from a faulty account of how such claims could be known, or because of the perceived failure of metaphysicians to fully address the question of how their claims could be known, if true.

Scott Shalkowski

REFERENCES AND RECOMMENDED READING

Loux, Michael J. 2006. *Metaphysics: A Contemporary Introduction.* 3rd ed. London: Routledge.
Sider, Theodore, John Hawthorne, and Dean W. Zimmerman, eds. 2008. *Contemporary Debates in Metaphysics.* Malden, MA: Blackwell.
van Inwagen, Peter, and Dean W. Zimmerman. 2008. *Metaphysics: The Big Questions.* 2nd ed. Malden, MA: Blackwell.

METHODOLOGICAL NATURALISM. Methodological naturalism (MN) is a highly controversial principle of scientific methodology. While multiple (and sometimes incompatible) definitions of MN have been given, the basic idea is that "by its very nature, science is obliged to leave out any appeal to the supernatural" (Haught 2004, 231). Methodological naturalism is not the same as philosophical naturalism (PN). PN makes the ontological claim that only the natural world exists. MN is compatible with the existence of nonnatural or supernatural entities, but it prohibits appeal to them within scientific theories and explanations.

Offering a more precise definition of MN is difficult because there is no philosophical consensus on what the "natural world" contains. There is a dispute between strict and broad naturalism (Goetz and Taliaferro 2008). Strict naturalists deny the existence of any irreducible **teleology** in nature, claiming that all phenomena can be explained by undirected causes operating by **chance** or necessity. For strict naturalists, MN could be used to exclude from science not only God but also intelligent causes allegedly operating within nature. Broad naturalists, however, allow that irreducible teleology may emerge in sufficiently complex systems (like brains), and so can allow that humans and other creatures do exhibit goal-directed behavior. For them, MN would exclude only supernatural **causation** from science.

The status of MN is also controversial, even among its defenders. Some defend it on a priori philosophical grounds, claiming that MN is a necessary condition for any activity to qualify as scientific. Others defend MN based on its a posteriori track record within science. And while some give MN an absolute and universal status, others see it as limited in application or merely as a defeasible rule of thumb.

If MN is restricted to standard *operations science*, which uses an inductive method to investigate the repeatable connections between secondary causes (as in a typical chemistry experiment), few will object to it, as there is no reason to appeal to supernatural (or intelligent) causation. However, MN is highly controversial when applied to *historical science*, which attempts to infer the best explanation of a singular event or state of affairs. This is particularly clear when historical science investigates questions of ultimate origins, like the origins of the universe, life, biological **information**, **consciousness**, and **morality**. In such cases, it is by no means clear why the best explanation could not be a supernatural cause.

In his 2005 Dover ruling, Judge John Jones used MN as an a priori reason to dismiss **intelligent design** (ID) as nonscience, arguing that "ID violates the centuries-old ground rules of science by invoking and permitting supernatural causation" (Jones 2005, 64). Defenders of ID made a number of responses. First, such an argument assumes that MN functions as a *demarcation criterion* for distinguishing science from nonscience. But as **Larry Laudan** argued (Laudan 1998), philosophers of science reject demarcation criteria because they are vulnerable to counterexamples, and as **Stephen Meyer** points out, "The real issue is not whether a theory is 'scientific' according to some abstract definition, but whether a theory is true, or supported by the evidence" (Meyer 2009, 432).

Second, both theist **Del Ratzsch** (2001) and atheist Bradley Monton (2009, chap. 2) have argued that if science is fully committed to MN, then it cannot claim to be a no-holds-barred search for the truth about the natural world, since it is logically possible that at least some aspects of the world are best explained by God (or a designer). If a pirate is searching an island for buried treasure but refuses to investigate some part of the island because the map says, "Here there be dragons," that is no reason to think the treasure is not there. Similarly, refusing to consider supernatural explanations means that if they are correct, science will never discover that truth.

A third response is that ID is not restricted to supernatural causes. ID argues only that scientists can infer *intelligent* causes, and these need not be supernatural: a designer might be human (e.g., archaeology), a machine (e.g., **artificial intelligence**), or an alien life form (e.g., the **SETI** project), and even a cosmic designer might be a teleological principle within nature rather than a supernatural deity. Thus, if MN only excludes supernatural causes, it cannot show that all design inferences are unscientific. But if MN excludes all intelligent causes, it has adopted the highly disputable strict naturalist understanding of nature.

Another major area of controversy is whether MN is neutral between **theism** (or design) and philosophical naturalism. Proponents of MN typically claim it is, because refusing to allow supernatural (or intelligent) causes in scientific study has no bearing on whether they exist. However, it is also frequently claimed that the success of science using MN does provide evidence of philosophical naturalism (Forrest 2000). The idea is that because we can explain so much of nature without appeal to God (or a designer), we have good reason to think that nature is all that exists.

A major problem with this argument is that even if MN is neutral as a matter of pure logic, in practice it encourages the conflation of the best explanation with the best *naturalistic* explanation. For example, within **origin of life** studies, MN will allow scientists to consider only explanations that appeal to chance, necessity, or some combination of the two. It could be that all of these explanations are poorly supported by the data, and thus that the best naturalistic explanation is still very improbable, while a theistic (or design) explanation is highly probable. The worry is that MN may create the illusion that naturalistic explanations have triumphed simply because more probable nonnaturalistic theories are excluded from consideration.

Also arguable is that the conjunction of MN with PN has two unwelcome consequences for naturalists (Dilley 2010). PN becomes a scientifically irrefutable thesis because the only scientific evidence that could count against it is evidence of God (or a designer), and that is excluded by MN. And PN cannot confidently claim to derive scientific support from data since MN permits only data that supports naturalistic theories, making **confirmation** of PN trivial. Interestingly, some proponents of MN claim to have refuted supernatural (or design) explanations, but it seems incoherent to maintain both that "God hypotheses are ineligible for disconfirmation *and* have been disconfirmed" (Dilley 2010, 127). If we seek to follow the evidence wherever it leads, we may find MN to be an artificial obstruction.

Angus J. L. Menuge

REFERENCES AND RECOMMENDED READING

Dilley, Stephen C. 2010. "Philosophical Naturalism and Methodological Naturalism: Strange Bedfellows?" *Philosophia Christi* 12 (1): 118–41.

Forrest, Barbara. 2000. "Methodological Naturalism and Philosophical Naturalism: Clarifying the Connection." *Philo* 3 (2): 7–29.

Goetz, Stewart, and Charles Taliaferro. 2008. *Naturalism*. Grand Rapids: Eerdmans.

Haught, John. 2004. "Darwin, Design, and Divine Providence." In *Debating Design*, ed. Michael Ruse and William Dembski. New York: Cambridge University Press.

Jones, John, III. 2005. *Kitzmiller v. Dover*. Memorandum Opinion. https://web.archive.org/web/20051221144316/http://pamd.uscourts.gov/kitzmiller/kitzmiller_342.pdf.

Laudan, Larry. 1998. "The Demise of the Demarcation Problem." In *But Is It Science? The Philosophical Question in the Creation/Evolution Controversy*, ed. Michael Ruse, 337–50. Buffalo, NY: Prometheus.

Meyer, Stephen C. 2009. *Signature in the Cell*. New York: HarperCollins.

Monton, Bradley. 2009. *Seeking God in Science: An Atheist Defends Intelligent Design*. Peterborough, ON: Broadview.

Ratzsch, Del. 2001. *Nature, Design, and Science*. Albany, NY: SUNY Press.

MEYER, STEPHEN C. Stephen C. Meyer (1958–) is an American philosopher of science and one of the architects of the modern theory of **intelligent design**, which he defines as the idea that "there are tell-tale features of living systems and the universe that are best explained by an intelligent cause … rather than by an undirected process" (Meyer 2009). Meyer has written a number of significant books and articles developing the theory. In addition to being a scholar, he is a public figure and has been interviewed frequently by the news media, has lectured around the world, and has appeared in numerous science documentaries.

Prior to attending graduate school, Meyer worked as a geophysicist for the Atlantic Richfield Company (ARCO) in Dallas, Texas, from 1981–85 in digital signal processing and seismic survey interpretation. Selected as a Rotary International Scholar, he received his PhD in the history and **philosophy of science** from Cambridge University in 1991. He subsequently served as a philosophy professor at Whitworth University from 1990 to 2002 and as a university professor in

the Conceptual Foundations of Science at Palm Beach Atlantic University from 2002 to 2005. Since 1996 he has directed the Center for Science and Culture at **Discovery Institute**, a program he cofounded with social scientist John G. West.

Meyer's most important works are *Signature in the Cell: DNA and the Evidence of Intelligent Design* (2009) and *Darwin's Doubt: The Explosive Origin of Animal Life and the Case for Intelligent Design* (2013). In *Signature in the Cell*, Meyer focused on the origin of the first life, arguing that a designing intelligence is the best explanation for the immense amounts of biological **information** encoded by **DNA**. In *Darwin's Doubt*, Meyer extended his argument to the development of animal life, especially the burst of biological **complexity** during what is known as the Cambrian explosion. In both books, Meyer framed the argument for intelligent design as an **inference to the best explanation**, and he provocatively argued that his theory of intelligent design follows the methodology for the historical sciences originally pioneered by Charles Lyell and **Charles Darwin**.

Although controversial, Meyer's work has been praised by a number of scholars who do not accept intelligent design, including Harvard geneticist George Church and noted atheist philosopher **Thomas Nagel**, who selected *Signature in the Cell* as one of the top books of the year in the *Times Literary Supplement* (Nagel 2011).

Meyer has stressed that in his view the theory of intelligent design is not based on religious faith, but he has gone on to say that it has positive *implications* for faith. In line with this idea, Meyer has explored the relationship between Christianity and science in a number of essays, arguing for what he calls a model of "qualified agreement" between science and Christianity (Meyer 2000).

Meyer also has taken an interest in science education policy. He has testified before state boards of education in Texas, Ohio, and Kansas relating to the development of science standards, and before the U.S. Civil Rights Commission on the subject of viewpoint discrimination in science education.

John G. West

REFERENCES AND RECOMMENDED READING

"Biography." StephenCMeyer.org. Accessed August 9, 2014. www.stephencmeyer.org/biography.php.

Klinghoffer, David, ed. 2010. *Signature of Controversy: Responses to Critics of "Signature in the Cell."* Seattle: Discovery Institute Press.

Meyer, Stephen C. 2000. "Qualified Agreement: Modern Science and the Return of the 'God Hypothesis.'" In *Science and Christianity: Four Views*, ed. Richard F. Carlson, 127–74. Downers Grove, IL: IVP Academic.

———. 2009. *Signature in the Cell: DNA and the Evidence of Intelligent Design*. New York: HarperOne.

———. 2013. *Darwin's Doubt: The Explosive Origin of Animal Life and the Case for Intelligent Design*. New York: HarperOne.

Nagel, Thomas. 2011. "Thomas Nagel and Stephen C. Meyer's *Signature in the Cell*." *Times Literary Supplement*. www.the-tls.co.uk/articles/public/thomas-nagel-and-stephen-c-meyers-signature-in-the-cell/.

Socrates in the City. 2013. "Stephen Meyer and Eric Metaxas Discuss *Darwin's Doubt* at Socrates in the City." www.youtube.com/watch?v=aFPhTDfcbrA.

MILLER, KENNETH R.

MILLER, KENNETH R. Kenneth R. Miller (1949–) is a cell biologist, author, and professor of biology at Brown University. Educated at Brown University (BSc, biology, 1970) and the University of Colorado (PhD, cell biology, 1974), Miller taught at Harvard University from 1974 to 1980, then moved to Brown University, where in 1986 he became full professor.

Miller's scientific work has focused on characterizing the structures of the photosynthetic apparatus. He is best known, however, for two other areas of work: (1) as coauthor, with science writer Joseph Levine, of one of the most widely adopted high school biology textbooks, *Biology* (multiple editions, beginning in 1990) and (2) contending as a theistic (Roman Catholic) advocate of evolution, originally against young-earth creationists (YECs), and later, **intelligent design** (ID) proponents. In the early 1980s, leading YEC Henry Morris of the **Institute for Creation Research** acknowledged that Miller was his most effective debate opponent. Miller quickly gained a reputation as an articulate and cheerful defender of evolution.

With the rise of the ID community in the early 1990s, Miller began to focus his critical energies on the most popular ID arguments, such as Michael Behe's concept of **irreducible complexity**. He also undertook a series of public debates with leading ID proponents, such as Behe and **William Dembski** (notably, in April 2002, at the American Museum of Natural History in New York City). Miller's first book specifically addressing the ID debate appeared in 1999: *Finding Darwin's God: A Scientist's Search for Common Ground between God and Evolution* (HarperCollins), which argued that, properly understood, evolutionary theory and Christian faith were fully compatible, and that ID reasoning prematurely foreclosed scientific inquiry by inserting an intervening God into the open puzzles of nature.

In 2005 Miller served as an expert witness for the ACLU and plaintiffs in the federal *Kitzmiller v. Dover Area School District* case, where teaching of ID was held by Judge John Jones to be unconstitutional. In his testimony, Miller critiqued the coherence of central ID notions such as irreducible complexity and defended the soundness of evolutionary theory. In 2009 Miller published his second book-length critical evaluation of ID and defense of evolution, *Only a Theory: Evolution and the Battle for America's Soul* (Viking). In this book, Miller again argued that apparent examples of irreducible complexity had been refuted by more extensive research; moreover, ID could not escape its connection to creationism, given that any designer must actualize his designs by bringing them into existence, an event that can only represent an act of creation as normally understood.

Paul Nelson

REFERENCES AND RECOMMENDED READING

Kitzmiller v. Dover Area School District. http://ncse.com/files/pub/legal/kitzmiller/trial_transcripts/2005_0926_day1_am.pdf and http://ncse.com/files/pub/legal/kitzmiller/trial_transcripts/2005_0926_day1_pm.pdf.

Miller, Kenneth R. 1999. *Finding Darwin's God: A Scientist's Search for Common Ground between God and Evolution*. New York: HarperCollins.

———. 2008. *Only a Theory: Evolution and the Battle for America's Soul*. New York: Viking.

NCSE. "Forum on 'Intelligent Design' Held at the American Museum of Natural History (April 23, 2002)." 2002. Transcripts at http://ncse.com/creationism/general/forum-intelligent-design-held-at-american-museum-natural-his.

MIND

MIND. Philosophers generally agree that the mind is that which thinks, understands, reasons, and feels. It is aware of the world through sensation and of itself through introspection. Mental states seem radically different from physical ones. Physical states are in time and space; thoughts are in time but do not seem to occupy space (or to occupy it in the same way). A thought is intrinsically subjective (it cannot be detached from its thinker), whereas neurons can be detached from a brain. Thoughts have intentionality: they are about something beyond themselves, and one can think of future events and even nonexistent entities like leprechauns. But physical states do not seem to be about anything, and future events and nonexistent entities cannot physically cause us to think of them.

One explanation of these contrasts is substance **dualism**, where a mental "substance" is understood very broadly to mean an enduring mental subject of some kind: it might be an emergent subject (Hasker 1999) or a Thomistic substantial form, rather than a substance in the strict Cartesian sense. Many philosophers see this mental substance as the **soul** (Goetz and Taliaferro 2011; Moreland 2014; Swinburne 2013).

For Christians, an attractive feature of substance dualism

is that it makes sense of the soul's existence between physical **death** and resurrection: if a soul's essence is its mental properties, it can exist without a body. The most common complaint about substance dualism is that it makes it difficult to understand how the mental and physical world causally interact (the **mind-body problem**). Dualists typically reply that we can have very good reason to think that a causal interaction occurs without knowing how it occurs (e.g., a seventeenth-century person had good reason to think low temperatures caused water to freeze without a molecular explanation).

Attempting to harmonize our understanding of human agency with modern science, most philosophers today embrace some version of **materialism** (or **physicalism**), according to which everything that exists depends exclusively on underlying physical entities such as particles. Eliminative materialists like Paul and Patricia Churchland (1998) claim that the familiar mental states of our commonsense self-understanding ("folk **psychology**") do not really exist and can be replaced by patterns of neural activation. Most materialists reject this view because it seems incompatible with the facts of **consciousness** and rationality. Reductive materialism claims one can identify mental states with physical or functional states of the brain. A recurring problem is that the latter states lack subjectivity and intentionality (Searle 1992).

Others defend nonreductive materialism (e.g., Searle 2007). This view admits that mental properties are different from typical physical properties but claims that mental properties are entirely determined by (supervene on or emerge from) physical "base" properties. A major problem for nonreductive materialism is that it apparently denies the existence of mental **causation**: the physical base properties exclude any causal contribution of the supervening mental properties (Kim 2010). Moreover, the nonreductive materialist has an interaction problem of the same kind as the substance dualist: since mental and physical properties are admitted to be very different, how could they affect each other?

Angus J. L. Menuge

REFERENCES AND RECOMMENDED READING

Churchland, Paul, and Patricia Churchland. 1998. *On the Contrary: Critical Essays, 1987–1997*. Cambridge, MA: MIT Press.
Goetz, Stewart, and Charles Taliaferro. 2011. *A Brief History of the Soul*. Malden, MA: Wiley.
Hasker, William. 1999. *The Emergent Self*. Ithaca, NY: Cornell University Press.
Kim, Jaegwon. 2010. *Philosophy of Mind*. 3rd ed. Boulder, CO: Westview.
Moreland, J. P. 2014. *The Soul*. Chicago: Moody.
Searle, John. 1992. *The Rediscovery of the Mind*. Cambridge, MA: MIT Press.
———. 2007. *Freedom and Neurobiology*. New York: Columbia University Press.
Swinburne, Richard. 2013. *Mind, Brain, and Free Will*. New York: Oxford University Press.

MIND-BODY PROBLEM. The mind-body problem has generated a great deal of attention in philosophy, especially in recent times. This is because of its place in wider debates related to Christian **theism** and atheism, free will and **morality**, the question of immortality, and the limits of scientific inquiry.

An enormously significant topic in philosophy, the central dispute revolves around the question: What is the relationship between the mind and the body? The mind refers to human **consciousness**, ideas, reasoning ability, memories, and imagination; the body refers to the physical stuff of the brain, such as neurons, cells, cortexes, and so forth. Traditionally, the brain (or body) has been regarded as a physical object, consisting of matter and energy, and subject to scientific laws; but the mind seems to be of a different order, a nonphysical, mental, spiritual entity, the seat of our consciousness, memories, and personal identity.

This commonsense distinction between the two inspired **René Descartes** (1596–1650) to develop his famous theory of substance (or Cartesian) **dualism**, the view that the mind and brain are two related but distinct entities. While the brain is a physical substance that has causal power over the mind, the mind is a mental substance that has causal power over the brain.

Substance dualism is opposed to **materialism**, the other main position about the mind-body relationship. Materialism, sometimes referred to as **physicalism**, is the view that the mind is either completely physical in nature or that it depends on the physical for its existence. Some philosophers take a strong view of materialism and argue for mind/brain identity—the view that the mind and the brain are the same thing, that **consciousness**, thoughts, and **logic** are sophisticated, complex physical operations of the brain, and although we do not yet fully understand how they work, we will in the future through further scientific research. Other materialists take a more moderate position, holding that mental activities might be nonphysical but are still produced by the brain and therefore are completely dependent on the brain. This view, sometimes called *epiphenomenalism*, also holds, counterintuitively, that mental events have no causal power over the brain.

Philosophers have taken quite a variety of positions in

between materialism and substance dualism, including **functionalism** and property dualism.

Dualists have defended their view with a number of arguments. A main one concerns the irreducible nature of mental properties, which are said to include **qualia**—those experiences, feelings, and perhaps beliefs that are available to us introspectively in consciousness. The irreducible nature of mental properties suggests that while the brain may be a necessary condition for mental activity in this life, it does not follow that it is also a sufficient condition.

This claim appeals to the logical principle that if two things have different properties, then they can't be the same thing. Descartes famously argued that the mind cannot be literally measured, weighed, or divided up, but the brain can. It makes no sense to talk about the weight of mental properties (such as an idea), but it does make sense to talk about the weight of the cortex. In addition, the experience of seeing red is qualitatively different from any brain state that might be correlated with it (see **Qualia**). This argument shows that the mind is of a different order than the brain and that it cannot be reduced to brain activity or to scientific causal explanations. Materialists respond to arguments of this type by noting that these differences may be only at the level of conceptual or descriptive analysis and that further study could reveal a much closer physical relationship between the mind and the brain.

The dualist also appeals to the argument from intentionality. This argument draws attention to a very peculiar property of mental states, our thoughts and ideas, a property not shared by physical objects. When we think of something such as our home, the ideas and pictures in our mind are said to have intentional content, that is, they are "about" or "of" something out there in the real world, the world outside the mind. This is true for most of our ideas, concepts, beliefs, and arguments. The dualist argues that intentionality cannot be explained in physical terms, because it makes no sense to say that the atomic or molecular structure of a physical object (e.g., brain cells) could be about another object distinct from it. Nor does it make much sense to say that a physical object could produce a nonphysical effect that would have as one of its features the phenomenon of intentionality.

When faced with recalcitrant features of the mind that seem to resist physical, scientific explanation, materialists often appeal to a kind of "scientific faith" argument. This argument is based on the claim that since we have encountered many things in the past (e.g., lightning) that we initially thought were inexplicable but for which we eventually did find scientific explanations, it will be the same with intentionality and indeed with the mind more generally. The dualist recognizes that the scientific faith argument is a good argument in general in science (e.g., when applied to lightning) but denies that it is a good argument when applied to intentionality, or to the mind more generally. This is because intentionality, unlike lightning, is not just another physical object and seems to have no basis in physical matter, such as atoms and causal laws.

A third argument offered by dualists might be called the *argument from free will*, an argument many hold to be decisive against any theory of materialism about the human mind. Free will may be defined as the ability of human beings to make a genuine choice between alternatives, a choice that is not determined by scientific laws operating on atomic or molecular particles or combinations of particles in the brain. Without genuine free will, morality would make no sense, and our notions of moral responsibility and punishment would also be compromised.

The dualist contends that since human beings have free will, materialism is false. This is a thorny problem for materialists, who are faced with saying that, since all our actions are rooted in our brains and central nervous systems, all our "choices" should be explicable in terms of scientific causal laws operating on matter and energy. We should be like sophisticated robots, whose very operation is determined by causal sequences operating according to scientific laws. In short, there seems no room for free will in a naturalistic universe. Materialists are only beginning to come to terms with the problem that free will creates for their view, with some prepared to deny that free will exists and others proposing various "compatibilist" theories (see **Compatibilism**).

Dualists have extended these various arguments for the irreducible nature of consciousness to support an argument for immortality, as Descartes did. Because the mind is nonphysical, it has a certain independence from the brain, and though the mind and the brain operate together in this life, there is no logical objection to saying that at bodily **death** the mind could survive. Since the mind also involves our consciousness and memories, this would also be an argument that our personal identity will be maintained in the afterlife. More generally then, mind/body dualists are likely to appeal to arguments of this sort to support a theistic view of reality, though a small number of thinkers in recent times have argued that materialism is compatible with Christian theism (see **Life after Death**).

Brendan Sweetman

REFERENCES AND RECOMMENDED READING

Descartes, René. *Meditations* (many editions).

Lowe, E. J. 2000. *An Introduction to the Philosophy of Mind.* Cambridge: Cambridge University Press.

Murphy, Nancey. 2006. *Bodies and Souls, or Spirited Bodies?* New York: Cambridge University Press.

Searle, John. 2006. *Freedom and Neurobiology.* New York: Columbia University Press.

Taliaferro, Charles. 1994. *Consciousness and the Mind of God.* New York: Cambridge University Press.

van Inwagen, Peter. 1983. *An Essay on Free Will.* Oxford: Clarendon.

MIRACLES. Thinkers have defined *miracles* in diverse ways. For **Augustine**, miracles are above nature; because nature is what God does, however, miracles are not truly against it. For Thomas Aquinas, miracles are divine acts that generate awe; they may exceed what nature can produce or may accomplish what nature can also produce but in a supernatural way.

An essay on miracles by **David Hume** (1711–76) shaped most subsequent discussion. Ignoring the definitions of his detractors (Burns 1981, 234–37), Hume innovatively defined miracles as violations of the **laws of nature**—which, he argued, cannot be violated. Hume's argument against miracles at this point merely plays with words, since even the **Enlightenment** scientists on whom he depended did not believe that the divine Legislator "violated" his own laws when he performed miracles (see Brooke 1991, 118).

Nevertheless, most scholars since Hume have defined miracles as "supernatural" events, identifiable partly because they differ from the ordinary course of nature. Some go further, defining miracles as events without plausible natural explanations; as the range of possible natural explanations increases, the field of naturally inexplicable events accordingly shrinks. Despite Hume's polemical target, however, his definition of "unnatural" miracles misses most biblical examples of miracles (see, e.g., Tucker 2005, 375–79). In many foundational biblical signs, God used nature to achieve extraordinary outcomes (e.g., Ex. 10:13; 14:21).

A definition of miracle that better encompasses biblical instances, held by many scholars today, is *special divine action* (see Gwynne 1996). "Special" in this case is a matter of degree, distinguishing miracles from God's *ordinary* activity in the course of nature. This definition overlaps with the biblical term *sign*: a divine action that differs from ordinary human experience in a manner dramatic enough to demand attention (and often decision).

Historic Christian Claims

Most New Testament scholars believe that Mark's gospel was the first one written; stories recounting miracles and exorcisms constitute roughly 40 percent of Mark's narrative. Likewise, they constitute about one-fifth of Acts, the earliest account of Jesus's first followers. Most proposed analogies are late (such as Apollonius of Tyana) or very limited (Eve 2002; Keener 2011a), though earlier biblical narratives such as accounts of Moses, Elijah, and Elisha provide models.

Virtually all substantive ancient sources about Jesus depict him as a miracle worker, and even ancient critics of his movement conceded that he performed signs. Most historical Jesus scholars today recognize that Jesus's contemporaries experienced him as miracle worker, however this is explained. Some suggest that recoveries involved psychogenic illnesses (see Capps 2008). Without ruling out this factor in some cases, the conditions for most of Jesus's reported cures, for example of blindness, differ significantly from cures under psychiatric treatment: they were public and immediate. His cures of blindness appear multiple times and are multiply attested, in the shared tradition called *Q* (Matt. 11:5//Luke 7:22), in Mark (8:25; 10:52), John (9:1–7), and Matthew (21:14). How many such psychogenic cases would Jesus have faced during his brief ministry in Galilee, and how would crowds have responded if the vast majority of cases of blindness, not psychogenically explained, refused to respond to his treatment?

Later hostile rabbis report that some of Jesus's followers continued to heal the sick. Church fathers offered their own eyewitness accounts of miracles, named non-Christians cured, and included accounts of raisings from **death**. Indeed, the leading known reasons for conversion to Christianity in the 300s were miracles and exorcisms (MacMullen 1984, 60–62). Dramatic accounts continue through history, particularly prominent in reports of groundbreaking mission (see Porterfield 2005; Keener 2011a, 264–599). Worldwide, a majority of Christians today affirm and pray for divine healing.

Hume against Miracles

Some seventeenth-century deists began to deny the possibility of miracles, sometimes citing mechanistic **physics** (see **Deism**). Ironically, **Isaac Newton** (1642–1727), whose mechanistic model of nature was most often invoked, and many other early English scientists affirmed biblical miracles, as did Newton's early followers. It was not scientific discoveries but a particular philosophic framework that led many circles to abandon belief in miracles.

Although other essays against miracles were more prominent in Hume's day, Hume's stature as a philosopher eventually made his essay against miracles the dominant one. Circles today that a priori deny the possibility of affirming miracles usually depend, knowingly or unknowingly, on Hume's argument.

Nevertheless, Hume's essay was controversial and has been debated since its publication (see Burns 1981, 176–246; Mullin 1996, 33). Although Hume's essay has its academic defenders (e.g., Fogelin 2003), a larger number of philosophers today have critiqued it severely (e.g., Earman 2000; Houston 1994; Johnson 1999; Swinburne 1970). Hume's essay on miracles is one of his least consistent works; Robert Burns has shown that many lacunae in his argument appear because he presupposes the fuller argument of earlier deists (1981, e.g., 72–73, 75–76, 89–93).

Although scholars debate the precise character of Hume's argument, all agree that it includes two major sections. First, Hume apparently argues that miracles are violations of the laws of nature and that such laws cannot be violated; thus, by fiat, he excludes them of definition. (Many complain about Hume's circular use of definitions here; see, e.g., Brown 1984, 94; Johnson 1999, 5–8, 19; Larmer 1988, 17–30, 37; 2014, 69–72, 101–4; Nichols 2002, 704; Taylor 1927, 7, 11.)

As Hume's critics have regularly complained, his assumption of a deity subject to created laws does not address actual theistic conceptions of the deity (Houston 1994, 133–34, 148, 160, 162; Smart 1969, 32–33). Indeed, on theistic assumptions, miracles may even be probable (e.g., Hamburger 1980, 601; Langtry 1990, 70; Otte 1996, 155–57; Swinburne 1989, 151; Ward 1985, 144–45). Moreover, Hume's attempt to rule out acceptance of miracles a priori cannot proceed empirically or on the basis of induction; he takes into account only very limited possible examples and too quickly excludes alternative ones. His deductive argument against miracles contradicts his own **epistemology**, which not only challenges deduction but even limits causal inferences (see, e.g., Brown 1984, 168; Gwynne 1996, 171; Larmer 1988, 38; 2014, 61–65; Taylor 1927, 29–36).

Hume's detractors today often further respond that modern physics treats laws as descriptions of nature rather than limitations on what is possible. (Modern theologians do vary among themselves regarding the relationship between nature and experiences deemed miraculous.) Some also suggest that just as nature's norms may differ under differing

conditions, such as black holes or superconductivity, special divine activity allows for special norms (Nichols 2002, 705). Hume's understanding of natural law interplays with what he considers uniform human experience (related to his second argument).

The second argument by Hume appeals to uniform (or at least standard) human experience to exclude the reliability of eyewitness claims that deviate from such experience. Most critics regard the argument as circular (e.g., Holder 1998, 57; Larmer 1988, 36). To argue against miracle testimony because miracles violate experience is circular; to argue against it because it is deemed rare is inconsistent with how we treat other rare events.

Hume claims that no witnesses of miracles meet his criteria for credibility, such as being highly reputable and of good sense. Many witnesses do in fact meet his criteria, except insofar as he questions the good sense of any who claim to witness miracles (Colwell 1983, 10). Since most witnesses themselves are aware of the natural improbability of their claims (Breggen 2002, 451–52), dismissing them as liars simply because of what they testify assumes what it claims to prove (see further Cramer 1988, 136–37; Phillips 1993, 35; Ward 2002, 745). One might then trust only those reports that confirmed one's prior beliefs (Weintraub 1996, 360).

One of Hume's supporting arguments, the exclusion of testimony from non-European cultures, can be dismissed today as reflecting a racist bias explicit in some of his other writings (Keener 2011b; Taliaferro and Hendrickson 2002; Ten 2002). His argument that claims from competing religions cancel each other assumes a solely apologetic motive for miracles. (Healing claims are more common in some religions, such as Hinduism and traditional religions, than in others.) Hume's extrapolation from spurious miracles reflects the false analogy fallacy, whereas a single demonstrated miracle would undercut his case.

On the basis of legal and mathematical **probability** models, detractors have long challenged Hume's wider skepticism of testimony's value (for early voices, see Dawid and Gillies 1989, 58; Earman 1993, 305; Sober 2004, 487, 491). In particular, multiple independent witnesses make testimony probable (see e.g., Earman 2000, 24–25; Holder 1998, 53; McGrew 2009, 641–42; Weintraub 1996: 371).

Hume extrapolated uniform human experience from a very small sample size (Mavrodes 1998, 176, 180), an error against which his own epistemology (Landesman 1997, 136–41) should have warned him. Without testimony from outside our immediate circle, we would know very little about the past or the rest of the world (Lawton 1960, 56; Licona 2008, 97, 129; Popper 1969, 21).

One of Hume's specific examples was the well-attested public cure of **Blaise Pascal**'s niece; the testimony meets most of Hume's own stated criteria. Yet because the healing was associated with Jansenists, who were too Catholic for Protestant tastes and too Augustinian for French Catholics, he could simply dismiss it. Since such a well-attested case is untrustworthy, he further argued, why should anyone believe less-attested cases such as those in antiquity? (Here he followed a deist line of argument; Burns 1981, 74–75.)

The Bar of Evidence

Hume sets the bar of evidence so high that very few historical events could meet it (see Hesse 1965, 40). A more neutral position is not to presuppose that miracles cannot happen, but to allow that they might, if evidence warrants and/or if evidence supports **theism** more generally. To exclude miracles on the grounds that they are divinely caused events is to work not with neutral assumptions but with specifically atheistic ones, thus stacking the deck. These assumptions are no less historically contingent than are religious ones (Gregory 2006).

Some critics stack the deck with insurmountable demands for evidence. For example, in some works, following Hume's logic, any reports that are inconceivable naturally are dismissed as obviously fabricated, whereas those that are conceivable naturally are dismissed as nonmiraculous (countered in Hambourger 1980, 600). Some critics reject any medically diagnosed case, claiming that the patient was under medical care and thus not miraculously cured, while also rejecting any case studies of those not under medical care, since this eliminates a medical diagnosis. Cures within recent years are deemed potentially temporary, but documentation often no longer exists for older cures. In other words, all evidence is ruled out from the start. Some early critiques of miracle reports, still cited today, dismissed significant evidence (see Opp 2005, 176–87).

Other critiques dismiss evidence for miracles even by promising that a purely natural explanation will emerge (sources in Mullin 1996, 42); while this promise might prove true in some cases, the approach is one that a priori rules out the admissibility of any evidence. A tacit admission of lack of counterargument, it is simply an inverted form of the "God-of-the-gaps" argument, which naturalists insist that theists not use (cf. Larmer 2014, 85–86; Plantinga 2009, 109, 112–13). When an insurmountable burden of proof is placed on theists and none on skeptics, an investigation cannot claim **objectivity**.

Critics often demand medical documentation for all cases (thus ruling out examples from many periods and cultures). Medical documentation is, however, sometimes available. For example, although the particularly rigorous standards at Lourdes are difficult today for almost any cure to meet, some of the cases there are very strong. When such documentation is produced, however, some critics reject it. Virtually any unexplained cure can be dismissed as simply an anomaly—leaving no evidence for discussion (Krippner and Achterberg 2000, 358).

Explanation only in terms of coincidence can become reductionistic. One scholar, for example, suggests that even if an occurrence might happen naturally only 1 in 10 million times, that explanation is more satisfactory than a miracle (Diamond 1973, 314–15, 323). Yet even David Hume recognized that coincidence can go only so far as an explanation when patterns mount (Hume 1985, 31–32). Clusters of cases today surrounding groundbreaking evangelism compound improbabilities.

Science and Miracles

The interests of science and theistic faith overlap, but their questions often differ (see Polkinghorne 1994, 1998). Verifying a person's impairments or lack thereof is within the purview of science; explaining cures requires interpretation, but interpretations will be complete only to the extent that the discipline's methods permit. For example, we might correctly describe a page in terms of the chemical composition of paper and ink, but the hands, the brain, the **mind**, and the social setting of the author reflect different levels of **causation**, all appropriate matters of study in their own spheres. Different orders of language may be necessary for different spheres (cf. Ramsey 1964, 23–26).

The question of miracles' possibility as *miracles* is not one of science but one of philosophy (of science and religion). Anomalous events occur (cf. Krippner and Achterberg 2000; McClenon 1994), but frameworks control their interpretation. Theists, for example, normally deem them miracles only in theistic contexts. Critics normally resist evidence that cannot fit reigning **paradigm**s until paradigm shifts occur (see, e.g., Kuhn 1970, 64–65, 107, 133, 169; Polanyi 1962, 138). Thus some scholars report fear of expressing faith or of publishing anomalies (cf. Ecklund 2010, 43–45; Matthews with Clark 1998, 58; Nichols 2002, 707). Although many scientists are Christians, hostility toward religion, often grounded in misinformation, appears disproportionately among scientists in some elite universities (Ecklund 2010).

Even when sufficient medical documentation demonstrates anomalous cures in theistic contexts, some reject its value without controlled studies. Controlled studies, however, look for predictable patterns, requiring the deity to participate as an actor in the study. Most forms of theism, however, view God as a personal agent, rendering problematic the sorts of predictions expected in such studies (cf. Polkinghorne and Beale 2009, 29; Ward 1985, 137; 2002, 746–47). The actions of personal agents, whether human or (a fortiori) divine, are not predictable in the same way chemical reactions are. Moreover, controlled studies cannot control for **prayer** outside the study. Worse, they are both difficult and unattempted in the settings (new evangelism contexts) where miracles are by far most often reported. (For other issues, see Brown 2012, 87–98.)

Because replicability and natural explanations are important in scientific publications, anomalies such as miracles are rarely published in such settings (Llewellyn 2008, 253). Yet different necessary disciplines require different epistemic approaches. Events in history, for example, are not, strictly speaking, replicable; nor are most events treated by journalism or law. Whereas most sciences rightly deal with basic natural phenomena that can be replicated by experiments or regular observation, replicability cannot be an epistemic criterion for unique events in history (Copleston 1972, 43–44; Gorsuch 2008, 284–85; Polkinghorne 2007, 34–35; Ward 2002, 744–47). Science observes patterns of regularity; history must give greater attention to particularities (Popper 1961, 143). Granted, one may often compare events with analogous *kinds* of events. Claiming that miracles do not meet this criterion, however, is possible only if one a priori dismisses all the other claims in the same category, that is, all other miracle claims (Swinburne 1970, 33–51).

Thus the typical scientific epistemology, while rightly indispensable in its sphere, cannot fully circumscribe the boundaries of experience. Indeed, an exclusively empirical epistemology is logically self-defeating. Hume admitted that he did not live by his strict epistemology outside his philosophic work (Taylor 1927, 24–25), and no one, including empiricists, evaluates all personal communications from trusted sources by demanding replicability.

Miracle Claims Today

Hume's argument from uniform human experience depends heavily on the alleged lack of credible eyewitness claims. Yet contrary to his assumptions based on his circle of experience, eyewitnesses from a variety of backgrounds often *do* offer such claims, most prominently in Africa, Asia, and Latin America. A 2006 Pew Forum survey (PewResearchCenter 2006) suggests hundreds of millions of healing claims in just 10 countries studied; this figure includes not only many Pentecostals and charismatics (cf. studies in Brown 2011), but more than one-third of "other Christians" surveyed. Even in the United States, 34 percent in a 2008 survey report that they have witnessed or experienced divine healing.

These claims cannot be simply dismissed as one religion's apologetic bias. For example, a 1981 study concluded that one-tenth of non-Christians in Chennai (then Madras), India, believed that they had been healed through prayers to Jesus. Moreover, healing experiences have proved sufficiently convincing to persuade millions of people to change ancestral beliefs. For example, healings have triggered movements of entire groups of people (such as many of the Nishi people in India or another movement in Nickerie, Suriname) to a new faith (Keener 2011a, 277, 509–10). On a more individual level, some reports from China, which was not included in the above-mentioned Pew survey, attribute between half and 90 percent of all the millions of new conversions in the twentieth century's final two decades to religious healing experiences (Tang 2005, 481; Währich-Oblau 2001, 92–93; 2011, 313).

The nature of miracle claims varies, but a surprising number of eyewitness claims recount dramatic experiences such as instant healings of blindness, in some cases caused by cataracts, and raisings from the dead, in a number of cases those believed dead for many hours (Keener 2011a, 508–79; 2015, 58–79). Eyewitnesses report instant miracles such as the instant disappearance of goiters (Keener 2011a, 745–46). Some reports come from physicians who reviewed medical documentation (e.g., Brown et al. 2010; Gardner 1983, 1986; Wilson 2008, 269–73; see further Brown 2012, 202–33; Keener 2011a, 714–25). One 2004 survey of US physicians even found that over half reported witnessing what they believed to be miracles (Keener 2011a, 721–22). The massive incidence of such claims from witnesses in a range of cultures and social stations appears problematic for Hume's argument about uniform human experience. Human experience on such matters hardly appears uniform.

Evaluation

Whether such claims represent genuine special divine action is debated based on the explanations assigned to such experiences. Emic explanations are those offered by the witnesses or their cultures. Etic explanations arise instead from external interpreters' categories, although these explanations, too, reflect **worldview** assumptions, whether allowing or disallowing supernatural causes.

Some claims reflect fraud, imagination, or denial. Misdiagnosis is common, and some recoveries inevitably prove faster than general medical estimates of recovery time. Medical documentation can be ambiguous; it is not always easily collected, and prior assumptions can shape interpretations. Philosophic a prioris determine the bar of evidence required; some critics rule out any measure of evidence, whereas some others grasp at very limited evidence.

Many illnesses are psychosomatic; some others (including even some dramatic disorders) may be genuine physical illnesses with psychological causes. Psychoimmunology has demonstrated the close connection in many cases between physical and psychological wholeness, and various studies of health and religion have suggested positive health factors in some religious practice. Theists usually allow that God can work through such causes.

Nevertheless, theists also usually argue that, if the possibility of theism is not ruled out, the possibility of more dramatic special divine action cannot be ruled out in many cases of spiritual cures. Where improbable anomalies cluster in given spiritual contexts (such as prayer in groundbreaking evangelism settings), their cumulative statistical improbability supports the likelihood of causes specific to these contexts.

One Christian researcher discovered that roughly 10 people in his immediate circle offered eyewitness claims of full-recovery raisings from the dead through prayer without medical intervention. Most of these had appeared dead for at least an hour and some for eight or more hours. Granted, occasionally people are deemed dead prematurely; but if more than 10 percent of people experience such merely apparent deaths in their immediate circle, an inordinate number of people are undoubtedly buried prematurely. Further, even on this generous estimate of a 1-in-10 likelihood of a given person's circle witnessing such a recovery, the odds of independently finding 10 such recoveries in one's circle would be roughly 1 in 10 billion. One should add that all these cases involved prayer; that none of these witnesses reported raisings not involving prayer or reported praying randomly over other dead persons; and the further coincidence that the researcher knew of other circles similar to his own (Keener 2011a, 662–63, 752–56; 2015, 79).

A variety of causes may thus stand behind various miracle claims, but the interpretation of many claims involves not only evidence but the assumptions through which the evidence is framed. Different cultural contexts make a range of options from credulity to skepticism appear plausible to various interpreters. What seems beyond debate, however, is that globally hundreds of millions of people sincerely believe they have experienced miracles.

Conclusion

Hume's argument against miracles is circular. His a priori stance against miracles became dominant in many academic circles but is now widely debated among philosophers. Meanwhile, hundreds of millions of people worldwide claim not only to believe in miracles but to have experienced them.

Craig Keener

REFERENCES AND RECOMMENDED READING

Beckwith, Francis J. 1989. *David Hume's Argument against Miracles: A Critical Analysis.* Lanham, MD.: University Press of America.

Brooke, John Hedley. 1991. *Science and Religion: Some Historical Perspectives.* Cambridge History of Science Series. New York: Cambridge University Press.

Brown, Candy Gunther, ed. 2011. *Global Pentecostal and Charismatic Healing.* Foreword by Harvey Cox. Oxford: Oxford University Press.

———. 2012. *Testing Prayer: Science and Healing.* Cambridge, MA: Harvard University Press.

Brown, Candy Gunther, Stephen C. Mory, Rebecca Williams, and Michael J. McClymond. 2010. "Study of the Therapeutic Effects of Proximal Intercessory Prayer (STEPP) on Auditory and Visual Impairments in Rural Mozambique." *Southern Medical Journal* 103 (September 9): 864–69.

Brown, Colin. 1984. *Miracles and the Critical Mind.* Grand Rapids: Eerdmans.

Burns, Robert M. 1981. *The Great Debate on Miracles: From Joseph Glanvill to David Hume.* Lewisburg, PA: Bucknell University Press.

Capps, Donald. 2008. *Jesus the Village Psychiatrist.* Louisville, KY: Westminster John Knox.

Colwell, Gary G. 1983. "Miracles and History." *Sophia* 22:9–14.

Copleston, Frederick. 1972. *Contemporary Philosophy: Studies of Logical Positivism and Existentialism.* Rev. ed. London: Search; Paramus, NJ: Newman.

Cramer, John A. 1988. "Miracles and David Hume." *Perspectives on Science and Christian Faith* 40 (September 3): 129–37.

Dawid, Philip, and Donald Gillies. 1989. "A Bayesian Analysis of Hume's Argument concerning Miracles." *Philosophical Quarterly* 39:57–65.

Diamond, Malcolm L. 1973. "Miracles." *Religious Studies* 9 (3): 307–24.

Earman, John. 1993. "Bayes, Hume, and Miracles." *Faith and Philosophy* 10 (3): 293–310.

———. 2000. *Hume's Abject Failure: The Argument against Miracles.* Oxford: Oxford University Press.

Ecklund, Elaine Howard. 2010. *Science vs. Religion: What Scientists Really Think.* Oxford: Oxford University Press.

Ellens, J. Harold, ed. 2008. *Religious and Spiritual Events.* Vol. 1 of *Miracles: God, Science, and Psychology in the Paranormal.* Westport, CT, and London: Praeger.

Eve, Eric. 2002. *The Jewish Context of Jesus' Miracles.* Journal for the Study of the New Testament: Supplement Series 231. Sheffield: Sheffield Academic Press.

Fogelin, Robert J. 2003. *A Defense of Hume on Miracles.* Princeton Monographs in Philosophy. Princeton, NJ: Princeton University Press.

Gardner, Rex. 1983. "Miracles of Healing in Anglo-Celtic Northumbria as Recorded by the Venerable Bede and His Contemporaries: A Reappraisal in the Light of Twentieth-Century Experience." *British Medical Journal* 287 (December 24–31): 1927–33.

———. 1986. *Healing Miracles: A Doctor Investigates.* London: Darton, Longman & Todd.

Geivett, R. Douglas, and Gary R. Habermas, eds. 1997. *In Defense of Miracles: A Comprehensive Case for God's Action in History.* Downers Grove, IL: InterVarsity.

Gorsuch, Richard L. 2008. "On the Limits of Scientific Investigation: Miracles and Intercessory Prayer." In *Religious and Spiritual Events*, vol. 1 of *Miracles: God, Science, and Psychology in the Paranormal*, ed. J. Harold Ellens, 280–99. Westport, CT, and London: Praeger.

Gregory, Brad S. 2006. "The Other Confessional History: On Secular Bias in the Study of Religion." *History and Theory* 45 (December 4): 132–49.

Gwynne, Paul. 1996. *Special Divine Action: Key Issues in the Contemporary Debate (1965–1995).* Tesi Gregoriana, Serie Teologia 12. Rome: Gregorian University Press.

Hambourger, Robert. 1980. "Belief in Miracles and Hume's Essay." *Nous* 14:587–604.

Hesse, Mary. 1965. "Miracles and the Laws of Nature." In *Miracles: Cambridge Studies in Their Philosophy and History*, ed. C. F. D. Moule, 33–42. New York: Morehouse-Barlow.

Holder, Rodney D. 1998. "Hume on Miracles: Bayesian Interpretation, Multiple Testimony, and the Existence of God." *British Journal for the Philosophy of Science* 49 (March 1): 49–65.

Houston, J. 1994. *Reported Miracles: A Critique of Hume.* Cambridge: Cambridge University Press.

Hume, David. 1985. *Of Miracles.* Introduction by Antony Flew. La Salle, IL: Open Court.

Johnson, David. 1999. *Hume, Holism, and Miracles.* Cornell Studies in the Philosophy of Religion. Ithaca, NY: Cornell University Press.

Kee, Howard Clark. 1983. *Miracle in the Early Christian World: A Study in Sociohistorical Method.* New Haven, CT: Yale University Press.

Keener, Craig S. 2011a. *Miracles: The Credibility of the New Testament Accounts.* 2 vols. Grand Rapids: Baker Academic.

———. 2011b. "A Reassessment of Hume's Case against Miracles in Light of Testimony from the Majority World Today." *Perspectives in Religious Studies* 38, no. 3 (Fall): 289–310.

———. 2015. "'The Dead Are Raised' (Matthew 11:5//Luke 7:22): Resuscitation Accounts in the Gospels and Eyewitness Testimony." *Bulletin for Biblical Research* 25 (1): 55–79.

Krippner, Stanley, and Jeanne Achterberg. 2000. "Anomalous Healing Experiences." In *Varieties of Anomalous Experience: Examining the Scientific Evidence*, ed. Etzel Cardeña, Steven Jay Lynn, and Stanley Krippner, 353–96. Washington, DC: American Psychological Association.

Kuhn, Thomas S. 1970. *The Structure of Scientific Revolutions.* 2nd ed. Chicago: University of Chicago Press.

Landesman, Charles. 1997. *An Introduction to Epistemology.* Cambridge, MA; Oxford: Blackwell.

Langtry, Bruce. 1990. "Hume, Probability, Lotteries, and Miracles." *Hume Studies* 16 (April 1): 67–74.

Larmer, Robert A. 1988. *Water into Wine? An Investigation of the Concept of Miracle.* Montreal: McGill-Queen's University Press.

———. 2014. *The Legitimacy of Miracle.* Lanham, MD: Rowman & Littlefield.

Lawton, John Stewart. 1960. *Miracles and Revelation.* New York: Association Press.

Licona, Michael R. 2008. "The Historicity of the Resurrection of Christ: Historiographical Considerations in the Light of Recent Debates." PhD diss. University of Pretoria.

Llewellyn, Russ. 2008. "Religious and Spiritual Miracle Events in Real-Life Experience." In *Religious and Spiritual Events*, vol. 1 of *Miracles: God, Science, and Psychology in the Paranormal*, ed. J. Harold Ellens, 241–63. Westport, CT, and London: Praeger.

MacMullen, Ramsay. 1984. *Christianizing the Roman Empire.* New Haven, CT: Yale University Press.

Matthews, Dale A., with Connie Clark. 1998. *The Faith Factor: Proof of the Healing Power of Prayer.* New York: Viking Penguin.

Mavrodes, George I. 1998. "David Hume and the Probability of Miracles." *International Journal for Philosophy of Religion* 43 (3): 167–82.

McClenon, James. 1994. *Wondrous Events: Foundations of Religious Belief.* Philadelphia: University of Pennsylvania Press.

McGrew, Timothy. 2009. "The Argument from Miracles: A Cumulative Case for the Resurrection of Jesus of Nazareth." In *The Blackwell Companion to Natural Theology*, ed. J. P. Moreland and William Lane Craig, 593–662. Malden, MA: Blackwell.

Mullin, Robert Bruce. 1996. *Miracles and the Modern Religious Imagination.* New Haven, CT: Yale University Press.

Nichols, Terence L. 2002. "Miracles in Science and Theology." *Zygon* 37 (3): 703–15.

Opp, James. 2005. *The Lord for the Body: Religion, Medicine, and Protestant Faith Healing in Canada, 1880–1930.* Montreal: McGill-Queen's University Press.

Otte, Richard. 1996. "Mackie's Treatment of Miracles." *International Journal for Philosophy of Religion* 39 (3): 151–58.

PewResearchCenter. 2006. "Spirit and Power: A 10-Country Survey of Pentecostals." PewResearchCenter. October 5. http://pewforum.org/survey/pentecostal.

Phillips, D. Z. 1993. "Miracles and Open-Door Epistemology." *Scottish Journal of Religious Studies* 14 (1): 33–40.

Pilch, John J. 2000. *Healing in the New Testament: Insights from Medical and Mediterranean Anthropology.* Minneapolis: Fortress.

Plantinga, Alvin. 2009. "Science and Religion: Why Does the Debate Continue?" In *The Religion and Science Debate: Why Does It Continue?* ed. Harold W. Attridge, 93–123. New Haven, CT: Yale University Press.

Polanyi, Michael. 1962. *Personal Knowledge: Towards a Post-critical Philosophy.* Rev. ed. Chicago: University of Chicago Press.

Polkinghorne, John. 1994. *The Faith of a Physicist: Reflections of a Bottom-Up Thinker.* Gifford Lectures, 1993–94. Minneapolis: Fortress.

———. 1998. *Belief in God in an Age of Science.* Terry Lectures. New Haven, CT: Yale University Press.

———. 2007. *Quantum Physics and Theology: An Unexpected Kinship.* New Haven, CT: Yale University Press.

Polkinghorne, John, and Nicholas Beale. 2009. *Questions of Truth: Fifty-One Responses to Questions about God, Science, and Belief.* Louisville, KY: Westminster John Knox.

Popper, Karl R. 1961. *The Poverty of Historicism.* 3rd ed. New York: Harper & Row.

———. 1969. *Conjectures and Refutations: The Growth of Scientific Knowledge.* 3rd rev. ed. London: Routledge and Kegan Paul.

Porterfield, Amanda. 2005. *Healing in the History of Christianity.* New York: Oxford University Press.

Ramsey, Ian T. 1964. "Miracles: An Exercise in Logical Mapwork." Inaugural lecture delivered before the University of Oxford, December 7, 1951. In *The Miracles and the Resurrection: Some Recent Studies by I. T. Ramsey, G. H. Boobyer, F. N. Davey, M. C. Perry, and Henry J. Cadbury*, 1–30. Theological Collections 3. London: SPCK.

Smart, Ninian. 1969. *Philosophers and Religious Truth.* 2nd ed. London: SCM.

Sober, Elliott. 2004. "A Modest Proposal." *Philosophy and Phenomenological Research* 68, no. 2 (March): 487–94.

Swinburne, Richard. 1970. *The Concept of Miracle.* London: Macmillan.

———. 1989. "Historical Evidence." In *Miracles*, ed. Richard Swinburne, 133–51. New York: Macmillan.

Taliaferro, Charles, and Anders Hendrickson. 2002. "Hume's Racism and His Case against the Miraculous." *Philosophia Christi* 4 (2): 427–41.

Tang, Edmond. 2005. "'Yellers' and Healers — Pentecostalism and the Study of Grassroots Christianity in China." In *Asian and Pentecostal: The Charismatic Face of Christianity in Asia*, ed. Allan Anderson and Edmond Tang, 467–86. Regnum Studies in Mission, *Asian Journal of Pentecostal Studies*. Ser. 3. Oxford: Regnum; Baguio City: APTS Press.

Taylor, A. E. 1927. *David Hume and the Miraculous.* Cambridge: Cambridge University Press.

Ten, C. L. 2002. "Hume's Racism and Miracles." *Journal of Value Inquiry* 36:101–7.

Theissen, Gerd. 1983. *The Miracle Stories of the Early Christian Tradition*, ed. John Riches; trans. Francis McDonagh. Philadelphia: Fortress.

Tucker, Aviezer. 2005. "Miracles, Historical Testimonies, and Probabilities." *History and Theory* 44 (October): 373–90.

Twelftree, Graham H., ed. 2011. *The Cambridge Companion to Miracles*. New York: Cambridge.

van der Breggen, Hendrik. 2002. "Hume's Scale: How Hume Counts a Miracle's Improbability Twice." *Philosophia Christi* 4 (2): 443–53.

Währich-Oblau, Claudia. 2001. "God Can Make Us Healthy Through and Through: On Prayers for the Sick and the Interpretation of Healing Experiences in Christian Churches in China and African Immigrant Congregations in Germany." *International Review of Mission* 90, no. 356/357 (January–April): 87–102.

———. 2011. "Material Salvation: Healing, Deliverance, and 'Breakthrough' in African Migrant Churches in Germany." In *Global Pentecostal and Charismatic Healing*, ed. Candy Gunther Brown, 61–80. Oxford: Oxford University Press.

Ward, Keith. 1985. "Miracles and Testimony." *Religious Studies* 21:134–45.

———. 2002. "Believing in Miracles." *Zygon* 37 (3): 741–50.

Weintraub, Ruth. 1996. "The Credibility of Miracles." *Philosophical Studies* 82:359–75.

Wilson, William P. 2008. "How Religious or Spiritual Miracle Events Happen Today." In *Religious and Spiritual Events*, vol. 1 of *Miracles: God, Science, and Psychology in the Paranormal*, ed. J. Harold Ellens, 264–79. Westport, CT, and London: Praeger.

MONISM

MONISM. According to *monism*, reality is one. One type of monism asserts that reality is one individual *thing*. The ancient Greek philosopher Parmenides of Elea (c. 515–450 BC) is traditionally thought to have been a monist of this sort. The British philosopher Francis Herbert Bradley (1846–1924) also held this view. **Pantheism**, the thesis that all of reality is one divine being, is an example of this sort of monism. Philosophers who are usually labeled pantheists include Plotinus (204/5–270), Sankara (788–820), **Baruch Spinoza** (1632–77), and Georg Wilhelm Friedrich Hegel (1770–1831).

In another type of monism, reality consists of one *kind* of thing (whether or not there is only one individual thing). The two most dominant views of this latter sort are **materialism**, according to which everything is material, and **idealism**, according to which everything is immaterial and mental. Hegel's individual monist theory is also an idealist monist theory, since he held that the one ultimate reality is fundamentally immaterial and mental in kind. But the individual *pluralist* theory of the ancient atomists is a materialist monist theory, since they held that many things exist but that they are all material things.

With respect to both types of monism (individual monism and kind monism), there can be corresponding dualist and pluralist theories. For instance, the atomistic materialists were individual pluralists (there are many individual things) and kind monists (each of these things is the same kind of thing—material).

Orthodox Christians cannot be individual monists, since they believe God is one being who created many other things. But some orthodox Christians are kind monists. These people are either idealists, like the philosopher George Berkeley (1685–1753) or materialists, like a number of contemporary Christian thinkers who believe that, though God is an immaterial being, the created order is entirely material. However, the traditional position of orthodox Christians has been that of "substance **dualism**," according to which creation contains two different kinds of substances or things—immaterial **mind**s and material objects, including bodies. This was **René Descartes**'s position. It was also the position taken by the great Christian thinker **Augustine** (354–430), following **Plato** (though without endorsing Plato's denigration of the body). Dualists like Descartes also affirm that immaterial minds and material bodies interact causally ("interactionist" substance dualism).

Many idealist and materialist monists consider this interactionist feature of substance dualism problematic on the grounds that it is inexplicable how an immaterial thing can interact causally with a material thing. This "problem of interaction" has become a standard reason to reject dualism in favor of one of these versions of monism. Today the dominant type of monism is materialism (aka **physicalism**), which is often affirmed on the grounds that it is best supported by contemporary science and simpler than dualism. But Christians continue to debate about whether materialism can accommodate the doctrine of **life after death**.

James Taylor

REFERENCES AND RECOMMENDED READING

Cooper, John W. 2000. *Body, Soul, and Life Everlasting: Biblical Anthropology and the Monism-Dualism Debate*. Grand Rapids: Eerdmans.

Koons, Robert C., and George Bealer, eds. 2010. *The Waning of Materialism*. New York: Oxford University Press.

van Inwagen, Peter. 2014. *Metaphysics*. 4th ed. Boulder, CO: Westview.

MONOD, JACQUES LUCIEN

MONOD, JACQUES LUCIEN. Jacques Lucien Monod (1910–76) received the Nobel Prize for medicine and physiology in 1965 along with François Jacob and Andre Lwoff for their seminal work on **gene** regulation. This work began with genetic analysis of bacteria linking phenotypical changes in carbohydrate metabolism to mutations in specific genes. It led to a model for the coregulation of gene expression of three proteins involved in lactose metabolism (beta-galactosidase, permease, and transacetylase). Known as the *lac operon*, their model postulated that a single repressor protein is allosterically modified by lactose to allow the simultaneous transcription of the three functional genes. Today these elegant and important experiments are used to introduce gene expression in nearly every introductory text on genetics or microbiology.

Born in Paris, France, Monod studied at the California Institute of Technology in 1936 as a Rockefeller Foundation fellow. He received his doctorate in 1941 from the University of Paris and continued his work and research throughout the Second World War and the Nazi occupation of France. He was an active participant in the French resistance movement along with his friend and colleague, Albert Camus. In spite of his political leftist leanings and his opposition to Nazi fascism, in 1948, after Communist authorities in Russia denounced the study of genetics, he publically defended the science of genetics in the resistance paper *Combat*.

In 1969 Monod presented the Robbins Lectures at Pomona College in California. In these lectures, he presented what he believed to be the philosophical and societal extensions of his work as a scientist. He subsequently published his ideas in the monograph *Chance and Necessity*. In this essay, he presented his view of the universe based on molecular biology and evolutionary processes and concluded famously that there is no plan and no intention in the universe. He asserted this as a fundamental postulate that he referred to as the postulate of **objectivity**. He concluded, "Man knows at last that he is alone in the universe's unfeeling immensity, out of which he emerged only by **chance**. His destiny is nowhere spelled out, nor is his duty" (Monod 1971).

With regard to the possibility of theistic evolution, Monod said in an interview, "I have no dispute with it, except one (which is not a scientific dispute, but a moral one). Namely, selection is the blindest and most cruel way of evolving new **species**." He declared, "I am surprised that a Christian would defend the idea that this is the process which God more or less set up in order to have evolution" (Gadsby 1980).

Monod's career is linked to the Pasteur Institute, which he joined in 1931 as an instructor. He was named as its head of laboratory in 1945, the head of the department of cellular biochemistry in 1954, and director general in 1971. In addition to the Nobel Prize, Monod received many other honors and awards, including those for his military service: Chevalier de la Légion d'Honneur, Croix de Guerre, and the Bronze Star Medal. He was a foreign member of the Royal Society and foreign member of the National Academy of Sciences.

Byron Noordewier

REFERENCES AND RECOMMENDED READING

Carroll, Sean B. 2013. *Brave Genius: A Scientist, a Philosopher, and Their Daring Adventures from the French Resistance to the Nobel Prize.* New York: Crown.

Crick, Francis. 1976. "Obituary of Jacques Monod." *Nature* 262:429–30.

Gadsby, W. Peter. 1980. "Jacques Monod and Theistic Evolution." *Creation* 3:18–19.

Monod, Jacques. 1971. *Chance and Necessity: An Essay on the Natural Philosophy of Modern Biology.* New York: Vintage.

Nobel Media. 2014a. "Jacques Monod—Biographical." Nobelprize.org. Accessed November 30, 2015. www.nobelprize.org/nobel_prizes/medicine/laureates/1965/monod-bio.html.

Nobel Media. 2014b. "Jacques Monod—Nobel Lecture: From Enzymatic Adaption to Allosteric Transitions." Nobelprize.org. Accessed November 30, 2015. www.nobelprize.org/nobel_prizes/medicine/laureates/1965/monod-lecture.html.

MORAL PSYCHOLOGY. Moral psychology is the scientific study concerned with the mental, emotional, behavioral, and social processes involved in the formation and expression of an individual's regard for the rights and welfare of others. The roots of the field of moral psychology are often traced to two social scientists, Jean Piaget (1896–1980) and Emile Durkheim (1858–1917), whose work (Durkheim 1925; Piaget 1932) directly addressed the development of moral persons. Two main twentieth-century approaches to moral development grew from these two figures: the cognitive developmental approach based on Piaget's work, and the character development approach based on Durkheim and others.

In the late 1950s, Lawrence Kohlberg (1927–87) emerged as a dominant figure in moral psychology. Building on Piaget's stages of cognitive development, Kohlberg laid out six stages of "moral judgment," in which persons construct increasingly complex and progressively more useful understandings of **morality**. Kohlberg categorized individuals' moral thought into stages based upon how they reasoned about the rights and responsibilities of the characters in various scenarios. Carol Gilligan (1982), among others, criticized Kohlberg for too narrow a focus on justice and for underestimating reasoning about care for the welfare of others (Snarey and Samuelson, 2008).

Even while cognitive developmental psychology has moved away from Piagetian stage theory, moral psychology has continued to utilize Kohlberg's stage theory while recognizing that it does not present a comprehensive picture of moral functioning, particularly in explaining moral action. More complex models have been developed (e.g., James Rest and colleagues' [1999] four-component model, Turiel's [2002] moral domain theory); a focus on the role of empathy, perspective taking, and emotional regulation in moral functioning has emerged (Eisenberg and Strayer 1987); consideration of the role of conscience in moral development has been examined (Konchanska and Aksan 2004); and a turn to more naturalistic models of the moral person has been explored (Walker and Pitts 1998), including the examination of the lives and development of moral exemplars (Colby and Damon 2010). Some have begun to focus on the formation of moral identity as a key for understanding moral action (Blasi 2004).

Recent trends in psychology have begun to exert influence on moral psychology as well. The positive psychology movement has identified a list of key character strengths and virtues that lead to human flourishing (Peterson and Seligman 2002), including moral virtues that place emphasis on the role of values, norms, and social expectations in moral functioning. Findings from evolutionary psychology, **anthropology**, and cognitive psychology have led to a new approach that emphasizes moral **intuition**s as a driving force in moral action (Haidt 2001). In this approach, moral reasoning is secondary (after the fact) to the more rapid gut-feelings (or moral intuitions) of the rightness or wrongness of a situation. Neuropsychology and brain-imaging studies have served to reinforce the role of these rapid, preconscious responses and have shown that moral deliberation and action are complex phenomena involving the coordination of emotional and reasoning processes.

Justin L. Barrett

REFERENCES AND RECOMMENDED READING

Blasi, A. 2004. "Moral Functioning: Moral Understanding and Personality." In *Moral Development, Self, and Identity*, ed. D. K. Lapsley and D. Narvaez. Mahwah, NJ: Lawrence Erlbaum.

Bloom, Paul. 2013. *Just Babies: The Origin of Good and Evil*. New York: Crow.

Colby, A., and W. Damon. 2010. *Some Do Care*. New York: Simon & Schuster.

Durkheim, E. 1925. *Moral Education: A Study in the Theory and Application of the Sociology of Education*. New York: Free Press.

Eisenberg, N., and J. Strayer. 1987. *Empathy and Its Development*. New York: Cambridge University Press.

Gilligan, C. 1982. *In a Different Voice*. Cambridge, MA: Harvard University Press.

Haidt, J. 2001. "The Emotional Dog and Its Rational Tail: A Social Intuitionist Approach to Moral Judgment." *Psychological Review* 108 (4): 814–34. doi:10.1037/0033–295X.108.4.814.

———. 2012. *The Righteous Mind: Why Good People Are Divided by Politics and Religion*. New York: Vintage.

Kochanska, G., and N. Aksan. 2004. "Conscience in Childhood: Past, Present, and Future." *Merrill-Palmer Quarterly* 50 (3): 299–310. doi:10.1353/mpq.2004.0020.

Lapsey, D. K. 1996. *Moral Psychology*. Boulder, CO: Westview.

Nadelhoffer, T., E. Nahmias, and S. Nichols, eds. 2010. *Moral Psychology: Historical and Contemporary Readings*. West Sussex, UK: Blackwell.

Peterson, C., and M. P. Seligman. 2004. *Character Strengths and Virtues: A Handbook and Classification*. New York: American Psychological Association.

Piaget, J. 1932. *The Moral Judgment of the Child*. New York: Free Press.

Rest, J., D. Narvaez, M. J. Bebeau, and S. J. Thoma. 1999. *Postconventional Moral Thinking: A Neo-Kohlbergian Approach*. Mahwah, NJ: Lawrence Erlbaum.

Snarey, John, and Peter Samuelson. 2008. "Moral Education in the Cognitive-Developmental Tradition: Lawrence Kohlberg's Revolutionary Ideas." In *Handbook of Moral and Character Education*, ed. L. Nucci and D. Narvaez, 53–79. New York: Routledge.

Turiel, E. 2002. *The Culture of Morality: Social Development, Context, and Conflict*. Cambridge: Cambridge University Press.

Walker, L. J., and R. C. Pitts. 1998. "Naturalistic Conceptions of Moral Maturity." *Developmental Psychology* 34 (3): 403–19. doi:10.1037/0012–1649.34.3.403.

MORALITY. The term *morality* derives from the Latin *moralis*, meaning customs or mores. Morality refers to beliefs, notions, or opinions about what behavior or decisions are good, bad, right, or wrong. Generally speaking, *ethics* is a synonym.

When used *descriptively*, morality refers to the ethical beliefs or customs of a person, group, or era. So, the sentence "The Callatians cannibalized their elderly dead" merely describes a certain moral state of affairs among an ancient people group without evaluating whether their behavior was right or wrong, good or bad. When used *normatively* or *prescriptively*, morality may be used to offer a prescription of certain beliefs and/or behaviors or assessment of the rightness or wrongness of certain beliefs and/or behaviors. Thus "The Callatian practice of cannibalism was morally abhorrent" states that the behavior of the people group was immoral or wrong.

Moral relativism is the reigning **paradigm** today, not only among academics but especially among the general populace. Moral relativism is the view that notions of right and wrong are matters of opinion—which may differ from person to person and culture to culture—and have no basis in objective reality. Morality, like popular thinking about beauty, is in the eye of the beholder. This view is problematic on any number of levels.

First, certain moral beliefs seem to be universal. The late political scientist James Q. Wilson, for instance, argued that every rational person and every culture shares a moral sensibility, or **intuition**, that the virtues of sympathy, fairness, self-control, and duty are universal moral norms. Gang members, corporate lawyers, Europeans, and Australian Aboriginals all seem to possess the idea that doing one's duty is required and that not doing one's duty, whatever that is, is reprehensible. Granted, the content of one's duty may differ from one person or culture to another, but that one should do one's duty, whatever it is, seems uncontestable across cultures.

Second, if there is no objective morality, the locutions "That is morally right" and "That is morally wrong" are purely matters of etiquette. One could never say that a belief or behavior is truly wrong; one could say that they are different from another person's or culture's beliefs or behavior. Yet the wanton killing of another human being seems to be more than a violation of custom; it is morally blameworthy. Hitler's annihilation of 6 million Jewish persons seems to be more than a breach of proper etiquette. Pedophilia is not only a violation of the Western moral code; it is a violation of an absolute moral law and is, therefore, everywhere and always wrong whether or not a person or culture believes it to be wrong. Rape is the abuse of another human being and not an unfortunate behavior among a certain subculture. These are all examples that point to absolute, objective moral laws, not just mores.

Third, if moral relativism is true, there is no place for moral reformers like Martin Luther King Jr., Desmond Tutu, or even Jesus. If there are no universal moral truths, there is no role for someone to call individuals or society to obey those truths. On a relativist model, morality is merely a social construct or a code of polite society. If this is true, then discrimination based on the color of one's skin cannot be universally wrong. If, however, prejudice based on ethnic or racial identity is a violation of basic human rights, then there must be some objective morality that is grounded in the **nature** of human beings as such. Surely racial justice is not merely a matter of social manners and customs but is part of the fabric of human morality, not to mention biblical **revelation**.

These problems raise the question of the sources of morality. Among nonrelativist morality there are essentially two sources of normative or prescriptive morality. On one hand, natural law theorists argue that moral norms are built into the nature of reality. They are unwritten moral norms, the observance of which contribute to human flourishing. Natural law morality has a long history beginning with **Aristotle** and Aquinas and evolving through **Immanuel Kant**, Hugo Grotius, Samuel Pufendorf, and **John Locke**.

Locke's *Two Treatises on Government* is a classic natural law text. On Locke's view, natural law is not dependent on divine revelation but has its source in human reason and grounded in basic human rights. The United States Declaration of Independence echoes Lockean natural law in its affirmation: "We hold these truths to be self-evident, that all men are created equal, that they are endowed by their Creator with certain unalienable Rights, that among these are Life, Liberty and the pursuit of Happiness." These rights are not discerned through analysis of the Bible, the Qur'an, or other religious documents but are self-evident truths, according to Locke.

More recently, legal theorists like John Finnis and Robert P. George have conceived of natural law that is grounded in certain incommensurable goods, such as life, knowledge, play, aesthetics, sociability or friendship, practical reasonableness, and religion. Finnis defines natural law as "the set of principles of practical reasonableness in ordering human life and human community" for human flourishing (Finnis 2011, 23). A moral life is one in which these goods are properly ordered by individuals and society. The protection of these goods is necessary for a just and moral society.

On the other hand, other nonrelativists find the ground of morality in biblical revelation, not human reason. Among Jewish ethicists, the Torah and the rabbinic interpretations of the Torah are normative. Among Christians, the Old and New Testaments comprise the normative or prescriptive revelation of God's moral will for humanity. The fathers of the early church, such as Clement of Alexandria, Cyprian, and Ambrose authored commentaries on the Bible's ethical teaching. The Reformers, such as **John Calvin** and Martin Luther, though somewhat skeptical of natural law because of the noetic effects of human depravity, found the Scriptures of the Old and New Testaments to be the basis of God's moral demands and the Christian's ethical duty.

General revelation and common grace make it clear that there is a moral law, but the content of that law must be made known through special revelation. So the apostle Paul says in Romans 1:20 (ESV), for example, "[God's] invisible attributes, namely, his eternal power and divine nature, have been clearly perceived, ever since the creation of the world, in the things that have been made." Nevertheless, the apostle spends much of the remainder of his letter to the Roman church outlining God's unique demands for followers of Jesus, including, "Do not be conformed to this world, but be transformed by the renewal of your **mind**, that by testing you may discern what is the will of God, what is good and acceptable and perfect" (12:2 ESV). Knowing God's prescriptive will, therefore, requires study of the biblical text.

One contemporary Christian ethicist, Oliver O'Donovan, has expressed it this way: "The foundations of **Christian ethics** must be evangelical foundations; or, to put it more simply, Christian ethics must arise from the gospel of Jesus Christ. Otherwise, it could not be Christian ethics" (O'Donovan 1994, 11). For O'Donovan and others in this tradition,

Christian morality must be grounded in the revelation of Jesus the Messiah and the canonical Christian Scriptures.

C. Ben Mitchell

REFERENCES AND RECOMMENDED READING

Beckwith, Frances J., and Greg Koukl. 1998. *Relativism: Feet Firmly Planted in Mid-Air.* Grand Rapids: Baker.
Fedler, Kyle D. 2009. *Exploring Christian Ethics: Biblical Foundations for Morality.* Louisville, KY: Westminster John Knox.
Feinberg, John S., and Paul Feinberg. 2010. *Ethics for a Brave New World.* 2nd ed. Wheaton, IL: Crossway.
Finnis, John. 2011. *Natural Law and Natural Rights.* 2nd ed. Oxford: Oxford University Press.
Kreeft, Peter. 1999. *A Refutation of Moral Relativism: Interviews with an Absolutist.* San Francisco: Ignatius.
McQuilkin, Robertson, and Paul Copan. 2014. *An Introduction to Biblical Ethics: Walking in the Way of Wisdom.* Downers Grove, IL: IVP Academic.
Mitchell, C. Ben. 2013. *Ethics and Moral Reasoning: A Student's Guide.* Wheaton, IL: Crossway.
O'Donovan, Oliver. 1994. *Resurrection and the Moral Order: An Outline for Evangelical Ethics.* 2nd ed. Grand Rapids: Eerdmans.
Pojman, Louis P. 2011. *Ethics: Discovering Right from Wrong.* Boston: Cengage Learning, 2011.
Wright, N. T. 2012. *After You Believe: Why Christian Character Matters.* New York: HarperOne.

MORELAND, J. P. James Porter Moreland (1948–) is the distinguished professor of philosophy at Talbot School of Theology, Biola University, in California. He has four earned degrees (a BS in chemistry from the University of Missouri, a ThM from Dallas Theological Seminary, an MA in philosophy from the University of California–Riverside, and a PhD in philosophy from the University of Southern California). His dissertation "Universals and the Qualities of Things: A Defense of Realism" was supervised by Dallas Willard, who was a formative influence on Moreland both as a philosopher and a Christian.

Moreland has coplanted three churches, served with Campus Crusade for Christ for 10 years, and spoken or debated on more than 200 college campuses. For eight years he served as a bioethicist for PersonaCare Nursing Homes, Inc. Although he is a top-flight philosopher, Moreland is well practiced at communicating to lay audiences.

He has made major contributions to several philosophical fields as they touch on the Christian **worldview**. He was a pioneer of the **intelligent design** movement (cf. Moreland 1987, 1989, 1994; Moreland and Nielsen 1993). A critic of **scientism** and **methodological naturalism**, Moreland defends the scientific status of creation science (cf. Moreland 1989, 1994), theistic science, and intelligent design theory

(cf. Moreland 2008). Moreland leans "heavily toward old-earth views" but takes theistic evolution "to be biblically inadequate and less than required by the relevant scientific considerations" (Moreland and Reynolds 1999, 142).

In the field of **natural theology** Moreland defends a wide range of theistic arguments, most notably the kalam argument, the teleological argument (where Moreland's argument from biological **information** prefigures the work of design theorists such as William A. Dembski and **Stephen C. Meyer**), axiological arguments from goodness and beauty, as well as arguments from **religious experience** and from the existence of the human **soul** (cf. Moreland, 1987, 2009a, 2009c, 2009d; Moreland and Craig 2003; Moreland and Nielsen 1993).

Moreland has addressed several issues relevant to ramified natural theology, especially the historicity of the New Testament (cf. Moreland 1987, 1995, 2009c) and the evidence for Jesus's resurrection (cf. Moreland 1987, 1998, 2009c). Moreland argues that the New Testament Gospels were written between the early AD 40s and late AD 50s, while Paul's letters date from AD 49–65. He concludes, "Within no longer than five years after the crucifixion, Jesus was being worshipped by monotheistic Jews as God Almighty," and "a high Christology goes back to Jesus of Nazareth himself" (Moreland 2009c, 109, 117).

In the philosophy of **mind**, Moreland defends (a Thomistic version of) mind-body **dualism** (cf. Moreland 2009b; Moreland and Craig 2003; Moreland and Roe 2000), **libertarian free will** (cf. Moreland and Craig 2003), and a Christian vision of the afterlife (cf. Moreland and Habermas 1998). He also advocates a specifically Christian version of intelligent design **psychology** over against evolutionary psychology (cf. Moreland 2007b).

Moreland brings a philosopher's clarity to the subjects of spiritual formation and Christian discipleship, where he emphasizes the need for Christians to worship God with their minds (cf. Moreland 1997a, 2007a; Moreland and Matlock 2005) and develops an intellectual approach to topics such as **prayer** and supernatural gifts (cf. Moreland 2007a, 2009c).

Peter S. Williams

REFERENCES AND RECOMMENDED READING

Gould, Paul M., and Richard Brian Davis, eds. 2014. *Loving God with Your Mind: Essays in Honor of J. P. Moreland.* Chicago: Moody.
Moreland, J. P. 1987. *Scaling the Secular City: A Defense of Christianity.* Grand Rapids: Baker.

———. 1989. *Christianity and the Nature of Science: A Philosophical Investigation*. Grand Rapids: Baker.

———, ed. 1994. *The Creation Hypothesis: Scientific Evidence for an Intelligent Designer*. Downers Grove, IL: InterVarsity.

———, ed. 1995. *Jesus under Fire: Modern Scholarship Reinvents the Historical Jesus*. Grand Rapids: Zondervan.

———. 1997a. *Love Your God with All Your Mind: The Role of Reason in the Life of the Soul*. Colorado Springs: NavPress.

———. 1997b. "Science, Miracles, Agency Theory and the God-of-the-Gaps." In *In Defence of Miracles: A Comprehensive Case for God's Action in History*, ed. R. Douglas Geivett and Gary R. Habermas. Leicester, UK: Apollos.

———. 1998. "The Explanatory Relevance of Libertarian Agency as a Model of Theistic Design." In *Mere Creation: Science, Faith and Intelligent Design*, ed. William A. Dembski. Downers Grove, IL: InterVarsity.

———. 2007a. *Kingdom Triangle*. Grand Rapids: Zondervan.

———. 2007b. "Intelligent Design and Evolutionary Psychology as Research Programs: A Comparison of Their Most Plausible Specifications." In *Intelligent Design: William A. Dembski and Michael Ruse in Dialogue*, ed. Robert B. Stewart. Minneapolis: Fortress.

———. 2008. "Intelligent Design and the Nature of Science." In *Intelligent Design 101*, ed. H. Wayne House. Grand Rapids: Kregel.

———. 2009a. *Consciousness and the Existence of God: A Theistic Argument*. London: Routledge.

———. 2009b. *The Recalcitrant Imago Dei: Human Persons and the Failure of Naturalism*. London: SCM.

———. 2009c. *The God Question: An Invitation to a Life of Meaning*. Eugene, OR: Harvest House.

———. 2009d. "The Argument from Consciousness." In *The Blackwell Companion to Natural Theology*, ed. William Lane Craig and J. P. Moreland. Oxford: Wiley-Blackwell.

———. 2012. "Four Degrees of Postmodernism." In *Come Let Us Reason: New Essays in Christian Apologetics*, ed. Paul Copan and William Lane Craig. Nashville: B&H Academic.

Moreland, J. P., and William Lane Craig. 2003. *Philosophical Foundations for a Christian Worldview*. Downers Grove, IL: InterVarsity.

Moreland, J. P., and Gary Habermas. 1998. *Beyond Death: Exploring the Evidence for Immortality*. Wheaton, IL: Crossway.

Moreland, J. P., and Mark Matlock. 2005. *Smart Faith: Loving Your God with All Your Mind*. Colorado Springs: Think.

Moreland, J. P., and Kai Nielsen. 1993. *Does God Exist? The Debate between Theists and Atheists*. Amherst, NY: Prometheus.

Moreland, J. P., and Scott B. Rae. 2000. *Body and Soul: Human Nature and the Crisis in Ethics*. Downers Grove, IL: InterVarsity.

Moreland, J. P., and John Mark Reynolds, eds. 1999. *Three Views on Creation and Evolution*. Grand Rapids: Zondervan.

Online Papers

Moreland, J. P. 1996. "Philosophical Apologetics, the Church, and Contemporary Culture." *Journal of the Evangelical Theological Society* 39, no. 1 (March): 123–40. www.etsjets.org/files/JETS-PDFs/39/39–1/39–1-pp123–140_JETS.pdf.

———. 2007. "The Historicity of the New Testament." Bethinking. www.bethinking.org/is-the-bible-reliable/the-historicity-of-the-new-testament.

———. "How Evangelicals Became Over-committed to the Bible and What Can Be Done about It." Accessed January 25, 2015. http://indiegospel.net/data/media/0/0/Ning_Media/blogs/1–1000/490-BibliolatryOvercommittmenttotheBible.pdf.

Websites

J. P. Moreland's Facebook page. www.facebook.com/pages/J-P-Moreland/118578028208045?sk=timeline&ref=page_internal.

J. P. Moreland's Talbot faculty page. www.talbot.edu/faculty/profile/jp_moreland/.

J. P. Moreland's website. www.jpmoreland.com.

Audio

"Apologist Interview: J. P. Moreland." 2010. Apologetics 315. September 6. www.apologetics315.com/2010/09/apologist-interview-jp-moreland.html.

Video

Williams, Peter S. "J. P. Moreland." YouTube. www.youtube.com/playlist?list=PLQhh3qcwVEWjPZDXV4NVvh68QwYeKY25F.

MORRIS, HENRY M. Henry M. Morris (1918–2006) is widely considered to be the father of the modern twentieth-century creationist movement. Morris is probably best known for the *Genesis Flood* (1961), a book coauthored with Dr. **John C. Whitcomb** that advocated **young-earth creationism** and flood **geology**, and for the **Institute for Creation Research** (ICR) that he founded in 1970. *The Genesis Flood* went through 29 printings, sold more than 200,000 copies, and was widely accepted by the evangelical community but strongly ridiculed by mainstream academia, the **American Scientific Affiliation**, and others. *The Genesis Flood*, ICR, and related material inspired many others to study, research, and defend or attack Morris's position, and also motivated the creation of organizations such as **Answers in Genesis** and the **National Center for Science Education**.

Henry Morris was born on October 6, 1918, grew up in Texas before and during the Great Depression, and later earned a BS with distinction in civil engineering from Rice University in 1939. He began his first thorough study of the biblical creation story after graduation while working as an engineer for the International Boundary and Water Commission. Morris was initially open to the idea of an old earth and evolution but could not reconcile these assertions with his reading of Scripture. He ultimately reconciled Scripture and science after being strongly influenced by writings by two self-taught creationists, **George McCready Price** and Harry Rimmer. Morris concluded that the biblical creation occurred in six days, the earth is young, and the appearance of the earth's age is primarily due to "flood geology."

Morris earned his MS and PhD in hydraulic engineering from the University of Minnesota in 1948 and 1950. Morris's impressive academic career began as an instructor at Rice University (1942–46), continued as an instructor and assistant professor at the University of Minnesota (1946–51), as a professor and department head of civil engineering at the University of Louisiana at Lafayette (1951–56) and acting dean of engineering (1956), as a professor of applied science in 1957 at Southern Illinois University, and finally as professor of hydraulic engineering and chairman for the Department of Civil Engineering at the Virginia Polytechnic

Institute and State University (Virginia Tech). Morris also attended two National Science Foundation Summer Institutes in 1959 and 1963.

He was granted honorary degrees from Bob Jones University and Liberty University, authored numerous technical journal articles and encyclopedia articles, as well as a graduate textbook, *Applied Hydraulics in Engineering* (1963; second edition with James M. Wiggert in 1972), and directed four PhD dissertations and 12 master's theses in engineering.

Morris's first apologetics book, *That You Might Believe*, impressed many, including theologians and scholars, and elevated Morris's status within the evangelical community, making it natural for him to respond to the publication of **Bernard Ramm**'s *The Christian View of Science and Scripture* (1954), which ridiculed the young-earth position and flood geology. *The Genesis Flood*, written by Dr. Morris and Dr. John C. Whitcomb, became the catalyst for the modern creation science movement. In 1963 Morris and others founded the Creation Research Society, and Morris continued his creationist writing and speaking, causing his influence to grow further. Tensions grew during the 1960s at Virginia Tech between Morris, certain faculty, and the dean of engineering, leading Morris to take a paid sabbatical leave and eventually a voluntary resignation that allowed him to focus full-time on creation research.

Morris cofounded Christian Heritage College (now San Diego Christian College) with Timothy LaHaye and created the Creation Science Research Center, which was reorganized as the Institute for Creation Research (ICR) in 1970. He was also the first president of the Transnational Association of Christian Schools and Colleges, an accrediting agency. Morris influenced culture, theologians, politicians, scientists, legislation, and litigations. Morris's best-known public debate was with **Kenneth Miller** at Brown University on April 10, 1981. ICR normally left debating in the hands of **Duane T. Gish**.

The scholar died on February 25, 2006, and was survived by his wife of 66 years, Mary Louise Morris, and five children, 17 grandchildren, and nine great-grandchildren.

Jonathan Fisher

REFERENCES AND RECOMMENDED READING

Morris, Henry M. (1946) 1978. *That You Might Believe*. 2nd ed. Chicago: Good Books.
Morris, Henry M., and John C. Whitcomb. 2011. *The Genesis Flood: The Biblical Record and Its Scientific Implications*. Phillipsburg, NJ: P&R.
NCSE. "Creationism Controversy." National Center for Science and Education. http://ncse.com/creationism/general/miller-morris-debate–1981.
Numbers, Ronald L. 1993. *The Creationists*. Berkeley: University of California Press.
Ramm, Bernard. 1978. *The Christian View of Science and Scripture*. Grand Rapids: Eerdmans.
Rudoren, J. 2006. "Henry M. Morris, 87, Dies; A Theorist of Creationism." *New York Times*. March 4. http://query.nytimes.com/gst/fullpage.html?res=9507EEDC1431F937A35750C0A9609C8B63.
Schudel, M. 2006. "Henry Morris: Intellectual Father of 'Creation Science.'" *Washington Post*. February 28. www.washingtonpost.com/wp-dyn/content/article/2006/02/28/AR2006022801716_pf.htm.

MULTIVERSE. A finite age of the universe (just under 14 billion years) and a finite **speed of light** (186,000 miles per second) set strong, fundamental limits on the farthest distances that humanity can possibly see. Cosmic microwave background radiation (CMBR) observed by scientists travels to Earth from regions approaching those fundamental limits. As scientists seek to understand the CMBR and other measurements of the observable region of the universe, their explanations increasingly include the existence of physical realms beyond those limits: a *multiverse*. While prominent in scientific explanations of the cosmos, the multiverse also affects philosophical and apologetic thinking.

While the term enjoys a more recent origin (within the last 150 years), the concept of the multiverse (multiple universes) extends into antiquity, as seen in many of the world's religions, including Christianity. In the last hundred years, scientific explanations of the universe have often employed a multiverse, but the character and nature of the multiverse have changed dramatically. Prior to the twentieth century, most scientific thought assumed the existence of only this physical universe. The advent and development of **big bang** cosmology during the past hundred years brought different conceptions of the multiverse. For example, as scientists sought to reconcile an expanding universe with the long-held notion of an eternal universe, they advanced the oscillating universe model, which postulated a multiverse resulting from an ongoing series of expansions and contractions. Current multiverse models usually invoke some aspect of inflation or quantum mechanics (or both).

Cosmologists classify multiverse models differently. For example, Brian Greene delineates nine separate classes while Max Tegmark posits only four. Regardless of the classification scheme, only three have a relatively close tether to actual measurements.

A Really Large Universe

Within the limits of human observation, evidence strongly points to an epoch of inflationary expansion early in the history of the universe. Regardless of how inflation might have worked, the existence of an inflationary epoch necessitates that the space, time, matter, and energy of the universe must extend far beyond those limits. This region beyond observation represents the least controversial form of a multiverse. Although it is technically correct to call this scenario a *multiverse* (these regions exist beyond our observable universe), scientists often reserve the term for the more radical ideas below.

Inflationary Bubble Universes

Scientists continue to seek understanding of how inflation might have worked in a way that explains the measurements of the observable universe. Virtually every reasonable model of inflation exhibits a few key characteristics. First, some "substance" (typically a scalar field that produces a false vacuum) drives the exponential expansion required for inflation. That substance decays to a lower energy state at some location that grows larger over time (like a bubble). Many other bubbles form via the same process. To reproduce scientists' observations, this universe must reside inside one of these bubbles; consequently, other universes of the multiverse exist inside the other bubbles.

The Quantum Multiverse

Quantum mechanics introduces scientific ideas that seem bizarre but enjoy strong experimental validation. One such notion is that quantum particles simultaneously exist in a superposition of many different states. When scientists calculate the expected results of an experiment, they perform mathematical operations on a wave function (that describes the superposition of states) and get a set of numbers that specify the probabilities of measuring the different outcomes of the experiment. So an experiment takes the superposition of states inherent in the wave function (which scientists cannot measure) and leads to a unique measurement of only one state. One interpretation of the reality behind this sequence argues that the experiment results in the manifestation of all the different states, but humans see only one outcome in this universe. The other outcomes manifest in other branches of the multiverse.

No known experimental or observational evidence demands the existence of a multiverse, although the most natural explanation of the cosmology data directly implies the existence of the "really large multiverse." In contrast, the "quantum multiverse" depends on a particular interpretation of quantum mechanics, but many other interpretations explain all the data without a multiverse. Similarly, the "inflationary bubble multiverse," while reasonable, relies on huge extrapolations—both incomplete and possibly incorrect—from known **physics**.

Multiverse Implications

Tentative evidence from quantum mechanics, inflationary big bang cosmology, **string theory**, and more provide enough plausibility that multiverse models belong in the arena of scientific investigation. The current scientific ambiguities in assessing multiverse models impact apologetic arguments for God's existence. Instead of focusing on the existence of a multiverse, the key question becomes, "Do multiverse models fit more comfortably in a Christian, theistic **worldview** or in an atheistic worldview of strict **naturalism**?" Three major areas where these two worldviews differ relate to the origin of the universe (**cosmological argument**), design in the universe (teleological argument), and **consciousness** (**argument from reason**).

Initially, multiverse models seemed to remove the basis for the second premise of the cosmological argument—namely, that the universe began to exist. For example, in inflationary big bang multiverses, this universe still has a beginning, but the mechanism for inflation produced new universes forever into the future. Cosmologists thought this process might extend forever into the past as well. If true, our universe would begin, but the multiverse would be eternal. Research eventually demonstrated that any inflationary multiverse model capable of explaining the universe must *also* have a beginning (Grossman 2012), further strengthening the cosmological argument for God's existence. Most cosmologists now agree that the physical realm (not just the universe, but the whole multiverse) began to exist.

Much evidence used in support of the teleological argument focuses on critical conditions for life in this universe that exhibit seemingly improbable fine-tuning (see **Fine-Tuning of the Universe and Solar System**). However, statistical arguments require assessing the probabilities *and* the sample size. The enormous increase in sample size provided by multiverse models (argued to be infinite in some cases) virtually ensures that any event with nonzero **probability** will happen somewhere. However, the large sample associated with the multiverse means that other improbable forms of life (such as Boltzmann brains—self-aware entities arising from the **quantum fluctuation**s occurring throughout space, *Matrix*-style simulations, etc.) also happen.

The possibility of other life forms changes the apologetic

emphasis from trying to explain the rarity of human life to one of explaining why humanity is not one of these other forms—especially since these other possibilities seem increasingly more common. Cosmologists work to construct multiverse models that eliminate the existence of these other life forms, but they must fine-tune the models to accomplish the task. Developing a suitable mechanism for generating a multiverse seems to require fine-tuning (Collins 2009). Consequently, whether the multiverse exists or not, the physical realm seems to be designed for humanity.

Multiverse models affect arguments that rely on humanity's rationale for trusting its ability to reason by *adding more chances* of assembling all the necessary components. Yet philosophers and scientists seeking to understand this ability describe a *hard or intractable problem of consciousness*—the difficulty (if not impossibility) of explaining human consciousness in terms of strictly physical processes. In light of the lack of such a mechanism, adding more **chance**s to assemble physical materials does not help to explain consciousness.

In sum, even if a type of multiverse exists, the latest research indicates it *began* to exist, which demonstrates evidence of design for humanity and seems to require a **mind** (that exists apart from the multiverse) to explain consciousness. Rather than supporting the case for an atheistic, naturalistic worldview, these results strongly argue for a theistic, supernatural worldview akin to Judeo-Christianity.

Jeff Zweerink

REFERENCES AND RECOMMENDED READING

Collins, Robin. 2009. "The Teleological Argument: An Exploration of the Fine-Tuning of the Universe." In *The Blackwell Companion to Natural Theology*, ed. W. L. Craig and J. P. Moreland. Oxford: Wiley-Blackwell.
Greene, Brian. 2001. *The Hidden Reality*. New York: Knopf.
Grossman, Lisa. 2012. "Why Physicists Can't Avoid a Creation Event." *New Scientist* 2847 (January 11): 6–7. www.newscientist.com/article/mg21328474.400-why-physicists-cant-avoid-a-creation-event.html?.
Krauss, Lawrence. 2012. *A Universe from Nothing*. New York: Free Press.
Tegmark, Max. 2014. *Our Mathematical Universe*. New York: Knopf.
Vilenkin, Alex. 2006. *Many Worlds in One*. New York: Hill and Wang.

MURPHY, NANCEY. Nancey Murphy (1951–) is a Christian philosopher who has contributed to both general discussions of the relationship between theology and science and detailed consideration of the relationship between Christianity and **neuroscience**. Murphy has argued that mid-twentieth-century developments in Anglo-American philosophy mark the beginning of a new postmodern era in thought (Murphy 1997). One of the central shifts in this purported transition is from modern foundationalism and **reductionism** to holism. Knowledge is no longer to be understood as a building constructed from beliefs ultimately resting on elusive but stable, noninferential foundations. This Cartesian picture is replaced by Quine's web of interdependent beliefs, within which each element depends on the whole that it partly constitutes.

In the case of scientific knowledge, the elements of the web are observations and experimental results, and the wholes are research programs or **paradigm**s (Kuhn 1996; Lakatos 1970). Scientific progress thus involves the ongoing development and replacement of these structures. Murphy takes **physicalism** to be the core ontological commitment of a progressive scientific research program. However, she writes, "If free will is an illusion and the highest of human intellectual and cultural achievements can … be counted as the mere outworking of the laws of **physics**, this is utterly devastating to our ordinary understanding of ourselves, and of course to theological accounts, as well" (Murphy 1998, 131).

Devastation is avoided, however, since in Murphy's version of nonreductive physicalism (emergent **monism**), the *ontological* reduction of persons to entirely physical entities need not entail the *causal* reduction of mental processes to those of physics and chemistry. Her antireductionist perspective entails that as one moves up through the hierarchy of sciences, one encounters novel entities from atoms all the way to conscious organisms. Such emergent entities are wholly constituted by elements described at lower levels while possessing distinctive, irreducible properties. For example, the shape of a paper airplane is an irreducible global property of the plane. This global property also determines the plane's aerodynamic performance and so plays a causal role in its behavior. This is a "downward" causal influence with respect to the parts of which the plane is composed, but it does not intervene in causal processes at lower levels.

Taking human mental properties to be just such global physical properties, Murphy's recent work has focused on accounting for such features as moral responsibility and mental **causation** in greater detail (Murphy 2006; Murphy and Brown 2007).

Murphy also considers the consequences of her postmodern holist view in theology (e.g., the relationship between liberalism and fundamentalism), ethics (e.g., irreducibility of ethics to biology), and the question of **divine action** in a physical world, which Murphy takes to be the ultimate case of downward causation (Murphy 2011; Murphy et al 2008). Murphy's perspective remains controversial. For example, the rejection of Cartesian foundationalism need not require the acceptance of holism (compare the modest foundationalism espoused by Reformed epistemologists like **Alvin Plantinga** and Nicholas Wolterstorff), and it is not clear that downward causation can be coherently and adequately understood in monistic terms.

Jonathan Loose

REFERENCES AND RECOMMENDED READING

Kuhn, Thomas S. 1996. *The Structure of Scientific Revolutions.* 3rd ed. Chicago: University of Chicago Press.

Lakatos, Imre. 1970. "Falsification and the Methodology of Scientific Research Programmes." In *Criticism and the Growth of Knowledge*, ed. Imre Lakatos and Ian Musgrave. Cambridge: Cambridge University Press.

Murphy, Nancey C. 1997. *Anglo-American Postmodernity: Philosophical Perspectives on Science, Religion and Ethics.* Boulder, CO: Westview.

———. 1998. "Nonreductive Physicalism: Philosophical Issues." In *Whatever Happened to the Soul? Scientific and Theological Portraits of Human Nature*, ed. Warren S. Brown, H. Newton Malony, and Nancey C. Murphy, 127–48. Minneapolis: Fortress.

———. 2006. *Bodies and Souls, or Spirited Bodies? Current Issues in Theology.* Cambridge: Cambridge University Press.

———. 2011. "Divine Action, Emergence and Scientific Explanation." In *The Cambridge Companion to Science and Religion*, 244–59. Cambridge: Cambridge University Press.

Murphy, Nancey C., and Warren S. Brown. 2007. *Did My Neurons Make Me Do It? Philosophical and Neurobiological Perspectives on Moral Responsibility and Free Will.* Oxford: Oxford University Press.

Murphy, Nancey C., Robert John Russell, and W. R. Stoeger. 2008. *Scientific Perspectives on Divine Action: Twenty Years of Challenge and Progress.* Rome: Vatican Observatory Press; Notre Dame, IN: Notre Dame Press.

MYSTERY. Perhaps appropriately, the notion of mystery is itself shrouded in ambiguity. Basically, it refers to the way certain realities escape merely rational understanding. But how these realities make such an escape, and how, if at all, they may be otherwise grasped, and what the significance of "mysteriousness" is for the intellect and for life—all of these questions can be construed quite differently within different contexts.

In popular usage—including that of professionals and journalists communicating scientific results to a wider audience—"mystery" often describes that which is not known or understood now, but the designation does not necessarily exclude comprehension in principle. To speak of the mystery or mysteries of Stonehenge or of **consciousness** is to acknowledge gaps, possibly very large and fundamental, in our grasp of these things at the level of natural causes, dynamics, and narratives; but these gaps might well be filled in eventually, given sufficient funding, insight, or effort. Mysteries are to be solved, after all.

The notion of "mystery" in the biblical and theological traditions, however, is more complex. In the New Testament, *mystçrion* often refers to the eschatological fulfillment of God's eternal purposes in Christ, which has been disclosed to—thus, in a sense, understood by—human beings, but which is not now or ever subject to human investigation, and so must be revealed by God and truly known only in the consummation (as in Eph. 3). "Mystery" also came to be applied to significant events in the life of Christ and to the sacramental axis of the church's liturgical existence.

When ambiguity threatens, clarification may be all that is necessary to avoid misinterpretation. Yet at a deeper level, the richer notion of mystery raises questions about what it means that some truths are beyond human understanding in principle; whether and how human beings can nevertheless know that which transcends the rational; and the reality and nature of divine **revelation**. "The Christian vision of things affirms the ultimate coherence of reality, so that the opacity of existence reflects a mystery, not an incoherence" (McGrath 2003, 98).

Maurice Lee

REFERENCES AND RECOMMENDED READING

Bornkamm, Gunther. 1964. "*Mystçrion.*" In *Theological Dictionary of the New Testament*, ed. Gerhard Kittel, 4:802–28. Grand Rapids: Eerdmans.

Catechism of the Catholic Church. 1997. 2nd ed. Vatican City State: Libreria Editrice Vaticana.

McGrath, Alister E. 2003. *A Scientific Theology.* Vol. 3. *Theory.* Grand Rapids: Eerdmans.

MYSTERY OF LIFE'S ORIGIN, THE. Published in 1984 by Charles Thaxton, **Walter Bradley**, and Roger Olsen, *The Mystery of Life's Origin: Reassessing Current Theories* is a scientific book that critiques prominent theories of the chemical **origin of life** and served as a seminal work early in the **intelligent design** (ID) movement.

The authors had strong technical credentials. Thaxton earned his PhD in physical chemistry from Iowa State University and did postdoctoral work at Harvard and Brandeis Universities. Bradley received a PhD in materials science from the University of Texas, Austin, and spent more than 25 years as a professor of mechanical engineering at Texas A&M and Baylor Universities. Olsen held a PhD in geochemistry from Colorado School of Mines, where he taught before becoming a research chemist with Rockwell International.

Originally published by Philosophical Library (which has published titles by more than 20 Nobel laureates, including

Albert Einstein), the book enjoyed favorable reviews in prestigious venues (Dose 1988; Jekel 1985) and became a bestselling college-level text on chemical evolution. As a review in *Yale Journal of Biology and Medicine* stated:

> To all who share the comfortable assumption that the scientific problems of abiogenesis are mostly resolved, this book will come as a real surprise. The authors have developed a critique of current hypotheses that is a synthesis of the concerns of many working in the field, combined with their own additional contributions.... The volume as a whole is devastating to a relaxed acceptance of current theories of abiogenesis ... and is strongly recommended to anyone interested in the problem of chemical and biological origins. (Jekel 1985)

The scientific problems surveyed include, among others, the following:

- Difficulties achieving prebiotic synthesis given the nonreducing composition of earth's early atmosphere
- "Destructive" chemical processes that would break down prebiotic organics
- The "continued shortening of the **time**" available for the origin of life on earth
- The fact that "True living cells are extraordinarily complex, well-orchestrated dynamic structures containing enzymes, **DNA**, phospholipids, carbohydrates, etc., to which so-called protocells bear only a superficial resemblance."
- The "observational limit" of "what has been accomplished in the laboratory by natural processes," and the necessity of "investigator interference" when "constructing biospecific macromolecules." (Thaxton et al. 1984)

Though written more than 30 years ago, many problems highlighted in the book persist. In 2007 Harvard chemist George Whitesides admitted he has "no idea" how "life emerged spontaneously from mixtures of molecules in the prebiotic Earth" (Whitesides 2007), and a 2009 paper in *Complexity* acknowledged, "Many different ideas are competing and none is available to provide a sufficiently plausible root to the first living organisms (Schuster 2009).

The book not only critiqued chemical theories of life's origins, but also offered possible solutions, including: (1) discovery of new natural laws, (2) **panspermia**, (3) directed panspermia, (4) a "creating intelligence within the cosmos," and (5) a "creating intelligence beyond the cosmos"

(Thaxton et al. 1984, p. 196). By proposing that life "can be accomplished only through what **Michael Polanyi** has called 'a profoundly informative intervention'" (Thaxton et al. 1984, p. 185), the authors set the stage for ID theorists who developed these arguments further, arguing that the complex and specified **information** in life can arise only through intelligent design (Dembski 1998; Meyer 2009).

Casey Luskin

REFERENCES AND RECOMMENDED READING

Dembski, William. 1998. *The Design Inference: Eliminating Chance through Small Probabilities.* Cambridge, MA: Cambridge University Press.

Dose, Klaus. 1988. "The Origin of Life: More Questions Than Answers." *Interdisciplinary Science Reviews* 13.

Jekel, James. 1985. "Review of *The Mystery of Life's Origin: Reassessing Current Theories.*" *Yale Journal of Biological Medicine* 58:407–8.

Meyer, Stephen C. 2009. *Signature in the Cell: DNA and the Evidence for Intelligent Design.* New York: HarperOne.

Schuster, Peter. 2009. "Origins of Life: Concepts, Data, and Debates." *Complexity* 15.

Thaxton, Charles, Walter Bradley, and Roger Olsen. 1984. *The Mystery of Life's Origin: Reassessing Current Theories.* Dallas: Lewis and Stanley.

Whitesides. George. 2007. "Revolutions in Chemistry: Priestley Medalist George M. Whitesides' Address." *Chemical and Engineering News* 85:12–17.

MYTHOLOGY. A myth is a story "about something significant" (Segal 2004, 5). It isn't necessarily the "false story" of colloquial usage. Although mythology doesn't map neatly onto modern conceptions of science, it can't be dismissed as mere fantasy or falsified science. **William Lane Craig** reports, "Whereas nineteenth-century scholars looked at ancient creation myths as a sort of crude proto-science, contemporary scholars tend more to the view that such stories were taken figuratively, not literally, by the people who told them" (Craig 2014, 39). As Robert A. Segal concludes, "Myths serve as *guides* to the world rather than as *depictions* of the world" (Segal 2004, 139).

Somewhat as the highly abstract London Underground Map guides people through London's underground system, a myth provides a narrative that helps people to understand themselves within the framework of a given **worldview** in imaginative and intellectual terms. As such, myths articulate truth-claims that can be critically assessed. For example, if we compare creation myths from ancient Babylon, China, Egypt, and Greece with the biblical creation myth, we discover points of similarity and difference:

- In all these myths there's a development from a cosmic order without life to one with life.

- As with the Babylonian and some Egyptian myths, the Bible attributes this development to divine intentionality rather than to nothing but natural processes.
- The Babylonian and biblical myths both represent the prelife cosmos as "water."
- The Babylonian and biblical myths both reference a divinity hovering over the "water."
- In the Bible (as in Egyptian cosmogony), the cosmic order *per se* (and not merely its present form with life) has a clear "beginning" (cf. Craig 2001; Craig and Copan 2004).
- Only the biblical myth is presented within a context of (trinitarian) monotheism rather than polytheism.
- Only in the Bible is the *existence and form* of the whole cosmic order, past and present, explained with reference to the intentional activity of an infinite, self-existent, wholly supernatural, personal divinity who transcends and created the entire cosmic order.
- Thus only within the biblical myth is reality as a whole clearly not a brute fact (because God, the uncreated Creator, isn't a brute fact).

Having carefully abstracted the worldviews of creation myths from the figurative language in which they are expressed, we can assess these worldviews in light of contemporary philosophical and scientific thinking. Philosophically, the Leibnizian form of the **cosmological argument** shows that we need more than a "brute fact" ultimate explanation, and that God is the necessarily existent foundation of reality (cf. Craig 2008).

Philosophically and scientifically we have good reason to think that the cosmos had a beginning a finite time ago (cf. Craig 2008; Holder 2013). As the atheist cosmologist Alexander Vilenkin states, "All the evidence we have says that the universe had a beginning" (Grossman 2012, 7).

So-called kalam versions of the cosmological argument build on the premise of a finite cosmic past to argue for God as the uncaused cause of physical reality (cf. Craig 2008; Williams 2013). Scientifically we see that the primeval cosmic order emerging from the **big bang** exhibited a "finely tuned" structure necessary but not sufficient for the **emergence** of life (cf. Abel et al. 2011; Craig 2008; Holder 2013; Meyer 2009). Likewise, water is a necessary but insufficient precondition for life. Taken together, these modern observations, arguments, and theories contradict the creation worldviews of Babylon, China, Egypt, and Greece but confirm the creation worldview of the Bible.

Peter S. Williams

REFERENCES AND RECOMMENDED READING

Abel, David L., Kurk K. Dunston, and Donald Johnson. 2011. *The First Gene: The Birth of Programming, Messaging and Formal Control*. New York: Longview Academic.

Craig, William Lane. 2001. *Time and Eternity: Exploring God's Relationship to Time*. Wheaton, IL: Crossway.

———. 2008. *Reasonable Faith: Christian Truth and Apologetics*. 3rd ed. Wheaton, IL: Crossway.

———. 2014. Interviewed in *Science and Religion: 5 Questions*, ed. Gregg D. Caruso. New York: Automatic.

Craig, William Lane, and Paul Copan. 2004. *Creation Out of Nothing: A Biblical, Philosophical, and Scientific Exploration*. Grand Rapids: Baker Academic.

Grant, Edward. 2007. *A History of Natural Philosophy: From the Ancient World to the Nineteenth Century*. Cambridge: Cambridge University Press.

Grossman, Lisa. 2012. "Death of the Eternal Cosmos." *New Scientist* 2847 (January 14): 6–7.

Holder, Rodney. 2013. *Big Bang, Big God: A Universe Designed for Life?* Oxford: Lion.

McGrath, Alister. 2014. "The Concept of Myth in Lewis' Thought." In Alister McGrath, *The Intellectual World of C. S. Lewis*. Oxford: Wiley-Blackwell.

Meyer, Stephen C. 2009. *Signature in the Cell: DNA and the Evidence for Intelligent Design*. New York: HarperOne.

Sedley, David. 2009. *Creationism and Its Critics in Antiquity*. Berkeley: University of California Press.

Segal, Robert A. 2004. *Myth: A Very Short Introduction*. Oxford: Oxford University Press.

Williams, Peter S. 2013. *A Faithful Guide to Philosophy: An Introduction to the Love of Wisdom*. Milton Keynes, UK: Paternoster.

———. 2014. "Comparing Creation Myths." Damaris. www.damaris.org/podcasts/897.

N

NAGEL, ERNEST. Ernest Nagel (1901–85) was one of the most influential philosophers of science of the mid-twentieth century, and surely the most wide-ranging, working in many areas, from the logical foundations of **mathematics** and the philosophy of **quantum physics** and relativity, to the methodology of the **social sciences** and historical **explanation**.

Born in 1901 in what later became Czechoslovakia, Nagel immigrated with his parents to the United States a decade later. He attended the City University of New York and earned his PhD from Columbia University in 1931, studying under John Dewey and Morris Cohen. His academic career, spent almost entirely at Columbia, spanned the analytical **philosophy of science** from the heyday of **logical positivism** in the 1930s to the debates about **objectivity** that emerged in the 1960s, and to the close attention to the particularities of the various sciences characterizing recent philosophy of science.

Skeptical of comprehensive theory building, Nagel was a penetrating critic of highly abstract accounts of inductive reasoning, **probability**, and **confirmation**. He was, however, a defender of the fundamental unity of reason, not just across the sciences, but in all human endeavors, as the sole route to knowledge. His musings on the historical and sociological constraints on scientific objectivity prefigure ideas to which **Thomas Kuhn** brought widespread attention decades later in *The Structure of Scientific Revolutions*, yet Nagel was an unflagging champion of the power of rational, empirical methods to discern objective truth. In Nagel's view, this austere naturalistic **epistemology** limited knowledge to the physical world and precluded rational belief in God, the **soul**, or a purpose for the universe.

Writing in periodicals like *The New Republic* and *Saturday Review*, Nagel advocated the application—on an experimental basis, of course—of **scientific method**s to social and political problems, manifesting a degree of confidence that would seem naive today. *An Introduction to Logic and the Scientific Method*, coauthored with his mentor Morris Cohen, was a widely used text for years. *Gödel's Proof* (coauthored with James Newman) still introduces nonspecialists to the famous incompleteness results.

Nagel's magnum opus, *The Structure of Science*, a near-encyclopedic examination of science explanation, defends and elaborates the deductive-nomological model as the basis of the logical unity of the sciences. It is richly informed by scientific detail and connections to broader philosophical issues. Its chapter on reduction is the definitive statement of the classic view. The book's discussion of the integration of teleological explanation in biology with the rest of science, together with its later elaboration in Nagel's Dewey Lectures, published in *Teleology Revisited*, is a seminal exploration of the issue. *The Structure of Science* similarly portrays the methods of the social sciences as essentially those of the physical sciences.

Recognitions Nagel received late in life include election to the National Academy of Sciences, an honor rarely accorded nonscientists. He died in 1985.

Donald Wacome

REFERENCES AND RECOMMENDED READING

Nagel, Ernest. 1954. *Sovereign Reason and Other Studies in the Philosophy of Science.* Glencoe, IL: Free Press.
———. 1955. "Naturalism Reconsidered." *Proceedings and Addresses of the American Philosophical Association* 28:5–17.
———. 1956. *Logic without Metaphysics and Other Essays in the Philosophy of Science.* Glencoe, IL: Free Press.
———. 1961. *The Structure of Science: Problems in the Logic of Scientific Explanation.* New York: Harcourt, Brace, World.
———. 1979. *Teleology Revisited and Other Essays in the Philosophy and History of Science.* New York: Columbia University Press.
Nagel, Ernest, and Morris R. Cohen. 1934. *An Introduction to Logic and Scientific Method.* New York: Harcourt, Brace, World.
Nagel, Ernest, and James R. Newman. 1958. *Gödel's Proof.* New York: New York University Press.

NAGEL, THOMAS. Thomas Nagel (1937–) is professor emeritus of philosophy and law at New York University. He was born to Jewish parents in Belgrade, Yugoslavia (Serbia). He lived in the United States from 1939 onward, and he became a naturalized US citizen in 1944. He received his doctoral degree in philosophy from Harvard in 1963. He specializes in political philosophy, ethics, **epistemology**, and philosophy of **mind**.

Nagel is an atheist who argues, in his well-known 1971 essay "The Absurd" (Nagel [1971] 1979) that the absurdity of human life, as he understands it, is a nonremovable feature of human existence that cannot be eliminated by adopting a different view of the world. This is contrary to the position of Christian apologists who hold that the absurdity of life without God is a reason for rejecting atheism.

However, Nagel has also been a consistent critic of philosophical **materialism** and, in particular, its attempt to house the mind within a materialist framework. This began with his essay "What Is It Like to Be a Bat?" (Nagel 1974). In that essay he argues that any third-person perspective on a person, such as might be provided by natural science, invariably leaves out the first-person perspective of that person. This argument was prefigured in **C. S. Lewis**'s essay "Meditation in a Toolshed," in which Lewis distinguished between "looking at" and "looking along" and claimed that a systematic preference for "looking at" as opposed to "looking along" breaks down when it comes to considering our own thinking, and consistently applied it would give us nothing to think about (Lewis 1970, 212–15).

In his book *The View from Nowhere* (1986), Nagel argues that **natural selection** only explains how creatures with vision or reason will survive, not how vision or reasoning are possible. We have many capacities, such as the capacity for higher **mathematics**, which would not have been any use to us in the hunter-gatherer stage. He thinks that the mere increase in the size of the brain would not be sufficient to explain these rational capacities. He does not accept a religious explanation of this, however, but simply says he has no explanation.

In *The Last Word* (1997), Nagel maintains that a Darwinian explanation of our faculties is "laughably inadequate"; he mentions a theological explanation and then claims that some things can't be explained because they have to enter into every explanation. In the same work, Nagel mentions the "fear of religion" (to which he himself confesses) as a reason for the overuse of Darwinian explanations and the insistence on materialism in explaining the mind.

In *Mind and Cosmos* (2012), he says that **intelligent design** (ID) advocates such as **Michael Behe** and **Stephen Meyer** do not deserve the harsh criticism that they have received. However, he does not argue for intelligent design. He offers an alternative to both design and Darwin, which is the existence of an inherent **teleology** in the natural world. Interestingly enough, this position seems to have an Aristotelian flavor to it, and many Aristotelian-Thomist philosophers have taken this position as a response to materialism, developing theistic arguments based on it. Nagel has been criticized by some for giving aid and comfort to ID advocates, but he is not one of their supporters.

Victor Reppert

REFERENCES AND RECOMMENDED READING

Lewis, C. S. 1970. "Meditation in a Toolshed." In *God in the Dock*. Grand Rapids: Eerdmans.

Nagel, Thomas. 1974. "What Is It Like to Be a Bat?" *Philosophical Review* 83, no. 4 (October): 435–50.

———. (1971) 1979. "The Absurd." In Thomas Nagel, *Mortal Questions*, 11–23. Cambridge: Cambridge University Press. Originally published in *Journal of Philosophy* (October).

———. 1986. *The View from Nowhere*. New York: Oxford University Press.

———. 1997. *The Last Word*. New York: Oxford University Press.

———. 2012. *Mind and Cosmos*. New York: Oxford University Press.

NATIONAL CENTER FOR SCIENCE EDUCATION (NCSE).

The National Center for Science Education (NCSE) is a 501(c)(3) not-for-profit organization based in Oakland, California. Founded in 1981 with the objective of the "defense of education in evolutionary theory," it later adopted other scientific causes, such as teaching the science of global **climate change**. The NCSE provides **information** and resources to schools, educators, parents, and others to promote quality public school education while maintaining a religiously neutral community united by the conviction to promote good science education based on science and the **scientific method**.

The NCSE grew out of the grassroots organization started in 1980 by Stanley L. Weinberg, a veteran high school teacher in New York and Iowa. Weinberg earned a bachelor's degree in biology from City College of New York (cum laude, 1933) and was inducted into Phi Beta Kappa, had graduate training at Columbia, and earned a master's degree from Northeast Missouri State (1971). Weinberg received numerous awards as well as authoring a high school biology textbook titled *Biology: An Inquiry into the Nature of Life*, which prompted controversy from the creationist community because of its strong presentation of evolution (NCSE, "Weinberg").

Weinberg, educators, and scientists were motivated to respond to the creationist resurgence during the late 1970s, in particular creationists' plan to influence local and state governments to require a balanced treatment to teach creation science as a competing theory to evolution science. Weinberg conceptualized and launched a citizen network of Committees of Correspondence around the country that were committed to providing a defense and response to young-earth creationist aims (Numbers 1993).

The Committees of Correspondence organized a quarterly publication called the *Creation/Evolution Journal* that was first published in the summer of 1980 and used to educate their members and promote their cause. In 1981 members of several Committees of Correspondence founded the National Center for Science Education (NCSE). In 1983 NCSE was incorporated and Weinberg was installed as the first president.

In 1986 the NCSE board received a grant from the Carnegie Foundation and other private foundations to open a national office, and the board hired Eugenie Scott as the executive director in 1987, a role she served in until 2014. (Scott was first motivated to support this cause after attending a debate between her mentor, James Gavan, and creationist **Duane Gish**.) Scott became a nationally recognized advocate, noted author, and activist for the cause of science and science education. Scott directed the NCSE to become the most influential organization in the battle over evolution (Dean 2013).

The NCSE continued to evolve their strategies as some in the creationist movement adopted and promoted **intelligent design** in an attempt to become more scientific—a strategy that ultimately failed in 2005 with the *Kitzmiller v. Dover Area School District* legal case. The NCSE played a pivotal role by supporting the ACLU with staff and expertise in defense against the Dover Area School District (Foerstel 2010). In 2012 the NCSE announced they would be engaged in efforts to keep climate change education and global warming issues safe from threats from special interests promoted by religious, secular, and business organizations. The NCSE has more than 5,000 members, including scientists, teachers, clergy, and citizens with diverse religious and political affiliations.

Jonathan Howard Fisher

REFERENCES AND RECOMMENDED READING

Dean, Cornelia. 2013. "Standard-Bearer in Evolution Fight, Eugenie C. Scott Fights the Teaching of Creationism in Schools." *New York Times.* September 2.
Foerstel, Herbert N. 2010. *Toxic Mix? A Handbook of Science and Politics.* Westport, CT: Greenwood Press/ABC-CLIO.
"National Center for Science Education." Wikipedia. Accessed August 31, 2015. https://en.wikipedia.org/wiki/National_Center_for_Science_Education.
NCSE. National Center for Science Education. http://ncse.com.
NCSE. "Weinberg, Stanley, NCSE Founder Dies." Accessed August 31, 2015. http://ncse.com/library-resource/stanley-weinberg-ncse-founder-dies.
Numbers, Ronald L. 1993. *The Creationists: The Evolution of Scientific Creationism.* Berkeley: University of California Press.
Weinberg, Stanley L. 1966. *Biology: An Inquiry into the Nature of Life.* Boston: Allyn and Bacon.

NATURAL LAW THEORY. Natural law theories in ethics fall into three broad categories: classical natural law theories like the one defended by Thomas Aquinas (Aquinas 1948); modern natural law theories like the one defended by **John Locke** (Locke 1980); and the "new natural law theory" developed in recent decades by Germain Grisez (Grisez 1965) and John Finnis (Finnis 1980). The latter two theories eschew the metaphysical foundations underlying classical natural law theory but differ in what they would put in place of those foundations.

Aquinas's classical natural law theory grounds ethics in human **nature**, where "nature" is understood in Aristotelian terms (see **Aristotle; Aristotle's Four Causes**). In particular, the theory presupposes a **metaphysics** of *essentialism* and immanent *teleology*.

The basic idea can be illustrated as follows. Consider a tree and its characteristic activities: sinking roots into the ground, drawing in water and nutrients through them, and so on. These are ends or outcomes *toward which* the tree tends, what it will do unless prevented (by damage, disease, or some other defect). They are, accordingly, instances of **teleology**, that is, directedness toward an end or goal. And these tendencies are not imposed from outside, the way a time-telling function is imposed by a watchmaker on the metal bits that make up a watch. Rather, the tendencies are *inherent* or *immanent in* the tree, just by virtue of being a tree. That is to say, they flow from the *essence* or *nature* of the tree.

What is true of trees is also true of animals. A lion, for example, will, given its nature, tend to develop traits like having sharp claws and powerful muscles, and will tend toward activities like hunting down prey and (in the case of a lioness) nurturing cubs. These are the ends toward which a lion is directed given its essence.

Now the ends toward which a thing naturally tends entail an objective standard of goodness or badness. A tree that, due to damage or disease, fails to sink deep roots or grow healthy leaves, is to that extent a bad tree, while a tree that realizes these ends is to that extent good. A lion that, due to disease, injury, or genetic defect, fails to develop strong muscles, hunt prey, or nourish its cubs will to that extent be a bad lion, while a lion that realizes these ends will to that extent be a good lion.

So far we are not talking about *moral* goodness and badness; the claim is not that a sickly tree or lazy lion is blameworthy. The sense of "good" and "bad" operative here is rather the one operative when we speak of a good or bad specimen, a good or bad instance of a kind of thing. It has to do with a thing's success or failure in living up to the standard inherent in the kind of thing it is.

Moral goodness or badness enters the picture with creatures capable of *freely choosing* to act in a way that either facilitates or frustrates the ends toward which their nature directs them, and which thereby either promotes or frustrates the realization of what is good for them. This brings us to human beings, who are *rational* animals and thus capable of such free action. Moral goodness or badness in human beings involves deliberate choice to act in a way that either facilitates or frustrates the ends inherent in human nature.

What are the ends defining what is good for us? A complete answer requires a systematic study of human nature, but a rudimentary understanding can be had by any human being. Aquinas speaks of our good as that toward which we have a *natural inclination* and which we know precisely because of the existence of such inclinations. He gives as examples goods common to all things (such as self-preservation), goods common to animals (such as sexual intercourse and child rearing), and goods unique to human beings (such as knowing God and living in society).

We know these as goods precisely insofar as we are naturally inclined to pursue them, just as a tree tends naturally to grow roots and a lion tends naturally to hunt prey (albeit they do not *rationally apprehend* their ends as goods). (Note that the sense of "natural" operative here differs from the sense in which Paul speaks in 1 Corinthians 2:14 [NASB] of the "natural person" [ESV] who regards the things of God as foolishness. The word translated "natural" in that passage has the sense of "sensual" or "unspiritual," which is not what Aquinas means by "natural.")

Importantly, a mere deep-seated desire does not constitute a "natural inclination" in Aquinas's sense. A sickly tree might grow deformed roots, and a genetically defective lioness might eat rather than nurture her cubs. However deeply ingrained, these are not natural tendencies in the relevant sense, but rather defects or deviations from natural tendencies. Similarly, human beings might because of psychological conditioning or genetic defect exhibit inclinations—a predisposition for alcoholism, say—that are not "natural" in the relevant sense, but instead are at odds with the ends nature has set for us. We know this not only from the fact that such aberrant inclinations are relatively rare in human beings, but also because they positively frustrate ends that nature has evidently put into us. Alcoholism, for example, frustrates the use of reason as well as damages bodily health.

The basic imperative nature has put into us is to pursue good and avoid evil, in the thin sense that we naturally only pursue what we *take to be* in *some* sense good and avoid what we *take to be* in some way bad. Aquinas calls this the "first precept" of the natural law. Even someone who pursues what he thinks is morally bad obeys this precept insofar as he takes the object of his action to be good in some other way. For instance, the drug addict who is ashamed of his addiction but nevertheless uses drugs believes it would be good to satisfy the craving he has at that moment.

Practical reasoning thus has for Aquinas the structure: (1) *Good is to be pursued and evil avoided*; (2) *X is good and Y is evil*; therefore (3) *X is to be pursued and Y avoided*. Aquinas takes (1) to be self-evident (given the thin sense of "good" and "evil" operative in the premise). The values of X and Y in premise (2), at least for the fundamental goods and evils, are revealed by our natural inclinations. For example, our natural inclinations tell us that truth is good and error bad, and therefore it follows that we should pursue truth and avoid error. Of course, many moral questions are more complicated than that, and even the application of a principle like "Pursue truth and avoid error" raises many questions. The casuistry of classical natural law theory works out the ramifications of these basic principles in a systematic way.

Locke's modern natural law theory rejects the Aristotelian metaphysical foundations of the classical approach. Locke grounds ethics instead in God's ownership of us, which Locke takes to be knowable by natural reason. Because we are God's "workmanship," to harm ourselves or other human beings is to damage God's property. The "new natural law theory" eschews both Aquinas's Aristotelian metaphysics and Locke's theological foundations. Echoing Kant, it grounds **morality** instead in a theory of practical reason. In particular the theory takes action to be intelligible only insofar as it is aimed at the realization of certain "basic goods" (such as life, knowledge, friendship, etc.) grasped as self-evidently desirable.

Needless to say, the Aristotelian metaphysics underlying classical natural law theory is even more controversial now than it was in Locke's day (which is one motivation for the "new natural law theory"). In particular, it is often suggested that modern science has undermined that metaphysics. However, its abiding defensibility and compatibility with science is urged by Thomists and may arguably find **confirmation** in the neo-Aristotelian "new essentialist" movement in contemporary metaphysics and **philosophy of science**.

Edward Feser

REFERENCES AND RECOMMENDED READING

Aquinas, Thomas. 1948. *Summa Theologica*. 5 vols. Trans. Fathers of the English Dominican Province. New York: Benziger.

Feser, Edward. 2007. *Locke*. Oxford: Oneworld.

———. 2009. *Aquinas*. Oxford: Oneworld.

———. 2014. *Scholastic Metaphysics: A Contemporary Introduction*. Heusenstamm, Ger.: Editiones Scholasticae/Transaction Books.

Finnis, John. 1980. *Natural Law and Natural Rights*. Oxford: Clarendon.

George, Robert P. 1999. *In Defense of Natural Law*. Oxford: Oxford University Press.

Grisez, Germain. 1965. "The First Principle of Practical Reason: A Commentary on the *Summa Theologiae*, 1–2 Question 94, Article 2." *Natural Law Forum* 10:168–201.

Lisska, Anthony J. 1996. *Aquinas's Theory of Natural Law: An Analytic Reconstruction*. Oxford: Clarendon.

Locke, John. 1980. *Second Treatise of Government*. Indianapolis: Hackett.

McInerny, Ralph. 1997. *Ethica Thomistica: The Moral Philosophy of Thomas Aquinas*. Rev. ed. Washington, DC: Catholic University of America Press.

Novotny, Daniel D., and Lukas Novak, eds. 2014. *Neo-Aristotelian Perspectives in Metaphysics*. London: Routledge.

Oderberg, David S. 2000. *Moral Theory: A Non-consequentialist Approach*. Oxford: Blackwell.

———. 2007. *Real Essentialism*. London: Routledge.

Waldron, Jeremy. 2002. *God, Locke, and Equality: Christian Foundations in Locke's Political Thought*. Cambridge: Cambridge University Press.

NATURAL PHILOSOPHY. Natural philosophy was one of the three traditional branches of philosophy (the others being **metaphysics** and ethics). It had a narrower meaning than today's concept of **science** since it was purely theoretical. A natural philosopher studied the causes of phenomena in the natural world and tried to explain them. Although *natural science* was long synonymous with *natural philosophy*, the term *natural scientist* did not exist until the nineteenth century.

The Scope of Natural Philosophy

Natural philosophy was concerned only with causes rather than observations — thus the traditional conception of **astronomy** as a branch of **mathematics** rather than natural philosophy. Astronomers observed the heavens and attempted to predict the motion of the planets. This was known as "saving the phenomena." Actually explaining how the universe worked and what caused the planets to move the way they did was in the realm of natural philosophy. Unfortunately, up until the seventeenth century, the explanations of the philosophers and the models of the astronomers were incompatible. The eccentric circles and epicycles that the Greeks used to describe the planets' orbits had no place in the philosophers' understanding of their underlying causes.

The archetypal work of natural philosophy is *The Physics* of **Aristotle**, which sought to explain the causes of motion. Aristotle did not delineate mathematical equations to describe how objects move. His aims were deeper but less precise. It was not until the fourteenth century that Thomas Bradwardine, later archbishop of Canterbury, produced an equation that described the Aristotelian theory of motion. Thereafter, the boundaries between mathematician and natural philosopher became increasingly blurred. Both **Galileo** and **Isaac Newton** considered themselves philosophers, but their official job title was professor of mathematics. Today it seems obvious that mathematical formulae can be used to describe complicated natural phenomena, but before Bradwardine, it was rarely attempted.

Natural Philosophy and Natural Theology

Up until the nineteenth century, natural philosophy explicitly consisted of the study of God's creation. Medieval Christians had tried to learn about God by examining his work. Twelfth-century theologians suggested the metaphor, popularized by Galileo, that the Bible and nature were two books, both written by God and so unable to conflict (see **Two Books Metaphor**). In the Middle Ages, natural philosophy became an essential prolegomenon for theologians. Anyone who wished to study theology at one of the new universities first had to spend several years obtaining a master of the arts degree, which included studying Aristotle's *Physics* and *On the Heavens* in depth.

In the early modern period, natural philosophy was extensively used to supply arguments for the existence of God, a practice known as **natural theology**. However, by the early nineteenth century, **Simon Laplace** explicitly broke the link between natural philosophy and theology when he told Napoleon he had no need for the hypothesis of God. Nonetheless, many nineteenth-century physicists, such as **Michael Faraday** and **James Clerk Maxwell** continued to view science as a religious imperative.

After the word *scientist* was coined in 1834, practitioners of science gradually stopped calling themselves philosophers. The term *natural philosophy*, which had always had competition with *natural science*, also fell away as professionalized scientists began to dominate the academy later in the nineteenth century.

James Hannam

REFERENCES AND RECOMMENDED READING

Aristotle. 1984. *The Complete Works of Aristotle: The Revised Oxford Translation*. Ed. Jonathan Barnes. Princeton: Princeton University Press.

Grant, Edward. 2007. *A History of Natural Philosophy: From the Ancient World to the Nineteenth Century*. Cambridge: Cambridge University Press.

Maier, Anneliese. 1982. *On the Threshold of Exact Science: Selected Writings of Anneliese Maier on Late Medieval Natural Philosophy*. Trans. Steven D. Sargent. Philadelphia: University of Pennsylvania Press.

NATURAL SELECTION

Scientific Overview

Natural selection is the mechanism proposed by **Charles Darwin** to explain the origin of **species**. The surprisingly simple but also deceptively subtle notion consists of three elements: (1) there is variability in natural populations; (2) some of this variability is heritable; and (3) some variants have qualities ("adaptations") that enable them to reproduce more effectively than others. Thus the best-adapted species increased in proportion, entailing, in the famous phrase of Herbert Spencer, "survival of the fittest."

Recent empirical and mathematical treatments would add a fourth condition for selection: population size must be large enough and environmental conditions must be consistent enough for the better-adapted variants to reliably reproduce more, as opposed to being overwhelmed by **chance** (or "genetic drift"). Therefore one modern definition of natural selection is simply "differential or non-random reproduction of genotypes" ("Evolution Notes").

A question that immediately arises is whether we have actually seen natural selection in operation, and if so, is it sufficient to account for the origin of species? Darwin clearly documented the ability of selection or differential reproduction to generate striking diversity via records of domestic breeding. Some breeds could even qualify for designation as different species.

He also observed unique, clustered groups of species on islands, which provide inferential grounds for believing selection acts without human-engineered breeding. Since then the operation of selection has been abundantly confirmed in both laboratory and field studies that have demonstrated modulation of both proportion and range of genotypic and phenotypic variants, or **gene**s and their traits (Endler 1986; Orr 2009).

But is selection sufficient to generate new species? In spite of Darwin's ambitious title — *On the Origin of Species by Means of Natural Selection* — the uncontroversial answer to this is no. For one thing, selection alone does not create novel traits. The process also requires mutation, sexual recombination, or other sources of new variation (which in combination with selection is referred to as the "Modern Synthesis"). This does not mean that selection makes little contribution to the **emergence** of complex cumulative traits, for "non-random reproduction" amplifies the probabilities

of a sequential series of changes building on each other, as opposed to the unlikely emergence by unmediated chance.

Richard Dawkins illustrates this concept with his famous "weasel" example. The **probability** of getting a monkey to type out "methinks it is like a weasel" involves 28 characters with 27 options (letters + spaces) for a probability of about 10^{-40}. It would take a computer randomly assembling the characters more time than there is in the universe. However, a program that selectively reproduces the closest randomly mutating variants can do this in a series of 50 or so generations, taking a matter of minutes. The problems, among others, are these: natural selection does not work toward a prespecified target, it does not reproduce one and only one "best" variant, and it is vulnerable to small populations and changing environments. More realistic models take between forever and a matter of minutes but still do much better than random variation alone.

Another reason that natural selection alone typically does not generate species is that under most circumstances variants must become geographically separated in order to develop biological mechanisms that prevent them from forming hybrids with other variants — a widely accepted criterion of speciation. Both field and lab studies have shown that such mechanisms can develop, sometimes influenced by changes in just a single gene. So although selection may be instrumental in speciation, for the above (and below) reasons, modern evolutionary theory posits "the origin of species by means of mutation, recombination, natural selection, drift, geographic isolation, and manifold other processes" (Laland et al. 2015).

Scientific/Philosophical Debates

In addition to the above questions about speciation, there has been a series of debates with scientific and philosophical import about natural selection itself (Sober 2004). One is whether the very idea is a truism or tautology, since "survival of the fittest" seems at face value to mean merely "reproductive success of those who succeed reproductively." But this isn't quite true, since natural selection entails reproductive success not just of those who happen to reproduce, but of those with heritable traits that reliably enhance reproduction in a particular environment. This is not a truism and cannot be the case unless all four of the above specific conditions are met.

Other questions involve the extent to which traits are effectively shaped by selection. The "neutralist — selectionist" controversy is over how much genetic variation is adaptive and therefore constrained by selection as opposed to neutral and subject to random drift. Another question—quite salient when applied to human traits like moral cognition or the capacity for **mathematics**—is whether it makes sense to try to tell an adaptive story for everything, or whether some traits don't confer any reproductive advantage at all (and may even be costly), but are nonadaptive "spandrels" or by-products of other traits. Still another debate is whether there is an overall arc or maybe even progressive directionality to evolutionary history that has been shaped by intrinsic constraints on selection or development, versus the claim that the history of life is a random, nonrepeatable wander buffeted by contingencies (Morris 2004).

Finally, there has been vigorous debate over the units and levels of selection. One aspect involves the replicating entities on which selection acts: just genes, other biological **information**, or even units of cultural information (see **Memes**). Another quite virulent controversy involves the scale of adaptations that confer reproductive success: in addition to individual traits, does selection operate at group or even species levels? (See Birch and Okasha 2015.)

Many of these (still debated) questions contribute to what may be the most provocative and enduring controversy of all: how we understand humans in light of selection. The overwhelming majority of biologists find the evidence for common descent of humanity persuasive. But ever since Darwin and his contemporary **Alfred Wallace** first proposed natural selection, right up until recent controversies over sociobiology and evolutionary **psychology**, there has been vigorous debate both within and outside biology over the extent to which selection shapes the central tendencies and/or range of human cognition and culture: whether it holds them—in **E. O. Wilson**'s famous phrase—"on a genetic leash" (see **Altruism**).

Theological Considerations

Many of the above questions have important theological implications. While these complex issues lie beyond the scope of a brief article, several misconceptions and over-simplifications can be corrected.

One widespread assertion is that "[Darwin's] great contribution was the final demolition of the idea that nature is the product of **intelligent design**" (Rachels 1999, 110). However, this is untrue on two counts. First, however their merits are construed, cosmological and physical fine-tuning arguments—both recent and dating to Darwin's time—are uninfluenced by standard notions of selection. Second, in

the biological realm, while selection constitutes a naturalistic alternative to divine interventionism, it says nothing about the structure or design of intrinsic biochemical, developmental, and environmental constraints that lawfully guide selection (Barrow et al. 2008).

Another claim is that human uniqueness is untenable in light of selection. While the question of taxonomic uniqueness is complex, selection does not settle it for two reasons. One, phylogenetic continuity need not entail phenotypic continuity: **common ancestry** does rule out strikingly *un*common traits. Second, some evolutionists suggest that selection actually illuminates human exceptionalism: insofar as our behavior transcends the imperatives of genetic replication (Dawkins 2006), the "genetic leash has broken."

Lastly, natural selection is viewed by some as exacerbating the problem of natural evil because "evil" is not just an intrusion into, but plays a fundamental role in, nature: Can a good God create through a process of ruthless struggle and selfish competition? Not to minimize the challenge of **theodicy** (see **Evil, Problem of**), but this claimed impact of selection may be oversimplified in two respects. First, there are manifold, emerging proposals for the crucial role of cooperation in the evolutionary process (Nowak and Coakley 2013). But even without these accounts, selection and competition ought not to be conflated. Competition is defined as mutual negative impacts on reproductive flourishing; recall that selection is simply differential reproduction, which can occur with no impact, or even mutually positive impact.

Of course the theory of universal common descent itself raises specific theological concerns for many Christians; however, it is not clear that the proposed mechanism of natural selection poses the often-asserted challenges to **theism**.

Jeffrey P. Schloss

REFERENCES AND RECOMMENDED READING

Barrow, John, Simon Conway Morris, Stephen Freeland, and Charles Harper, eds. 2008. *Fitness of the Cosmos for Life: Biochemistry and Fine-Tuning.* Cambridge: Cambridge University Press.

Birch, Jonathan, and Samir Okasha. 2015. "Kin Selection and Its Critics." *BioScience* 65 (1): 22–32.

Dawkins, Richard. 2006. *The Selfish Gene: 30th Anniversary Edition.* Oxford: Oxford University Press.

Endler, John. 1986. *Natural Selection in the Wild.* Princeton, NJ: Princeton University Press.

"Evolution Notes." www.planet.botany.uwc.ac.za/NISL/Evo_primer/Doc/EVO_NOTE.93A.doc.

Laland, Kevin N., Tobias Uller, Marcus W. Feldman, et al. 2015. "The Extended Evolutionary Synthesis: Its Structure, Assumptions and Predictions." *Proceedings of the Royal Society, B* 282:20151019.

Morris, S. Conway. 2004. *Life's Solution: Inevitable Humans in a Lonely Universe.* Cambridge: Cambridge University Press.

Nowak, Martin, and Sarah Coakley, eds. 2013. *Evolution, Games and God: The Principle of Cooperation.* Cambridge, MA: Harvard University Press.

Orr, H. Allen. 2009. "Testing Natural Selection with Genetics." *Scientific American* 300:44–51.

Rachels, James. 1999. *Created from Animals: The Moral Implications of Darwinism.* Oxford: Oxford University Press.

Sober, Elliot. 2004. *The Nature of Selection: Evolutionary Theory in Philosophical Focus.* Cambridge, MA: MIT Press.

NATURAL THEOLOGY. Natural theology is generally understood to be a systematic inquiry into what can be known about God apart from what God has specially revealed. There are traditions of natural theology outside of Christianity (and even outside of monotheism), but this article will confine itself to the Christian tradition.

Traditionally, natural theology is focused on arguments for the existence and nature of God drawn from the natural world (like cosmological and teleological arguments) or from reason (like the ontological argument). These continue to have varying degrees of popularity, and other articles will examine them specifically (see **Reason, Argument from**; **Cosmological Argument**; **Design Argument**). This article looks at the practice of natural theology more generally.

Natural theology in the Christian tradition is often traced back to Anselm in the eleventh century. He gave an influential version of the ontological argument for the existence of God, but it might not be quite right to see this as an example of reasoning independent of special **revelation**. Anselm wrote, *Credo ut intelligam* — "I believe in order to understand." The point of this methodological commitment was not **fideism** (belief ungrounded on and even in spite of reason). Rather, it was that faith is the starting point for working out Christian understanding. That is, faith provides a stock of beliefs through revelation (e.g., God exists, the incarnate Christ is fully God and fully human). These are then worked out through reason; they are shown to be plausible and rational in the thought system of the day.

Thomas Aquinas in the thirteenth century had a better claim to founding Christian natural theology. He defended the notion that we can "know" things by faith, but this is a different species of knowledge than what we can "know" by reason, and he was concerned not to confuse the two. Thomas said that we "believe" those things to be true which are known by faith, and we "see" those things to be true which are known by reason. He held that there are some things that we can only believe by faith — for example, that God is a **Trinity**. This is revealed to us, and nothing in reason

will contradict it, but neither can it be shown by reason to be true. There are other points of revelation, he thought, that can also be demonstrated by reason — God's existence and God's role as creator, for example. Some Christians will never work through the rational proofs for these and will only ever accept them as articles of revealed faith. But for the one who does see them by reason, they cannot only be articles of faith.

Sometimes the solution of Aquinas is called the *Thomistic synthesis*, but this is misleading in a way, because what he did was not to synthesize theology and philosophy/science into one discipline, but to clearly carve out separate domains for them. They will not contradict each other when done properly, but they are separate ways to the truth. Aquinas held together these two separate ways to produce one coherent system of knowledge (hence the appropriateness of the term *synthesis*), but later Christian thinkers would not be as concerned to do so. Hence the two ways of knowing began to produce very different results, which even if not strictly contradictory yielded very different portraits of God. The God revealed in some parts of the Bible may appear to be a premodern, anthropomorphized figure; reason throughout the modern period produced a very different concept: the "God of the philosophers." Jesus as the incarnate Son of God is absent from the latter, and in that tradition he had no other role than a good moral teacher. Christology is given no relevance in the natural theology of the period, and we are left with a generic **theism**.

Here we see the relevance of Karl Barth's criticism of natural theology. From his perspective, natural theologians have bought into the separation of faith and reason, and the distinctiveness of Christianity is left out of the equation. Modern philosophers sought certainty for their beliefs, and the path to certainty came not through stories that had been passed down, but by the application of reason. Descartes thought he was providing a valuable service to theology by giving belief in God and the immortality of the **soul** a certain foundation in philosophical reason. Others see that move as reducing Aquinas's Christian theism to philosophical theism, which would become **deism**, and then atheism. In this objection, natural theology divorced from revelation is inherently unstable and incapable of justifying Christian faith.

There is a further development of this objection. When reason becomes the only acceptable foundation for belief, **religious experience** is no longer deemed adequate for grounding faith. But some claim that there is something fundamentally wrong with eliminating this subjective element. Contemporary philosopher of religion Paul Moser claims that natural theology treats God as an object, similar to the objects that natural science investigates. In so doing, the arguments of natural theology fail to detect the personal Being who is the God revealed to Abraham, Paul, and (most significantly) Jesus. Instead, the appropriate cognitive basis for the Christian faith is found in the relationship one can have with God through God's intervening personal Spirit. According to Moser, the Christian God's desire for people is not merely intellectual or cognitive **information**; rather, God desires moral transformation.

Arguments from natural theology offer evidence of a God who is static and reveals himself independently of humans' volitional attitudes toward him. But this is not the God Christians should be looking for. The Christian God conceals himself in response to human volitional resistance because God is noncoercive and desires that we learn to love unselfishly as God does. The true God is not revealed in the "spectator evidence" of natural theology but is made known to us only as we enter into relationship with God. And God enters into relationship with us only if we are willing to undergo the moral transformation God desires for us—namely, to become perfectly loving toward all people, even one's enemies, because that is the nature of God.

Moser's is a powerful argument from a subjective Christian perspective, but critics will object that he does not leave enough room for the role of objective evidence. Could it be that the traditional arguments do have value for some in making it seem plausible that there could be such a being as God? Reason might help to clear away some of the objections that people have to belief in God. Then, perhaps, once someone accepts the possibility of there being something supernatural, she or he is more willing to seek relationship with the kind of God Moser describes. In this way, natural theology could open the door to belief in the Christian God, even if it cannot by itself prove the existence of this God.

J. B. Stump

REFERENCES AND RECOMMENDED READING

Craig, William Lane, and J. P. Moreland, eds. 2009. *The Blackwell Companion to Natural Theology.* Malden, MA: Wiley-Blackwell.

Moser, Paul. 2012. "Religious Epistemology Personified: God without Natural Theology." In *The Blackwell Companion to Science and Christianity,* ed. J. B. Stump and Alan G. Padgett. Malden, MA: Wiley-Blackwell.

Stump, J. B. 2012. "Natural Theology after Modernism." In *The Blackwell Companion to Science and Christianity,* ed. J. B. Stump and Alan G. Padgett. Malden, MA: Wiley-Blackwell.

NATURALISM. The concept of naturalism generates a variety of responses or understandings among philosophers and scientists. This article discusses philosophical naturalism first, followed by what scientists refer to as **methodological naturalism**, as sometimes included in discussions of the **scientific method**.

A person who does not affirm the supernatural—God, gods, ghosts, immaterial souls, spirits—is a person who affirms naturalism. For naturalists, nature is all there is. And if it is not science, then it is nonscience (i.e., nonsense). Most naturalists put stock in empirical, evidence-based ways of justifying opinions about what is real; this is exemplified by science (see **Scientism**). Naturalists think such beliefs are more reliable and objective than those based on **intuition**, various kinds of **revelation**, sacred texts, religious authority, or reports by people claiming to have had **religious experience**s.

Some naturalism adherents believe that science reveals a single manifold or existence (called *nature*) that contains an unbound (so far) plethora of interconnected phenomena involving great spans in size, mass, and time—from the submicroscopic to the extent of the cosmos, from the minute electron to the galaxies, and from the Planck time (10^{-43} seconds) to the age of the universe (4×10^{17} seconds). This is nature, and this is all that is, according to naturalists.

Naturalism as a metaphysical philosophical construct attempts to give a well-defined and valid account of what its adherents consider "all of reality." Its methodology is centered on what naturalists call a strong commitment to **objectivity** and explanatory openness or clarity. They view supernaturalism as clinging to nonscientific, nonempirical justifications for beliefs—the opposite of objectivity.

A naturalist affirms science's finding no evidence for a supernatural God, no evidence for an immaterial **soul** or mental agent supervising the body and brain (see **Mind-Body Problem**). A person is seen to be simply a natural phenomenon. In short, naturalism is a philosophy, a metaphysical system of beliefs about the universe and the place of humanity in the universe, a universe completely and adequately described by science and nothing else.

The foregoing is rejected by Christian believers. Christians active in the sciences generally agree with the scientific method, and a number subscribe to a kind of naturalism—but to a different form, a naturalism that dictates their scientific approach but not their metaphysical commitments. For better or worse, this form of naturalism is called ***methodological naturalism*** and is to be clearly distinguished from what has been described above, which is referred to as metaphysical naturalism.

In terms of doing science, the methodological naturalist has the same attitude about conducting scientific research as does the metaphysical naturalist. But for the methodological naturalist, there are differences. First, that person is subscribing to a method—a strategy in acquiring and assessing scientific **information**—but not to an overall philosophy. That person does not necessarily dismiss supernaturalism, especially the existence of God, the Father of our Lord Jesus Christ. The methodological naturalist who is a Christian does not see nature and science's understanding of nature as "all there is." For that person, there is "more than meets the eye," more than can be empirically investigated, more than can be quantified with numbers. And this "more than" reality is as real or more real than what scientists can discover in and out of the laboratory and includes essentially all religious knowledge.

The idea of methodological naturalism (MN) recognizes that since the advent of modern science in Europe sometime around the 1400s–1500s, the scientific method has emphasized investigative methods and ideas that refer to concepts that can be empirically investigated (observed) in some sort of a laboratory, including natural environments; this also includes historical investigations. The basic theories, laws, and equations of science do not refer in any way to God, the supernatural, or miracles. The *methods* of science are naturalistic, and hence the scientific method is said to be *methodologically* naturalistic, *methodologically* atheistic, or *methodologically* agnostic. Perhaps MN is not the ideal way to refer to this aspect of the scientific method. But this is the designation that has been adopted, and people engaged in the scientific enterprise understand its meaning.

The concept of naturalism has received some commentary from a number of scientists. Active research scientists tend to be content with associating the scientific method as they practice it with MN. However, certain scholars in other fields have reacted to MN in a variety of ways. Phillip Johnson has written a number of books in which he is highly critical of current evolutionary biology. In several places he has written that neo-Darwinism is an atheistic system of thought (see **Darwinism**), and hence he understands the philosophical underpinnings of evolutionary biology to be philosophical naturalism (Johnson 1991). In response **Nancey Murphy** (1993) has written that Johnson is wrong when he conflates evolutionary science with naturalistic philosophy and that he does not recognize the difference between MN and philosophical naturalism.

Another important Christian contributor to the scientific method and its relation to philosophy and **metaphysics** is **Alvin Plantinga** in his book *Where the Conflict Really Lies* (2011). Plantinga, like Johnson, is interested in the relationship between evolutionary biology and naturalism. But unlike Johnson, Plantinga does not insist that evolutionary biology necessarily implies naturalism, but rather concludes that evolutionary biology does not entail naturalism. He sees no problem with the science of evolution itself but with evolutionary science combining with naturalism in such a way that they together form an inseparable package. He strongly objects to that pairing. He maintains that evolutionary science by itself does not deny, for instance, that humans were created by God. Naturalists conclude that humans have not been created in God's image precisely because there is no God. Plantinga says that this is a wrong and unnecessary extrapolation of evolutionary science that has no scientific (or metaphysical) validity.

Furthermore, Plantinga finds no conflict between the scientific conclusions of the earth and the cosmos being multibillions of years old and the evolutionary development of life on earth. It is only when Plantinga sees an ill-advised extrapolation of empirical science to imply atheistic naturalism that he raises objections.

Richard F. Carlson

REFERENCES AND RECOMMENDED READING

Johnson, Phillip. 1991. *Darwin on Trial*. Downers Grove, IL: InterVarsity.
Murphy, Nancey. 1993. "Phillip Johnson on Trial." *Perspectives on Science and Christian Faith*. 45:26–36.
Plantinga, Alvin. 2011. *Where the Conflict Really Lies: Science, Religion, and Naturalism*. New York: Oxford University Press.

NATURALISTIC FALLACY. How are moral and natural facts related? Hume's famous dictum that it is impossible to derive an "ought" from an "is" seems to suggest that it is a fallacy to try to equate moral and descriptive facts. G. E. Moore's 1903 *Principia Ethica* both founds the contemporary study of metaethics and agrees with this suggestion, introducing what he terms the naturalistic fallacy to describe a formal error that is committed in any attempt to equate moral and descriptive facts. The name that Moore chose for this fallacy suggests that it would apply to natural facts alone, but he meant it to apply to any description of moral facts, whether given in natural *or* divine terms (Moore 1903).

Moore supports his claim with his Open Question Argument (OQA), which purports to show that the "good" is indefinable. According to the OQA, successful definitions entail that questions about instances will have a particular feature. Yet questions about instances of "the good" do not have this feature, and so "the good" has no successful definition. Specifically, the OQA holds that if one type of thing, X (e.g., a bachelor), can be defined as another type of thing, Y (unmarried), then the question of whether a particular x (e.g., bachelor George) is also a particular y (an unmarried man) has the feature of being *closed*. This is because the answer is given in the definition of the term (*bachelor*). By contrast, in the absence of clear definition, questions remain *open*. For example, if George is a scientist, then the question of whether he is a physicist is *open*, since the definition of *scientist* is not adequate to determine that. Moore argued that questions about whether an act is "good" are always open, and hence no purported definition of "good" is adequate.

A century of metaethical work has provided trenchant criticisms of Moore's OQA and his formal, naturalistic fallacy, yet for some, "it seems impossible to deny that Moore was on to something" (Darwall et al. 1992, 115). What might this be? There is no uncontroversially successful naturalistic account of the characteristic motivational and normative qualities of moral facts (see Garcia and King 2009 for the debate). According to atheist J. L. Mackie, these characteristics render moral facts "queer," and the only proper response is to deny their very existence (Mackie 1977).

In contrast, many theists find a harmonious explanatory relationship between the characteristics of God and the reality of moral facts. For example, it may be claimed that a thing is *good* to the extent that it is similar to the necessarily good nature of a loving God, while an action is *right* if it is consistent with the commands flowing from that nature (Adams 1999). Thus the naturalistic fallacy may be "on to" **naturalism**'s disadvantage as compared with **theism** in accounting for moral facts. In short, we can "derive an ought," but only from a "*divine is*."

If the OQA were accepted, Moore's naturalistic fallacy would present a different kind of problem for naturalism. Moral facts would turn out to be empirically undetectable features of the natural world. The naturalist takes cognitive faculties to be the product of unguided evolutionary processes that are *insensitive* to such facts. Hence if naturalism were true and the OQA were sound, then moral knowledge would be impossible.

Jonathan Loose

REFERENCES AND RECOMMENDED READING

Adams, Robert Merrihew. 1999. *Finite and Infinite Goods: A Framework for Ethics*. Oxford: Oxford University Press.

Darwall, Steven, Allan Gibbard, and Peter Railton. 1992. "Towards *fin de siecle* Ethics: Some Trends." *Philosophical Review* 101:115–89.

Garcia, Robert K. and Nathan L. King, eds. 2009. *Is Goodness without God Good Enough? A Debate on Faith, Secularism and Ethics*. Plymouth, UK: Rowman & Littlefield.

Mackie, John Leslie. 1977. *Ethics: Inventing Right and Wrong*. New York: Penguin.

Moore, G. E. 1903. *Principia Ethica*. Cambridge, UK: Cambridge University Press.

NATURALISTIC THEORIES OF RELIGION. Naturalistic interpretations of religion generally stipulate (1) the unreality of transcendent powers of religions, and (2) the possibility of explaining the belief in these powers and their alleged effects (e.g., **miracles**) without going beyond the physical, social, and psychological aspects of human beings. These theories recognize only material realities, excluding all ideas of spirits, gods, **soul**s, and the like. For instance, E. B. Tylor, an early advocate of the evolution of religion, ruled out the possibility of "supernatural aid or **revelation**" in the religions that he studied (Tylor 1989, 427).

Philosophical assumptions. These theories were erected in the nineteenth and early twentieth centuries, and even though in polemical settings today they are frequently referred to as true, there are few if any attempts at creating new versions or defending the older ones. At their time of origin, there was enough philosophical support for atheism in the academic world that one could assume it, at least tacitly, as a basis for further application. For example, the philosopher Ludwig Feuerbach (1841) had designated God as a fictional projection of idealized human properties such as love, power, or wisdom. Many proponents of naturalistic theories accepted an atheistic position as given, and thus point 1 above, the unreality of transcendent powers, was axiomatic.

Point 2, the sufficiency of materialistic explanations, is a corollary of point 1, but its plausibility depends on the success of the materialistic explanations. In the quest for explanations, questions of the origin, nature, and function of religion became entangled with each other and led to a common concern: Why would human beings embellish their cultures with apparently unnecessary beliefs and practices? A fundamental problem with materialistic interpretations is their claim to exclusivity. The fact that a certain aspect of a religion can be explained materialistically does not rule out a simultaneous spiritual, supernatural reality.

Magic. Some theories emphasize that human beings want to take an active part in repulsing common threats, such as illness, drought, accidents, or marauding neighbors. Accordingly, various writers (e.g., Frazer 1911; Graebner 1924) have argued there was an anticipatory stage in human religious development that is characterized by the attempts to practice "magic," defined as *the manipulation of spiritual forces in order to bring about a desired end.*

According to the earlier writings of K. T. Preuss (1904–5), the first human beings manifested *Urdummheit,* "original stupidity." Their actions were akin to those of a child who scolds a rock over which he has just tripped. Since neither inconvenient rocks nor more serious calamities responded to mere words, they refined their thinking, stipulating a specific magical force—often called *mana* (Codrington 1891, 108–10)—and the need for increasingly complex magical rituals. The writers who held to this thesis believed that magic was not properly religious and that people turned away from it toward religion when they recognized that even these more sophisticated forms of magic did not work. However, the practice of magic in the technical sense (manipulation of forces to an end) has persisted right up to monotheistic religion, where one still finds people performing rituals primarily to protect themselves from evil occurrences.

Animism. E. B. Tylor (1989) and his followers did not accept the idea of an early magic-oriented phase in human culture. They argued that from the earliest beginnings right up to the present, all religions are concerned with spirit beings that differ only in quantity and magnitude. Wherever human culture evolved to a certain point, people came to realize that they consisted of two parts, their physical bodies and their souls or spirits. They observed that the soul is really the part that makes a person alive; if the soul departs from the body for a while, the person is in a state of short-term **death** (sleep), during which the soul can wander around and even visit other people. If the soul leaves a body permanently, the body is dead, but the soul is still present in the surrounding world. This line of reasoning affirmed that what applies to one person must apply to all, and then, just a short step further, affirmed that similar spirits must give life to animals and plants as well, filling the world with numerous spirit beings.

Tylor claimed that this animism was the first religion of human beings. Eventually some of the spirits were considered to be greater than others and became gods. From there, one god may have become elevated over the others, and finally this superior god may have turned into the supreme God of monotheistic religion. However, according to Tylor, the God of monotheism is still only a highly inflated spirit emerging out of the fantasies of animism.

Manism and naturism. Other naturalistic theories took still different starting points. Herbert Spencer (1921) proposed that it was specifically the fear of the ghosts of departed ancestors that awakened the human religious impulse, a theory called *manism* from the Latin word *manes,* for "ghost." Another theory was defended by John Muir (1872), who theorized that religion began when people started to think of natural phenomena (sunshine, rain, thunder, earthquakes, etc.) as being caused by gods and goddesses who had specific provenance of these items in nature.

Social theories. Numerous authors have described religion as an institution within society for the benefit of society. For example, **Émile Durkheim** (1912), the French pioneer of academic sociology, propounded this conclusion. He did so by declaring totemism (the division of a tribe into various clans) to be the original religion of human beings and attempting to show how totemism made a unified and harmonious society possible. Even though there was little content in his work on religion that was grounded in facts and correct interpretations, he inspired others to pursue the social function of religion. Claude Lévi-Strauss (1955) contended that similar conceptual structures undergird social institutions (structuralism).

Psychological theories. As is well-known, **Sigmund Freud** (1918) considered religion to be an impediment to the psychological welfare of human beings as a consequence of some archetypal violation of sexual taboos. Other writers (e.g., Rudolf Otto 1923) took a positive approach in emphasizing the personal, subjective experience that a person might report in an encounter with transcendence.

Even when naturalistic theories were popular, they were not unanimously accepted in the academic world. American scholars, following Franz Boas (1938), did not generally believe that there could ever be enough evidence to support a grand theory of religion. Others (Lang 1898; Schmidt 1935) believed that there was sufficient evidence, but that it pointed away from naturalistic theories.

Winfried Corduan

REFERENCES AND RECOMMENDED READING

Boas, Franz. 1938. *The Mind of Primitive Man.* Rev. ed. New York: Macmillan.
Codrington, C. H. 1891. *The Melanesians.* Oxford: Clarendon.
Durkheim, Émile. 1912. *The Elementary Forms of Religious Life.* Oxford: Oxford University Press.
Feuerbach, Ludwig. 1841, English trans. 1854. *The Essence of Christianity.* New York: Oxford University Press.
Frazer, J. G. 1911. *The Golden Bough.* New York: Macmillan.
Freud, Sigmund. 1918. *Totem and Taboo.* New York: Moffat.
Graebner, Fritz. 1924. *Das Weltbild der Primitiven.* Munich: Reinhardt.
Lang, Andrew. 1898. *The Making of Religion.* London: Longmans, Green.

Lévi-Strauss, Claude. 1955. *Tristes Tropiques*. Trans. John Weightman and Doreen Weightman. New York: Penguin.
Malinowsky, Bronislaw. 1948. *Magic, Science and Religion*. Garden City, NY: Doubleday Anchor.
Muir, John. 1872. *Original Sanskrit Texts on the Origin and History of the People of India*. Vol. 5. London: Trübner.
Otto, Rudolf. 1923. *The Idea of the Holy*. New York: Oxford University Press.
Preuss, K. T. 1904–5. "Der Ursprung der Religion und Kunst. Vorläufige Mitteilungen." *Globus* 86 (1904): 321–92; 87 (1905): 333–419.
Schmidt, Wilhelm. 1935. *The Origin and Growth of Religion*. Trans. H. J. Rose. 2nd ed. New York: Humanities.
Spencer, Herbert. 1921. *The Principles of Sociology*. 3rd ed. London: Appleton.
Tylor, Edward B. 1989. *Primitive Culture*. Vol. 1. 2nd ed. New York: Holt.

NATURALIZED EPISTEMOLOGY. Naturalized epistemology may be characterized as an epistemology (which is defined as the study of the nature of knowledge and justification) that only makes reference to "scientifically respectable" properties. This definition is, at best, unilluminating since what it means to be scientifically respectable is inescapably vague.

The best way to understand naturalized epistemology is through paradigmatic examples of naturalistic notions. Concepts used in this family of epistemological theories include things like reliability and lawful causal connections. This is because, in theory, we can use the tools of science to measure things like reliability or whether a causal chain obtains between a belief and a relevant fact. So if knowledge is defined broadly as justified true belief, a concept like justification, if it is to be scientifically respectable, must be reducible to reliability, causality, or something of this sort.

What a naturalized epistemology leaves behind are concepts that are known a priori (i.e., prior to or independent of experience) as first epistemic principles and deontic concepts, which presuppose epistemic obligations (e.g., to embrace as many true beliefs as possible while rejecting as many false beliefs as possible), since these are not measurable by the tools of science. In fact, for most naturalists, there are no purely epistemic facts at all but only nonepistemic (natural) facts to which the epistemic facts are reducible without remainder. The epistemic facts are, on these views, mere philosophical holdouts from antiquated ontologies—that is, metaphysical categories like "substance" or "essence."

Epistemological **naturalism** comes in a variety of views. Willard Van Orman Quine's work is the *locus classicus* of the topic, in which he stated, "Epistemology, or something like it, simply falls into place as a chapter of **psychology** and hence natural science" (Quine 1969, 82–83). The idea is that the project of trying to analyze the concept of knowledge a priori has failed. Instead, we should replace this project with a scientific study of the ways in which we do in fact form beliefs.

One difficulty here for the Quinean view is that it is not clear that this is even something like epistemology. We want to know not just *how* we actually form beliefs (i.e., descriptively), but how we *should* form beliefs (i.e., prescriptively) and, more importantly, what it is for a belief to rise to the ideal of being rationally justified or even qualifying as "knowledge." Arguably the tools of psychology are inadequate to discover what makes for the epistemic ideals.

Though influential, Quine's work has not engendered many adherents to a specifically Quinean view. However, views that approximate the Quinean extreme have become the major, if not dominant, views in contemporary epistemology. Alvin Goldman is rightly seen as the popularizer of this sort of approach, which is typically externalist (see **Epistemology**) in character. Earlier he argued for a causal theory of knowing where there must be a proper causal chain from the fact known to the knower (Goldman 1967). He later adjusted to a reliabilist theory of justification, according to which a belief is justified if it is produced by a reliable belief-forming process. Both of these views fall within the family of naturalized epistemologies.

Although **Alvin Plantinga** is a staunch defender of Christian **theism**, his epistemological views would also fall under the broader category of a naturalized epistemology. This is because warrant (which is whatever makes the difference between mere true belief and knowledge) for Plantinga has crucially to do with properly functioning cognitive faculties and, like reliability and causality, proper function is, in principle, scientifically testable. In addition to this, his account makes no reference to deontic concepts or concepts known a priori.

However, though Plantinga's epistemological account is, in a broad sense, naturalistic, this is no boon for metaphysical naturalism. Plantinga argues that "naturalistic epistemology flourishes best in the garden of supernaturalistic metaphysics" (Plantinga 1993, 237; see also **Evolutionary Argument against Naturalism**). This is because apart from theism there is no guarantee that our cognitive faculties are aimed at producing true beliefs. Thus, somewhat ironically, a naturalized epistemology of this sort favors a nonnatural ontology (i.e., theism).

Travis M. Dickinson

REFERENCES AND RECOMMENDED READING

Goldman, Alvin. 1967. "A Causal Theory of Knowing." *Journal of Philosophy* 64 (12): 357–72.

———. 1979. "What Is Justified Belief?" In *Justification and Knowledge: New Studies in Epistemology*, ed. G. Pappas, 1–23. Dordrecht: Reidel.

Plantinga, Alvin. 1993. *Warrant and Proper Function.* New York: Oxford University Press.

Quine, W. V. O. 1969. *Ontological Relativity and Other Essays.* New York: Columbia University Press.

NATURE. From a scientific perspective, nature refers to the entire physical universe, including the physical laws that govern it. The physical universe includes matter, energy, space, and time. Nature is often also used in a narrower sense to mean outdoor areas that are either largely untouched by human hands or only minimally tended by humans.

From a biblical perspective, nature is the realm created by God for human beings to live in until their physical **death**. The physical universe was created by God/Christ (e.g., Gen. 1:1; John 1:3), and it is subject to the laws that God created to govern the behavior of all its matter, energy, space, and time. God is distinct and separate from nature since a created object is different from the Creator (Rom. 1:20, 25), and God is sovereign over all aspects of nature from the moment he created it until the moment he will end this physical universe (Acts 17:24; 2 Peter 3:10–12).

Within the realm of nature, we know of only one type of creature God created that is both physical (i.e., of this physical universe) and spiritual, namely, human beings (Gen. 1:27; 2:7; Eccl. 3:11; 12:6–7). The term *nature* is typically limited to this physical universe and is not typically taken to include the spiritual realm of God and the angels, although the Bible clearly teaches that angels and heaven were also created by God/God's Word (John 1:3).

The Bible teaches that nature is a reliable source of truth about God (Ps. 19:1–2; Rom. 1:20), and there are many instances in the Bible where God uses something from nature to teach truth (e.g., Ps. 19:1–2; Prov. 6:6–8; Isa. 28:23–29; Matt. 6:26–30). As such, the record of nature is part of God's *general* **revelation** about himself to all human beings. Being part of his general revelation, the facts of nature cannot be in conflict with the words and meaning of the *specific revelation* given in Scripture, since God is the source of both. Rather, studying nature can strengthen faith in God. (See, e.g., Abraham's profession of faith after God told him to try counting the stars in Gen. 15 and Rom. 4.) Nature reveals many things about God, including his existence, glory, power, wisdom, knowledge, understanding, eternality, care for his creatures, and love for humankind (Job 38–39; Ps. 19; Matt. 5:45; 6:26–30; Rom. 1:19–20).

God gave **Adam and Eve** authority over the earth (Gen. 1:28) and, by extension, human beings have been given authority by God to explore, test, and discover the physical laws governing nature by making observations and conducting controlled experiments (e.g., King Solomon's wisdom led him to discover many things about nature: 1 Kings 4:33; Prov. 25:2).

This God-granted authority and ability to discover the **laws of nature** has proven to be of immense help in carrying out the commission given to human beings in Genesis 1 to manage the resources of the earth for the benefit of all **species**, including themselves. For example, humanity's discovery of the laws of electrodynamics (Maxwell's equations) sparked a technological revolution that continues to raise the standard of living of people all over the world. Note that human beings have not been given the same authority over the spiritual realm, which presents a challenge in attempts to apply the **scientific method** to spiritual matters, since humans cannot presume to conduct controlled experiments on spiritual things or beings, although we can make observations about them.

Far from being typically uninvolved, God is continually involved in every aspect of the behavior of the natural world, upholding the physical laws that govern the typical behavior of nature (Ps. 104:4; Matt. 5:45; Heb. 1:3). Having created the physical universe and the laws that govern it, God is sovereign over nature. He can and does act in the natural world in ways that sometimes override its typical physical laws when he performs certain **miracles**. In these instances, it becomes eminently clear that the physical universe (nature), while it can appear to function as a closed system, does not always function as a closed system would, and explicitly supernatural events occur when any being from the spiritual realm exerts influence over the physical realm so as to cause a change from the natural order of things in this universe.

Because of the principle that nature reveals truths about God's character (Rom. 1:20), Scripture often portrays biblical heroes using a personal experience of nature as a tool to seek God. It was while Abraham was counting the stars (as God had commanded him) that he "believed God, and it was credited to him as righteousness" (Rom. 4:3; cf. Gen. 15:5–6). Moses fasted and received the Ten Commandments on a mountain. Jesus taught in the open air atop a hill or mountain, he fasted in the wilderness, and he often slipped away to the wilderness, garden, or a mountain to pray.

Erica W. Carlson

REFERENCES AND RECOMMENDED READING

Genesis 1–2
Psalm 19
Romans 1
Ross, Hugh. 2008. *Why the Universe Is the Way It Is.* Grand Rapids: Baker.

NEAR-DEATH EXPERIENCES. In recent years, few religious topics have captivated public attention more than near-death experiences (NDEs). At least two key aspects are of importance to Christians here—the question of evidence along with the challenging **worldview** issues raised by some who claim such experiences, both of which will concern us briefly.

Of far more evidential interest than the innumerable reports of looking down on one's incapacitated body, traveling down a corridor, and experiencing a beautiful light are the accounts of persons who claim to have witnessed things during the first phase of their experience that could later be verified. Almost without exception, these reports concern objects and events in this world rather than those in the more heavenly phase of some NDEs.

Of course, many religions and philosophies propose the existence of some sort of afterlife, so even evidenced phenomena do not prove the superiority of Christianity. But they may argue strongly against philosophical positions like **naturalism** that deny an afterlife altogether. Further, NDEs may provide pastoral or other practical considerations regarding at least the existence of **life after death**. These are a couple of potential benefits that NDEs may introduce. But since the personal, rather subjective portions of these testimonies are mostly insufficient to argue the case, evidenced claims are crucial.

Over the years, dozens of evidenced NDE accounts have been reported, ranging from those that provide mild support all the way to others with strong evidence of several varieties. What might the strongest cases so far look like? That probably depends on the appeal that different sorts of circumstances have on different researchers.

For example, some who had NDEs were blind both before and after their experience, while reporting sight during it. A few were underwater for significant periods of time, with each still correctly describing events in their vicinity during their experience. Even more evidential, others had no measurable heartbeat or brain activity but nonetheless correctly supplied verifiable details during those moments. More rarely, others reported accurately certain events a distance away from their immediate locations, things they could not have seen from their position even if they were totally conscious and doing well (see Holden 2009, chap. 9, and Habermas and Moreland 1998 for anecdotal evidence).

So there are undoubtedly a large number and range of reported NDEs that include evidence of various sorts. Moreover, different researchers have applied different kinds of cross-checks and balances to the data in order to detect as thoroughly as possible any occurrences of witness error.

Instances of the latter include cardiologist Michael Sabom's comparison of NDE reports to 25 control accounts of medical patients who were in similar circumstances but without reporting NDEs (Sabom 1998, 84–86). Counseling professor Holden employed several methods, including excluding from her study both popular as well as autobiographical reports, plus evaluating only those accounts that arose from near-death episodes. She also devised a way to rank as closely as possible the stronger from the weaker cases, and to separate completely accurate reports from those containing some error and those with large amounts of flawed material (Holden 2009, 193–97).

By each of these means, including both the reports themselves plus the application of various examinations, it certainly seems as though many of these evidential accounts reliably report **consciousness** beyond at least the initial moments of near-death states. So naturalism appears to have been dealt a serious blow at this point. But what about the very difficult questions that are raised for the Christian worldview in the process?

Worldview Questions

Near-death experiences certainly raise some difficult questions for believers. Most people who have NDEs report chiefly positive experiences, even if they are atheists or members of another religion. Few report judgment of any traditional sort. Moreover, the common interpretation drawn by many seems to be some sort of syncretistic universalism, with all religions providing ways to God. Occultic connections also emerge here and there. If NDEs are well evidenced, what should be concluded concerning these various conundrums?

Initially, each question here can be addressed individually, though we cannot work through them in the context of a single article (Habermas and Moreland 1998, 178–83). But just to comment briefly on one of the major concerns, why are not more negative NDEs reported? Although seemingly not given as much press, many NDE studies have still indicated a fair number of undesirable experiences. For example, Nancy Bush reports that in a dozen NDE studies that included 1,369 experiences, 23 percent were negative. The specific numbers of undesirable cases ranged from 12 percent to fully 60 percent, with some described as "terrifying." Surprisingly, in three studies the percentages of negative experiences ranged from just below 50 percent to 60 percent (Bush 2009, 66–71).

Pointing to the possibility of some underreporting here as well, Bush points out, "People who have had a terrible NDE are notoriously reluctant to talk." As another researcher reported rather honestly concerning the early NDE studies, researchers did not attempt to locate these terrifying reports specifically because they did not want to know about them (Bush 2009, 70–71).

Yet overall there is a much further-reaching consideration that largely appears to nullify the force of these tough worldview questions. I began by arguing that only the evidenced data should be utilized when considering the force of NDEs, since other reports are just too subjective. That principle applies quite specifically at this point.

Again, the evidenced considerations are almost all reports from this world regarding observed events during the NDE experience. But these major worldview questions involve otherworldly reports devoid of such data. Therefore, without this evidence, we cannot distinguish between these "he said–she said" types of sectarian reports. In other words, how do we distinguish between competing religious views on the grounds of unevidenced NDE interpretations alone? After all, there are no tests for the presence of angels. If it follows that we cannot make such moves, then these worldview questions must be settled on other grounds.

Gary R. Habermas

REFERENCES AND RECOMMENDED READING

Bush, Nancy Evans. 2009. "Distressing Western Near-Death Experiences: Finding a Way through the Abyss." In *The Handbook of Near-Death Experiences: Thirty Years of Investigation*, ed. Janice Miner Holden, Bruce Greyson, and Debbie James. Santa Barbara, CA: Praeger.

Habermas, Gary R., and J. P. Moreland. 1998. *Beyond Death: Exploring the Evidence for Immortality*. Wheaton, IL: Crossway.

Holden, Janice Miner. 2009. "Veridical Perception in Near-Death Experiences." In *The Handbook of Near-Death Experiences: Thirty Years of Investigation*, ed. Janice Miner Holden, Bruce Greyson, and Debbie James. Santa Barbara, CA: Praeger.

Sabom, Michael B. 1981. *Recollections of Death: A Medical Investigation*. New York: HarperCollins.

———. 1998. *Light and Death: One Doctor's Fascinating Account of Near-Death Experiences*. Grand Rapids: Zondervan.

NECESSITY AND CONTINGENCY. Matters of necessity and contingency have always held great fascination because they raise foundational questions concerning the nature of **causation**, the structure or architecture of the universe, the nature of **logic** and **mathematics**, the question of progress in nature, and the nature of God. Although the concepts are also employed in modal logic to explore the logical relationships between propositions, they are most relevant in the area of Christianity and **science** when applied to the question of God's existence, to empirical study of the natural world, and to the nature of science and causation.

The concepts are at the center of the **cosmological argument** for the existence of God, especially the version defended by Thomas Aquinas. This argument is sometimes referred to as the "argument from contingency," and the concept of contingency is meant to convey the idea of "being dependent on" rather than being necessary or nondependent. Aquinas argued that when we seek the ultimate cause of the universe and not just the local cause, which would be yet another physical event, we realize that this cause must be outside the universe. He developed the argument by appeal to the concepts of contingent and necessary being.

A contingent being, or a contingent event, is a being or an event that is not the cause of itself, whose existence must come from outside itself. A necessary being is a being that has always existed and so does not need a cause. A series of contingent events linked together by cause and effect would be a contingent series; the universe is made up of individual events, none of which is the cause of itself and so is a contingent series. Aquinas held that a series of events like this requires an ultimate explanation for its existence, no matter how many members are in the series. We can explain the local cause of any particular event, or sequence of events, by invoking prior causes in the series, but according to Aquinas, this will not help us to explain the existence of the whole series or why a series exists at all. So it is therefore reasonable to conclude that there must be a necessary being. Otherwise, no contingent series can get started in an ultimate sense.

Unlike some contemporary versions of the cosmological argument, Aquinas did not think that an infinite series of physical events is a logical impossibility, but he thought that because such a series is contingent, it would still need a cause from outside the series. This would have to be a necessary cause, because if it too were contingent, we would still need to explain how it came into existence.

A key feature of this argument is that the notion of necessity is not simply postulated, nor does Aquinas assume at the beginning that the concept of necessity is intelligible. The argument begins with the existence of a contingent being, or contingent events, and reasons backward logically to the conclusion that there must be a necessary being, no matter how unusual this concept may appear or how difficult it is for us to grasp.

There must be a necessary being, because logically there are only two possible answers to the question of how a series of contingent beings such as the universe got here. The first is to argue that it was brought about by a contingent being or cause, or series of causes. But this is unsatisfactory because one can always ask what caused this contingent being, and so forth. The second is to argue that there must be a necessary being who started off all contingent events and who does not himself need a cause. Otherwise, there would be no way to explain the existence of the universe.

The argument points to a necessary intelligence behind the universe, rather than to a beginning that has no cause, an infinite past that has no cause, or either a beginning or infinite past that have only a contingent cause, all atheistic responses that critics of the cosmological argument have proposed. The argument from contingency also becomes the basis to develop further arguments for the attributes of God, such as omnipotence, omniscience, omnibenevolence, and the like. God is also said to be metaphysically necessary in that his essence is his existence, a claim that is also the foundation for the ontological argument, though there is debate over whether God's existence is also logically necessary (i.e., whether God's nonexistence is a logical impossibility).

The concept of necessity is also relevant to some versions of the **design argument** because it is raised when we ask the question: Which events and happenings in our universe have to be the way they are and could not be otherwise? For example, could the scientific laws that we discover in nature and that make science possible be otherwise than they are? Might the laws of logic or the theorems of mathematics have been different? Is it possible for events in the universe to have unfolded differently than the way they did in fact unfold?

A further related question is whether there is any **chance** operating in the process of causation and also how chance and necessity are related. Is there a significant element of chance operating in nature; for instance, is it the case, as **Stephen J. Gould** has argued, that if we were to rerun history ("the tape of life"), we would end up with different **species** than the ones we have now and very likely no species of *Homo sapiens*?

Christian theists have argued that the consistency of the **laws of nature** and the progressive direction evident in **evolution** are arguments against there being a significant element of chance and contingency in nature, that there are some features of the universe that are necessary, such as scientific laws and the laws of logic and mathematics, all of which make not only science possible but medicine, **technology**, and even life itself. Moreover, this necessity is itself an argument for design in nature, because it prompts us to reflect on the question of how such necessity got into nature if the universe came about by accident. The argument that there is no necessity runs contrary to much of the evidence we have from our study of the universe, from our work in reason and logic, and from the general intelligibility of reality to the human **mind**.

Brendan Sweetman

REFERENCES AND RECOMMENDED READING

Plantinga, Alvin. 1979. *The Nature of Necessity.* New York: Oxford University Press.
Sweetman, Brendan. 2015. *Evolution, Chance and God.* New York: Bloomsbury.
Swinburne, Richard. 2004. *The Existence of God.* New York: Oxford University Press.
Thomas Aquinas. 1998. *Selected Writings.* Ed. Ralph McInerny. New York: Penguin.

NEO-DARWINIAN SYNTHESIS. The neo-Darwinian synthesis, also called *neo-Darwinism* or the *modern evolutionary synthesis*, is the dominant model of evolution within the biological sciences. It was initially developed during the 1930s and 1940s by evolutionary biologists such as Ernst Mayr, Theodosius Dobzhansky, Julian Huxley, and George Gaylord Simpson. Neo-Darwinism involves three primary claims (Meyer and Keas 2003):

1. Populations change gradually over **time** through descent with modification.
2. All life is related through universal **common ancestry**.
3. **Natural selection** acting on random genetic mutations was the driving mechanism building the **complexity** of living organisms.

The first two elements of neo-Darwinism (change over time or common ancestry) were discussed prior to Darwin. But Darwin (along with **Alfred Russel Wallace**) was the first to propose a general theory of evolution where the primary mechanism was natural selection gradually acting on random variation. This model became known as *Darwinian evolution*.

However, Darwin was unaware of the biological mechanisms by which variation arose and did not understand how traits were passed from parent to offspring. After Darwin it was shown that traits are inherited through **gene**s, and that variation can arise through mutations in **DNA**, the molecule that carries genes. Darwin's supporters then updated his theories to incorporate modern discoveries about population genetics and DNA, creating a new model known as *neo-Darwinism*. As Peter Bowler explains, "The fund of variability built up by mutation and retained by sexual reproduction provided the 'random' variation which Darwin and the neo-Darwinians had assumed to be the raw material of selection" (Bowler 2003).

Monroe Strickberger's textbook *Evolution* thus equates neo-Darwinism with the "modern synthesis," defining it as "a change in the frequencies of genes introduced by mutation, with natural selection considered as the most important, although not the only, cause for such changes" (Strickberger 2000). Similarly, Douglas Futuyma's textbook *Evolution* defines neo-Darwinism as "the modern belief that natural selection, acting on randomly generated genetic variation, is a major, but not the sole, cause of evolution" (Futuyma 2009). Thus, under neo-Darwinism, other apparently unguided evolutionary mechanisms like genetic drift are at work but are minor when compared to selection in generating adaptive biological features.

While neo-Darwinism is the dominant **paradigm** for explaining biological origins within the scientific community, in recent years questions have arisen about whether the synthesis remains viable, focusing on the ability of the mutation-selection mechanism to generate biological novelty. Over 900 PhD scientists have signed a statement expressing their skepticism of modern evolutionary theory's "claims for the ability of **random mutation** and natural selection to account for the complexity of life," and urge that "careful examination of the evidence for Darwinian theory should be encouraged" (*A Scientific Dissent from Darwinism*). In 2012 Oxford University Press published a book by the atheist philosopher **Thomas Nagel** with the subtitle *Why the Materialist Neo-Darwinian Conception of Nature Is Almost Certainly False* (Nagel 2012).

Many mainstream scientific articles have challenged central tenets of neo-Darwinism. Many of these scientists still accept a naturalistic evolutionary paradigm but are skeptical that neo-Darwinian mechanisms can create new complex biological functionality.

An article in *Trends in Ecology and Evolution* acknowledges a "healthy debate concerning the sufficiency of neo-Darwinian theory to explain macroevolution" (Bell 2008), and an article in *Theory in Biosciences* maintains that neo-Darwinian theory has not fully accounted for the origin of novel features and biological complexity:

> While we already have a quite good understanding of how organisms adapt to the environment, much less is known about the mechanisms behind the origin of evolutionary novelties, a process that is arguably different from adaptation. Despite Darwin's undeniable merits, explaining how the enormous complexity and diversity of living beings on our planet originated remains one of the greatest challenges of biology. (Theißen 2009)

Lynn Margulis, a member of the U.S. National Academy of Sciences until her death in 2011, was a notorious critic of the power of the mutation-selection mechanism undergirding neo-Darwinism:

> Natural selection is of critical importance to the evolutionary process. But this Darwinian claim to explain all of evolution is a popular half-truth whose lack of explicative power is compensated for only by the religious ferocity of its rhetoric. Although random mutations influenced the course of evolution, their influence was mainly by loss, alteration, and refinement. One mutation confers resistance to malaria but also makes happy blood cells into the deficient oxygen carriers of sickle cell anemics. Another converts a gorgeous newborn into a cystic fibrosis patient or a victim of early onset diabetes. One mutation causes a flighty red-eyed fruit fly to fail to take wing. Never, however, did that one mutation make a wing, a fruit, a woody stem, or a claw appear. Mutations, in summary, tend to induce sickness, death, or deficiencies. No evidence in the vast literature of heredity changes shows unambiguous evidence that random mutation itself, even with geographical isolation of populations, leads to speciation. (Margulis and Sagan 2002)

Elsewhere she stated, "Neo-Darwinists say that new **species** emerge when mutations occur and modify an organism.... I believed it until I looked for evidence" (Margulis 2011).

In 2008 influential biologists gathered in Altenberg, Austria, to discuss insufficiencies in the neo-Darwinian synthesis. According to *Nature*, they believed that "the modern synthesis is remarkably good at modeling the survival of the fittest, but not good at modeling the arrival of the fittest" and "the origin of wings and the invasion of the land ... are things that evolutionary theory has told us little about" (Whitfield 2008). The same year, historian of science and evolutionary biologist William Provine contended before the History of Science Society that "every assertion of the evolutionary synthesis below is false":

> 1. Natural selection was the primary mechanism at every level of the evolutionary process. Natural selection caused genetic adaptation.... 4. Evolution of phenotypic characters such as eyes and ears, etc., was a good guide to protein evolution.... 5. Protein evolution was a good guide to DNA sequence evolution.... 6. Recombination was far more important than mutation in evolution. 7. Macroevolution was a simple extension of microevolution. 8. Definition of "species" was clear.... 9. Speciation was understood in principle. 10. Evolution is a process of sharing common ancestors back to the origin of life, or in other words, evolution produces a tree of life.... 13. The evolutionary synthesis was actually a synthesis. (Provine 2008)

The following year, an article in *Trends in Genetics* stated that breakdowns in core neo-Darwinian tenets, such as the "traditional concept of the tree of life" or the view that "natural selection is the main driving force of evolution," indicate that "the modern synthesis has crumbled, apparently, beyond repair" and concluded, "Not to mince words, the modern synthesis is gone" (Koonin 2009).

This article is on the neo-Darwinian synthesis. While many of the scientists and scholars discussed herein are skeptical of neo-Darwinism, they are not challenging the overall view that some form of naturalistic macroevolution is correct. Nonetheless, skepticism toward the neo-Darwinian synthesis is becoming more common, so much so that in 2014 the world's top scientific journal, *Nature*, printed opposing articles debating whether modern neo-Darwinian theory needs a "rethink." One article responded, "No, all is well" (Wray and Hoekstra 2014), and defended the neo-Darwinian consensus. Another group of biologists answered, "Yes, urgently," and proposed an extended evolutionary synthesis (EES) to replace neo-Darwinism. The latter group also noted that evolutionary biologists sometimes suppress their own criticisms of neo-Darwinism to avoid the appearance of lending support to **intelligent design**:

> The number of biologists calling for change in how evolution is conceptualized is growing rapidly.... Yet the mere mention of the EES often evokes an emotional, even hostile, reaction among evolutionary biologists. Too often, vital discussions descend into acrimony, with accusations of muddle or misrepresentation. Perhaps haunted by the spectre of intelligent design, evolutionary biologists wish to show a united front to those hostile to science. (Laland et al. 2014)

Similarly, in *What Darwin Got Wrong*, cognitive scientists Jerry Fodor and Massimo Piattelli-Palmarini contend, "There is something wrong—quite possibly fatally wrong—with the theory of natural selection," and lament that "neo-Darwinism is taken as axiomatic; it goes literally unquestioned. A view that looks to contradict it, either directly or by implication is ipso facto rejected, however plausible it may otherwise seem. Entire departments, journals and research centres now work on this principle." They continue, "We've been told by more than one of our colleagues that, even if Darwin was substantially wrong to claim that natural selection is the mechanism of evolution, nonetheless we shouldn't say so. Not, anyhow, in public" (Fodor and Piattelli-Palmarini 2010).

Given the pressures faced by critics of the modern synthesis, it's unsurprising that neo-Darwinism still has many prominent defenders and remains the dominant viewpoint. In a 2015 essay, Douglas Futuyma explains that "some biologists have expressed doubt that the synthetic theory, based principally on mutation, genetic variation, and natural selection, adequately accounts for macroevolution," but in his view no "paradigm shift" is needed because the evidence "can mostly be interpreted within the framework of the Synthetic Theory" (Futuyma 2015). Undoubtedly these debates will continue into the future.

Casey Luskin

REFERENCES AND RECOMMENDED READING

Bell, Michael A. 2008. "Gould's Most Cherished Concept." *Trends in Ecology and Evolution* 23:121–22.

Bowler, Peter J. 2003. *Evolution: The History of an Idea*. 3rd ed. Berkeley: University of California Press.

Fodor, Jerry, and Massimo Piattelli-Palmarini. 2010. *What Darwin Got Wrong*. New York: Farrar, Straus, and Giroux.

Futuyma, Douglas J. 2009. *Evolution*. Sunderland, MA: Sinauer.

———. 2015. "Can Modern Evolutionary Theory Explain Macroevolution?" In *Macroevolution: Explanation, Interpretation and Evidence*, ed. Emanuele Serrelli and Nathalie Gontier. Vol. 2. Cham, Ger.: Springer-Verlag.

Koonin, Eugene. 2009. "The *Origin* at 150: Is a New Evolutionary Synthesis in Sight?" *Trends in Genetics* 25:473–75.

Laland, Kevin, Tobias Uller, et al. 2014. "Does Evolutionary Theory Need a Rethink? Yes, Urgently." *Nature* 514 (October 9): 161–64.

Margulis, Lynn. 2011. "Lynn Margulis: Q + A." *Discover Magazine* (April).

Margulis, Lynn, and Dorion Sagan. 2002. *Acquiring Genomes: A Theory of the Origins of the Species.* New York: Basic Books.

Meyer, Stephen C., and Mike Keas. 2003. "The Meanings of Evolution." In *Darwinism, Design, and Public Education,* ed. J. A. Campbell and Stephen C. Meyer. East Lansing: Michigan State University Press.

Nagel, Thomas. 2012. *Mind and Cosmos: Why the Materialist Neo-Darwinian Conception of Nature Is Almost Certainly False.* Oxford: Oxford University Press.

Provine, William. 2008. "Random Drift and the Evolutionary Synthesis." History of Science Society HSS Abstracts. https://web.archive.org/web/20131010003728/www.hssonline.org/Meeting/oldmeetings/archiveprogs/2008archiveMeeting/2008HSSAbstracts.html.

"A Scientific Dissent from Darwinism." Dissent from Darwin. Accessed August 30, 2016. www.dissentfromdarwin.org.

Strickberger, Monroe W. 2000. *Evolution.* 3rd ed. London: Jones & Bartlett.

Theißen, Günter. 2009. "Saltational Evolution: Hopeful Monsters Are Here to Stay." *Theory in Biosciences* 128:43–51.

Whitfield, John. 2008. "Biological Theory: Postmodern Evolution?" *Nature* 455 (September 17): 281–84.

NEUROSCIENCE. Neuroscience is the scientific study of the nervous system. It encompasses molecular, cellular, systems, and cognitive aspects of neurobiology. It also entails psychophysics, computational modeling, and the study of diseases of the nervous system. Modern neuroscience has deep roots in biology, but it is an interdisciplinary science, drawing from **psychology**, chemistry, medicine, genetics, computer science, **mathematics**, linguistics, engineering, and philosophy. Neuroscientists study the nervous system at a broad range of scales, from molecular and cellular processes to functional imaging of the entire nervous system.

History

The earliest record of neuroscientific observation was the recognition of the euphoric effect of poppy plants noted in Sumerian tablets. The earliest reference to the brain is the Egyptian hieroglyph for *brain*, which appears eight times in the seventeenth-century BC Edwin Smith Papyrus. Hippocrates, in the fourth century BC, described the brain as involved in sensation and as the seat of intelligence, and he provided the first description of a neurological disease — epilepsy. While some ancient authors (such as Hippocrates and Pythagorean Alcmaeon of Croton in the sixth century BC) regarded the brain as the seat of the **mind, Aristotle** regarded the heart as the seat of the intellect and the brain as a cooling mechanism for the blood.

By the end of the first millennium AD, the cranial nerves were well described, and the camera-like nature of the eye was recognized. In the sixteenth century, Vesalius's anatomy texts

revolutionized the understanding of neuroanatomy, and he described hydrocephalus. Much finer detail in neuroanatomy was worked out in the seventeenth and eighteenth centuries, with development of microscopy, and circulation of blood and cerebrospinal fluid was described in terms recognizable to modern neuroscientists.

The nineteenth century saw an explosion of neurobiological research, with recognition of cerebral localization for speech and somatic functions such as motor control. Development of radiology, pneumoencephalography and cerebral angiography in the early twentieth century allowed clinical study of the living brain, and the work of Sherrington, Golgi, Ramon y Cajal, Eccles, and many others brought the dawn of modern neuroscience with studies of synapses and cerebral electrophysiology. The US government announced 1990 as "The Decade of the Brain," and in 2013 President Barack Obama announced the Human Brain Project.

Conceptual Issues

Despite the extraordinary accomplishments of the basic and clinical neurosciences, a number of conceptual problems have plagued modern neuroscience. Cognitive neuroscience has been hampered by what philosopher of mind David Chalmers has called the "hard problem of **consciousness**."

The hard problem is the problem of explaining the first person experience — the "I" — of **consciousness**. The remarkable advances in neuroscience have failed to provide any plausible account for the subjective nature of experience. It is unclear how the extraordinarily detailed knowledge about third-person objective facts of neuroscience — molecular and cellular neurobiology, neuroanatomy, and neurophysiology — can account for the fact that consciousness is *experienced* in the first person. Philosopher Joseph Levine has described this chasm between neuroscience and an understanding of the basis for subjective experience as "the explanatory gap" of modern neuroscience.

Metaphysical Perspectives

The explanatory gap between neuroscience and subjective experience is a relatively new problem, emerging in the seventeenth century with the materialist-mechanical philosophy of **Descartes**, **Bacon**, and Hobbes. Mechanical philosophers put aside the hylomorphic **metaphysics** of Aristotle and Aquinas, who described the **soul** as the substantial form of the body. In the traditional Aristotelian-Thomist view, the salient powers of the mind, such as first-person experience, were readily explained using the four causes — material, efficient, formal, and final (see **Aristotle's Four Causes**). Mechanical philosophers in the seventeenth century denied the relevance of final and formal causes, and attempted to explain mental powers via material and efficient causes, effectively reducing the mind to a machine—a machine made of meat. This materialist perspective remains embedded in working neuroscience despite its profound conceptual confusion.

Specific Conceptual Problems in Cognitive Neuroscience

Intentionality

In the nineteenth century, philosopher Franz Brentano observed that consciousness is invariably characterized by intentionality, which is the "aboutness" of a thought. Each of our thoughts is *about* something—about our neighbor, about justice, or about God, for example. Intentionality is the hallmark of the mind, yet material things are never "about" anything in themselves.

How does intentionality arise? The traditional Thomist understanding of the mind explained intentionality without difficulty, as the grasping by the soul of the substantial and accidental forms of the object. In this perspective, intentionality is a manifestation of **teleology**. Materialist metaphysics has excluded teleology from nature and, in doing so, has rendered intentionality unintelligible.

Qualia

Another hallmark of conscious experience is its subjective qualities, also known as *qualia*. We have first-person experience, yet nothing in the materialist explanation of the natural world accounts for subjectivity. Materialist mechanical philosophy strips matter of subjective qualities; therefore **materialism** is by stipulation unable to account for subjective experience. The Thomist understanding of psychology posits qualia as aspects of the formal cause of mental powers.

Mental Representation

John Locke's doctrine of mental representation—that when we think we think of the idea we have in our mind, rather than having direct comprehension of the object of our thought—dovetailed neatly with the emerging materialist mechanical philosophy of the seventeenth century. This Lockean view of thought leaves us without reliable knowledge of reality as it is—we cannot check mental representations against reality in any meaningful way, because any check on the representation must itself be a representation. Despite the

Kantian efforts to repair this breech in our confidence in reason, the problem of mental representation—the problem of how it is that we can know reality and not just know our mental representation of reality—continues to plague cognitive neuroscience. In Thomist psychology, knowledge of reality was by direct incorporation of the intelligible **species** (the form) of the object in the mind.

Mereological Fallacy

Another conceptual confusion in neuroscience is the mereological fallacy. The mereological fallacy is the unwarranted attribution of attributes of the whole to its parts. Neuroscientist Max Bennett and philosopher Peter Hacker have pointed out that the very common claim in neuroscience that the brain "sees" or the brain "understands" or the brain "chooses" and so forth commits the mereological fallacy. Only a *person* sees or understands or chooses. There are indeed brain processes that *correlate* with seeing and understanding and choosing, but the brain itself is an organ and has neither sight nor understanding nor choice in itself.

Denial of Free Will

Some neuroscientists have claimed that neuroscience supports the view that free will does not exist. They cite research that demonstrates that cortical brain activity in humans may occur several seconds before subjects are aware of having made a decision. The implication they draw from this is that free will is an illusion; our decisions are determined entirely by material processes in our brain.

Many scientists and philosophers have noted that this interpretation misrepresents the science. The pioneer in this research, **Benjamin Libet**, asserted that his research *confirmed* free will; he found that subjects were able to veto or change decisions after the preliminary unconscious cortical activity was measured. Other investigators and philosophers have noted that the deterministic interpretation of Libet's work grossly oversimplifies the process of decision making and does not exclude free will.

Evolution of Consciousness

Evolutionary theories of the mind are deeply problematic. While materialists have tried with dubious success to explain biological adaptation in Darwinian terms of random heritable variation and **natural selection**, consciousness cannot have a Darwinian origin. Consciousness is a subjective property, with no necessary manifestation in objective behavior. Natural selection couldn't select for consciousness because the *behavior* of a sentient organism would be indistinguishable from behavior of an identical organism that was nonsentient.

Conclusion

Despite the remarkable advances in neurobiology in the past century and a half, neuroscience remains saddled with a profound conceptual albatross. Materialistic mechanical philosophy precludes an adequate understanding of the salient powers of the mind. These failures are due to the materialist metaphysical predicates of modern neuroscience, and cognitive neuroscience remains hampered by the profound conceptual confusion characteristic of the materialist perspective.

Michael Egnor

REFERENCES AND RECOMMENDED READING

Adler, Mortimer. 1982. *Angels and Us.* New York: Macmillan.

———. 1985. *Ten Philosophical Mistakes.* New York: Touchstone.

Bennett, M. R., and P. M. S. Hacker. 2007. *Philosophical Foundations of Neuroscience.* New York: Columbia University Press.

———. 2013. *History of Cognitive Neuroscience.* West Sussex, UK: Wiley-Blackwell.

Bennett, M. R., P. M. S. Hacker, D. Dennet, and J. Searle. 2007. *Neuroscience and Philosophy: Brain, Mind and Language.* New York: Columbia University Press.

Feser, Edward. 2005a. *Aquinas: A Beginner's Guide.* Oxford: Oneworld.

———. 2005b. *Philosophy of Mind: A Beginner's Guide.* Oxford: Oneworld.

Gilson, Etienne. 1956. *The Christian Philosophy of St. Thomas Aquinas.* New York: Random House.

Kandel, Eric, and James Schwartz. 2012. *Principles of Neural Science.* 5th ed. New York: McGraw-Hill Professional.

Libet, Benjamin. 2004. *Mind Time: The Temporal Factor in Consciousness.* Cambridge, MA: Harvard University Press.

NEW ATHEISM. New Atheists (neo-atheists) embrace a conflict model of the relationship between science and religion, seeing themselves as championing a **worldview** based on evidence and therefore opposed to religion, which they consider "the greatest threat to rationality and scientific progress" because they think religion demands "irrationality … as a sacred duty" (Dennett 2008). Neo-atheists consequently believe that "religion is not only wrong; it's evil" (Wolf 2006). The "New Atheist" label comes from agnostic Gary Wolf's 2006 *Wired* magazine article "The Church of the Non-believers," a title that suggests the New Atheism is an antireligious mirror image of religious fundamentalism.

The New Atheism was conceived as terrorists flew passenger jets into the Twin Towers in New York on September 11, 2001: "It is no coincidence that **Sam Harris** began writing *The End of Faith* the day after 9/11" (Bullivant 2012, 115). Sales of *The End of Faith* revealed a public appetite

for antireligious polemic, heralding a slew of popular books including the following: **Richard Dawkins**, *The God Delusion* (2006); **Daniel Dennett**, *Breaking the Spell* (2007); A. C. Grayling, *Against All Gods* (2007) and *The God Argument* (2013); Sam Harris, *The Moral Landscape* (2010); Christopher Hitchens, *God Is Not Great* (2007); Lawrence M. Krauss, *A Universe from Nothing* (2012); Michel Onfray, *In Defense of Atheism* (2007); Victor J. Stenger, *The New Atheism* (2009); and Peter Boghossian, *A Manual for Creating Atheists* (2013).

Onfray admits, "Never more than today has there been such evidence of vitality in … religious thinking, proof that God is not dead …" (Onfray 2007, 37). Moreover, observes David Fergusson, "much modern atheism is … not merely dismissive of religion but angry and frustrated by its re-emergence as a powerful social force" (Ferguson 2011, 7). **Alister McGrath** talks of the subsequent "crisis of confidence … gripping atheism" (McGrath 2013). *The End of Faith*'s subtitle—*Religion, Terror and the Future of Reason*—encapsulates the New Atheist reaction: scapegoating Abrahamic religion for social evils, among which the presumed irrationality of "faith" is the primary culprit.

Neo-atheism is characterized by "the blind faith that all faith is blind faith" (Lennox 2011, 56). Thus Richard Dawkins believes, "Non-fundamentalist, 'sensible' religion … is making the world safe for fundamentalism by teaching … that unquestioned faith is a virtue" (Dawkins 2006, 286). This misunderstanding is a corollary of New Atheism's **scientism**. Indeed, one can define neo-atheism as "the combination of scientism, scientific **materialism**, and antireligious activism." Despite rejecting moral objectivism and/or **libertarian free will**, the New Atheists portray themselves in an ethical struggle against the irrationality of religion. This self-contradictory framework offers adherents a sense of moral and intellectual superiority, community, meaning, purpose, and identity (cf. Williams 2010).

The New Atheists' works are laced with logical fallacies and factual errors. David Bentley Hart judges the New Atheism to consist "entirely of vacuous arguments afloat on oceans of historical ignorance" (Hart 2009, 4), chastising neo-atheists for "a formidable collection of conceptual and historical errors" (19). For example, Richard Dawkins says the biblical Gospels are fictional works with numerous contemporary competitors! New Atheists parrot many other skeptical views rejected by mainstream scholarship, including the myth of the warfare between science and religion, and doubt about Jesus's historicity and the idea that pagan **mythology** shaped Christology. Moreover, as Lennox observes, there is "no serious attempt by any of the New Atheists to engage with the evidence for the **resurrection of Jesus** Christ" (Lennox 2011, 188). Contrary to their professed interest in evidence, the New Atheists ignore the historical case for Jesus's resurrection (cf. Craig 2008; Licona 2010; Wright 2003) by appealing to **David Hume**'s discredited arguments against **miracles** (cf. Craig 2008; Larmer 2014).

James E. Taylor is surprised that "none of [the New Atheists] addresses either theistic or atheistic arguments to any great extent" (Taylor 2010). Indeed, they generally deal with arguments against **naturalism** and for **theism** by misrepresenting or ignoring them. **Alvin Plantinga** complains, "Dennett … doesn't know anything about contemporary analytic **philosophy of religion**, but that doesn't stop him from making public declarations on the subject" (Plantinga 2011, 49). When it comes to **natural theology**, Dennett punts to Dawkins: "I give short shrift to the task of rebutting the standard arguments for the existence of God [in *Breaking the Spell*], so I welcome the … demolitions that Dawkins has assembled" (Dennett 2006).

This is a case of the blind leading the blind. As Taylor comments, "Dawkins … has been criticized for engaging in an overly cursory evaluation of theistic arguments and for ignoring the philosophical literature in natural theology" (Taylor 2010). Moreover, as Jeremy Pierce notes, Dawkins "regularly commits easy-to-spot fallacies" (Pierce 2006). James Hannam describes *The God Delusion* as "under-researched" and "under-argued," and observes, "The treatment of the traditional proofs of God's existence is largely an attack on straw men.… This refusal to engage with the serious literature is evident throughout" (Hannam 2006).

Dennett portrays Dawkins "flattening all the serious arguments *for* the existence of God" (Dennett 2006). *The God Delusion* is the most extensive New Atheist rebuttal of natural theology; but whereas Dawkins devotes 37 pages to 10 theistic arguments, Plantinga once discussed "a couple of dozen or so" theistic arguments (cf. Plantinga 2006).

Of the nine positive arguments defended in *The Blackwell Companion to Natural Theology* (Craig and Moreland 2012), only five appear in *The God Delusion*. As Chuck Edwards muses, "Dawkins shows that he is totally unfamiliar with the wealth of literature on the subject" (Edwards 2007). Hence, even if Dawkins offered the decisive refutations Dennett imagines, *The God Delusion* wouldn't merit P. Z. Myers's appraisal as "a thorough overview" (Myers 2006). However, Dawkins doesn't rebut the arguments he considers (mainly because he doesn't understand them).

As **William Lane Craig** concludes, the objections raised by Dawkins to these arguments "are not even injurious, much less deadly" (Craig 2009, 30). Barney Zwartz thinks Dawkins "is spectacularly inept when it comes to the traditional philosophical arguments for God" (Zwartz 2006). Plantinga writes that many of Dawkins's arguments in *The God Delusion* "would receive a failing grade in a sophomore philosophy class" (Plantinga 2007). Indeed, Plantinga castigates the New Atheists for "their close-mindedness, their reluctance to consider evidence, and their resort to ridicule, mockery, and misrepresentation in the place of serious argument" (Lennox 2011). Paul Copan likewise decries their "sloppily argued attacks" (Copan and Craig 2009, vii), which he considers "remarkably out of touch with [contemporary] sophisticated theistic arguments for God's existence" (Copan 2008). Craig warns that the "New Atheism is just an imposture, a bluff really that preys upon the naive and the uninformed" (Craig 2014).

Many atheists distance themselves from the New Atheism. For example, Julian Baggini critiques their tone as "counterproductive" (Baggini 2009). Daniel Came warns, "There isn't much in the way of serious argumentation in the New Atheists' dialectical arsenal" (Came 2011). **Thomas Nagel** observes, "Dawkins dismisses, with contemptuous flippancy, the traditional … arguments for the existence of God.… I found these attempts at philosophy … particularly weak" (Nagel 2006). Massimo Pigliucci critiques the New Atheism for its scientism and describes *The God Delusion* as a "historically badly informed polemic" (Pigliucci 2013). **Michael Ruse** comments, "Dawkins is brazen in his ignorance of philosophy and theology (not to mention the history of science)," and laments, "It is not that the [new] atheists are having a field day because of the brilliance and novelty of their thinking. Frankly … the material being churned out is second rate. And that is a euphemism for 'downright awful'" (Ruse 2007).

Peter S. Williams

REFERENCES AND RECOMMENDED READING

Baggini, Julian. 2009. "The New Atheist Movement Is Destructive." Tiden Etterpå. http://fritanke.no/index.php?page=vis_nyhet&NyhetID=8484.

Boghossian, Peter. 2013. *A Manual for Creating Atheists*. Durham, NC: Pitchstone.

Bullivant, Stephen. 2012. "The New Atheism and Sociology." In *Religion and the New Atheism: A Critical Appraisal*, ed. Amarnath Amarasingam. Chicago: Haymarket.

Came, Daniel. 2011. "Richard Dawkins's Refusal to Debate Is Cynical and Anti-intellectualist." *The Guardian*. www.theguardian.com/commentisfree/belief/2011/oct/22/richard-dawkins-refusal-debate-william-lane-craig.

Copan, Paul. 2008. "Interview with Paul Copan: Is Yahweh a Moral Monster?" *EPS Blog.* April 7. www.epsociety.org/blog/2008/04/interview-with-paul -copan-is-yahweh.asp.

Copan, Paul, and William Lane Craig, eds. 2009. *Contending with Christianity's Critics: Answering New Atheists and Other Objectors.* Nashville: B&H Academic.

Craig, William Lane. 2008. *Reasonable Faith: Christian Truth and Apologetics.* 3rd ed. Wheaton, IL: Crossway.

———. 2009. "Richard Dawkins on Arguments for God." In *God Is Great, God Is Good: Why Believing in God Is Reasonable and Responsible*, ed. William Lane Craig and Chad Meister. Downers Grove, IL: IVP.

———. 2010. "The New Atheism and Five Arguments for God." *Reasonable Faith.* www.reasonablefaith.org/the-new-atheism-and-five-arguments-for-god.

———. 2014. "What's New with 'The WLC'?" *Reasonable Faith Podcast.* September 21. www.reasonablefaith.org/whats-new-with-the-wlc.

Craig, William Lane, and J. P. Moreland, eds. 2012. *The Blackwell Companion to Natural Theology.* Malden, MA: Wiley-Blackwell.

Dawkins, Richard. 2006. *The God Delusion.* New York: Mariner.

Dennett, Daniel. 2006. "Review of Richard Dawkins' *The God Delusion* for *Free Inquiry*." October 10. www.philvaz.com/apologetics/DawkinsGod DelusionReviewFreeInquiry.pdf.

———. 2007. *Breaking the Spell: Religion as a Natural Phenomenon.* London: Penguin.

Dennett, Daniel, and Robert Winston. 2008. "Is Religion a Threat to Rationality and Science?" *The Guardian.* April 22. www.theguardian.com/education/ 2008/apr/22/highereducation.uk5.

Edwards, Chuck. 2007. "Dawkins' Delusional Arguments against God." Summit Ministries. April 24. www.summit.org/resource/tc/archive/0407/.

Fergusson, David. 2011. *Faith and Its Critics: A Conversation.* Oxford: Oxford University Press.

Ganssle, Gregory E. 2009. *A Reasonable God: Engaging the New Face of Atheism.* Waco, TX: Baylor University Press.

Gilson, Tom, and Carson Weitnauer, eds. 2013. *True Reason: Confronting the Irrationality of the New Atheism.* Grand Rapids: Kregel.

Glass, David H. 2012. *Atheism's New Clothes: Exploring and Exposing the Claims of the New Atheists.* Nottingham, UK: Apollos.

Grant, Edward. 2007. *A History of Natural Philosophy: From the Ancient World to the Nineteenth Century.* Cambridge: Cambridge University Press.

Grayling, A. C. 2007. *Against All Gods.* London: Oberon.

———. 2013. *The God Argument.* New York: Bloomsbury.

Hannam, James. 2006. "*The God Delusion* by Richard Dawkins." Bede's Library. www.bede.org.uk/goddelusion.htm.

Harris, Sam. 2004. *The End of Faith: Terror and the Future of Reason.* New York: W. W. Norton.

———. 2010. *The Moral Landscape.* New York: Free Press.

Hart, David Bentley. 2009. *Atheist Delusions: The Christian Revolution and Its Fashionable Enemies.* New Haven, CT: Yale University Press.

Hitchens, Christopher. 2007. *God Is Not Great.* London: Atlantic.

Krauss, Lawrence M. 2012. *A Universe from Nothing.* New York: Free Press.

Larmer, Robert A. 2014. *The Legitimacy of Miracle.* Lanham, MD: Lexington.

Lennox, John. 2011. *Gunning for God: Why the New Atheists Are Missing the Target.* Oxford: Lion.

Licona, Michael R. 2010. *The Resurrection of Jesus: A New Historiographical Approach.* Nottingham, UK: Apollos.

McGrath, Alister. 2013. "The Spell of the Meme." St Edmund's College. www. st-edmunds.cam.ac.uk/faraday/issues/McGrath%20RSA%20Lecture%20 13-03-06.pdf.

Myers, P. Z. 2006. "Bad Religion." Richard Dawkins Foundation. http:// richarddawkins.net/article,211,Bad-Religion,PZ-Myers-Seed-Magazine.

Nagel, Thomas. 2006. "Fear of Religion." *New Republic.* October 23. www .tnr.com/article/the-fear-religion.

Onfray, Michel. 2007. *In Defense of Atheism: The Case against Christianity, Judaism and Islam.* London: Serpent's Tail.

Pierce, Jeremy. 2006. "Dawkins Review." The Prosblogion. http://prosblogion .ektopos.com/archives/2006/10/dawkins-review.html.

Pigliucci, Massimo. 2013. "New Atheism and the Scientistic Turn in the Atheism Movement." *Midwest Studies in Philosophy* 37. http://philpapers.org/ archive/PIGNAA.pdf.

Plantinga, Alvin. 2006. "Two Dozen or So Theistic Arguments." http://appeared toblogly.files.wordpress.com/2011/05/plantinga-alvin-22two-dozen-or -so-theistic-arguments221.pdf.

———. 2007. "The Dawkins Confusion." *Christianity Today*, March–April www.christianitytoday.com/bc/2007/002/1.21.html.

———. 2011. *Where the Conflict Really Lies: Science, Religion, and Naturalism.* New York: Oxford University Press.

Ruse, Michael. 2007. "*The God Delusion.*" *Isis* 98, no. 4 (December).

Stenger, Victor J. 2009. *The New Atheism.* Amherst, NY: Prometheus.

Stewart, Robert B., ed. 2008. *The Future of Atheism: Alister McGrath and Daniel Dennett in Dialogue.* London: SPCK.

Taylor, James E. 2010. "The New Atheists." *Internet Encyclopedia of Philosophy.* www.iep.utm.edu/n-atheis/.

Ward, Keith. 2008. *Why There Almost Certainly Is a God: Doubting Dawkins.* Oxford: Lion.

Williams, Peter S. 2004. *I Wish I Could Believe in Meaning: A Response to Nihilism.* Southampton, UK: Damaris.

———. 2009. *A Sceptic's Guide to Atheism: God Is Not Dead.* Milton Keynes, UK: Paternoster.

———. 2010. "The Emperor's Incoherent New Clothes—Pointing the Finger at Dawkins' Atheism." *Think* 9:29–33.

———. 2011. *Understanding Jesus: Five Ways to Spiritual Enlightenment.* Milton Keynes, UK: Paternoster.

———. 2013a. *A Faithful Guide to Philosophy: A Christian Introduction to the Love of Wisdom.* Milton Keynes, UK: Paternoster.

———. 2013b. *C. S. Lewis vs. the New Atheists.* Milton Keynes, UK: Paternoster.

Wolf, Gary. 2006. "The Church of the Non-believers." *Wired* 14 (11). www .wired.com/wired/archive/14.11/atheism.html.

Wright, N. T. 2003. *The Resurrection of the Son of God.* London: SPCK.

Zwartz, Barney. 2006. "The God Delusion." Richard Dawkins Foundation. http://richarddawkins.net/articles/366-the-god-delusion-review.

Video

Williams, Peter S. "Concerning the New Atheism." YouTube. www.youtube .com/playlist?list=PLQhh3qcwVEWifP3P_gIS8MMsRXLOGDiG_.

NEWTON, ISAAC. Sir Isaac Newton (1643–1727) was a philosopher, mathematician, physicist, and astronomer, a towering figure in the history of science. He played a key role in the unfolding of the **Scientific Revolution**. Even after more than three centuries of scientific advance, including the rise of quantum mechanics and Einsteinian relativity, Newtonian **physics** continue to be applicable to numerous physical phenomena in the world, especially in the areas of kinematics, fluid dynamics, optics, and spacecraft navigation. In 1687 he published *Philosophiae Naturalis Principia Mathematica* (Mathematical Principles of **Natural Philosophy**), commonly referred to as the *Principia*, which many hold to be the most influential scientific work in physics and among the greatest in all of science.

Isaac Newton was born in an Anglican family on January

4, 1643, in Woolsthorpe, England, and died March 31, 1727, in London. His father (bearing the same name as Isaac) was a successful farmer who died three months before Isaac was born. After his mother raised him alone for his first three years, she married the rector of a nearby parish, the Reverend Barnabus Smith, and left Isaac under the care of his grandmother until age 12 when she once again took him under her care after her second husband died. He entered Trinity College at the University of Cambridge at age 18.

During his years at Cambridge, Newton studied philosophy and developed a strong interest in questions of nature that would inform his later ideas and revolutionary work in **mathematics** and physics. The Scientific Revolution had begun with the earlier work of **Nicholas Copernicus**, who proposed a heliocentric (sun-centered) universe, and **Johannes Kepler** and **Galileo Galilei**, who expanded significantly on this new view of the universe.

Newton's time at Cambridge was cut short when the Great Plague that was moving throughout Europe reached Cambridge and the university was forced to close. Newton narrowly escaped the clutches of the disease by returning home to continue his studies privately. It was during the following year and a half that Newton conceived of and worked out his most influential and far-reaching ideas, including the invention of calculus, development of his theory of optics, light, and color, and detailed calculation of planetary motion. Much of his accomplishment during this brief period of intense scientific outpouring was not formally shared with the world until many years later with the publication of his *Principia* in 1687.

In 1667, after the plague had run its course, Newton returned to Cambridge to work on his master of arts degree. He was made a fellow of the university, which came with the requirement that he take a vow of celibacy and recognize doctrinal articles of the Church of England. In addition to this, King Charles II created a law requiring all graduates to receive ordination upon graduation, and Isaac considered withdrawing from his studies to avoid this duty. Later, exemption was provided to members of Trinity College, and so Isaac graduated free of this requirement.

In 1668 he designed and constructed the first reflecting telescope, an aid to his developing theory of optics. He completed his degree in 1669 and, in 1671, was requested by the Royal Society to demonstrate the operation of his telescope, after which he published his work in optics and light, the content of which was later to be included in his book *Opticks: Or, a Treatise of the Reflections, Refractions, Inflections and Colours of Light*. Newton became widely

recognized for his genius, and shortly after completion of his master's degree, he was appointed the Lucasian Chair at Cambridge University.

Newton's work in optics came under strong criticism from Robert Hooke, a fellow member of the Royal Society. Newton's theory held that light consisted of discrete corpuscles, or particles, and that white light was a composite of all colors in the natural spectrum. Hooke believed that light consisted of waves, a view that was shared by Christiaan Huygens and other contemporaries.

Newton did not handle criticism well, sometimes flying into a rage. In the coming months, his relationship with Hooke became increasingly bitter and rivalrous, and he would have resigned from the Royal Society but for the encouragement of several colleagues. Newton's relationship with Hooke continued to deteriorate in coming years, and he was eventually to suffer a severe nervous breakdown in 1678, thereafter retreating from public intellectual life for six years.

During this time of isolation, Newton continued to develop his work in gravitation and planetary motion. Robert Hooke wrote him a letter in 1679, speculating about the possibility that the motions of the planets might be explained by a gravitational force dependent on the inverse square of the distance between the bodies. In 1684 Hooke discussed his idea of gravitation with Edmund Halley and Christopher Wren, both of whom were impressed by the idea but insisted that it required a complete mathematical treatment.

Later that year, Halley visited Newton and learned of his conclusion that the inverse square distance dependence of the gravitational force leads to elliptical planetary orbits consistent with Kepler's earlier measurements. Halley encouraged him to publish his findings, and soon thereafter Newton wrote his *Principia* and published it in 1687. Hooke would later accuse Newton of plagiarizing his inverse square idea, but Newton insisted that he had developed the idea earlier during his hiatus from Cambridge University.

The significant impact of the *Principia* on the development of science to this day is hard to overstate. Book 1 defined the basic concepts of mass and force, and presented his three celebrated laws of kinematic motion: (1) a body in uniform linear motion will remain so unless acted on by an external force; (2) an external force applied to a body results in its acceleration, with a value proportional to the ratio of the force to the mass; and (3) for every action (applied force) there is an equal and opposite reaction (force). With these three laws, Newton was able to successfully provide a solution to the majority of physical phenomena and unanswered questions of his day, and his ideas continue to form the bedrock of today's classical physics.

Book 2 presented a new scientific philosophy and methodology that was universal and far-reaching, later to replace Cartesianism. Newton asserted that scientific **explanation** of any natural phenomenon should be based only on those natural causes that are true and sufficient to explain the phenomenon; that the same effects should be attributed to the same causes; that the specific qualities of a body are to be understood as universal; and that scientific explanations based on the observations are to be accepted as accurate until other observations arise that contradict them. This new methodology embraced **objectivity** as core principle to scientific inquiry, an attitude that has been valued and celebrated down to the present day.

Book 3 explored numerous applications of his physical propositions, which included an explanation of the tides and a detailed analysis of lunar motion. They successfully explained the subtle gravitational influence planets have on each other, the oblate spheroidal shape of the rotating earth, the detailed motion of the moon, the precession of the equinoxes, the return of Halley's Comet, and numerous other unsolved problems of his day.

Newton's religious beliefs developed over time along with his systematic study of physical nature. To Newton the existence of God was undeniable, evidenced by the majesty and grandeur of the universe. He was not a strict deist, as were some of his contemporaries, including Leibniz. He believed not only that God was the master architect of the created order, but that his continual intervention was necessary, for example, to maintain the mysterious "action at a distance" behavior of gravity through the void of space and maintaining the planets in their orbits.

Today many scholars consider Newton's beliefs to be best described as Arian, since he did not hold to **the Trinity** or to the divinity of Christ, while others consider him a deist strongly influenced by Christianity. In the latter decades of Newton's life, he wrote voluminously on the Scriptures, developing what he believed was a literal and proper interpretation of the Bible, and searching for hidden messages and for scientific truths in it. He studied and wrote several religious tracts and treatises on prophecy, and even on estimates of when the world might end. In fact, Newton wrote more on religion and the Scriptures than he did on mathematics and physics, though today he is solely remembered and revered for his work on the latter.

As a result of the "mechanical universe" unveiled by Newton's laws, many in his day and later came to embrace a deterministic **worldview** based on a strict cause-and-effect relationship for all microscopic physical phenomena. Thus one could (in principle) predict the future if at a particular instant in time the mass, position, and velocity of each particle in the universe were known with infinite accuracy. While no one has ever seriously considered this knowledge to be possible for any being but God, the view has nevertheless through the years caused questions of free will and **divine action** to be probed with great intensity. In modern-day science (especially with the advent of **chaos theory** and quantum mechanics), physicists do not embrace such a strictly deterministic viewpoint of nature.

Warren F. Rogers

REFERENCES AND RECOMMENDED READING

Christianson, Gale E. 1996. *Isaac Newton and the Scientific Revolution.* New York: Oxford University Press.
Dolnick, Edward. 2012. *The Clockwork Universe: Isaac Newton, the Royal Society, and the Birth of the Modern World.* New York: HarperPerennial.
Gleick, James. 2004. *Isaac Newton.* London: Vintage.
Holton, Gerald. 1988. *Thematic Origins of Scientific Thought: Kepler to Einstein.* Cambridge, MA: Harvard University Press.
Newton, Isaac. 1687. *Philosophiae Naturalis Principia Mathematica.*
Segré, Emilio. 2007. *From Falling Bodies to Radio Waves: Classical Physicists and Their Discoveries.* New York: Dover.

NOAH'S ARK. The vessel described in Genesis 6 as the vehicle God instructed Noah to build is commonly referred to as Noah's ark. The Hebrew word for Noah's ark in the Old Testament is *teba*. *Teba* also is used to refer to the small vessel that hid Moses in the Nile River reeds. The purpose of Noah's ark was to rescue Noah and his family and, through them, humanity from rampant evil so malignant that it threatened the future of the world.

More than 200 flood stories exist in the lore of ancient and primitive civilizations. The majority mention a large vessel that saved humanity from **extinction**. For example, the Babylonian flood poem (*Gilgamesh Epic*) describes a ship measuring about 200 feet by 200 feet by 200 feet.

Genesis 6 describes the design details for the ark's construction. It was to measure 300 cubits long by 50 cubits wide by 30 cubits high. Estimates of the cubit's length vary from 17.5 inches to 36 inches. However, most scholars agree it was somewhere in the neighborhood of 18–20 inches. Thus the ark most likely measured 475 feet x 79 feet x 47 feet. It included three decks, a side entrance, and a roof elevated above a cubit-high opening all around. The main construction material is described in the text as gopher wood, smeared inside and out with pitch. While this wood type remains a **mystery**, its tensile strength must exceed that of oak, given the boat's dimensions. Any wood of lesser quality likely would have suffered stress fractures.

The folklore surrounding the ark often includes the idea that animals from all over the earth were housed in the ark. Although the English Bible seems to imply that the ark did hold all of the earth's land-dwelling animals, the Hebrew nouns likely indicate otherwise. The *basar, behema, hayya, nepesh, op, remes,* and *sippor* include all the tamable animals with which humans at that time would have had contact. The Levitical law indicates that only animals in this category can be behaviorally impacted by human evil. Thus the restart of human civilization after **the flood** required the destruction of all humans (other than Noah and his family) and all the tamable animals associated with human wickedness (other than the creatures Noah rescued via the ark).

Given this limitation on the kinds of animals rescued, the ark would have been sufficiently large to accommodate them along with all the food, water, and supplies necessary to sustain them for 13 months. Also, eight people would be enough to care for the animals. Given the hundred-year building, planning, and preparation time (Gen. 5:32; 7:6; 11:10), Noah and his family may well have adapted and installed certain labor-saving devices. Dumb waiters, carts, chutes, and rails, constructed out of wood and controlled by ropes, would have greatly streamlined their work as animal keepers.

Through the years, multiple claims of recovered ark artifacts have been made, but none to date has any plausibility. This lack of artifacts has caused some scholars to doubt the reality of the ark. However, no ark artifacts should be expected. Poorly dated wood fragments found at the mid to upper elevations of Mount Ararat must be viewed with skepticism. Genesis 8:4 reports that the ark came to rest on "the mountains of Ararat," not on Mount Ararat itself. The region encompassed by this mountain range covers more than 100,000 square miles. Based on geographical clues, it seems most likely the ark came to rest on the foothills some 200 miles southwest of Mount Ararat, not far north of the ancient city of Nineveh.

If this location (or a similar one) is correct, the **chance**s of finding any remnants of the boat would be virtually nil. The ark's high-quality cut timbers would have been too valuable for the postflood peoples, perhaps Noah's own family, to ignore as they worked to rebuild their homes and cities. Of course, given climate and other factors, that wood would have long ago decayed.

Hugh Ross

REFERENCES AND RECOMMENDED READING

Edridge, Anthony L. 2012. *After the Beginning: Creation Revealed in Science and Scripture,* 121–73. Bloomington, IN: WestBow.
Ross, Allen P. 1988. *Creation and Blessing: A Guide to the Study and Exposition of Genesis.* 188–200. Grand Rapids: Baker.
Ross, Hugh. 2014. *Navigating Genesis: A Scientist's Journey through Genesis 1–11,* 131–82. Covina, CA: RTB Press.

NOMINALISM. Nominalism is either the thesis that everything is a specific thing—a particular—or else the thesis that everything is concrete. The first is inconsistent with the existence of universals—things that can have multiple instances and may be "wholly present" at more than one spatiotemporal location, such as the universal of being red. The second is inconsistent with the existence of abstract objects—universals (according to some people, "Platonist" theories of universals), propositions, and mathematical objects—but consistent with the existence of "Aristotelian" universals that exist only where and when there are concrete instances.

When universals are rejected, alternative accounts are often given about the nature of attribution. Different kinds of answers are proposed to questions like "What does it mean for an object, O, to be red?" Among them are the following:

1. Trope theory: O is red because of the existence of a particular: O's redness.
2. Predicate nominalism: O is red because the predicate "red" applies to it.
3. Concept nominalism: O is red because it falls under the concept *red.*
4. Class nominalism: O is red because it belongs to the class of all (and only) red things.
5. Resemblance nominalism: O is red because it resembles other red things.

These forms of nominalism, along with the Platonism against which they stand, assume that the question "What is it to be red" is, most fundamentally, a philosophical question to which the answer is philosophical in nature. Nominalism can also take the form of rejecting all of these philosophical answers and treat the question as a scientific question, the answer to which makes no reference at all to the alternatives above. A scientific answer might refer to the character of light, the characters of pigments, or various absorptive and reflective characteristics of red things.

Propositions are typically thought to be abstract objects that can possess truth values and stand in logical relations to each other. Nominalism about propositions is the claim that there are no abstract truth bearers. Nominalists either propose concrete objects as truth bearers, or else they propose alternative ways of understanding phrases that seem to refer to abstract propositions.

Mathematical nominalism is the denial of the existence of mathematical objects, such as numbers, sets, and functions. Mathematical fictionalism is a form of nominalism that treats typical mathematical claims as false, because there are no mathematical objects to which, for instance, numerals refer. So, even though "7 is odd" seems to refer to the number seven and state that it is odd, the mathematical fictionalist maintains that there is no number seven, and so "7 is odd" is false.

Modal structuralism is the thesis that **mathematics** is about the possible existence of various concrete structures instead of about the actual existence of abstract structures. Therefore what appears to be thought, talk, and proof about how things are abstractly is really thought, talk, and proof about how concrete things *could* be. All other forms of mathematical nominalism are variations on these themes: either mathematics is about what it seems to be about but is false because the appropriate objects do not exist, or else mathematics is not really about abstract objects but things that do or could exist, rendering typical mathematical claims true (see **Mathematics**).

Scientific theory and practice is unaffected by the issues that divide nominalists and Platonists, since these are philosophical rather than scientific positions. Some Platonists argue, however, that the best way to understand important features of scientific explanations is by rejecting mathematical nominalism. Some recent versions of the indispensability argument for mathematical objects rest on this claim about the interpretation of the use of mathematics in scientific theories and explanations.

Scott Shalkowski

REFERENCES AND RECOMMENDED READING

Azzouni, Jody. 2004. *Deflating Existential Consequence: A Case for Nominalism.* New York: Oxford University Press.
Balaguer, Mark. 1998. *Platonism and Anti-Platonism in Mathematics.* New York: Oxford University Press.
Goodman, Nelson. 1972. "A World of Individuals." In Nelson Goodman, *Problems and Projects.* New York: Bobbs-Merrill.
Loux, Michael J. 2006. *Metaphysics: A Contemporary Introduction.* 3rd ed. London: Routledge.

NON-OVERLAPPING MAGISTERIA (NOMA).
Ian Barbour provided the standard typology of ways that

science and religion might be related to each other: conflict, independence, dialogue, and integration. Non-overlapping magisteria (NOMA) is a radical version of independence between science and religion developed by American evolutionary biologist Stephen Jay Gould.

The word *magisteria* comes from the Latin *magister*, meaning "teacher." Gould uses the word to mean "areas of teaching" and claims that the magisterium of science should be restricted to the empirical realm of facts, and the magisterium of religion should be restricted to questions of ultimate meaning and values. Gould himself was a religious agnostic but hoped the NOMA approach to science and religion would help to reduce or eliminate what he saw as the increasing acrimony between science and religion.

Gould's theory is more sophisticated than sometimes presented. He admits that there is contact between these two different magisteria, and even that they are absolutely inseparable, while still maintaining that they are utterly different (Gould 1999, 65–67). He cites the different attitudes of two twentieth-century popes on the topic of **human evolution** as an example of how his approach should and should not work in practice.

The first is the negative model: Pope Pius XII issued an encyclical in 1950 titled *Humani Generis*. In it he admits that it may be permitted for scientists to investigate the origins of the human body along the lines suggested by evolution, but that the Catholic faith obliges us to regard the human **soul** as an immediate creation by God. Furthermore, science cannot trump the teaching of Scripture that all human beings are descended from Adam. It is clear that even if Pius allows some room for scientific inquiry to proceed according to its own rules, it is the church that gets to determine how much room science has.

Pope John Paul II seemed to reverse the authority in that sphere of inquiry. In his 1996 "Message to the Pontifical Academy of Sciences on Evolution," he acknowledges that since Pius's 1950 encyclical, the data for evolution has become impossible to resist. And he concedes that science can determine the bounds of acceptable biblical interpretation by showing when some interpretations are wrong. Gould interprets John Paul's mandate of setting proper limits on biblical interpretation and theology as carving out an independent sphere for science.

Critics of NOMA stress that a religious system—and Christianity in particular—will entail claims about what exists in the empirical realm. For example, a universe in which God exists and performs **miracles** will have a different empirical reality than a universe in which he does not (see **Miracles**). And the life, death, and resurrection of Jesus Christ as described in the Gospels is just as open to historical research and empirical study as any other claim in history (see **Resurrection of Jesus**). If these critics are correct, there will necessarily be some overlap between the magisteria of science and religion, in conflict with the NOMA suggestion.

J. B. Stump

REFERENCE AND RECOMMENDED READING

Gould, Stephen Jay. 1999. *Rocks of Ages*. New York: Ballantine.

NUMBERS, RONALD L. A leading historian of science and religion, Ronald Numbers (1942–) was born into a Seventh-day Adventist minister's family. After receiving a BA in **mathematics** and **physics** from Southern Missionary College and an MA in history from Florida State University, he earned his PhD in history from the University of California, Berkeley, in 1969.

Beginning his career at Andrews University (1969–70) and Loma Linda University (1970–74), he distinguished himself at the University of Wisconsin-Madison from 1974 to 2014 and held various appointments, including chairing the departments of the History of Medicine (1977–81) and Medical History and **Bioethics** (1999–2003), and retiring as the Hilldale Professor of the History of Science and Medicine Emeritus.

Numbers's conservative religious upbringing and early education combined with his undergraduate work in mathematics and physics to shape the interests of his historical pursuits. They also provided the personal spiritual crisis seeming to motivate his ongoing interest in the intersection of faith and science, particularly with regard to evolution and creation. As a graduate student at Berkeley, Numbers recounts being confronted with a much older age of the earth than his early training had allowed, in a way he could not reject. As a result of the crack in his childhood beliefs, in his words, he "quickly, though not painlessly, slid down the proverbial slippery slope toward unbelief" (Numbers 2006, 13). It also motivated him to consciously treat all advocates of all positions with respect, especially those conservatives with religious, young-earth views.

Numerous societies and foundations have recognized Numbers for his scholarship and achievements with awards, fellowships, and invitations as diverse as the Albert C. Outler Prize from the American Society of Church History for his publication of *The Creationists* (1992), to the Benjamin Rush Award from the American Psychiatric Association (2000) for his contributions to the history of psychiatry.

Numbers's prolific career includes more than 25 books he has written or edited and numerous articles and addresses. The history of medicine provided an early interest, but his later work has focused largely on the history of creationism with regard to science, with particular interest in the controversies in fundamentalist/evangelical circles regarding **Darwinism** and antievolution movements. This subject is the focus of his signature work, *The Creationists: From Scientific Creationism to Intelligent Design*. He has also been editor or consulting editor or on the editorial board for numerous publications, including *Isis* (1994–99) and the *Cambridge History of Science* with David Lindberg.

He has served as president of the History of Science Society (2000–2001), the American Society of Church History (1999–2000), and the International Union of History and **Philosophy of Science** in the Division of History of Science and Technology (2005–9).

John Soden

REFERENCES AND RECOMMENDED READING

Numbers, Ronald L. 2000. "The Most Important Biblical Discovery of Our Time: William Henry Green and the Demise of Ussher's Chronology." *Church History* 69 (2): 257–76.
———. 2006. *The Creationists: From Scientific Creationism to Intelligent Design*. Exp. ed. Cambridge, MA: Harvard University Press.

O

OBJECTIVITY. Objectivity is typically contrasted with subjectivity. Objectivity is a matter of how things are in themselves while subjectivity is how things appear to be to some perceiver or thinker. According to most orthodox ways of thinking about much of reality, to the degree that things exist objectively, that existence is not dependent on an acting, perceiving, or thinking subject. The objectivity/subjectivity distinction is the reality/appearance distinction.

Psychology exposes the limitation of this characterization. There are objective facts about subjectivity. One can be genuinely, objectively in pain or in some other mental state. Objectivity is a matter of how things both are and are discoverable, contrasted with *mere* appearance. Those matters amenable to discovery may themselves have been the result of construction or creation. Novels are available for discovery, even though they are the products of creative **mind**s.

John Locke famously distinguished the **primary and secondary qualities** of objects. Primary qualities were to be the objective characteristics that objects have in themselves, such as extension, mass, motion, and number. Secondary qualities involve the sensations caused by objects, such as perceived colors, sounds, tastes, smells, and textures. Being measurable to greater degrees, primary qualities became the focus of much of physical science. Assuming that objective reality is not genuinely contradictory, the same state of the water may appear to be hot to one but cold to another, depending on the conditions of those observers. Similar observations arise regarding the other senses.

Philosophical issues of objectivity concern not only whether subjectivity is involved in some state of affairs, but also whether the relevant reality is *ultimately* subjective or mind dependent. Bishop George Berkeley rejected **materialism** because, he maintained, everything is ultimately an idea. Matters we regard as objective are those that are not matters of creaturely subjectivity, but are discoverable matters of God's mind. Berkeley thought that God's subjective states are what they are regardless of what nondivine creatures take them to be.

Some ethical theories, such as hedonic utilitarianism, treat the fundamentals of morals as ultimately subjective (states of pleasure and pain), but the facts of **morality** as objective, since it is not a matter of mere preference whether one action or policy maximizes pleasure or not. More thorough subjectivist ethical theories construe moral claims either as equivalent to one's approval or disapproval of some state or action, or else they merely express, rather than report, one's attitudes about that state or action. "Objectivist" theories of morality, by contrast, treat most moral claims as reports about a moral reality that has its character independently of anyone's judgments or attitudes about it.

Though objectivity is not typically treated as a matter of knowledge or belief, it is often associated with intersubjectivity, though it does not require it. Intersubjective agreement is often used as a means of testing or confirming the objective correctness of a judgment. That others, from their different respective vantage points, observe or conclude the same thing is evidence that an appearance or a conclusion arises from interaction with some state of affairs that is not largely of one's own construction or imagination.

Scott Shalkowski

REFERENCES AND RECOMMENDED READING

Brock, Stuart, and Edwin Mares. 2007. *Realism and Anti-realism.* Montreal: McGill-Queen's University Press.

Reiss, Julian, and Jan Sprenger. 2014. "Scientific Objectivity." In *Stanford Encyclopedia of Philosophy*, ed. Edward N. Zalta. Fall. http://plato.stanford .edu/archives/fall2014/entries/scientific-objectivity/.

OCCAM'S RAZOR. Occam's (or Ockham's) razor is a heuristic principle traditionally attributed to Franciscan logician William of Occam (c. 1280–c. 1349), who wrote, "Plurality should not be posited without necessity." French Dominican theologian and philosopher Durand de Saint-Pourçain used the razor before Occam, but Occam became associated with the principle due to his frequent mention and application of it.

The first known use of the term *Occam's razor* occurred in 1852 in the work of the British mathematician William Rowan Hamilton. Today the razor is best known via the paraphrase by the seventeenth-century scholar John Ponce: "Entities are not to be multiplied beyond what is necessary." A similar principle of parsimony can be seen in the thought of Thomas Aquinas, who wrote, "It is superfluous to suppose that what can be accounted for by a few principles has been produced by many" (Aquinas 1274).

Encyclopaedia Brittanica incorrectly states that Occam's razor gives "precedence to simplicity; of two competing theories, the simpler explanation of an entity is to be preferred" (Duignan 2014). Instead, explanatory adequacy is morc important than cxplanatory simplicity; a complex but adequate explanation is obviously preferable to a simpler but inadequate explanation.

One might think of Occam's razor as consisting of *two* "blades"—the first has a preference for explanatory adequacy while the subordinate second blade has a preference for explanatory simplicity, but with an "all things being equal" condition attached. Occam's razor can thus be expressed as the principle that when seeking to explain some data set X, one should (a) eliminate inadequate explanations and (b) eliminate needlessly complex explanations. That is, one should seek the simplest adequate explanation. While the razor helps us to avoid inadequate explanations and unwarranted beliefs, it may not allow us to settle on a uniquely "best" explanation.

Occam's razor raises questions about simplicity. Simplicity in terms of the number of entities posited differs from simplicity in terms of the number of ontological types posited. Only in the first sense of simplicity is God a simpler explanation of cosmic fine-tuning than a **multiverse**. Occam's razor also raises questions about our criteria for explanatory adequacy. Especially noteworthy is the role played by principles of epistemic trust in explanatory adequacy (cf. Swinburne 2010). For example, George Berkeley used Occam's razor to eliminate matter as an unnecessary plurality, but doing so ignored the properly basic status of belief in physical reality. Likewise, Reformed epistemologists argue that one need not adopt Aquinas's procedure of using theistic arguments in order to have a warranted belief in God, even though **naturalism** is simpler than **theism** (cf. Plantinga 2000; Plantinga and Wolterstorff 1983).

Peter S. Williams

REFERENCES AND RECOMMENDED READING

Carroll, Robert T. "Occam's Razor." Accessed October 11, 2016. *The Skeptic's Dictionary.* http://skepdic.com/occam.html.

Duignan, Brian. 2015. "Occam's Razor." *Encyclopaedia Brittanica.* Accessed October 11, 2016. www.britannica.com/EBchecked/topic/424706/Occams-razor. Last updated June 4, 2015.

Kaye, Sharon. "William of Ockham." *Internet Encyclopedia of Philosophy.* Accessed October 11, 2016. www.iep.utm.edu/ockham/#H2.

"Occam's Razor." *RationalWiki.* Accessed October 11, 2016. http://rationalwiki.org/wiki/Occam's_razor.

Plantinga, Alvin. 2000. *Warranted Christian Belief.* New York: Oxford University Press.

Plantinga, Alvin, and Nicholas Wolterstorff, eds. 1983. *Faith and Rationality: Reason and Belief in God.* Notre Dame, IN: University of Notre Dame Press.

Swinburne, Richard. 2010. *Is There a God?* New York: Oxford University Press.

Thomas Aquinas. 1274. *Summa Theologica.* New Advent. www.newadvent.org/summa/1002.htm.

Warburton, Nigel. 2007. *Thinking from A to Z.* 3rd ed. London: Routledge.

OCCASIONALISM. Occasionalism is a theory about the mode of God's providential action in the natural realm. As with most philosophical ideas, it comes in a variety of forms. In its strongest form, occasionalism maintains that all created entities, whether inanimate or sentient, are devoid of the power to cause anything, so God is the only genuine causal agent.

In this strong form, physical objects do not cause effects in other physical objects or in **mind**s; minds do not cause effects in the material world or in other minds; and individual minds do not even cause effects within themselves. Instead, it is God's direct action that is responsible for everything: when one billiard ball strikes another, it provides an occasion for God to move the second ball in accordance with regularities he has prescribed. When you drink your morning coffee, the liquid on your tongue is merely the occasion for God to cause your relevant perception of taste; when you exercise your will to walk outside to get your mail, it is an occasion for God to move your legs and give your mind the sensation of walking and motion; even following a progression of thoughts in your mind provides the occasion for God to cause that succession of ideas.

Needless to say, many who are inclined to embrace occasionalism as an account of body-body and mind-body **causation** balk at the idea that God causes the succession of ideas in our minds—though the American philosopher-theologian Jonathan Edwards (1703–58) held this strong view (see Wainwright 2012). More common is a restricted form of occasionalism maintaining that God is the sole active cause of everything in that part of the universe not subject to the free choices of finite sentient beings, whose freedom of thought and will lead to decisions to act that become the occasion for God's causal realization of those actions in the world.

Precedent for an occasionalist understanding of **providence** is found in both the Bible and the Qur'an (see such biblical passages as Job 38:25–30, 39–41; Ps. 148:3–10; Isa. 26:12; Acts 17:27–28; Col. 1:16–17; Heb. 1:3; 11:3; for the Qur'an, see, e.g., *Surah* 13:2–5) and throughout the history of Judeo-Christian and Islamic thought. It has sometimes been argued that the dominance of occasionalism in Islamic thought, particularly through the influence of al-Ghazali (1058–1111), led to the decline of **natural philosophy** in

Islam and its failure to sustain a tradition leading to the development of modern science (see, e.g., Grant 2004, 237).

To place the blame for this on the mode of **divine action** rather than differences between Judeo-Christian and Islamic conceptions of God and the relationship of religion to the state, however, is a mistake. While the God of the Bible is unchanging in his moral character and both constant and faithful in his care for the created order and love toward humanity, Islam casts Allah as an absolute divine power whose will can be arbitrary or capricious, leading to a fatalistic attitude toward human life. It was this view of God as absolute and arbitrary power, combined with control of the state by Islamic clerics who feared that the study of logic, **mathematics**, and natural philosophy would strip students of their religion, that led to the suppression of such studies and the demise of natural philosophy under Islam. Occasionalism, as its preferred conception of divine action, bears no substantial blame.

In the West, general philosophical considerations regarding the nature of causal relations led to the rise of occasionalism as a theory of causation in seventeenth- and eighteenth-century philosophy (Adams 1973; Clatterbaugh 1999; Downing 2004; Freddoso 1988; Lee 2008; Nadler 1993, 1996; Schmaltz 2008; Wainwright 2012). Seminal in this regard was the influence of **René Descartes** (1596–1650) and subsequent Cartesian philosophers such as Johannes Clauberg (1622–65), Géraud de Cordemoy (1626–84), Arnold Geulincx (1624–69), Louis de la Forge (1632–66), and, most notably, Nicolas Malebranche (1638–1715).

While influenced by Malebranche, George Berkeley's (1685–1753) occasionalism followed from his immaterialist idealism (see **Idealism**), since physical objects conceived as collections of ideas were passive and devoid of intrinsic causal powers. Unlike Jonathan Edwards, whose occasionalist idealism was derivative of his extreme Calvinism, however, Berkeley regarded finite spiritual beings as causally active in their own right (Adams 1973; Lee 2008; Wainwright 2012). Occasionalist arguments also strongly influenced **David Hume**'s (1711–76) account of causation (Nadler 1996).

Occasionalism continues to be debated among philosophers and theologians as a theory of causation and mode of divine action (Freddoso 1991, 1994; Kvanvig and McCann 1988; McCann and Kvanvig 1991; Morris 1988; Quinn 1988). More recently, this debate has shifted toward the causal implications of quantum theory (see **Quantum Theory, Interpretations of**), with some philosophers arguing that occasionalism is the only viable conception of providential action in light of the causal incompleteness of nature that

quantum theory reveals, and others resisting this inference (Gordon 1998, 2011, 2013; Plantinga 2011, 2014; Pollard 1958; Pruss 2006; Russell et al. 2001; Saunders 2002).

Bruce L. Gordon

REFERENCES AND RECOMMENDED READING

Adams, Robert. 1973. "Berkeley's 'Notion' of Spiritual Substance." *Archiv für Geschichte der Philosophie* 55:47–69.
Clatterbaugh, K. 1999. *The Causation Debate in Modern Philosophy, 1637–1739.* New York: Routledge.
Downing, Lisa. 2004. "George Berkeley." In *Stanford Encyclopedia of Philosophy*, ed. Edward N. Zalta. http://plato.stanford.edu/archives/win2004/entries/berkeley/.
Freddoso, Alfred. 1988. "Medieval Aristotelianism and the Case against Secondary Causation in Nature." In *Divine and Human Action: Essays in the Metaphysics of Theism*, ed. Thomas V. Morris, 74–118. Ithaca, NY: Cornell University Press.
———. 1991. "God's General Concurrence with Secondary Causes: Why Conservation Is Not Enough." *Philosophical Perspectives* 5:553–85.
———. 1994. "God's General Concurrence with Secondary Causes: Pitfalls and Prospects." *American Catholic Philosophical Quarterly* 67:131–56.
Gordon, Bruce. 1998. "Quantum Statistical Mechanics and the Ghosts of Modality." PhD diss., Northwestern University.
———. 2011. "A Quantum-Theoretic Argument against Naturalism." In *The Nature of Nature: Examining the Role of Naturalism in Science*, eds. Bruce L. Gordon and William A. Dembski, 79–114. Wilmington, DE: ISI Books.
———. 2013. "In Defense of Uniformitarianism." *Perspectives on Science and Christian Faith* 65:79–86.
Grant, Edward. 2004. *Science and Religion, 400 B.C. to A.D. 1550: From Aristotle to Copernicus.* Baltimore: Johns Hopkins University Press.
Kvanvig, Jonathan, and McCann, Hugh. 1988. "Divine Conservation and the Persistence of the World." In *Divine and Human Action: Essays in the Metaphysics of Theism*, ed. Thomas V. Morris, 13–49. Ithaca, NY: Cornell University Press.
Lee, Sukjae. 2008. "Occasionalism." In *Stanford Encyclopedia of Philosophy*, ed. Edward N. Zalta. http://plato.stanford.edu/entries/occasionalism/.
McCann, Hugh J., and Jonathan L. Kvanvig. 1991. "The Occasionalist Proselytizer: A Modified Catechism." *Philosophical Perspectives* 5:587–615.
Morris, Thomas V., ed. 1988. *Divine and Human Action: Essays in the Metaphysics of Theism*. Ithaca, NY: Cornell University Press.
Nadler, Steven, ed. 1993. *Causation in Early Modern Philosophy.* University Park: Penn State University Press.
———. 1996. "'No Necessary Connection': The Medieval Roots of the Occasionalist Roots of Hume." *The Monist* 79:448–66.
Plantinga, Alvin C. 2011. *Where the Conflict Really Lies: Science, Religion, and Naturalism.* New York: Oxford University Press.
———. 2014. "Law, Cause, and Occasionalism." Paper presented at "Faith and Reason: Themes from Swinburne Conference," West Lafayette, Indiana, Purdue University. September 26.
Pollard, William G. 1958. *Chance and Providence: God's Action in a World Governed by Scientific Law.* London: Faber and Faber.
Pruss, Alexander. 2006. *The Principle of Sufficient Reason: A Reassessment.* Cambridge: Cambridge University Press.
Quinn, Philip L. 1988. "Divine Conservation, Secondary Causes, and Occasionalism." In *Divine and Human Action: Essays in the Metaphysics of Theism*, ed. Thomas V. Morris, 50–73. Ithaca, NY: Cornell University Press.
Russell, R. J., P. Clayton, K. Wegter-McNelly, and J. Polkinghorne. 2001. *Quantum Mechanics: Scientific Perspectives on Divine Action.* Notre Dame, IN: University of Notre Dame Press.
Saunders, Nicholas. 2002. *Divine Action and Modern Science.* Cambridge: Cambridge University Press.
Schmaltz, Tad. 2008. *Descartes on Causation.* Oxford: Oxford University Press.

Wainwright, William. 2012. "Jonathan Edwards." In *Stanford Encyclopedia of Philosophy*, ed. Edward N. Zalta. http://plato.stanford.edu/entries/edwards/#2.2.

OPEN THEISM.

OPEN THEISM. Open theism (sometimes called *free-will theism*) is the view that God does not (or cannot) have complete foreknowledge; specifically, God cannot know the truth value of future contingent propositions (e.g., "It will rain tomorrow in Boston"; "The president of the USA in 2024 will be a woman").

The primary motivation for open theism is to provide a solution to the dilemma of divine foreknowledge and human free will (Basinger 1996; Boyd 2001; Pinnock 1994, 121). Others have come to open theism from a philosophical position according to which future contingent propositions have no truth value, or if they do, the truth values cannot be known (Hasker 1989; Swinburne 1993, 1994; Hasker 1989). In either case it is said that the future is "open" to God, that in many respects (aside from God's decretive will, as is revealed in prophecy or God's promises) the future could go in many different ways, thus allowing humans the privilege of cooperating with God in determining the future. Open theists insist this view is consistent with divine omniscience: If future contingents cannot be known, then the fact that even God can't know them doesn't count against God's omniscience.

Open theism rests on five claims: (1) Time is dynamic (A-theoretic), not static (B-theoretic); therefore the future does not exist on a par with the present. Thus open theism is incompatible with the four-dimensional "block" space-time of relativity theory. (2) God is temporal, not timeless; that is, God experiences temporal succession and is not "above" or "outside" of time. (3) Human free will is libertarian, not compatibilist; **libertarian free will** is incompatible with any global physical or theological **determinism** (although certain actions of a libertarian agent might indeed be determined, at least some morally significant actions are not). (4) If God's foreknowledge is complete, then future events are determined and human freedom is not libertarian. (5) The only way out of determinism is to deny that God knows future contingents. Denying any of these claims undercuts the open theism position.

The claim that God does not know future contingents is quite controversial. Open **theism** was rejected by the Evangelical Theological Society in 2001 when the society adopted a resolution affirming that "the Bible clearly teaches that God has complete, accurate and infallible knowledge of all events past, present and future, including all future decisions and actions of free moral agents." Evangelical theologians thus reject (at least) claim 5 on grounds of a traditional orthodox understanding of God's attributes based on biblical exegesis (Ware 2000). Some also would reject some or all of claims 1 through 4, opting instead to defend static time and a timeless God (Helm 2011), or defending **compatibilism** against libertarianism (Helm 2001).

Some philosophers also reject open theism by rejecting claim 4. They note that throughout church history, several rather sophisticated solutions to the foreknowledge/freedom dilemma have been proposed (Craig 2001; Plantinga 1986; Zagzebski 1991). These proposals attempt to demonstrate how future contingents can have truth value and how God can have foreknowledge without thereby threatening human freedom.

Garrett J. DeWeese

REFERENCES AND RECOMMENDED READING

Basinger, David. 1996. *The Case for Freewill Theism: A Philosophical Assessment.* Downers Grove, IL: InterVarsity.
Boyd, Gregory A. 2001. "The Open Theism View." In *Divine Foreknowledge: Four Views*, ed. James K. Beilby and Paul K. Eddy. Downers Grove, IL: InterVarsity.
Craig, William Lane. 2001. "Middle Knowledge, Truth-Makers, and the Grounding Objection." *Faith and Philosophy* 18:337–52.
Hasker, William. 1989. *God, Time, and Knowledge.* Ithaca, NY: Cornell University Press.
Helm, Paul. 2001. "The Augustinian/Calvinist View." In *Divine Foreknowledge: Four Views*, eds. James K. Beilby and Paul K. Eddy. Downers Grove, IL: InterVarsity.
———. 2011. *Eternal God: A Study of God without Time.* 2nd ed. New York: Oxford University Press.
Pinnock, Clark. 1994. "Systematic Theology." In *The Openness of God: A Biblical Challenge to the Traditional Understanding of God*, ed. Clark Pinnock et al. Downers Grove, IL: InterVarsity.
Plantinga, Alvin. 1986. "On Ockham's Way Out." *Faith and Philosophy* 3:235–69.
Swinburne, Richard. 1993. *The Coherence of Theism.* Rev. ed. Oxford: Clarendon.
———. 1994. *The Christian God.* Oxford: Oxford University Press.
Ware, Bruce A. 2000. *God's Lesser Glory: The Diminished God of Open Theism.* Wheaton, IL: Crossway.
Zagzebski, Linda. 1991. *The Dilemma of Freedom and Foreknowledge.* New York: Oxford University Press.

ORESME, NICOLE.

ORESME, NICOLE. Nicole Oresme (c. 1320–82) was one of the foremost mathematicians and natural philosophers of the fourteenth century. He developed geometrical methods in **mathematics** and considered whether the earth might be rotating.

Life and Career

Oresme was born in Normandy, France. Given that he studied at the University of Paris on a scholarship for poor students, he was probably of humble origins. It is likely that he was taught by Jean Buridan, the rector of the university and a celebrated natural philosopher. After obtaining a master of arts degree, Oresme went on to study in the theology faculty of the university where he achieved his doctorate by 1356. In the same year, he became head of the College of Navarre. At about this time, Oresme became involved with the court as a royal counselor and chaplain. From 1362 he was appointed to a number of church positions on the basis of his value to King Charles V of France, culminating with the bishopric of Lisieux in 1377. He died in 1382.

Natural Philosophy

Oresme built on the work of Buridan in several areas of **natural philosophy**. For instance, Buridan had considered whether the earth was rotating. He concluded that it was not because an arrow fired vertically into the air lands where it was fired. Oresme correctly noted that this does not show that the earth is not moving because the arrow carries with it the motion of the earth.

As a theologian, Oresme also looked in the Bible for an answer. He concluded that most passages that suggest a stationary earth are just using everyday language. Such a "passage conforms to the normal use of popular speech just as it does in many other places … which are not to be taken literally" (Grant 1974, 67). However, he decided that in the case of Psalm 93:1 ("The world is established; it shall never be moved" [ESV]), a literal interpretation was to be preferred. Thus he concluded that the earth does not rotate. Nonetheless, he had shown that observation alone could not determine this question either way.

Mathematical and Musical Work

The mean speed theory, which allowed the distance traveled by a uniformly accelerating object to be calculated, had been developed in Oxford in the early fourteenth century. Oresme developed a way to prove the mean speed theory with a graph and showed how such techniques could be used to model the real world three centuries before **René Descartes** popularized graphs. Oresme was also extremely interested in ratios and musical intervals.

Legacy

Unusual for his time, Oresme did not write exclusively in Latin. He translated several scientific treatises into French for the benefit of the king, originating much of the scientific vocabulary of that language. However, although his work on the mean speed theorem was used by Galileo (see **Galilei,**

Galileo), the reputation of Oresme faded along with many other medieval philosophers during the early modern period.

James Hannam

REFERENCES AND RECOMMENDED READING

Clagett, Marshall. 1968. *Nicole Oresme and the Medieval Geometry of Qualities and Motions*. Madison: University of Wisconsin Press.
———. 1970. "Oresme, Nicole." In *Dictionary of Scientific Biography*, ed. Charles Coulston Gillispie. New York: Scribner.
Grant, Edward. 1974. *A Source Book in Medieval Science*. Cambridge, MA: Harvard University Press.

ORIGINAL SIN. The Western doctrine of original sin describes how all humanity, by dint of Adam's primal sin, is born ruptured from God, culpably so, and saddled with an abominable, incurable, and innate moral corruption (**the fall** is also part of original sin, but we focus here on "originated" or *inherited* sin).

This doctrine is significant not only in identifying the precondition for the inestimable blessings of salvation, but also in its coherence with many other doctrines—like a thread in a seamless garment (see Reeves and Madueme 2014). Recent scientific developments, however, raise a host of questions concerning our understanding of original sin, questions ranging from Adam's historicity to a radical rethinking of the nature of sin.

Evolutionary accounts of human origins render the historical reality of Adam highly implausible and offer a different narrative for behavior, one that reduces human behaviors to genetic adaptations emerging from the evolutionary process. What Christians interpret as clear instances of sin (e.g., envy, rape, genocide) are demoted to evolutionary by-products of **natural selection** (e.g., see Buller 2005; Dawkins 2006; Wilson 1978). Studies in **neuroscience** trace flagrant immoral activity, including psychopathic and antisocial behavior, to impairments in the brain (e.g., Rafter 2008; Raine 2013). In behavioral genetics, specific traits of behavior are the product of genetic and environmental factors (e.g., see Rutter 2006; Sesardic 2005); rarely, genetic factors seem to be the *sole* cause of criminal behavior (Brunner et al. 1993).

While this literature is hardly monolithic—one finds cautionary voices across each of these secular disciplines (e.g., in behavioral genetics, see Wasserman and Wachbroit 2004)—the tendency is for older language of sin to be subsumed under biological categories. Hamartiology *just is* biology.

What should we make of these scientific proposals? Among Christian scholars, three positions are recognizable. The first—call it "strong biologism"—tends to view originated sin as a *natural* part of the human story, an evolved, inherited biological capacity for selfishness, violence, aggression, and the like (e.g., Williams 2001). Others, less controversially, reinterpret originated sin as **genes** plus environment, a "weak biologism" that recognizes notable nonbiological dimensions to moral predispositions (e.g., Deane-Drummond 2009; Korsmeyer 1998; Messer 2007). The last group acknowledges these evolutionary predispositions yet denies their sinfulness—by the lights of this "suprabiologism," only conscious, willful disobedience counts as *sin* (see Edwards 1998, 1999).

But theological difficulties attend these explorations in evolutionary hamartiology. The key problem is that sin becomes *intrinsic* to human beings, a biological not theological predicament (raising a vexing christological question: Does the full humanity of Jesus undermine his impeccability?). The distinction between "moral" and "natural" evil collapses, so that it is unclear how one justifies the very idea of moral responsibility (for if human disobedience has ultimate evolutionary or genetic causes, then is moral *agency* a mirage?). These conundrums are not far removed from debates over the implications of biblical authority for science-faith dialogue. In the end, it is precisely the salience of such questions that guarantees that the doctrine of original sin will generate a dynamic research agenda for the future.

Hans Madueme

REFERENCES AND RECOMMENDED READING

Brunner, H. G., M. R. Nelen, P. van Zandvoort, et al. 1993. "X-Linked Borderline Mental Retardation with Prominent Behavioral Disturbance: Phenotype, Genetic Localization, and Evidence for Disturbed Monoamine Metabolism." *American Journal of Human Genetics* 52 (6):1032–39.

Buller, David J. 2005. *Adapting Minds: Evolutionary Psychology and the Persistent Quest for Human Nature.* Cambridge, MA: MIT Press.

Dawkins, Richard. 2006. *The Selfish Gene: 30th Anniversary Edition.* Oxford: Oxford University Press.

Deane-Drummond, Celia. 2009. *Christ and Evolution: Wonder and Wisdom.* Minneapolis: Fortress.

Domning, Daryl, and Monika Hellwig. 2006. *Original Selfishness: Original Sin and Evil in the Light of Evolution.* Burlington, VT: Ashgate.

Edwards, Denis. 1998. "Original Sin and Saving Grace in Evolutionary Context." In *Evolutionary and Molecular Biology: Scientific Perspectives on Divine Action,* ed. Robert J. Russell, William R. Stoeger, and Francisco Ayala, 377–92. Notre Dame, IN: University of Notre Dame Press.

———. 1999. *The God of Evolution: A Trinitarian Theology.* Mahwah, NJ: Paulist.

Korsmeyer, Jerry. 1998. *Evolution and Eden: Balancing Original Sin and Contemporary Science.* New York: Paulist.

Madueme, Hans. 2014. "'The Most Vulnerable Part of the Whole Christian Account': Original Sin and Modern Science." In *Adam, the Fall, and Original Sin: Theological, Biblical, and Scientific Perspectives,* ed. Hans Madueme and Michael Reeves, 225–49. Grand Rapids: Baker Academic.

Messer, Neil. 2007. *Selfish Genes and Christian Ethics: Theological and Ethical Reflections on Evolutionary Biology.* London: SCM.

Rafter, Nicole. 2008. *The Criminal Brain: Understanding Biological Theories of Crime.* New York: New York University Press.

Raine, Adrian. 2013. *The Anatomy of Violence: The Biological Roots of Crime.* New York: Pantheon.

Reeves, Michael, and Hans Madueme. 2014. "Threads in a Seamless Garment: Original Sin in Systematic Theology." In *Adam, the Fall, and Original Sin: Theological, Biblical, and Scientific Perspectives,* ed. Hans Madueme and Michael Reeves, 209–24. Grand Rapids: Baker Academic.

Rutter, Michael. 2006. *Genes and Behavior: Nature-Nurture Interplay Explained.* Malden, MA: Blackwell.

Sesardic, Neven. 2005. *Making Sense of Heritability.* Cambridge: Cambridge University Press.

Wasserman, David, and Robert Wachbroit, eds. 2001. *Genetics and Criminal Behavior.* Cambridge: Cambridge University Press.

Williams, Patricia. 2001. *Doing without Adam and Eve: Sociobiology and Original Sin.* Minneapolis: Fortress.

Wilson, E. O. 1978. *On Human Nature.* Cambridge, MA: Harvard University Press.

ORIGINS OF SCIENCE. Modern science undisputedly developed in the Christian West. But it is an open question whether that was an accident of history or whether there was something inherent in and unique to the Christian context that allowed modern scientific thinking to develop there. Other cultures seemed to have been further along the road of scientific accomplishment in the ancient world. But their attempts at birthing modern science were "stillborn," to use the phrase of **Stanley Jaki**. Why was viable science birthed in Christianized Europe of the sixteenth and seventeenth centuries?

The history of science emerged as a professional academic discipline largely in connection to this question about the rise of modern science. The twentieth century produced a considerable body of work on the topic, and there are many facets to the story. The focus of this entry is limited to the contentious point of just how much influence Christianity had on the development of modern science.

At the beginning of the twentieth century, some claimed that it was in spite of the influence of Christianity, rather than because of it, that science developed within a Christian context. Such sentiments suggest that it would have been easier for science to develop in a place like China where there was an older civilization, a larger population from which to draw scientific genius, and even technological innovations like a movable-type printing press, the magnetic compass, and gunpowder that predated their counterparts in Europe. India, like China, had ancient civilizations with large numbers of people, and may very well lay claim to significant innovations in **mathematics**. So why didn't India or China come to discover heliocentrism, the laws of motion, or the periodic table of elements?

Joseph Needham, an expert on the history of science in China, argued that a large part of the answer could be found in differing social and governmental structures in China. But he also gave a significant place to Chinese culture's conception of the divine, specifically that it did not revolve around a personal God who had imposed order and rationality on the natural world.

In addition, a factor noted by Dutch historian of science Reijer Hooykaas was the biblical **worldview**'s effect of demythologizing nature. For most cultures in the ancient Near East, the natural world was filled with personal spirits. The spirits' whims determined the course of nature; hence there was little motivation for studying the workings of nature. But in the Hebrew tradition, a personal God stood outside of nature and created it. For the Hebrews, nature itself was impersonal and could be expected to follow statable natural laws. Thus people might profitably learn new knowledge by studying nature and figuring out how it works. The Hebrew Creator, who fashioned human beings in the **image of God**, also provided a basis for rationality in nature.

Yet Christians share a monotheistic tradition with Jews and Muslims. So why didn't this tradition spur the development of modern science among these other religious cultures? In the Middle Ages, Jewish and Muslim cultures were further advanced and must be credited with preserving the works of the ancient Greeks, which proved important for the European Renaissance.

According to Hooykaas, the Protestant Reformation provides the key to understanding the significance of Christianity for modern science's development. The Reformation provided an additional impetus to throw off submission to authority that had controlled much thinking in the Middle Ages. A key example for Hooykaas on this point is **Johannes Kepler**, with his unwillingness to bow to the rationalist conception of the traditional authorities that the heavenly bodies must move in perfect circles. Instead, Kepler allowed the anomaly of eight minutes of arc in the observed orbit of Mars to force him to abandon the dogma of circularity. The Reformation attitude of not blindly following authority gave Kepler the permission to see the data for what it was, rather than for what it had been said to be.

Historian Toby Huff also recognizes this inherently rebellious attitude of science. However, he is less sympathetic to Christianity's role in the development of this attitude. He argues instead that the essential ingredient for the development of modern science was the existence of "neutral spaces" in society within which discussion of ideas could take place free from political and religious censors.

In Huff's view, modern science did not develop in the East or in Muslim cultures because they lacked institutional supports for the development of neutral spaces of inquiry.

In the West the development of science had to overcome the culture's Christian framework, according to Huff, and this was accomplished through the institution of universities and their incorporation of Aristotelian **metaphysics** that displaced the centrality of the Christian worldview. Universities gradually led to a separation between the sacred and the secular, and legal protection was thus afforded to secular thinking that was not available in Chinese, Indian, or Islamic cultures.

Stephen Gaukroger has argued that speaking of neutral spaces of inquiry in the early modern period is anachronistic, however. It presumes that the goal of scientific inquiry at that time is the same as we find it to be today, namely, the pursuit of truth. But in the early modern period in the West, science (or what was then called **natural philosophy**) was valued for its usefulness rather than its truth. And in that time period, its usefulness was measured by its service to Christianity. Gaukroger develops in rigorous detail the thesis that Christianity played a central role in the development of natural philosophy by legitimizing it as theology's "handmaiden." In broad strokes, the argument runs as follows.

In the thirteenth century, Aquinas had carved out a separate sphere for natural philosophy by allowing it to provide justification and demonstration of the truths of **revelation**. But when the Aristotelianism on which Aquinas's natural philosophy rested was called into question, natural philosophy had to be transformed to maintain its position of reinforcing theology. Natural philosophers and theologians developed the **two books metaphor**, according to which God revealed himself in his Word (the Bible) and in his world (the created order). As such, the two domains were able to operate independently in support of each other. Natural philosophy thus began as a handmaiden but became more of an equal, and it did so because of the theological imperative to study God's book of nature.

In this understanding, the attention paid to natural philosophy by the Christian West was a direct result of its theology. That natural philosophy became the more narrowly focused discipline of modern science does not belie the fact that it has Christian roots.

James B. Stump

REFERENCES AND RECOMMENDED READING

Gaukroger, Stephen. 2006. *The Emergence of a Scientific Culture: Science and the Shaping of Modernity 1210–1685.* Oxford: Oxford University Press.

Hooykaas, Reijer. 1972. *Religion and the Rise of Modern Science.* Grand Rapids: Eerdmans.

Huff, Toby, 2003. *The Rise of Early Modern Science: Islam, China, and the West.* 2nd ed. Cambridge: Cambridge University Press.

Jaki, Stanley L. 2000. *The Savior of Science*. Grand Rapids: Eerdmans.
Needham, Joseph. 1978. *The Shorter Science and Civilisation in China: An Abridgement of Joseph Needham's Original Text*. Ed. Colin A. Ronan. Vol. 1. Cambridge: Cambridge University Press.

ORR, JAMES. Born in Glasgow, Scotland, on April 11, 1844, Orr was raised by relatives after his parents died when he was a young boy. Intent on entering the ministry in the United Presbyterian Church, he enrolled in Glasgow University in 1865. In 1870 he earned an MA degree in philosophy and two years later a bachelor of divinity degree. In 1873 he became pastor of East Bank United Presbyterian Church in Hawick, Roxburghshire. Glasgow awarded him a doctor of divinity degree in 1885.

Orr became a professor of church history at the United Presbyterian College in Edinburgh in 1891. After the union between the United Presbyterian and the Free Church of Scotland, he became professor of apologetics and dogmatics at the United Free Church College in Glasgow in 1900 (Scorgie 1988).

Orr's 1893 work, *The Christian View of God and the World*, established his international reputation as an evangelical theologian. In this work, Orr contended that Christianity was not a philosophy but an entire world-and-life view. Orr pointed to how well Christianity resonated with both reason and human experience as evidence of its truthfulness. Orr not only promoted evangelical theology but also criticized liberal Protestantism. In *The Ritschlian Theology and the Evangelical Faith* (1897) and *The Progress of Dogma* (1901), Orr critiqued two of liberalisms most influential theologians, Albrecht Ritschl and Adolf Harnack.

Although an evangelical and proponent of Reformed theology, Orr was not bound by the strictest expression of conservative orthodoxy in his day. For instance, he helped write the Declaratory Act of 1879 in the United Presbyterian Church. This statement softened the denomination's expectations that its ministers would affirm a strict subscription to the Westminster Confession of Faith. He was also hesitant to insist that the doctrine of biblical inerrancy was a fundamental tenet of Christian orthodoxy (Bebbington 2006; Scorgie 1988).

Like many intellectuals in the late nineteenth century, Orr surmised that **Darwinism** posed a critical threat to evangelical Protestant theological convictions. While rejecting a purely naturalistic theory of the origins of life, Orr acknowledged that some form of the evolutionary development of organic life was extremely probable. He advocated a theistic view of evolution that considered evolution the divine method of creation.

According to Orr, Scripture taught that all of life derived from God. But he eschewed positions that considered a so-called literal interpretation of the Genesis account of creation essential to Christian orthodoxy. He also believed that there may have been some sort of genetic link between humanity and lower **species** that preceded the historical Adam (Hinson 1981; McGrath 1999). But his theological synthesis still sought to preserve the historic Christian doctrine that humans were created in the **image of God** and endowed with certain attributes that set them apart from the rest of creation.

Orr also affirmed a classically Augustinian view of **original sin**. In 1903 he gave the Stone Lectures at Princeton Seminary. Published in 1905 as *God's Image in Man and Its Defacement in the Light of Modern Denials*, Orr attributed the *imago Dei* to divine interventions in the evolutionary process. Orr also contributed four essays to *The Fundamentals* (1910–15), including one titled "Science and the Christian Faith." The fact that a theologian who advocated theistic evolution was included in a publication designed to rally support for the fundamentals of the faith indicates that conservative Protestants in the larger transatlantic community in the late nineteenth and early twentieth centuries embraced a wide variety of positions toward evolution (Livingstone 1987; Scorgie 1988).

In addition to his theological treatises, Orr edited several Presbyterian periodicals and served as the general editor of the *International Standard Bible Encyclopedia*. He died of heart disease on September 6, 1913 in Glasgow (Bebbington 2006).

P. C. Kemeny

REFERENCES AND RECOMMENDED READING

Bebbington, David W. 2006. "Orr, James (1844–1913)." *Oxford Dictionary of National Biography*. www.oxforddnb.com/view/article/41222.
Hinson, E. Glenn. 1981. "Neo-Fundamentalism: An Interpretation and Critique." *Baptist History and Heritage* 16 (2): 33–42.
Livingstone, David N. 1987. *Darwin's Forgotten Defenders: The Encounter between Evangelical Theology and Evolutionary Thought*. Grand Rapids: Eerdmans.
McGrath, Gavin Basil. 1999. "James Orr's Endorsement of Theistic Evolution." *Perspectives on Science and Christian Faith* 51 (2): 114–20.
Orr, James. 1893. *The Christian View of God and the World, as Centering in the Incarnation*. Edinburgh: A. Elliot.
———. 1897. *The Ritschlian Theology and the Evangelical Faith*. London: Hodder and Stoughton.
———. 1901. *The Progress of Dogma*. London: Hodder and Stoughton.
———. 1905. *God's Image in Man and Its Defacement in the Light of Modern Denials*. London: Hodder and Stoughton.
———. 1911a. "The Early Narratives of Genesis." In *The Fundamentals: A Testimony to the Truth*, eds. A. C. Dixon and R. A. Torrey, 6:85–97. Chicago: Testimony.
———. 1911b. "Science and the Christian Faith," In *The Fundamentals: A Testimony to the Truth*, eds. A. C. Dixon and R. A. Torrey, 4:91–104. Chicago: Testimony.
Scorgie, Glen G. 1988. *A Call for Continuity: The Theological Contribution of James Orr*. Macon, GA: Mercer University Press.

P

PALEONTOLOGY. Paleontology is a scientific discipline at the intersection of geology and biology concerned with the study of ancient life on the earth. The term is derived from the Greek *palaios* (ancient), *onta* (thing or being), and *logia* (discourse). The materials of paleontology are primarily the preserved remains of animals and plants enclosed in sedimentary rocks. Fossil remains may include the hard parts of organisms, such as shell or bone (composed of original or replacement minerals); mummified tissue, carbonized residue, or impressions of soft parts; and traces such as burrows, tracks, and footprints.

In popular culture, paleontologists are imagined to roam the globe searching for awe-inspiring creatures to be displayed in museums or featured in television documentaries. Pioneering paleontologists of the nineteenth century were preoccupied with the discovery and classification of fossil organisms according to Linnaean taxonomy, insofar as individual fossils could be related to living or known organisms. Over time the scope of paleontology has grown with the establishment of several subdisciplines with applications to evolutionary studies, climate change, and energy exploration.

Paleontological research falls into much the same categories as zoological, botanical, and ecological studies of living creatures:

Vertebrate paleontology is devoted to animals of phylum *Chordata*, including sharks, bony fishes, and tetrapods such as turtles, snakes, dinosaurs, birds, and mammals.

Invertebrate paleontology covers animals lacking a vertebral column, such as mollusks, arthropods, and cnidarians (i.e., coral, jellyfish).

Micropaleontology addresses single-celled organisms such as foraminifers, diatoms, and radiolarians.

Paleobotany is the study of fossil plants.

Palynology is a specialized micropaleontology devoted to pollen and spores of plants and algae.

Paleobiology (also known as *geobiology*) applies biological principles to theoretical questions of how animals lived. Using clues from living organisms, paleobiologists ask questions about the functions of skeletal parts or the physiology (unpreserved

soft parts) of extinct organisms—for example, modeling the kind of cardiovascular system required to circulate blood throughout gigantic sauropod dinosaurs or determining if a particular species of trilobite crawled on the seafloor or could swim.

Paleoichnology, the study of tracks, footprints, trails, and burrows of organisms, addresses questions of mobility and even social behavior of organisms.

Taphonomy is the study of decomposition, disarticulation, or other changes that occur in the fossilization process.

How individual fossil species and assemblages of fossils relate to their environment is the purview of *paleoecology*. By comparison to similar extant species and communities, fossils can be related to specific environments, such as marine reefs, deep sea floors, or wetland forests.

Principles of ecology can be applied to extremely rich fossil beds, known as *Lagerstätten* (Ger. for "mother lode"), to reconstruct ancient communities in detail (food webs, population dynamics, community succession). For example, a diverse assemblage of invertebrates in the Burgess Shale exposed in the Canadian Rockies reveals an early, diverse marine ecosystem of the Cambrian period (c. 515 million years ago). Abundant plant and animal fossils preserved in coal beds and ironstone concretions at Mazon Creek, Illinois, lived in coastal swamp and bay environments during the Pennsylvanian period (c. 300 million years ago). The La Brea tar pits in Los Angeles trapped animals that lived in the region over a period of 40,000 to 8,000 years ago. The oxygen isotope chemistry of fossil shells can be related to the temperature of water in which the organism lived, providing a tool to evaluate climate change in the past.

Biostratigraphy involves the use of fossils to correlate strata (unique layers of rock) and assess chronological relationships. According to the stratigraphic principle of faunal succession, the overall vertical sequence of sedimentary rocks in the earth's crust contains a parallel succession of unique fossils, representing different species living on the earth through geologic history. Index fossils are organisms that were readily preserved, abundant, widely distributed, and existed in earth history for only hundreds of thousands to not more than a few million years. The first and last appearances of index fossils and overlapping index fossil ranges in the same strata can be used to create time markers to correlate strata across wide regions and in many cases between continents.

Biotic succession was recognized and used successfully in the early nineteenth century, before Darwinian evolution was proposed as an explanation for the changes in species and the diversity of life. **Radiometric dating** of rocks containing fossils, such as layers of volcanic ash in sedimentary strata, provides a means of calibrating index fossil zones to an absolute time scale. Biostratigraphy is applied widely in the energy industry to correlate and subdivide petroleum-bearing strata based on the content of microfossils in drilled cores and cuttings (fragments of rocks recovered during drilling).

Paleontology provides important evidence for the evolution of life on earth. As they developed the principle of biotic succession, nineteenth-century geologists recognized that increasingly older strata contained fewer and fewer species that resembled modern forms (see **Extinction**). They discovered an apparent pattern of increasing complexity through time; oldest rocks contained only invertebrate forms followed by the successive appearances of fish, amphibians, reptiles, mammals, and finally birds. Each of those groups exhibit patterns of diversification, and detailed evolutionary lineages (phylogenies) are evident within them. For example, modern horses, rhinoceroses, and tapirs represent the three extant families of the order *Perissodactyla*.

The fossil record contains some 14 additional extinct families, including the titanotheres. The succession of perissodactyls in the rock record, especially well preserved in early Cenozoic strata of the Dakota Badlands, shows that each family emerged and diversified (new species added over time) from a small group of very similar primitive animals, including *Hyracotherium* (the earliest known ancestor of modern horses). In most cases, paleontologists are careful not to infer direct ancestry between related fossils in a succession of strata because the dynamic nature of the earth and specific conditions required for burying and preserving fossils work against leaving a complete record of every organism that lived in the past. However, paleontologists interpret common ancestry between contemporary or successive species and show that the fossil record of diversification is consistent with the evolutionary paradigm.

Cladistics is a method of grouping organisms by reference to one or more shared, unique characteristics inherited from the group's last common ancestor. Very precise transitions between species are recognized by both gradual and more sudden changes in form. Examples of gradual change include changes in morphology and size of marine microfossils and the increase in the number of thoracic segments of trilobites upward in stratigraphic successions. Alternatively, another pattern observed in the fossil record, described as **punctuated equilibrium**, involves little change in a species over its range (stasis), followed by extinction and rapid replacement of the species by a similar but slightly changed species without transitional forms (see **Fossil Record**).

Various intersections between paleontology and Christian thought are evident in the early development of the science and continue today. After fossils were recognized as relics of ancient life, seventeenth- to early nineteenth-century European scientists, including Steno (1638–86), Hooke (1635–1703), Buffon (1707–88), and Cuvier (1769–1832) held paradigms of earth history that were shaped by biblical accounts. Their various catastrophist interpretations had little in common with modern young-earth creationism and flood geology (see **Creationism, Young-Earth**).

Catastrophists shared the presupposition that successions of fossils and geological epochs represented multiple creations punctuated by upheavals and extinctions, revealing God's work of building and perfecting the earth, leading to the creation of humankind. This view raised theological concerns about how past creations could be less than perfect and why God would create species only for them to go extinct.

Rejecting the evolutionary paradigm, young-earth creationists interpret fossil succession as a record of mass destruction during the **Genesis flood**. Their critique typically points to gaps in the fossil record (missing transitional forms) or questions evolutionary lineages as nothing more than subjective inference by paleontologists. Succession patterns are interpreted as the sequential destruction of preflood ecosystems. Creationists propose baraminology as a new classification of fossil and living species according to created kinds, following from the creation account of Genesis 1.

Intelligent design and **progressive creation** advocates typically accept the standard geologic ages attributed to the fossil record but argue that **natural selection** provides insufficient explanation for apparently sudden appearances of novel features, body plans, and fully developed communities, such as the Burgess Fauna (see **Cambrian Explosion**). Progressive creationists argue that observed patterns of punctuated equilibrium are consistent with distinct acts of species creation.

Stephen O. Moshier

REFERENCES AND RECOMMENDED READING

Fortey, Richard A. 2001. *Trilobite: Eyewitness to Evolution.* New York: Vantage.

Gish, Duane T. 1985. *Evolution: The Challenge of the Fossil Record.* El Cajon, CA: Creation Life.

Gohau, Gabriel. 1990. *A History of Geology.* New Brunswick, NJ: Rutgers University Press.

Meyer, Stephen C. 2013. *Darwin's Doubt: The Explosive Origin of Animal Life and the Case for Intelligent Design.* New York: HarperOne.

Prothero, Donald R. 2013. *Bringing Fossils to Life: An Introduction to Paleobiology.* 3rd ed. New York: Columbia University Press.

Rudwick, Martin J. S. 1976. *The Meaning of Fossils: Episodes in the History of Palaeontology.* 2nd ed. Chicago: University of Chicago Press.

PALEY, WILLIAM. William Paley (1743–1805) was a prominent British philosopher and Anglican clergyman. He was educated at Christ's College, Cambridge, where he later taught. While he is primarily remembered as a paragon of British natural theology and the author of *Natural Theology* (1802), Paley wrote several other well-received books, including a work of utilitarian ethics in 1785 (*The Principles of Moral and Political Philosophy*), a book defending the historicity and Pauline authorship of Paul's epistles in 1790 (*Horae Paulinae*), and an apologetic for Christianity in 1794 (*A View of the Evidences of Christianity*).

Natural Theology begins with a famous thought experiment. Paley noticed that if a man walking across a heath were to stumble across a stone, he would not necessarily attribute it to design. But if a man stumbled across a watch, he would. Paley attributed the difference to the purposeful arrangement of parts that the watch displays. Unlike the stone, it contains several parts ordered toward an end or function. Paley argued that because the natural world itself contains even more complex arrangements of parts for purposes—a fact he details with copious examples—we should likewise attribute these features of the natural world to a designer.

Readers have typically seen Paley as offering an analogical argument. An eye has parts arranged like a telescope; so the eye, like the telescope, probably also has a designer. This reading has led to the charge that David Hume (1711–76) demolished Paley's reasoning before Paley ever wrote. In *Dialogues Concerning Natural Religion* (1779), Hume argued that analogical arguments are only as strong as the analogy. Yet surely there are many differences between a telescope and an eye (their material composition, their ability to reproduce, etc.).

But more recently, philosopher of biology Elliott Sober (2000) has argued that Paley's argument is an inference to the best explanation, a type of argument common in the historical sciences. Paley considered the phenomenon of parts arranged for an adaptive purpose. He gathered various explanations (chance and design) and concluded that design was the best available explanation. Nowadays, of course, Paley would also have to consider Darwin's explanation—the explanation Sober favors.

However, it should be noted that Paley's argument can also be given a deductive reading (e.g., Oppy 2002). Several features of Paley's argument make a deductive reading plausible. Paley uses the language of "proof," "demonstration," and "implication." His conclusions do not seem to be probabilistic or tentative but instead include language like "certain," "inevitable," and "invincible." Furthermore, Paley seemed at pains to show that his argument avoided Hume's criticisms of analogical arguments. For instance, Paley (2006, 35–37) claimed that the presence of useless organs in an organism does not weaken the case for design based on the parts that are purposefully arranged, which clearly would weaken the case for design if Paley's argument were analogical. Given these features, perhaps the default construal of Paley's argument should be deductive.

Paley's works continued to be required reading in England for decades after he was laid to rest in Carlisle Cathedral in 1805.

Logan Paul Gage

REFERENCES AND RECOMMENDED READING

Oppy, Graham. 2002. "Paley's Argument for Design." *Philo* 5 (2): 161–73.

Paley, William, and Matthew D. Eddy. 2006. *Natural Theology.* New York: Oxford University Press.

Sober, Elliott. 2000. *Philosophy of Biology.* 2nd ed. Boulder, CO: Westview.

PANNENBERG, WOLFHART. Wolfhart Pannenberg (1928–2014) is one of the most prolific German theologians of the twentieth century. One way of understanding his immense theological accomplishments as they relate to science is through the metaphor of a bridge. Pannenberg's thought is as one long, concerted effort to bridge the gap between theology and the sciences in order to address the modern tendency of theologians to withdraw from the arena of secular reason. More specifically, he sought to overcome revelation's seclusion from reason by locating an overlapping center between the hard sciences and the science of God's self-revelation.

A constituent feature of this project is Pannenberg's understanding of theology no longer as *sapientia* ("wisdom") only, but as *scientia inter alia scientias* ("a science among other sciences"). Theology is in no way an inferior science. Divine revelation is historical and indirect—by which he means that God discloses himself in the *interpretation* of historical acts—and is therefore capable of being maintained in the court of the secular sciences. For Pannenberg, every science makes claims, which although not false, always remain provisional, yet theologically relevant. Since theology is no less epistemologically viable than the other sciences, Pannenberg contends that theology and science can function as suitable dialogue partners.

Insofar as the sciences are ascribed the same provisional status as theology, they both make claims about a reality beyond total comprehension until history finishes its course. It is by placing theology alongside the sciences that Pannenberg puts into question the apodictic character of the modern sciences themselves, thus opening them up for further consideration in light of theology. For Pannenberg this involves theological expansion on modern science's provisional claims—what he calls "critical appropriation."

Pannenberg's work of building bridges between the natural sciences and theology is characterized by (1) his understanding of the contingency of all things, (2) his coordination of field theory with the work of the Holy Spirit, and (3) the role of the eschatological future. He places great stress on the contingency of the universe, underwriting contingency with both theology, through the doctrine of continuous creation, and science, through the general instability of scientific laws.

In critical appropriation of the phenomenon of inertia, Pannenberg posits the potential existence of a field of forces, which he identifies with the Holy Spirit. Scientific hypotheses identify general laws because God acts with regularity, but as both necessary and free, he is not bound to continue acting the same way but can act differently at any time, such that perceived laws fade into indeterminate patterns. This theologically enhanced understanding of the world serves to illustrate Pannenberg's assertion of the simultaneity of scientific theories and the divine determination.

The natural regularities, which are conceived of as laws, can find confirmation only in the eschatological future Pannenberg describes as the culmination of the created order. The "lawness" of phenomena cannot be determined until the totality of history can be perceived. Pannenberg identifies this future as the confirmation of the all-determining power, the God revealed in Christ.

Pannenberg also applies his method of critical appropriation to the social sciences. He responds to the contention of

Feuerbachian threads of modernity that theology is merely anthropology by laying theological claim to the data of human phenomena collected from secular anthropology (see also **Freud, Sigmund**). For Pannenberg, this scientific form of theological anthropology functions to ground religion, and thus God, as indispensable to humanness. Nevertheless, God cannot be discerned fully until the culmination of history. Human experience can only be anticipatory of God as the all-determining reality. Theology therefore, while justified as scientific, remains provisional.

Alexander H. Pierce

REFERENCES AND RECOMMENDED READING

Albright, Carol Rausch, and Joel Haugen, eds. 1999. *Beginning with the End: God, Science, and Wolfhart Pannenberg.* Chicago: Open Court.
Pannenberg, Wolfhart. 1968. *Revelation as History.* Trans. D. Granskou. New York: Macmillan.
———. 1970. *What Is Man? Anthropology in the Theological Perspective.* Minneapolis: Fortress.
———. 1976. *Theology and the Philosophy of Science.* Trans. Francis McDonagh. Philadelphia: Westminster John Knox.
———. 1983. *Anthropology in Theological Perspective.* Trans. Matthew J. O'Connell. Philadelphia: Westminster John Knox.
———. 1993. *Toward a Theology of Nature: Essays on Science and Faith.* Ed. Ted Peters. Louisville, KY: Westminster John Knox.
———. 2008. *The Historicity of Nature: Essays on Science and Theology.* Ed. Niels Henrik Gregersen. West Conshohocken, PA: Templeton Foundation Press.

PANSPERMIA. Panspermia refers to the spread of genetic information and life by transportation throughout the galaxy, from planet to planet and from star to star. This transportation is variously attributed to spores carried on stellar winds, to comets that pass out of our solar system, or occasionally, to directed intelligence. Its cause may not be clear, but its effects are undisputed: the spatial ubiquity and the temporal development of ecosystems.

Panspermia is not a theory about the origin of life (OOL)—despite many critics who dismiss it for being a cryptic OOL—nor is it antireligious, nor even about intelligent extraterrestrials (ET), but principally about the viable transport of microbial life through space. As an alternative explanation for the fossil record, however, it directly competes with the two dominant theories of the history of life: Darwinian evolution (DE; see **Darwinism**), and **young-earth creationism** (YEC). Both theistic and atheistic versions of DE agree that life was spatially limited to and temporally developed on Earth alone, while YEC agrees only with spatial limits, denying temporal development.

The spatial limitation is not a necessary feature of either

DE or YEC, for nothing in DE prevents life from spreading to Mars, say, by contamination from the many NASA rovers, and likewise, nothing in Genesis prohibits the creation or even the spread of life to other planets, as many theologians have claimed in the past four centuries. So the principle argument against panspermia has been practical—could life survive the long transit through space? Recent scientific discoveries have answered this question in the affirmative, removing the major objection.

The minor objection regarding temporal development is more philosophical. Panspermia makes the fossil record an account of Earth arrivals, destroying the justification for DE as "the better of two bad options." Likewise, extraterrestrial fossils undermine the YEC flood explanation for a recent origin, supporting the existence of "deep time."

Consequently, panspermia is often attacked as a transparent attempt to avoid the OOL problem by outsourcing it to other planets. When Darwinian evolutionists make this argument, they acknowledge just how powerfully panspermia contradicts DE, and are attempting to deflect the criticism. When YEC make this argument, they imply that panspermia is a type of DE and hence properly rejected. Most panspermians refuse to give any theory of OOL, however, whether they are theists or atheists. Some atheists, such as physical chemist Svante Arrhenius (1908) or astronomer **Fred Hoyle** (1981), argue that the universe is infinite in time and extent, and thus OOL vanishes in the mists of eternity. Theists such as Lord Kelvin (1871) argue that OOL ultimately derives from God, just not on Earth. Still others, such as Richard Hoover (2011), argue that OOL may have originated on Earth, but has long since escaped its terrestrial bonds. But all agree OOL remains a separate assumption.

Likewise, panspermia must be carefully separated from ET theories. Michael Crowe (Crowe and Dowd 2013) documented the last six centuries of the ET debate, showing how the Aristotelian model was transferred to the heavens by **Copernicus**, resulting in a two-century consensus that intelligent ET were ubiquitous and numerous; so, for example, William Whiston (1716) and Johann Lambert (1765) proposed intelligent inhabitants of comets. This analogy between Earth and other astronomical bodies came under attack by philosophers such as G. W. F. Hegel (1827), whose influential critique along with better observations of comets and planets in the early decades of the twentieth century reversed the consensus by finding the heavens inhospitable to life.

Only after the discovery of microbes by Louis Pasteur in the late 1800s did panspermia emerge when Richard Proctor

(1870) argued (contra Hegel) that microbes were versatile enough to live on Mars or Venus. A year later, Lord Kelvin (1871) and, independently, Herman von Helmholtz (1875) argued that these microbes could be transported through space as an alternative to DE. The debate about planetary habitability continues to this day but should not obscure the separate panspermia thesis that microbes can traverse the expanses of space.

Early work on panspermia involved collecting meteorites and examining them for life. Particularly intriguing were rare carbonaceous chondrite (CC) meteorites with large amounts of carbon, water, and clays. J. J. Berzelius (1834) found organic material on the Alais CC but was not able to determine if it was extraterrestrial. Louis Pasteur (1864) attempted to cultivate microbes from the Orgeuil CC but without success. Despite these failures, both Kelvin and Helmholz were convinced that CC carried life to Earth.

Panspermia received a boost in the twentieth century when Arrhenius argued that microbes need not arrive on meteorites, but spores could be wafted in by stellar winds. Hoyle reported infrared spectroscopic observations of clouds of spores in the Trapezium Nebula (1977), and later, evidence for diatoms as well (1984), but without much community acceptance. Panspermia returned when George Claus and Bartholomew Nagy reported (1961) on microscopic examination of Orgeuil CC, finding "organized elements" of microbial fossils. Confirmation quickly followed (1963), along with unjust accusations of fraudulent tampering with the meteorite (1964). The controversy delegitimized panspermia, destroyed careers, and led to a ban on publication for 20 years.

Most recently panspermia revived with David McKay's (1996) analysis of biological features in Martian meteorite ALH84001. The DE consensus was restored after NASA rejected McKay's analysis, but not before Richard Hoover began to look at CC with an electron microscope (1998). His photomicrographs of microbial fossils from all available CC were detailed enough to identify genus and species from every cyanobacterial family (2011). Stones of a CC that fell in Sri Lanka (2012) expand the list to include eukaryotic diatoms, as Hoyle predicted.

These discoveries show that panspermia remains a viable theory, first, because it changes the scientific perspective of Earth-centered life. Since CC are thought to be comet fragments, and cyanobacteria are the only organism known that can both photosynthesize carbohydrates and fix nitrogen, then these fossils are consistent with the only organism capable of pioneering growth in sterile, pristine comets. Life could then bioengineer them with polysaccharides to increase their tensile strength and heat absorption, as well as with magnetite nanoparticles to provide thermal regulation (Sheldon and Hoover 2012). And since comets disintegrate in orbit, releasing dust that other comets collect, life can migrate onto hyperbolic or extra-solar comets that travel from star to star. Therefore cyanobacterial ecosystems do not require planets in habitability zones but can make any star a home.

Panspermia remains a viable theory, second, because it removes one of the two pillars of DE. Since genes have few copying errors and high sensitivity to damaging mutations, the "genetic drift" hypothesis of DE is arguably unlikely and presently unobservable. Cyanobacteria are found to carry large virus loads, including fragments of DNA from previous hosts; novel DNA could thus be transferred horizontally between species and locations. Therefore the fossil record and the appearance of novel DNA on Earth throughout its history could arguably be due to contamination from meteoritic cyanobacteria rather than DE.

Robert Sheldon

REFERENCES AND RECOMMENDED READING

Anders, E., et al. 1964. "Contaminated Meteorite." *Science* 146 (3648): 1157–61.

Arrhenius, Svante. 1908. *Worlds in the Making: The Evolution of the Universe.* Transl. H. Borns. New York: Harper and Bros.

Berzelius, J. J. 1834. "Über Meteorsteine, 4. Meteorstein von Alais." *Annual Review of Physical Chemistry* 33: 113–23.

———. 1836. "On Meteoric Stones." *London and Edinburg Philosophical Magazine and Journal of Science* LXXX.

Claus, G., and B. Nagy. 1961. "A Microbiological Examination of Some Carbonaceous Chondrites." *Nature* 192: 594–96.

Crowe, M., and M. F. Dowd. 2013. "The Extraterrestrial Life Debate from Antiquity to 1900." In *Astrobiology, History and Society.* Ed. D. Vakoch. Berlin: Springer Verlag.

Hegel, G. W. F. 2002. *Vorlesungen über die Philosophie der Natur Berlin 1819/20.* Ed. Martin Bondelli and Hoo Nam Seelman. Vol. 10: 65–67. Hamburg: Meiner.

Helmholtz, Herman. 1908. "On the Origin of the Planetary System (1875)." In *Popular Lectures on Scientific Subjects.* Transl. E. Atkinson. London: Longmans Green & Co., 129.

Hoover, Richard B., et al. 1986. "Diatoms on Earth, Comets, Europa, and in Interstellar Space." *Earth, Moon, and Planets* 35: 19–45.

Hoover, Richard B. 1997. "Meteorites, Microfossils and Exobiology." In *Instruments, Methods, and Missions for the Investigation of Extraterrestrial Microorganisms.* Proceedings of SPIE 3111: 115–36.

———. 2011. "Fossils of Cyanobacteria in Cl1 Carbonaceous Meteorites." *Journal of Cosmology* 13 (March): 102.

Hoyle, F., and Wickramasinghe, N. C. 1978. *Lifecloud: The Origin of Life in the Galaxy.* London: J.M. Dent.

Hoyle, Fred, 1984. *Evolution from Space: A Theory of Cosmic Creationism,* New York: Simon & Schuster.

Lambert, Johann, 1976. *Cosmological Letters on the Arrangement of the World Edifice (1765).* Transl. S. L. Jaki. New York: Science History Publications: 72–73.

McKay, David S., et al. 1996. "Search for Past Life on Mars: Possible Relic Biogenic Activity in Martian Meteorite ALH84001." *Science* 273 (5277): 924–30.

Nagy, B., et al. 1963. "Electron Probe Microanalysis of Organized Elements in the Orgueil Meteorite." *Nature* 198: 121–25.

Proctor, Richard. 1870. *Other Worlds Than Ours.* London: Spottiswoode and Co.

Sheldon, M. I., and R. B. Sheldon. 2015. "Arrhenius Reconsidered: Astrophysical Jets and the Spread of Spores." In *Instruments, Methods, and Missions for the Investigation of Extraterrestrial Microorganisms.* Proceedings of SPIE 9606: 28.

Sheldon, R. B., and R. B. Hoover. 2012. "Carbonaceous Chondrites as Bioengineered Comets." In *Instruments, Methods, and Missions for Astrobiology.* Ed. Richard B. Hoover, Gilbert V. Levin, and Alexei Y. Rosanov. Proceedings of SPIE 8521: 36.

Thomson, William Baron Kelvin. 1894. "Presidential Address to the British Association for the Advancement of Science (Edinburgh, August, 1871)." In *Popular Lectures and Addresses,* 132–205. London: Macmillan & Co.

Wallis, J., et al., 2013. "The Polonnaruwa Meteorite: Oxygen Isotope, Crystalline and Biological Composition." *Journal of Cosmology* 22 (2). n.p.

Whiston, William. 1715. *Astronomical Lectures Read in the Public Schools at Cambridge.* London, 1728. Facsimile reprint, New York, 1972. (First Latin ed., Cambridge, 1707; first English ed., 1715.)

PANTHEISM, PANENTHEISM.

Pantheism and panentheism are often confused. But both reject theism, the worldview that asserts that the Creator is an infinite personal being who is metaphysically separate from the finite creation, which he brought forth out of nothing by his omnipotent power.

Pantheism admits of several schools. All forms deny (1) the personality of God and (2) the transcendence of God, and (3) that the cosmos was created. Some forms of pantheism are nondualistic. Hindu philosopher Sankara, for example, defended a nondualistic reading of the Hindu scriptures, arguing that the self and Brahman are one and identical. This is "the one without second."

The contemporary philosopher Ken Wilber has developed a multidisciplinary form of nondualistic pantheism in his many books. Baruch Spinoza's philosophically derived pantheism argues for one Substance, which can be viewed as God or nature. Either way, this is not the covenantal God of his Jewish heritage.

Some are led into pantheism by the concept of God as infinite. Consider the use of the word *is*. The *is* of *identity* equates X and Y. That is, they are the same thing. A triangle *is* a three-sided figure. So, if God is infinite, then God is everything because he is infinite. This denies that God has character, one that possesses some attributes (e.g., personality) and lacks others (e.g., evil).

The Bible speaks of God in terms of *the is of predication.* "This apple is red." Redness and apple-ness are not identical. God is loving, faithful, just, and more. These are his attributes, what can be predicated of him. Therefore, instead of affirming that "God is infinite" (*the* is *of identity*), it is more biblical to speak of God in terms of *the* is *of adverbial predication*. To wit, God is *infinitely* good (not finitely good), *infinitely* powerful (not finitely powerful), *infinitely* knowing (not limited by ignorance), and so on.

Panentheism, pantheism's cousin, grants God transcendence. Cosmos and deity are not one. The world is in God, and God is in the world. According to this view, God is to the world what the soul is to the body (on a dualistic account). God is distinct from the world but not the Lord over it. Taking its inspiration from Hegel, process philosophy asserts that God and the world are interdependent; each changes in response to the other. Unlike theism, the God of panentheism is neither self-existent (see Acts 17:25) nor the creator of all else outside of himself (Gen. 1:1). Some modern theologians (e.g., the late W. Pannenberg) are panentheists.

Modern cosmology, specifically the need for a cause of the universe, can be seen to undermine both pantheism and panentheism.

Douglas Groothuis

REFERENCES AND RECOMMENDED READING

Cooper, John W. 2007. *Panentheism: The Other God of the Philosophers: From Plato to the Present.* Downers Grove, IL: IVP.

Geisler, N., and David Clark. 2004. *Apologetics in the New Age: A Christian Critique of Pantheism.* Eugene, OR: Wipf and Stock.

PARADIGM. In science and religion circles, the word *paradigm* was made famous by Thomas Kuhn's seminal book *The Structure of Scientific Revolutions* (1962). After being criticized for using "paradigm" ambiguously, Kuhn wrote a "postscript" to *Structure* seven years later to clarify the term (cf. Masterman [1965] 1970). This postscript serves as the touchstone for Kuhn's understanding of "paradigm" both in *Structure* and later writings (e.g., Kuhn 2000).

In the postscript, Kuhn elucidates narrow and broad senses of "paradigm," which he labels "exemplars" and "disciplinary matrix," respectively. "Exemplars" are "the concrete puzzle-solutions which, employed as models or examples, can replace explicit rules as a basis for the solution of the remaining puzzles of normal science" (Kuhn [1962] 1996, 175; cf. 187). "Normal science," as Kuhn calls it, is a phase in which a scientific community has achieved consensus about a solution to a perplexing problem. An exemplar *is* this solution. It is not a set of explicit rules, nor is it an abstractly stated theory or law, but rather a concrete instance of success. Exemplars thus epitomize a community's view of the proper way to conduct present and future research in a particular area of science.

By way of example, consider **Charles Darwin**'s ostensible solution to the problem of the origin of species. Rather than invoking providence or direct divine design, Darwin argued that **common ancestry** and **natural selection** explain the rise and relatedness of flora and fauna. A number of scientists, especially younger ones, felt that this "naturalistic" exemplar gave a concrete explanation (or solution) to a long-standing mystery. Moreover, they thought that Darwin's solution provided a model for further research. A "naturalized" approach to organic history, centered on common ancestry and natural selection, promised to open new vistas of research in taxonomy, embryology, migration, human origins, psychology, and so on (cf. Darwin 1859, 486–88; Gillespie 1979).

The second meaning of "paradigm" is "disciplinary matrix." A disciplinary matrix is a "constellation" of key "beliefs, values, techniques, and so on shared by the members of a given community" (Kuhn [1962] 1996, 175). A disciplinary matrix is the broad umbrella that not only includes a given exemplar but also symbolic generalizations, metaphysical models, and values. Symbolic generalizations are formalizable universal propositions accepted by a given community—for example, natural laws or fundamental equations of theories (Hoyningen-Huene 1993, 145). Metaphysical models include claims about the way nature is—for example, that "all perceptible phenomena" are due to "matter and force" rather than, say, "neutral atoms in the void" (Kuhn [1962] 1996, 184).

Finally, values include concepts like coherence, simplicity, fruitfulness, and compatibility with other theories. They can be used to judge a specific application of a theory or a whole theory itself. Values can also be widely shared across communities, although specific communities may apply them in divergent ways. Collectively, the elements that comprise a disciplinary matrix shape a scientific community's goals, methods, experimental techniques, standards of evidence, interpretation of data, direction of research, legitimate solutions to research puzzles, and so on.

By way of example, the conflict between Darwinism and **intelligent design** can be seen in part as a reflection of differing exemplars and disciplinary matrixes. These differences influence each camp's assessment about whether intelligent agency is a proper scientific solution to the puzzle of the origin of living creatures. Is an agent's volition a legitimate explanation within science? Or should science limit itself to only secondary or natural causes? The answer to these (and other) questions often depends on deep, matrix-level commitments (cf. Gillespie 1979).

Stephen Dilley

REFERENCES AND RECOMMENDED READING

Darwin, Charles. 1859. *On the Origin of Species by Means of Natural Selection, or the Preservation of Favoured Races in the Struggle for Life*. London: John Murray.
Gillespie, Neal. 1979. *Charles Darwin and the Problem of Creation*. Chicago: University of Chicago Press.
Hoyningen-Huene, Paul. 1993. *Reconstructing Scientific Revolutions*. Chicago: University of Chicago Press.
Kuhn, Thomas. (1962) 1996. *The Structure of Scientific Revolutions*. 3rd ed. Chicago: University of Chicago Press.
———. 2000. *The Road Since Structure*. Ed. James Conant and John Haugeland. Chicago: University of Chicago Press.
Masterman, Margaret. (1965) 1970. "The Nature of a Paradigm." In *Criticism and the Growth of Knowledge*, ed. Imre Lakatos and Alan Musgrave, 59–89. Cambridge: Cambridge University Press.

PARADOX. A *paradox* is a truth claim that is well supported and yet difficult to believe. It is well supported because there is an apparently good argument for it, and it is difficult to believe because it seems logically contradictory, incoherent, or contrary to commonsense.

One type of paradox is a conjunction of propositions that are individually plausible but jointly logically inconsistent. One can solve this kind of paradox only by denying at least one of the propositions. What is paradoxical about this type of conjunction is the need to reject a proposition that seemed initially plausible. An example of a paradox in this category is the paradox of freedom and determinism: (1) free will exists; (2) free will exists only if determinism is false; (3) determinism is true. The conjunction of these three propositions would create a paradox for someone who had a reason to affirm each of them and yet recognized that their conjunction entails the contradiction that determinism is false and determinism is true. Three different philosophical solutions to the problem of freedom and determinism (libertarianism, hard determinism, and soft determinism) can be defined in terms of three possible ways to affirm two of these propositions while denying the third.

Another type of paradox is a well-supported claim that is apparently but not obviously false or contradictory. This kind of paradox can be solved in either of two different ways. One way involves determining that the problematic claim is in fact false or contradictory and then explaining what

is deficient about the argument on which it is based. The other way is to affirm that the claim is true and the argument for it adequate, and then to explain away its apparent falsity or inconsistency.

Two examples of this sort of paradox are the physical theory of wave-particle duality and the orthodox Christian doctrine of the **incarnation**. The former is an apparently well-supported scientific theory, and the latter is an apparently well-supported theological thesis. But both claims are also paradoxical and apparently contradictory. What makes the theory of wave-particle duality apparently contradictory is that the ordinary concept of a wave and the ordinary concept of a particle seem to be logically mutually exclusive (i.e., it seems that nothing can be both a wave and a particle). What can make the doctrine of the incarnation apparently contradictory is that it can seem that it is logically impossible for one person to be both fully divine and fully human, on the grounds that these two properties are logically mutually exclusive.

In spite of these apparent inconsistencies, physicists continue to affirm the former theory and theologians continue to affirm the latter doctrine. These affirmations are rational if it is rational to affirm a proposition that is both well supported and not obviously false. Moreover, scientists and theologians can strengthen the rationality of their affirmations by showing that there is no good reason for thinking that the claim in question is actually contradictory and not just apparently contradictory.

Paradoxes can be intriguing because they can be difficult to solve. And they can be serious because they involve important matters of human concern. Their persistence provides ongoing and interesting challenges for philosophers, scientists, theologians, and others.

James Taylor

REFERENCES AND RECOMMENDED READING

Hepburn, Ronald W. 1958. *Christianity and Paradox*. New York: Pegasus.
Morris, Thomas V. 1986. *The Logic of God Incarnate*. Ithaca, NY: Cornell University Press.
Sainsbury, R. M. 2009. *Paradoxes*. 3rd ed. Cambridge: Cambridge University Press.

PASCAL, BLAISE. One of the scientific revolution's most creative and intuitive thinkers was also one of Christianity's most passionate and unique apologists. Frenchman Blaise Pascal (1623–62) was one of seventeenth-century Europe's quintessential Renaissance men. In the short span of his life (only 39 years), he worked and served as a mathematician, physicist, inventor, polemicist, and a Christian philosopher-theologian (Audi 1995; "Pascal" 1986).

Mathematician, Experimental Scientist, and Inventor

Throughout his adult life, Pascal made important contributions to the field of mathematics (Popkin 1972, 1992). His fertile mind laid the foundations for infinitesimal calculus, integral calculus, and the calculus of probabilities. The German mathematician and philosopher Gottfried Wilhelm Leibniz (1646–1716) credited Pascal's infinitesimal analysis with inspiring his own development of calculus. Pascal also contributed to the study of geometry and number theory. Philosopher Richard H. Popkin says of him: "Pascal's analysis of the nature of mathematical systems seems to be closer to twentieth-century mathematical logic than that of any of his contemporaries" (Popkin 1992, 210).

Pascal was also considered a first-rate experimental scientist. He diligently practiced the then-emerging scientific method by rigorously testing, verifying, and/or falsifying his observations and conclusions. Many people credit his original physics experiments on air pressure and the nature of vacuums as fundamental for the development of hydrodynamics and hydrostatics.

Like all great inventors, Pascal's technological intuition and productive imagination placed him far ahead of his time. His creative experimentation produced many inventions—his most famous being the first digital calculator or adding machine. This breakthrough is considered one of the first applied achievements of the early Scientific Revolution and the precursor to the modern computer (Popkin 1992).

Philosopher of Science

Pascal had an astute appreciation for the "new science" that had been birthed and nurtured in seventeenth-century Europe. An avid supporter of the views of **Copernicus** and **Galileo**, he argued that respect for authority should not take precedence over analytic reasoning and scientific experimentation. He explored the nature of the scientific method and specifically addressed the importance of experimental data and the need to develop sound explanatory hypotheses. He asserted that as scientists continue to explore nature's mysteries, newer and more updated hypotheses would replace presently accepted ones.

Recognition of the limits of science also marked Pascal's cutting-edge thinking. He believed that while scientific

theories can be confirmed or falsified, they can never be fully established—a position, Popkin points out, quite similar to the one advocated by the eminent twentieth-century philosopher of science Karl Popper (Popkin 1992). Pascal recognized that scientific progress had not changed human nature for the good, and that the process by which human beings form their basic beliefs is rarely a purely rational or empirical one. Contemporary Christian philosopher Peter Kreeft said of Pascal, "He knew the power of science but also its impotence to make us wise or happy or good" (Kreeft 1993).

As a founding father of the new science, Pascal's achievements mark him as one of the most advanced scientists of his time. As a Christian thinker, his writings provide a penetrating and provocative analysis of the broader Christian world- and life view.

Kenneth Richard Samples

REFERENCES AND RECOMMENDED READING

Audi, Robert, ed. 1995. "Blaise Pascal." In *The Cambridge Dictionary of Philosophy*, 562–63. Cambridge: Cambridge University Press.
Kreeft, Peter. 1993. *Christianity for Modern Pagans: Pascal's Pensées Edited, Outlined and Explained.* San Francisco: Ignatius.
Morris, Thomas V. 1992. *Making Sense of It All: Pascal and the Meaning of Life.* Grand Rapids: Eerdmans.
"Pascal." 1986. In *The New Encyclopaedia Britannica*, 25:452–54. Chicago: Encyclopaedia Britannica.
Popkin, Richard H. 1972. "Blaise Pascal." In *The Encyclopedia of Philosophy*, ed. Paul Edwards, 6:51–55. New York: Macmillan.
———. 1992. "Blaise Pascal." In *Great Thinkers of the Western World*, ed. Ian P. McGreal, 209–12. New York: HarperCollins.

PASCAL'S WAGER. A polymath who made important contributions to physics, mathematics, and philosophy, Blaise Pascal is perhaps best known for his famous "wager" about God. The background to his wager was a set of arguments or purported proofs that had developed for God's existence, such as Anselm's ontological argument, Aquinas's Five Ways, Descartes's causal argument, and others (see **Natural Theology**). These arguments were supposed to be so intellectually compelling that God's existence could only be denied on pain of irrationality.

Although many Christians still claim that arguments from nature are strong enough to prove the existence of God to anyone who will consider the evidence objectively, Pascal said, "The evidence of God in nature is not of this kind." God does not unambiguously declare his existence; instead, the evidence is of a God who hides himself from anyone not seeking him wholeheartedly. Pascal says, "Wishing to appear openly to those who seek him with all their heart and hidden from those who shun him with all their heart, he has qualified our knowledge of him by giving signs which can be seen by those who seek him and not by those who do not." The matter of belief in God is not a question of having sufficient evidence or scientific proof; Pascal thought God never meant for it to be (see **Reductionism**; **Scientism**).

Instead of the traditional arguments, Pascal offered a pragmatic reason for believing in God in the form of a wager. He said, "I should be much more afraid of being mistaken and then finding out that Christianity is true than of being mistaken in believing it to be true." This is the essence of the wager. While Pascal was aware of other religions, he thought that the fulfillment of Old Testament prophecies in the life of Jesus, as well as Christianity's testimony about our fallen human nature, made it the only religious option worth serious consideration.

The wager states that if Christianity is false, it will not make much overall difference whether we accept it or not. We may gain some things by believing it, such as comfort and peace during suffering, but we will also be denied certain pleasures because of Christianity's moral demands. In all, Pascal considered the gains and losses to be nearly balanced.

Alternatively, if we reject Christ, we may lose the hope offered by faith, but we will make up some of that lost ground with the freedom we would have to pursue pleasure. Thus overall we do not stand to gain or lose much either way if Christianity is false. However, if it is true and we reject it, we suffer immeasurable loss because we have rejected the only possible means offered to us by God for everlasting happiness. On the other hand, if Christianity is true and we accept it, then we gain eternal life and infinite joy as our reward. Thus the prudent gambler, when faced with these possible outcomes, ought to wager in favor of God's existence since there is potentially infinite gain if we wager for God and win, and potentially infinite loss if we wager against God and lose.

Even though it amounts to something far less than certainty or proof, Pascal thought the reasons were compelling enough to make wagering for God the only wise and practical choice.

Bradley Sickler

REFERENCES AND RECOMMENDED READING

Brown, Geoffrey. 1984. "A Defence of Pascal's Wager." *Religious Studies* 20:465–79.

Groothuis, Douglas. 2001. "Are All Bets Off? A Defense of Pascal's Wager." *Philosophia Christi* 3 (2): 517–23.

Hájek, Alan. 2012. "Blaise and Bayes." In *Probability in the Philosophy of Religion*, ed. Jake Chandler and Victoria S. Harrison, 167–86. Oxford: Oxford University Press.

Jordan, Jeff, ed. 1994. *Gambling on God: Essays on Pascal's Wager*. Lanham, MD: Rowman & Littlefield.

Kreeft, Peter. 1993. *Christianity for Modern Pagans: Pascal's Pensées*. San Francisco: Ignatius.

Monton, Bradley. 2011. "Mixed Strategies Can't Evade Pascal's Wager." *Analysis* 71:642–45.

PEACOCKE, ARTHUR R. Arthur Peacocke (1924–2006) was a biochemist-theologian whose ideas shape contemporary scholarly science and religion dialogue. After completing his doctorate in physical chemistry, Peacocke began his academic career at the University of Birmingham, where he studied how solution conditions and gamma radiation affect DNA's structure and undertook theological studies that led to his 1971 Anglican ordination. By then he had moved to Oxford, where he investigated biomolecule-ligand interactions and increasingly devoted himself to various initiatives in science and religion.

Peacocke served as an important mentor and inspiration for a generation of science and religion thinkers by cofounding the Science and Religion Forum, European Society for the Study of Science and Theology (ESSSAT), and the Society of Ordained Scientists, directing Oxford's Ian Ramsey Center, and stimulating scholarly discourse through 18 books and numerous articles and talks.

Although Peacocke's ideas were first outlined in *Science and the Christian Experiment* (1971), his prominence dates from his Bampton lectures on *Creation and the World of Science* (1978, 2004). Therein he outlined how Christian theology might be impacted by science's picture of a chaotic yet orderly and structured universe. Since his proposals represented an intellectually rigorous alternative to special creationism and the extreme **materialism** and **reductionism** of writers like **Jacques Monod**, Peacocke emerged as the preeminent theistic evolutionist of the late twentieth century, a status solidified through *God and the New Biology* (1987), *Theology for a Scientific Age* (1993), *Paths from Science towards God* (2001), *Evolution: The Disguised Friend of Faith?* (2004c), and *All That Is: A Naturalistic Faith for the Twenty-First Century* (Peacocke and Clayton 2007).

Peacocke thought Christian theology would become culturally irrelevant unless it adopted a "naturalistic" faith that agreed with science's credible picture of the world while remaining grounded in Christian orthodoxy. This was possible since both science and theology use inference to the best explanation and employ imperfect and revisable concepts and models to describe objective realities. For Peacocke, then, science functions as a "path towards God" by indicating whether and how Christian doctrine might be re-envisioned.

Personally, Peacocke advocated an *emergentist-naturalistic-panentheistic* vision of God and nature in which divine creation is not an alternative to natural processes but rather coincident with them. Specifically, God set the universe's initial conditions and laws, upholds them as they run their course, and uses chaotic and chance-laden processes (like evolution) to actuate the divine purpose from among contingent possibilities.

While accepting science's physicalist description of the cosmos and the usefulness of reductionist models, Peacocke also argued that nature displayed emergent properties, both in terms of higher-level systems (like ecosystems) possessing properties that are irreducible to lower-level ones (like organisms) and in the ability of higher systems to influence how lower ones behave through whole-part constraints. For Peacocke, this explains how God acts on the world while respecting its autonomy and remaining immanent to its operations and travails. Further, Christ is an emergent, illustrating what God intends to bring forth from evolution-derived humanity, with his incarnation an example of God's top-down acting in the world.

Peacocke's efforts at reconciling science and religion were recognized by the 2001 Templeton Prize for Progress in Religion. However, his naturalistic views of miracles and other doctrines meant that his ideas were less influential in fundamentalist and evangelical circles while his commitment to creedal orthodoxy meant he did not go far enough for more radically naturalistic scholars.

Stephen Contakes

REFERENCES AND RECOMMENDED READING

Barbour, Ian G. 2008. "Remembering Arthur Peacocke: A Personal Reflection." *Zygon* 43 (1): 89–102.

Brooke, John Hedley. 2007. "Arthur Peacocke: An Appreciation." *Reviews in Science and Religion* 49 (May): 8–13.

Deane-Drummond, Celia. 2007. "Arthur Peacocke: A Personal Testimony." *Reviews in Science and Religion* 49 (May): 13–16.

Eaves, Lindon. 1991. "Adequacy or Orthodoxy? Choosing Sides at the Frontier." *Zygon* 26 (4): 495–503.

Gregersen, Niels Henrik. "Arthur Peacocke in Memoriam (1924–2006)." *Theology and Science* 5 (1): 5–7.

Hefner, Philip. 2007. "Arthur Peacocke: A Compleat Man." *Theology and Science* 5 (1): 9–11.

McGrath, Alister. 2010. "Arthur Peacocke (1924–2006)." In *Science and Religion: A New Introduction*, 209–12. 2nd ed. Chichester, West Sussex, UK: Wiley-Blackwell.

Murphy, Nancey. 2008. "Arthur Peacocke's Naturalistic Christian Faith for the Twenty-First Century: A Brief Introduction." *Zygon* 43 (1): 67–73.

Peacocke, A. R. 1971. *Science and the Christian Experiment.* London and New York: Oxford University Press.

———. 1984. *Intimations of Reality: Critical Realism in Science and Religion.* Mendenhall Lectures. Notre Dame, IN: University of Notre Dame Press for Depauw University.

———. 1987. *God and the New Biology.* New York: HarperCollins.

———. 1991. "From DNA to Dean." *Zygon* 26 (4): 477–93.

———. 1993. *Theology for a Scientific Age: Being and Becoming—Natural, Divine, and Human.* Theology and the Sciences. Minneapolis: Fortress.

———. 1994. "The Religion of a Scientist: Explorations into Reality (*Religio Philosophi Naturalis*)." *Zygon* 29 (4): 639–59.

———. 2001. *Paths from Science towards God: The End of All Our Exploring.* Oxford: Oneworld.

———. 2004a. Reprint of 1978 Bampton Lecture. *Creation and the World of Science: The Re-shaping of Belief.* Oxford: Oxford University Press.

———. 2004b. " 'The End of All Our Exploring' in Science and Theology." *Zygon* 39 (2): 413–29.

———. 2004c. *Evolution: The Disguised Friend of Faith? Selected Essays.* Philadelphia: Templeton Foundation Press.

Peacocke, Arthur R., and Philip Clayton. 2007. *All That Is: A Naturalistic Faith for the Twenty-First Century: A Theological Proposal with Responses from Leading Thinkers in the Religion-Science Dialogue.* Theology and the Sciences. Minneapolis: Fortress.

Polkinghorne, J. C. 1996. *Scientists as Theologians: A Comparison of the Writings of Ian Barbour, Arthur Peacocke and John Polkinghorne.* London: SPCK.

Russell, Robert John. 1991. "The Theological-Scientific Vision of Arthur Peacocke." *Zygon* 26 (4): 505–17.

———. 2007. "Ringing the Changes: In Tribute to Arthur R. Peacocke." *Theology and Science* 5 (1): 17–19.

Smedes, T. A. "Arthur Peacocke. 2012." In *The Blackwell Companion to Science and Christianity*, ed. J. B. Stump and Alan G. Padgett, 589–99. Chichester, West Sussex, UK: Wiley-Blackwell.

Woloschak, Gayle E. 2008. "Chance and Necessity in Arthur Peacocke's Scientific Work." *Zygon* 43 (1): 75–87.

PERSON. *Person* (from Lat., *persona*, a reference to an actor's mask), philosophically speaking, refers to a rational, independent, and autonomous agent. These agents may or may not have a body. For **Plato**, for instance, the soul is the immortal aspect of the person that survives the death of the physical body. Contrariwise, for **Aristotle**, the soul is the "form of the body" and cannot exist apart from it.

One school of thought that prioritizes the notion of person is called *personalism*. According to the personalist account of Christian Smith, a person is

> the particular kind of being that under proper conditions is capable of developing into (or has developed into) a conscious, reflective, embodied, self-transcending center of subjective experience, durable identity, moral commitment, and social communication who—as the efficient cause of

his or her responsible actions and interactions—exercises complex capacities for agency and intersubjectivity in order to develop and sustain his or her own incommunicable self in loving relationships with other personal selves and with the nonpersonal world. (Smith 2015, 35)

This holistic and robust definition of what it means to be a person is a helpful starting point.

Person also has a long history in theological discourse, especially in the christological debates of the early church. Orthodox Christians affirm that each member of the Trinity is a person. Those three persons—Father, Son, and Holy Spirit—are one God. The Bible also speaks of other persons, including angelic persons and human persons. The early Christian apologist Tertullian (c. AD 155–240) was the first to use the terms *substance* and *person* to define God. Later, in the sixth century, the statesman and philosopher Boethius defined a person as "an individual substance of a rational nature."

According to biblical theology, human persons are embodied from conception onward. At conception at least one genetically unique human person is formed (twinning may occur during the first two weeks of pregnancy). So the psalmist offers a hymn to God in Psalm 139:

> You created my inmost being; you knit me together in my mother's womb.
>
> I praise you because I am fearfully and wonderfully made; your works are wonderful, I know that full well.
>
> My frame was not hidden from you when I was made in the secret place, when I was woven together in the depths of the earth.
>
> Your eyes saw my unformed body; all the days ordained for me were written in your book before one of them came to be. (vv. 13–16)

Human persons are, however, the only persons who are made in the *imago Dei* (image of God). Thus Jesus—fully God and fully human—is the "image of the invisible God, the firstborn over all creation" (Col. 1:15). Likewise, according to Genesis, "God created mankind in his own image, in the image of God he created them; male and female he created them" (Gen. 1:27). (See **Consciousness**; **Image of God**; **Life after Death**; **Mind**; **Sentience**; **Soul**.)

C. Ben Mitchell

REFERENCES AND RECOMMENDED READING

Cooper, John W. 2000. *Body, Soul and Life Everlasting: Biblical Anthropology and the Monism-Dualism Debate*. Grand Rapids: Eerdmans.

Cortez, Marc. 2016. *Christological Anthropology in Historical Perspective*. Grand Rapids: Zondervan.

Rudman, Stanley. 2008. *Concept of Person and Christian Ethics*. Cambridge: Cambridge University Press.

Smith, Christian. 2011. *What Is a Person? Rethinking Humanity, Social Life, and the Moral Good from the Person Up*. Chicago: University of Chicago Press.

———. 2015. *To Flourish or Destruct: A Personalist Theory of Human Goods, Motivations, Failure, and Evil*. Chicago: University of Chicago Press.

Van Huyssteen, J. Wentzel, and Erik P. Wiebe. 2011. *In Search of Self: Interdisciplinary Perspectives on Personhood*. Grand Rapids: Eerdmans.

PHILOSOPHY OF RELIGION. The philosophy of religion is the philosophical investigation of the content and central truth claims of religious traditions. Questions addressed in this area are of central and enduring human significance and include the existence and nature of God (see **Existence of God**), evil (see **Evil, Problem of**), **morality**, religious language, **religious experience**, **miracles**, **life after death**, religious diversity and the relationships between faith, reason and science. As such, philosophy of religion may be the most active and energetic of all contemporary areas of philosophical enquiry. (For the claim that philosophy of religion has the largest number of societies, journals, conferences, and publishing houses dedicated to it of any area of philosophical enquiry, see Taliaferro 2009, 1.)

All areas of philosophy are involved in philosophy of religion. **Metaphysics** is concerned with the nature and structure of reality and is thus relevant to central debates, such as that between naturalism and theism. **Epistemology** addresses the nature of knowledge, taking a central place in discussions of the justification or warrant for belief in God. Questions of the relationship between God and morality draw on issues in value theory and ethics.

Explanation of the relationship between science and religion is an important project connecting the philosophy of religion with both philosophy of science and a range of other disciplines. The philosophy of religion also makes an increasing contribution to cross-cultural dialogue through investigation of the world's panoply of concepts of divinity. However, the historic and contemporary focus of Western philosophy of religion remains on theism, "the philosophy of God, according to which God is the creator and sustainer of the cosmos, all good, omnipresent, eternal or everlasting, omnipotent, omniscient, existing necessarily … and provident" (Taliaferro et al. 2013, 1–7). Christian theists add such concepts as **Trinity** and **incarnation** to this list.

The field has a long past, beginning in a Greek sense of wonder expressed first in religious ritual and language and subsequently in the separate emergence of philosophical reflection that infused language with belief. Later nonreligious understandings of the world prompted early arguments for the existence of God, such as those recorded by Plato (Boys-Stones 2009).

Christianity later came to dominate a Roman world pervaded by Greek philosophy, and the subsequent attempt to correct and integrate Greek thinking with Christian doctrine produced a millennium of interwoven theological and philosophical discussion addressing arguments about the nature and existence of God and the relationship between faith and reason.

The Renaissance brought a resistance to religious authority, paving the way for a renewed philosophical independence as well as for the Reformation (see **Science and the Reformation**), modern science, and later modern philosophy, which included philosophy of religion as a distinct subfield.

The question of God's interaction with nature was uppermost for seventeenth-century thinkers such as the Cambridge Platonist Ralph Cudworth (1617–88) (Anstey 2009), who was to coin the terms *philosophy of religion* and *theism* in English (Taliaferro 2005, 12). The field developed within the intellectual ferment of the seventeenth and eighteenth centuries, including both the religiously constructive tradition of Descartes, Locke, Leibniz, and Berkeley, and the skeptical contributions of Spinoza and Hume.

This ferment produced renewed philosophical defenses of traditional belief, **deism** (understood as theism without revealed religion), and unbelief. The work of Hume, Kant, and Hegel (1730–1830) took philosophy of religion into the nineteenth century, emphasizing "a study of religion … at once free from functional dependence upon any theology, sensitive to the full power of the skeptical challenge in its religious implications, and thoroughly philosophical in nature" (Collins 1967).

Hume and Kant attacked the traditional proofs of God's existence, producing the widespread, if temporary, belief that natural theology was damaged beyond repair. While Hume's skepticism would inaugurate a tradition of suspicion involving the search for occult motives for religious belief, metaphysical skepticism itself would continue in materialist, positivist, and naturalist movements that assumed themselves sanctioned by science (Taliaferro 2009; Westphal 2010). Kant sought to reduce religion to morality and to catalyze an idealist tradition founded on his claim that the objects of human thought are appearances and not things in themselves.

The idealist tradition continued into the twentieth century, offering a position close enough to theism to prompt

attacks from philosophical atheists such as G. E. Moore and Bertrand Russell, while Ayer's positivist movement rose to challenge theism, proclaiming the meaninglessness of religious and metaphysical language. Positivism's collapse in the second half of the century contributed to an explosion of interest in philosophy of religion and a widening of its scope.

Along with important developments in religious epistemology, the philosophy of God returned to prominence with attention focused on the divine attributes and an energetic focus on natural theology that continues to the present day (Moreland and Craig 2009). This growth in mainstream analytic philosophy of religion has been accompanied by the rise of a Continental stream focused on phenomenological methods and emphasizing lived experience over esoteric argument. Increasing confluence of these streams suggests growing mutual enrichment.

The need to understand the "tumultuous, many-faceted, and confusing" (Plantinga 2014) relationship between religion and science represents an important project for the philosophy of religion. Approaches have typically been classified according to **Ian Barbour**'s fourfold scheme of conflict, independence, dialogue, and integration (Barbour 1997). Nineteenth-century proponents of conflict or even war held that science and religion address some of the same questions in incompatible ways such that religious modes of thought must inevitably give way. In sharp contrast, the independence view holds that the subject matters of science and religion do not intersect at all.

Between these extremes a dialogue approach seeks fruitful points of contact in areas such as the presuppositions of scientific activity. For example, long-term consideration of the Christian doctrine of creation produced the belief that the world can be known through empirical investigation rather than through intellectual reflection as the Greeks had previously supposed (Mascall 1956). Beyond points of contact lies full integration. For example, natural theology draws on scientific investigation while making use of distinct but complementary methods and aims. Current versions of the teleological argument based on the supposed fine-tuning of physical constants show that developments in science continue to provide natural theology with new resources (Collins 2009).

Recent contributions to this discussion break down Barbour's classification by emphasizing that the source of much perceived conflict is found in the attempted marriage of modern science with naturalism. **Thomas Nagel** does not wish to entertain theism but emphasizes that the exclusion of mind and purpose from scientific explanations assures not only their astonishing success, but also their powerlessness to supply a comprehensive account of reality. Nagel takes contemporary empirical arguments for the necessity of design in nature to be one indicator of the insufficiency of a naturalist view of reality (Nagel 2012).

In a further substantial contribution, **Alvin Plantinga** argues that deep concord exists between science and theism, and much presumed conflict evaporates when unnecessary naturalistic assumptions are identified and rejected. He also argues that if one accepts both naturalism and biological evolution, the reliability of human cognitive faculties is undermined, along with the truth claims they produce (Plantinga 2011). Thus a conflict exists between science and naturalistic belief.

These contributions emphasize the ongoing, important, and distinctive contribution made by work in philosophy of religion to central areas of contemporary thought and Christian belief.

Jonathan Loose

REFERENCES AND RECOMMENDED READING

Anstey, Peter. 2009. "Early Modern Philosophy of Religion: An Introduction." In *Early Modern Philosophy of Religion*, ed. Graham Oppy and N. N. Trakakis, 1–18. Durham, UK: Acumen.

Barbour, Ian. 1997. *Religion and Science: Historical and Contemporary Issues.* San Francisco: Harper.

Boys-Stones, George. 2009. "Ancient Philosophy of Religion: An Introduction." In *Ancient Philosophy of Religion*, ed. Graham Oppy and N. N. Trakakis, 1–22. Durham, UK: Acumen.

Collins, James. 1967. *The Emergence of Philosophy of Religion.* New Haven, CT: Yale University Press.

Collins, Robin. 2009. "The Teleological Argument: An Exploration of the Fine-Tuning of the Universe." In *The Blackwell Companion to Natural Theology*, 202–81. West Sussex, UK: Wiley-Blackwell.

Mascall, E. L. 1956. *Christian Theology and Natural Science.* New York: Ronald.

Moreland, J. P., and William Lane Craig. 2009. *The Blackwell Companion to Natural Theology.* West Sussex, UK: Wiley-Blackwell.

Nagel, Thomas. 2012. *Mind and Cosmos.* Oxford: Oxford University Press.

Plantinga, Alvin. 2011. *Where the Conflict Really Lies.* Oxford: Oxford University Press.

Taliaferro, Charles. 2005. *Evidence and Faith.* Cambridge: Cambridge University Press.

———. 2014. "Religion and Science." In *Stanford Encyclopedia of Philosophy*, ed. Edward N. Zalta. Spring. http://plato.stanford.edu/archives/spr2014/entries/religion-science/.

———. 2009. "Twentieth-Century Philosophy of Religion: An Introduction." In *Twentieth-Century Philosophy of Religion*, ed. Graham Oppy and N. N. Trakakis, 1–12. Durham, UK: Acumen.

Taliaferro, Charles, Victoria S. Harrison, and Stewart Goetz, eds. 2013. *The Routledge Companion to Theism.* Introduction."" –New York: Routledge.

Westphal, Merold. 2010. "The Emergence of Modern Philosophy of Religion." In *A Companion to Philosophy of Religion*, ed. Paul C. Quinn and Charles Taliaferro, 133–40. Oxford: Blackwell.

PHILOSOPHY OF SCIENCE. While always a subject of great importance, the philosophy of science has garnered renewed attention in the past 50 years, due in part to the great success of the **scientific method** in discovering how the physical universe works and in practical application in many areas of human life, such as technology, travel, communications, and medicine.

The accomplishments of science appear to give it a type of hegemony over modern life and culture, and this development has prompted philosophers, including Christian philosophers, to examine the discipline more closely. The philosophy of science therefore raises foundational questions with regard to such issues as the definition of science and its method of inquiry, the truth status of scientific theories, whether science gives us objective knowledge of the real world, the difference between science and nonscience, the limits of science, and its relationship to other forms of inquiry, such as philosophy, theology, religion, and **ethics**.

Science is distinctive in its method of inquiry, which may be characterized as the study of the physical realm by means of the gathering of facts and data based on empirical observation, confirmation through experimentation, and propounding and testing hypotheses and theories to explain phenomena.

Arriving at a definition of science that covers all types of scientific theories and claims has proved notoriously difficult, but it is important to note that science should not be understood as equivalent to or as the definition of the "rational" or the "reasonable," a key point in the discussion of its relationship with religion. The realm of the rational is broader than that of the scientific, which means that a claim or theory can be supported by reasons and accepted as true even if it is not subjected to scientific testing—for example, an argument for God's existence or an argument for a moral conclusion. This point is important because it frustrates those thinkers, beginning with the movement of **logical positivism**, who attempt to equate the domain of the rational or the logical with the domain of the scientific as a way of undermining religious and sometimes ethical claims.

A related concern is whether the scientific method yields objective truth about reality, and if so, about which parts of reality. While most practicing scientists would be realists about the nature of knowledge and would hold that the discoveries of science tell us the way the world really is, the discipline of science has not been unaffected by the movement of **antirealism** that has dominated the discussion of the philosophical foundations of knowledge in the twentieth century. Indeed, this is an influential view in current philosophy of science—an understanding that all knowledge, including scientific knowledge, involves a human perspective that compromises objectivity to some extent, and so science does not in fact describe the way the world really is in itself.

Needless to say, while many thinkers will accept and sometimes welcome such a view in religion, philosophy, and ethics, they are reluctant to accept it in science, and so are open to a charge of inconsistency. Various arguments have been proposed for why we should accept scientific theories and claims even if we think they fall short of objective truth, including **instrumentalism**—the view that a theory should be regarded as a useful, practical instrument in our present attempts to understand the physical realm until a better theory comes along.

Such considerations have contributed to a growing realization that it is problematic to assert that a scientific theory is objectively true. While we can say that a scientific theory may be the best theory we currently have, we must acknowledge that it could be seriously modified, even abandoned, in the light of further evidence. This position is usually defended by appeal to two arguments.

The first argument is based on the history of science, with many theories now abandoned that were once regarded as true—for instance, the humors of medieval medicine, the existence of phlogiston as an element released in combustion, and the electromagnetic ether that was supposed to surround the earth. The same will likely be true for some of our current theories.

The second argument points out that many theories are underdetermined by the evidence offered to support them. Examples often cited in support of this argument include evolution, theories in particle physics, such as **string theory**, and theories about the structure of the universe, such as those concerning black holes and cosmic inflation.

These arguments in the philosophy of science serve as a caution that, despite great confidence in the scientific approach, there is considerable uncertainty behind many theories. These arguments also chasten us not to be too quick to claim that science is close to unraveling the deepest mysteries of life and the universe. While being strong supporters of the discipline of science, Christian philosophers welcome insights in the philosophy of science because they place science in proper perspective and inspire thinkers in

both science and religion to work together in an attempt to understand more fully God's creation.

Along these lines, philosophy of science raises the question of the limits of scientific inquiry. Science studies the physical realm, and the scientific method appears to be limited to this realm. This should not be taken as a criticism of the scientific method, but rather as a recognition that there are some areas of inquiry, including those dealing with significant questions in human life, that are not within its domain. These would include key questions of religion and ethics, as well as questions about the origin of the universe, the origin of the laws of physics, and the nature of human consciousness.

Such an understanding is behind famous arguments for God's existence in the Christian tradition, such as the cosmological argument, which is based on the idea that science cannot in principle answer the question about the ultimate cause of things, why anything exists at all. Science also runs up against its limit in the area of ethics. For instance, the scientific method can discover how technically to harvest embryonic stem cells but cannot address the moral questions raised by this practice, questions outside of its domain. The areas where science reaches its limits are often the subject of dispute, with some claiming that topics like the **origin of life** and of **consciousness** are well within its purview; some thinkers have even proposed scientific accounts of the origin of religion and ethics.

The distinction between methodological and metaphysical **naturalism** has often been invoked as a way of addressing the overreach of science and of illustrating the limits of scientific inquiry. **Methodological naturalism** is the view that when doing science, only physical, testable explanations should be considered and pursued, whereas metaphysical naturalism describes the atheistic view that the only type of explanation we should ever consider for any question is a scientific one, because only natural, physical causes exist.

Although methodological naturalism is itself subject to criticism (Plantinga 2001), many Christian thinkers have drawn upon this distinction in their attempts to critique the conflict model of the relationship between religion and science by showing that it is not religion and science that are in conflict but religion and metaphysical naturalism masquerading as science. This argument has become important in many contemporary discussions because metaphysical naturalism has become popular within some sections of the academic community, yet science must be clearly distinguished from metaphysical naturalism because science as a discipline does not claim that all questions have scientific explanations.

This latter claim is a philosophical, not a scientific, one, a confusion perpetrated by many thinkers and one that has spread confusion among the general public who often mistakenly think that science and metaphysical naturalism are equivalent. Moreover, an increasing number of Christian thinkers argue that in the debate between theism and naturalism, scientific evidence in various areas such as cosmology, molecular biology, and the study of consciousness better supports a religious understanding of reality.

Brendan Sweetman

REFERENCES AND RECOMMENDED READING

De Vries, Paul. 1986. "Naturalism in the Natural Sciences: A Christian Perspective." *Christian Scholar's Review* 15:388–96.
Okasha, Samir. 2002. *Philosophy of Science.* London: Oxford University Press.
Plantinga, Alvin. 2011. *Where the Conflict Really Lies: Science, Religion and Naturalism.* New York: Oxford University Press.
Ratzsch, Del. 2000. *Science and Its Limits.* Downers Grove, IL: InterVarsity.
Sweetman, Brendan. 2010. *Religion and Science: An Introduction.* New York: Continuum.

PHYSICALISM. The term *physicalism* denotes the claim that, in some sense, everything is physical. Although typically used interchangeably with "materialism," it avoids any connotation of an outdated physics. The claim that even minds and mental properties are entirely physical is jarring, and debates about the adequacy of physicalism are found most often within the philosophy of mind. We might thus understand the physicalist project in Jaegwon Kim's words:

> The shared project of the majority of those who have worked on the mind-body project over the past few decades has been to find a way of accommodating the mental within a principled physicalist scheme, while at the same time preserving it as something distinctive — that is, without losing what we value, or find special, in our nature as creatures with minds. (Kim 1998, 2)

Early use of the term *physicalism* is found among twentieth-century logical positivist thinkers such as Carnap, Hempel, and Ayer, who embraced the term as a component of their philosophical behaviorism. They held that psychology is ultimately reducible to physics and that statements about mental states are translatable into statements about behaviors or dispositions to behave. For example, pain is nothing more than the disposition to exhibit pain behavior in certain conditions. Adopting this implausible view seemed to require one to "feign anesthesia" — a phrase coined by I. A. Richards (quoted in Ayer 1964, 101).

Serious challenges in the 1950s and 1960s included Chisholm's demonstration that attempts to reduce mental statements to behavioral ones are circular, requiring further mental statements to be invoked (Chisholm 1957, chap. 11). The eventual demise of behaviorism left the field open for its natural successor, functionalism (see **Functionalism**), and for other reductionist theories. The term "*physicalism*" is sometimes used in a narrow sense to apply to one of these: the so-called type-type identity theory (Block 1980).

Instead of identifying mental statements with behavioral ones, *type-type* identity theory considers types of mental state (e.g., pain) to be identical with types of neurophysiological state (e.g., an electrochemical process in a neural structure) (Feigl 1958; Smart 1959). However, type-type theory cannot accommodate the reasonable claim that creatures with distinct neurophysiology (e.g., a mouse or a person) must be capable of being in the same mental state (e.g., pain). This is the problem of multiple realizability (Fodor 1974).

An alternative that overcomes this problem is the *token-token* theory. This theory holds that while mental state types are in fact irreducible, each *token* of the state (e.g., each particular instance of pain) is identical with some neurophysiological state or other. Hence the same type of mental state may be realized in qualitatively different physical systems. However, the token view fails to explain what holds these instances of mental states together as tokens of the same type. Thus, in seeking to avoid the multiple realization problem for mental state types, token-token theory undermines their very existence. Eliminativism embraces and extends this conclusion, arguing that intentional mental states are part of a superseded theory of intelligent behavior and should thus be eliminated (Churchland 1984): this view is typically taken to be self-refuting.

Donald Davidson brought to prominence the notion of *supervenience*, which has become central to discussions of physicalism, and defined it minimally as follows: "There cannot be two events alike in all physical respects but differing in some mental respect" (Davidson 1970, 214). David Lewis famously illustrates supervenience in terms of the connection between the global properties of a dot-matrix picture (such as its symmetry) and the arrangement of the individual dots that make it up: "No two pictures could differ in their global properties without differing, somewhere, in whether there is or there isn't a dot" (Lewis 1986, 14).

Supervenience physicalism is thus a relation of necessary covariation between mental and physical properties and is normally construed in terms of one-way dependence of the mental on the physical. However, supervenience often fails to explain the connection it describes, and some formulations are consistent with property dualism (the view that a human being is one material substance with both physical and mental properties). Hence supervenience does not offer a complete account of physicalism but is nevertheless suggestive of nonreductive accounts that might avoid problems with identity and preserve the mental from elimination.

Some Christian scholars consider that a broadly scientific outlook requires participation in the physicalist project and that to accept physicalism in relation to human minds and mental properties can be theologically benign. Such thinkers challenge the reductive tendencies that are devastating to both commonsense and theological accounts of human persons, and they explore nonreductive versions of physicalism instead.

These proposals must establish that causally efficacious mental properties are distinct from physical properties while being entirely dependent on and realized by them. Lynne Baker offers a non-reductive account based on the claim that pairs of objects can remain distinct despite being wholly physical and perfectly coincident. According to Baker, such objects may exist in a relationship of constitution, where *constitution is not identity*. In order to be in a constitutional relationship, objects must differ in one or more essential properties, and Baker argues that human persons and their bodies do differ in this way. She thus claims that human persons are *constituted by* rather than identical to their human bodies, and because of this it is coherent to hold that we are wholly physical objects perfectly coinciding with our bodies while remaining irreducible to them (Baker 2000). However, it is very difficult to maintain positions such as this while avoiding both the Scylla of dualism and the Charybdis of reductionism. For example, constitution may turn out to be nothing more than coincidence (Wasserman 2004).

Stepping back, Daniel Stoljar assesses the numerous interpretations and failures of physicalism, concluding that "physicalism has no formulation on which it is both true and deserving of the name" (Stoljar 2010). This raises the question of why the physicalist project should be pursued.

Perhaps there are overwhelming arguments for physicalism despite difficulties of formulation. This is not the case. For example, it is common for physicalists to argue from the claim that all causes are physical causes (the "causal closure of the physical") to the conclusion that mental events supervene on physical events in a way that guarantees the truth of physicalism. However, even if causal closure could be established, the soundness of this argument is questionable. For example, it may be compatible with the conclusion that mental properties are causally effete, *non-physical* entities (epiphenomenalism).

In contrast, the arguments against physicalism are more diverse and difficult to deal with given the features of minds and mental properties to which they refer. Perhaps most significant among these are arguments from the intrinsic qualitative feel of mental states (**qualia**) (Jackson 1986; Nagel 1974). Stoljar concludes that the standards of evidence required to persuade someone of the truth of physicalism are typically low since "we live in an overwhelmingly physicalist or materialist intellectual culture" (Stoljar 2015).

Physicalism has thus proved difficult both to specify and to support, and its persistence may be largely explained by favorable cultural winds. Given this, other Christian scholars see the existence of minds and mental properties as evidence against both the physicalist project and the larger naturalist cultural narrative that carries it forward. On this view, physicalism is an expression of a "scientistic philosophical monism" (Moreland 2009) that is antithetical to theism and not required by science. The recalcitrance of the mental in the face of physicalism is thus taken to be evidence of naturalism's inadequacy in comparison to theism.

Jonathan Loose

REFERENCES AND RECOMMENDED READING

Ayer, A. J. 1964. "The Concept of a Person." In *The Concept of a Person and Other Essays*. London: Macmillan.

Baker, Lynne Rudder. 2000. *Persons and Bodies: A Constitution View*. Cambridge: Cambridge University Press.

Block, Ned. 1980. "Troubles with Functionalism." In *Readings in the Philosophy of Psychology*, ed. Ned Block. Cambridge, MA: Harvard University Press.

Chisholm, Roderick M. 1957. *Perceiving: A Philosophical Study*. Contemporary Philosophy Series. Ithaca, NY: Cornell University Press.

Churchland, Paul M. 1984. *Matter and Consciousness*. Cambridge, MA: MIT Press.

Davidson, D. 1970. "Mental Events." In *Essays on Actions and Events*, ed. B. Vermazen and and M. B. Hintikka. Oxford: Oxford University Press.

Feigl, Herbert. 1958. "The 'Mental' and the 'Physical.'" In *Concepts, Theories, and the Mind-Body Problem*, ed. Herbert Feigl, Michael Scriven, and Grover Maxwell. Studies in the Philosophy of Science. Minneapolis: Minnesota University Press.

Fodor, Jerry. 1974. "Special Sciences: Or the Disunity of Science as a Working Hypothesis." *Synthese* 28:97–115.

Jackson, Frank. 1986. "What Mary Didn't Know." *Journal of Philosophy* 83:291–95.

Kim, Jaegwon. 1998. *Mind in a Physical World*. Cambridge, MA: MIT Press.

Lewis, D. 1986. *On the Plurality of Worlds*. Oxford: Blackwell.

Moreland, J. P. 2009. *The Recalcitrant Imago Dei: Human Persons and the Failure of Naturalism*. London: SCM.

Nagel, Thomas. 1974. "What Is It Like to Be a Bat?" *Philosophical Review* 4:435–50.

Smart, J. J. C. 1959. "Sensations and Brain Processes." *Philosophical Review* 68:141–56.

Stoljar, Daniel. 2010. *Physicalism*. London: Routledge.
———. 2015. "Physicalism." In *Stanford Encyclopedia of Philosophy*, ed. Edward N. Zalta. Spring. http://plato.stanford.edu/archives/spr2015/entries/physicalism/.
Wasserman, Ryan. 2004. "The Constitution Question." *Nous* 38, no. 4 (January): 693–710.

PHYSICS. Physics is the branch of science that most generally tries to understand the fundamental principles that govern the universe. It is often described as the natural science that involves the study of matter and its motion through space and time, along with related concepts such as energy and force. With the inclusion of astronomy, it can be argued that physics is the oldest of all the sciences.

The subjects of physics are often divided into two broad categories: classical physics and modern physics. Classical physics deals with subjects that were developed primarily before the twentieth century and includes mechanics, thermodynamics, and electromagnetism. Near the end of the nineteenth century, some physicists believed that the study of basic science was nearing a completion, as these subjects tended to describe almost all known phenomena. However, unexpected discoveries in the early twentieth century radically changed our view of the universe and led to the development of many of the subjects now described as modern physics, which include special relativity, general relativity, and quantum physics.

The word *physics* comes from the Greek *physikē*, "belonging to nature." Before the seventeenth century, physics was a part of natural philosophy that included chemistry, biology, and mathematics, and was primarily practiced based on human reasoning rather than observation and experimentation. Our current understanding of science and physics developed during the Scientific Revolution of the seventeenth century when a distinction arose between the philosophers of science who based many of their conclusions simply on reason or beauty, and the mathematicians and physicists who developed their ideas based on observations.

There are many fields of physics. Some of the major branches include astrophysics, condensed matter physics, atomic physics, optical physics, nuclear physics, and particle physics. Cross-disciplinary physics include biophysics and geophysics. In addition, each field of physics is often divided into theoretical or experimental realms. Although theoreticians and experimentalists often work closely together, theoretical physicists tend to develop and refine mathematical theories that describe the universe while experimental physicists tend to perform observations to test or refute these theories. Comparisons between theoretical ideas and experimental results lead to confirmation of theories and development of new theories.

All theories in physics must be testable to be confirmed or refuted. In fact, the known "facts" about our physical universe are really a synopsis of the results of experiments that have been performed, usually many times, and give a description of how nature operates. Viable theories must not only provide qualitative predictions but actual quantitative predictions that can be accurately tested.

Principles of physics are considered meaningful only if they can be expressed by mathematical equations. For centuries, scientists, philosophers, and theologians have marveled that the universe is described by the precision inherent in mathematics. Theists point out that a mathematical description of the universe clearly points to the character of the Creator. For example, **Galileo Galilei** asserted, "Mathematics is the language with which God has written the universe" ("Galileo Galilei").

Even nontheists are amazed at our ability to use mathematics to explain the universe. Physicists and Nobel laureate Eugene Wigner wrote, "The miracle of the appropriateness of the language of mathematics for the formulation of the laws of physics is a wonderful gift which we neither understand nor deserve" (1960, 14). The mathematical laws of physics give convincing evidence that the universe is intelligently designed.

Michael G. Strauss

REFERENCES AND RECOMMENDED READING
"Galileo Galilei." Refspace. Accessed October 17, 2016. http://refspace.com/quotes/Galileo_Galilei/mathematics.
Giancoli, Douglas. 2014. *Physics: Principles with Applications*. 7th ed. San Francisco: Pearson.
Kepler, Johannes. 1601. *New Astronomy*.
Wigner, Eugene. 1960. "The Unreasonable Effectiveness of Mathematics in the Physical Sciences." *Communications on Pure and Applied Mathematics* 13:1–14.

PI IN THE BIBLE. The Greek letter pi (π) represents the ratio of the circumference of a circle to its diameter. The value of π is approximately 3.14159265358979 (to 15 digits). All decimal or fractional expressions of its value are, of necessity, approximations, since pi is an irrational number, that is, a number that cannot be represented by the ratio of integers so that its decimal representation has an infinite number of digits.

In the account of the great bronze sea of Solomon's temple found in 1 Kings 7:23 and in 2 Chronicles 4:2–5, we read: "He [Huram of Tyre, Solomon's master builder] made the Sea of cast metal, circular in shape, measuring ten cubits from rim to rim and five cubits high. It took a line of thirty cubits to measure around it." It appears from this text that the Bible declares (at least indirectly) that pi is exactly three.

Some critics of the Bible have seized on this putative inaccuracy to attack belief in biblical inerrancy. Biblical commentators have offered various responses. Their answers range from that of Rabbi Eliyahu (The Gaon of Vilna), a famous eighteenth-century Talmudic scholar who argued that the text contains a gematria (a number code based on the value of the letters in the text) that hides a much more accurate approximation for pi of 3 x 111/106 = 3.141509, to others who point out that the Hebrew text uses approximate values frequently, rounding to the nearest convenient unit.

Other commentators suggest that the "circumference" in the account may refer to the perimeter of the basin under the lip that was a hand's breadth in thickness, that is, approximately 4 inches (1 Kings 7:26). Thus, if the latter case obtains, the circumference of 30 cubits (approximately 45 feet or 13.716 m) would correspond to a diameter of approximately 14 feet 3.9 inches (4.37 m), or less by about 2 handbreadths (8 inches or 20 cm) of the wall's thickness than the 10 cubits brim to brim as recounted in the text.

On the other hand, the significance of the quantitative discussion may lie, not in the accuracy of the report but in its use of the appropriate precision. In the practice of modern quantitative science, data are reported to a given number of significant figures and are indicated by various conventions of notation. In the biblical text, the diameter of the basin is reported as 10 cubits, to a precision of one significant figure. Thus modern scientific practice requires that all factors be of the same precision, suggesting that one should use a value of 3 for pi in all computations of one significant figure. Since a fractional representation of an irrational number is always a somewhat inexact approximation, three is the appropriate level of precision called for in the present case, presaging modern scientific practice.

All such discussions may be empty speculation, however, and it may instead be that the reader's mathematical interpretation reveals more about the reader's presuppositions than the accuracy of the exegesis of the text itself.

Samuel E. Matteson

REFERENCES AND RECOMMENDED READING

Beckman, Petr. 1976. *A History of Pi*. New York: St. Martin's Griffin.

PLANTINGA, ALVIN. Alvin Carl Plantinga (1932–) is an American philosopher of religion writing in the analytic style who is widely regarded to be among the most influential philosophers of the twentieth century. Born in Ann Arbor, Michigan, into a Dutch Reformed family that took their religious beliefs very seriously, Plantinga studied at Calvin College (AB, 1954), the University of Michigan (MA, 1955), and Yale University (PhD, 1958). He has held academic positions at Wayne State (1958–63), Calvin College (1963–82), and Notre Dame (1982–present).

Plantinga retired in 2010 and currently is the John A. O'Brien Professor of Philosophy Emeritus at the University of Notre Dame and is the inaugural holder of the Jellema Chair in Philosophy at Calvin College. He has done groundbreaking work in **metaphysics**, **epistemology**, and **philosophy of religion**. Plantinga's involvement in the science-religion dialogue originated from his work on the nature of Christian scholarship.

The Nature of Christian Scholarship

One of the dominant themes of Plantinga's upbringing, one that is woven through nearly all of his academic work, is that there is no such thing as a serious, substantial, and relatively complete intellectual endeavor that is religiously neutral. In other words, since the rejection or acceptance of religious beliefs is fundamental to all reasonably complete academic endeavors, it is pointless to try to assume a position of religious neutrality in academic pursuits. Since religious neutrality is impossible, Christians can and should bring their religious beliefs into conversation with their philosophical and scientific work. Along these lines, in "Advice to Christian Philosophers" (1984), Plantinga encourages the Christian academic community to do their work as Christians and not to be constrained by the broader academic community's standards for what constitutes good scholarship, worthwhile academic inquiry, or a suitable explanation.

In the arena of science, Plantinga's advice runs contrary to the long-standing assumption that true science must assume methodological naturalism—religious beliefs must be ignored and not allowed to shape or direct scientific explanations in any way. Plantinga's response is that such an approach might make sense from a certain perspective, but from a Christian perspective, the sensible approach would be to pursue science using all that we know, including our theological beliefs.

Some who object to Plantinga's argument do so because they assume that theological beliefs cannot amount to knowledge—they are not universally held, are not based on arguments or evidence, or are the result of wish fulfillment. Plantinga has spent a good portion of his academic career refuting these sorts of objections, most fully in *Warranted Christian Belief* (2000).

Evolution and Intelligent Design

Plantinga has been labeled a defender of **intelligent design** and a member of the ID movement. The first of these is, with some clarification, straightforwardly true; the second is dubious at best. In a response to **Michael Ruse**, who labels Plantinga an "open enthusiast of intelligent design" (Ruse 2010, 56), Plantinga responds: "Like any Christian (and indeed any theist), I believe that the world has been created by God, and hence 'intelligently designed.' The hallmark of intelligent design, however, is the claim that this can be shown scientifically; I'm dubious about that" (Plantinga 2010, 57).

So, while Plantinga accepts at least some of the ID movement's critique of current evolutionary theory, he rejects their claims to be able to demonstrate that the world has been created by an intelligent designer. His stance is therefore likely to please neither the staunch evolutionary biologist nor the unswerving member of the ID movement. Consequently, on this issue (as on others), Plantinga finds himself in the proverbial "middle of the road, getting hit by trucks moving in both directions."

The Evolutionary Argument against Naturalism

One of Plantinga's most controversial contributions to the science-religion dialogue comes in the form of an **evolutionary argument against naturalism** (the view that there is no such thing as God or anything like God and that nature is the sum total of reality). In brief, Plantinga argues that the probability that humans would have developed truth-aimed, reliable belief-producing mechanisms, given naturalism and contemporary evolutionary theory, is low. This is because, given naturalism, it is difficult to see how the content of a belief (or the proposition associated with the belief) enters the causal chain leading to adaptive behavior. The naturalist who comes to accept this implication of naturalism and evolution acquires a defeater for her or his belief that unguided evolution has produced truth-aimed, reliable cognitive faculties.

This defeater, then, gives the naturalist a defeater for all other beliefs she or he has, including naturalism itself. Hence naturalism is self-defeating.

One should not mistake Plantinga's argument for an argument against either the *fact* that humans have reliable cognitive faculties or the concept of evolution. Plantinga, of course, accepts that humans have reliable cognitive faculties; he denies that they are the product of unguided evolution. And his argument does not address evolution *simpliciter*. There is no problem, according to Plantinga, with *divinely guided* evolution producing reliable cognitive faculties. The problem arises from the conjunction of naturalism and evolution.

Where the Conflict Really Lies

Where the Conflict Really Lies: Science, Religion, and Naturalism (2011) is Plantinga's first book-length discussion of science and religious belief. In it his deliberately controversial thesis is meant to undermine the popular belief that science sits comfortably with metaphysical naturalism but uneasily with theistic belief. He argues for quite the opposite: "There is superficial conflict, but deep concord between science and theistic religion, but superficial concord but deep conflict between science and naturalism" (2011, ix).

It is important to note that Plantinga is using the term "*conflict*" in a philosophical sense. There, of course, has been conflict (in a certain sense) between science and religion at the sociological or historical levels. Plantinga's claim is therefore best understood as meaning there need be no enmity between science and religion; one can be an enthusiastic proponent of both, and accepting or valuing one doesn't give a person a reason to reject the other.

To make his case, Plantinga surveys the alleged conflicts between science and divine action in the world and argues that these arguments only make sense if it is assumed that the natural world is a closed system of cause and effect. Consequently, the conflict is not between science and religious belief but between metaphysical naturalism and religious belief. And the conflict between evolutionary psychology and religious belief is superficial at best and does not give religious believers a defeater for their religious beliefs. On the other hand, while there are scientific arguments—fine-tuning arguments, for example—that provide at least "mild support" for theistic belief, Plantinga argues that his evolutionary argument against naturalism shows that there is deep and substantial conflict between science and naturalism.

James Beilby

REFERENCES AND RECOMMENDED READING

Dennett, Daniel C., and Alvin Plantinga. 2010. *Science and Religion: Are They Compatible?* Point/Counterpoint Series. New York: Oxford University Press.

Plantinga, Alvin. 1984. "Advice to Christian Philosophers." *Faith and Philosophy* 1, no. 3 (July): 253–71.

———. 1991a. "Evolution, Neutrality, and Antecedent Probability: A Reply to Van Til and McMullin." *Christian Scholar's Review* 21, no. 1 (September): 80–109.

———. 1991b. "When Faith and Reason Clash: Evolution and the Bible." *Christian Scholar's Review* 21, no. 1 (September): 8–32.

———. 1992. "On Rejecting the Theory of Common Ancestry." *Perspectives on Science and Christian Faith* 44, no. 4 (December): 258–63.

———. 1996. "Science: Augustinian or Duhemian." *Faith and Philosophy* 13, no. 3 (July): 368–94.

———. 1997. "Methodological Naturalism." *Perspectives on Science and Christian Faith* 49 (September):143–54.

———. 2000. *Warranted Christian Belief.* New York: Oxford University Press.

———. 2010. "Evolution, Shibboleths, and Philosophers." *Chronicle of Higher Education* (April 11): www.chronicle.com/article/Evolution-Shibboleths-and/64990/.

———. 2011. *Where the Conflict Really Lies: Science, Religion, and Naturalism.* New York: Oxford University Press.

———. 2014. "Religion and Science." In *Stanford Encyclopedia of Philosophy,* ed. Edward N. Zalta. Spring. http://plato.stanford.edu/archives/spr2014/entries/religion-science/.

Ruse, Michael. 2010. "Philosophers Rip Darwin." *Chronicle of Higher Education.* March 7. http://chronicle.com/article/What-Darwins-Doubters-Get/64457/.

PLATO. It is difficult to think of a more important figure in Western intellectual thought than Plato (429–347 BC). **Alfred North Whitehead** famously characterized all of Western philosophy as a series of footnotes to Plato. This may be a bit overstated, but it does underscore the point that Plato asked virtually all the big philosophical questions in some form or other, and we have indeed been attempting answers ever since.

The most important feature of the early life of Plato is his discipleship to Socrates. Since philosophical musing requires significant time and means, Socrates's students were almost always children of wealthy aristocrats. Plato was no exception, having been born into a very wealthy Athenian family. His given name was Aristocles, but at some early point in his life, he came to be known by the nickname Plato (which simply means "broad"). No one knows what elicited the moniker, or whether it is complimentary or pejorative. Suggestions include his physique, his literary abilities, and even perhaps a disproportionate forehead.

Plato is the primary reason why we know as much as we do about Socrates, since Socrates had no recorded writings and since Socrates features as the primary character in most of Plato's dialogues. Without Plato's immortalizing of Socrates, he would perhaps be among the obscure but important philosophers who preceded him—the so-called

pre-Socratics, for whom we have very few extant writings. By contrast, Plato's philosophical writings have, so far as we know, survived in their entirety.

There is significant disagreement about how accurately Socrates is portrayed by Plato. Plato almost certainly took liberties, but we seem to get at least a portrait of the sort of man and the sort of philosopher he was. A more pronounced but related difficulty is discerning when Plato is offering his own views in the mouth of Socrates and other speakers. Historically Plato's early dialogues (e.g., *Euthyphro, Apology, Crito*) are seen as extremely Socratic, perhaps recounting actual conversations. His middle dialogues (e.g., *Republic, Symposium, Phaedo*) still have Socrates as the main spokesperson but are likely a development of Plato's own views, and they are where we get most of what we call "Platonism." In his late dialogues (e.g., *Timaeus, Sophist, Laws*), Plato seems decidedly to move beyond his teacher and even what we call Platonism, including a possible refutation of his famous theory of the forms. For example, in the *Timaeus*, Socrates is present in the dialogue, but he is not the main spokesperson and, in the *Laws*, Socrates is entirely absent, as is any defense of the theory of the forms. However, pinpointing just what Plato actually believed is a vexing task.

Plato's philosophical writings are all in dialogue form. These typically (especially the early and many of the middle dialogues) pick up on a philosophical conversation between Socrates and some interlocutor or group of interlocutors about the nature of certain concepts, such as virtue, holiness, knowledge, or justice. Socrates typically outwits the interlocutor, sometimes to the extent that he arrives at no answer at all, but only a state of *aporia*—a state of confusion or contradiction.

Sometime after the execution of Socrates in 399 BC, Plato founded a school in Athens known as the Academy, which is the precursor for our modern university. Here students, including the likes of Aristotle, would come to pursue philosophical study, broadly construed.

Though Plato is sometimes pictured as a first philosopher, he definitely inherited philosophical ideas from those who came before him. The philosophically rich pre-Socratic age had given way to the skepticism and nihilism of the Sophists, the frequent object of Socrates's ire. Plato was able to synthesize several streams of pre-Socratic thought that had theretofore stymied the progress of science and intellectual thought. Parmenides asserted that there was no such thing as motion, and Zeno seemed to prove this with various insoluble paradoxes. On the other hand, Heraclitus had argued that everything is in motion, illustrated well by his famous slogan "No man ever steps in the same river twice." A river is constantly changing with its pulsing flow. This presents a descriptive problem since perhaps there are vague and fuzzy generalities true of a river, such as that "the Nile River is in Egypt," but there don't seem to be precise and determinate truths about the Nile (such as its exact location or the precise volume of water it contains), given that these facts are constantly in flux. Heraclitus thought all of reality is like the river to some degree or other (see **Process Philosophy**).

On both views, there is no ability to do science, because with no motion, there is no discovery. Or with no stability, our knowledge of the world is simply illusory.

Plato's metaphysics cut this Gordian knot by seeing reality according to his two-worlds hypothesis. Plato, in effect, agreed with Heraclitus about the ever-changing flux of reality but thought that this is only true of the visible or sensible world (i.e., the world of material objects that must be experienced with our five senses). The world of sensible objects is in a constant state of change and becoming. However, Plato, in effect, agreed with Parmenides that there is a reality that is eternally fixed. This is the intelligible world or the world of the forms.

The relation between these two worlds is that the sensible world is but an ever-changing dim reflection of the world of the forms. Sensible objects are said to participate in the forms. Apples, for example, come in a variety of sizes and colors, and all varieties taste somewhat different. However, despite having marked differences in terms of properties, there is some underlying "appleness" that each has to varying degrees. The apple, as a material object, is in a constant state of growth and decay, concluding with rotting and finally disintegrating. At some point in this process, it ceases to have appleness. Apples decay, but appleness is, for Plato, the form that exists eternally and in a state of perfection, in which apples participate, so long as they remain apples.

Given the stability of the world of the forms, we are able to have knowledge (see **Epistemology**). How do we do this if we cannot sense the forms? Plato's novel view is that we grasp the forms by a process of recollection from a time before we were born and lived among the forms. This recollection is brought on by intense abstract philosophical work. Plato thought that we, in a way, ought to break free from the sensible world, or at least our fixation with it, and come to see the greatness and beauty of the world of the forms. This is illustrated by his famous allegory of the cave in the *Republic*.

Knowledge of the sensible world remains somewhat elusive for Plato, given that one cannot say perfectly accurate things about the flux. Scientific reasoning is probably most like what Plato, in the *Timaeus*, calls "a likely story." A likely story is an account that is to some degree metaphorical but illuminates deep truths about some feature of reality. Consider the experience of the beauty of one's beloved. It seems wholly insufficient to give a factual description of this beauty. But when Romeo says "Juliet is the sun," we are able to understand in a deep way the experience Romeo is having.

This storytelling is the best we can do when it comes to describing the sensible world, and thus this is the best we can do when we do science. This is not to have a low view of science, since a likely story will illuminate deep truths about the world. And, moreover, science can progress, since our stories can get, in a way, likelier. When it comes to our current scientific theories, the Platonist might think that we have scientific stories that are likelier than the stories of the past that help us to grasp better some feature of the world, even though we will never reach any kind of absolute or perfect knowledge of sensible and material reality given its transitory nature. History's large repository of false scientific theories suggests that this picture is perhaps not too far afield.

Though Plato's views, in a variety of respects, are clearly inconsistent with an overall Christian view, his ideas have influenced many Christian thinkers (perhaps especially **Augustine**). In Plato we have arguments for an intelligently designed universe, an eternal reality beyond this contingent world, an immortal soul that outlives the body, and the reality and absoluteness of properties like justice, beauty, and moral goodness. These all have made Plato a rich source from which the discerning Christian can draw.

Travis M. Dickinson

REFERENCES AND RECOMMENDED READING

Annas, Julia. 2003. *Plato: A Very Short Introduction.* Oxford: Oxford University Press.
Fine, Gail, ed. 2008. *The Oxford Handbook of Plato.* Oxford: Oxford University Press.
Kraut, Richard, ed. 1992. *The Cambridge Companion to Plato.* Cambridge: Cambridge University Press.
———. 2008. *How to Read Plato.* London: Granta.
Reynolds, John Mark. 2009. *When Athens Met Jerusalem: An Introduction to Classical and Christian Thought.* Downers Grove, IL: IVP.

POLANYI, MICHAEL. Michael Polanyi (1891–1976) was an Anglo-Hungarian polymath known for contributions to physical chemistry and philosophy. Trained as a doctor, he served as a medical officer in the Austro-Hungarian army during the Great War. After a medical leave enabled him to complete a paper on the adsorption of gases, he was awarded a PhD in chemistry by the University of Budapest and appointed to its faculty. In 1919 the Jewish-born Polanyi converted to Catholicism after reading Tolstoy's *Confessions* and Dostoyevsky's *Grand Inquisitor*; shortly thereafter he immigrated to Germany.

While at the Kaiser Wilhelm Institute and subsequently the University of Manchester, Polanyi developed the principles of fiber X-ray diffraction, dislocation models for solid mechanics, and (along with Henry Erying) the field of chemical reaction dynamics. Two Nobelists studied under Polanyi, Eugene Wigner and Melvin Calvin, and his Nobelist son, John, studied under another former student.

Today Polanyi is best remembered for his contributions to epistemology, the sociology of science, and economics. Overall, the twin thrusts of Polanyi's efforts in these areas involved legitimizing faith and values as real knowledge and defending economic and scientific freedom. The latter derived from his travels to the USSR, which convinced him of the inefficiency of socialist economic systems.

When socialists proposed that British science and economics be subjected to centralized government control, Polanyi argued that the introduction of socialist control measures into complex difficult-to-predict enterprises like science and the market would introduce inefficiencies and stymie progress. Instead "polycentric" systems in which decision making was distributed over many entities were needed: for instance, science should be left to the initiative of individual scientists and economic decisions to a multitude of individual managers. However, Polanyi did not believe the economy should be wholly unregulated; instead, he espoused monetarist views (1945, 2014).

Polanyi was concerned that the misunderstanding of science as the impersonal pursuit of knowledge stunted mankind's ability to pursue genuine knowledge, in part by dismissing morality and spirituality. Influenced by his experience as a scientist and ideas from Gestalt psychology, Polanyi countered that knowledge is not developed by impersonal analysis of scientific data. In *Personal Knowledge* (1958) and *The Tacit Dimension* (1966), Polanyi stressed the importance of "tacit" knowledge—things that "we know but cannot tell" (Polanyi 1962b, 601)—which is gained by "indwelling" practices in communities. For Polanyi, knowing is holistic and personal; thus epistemologies that overemphasize the distinction between subjects and objects

hamper humanity's ability to grasp the "comprehensive meaning" revealed by the "particulars" (Polanyi 1946; 1966, 34; Polanyi and Grene 1969).

Although Polanyi was not primarily concerned with science and religion, he recognized his epistemology's promise for bringing science and religion together (1963), and his views influenced Ian Barbour, T. F. Torrance, John Polkinghorne, and John Haught (Russell 2008–9). He was also an important early emergentist, holding that life cannot be ontologically reduced to chemistry and physics since higher "levels of reality" (notably consciousness) control lower-level ones (like physics and chemistry) by imposing boundary conditions on their behavior (Polanyi 1965, 1968, 1970). However, Polanyi rejected the neo-Darwinian synthesis in favor of Teilhard de Chardin's teleological views (Polanyi 1963), and Philip Clayton has criticized his emergentism as based on a flawed neovitalist biology (Clayton 2002–3).

Christian theologians have also been attracted to Polanyi's epistemology as an alternative to positivism and postmodernism. Indeed, Polanyi himself recognized that his epistemology finds consonance with the traditional Christian conceptions of a life-apprehending faith seeking understanding in community (1961).

Stephen Contakes

REFERENCES AND RECOMMENDED READING

Apczynski, John V. 1977. *Doers of the Word: Toward a Foundational Theology Based on the Thought of Michael Polanyi*. American Academy of Religion Dissertation Series 18. Missoula, MT: Scholars Press/American Academy of Religion.

Clayton, Philip. 2002–3. "Emergence, Supervenience, and Personal Knowledge." *Tradition & Discovery* 29 (3). 8–19.

Foster, Durwood. 2008–9. "Michael and Paulus: A Dynamic Uncoordinated Duo." *Tradition & Discovery* 35 (3): 21–39.

Gelwick, Richard. 1977. *The Way of Discovery: An Introduction to the Thought of Michael Polanyi*. New York: Oxford University Press.

———. 2008–9. "The Christian Encounter of Paul Tillich and Michael Polanyi." *Tradition & Discovery* 35 (3): 7–20.

Hodgkin, R. A., and Eugene P. Wigner. 1977. "Michael Polanyi, 1891–1976." *Biographical Memoirs of Fellows of the Royal Society* 23:421–48.

Jaeger, Lydia. 2010. *Einstein, Polanyi, and the Laws of Nature*. West Conshohocken, PA: Templeton.

Manno, Bruno V. 1974. "Michael Polanyi on the Problem of Science and Religion." *Zygon* 9 (1): 44–56.

Mitchell, Mark T. 2006. *Michael Polanyi: The Art of Knowing*. Library of Modern Thinkers. Wilmington, DE: ISI Books.

Mullins, Phil. 1982. "The Spectrum of Meaning—Polanyian Perspectives on Science and Religion." *Zygon* 17 (1): 3–8.

Nye, M. J. 2002. "Michael Polanyi (1891–1976)." *HYLE—International Journal for the Philosophy of Chemistry* 8 (2): 123–27.

———. 2011. *Michael Polanyi and His Generation: Origins of the Social Construction of Science*. Chicago: University of Chicago Press.

Polanyi, Michael. 1932. *Atomic Reactions*. London: Williams & Norgate.

———. 1936. *U.S.S.R. Economics: Fundamental Data, System and Spirit*. Manchester, UK: Manchester University Press.

———. (1940) 2014. "Unemployment and Money: The Principles Involved." www.youtube.com/watch?v=wFm_ORFfp9U.

———. 1944. *Patent Reform: A Plan for Encouraging the Application of Inventions*. n.p.

———. 1945. *Full Employment and Free Trade*. Cambridge: Cambridge University Press.

———. 1946. *Science, Faith and Society*. Riddell Memorial Lectures. London: Oxford University Press.

———. 1956. *The Magic of Marxism and the Next Stage of History*. Manchester, UK: Committee on Science and Freedom.

———. 1958. *Personal Knowledge: Towards a Post-critical Philosophy*. Chicago: University of Chicago Press.

———. 1959. *The Study of Man*. Lindsay Memorial Lectures. London: Routledge and Kegan Paul.

———. 1960. *Beyond Nihilism*. Arthur Stanley Eddington Memorial Lecture. Cambridge: Cambridge University Press.

———. 1961. "Faith and Reason." *The Journal of Religion* 41, no. 4 (October): 237–47.

———. 1962a. "My Time with X-Rays and Crystals." In *Fifty Years of X-Ray Diffraction. Dedicated to the International Union of Crystallography on the Occasion of the Commemoration Meeting in Munich, July 1962*, ed. Peter Paul Ewald, 629–36. Utrecht: International Union of Crystallography/A. Oosthoek's Uitgeversmij.

———. 1962b. "Tacit Knowing: Its Bearing on Some Problems of Philosophy." *Reviews of Modern Physics* 34, no. 4 (October): 601–16.

———. 1963. "Science and Religion: Separate Dimensions or Common Ground?" *Philosophy Today* 7, no. 1 (Spring): 4–14.

———. 1965. "Levels of Reality." Lecture delivered at Wesleyan University, Middletown, CT. November 11.

———. 1966. *The Tacit Dimension*. Terry Lectures. Garden City, NY: Doubleday.

———. 1968. "Life's Irreducible Structure: Live Mechanisms and Information in DNA Are Boundary Conditions with a Sequence of Boundaries above Them." *Science* 160, no. 3834 (June 21): 1308–12.

———. 1970. "Transcendence and Self-Transcendence." *Soundings* 53, no. 1 (Spring): 88–94.

———. 1974. *Scientific Thought and Social Reality: Essays*. Psychological Issues. New York: International Universities Press.

———. 1975. *The Contempt of Freedom: The Russian Experiment and After*. History, Philosophy and Sociology of Science. New York: Arno.

———. 1998. *The Logic of Liberty: Reflections and Rejoinders*. Indianapolis: Liberty Fund.

Polanyi, Michael, and R. T. Allen. 1997. *Society, Economics and Philosophy: Selected Papers*. New Brunswick, NJ: Transaction.

Polanyi, Michael, and Marjorie Grene. 1969. *Knowing and Being: Essays*. London: Routledge and Kegan Paul.

Polanyi, Michael, and Harry Prosch. 1975. *Meaning*. Chicago: University of Chicago Press.

Prosch, Harry. 1986. *Michael Polanyi: A Critical Exposition*. SUNY Series in Cultural Perspectives. Albany, NY: SUNY Press.

Rae, Murray. 2012. *Critical Conversations: Michael Polanyi and Christian Theology*. Eugene, OR: Pickwick.

Russell, Robert John. 2008–9. "Polanyi's Gift to 'Theology and Science.'" *Tradition & Discovery* 35 (3): 40–47.

Scott, Drusilla. 1995. *Everyman Revived: The Common Sense of Michael Polanyi*. Grand Rapids: Eerdmans.

Scott, William T., and Martin X. Moleski. 2005. *Michael Polanyi: Scientist and Philosopher*. Oxford: Oxford University Press.

Torrance, Thomas F. 1980. *Belief in Science and in Christian Life: The Relevance of Michael Polanyi's Thought for Christian Faith and Life*. Edinburgh: Handsel.

———. 2000. "Michael Polanyi and the Christian Faith—a Personal Report." *Tradition & Discovery* 27 (2): 26–32.

POLKINGHORNE, JOHN. The Reverend Dr. John Charlton Polkinghorne, KBE, FRS was born on October 16, 1930. He is an English theoretical physicist, theologian, Anglican priest, and writer. He is regarded as a leader in the field of communicating the relationship between science and theology. Professionally he was professor of mathematical physics at Cambridge University from 1968 to 1979, resigning his chair at that point to study for the Anglican priesthood. He became an ordained Anglican priest in 1982 and took up parish ministry. Then from 1988 to his retirement in 1996, he was president of Queens College, Cambridge.

A small sampling of his awards and honors include being installed as a Knight Commander of the British Empire (KBE) in 1997 and receiving the Templeton Prize for his contributions to the understanding of the relationship of science and theology in 2002. He has the distinct honor of being the only member of the Royal Society who is also ordained clergy, and he is a founding member of the Society of Ordained Scientists and the first president of the International Society for Science and Religion.

Polkinghorne's concern has centered on investigating the compatibility of science and religion. He has spoken worldwide, and his writings include five books in his research field of particle physics and more than 25 books on science and religion. A small sampling of his widely read books include *One World* (1986), *Science and Creation* (1988), *The Way the World Is: The Christian Perspective of a Scientist* (1983), *Science and Providence* (1990), *Reason and Reality* (1991), *Quarks, Chaos and Christianity* (1994), *The Work of Love* (ed., 2001), *The God of Hope and the End of the World* (2002), *Quantum Physics and Theology* (2007), and *Testing Scripture* (2010). His books are generally moderately short in length, as he employs an economy of words to clearly and elegantly convey his ideas.

Polkinghorne has consistently maintained the position that science and Christianity are cousins, each different, yet each seeking truth. As a result, he sees the two enterprises as compatible. And even though different, each can inform the other in appropriate situations.

One of Polkinghorne's high honors was to be invited to deliver the Gifford Lectures in 1993–94, which subsequently were published as his longest book, *The Faith of a Physicist: Reflections of a Bottom-Up Thinker* (1994). The book jacket reads:

Polkinghorne ... here explores just what rational grounds there could be for Christian beliefs, maintaining that the quest for motivated understanding is a common concern shared by scientists and religious thinkers alike.... [He] organizes his inquiry around the Nicene Creed, an early statement that continues to summarize Christian beliefs. He applies to each of its tenets the question, "What is the evidence that makes you think this might be true?"

Polkinghorne describes his position as that of critical reason and maintains that science and religion address aspects of the same reality. He sometimes finds Christianity too good to be true but then thinks to himself, *"All right then, deny it"*—and knows he will never do this (2007, 107).

Richard F. Carlson

REFERENCES AND RECOMMENDED READING

Polkinghorne, John. 1988. *Science and Creation.* Boston: New Science Library.
———. 1994. *The Faith of a Physicist: Reflections of a Bottom-Up Thinker.* Princeton: Princeton University Press.
———. 2007. *From Physicist to Priest, An Autobiography.* London: SPCK.

POPPER, KARL. Sir Karl Popper (1902–94) started his career on the fringes of the Vienna Circle of philosophers who developed **logical positivism**. Having Jewish parents (though baptized Lutherans), he emigrated to New Zealand in 1937 during the rise of Nazism, where he formed a significant friendship with the Nobel Prize–winning Christian neurophysiologist Sir John Eccles. In 1946 he came to the London School of Economics, where he remained for the rest of his career.

The logical positivists restricted real knowledge to the observable and measurable. For any statement to count as science, and indeed to have any meaning at all, one must be able to verify it—that is, conduct an observation or experiment that shows it. The logical positivists denied that statements about God are meaningful because they are not verifiable in this way. It is not just that "God exists" is a false statement; it simply has no meaning. Ethical statements such as "You shall not steal" are likewise meaningless.

Popper challenged logical positivism on the grounds that no amount of measurement can verify general laws, which are what science deals in. Popper argued in contrast that scientific laws can only be falsified (Popper [1959] 1990, esp. 40–41). The statement "All swans are white," which is universal like

a scientific law, can only be verified by observing all swans in the universe, an impossible task. Observation of a single black swan would immediately falsify it. Interestingly, Popper thought that the statement "God exists" cannot be falsified, but he was more restrained than his logical positivist predecessors. Though the statement "God exists" is not a scientific statement, this does not make it a meaningless statement. Popper also thought that ethical questions are not scientific, but it can still be meaningful to say, "You shall not steal." Science just says nothing about these subjects.

According to Popper, all scientific theories are tentative because they are potentially falsifiable. Scientific progress comes through learning from past mistakes, falsifying theories, and presenting alternatives for criticism. All we ever have are provisional conjectures: "The old scientific idea of *epistēmē*—of absolutely certain, demonstrable knowledge—has proved to be an idol. The demand for scientific objectivity makes it inevitable that every scientific statement must remain *tentative for ever*" (Popper [1959] 1990, 280). Ironically, he concluded, "Only in our subjective experiences of conviction, in our subjective faith, can we be 'absolutely certain'" (ibid.).

According to Popper, for a postulate to have the status of a scientific theory, it should involve the repeatability of experiments (and hence be truly falsifiable) and should be predictive. On these grounds, Popper at first did not regard cosmology and biological evolution as scientific theories, though he later changed his mind on this point.

In practice, scientists do not discard theories at the first hint of falsification and are more optimistic than Popper would have them. Popper's pupil **Imre Lakatos** perhaps better captures the way science makes genuine progress with his "methodology of scientific research programmes" (and better than **Thomas Kuhn**'s "incommensurable paradigms"). Nevertheless, falsification remains an important criterion, and modern science does indeed demonstrate a process of self-correction at work, as Popper required. Witness the ability of special and general relativity to explain data that had, at least naively, falsified classical Newtonian mechanics.

The work of Popper and others helps dispel the simplistic notion that science is inhuman in its objectivity, relying solely on experimental evidence, and assured in its results. Value judgments are involved, and it is perhaps closer to religion than one might at first have thought. Popper wrote, "I am inclined to think that scientific discovery is impossible without faith in ideas which are of a purely speculative kind, and sometimes even quite hazy; a faith which is completely unwarranted from the point of view of science, and which, to that extent, is 'metaphysical'" (Popper [1959] 1990, 38).

Popper was also critical of **reductionism**, the idea that there is a hierarchy of sciences such that higher levels in the hierarchy can be reduced to lower levels, for example, biology to chemistry and chemistry to physics. While reduction is invaluable methodologically, "as a philosophy reduction is a failure" (Popper 1974, 269). However, that failure is important in leading to the recognition of emergence and emergent properties (268–69).

Supremely, Popper recognized that the human mind cannot be reduced simply to physical processes, and this insight led him to a form of mind-body dualism, which he called "psychophysical interactionism" (Popper 1974, 275). Interaction occurs between three worlds, whereby emergence and "downward causation" come into play:

World 1, the world of physical objects;

World 2, the world of subjective experiences; and

World 3, comprising the products of the human mind (Popper 1977, 15–16, 36–50; 1974, 274–75).

Materialism and epiphenomenalism are thus self-defeating because they imply that our decisions and actions are decided by purely physical processes, rather than by arguments and reasons (1977, 74–81). Determinism suffers from a similar problem. Determinism, if true, cannot be argued, since any argument is presumably itself determined by purely physical processes, as are any opposing arguments (Popper 1979, 223–24).

Gilbert Ryle famously argued that the "'dogma of the Ghost in the Machine' ... is entirely false, and false not in detail but in principle" (Ryle 1990, 17). In contrast, Popper boldly stated: "I believe in the ghost in the machine" (Popper 1977, 105).

Popper believed that moral concepts are dependent on language. While animals may have a degree of consciousness, "only a man can make an effort to become a better man; to master his fears, his laziness, his selfishness; to get over his lack of self-control" (Popper 1977, 144). Popper's concept of three worlds has been developed in more recent times by George Ellis (Ellis 2007, 126–35).

Rodney Holder

REFERENCES AND RECOMMENDED READING

Ellis, G. F. R. 2007. "Science, Complexity, and the Nature of Existence." In *Evolution and Emergence: Systems, Organisms, Persons*, ed. Nancey Murphy and William R. Stoeger. Oxford: Oxford University Press.

Holder, Rodney D. (1993) 2008. *Nothing but Atoms and Molecules? Probing the Limits of Science.* Cambridge, UK: Faraday Institute for Science and Religion; Crowborough, UK: Monarch.
Popper, Karl R. (1959) 1990. *The Logic of Scientific Discovery.* London: Unwin Hyman. First German ed., *Logik der Forschung*, 1934.
———. 1974. "Scientific Reduction and the Essential Incompleteness of All Science." In *Studies in the Philosophy of Biology: Reduction and Related Problems*, ed. F. J. Ayala and T. Dobzhansky. London: Macmillan.
———. 1977. Part 1 of *The Self and Its Brain*, Karl R. Popper and John C. Eccles. Berlin: Springer International.
———. 1979. *Objective Knowledge: An Evolutionary Approach.* Rev. ed. Oxford: Oxford University Press.
Ryle, Gilbert. 1990. *The Concept of Mind.* London: Penguin.

POSTMODERNISM. While postmodernism is difficult to define, there are a number of common themes running through it. (1) Postmoderns reject the dominant Enlightenment worldview of modernism, (2) a rejection of the possibility that humans are impartial, objective, and unsituated observers; rather, advocates of postmodernism affirm humans as radically situated.

(3) The meaning of statements is not to be found through reference to objects in the external world, but rather intertextually. Ferdinand de Saussure and the later poststructuralists see meaning as a matter of internal relation rather than external reference. (4) Truth itself is socially constructed, though some postmoderns don't want to go quite this far; the rough idea is that radical human situatedness leads toward the social construction of truth.

(5) Postmoderns have significant doubts whether there is an enduring and substantial self; for many postmoderns the self is a construct.

(6) Texts are inherently unstable (due to their untethering from the external world), and they never disclose full meaning; as Jacques Derrida puts it, there is a denial of full presence (meaning).

(7) Methodological objectivity is humanly impossible; all knowledge is radically perspectival. (8) Following the lead of Michel Foucault, postmoderns consider all truth claims to be ideological and oppressive; such claims are part of the long history of Western imperialism and subjugation. (9) Many postmoderns reject both external realism (the idea that the world exists independently of our representations of it) and the correspondence theory of truth (the idea that truth entails a matchup or correspondence between a belief or proposition and actual reality).

(10) Following Jean-François Lyotard, postmoderns share a general incredulity toward metanarratives; such overarching narratives are seen as epistemically overconfident (we simply

cannot know things of this scale) and as ideologically oppressive. (11) Derrida and others have seen the traditional Western reliance on human reason as logocentric, which presupposes a view of **metaphysics** and the possibility of full presence or meaning, as Plato, René Descartes, and others asserted. (12) Traditional narratives (such as Marxism, modernism, and perhaps Christianity) are seen as oppressive, as they exclude and marginalize those living on the fringes of society and make no space for them in the modern academic conversation.

It is not always clear what evangelical scholars should make of postmodernism's various claims. Evangelicals will differ as to how best to respond to postmodernism, with their response being based on two key factors: (1) how broadly they define postmodernism and (2) how much confidence they have in the project of natural theology, as much postmodern thought undermines a general confidence in unaided human reason.

I suggest that a sufficiently modest and chastened postmodernism is compatible with Christianity and the human cognitive situation. Claims 1 and 2 above can be partly endorsed, but Christians can still affirm that biased, fallen humans can have genuine, albeit limited, knowledge ("we know in part" [1 Cor. 13:9]) and that certain fundamental laws of logic or rationality are inescapable (i.e., to reject them is to use them).

Claims 7 and 8 both have a measure of truth: as Christians we do speak from a particular vantage point and often lack objectivity, but the standard postmodern position excludes any possibility of objective divine revelation, which we would not, and postmodernism itself takes a particular perspective and purportedly makes an objective assessment about, say, the Enlightenment or modernism.

Finally, texts do have some degree of instability (claim 6), and claim 12 is partly correct, although we could add that the accidents of history (that is, particular events that happened but didn't have to), such as the oppressive Inquisition, are not intrinsic to the Christian faith. The other claims, 3–5 and 9–11, are generally deserving of carefully considered rejection, both for philosophical reasons and for being incompatible with historic Christianity. Postmodernism in its more modest guises is compatible with the scientific enterprise, but for those postmoderns who are committed antirealists, compatibility with science is lacking.

Stewart E. Kelly

REFERENCES AND RECOMMENDED READING

Carson, D. A. 2002. "Domesticating the Gospel: A Review of Stanley J. Grenz's *Renewing the Center*." *Southern Baptist Journal of Theology* 6, no. 4 (Winter): 82–97.

Kelly, Stewart E. 2011. *Truth Considered and Applied.* Nashville: B&H Academic.
Rosenau, Pauline. 1991. *Post-modernism and the Social Sciences.* Princeton: Princeton University Press.
Smith, James K. A. 2006. *Who's Afraid of Postmodernism?* 2nd ed. Grand Rapids: Baker Academic.
Vanhoozer, Kevin. 2009. *Is There a Meaning in This Text?* Grand Rapids: Zondervan.

PRAYER. Simone Weil (1909–43), the Jewish-Christian thinker, captures the essence of prayer in her concept of prayer as "paying attention to God" (Weil 2009, 57). In recent evangelical tradition, this paying attention to God is sometimes summed up in the acronym ACTS (adoration, confession, thanksgiving, and supplication).

Each of these practices has biblical warrant (Pss. 51; 143:1–2; 145:1–2; Eph. 6:19–20; Phil. 4:6). The list, however, is incomplete in the light of the biblical witness. Lament is a missing practice, for instance; around a third of the psalms are laments that cry out to God for redress in contexts of suffering, oppression, or threats by others (e.g., Ps. 13). Also, of these practices, supplication or petition raises acute questions about its credibility in societies dominated by scientific ways of knowing. The psalmist confessed that he loved the Lord because the Lord answered his prayer (Ps. 116:1). Is this confession still possible in a culture so shaped by the scientific outlook? To that question we shall turn, but first the biblical testimony needs to be considered.

The Biblical Testimony

Petitioning God is a biblical practice, as can be seen in the following passages that are indicative rather than exhaustive. In 1 Kings 18:36–38 the prophet Elijah calls on the living God to answer by fire so that the false prophets of Baal might be discredited. The fire falls. In 2 Kings 20:1–6 the deathly ill King Hezekiah petitions God for more life. He is granted another 15 years. Turning to the New Testament, Jesus taught disciples to petition God as their heavenly Father in the famous Lord's Prayer (Matt. 6:9–13). The apostle Paul asks the Corinthians to help him by supplicating God on his behalf in 2 Corinthians 1:9–11. In James 5:17–18 we find the example of Elijah's successful praying for rain in a drought-stricken landscape. In this light, James claims that the prayer of a righteous person is effective (5:16).

The biblical witness is clear. The living God answers prayer. Even so, a feature of biblical writing must be noted. Biblical literature is nonpostulational (i.e., does not offer a theory). The Scriptures do not explore how things work or the essence of things. In other words, the Scriptures presuppose a metaphysic but don't present one. At this point, perhaps surprisingly, Enlightenment philosopher **Immanuel Kant** (d. 1804) may be of help.

The Transcendental Question

Kant crafted a form of question that is of particular relevance to our topic. This form of question is known as a transcendental question. It asks, what else must be true if X or Y is true? So regarding prayer, the question is, what else must be true about God and creation for the prayer of a righteous person to be effective, as in James 5? Likewise, what else must be true about God and creation for Christian behavior to hasten the day of the Lord, as in 2 Peter 3?

In exploring the transcendental question, two metaphors come into view that may help clarify alternatives. There are those whose understanding of God could be described in terms of the ideal composer. This composer not only creates the score in eternity but has the power as creation's sovereign to control the performance of all the players and the conductor in time. In other words, the perfect composer exercises a meticulous providence over nature and history (e.g., Paul Helm). With regard to prayer, God has timelessly determined both the petition and the answer. This would be a classic theistic approach.

Not so for others. The everlasting God is more like the ideal leader of a jazz band. He will play what he has determined to play in any possible universe. He is sovereign, after all. However, there is room for improvisation and divine responsiveness to human behavior. This behavior could surprise even God on occasion. God's providence is general rather than meticulous (e.g., John Sanders). This would be an **open theism** answer.

While we could mention other approaches, such as the dual affirmation of meticulous divine sovereignty and libertarian human freedom in prayer (e.g., **William Lane Craig**), the two approaches discussed above take divine sovereignty and the efficacy of prayer seriously but differ in their respective construal of God's relation to time and the logical possibilities that attend divine omnipotence and omniscience.

Prayer, Experiment, and the Scientific Outlook

There are those who argue that the scientific outlook presupposes a closed universe of cause and effect, allowing for no supernaturalism or divine action in the world (e.g., **Richard Dawkins**). Natural laws rule. Others, however, would argue that such a view is not strictly scientific (e.g., **John Lennox**).

It assumes a materialist metaphysic. As for natural laws, this refers to what is statistically usually the case.

The descriptor "law(s)" can be misleading here. On this view, an open universe is not antithetical to a scientific outlook that is epistemologically humble rather than imperialistic — that is, the laws of nature inform us how the world will operate unless a divine agent specially acts in it. In a universe that is a creation of God, natural law becomes another name for the faithfulness of its living Creator, who sustains it in being. **Augustine** (d. 430) has wisdom to contribute on this matter. He argued that **miracles** — and I would add divine answers to prayer — are not contrary to nature but to what we know of nature (*Contra Faustus* 26.3).

Scientific practices are conducted by persons with worldviews (or metaphysics) either held explicitly or tacitly. Some worldviews allow answers to prayers, while in others, to expect an answer is sheer foolishness. As philosopher William Halverson has argued, the divide between naturalistic and nonnaturalistic worldviews is the fundamental one. He contends, "It may be helpful to bear in mind from the beginning, however, that one theme that underlies nearly all philosophical discussion is the perpetual conflict between *naturalistic* and *nonnaturalistic* world views" (Halverson 1981, 414–15, emphasis in original).

Some scientists have endeavored to approach the question of the efficacy of petitionary prayer in an experimental way. Francis Galton (d. 1911) published a study on the subject of prayer and stillbirths in the *Fortnightly Review* in 1872 (Brümmer 2008, 9). He concluded that prayer made no statistical difference. A controversial 1998 study by Randolph Byrd of some 393 patients with coronary issues based at the San Francisco General Hospital suggested a positive result for intercessory prayer. However, a massive Harvard Medical School study (*Study of the Therapeutic Effects of Intercessory Prayer* or STEP) concluded in 2006 that intercessory prayer by third parties for some 1,802 patients had overall a negative rather than even a neutral outcome. This study took 10 years and cost $2.4 million. Each of these studies begs its own set of questions, especially at the levels of assumptions and methodology (Fung and Fung 2009, 43–44).

From a biblical perspective, it is hard to justify the experimental approach. Magic is never far below the surface in human nature. Magic is about finding a technique that can manipulate supernatural forces for benefit (white magic) or harm (black magic). The God of scriptural depiction is not open to manipulation as Simon Magus found out (Acts 8:9–24). Arguably one reason that prayers are not always answered as one would wish is both to keep the petitioner from magic and his or her relation to God personal rather than mechanical. The living God of the psalmist still answers prayer but has a mind of his own (Rom. 11:33–36).

Graham Cole

REFERENCES AND RECOMMENDED READING

Augustine. *Contra Faustam, Book 26*. www.newadvent.org/fathers/140626.htm. Accessed December 10, 2016.

Brümmer, V. 2008. *What Are We Doing When We Pray? On Prayer and the Nature of Faith*. Rev. and exp. Burlington, VT: Ashgate.

Fung, G., and Fung, C. 2009. "What Do Prayer Studies Prove?" *Christianity Today* 53:5 (May): 43–44.

Halverson, W. H. 1981. *A Concise Introduction to Philosophy*. 4th ed. Boston: McGraw-Hill.

"Review of Intercessory Prayer Studies." Intercessory Prayer Studies. Accessed November 26, 2014. www.intercessoryprayerstudies.com.

Weil, S. 2009. *Waiting for God*. New York: HarperCollins.

PRICE, GEORGE MCCREADY. Born in rural New Brunswick, Canada, George McCready Price (1870–1963) was raised on a farm and as a youth followed his mother into the Seventh-day Adventist Church. After high school, he worked for several years selling Adventist literature in eastern Canada. In 1891 he enrolled in Battle Creek College but left after two years without a degree. After selling books for two more years, he completed a one-year teacher training course at Provincial Normal School of New Brunswick, where he took several courses in the natural sciences. He then began a series of teaching positions at various Canadian high schools and Adventist institutions (Numbers 2006).

While teaching in Tracadie, New Brunswick, in 1899, a local physician befriended Price and introduced him to Darwinism. After studying several Darwinist works, Price grew convinced that the entire evolutionary scheme pivoted on what he perceived as their faulty understanding of the geological record (Price 1941). In 1902 he penned *Outlines of Modern Christianity and Modern Science*. It was the first of more than two dozen books and hundreds of articles advocating what he described as "flood geology" (Numbers 2006). While many Protestants who rejected Darwinism in the early twentieth century did so on theological grounds, Price attempted to resist evolution for scientific reasons.

Price's "flood geology" offered a wholly different interpretation of the geological timescale and the succession of strata than was universally accepted among geologists. Instead, he proposed a single succession of strata that covered the whole earth. The Noahic flood described in Genesis, Price insisted,

created the entire fossil record. Since the fossils could not be dated sequentially, Price asserted, the geological evidence not only supported his deluge model but also disproved an evolutionary history of life on earth. By his reasoning, the world is some 6,000 years old (Numbers 1998, 2006).

Although he pointed to geological evidence to support his views, Price's Adventist theological commitments also shaped his position. The Seventh-day Adventist Church had emerged in the aftermath of the mid-nineteenth-century apocalyptic preacher William Miller's unsuccessful predictions regarding the imminent return of Christ.

Led by the prophetess Ellen G. White (1827–1915), Seventh-day Adventists shared Miller's convictions regarding the imminent second coming of Christ. According to their interpretation of the fourth commandment, Adventists also believed that Christians should worship on Saturdays, which was the Sabbath day in the Old Testament, because it was a memorial to a literal six-day creation. Adventists considered the writings of White as authoritative as the Bible.

When White reportedly received a divine vision that carried her back to the first week of creation and demonstrated to her that each day of creation was a period of 24 hours, Adventists considered a literal six-day interpretation of Genesis an irrefutable truth (Numbers 2006; Price 1941). Consequently, Price's "flood geology" not only put him at odds with geologists in his day but also with many conservative Protestants who advocated either a day-age or gap theory. The former interpreted the days of Genesis 1 to represent vast periods of time, while the latter differentiated a creation "in the beginning" from a subsequent Edenic creation in six literal days. Price considered both views as erroneous as evolution (Numbers 1998, 2006).

Price gained the attention of the larger fundamentalist community as conservative Protestants launched their campaign against evolution in the late 1910s. Works such as *Q.E.D.: Or, New Light on the Doctrine of Creation* (1917) and especially *The New Geology* (1923) further extended Price's popularity.

Although Price was considered an amateur by scientists, William Jennings Bryan invited him to serve as an expert witness at the 1925 Scopes trial. Because he was teaching in England at the time, however, Price was unable to attend. After Bryan offered a rather muddled explanation of "flood geology" during the trial and acknowledged during cross-examination that he did not personally believe in an interpretation of Genesis of six 24-hour days, Price felt that Bryan had betrayed the antievolution movement.

While the Scopes trial may have been a setback for the antievolution cause, the popularity of Price's "flood geology" continued to grow as did his publications promoting his theory. Price died at the age of 93 on January 24, 1963. His controversial views on geology as well as Genesis inspired a subsequent generation of fundamentalist scientists and theologians as evidenced by the establishment of the Creation Research Society in 1963 and the current popularity of scientific creationism (Numbers 1998, 2006).

P. C. Kemeny

REFERENCES AND RECOMMENDED READING

Price, George McCready. 1902. *Outlines of Modern Christianity and Modern Science.* Oakland, CA: Pacific.
———. 1917. *Q.E.D.: Or, New Light on the Doctrine of Creation.* New York: Revell.
———. 1923. *The New Geology: A Textbook for Colleges, Normal Schools, and Training Schools; and for the General Reader.* Mountain View, CA: Pacific.
———. 1941. "Some Early Experiences with Evolutionary Geology." *Bulletin of Deluge Geology and Related Sciences* 1 (4): 77–92.
Numbers, Ronald L. 1998. *Darwinism Comes to America.* Cambridge, MA: Harvard University Press.
———. 2006. *The Creationists: From Scientific Creationism to Intelligent Design.* Exp. ed. Cambridge, MA: Harvard University Press.

PROBABILITY. Probability refers to the likelihood that a particular event will occur, while probability theory is the formal mathematics underlying the calculation of probabilities. Probability can give a quantifiable calculation or estimation of the likelihood that an event will occur.

Probability is usually described as a number from 0 to 1 with 0 indicating the event will not happen and 1 indicating the event must happen. If a correctly weighted coin is tossed in the air, the probability of getting heads on any single try is 1/2.

There are two primary interpretations regarding the fundamental nature of probabilities: objectivists and subjectivists. An objectivist's approach deals only with well-defined random events, while the subjectivist's approach assigns probability more as a degree of belief regarding an event.

The most standard and common interpretation is the frequentist probability interpretation, which is the classic objectivist approach. The probability is defined as the relative frequency of an event compared with the entire sample space. For example, the sample space of a six-sided die consists of all six possibilities, and the probability that any one side is face up for any single roll is 1/6. For independent events, probabilities can simply be multiplied. The probability of rolling a 1 on a six-sided die is 1/6; so the probability of rolling two 1s is 1/6 x 1/6 or 1/36.

Developing some of the mathematical formalism of probability theory may be helpful here. $P(A)$ is defined as the probability for event A to occur. If two events—say, A and B—are independent, then the probability of both occurring is $P(A \cap B) = P(A)P(B)$. This was illustrated above when discussing the probability of rolling two 1s with six-sided dice.

The probability of either of two events, A or B, occurring is given by $P(A \cup B) = P(A) + P(B)$. An example is the probability of rolling a 1 or a 2 with a single six-sided die is 1/6 + 1/6 = 1/3. An important principle in probability theory is the conditional probability. What is the probability that an event A will occur given the fact that event B has already occurred? This is written as $P(A|B)$. If you live in a Christian household, the probability that you will get a present (say, event A) is much higher if it is December 25 (event B) than if it is some arbitrary date. Formally, $P(A|B) = P(A \cap B)/P(B)$. Another important concept is the inverse probability. The inverse probability for $P(A|B)$ is $P(B|A)$. It is a common misperception that if $P(A|B)$ is large, then so is $P(B|A)$. But this is not necessarily true and is often false. Just because the probability that you will get a present is high if the date is December 25, this does not necessarily mean that the probability is high that the date is December 25 just because you have received a present.

The most common subjectivist approach to probability is Bayesian probability, though Bayesian probability can be interpreted within a frequentist framework. In the eighteenth century, Thomas Bayes provided the first mathematical treatment of his idea in a paper titled "An Essay towards Solving a Problem in the Doctrine of Chances," and Pierre-Laplace later generalized his theorem. Bayes's approach uses conditional probabilities and previous knowledge (prior probabilities) to determine a posterior probability. The subjectivist interpretation of **Bayes' theorem** is that it provides a level of the degree of belief in an axiom given all of the available evidence. One of the principle characteristics of the mathematics of Bayes' theorem is the formalism to calculate $P(B|A)$ given $P(A|B)$, $P(B)$, and $P(A)$.

Both theists and nontheists tend to use probabilistic arguments to support their views. The fine-tuning argument indirectly appeals to the low probability of a universe that can support life as evidence that a deity exists, while nontheists like Bill Jefferys and Michael Ikeda claim that Bayesian analysis undermines the use of fine-tuning as an argument for God (see **Fine-Tuning of the Universe and Solar System**; Ikeda and Jefferys 2006). Proponents of intelligent design combine low probability with specified complexity to design a filter that determines whether the most likely explanation for something should be attributed to design (Dembski 1998). In response, nontheists often claim that "improbable things happen all the time" and we should not be surprised to observe improbable events (Hand 2014a). Theists respond that their appeal is not simply to low-probability events but to low-probability events with specified complexity.

When appealing to probability, the apologists mentioned above tend to use subjective probabilities, which have more flexibility than a strict objectivist approach. Although the mathematics of probability theory is precise, the interpretations and assumptions are not, and probability theory cannot give an unambiguous proof for or against the existence of God.

The claims made by the proponents of a certain probability calculation may be overblown. For instance, in the Jefferys-Ikeda approach, the authors attempt only to discredit the weak anthropic principle and make no distinction between a universe with finely tuned parameters that allow life to exist and one with a broad range of life-friendly parameters. They use a Bayesian technique but make no use of any prior information, and their conclusion is ultimately based on the assumption that a deity could actually make a universe that is inhospitable to life, but in which life is supernaturally sustained anyway. This reasoning leads to the preposterous claim that the anthropic principle makes God less likely—not more likely—since a probability denominator with natural universes only is smaller than a probability denominator with natural plus supernatural universes.

Probability calculations are formally used by corporations to make business decisions and informally used by almost everyone to make everyday decisions. A person who asks which commuter route will have less traffic given that there is an accident on the usual route is using information he has to make a decision based on probability. Used carefully and with appropriate caveats, probability calculations can give credence to theistic arguments. A case can be made that the resurrection of Jesus is the most probable explanation for the events surrounding the first-century development of Christianity or that the evidence for the resurrection increases the probability for theism (Miller 2012). Rough probability calculations also show the unlikelihood of finding a planet that can support higher life forms given the size of the one known universe, citing the appropriate caveat (Ross 2004).

Michael G. Strauss

REFERENCES AND RECOMMENDED READING

Dembski, William A. 1998. *The Design Inference: Eliminating Chance through Small Probabilities.* Cambridge: Cambridge University Press.
Hand, David. 2014a. *The Improbability Principle: Why Coincidences, Miracles, and Rare Events Happen Every Day.* New York: Scientific American/Farrar, Straus and Giroux.
———. 2014b. "It's Not Actually a Miracle: Five Reasons Why Absurdly Improbable Things Happen All the Time." Slate. www.slate.com/articles/health_and_science/science/2014/02/the_improbability_principle_rare_events_and_coincidences_happen_all_the.html.
Ikeda, Michael, and Bill Jefferys. 2006. "The Anthropic Principle Does Not Support Supernaturalism." University of Texas. Accessed October 17, 2016. http://quasar.as.utexas.edu/anthropic.html.
Miller, Calum. 2012. *Calum Miller's Blog.* Accessed December 2014. http://calumsblog.com/2012/02/18/resurrection-for-theism/.
Ross, Hugh. 2004. "Probability for Life on Earth." Reasons To Believe. May 6. www.reasons.org/articles/probability-for-life-on-earth-apr–2004.

PROCESS PHILOSOPHY. If all the major schools of metaphysics can be traced to the pre-Socratics, then process philosophy finds its roots in Heraclitus of Ephesus (ca. 540–480 BC). There are raucous polarities in these ancient philosophers, and Heraclitus took one extreme: everything—or just about everything—is in a state of change. Fluctuation is the norm. You cannot step into the same river twice, since it is not a static entity but a flow of events. The forces of nature are in "strife" with each other, and "war is the father of all and king of all."

Process philosophy extends and modifies this perspective by viewing reality as an evolutionary process. Unlike Heraclitus's nonpurposive and violent flux, process philosophers trade on the idea of development or result. They extend evolutionary ideas taken from **Darwinism**—which denied the stasis or forms of species—and extend them to the entire cosmos, and even to God himself. Process philosophers deem God a changing and finite entity not totally distinct from the cosmos and who did not create the world out of nothing. This is pantheism.

Process thinkers often claim Hegel as their forefather. But process philosophy was formulated more specifically by the philosopher and mathematician **Alfred North Whitehead** (1861–1947) in his *Process and Reality* (1929). He challenged traditional notions of reality as static, saying that the basic structures of being were unchanging substances or essences. Whitehead argued that the emphasis on "being" supplanted the reality of "becoming." Whitehead, and subsequent process philosophers, such as Charles Hartshorne, John Cobb, and David Ray Griffin, highlighted the dynamic nature of reality, its changeableness. Rather than deeming being as primary and becoming as secondary (since substances ground their changing attributes or qualities), process thought reverses the ontological order. Becoming is the central category of existence.

Process philosophers also tend to hold to panentheism. As opposed to pantheism (everything is divine), panentheism claims that the world is in God and God is in the world in an ongoing process of mutual interaction and evolution.

Process philosophers believe they are in the stream of scientific progress. Just as Darwin replaced static forms in biology (**species**) with a process of natural selection, and just as **quantum physics** broke up the notion of a simple world of static substances, so process philosophy applies the category of process to broader philosophical and theological questions.

The claims to be scientific notwithstanding, process thought does not jibe with the prerequisites of science. Processes are evident in reality, but so are the constants that govern them. Static realities include the periodic table, mathematical truths, and the cosmological constant, which are necessary for life in the universe.

Moreover, modern cosmology affirms that the universe began a finite time ago (see **Big Bang Theory**). This adds credibility to creation ex nihilo and not to the process understanding of both God and the universe being coeternal and mutually dependent. Physics reveals a universe fine-tuned on a razor's edge for life. The finite and evolving god of classical process philosophy is not up for this grand cosmic task, especially since these conditions were front-loaded into the big bang. This evidence from modern science supports theism and undermines key ideas in process philosophy.

Douglas Groothuis

REFERENCES AND RECOMMENDED READING

Henry, Carl F. H. 1983. "The Resurgence of Process Philosophy." *God, Revelation, and Authority*. Vol. 6. Waco, TX: Word.
Whitehead, Alfred North. 1979. *Process and Reality*. 2nd ed. New York: Free Press.

PROGRESSIVE CREATION. The central tenet of progressive creation holds that God miraculously intervened at different times and in different ways over Earth's long history to introduce new life forms. The term *progressive* describes the observation that life becomes more diverse, complex, and advanced with time and changing conditions. The physical creation process begins with the origin of the first life forms and culminates with the creation of human beings.

While progressive creationists differ on some points, most would agree that Earth's mass speciation events—when huge numbers of diverse species appear almost simultaneously in the fossil record—occur by God's intervention. These major creation events are separated by long periods of biological stasis, during which life undergoes only microevolutionary changes. In other words, progressive creation affirms that microevolution, but not macroevolution, occurs throughout the history of life on Earth. According to this view, the Creator designed genetics in such a way as to allow creatures to adapt, within limits, to both environmental changes and challenges from invasive species.

Progressive creation rejects universal common descent, the notion that all life descends by natural processes along an uninterrupted continuum from a last universal common ancestor (LUCA). Most advocates of progressive creation would also reject, for example, the idea that all hominids, including Neanderthals and humans, share a common ancestor or that birds and dinosaurs share a common ancestor.

Historically, the progressive creation perspective dates back to the eighteenth century. Anatomist Georges Cuvier and naturalist Alcide d'Orbigny advanced progressive creation ideas in their writings. Nineteenth-century geologist Hugh Miller and naturalist Louis Agassiz also wrote extensively in defense of progressive creation, as did Russell Mixter in the early part of the twentieth century.

Advocates of progressive creation consider Genesis 1 a chronological overview, or summary, of God's creative acts, including the introduction of increasingly advanced life forms over time. They affirm the Genesis 1 declaration that created "kinds" reproduce after their own kind rather than morphing into distinctly different kinds.

Progressive creation accepts the record of life's history and of Earth's geologic history that emerges from mainstream scientific research. It differs, however, from widely held views on the *means* by which life emerges and the *degree* to which life changes by strictly natural processes. Nevertheless, because of this agreement with the fossil sequence and age measurements, some creationists disparage progressive creation as a "compromised" position (Ham 2014; Ham et al. 2006).

Proponents of progressive creation, such as John Lennox, Robert Newman, and Vern Poythress, would respond that an examination of all biblical passages on creation, not just the first two chapters of Genesis, and an interpretation of those passages as literal and consistent revelation from God, supports their stance on Earth's and life's history.

Hugh Ross

REFERENCES AND RECOMMENDED READING

Ham, Ken. 2014. "Hugh Ross Twists the Bible to Fit Man's Fallible Opinions." *Ken Ham*. Answers in Genesis. September 27. https://answersingenesis.org/blogs/ken-ham/2014/09/27/hugh-ross-twists-the-bible-to-fit-mans-fallible-opinions/.

Ham, Ken, Mike Riddle, Bodie Hodge, et al. 2006. *War of the Worldviews: Powerful Answers for an Evolutionized Culture*. Ed. David Menton, Jason Lisle, Terry Mortenson, and Georgia Purdom. Forest, AR: New Leaf.

Lennox, John C. 2011. *Seven Days That Divide the World*. Grand Rapids: Zondervan.

Newman, Robert C., and Eckelmann, Herman J., Jr. 1977. *Genesis One and the Origin of the Earth*. Grand Rapids: Baker.

Poythress, Vern. 2006. *Redeeming Science*. Wheaton, IL: Crossway.

Ross, Hugh. 2015. *A Matter of Days*. 2nd exp. ed. Covina, CA: RTB Press.

PROVIDENCE. Although the specific term "*providence*" (Lat., *providential*; Gk., *pronoia*) plays little role in the Bible, its use in later Christian tradition seeks to conceptualize the biblical picture of God's care and guidance of his creation and of individual creatures.

John of Damascus, in the eighth century, defined providence as "the solicitude which God has for existing things" and "the will of God by which all existing things receive suitable guidance through to their end" (John of Damascus 1958, 43). John's language is usually traced to *On the Nature of Man* of Nemesius of Emesa in the fourth century; like many other Christian writers of this era, Nemesius was especially interested in refuting providence-denying deistic and atheistic philosophies such as Epicureanism.

Thomas Aquinas, in the thirteenth century, reflecting on what makes for the good of creatures, found it necessary "that a plan for the ordering of things to their end should preexist in God's mind. And this plan ... is providence, properly speaking" (2006, 1.21.1, 88).

John Calvin, in the sixteenth century, noted that by a "special providence" God "sustains, nourishes, and cares for everything he has made," and "as keeper of the keys, governs all events" (Calvin 1960, 1.16.1, 4).

Providence, then, is a way of construing God's relation to the world and to its history in terms of his care for the world and its constituents' continuing existence and well-being and his guiding of the world and its constituents toward a particular end or destiny. Providence, however, is not simply the same thing as predestination; the notion of providence emphasizes not so much God's decision making or even foreknowledge as his incomparably close involvement in the trajectories of his creatures. Calvin adds that providence "pertains no less to God's hands" — or, we might say "hands-on" — "than to his eyes" (Calvin 1960, 1.16.4). Nor

is providence identical to creation, although in the Christian tradition the two ideas are deeply linked, and systematic treatments of doctrine almost always include providence as part of the locus on creation.

Some modern theological interpretations of providence have thematized the importance of the doctrine of the Trinity for specifying the end toward which creatures are directed by God, taking their cue from the biblical confession that the fulfillment of God's purposes for all creation are to be found in Jesus Christ, that God will "bring unity to all things in heaven and on earth under Christ" (Eph. 1:10), that through the Son he will "reconcile to himself all things, whether things on earth or things in heaven" (Col. 1:20). In the obedient, crucified, risen, Spirit-filled Christ, we are permitted to see the destiny God has for his creation: redemption and renewal for God's eternal reign of love. Yet even the knowledge of that revelation does not give human beings a "God's-eye" view of providence that would enable them to grasp how God's will in Christ through the Spirit is being worked out in the smallest of details, in the twists and turns of daily living.

It is, of course, not just with regard to the dialogue between Christianity and science that the doctrine of providence has generated difficult problems. The pervasiveness and power of evil, suffering, and death — abstractly considered, not to mention the devastating effects they have on actual lives — have perpetually raised doubts about the reality of God's providence and the coherence of the claim.

Attempted answers to these doubts at the intellectual level range from insisting on the inscrutability of God's purposes to placing limitations on the scope or efficacy of divine providence, to proposing the eschatological redemption of all things as God's ultimate way of dealing with evil. But scientific ways of understanding the world have also highlighted tensions with the doctrine of providence. If God is actively and sovereignly involved in the continuing well-being and destiny of his creatures, then where does that leave creaturely agency, freedom, and responsibility? How can the operation of "natural laws," the predictability of future events based on past regularities, and the transparency of the world's mechanisms to rational explication be compatible with a determinative, teleological divine causality which is not part, and not even the totality, of these systems? In a universe seemingly dominated by extinction rather than persistence, with movement seemingly characterized more by cycles and accidents than by direction and intention, does the concept of providence say anything true or add anything useful to our apprehension of reality?

Some have suggested that modern scientific interpretations of world occurrences have narrowed the focus of explanation to what, in the classical tradition stemming from Aristotle, were called *material and efficient causes* (see **Aristotle's Four Causes**). Such narrowing, by excluding consideration of final causes and by giving "chance" or randomness metaphysical, instead of merely epistemological, significance, ends up excluding purposes, goals, and ends—especially transcendent or divine ones—as contributing to our understanding of how nature works.

Yet to reverse the trend and to reappropriate divine teleology would still leave hanging questions about the integration of providence into an approach to knowledge deeply shaped by science's **methodological naturalism**, without either reducing God's care and guidance to merely another aspect of the world or to depending on supernatural "gaps" in the network of empirical causes and effects to preserve room for God's work (see **God of the Gaps**).

One attempt at such integration, given influential expression by Thomas Aquinas, distinguishes between God's primary causality—that by which he creates the universe, sustains it in existence, and guides it toward its destiny—and creatures' secondary causality—that by which creatures act on each other and themselves with true, if dependent, agency. These causalities are noncompetitive, their subjects being on totally different ontological "levels," even as their objects are indeed the same—namely, the molecules and bodies and forces of this world. Thus, rather than interfering with one another, they somehow interpenetrate to give rise to natural dynamisms and events that are "going somewhere" (also cf. Tanner 2001).

In light of the conundrums presented by twentieth-century quantum physics, another, intellectually risky possibility might be to see what appears to be constitutive, and not merely experimental, indeterminacy at the very foundations of physical reality as exposing to us the "joints" at which God is providentially at work in the world at the lowest level, as it were (Murphy 1995).

The ways in which providence is understood and embraced are not merely speculative. Beliefs about providence are expressed and applied in everyday prayer, worship, counseling, and other forms of piety. Thus to be able to account for providence not as a naïve fiction or as a cheerful but ultimately empty interpretation pasted onto a world ruled by chance, but rather as the truth about God and the world of God's creation, is of considerable relevance in a scientific age.

Maurice Lee

REFERENCES AND RECOMMENDED READING

Aquinas, T. 2006. *Summa Theologiae*, Vol. 5 (1a. 19–26). Ed. T. Gilby. Cambridge: Cambridge University Press.
Calvin, J. 1960. *Institutes of the Christian Religion*. Library of Christian Classics, vols. 20–21. Ed. J. McNeill. Trans. F. Battles. Louisville, KY: Westminster.
John of Damascus. 1958. *An Exact Exposition of the Orthodox Faith*. In *Writings*, trans. Frederic H. Chase Jr. The Fathers of the Church, vol. 37. Washington, DC: Catholic University of America Press.
Murphy, F. A., and P. G. Ziegler, eds. 2009. *The Providence of God*. London: T&T Clark.
Murphy, N. 1995. "Divine Action in the Natural Order: Buridan's Ass and Schrödinger's Cat." In *Chaos and Complexity: Scientific Perspectives on Divine Action*, ed. Robert John Russell, Nancey Murphy, and Arthur R. Peacocke. Vatican City: Vatican Observatory Publications.
Pannenberg, W. 1994. *Systematic Theology*. Vol. 2. Grand Rapids: Eerdmans.
Tanner, K. 2001. *Jesus, Humanity and the Trinity: A Brief Systematic Theology*. Minneapolis: Fortress.

PSEUDOGENES. Pseudogenes are stretches of DNA that resemble a functional gene but appear unable to produce an mRNA transcript capable of being translated into a protein. Under an evolutionary view, they are often regarded as "junk" sequences of DNA that were originally derived from functional genes but have been rendered nonfunctional by mutation (Ashurst and Collins 2003; Balakirev and Ayala 2003). Pseudogenes fall into three main categories:

- *Processed pseudogenes* lack introns and a promoter sequence. They are thought to arise after a "processed" mRNA transcript that had its introns and other noncoding sequences removed but was then inserted, or retrotransposed, back into DNA.
- *Nonprocessed pseudogenes* are thought to arise as duplicates of functional genes. They are structured like normal genes—having introns, exons, and promoter sequences—but due to mutation may be unable to yield a translatable mRNA transcript.
- *Unitary pseudogenes* also have a normal genetic structure but are not the duplicate of another gene. They typically cannot yield a translatable mRNA transcript apparently due to some mutation, like a premature stop codon.

The first pseudogene was reported in 1977 in an African frog (Jacq et al. 1977). In 2012 it was estimated that the human genome contains over 11,000 pseudogenes (ENCODE 2012). The implications of pseudogenes for biological origins have been debated by atheistic evolutionists, theistic evolutionists, creationists, and proponents of intelligent design.

Typifying the view of many nonreligious biologists, Richard Dawkins writes, "Genomes are littered with nonfunctional pseudogenes, faulty duplicates of functional genes that do nothing" (2004, 99). Though Dawkins maintains they have no *biological* function, in his view, "what pseudogenes are useful for is embarrassing creationists. It stretches even their creative ingenuity to make up a convincing reason why an intelligent designer should have created a pseudogene … unless he was deliberately setting out to fool us" (Dawkins 2009, 332).

Sounding much like Dawkins, theistic evolutionary biologist Kenneth Miller writes, "The human genome is littered with pseudogenes" that "cannot be attributed to anything that resembles intelligent design" (Miller 1994, 32). Likewise, theistic evolutionists Francis Collins and Karl Giberson write in *The Language of Science and Faith* that pseudogenes are "broken," and it is "not remotely plausible" that "God inserted a piece of broken DNA into our genomes." In their view, pseudogenes shared across different species establish "conclusively that the data fits a model of evolution from a common ancestor" (Giberson and Collins 2011, 43).

Proponents of intelligent design hold different viewpoints on pseudogenes. Some, like biochemist Michael Behe, cite pseudogenes as evidence for common ancestry (Behe 2007). Others, like biologist Jonathan Wells, in his book *The Myth of Junk DNA*, cite "growing evidence that many pseudogenes are not functionless, after all" (Wells 2011, 48).

Similarly, creationist biologist Jeffrey Tomkins maintains that "copious amounts of new research—now publicly available in a variety of online databases and described in research publications—are rapidly showing how pseudogenes are not only functional, but key to organism survival," showing "pervasive functionality and incredible bioengineering—the product of an omnipotent and wise Creator" (Tomkins 2013, 9).

Scientists critical of neo-Darwinian evolution recognize that there are many pseudogenes for which functions are not yet known. However, given the nascent nature of genomic research, they urge a "wait and see" approach, arguing that it is premature to conclude that pseudogenes are nonfunctional.

For example, during the 2005 *Kitzmiller v. Dover* trial, Kenneth Miller testified that the human beta-globin pseudogene is "broken" because "it has a series of molecular errors that render the gene non-functional." Since humans, chimpanzees, and gorillas share "matching mistakes" in the pseudogene, he told the court, this "leads us to just one conclusion … that these three species share a common ancestor" (Miller 2005). However, a 2013 study in *Genome Biology and Evolution* reported that the beta-globin pseudogene *is* functional (Moleirinho et al. 2013).

Humans have six copies of the beta-globin gene. Five produce beta-globin proteins, but the sixth, the pseudogene copy, has a premature stop codon that prevents translation. The researchers compared all six genes across humans and chimpanzees and found that the beta-globin pseudogene exhibits fewer differences than would be expected if it were nonfunctional and accumulating random mutations at a constant rate. This "conserved" sequence suggests that the beta-globin pseudogene has a selectable function, making it less tolerant of mutations.

The beta-globin pseudogene's inability to produce a translatable RNA transcript does not preclude it from being functional. The researchers argue that the pseudogene works as an on-off switch, regulating expression of protein-coding beta-globin genes during embryonic development. Indeed, there are multiple ways pseudogenes can regulate gene expression.

In RNA interference, a pseudogene yields an "anti-sense" RNA transcript that cannot produce a protein but can bind with transcripts of protein-coding versions of the gene. When such binding occurs, the protein-coding transcript cannot be translated, reducing protein production (Tam et al. 2008).

In target mimicry, small RNAs bind to a protein-coding mRNA transcript, inhibiting translation. If a pseudogene produces decoy mRNA transcripts that mimic the "target" sequence of the protein-coding counterparts, these small RNAs can bind to the pseudogene transcripts instead. This prevents inhibition of translation, increasing protein production (Poliseno et al. 2010).

Though Dawkins claims pseudogenes "are never transcribed or translated" (Dawkins 2009), they can yield functional RNA transcripts, functional proteins, or perform a function without producing any transcript. A 2012 paper in *Science Signaling* noted that although "pseudogenes have long been dismissed as junk DNA," recent advances have established that "the DNA of a pseudogene, the RNA transcribed from a pseudogene, or the protein translated from a pseudogene can have multiple, diverse functions and that these functions can affect not only their parental genes but also unrelated genes." The paper concludes that "pseudogenes have emerged as a previously unappreciated class of sophisticated modulators of gene expression (Poliseno 2012). A 2011 paper in the journal *RNA* concurs: "Pseudogenes have long been labeled as 'junk' DNA, failed copies of genes that arise during the evolution of genomes. However, recent results are challenging this moniker; indeed, some pseudogenes appear to harbor the potential to regulate their protein-coding cousins" (Pink et al. 2011).

Likewise, a 2012 paper in *RNA Biology* says, "Pseudogenes were long considered as junk genomic DNA," but "pseudogene regulation is widespread in eukaryotes" (Wen et al. 2012). Indeed, specific functions for many pseudogenes have been discovered (Hirotsune et al. 2003; Pain et al. 2005; Tam et al. 2008; Zhang et al. 2006; Zheng and Gerstein 2007), with one project reporting 863 human pseudogenes (out of an estimated 11,224 pseudogenes) that are "transcribed and associated with active chromatin" (ENCODE 2012).

Skeptics of Darwinian evolution argue that the evolutionary assumption that DNA elements such as pseudogenes are "junk" is a "science stopper" (Wells 2011, 107), which has "hindered the progress of science" (Luskin 2014, 46). One paper in *Science* notes, "the term 'junk DNA' for many years repelled mainstream researchers from studying noncoding DNA" (Makalowski 2003). Because a pseudogene may only function in specific tissues and/or only during particular stages of development, their true functions may be difficult to detect. The aforementioned *RNA Biology* paper concludes, "The study of functional pseudogenes is just at the beginning" and predicts that "more and more functional pseudogenes will be discovered as novel biological technologies are developed in the future" (Wen et al. 2012). When we carefully study pseudogenes, we often find function. One paper in *Annual Review of Genetics* observed, "Pseudogenes that have been suitably investigated often exhibit functional roles" (Balakirev and Ayala 2003).

At these early stages of research, the precise functions of many pseudogenes remain unknown. For example, the vitamin C "gulo" pseudogene, a unitary pseudogene shared by humans and many primates, is not yet known to function, which is probably why it has become a popular argument against intelligent design among evolutionary creationists (Giberson and Collins 2011; Venema 2012). Prior to 2013, however, the same could have been said about the beta-globin pseudogene, now known to have function. This suggests it may be wisest to adopt a "wait and see" approach, letting the evidence determine our conclusions. Those who argue that pseudogenes are the "silver bullet" (Venema 2012) evidence for evolution may overstate the evidence.

Casey Luskin

REFERENCES AND RECOMMENDED READING

Ashurst, J. L., and J. E. Collins. 2003. "Gene Annotation: Prediction and Testing." *Annual Review of Genomics and Human Genetics* 4:69–88.
Balakirev, Evgeniy S., and Francisco J. Ayala. 2003. "Pseudogenes: Are They 'Junk' or Functional DNA?" *Annual Review of Genetics* 37:123–51.
Behe, Michael. 2007. *The Edge of Evolution: The Search for the Limits of Darwinism.* New York: Free Press.
Dawkins, Richard. 2004. *A Devil's Chaplain: Reflections on Hope, Lies, Science, and Love.* New York: Mariner.
———. 2009. *The Greatest Show on Earth.* New York: Free Press.
ENCODE Project Consortium. 2012. "An Integrated Encyclopedia of DNA Elements in the Human Genome." *Nature* 489:57–74.
Giberson, Karl, and Francis Collins. 2011. *The Language of Science and Faith: Straight Answers to Genuine Questions.* Downers Grove, IL: InterVarsity.
Hirotsune, S., N. Yoshida, A. Chen, et al. 2003. "An Expressed Pseudogene Regulates the Messenger-RNA Stability of Its Homologous Coding Gene." *Nature* 423:91–96.
Jacq, C., J. R. Miller, and G. G. Brownlee. 1977. "A Pseudogene Structure in 5S DNA of *Xenopus laevis*." *Cell* 12:109–20.
Luskin, Casey. 2014. "The Top Ten Scientific Problems with Biological and Chemical Evolution." In *More Than Myth?* Ed. Robert Stackpole and Paul Brown. Leicester, UK: Chartwell Press.
Makalowski, Wojciech. 2003. "Not Junk After All." *Science* 300:1246–47.
Miller, Kenneth. 1994. "Life's Grand Design." *Technology Review* 97:24–32.
———. 2005. Testimony in *Kitzmiller v. Dover Area School District.* 400 F. Supp 2d 707 (M.D. Pa. 2005).
Moleirinho, A., S. Seixas, A. M. Lopes, et al. 2013. "Evolutionary Constraints in the β-Globin Cluster: The Signature of Purifying Selection at the δ-Globin (HBD) Locus and Its Role in Developmental Gene Regulation." *Genome Biology and Evolution* 5:559–71.
Pain, D., G. W. Chim, C. Strassel, and D. M. Kemp. 2005. "Multiple Retropseudogenes from Pluripotent Cell-Specific Gene Expression Indicates a Potential Signature for Novel Gene Identification." *Journal of Biological Chemistry* 280:6265–68.
Pink, R. C., K. Wicks, D. P. Caley, et al. 2011. "Pseudogenes: Pseudo-functional or Key Regulators in Health and Disease?" *RNA* 17:792–98.
Poliseno, Laura. 2012. "Pseudogenes: Newly Discovered Players in Human Cancer." *Science Signaling* 5, no. 242 (September 18): re5.
Poliseno, L., L. Salmena, J. Zhang, et al. 2010. "A Coding-Independent Function of Gene and Pseudogene mRNAs Regulates Tumour Biology." *Nature* 465:1033–38.
Tam, O. H., A. A. Aravin, P. Stein, et al. 2008. "Pseudogene-Derived Small Interfering RNAs Regulate Gene Expression in Mouse Oocytes." *Nature* 453:534–38.
Tomkins, Jeffrey. 2013. "Pseudogenes Are Functional, Not Genomic Fossils." *Acts & Facts* 42:9.
Venema, Dennis. 2012. "Is There 'Junk' in Your Genome? Part 4." BioLogos Forum. Accessed September 16, 2014. http://biologos.org/blog/understanding-evolution-is-there-junk-in-your-genome-part-4.
Wells, Jonathan. 2011. *The Myth of Junk DNA.* Seattle, WA: Discovery Institute Press.
Wen, Y. Z., L. L. Zheng, L. H. Qu, et al. 2012. "Pseudogenes Are Not Pseudo Any More." *RNA Biology* 9:27–32.
Zhang, J., X. Wang, M. Li, et al. 2006. "NANOGP8 Is a Retrogene Expressed in Cancers." *FEBS Journal* 273 (8): 1723–30.
Zheng, D., and M. B. Gerstein. 2007. "The Ambiguous Boundary between Genes and Pseudogenes: The Dead Rise Up, or Do They?" *Trends in Genetics* 23:219–24.

PSEUDOSCIENCE. Pseudoscience is a belief or methodology that claims to be built on scientific foundations but does not adhere to accepted scientific practices or reliable testing. Because science and pseudoscience are broad categories with blurry edges, the boundary between science and pseudoscience is not always easy to conclusively define. Philosopher of science **Karl Popper** suggested that true science is falsifiable while pseudoscientific ideas are not falsifiable and refuse to entertain the possibility that they may be wrong. The science historian and skeptic Michael Shermer has suggested that pseudoscientific beliefs can be identified by whether or not the scientific community adopts them and incorporates them into research that produces useful knowledge (Shermer 2011).

Most pseudoscience beliefs will share certain characteristics, though not all such characteristics will be found in every pseudoscientific idea.

- Observations, evidence, and facts are reinterpreted in order to confirm a previously determined conclusion. Proponents of pseudoscientific ideas will continue to adhere to their beliefs despite any contrary evidence.
- Confirmation is overemphasized while little mention is made of refutation. Those who adhere to a particular pseudoscientific idea will quickly embrace any evidence that seems to support their belief but will ignore, dismiss, or reformulate observations or evidence that contradicts their belief.
- Pseudoscientific ideas are often promoted and shaped by individuals with strong personalities who are outside of the mainstream scientific community. Because their ideas do not stand up to scientific scrutiny, they are usually presented directly to the public, bypassing the normal scientific channels.
- Pseudoscientific beliefs tend to remain stagnant over time with little change or refinement due to new information. Because contradictory evidence is dismissed, little progress is made in revising and reformulating ideas as additional information is gathered.
- Many pseudoscientific ideas are vague or exaggerated. Proponents of the ideas will often claim extraordinary results or conclusions that cannot be independently confirmed or tested.

Because proponents of pseudoscientific ideas will systematically choose to embrace the observations that support their ideas and ignore the evidence refuting their beliefs, a pseudoscientific idea can often be exposed by understanding the facts and reasons that cause opponents to dismiss it. Simply exploring the full body of evidence can refute most pseudoscientific ideas.

Some pseudoscientific ideas seem viable because only part of a multifaceted process is presented. For instance, some Christians have claimed that the amount of salt and other minerals in the oceans is far less than would be expected if the earth were about 4.5 billion years old. However, the mineral content of oceans is a complex problem involving erosion, tectonic activity, and other processes. Unless all processes and their variation are taken into account, any conclusions drawn by observing the mineral content of the ocean are likely to be inaccurate. At other times, pseudoscientific ideas will be supported by research that has been shown to be discredited or superseded, and such false conclusions can be discarded by looking at more accurate and recent research.

Christians sometimes use pseudoscientific methods to support their beliefs, and they sometimes embrace pseudoscientific ideas presented as truth. If Christians are to follow the God of truth, however, it is important to be able to distinguish ideas that have solid evidence supporting them from those that do not, and to understand some of the methods employed to present false ideas as scientific and valid.

Michael G. Strauss

REFERENCES AND RECOMMENDED READING

Popper, Karl. 1963. *Conjectures and Refutations*. London: Routledge and Kegan Paul.
Shermer, Michael. 2011. "What Is Pseudoscience?" *Scientific American* (September 1): 92.

↜ PSYCHOANALYSIS (Critical View). Psychoanalysis is a therapeutic approach to curing mental health problems developed by **Sigmund Freud** in the late nineteenth and early twentieth centuries. Freud synthesized a number of ideas from philosophy and contemporary methods for healing "hysteria" to create a theoretical perspective describing the structure and functioning of the human mind.

The development of psychoanalysis is unique compared to other psychological theories of this period. While most emerging theories of psychology were being developed from the use of experiments within academic settings, psychoanalysis emerged from practical fieldwork. This unconventional beginning allowed for a more relaxed and broad approach to understanding human behavior and mental processes (Hergenhahn and Henley 2014). Freud's basic ideas for psychoanalysis evolved over time, but its core elements can be found in the books and papers he published, such as *The Origin and Development of Psycho-Analysis* (1910), *Civilization and Its Discontents* (1930), and his seminal work titled *The Interpretation of Dreams* (1900). These and other works demonstrate the many different elements Freud believed created one's conscious and unconscious experience.

Freud is not the only contributor to psychoanalytical thought. He inspired a number of thinkers who extended his ideas and incorporated them into their own approach to psychoanalysis. These contributors include his daughter Anna Freud, as well as Alfred Adler, Carl Jung, Erik Erikson, and Karen Horney to name just a few (Berger 2011). The psychoanalytical approach persists today in some form or another. One organization promoting and continuing the work of psychoanalytical theory is the American Psychoanalytic Association. This group continues to do research on psychoanalytical ideas and promotes its practice within the United States and Canada. Some new movements building on psychoanalysis include neuropsychoanalysis, which is a combination of advances made in neurology and the core elements of psychoanalysis. Thus it is an attempt to understand how particular brain areas and functions relate to ideas such as repression, memory, and dreams (American Psychoanalytic Association 2016).

While the practice of psychoanalysis varies among those who use it (i.e., one might be more Jungian, Freudian, or reliant on theories considered psychodynamic in nature), they adhere to a common set of ideas. First, psychoanalysis is built on the idea that patients can explore unconscious thoughts to relieve anxiety. Because anxious thoughts are unconscious in nature, they cannot be directly manipulated to relieve the psychological distress they cause.

When this anxiety builds up to an intolerable point, it must be released in some way, and the way it is released is often in negative, unhealthy behavior. To assist patients in feeling at ease and being willing to explore their unconscious feelings, clients are asked to simply relax and talk to the therapist, articulating whatever comes to their minds. This is why psychoanalysis is often referred to as "insight therapy" as well as the "talking cure." By talking freely and discussing what comes to mind, clients reveal subconscious trends that the therapist interprets. Once clients understand the source of their negative feelings and behaviors, these negative psychological experiences dissipate and clients are healed (Freud 1904; Mitchell and Black 1996). The clients become free from disordered emotional and behavioral symptoms at that point.

In addition to this general understanding of unconscious forces and the need to release anxiety, most psychoanalysts believe personalities are determined by a number of early childhood experiences. These childhood experiences require people to pass through a number of stages, and if these stages are not successfully completed, the individual becomes psychologically "stuck," causing him or her to function in abnormal ways. For instance, the first stage individuals must learn to navigate is the oral stage. The oral stage is characterized by the individual's need to explore the world with his mouth. This exploration brings the individual an unconscious sense of pleasure. Within the context of normal development, the individual will transition out of this stage to the next. However, if an individual does not transition from the oral stage, he becomes fixated and this fixation manifests itself in a multitude of behaviors throughout life. Examples of such behaviors may include overeating, always putting things in one's mouth, or smoking (Griggs 2006).

In summary, the psychoanalytic tradition assumes all mental distress is caused by an excess of anxiety subconsciously accumulated in that part of the mind one cannot directly access. This unconscious anxiety manifests itself in particular behaviors, thoughts, and emotions, masking the latent and more important meaning behind these manifestations. The manner in which one handles this unconscious anxiety is connected with childhood experience, and only when one is made consciously aware of the latent meaning will one be able to function normally.

Psychoanalysis can be critiqued from a scientific and theological perspective. Scientifically, psychoanalytic theory suffers from the fact that it fails in at least one of the two major functions expected of a scientific theory. Any scientific theory should provide an organized way of understanding empirical observations as well as act as a guide for any future observations. This second function depends on a theory's ability to generate confirmable propositions.

These propositions are tested through experimentation. Psychoanalytic theory does a good job of organizing the ideas Freud drew from to develop psychoanalysis but does not provide a means for developing testable hypotheses. Thus the psychoanalytic tradition, at least as Freud presents it, is often convicted of not being falsifiable.

Philosopher of science Karl Popper criticized Freud's work for that very reason (Popper [1935] 2002). It can be argued that in the psychoanalytic tradition there is less prediction of behaviors occurring than what might be labeled as "postprediction"—attempts to explain events after they have occurred rather than predicting what results will occur following particular events (Hergenhahn and Henley 2014).

Additionally, the groundwork on which psychoanalysis

is built is derived from poor data collection techniques. The primary data source Freud used for the development of psychoanalysis came from middle-class Viennese women. These women were his patients. Freud applied no experimental controls for selection, and therefore no randomization or attempts to represent a greater population were used. Thus much of what is considered seminal in psychoanalysis is not generalizable from a purely scientific perspective.

Theologically, first, psychoanalysis assumes a deterministic understanding of human behavior. The assumption underlying psychoanalysis is that behavior, thinking, and emotion are determined by early childhood experience, ignoring the concept of free will (or for some with another theological persuasion, "personal responsibility"). As God told Cain, "If you do well, will not your countenance be lifted up? And if you do not do well, sin is crouching at the door; and its desire is for you, but you must master it" (Gen. 4:7 NASB). Eliminating free will implies that human beings are never truly capable of love and that they are not culpable for sinful behaviors.

According to this theory, all behavior extends from some psychological determinant. Even virtuous behavior is said to have its roots in some unconscious psychological drive. For example, the soldier choosing to bravely go into battle does so because he uses the defense mechanism of sublimation to transfer his aggressive behaviors into an acceptable profession. The woman choosing to love and care for her elderly male neighbor does so because she has subconscious unresolved issues with her deceased father, not because she exhibits Christian charity.

For the psychoanalyst, all behavior is psychologically determined; it is never freely chosen. Of course, this is a problem for a Christian anthropology, because Scripture demonstrates that human beings are created with a free will, and the fact that they misuse their free will leads to the unfolding narrative of why Christ comes as the Savior for all humanity. In Genesis 3 we read that Adam and Eve were tempted and used their free will to defy the one command God gave them. As the Westminster Larger Catechism states, "Our first parents being left to the freedom of their own will, through the temptation of Satan, transgressed the commandment of God in eating the forbidden fruit; and thereby fell from the estate of innocency wherein they were created" (q. 21). God told them not to eat the fruit from the tree of the knowledge of good and evil. The consequences of this "choice" are outlined in Genesis 3, describing how people will live in a world impacted by the choice to disobey God.

A second theological problem with psychoanalysis is its emphasis on pleasure as the primary motivating force in human behavior (i.e., Freud believed the pleasure principle motivated our behavior because of the id's constant drive for fulfillment). Recall that according to this theory, we develop through a number of stages, beginning with the oral stage and progressing through the anal, phallic, latent, and ultimately the genital stage.

This approach proposes that pleasure is acquired through different areas of the body (i.e., the oral stage draws pleasure through the mouth, the anal through control of one's bowel movements, the phallic and genital through one's sex organ, and of course the latent stage—as just what it implies—where there is little sexual motivation); therefore pleasure motivates certain behaviors. If one does not successfully move through these stages, one fixates on them, thus negatively impacting future behavior. An individual stuck in the phallic stage of development, for example, may be a habitual masturbator or sexual deviant. The pleasure principle is the determining force in all unconscious human experience according to psychoanalytic theory.

In the Christian understanding, humans are motivated—whether for good or ill—by love for something. While one could agree with Freud to some extent that the drive for physical pleasure is involved, this is too narrow and reductionistic a view of how humans operate.

In the writings of **Augustine** of Hippo, one reads frequently that love is the motivating force in the lives of people, and when love is disordered, sin emerges. St. Augustine believes that human beings are motivated to pursue what they believe is good, beautiful, and true. However, instead of loving God first (the ultimate locus of the good, beautiful, and true) and our neighbor as ourselves, we love in a disordered way, thus causing pathological behaviors. For example, Augustine says in the *Confessions* (13.9), "My weight is my love, and by it I am carried wheresoever I am carried"—his point being that even within the pathological, it is not so much physical pleasure motivating behavior as it is love. This distinction is connected to the fact that Freud was influenced by **Charles Darwin** and saw human behavior as nothing more than complex animal behavior, whereas Augustine viewed human beings as different in kind than animals. This idea of the uniqueness of the human person is lost in many psychological theories, including this one (Johnson 2007; see **Darwinism**).

A third theological problem with psychoanalysis is its strong, unbalanced emphasis on the mind. Psychoanalysis tends to see people as primarily psychological, ignoring a more holistic understanding of the human person. A Christian anthropology understands that human behavior and mental experience are impacted by more than just mental conscious and unconscious forces. Human beings are physical, cognitive, emotional, moral, relational, and spiritual creatures. Each of these spheres of human anthropology interacts with the others and impacts the whole person.

With psychoanalysis, people are described as mostly psyche with a tendency to view psyche as more important than the body in which one is "trapped." This idea is reflective of Cartesian and Platonic thought as well as strong gnostic themes (see **Descartes, René**; **Soul, The**). Within these philosophies it is believed that persons are healed or enlightened when they come to know themselves (and the "self" is that internal psychological element of who one is). This emphasis on self reflects tenets of Gnostic philosophy, ignoring a more holistic Christian understanding of the person.

Psychoanalysis and its parent psychoanalytic theory can be a complex system used to explore the human soul. However, there are implications that any Christian attempting to understand this theory needs to consider. While Freud certainly opened up the conversation on what we consciously and unconsciously experience, he did so by drawing on reductionistic, deterministic philosophies that ignore the wisdom of the Judeo-Christian faith (see **Determinism**; **Reductionism**).

Dominick D. Hankle

REFERENCES AND RECOMMENDED READING

APA. 2016. "About Psychoanalysis." American Psychoanalytic Association. www.apsa.org/content/about-psychoanalysis.
Berger, J. M. 2011. *Personality.* 8th ed. Belmont, CA: Wadsworth.
Freud, S. 1904. *Psychopathology of Everyday Life.* New York: Macmillan; London: Fisher Unwin.
———. 1995. *The Basic Writings of Sigmund Freud.* Trans. A. A. Brill. New York: Random House.
Griggs, R. 2006. *Psychology: A Concise Introduction.* New York: Worth.
Hergenhahn, B. R., and T. B. Henley. 2014. *An Introduction to the History of Psychology.* 7th ed. Belmont, CA: Wadsworth.
Johnson, E. L. 2007. *Foundations for Soul Care: A Christian Psychology Proposal.* Downers Grove, IL: InterVarsity.
Mitchell, S. A., and M. J. Black. 1996. *Freud and Beyond: A History of Modern Psychoanalytic Thought.* New York: HarperCollins.
Popper, K. (1935) 2002. *The Logic of Scientific Discovery.* New York: Routledge.

✦ PSYCHOANALYSIS (Supportive View).

Within the allied mental health professions, psychoanalysis represents perhaps the most controversial approach to psychotherapy and counseling. The tent of psychoanalytic theories and therapies is quite vast, including such varied but related approaches as classical psychoanalysis, object relations, self-psychology, and more contemporary variations (e.g., relational psychoanalysis, brief dynamic psychotherapy, attachment-based psychotherapy, and accelerated experiential dynamic psychotherapy). Collectively, these approaches are referred to as *psychoanalytic* or *psychodynamic*—terms that contemporary psychoanalytic scholars (e.g., Nancy McWilliams and Jonathan Shedler) use interchangeably (Bland and Strawn 2014).

Defining features. According to Narramore, the defining features of psychoanalytic *theory* are the following key ideas:

> [1] unconscious mental processes exist; [2] all human behavior is motivated and purposeful; [3] past experiences influence current adjustments and reactions; [4] personality functioning is inherently conflictual, and these conflicts can be understood on the basis of hypothetical mental structures such as id, ego, and superego; [5] psychological processes involve various quantities of energy, strength, or force; and [6] human behavior is influenced by interaction with the environment. (1999, 932)

Similarly, according to psychoanalytic scholars (e.g., Blagys and Hilsenroth 2000; Shedler 2010), the defining features of psychoanalytic *technique* are its: (1) emphasis on emotional experience and expression; (2) exploration of typically avoided, distress-eliciting thoughts and feelings; (3) identification of recurrent life themes and patterns; (4) discussion of past experiences through a developmentally contextualized lens; (5) focus on interpersonal relationships and dynamics; (6) emphasis on the relationship between the patient and mental health professional; and (7) exploration of fantasies, dreams, and wishes.

As McWilliams (2004) has noted, the broad family of psychoanalytic therapies can be conceptualized along a continuum, ranging from classical psychoanalysis on one end (e.g., usually involving an extended period of four or five sessions per week), through long-term psychodynamic psychotherapy in the middle (e.g., usually involving an extended period of one or two sessions per week), to short-term/brief dynamic psychotherapy at the other end (e.g., usually involving a time-limited period of highly focused sessions; see McWilliams 2004; Rizzuto and Shafranske 2013; Safran 2012 for reviews).

Research support. With regard to psychoanalytic *techniques*, the best available research evidence suggests that psychodynamic psychotherapies are as equally efficacious as other psychotherapeutic treatments (e.g., cognitive-behavioral therapies [CBT]) and are more efficacious than inactive comparison groups (e.g., people who receive no psychotherapeutic treatment; Abbass et al. 2006; Edwards and Davis 2013; Gerber et al. 2011; Leichsenring et al. 2004). However, a few psychoanalytic therapies have some evidence supporting their efficacy in treating specific mental disorders, namely, short-term psychodynamic psychotherapy for depression, psychoanalytic psychotherapy for panic disorder, and transference-focused psychotherapy for borderline personality disorder (Clarkin et al. 2007; Gabbard and Bennett 2006; Giesen-Bloo et al. 2006; Milrod et al. 2007; see Society of Clinical Psychology). Also, as Edwards and Davis (2013, 142–43) explained:

> The evidence-based Principles of Systematic Treatment Selection prescribe that insight-oriented, relationship-focused interventions (e.g., [psychoanalytic techniques]) are most likely to be effective with individuals who have an internalizing coping style (i.e., tend to internalize blame, to be introverted, and to cope by turning inwardly). In contrast, skill-building and symptom-removal interventions (e.g., CBT) are more likely to be effective with individuals who have an externalizing coping style (i.e., tend to externalize blame, to be extroverted, and to cope by acting outwardly). (See also Norcross, 2011.)

In terms of psychoanalytic *theories*, numerous psychoanalytic ideas have received little to no empirical support, whereas several others have received extensive and robust empirical support. For example, many of Freud's ideas have generally been deemed unfalsifiable and thus essentially discredited scientifically, such as his theories about psychosexual development (e.g., his psychosexual stage theory, including his ideas about infantile sexuality and the Oedipus complex), sexuality (e.g., his ideas about the etiology of homosexuality), and gender identity (e.g., his ideas about castration anxiety and penis envy; Hall et al. 1998). In contrast, there now is extensive and robust empirical support for several ideas that originated in the scholarly psychoanalytic literature. Several of those ideas will now be highlighted.

First, as Sigmund Freud (1900, 1915) proposed, a large portion of humans' mental activity occurs outside conscious awareness (Hassin et al. 2005; Kihlstrom 2008; Sherman et al. 2014). Likewise, as Freud and his daughter Anna argued (e.g., Freud 1936; Freud 1894), people routinely use nonconscious defense mechanisms (e.g., denial, reaction formation,

isolation) to self-regulate and protect against anxiety and threats to self-esteem (Baumeister et al. 1998; Burnette et al. 2013; Cramer 1998, 2000; Papies and Aarts 2011). Also, as Freud emphasized (e.g., Breuer and Freud 1895; Freud 1900, 1923), the mind, brain/body, and relationships are deeply intertwined and reciprocally influence each other (Cozolino 2014; Siegel 2012a, 2012b).

In addition, as psychoanalytic theorists asserted (e.g., Alexander and French 1946; Breuer and Freud 1895; Freud 1915–17), psychotherapeutic change centrally involves the patient(s) having corrective emotional experiences in psychotherapy (Fosha et al. 2009; Schore 2012; Siegel and Solomon 2014). Furthermore, resonating with what psychoanalytic theorists argued (e.g., Breuer and Freud 1895; Freud 1915–17; Greenson 1967), there now is demonstrable research evidence of the following:

- "The therapy relationship makes substantial and consistent contributions to psychotherapy outcome independent of the type of treatment" (Norcross and Wampold 2011, 98).
- "The therapy relationship accounts for why clients improve (or fail to improve) at least as much as the particular treatment method" (Norcross and Wampold, 2011, 98).
- The elements of a therapy relationship that are most demonstrably effective in promoting positive psychotherapy outcomes are empathy, the working alliance (in both individual and family therapy), and cohesion (in group therapy; see Norcross 2011 for reviews).

Moreover, a wide variety of other psychoanalytic ideas now have so much empirical evidence they are considered well established. These ideas include (1) the idea that humans develop mental representations of themselves, others, and the world, and these mental representations shape how people think, feel, behave, and make sense of their lives; (2) the proposal that early childhood experiences have a disproportionately large impact on people's emotional, behavioral, and social functioning throughout the lifespan; (3) the notion that affect-regulation and self-regulation capacities are centrally important markers of and contributors toward health and well-being; (4) the belief that mental and physical health are deeply intertwined; and (5) the theory that, throughout their lives, humans are fundamentally motivated to develop and maintain close attachment relationships (e.g., a network of people who serve as a safe haven during times of distress and a secure base from which to explore one's psychosocial environment; see Cassidy and Shaver 2008; Cozolino 2014; Gross 2013; Siegel 2012a, 2012b; Sroufe et al. 2005; Suls et al. 2010; Vohs and Baumeister 2011 for reviews). In sum, within the scholarly literature, several psychoanalytic ideas are now widely accepted as scientific facts.

Christianity and psychoanalysis. Nevertheless, within the scientific community and within Western society more broadly, there is a popularized notion that psychoanalytic theories and techniques are empirically unsupported or even outright discredited (e.g., Anestis et al. 2011; Shedler 2010; Weinberger and Westen 2001). Such a view is especially pronounced among Christians (Jones et al. 2011), perhaps partly due to the ongoing influence of popular Christian books that criticized psychology generally and psychoanalysis particularly (e.g., Adams 1970, 1986).

In fact, practically since the inception of psychoanalysis in the late nineteenth century, there has been a mutual suspicion between Christianity and psychoanalysis (Bland and Strawn 2014). Christians' suspicion of psychoanalysis tends to center on three themes: "(1) the [classical psychoanalytic] emphasis on sexual and aggressive drives as the motivational bases for behavior, (2) the deterministic and naturalistic assumptions of the model, and (3) the direct attacks on religion Freud made in his later writings" (Jones et al. 2011, 94; e.g., Freud 1927, 1930, 1938; see **Freud, Sigmund**).

However, in the past few decades, Christian scholars and mental health professionals have increasingly explored the integration of Christianity and psychoanalysis (Bland and Strawn 2014; Edwards and Davis 2013; Hoffman 2011; Jones et al. 2011). Interestingly, this increased openness of Christians to psychoanalysis has coincided with a correspondingly increased openness of psychoanalysis to religion/spirituality (Hoffman and Strawn 2008; Jones 1991; McDargh 1983; Rizzuto and Shafranske 2013; Spero 1992).

Epistemologically, such reciprocal increases in openness are perhaps undergirded by a cultural and scientific shift toward esteeming *consilience* — that is, valuing efforts to foster a "'jumping together' of knowledge by the linking of facts and fact-based theory across disciplines to create a common groundwork of explanation" (Wilson 1998, 8). True to Wilson's vision that there is an "intrinsic unity of knowledge" and "consilience is the key to [its] unification" (8), Christian and psychoanalytic scholars have begun articulating a variety of resonances and convergences between the Christian and psychoanalytic paradigms. Below we highlight a few of these places of resonance and convergence.

Addressing worldview-related concerns. However, before proceeding, it is important to address some worldview-related concerns that Christians often have about psychoanalytic theories (see Jones et al. 2011 for a review). For instance, as Edwards and Davis have emphasized, psychoanalytic theories "emphasize ideals of autonomy, self-determination, and personal fulfillment, whereas traditional Christian theology emphasizes ideals of depending on God, being led by the Holy Spirit, and finding fulfillment through Christlike service" (2013, 122–23).

Likewise, classical psychoanalytic theories are often criticized as holding an overly mechanistic, naturalistic, deterministic, and reductionistic view of human personhood and behavior (Bland and Strawn 2014; Hall et al. 1998; Jones et al. 2011). For example, Freud (1905) argued that personality is roughly fixed by age five years, yet a traditional Christian view holds that sanctification (i.e., holistic spiritual and personality change toward increasing Christlikeness; Gal. 5:22–23; Eph. 4:22–25) occurs across a Christian's lifetime (Johnson 1999).

Nonetheless, even as Christians strive to interpret a biblical text within that text's historical and cultural context (see **Hermeneutics**), so it is incumbent upon Christians to interpret psychoanalytic theories within those theories' historical and cultural context as well. That is, Christians must recognize that psychoanalytic theories were proposed within a historical and cultural context of modernism, positivism, and naturalism — the philosophical systems that pervaded Western science and culture during the late nineteenth and early twentieth centuries. However, as psychoanalysis has continued to evolve in the post-Freudian era, psychoanalytic theories have increasingly adopted more nuanced philosophical assumptions (e.g., postmodern, postcritical, postpositivist, and postmaterialist views; Bland and Strawn 2014). For example, in the past few decades, even as Christian theology has adopted a more relational and systemic orientation (Shults 2003), there has concurrently been a more relational and systemic orientation in the psychoanalytic literature as well (Bland and Strawn 2014; Hoffman 2011).

Resonance and convergence between the Christian and psychoanalytic paradigms. Several Christian and psychoanalytic authors have articulated myriad places of resonance and convergence between the Christian and psychoanalytic paradigms (e.g., Bland and Strawn 2014; Hoffman 2011; Jones et al. 2011; Narramore 1999). Here we will highlight a few.

First, the psychoanalytic notion that humans routinely use

unconscious defense mechanisms to avoid distressing thoughts and feelings (Freud 1936; Freud 1894) is resonant with the biblical notion that humans are innately self-deceptive (Ps. 139:23; Jer. 17:9; Narramore 1999). In fact, there is now an extensive scientific research base supporting this biblical claim (see Alicke and Sedikides 2011 for a review).

On a more positive note, the psychoanalytic assertion that all behavior is purposeful, goal-directed, and motivated is convergent with "a biblical view of human nature that sees individuals as intelligent, self-determining, social persons created in the image of God" (Narramore 1999, 935). Likewise, the psychoanalytic conceptualization of people as comprised of a reciprocally interacting mind and brain/body is resonant with a traditional biblical view that humans are comprised of a reciprocally interacting mind, body, heart, soul, and spirit (Finger 1989; Deut. 6:5; Mark 12:30; 1 Thess. 5:23).

Christian and psychoanalytic paradigms also converge in esteeming loving, empathic relationships as a core marker and contributor toward human health and well-being (e.g., Bland and Strawn 2014; Fromm 1956; Hoffman 2011; Norcross 2011; Deut. 6; Matt. 22:37–38; 1 Cor. 13; Eph. 3:14–21). In addition, Christian and psychoanalytic paradigms share a resonant goal of facilitating deep-level growth and transformation. In fact, several psychoanalytic writers have championed psychoanalysis as a powerful conduit for Christ to heal, redeem, and sanctify people (Bland and Strawn 2014; Edwards and Davis 2013; Hoffman 2011; Rom. 6–8, 12; Gal. 5; Eph. 4:17–32; Phil. 2:12–15).

Conclusion. In conclusion, we advocate for the integration of Christianity and psychoanalysis in ways that honor each paradigm's respective differences and promote their reflective linkage. Indeed, Siegel has defined *integration* as "the linkage of differentiated elements" (2012a, 464) and argued that integration is a fundamental mechanism and marker of health (Siegel 2012a, 2012b).

Thus we assert that, as Christian and psychoanalytic scholars strive toward celebrating their respective differences and promoting their reflective linkage, each field will individually and collectively achieve ever-increasing scholarly vitality, even as they individually and collectively achieve greater scientific understanding (cf. Siegel 2012a, 2012b; Wilson 1998). In short, echoing Hoffman's (2011) resounding recent call, the present authors urge aspiring toward increased "mutual recognition" (Hoffman 2011, 1) of the Christian faith and psychoanalysis.

Edward B. Davis and Andrew D. Cuthbert

REFERENCES AND RECOMMENDED READING

Abbass, A. A., J. T. Hancock, J. Henderson, and S. Kisely. 2006. "Short-Term Psychodynamic Psychotherapies for Common Mental Disorders." *Cochrane Database of Systematic Reviews* 4, no. CD004687.

Adams, J. E. 1970. *Competent to Counsel.* Grand Rapids: Zondervan.

———. 1986. *The Christian Counselor's Manual.* Grand Rapids: Zondervan.

Alexander, F., and T. M. French. 1946. *Psychoanalytic Psychotherapy: Principles and Applications.* New York: Ronald.

Alicke, M. D., and C. Sedikides, eds. 2011. *Handbook of Self-Enhancement and Self-Protection.* New York: Guilford.

Anestis, M. D., J. C. Anestis, and S. O. Lilienfeld. 2011. "When It Comes to Evaluating Psychodynamic Therapy, the Devil Is in the Details." *American Psychologist* 66:149–50.

Baumeister, R. F., K. Dale, and K. L. Sommer. 1998. "Freudian Defense Mechanisms and Empirical Findings in Modern Social Psychology: Reaction Formation, Projection, Displacement, Undoing, Isolation, Sublimation, and Denial." *Journal of Personality* 66:1081–1124.

Blagys, M. D., and M. J. Hilsenroth. 2000. "Distinctive Features of Short-Term Psychodynamic-Interpersonal Psychotherapy: A Review of the Comparative Psychotherapy Process Literature." *Clinical Psychology: Science and Practice* 7:167–88.

Bland, E. D., and B. D. Strawn. 2014. *Christianity and Psychoanalysis: A New Conversation.* Downers Grove, IL: IVP.

Breuer, J., and S. Freud. 1895. "Studies on Hysteria." In *The Standard Edition of the Complete Psychological Works of Sigmund Freud,* ed. J. Strachey, A. Strachey, and A. Tyson. Vol. 2. London: Hogarth.

Burnette, J. L., E. H. O'Boyle, E. M. VanEpps, J. M. Pollack, and E. J. Finkel. 2013. "Mind-Sets Matter: A Meta-analytic Review of Implicit Theories and Self-Regulation." *Psychological Bulletin* 139:655–701.

Cassidy, J., and P. R. Shaver, eds. 2008. *Handbook of Attachment: Theory, Research, and Clinical Applications.* 2nd ed. New York: Guilford.

Clarkin, J. F., K. N. Levy, M. F. Lenzenweger, and O. F. Kernberg. 2007. "Evaluating Three Treatments for Borderline Personality Disorder: A Multiwave Study." *American Journal of Psychiatry* 164:922–28.

Cozolino, L. 2014. "The Neuroscience of Human Relationships: Attachment and the Developing Social Brain." 2nd ed. New York: W. W. Norton.

Cramer, P. 1998. "Defensiveness and Defense Mechanisms." *Journal of Personality* 66:879–94.

———. 2000. "Defense Mechanisms in Psychology Today." *American Psychologist* 55:637–46.

Edwards, K. J., and E. B. Davis. 2013. "Evidence-Based Principles from Psychodynamic and Process-Experiential Psychotherapies." In *Evidence-Based Practices for Christian Counseling and Psychotherapy,* ed. E. L. Worthington Jr., E. L. Johnson, J. N. Hook, and J. D. Aten, 122–45. Downers Grove, IL: IVP.

Finger, T. N. 1989. *Christian Theology: An Eschatological Approach.* Vol. 2. Scottdale, PA: Herald.

Fosha, D., D. J. Siegel, and M. Solomon, eds. 2009. *The Healing Power of Emotion: Affective Neuroscience, Development, and Clinical Practice.* New York: W. W. Norton.

Freud, A. 1936. *The Ego and the Mechanisms of Defense.* London: Hogarth.

Freud, S. 1894. "The Neuro-psychoses of Defense." In *The Standard Edition of the Complete Psychological Works of Sigmund Freud,* ed. J. Strachey, A. Strachey, and A. Tyson, 3:45–61. London: Hogarth.

———. 1900. "The Interpretation of Dreams." In *The Standard Edition of the Complete Psychological Works of Sigmund Freud,* ed. J. Strachey, A. Strachey, and A. Tyson, vols. 4–5, pp. 1–626. London: Hogarth.

———. 1905. "Three Essays on the Theory of Sexuality." In *The Standard Edition of the Complete Psychological Works of Sigmund Freud,* ed. J. Strachey, A. Strachey, and A. Tyson, 7:125–245. London: Hogarth.

———. 1915. "The Unconscious." In *The Standard Edition of the Complete Psychological Works of Sigmund Freud,* ed. J. Strachey, A. Strachey, and A. Tyson, 14:166–215. London: Hogarth.

———. 1915–17. "Introductory Lectures on Psychoanalysis." In *The Standard Edition of the Complete Psychological Works of Sigmund Freud*, ed. J. Strachey, A. Strachey, and A. Tyson, vols. 15–16. London: Hogarth.

———. 1923. "The Ego and the Id." In *The Standard Edition of the Complete Psychological Works of Sigmund Freud*, ed. J. Strachey, A. Strachey, and A. Tyson, 19:1–66. London: Hogarth.

———. 1927. "The Future of an Illusion." In *The Standard Edition of the Complete Psychological Works of Sigmund Freud*, ed. J. Strachey, A. Strachey, and A. Tyson, 21:34–63. London: Hogarth.

———. 1930. "Civilization and Its Discontents." In *The Standard Edition of the Complete Psychological Works of Sigmund Freud*, ed. J. Strachey, A. Strachey, and A. Tyson, 21:59–145. London: Hogarth.

———. 1938. "Moses and Monotheism." In *The Standard Edition of the Complete Psychological Works of Sigmund Freud*, ed. J. Strachey, A. Strachey, and A. Tyson, 23:3–137. London: Hogarth.

Fromm, E. 1956. *The Art of Loving.* New York: Harper & Brothers.

Gabbard, G. O., and T. J. Bennett. 2006. "Psychoanalytic and Psychodynamic Psychotherapy for Depression and Dysthymia." In *The American Psychiatric Publishing Textbook of Mood Disorders*, ed. D. J. Stein, D. J. Kupfer, and A. F. Schatzberg, 389–404. Arlington, VA: American Psychiatric Publishing.

Gerber, A. J., J. H. Kocsis, B. L. Milrod, et al. 2011. "A Quality-Based Review of Randomized Controlled Trials of Psychodynamic Psychotherapy." *American Journal of Psychiatry* 168:19–28.

Giesen-Bloo, J., R. van Dyck, P. Spinhoven, et al. 2006. "Outpatient Psychotherapy for Borderline Personality Disorder: Randomized Trial of Schema-Focused Therapy vs. Transference-Focused Psychotherapy." *Archives of General Psychiatry* 63:649–58.

Greenson, R. R. 1967. *The Technique and Practice of Psychoanalysis.* New York: International Universities Press.

Gross, J., ed. 2013. *Handbook of Emotion Regulation.* 2nd ed. New York: Guilford.

Hall, C. S., G. Lindzey, and J. B. Campbell. 1998. *Theories of Personality.* 4th ed. Hoboken, NJ: Wiley.

Harwood, T. M., L. E. Beutler, O. B. Williams, and R. S. Stegman. 2011. "Identifying Treatment-Relevant Assessment: Systematic Treatment Selection/Innerlife." In *Integrative Assessment of Adult Personality*, ed. T. M. Harwood, L. E. Beutler, G. Groth-Marnat, 61–79. 3rd ed. New York: Guilford.

Hassin, R. R., J. S. Uleman, and J. A. Bargh, eds. 2005. *The New Unconscious.* New York: Oxford University Press.

Hoffman, M. T. 2011. *Toward Mutual Recognition: Relational Psychoanalysis and the Christian Narrative.* New York: Routledge.

Hoffman, M. T., and B. D. Strawn, eds. 2008. "Transformation: Psychoanalysis and Religion in Dialogue." Special issue. *Psychoanalytic Inquiry* 28 (5).

Johnson, E. L. 1999. "Sanctification." In *Baker Encyclopedia of Psychology and Counseling*, ed. D. G. Benner and P. C. Hill, 1050–51. 2nd ed. Grand Rapids: Baker.

Jones, J. W. 1991. *Contemporary Psychoanalysis and Religion.* New Haven, CT: Yale University Press.

Jones, S. L., R. Watson, and R. E. Butman. 2011. "Classical Psychoanalysis." In *Modern Psychotherapies*, ed. S. L. Jones and R. E. Butman, 94–134. 2nd ed. Downers Grove, IL: IVP.

Kihlstrom, J. F. 2008. "The Psychological Unconscious." In *Handbook of Personality*, ed. O. P. John, R. W. Robins, and L. A. Pervin, 583–602. 3rd ed. New York: Guilford.

Leichsenring, F., S. Rabung, and E. Leibing. 2004. "The Efficacy of Short-Term Psychodynamic Psychotherapy in Specific Psychiatric Disorders: A Meta-analysis." *Archives of General Psychiatry* 61:1208–16.

McWilliams, N. 2004. *Psychoanalytic Psychotherapy.* New York: Guilford.

McDargh, J. 1983. *Psychoanalytic Object Relations Theory and the Study of Religion.* Lanham, MD: University Press of America.

Milrod, B., A. C. Leon, F. Busch, et al. 2007. "A Randomized Controlled Clinical Trial of Psychoanalytic Psychotherapy for Panic Disorder." *American Journal of Psychiatry* 164:265–72.

Narramore, S. B. 1999. "Psychoanalytic Psychology." In *Baker Encyclopedia of*

Psychology and Counseling, ed. D. G. Benner and P. C. Hill, 932–35. 2nd ed. Grand Rapids: Baker.

Norcross, J. C., ed. 2011. *Psychotherapy Relationships That Work: Evidence-Based Responsiveness.* 2nd ed. New York: Oxford University Press.

Norcross, J. C., and B. E. Wampold. 2011. "Evidence-Based Therapy Relationships: Research Conclusions and Clinical Practices." *Psychotherapy* 48:98–102.

Papies, E. K., and H. Aarts. 2011. "Nonconscious Self-Regulation, or the Automatic Pilot of Human Behavior." In *Handbook of Self-Regulation: Research, Theory, and Applications*, ed. K. D. Vohs and R. F. Baumeister, 125–42. 2nd ed. New York: Guilford.

Rizzuto, A.-M., and E. P. Shafranske. 2013. "Addressing Religion and Spirituality in Treatment from a Psychodynamic Perspective." In *APA Handbook of Psychology, Religion, and Spirituality*, vol. 2, *An Applied Psychology of Religion and Spirituality*, ed. K. I. Pargament, 125–46. Washington, DC: American Psychological Association.

Safran, J. D. 2012. *Psychoanalysis and Psychoanalytic Therapies.* Washington, DC: American Psychological Association.

Schore, A. N. 2012. *The Science of the Art of Psychotherapy.* New York: W. W. Norton.

Shedler, J. 2010. "The Efficacy of Psychodynamic Psychotherapy." *American Psychologist* 65:98–109.

Sherman, J. W., B. Gawronski, and Y. Trope, eds. 2014. *Dual-Process Theories of the Social Mind.* New York: Guilford.

Shults, F. L. 2003. *Reforming Theological Anthropology: After the Philosophical Turn to Relationality.* Grand Rapids: Eerdmans.

Siegel, D. J. 2012a. *The Developing Mind: How Relationships and the Brain Interact to Shape Who We Are.* 2nd ed. New York: Guilford.

———. 2012b. *Pocket Guide to Interpersonal Neurobiology: An Integrative Handbook of the Mind.* New York: W. W. Norton.

Siegel, D. J., and M. Solomon, eds. 2014. *Healing Moments in Psychotherapy.* New York: W. W. Norton.

Society of Clinical Psychology. "Research-Supported Psychological Treatments." Society of Clinical Psychology. Accessed October 17, 2016. www.div12.org/psychological-treatments/.

Spero. M. H. 1992. *Religious Objects as Psychological Structures: A Critical Integration of Object Relations Theory, Psychotherapy, and Judaism.* Chicago: University of Chicago Press.

Sroufe, L. A., B. Egeland, E. A. Carlson, and W. A. Collins. 2005. *The Development of the Person.* New York: Guilford.

Suls, J. M., K. W. Davidson, and R. M. Kaplan, eds. 2010. *Handbook of Health Psychology and Behavioral Medicine.* New York: Guilford.

Vohs, K. D., and R. F. Baumeister, eds. 2011. *Handbook of Self-Regulation: Research, Theory, and Applications.* 2nd ed. New York: Guilford.

Weinberger, J., and D. Westen. 2001. "Science and Psychodynamics: From Arguments about Freud to Data." *Psychological Inquiry* 12:129–66.

Wilson, E. O. 1998. *Consilience: The Unity of Knowledge.* New York: Vintage.

PSYCHOLOGY. Modern psychology is typically defined as the scientific study of thought and behavior and is a diverse discipline including research ranging from neuropsychology to social psychology and including varied applications such as educational, sports, and clinical psychology.

Modern psychology originated in the late 1800s and adopted the philosophy of materialistic naturalism from the natural sciences. This philosophy led to the goal of describing, explaining, and predicting thought and behavior from a secular perspective. A materialistic philosophy also determined that the empirical method be employed by psychology. Psychology investigates phenomena through the formation of theories, the collection of empirical data to test theories, and the interpretation of patterns derived from statistical analyses of the empirical data. Studies are designed and conducted as falsifiable and replicable so that other researchers can verify findings. Ultimately the use of empirical methodology is intended to eliminate the subjective nature of psychological investigations and result in objective certainty. This drive for objective certainty remains a strong, directive force in the field today.

Psychology has flourished under its current model and has produced an impressive amount of information covering intelligence, memory, neuronal functioning, aggression, conformity, attitudes, depression, interpersonal relationships, and other topics too numerous to mention. Psychology will likely continue to play a fundamental role in areas such as education, business, economics, management, and leadership. The value of psychological research is self-evident, and the benefit to humanity is unquestioned. However, the philosophy underlying modern psychology is not without its weaknesses.

Despite its reliance on the observable, much of the field investigates immaterial phenomena, what Christians might call the soul. Central concepts of psychological research are not observable (e.g., attitudes, intelligence, emotions), meaning observable substitutes or operational constructs must be used in research. For instance, the gap between the object to be studied, intelligence, and the object actually studied, the score on a test, means that the certainty based on empirical results is reduced. The move toward qualitative research methods to help bridge this gap has been minimal to this point.

More problematic is the lack of understanding concerning the connection between research concepts and metaphysical assumptions within empirical research. For instance, to investigate social maturation, one must define the term that rests on a larger definition of what the mature person is. The connection between research concepts and the nature and purpose of humanity is largely ignored and overwhelmingly answered from a materialistic perspective. For example, it is more than problematic that God is excluded from modern psychology, given that Christians understand humans to be created in the image of God. If the implicit human nature assumptions of researchers are inaccurate, then research designed and conducted by them is deficient to some degree and can be improved.

The commitment to the empirical method and a materialistic philosophy means that the major issue with modern psychology is what is left out. A Christian philosophical model of the person can be used to suggest philosophical and methodological improvements. For instance, rather than understanding the person as simply egoistic, the Christian view can offer a richer and more accurate understanding of people within a creation/fall/redemption/consummation framework. Seeing the person as more complex and holistic compared to a materialistic view should also result in the recognition of the need for methods of investigation beyond the empirical. A foundationally Christian psychology calls for a broadening of philosophical definitions of the person and for a broadening of the methods used to investigate the person.

C. Eric Jones

REFERENCES AND RECOMMENDED READING

Evans, C. S. 2002. *Preserving the Person.* Vancouver: Regent College Publishing.
Jones, Charles E., and Eric L. Johnson. 2012. "A Christian's Guide to Psychology." In *Omnibus VI: The Modern World*, ed. Gene Veith, Douglas Wilson, and Tyler Fisher, 3–12. Lancaster, PA: Veritas.
Slife, Brent, Jeffrey Reber, and Frank Richardson. 2005. *Critical Thinking about Psychology.* Washington, DC: APA Publishing.

PSYCHOLOGY, EVOLUTIONARY. Evolutionary psychology is the systematic attempt to apply evolutionary theory to cognition and behavior in humans and other animals. While Darwin (1859) was concerned to explain the variety of physical adaptations possessed by different biological species, his later work (Darwin 1871) also includes accounts of the origins of our psychological capacities, like our moral sense and linguistic abilities.

Although Darwin proposed that variation and natural selection were sufficient to explain living creatures, he offered no mechanism. In the 1930s and 1940s, scientists synthesized Darwin's view with Mendelian genetics and then, in the 1950s, discovered that DNA contains the genetic information that explains heritable traits. Biologists then pursued the idea that random mutations and other undirected changes to DNA combined with natural selection to explain the diversity of life. In a landmark work, E. O. Wilson (1975) applied the same approach to explaining behavior. More recently, evolutionary psychology has emerged as a cross-disciplinary field that proposes evolutionary explanations of specific cognitive capacities on the assumption that they are adaptations or by-products of adaptive features.

A crude proposal (sometimes called *genetic determinism*) is that genes alone determine the psychological states and behaviors of creatures. An obvious problem is that culture and tradition affect us independently of genes: genetically identical twins raised in different cultures will have different ideas and perform different actions. As Richard Lewontin notes, it is not credible that "since 99 percent of Finns are Lutheran, they must have a gene for it" (Lewontin 1991, 94). Another concern is that simplistic explanations that appeal to a gene "for" a particular behavior are typically made on the basis of speculations about our ancestors and cannot be confirmed by the genetic evidence. Lewontin complains:

> No one has ever measured in any human population the actual reproductive advantage or disadvantage of any human behavior. All of the sociobiological explanations of the evolution of human behavior are like Rudyard Kipling's *Just So* stories of how the camel got his hump and the elephant got his trunk. They are just stories. (Lewontin 1991, 100; see **Just-So Stories**)

Most evolutionary psychologists therefore conclude that what genes explain is at most our cognitive *capacities* rather than the specific content of our thoughts or specific behaviors. A leading proponent of this view is Steven Pinker, according to whom the mind is a collection of specialized modules "designed by natural selection to solve the kinds of problems our ancestors faced in their foraging way of life" (Pinker 1997, 21). Since each of these modules is an independent adaptation, Pinker maintains there is no reason to believe in a single, supervisory self that oversees all of the modules (see **Natural Selection**). Rather, since we have only one body and its behavior must be controlled consistently, the "self" is a useful illusion that helps to coordinate the modules (Pinker 1997, 144).

Others, like Richard Dawkins (1989) and Susan Blackmore (1999), argue that we can account for the content of people's thoughts by supplementing genes (biological replicators) with *memes* (cultural replicators). According to Dawkins, "Examples of memes are tunes, ideas, catch phrases, clothes, fashions, ways of making pots or of building arches. Just as genes propagate themselves in the gene pool by leaping from body to body ... so memes propagate themselves in the meme pool by leaping from brain to brain via ... imitation" (Dawkins 1989, 192).

Memes can also be combined in *memeplexes*, collections of associated memes that replicate together (e.g., baseball memes). One advantage of memes is that they can solve puzzles that confront an exclusively genetic theory: while altruism is hard to square with a purely genetic account, there is no reason why an altruism meme could not be propagated.

Both genetic and memetic accounts have been used to give naturalistic accounts of religion. Dennett has argued that belief in God is simply a by-product of a Hyperactive Agency Detection Device (Dennett 2006, 108–9). And Richard Dawkins has compared belief in God to a mind-virus (a delusory collection of memes): "Natural selection builds child brains with a tendency to believe whatever their parents and tribal elders tell them. Such trusting obedience is valuable for survival: the analogue of steering by the moon for a moth. But the flip-side of trusting obedience is slavish gullibility. The inevitable by-product is vulnerability to infection by mind viruses" (Dawkins 2006, 176).

Two major concerns with such accounts are that they assume without argument that theistic belief is false and that they could also be applied to materialism. Alister McGrath points out, "If all ideas are memes or the effects of memes, Dawkins is left in the decidedly uncomfortable position of having to accept that his own ideas must be recognized as the effects of memes" (McGrath 2005, 124).

A more general worry about naturalistic evolutionary psychology is that it undermines confidence in human rationality. C. S. Lewis (1960, chap. 3) and Alvin Plantinga (1993, chap. 12; 2011, chap. 10) have developed what is known as the **evolutionary argument against naturalism** or the **argument from reason** (Reppert 2009). This argument aims to show that if human reasoning arose from naturalistic evolution, it cannot be relied on for truth. If we are simply the result of naturalistic evolution, then most likely epiphenomenalism is true (our thoughts have no effect on our behavior). This is because natural selection can only operate on our behavioral responses, and these can be refined indefinitely without requiring thought (a good analogy here is the improvement in strategy of computer games with self-adjusting algorithms). But then there is no reason to expect any thoughts that do emerge to be reliable: so long as our bodies run away from lions, it does not matter if we believe they are shrubs.

But suppose epiphenomenalism is false and beliefs are selected as causes of behavior. Still, what matters is that the behavior caused is adaptive, not that the beliefs are true; so it is still likely that our beliefs are unreliable. Thus, whether or not epiphenomenalism is true, we can have no confidence in any theory derived by reasoning, including naturalistic evolutionary psychology, so it undermines itself. Indeed, Pinker concedes that "our brains were shaped for fitness, not for truth" (Pinker 1997, 305). By contrast, Christian theists can argue that our minds are reliable because we are specially made in the image of a rational God.

Angus J. L. Menuge

REFERENCES AND RECOMMENDED READING

Blackmore, Susan. 1999. *The Meme Machine.* Oxford: Oxford University Press.

Darwin, Charles. 1859. *On the Origin of Species.* London: John Murray.

———. 1871. *The Descent of Man and Selection in Relation to Sex.* London: John Murray.

Dawkins, Richard. 1989. *The Selfish Gene.* Oxford: Oxford University Press.

———. 2008. *The God Delusion.* New York: Houghton Mifflin.

Dennett, Daniel. 2006. *Breaking the Spell: Religion as a Natural Phenomenon.* New York: Viking.

Lewis, C. S. 1960. *Miracles.* 2nd ed. New York: Macmillan.

Lewontin, Richard. 1991. *Biology as Ideology: The Doctrine of DNA.* New York: HarperCollins.

McGrath, Alister. 2005. *Dawkins' God: Genes, Memes, and the Meaning of Life.* Oxford: Blackwell.

Pinker, Steven. 1997. *How the Mind Works.* New York: W. W. Norton.

Plantinga, Alvin. 1993. *Warrant and Proper Function.* New York: Oxford University Press.

———. 2011. *Where the Conflict Really Lies.* New York: Oxford University Press.

Reppert, Victor. 2009. "The Argument from Reason." In *The Blackwell Companion to Natural Theology*, ed. William Lane Craig and J. P. Moreland, 344–90. Malden, MA: Wiley-Blackwell.

Wilson, E. O. 1975. *Sociobiology: The New Synthesis.* Cambridge, MA: Harvard University Press.

PSYCHOLOGY OF RELIGION. Division 36 of the American Psychological Association is the Society for the Psychology of Religion and Spirituality. The division has a threefold purpose:

> It promotes the application of psychological research methods and interpretive frameworks to diverse forms of religion and spirituality; encourages the incorporation of the results of such work into clinical and other applied settings; and fosters constructive dialogue and interchange between psychological study and practice on the one hand and between religious perspectives and institutions on the other. (APA 2014)

This division supports psychologists interested in researching topics related to the psychological nature of religion and spirituality as well as those interested in finding appropriate ways to apply their results. Because religion and spirituality are not easily described in concrete terms, most of the definitions utilized in research tend to satisfy only those who craft them (Yinger 1967, 18). However, psychologists are encouraged by their work in this area because of its contributions to topics such as conversion, spiritual development, mystical experience, and the impact of religious practice on health and well-being (Paloutzian 1996).

Historically the study of the psychology of religion had success in the first third of the twentieth century but then fell out of vogue for more than 40 years (Paloutzian and Park 2005). Early researchers included Edwin Starbuck, who in 1899 explored religious behaviors in his book *Psychology of Religion.* William James explored the psychology of religion in his 1902 publication *The Varieties of Religious Experience.* Many of the topics covered in his book continue to be explored today.

Other psychologists, such as Sigmund Freud and Carl Jung, explored religious phenomena. However, as the push for more empirical and statistical approaches grew in psychology and the adversarial relationship of science and religion intensified, the interest in the psychology of religion diminished. Much of this had to do with the growing trend to "explain away" religion instead of describing the psychological nature of the experience. But a number of factors have led to a reemergence of interest in this area of psychology. Since the 1970s, the development of pastoral counseling as well as religious schools establishing psychology programs has grown. As Paloutzian (1996) notes, psychologists have rediscovered an interest in the relationship between religion and mental health, authoritarianism and its relation to religious fundamentalism, and new, meaningful dialogues between religion and psychology.

Christians will find this area of psychology both challenging and rewarding. Historically, psychologists have been dismissive of religious experience. Freud's *The Future of an Illusion* finds religion to be a neurotic response to anxiety. G. Stanley Hall's work in genetic psychology proposes that Christianity needs restructuring to match current findings in science and evolutionary theory (Nelson 2009). Yet today psychologists find that spiritual interventions are a powerful tool in therapeutic work (Sperry 2012). Christians can contribute greatly in this area because of their rich heritage in soul care.

Dominick D. Hankle

REFERENCES AND RECOMMENDED READING

Allport, G. W. 1950. *The Individual and His Religion.* New York: Macmillan.

APA. 2014. "Society for the Psychology of Religion and Spirituality." American Psychological Association. www.apa.org/about/division/div36.aspx.

James, W. (1902) 1985. *The Varieties of Religious Experience.* Cambridge, MA: Harvard University Press.

Nelson, J. M. 2009. *Psychology, Religion, and Spirituality.* New York: Springer.

Paloutzian, R. F. 1996. *Invitation to the Psychology of Religion.* 2nd ed. Needham Heights, MA: Allyn & Bacon.

Paloutzian, R. F., and C. L. Park. 2005. "Integrative Themes in the Current Science of the Psychology of Religion. In *Handbook of the Psychology of Religion and Spirituality*, ed. R. F. Paloutzian and C. L. Park, 3–20. New York: Guilford.

Sperry, L. 2012. *Spirituality in Clinical Practice: Theory and Practice of Spiritually Oriented Psychotherapy.* 2nd ed. New York: Routledge.

Wulff, D. W. 1991. *Psychology of Religion: Classic and Contemporary Views.* New York: Wiley.

Yinger, J. M. 1967. "Pluralism, Religion, and Secularism." *Journal for the Scientific Study of Religion* 6:17–28.

PTOLEMY, CLAUDIUS. Claudius Ptolemy (c. AD 100–c. 170) lived in Alexandria, but we know nothing of his life apart from the scant details that can be gleaned from his writings. He was a mathematician who reworked and enhanced the best astronomy, optics, and geography of his time. Philosophically, he was a follower of Aristotle and almost certainly a pagan.

Astronomy

Ptolemy's most celebrated work was *The Mathematical Synthesis*, better known by its Arabic name *Almagest*, or "The Great." This title was adopted by Christian authors when *Almagest* was translated into Latin during the twelfth century.

Almagest incorporated the most important material from earlier Greek mathematical astronomy. This rendered the previous works obsolete and is likely to be the reason so few of them are preserved. As well as refining the work of earlier astronomers like Hipparchus, Ptolemy added further improvements of his own. In common with most ancient Greeks, Ptolemy believed that the seven planets (the sun, moon, Mercury, Venus, Mars, Jupiter, and Saturn) orbited a spherical Earth. Natural philosophers demanded that the planets moved around Earth with a uniform circular motion.

Unfortunately, empirical astronomers had long recognized that the planets' motions are not as regular as theory demanded. Therefore, mathematicians developed various techniques to model the observed motions of the planets using combinations of circles. These included epicycles (smaller circles rotating on the edge of larger ones) and eccentric orbits (where the center of the orbit was offset from Earth itself). Ptolemy introduced equant points (off-center points from which the uniformity of a planet's circular motion was determined) that allowed him to further refine the model.

The net effect was that Ptolemy's model was very complicated but also accurate almost up to the limit of observations available at the time. His work was further improved by Arab and Christian astronomers in an attempt to simplify its mechanics. During the Middle Ages, a number of simple handbooks, such as the *Sphere* of John Sacrobosco, were produced for students that covered the basics of Ptolemy's model without the difficult mathematics. In the sixteenth century, Copernicus amended Ptolemy's model by placing the sun at the center of his system, but used similar mathematical techniques. *Almagest* finally fell from favor when Johannes Kepler demonstrated that elliptical orbits around the sun were both more elegant and more accurate than the circular astronomy of Ptolemy and Copernicus.

Geography

Ptolemy's *Geography* used a spherical projection to map the surface of Earth onto a flat piece of paper. It was not translated into Latin until the fifteenth century when its utility was quickly recognized. However, relying on ancient Greek travelers meant that Ptolemy was frequently inaccurate and, of course, knew nothing of the Americas. He also underestimated the size of Earth, which provided Columbus with encouragement that it was possible to sail westward to the East Indies.

Other works of Ptolemy include his astrological handbook, *Tetrabiblios*, which lent much intellectual credibility to astrology in the Middle Ages and Renaissance; his *Harmonics* on musical theory; and his *Optics*, which provided a mathematical treatment of the propagation of light. This later work is extant only as a medieval Latin translation of an Arabic text. The Greek original has been lost.

James Hannam

REFERENCES AND RECOMMENDED READING

Linton, C. M. 2004. *Eudoxus to Einstein: A History of Mathematical Astronomy.* Cambridge: Cambridge University Press.

Ptolemy, Claudius. 1984. *Ptolemy's Almagest.* Trans. G. J. Toomer. London: Duckworth.

———. 2000. *Ptolemy's Geography: An Annotated Translation of the Theoretical Chapters.* Trans. J. Lennart Berggren and Alexander Jones. Princeton, NJ: Princeton University Press.

PUNCTUATED EQUILIBRIUM. First developed by Stephen Jay Gould and Niles Eldredge, the punctuated equilibrium model of evolution attempts to explain a common pattern in the fossil record where new species appear abruptly without transitional precursors. Though the model affirms the importance of natural selection, punctuated equilibrium stands in contrast with Darwinian gradualism because it proposes that populations exhibit "stasis" (remaining unchanged for long periods of time), punctuated by short periods of rapid evolutionary change during which new species may merge (Eldredge and Gould 1972; Gould 2002, 2007).

A major factor behind the model's development was the recurrence of the abrupt appearance of new species in the fossil record without fossil evidence showing a gradual origin. As Gould put it, "The extreme rarity of transitional forms in the fossil record persists as the trade secret of paleontology"

(Gould 1977). Under punctuated equilibrium, fossil "gaps" are said to be "the logical and expected result of the allopatric model of speciation" (Schopf 1972) because "changes in populations might occur too rapidly to leave many transitional fossils" (National Academy of Sciences 1998).

Under allopatric speciation, a portion of a population becomes geographically isolated and this "daughter population" changes in response to new selection pressures in an alternate environment. Eldredge and Gould argue, "Allopatric (or geographic) speciation suggests … if new species arise very rapidly in small, peripherally isolated populations, then the expectation of insensibly graded fossils is a chimera. A new species does not evolve in the area of its ancestors; it does not arise from the slow transformation of all its forbears. Many breaks in the fossil record are real" (Eldredge and Gould 1972).

According to Gould, punctuated equilibrium also implies that a major driving force behind macroevolutionary patterns is not competition between individual organisms but rather competition between species, or "species selection" (Gould 2002). Just as neo-Darwinism holds that natural selection proliferates fit individuals, punctuated equilibrium proposes that some species will "survive" (i.e., avoid extinction) and "reproduce" (i.e., undergo more speciation events) more frequently than others, thereby diversifying into larger clades.

Multiple challenges have been raised against punctuated equilibrium. Classical Darwinism held that larger populations and long periods of time increase the chances that favorable variations will arise (Darwin 1859). But punctuated equilibrium compresses evolutionary change into small populations and short periods of time, affording fewer opportunities for beneficial mutations to occur (Luskin 2008; Meyer 2013).

Critics also argue that the model demands unlikely finely tuned circumstances where populations are just large enough to generate novel traits but just small enough that transitional representatives are unlikely to fossilize (Luskin 2008; Meyer 2013). As Thomas J. M. Schopf explains, punctuated equilibrium requires "populations large enough to be reasonably variable, but small enough to permit large changes in gene frequencies due to random drift" (Schopf 1972).

Debates over punctuated equilibrium have led to disagreements among evolutionary scientists. Some paleontologists, aware of the lack of transitional fossils, favor this model (Stanley 1981, 1998), but other influential biologists oppose punctuated equilibrium because it apparently conflicts with gradualism—a basic premise of neo-Darwinism (see **Neo-Darwinian Synthesis**; Dawkins 1996).

Other critics observe that punctuated equilibrium cannot explain the abrupt origin of higher taxa, as in the Cambrian explosion (Valentine and Erwin 1987). Still others maintain that "genetic mechanisms that have been proposed to explain the abrupt appearance and prolonged stasis of many species are conspicuously lacking in empirical support" (Charlesworth et al. 1982). Even Gould and Eldredge admitted, "Continuing unhappiness, justified this time, focuses upon claims that speciation causes significant morphological change, for no validation of such a position has emerged" (Gould and Eldredge 1993).

After intense debates, critics affectionately called punctuated equilibrium "evolution by jerks" (Turner 1984), leading Gould to riposte that gradualists who opposed his theory advocated "evolution by creeps" (Rose 2006).

Casey Luskin

REFERENCES AND RECOMMENDED READING

Charlesworth, Brian, Russell Lande, and Montgomery Slatkin. 1982. "A Neo-Darwinian Commentary on Macroevolution." *Evolution* 36:474–98.

Darwin, Charles. 1859. *The Origin of Species.* "Chapter 6: Difficulties on Theories." Literature.org. www.literature.org/authors/darwin-charles/the-origin-of-species/chapter-06.html.

Dawkins, Richard. 1996. *The Blind Watchmaker.* New York: W. W. Norton.

Eldredge, Niles, and Stephen Jay Gould. 1972. "Punctuated Equilibria: An Alternative to Phyletic Gradualism." In *Models in Paleobiology*, ed. Thomas J. M. Schopf, 82–115. San Francisco: Freeman, Cooper.

Gould, Stephen Jay. 1977. "Evolution's Erratic Pace." *Natural History* 86 (May): 12–16.

———. 2002. *The Structure of Evolutionary Theory.* Cambridge, MA: Belknap.

———. 2007. *Punctuated Equilibrium.* Cambridge, MA: Belknap.

Gould, Stephen Jay, and Niles Eldredge. 1993. "Punctuated Equilibrium Comes of Age." *Nature* 366:223–27.

Luskin, Casey. 2004. "Punctuated Equilibrium and Patterns from the Fossil Record." Intelligent Design and Evolution Awareness (IDEA) Center. September 18. www.ideacenter.org/contentmgr/showdetails.php/id/1232.

———. 2008. "Finding Intelligent Design in Nature." In *Intelligent Design 101: Leading Experts Explain the Key Issues*, ed. H. Wayne House, 67–112. Grand Rapids: Kregel.

Meyer, Stephen C. 2013. *Darwin's Doubt: The Explosive Origin of Animal Life and the Case for Intelligent Design.* New York: HarperOne.

National Academy of Sciences. 1998. *Teaching about Evolution and the Nature of Science.* Washington, DC: National Academy Press.

Rose, Steven. 2006. *The Richness of Life: The Essential Stephen Jay Gould.* New York: W. W. Norton.

Schopf, Thomas J. M. 1972. Editorial introduction to Niles Eldredge and Stephen Jay Gould, "Punctuated Equilibria: An Alternative to Phyletic Gradualism." In *Models in Paleobiology*, ed. Thomas J. M. Schopf. San Francisco: Freeman, Cooper.

Stanley, Steven M. 1981. *The New Evolutionary Timetable: Fossils, Genes, and the Origin of Species.* New York: Basic Books.

———. 1998. *Macroevolution: Pattern and Process.* Baltimore: Johns Hopkins University Press.

Turner, John. 1984. "Why We Need Evolution by Jerks." *New Scientist* 1396 (February 9): 34–35.

Valentine, James W., and Douglas H. Erwin. 1987. "Interpreting Great Developmental Experiments: The Fossil Record." In *Development as an Evolutionary Process*, ed. R. A. Raff and E. C. Raff, 71–107. New York: Liss.

Q

QUALIA. *Qualia* is a plural noun (singular *quale*) that refers to the subjective qualities of conscious experiences, such as the sensation of red or the feeling of pain. Pain appears to have intrinsically personal qualities (qualia), and hence it feels like something to experience pain. On the face of it, qualia cannot be shared: while John may feel a pain similar to Jane's, John cannot experience Jane's pain in the way Jane does.

Some philosophers (e.g., Block 1978; Chalmers 1997; Kim 2007) argue that qualia pose a serious problem for physicalist accounts of the **mind**. **Physicalism** is generally committed to **supervenience** and causal closure. *Supervenience* means that the mental is entirely determined by the physical, so that it is impossible for two individuals to be alike in all physical respects but different in some mental respect. *Causal closure* means that every physical effect has a sufficient physical cause. And *physical* typically means recognized as a real entity by a physical science.

One problem is that all physical properties are impersonal, but qualia are intrinsically personal. If qualia are not physical, then physicalism cannot predict or explain their existence or character. Although some physicalists dispute this, it seems there are metaphysically possible worlds with individuals physically identical to us who are *zombies* (qualia are absent) or *inverts* (qualia are inverted so they feel pleasure when we feel pain, etc.), both of which entail that supervenience is false (Chalmers 1997). And physicalists would have to declare qualia *epiphenomenal* (causally powerless) since if they have effects, they violate the causal closure of the physical (Kim 1998). This entails, implausibly, that feeling pain does not make someone grimace or cry out.

Frank Jackson (1982) uses qualia to argue that physicalism cannot account for our gaining a special kind of knowledge through experience. In his example, Mary is imprisoned in a black and white room, but learns everything there is to know about the **physics** and neurophysiology of color vision. When Mary is released, she sees a red rose for the first time and appears to learn something new: what it is like to see red (to have red qualia). If so, Mary's experience of red confers knowledge that is not physical knowledge.

One physicalist response (Lewis 1990) is that Mary acquires a new ability (e.g., to recognize red things) but no new factual knowledge. But is her recognition conscious? If so, it will involve qualia, making the account circular. If not, it could be implemented by an unconscious robot that detects color by its physical wavelength but has no red qualia at all. A recurring problem for physicalist accounts of **consciousness** is their apparent implication that qualia do not exist.

Angus J. L. Menuge

REFERENCES AND RECOMMENDED READING

Block, Ned. 1978. *Troubles with Functionalism.* Minnesota Studies in the Philosophy of Science 9:261–325. Minneapolis: University of Minnesota Press.
Chalmers, David. 1997. *The Conscious Mind.* New York: Oxford University Press.
Jackson, Frank. 1982. "Epiphenomenal Qualia." *Philosophical Quarterly* 32:127–36.
Kim, Jaegwon. 1998. *Mind in a Physical World.* Cambridge, MA: MIT Press.
———. 2007. *Physicalism, or Something Near Enough.* Princeton, NJ: Princeton University Press.
Lewis, David. 1990. "What Experience Teaches." In *Mind and Cognition: A Reader.* Ed. W. Lycan. Oxford: Blackwell.

QUALITIES, PRIMARY AND SECONDARY.

The philosopher **John Locke** (1632–1704) developed a distinction between the *primary and secondary qualities* of perceptual objects (Locke 1979). Earlier philosophers and scientists made similar distinctions. Among them were the ancient atomists, **Galileo** (1564–1642), **Descartes** (1596–1650), and Locke's mentor **Boyle** (1627–91). Some later philosophers disputed Locke's distinction, including **Leibniz** (1646–1716), Berkeley (1685–1753), Reid (1710–96), and **Kant** (1724–1804). **Whitehead** (1861–1947) objected to the "bifurcation of nature" created by the distinction (Whitehead 2011).

Locke distinguished the "primary" sensible qualities of physical objects from their "secondary" sensible qualities. He characterized the primary qualities of objects as qualities that exist in the objects themselves—independently of their being perceived. He said our "ideas" of the primary qualities of objects (the sensations we have of those qualities) *resemble* those qualities. Examples of primary qualities are taking up space, being in motion or at rest, number, solidity, texture, size, and shape. Locke held that these qualities are objective in the sense of being **mind**-independent. That is, they exist in the objects whether the objects are perceived or not.

Moreover, primary qualities are quantifiable—mathematically describable. So they are the qualities of objects that are subject to scientific description.

Locke characterized the secondary qualities of objects as powers in the objects that produce ideas in us as a result of the interaction of the primary qualities of objects and our perceptual faculties. These ideas include our sensations of the color, smell, taste, sound, and temperature of objects. According to Locke, they do not resemble anything in the objects themselves but are subjective in the sense of being mind-dependent. That is, they exist only in the minds of perceivers and cease to exist when the object is unperceived. On Locke's view, secondary qualities are not quantifiable; they are purely qualitative and so not subject to mathematical scientific description.

A good way to illustrate Locke's distinction between primary and secondary qualities is to consider the well-known question, "If a tree falls in a forest and no one is around to hear it, does it make a sound?" Given Locke's theory, the correct answer is no if "sound" refers to the characteristic sort of conscious auditory sensation that a properly functioning auditor would typically experience in such circumstances. The reason for this negative answer is that such a sensation depends for its existence on an appropriate interaction between the sound waves produced by the falling tree (which are objective, primary qualities of the tree) and the auditory system of a perceiver. So though sound *waves* would exist in the hypothetical situation posed by the question, the sensation of *sound* would not.

Subsequent philosophical criticism of Locke's distinction took various forms. On the one hand, Berkeley (and others such as Leibniz and Kant) denied the distinction on the grounds that *all* the qualities of perceptual objects are mind-dependent (see Berkeley 1979). On the other hand, Reid affirmed the distinction but denied that perceptual objects have mind-dependent qualities (see Reid 2014). He held that primary qualities are intrinsic properties and secondary qualities are relational properties of objects.

James Taylor

REFERENCES AND RECOMMENDED READING

Berkeley, George. 1979. *Three Dialogues between Hylas and Philonous.* Indianapolis: Hackett.

Locke, John. 1979. *An Essay concerning Human Understanding.* Oxford: Oxford University Press.

Reid, Thomas. 2014. *Essays on the Intellectual Powers of Man.* Charleston, SC: Nabu.

Whitehead, A. N. 2011. *Science and the Modern World.* Cambridge, UK: Cambridge University Press.

QUANTUM FLUCTUATION. Some scientists invoke principles such as a quantum fluctuation, the **Heisenberg uncertainty principle**, the vacuum (nothingness), and zero energy for the entire cosmos, which together serve as a possible scientific picture for the beginning of our universe.

Quantum mechanics principally addresses microscopic phenomena—atoms, nuclei, and subatomic particles. At this infinitesimal scale, matter acts differently than at the macroscopic scale. In particular, the deterministic world of physical interactions with a definite outcome is replaced in the microscopic quantum world by a range of possible outcomes, each of which has some **probability** of occurring.

Associated with this is the Heisenberg uncertainty principle, which maintains that certain pairs of conjugate variables, such as momentum and position of a particle, or energy and time elapsed for an interaction, cannot in principle be known simultaneously with arbitrary precision. This principle allows particle-antiparticle pairs (virtual particles) to appear for brief moments then disappear, apparently from the space-time vacuum of our universe. This principle has also been invoked by some scientists as the key to the question of what happened at the initiation of our universe according to cosmological inflationary theory.

A way to picture this is the following simple example. Think of a smooth bowl made in the shape of a segment of a thin sphere, with a marble resting at the bottom. Once the marble stops moving, it will remain at rest at the bottom. No surprise there. Replace the marble by a microscopic particle, maybe a proton at the bottom of the bowl. Close examination reveals that it will not be exactly at rest (resulting in a precise determination of its position) because of the truth described by the uncertainty principle. Rather, it will undergo some random jittery motion, and hence exhibit some energy of motion. This is called *zero-point energy*, and if the bowl is small enough, the energy can be enormous—even enough to initiate the cosmos through a **big bang** and thereby result in the initial particles in the universe being formed. Zero-point energy motion is a vacuum fluctuation called a *quantum fluctuation* and is an important part of current ideas in the **physics** of cosmology that account for how the universe arose in a vacuum whose overall energy was zero.

Currently this is a speculative proposition, but if it is demonstrated to be likely, it will be an example of a theory usually useful for microscopic phenomena being applied to the cosmos, clearly a macroscopic entity. And there is the question of whether this idea is consonant with the theological understanding of **creation**. One problem with this proposal is that all known quantum fluctuations appear within the space-time fabric of our universe, and it is unknown if similar phenomena can be produced apart from this framework.

Richard F. Carlson

REFERENCES AND RECOMMENDED READING

Copan, Paul, and William Lane Craig. 2004. *Creation Out of Nothing: A Biblical, Philosophical, and Scientific Exploration.* Grand Rapids: Baker.

Davies, Paul. 1992. *The Mind of God.* New York: Simon & Schuster.

Isham, C. J. 1988. "Creation of the Universe as a Quantum Process." In *Physics, Philosophy and Theology: A Common Quest for Understanding.* Eds. Robert John Russell, William R. Stoeger, and George V. Coyne. Notre Dame, IN: Notre Dame Press.

Polkinghorne, John. 2002. *Quantum Theory: A Very Short Introduction.* Oxford: Oxford University Press.

Strassler, Matt. 2012. "Of Particular Significance: Quantum Fluctuations and Their Energy." April. Accessed September 27, 2016. http://facebook.com/ProfMattStrassler.

QUANTUM PHYSICS. Quantum physics, or quantum mechanics, is the branch of physics that describes properties of matter and energy at small size scales, approximately the size of atoms (10^{-10} m) or smaller. Quantum mechanical principles actually apply at all size scales, including macroscopic scales, but the deviations between the predictions of non−quantum mechanical physics (classical physics) and quantum physics are only noticeable at or below nanoscopic scales. A few macroscopic phenomena, such as superfluidity and superconductivity, can only be explained using quantum mechanical principles.

The word *quantum* comes from the Latin for "how much" and refers to the fact that certain aspects of nature can take on only specific discrete values rather than continuous values. A flight of steps, in which you can only stand at discrete heights on each step, might serve as a crude illustration of a quantized system, whereas an inclined ramp in which you could stand at any height would be a classical nonquantized, or analog, system.

The foundations of quantum mechanics were developed in the early twentieth century by studying electromagnetic radiation and atomic spectra. Nineteenth-century experiments, such as Young's double slit experiment, had shown that electromagnetic radiation is a wave phenomenon, comprised of oscillating electric and magnetic fields. However, this explanation of light could not adequately describe the known relationship between temperature and emitted wavelength of a so-called black body, an object that absorbs all incidental electromagnetic radiation.

Max Planck proposed that to solve the black-body radiation problem, the process of radiation absorption and emission must occur at only certain discrete energies, depending on the wavelength of the light. Planck did not assign any physical reality to these quanta, but saw his hypothesis as a mathematical trick that correctly matched his calculations to the experimental observations. However, in 1905 **Albert Einstein** used Planck's quanta to correctly describe the photoelectric effect in which light shining on a metal surface would eject electrons from the surface. Einstein interpreted these quanta as physically real "particles" of light now called *photons.*

Atomic experiments and observation of atomic spectra also exhibited discrete properties that were eventually interpreted within the construct of quantum mechanics. Energy, angular momentum, and other properties of atoms and subatomic particles were shown to only be able to take on quantized values. Some fundamental properties of particles, such as spin, were shown to be purely quantum mechanical phenomena.

Up until the 1920s, an early less-sophisticated form of quantum physics was developed, but in the mid-1920s and beyond, quantum theory was reformulated into a broader and more refined theory by physicists such as Werner Heisenberg, Max Born, Louis de Broglie, Erwin Schrödinger, Wolfgang Pauli, and Satyendra Bose.

The formal **mathematics** of quantum physics incorporates complex wave functions that describe the state, or properties, of a system, and that evolve over time. The wave function can be used to calculate the outcome of experiments done on the system. The calculations provide a precise prediction regarding the **probability** for the possible experimental outcomes. The predictions are inherently probabilistic in that the result of any single experiment cannot be determined beforehand. However, quantum mechanics is completely successful in that the actual outcome of experiments corresponds exactly with the predicted results on a statistical basis.

Many of the features of quantum mechanical systems seem to violate our everyday experience of how things should operate. For instance, the wave function that describes the position of a particle seems to indicate that the particle can exist at multiple locations before it is measured. Upon measurement the particle will be found at only one of the possible locations. Historically this has been described as the act of the measurement collapsing the wave function into one of its possible states. The reality of the particle's location before measurement is undetermined, and there has been much discussion about how exactly to interpret the meaning of the wave function before a measurement is made. But the mathematics can certainly be interpreted as the particle being in multiple locations simultaneously before its position is measured.

One of the most well-known strange features of quantum physics is the wave-particle duality. Every fundamental particle in nature can act as either a wave or a particle with properties that are, in part, determined by the choice of how an observation is made. For instance, when coherent waves are directed at two small openings, or slits, a diffraction pattern is observed that is characteristic of waves only. When particles are directed at the two slits, a different pattern is observed. If the two-slit experiment is performed with electrons that are often considered to be particles, a diffraction pattern that can only be caused by waves is observed. It's as if each electron went through both slits.

If the same experiment is done but an apparatus is set up to determine which slit each electron actually goes through, then the observed pattern changes to show a pattern characteristic of particles. In other words, when the observer does not know which slit the electron goes through, it's as if the electron went through both slits and a wave pattern is seen, but when the observer does know which slit the electron goes through, it's as if the electron goes through only one slit and a particle pattern is seen (Gribbon 1984; Wolf 2010). This interaction between the observer and the observation is an intriguing feature of quantum mechanical systems.

Within quantum mechanics, certain physical properties cannot simultaneously be known to an arbitrary precision. For instance, the more accurately the position of a particle is known, the less accurately its momentum can be known. Werner Heisenberg developed this "uncertainty principle" in 1927.

The uncertainty principle seems to be a more fundamental property of nature than simply how well certain aspects of nature can be measured. It seems to relate to some inherent property of nature. For instance, the uncertainty principle gives a relationship between energy and time just as it does between position and momentum. In essence, the principle of **conservation of energy** can be violated if the violation occurs in such an extremely short period of time so that the two quantities cannot be, in some abstract sense, accurately measured together. This uncertainty principle has an actual physical manifestation when "virtual" particles appear in a vacuum, apparently out of nothing, for a fraction of a second.

Such virtual particles are real and play an important role in particle physics calculations and measurement.

The principle of quantum entanglement is a central feature of quantum physics and deals with the relationship of multiple particles with overlapping wave functions. A classic example of entanglement is the EPR (Einstein-Podolsky-Rosen) **paradox**. In this experiment, two particles are initially set up so that the sum of their spins must be zero—if one particle has a spin of positive one-half, the other must have a spin of minus one-half. The two particles are then separated by a long distance without measuring the spins of either particle.

Now, according to the quantum-mechanical wave function, before any measurement both particles are in a superposition of both spin states. That is, each particle is a mixture of both spins with only a known probability of which of the two spins should be measured. However, when the spin of one of the particles is measured (say, to be positive one-half), then the spin of the other is immediately set to the other value (say, negative one-half). The particles may be separated by a long distance; indeed, they could possibly be light-years away from each other. And though neither particle has a well-defined spin state, the moment one of the particles is measured to have one spin state, the other particle is immediately forced to have the other spin state. It is as if the two particles can communicate instantaneously across vast distances. The two particles are said to be entangled.

It has been shown that this instantaneous collapse of the wave functions simultaneously cannot be used to send **information** from one particle to the other faster than the **speed of light** so that the **special theory of relativity** is not violated, but still it seems strange that apparently the two particles are instantaneously connected across a large distance by their wave functions.

Scientists and philosophers have proposed different interpretations of what the mathematics of quantum mechanics tells us about the reality of nature. The underlying wave function cannot be measured, so various ideas have been proposed about its meaning and ramifications, and about what role the observer actually plays in determining the outcome of experiments.

The Copenhagen interpretation, proposed by Werner Heisenberg and **Niels Bohr**, is held by the majority of physicists. The Copenhagen interpretation claims that the only meaningful questions are those that can be answered by experiment, and that there are no philosophical implications of the underlying mathematics. The "many worlds interpretation" claims that every time a measurement is made, all possible outcomes actually occur by the splitting of the universe into multiple universes, each with a different outcome.

Some scientists have advocated that certain features of quantum physics are sufficient to bring our universe into existence from nothing. **Quantum fluctuations** allow particles to apparently pop into existence from nothing, and the probabilistic nature of quantum mechanics proposes that particular quantum events are uncaused. Together this seems to allow an uncaused beginning of the universe from nothing. However, there are severe restrictions to these principles that would prohibit such an uncaused event. Quantum fluctuations are only known to occur within the space-time fabric of our universe. They require the underlying structure of the universe and so cannot be advocated as a cause of our universe. In addition, it is somewhat presumptuous to argue that quantum events are uncaused.

It is certainly possible that the complete picture has not been determined. Indeed, some theories propose that there are underlying principles that have not yet been discovered that would give rise to the cause of individual events. But even apart from this possibility, the very principles of quantum mechanics are the cause of every quantum mechanical event. It is misleading to say an event has no cause when, indeed, the precise and unalterable **laws of nature** cause the event to occur.

The probabilistic predictions of quantum physics have shown to be so accurate that all scientists accept quantum mechanics as the correct theory of how the universe operates. In fact, it turns out that the strange properties of quantum mechanics are actually required if life is to exist in the universe. The Pauli exclusion principle, which states that no two fermions can be in the same exact quantum state, provides the driving force behind the structure of the periodic table, and ultimately the chemistry of life. Virtual particles inside the proton give the proton's mass its finely tuned value, which is necessary to critically balance the forces in nature. The properties of quantum physics seem to be part of the exquisite design observed in so many different aspects of our universe.

Michael G. Strauss

REFERENCES AND RECOMMENDED READING

Gribbon, John. 1984. *In Search of Schrödinger's Cat: Quantum Physics and Reality.* New York: Bantam.
Rosenblum, Bruce, and Fred Kuttner. 2011. *Quantum Enigma: Physics Encounters Consciousness.* 2nd ed. New York: Oxford University Press.
Styer, Daniel F. 2000. *The Strange World of Quantum Mechanics.* Cambridge, UK: Cambridge University Press.
Wolf, Fred Alan. 2010. "Dr. Quantum—Double Slit Experiment." Accessed October 20, 2016. www.youtube.com/watch?v=Q1YqgPAtzho.

QUANTUM THEORY, INTERPRETATIONS OF.

Quantum mechanics is the mathematical theory describing the behavior of reality at the atomic and subatomic level. At dimensions this small, the world behaves very differently than the world of our ordinary experience. Quantum mechanics handles this strange behavior by setting aside classical conceptions of motion and the interaction of bodies (see **Isaac Newton**) and introducing acts of measurement and probabilities for observational outcomes in an *irreducible* way that is not ameliorated by appealing to our limited knowledge.

The state of a quantum system is described by an abstract mathematical object called a *wave function* (Ney and Albert 2013). As long as the system is not being measured, this wave function develops deterministically through time, but it only specifies the **probability** that various observables (like position or momentum) will, when measured, have a particular value. Furthermore, not *all* such probabilities can equal zero or one (i.e., be absolutely determinate—see **Heisenberg's Uncertainty Principle**). Such measurement results are irreducibly probabilistic: no sufficient condition exists for one value being observed rather than another permitted by the wave function.

This way of describing physical systems has further paradoxical consequences. **Albert Einstein** (1879–1955), Boris Podolsky (1896–1966), and Nathan Rosen (1909–95) argued in 1935 that the quantum description of physical systems was incomplete because there existed elements of reality it did not recognize (the so-called *EPR paradox*). **Niels Bohr** (1885–1962) countered that EPR missed the point of quantum-mechanical descriptions by ignoring the different contexts of measurement (Bohr 1935). John Bell's (1928–90) work (Bell 1964, 1966) and subsequent experimental tests (Aspect, Dalibard, and Roger 1982; Aspect, Grangier, and Roger 1981, 1982; Rowe et al. 2001), showed that Bohr was correct and Einstein wrong about quantum theory's completeness.

But this result leaves physical reality incomplete: the universe is shot through with mathematically predictable nonlocal (instantaneous) correlations with no physical causes (Bell 1981; Bub 1997; Clifton 1996; Cushing and McMullin 1989; Gordon 2011; Halvorson 2001; Herbert 1985; Maudlin 2002; Rae 2004; Redhead 1987; Wheeler 1983). Nonlocality runs even deeper because it extends to *isolated* quanta too (Shuntaro et al. 2014; for background, see Halvorson and Clifton 2002; Hegerfeldt 1974; Malament 1996). But the failure of particles to have locations apart from measurement implies their nonexistence when unobserved and renders microphysical *reality* deeply problematic.

How then do we understand the transition between the microscopic and the macroscopic world? This leads to *the measurement problem*, the second famous **paradox** of quantum theory, first detailed in Erwin Schrödinger's (1887–1961) famous "cat paradox" paper (1935), (see **Schrödinger's Cat**). He argued that all unobserved quantum systems hover between existence and nonexistence and—since quantum superpositions (think of waves passing through each other) percolate upward—anything macroscopic is always in a statistically dampened superposition of states (Bacciagaluppi 2012; Joos et al. 2003; Landsman 2007; Schlosshauer 2007; Zurek 1991). Indeed, under special conditions in the laboratory, overt *macroscopic* superpositions can be created (Dunningham et al. 2006; Lambert 2008). Nothing subject to a quantum description *ever* has simultaneously determinate values for *all* its associated properties, a state of affairs that problematizes the materiality of the physical world.

How is it even possible for the world to be this way? We consider three prominent interpretations of quantum theory—the Copenhagen interpretation, Bohmian mechanics, and the many worlds interpretation—that offer an answer to this question, but contend that only a theistic variant of the Copenhagen interpretation makes sense of quantum reality.

The Copenhagen interpretation (Bohr 1934, 1958; Bub 1997, 189–211; Faye 2014; Healey 1989; Heisenberg 1958, 1967; Murdoch 1987; van Fraassen 1991; von Neumann 1932; Wheeler 1983; Wigner 1961) is hardly monolithic, but its advocates generally adhere to variations on the following principles: (1) quantum theory is complete and physical reality is irreducibly indeterministic; (2) the square of the amplitude of the wave function gives the probability of associated measurement outcomes (the Born rule); (3) quantum measurements presuppose a classical world of measurement devices; (4) quantum mechanics should recover the predictions of classical mechanics when large numbers of quanta are involved (Bohm 1952, 31)—a modified version of the "correspondence principle" advocated by Bohr (Bokulich 2010); (5) for noncommuting observables the measurement process is *contextual* since mutually exclusive (*complementary*) experimental arrangements are required (this is Bohr's "principle of complementarity"); and (6) not all systems can be treated as quantum mechanical *simultaneously* because the measurement apparatus requires classical treatment.

Within a strictly physical framework, these principles

require denying the **principle of sufficient reason**—the general maxim that every contingent event has an explanation (see **Sufficient Reason, Principle of**). This undermines scientific explanation (Pruss 2006, 2009) by requiring countless physical events with no cause. Since we evaluate scientific explanations by comparing them with their competitors, and "no explanation" is now an inscrutable alternative to all proposed explanations, we have no defense for the claim that science explains anything. So to avoid killing science, the Copenhagen interpretation needs recourse to a *nonphysical causality* that grounds quantum outcomes. This transcendent requirement comports well with an occasionalist conception of divine **providence** and idealist **metaphysics** (see **Occasionalism** and **Idealism**; elaborated on in Gordon 2011, 2013).

Another interpretation is the De Broglie-Bohm nonlocal hidden variable theory or "Bohmian mechanics" (Bell 1984; Bohm 1952, 1980; Bohm and Hiley 1993; Cushing 1994; Cushing et al. 1996; Goldstein 2013; Saunders 1999). It tries to restore causality to quantum phenomena by privileging position and introducing a pilot wave or a quantum potential field giving determinate trajectories to all of the constituents of quantum systems.

It faces intractable difficulties. First, neither the potential field nor the pilot wave carries energy momentum, so they act in a way that is both undetectable and nonmechanical and cannot in principle provide a causal explanation for particle interactions. Second, when Bohmian mechanics is extended to relativistic fields (a) quanta associated with relativistic pilot waves can travel faster than light and backward in time; (b) particle number does not vary in field interactions as standard theory predicts and observation confirms; (c) unlike its orthodox counterpart, Bohmian field theory does not predict the existence of antimatter; and (d) relativistic Bohmian fields reintroduce the measurement problem and make it unsolvable (see Saunders 1999). The interpretation fails.

Finally, there is the "many worlds interpretation" (MWI) (Albert 1992, 112–33; Baggott 2013, 211–21; Deutsch 1999; DeWitt and Graham 1973; Everett 1957; Saunders 1999; Saunders et al. 2010; Vaidman 2014; Wallace 2003). It denies wave-function collapse, claiming that every possible quantum outcome in the history of the universe has been realized in different branches of the "universal wave function." Everything that can happen, quantum-mechanically speaking, has happened and will happen, but we only ever observe outcomes in branches of the wave function that lie in the past of the relevant version of our innumerable selves.

Aside from implausibility and the perfect mess it makes in Christian theology of human identity and moral responsibility, the doctrines of the **incarnation** and the atonement, and individual and corporate **eschatology**, the MWI faces intractable difficulties. First, there is potentially an infinite variety of ways to express the universal wave function as a superposition of component waves, and the branching that takes place depends on which expression (basis) is chosen. How should the universal wave function be built, then? This difficulty, known as the "preferred basis problem," reveals the mathematical arbitrariness of the potentially infinite branching processes that do not reflect any physical reality.

Second, suppose that a quantum event has two possible outcomes with unequal probabilities. Since, according to the MWI, *both outcomes occur* in different branches of the universal wave function, how can their probabilities be different? Doesn't *everything* happen with absolute certainty and thus **probability** one? If we follow the suggestion of Deutsch (1999) and Wallace (2003) by saying that quantum probabilities reflect how we should decide to bet about which universe we will find ourselves in, then, as David Baker (2007) has argued, we land in vicious circularity: talk of probabilities in the many worlds scenario assumes the existence of a preferred basis that comes about only through decoherence of the wave function, which is itself an irreducibly probabilistic phenomenon.

Furthermore, to paraphrase David Albert (2010), what needs to be explained about quantum theory is the empirical frequency of the outcomes we observe, not why, if we held radically different convictions about the nature of the world than we actually do, we would still place bets in accordance with the Born rule. So the MWI fails for multiple reasons (but see Saunders et al. 2010 for extensive polemics).

The Copenhagen interpretation stands alone as technically adequate but metaphysically incomplete. As noted, this creates a fertile field for the metaphysics of **divine action**.

Bruce L. Gordon

REFERENCES AND RECOMMENDED READING

Albert, David Z. 1992. *Quantum Mechanics and Experience*. Cambridge, MA: Harvard University Press.

———. 2010. "Probability in the Everett Picture." In *Many Worlds? Everett, Quantum Theory, and Reality*. Eds. Simon Saunders, Jonathan Barrett, Adrian Kent, and David Wallace, 355–68. Oxford: Oxford University Press.

Aspect, A., J. Dalibard, and G. Roger. 1982. "Experimental Tests of Bell's Inequalities Using Time-Varying Analyzers." *Physical Review Letters* 49:1804–7.

Aspect, A., P. Grangier, and G. Roger. 1981. "Experimental Tests of Realistic Theories via Bell's Theorem." *Physical Review Letters* 47:460–67.

———. 1982. "Experimental Realization of Einstein-Podolsky-Rosen-Bohm Gedanken-Experiment: A New Violation of Bell's Inequalities." *Physical Review Letters* 48:91–94.

Bacciagaluppi, Guido. 2012. "The Role of Decoherence in Quantum Mechanics." *Stanford Encyclopedia of Philosophy*. Ed. Edward N. Zalta. http://plato.stanford.edu/entries/qm-decoherence/.

Baggott, Jim. 2013. *Farewell to Reality: How Modern Physics Has Betrayed the Search for Scientific Truth*. New York: Pegasus Books, 27–28.

Baker, David J. 2007. "Measurement Outcomes and Probability in Everettian Quantum Mechanics." *Studies in History and Philosophy of Modern Physics* 38:153–69.

Bell, John S. 1964. "On the Einstein-Podolsen-Rosen Paradox." Repr. in J. S. Bell, *Speakable and Unspeakable in Quantum Mechanics*, 14–21. Cambridge, UK: Cambridge University Press, 1987.

———. 1966. "On the Problem of Hidden Variables in Quantum Mechanics." Repr. in J. S. Bell, *Speakable and Unspeakable in Quantum Mechanics*, 1–13. Cambridge, UK: Cambridge University Press, 1987.

———. 1981. "Bertmann's Socks and the Nature of Reality." Repr. In J. S. Bell, *Speakable and Unspeakable in Quantum Mechanics*, 139–58. Cambridge, UK: Cambridge University Press, 1987.

———. 1984. "Beables for Quantum Field Theory." CERN-TH.4035/84. Repr. In J. S. Bell, *Speakable and Unspeakable in Quantum Mechanics*, 173–80. Cambridge, UK: Cambridge University Press, 1987.

Bohm, David. 1952. "A Suggested Interpretation of the Quantum Theory in Terms of 'Hidden' Variables, I and II." *Physical Review* 85:166–93.

———. 1980. *Wholeness and the Implicate Order*. London: Routledge.

Bohm, D., and B. J. Hiley. 1993. *The Undivided Universe: An Ontological Interpretation of Quantum Theory*. London: Routledge.

Bohr, Niels. 1934. *Atomic Theory and the Description of Nature*. Cambridge, UK: Cambridge University Press.

———. 1935. "Can Quantum-Mechanical Description of Physical Reality Be Considered Complete?" *Physical Review* 48:696–702.

———. 1958. *Essays 1932–1957 on Atomic Physics and Human Knowledge*. Woodbridge, CT: Ox Bow Press.

Bokulich, Alisa. 2010. "Bohr's Correspondence Principle." In *Stanford Encyclopedia of Philosophy*. Ed. Edward N. Zalta. Winter. http://plato.stanford.edu/entries/bohr-correspondence/#BacSciCon.

Bub, Jeffrey. 1997. *Interpreting the Quantum World*. Cambridge, UK: Cambridge University Press.

Clifton, Robert, ed. 1996. *Perspectives on Quantum Reality: Non-relativistic, Relativistic, and Field-Theoretic*. Dordrecht, Neth.: Kluwer Academic.

Cushing, James T. 1994. *Quantum Mechanics: Historical Contingency and the Copenhagen Hegemony*. Chicago: University of Chicago Press.

Cushing, James T., Arthur I. Fine, and Sheldon Goldstein, eds. 1996. *Bohmian Mechanics and Quantum Theory: An Appraisal*. Dordrecht, Neth.: Kluwer Academic.

Cushing, James T., and Ernan McMullin, eds. 1989. *Philosophical Consequences of Quantum Theory: Reflections on Bell's Theorem*. Notre Dame, IN: University of Notre Dame Press.

Deutsch, David. 1999. "Quantum Theory of Probability and Decisions." *Proceedings of the Royal Society of London, A* 455:3129–37.

DeWitt, B., and N. Graham, eds. 1973. *The Many-Worlds Interpretation of Quantum Mechanics*. Princeton, NJ: Princeton University Press.

Dunningham, J. A., K. Burnett, R. Roth, and W. D. Phillips. 2006. "Creation of Macroscopic Superposition States from Arrays of Bose-Einstein Condensates." *New Journal of Physics* 8:182–88. http://iopscience.iop.org/1367-2630/8/9/182/fulltext/.

Einstein, A., B. Podolsky, and N. Rosen. 1935. "Can Quantum-Mechanical Description of Physical Reality Be Considered Complete?" *Physical Review* 47:777–80.

Everett, Hugh, III. 1957. "'Relative State' Formulation of Quantum Mechanics." *Reviews of Modern Physics* 29:454–62.

Faye, Jan. 2014. "Copenhagen Interpretation of Quantum Mechanics." In *Stanford Encyclopedia of Philosophy*. Ed. Edward N. Zalta. Fall. http://plato.stanford.edu/entries/qm-copenhagen/.

Fine, Arthur I. 1986. *The Shaky Game: Einstein, Realism, and Quantum Theory.* Chicago: University of Chicago Press.

———. 2013. "The Einstein-Podolsky-Rosen Argument in Quantum Theory." In *Stanford Encyclopedia of Philosophy*. Ed. Edward N. Zalta, ed. Winter. http://plato.stanford.edu/entries/qt-epr/.

Goldstein, Sheldon. 2013. "Bohmian Mechanics." In *Stanford Encyclopedia of Philosophy*. Ed. Edward N. Zalta. Spring. http://plato.stanford.edu/entries/qm-bohm/.

Gordon, Bruce. 2011. "A Quantum-Theoretic Argument against Naturalism." In *The Nature of Nature: Examining the Role of Naturalism in Science*. Eds. Bruce L. Gordon and William A. Dembski, 179–214. Wilmington, DE: ISI Books.

———. 2013. "In Defense of Uniformitarianism." *Perspectives on Science and Christian Faith* 65 (2): 79–86.

———. Forthcoming. "The Necessity of Sufficiency: The Argument from the Incompleteness of Nature." In *Two Dozen (or So) Arguments for God: The Plantinga Project*. Eds. Jerry Walls and Trent Dougherty. Oxford: Oxford University Press.

Halvorson, Hans. 2001. "Reeh-Schlieder Defeats Newton-Wigner: On Alternative Localization Schemes in Relativistic Quantum Field Theory." *Philosophy of Science* 68:111–33.

Halvorson, H., and R. Clifton. 2002. "No Place for Particles in Relativistic Quantum Theories?" *Philosophy of Science* 69:1–28.

Healey, Richard. 1989. *The Philosophy of Quantum Mechanics*. Cambridge, UK: Cambridge University Press.

Hegerfeldt, G. C. 1974. "Remark on Causality and Particle Localization." *Physical Review D* 10:3320–21.

Heisenberg, Werner. 1958. *Physics and Philosophy: The Revolution in Modern Science*. New York: Harper & Row.

———. 1967. "Quantum Theory and Its Interpretation." In *Niels Bohr: His Life and Work as Seen by His Friends and Colleagues*. Ed. S. Rozental. New York: Wiley Interscience.

Herbert, Nick. 1985. *Quantum Reality: Beyond the New Physics*. New York: Anchor Books.

Joos, E., H. D. Zeh, C. Kiefer, et al., eds. 2003. *Decoherence and the Appearance of a Classical World in Quantum Theory*. 2nd ed. Berlin: Springer.

Lambert, Joey. 2008. "The Physics of Superconducting Quantum Interference Devices." December 8. www.physics.drexel.edu/-bob/Term_Reports/Joe_Lambert_3.pdf.

Landsman, N. P. 2007. "Between Classical and Quantum." Ed. Jeremy Butterfield and John Earman. *Handbook of the Philosophy of Physics*, Part A. Amsterdam: Elsevier, 417–533.

Malament, David. 1996. "In Defense of Dogma: Why There Cannot Be a Relativistic Quantum Mechanics of (Localizable) Particles." In *Perspectives on Quantum Reality: Non-relativistic, Relativistic, and Field-Theoretic*. Ed. Robert Clifton, 1–9. Dordrecht, Neth.: Kluwer Academic.

Maudlin, Tim. 2002. *Quantum Non-locality and Relativity*. 2nd ed. Oxford: Blackwell.

Murdoch, Dugald. 1987. *Niels Bohr's Philosophy of Physics*. Cambridge, UK: Cambridge University Press.

Ney, Alyssa, and David Albert, eds. 2013. *The Wave Function: Essays on the Metaphysics of Quantum Mechanics*. Oxford: Oxford University Press.

Pruss, Alexander. 2006. *The Principle of Sufficient Reason: A Reassessment*. Cambridge, UK: Cambridge University Press.

———. 2009. "Leibnizian Cosmological Arguments." In *The Blackwell Companion to Natural Theology*. Eds. William L. Craig and J. P. Moreland, 24–100. Oxford: Blackwell.

Rae, Alistair. 2004. *Quantum Physics: Illusion or Reality?* 2nd ed. Cambridge, UK: Cambridge University Press.

Redhead, Michael. 1987. *Incompleteness, Nonlocality, and Realism: A Prolegomenon to the Philosophy of Quantum Mechanics*. Oxford: Clarendon.

Rowe, M. A., D. Kielpinski, V. Meyer, et al. 2001. "Experimental Violation of a Bell's Inequality with Efficient Detection." *Nature* 409:791–94.

Saunders, Simon. 1999. "The 'Beables' of Relativistic Pilot Wave Theory." In *From Physics to Philosophy*. Eds. Jeremy Butterfield and Constantine Pagonis, 71–89. Cambridge, UK: Cambridge University Press.

———. 2014. "Physics." Eds. Martin Curd and Stathis Psillos, 645–58. *The Routledge Companion to Philosophy of Science*, 2nd Ed. New York: Routledge.

Saunders, Simon, Jonathan Barrett, Adrian Kent, and David Wallace. 2010. *Many Worlds? Everett, Quantum Theory, and Reality*. Oxford: Oxford University Press.

Schlosshauer, Maximilian. 2007. *Decoherence and the Quantum-to-Classical Transition*. Berlin: Springer-Verlag.

Schrödinger, Erwin. 1935. "Die gegenwärtige Situation in der Quantenmechanik." *Naturwissenschaften* 23:807–12, 823–28, 844–49.

Shuntaro, Maria Fuwa, Takeda Marcin Zwierz, Howard M. Wiseman, et al. 2014. "Experimental Proof of Nonlocal Wavefunction Collapse for a Single Particle Using Homodyne Measurement." December 25. http://arxiv.org/pdf/1412.7790v1.pdf.

Vaidman, Lev. 2014. "Many Worlds Interpretation of Quantum Mechanics." In *Stanford Encyclopedia of Philosophy*. Ed. Edward N. Zalta. http://plato.stanford.edu/entries/qm-manyworlds/. http://plato.stanford.edu/entries/qm-manyworlds/.

van Fraassen, Bas. 1991. *Quantum Mechanics: An Empiricist View*. Oxford: Clarendon Press.

von Neumann, John. 1932. *Mathematische Grundlagen der Quantenmechanik*. Berlin: Springer. Trans. R. T. Beyer as *Mathematical Foundations of Quantum Mechanics*. Princeton: Princeton University Press, 1955.

Wallace, David. 2003. "Everettian Rationality." *Studies in History and Philosophy of Modern Physics* 34:87–105.

Wheeler, John A. 1983. "Law without Law." In John A. Wheeler and Wojciech H. Surek, eds., *Quantum Theory and Measurement*, 182–213. Princeton: Princeton University Press.

Wigner, Eugene. 1961. "Remarks on the Mind-Body Question." In *The Scientist Speculates*. Ed. I. J. Good. London: Heinemann.

Zurek, W. H. 1991. "Decoherence and the Transition from Quantum to Classical—Revisited." Available at: hccp://arxiv.org/pdf/quant-ph/0306072.

QUANTUM VACUUM STATE. The quantum vacuum state is the lowest possible energy state of any given system, sometimes also called the *ground state*. The quantum vacuum state exhibits **quantum fluctuation**s due to the **Heisenberg uncertainty principle**. For example, in the ground state of a quantum mechanical harmonic oscillator (think of a ball sitting at the bottom of a bowl), the position of the particle fluctuates. One consequence is that all particles, even in their ground state, display quantum fluctuations in their position (i.e., they wiggle).

When considering a system that can have different numbers of particles, the quantum vacuum state is typically the one with no particles in it. However, this quantum vacuum state should not be thought of as "nothing," or even as "empty space" with nothing in it. The quantum vacuum state is not the same thing as nothing, since it requires **space and time**, and also that the physical laws (including quantum mechanics) governing the quantum vacuum are in place. Neither should the quantum vacuum state be thought of as empty space. For example, in the quantum vacuum state associated with the intervening space between the air molecules in a room, particle-antiparticle pairs are continually popping in and out of existence, a process called *pair creation* and *pair annihilation*. (An antiparticle is the exact copy of the corresponding particle but with opposite charge. For example, the antiparticle of the electron is the positron.)

These quantum fluctuations of particle-antiparticle pairs being created and annihilated are continually happening all around and within us, and throughout the universe. One of the reasons we know this is because it affects atomic energy levels in a measurable way, called the *Lamb shift*.

Because they are so short-lived, particle-antiparticle pairs are often referred to as virtual particles. The higher the mass of the particle-antiparticle pair, the shorter its average lifetime. This is because particles that have mass (such as the protons, neutrons, and electrons that make up regular atoms) also have energy, as expressed in **Einstein**'s famous relation $E = mc^2$. Because mass is a form of energy, it costs energy to form a particle-antiparticle pair.

While this may appear on the surface to violate energy conservation, at the quantum level, these fluctuations in energy are governed by a type of Heisenberg uncertainty relation between energy and time. The larger the energy cost to create a particle-antiparticle pair (i.e., the higher the mass of the virtual particles), the quicker the two will recombine on average. The energy cost times the average recombination time is controlled by the Planck constant. Note that these particle-antiparticle pairs are not coming into existence from nothing—their existence depends on the existence of the quantum vacuum state itself.

Some have championed the idea that perhaps our physical universe began as a similar type of quantum fluctuation out of a presumed preexisting quantum vacuum state. This theoretical idea has not yet been vetted by observation and experiment. The idea does not propose an explanation for the beginning of the universe so much as push the problem further back in time and raise the question, "What is the cause of the preexisting quantum vacuum state?" While quantum fluctuations of a quantum vacuum state can (temporarily) generate particles, there are some difficulties with applying this concept to the universe as a whole:

1. Heisenberg's uncertainty principle *highly constrains this idea*. As explained above, even particles created through quantum fluctuations must obey the quantum version of energy conservation contained in the energy-time Heisenberg uncertainty relation. Any quantum fluctuation that costs energy has to go away within a time interval that is less than 10 percent of Planck's constant divided by the energy cost of the fluctuation.

While one could possibly conceive of the total energy of the universe being an exceedingly small number (by counting, for example, particles with mass as positive energy but the gravitational attraction between them as negative energy), note that the energy in question is not necessarily the total energy of the universe as is often discussed, but is actually the *difference* in energy between the presupposed initial quantum state and the current total energy of the universe. (For example, because of the energy cost of producing the mass associated with a virtual electron-positron pair, those virtual particle pairs can exist for at most 3×10^{-22} seconds. To treat a roughly 14-billion-year-old universe as a quantum fluctuation, the energy-time Heisenberg uncertainty relation would require that the energy cost of the fluctuation be less than about 7.5×10^{-34} electron-volts. Note that the energy required for a typical adult to walk up one single stair step is about a trillion trillion trillion trillion million times larger than this.)

With that in mind, it becomes clear that this idea concerns not so much the beginning of the universe as the beginning of the epoch of expansion of the universe.

2. *There must be preexisting time, space, and physical laws.* A preexisting quantum vacuum state requires that the physical space to house the state already exists, that time already exists, and that physical laws including quantum mechanics are already in operation. Note that quantum fluctuations happen with a certain **probability** per segment of time that passes, and without the passage of time, any quantum fluctuation has zero probability of occurring. In the case of the universe as a whole, space and time are intimately linked so that any beginning to the universe would also mark the beginning of the time dimension of this universe, and prior to this event there would be no time in which a quantum fluctuation could happen.

3. *Quantum mechanics itself may not apply to a supposed preexisting state.* We do not know whether any of the physical laws that we currently understand applies before the universe was 10^{-43} seconds old, and this includes quantum mechanics. This is consistent with Hebrews 11:3, which states that "what is seen was not made out of what was visible."

Erica W. Carlson

REFERENCES AND RECOMMENDED READING

Cohen-Tannoudji, Claude, and Bernard Diu. 1991. *Quantum Mechanics*. New York: Wiley.

Polkinghorne, John. 1986. *The Quantum World*. Princeton, NJ: Princeton University Press.

Tryon, Edward P. 1973. "Is the Universe a Vacuum Fluctuation?" *Nature* 246:396–97.

QUINE, WILLARD V. O. Willard Van Orman Quine (1908–2000) was an American analytic philosopher and logician who earned his doctorate at Harvard University in 1932 and, after postdoctoral work, was appointed in 1936 to the philosophy faculty of Harvard, where he remained for his entire career. His core philosophical orientation, which is both relativistic and pragmatic, was strongly influenced by the empiricist tradition and American pragmatism, but most formatively by the **logical positivism** of the Vienna Circle.

In his work on **logic** and the philosophy of logic, Quine is best known for developing a system akin to Russell's (Russell 1905) in which singular terms can be eliminated, for his work in the foundations of set theory avoiding Russell's **paradox** without recourse to Russell's theory of types (see **Russell, Bertrand**), and for his critique and rejection of the formal logic of possibility and necessity (quantified modal logic). Quine's criticisms of quantified modal logic have in turn been critiqued and rejected by **Alvin Plantinga** (1974, 222–51; see also the discussion in Taylor 1998, 181–257). Beyond this, as we will briefly discuss, Quine's most philosophically influential ideas are his rejection of the analytic-synthetic distinction, his arguments for the indeterminacy of translation and inscrutability of reference, and his naturalization of **epistemology**.

In his paper "Two Dogmas of **Empiricism**" (Quine 1953, 20–46), Quine rejects two earlier pillars of empiricism, namely, the analytic-synthetic distinction and the kind of **reductionism** associated with the positivist **verification principle**. In respect of the former—the distinction between analytic statements like "All bachelors are unmarried males," which are true by definition, and synthetic statements like "The lightbulb is fluorescent," in which the predicate adds something not definitionally contained in the subject—Quine argues that it is not possible to give a noncircular explanation of the concept of analyticity as grounded in meaning *alone* by way of contrast with synthetic statements that are grounded in fact: "Truth in general depends on both language and extra-linguistic fact" (1953, 36).

With respect to verificationism, furthermore, Quine argues that if we affirm that the meaning of a statement is its method of **confirmation** or disconfirmation, we are confronted with the difficulty that no statement is confirmed or disconfirmed in isolation. Rather, "our statements about the external world face the tribunal of sense experience … as a corporate body" (1953, 41). On this holistic basis, he argues that whether a statement is confirmed or not is radically underdetermined—that is, its truth or falsity is undecidable on the basis of any possible evidence—and "any statement can be held true come what may, if we make drastic enough adjustments elsewhere in the system" (1953, 43). While this contention is either trivially true or spectacularly false (see **Duhem-Quine Thesis** and **Underdetermination** for discussion), it has the effect of blurring the boundary between **metaphysics** and natural science and, for empiricists, shifting rational assessment in a pragmatic direction.

In light of such holist claims, Quine famously argued that mutually incompatible but empirically equivalent translation manuals always exist between languages, rendering translation indeterminate (Quine 1960; 1969, 26–68). He extended this conclusion into the home language of the translator, leading to his thesis of the inscrutability of reference and the complete relativization of ontology (Davidson 1984; Quine 1969, 26–68). Hilary Putnam (1980) similarly eschewed realism in science or talk about the world, arguing that treatment of scientific theories and natural languages as formal systems demonstrates (via the Löwenheim-Skolem theorems in model theory) that ontology is only determinate up to an isomorphism, which, in plain language, is to say that every formal theory has unintended interpretations that leave all of the sentences of the theory true.

From this formal standpoint, then, our talk about the world is underdetermined to the point of complete arbitrariness: since every theory has unintended interpretations in which all its statements are still true, it is impossible to fix the reference of *any* term at all. Taken at face value, both Quine's and Putnam's arguments are self-defeating, for they imply that our speech has no determinate content, a consequence from which their own arguments are not exempt. Putnam's argument also relies on the dubious claim that all human discourse about the world is expressible in the formalism of first-order logic (with associated model-theoretic consequences). This reduction has never been achieved, and there is little reason to think it is possible.

Furthermore, Quine's **naturalized epistemology** (see below) and Putnam's assertion that our language cannot be grounded in the world by the intentionality (aboutness) of our mental states or by causal theories of reference—since these either postulate "mysterious powers" that are unscientific (Putnam 1980, 474) or just add "more *theory*" to be formalized and rendered referentially indeterminate (477)—require successful physicalist and formalist reductions of language and cognition that do not yet exist and which most philosophers regard as chimerical, and they also evince a scientific materialist mind-set that is deprived of determinate cognitive content by the very argumentation seeking to justify it.

This leads us, finally, to Quine's naturalized epistemology (1969, 69–90, 114–38). Quine argues that the old epistemology—conceived as philosophical justification—has failed in its attempt to ground science on something firmer than science itself and should therefore simply be replaced by a scientific account of how human cognition operates to produce reliable beliefs (Goldman 1986; Kornblith 1985). But as James Harris (1992, 123–42) and Harvey Siegel (1984) point out, reducing epistemology to behaviorist **psychology**, as Quine does, presupposes a causal theory of perception that cannot be justified as reliable by the psychological explanations that assume it.

So any meta-scientific proposal that epistemology should be naturalized must be justified by extra-scientific reasoning, which leads to the rejection of naturalized epistemology as conceived by Quine, since it eschews this kind of justification. This is not to say that psychology has nothing to contribute to epistemology, of course, just that it cannot do so apart from philosophy. In fact, the evolutionary argument Quine invokes to ground induction (1969, 90, 126–28) is undermined by the context of philosophical naturalism in which it is proposed. Contrary to Quine's orientation, as Plantinga convincingly argues, "naturalistic epistemology flourishes best in the garden of supernaturalistic metaphysics" (Plantinga 1993, 237; see also Plantinga 2011a, 2011b; Koons 2011; **Evolutionary Argument against Naturalism**; **Intelligibility of the Universe**; **Naturalized Epistemology**).

Bruce L. Gordon

REFERENCES AND RECOMMENDED READING

Barrett, R. B., and R. F. Gibson, eds. 1990. *Perspectives on Quine.* Oxford: Blackwell.

Davidson, Donald. 1984. "The Inscrutability of Reference." In Donald Davidson, *Inquiries into Truth and Interpretation.* Oxford: Clarendon.

Goldman, A. I. 1986. *Epistemology and Cognition.* Cambridge, MA: Harvard University Press.

Harris, J. F. 1992. *Against Relativism: A Philosophical Defense of Method.* La Salle, IL: Open Court.

Koons, R. C. 2011. "The Incompatibility of Naturalism and Scientific Realism." In *The Nature of Nature: Examining the Role of Naturalism in Science.* Eds. B. L. Gordon and W. A. Dembski, 215–27. Wilmington, DE: ISI Books.

Kornblith, H., ed. 1985. *Naturalizing Epistemology.* Cambridge, MA: MIT Press.

Plantinga, A. 1974. *The Nature of Necessity.* Oxford: Clarendon.

———. 1993. *Warrant and Proper Function.* New York: Oxford University Press.

———. 2011a. "Evolution versus Naturalism." In *The Nature of Nature: Examining the Role of Naturalism in Science.* Eds. B. L. Gordon and W. A. Dembski, 137–51. Wilmington, DE: ISI Books.

———. 2011b. *Where the Conflict Really Lies: Science, Religion and Naturalism.* New York: Oxford University Press.

Putnam, H. 1980. "Models and Reality." *Journal of Symbolic Logic* 45:464–82.

Quine, W. V. O. 1940. *Mathematical Logic.* Cambridge, MA: Harvard University Press.

———. 1941. *Elementary Logic.* Cambridge, MA: Harvard University Press.

———. 1950. *Methods of Logic.* Cambridge, MA: Harvard University Press.

———. 1953. *From a Logical Point of View.* Cambridge, MA: Harvard University Press.

———. 1960. *Word and Object.* Cambridge, MA: MIT Press.

———. 1963. *Set Theory and Its Logic.* Cambridge, MA: Belknap.

———. 1966. *The Ways of Paradox and Other Essays.* Cambridge, MA: Harvard University Press.

———. 1969. *Ontological Relativity and Other Essays.* New York: Columbia University Press.

———. 1970. *Philosophy of Logic.* Cambridge, MA: Harvard University Press.

———. 1981. *Theories and Things.* Cambridge, MA: Belknap Press/Harvard University Press.

———. 1990. *Pursuit of Truth.* Cambridge, MA: Harvard University Press.

———. 1995. *From Stimulus to Science.* Cambridge, MA: Harvard University Press.

Romanos, G. D. 1983. *Quine and Analytic Philosophy: The Language of Language.* Cambridge, MA: MIT Press.

Russell, B. 1905. "On Denoting." *Mind* 14:479–93.

Schilpp, P. A., and L. E. Hahn, eds. 1986. *The Philosophy of W. V. Quine.* La Salle, IL: Open Court.

Siegel, H. 1984. "Empirical Psychology, Naturalized Epistemology, and First Philosophy." *Philosophy of Science* 51:667–76.

Taylor, K. 1998. *Truth and Meaning: An Introduction to the Philosophy of Language.* Oxford: Blackwell.

R

RADIOMETRIC DATING. Radiometric dating refers to analyses of naturally occurring materials and human artifacts that rely on measurements of radioactive atoms, or the products of radioactivity, to quantify the passage of **time**.

The first radiometric dating techniques were developed in the early twentieth century, shortly after the discovery of radioactivity by Henri Becquerel in 1896, and applied to rocks and minerals from the earth's crust. Since that time, many different radiometric methods have been devised and applied to hundreds of thousands of samples of rock, minerals, tissue, bone, water, archaeological artifacts, and even starlight. Ages determined for earth materials consistently fall within a range of zero (modern) to roughly four and a half billion years. The oldest rocks from the earth's crust are found in Western Australia and date their formation to approximately 4.4 billion years ago. The oldest meteorites, thought to represent debris solidified shortly after the birth of our solar system, date to approximately 4.6 billion years ago.

Radioactivity arises from an unstable combination of neutrons and protons in the nucleus of an atom. For a particular element, the number of protons is constant, but the number of neutrons can vary. Atoms of the same element (same number of protons) with different numbers of neutrons are called *isotopes*. Using carbon as an example, every atom of carbon has six protons, but the number of neutrons varies. Isotopes of carbon with six, seven, or eight neutrons have atomic masses of 12, 13, and 14, respectively. Carbon-12 and carbon-13 are stable. Carbon-14 (radiocarbon) is not, and radioactively decays. During decay, the number of protons and neutrons changes, resulting in a new element called the *daughter isotope* (the original is called the *parent isotope*). In some cases, such as carbon-14, the decay happens in a single step to produce a stable daughter isotope (nitrogen-14). In others, such as uranium-238, decay produces a series of unstable daughter isotopes before producing a stable form (lead-206).

The rate of decay for a particular radioactive isotope is described by its half-life, the amount of time it takes for half of the atoms to undergo radioactive decay. If we start with 1,000 radioactive atoms, after one half-life, there will be 500; after an equal amount of time passes (a second half-life) there will be 250; after a third half-life, 125; and so on. The more unstable the nuclear configuration, the shorter the half-life. Highly unstable forms can have half-lives of less than a microsecond,

while others have half-lives of billions of years. Radioactive isotopes useful for dating typically have half-lives of at least several years (for dating samples years to decades old) to billions of years (for samples millions of years or older). As an example, lead-210, with a half-life of 22 years, is useful for dating sediments accumulated in modern lakes over the last century. In older samples, there is too little lead-210 left to measure. Uranium-238, with a half-life of 4.5 billion years, is useful for dating rocks millions to billions of years in age.

If the initial concentration (or activity) of a radioactive isotope is known, the half-life can be used to calculate how much time was required for the initial concentration to decay to its present level. If the initial concentration is not known, a combination of the parent and daughter isotopes can be used. When a rock solidifies from a magma (melted rock), crystals form that include some elements and exclude others. In a magma, uranium and lead freely mix, but as crystals form, minerals like zircon incorporate uranium and exclude lead, setting the radiometric "clock" to zero.

Over time lead builds up inside the solid crystal as uranium decays. The ratio of uranium to lead can then be used to calculate how much time had to pass to reach the current ratio. This is why many radiometric dating methods are identified by a parent-daughter pair, such as the uranium-lead (U-Pb), or potassium-argon (K-Ar) methods. If daughter isotopes were incorporated in the sample at the time of formation, a simple parent-daughter ratio will yield an age that is too old. In this case, a more complex method is employed using multiple samples from the same source, with plots of isotope ratios yielding the concentration of daughter isotopes at the start and the age of the samples. These are called *isochrons* (*iso* = equal, *chron* = time) because samples of equal age plot along the same line. Scientists who use radiometric dating are careful to incorporate all relevant data and initial conditions into their age determination.

The accuracy of radiometric dating is dependent on the absence of leakage of parent or daughter isotopes in or out of the sample over time (it is a closed system), and on radioactive decay rates being constant. Intense heating is known to allow migration of atoms in and out of minerals, so metamorphic rocks are typically avoided for dating purposes (unless wanting to know the timing of heating). An isochron that fails to produce a straight line is one way that a geochronologist (geologist who measures ages) might recognize leakage.

The assumption of constant decay rates has been called into doubt by young-earth advocates with claims that rates were likely much faster in the past. There are several ways, however, of testing both the constancy of decay rates and the reliability of radiometric dating. For time spans of a few thousand years, radiometric dates for samples collected from ancient volcanic eruptions can be compared with known eruption dates. Radiometric dates of samples from the Mount Vesuvius eruption that buried Pompeii match the reported AD 79 date to within a few years. For samples dating in the millions of years, the rate of ocean spreading at places like the Mid-Atlantic Ridge can be calculated using the radiometric age of ocean crust and distance from the ridge, with real-time measurements using GPS **technology**.

If decay rates were much faster in the past, calculated and measured rates should not match. Significantly, both the calculated rate using radiometric ages of ocean crust and satellite measurements of the speed at which North America and Africa are separating is approximately 1 inch per year.

Commonly used isotopes and types of samples:

Radiometric Technique	Half-Life (Years)	Range of Ages (Years)	Sample Types
Uranium-Lead	4.5 billion	1 million to 4.5 billion	Igneous minerals
Rubidium-Strontium	28 billion	60 million to 4.5 billion	Igneous minerals
Potassium-Argon	1.3 billion	3 million to 4.5 billion	Igneous minerals
Argon-Argon*	1.3 billion	About 2,000 to 4.5 billion	Igneous minerals
Uranium series	75,000	A few centuries to 400,000	Corals, cave deposits
Carbon-14	5730	About 50 to 45,000	Tree rings, bones, carbon material
Lead-210	22	50 to 100	Recent sediments

*Employs two different isotopes of argon

Radiocarbon

Carbon-14 gets more attention than other radioactive isotopes in part because its half-life of 5,730 years makes it ideal for dating archaeological specimens going back several tens of thousands of years. It has been employed to successfully date a number of biblical artifacts, including wood from Hezekiah's water supply tunnel beneath Jerusalem. It also provides another unique opportunity to test competing claims of constant versus variable decay rates.

In one study in Lake Suigetsu, Japan, lake bottom cores were collected that contained thousands of sediment layers that appear to be annual deposits (called *varves*). If each layer represents one year and carbon-14 decay rates have been constant, a plot of carbon-14 compared to varve count should show a relatively steady decline along a predictable trajectory. Variable decay rates or sediment deposition would be equally identifiable with departures from this expected trend. The actual data fits expectations for constant decay rates and annual deposition of sediment through 45,000 layers (below which the carbon-14 content becomes too low to accurately detect).

In figure 1, when the amount of radiocarbon in the mammoth bone is placed on the varve count line, the time in the past when the mammoth lived is obtained from the varve count. The figure shows the linear trend of carbon-14 in sediment layers from two lakes, and where the wood from Hezekiah's tunnel falls. It also shows the amount of radiocarbon in a mammoth bone, demonstrating that when the radiocarbon date of the bone is placed on the varve count line, the time in the past when the mammoth lived is obtained from the varve count. The radiocarbon correspondence with the varve counts shows an unbroken history of the earth for about the last 50,000 years.

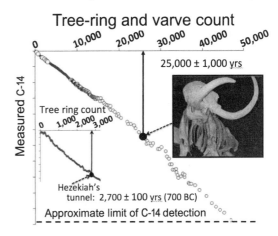

Figure 1. H. Kitagawa and J. van der Plicht, "Atmospheric Radiocarbon Calibration beyond 11,900 Cal BP from Lake Suigetsu Laminated Sediments." *Radiocarbon* 42 (2000): 370–81.

Ken Wolgemuth

REFERENCES AND RECOMMENDED READING

Dalrymple, G. Brent. 2000. "Radiometric Dating Does Work!" *Reports of the National Center for Science Education* 20 (May–June): 14–19. https://ncse.com/library-resource/radiometric-dating-does-work.

———. 2004. *Ancient Earth, Ancient Skies: The Age of Earth and Its Cosmic Surroundings.* Stanford, CA: Stanford University Press.

Davidson, Gregg, and Ken Wolgemuth. 2012. "How Old Is the Earth? What God's Creation Professes." *Christian Research Journal* 35 (1): 54–57.

Frumkin, A., A. Shimron, and J. Rosenbaum. 2003. "Radiometric Dating of the Siloam Tunnel, Jerusalem." *Nature* 425:169–71.

Tian, J., T. A. Brown, and F. S. Hu. 2005. "Comparison of Varve and 14C Chronologies from Steel Lake, Minnesota, USA." *The Holocene* 15:510–17.

Wiens, Roger C. 2002. "Radiometric Dating: A Christian Perspective." American Scientific Affliation. www.asa3.org/ASA/resources/Wiens.html.

RAMM, BERNARD. Baptist theologian Bernard Ramm (1916–92) has been ranked with Carl F. H. Henry as "one of the foremost American evangelical theologians of the twentieth century" (Vanhoozer 1993, 292). Although he wrote 20 books on many different subjects, probably none has been more influential than *The Christian View of Science and Scripture* (1954). The book grew out of a course he taught at the Bible Institute of Los Angeles (now Biola University) not long after World War II, while he was completing doctoral work in **philosophy of science** at the University of Southern California.

Ramm sought an alternative to the fundamentalist tendency to circle the wagons and the modernist tendency to dismiss the Bible in response to science. He spoke frankly of "two traditions in Bible and science" emerging from the nineteenth century. One was "the ignoble tradition, which has taken a most unwholesome attitude toward science" and relies on poor scholarship, while the other was "a noble tradition in Bible and science, and this is the tradition of the great evangelical Christians … who have taken great care to learn the facts of science and Scripture." He lamented that "the noble tradition" was not "the major tradition in evangelicalism in the twentieth century. Both a narrow evangelical Biblicism, and its narrow theology, buried the noble tradition" (Ramm 1954, unpaginated preface).

Young-earth creationism had not yet become popular, but Ramm knew about **George McCready Price** and steered far clear of his ideas. Most conservative Protestant institutions at that time taught the gap theory, an old-earth interpretation of Genesis that had been widely accepted since the mid-nineteenth century but could no longer give a satisfactory account of geological data. Ramm hoped to persuade readers to abandon that approach in favor of what he called "**concordism** because it seeks a harmony of the geologic record and the days of Genesis interpreted as long periods of time." He also called his view **progressive creation**, emphasizing that it "is not theistic evolution which calls for creation from within with no acts *de novo*." Nevertheless, he spoke positively of "a sure but slender thread of theistic evolutionists" among evangelicals (Ramm 1954, 211, 227–28, 284).

Ramm's measured conclusions divided conservative Protestants into progressive and reactionary groups. The positive reception he garnered from several influential members of the **American Scientific Affiliation**, an organization of evangelical scientists that Ramm had joined in the late 1940s, led other members to leave the organization in the early 1960s, when **Henry M. Morris** reinvigorated Price's views in *The Genesis Flood* (1961), the book he co-authored with **John C. Whitcomb**, that launched the modern creationist movement. Despite the considerable success of creationism, approaches similar to Ramm's concordism continue to find substantial support among conservative Protestants; twenty-first-century proponents include John Jefferson Davis, **William Dembski**, and **Hugh Ross**.

Edward B. Davis

REFERENCES AND RECOMMENDED READING

Hearn, Walter. 1979. "An Interview with Bernard Ramm and Alta Ramm." *Journal of the American Scientific Affiliation* 31:179–86.

Ramm, Bernard. 1954. *The Christian View of Science and Scripture.* Grand Rapids: Eerdmans.

Vanhoozer, Kevin J. 1993. "Bernard Ramm." In *Handbook of Evangelical Theologians.* Ed. Walter A. Elwell, 290–306. Grand Rapids: Baker.

RANDOM MUTATION. All organisms, and organism-like entities such as viruses, make copies of their nucleic acid genomes in the process of replication. Despite a high degree of fidelity in genome replication, progeny genomes are seldom identical to the parental (template) sequence. For example, it is now known that for humans, on the order of 100 replication errors are made each generation when our 3 billion **DNA** base pairs are copied—an error rate far less than 1% but nonetheless not absolutely perfect.

Any difference between parental and offspring sequences is known as a *mutation* (from Latin *mutare*, "to change"). Mutations may arise from several distinct processes. A *point* mutation can arise if a single DNA base is incorrectly paired during chromosome replication. Incorrect pairing can arise if DNA bases are damaged (by chemicals or ultraviolet light), or by a natural process known as tautomerization, where hydrogen atoms transiently change position within the DNA base itself (Berg et al. 2002). Both damage and tautomerization produce changes in DNA base pairing affinity, which may lead to mismatched base pairs during chromosome replication. Other mutation types include the *deletion* of numerous DNA base pairs in one event; conversely, *duplication* mutations may erroneously insert extra copies of a DNA sequence into a progeny genome.

Errors in how chromosome copies separate during cell division can lead to the duplication or deletion of entire chromosomes. Other events are possible: mobile genetic elements (*transposons*) insert their small genome into the genome of their hosts (an example of an *insertion* mutation). Large-scale chromosome breakage and rejoining may lead to *inversion* or *translocation* mutations. Taken together, many physical events can lead to changes in DNA sequence between parent and offspring, and all fall under the general definition of *mutation*.

Biologists commonly refer to mutations as *random*. In this context, *random* has two, and only two, specific meanings (Futuyma 2013). The first is that mutation is a *stochastic* event. This means that for any given DNA sequence, it is possible to measure (and later, predict) the mutation frequency for a large number of replication events. Whether a particular progeny sequence will contain a mutation, however, cannot be determined in advance. In this sense, mutation is analogous to radioactive decay: the aggregate properties of a large population (DNA sequences or atoms) is readily predictable (by mutation frequency or half-life), but individual properties cannot be predicted in advance (whether an individual DNA sequence will contain a mutation following replication, or when an individual atom will undergo radioactive decay).

The second, and more important meaning, is that mutations arise independently of how useful they are to an organism in its particular environment. The environment, then, does not influence the **probability** that an advantageous mutation will occur. The first evidence that the environment does not influence the probability of an advantageous mutation was observed by the seminal work of Lederberg and Lederberg (1952). In their experiment, they exposed bacteria to the antibiotic penicillin and noted that rare variants were resistant to its bactericidal effects. Through careful work, they were able to determine that the mutations that led to antibiotic resistance were present within the population of bacteria before it was exposed to the antibiotic. As such, the antibiotic was selecting for preexisting mutations that conferred resistance, not favoring the production of new,

advantageous, mutations. Subsequent work in this area in the decades since has yet to demonstrate a case where the environment caused specific mutations, advantageous or not.

It is important to note that the randomness of mutation in the biological sense does not extend to other common definitions of random. For example, random can mean "unbiased": a random number generator is a stochastic mechanism that produces an unbiased string of numbers. Biologically, mutations are not random in this sense. It is known that different genome regions are not equally prone to mutation, and that the various kinds of mutation events are not equally probable. The physical properties of DNA influence mutation events in many ways that introduce biases. For example, highly repetitive DNA (where a short sequence of DNA is repeated several times in tandem) is much more prone to duplication mutations than is nonrepetitive DNA.

As repetitive DNA is replicated, it is possible that the newly copied strand will slip backward relative to the template strand, but re-pair with it due to the repetitive matched sequences. Such slippage and re-pairing means that a section of the newly copied strand loops out from the template as an unpaired region, and the new strand recopies sequence from the template strand. The end result in the new strand is a further duplication of the repeated DNA sequence.

Nonrepetitive DNA, in contrast, will not readily form such single stranded loops and re-pair since such a structure would not be stabilized through repeated sequences. A second example is the elevated mutation rate at what are known as CpG dinucleotides: a cytosine followed by a guanine on the same DNA strand (Duncan and Miller, 1980). The *p* between the *C* and the *G* is used to indicate the phosphate bond connecting them, and distinguish this structure from a cytosine paired with a guanine on the opposite strand (i.e., a CG base pair). In CpG dinucleotides the cytosine is commonly methylated. Methylated cytosine readily undergoes a deamination reaction (the loss of an amine group), the product of which happens to be thymine, one of the other DNA bases. Because such a newly produced thymine appears as a "normal" DNA base, it is not readily recognized by DNA repair enzymes as a mutation. Because of these physical properties, the C in a CpG dinucleotide is much more susceptible to mutation to a T (thymine) than are other DNA bases.

Other examples could be given: transposons have long been known to prefer certain insertion sites over others; the mutation rate is known to vary slightly for different regions within individual **gene**s or between genes. As such, it would be inappropriate to describe mutation as random in the sense of "equally probable" or "evenly distributed." Moreover, the randomness of mutation does not mean that the environment has no effect on mutations: the presence of chemicals or radiation can increase the mutation rate in general, but still not direct the production of advantageous mutations specifically.

Similarly, in some bacteria environmental stress (such as excess heat or lack of resources) can elevate mutation rates in general (which increases the probability that at least some mutated progeny will have advantageous mutations). Even in such cases, however, the resulting mutations are random in the biological sense; they are produced through a stochastic process that does not "foresee" which particular mutations will be an advantage. Rather, random mutation followed by **natural selection** is the mechanism by which adaptation occurs.

Finally, it is important to understand that "random" in the biological sense does not mean "without **teleology**" or "without purpose." Science is restricted to cause-and-effect relationships within the natural world and is blind to non-scientific questions of meaning and purpose. Therefore the scientific demonstration that a physical process is stochastic does not indicate that it is purposeless, since such a conclusion goes beyond what science can demonstrate. Indeed, humans routinely use stochastic processes (such as random number generators) for specific intended purposes (such as mathematic modeling). Thus the scientific demonstration that a process is stochastic should not be conflated with an ateleological or dysteleological interpretation of that process.

Dennis R. Venema

REFERENCES AND RECOMMENDED READING

Berg, J. M., J. L. Tymoczko, and L. Stryer. 2002. *Biochemistry*. 5th ed. New York: W. H. Freeman.

Duncan, B. K., and J. H. Miller. 1980. "Mutagenic Deamination of Cytosine Residues in DNA." *Nature* 287:560–61.

Futuyma, D. J. 2013. *Evolution*. 3rd ed. Sunderland, MA: Sinauer.

Lederberg, J., and E. M. Lederberg. 1952. "Replica Plating and Indirect Selection of Bacterial Mutants." *Journal of Bacteriology* 63:399–406.

Loewe, L. 2008. "Genetic Mutation." *Nature Education* 1:113.

RATZSCH, DEL. Del Ratzsch (1945–) earned his PhD in philosophy from the University of Massachusetts. He is professor of philosophy (emeritus) at Calvin College, where he taught for almost 35 years, authoring or coauthoring four books as well as dozens of journal articles and book chapters.

While **philosophy of science** was not Ratzsch's primary focus in graduate school, he was soon drawn to it, becoming one of the foremost philosophers of science within the Society of Christian Philosophers (SCP). He has lectured in several countries, but was especially active in China, teaching seminars for Chinese students at Wuhan University and codirecting large conferences of Christian academics in Beijing. His *Science and Its Limits* (2000), which was translated into four languages, is considered by many to be the best introduction to academic philosophy of science from a Christian perspective.

Ratzsch's publications mostly focused on issues at the intersection of science and religion, including work on the **laws of nature** (1987), **naturalism** (2004), and the use of design concepts in science (2001). Grants from the National Science Foundation, the National Endowment for the Humanities, the Pew Foundation, and others were used to stimulate interest in these topics in several countries. Ratzsch is best known, however, for his work on controversies involving creationism, evolution, and **intelligent design**. In *The Battle of Beginnings* (1996), he argues that both sides of the creation-evolution debate tend to misunderstand and misrepresent the other, making progress on the issue extremely difficult. He also reveals the tendency of both sides to impose their own view of the nature of science in order to gain a rhetorical advantage.

Ratzsch has been influential on the intelligent design movement since the mid-1990s, though he is more of a "friendly critic" than a proponent. While he argued that it is possible in principle to rightly detect design in nature, he believes that the ID movement has not yet provided sufficient evidence to meet its burden of proof. In particular, he showed that **William Dembski**'s **specified complexity** is not a sufficient condition for detecting design (Ratzsch 2001). On the other hand, Ratzsch has argued that many of the criticisms leveled against ID are faulty and that **divine action** in nature ought not be considered unscientific by definition. In short, Ratzsch supports some of the core principles of ID but does not think that ID has proven itself in practice.

Through the influence of the SCP, academic philosophy in the English-speaking world is far more open to **theism** than it was a half-century ago. Ratzsch was one of a very small number of philosophers of science involved in this turnaround. He continues to have a strong and lasting influence on a new generation of Christian academics specializing in the philosophy of science.

Jeffrey Koperski

REFERENCES AND RECOMMENDED READING

Ratzsch, Del. 1987. "Nomo(theo)logical Necessity." *Faith and Philosophy* 4 (4): 383–402.

———. 1996. *The Battle of Beginnings: Why Neither Side Is Winning the Creation-Evolution Debate.* Downers Grove, IL: InterVarsity.

———. 2000. *Science and Its Limits: The Natural Sciences in Christian Perspective.* 2nd ed. Downers Grove, IL: InterVarsity.

———. 2001. *Nature, Design, and Science.* Albany, NY: SUNY Press.

———. 2004. "Natural Theology, Methodological Naturalism, and 'Turtles All the Way Down.'" *Faith and Philosophy* 21 (4): 436–55.

REALISM AND ANTIREALISM.

REALISM AND ANTIREALISM. The question of whether the human **mind** can gain knowledge of reality has been one of the central preoccupations of philosophers. Realism and antirealism represent the two broad positions on this question. Realism is the default, commonsense view, the view that the human mind in the act of knowing does grasp essential truths about reality outside of the mind (extramental reality), that the mind can come to have knowledge of things as they are in themselves. This view was held by most major philosophers up until at least the time of **John Locke**. The views of the majority of traditional Christian thinkers, as well as the official teachings of the various religious denominations, were based on a realist understanding of knowledge with regard to such matters as the nature of God, articulations of religious doctrines, and religious **morality**, accounts of which were proposed as objectively true and regarded as largely independent of opinions, biases, or cultural influences.

With the distinction between **primary and secondary qualities**, Locke was the first thinker to seriously introduce an antirealist theory of knowledge. This is the view that the human mind in the act of knowing modifies or distorts the objects of knowledge, and consequently the mind does not come to know reality as it really is but only as it appears to human observers. This view can be better understood by imagining that there is a kind of filter in the human mind that our perceptions and experiences about the world pass through, and which thereby distorts our claims to knowledge.

Another way of making this point is to say that all knowledge claims involve a human perspective that compromises their **objectivity**. Various philosophers then proposed different accounts of how the "filter" is supposed to work (e.g., **Kant**, Heidegger, Derrida, **Quine**). Initially, it was thought that all human beings shared the same type of filter, and so some semblance of objectivity could be maintained, but in recent philosophy a more radical form of antirealism has become prominent. This is based on the claim that the human perspective on knowledge is significantly influenced by one's cultural upbringing, conceptual scheme, language, historical era, even gender, and so knowledge would then be relative to each group, or even each individual.

In the face of the widespread influence of antirealism in the twentieth century, realist, orthodox approaches to Christian doctrine and ethics have come under severe criticism. One thinker whose work was especially influential was the English philosopher John Hick who used the well-known metaphor of the blind men who each provide inadequate descriptions of an elephant to illustrate an antirealist (Kantian) approach to the question of religious pluralism. Antirealist influences of this sort have made significant ground in recent Christian theology and have defined the responses of many pastors and churches to questions of biblical interpretation, to theological descriptions of the nature of God, as well as to moral and cultural questions.

However, antirealist theories have been plagued by two familiar problems. The first is that no antirealist philosopher has been able to move beyond an abstract statement of antirealism to show in a concrete, convincing way how the filter in the mind works, to show how language or culture, for example, compromise the mind's ability to know reality. The second problem is one of contradiction: the antirealist argues that every knowledge claim is filtered, yet his own description of the nature of knowledge is supposed to be objectively true and so not subject to the filtering process. If it is not subject to the filter, it is contradictory; if it is subject to the filter, it cannot be regarded as an objective claim and so would be question-begging.

Brendan Sweetman

REFERENCES AND RECOMMENDED READING

Brock, Stuart, and Edwin Mares. 2007. *Realism and Anti-realism.* Montreal: McGill-Queen's University Press.

Hick, John. 2005. *An Interpretation of Religion.* New Haven, CT: Yale University Press.

McLaren, Brian. 2011. *A New Kind of Christianity.* San Francisco: HarperOne.

Putnam, Hilary. 1988. *The Many Faces of Realism.* Peru, IL: Open Court.

REASON, ARGUMENT FROM.

REASON, ARGUMENT FROM. The argument from reason is a name applied to an argument, or a group of arguments, that attempts to make a case against a naturalistic philosophy by pointing out that such a philosophy undercuts the claim to hold rational beliefs. The argument is best known in the writings of **C. S. Lewis** but is considerably older. Some have actually found this line of argumentation as far back as **Plato**, and a version of it is found in **Immanuel Kant**.

What these arguments invariably target are doctrines known as **naturalism**, **materialism**, or **physicalism**. All of these concepts are notoriously difficult to define. What seems to be common to all of these doctrines is the idea that at the basis of reality are elements that are entirely nonmental in nature.

We can begin thinking about this by contrasting two different types of explanation. One type of explanation is what might be provided by how we could explain the movement of rocks down a mountain in an avalanche. If I am standing at the bottom of the mountain, we can expect the rocks to move where they do without regard to whether my head is in their path or not. They will not deliberately move to hit my head, neither will they move to avoid it. They will do what the laws of **physics** require that they do, and if my head is in the wrong place at the wrong time, it will be hit, and otherwise it will not be hit. The process is an inherently blind one.

Consider, by contrast, how we might explain what happens when I decide to vote for a certain candidate for president. I weigh the options and choose the candidate who is most likely to do what I want to see done in the country for the next four years. The action of voting for one candidate or the other is one filled with intention and purpose. I know what the choice is about, I have a goal in mind when voting, and I perform the act of voting with the intent to achieve a certain result.

If we look at the world from a naturalistic perspective, we are always looking to find nonmental explanations even behind the mental explanations that we offer. Take, for example, **Einstein** developing his theory of relativity. If a naturalistic view of the world is correct, then we can — and must — explain the development of Einstein's theory in mental terms, in terms of certain mathematical relationships obtaining, and so forth. But Einstein's brain is, according to the naturalist, entirely the result of a purely nonintentional process of random variation and **natural selection** (see **Evolutionary Argument against Naturalism**). The appearance of intention and design is explained by an underlying blind process that not only produced Einstein's brain, but also the processes in his brain, which are the result of particles operating as blindly as the rocks falling down the mountain and either hitting or not hitting my head at the bottom.

Contrast this with a theistic view. On such a view, there may be particles that follow the laws of physics, but those laws are in place because they were built into creation by God. Presumably, if God had wanted there to be other laws of physics, he could have made a world with laws of physics very different than the ones that we see. So on the theistic view we see the opposite of naturalism. Even what seems on one level to be completely explained in terms of the nonmental has a mental explanation.

The argument from reason tries to show that if the world were as the naturalist or materialist or physicalist says that it is, then no one can be rational in believing that it is so. Rational beliefs must, according to the argument, have rational causes, but naturalism holds that in the final analysis, all causes are nonrational causes. But if this is so, then human beings really don't reason, and if they don't reason, they don't do science either. So, the very naturalistic **worldview** that is supposed to be based on science is actually a view that renders science impossible.

In the original 1947 edition of his book *Miracles: A Preliminary Study*, Lewis presented a version of the argument from reason that can be formalized as follows.

1. If naturalism is true, then all thoughts, including the thought "naturalism is true," can be fully explained as the result of irrational causes.
2. If all thoughts are the result of irrational causes, then all thoughts are invalid, and science is impossible.
3. If all thoughts are invalid, and science is impossible, then no one is justified in believing that naturalism is true.
4. Therefore naturalism should be rejected.

In explaining why this is problematic for a naturalistic view, it has been argued (Reppert, 2003, 2009) that a naturalistic view requires three elements. First, the system of "natural" or "physical" events must be causally closed. Second, whatever happens in the world at some level other than the physical level must supervene on the physical (see **Emergence**, **Supervenience**). What that means is that given the state of the physical, the other levels cannot differ. Two possible worlds cannot be physically identical but mentally different. Third, the physical has to be mechanistic, and by this I mean that "mental" facts cannot enter into the explanation of reality at the basic level. If the basic level has no room for mental states, and all the other levels are the way they are because the basic level is the way it is, then whether there are reasons for a belief or not is irrelevant to the question of what mental states, if any, a person is in.

Discussion of this line of argument has progressed in

various ways. One lesser-known early development was a defense of Lewis by Eric Mascall (1957) against Elizabeth Anscombe prior to Lewis's own revision of the argument. J. R. Lucas (1973) developed an argument centered around **Gödel's theorem**—an argument that was inspired by Lewis's argument—but interestingly enough Gödel himself developed the same implications in an unpublished paper. William Hasker also developed a version of the argument (1973, 1999). Reppert would write "The Lewis-Anscombe Controversy" (1989) and further develop and defend Lewis's argument (2003, 2009). The argument from reason has been criticized by thinkers such as **Antony Flew**, Jim Lippard, Keith Parsons, Theodore Drange, and Richard Carrier.

Victor Reppert

REFERENCES AND RECOMMENDED READING

Hasker, William. 1973. "The Transcendental Refutation of Determinism." *Southern Journal of Philosophy* 11:175–83.
———. 1999. *The Emergent Self.* Ithaca, NY: Cornell University Press.
Lewis, C. S. 1978. *Miracles: A Preliminary Study.* 2nd ed. New York: Macmillan.
Lucas, J. R. 1973. *Freedom of the Will.* Oxford: Clarendon.
Mascall, E. L. 1957. *Christian Theology and Natural Science: Some Questions in Their Relations.* London: Longmans, Green.
Reppert, Victor. 1989. "The Lewis-Anscombe Controversy: A Discussion of the Issues." *Christian Scholar's Review* 19 (September): 32–48.
———. 2003. *C. S. Lewis's Dangerous Idea: In Defense of the Argument from Reason.* Downers Grove, IL: InterVarsity.
———. 2009. "The Argument from Reason." In *The Blackwell Companion to Natural Theology.* Eds. William Lane Craig and J. P. Moreland. Malden, MA: Wiley-Blackwell.

REASONS TO BELIEVE. Reasons to Believe (RTB) is a science apologetics ministry founded by astronomer **Hugh Ross** in 1986 and based in Covina, California. Its mission is to spread the Christian gospel by demonstrating that sound reason and scientific research consistently support, rather than erode, confidence in the truth of the Bible and faith in the personal, transcendent God revealed in both Scripture and nature.

RTB comprises a team of research scholars—Hugh Ross, president; Fazale Rana, biochemist, vice president of research and apologetics; Jeffrey Zweerink, astrophysicist, research scholar; Anjeanette "AJ" Roberts, molecular biologist; and Kenneth Samples, philosopher-theologian, senior research scholar—who address audiences internationally on a variety of science-faith topics. Along with a locally based support staff, RTB strives for global impact with its growing lists of visiting scholars, apologetics community members, and nearly 50 national and international chapters all working in concert to help strengthen believers' faith and remove nonbelievers' stumbling blocks to faith.

Operating with a belief that science and faith are allies, not enemies, RTB employs a *constructive integration* approach to general **revelation** (science) and special revelation (Scripture). As such, RTB holds a moderate *concordist*, old-earth creation view, which seeks general agreement between properly interpreted Scripture passages that describe some aspect of the natural realm and established, well-understood scientific data. Ongoing development of a scientifically testable creation model distinguishes RTB from other creationist organizations and challenges skeptical scientists to consider the veracity of the Christian faith. That biblically derived model includes predictions about the origin of the universe, of **life**, and of humanity.

RTB scholars have spoken on more than 300 campuses in the United States and abroad and have written more than 20 books that explain aspects of the creation model. RTB's website features updated content, including a considerable archive of "Today's New Reason to Believe" articles among its many video, audio, podcast, and other resources. RTB scholars appear regularly on international television and radio programs, speak at churches of all sizes and denominational affiliations, and participate in and/or host apologetics conferences.

Ministry imperatives include engaging skeptics, equipping believers, and empowering the church with the truth of the gospel and doing so with gentleness, respect, and a clear conscience. Part of the equipping includes Reasons Institute, one of RTB's two educational arms, which offers university-level courses in science apologetics for personal enrichment, a certificate in science apologetics, or college credit. Reasons Academy (for K–12), the second arm, brings research in the constructive integration of the Bible and science into the classroom, co-op, or homeschool.

RTB publishes its statement of faith on its website (reasons.org) and endorses the Chicago Statement on Biblical Inerrancy.

Joe Aguirre

REFERENCES AND RECOMMENDED READING

"Reasons to Believe." 2014. *Wikipedia.* Accessed December 30, 2014. http://en.wikipedia.org/wiki/Reasons_To_Believe.
Reasons to Believe official website. www.reasons.org.

REDUCTIONISM. Finding either explicit or tacit reductionism—that is, reducing qualities of some entity to qualities described in terms of constituent parts—in contemporary interpretations of scientific theories is common. Often the constituents are taken to be the fundamental particles of **physics** (and sometimes chemistry). Reductionism is perhaps most notable in physicalist theories of **mind**, where mental properties are "reduced" to physical properties of (constituents of) the brain, thereby eliminating or explaining away minds as immaterial entities (see **Physicalism**).

Currently, five different types of reduction are relevant to mind-body debates: (1) *Individual ontological reduction*: one object (a macro-object like the person) is identified with another object (e.g., a physical simple or mereological compound such as the brain or body). (2) *Property ontological reduction*: one property (heat) is identified with another property (mean kinetic energy). (3) *Linguistic reduction*: one word or concept (*pain*) is defined as or analyzed in terms of another word or concept (*the tendency to grimace when stuck with a pin*). (4) *Causal reduction*: the causal activity of the reduced entity is entirely explained in terms of the causal activity of the reducing entity. (5) *Theoretical* or *explanatory reduction*: one theory or law is reduced to another by biconditional bridge principles.

Individual ontological reduction is affirmed by virtually all physicalists. Property reduction is affirmed by type identity physicalists and eschewed by token physicalists and eliminativists. There is a debate about whether or not functionalists accept property reduction (see below), but apart from emergent supervenient physicalists (see below), all physicalists believe that in the actual world all the properties exemplified by persons are physical properties in some sense or another. Causal reduction is hotly disputed by physicalists. Part of the debate involves the causal closure of the physical and the reality of so-called top-down **causation**. It is safe to say that, currently, most physicalists follow Jaegwon Kim and **John Searle** and accept causal reduction. Linguistic reduction is no longer a main part of the debate since the demise of philosophical **behaviorism** and positivist theories of meaning. Theoretical reduction, finally, is employed in classifications of physicalism and, unless otherwise indicated, descriptions of reductive vs. nonreductive physicalism should be understood to employ it.

Currently, the main version of reductive physicalism is type identity physicalism. Type identity physicalists accept explanatory reduction and, on that basis, property ontological reduction. On this view, mental properties are identical to physical properties, so that identity statements asserting the relevant identities are construed as contingent identity statements employing different yet co-referring expressions (e.g., *pain* contingently identifies the same brain state as the expression *C-fibers firing*). The truth of these identity statements is an empirical discovery, and the statements are theoretical identities.

Two main objections seem decisive against type identity physicalism. First, it is obvious that mental and physical properties are different from each other. For example, the thought of a green field is not a green region in the brain; more generally, mental states do not have spatial location or extension while those properties are essential to physical things. Physicalists have not met the burden of proof required to overturn these deeply ingrained **intuition**s. Physicalists respond that in other cases of identity (e.g., heat is mean molecular kinetic energy), our intuitions about nonidentity turned out to be wrong, and the same is true in the case of mental properties. But for two reasons, this response fails. For one thing, these other cases of alleged property identities are most likely cases of correlation of properties.

Second, as Saul Kripke argued, we can easily explain why our intuitions were mistaken in the other cases, but a similar insight does not appear in the case of mental properties (Kripke 1972). Since there is a distinction between what heat is (mean kinetic energy) and how it appears to us (as being warm), our intuitions about nonidentity confused appearance with reality. But since mental properties such as painfulness are identical to the way they appear, no such source of confusion is available. Thus intuitions about the nonidentity of mental and physical properties remain justified.

The second difficulty with type identity theory is called the *multiple realization problem*: it seems obvious that humans, dogs, Vulcans, and a potentially infinite number of organisms with different physical states can all be in pain; thus the mental kind is not identical to a physical kind.

Largely in response to the multiple realization problem, a version of (allegedly) nonreductive physicalism—**functionalism**—has become the prominent current version of physicalism. Functionalists employ a "topic neutral" description of mental properties/states in terms of bodily inputs, behavioral outputs, and other mental state outputs. Mental properties thus are reduced to body/brain functions.

There are serious difficulties with functionalism. First, there are problems regarding absent or inverted qualia (see **Qualia**). Qualia arguments turn on the observation that mental kinds are essentially characterized by their intrinsic properties and only accidentally characterized by their extrinsic functional relations.

Further, there is no clear sense as to what the "realization relation" is that is available to a strict physicalist. Realization is not a relation that figures into chemistry and physics. Moreover, when physicalists characterize the realization relation in terms of **paradigm** cases, they select artifacts and appeal to mental notions such as intentions, values, goals, and agent production in their characterization (Papineau 1995). If the objective is to characterize realization in nonmental terms, this will hardly do.

In summary, whatever the merits of reductionism in other theoretical areas, it seems dubious when applied to the **mind-body problem**.

J. P. Moreland

REFERENCES AND RECOMMENDED READING

Hasker, William. 1999. *The Emergent Self.* Ithaca, NY: Cornell University Press.
Horst, Steven. 2007. *Beyond Reductionism.* New York: Oxford University Press.
Kripke, Sail. 1972. *Naming and Necessity.* Cambridge, MA: Harvard University Press.
Moreland, J. P. 2008. *Consciousness and the Existence of God.* London: Routledge.
Papineau, David. 1995. "Arguments for Supervenience and Physical Realization." In *Supervenience: New Essays.* Eds. Elias E. Savellos and Umit D. Yalcin. Cambridge: Cambridge University Press.

REICHENBACH, HANS. Hans Reichenbach (1891–1953) was a leading philosopher of science in the first half of the twentieth century and founder of the Berlin Circle—a group of logical empiricists that included **Carl Hempel**, Kurt Grelling, Richard von Mises, and David Hilbert—that was the German counterpart to the Vienna Circle logical positivists (see **Logical Positivism**).

Born of Jewish parents in Hamburg, Germany, Reichenbach entered engineering school in Stuttgart in 1910, but left after a year to pursue studies in **mathematics**, **physics**, and philosophy that took him to universities in Berlin, Göttingen, Munich, and Erlangen. Among his notable teachers during this time were the physicists **Albert Einstein**, Max Planck, and Arnold Sommerfeld; the mathematicians David Hilbert, Max Noether, and Emmy Noether; and the neo-Kantian philosopher Ernst Cassirer. In 1915 he received his doctorate from the University of Erlangen for a dissertation on the philosophical foundations of **probability** theory.

Reichenbach served briefly in World War I on the Russian front, but was removed from active duty due to illness, returning to Berlin where he worked as a physicist and engineer for three years while attending Albert Einstein's lectures on the theory of relativity. In 1920 he published *Relativitätstheorie und Erkenntnis apriori (The Theory of Relativity and A Priori Knowledge)*, a philosophical treatise critiquing the Kantian synthetic a priori on the basis of relativistic physics, especially the notion that **space and time** are a priori forms of cognition.

Reichenbach's work in the philosophy of physics continued throughout the 1920s. In 1926, with the help of Max von Laue, Max Planck, and the vigorous support of Einstein, Reichenbach was appointed to a teaching position in **natural philosophy** at the University of Berlin, where he remained until 1933. During this time, he established the Berlin Circle, founded the journal *Erkenntnis (Knowledge)* with **Rudolf Carnap** (1891–1970), and wrote *Philosophie der Raum-Zeit-Lehre (The Philosophy of Space and Time)* and *Atom und Kosmos: Das physikalische Weltbild der Gegenwart (Atom and Cosmos: The World of Modern Physics)*. The former was a highly influential text on the foundations of geometry, the theory of time, the consequences of Einstein's special and general theories of relativity, and general issues in the **philosophy of science**.

When Hitler came to power in 1933, Reichenbach fled Berlin for Istanbul, heading the philosophy department at the University of Istanbul from 1933 to 1938. While there, he wrote two books, *Wahrscheinlichkeitslehre: Eine Untersuchung über die Logischen und Mathematischen Grundlagen der Wahrscheinlichkeitsrechnung (The Theory of Probability: An Inquiry into the Logical and Mathematical Foundations of the Calculus of Probability)*, which was published in 1935, and *Experience and Prediction: An Analysis of the Foundations and the Structure of Knowledge*, which was published by University of Chicago Press in 1938, the year he moved from Istanbul to a professorship at the University of California at Los Angeles, a position he held until his death in 1953.

Reichenbach's treatise on probability focused on its meaning and applications, defending a frequentist interpretation and attempting to establish consistent rules for deriving new probabilities from given probabilities and for assigning probabilities in situations where none are given, all with the goal of clarifying induction and establishing a pragmatic basis for scientific knowledge. This work, along with *Experience and Prediction*, moved him away from the logical reductions to sense-data characteristic of positivism and toward probabilistic and conventionalist coordinations of language with physical circumstances more antifoundationalist and pragmatist in spirit.

This latter work contains Reichenbach's famous distinction between the context of discovery and the context of justification. Using mathematics as an illustration, he emphasizes that deductive mathematical relations are what they are, but how we first come to find them is a subjective matter of **psychology** (1938, 36–37). He contends that we must make the same distinction moving inductively from facts to theories. So the distinction is between the objective (deductive or inductive) relationship between premises and conclusions (the context of justification) and the various subjective means (context of discovery) by which this relationship is noticed (Glymour 2012, §3).

Several of Reichenbach's later works (1944, 1951, 1954, 1956), the last two of which were published posthumously, deal respectively with the philosophy of quantum mechanics, his "scientific philosophy" in general (touching on questions of free will and ethics), a counterfactual analysis of natural laws and modalities, and time asymmetry in different contexts of physical theory (mechanics, statistical thermodynamics, and quantum physics).

Reichenbach's philosophy of quantum mechanics gives a standard discussion of the formalism of the theory, but its treatment of the causal anomalies of quantum theory is badly dated, and his "resolution" of them involves adopting an idiosyncratic 3-valued **logic** for which he provides neither axioms nor inference rules. His "scientific philosophy" is also an artifact of the positivist era and largely discredited, involving a naive attempt to reconcile free will with a materialist conception of the world and an essentially emotivist theory of ethics similar to Charles Stevenson's (Stevenson 1944). His work on modality and subjunctive conditionals (Reichenbach 1954), while clarified substantially by **Wesley Salmon**'s expository foreword in its 1977 reissue, had little influence.

Finally, Reichenbach's work on the asymmetry of time (1956), which introduces a common cause principle used to distinguish various causal structures, has been impactful in discussions of causality in physics (Arntzenius 2010).

In conclusion, then, Reichenbach was one of the most important empiricist philosophers of the twentieth century, and while only a handful of his efforts have withstood the test of time, his formative influence on the interdisciplinary character and rigorous nature of contemporary philosophy of science is felt throughout the discipline.

Bruce L. Gordon

REFERENCES AND RECOMMENDED READING

Arntzenius, Frank. 2010. "Reichenbach's Common Cause Principle." In *Stanford Encyclopedia of Philosophy*. Ed. Edward N. Zalta. Fall. http://plato.stanford.edu/entries/physics-Rpcc/#3.2.

Glymour, Clark. 2012. "Hans Reichenbach." In *Stanford Encyclopedia of Philosophy*. Ed. Edward N. Zalta. Winter. http://plato.stanford.edu/entries/reichenbach/.
Reichenbach, Hans. 1920. *Relativitätstheorie und Erkenntnis apriori*. Berlin: Springer. English trans. and intro. by M. Reichenbach as *The Theory of Relativity and A Priori Knowledge*. Berkeley: University of California Press, 1965.
———. 1928. *Philosophie der Raum-Zeit-Lehre*. Berlin and Leipzig: Walter de Gruyter. English trans. by M. Reichenbach and J. Freund as *The Philosophy of Space and Time*. New York: Dover, 1957.
———. 1930. *Atom und Kosmos: Das physikalische Weltbild der Gegenwart*. Berlin: Deutsche Buch-Gemeinschaft. English trans. by H. Reichenbach as *Atom and Cosmos: The World of Modern Physics*. London: George Allen & Unwin, 1930.
———. 1935. *Wahrscheinlichkeitslehre: Eine Untersuchung über die Logischen und Mathematischen Grundlagen der Wahrscheinlichkeitsrechnung*. Leiden: Sijthoff. English trans. by E. Hutten and M. Reichenbach as *The Theory of Probability: An Inquiry into the Logical and Mathematical Foundations of the Calculus of Probability*. Berkeley: University of California Press, 1949.
———. 1938. *Experience and Prediction: An Analysis of the Foundations and the Structure of Knowledge*. Chicago: University of Chicago Press.
———. (1944) 1998. *Philosophic Foundations of Quantum Mechanics*. New York: Dover.
———. 1947. *Elements of Symbolic Logic*. New York: Macmillan.
———. 1949. "The Philosophical Significance of the Theory of Relativity." In *Albert Einstein: Philosopher-Scientist*. Ed. P. Schilpp, 287–311. La Salle, IL: Open Court.
———. 1951. *The Rise of Scientific Philosophy*. Berkeley: University of California Press.
———. 1954. *Nomological Statements and Admissible Operations*. Dordrecht: North Holland. Reissued as *Laws, Modalities, and Counterfactuals*. Berkeley: University of California Press, 1977.
———. 1956. *The Direction of Time*. Berkeley: University of California Press.
Salmon, Wesley. 1977. "The Philosophy of Hans Reichenbach," in *Hans Reichenbach: Logical Empiricist*. Ed. W. Salmon, 1–84. Dordrecht: D. Reidel.
Stevenson, Charles L. 1944. *Ethics and Language*. New Haven, CT: Yale University Press.

RELATIVITY, GENERAL THEORY OF.

The general theory of relativity, developed by **Albert Einstein** between 1907 and 1915, describes gravitation, specifically how mass interacts with the space-time fabric of the universe. General relativity makes several predictions that have been confirmed and that differ from Newton's universal gravitational law.

One of the foundational principles of general relativity is the equivalence principle, which equates the gravitational mass of an object with its inertial mass. As such, all of the observations made by a person influenced by a gravitational force, say, on the surface of a planet, are identical to those made by a person in an accelerating reference frame. As an example, suppose a person were placed in a room with no windows or doors. The person noticed that all objects fell to the floor with a constant acceleration of 10 meters per second squared. According to the equivalence principle, this could be caused either because the room was on a planet with a gravitational constant of 10 meters per second squared or because the elevator was accelerating "upward" at 10 meters per second squared. No experiment the person performed could distinguish the difference between the two situations.

Einstein realized that the equivalence between gravity and acceleration could be described by the geometry of space-time. In effect, objects with mass warp the **space and time** around them and the shape of space-time determines the motion of objects. Objects move along geodesics in space-time that differ from Euclidean geometry. An example of a geodesic is the shortest distance between two points on a globe. For instance, to go from New York to Paris, a flat map would seem to indicate that the shortest distance is obtained by going directly east. But a globe reveals that the shortest distance is a path called the *great circle route* that travels far north over Greenland then drops south into France. As space-time is curved by massive objects, a number of geometric consequences occur.

The first prediction of general relativity that was shown to be true involved the anomalous shift of the perihelion of the planet Mercury—the planet closest to the sun. This phenomenon, in which Mercury orbits in a slightly shifting rosette-like pattern, was known before Einstein developed his theory but was not accurately explained by Newton's law of gravity, which predicted a more nearly fixed elliptical orbit. Other predictions of general relativity that have been observed include gravitational lensing in which the massive gravitational field from large objects actually bends light traveling from distant galaxies, and gravitational red shift in which the expansion of space-time shifts the wavelength of light. In addition, general relativity predicts that time will slow down for an observer in a stronger gravitational field compared to one in a weaker gravitational field. Such an effect has been observed in very precise measurements.

General relativity also predicts that objects should produce distortions of the geometry of space-time known as gravitational waves. Such waves have now been observed and give even more evidence for the validity of general relativity (Abbot et al. 2016). General relativity describes black holes as well. A black hole is a region of space with enough mass concentrated into it so that a huge gravitational force is produced. This force of gravity is so strong that nothing can escape its gravitational pull, not even light. Consequently, the space around this concentration of mass would appear dark with no light emitted from it.

The general theory of relativity has been extensively tested and so far has been found to make extremely accurate predictions. However, despite its extreme success, there is, as of yet,

no theory of gravity that is also compatible with the very successful theory of quantum mechanics (see **Quantum Physics**).

Michael G. Strauss

REFERENCES AND RECOMMENDED READING

Abbott, B. P., R. Abbott, T. D. Abbott, et al. 2016. "Observation of Gravitational Waves from a Binary Black Hole." LIGO Scientific Collaboration and Virgo Collaboration. *Physical Review Letters* 116 (February 12): 061102.
Einstein, Albert. 1920. *Relativity, the Special and General Theory*. New York: Henry Holt.
Geroch, Robert. 1981. *General Relativity from A to B*. Chicago: Chicago University Press.

RELATIVITY, SPECIAL THEORY OF. The special theory of relativity was developed by **Albert Einstein** and published in 1905. It describes the relationship of **space and time** between two different inertial reference frames, that is, two different frames of reference that are moving at constant speed with respect to each other, but not accelerating with respect to each other. The theory is called the *special* theory because of the limitation that the reference frames are inertial, while the *general* **theory of relativity** discards that restriction.

There are two foundational postulates in special relativity that give rise to a number of nonintuitive results regarding space and time. All predictions of special relativity have been experimentally verified. The two postulates are (1) the laws of **physics** are identical in all inertial reference frames, and (2) the **speed of light** in a vacuum is the same for all observers, regardless of the speed of the source of the light or the speed of the observer. (The speed of light in a vacuum is approximately 300 million meters per second or 186,000 miles per second.) The second postulate was made by Einstein because the theories of Newtonian mechanics and Maxwell's electromagnetism were incompatible and because there seemed to be no unique reference frame in which Maxwell's equations were valid.

The consequences of these two postulates have changed our understanding of space and time. Some of the consequences include the ideas of simultaneity, time dilation, length contraction, the equivalence of mass and energy, the addition of velocities, and the maximum speed limit in the universe.

Two events that occur simultaneously in one reference frame will not occur simultaneously in a different inertial reference frame. Consequently, the idea of an absolute time scale is not meaningful in our universe.

When an observer observes another reference frame moving with respect to her, two things will appear to change. The length of objects will shorten (length contraction) in the direction parallel to the direction of motion, and the time interval between events will lengthen (time dilation). It is as if some length is exchanged for some time interval. The observer in the "moving" frame will not notice these effects. They will only be visible by the observer in the "stationary" frame of reference.

Special relativity implies that no object with a mass can ever reach the speed of light in a vacuum and every object without mass will always travel at that speed. This universal speed limit imposes severe limitations on the extent to which any life-form can travel throughout the universe. The nearest star to the earth is about 4.2 light-years away, meaning that the minimum amount of time it would take to reach the nearest star, traveling at the speed of light, would be 4.2 years. The fastest spaceship humans have ever launched traveled about 0.005 percent of the speed of light.

Speeds must be added using ideas of Lorentz transformations rather than Galilean transformations. For instance, if a spaceship were traveling at 50 percent of the speed of light relative to a "stationary" observer and a cannon attached to the spaceship shot a projectile forward at a speed of 50 percent of the speed of light relative to the spaceship, the observer would not measure the speed of the projectile as equal to the speed of light but equal to something somewhat less than that speed.

Relativistic effects as described above occur at all speeds but are not noticeable at speeds usually attained by humans. A general rule of thumb is that they only become noticeable when two reference frames are moving at a relative speed of about 10 percent of the speed of light. At such speeds, relativistic effects give corrections to nonrelativistic calculations of about 0.5 percent. At 50 percent of the speed of light, relativistic effects give about 16 percent corrections, and at 90 percent of the speed of light they correct the nonrelativistic calculations by about a factor of 2.2.

Special relativity also provides the famous equation $E=mc^2$ where E is energy, m is mass, and c is the speed of light in a vacuum. The interpretation of this equation is that mass is equal to energy, or sometimes stated that mass is a form of energy.

Some of the implications of special relativity can be relevant when trying to explain God's characteristics to a nontheist. For example, because elapsed time is dependent on speed, an object traveling at the speed of light does not have any time pass in relation to a stationary observer. In other words, if you could actually travel at the speed of light, you could be everywhere in the universe at the same time. Since an object confined to the laws of physics can, in theory, be everywhere at one time, then the omnipresence of a deity not bound by the laws of physics seems to be easily comprehensible. In any case, the special theory of relativity with its implications about the relativity of space and time requires that we give credence to the possibility of a being with an ability to maximally manipulate space and time.

Michael G. Strauss

REFERENCES AND RECOMMENDED READING

Craig, William Lane. 1990. "God and Real Time." *Religious Studies* 26:335–47. www.reasonablefaith.org/god-and-real-time.
———. 1994. "The Special Theory of Relativity and Theories of Divine Eternity." *Faith and Philosophy* 11:19–37. www.reasonablefaith.org/the-special-theory-of-relativity-and-theories-of-divine-eternity.
Giancoli, Douglas. 2014. *Physics: Principles with Applications.* 7th ed. San Francisco: Pearson.
Taylor, Edwin, and John Wheeler. 1992. *Spacetime Physics.* New York: Macmillan.

RELIGION. Religion can be defined as a set of beliefs and practices bound up with the core of a person's **worldview**, intended to facilitate a connection to some form of transcendence. Before explaining the components of this definition, some comments on definitions of religion in general are in order.

This definition does not prescribe what a religion should be, but tries to bring under one descriptive umbrella as many of the systems of belief and practice that we usually call "religions" as possible. Many cultures do not have a term that translates directly as "religion," so it is somewhat artificial to single out one aspect of their culture that, for them, is simply a part of the total order of their lives. For example, South Asian cultures often refer to a religion as the *dharma*, the "way," which encompasses both societal and spiritual norms.

Some writers contend that "religion" cannot be defined. For some of them, the variations among what we call "religions" are so overwhelming that we cannot group them all together on the basis of a common core (Hopfe 1994, 4–5; James 1902). Still, a summary of its most frequent meanings seems to be useful. Others (e.g., Spiegelberg 1956) claim that the subject matter of religion is too sacred or too deep to be captured by human concepts without doing damage to it. Typically, such writers violate their own precept and go on to write at length on the ineffable nature of religion by substituting a thoroughly ambiguous term. For example, Spiegelberg insists that to define religion "would be a fatal error, for religion is utterly indefinable, as is its object" (1956, 7). He goes on to say that religions occupy themselves with the "Miracle of Being," which he declares to be "supralogical," and which therefore "has the advantage of certainty" (1956, 22), a claim that can neither be supported nor refuted due to its lack of meaningful content.

Paul Tillich's concept of religion as "ultimate concern" is similar in certain respects (Tillich 1951, 11–15). He elevates the ultimate concern of Christian theology above all others because it is "that which determines our being and not-being" (1951, 14). He points to God as the proper ultimate concern for Christians, but emphasizes that there are many improper objects of ultimate concern, such as nationalist ideologies, which thus constitute religions, albeit idolatrous ones (1951, 13). The problem with such a broad definition is that it is no longer possible to maintain the distinction between religion and nonreligion.

The definition of religion at the outset of this article included the concept of transcendence. An entity is transcendent when it surpasses the limits of our finite existence. For example, the Christian doctrine of God's transcendence implies that since God is infinite, he exceeds the properties of his creation in all of his attributes. By saying that a religion is concerned with something transcendent, we do not intend to say that all religions refer to one identical transcendent reality, as John Hick does with his concept of "The Real." The point is that a religion will have some aspect, entity, or goal (real or unreal) that can be classified as transcendent.

Transcendence can take on many forms. It may show up as God or gods, a spirit world, an inner Self, or even paradoxically something that is entirely immanent, the opposite of transcendence in the dictionary. Such is the case with **pantheism**, the worldview according to which God and the world are identical (thus constituting ultimate immanence), while God also has attributes of transcendence that exceed those of the world, such as **infinity**, eternity, or immutability.

By insisting that religions contain an element of transcendence, we are able to put a restraint on what counts as religion. Some writers define religion in terms of whatever constitutes the "pivotal value" (Monk et al. 1973, 3) in a person's life. However, similar to Tillich, that term could leave the door open to ideologies such as communism that are intentionally materialistic, atheistic, and antireligious qualifying as religions. The pivotal value of a religion must be transcendent, and thus we maintain the required distinction.

We must also reverse that point and say that the transcendental value of a religion must be pivotal. A genuine religion must reside at the core of a person's worldview. By "worldview" we mean the fundamental conceptual framework of categories that help us make sense of our existence. Our response to issues such as how we perceive the world around us, how we make ethical decisions, or why our lives have significance are guided by our worldviews. A religious worldview does so by directing a person to an object of transcendence. Thereby religion reassures people that whatever misery may disturb their present lives is not the final word on the subject. For example, the guilt incurred by sin, the restraints of a corruptible material body, or the inability to cope with the crises of life can be approached more successfully from the perspective of a transcendent outlook. The details vary, of course. Not all religions are salvation oriented, but they all address serious issues with a transcendent factor.

The above observation leads us to make another important distinction, namely, between a full religion and fragments of religious concepts. It is possible (and probably happens quite often) that someone may affirm a belief that has originated in a religion without subscribing to the religion as a whole. For example, believing that people ought to keep the Ten Commandments is an appropriation of a religious concept, but if this belief has no further religious connections, it would be inappropriate to say that such a single, isolated belief constitutes a religion. A person whose basic understanding of the universe is materialistic and whose goal in life is to acquire material wealth, but who also happens to allow for the **existence of God** without further impact on his existence, can hardly be said to be religious.

We also need to stress that an adequate understanding of a religion includes certain beliefs that can be expressed in statements that are either true or false. It is not necessary to expect that everything about a transcendent entity can be put into words, but if nothing can be said, nothing can be believed. Christians do not believe that they fully comprehend God, but they do believe that they have some true knowledge of him. Advaita Hinduism holds that the highest reality, Brahman, has no attributes or forms (*Brahman nirguna*), but makes the proviso that it can be spoken of as though it had attributes (*Brahman saguna*).

Religious practices usually create a life-world that exceeds its minimum requirements and carries cultural expressions with it. There are the direct human actions, such as praying, chanting, singing, sacrificing a chicken, making a pilgrimage, fasting, meditating, and so forth. In addition, a religion typically has its own physical and cultural conventions, ranging from sitting on pews in a building with a steeple while singing from a hymnal to meditating underneath a lone tree in the desert to performing a rain dance. The combination of the practices and their surrounding setting are called the religion's *cultus*. The preservation of a cultus requires that most religions can function only within the context of a community, but if it were not for individual expressions of a religion, there could be no reform or revival (see **Science and Theology**).

Winfried Corduan

REFERENCES AND RECOMMENDED READING

Hopfe, Lewis. 1994. *Religions of the World*. 6th ed. New York: Macmillan.
James, William. 1902. *The Varieties of Religious Experience: A Study in Human Nature*. London: Longmans, Green.
Monk, Robert C., Walter C. Hofheinz, Kenneth T. Lawrence, et al. 1973. *Exploring Religious Meaning*. Englewood Cliffs, NJ: Prentice Hall.
Spiegelberg, Frederic. 1956. *Living Religions of the World*. Englewood Cliffs, NJ: Prentice Hall.
Tillich, Paul. 1951. *Systematic Theology*. Vol. 1. Chicago: University of Chicago Press.

RELIGIOUS EXPERIENCE. A religious experience can be characterized as an experience that is understood by the person as having religious meaning and being of a reality that is beyond the person. In a broad sense, religious experience refers to any experience of the sacred within a religious context, including religious feelings, visions, and mystical and numinous experiences. Such an experience is generally intensely personal, and it often occurs in the midst of religious practices such as **prayer**, meditation, worship, chanting, or other religious rituals. Different schemas have been used to describe and classify the diverse types of religious experience. One such schema distinguishes three categories of experience: regenerative, charismatic, and mystical.

A *regenerative religious experience* is one in which the experiencer undergoes a life transformation or conversion. Through such experiences, individuals often find their lives to be changed, filled with meaning and purpose, and full of love, compassion, and hope. Another facet of the regenerative experience is moral transformation. In this case, prior to the experience, the individual may feel a sense of sin, guilt, or the inability to do what she or he knows to be morally appropriate. Upon having the regenerative religious experience, the person senses that sin and guilt have been removed and a new vision of goodness is seen and pursued.

Another category of religious experience is *charismatic*

experience. With this experience, special abilities, gifts, or blessings are manifested. Such experiences may include healing, speaking in tongues, prophesying, dreaming, and having visions. While charismatic experiences are described in the Bible, they are not limited to the Judeo-Christian tradition.

Mystical experience is a third category. **William James** (1842–1910) attributed to such experiences four distinct characteristics (James 1902, 370–72):

ineffability—the experience cannot be adequately described, if at all;

noetic quality—the experiencer believes that he has learned something important from the experience;

transiency—the experience is temporary and the experiencer soon returns to a "normal" state of mind; and

passivity—the experience occurs without conscious decision or control, and it cannot be brought to happen at will.

Rudolf Otto (1869–1937) described a particular type of mystical experience as a *mysterium tremendum*. He noted that such an experience sometimes comes "sweeping like a gentle tide, pervading the **mind** with a tranquil mood of deepest worship." It may also "burst in sudden eruption up from the depths of the **soul** with spasms and convulsions, or lead to the strangest excitements, to intoxicated frenzy, to transport, and to ecstasy." With these experiences, the individual may feel an "absolute overpoweringness" or a sense of "fear" and "dread" or an alluring "awe" that is "beautiful and pure and glorious" (Otto 1923, 12–23).

Mystical experiences may be focused on some particular individual, such as Jesus or Krishna, or on some object, such as an icon or statue. Or there may be no identified object in the experience. Yet they commonly reflect an encounter with an "other"—a separate self or will or power that forces itself on the **consciousness** of the experiencer, unexpectedly and profoundly.

Those having religious experiences generally take them to be authentic experiences of an actual reality beyond themselves. Is it reasonable to agree with them? To put the question differently, do such experiences provide reasons for religious belief? Or are there naturalistic explanations for religious experience? Work in the sciences—both the **social sciences** and physical sciences—has attempted to answer these questions. Two scientific approaches to religious experience will be considered here.

First, there are various psychological explanations of

religious experience. **Sigmund Freud** (1856–1939) argued that feelings of helplessness and fear in childhood foster a desire for fatherly, loving protection. This desire, or wish, for a protective figure carries on into adulthood and demands a greater, more powerful being than a human father. Two further desires are prominent: the substantiation of universal justice and a continuation of our own existence after **death**. According to Freud, these combined wishes are satisfied through the illusion of divine **Providence**, belief in, and even experience of, such a divine reality. Freud's wish fulfillment hypothesis of religious experience was primarily directed at theistic religion in which a heavenly father replaced an earthly one as provider. But it can apply to all types of religious experience, with the conclusion that such experiences are psychological projections that fulfill certain fundamental human needs and longings.

Second, while it may well be true that a particular religious experience is brought about by certain needs and desires, Freud's conclusion does not necessarily follow. Suppose that one believes in the existence of a personal and powerful God because of a deep-seated need for a heavenly Father. Does that prove that a personal and powerful God does not exist? It seems not. Perhaps we were created with such a need. Indeed, this is precisely what many Jews, Christians, Muslims, and Hindus actually believe and is how they interpret passages in their sacred Scriptures that refer to God as Father, Provider, Protector, and so on.

Looking at the physical sciences, recent work in **neuroscience** has led to a field of study dubbed "neurotheology," which bridges the fields of neuroscience and theology. One type of question raised in neurotheology concerns the ontological status of religious experiences. Some affirm that neurological explanations of religious experiences discredit them or demonstrate their nonveridical or delusional nature. Brain events that occur during religious experiences are similar to, or even identical with, the types of brain events that occur when having seizures or when induced with drugs. Some have concluded that therefore religious experiences are nothing more than physical brain events; there need not be a reality beyond the brain that produced them.

However, as many philosophers have pointed out, all experiences have a corresponding neurological state. Thus it is a fallacy to claim that an experience is illusory or delusional because there is a corresponding brain event. Following this fallacious line of thought would lead one to conclude that all sensory experiences are illusory or delusional since they all have a corresponding brain state.

From whatever perspective they are studied or experienced, perhaps because of their unusual and sometimes outlandish manifestations, religious experiences continue to capture the attention of religious believers and skeptics alike.

Chad Meister

REFERENCES AND RECOMMENDED READING
Alston, William. 1991. *Perceiving God*. Ithaca, NY: Cornell University Press.
Donovan, Peter. 1979. *Interpreting Religious Experience*. New York: Seabury.
Freud, Sigmund. (1927) 1989. *The Future of an Illusion*. Trans. James Strachey. New York: W. W. Norton.
Griffith-Dickson, Gwen. 2000. *Human and Divine: An Introduction to the Philosophy of Religious Experience*. London: Duckworth.
James, William. 1902. *The Varieties of Religious Experience*. New York: Modern Library.
Jantzen, Grace. 1995. *Power, Gender and Christian Mysticism*. Cambridge: Cambridge University Press.
Moser, Paul. 2008. *The Elusive God: Reorienting Religious Epistemology*. New York: Cambridge University Press.
Otto, Rudolf. 1923. *The Idea of the Holy*. Oxford: Oxford University Press.

RESURRECTION OF JESUS. For Christian **theism**, no subject surpasses the resurrection of Jesus in terms of its uniqueness, significance, and versatility. Whether addressing the heart of soteriology via its message of the gospel's content, the believer's ultimate hope of eternal life, or the sheer evidential force of its multifaceted historical argument, the resurrection of Jesus remains Christianity's central teaching.

Theological Importance and Significance

Contemporary theologians, whatever their theological inclinations, generally agree that Jesus's resurrection from the dead occupies the very heart of Christianity. Strangely enough, even those scholars who tend to reject this literal event still usually insist on its centrality.

Jesus's resurrection is mentioned in more than 300 New Testament verses. No author sums up the matter more clearly than does the apostle Paul. As he states in an ever-rising crescendo, if Christ was not raised from the dead, then Christian preaching is vain, as is our faith. Further, without the resurrection, believers would still be lost in their sins. It follows, then, that there would be no Christian hope for our loved ones who had died in Christ either. In sum, if this depressing picture of no resurrection represents the extent of our confidence, then we are surely the most pitiable and forlorn of all persons (1 Cor. 15:12–19).

However, Paul continues, the entire picture is exactly reversed if Christ has indeed been raised from the dead. At the head of the list is that Jesus's resurrection ensures the believer's own resurrection (1 Cor. 15:20–23). In fact, apart from a resurrection, we may as well live for the sake of present pleasures until we die, for there is no foundation for anything further (v. 32). Thus everything from theology to apologetics to practice clearly stands or falls with this event.

Paul is not alone in this stance. From the earliest traditions contained in Paul's epistles (which actually predate his teachings) through the remainder of the New Testament, this is the overall message and approach. The risen Christ is clearly the center of the gospel proclamation (Rom. 4:24–25; 10:9). As the chief sign indicating that Jesus's message is true (Matt. 12:38–40; 16:1–4; Luke 24:46–47), this event evidences the truth of the Christian proclamation (Acts 2:22–24; 17:29–31; Rom. 1:3–4). Moreover, the resurrection is the pattern for both the believer's risen life, as well as the new life we live now (1 John 3:2–3), providing the greatest joy even in spite of suffering and persecution (1 Peter 1:3–9).

In short, Jesus's resurrection from the dead grounds the entire breadth of Christian theism. It provides the basis for the most central tenets of faith, as well as the reasoning and foundation not only for its truth, but also for practicing its disciplines in our present lives. But did this event occur literally in history?

The Historicity Of Jesus's Resurrection: The Minimal Facts Method

The minimal facts method is an approach to arguing for the historicity of the resurrection. Surveying the historical landscape surrounding the **death** and resurrection of Jesus, a handful of particular facts are distinguished as especially well-established according to recent scholars. These historical facts are confirmed by multiple factual considerations, whether historical, medical, or archaeological. As a result, these events are recognized as historical by the vast majority of even skeptical scholars who study them. These "minimal" facts are the ones that form the groundwork for the historicity of the resurrection. The specific minimal facts employed vary from scholar to scholar. To bolster the case for the resurrection, some condense the number utilized from approximately a dozen to between just three and seven in order to make the strongest case.

Choosing simply five of these facts, we could highlight (1) the death of Jesus by crucifixion, (2) followed by Jesus's disciples having experiences that they were totally convinced were appearances of their risen Lord. (3) These disciples preached and taught this message very early after the events themselves. (4) James, the previously unbelieving brother of

Jesus, also had an experience that he, too, thought was an appearance of the risen Jesus. (5) Last, Saul the persecutor was also convinced that he likewise had seen the risen Christ.

If additional minimal facts were desired or deemed useful, these could include the transformations of these early disciples into followers who were more than willing to die for their conviction that they had seen the resurrected Jesus, as well as the centrality of this message. Other data could also be mentioned in this category of widely accepted historical facts.

These particulars can also argue decisively against each of the major naturalistic responses to these facts. In other words, even this reduced list of critically recognized **information** is sufficient to constitute a strong argument for the resurrection, as well as revealing the inadequacies of alternative responses. Further, this can all be done with a minimum amount of data that are so exceptionally well-established that virtually all critical scholars recognize their historicity (see Habermas 2003, chap. 1). This sort of method has perplexed some skeptical scholars, who have designated this approach as the strongest angle yet on the resurrection argument.

Scientific and Philosophical Rejoinders to the Resurrection Evidence

The most common response to the minimal facts approach is not to question the historical foundation itself, which is a concession to its strength. Rather, the chief route (especially among naturalists) is to question the assumed miraculous nature of the event and to assert that **miracles** are either impossible or at least highly unlikely (see **Miracles**). It is also charged that such events are never observed today, or that extraordinary evidence is necessary in order to show that exceptional events have occurred.

These charges often share the assumption that miracles are contrary to nature's laws and cannot be admitted, no matter what evidence is produced for them. Sometimes it is added that no other response is even necessary, given the bombastic nature of the claims. However, several responses can be made here briefly.

Actually, it is not even argued in the minimal facts context that Jesus's resurrection is a miracle. Critics may simply be getting ahead of themselves by inferring that a tighter connection exists here than actually does. It is often argued that a historical case may only show that certain events happened, not that God acted by causing the events—that would involve a theological or philosophical argument from the data. The minimal facts approach is a historical method, so our interest here is whether the historical events in question actually occurred: Did Jesus die by crucifixion and was he seen later? If these events occurred, then the subsequent issues of the nature and extent of God's involvement can be addressed. The latter involves subjects like the truth of Jesus's teachings, as to whether he made claims to deity as well as to being the only path to God, his other miracles, and why only Jesus was raised from the dead and seen on many occasions. But the minimal facts method per se addresses the strictly historical points of the facts that are conceded by virtually all scholars dealing with this subject.

Thus the "miracles are impossible" sort of objection may be a moot point. Neither is this response simply a tricky move to divert the discussion. Here's the twofold question that must be answered: Did Jesus die? Then, was he actually seen again afterward? These historical issues are all that we are attempting to answer via the minimal facts method. Far from smuggling in an assumption of miracles, we have not even posed whether the resurrection is an act of God.

What about the assertion that incredible events such as those recorded in the New Testament are not observed today? Regardless of whether these events are considered to be miracles, this subject has changed significantly in recent years. Many relevant studies have been released in both religious and nonreligious contexts. In fact, a huge number of cases have emerged that parallel quite closely New Testament healings, with dozens even buttressed by both pre- and post-MRIs, CT scans, and X-ray evidence (Keener 2011; see esp. 1:428, 431–32, 435, 440, 463, 491, 503; 2:680, 682n206). This wealth of available data even caused Cambridge University's Richard Bauckham to exclaim, "So who's afraid of David Hume now?" (Keener 2011, vol. 2, back cover endorsement).

Moreover, several recent surveys have shown that a majority of physicians now exhibit positive beliefs concerning scientifically inexplicable medical healings. In one such study, 70 percent of more than 1,100 physicians accepted the possibility of miracles at a rate lagging just slightly behind the general public (HCD Research 2008). Two years later the percentage among another group of over 1,000 physicians was 75 percent (HCD Research 2010).

What about the exceptional evidence that skeptics demand for such claims? Besides the medical data just mentioned, if the more than 100 well-evidenced near-death experiences (NDEs) reveal the likely presence of at least some **consciousness** beyond the initial cessation of measurable heart and brain activity, this would provide evidence for the possibility of Jesus's resurrection (Habermas and Moreland 2004) (see

Near-Death Experiences). For if verified post-near-death awareness already indicates the likelihood of some minimal afterlife realm, and perhaps even far more, then critical scholars should not claim that Jesus's afterlife appearances are impossible.

In sum, the resurrection of Jesus is far from a ridiculous event that only the uneducated believe. Strong historical evidence drawn directly from the critically admitted facts, along with recent data favoring both medical healings as well as NDEs, indicate that we should be much more open to such events. A priori rejections are out of place.

Gary R. Habermas

REFERENCES AND RECOMMENDED READING

Habermas, Gary R. 2003. *The Risen Jesus and Future Hope.* Lanham, MD: Rowman & Littlefield.

Habermas, Gary R., and J. P. Moreland. 2004. *Beyond Death: Exploring the Evidence for Immortality.* Eugene, OR: Wipf and Stock.

HCD Research. 2008. "Religion and Miracles: Doctors and General Public Share Similar Views; Majority of Both Groups Believe in Miracles and Similar Religious Practices." HCD Research. http://204.12.61.19/News/MediacurvesRelease.cfm?M=228.

———. 2010. "National Study: Majority of Physicians Still Believe Miracles Can Occur Today." HCD Research. http://204.12.61.19/news/Mediacurves Release.cfm?M=566.

Keener, Craig. 2011. *Miracles: The Credibility of the New Testament Accounts.* 2 vols. Grand Rapids: Baker Academic.

REVELATION. The most general definition of *revelation* is knowledge received as a gift that stands in need of being understood (Gunton 1995). Christians understand that the ultimate giver of this gift is the triune God. Revelation is mediated through nature, human beings, reading Scripture, and other means.

General and Special Revelation

Theologians usually distinguish *general revelation* (sometimes called *natural revelation*) and *special revelation* (sometimes called *specific revelation*). General revelation is the knowledge of God that is disclosed through nature. This category is usually thought to include very general knowledge about God's power, deity, and so forth. Special revelation is the specific, highly detailed knowledge about God, redemption, and Jesus, the Messiah, found in biblical texts. The doctrine of **providence** would be an example of special revelation.

Creation Revelation

A third, much less discussed subcategory of general revelation is called *creation revelation* (Bavinck 2003, 341–42;

Goheen 1996): specific, detailed knowledge about creation revealed through creation. Theologians typically focus on knowledge of God and therefore rarely discuss creation revelation. In contrast, natural philosophers, such as Albert Magnus, Thomas Aquinas's teacher; **Galileo Galilei**; **Robert Boyle**; and **Isaac Newton**, generally have been very interested in and written much more about creation revelation (the term *scientist* was coined in the nineteenth century and replaced the term *natural philosopher*; one can say that natural philosophers were the scientists of their times). As an example, Galileo wrote that he was "*led by the hand*" in his studies of motion "to the investigation of naturally accelerated motion *by consideration of custom and procedure of nature herself in all her other works*, in the performance of which she habitually employs the first, simplest, and easiest means" (Galilei 1974, 153, emphasis added). Similarly Johannes Kepler wrote, "As we astronomers are priests of the highest God in regard to the book of nature, we are bound to think of the praise of God and not of the glory of our own capacities.... Those laws are within the grasp of the human **mind**; God wanted us to recognize them by creating us after his own image so that we could share in his own thoughts" (Baumgardt 1951, 44, 50).

The biblical basis for creation revelation lies in such passages as Isaiah 28:23–29, where farmers learn farming from working the soil and observing what happens, and Genesis 2:19–20 and 1 Kings 4:29–33, where Adam and Solomon studied and named animals, birds, fish, and other creatures (in the ancient Near East one cannot accurately name something without first knowing the thing, so Adam and Solomon would have had to closely observe creatures before they could name them). In Psalm 104 we find the psalmist praising God for works ranging from grass growing to sustaining streams flowing to homes for animals to the cycles of day/night and the seasons. This psalm is filled with knowledge learned from observing and experiencing creation (cf. Job 12:7–8).

Revelation and Science

One implication is that scientific investigation is an exploration of creation that is a form of creation revelation. Modern Western societies do not associate the sciences with revelation; rather, the sciences and revelation tend to be treated as opposites. One reason for this is that the authority of the Bible often is thought to contrast with the openness of scientific exploration. The former somehow bypasses our human faculties, whereas the latter crucially depends on

them. Special revelation is often thought of as something that must be accepted completely apart from reason and experience, whereas scientific knowledge is only accepted after the stringent application of reason and experience. However, there is less contrast between scientific investigation (creation revelation) and our working with special revelation than is often realized.

First, knowledge gained through the Bible is mediated through practices such as worship, **prayer**, and interpretation; through attempting to live out that revelation to the best of our understanding; through Christian communities coming to an understanding of biblical texts; through the formation and interpretation of creeds; and so forth. Both special revelation and creation revelation are mediated through practices that involve reason and experience.

Second, although scientific inquiry is an open practice, it also relies on a form of provisional authority in the form of authority given to nature, scientists, or societies. For instance, a scientist has to give some kind of provisional authority or trust to other scientists to be able to evaluate their published research appropriately. Although reasons may surface later to withdraw this grant of authority, the kinds of data scientists collect cannot have any evidentiary status in the absence of some such granting of provisional authority. Both special revelation and creation revelation require granting provisional authority if any discovery or learning is to take place.

Third, special revelation and creation revelation are not opposites, but work synergistically. Philosopher of religion and theologian Colin Gunton pointed out that "Revelation speaks to and constitutes human reason, but in such a way as to liberate the energies that are inherent in created rationality" (1993, 212). For example, creation revelation enables human engagement with and discovery of creation's contingent rationality. Scientists study phenomena, uncover and interpret facts and relationships, and find "food for thought." Something similar happens with the study of the Bible. The latter adds forms of human thought and action that would not be available when relying on creation revelation alone. Special revelation also speaks to and shapes human reason when we are open to listening to, struggling with, coming to understand, and learning from it. Both scientific and biblical forms of inquiry are open-ended dialogues.

Finally, the role of the Holy Spirit is crucial to all forms of revelation. The Son is the giver of all forms of revelation through the Spirit. Moreover, it is the Spirit who gives scientists the ability to recognize and grasp knowledge about creation by coming under a form of provisional authority when conforming their thinking to nature. Likewise, it is the Spirit who gives readers of the Scriptures the ability to grasp knowledge about special revelation and come under its authority (John 16:13). The Spirit may work through different means that are best suited for general, creation, or special revelation; there is no mediation-free access to creation or the Bible. For example, basic reliability of reason and sense experience are good gifts of the Spirit, and it is the Spirit who enables us to use those gifts in ways that are appropriate to the study and interpretation of creation or appropriate to the study and interpretation of biblical texts (however, it is humans who use those gifts in more or less responsible ways when we engage in these activities).

The reason-revelation dichotomy underlying worries about revelation and scientific inquiry is a distinctly modern one (Turner 1986). Classical Greek natural philosophers operated with a largely seamless relationship between reason and revelation. While it is the case that some early Christian theologians made strong distinctions between reason and revelation (e.g., Tertullian), far more often one sees these early theologians grappling with biblical texts as reason *and* revelation as they seek to understand the Bible and its implications. Medieval European thinkers likewise conceived of reason and revelation being inseparable.

The justifications biblical authors produced often were not empirical in the sense we expect for the natural sciences (e.g., truth telling and argument sometimes took the form of poetry and parables). Nevertheless, their justifications often are the results of argumentation and the interpretation of experience as so much of the rationality of life is. As Eric Osborne notes, the early Christian following of the rule of faith involved the life and practice of the Christian communities as much as it was interpretation of the Bible. As such, it was inseparable from reason: the rule was used to make room for reason in the life of the church as much as it was an exercise of reason (Osborne 1989). Revelation as gift underlies scientific practice as much as it does religious practice.

Robert C. Bishop

REFERENCES AND RECOMMENDED READING

Baumgardt, C. 1951. *Johannes Kepler: Life and Letters.* New York: Philosophical Library.
Bavinck, H. 2003. *Reformed Dogmatics.* Vol. 1, *Prolegomena.* Ed. John Bolt. Trans. John Vriend. Grand Rapids: Baker Academic.
Galilei, G. 1974. *Two New Sciences, Including Centers of Gravity and Force of Percussion.* Ed. and trans. Stillman Drake. Madison: University of Wisconsin Press.
Goheen, M. 1996. "Scriptural Revelation, Creational Revelation and Natural Science: The Issue." In *Facets of Faith and Science.* Vol. 4, *Interpreting God's Action in the World.* Ed. Jitse M. Van der Meer, 331–43. Lanham, MD: University Press of America.
Gunton, C. 1993. *The One, the Three and the Many: God, Creation and the Culture of Modernity.* The 1992 Bampton Lectures. Cambridge: Cambridge University Press.
———. 1995. *A Brief Theology of Revelation.* London: T&T Clark.
Osborn, E. R. 1989. "Reason and the Rule of Faith in the Second Century AD." In *The Making of Orthodoxy: Essays in Honor of Henry Chadwick.* Ed. Rowan Williams, 40–61. Cambridge: Cambridge University Press.
Turner, J. 1986. *Without God, without Creed: The Origins of Unbelief in America.* Baltimore: Johns Hopkins University Press.

ROSS, HUGH. Hugh Ross (1945–) is an astronomer, pastor, and founder of **Reasons to Believe** (RTB), a science apologetics ministry whose mission is "to spread the Christian gospel by demonstrating that sound reason and scientific research—including the very latest discoveries—consistently support, rather than erode, confidence in the truth of the Bible and faith in the personal, transcendent God revealed in both Scripture and nature" (RTB).

Born in Montreal and raised in Vancouver, Canada, Ross earned an undergraduate degree in **physics** from the University of British Columbia and a PhD in **astronomy** from the University of Toronto. Postdoctoral studies on quasars brought him (in the early 1970s) to the California Institute of Technology in Pasadena, the city from which he would launch RTB in 1986.

Ongoing development of a scientifically testable creation model ranks as Ross's seminal contribution to the Christian apologetics enterprise. The model aims to meet all the scientific requirements—detailed, specific, adaptable, falsifiable, and predictive. It provides a framework that challenges secular scientists to rethink the philosophical **paradigm** of **non-overlapping magisteria** (NOMA) in favor of a compatible, organic union of science and faith.

Ross's *constructive integration* approach incorporates the classical historic Christian "two books" view of the harmony between general **revelation** (science) and special revelation (Scripture). He adopts a *concordist* view, which seeks general agreement between properly interpreted Scripture passages that describe some aspect of the natural realm and established, well-understood scientific data (see **Concordism**; **Two Books Metaphor**).

Across the spectrum of creationist views, Ross subscribes to day-age, old-earth creation (see **Days of Creation**; **Old-Earth Creationism**). As such, his position is to be distinguished from, among others, **young-earth creationism**, **evolutionary**

creationism, and the **intelligent design** movement. Ross and his staff of research scholars at RTB endorse the Chicago Statement on Biblical Inerrancy.

Critics, both atheists and Christians, assert that Ross "reads science into Scripture" where it is unwarranted. Others find fault with his proposal that God's transdimensionality may resolve difficult theological concepts such as **the Trinity** and predestination versus free will. However, Ross's views are endorsed by many evangelical leaders and pastors as aligned with Christian orthodoxy.

Ross has addressed students and faculty on more than 300 campuses in the United States and abroad on a wide variety of science-faith topics. He has written many books, including *The Fingerprint of God, The Creator and the Cosmos, Beyond the Cosmos, A Matter of Days, Creation as Science, Why the Universe Is the Way It Is, More Than a Theory, Hidden Treasures in the Book of Job, Improbable Planet,* and *Navigating Genesis.* Ross has been nominated for the Templeton Prize, and in 2012 he won the Trotter Prize, delivering the Trotter Lecture at Texas A&M University titled "Theistic Implications of Big Bang Cosmology."

Motivated by the Great Commission, Ross and his ministry (now located in Covina, California) use science as a bridge to reach nonbelievers with the truth of the gospel. RTB's guiding biblical imperative is to "revere Christ as Lord. Always be prepared to give an answer to everyone who asks you to give the reason for the hope that you have. But do this with gentleness and respect, keeping a clear conscience" (1 Peter 3:15–16).

Joe Aguirre

REFERENCES AND RECOMMENDED READING

Reasons to Believe. "Mission and Beliefs." Accessed November 16, 2015. www.reasons.org/about/our-mission. See also www.reasons.org/about/who-we-are/hugh-ross.
Ross, Hugh. 1991. *The Fingerprint of God.* Orange, CA: Promise.
———. 1993. *The Creator and the Cosmos.* 3rd exp. ed. Colorado Springs: NavPress.
———. 1999. *Beyond the Cosmos.* 2nd exp. ed. Colorado Springs: NavPress.
———. 2001. "Beyond the Stars: An Astronomer's Quest." In *The Day I Met God: Extraordinary Stories of Life-Changing Miracles.* Eds. Jim and Karen Covell and Victorya Michaels Rogers, 47–51. Sisters, OR: Multnomah.
———. 2006a. *Creation as Science.* Colorado Springs: NavPress.
———. 2006b. "Why I Believe in the Miracle of Divine Creation." In *Why I Am a Christian: Leading Thinkers Explain Why They Believe.* Ed. Norman L. Geisler, 135–59. Grand Rapids: Baker.
———. 2008. *Why the Universe Is the Way It Is.* Grand Rapids: Baker.
———. 2009. *More Than a Theory.* Grand Rapids: Baker.
———. 2011. *Hidden Treasures in the Book of Job.* Grand Rapids: Baker.
———. 2014. *Navigating Genesis.* Covina, CA: RTB Press.
———. 2015. *A Matter of Days.* 2nd exp. ed. Covina, CA: RTB Press.

RUSE, MICHAEL. Michael Ruse (1940–) is a historian of biology and the Lucyle T. Werkmeister Professor of Philosophy at Florida State University. Though an atheist, he was raised as a conservative Quaker in the United Kingdom, where he was educated at private Quaker schools. Ruse then attended Bristol University (BA, 1962), McMaster University (MA, 1965), and Bristol University (PhD in philosophy, 1970).

Beginning his academic training in **mathematics**, Ruse moved into the **philosophy of science**, and after earning his doctorate, he became one of the founders of the philosophical discipline now known as the philosophy of biology. While teaching philosophy, the history of science, and zoology at the University of Guelph in Ontario (from 1965 to 2000), Ruse published an influential series of books, including *The Philosophy of Biology* (1973), *The Darwinian Revolution* (1979), *Darwinism Defended* (1982), and *Taking Darwin Seriously* (1986); here he staked out the positions he has consistently maintained since, such as the centrality of **natural selection** to biological explanation, the evolutionary (or naturalistic) grounding of ethics, and the supremacy of materialist understanding of origins over creationist or theistic interpretations.

In the last capacity — i.e., as a philosophical defender of neo-Darwinian evolutionary theory — Ruse was enlisted by the American Civil Liberties Union to serve as an expert witness on the philosophy of science in the 1981 federal trial *McLean v. Arkansas,* in which the constitutionality of Arkansas's so-called balanced treatment law, Act 590, about the teaching of evolution and creationism, was under scrutiny. Ruse's testimony about the nature of science, incorporated into Judge William Overton's ruling overturning the law, brought harsh criticism from other philosophers of science (notably, Philip Quinn, **Larry Laudan**, and Barry Gross), commencing a debate about the proper role of philosophers of science in public policy controversies that continues today.

Ruse's critics argued that his Arkansas testimony misrepresented the **complexity** of demarcating science from other parts of human knowledge and inquiry by promulgating an erroneous positivist definition that was philosophically indefensible (see **Creationism, Intelligent Design, and the Courts; Demarcation, Problem of; Logical Positivism; Philosophy of Science**). In response, Ruse contended that his testimony was governed not by the broad standards of the seminar room, but rather by the much narrower context of legal disputes, where bright and clear criteria are required—a position he later challenged himself in a 1993 lecture to the American Association for the Advancement of Science (Ruse 1993). (Many of the relevant writings arising from this debate can be found in Ruse 1988.) In 1986 Ruse and colleague David Hull founded the journal *Biology & Philosophy*, which Ruse edited until 2000, surrendering his editorship upon his move to Florida State University, where he assumed the Lucyle T. Werkmeister chair of philosophy (2000–).

Although himself an atheist, Ruse has collaborated with intelligent design theorists like **William Dembski** in editing an anthology on the design debate (Dembski and Ruse 2004), and has been an outspoken critic of the "**New Atheists**," calling their position "a bloody disaster" and "doing terrible political damage to the cause of Creationism fighting." For a comprehensive personal account of Ruse's career and interests, see his interview with Clifford Sosis (Sosis 2015).

Paul Nelson

REFERENCES AND RECOMMENDED READING

Dembski, W., and M. Ruse, eds. 2004. *Debating Design: From Darwin to DNA* (Cambridge: Cambridge University Press).

Ruse, M., ed. 1988. *But Is It Science? The Philosophical Question in the Creation/ Evolution Controversy.* Buffalo, NY: Prometheus.

———. 1993. Lecture to the Annual Meeting of the American Association for the Advancement of Science, at the symposium "The New Antievolutionism." Boston. February 13. www.arn.org/docs/orpages/or151/mr93tran.htm.

Sosis, Clifford. 2015. "What Is It Like to Be a Philosopher? Interview with Michael Ruse." www.whatisitliketobeaphilosopher.com/michaelruse.

RUSSELL, BERTRAND. Bertrand Arthur William Russell (1872–1970) was a well-known British philosopher, logician, social and political activist, and man of letters. He was born into an aristocratic family, orphaned at the age of four, raised by his grandmother, and educated at home with the help of private tutors. He studied **mathematics** and philosophy at Cambridge University from 1890 to 1893 and, after a brief flirtation with British **idealism**, led a revolt against it, becoming one of the founders of modern analytic philosophy along with his German predecessor Gottlob Frege (1848–1925), his British contemporary G. E. Moore (1873–1958), and his Austrian protégé **Ludwig Wittgenstein** (1889–1951).

For his work with **Alfred North Whitehead** (1861–1947) on the *Principia Mathematica* (1910–13), Russell is recognized as one of the premier logicians of the twentieth century. His writings have had a profound influence on developments in logic, set theory, computer science, **artificial intelligence**, **cognitive science**, linguistics, and philosophy—in the last

case, most especially in the philosophy of mathematics, philosophy of logic, philosophy of language, **metaphysics**, and **epistemology**. In the philosophy of language, his seminal essay "On Denoting" (1905) continues to be a focal point of discussion and is universally recognized as a **paradigm** of the analytic method.

But Russell was also passionately involved in politics and social reform and wrote extensively and popularly on such issues as war, pacifism, nuclear disarmament, sexual ethics, happiness, and religion. In this latter regard, his most famous student, the philosopher Ludwig Wittgenstein, once amusingly remarked that "Russell's works should be bound in two colors: those dealing with mathematical **logic** in red—and all students of philosophy should read them; those dealing with ethics and politics in blue—and no one should be allowed to read them" (Monk 1990, 471).

Russell's views on **morality** and religion will be treated briefly at the end of this discussion; in the meantime, note that, among his varied and voluminous writings, his most philosophically important works are generally regarded to be *A Critical Exposition of the Philosophy of Leibniz* (1900), *The Principles of Mathematics* (1903a), *Principia Mathematica* (3 vols., with A. N. Whitehead, 1910–13), *The Problems of Philosophy* (1912), *Our Knowledge of the External World* (1914), *The Analysis of Mind* (1921), *The Analysis of Matter* (1927), *An Inquiry into Meaning and Truth* (1940), *Human Knowledge: Its Scope and Limits* (1948), and the collection of essays *Logic and Knowledge* (1956).

Russell was elected a fellow of the Royal Society of London in 1908, named the third Earl Russell in 1931 after the death of his brother Frank, received the Order of Merit from the king of England in 1949, and was awarded the Nobel Prize in Literature in 1950 "in recognition of his varied and significant writings in which he champions humanitarian ideals and freedom of thought" (Nobel Prizes and Laureates).

When Russell went to Cambridge as an undergraduate in 1890, he came under the influence of neo-Hegelianism and flirted with John McTaggart's (1866–1925) form of idealism, but he abandoned it when he discovered it could not be extended consistently in a purely logical way to deal with problems in the foundations of mathematics. He then moved to an extreme form of Platonic realism, adumbrated in his book *A Critical Exposition of the Philosophy of Leibniz* (1900) and more fully expressed in *The Principles of Mathematics* (1903a). This latter work was a seminal treatise for the logicist school in the philosophy of mathematics, which held that the whole of pure mathematics is deductively derivable from logical principles, so the foundations of mathematics ultimately rest on logic.

Under the influence of his mentor, Alfred North Whitehead, Russell soon moved away from his extreme Platonism to the view that mathematical entities are logical constructions, that is, they do not exist as imperceptible real entities, but rather mathematical truths are translatable into logical truths and the whole of pure mathematics is merely a development from logic. When we discuss the arithmetical properties of a number, for instance, we are not discussing a Platonic entity; rather, we are talking about the properties of a certain class of classes of things, the members of which can be set into one-to-one correspondence with the members of a given class. Working out the details of this program, the end result of which was the three volumes of the *Principia Mathematica*, took Russell and Whitehead a full decade.

Achieving the requisite derivation of mathematics from logic required a great deal of inventiveness and the articulation and appropriation of some controversial ideas, such as the theory of types and the axiom of **infinity**. The theory of types was devised as a way around a **paradox** Russell had discovered in the theory of sets (classes) in 1901. Russell's paradox, as it is called, arises from asking whether the class of all classes that are not members of themselves (as, for example, the set of all dogs, which is not itself a dog) is a member of itself. If it is, then it is not, and if it is not, then it is, so either way a contradiction arises. This means there can be no such set, which tells us that not every intelligible property defines a class.

This realization pushed set theory toward an extensional understanding of sets—conceiving of them as identified by their members rather than defined by specifying conditions—and led Russell to his (simple) theory of types, which stratified the universe of objects into multiple levels and prohibited reference to a set containing an object when defining that object, so as to circumvent self-referential paradoxes: the first level (type) contains only individuals, the next collections of individuals, the next collections of collections of individuals, and so on.

Russell later provided a more complicated stratification scheme in his ramified theory of types. Russell also put forward the axiom of infinity—which postulated the existence of an infinite number of objects—to guarantee an infinite number of individuals of the lowest type. Metaphysically speaking, the idea that there exists, actually and not just potentially, an infinite set of individuals is quite controversial (Hilbert 1926; see also the discussion of the kalam argument in **Cosmological Argument** and the discussion of various views on the relationship between God and abstract objects in Gould 2014).

Later on, the whole logicist project came into question when Kurt Gödel (1906–78) demonstrated, roughly speaking, that consistent axiomatic systems, like that of the *Principia*, which are strong enough to serve as a foundation for arithmetic, must be incomplete in the sense that there are mathematical truths expressible in them that are not derivable from the axioms (Gödel 1931; see **Gödel's Theorem**).

The logical constructionism of Russell's philosophy of mathematics extended to his work in epistemology, philosophy of **mind**, philosophy of language, and **philosophy of science**. For example, in *Our Knowledge of the External World* (1914), Russell attempts to construct physical objects out of complex sets of sense data. In *The Analysis of Mind* (1921), Russell does not interpret the mind as the substantial recipient of sense data, but rather as the complex pattern of the data itself, leading to a form of neutral **monism** in which matter and mind are differently constructed "events," neither of which can be classified as either material or mental substances (see also Russell 1927).

Russell was also concerned with the relationship between the mind and the world as mediated by language, and thought that when the real as opposed to the apparent structure of human language was made explicit, there would be a structure-preserving correspondence between language and reality. This **intuition** was spelled out in his advocacy of logical **atomism**—a view also defended, for different reasons, by Ludwig Wittgenstein in his *Tractatus Logico-Philosophicus* (1921)—in which every statement, no matter how complex, was a truth-function of atomic statements reporting atomic facts about the content of experience that were not further analyzable and were logically independent of each other.

This programmatic **empiricism**, which was central to **logical positivism** and culminated in **Rudolf Carnap**'s (1891–1970) treatise *The Logical Structure of the World* (1928) and Alfred Ayer's (1910–89) book *Language, Truth, and Logic* (1936), was recognized to be untenable and abandoned in the 1950s (see **Duhem-Quine Thesis**; **Empiricism**; **Logical Positivism**; and **Underdetermination**), though Russell was still working on a viable formulation of these ideas in his *An Inquiry into Meaning and Truth* (1940). The broadest and most accessible synthesis of his approach to questions in metaphysics, epistemology, philosophy of language, and philosophy of science can be found in his 1948 book *Human Knowledge: Its Scope and Limits*.

Russell was also, of course, known as a man of letters, and he wrote extensively and popularly on politics, ethics, and religion. His inclinations in politics were left-leaning and pacifist (Russell 1896, 1916a, 1916b, 1920, 1959a) and more than once landed him in jail, and his advocacy of eugenics, along with moral views that were largely libertine and religious views that were atheistic (Russell 1903b, 1925, 1929, 1930, 1931, 1932, 1935, 1957), cost him an academic appointment to the City College of New York in 1940.

Apart from a fleeting moment in his youth when he thought the ontological argument was valid, Russell held throughout his life that the existence of God and personal immortality were mere logical possibilities of exceeding improbability and that no sufficient ground for believing them could be found in any aspect of human experience. Rather, the tragic romanticism of his 1903 essay "A Free Man's Worship" was his lifelong outlook:

> That Man is the product of causes which had no prevision of the end they were achieving; that his origin, his growth, his hopes and fears, his loves and his beliefs, are but the outcome of accidental collocations of atoms; that no fire, no heroism, no intensity of thought and feeling, can preserve an individual life beyond the grave; that all the labors of the ages, all the devotion, all the inspiration, all the noonday brightness of human genius, are destined to **extinction** in the vast death of the solar system, and that the whole temple of Man's achievement must inevitably be buried beneath the debris of a universe in ruins—all of these things, if not quite beyond dispute, are yet so nearly certain, that no philosophy which rejects them can hope to stand. Only within the scaffolding of these truths, only on the firm foundation of unyielding despair, can the soul's habitation henceforth be safely built. (1903b, 416)

That this view, as an instance of metaphysical naturalism, is epistemically self-defeating seems ironically to have escaped Russell's notice—for if all human thought is "but the outcome of accidental collocations of atoms," then his own thought is no exception, and there is no basis for thinking it to be "nearly certain," let alone true (see **Evolutionary Argument against Naturalism** and **Naturalism**; also see Plantinga 2011, 307–50).

But Russell went much further than this, arguing that religious belief was not only rationally indefensible, but actually inhibitory of human progress and irreconcilable with a scientific view of the world (Russell 1931, 1935, 1957). His

stance on these issues might best be characterized as a more genteel and better argued version of the claims associated with the New Atheists (see **New Atheism**). Even so, his stance is contrary to the evidence of history and philosophically deficient, for theistic belief in general and Christianity in particular provided both warrant and historical impetus to the rise of science (see **Intelligibility of the Universe**; also Gordon 2011; Hannam 2011; Plantinga 2011, 255–303), and the enterprise of natural theology is alive and well (see **Natural Theology**; also Craig and Moreland 2009; Dougherty and Walls, forthcoming).

Bruce L. Gordon

REFERENCES AND RECOMMENDED READING

Ayer, Alfred J. (1936) 1971. *Language, Truth, and Logic.* London: Penguin.
Carnap, Rudolf. (1928) 1969. *Der Logische Aufbau der Welt* (The Logical Structure of the World). Berkeley: University of California Press.
Clark, Ronald W. 1975. *The Life of Bertrand Russell.* New York: Penguin.
Craig, William Lane, and J. P. Moreland, eds. 2009. *The Blackwell Companion to Natural Theology.* Oxford: Blackwell.
Dougherty, Trent, and Jerry Walls. Forthcoming. *Two Dozen (or So) Arguments for God: The Plantinga Project.* Oxford: Oxford University Press.
Gödel, Kurt. 1931. "Über formal unentscheidbare Sätze der *Principia Mathematica* und verwandter Systeme I." *Monatshefte für Mathematik und Physik* 38:173–98.
Gordon, Bruce L. 2011. "The Rise of Naturalism and Its Problematic Role in Science and Culture." In *The Nature of Nature: Examining the Role of Naturalism in Science.* Eds. Bruce L. Gordon and William A. Dembski, 3–61. Wilmington, DE: ISI Books.
Gould, Paul, ed. 2014. *Beyond the Control of God? Six Views on the Problem of God and Abstract Objects.* New York: Bloomsbury Academic.
Hannam, James. 2011. *The Genesis of Science: How the Christian Middle Ages Launched the Scientific Revolution.* Washington, DC: Regnery.
Hilbert, David. 1926. "On the Infinite." *Mathematische Annalen* 95:161–90. Repr. in *Philosophy of Mathematics: Selected Readings.* Eds. Paul Benacerraf and Hilary Putnam; trans. E. Putnam and G. J. Massey, 183–201. 2nd ed. Cambridge: Cambridge University Press, 1983.
Monk, Ray. 1990. *Ludwig Wittgenstein: The Duty of Genius.* New York: Free Press.
———. 1996. *Bertrand Russell: The Spirit of Solitude 1872–1921.* New York: Free Press.
———. 2001. *Bertrand Russell: The Ghost of Madness 1921–1970.* New York: Free Press.
Nobel Prizes and Laureates. "The Nobel Prize in Literature 1950." Nobelprize.org. Accessed October 21, 2016. www.nobelprize.org/nobel_prizes/literature/laureates/1950/index.html.
Plantinga, Alvin. 2011. *Where the Conflict Really Lies: Science, Religion, and Naturalism.* New York: Oxford University Press.
Russell, Bertrand. (1896) 1965. *German Social Democracy.* London: Allen & Unwin.
———. (1897) 2007. *An Essay on the Foundations of Geometry.* New York: Cosimo.
———. (1900) 1958. *A Critical Exposition of the Philosophy of Leibniz.* London: Allen & Unwin.
———. (1903a) 2000. *The Principles of Mathematics.* London: Routledge.
———. 1903b. "A Free Man's Worship." *Independent Review* 1:415–24.
———. 1905. "On Denoting." *Mind* 14:479–93.
———. 1912. *The Problems of Philosophy.* Cambridge: Home University Library.
———. (1914) 1993. *Our Knowledge of the External World.* London: Routledge.

———. (1916a) 1917. *Justice in War-Time*. Chicago: Open Court.

———. (1916b) 1980. *Principles of Social Reconstruction*. London: Unwin Paperbacks.

———. 1919. *Introduction to Mathematical Philosophy*. London: Allen & Unwin.

———. 1920. *The Practice and Theory of Bolshevism*. London: Allen & Unwin.

———. 1921. *The Analysis of Mind*. London: Allen & Unwin.

———. 1925. *What I Believe*. London: Kegan Paul, Trench, Trubner & Co.

———. 1927. *The Analysis of Matter*. New York: Harcourt, Brace.

———. 1929. *Marriage and Morals*. London: Allen & Unwin.

———. 1930. *The Conquest of Happiness*. New York: Horace Liveright.

———. 1931. *The Scientific Outlook*. London: Allen & Unwin.

———. (1932) 2009. *Education and the Social Order*. London: Routledge.

———. (1935) 1997. *Religion and Science*. Oxford: Oxford University Press.

———. (1940) 1950. *An Inquiry into Meaning and Truth*. London: Allen & Unwin.

———. (1945) 1993. *A History of Western Philosophy*. London: Routledge.

———. 1946. *Physics and Experience*. Cambridge: Cambridge University Press.

———. (1948) 1993. *Human Knowledge: Its Scope and Limits*. London: Routledge.

———. 1956. *Logic and Knowledge*. Ed. R. C. Marsh. London: Allen & Unwin.

———. 1957. *Why I Am Not a Christian*. Ed. Paul Edwards. London: Allen & Unwin.

———. 1959a. *Common Sense and Nuclear Warfare*. London: Allen & Unwin.

———. 1959b. *My Philosophical Development*. New York: Simon & Schuster.

———. 1961. *The Basic Writings of Bertrand Russell*. Eds. L. E. Denonn and R. E. Egner. New York: Simon & Schuster.

———. 1967, 1968, 1969. *The Autobiography of Bertrand Russell*. 3 vols. New York: Little, Brown.

Russell, Bertrand, and Alfred North Whitehead. 1910, 1912, 1913. *Principia Mathematica*. 3 vols. Cambridge: Cambridge University Press.

Wittgenstein, Ludwig. (1921) 1961. *Tractatus Logico-Philosophicus*. London: Routledge and Kegan Paul.

Wood, Alan. 1959. "Russell's Philosophy: A Study of Its Development." Appendix to Bertrand Russell, *My Philosophical Development*, 255–77. New York: Simon & Schuster.

RUSSELL, ROBERT. Theologian and physicist Robert John Russell (1946–), founding director of The Center for Theology and the Natural Sciences (Berkeley, California), is arguably the most important contemporary Protestant scholar of Christianity and science. Although he is not an evangelical, an orthodox understanding of creation, **resurrection**, and **eschatology** has shaped all of his work. As an organizer and facilitator of conversations about theology and science, he has often brought world-class scientists into close contact with leading theologians, historians, and philosophers, all with the goal of producing comprehensive publications that develop creative new ideas about some of the hardest issues facing all Christians who take modern science seriously.

The largest project focused on **divine action** in various sciences, resulting in five full-length anthologies that provide crucial background for Russell's single most important idea, Non-Interventionist Objective Divine Action (NIODA). According to Russell, owing to conceptual changes in science and philosophy in the past two centuries, "*we can now*

understand special providence as the objective acts of God in nature and history and we can understand these acts in a non-interventionist manner consistent with science" (Russell 1997, 45, italics in original). Although some divine acts, including the resurrection, still fall outside this scheme, Russell believes that NIODA helps us understand most divine action while avoiding both horns of an old theological dilemma—either requiring God to act contrary to natural laws, or else reducing divine action to a purely subjective category.

Russell prepared carefully to tackle questions of this nature and magnitude. After undergraduate study in **physics**, religion, and music at Stanford University, he studied theology at the Pacific School of Religion, leading to his ordination in the United Church of Christ, before completing doctoral work at the University of California, Santa Cruz, studying condensed matter physics with Frank Bridges. He then spent three years teaching physics at Carleton College (Minnesota), where he developed a close relationship with **Ian Barbour**, the prime mover behind the modern dialogue of science and religion (Peters 2006, 6).

Although his personal and intellectual debt to Barbour is considerable, Russell has never been a proponent of Barbour's process **theism**. Nor has he embraced the separation of religion from science encapsulated by Langdon Gilkey's "two languages" approach. Both of these perspectives are especially clear from Russell's book *Cosmology: From Alpha to Omega* (2008), an updated edition of earlier essays bringing Trinitarian theology to bear on cosmology, **mathematics**, quantum mechanics, evolution, **theodicy**, and eschatology in highly original ways. In the book, Russell advances what he calls the "creative mutual interaction" of theology and science, paying careful attention to both "consonance *and* dissonance" as part of that interaction (Russell 2008, 9–11, italics in original).

Edward B. Davis

REFERENCES AND RECOMMENDED READING

Peters, Ted. 2006. "Robert John Russell's Contribution to the Theology and Science Dialogue." In *God's Action in Nature's World*. Eds. Ted Peters and Nathan Hallanger, 1–18. Aldershot, UK: Ashgate.

Russell, Robert John. 1997. "Does the 'God Who *Acts*' Really *Act*? New Approaches to Divine Action in Light of Science." *Theology Today* 54:43–65.

———. 2008. *Cosmology: From Alpha to Omega*. Minneapolis: Fortress.

RYLE, GILBERT. Gilbert Ryle (1900–1976) was an influential British philosopher associated with the "ordinary language" philosophy of those such as **Ludwig Wittgenstein**.

This association is due to Ryle's thesis that many of the problems in philosophy are merely philosophical confusions that arise through the assimilation or misapplication of categorically different terms. According to Ryle, these confusions can only be resolved by a careful analysis of the **logic** and use of language.

Ryle was a prolific writer focusing mainly on meaning and reference. His book *The Concept of Mind* (1949) was widely read and written about for the first decade after its publication. It remains a modern classic. The first aim of the book is to attack substance **dualism**, according to which human persons are comprised of a physical body and a nonphysical **mind** or **soul** (see **Dualism**; **Soul**). Ryle referred to this as "Descartes' Myth" and the "ghost in the machine." Even though Ryle's portrayal of Descartes's view of human persons is contested, the phrase remains popular (see **Descartes, René**).

According to Ryle, the idea of substance dualism is absurd. True to his emphasis on language, Ryle argued that philosophical debates concerning the nature of the mind and the relation between mind and body were the result of a "category mistake" that led many to mistakenly treat statements about mental phenomena in the same way as statements about physical phenomena. This is to assume that mind and body are both governed by mechanical laws, which is absurd. Nonphysical minds have no levers or gears. For Ryle there are no nonphysical objects. Ordinary talk of mind is actually talk of physical objects and physical happenings.

The second aim in *The Concept of Mind* is to provide a positive project of "charting the logical geography" of the many concepts used in referring to the mind. Again the emphasis on language is dominant. Although Ryle considered his project neutral on the nature of human persons, many philosophers have described Ryle's view of the human person as behaviorist as well as verificationist.

At times Ryle seems to reduce the human mind to human behavior. For example, faced with the problem of knowing what another person's mental life is like, Ryle suggested it is a matter of "how we establish, and how we apply, certain sorts of lawlike propositions about the overt and the silent behavior of persons" (1949, 169). Accordingly, knowledge of the mental lives of others is gained through knowledge of their behavior.

A careful reading of Ryle, however, reveals that at some points he did advance **behaviorism** and at other points he rejected it. It is fair to say that Ryle gave little attention to the significance of reflective experiences, such as the experience of pain. Such mental events are not reducible to behavior, as one can be in pain and not act like it or, conversely, exhibit pain behavior while not actually experiencing any pain.

Toward the latter part of Ryle's career, he produced considerable work on **Plato**. Yet his work on the philosophy of mind remains his most influential contribution, which is apparent in contemporary functionalist theories of consciousness (see **Consciousness**; **Functionalism**).

Brandon L. Rickabaugh

REFERENCES AND RECOMMENDED READING

Lyons, William E. 1980. *Gilbert Ryle: An Introduction to His Philosophy*. Brighton/Atlantic Highlands, NJ: Harvester/Humanities.

Mabbott, J. D. 1976. "Gilbert Ryle: A Tribute." Repr. in *Aspects of Mind: Gilbert Ryle*. Ed. René Meyer, 221–25. Cambridge: Oxford, 1993.

Magee, Brian. 1971. "Conversation with Gilbert Ryle." In Brian Magee, *Modern British Philosophy*. London: Secker & Warburg.

Ryle, Gilbert. 1931–32. "Systematically Misleading Expressions." *Proceedings of the Aristotelian Society* 32:139–70.

———. 1945. "Philosophical Arguments." Inaugural lecture as Waynflete Professor of Metaphysical Philosophy, Oxford. Repr. in Ryle, *Collected Papers*, 2:194–211. London: Hutchinson, 1971.

———. 1945–46. "Knowing How and Knowing That." *Proceedings of the Aristotelian Society* 46:1–16.

———. 1949. *The Concept of Mind*. London: Hutchinson.

———. 1950–51. "Heterologicality." *Analysis* 11:61–69.

———. 1954. *Dilemmas: The Tarner Lectures*. Cambridge: Cambridge University Press.

———. 1961. "Use, Usage, and Meaning." *Proceedings of the Aristotelian Society*, supp. 35:223–30.

———. 1966. *Plato's Progress*. Cambridge: Cambridge University Press.

———. 1971. *Collected Papers*. 2 vols. London: Hutchinson.

———. 1979. *On Thinking*. Ed. K. Kolenda. Oxford: Blackwell.

Wood, O. P., and G. Pitcher. 1970. *Ryle, Modern Studies in Philosophy*. Ed. A. Rorty. London: Macmillan.

S

SAGAN, CARL. Carl Sagan (1934–96) was an American scientist and educator. He is best known as cocreator and host of the 1980 PBS miniseries *Cosmos*, which brought an infectious enthusiasm for **astronomy** into millions of living rooms, as well as for his popular writings about science.

Sagan was born and raised in Brooklyn, New York, and earned his PhD from the University of Chicago in 1960. He was briefly a professor at Harvard University and then spent nearly three decades as a professor at Cornell University in Ithaca, New York. He was on the science teams of many NASA spacecraft missions and made a number of contributions to the study of planetary surfaces and atmospheres, but his most lasting scientific contributions stemmed from his pioneering work on astrobiology, the study of life away from Earth. Sagan contemplated the habitability of Jupiter's clouds and Europa's oceans, and performed laboratory experiments on organic compounds in an attempt to evaluate the possibility of prebiotic chemistry on the surface of Titan.

Sagan was a proponent of the search for signs of intelligent life elsewhere in the universe. He was instrumental in placing plaques aboard the *Pioneer* and *Voyager* spacecraft containing greetings and other **information** about humanity in the hope that intelligent beings might someday find and decipher them.

Sagan wrote popular books about astronomy throughout the 1970s, but his career reached a turning point when he cowrote and hosted *Cosmos*, a 13-part miniseries that premiered on PBS in 1980. *Cosmos* was a panoramic introduction to astronomical concepts including Earth, life, and the universe. It has since been cited as an inspiration by many scientists of succeeding generations and has been seen by more than 500 million people.

In 1985 Sagan published a novel, *Contact*, which imagined the societal effects of communication between humans and an alien civilization. *Contact* was made into a film starring Jodie Foster in 1997, the year after Sagan's death from complications of myelodysplasia.

Sagan evocatively expressed the implications of stellar nucleosynthesis by calling humans "star stuff," and he rhapsodized about the smallness and isolation of Earth by calling it a "pale blue dot." The latter appeared in a 1994 book, *Pale Blue Dot*, which extensively contemplated the place of humanity within the cosmos. Sagan's 1995 book *The Demon-Haunted World* set forth the **scientific method** as the essential means for advancing human knowledge and offered a critique of superstition and **pseudoscience** as well as of organized religion. As an illustration of claims that place themselves outside the realm of science, with a particular eye toward the **existence of God**, Sagan's "dragon in my garage" is a more detailed version of **Bertrand Russell**'s classic "teapot in outer space."

Sagan was known for enthusiastically pronouncing the word *billions* as he described the vastness of the universe, though he claimed never to have used the signature phrase "billions and billions," which may owe more to parodies of Sagan by comedian Johnny Carson than to Sagan himself.

This scholar was a prominent critic of Christianity and other religions. He felt that the existence of a personal God was not credible in the absence of rigorous **scientific proof**, per his dictum that "extraordinary claims require extraordinary evidence," and he was unapologetic about incorporating this belief into his outlook as a scientist (see **Scientism**). Christians sometimes protested the fairness of his critiques of historical and contemporary Christianity, and creationists were further perturbed by Sagan's embrace of **biological evolution** and the great **age of the universe**. On the other hand, although the opening lines of *Cosmos* ("The cosmos is all that is or ever was or ever will be") have been taken as an archetypal statement of philosophical **naturalism**, Sagan acknowledged that the nonexistence of God can never be proved.

Matthew Tiscareno

REFERENCES AND RECOMMENDED READING

Sagan, Carl. 1994. *Pale Blue Dot*. New York: Random House.
———. 1995. *The Demon-Haunted World*. New York: Random House.

SALMON, WESLEY. Wesley Salmon (1925–2001) was an accomplished philosopher of science who made important contributions to discussions of **causation**, explanation, **probability**, scientific **confirmation**, and induction. Salmon did his doctoral work at the University of California–Los Angeles under **Hans Reichenbach** and would eventually settle at the University of Pittsburgh, a school (especially during his tenure) known for excellence in the history and **philosophy of science**.

One significant project of Salmon's was to seek a balance between the logical empiricists, who touted **objectivity** and deduction, and **Thomas Kuhn**'s historical philosophy of science, which emphasized the subjectivity of theory choice. At times two rival theories may compete to explain the same set of observations, for example, the corpuscular and wave theories of light, and Salmon sought to provide a way to resolve disputes between such rivals based on Bayesian analysis and careful attention to the role of prior probabilities. His approach avoided the extreme subjectivism of Kuhn and the deductive certainty of logical empiricists by offering a "Bayesian algorithm for theory preference" based on considerations of plausibility (see **Bayes' Theorem**).

Questions of causality were also central to Salmon's work. Salmon thought a proper understanding of causation was central to successful scientific explanations. In particular Salmon rejected **Carl Hempel**'s "covering law" model with its use of deductive-nomological (DN) and inductive-statistical (IS) approaches that made causality secondary to explanation. Causation is often thought of as a relation between a pair of events, A and B, that manifest a regular pattern of A-type events being followed by B-type events. Rejecting such event-based (as well as counterfactual) accounts, Salmon made causation a function of causal processes affecting each other through interaction. To accomplish this he made "mark transmission" the indicator of a causal process, and change or modification of characteristics as an indicator of interaction (see **Aristotle's Four Causes**; **Causation**).

Mark transmission is meant to distinguish genuine causal processes from pseudoprocesses. A genuine causal process is capable of propagating a mark over time, where a mark is a modification to the object, such as a scuff on a baseball. A moving baseball, as opposed to the pseudoprocess of a shadow moving across a wall, is a genuine causal process because the mark or alteration can be permanently transmitted in the case of the baseball but not in the case of the shadow. When a genuine causal process, like the flight of the ball, is altered by another causal process, like the swinging of a bat, there is interaction and we can say causation has occurred. In particular, following Phil Dowe, Salmon argued that in the case of genuine causal interaction there will be transmission or alteration of a conserved quantity, such as mass-energy, charge, or momentum.

Wesley Salmon was one of the most influential of the twentieth-century philosophers of science, and one of the most widely published with over 100 professional articles and numerous books to his credit. While his ideas have been widely debated, Salmon left a lasting impression on twentieth-century philosophy of science.

Bradley Sickler

REFERENCES AND RECOMMENDED READING

Dowe, Phil. 2000. *Physical Causation*. Cambridge: Cambridge University Press.

Hempel, Carl. 1965. *Aspects of Scientific Explanation and Other Essays in the Philosophy of Science*. New York: Free Press.

Kuhn, Thomas. (1962) 1970. *The Structure of Scientific Revolutions*. 2nd ed. with postscript. Chicago: University of Chicago Press.

Salmon, Wesley. 1971. "Statistical Explanation and Statistical Relevance." In *Statistical Explanation and Statistical Relevance*. Ed. W. Salmon, 29–87. Pittsburgh: University of Pittsburgh Press.

———. 1984. *Scientific Explanation and the Causal Structure of the World*. Princeton, NJ: Princeton University Press.

———. 1994. "Causality without Counterfactuals." *Philosophy of Science* 61:297–312.

———. 1998. *Causality and Explanation*. New York: Oxford University Press.

SCHAEFER, HENRY F. "Fritz" Schaefer (1944–) is Graham Perdue Professor of Chemistry at the University of Georgia where he directs the Center for Computational Quantum Chemistry (CCQC). Born in Grand Rapids, Michigan, Schaefer received his BS in chemical **physics** from Massachusetts Institute of Technology in 1966 and a PhD in the same subject from Stanford University three years later. This work was based on computational studies of the electronic structure of light atoms and diatomic molecules. He began his academic career at the University of California–Berkeley in 1969, where he established a computational chemistry research program focused on conducting rigorous electronic structure calculations that accounted for electron correlation (i.e., electron-electron interactions). His success was such that he was recruited as the inaugural director of the Institute for Theoretical Chemistry at the University of Texas–Austin in 1979 and to his current position at the University of Georgia in 1987.

Schaefer's prolific and award-winning scientific output of more than 1,400 papers and books is characterized by thoroughness, methodological rigor, and engagement with experimental findings. His 1969 prediction of methylene's bent structure in opposition to the linear structure assigned by the eminent spectroscopist Gerhard Hertzberg is characteristic of his willingness to use rigorous calculations to challenge questionable experimental findings and helped establish the field of quantum chemistry's utility for making accurate predictions and interpreting experiments after subsequent experimental work proved Schaefer correct (Murphy 2006; Richards 1979; Schaefer 1986).

In addition to his research, Schaefer contributed to quantum chemistry's development through his over 100 PhD students and nearly 50 postdoctoral researchers (Schaefer 2010), his authoritative monographs in the field (1977a, 1977c, 1984), the PSI quantum chemistry software (Turney et al. 2012), and his longstanding service as editor of *Molecular Physics* and president of the World Association of Theoretical and Computational Chemists.

Schaefer is well known in both the chemistry and Christian communities for his serious Christian faith and his willingness to address science-faith issues. In addition to teaching a freshman seminar on science and Christianity and engaging in unobtrusive Christian witness (Crawford 2010; Harris 2010), Schaefer delivered over 350 lectures on science-faith issues since 1984. These have been published as *Science and Christianity: Conflict of Coherence?* (2003, 2010) but many are also available through various apologetics ministry websites (e.g., Schaefer's Virtual Office).

Schaefer's overall thrust is to present Christianity as both deeply satisfying and intellectually reasonable while critiquing cultural and intellectual movements that co-opt science to promote atheist views of reality. In a highly personal and colloquial style, he describes his personal faith journey, answers common questions about Christianity, gives advice for seekers of truth, explores past and present scientists' beliefs, describes his dialogue with the atheist physicist **Steven Weinberg**, evaluates the theological significance of the **big bang** and Hartle-Hawking proposal, critiques **postmodernism**, exhorts us to heed **C. S. Lewis**'s warnings about **scientism**, and discusses his skepticism about scientific accounts of life's origin and his belief in a designer.

Although Schaefer considers debates over evolution of secondary importance to his faith, he is a fellow of the **Discovery Institute** and has been a prominent supporter of the **intelligent design** (ID) movement (Forest and Gross 2007, 18–22), which made much of speculation that he was a five-time Nobel Prize nominee. Significantly, Schaefer participated in the 1996 "mere creation" ID conference (1998), signed the scientific dissent from **Darwinism**, and advocated for "teach the controversy" efforts in Cobb County, Georgia (2002).

Schaefer's technical contributions to science-faith dialogue include exploring the consonance between Christianity and **chaos theory** (Allen and Schaefer 2006) and the implications of anthropic coincidences for chemistry (Allen and Schaefer 2010) in semitechnical papers coauthored with his CCQC collaborator Wesley Allen.

Stephen Contakes

REFERENCES AND RECOMMENDED READING

Allen, Wesley D., and Henry F. Schaefer III. 2006. "Complexity, Chaos and God." In *Darwin's Nemesis: Phillip Johnson and the Intelligent Design Movement.* Ed. William A. Dembski, 276–303. Downers Grove, IL: IVP Academic.

———. 2010. "Counterfactual Quantum Chemistry of Water." In *Water and Life: The Unique Properties of H_2O.* Boca Raton, FL: CRC.

Basour, J. 2006. "Review of *Science and Christianity: Conflict or Coherence?* by Henry F. Schaefer III." *Science and Christian Belief* 18 (1): 95–96.

"Biography of Fritz Schaefer." 2004. *Journal of Physical Chemistry A* 108, no. 15 (April 1): 2805–7.

Crawford, T. Daniel. 2010. "The Life and Science of Fritz Schaefer." *Molecular Physics* 108, no. 19–20 (October 10): 2439–45.

Crawford, T. Daniel, and C. David Sherrill. 2009. "A Special Issue of Molecular Physics Honoring Prof. Henry F. Schaefer III." *Molecular Physics* 107, no. 8–12 (April 20): 711.

"Curriculum Vitae of Fritz Schaefer." 2004. *Journal of Physical Chemistry A* 108, no. 15 (April 1): 2810–17.

Fisher, David. 2004. "Review of *Science and Christianity: Conflict or Coherence?* by Henry F. Schaefer III." *Perspectives on Science and Christian Faith* 56 (2). www.asa3.org/ASA/BookReviews2000-present/6–04.html.

Forrest, Barbara, and Paul R. Gross. 2007. *Creationism's Trojan Horse: The Wedge of Intelligent Design.* New York: Oxford University Press.

Garrison, Barbara J., Gustavo E. Scuseria, and David R. Yarkony. 2004. "Dedication to Fritz Schaefer." *Journal of Physical Chemistry A* 108, no. 15 (April 1): 2803–4.

Harris, Robert A. 2010. "A Unique Friendship." *Molecular Physics* 108, no. 19–20 (October 10): 2447–48.

Hearn, Walter R., and Henry F. Schaefer III. 2001. "ASAer Profile on Fritz Schaefer." *ASA Newsletter* 43, no. 5 (September–October). www.asa3.org/ASA/newsletter/SEPOCT01.htm.

IAQMS. "Henry F. Schaefer III." International Academy of Quantum Molecular Science. Accessed October 26, 2016. www.iaqms.org/members/schaefer.php.

Murphy, John. 2006. "Leading the Computational Chemistry Field." *Scientific Computing World* 5 (August–September). www.scientific-computing.com/features/feature.php?feature_id=6.

Richards, Graham. 1979. "The Third Age of Quantum Chemistry." *Nature* 278: 507.

Rienstra-Kiracofe, Jonathan C. 2004. "God Is in the Details: A Scientist Affirms His Faith (Review of *Science and Christianity: Conflict or Coherence?* by Henry F. Schaefer III)." *Books and Culture: A Christian Review* (February). www.booksandculture.com/articles/webexclusives/2004/february/040223a.html?paging=off.

Schaefer, Henry F., III, ed. 1977a. *Applications of Electronic Structure Theory.* Modern Theoretical Chemistry 4. New York: Plenum.

———. 1977b. "The Fuzzy Interface between Surface Chemistry, Heterogeneous Catalysis, and Organometallic Chemistry." *Accounts of Chemical Research* 10 (8): 287–93.

———, ed. 1977c. *Methods of Electronic Structure Theory.* Modern Theoretical Chemistry 3. New York: Plenum.

———. 1984. *Quantum Chemistry: The Development of Ab Initio Methods in Molecular Electronic Structure Theory.* Oxford Science Publications. Oxford: Clarendon.

———. 1986. "Methylene: A Paradigm for Computational Quantum Chemistry." *Science* 231, no. 4742 (March 7): 1100–1107.

———. 1988. Foreword to *Mere Creation: Science, Faith and Intelligent Design.* Ed. William A. Dembski. Downers Grove, IL: InterVarsity.

———. 1997. "The Reachable Dream: Some Steps toward the Realization of Molecular Quantum Mechanics by Computer." *Journal of Molecular Structure: THEOCHEM* 398–99, no. 1–3 (June 30): 199–209.

———. 1998. "Foreword." In *Mere Creation: Science, Faith and Intelligent Design.* Ed. William A. Dembski, 9–12. Downers Grove, IL: InterVarsity Press.

———. 2001. "Computers and Molecular Quantum Mechanics: 1965–2001, a Personal Perspective." *Journal of Molecular Structure: THEOCHEM* 573, no. 1–3 (October 26): 129–37.

———. 2002. "Standard Evolutionary Theory Has Its Shortcomings." *Atlanta Journal Constitution.* September 28.

———. 2003. *Science and Christianity: Conflict or Coherence?* Watkinsville, GA: Apollos Trust.

———. 2004. "Science and Christianity: Conflict or Coherence?" In *Reading God's World.* Ed. Angus J. L. Menuge, 119–56. St. Louis, MO: Concordia.

———. 2005. "Review of *Who Is Adam?* by Fazale Rana and Hugh Ross." *Perspectives on Science and Christian Faith* 57 (4): 325.

———. 2010. *Science and Christianity: Conflict or Coherence?* 6th rev. ed. Athens: University of Georgia.

———. "Dr. Henry F. 'Fritz' Schaefer, III. Virtual Office." Leadership U. Accessed October 25, 2016. www.leaderu.com/offices/schaefer/.

Schaefer, Henry F., III, and Louis F. Rodrigues. 2010. "Henry F. Schaefer." In *Open Questions: Diverse Thinkers Discuss God, Religion, and Faith,* 287–94. Santa Barbara, CA: Praeger.

Swamidass, S. Joshua, and Shoba Spencer. 2008. "A Chemist and God: Henry Schaefer Sees a Natural Nexus between Faith and Science." *World* (October 18). www.worldmag.com/2008/10/a_chemist_and_god.

Turney, Justin M., Andrew C. Simmonett, Robert M. Parrish, et al. 2012. "PSI4: An Open-Source Ab Initio Electronic Structure Program." *Wiley Interdisciplinary Reviews: Computational Molecular Science* 2 (4): 556–65.

SCHRÖDINGER'S CAT. Schrödinger's Cat is a thought experiment proposed by physicist Erwin Schrödinger (1887–1961) in an attempt to understand and wrestle with some of the implications of the theory of quantum mechanics. Within the mathematical theory of quantum mechanics that accurately describes all experimental observations made, an object can be in a superposition of multiple states. This means that the **mathematics** that describe a subatomic particle seem to imply it exists with two different sets of properties at the same time. It's as if a coin could simultaneously be showing both heads and tails. Although any attempt to measure an object will always find the object in only one unique state (heads, for instance), the mathematics of the theory seems to indicate that before the measurement the object actually exists in both states.

Schrödinger proposed a scenario with a cat placed in an enclosed box isolated from the outside world. Also, a single quantum mechanical object like an atom that could be in one of two states is placed in the box with the cat. A mechanism would be set up so that if the atom were in one state the cat would be killed, and if the atom were in the other state the cat would not be killed. For example, a vial of hydrocyanic acid could be in the box that would shatter and kill the cat if the atom were in one state but would stay intact if the atom were in the other state. According to the prevailing Copenhagen interpretation of quantum mechanics, the atom would be in a superposition of both states until some kind of measurement were performed. Consequently, it would seem that the mechanism that could kill the cat, which is coupled to the atom, would also be in a superposition of both states (the vial broken but not broken), and therefore the cat would be both dead and alive at the same time. It seems, then, that the indeterminacy intrinsic to the microscopic world of quantum mechanics is transferred to the macroscopic cat.

This thought experiment is used as a talking point to try to explain and understand the meaning of the quantum mechanical calculations. What is required for the wave function that describes the object to collapse into one of its possible states? Does it require a macroscopic measuring device (such as the vial), or a sentient being (such as the cat or the person who ultimately opens the box)?

One interpretation of quantum mechanics, the *many worlds hypothesis*, proposes that both possibilities actually happen and two alternate realities are spawned, one where the cat is alive and one where the cat is dead. Another interpretation, the *ensemble interpretation*, states that the wave function describing the atom is only a statistical device and doesn't have any basis in the single reality of one atom. One theological proposal is that God is the ultimate observer of everything in nature, and that his sentient observation is ultimately responsible for the collapse of the wave function.

Whatever the actual relationship between the mathematics of quantum mechanics and the precise and accurate predictions made by the theory, the Schrödinger's Cat thought experiment serves as an intriguing illustration of, and point of discussion about, the interaction between the probabilities intrinsic to the mathematics of quantum mechanics and the definitive results of observational experiments.

Michael G. Strauss

REFERENCES AND RECOMMENDED READING

Gribbin, John. 1984. *In Search of Schrödinger's Cat.* New York: Bantam.
Polkinghorne, John. 1986. *The Quantum World.* Princeton, NJ: Princeton University Press.

SCHROEDER, GERALD L. Physicist and author Gerald L. Schroeder currently lectures at Aish HaTorah College of Jewish Studies in Jerusalem. Schroeder earned a PhD in the combined fields of nuclear **physics** and earth and planetary sciences in 1965 from the Massachusetts Institute of Technology (MIT). In 1971, after serving on the MIT physics faculty as well as on the U.S. Atomic Energy Commission, he emigrated to Israel where he continued his research at the Weizmann Institute of Science, the Volcani Research Institute, and the Hebrew University of Jerusalem.

Schroeder is best known for his books integrating belief in God, the Torah, the Talmud, the Midrash, and the Kabbalah with mainstream scientific understandings of big bang cosmology (see **Big Bang Theory**) and with Einstein's theory of relativity. His published books include *Genesis and the Big Bang* (1990), *The Science of God* (1997), *The Hidden Face of God* (2002), and *God according to God* (2009). In 2012 Schroeder was awarded the Trotter Prize by Texas A&M University's College of Science. His Trotter Prize lecture, "Genesis and the Big Bang," can be accessed at *science.tamu.edu/trotter.*

In his writings and lectures, Schroeder demonstrates the clarity and extensiveness of Old Testament references to big bang cosmology. He cites the commentaries of ancient Jewish theologians, especially Nachmanides and Maimonides, to show that the big bang theory for the origin and history of the universe is not merely an example of twentieth-century interpretative hindsight but, rather, a biblical doctrine well understood by Bible scholars for many hundreds of years. Given its demonstrated predictive power, Schroeder concludes that the Old Testament is the inspired Word of God.

Schroeder has drawn both praise and criticism for his attempts to reconcile the chronology of creation, as set forth in Genesis 1, with the scientific record for the origin and history of the universe, Earth, and Earth's life. He has garnered praise for showing that the order of creation events described in Genesis 1 matches the order observed in the established scientific record. Criticism arises from his attempts to reconcile the 13.8-billion-year history of the universe with the six creation "days" (taken as 24-hour days) in Genesis 1. He combines complex numerical analysis derived from mystical Jewish commentaries with the space-time stretching effect derived from Einstein's theory of relativity to show that the Genesis creation "days" represent progressively shorter time periods.

In broad outline, Schroeder's chronology for Genesis 1 seems to parallel that of most day-age creationists. The major difference between his view and theirs lies in his attempt to provide precise dates for the boundaries between the six creation days—boundaries based on his numerical methods.

He also differs with many, though not all, day-age creationists in placing the cosmic beginning, the big bang, at the start of creation day 1 rather than prior to day 1, which most creationists would say focuses specifically on planet Earth.

Schroeder is married, with children and grandchildren. His wife, Barbara Sofer, is a columnist for the *Jerusalem Post* and serves as the director of public relations for Hadassah Medical Center in Jerusalem.

Hugh Ross

REFERENCES AND RECOMMENDED READING

Schroeder, Gerald L. 1990. *Genesis and the Big Bang: The Discovery of Harmony between Modern Science and the Bible.* New York: Bantam Books.
———. 1997. *The Science of God: Convergence of Scientific and Biblical Wisdom.* New York: Free Press.
———. 2002. *The Hidden Face of God: Science Reveals the Ultimate Truth.* New York: Free Press.
———. 2009. *God according to God: A Scientist Discovers We've Been Wrong About God All Along.* New York: HarperCollins.

SCIENCE. Science, from the Latin *scientia*, means "knowledge." The scope and methods of science have evolved through the centuries and are still debated today. Originally *scientia* meant a particular quality of knowledge, namely, certain knowledge resulting from valid deductive **logic** applied to self-evidently true axioms and unassailable first principles.

Because *scientia* was a quality rather than a domain of knowledge, it was sought in every domain, including **mathematics**, natural science, ethics, and philosophy. But the contemporary meaning of science is focused on a particular domain—namely, knowledge of the physical world. The study of the natural world was previously called **natural philosophy**, situating it as a branch of the humanities, and the concept of the sciences as something distinct from the humanities took several centuries to develop.

The transition began with the **Scientific Revolution**, led by the philosophical work of **Francis Bacon** and the experimental and observational methods of **Galileo Galilei**. In the 1830s, the word *scientist* was coined by members of the British Association for the Advancement of Science and popularized by **William Whewell**. The *Oxford English Dictionary* notes that a new meaning for science had developed by the 1860s as physical and experimental knowledge to the exclusion of theological and metaphysical knowledge, and its 1987 supplement remarks that "this is now the dominant sense in ordinary use." Although there were impressive developments in logic, mathematics, science, and **technology** in China, India, Egypt, and elsewhere, here the emphasis is on the West.

The archetypical questions of classical natural philosophy were "What are things made of?" and "What is the path of moving objects?" Those questions were surprisingly difficult and took over two millennia to answer satisfactorily.

But underlying the specific questions of natural philosophers was the more basic question about how scientific thinking works. What inputs are required to reach true conclusions about the physical world? In other words, what must go in so that scientific conclusions can come out? This methodological question also proved to be surprisingly difficult. Three resources are needed: presuppositions, evidence, and logic.

Presuppositions are indispensable for science to connect personal sensory perceptions and external physical objects. Accordingly, the basic presuppositions of science are that the physical world is real and orderly and that we humans find it substantially comprehensible—particularly because of endowments of generally reliable sense perceptions. For instance, even the simple statement "I am patting my cat," when construed in an ordinary realist manner, implicates real physical objects and my reliable sensory endowments. However, the ancient skeptics Pyrrho of Elis and Sextus Empiricus were unwilling to grant these presuppositions, so they suspended judgment.

By contrast, Albertus Magnus in the 1200s was confident that we can have certain demonstrations about physical objects, given his commonsense presuppositions about a real and orderly physical world and adequate human endowments. One example: Magnus concluded that it is necessary that a person is sitting if someone sees that person sitting (Gauch 2012, 74). Likewise, Thomas Reid (1710–96) was as certain that the city of Rome exists as he was of any proposition in Euclid's geometry (Gauch 2012, 46). Many great scientists have grounded science in an initial appeal to common sense.

Evidence had long come from careful observations of nature. But in the 1200s, Roger Bacon and especially Robert Grosseteste emphasized that experiments could expand the opportunities to see what happens under different conditions than what nature provides, thereby allowing better discrimination among competing hypotheses. Development of telescopes, microscopes, and other instruments expanded scientists' observational powers.

Deductive logic reasons from given axioms to derived theorems or from general principles to particular instances, whereas inductive logic reasons from particulars to generalities.

Deductive reasoning yields necessary conclusions, whereas inductive reasoning yields probable conclusions. Science needs both. **Aristotle** had two versions of science that he never adequately connected. His ideal or mature science is rationalist, deriving extensive knowledge deductively from a small number of first principles. Its implicit standard was geometry.

But Aristotle's actual science is empiricist, featuring careful observations of stars and animals and such, as well as inductive generalizations from the data. His inductive-deductive method used induction from observations to infer general principles, deductions from those principles to check the principles with further observations, and additional cycles of induction and deduction to continue the advance of knowledge. This interaction between physical evidence and mental model remains the core of scientific inquiry. The emergence of **statistics**, including the seminal contributions by Thomas Bayes (1701–61) who developed **Bayes' Theorem**, improved inductive logic enormously, especially after computers became readily available in the 1960s.

Presuppositions, evidence, and logic are the basis of scientific thinking. Between 1200 and 1600, long after Aristotle, these three were developed into a robust foundation for the Scientific Revolution. But no subset of these three resources works. The rationalists sought truth from reason or logic, and the empiricists sought truth from experience or evidence, but both of those projects are incomplete for natural science.

Between 1920 and 1960, logical positivists attempted to combine reason and experience in a hard, no-nonsense version of science that rejected **metaphysics** and empirically unprovable presuppositions (see **Empiricism** and **Logical Positivism**). Although this school achieved nearly universal consensus for a few decades, its eventual demise was rapid. The divorce from metaphysics was costly because it disconnected science from its grounding in common sense. Also, the logical positivists had an overly automatic or mechanical view of the scientific process, whereas other scholars were much more sanguine about the human face of science.

A distinctive interest that many Christians bring to science is the relationship between science and Christianity (or other **worldview**s). Most pointedly, is there scientific evidence for supernatural causes and/or for God? Christians are quite divided over this. Some Christians marshal evidence and present God's work in the world as a scientific theory (examples include young-earth creationism and progressive creationism; see **Creationism, Young-Earth** and **Progressive Creation**). The **intelligent design** movement similarly aims to prove the existence of intelligent (likely supernatural) causes, though it does not name God explicitly.

On the other hand, some object that **methodological naturalism** limits the purview of science to physical objects and events, and that any consideration of supernatural causes (though it is often informed by science) necessarily occupies the realm of philosophy and theology and cannot claim the attributes of **scientific proof**. On theological grounds, some Christians object that the generic **theism** defended by **natural theology** is too thin to provide any real benefit, even if such arguments are deemed successful—although the relatively recent discipline of ramified natural theology does concern major tenets of distinctively Christian theism. Others suggest that the Bible itself leads us to expect that God would not make his existence demonstrable through clear scientific proof (see **Hiddenness of God**).

The boundaries between science and other pursuits of knowledge, and the importance of avoiding errors such as **scientism**, have been discussed in position papers from leading scientific organizations including the American Association for the Advancement of Science, the National Science Foundation, the National Academies of Science, and their counterparts in many nations. These documents are admirably thoughtful and merit careful consideration.

The question of science's proper boundaries will continue to be important for the purposes of ensuring that scientific practice (not to mention the public's understanding of science) is free from inordinate bias, whether proreligious or antireligious. Also important is the question of relevant and legitimate resources for ambitious worldview inquiries, including whether God exists (see **God, Existence of**). A plausible posture, at least for Christians, is that the most satisfactory and reliable answers to worldview questions will require the combined resources of science, philosophy, and theology, rather than the limited resources of any single one of these disciplines.

Hugh G. Gauch Jr. and Matthew S. Tiscareno

REFERENCES AND RECOMMENDED READING

AAAS. 1989. *Science for All Americans*. Washington, DC: American Association for the Advancement of Science.
———. 1990. *The Liberal Art of Science*. Washington, DC: American Association for the Advancement of Science.
Ecklund, E. H. 2010. *Science vs. Religion: What Scientists Really Think*. Oxford: Oxford University Press.
Gauch, H. G., Jr. 2012. *Scientific Method in Brief*. Cambridge: Cambridge University Press.
———. 2013. "The Methodology of Ramified Natural Theology." *Philosophia Christi* 15:283–98.
Lindberg, D. C. 2007. *The Beginnings of Western Science*. 2nd ed. Chicago: University of Chicago Press.
Plantinga, A. 2011. *Where the Conflict Really Lies: Science, Religion, and Naturalism*. Oxford: Oxford University Press.

SCIENCE, LIMITS OF. The natural sciences make important contributions to human knowledge and welfare, but given their astonishing progress over the centuries, it is easy to overestimate their powers. It is not uncommon to read that the only knowledge that matters is scientific knowledge or that **scientific method**s are the only reliable means to knowledge (see **Scientism**). A more reasonable view of the sciences recognizes both the power and limits of scientific investigation (Gauch 2012). This entry will focus on the natural sciences, hereafter referred to as "sciences."

Presuppositions for Science

The starkest as well as most easily overlooked limitation of scientific inquiry involves the basic presuppositions making such inquiry possible. Perhaps the least recognized of these presuppositions is that truth exists. The kind of truth the sciences seek is provisional in the sense that it is conditioned by what is currently known. It is also conditioned by the commitment to empirical methods. Such methods cannot produce absolute certainty because this requires empirical omniscience: Scientists would have to collect all possible relevant evidence and understand all possible influences on a phenomenon to achieve—or at least nearly achieve—absolute certainty about it. Scientific methods are designed to tell us what we can know about things right now to the best of our ability. Scientists thus remain open to new discoveries that can prompt them to revise their current views on a given subject.

Scientific inquiry also presupposes the existence of a mind-independent world. Empirical methods presuppose an actual reality to be discovered and measured that would be there even if nobody was looking (e.g., electrons would have the mass they do even if we were unaware of their existence).

In a more obvious way, scientific methods presuppose the inescapability of logical laws (see **Logic**) as well as the basic reliability of reason and sense experience. Conducting a controlled experiment depends on reason in terms of working out the implications of a hypothesis or model, planning a design, thinking things through, and so forth. Moreover, observation is only meaningful if sense experience is trustworthy as a means for gaining knowledge.

There is no requirement that reason or sense experience be perfect (otherwise knowledge would be impossible), just basically reliable.

Furthermore, sense experience is tied to a material reality that can be engaged. Not that human sense experience must only be of physical reality—for example, Christians sense the presence of the Holy Spirit testifying that we are children of the Father (Rom. 8:15–16). Rather, the kinds of sense experiences scientific investigation relies on presuppose a genuine physical world to observe.

Applying scientific methods to study nature also presupposes the uniformity of nature, the idea that natural laws and the processes that scientists study are the same everywhere and at every time. For example, electricity and magnetism work the same in North America as in Africa as in South America, throughout our solar system, galaxy, and universe. Moreover, these forces have worked the same in the past as they do today and will continue to do so. Exploring **laws of nature** presupposes that nature has this kind of uniformity (see **Uniformitarianism**).

Furthermore, scientific investigation presupposes that nature is intelligible. No matter how uniform and persistent nature's patterns, if it were not possible to make sense of those patterns, scientific investigation would be impossible.

Demonstrating Science's Presuppositions

Without these presuppositions, scientific inquiry is a nonstarter; indeed, no forms of human inquiry are possible without such presuppositions. Yet scientific methods themselves cannot be used to demonstrate the truth of these presuppositions. Attempting to do so commits the circular argument fallacy, assuming what one wishes to demonstrate. Science must assume that these presuppositions are well justified and see where its inquiry leads in light of these commitments.

Because of any kind of human inquiry's reliance on basic presuppositions, the kind of evidentialist **epistemology** exemplified by W. K. Clifford—"It is wrong, always, everywhere, and for anyone to believe anything upon insufficient evidence" (1901, 183)—is incoherent. We cannot produce "sufficient evidence" for the basic reliability of reason and sense experience without already presupposing that reliability. Hence the evidence to which Clifford would appeal only makes sense in light of certain presuppositions. Additionally, no one believes these presuppositions based on the kind of evidence Clifford demands; instead, we discover and assess evidence based on them. Scientism—the view that only scientific methods can produce knowledge

and only scientific knowledge is genuine—founders in a similar way.

Presuppositions can only be motivated or justified as elements of a larger philosophical or theological view. So the sciences are dependent on deep, underlying philosophical commitments just like any other human inquiry—or, indeed, anything worthwhile in life. In this sense, the sciences are in a position of trust not unlike religious commitment.

Therefore scientific methods have a significant limitation: they rely on presuppositions we come to understand through philosophical and theological ways of knowing. Relatedly, the sciences represent some, but not the only, ways of knowing. Scientific methods may be the best way to discover knowledge about nature, but they are not the only way. Nor are they the only way of knowing in general, as there are historical, philosophical, and aesthetic ways of knowing, among others.

In addition, scientific methods are not designed to detect or uncover meaning. They are designed to explore physical reality, which they do effectively. Physical properties and processes studied by the sciences do not discover purposes, judgments, and the like—nor do they produce language for reasoning and articulating experience. Purposes, values, meanings, declarations, arguments, and such do not exist in the subatomic, chemical, and biological domains. They exist in the domain of human **consciousness**. Even scientific theories, which scientific methods help to formulate and probe, are meanings that humans must sort through as understandings of the natural world.

Science as Self-Limiting

In sum, since scientific methods are designed to probe physical reality, they are limited to that reality. This self-limitation has been part of the power of the sciences to discover tremendous knowledge about nature while also serving as a natural, appropriate boundary (Gauch 2012).

Therefore any scientific investigation involves more than merely "scientific methods," "data," and "analysis." Without the purposes, values, and meanings that humans bring to the processes of investigation, scientific methods could not exist or be able to contribute to our understanding of nonphysical things. Furthermore, to categorize purposes, values, and meanings as "subjective" or "less real" because they are not physical is to (a) fall into a philosophical view called *metaphysical naturalism*, where nature—the physical—is all that genuinely objectively exists, and (b) fail to notice how much the sciences depend on the nonphysical for their existence and success. With an understanding of the **limits of science**, we can see such dependency more clearly.

The self-limitation of scientific methods' focus on physical reality underlies **methodological naturalism**, which has been an important part of the sciences but is also motivated theologically (Bishop 2013), since self-limitation to physical phenomena does not necessitate there being nothing beyond the physical. Rather, this self-limitation—along with the sciences themselves—can be seen as dependent on the non-physical: the purposes, values, and meanings that make the existence and pursuit of scientific inquiry possible.

Robert C. Bishop

REFERENCES AND RECOMMENDED READING

Bishop, R. C. 2013. "God and Methodological Naturalism in the Scientific Revolution and Beyond." *Perspectives on Science and Christian Faith* 65:10–23.
Clifford, W. K. 1901. *Lectures and Essays.* London: Macmillan.
Gauch, H. 2012. *Scientific Method in Brief.* Cambridge: Cambridge University Press.

SCIENCE, PRESUPPOSITIONS OF. Many people, including some famous physicists, are unaware that science requires philosophical presuppositions to be a properly grounded rational pursuit. Those presuppositions are themselves either self-evident or require support by inquiry beyond science. "Philosophy is dead," Stephen Hawking and Leonard Mlodinow announced in their bestseller (Hawking and Mlodinow 2010, 5), because it "has not kept up with modern developments in science."

Although science has overturned some philosophical ideas about space, time, and other aspects of existence, such episodes don't justify declaring the death of an entire discipline. Moreover, the very statement "Philosophy is dead" is philosophical, not scientific, and thus self-defeating in this context. It is as self-refuting as saying, "I can't speak a word of English." Scientists are not exempt from the logical (philosophical) rule of "a self-refuting claim cannot be true." Such a rule (like the assertion "Philosophy is dead") cannot be justified by performing experiments or engaging in other modes of scientific inquiry. This logical rule is self-evident, and science depends on such philosophical insight.

Hawking and Mlodinow further illustrate, unwittingly, how philosophy is *alive* in the presuppositional background of science when they write, "Because there is a law like gravity, the universe can and will create itself from nothing" (Hawking and Mlodinow 2010, 180). Something can't cause itself to come into existence because it would have to exist already to have causal powers. So their assertion is self-contradictory. Furthermore, a natural law like gravity is not "nothing." This is either an equivocation on the term *nothing*, or a contradiction (Keas 2013). Scientists necessarily engage in irrationality when they propose theories that violate the philosophical principle of internal coherence (i.e., avoiding self-contradiction). Hawking has made profound discoveries despite his rationality-defying **scientism**, which assumes philosophy is obsolete. He has made these discoveries while making use of logical principles (such as internal coherence) that fall under the purview of philosophy.

Contrast Hawking and Mlodinow's naive scientism with **Johannes Kepler**'s (1571–1630) philosophical-theological presuppositions. Kepler, celebrated in **astronomy** textbooks for his three laws of planetary motion, contrasted his mathematical analysis of nature with **Aristotle**, "who did not believe that the World had been created and thus could not recognize the power of these quantitative figures as archetypes [i.e., design plans for the material world], because without an architect there is no such power in them to make anything" physical. Yet, Kepler argued, a mathematical study of celestial **physics** "is acceptable to me and to all Christians, since our Faith holds that the World, which had no previous existence, was created by God in weight, measure, and number, that is in accordance with ideas coeternal with Him" (Kepler 1997, 115).

Kepler presupposed that mathematical ideas exist eternally in the divine **mind** and that God freely selected some of these mathematical rules to govern his creation. Kepler's Christian philosophical presuppositions thus aided him in discovering natural laws. Had Hawking and Mlodinow been committed to Kepler's **philosophy of science**, they would have avoided self-contradictory statements about the universe coming from nothing.

Historians of science have documented (Keas 2013) how Christian theology assisted in the establishment of philosophical presuppositions that helped justify observational and other **scientific method**s. The Christian belief in divine freedom undercut the view established by **Plato** and Aristotle that the structure of the cosmos is a necessary one. Christians insisted that God could have created a universe quite different from the one Aristotle imagined, and so they concluded that multiple-hypothesis testing by experiment and other observational techniques is an effective way to determine which set of natural laws God actually created (Davis 1999). Without such a presupposition, it is difficult to justify the scientific enterprise.

Christianity cultivated both humility and confidence in human knowledge. Confidence derives from the orderliness of God's world designed for discovery by his human image bearers. However, the Christian doctrine of **the fall** of **Adam and Eve** (and our status as finite creatures) provides an **explanation** for the difficulty of human reason in achieving certainty about the cosmos, with a consequent emphasis on the testing of hypotheses. Many medieval and early modern scientists presupposed this balance of confidence and humility (Harrison 2007).

To extend this historical survey of science's philosophical presuppositions to additional contemporary analysis of this subject, the moral rules presupposed by science are important. Ethics, a branch of philosophy, analyzes **morality**, including moral rules important for the truth-oriented trajectory of scientific research. For instance, scientists ought to honestly evaluate and report all data relevant to their work, rather than deal only with data friendly to their preferred theories. The success of science depends on scientists operating in harmony with such ethical presuppositions.

Ethics, which fits within the philosophical study of value (axiology), is related to the truth-indicating values called *theoretical virtues*, which scientists presuppose in their work. Indeed, the best theories in most academic disciplines exhibit many of the same theoretical virtues. These virtuous traits indicate that a theory is likely true, and usually include evidential accuracy, causal adequacy, conceptual clarity, internal coherence (lacking in the Hawking-Mlodinow theory above), universal coherence, scope, elegance, simplicity, relative lack of ad hoc modification, predictive success, fruitfulness, and applicability.

Yet other philosophical (metaphysical and epistemological) presuppositions and questions are resident in and beneath the theoretical virtues. Are theoretical virtues truth indicative or merely pragmatic? What is **causation**? Why are elegant, simple theories more likely to be true than ugly, complicated ones? Do naturalistic presuppositions (see **Methodological Naturalism**) preclude recognition of certain truths about nature? Scientists should not try to saw off the branches of philosophy on which they sit (Plantinga 2011).

Although the identification, characterization, and ranking of the theoretical virtues are debated by philosophers (Lacey 1999, 52–53; McMullin 2012, 697–99) and by participants in specific theoretical disputes, many scholars agree that these virtues help us to infer which rival theory is the best explanation (Kuhn 1977, 321–22; Lipton 2004, 122–23; see **Inference to the Best Explanation**). Historical and philosophical studies of widely accepted theories, especially in the natural sciences (Doppelt 2007, 96–118), have helped us to recognize, refine, and more skillfully apply these rational tools in all theory-making enterprises across the disciplines. This illustrates how many of the widely recognized philosophical presuppositions of science also guide inquiry in other academic fields.

Christian theology has resources to help us make sense of the philosophical presuppositions of science (Plantinga 2011), many of which direct the search for truth across all fields. Although we lack space to develop this point further (see Keas forthcoming), we have seen how Kepler understood some of this four centuries ago. It is a tragedy that some famous physicists, like Hawking and Mlodinow, despite their great admiration for Kepler, have tried to cut themselves off from the philosophical presuppositions (and associated theological insights) on which he grounded science as a rational enterprise.

Michael N. Keas

REFERENCES AND RECOMMENDED READING

Davis, Edward. 1999. "Christianity and Early Modern Science: The Foster Thesis Reconsidered." In *Evangelicals and Science in Historical Perspective*. Eds. David Livingstone et al., 75–95. New York: Oxford University Press.

Doppelt, G. 2007. "Reconstructing Scientific Realism to Rebut the Pessimistic Meta-induction." *Philosophy of Science* 74:96–118.

Harrison, Peter. 2007. *The Fall of Man and the Foundations of Science*. Cambridge: Cambridge University Press.

Hawking, Stephen, and Leonard Mlodinow. 2010. *The Grand Design*. New York: Bantam.

Keas, Michael. 2013. "In the Beginning: Episodes in the Origin and Development of Science." *Salvo* 26:6–12. http://salvomag.com/new/articles/salvo26-science-faith/in-the-beginning.php.

Kepler, Johannes. 1997. *The Harmony of the World*. Trans. E. J. Aiton et al. Philadelphia: American Philosophical Society.

Kuhn, Thomas. 1977. "Objectivity, Value Judgment, and Theory Choice." In *The Essential Tension*. Ed. Thomas Kuhn, 310–39. Chicago: University of Chicago.

Lacey, Hugh. 1999. *Is Science Value Free? Values and Scientific Understanding*. London: Routledge.

Lipton, Peter. 2004. *Inference to the Best Explanation*. 2nd ed. London: Routledge.

McMullin, Ernan. 2012. "Values in Science." *Zygon* 47:686–709.

Plantinga, Alvin. 2011. *Where the Conflict Really Lies*. New York: Oxford University Press.

SCIENCE, TEACHING OF.

SCIENCE, TEACHING OF. Beyond having an obligation to his or her students to teach as well as possible, the Christian teacher of science has the added duty of teaching in the service of Christ (Col. 3:23–24). This leads to the much-debated task of *biblical integration*. So the Christian science teacher must not only be well versed in the history and **philosophy of science** and the general workings of

God's physical creation but must also have a clear view of her or his own understanding about where to carve the universe at its natural/supernatural and material/immaterial joints, although the details of this can differ among committed Christians.

Integration can be accomplished both by stressing how creation declares the glory of God and by defending a proper formulation of science, properly distinguishing it from **naturalism**, **materialism**, and **scientism**. Challenging students to look at the physical world not as a brute fact but as the handiwork of their heavenly Father and worthy of study for that sake alone can lead them to new and deeper ways of praising and honoring him.

Lessons that accomplish this might reference the finetuning of physical constants—not to mention properties of water or proximity to the sun and moon—that allow Earth to be a "privileged planet," or the remarkably complex and information-rich molecular machinery of the living cell, noting that naturalists themselves use design language when speaking of cells as "factories" or brains as "computerlike." For instance, "Teleological thinking has been steadfastly resisted by modern biology. And yet, in nearly every area of research biologists are hard pressed to find language that does not impute purposiveness to living forms" (Lenoir 1992, ix). Of course, lessons should not fail to consider that Christianity also offers fruitful guidelines and boundaries for doing science and using **technology** ethically and for the benefit of our neighbors, and in caring for creation.

Moreland (2003), however, believes that integration must go beyond a simple "doxology" approach. Since **the Enlightenment**, a thoroughgoing metaphysical naturalism has given "science" epistemic authority in Western culture. The Christian science teacher should lose no opportunity to point out that a proper formulation of science and the **scientific method** does not necessarily presuppose a metaphysical naturalism, that strong materialism is an unwarranted reduction, and that scientism is not science but instead is a philosophical position not discovered by simple observation and experimentation.

The Christian science teacher laboring at a secular institution can do this as well, within limitations, using a minimalist approach (Plantinga 2011). The teacher can teach the naturalistic explanations given in the textbook, while exposing unwarranted reductions and humbly pointing out their weaknesses in a nonsectarian manner, and pointing out that the human activity we call "science" practically does not, and indeed metaphysically cannot, explain everything.

Textbooks provide another opportunity to contend for a more balanced approach. Chapter 1 in most science textbooks usually contains a rudimentary and amateurish history and philosophy of science (McComas 1998) that bears at least a classroom discussion, if not outright correction. The history of science can also be integrated into a curriculum, as many prominent scientists were at least theists, and some, like Faraday and Maxwell, were quite evangelical.

Thus it is possible to teach the natural sciences in such a way so as not inadvertently to create more accidental naturalists, but to reproduce scholars who are trained in detecting the subtle influences of naturalism and materialism in their textbooks, their culture, and the media, and who value God's material and immaterial creation in a manner that honors him.

Mark A. Pichaj

REFERENCES AND RECOMMENDED READING

Barbour, Ian. 1997. *Religion and Science: Historical and Contemporary Issues.* New York: HarperOne.
Bloom, John A. 2015. *The Natural Sciences: A Student's Guide.* Reclaiming the Christian Intellectual Tradition. Ed. David S. Dockery. Wheaton, IL: Crossway.
Brush, Nigel. 2005. *The Limitations of Scientific Truth: Why Science Can't Answer Life's Ultimate Questions.* Grand Rapids: Kregel.
Cohen, I. Bernard, ed. 1990. *Puritanism and the Rise of Modern Science: The Merton Thesis.* Rutgers University Press.
Hunter, Cornelius G. 2007. *Science's Blind Spot: The Unseen Religion of Scientific Naturalism.* Grand Rapids: Brazos.
Lennox, John C. 2009. *God's Undertaker: Has Science Buried God?* Oxford: Lion.
Lenoir, Timothy. 1992. *The Strategy of Life.* Chicago: University of Chicago Press.
McComas, William F., ed. 1998. *The Nature of Science in Science Education.* Leiden: Kluwer Academic. Online adaptation, "The Principal Elements of the Nature of Science: Dispelling the Myths." http://i.e teoria.ru/u/39/95 da7cd0c811e495c88addfed12f18/-/TheMythsOfScience.pdf.
Moreland, J. P. 1989. *Christianity and the Nature of Science: A Philosophical Investigation.* Grand Rapids: Baker.
———. 2003. "Academic Integration and Christian Scholarship." In *Philosophy: Christian Perspectives for the New Millennium.* Eds. Paul Copan, Scott B. Luley, and Stan W. Wallace. Dallas and Norcross, GA: CLM/RZIM.
Pearcey, Nancy R., and Charles B. Thaxton. 1994. *The Soul of Science: Christian Faith & Natural Philosophy.* Wheaton, IL: Crossway.
Plantinga, Alvin. 2011. *Where the Conflict Really Lies: Science, Religion, and Naturalism.* Oxford: Oxford University Press.
Wiker, Benjamin, and Jonathan Witt. 2006. *A Meaningful World: How the Arts and Sciences Reveal the Genius of Nature.* Downers Grove, IL: IVP Academic.

SCIENCE, VOCATION OF. Although modern usage of the word *vocation* can simply mean an occupation, the original idea of a vocation was developed within Christianity and referred to a unique calling by God.

In the context of science and vocation, the seminal work

devoted to this subject is arguably the text of a lecture given by the German philosopher and political economist Max Weber in 1918 at the University of Munich and published by Dunker & Humboldt in 1919. Titled "Science as Vocation," this speech touches on the political and economic realities of pursuing a career in science in Germany and in the United States in the early twentieth century, as well as the intrinsic value of scientific inquiry compared with other academic and artistic disciplines. It includes discussion on the role of religion in contemporary life and on the disenchantment of our rationalized and intellectualized world (Weber 1946).

Weber pointed out that scientists in the Middle Ages and Reformation periods believed they were doing God's task by understanding nature and were showing a path to God. However, he then stated, "Who ... still believes that the findings of **astronomy**, biology, **physics**, or chemistry could teach us anything about the meaning of the world?" (Weber 1946, 8). He then argued that even though science does not give the way to God or even the way to happiness, it still has something to contribute to practical and personal life. Weber lists three aspects of science that make it a true "vocation."

> Science contributes to the **technology** of controlling life by calculating external objects as well as man's activity.
> Science can contribute ... methods of thinking, the tools and the training for thought.
> The contribution of science does not reach its limit with this. We are in a position to help you to a third objective: to gain clarity of thought. (Weber 1946, 13)

Although Weber dismissed the early scientists' belief that science is a vocation and calling because it shows a path to God, that idea cannot be so easily discarded. The apostle Paul writes in Romans 1:20, "For since the creation of the world God's invisible qualities—his eternal power and divine nature—have been clearly seen, being understood from what has been made, so that people are without excuse." King David writes in Psalm 19:1, "The heavens declare the glory of God; the skies proclaim the work of his hands." Later in the Psalms, we read, "Great are the works of the LORD; they are pondered by all who delight in them" (Ps. 111:2).

These and other biblical passages indicate that God's character can be seen by observing nature. A scientist studying the workings of the universe should clearly be able to see the hand of God and even observe specific qualities

about God's being. As an example, observations that have led to our understanding of the **origin of the universe** indicate that the cause of this universe must be transcendent, a clear characteristic of God. Observations of **fine-tuning** and design of the universe lead to the **anthropic principle** that indicates humans have a special place in the universe. Biblical proclamations and modern discoveries support the idea that a career in science can be a vocation indeed.

Michael G. Strauss

REFERENCES AND RECOMMENDED READING

Weber, Max. (1919) 1946. *From Max Weber: Essays in Sociology.* Trans. and eds. H. H. Gerth and C. Wright Mills. New York: Oxford University Press. http://anthropos-lab.net/wp/wp-content/uploads/2011/12/Weber-Science-as-a-Vocation.pdf.

SCIENCE AND THE BIBLE. How to relate the Bible and the sciences is a central theme in science-Christianity discussions. This relationship is not as straightforward as many of these discussions presuppose, however. God is the source of both the Bible and creation (see **Two Books Metaphor**) and all things are reconciled in Christ (Col. 1:20). So Christians may proceed with confidence and humility in exploring the relationship between the Bible and the sciences, confident because we have the sure promise that all things are reconciled in the one through whom all things were made and are being redeemed, and humble because we are not certain about the ultimate shape that reconciliation between the Bible and the sciences takes. There are two broad approaches to exploring this reconciliation: *concordism* and *nonconcordism*.

Concordism

Concordism is an interpretive framework presupposing biblical and scientific statements are directly correlated. The idea is that biblical statements have scientific import, so we should expect implications for the actual content of the sciences. One example of concordist readings of biblical texts would be interpreting Genesis 1 as describing the exact sequence and timing of the origin of the world in the span of six calendar days (e.g., Morris 1976). A second example would be a day-age interpretation of Genesis 1 in which the "days" correspond to geological ages. Though strikingly different, both of these concordist interpretations take possible scientific implications of the text very seriously.

The strengths of concordist interpretations are that they seek to deal authentically with an authoritative text, to establish relevance of the Bible for science-saturated societies, and to generally present what appear to be clear, understandable readings of biblical texts.

There are also significant objections to concordist interpretations. First, concordist readings of Scripture only became possible with the development of modern Western standards for how to conceive science and history, so they are relatively recent developments in terms of biblical hermeneutics. Nothing corresponding to concordism existed in the first few centuries of Christian interpretation of the Bible (Bouteneff 2008; Harrison 1998; Hauser and Watson 2008, 2009).

Second, much is made of "face value," "plain sense," or "literal" interpretations of biblical texts, such as Genesis 1, in some Christian circles, yet concordist readings do not always take biblical texts at face value. Instead, they seek a modern scientific interpretation of biblical texts. Such interpretations are often foreign to the ancient historical context of the original authors and audience of the texts.

A third related objection is that although concordist readings seek to treat the Bible as authoritative, such interpretations may privilege a form of scientific harmony over other meanings. In response, many argue that the authority of biblical texts ought to lie in their meanings in their historical context, not in the context of modern science. Sometimes concordists respond to such objections by maintaining that the Holy Spirit could have superintended such meanings knowing the relevance they would have for future generations (see discussion in Howell 2003).

This leads to a fourth major worry for concordism: By demanding some form of direct implication between biblical texts and scientific claims, Christians can presuppose **scientism**, which is the view that interpretations must be "scientific" to count because only scientific content and understanding ultimately matter. Concordist interpretations can be preoccupied with "being scientific," thus tacitly drawing on Enlightenment assumptions and standards for how historical and scientific texts function. Arguably the reason for pursuing concordist readings has more to do with changes in Western ideals about what counts as knowledge and various modern apologetic concerns than anything else (e.g., Turner 1986).

Nonconcordism

Nonconcordism is an interpretive framework where correlations or parallels between biblical and scientific statements are not required—no scientific implications of biblical statements are presupposed. Nonconcordist interpretations do not necessarily spiritualize or allegorize biblical texts, however, as that would evade concrete realities the texts address. Instead, nonconcordist interpretations generally take biblical texts on their own terms within their historical and cultural context to understand the realities they address. Such interpretations typically focus on what the original authors and audience would have understood those texts to mean.

An example of a nonconcordist interpretive framework would be the literary framework hypothesis where Genesis 1 establishes the creation kingdoms in days 1 through 3 while days 4 through 6 establish the production of creature kings (e.g., Kline 1996). Another example would be reading Genesis 1 as having the structure of a temple dedication text where the creation is God's temple (e.g., Walton 2009).

Strengths of nonconcordist interpretations are that they seek to deal seriously with an authoritative text, generally practice the Reformation principle that Scripture interprets Scripture, usually avoid "Bible-science" controversies, and make it possible for theology and the sciences to learn from each other without placing either in a straitjacket.

There are objections to nonconcordist interpretations as well. First is the potential lack of relevance of such interpretations for societies dominated by scientific thinking. Those who seek to engage in a scientifically relevant brand of apologetics (e.g., **Reasons to Believe**) do not find nonconcordist frameworks helpful to their cause. Second, sometimes it is argued that nonconcordist interpretations avoid scientific controversies precisely because they do not take the biblical texts as authoritative. This objection is countered by the point that biblical authority is rooted in the authors' meanings in their historical context rather than in modern Western contexts.

A third, and perhaps most pressing, objection is that nonconcordist frameworks seem to provide few constraints on biblical interpretation. Under concordist frameworks, something like a "literal" approach to texts or a correspondence between "days" and ages constrain the range of biblical interpretation of Genesis 1, for instance. Nonconcordist frameworks appear to allow almost any readings of the texts (including overspiritualizing and allegorizing texts, an objection to the church father Origen's interpretations that has reverberated throughout the history of biblical interpretation).

The worry is that interpreters might opt for spiritualizing biblical texts or looking for metaphorical interpretations too quickly in the face of scientific knowledge. This would be letting science have too much influence in biblical interpretation. The dangers of undue scientific influence in biblical interpretation are always present in a science-saturated age. Proponents of nonconcordist interpretations respond by arguing that authorial intentions and historical and cultural contexts generate sufficient constraints to shield against undue scientific influences. Nonconcordists generally do not find these responses compelling.

Reconciliation and Relationship

Returning to Colossians 1:20, the implication of all things being reconciled in Christ is that there should be an appropriate, fruitful relationship between the Bible and the sciences. We know from human relationships, say, between friends or husband and wife, that relationships can be carried out well or poorly. Relationships have quarrels and reconciliations, mutual help and enjoyment, and so on. Through such dynamics, a husband and wife learn about and from each other, develop as persons, and play important roles in each other's growth. So it should be with the Bible-science relationship where biblical interpretations and scientific interpretations of creation are conversant with each other, cooperate with each other, and aid each other while also following their own developmental paths. Just as in human relationships, working out an appropriate balance is an important and ongoing part of any healthy relationship. The relationship between the Bible and the sciences is no different.

Robert C. Bishop

REFERENCES AND RECOMMENDED READING

Bouteneff, P. 2008. *Beginnings: Ancient Christian Readings of the Biblical Creation Narratives.* Grand Rapids: Baker Academic.
Harrison, P. 1998. *The Bible, Protestantism and the Rise of Natural Science.* Cambridge: Cambridge University Press.
Hauser, A., and D. Watson, eds. 2008. *A History of Biblical Interpretation.* Vol. 1, *The Ancient Period.* Grand Rapids: Eerdmans.
———. 2009. *A History of Biblical Interpretation.* Vol. 2, *The Medieval through the Reformation Periods.* Grand Rapids: Eerdmans.
Howell, K. J. 2003. *God's Two Books: Copernican Cosmology and Biblical Interpretation in Early Modern Science.* Notre Dame, IN: University of Notre Dame Press.
Kline, M. G. 1996. "Space and Time in the Genesis Cosmogony." *Perspectives on Science & Christian Faith* 48:2–15.
Morris, H. M. 1976. *The Genesis Record: A Scientific and Devotional Commentary on the Book of Beginnings.* Grand Rapids: Baker.
Turner, J. 1986. *Without God, without Creed: The Origins of Unbelief in America.* Baltimore: Johns Hopkins University Press.
Walton, J. H. 2009. *The Lost World of Genesis One: Ancient Cosmology and the Origins Debate.* Downers Grove, IL: InterVarsity.

SCIENCE AND THE CHURCH FATHERS. The science with which early Christians had to deal was a branch of philosophy built on the so-called natural books of **Aristotle**. Unlike modern science, Aristotle's work was highly speculative and had almost no practical applications. Furthermore, we now know that the majority of its conclusions were wrong. Greek **mathematics**, especially geometry, was of more lasting value and remained a basic element of education even once Christianity became the official religion of the Roman Empire.

The Early Church Fathers and Science

Given its peripheral relationship to theology, the earliest Christian writers had little to say about science. Some, such as Justin Martyr, were comfortable with Greek philosophy. Others, like Tertullian, were notoriously hostile. "What," he asked, "has Athens [pagan philosophy] to do with Jerusalem [Christian theology]?" With this question, he seemed to have rejected all the fruits of pagan learning and even rejected reason. However, his concern was with pagan ethics rather than **natural philosophy**. He simply was not interested in science.

Tertullian's ambivalence was shared by many Christian writers. Science was a minority interest, and there were not many reasons for apologists or theologians to engage with it. Where it could be useful was in biblical interpretation, and the Alexandrian fathers of the third century had more to say about the subject in this context. Origen thought that mathematical disciplines like **astronomy** and geometry were useful tools for exegesis. He compared pagan learning to the gold of the Egyptians that the Hebrews had taken with them at the exodus. Christians should simply take those parts of Greek science that were useful and ignore the rest. Origen's near-contemporary Clement of Alexandria put this advice into practice as he drew freely on pagan philosophers in his theological writing.

The risk that commentaries on Scripture might become redundant if they were based on science that was itself in error was recognized by other church fathers, such as Basil, bishop of Caesarea. His *Homilies of the Hexaemeron* (the six **days of creation**) shows that he is both well-versed in Greek science and unwilling to take hostages to fortune in his interpretations. For instance, he explains the Greek model of the cosmos in some detail but does not state that it is true. Instead, he urges Christians to raise their eyes above the exact details of how the world works to the glory of its creator. Basil makes much of the fact that Greek thinkers frequently disagreed about fundamental questions. As a mere spectator to their arguments, he quickly deduced he could not rely on any of them.

Opposition to Christianity

Also during the third century, Christianity became influential enough to provoke a hostile response. Neoplatonism, a blend of the philosophy of **Plato** with magical and theological thinking, became the dominant school of pagan thought. Some of its major figures, such as Porphyry (whose polemical works were banned by the Christian Roman Empire), were actively antagonistic toward Christianity. However, Neoplatonism was a mystical creed that was far removed from the natural science of Aristotle. The philosophy that the later church fathers found themselves opposing looked nothing like what we think of as science today.

Neoplatonic opposition to Christianity provoked a reaction from the authorities once the Roman Empire became officially Christian in the fourth century. Pagan philosophers had set up shop in Athens, then something of a backwater city, to reestablish the ancient academy of Plato, which had been closed down by the Romans in 86 BC. This new school was eventually shut on the orders of the emperor Justinian in AD 529 as part of his campaign to Christianize the empire.

The Latin Fathers

In the Western Empire, where Latin rather than Greek was the common language, only the most educated had direct access to the works of philosophers and mathematicians like Aristotle and Ptolemy (see **Claudius Ptolemy**). This means that relatively few of the Latin fathers interacted closely with Greek science. A few of those that did, however, made some egregious mistakes. Lactantius, whose *Divine Institutes* was an attempt to set out a complete Christian apologia, mocked Greek philosophers for believing that the earth is a sphere.

Augustine of Hippo was a better judge. In his *Confessions*, he tells how he resisted the blandishments of the Manicheans because he found their astronomy so laughable. Augustine recognized the achievements of ancient astronomers — for instance, their ability to predict eclipses — while rejecting the ability of astrologers to predict the future. He used his scientific knowledge to add nuance to his biblical interpretation and was also concerned that Christians might be exposed to ridicule if they lacked sufficient education in science. "It is a disgraceful and dangerous thing," he

warned in his *Literal Meaning of Genesis*, "for a pagan to hear a Christian, presumably giving the meaning of Holy Scripture, talking nonsense on these topics" (Augustine 1982, 42 [1:19]). Consequently, Augustine read the Scriptures in the light of the best science available to him.

Unfortunately, Augustine's work is therefore somewhat compromised by the inaccuracies of the pagan thinkers he is using in order to understand Holy Scripture. For example, he interpreted the reference to the waters above the **firmament** in Genesis 1:6–7 through the medium of Aristotle's theory of the elements. The waters above the firmament led Christian thinkers to postulate that there were three heavens: the outermost empyrean where God and his angels dwell; the crystalline watery heaven; and below that, the firmament containing the visible stars. Thus biblical interpretations based on whatever happens to be the latest science of the time are always vulnerable to that science later being proven wrong.

Late Antiquity

By the sixth century, paganism was rapidly fading from view. At this stage, even the teachers of philosophy in Alexandria could be Christians. The foremost of these was John Philoponus. His refinements of Alexandrian **physics** represented considerable scientific progress. For instance, he is the first writer to note that heavy objects fall at much the same speed as light objects. This is contrary to one of Aristotle's axioms, and yet the converse is easily demonstrated.

Philoponus also developed one of the earliest versions of impetus theory to explain the motion of projectiles. He actively engaged with pagan natural philosophers such as Simplicius, one of those whom Justinian had dispossessed from the school in Athens. However, the possible flowering of science in Alexandria from the cross-pollination of Christianity and philosophy did not take place because the city was shortly thereafter conquered first by the Persians and then by Islamic invaders.

In the Latin-speaking West, the Roman Empire was extinguished by barbarian tribes from Germany. Christian Romans sought employment with the new kings. Among them was Boethius who was acutely conscious that the old world was coming to an end. He sought to translate the works of Aristotle, as well as primers on arithmetic and geometry, into Latin so that Greek learning might be preserved. Unfortunately, he was executed by the barbarian king he served before his project could be completed. Later Latin fathers, such as Isidore of Seville and the Venerable Bede, had to draw on Roman encyclopedias such as the

Natural History of Pliny the Elder. This meant that only a modicum of scientific and mathematic knowledge was preserved in the West until Greek learning was rediscovered in the twelfth century.

James Hannam

REFERENCES AND RECOMMENDED READING

Augustine. 1982. *The Literal Meaning of Genesis.* Vol. 1. Trans. John Hammond Taylor. New York: Newman.

Cameron, Alan. 1969. "The Last Days of the Academy at Athens." *Proceedings of the Cambridge Philological Society*, new ser., 195 (15): 7–29.

Lindberg, David. 2000. "Science and the Early Church." In *The Scientific Enterprise in Antiquity and the Middle Ages.* Ed. Michael Shank, 125–46. Chicago: University of Chicago Press.

———. 2008. *The Beginnings of Western Science: The European Scientific Tradition in Philosophical, Religious, and Institutional Context, Prehistory to A.D. 1450.* Chicago: University of Chicago Press.

Sorabji, Richard, ed. 1987. *Philoponus and the Rejection of Aristotelian Science.* London: Duckworth.

SCIENCE AND FUNDAMENTALISM. The nineteenth century was a dynamic period in the history of science, and new discoveries and theories posed unprecedented challenges to Christians who sought to correlate these developments with their understanding of biblical **revelation**—a process that proved more complex than anyone could have predicted. Throughout the century, Christians were confronted with two issues in particular that many regarded as serious threats to the credibility of the Genesis account of creation.

The first challenge involved the age of the universe and planet Earth—and by extension, how long human beings had existed. Beginning with the speculations of Emmanuel Swendenborg (1688–1772), and later popularized by **Immanuel Kant** (1724–1804), the nebular hypothesis posited an alternative to the instantaneous creation of the solar system with a process that required eons of time. The theory was slow to gain traction, but by the 1820s, due primarily to the work of French astronomer **Pierre-Simon Laplace** (1749–1827), the nebular hypothesis was generally accepted.

At the same time, many naturalists were making the case that Earth, like the rest of the solar system, was also far older than the few thousand years that a strict literalistic reading of Genesis inferred. Based initially on the discoveries of James Hutton (1726–97), by the turn of the nineteenth century, some geologists were arguing for **uniformitarianism**, the theory that the same natural laws and processes that operate throughout the universe apply also to Earth. The case for uniformitarianism was bolstered in the early 1830s

when Charles Lyell (1797–1875) published a multivolume series, *Principles of Geology*, in which he argued that Earth was in a state of perpetual change, eroding and reforming continuously over millions of years. This was significant in that uniformitarianism challenged the accepted theory of catastrophism, which held that Noah's flood had drastically altered the earth's ecosystem and was responsible for many of its geological features. Based on the new **information** gleaned from **cosmology** and **geology**, an increasing number of naturalists concluded that life on earth, including human life, had existed far longer than the 6,000 years that the biblical genealogies seemed to indicate.

Questions concerning the age of the earth were not necessarily problematical at the time because many Christians believed old-earth theories could be reconciled with the Genesis creation account. Among fundamentalist Christians (as conservatives and evangelicals were commonly called at the time), two theories of geology and the age of the earth emerged. The gap theory allowed for an indeterminate period of time between Genesis 1:1 and 1:2, which accounted for the formation of the stars and planets over long periods of time while still holding to six literal 24-hour days in which God reshaped the earth and created all life-forms only a few thousand years ago.

The two most notable proponents of the gap theory were the Reverend Dr. William Buckland (1784–1856), an English theologian, eminent geologist, paleontologist, and member of the Royal Society, and Thomas Chalmers (1780–1847), a Scottish minister, theology professor, political economist, and premier natural theologian of his day. The gap theory was later popularized in the *Scofield Reference Bible* (1909), which followed the chronology of Bishop **James Ussher** in dating the creation of **Adam and Eve** to 4004 BC.

A more popular alternative, the day-age theory, held that the six **days of creation** were not literal 24-hour days but indeterminate geological epochs. Therefore the universe could be millions of years old, and some animal life, including **dinosaurs** and other extinct **species**, could have existed for millions of years prior to the creation of human beings. The day-age theory was promoted by many notable naturalists, including Scottish geologist and evangelical Christian Hugh Miller (1802–56). Based on his examination of fossils, Miller was convinced that Earth had been inhabited by many homologous species that had gone extinct over time, but he doubted that later species were descended from earlier ones. Although undoubtedly many Christians still believed in a young earth and the recent creation of mankind based on a strict literalistic interpretation of Genesis 1–3, by the late nineteenth century many, if not most, educated Christians held that the Bible allowed for an ancient earth and even pre-Edenic life.

Far more alarming to many Christians was the challenge posed by **Charles Darwin**'s theory of **evolution**. According to Darwin, all life-forms, including human beings, evolved over millions of years via the aegis of common descent and **natural selection**, a process devoid of any hint of divine **teleology**. Not only did Darwin's theory undermine the literal "plain sense" meaning of the Genesis narrative, but it also called into question many core theological doctrines of the historic Christian faith, not least of all the historicity of Adam and the doctrine of **the fall**.

With the publication of *On the Origin of Species* (1859) and *The Descent of Man* (1871), Darwin shattered the traditional religious consensus in Europe and America. As his theory related to human beings, Darwin's stated goal was to "overthrow the dogma of separate creations" as it related to all living species, including humanity. Like all other creatures, human beings are the product of genetic mutations, natural selection, and "survival-of-the-fittest." In the process, Darwin put forth a naturalistic view of human origins in which he speculated that modern man is descended from "a hairy quadruped" that itself evolved over tens of millions of years from lower life-forms. The implication was clear: human beings are but highly evolved animals, not special creations endowed with the *imago Dei*, the **image of God**.

On the issue of evolution, Christian reactions were mixed. Most fundamentalists were skeptical, while liberal/modernist Christians who took a more critical view of the Bible readily accepted the theory. Many Christians suspected that the ramifications of **Darwinism** were potentially ruinous for the Christian faith. Although not necessarily atheistic, at the very least Darwinism undermined any reason to believe in a *theistic* God—although one might still hold to a *deistic* God who started the whole evolutionary process. Indeed, many evolutionists asserted from the outset that Darwin's theory destroyed any real basis for believing in God. As Sir Julian Huxley famously stated, "Darwinism removed the whole idea of God as the creator of organisms from the sphere of rational discussion." Conversely, others contended that Darwinism didn't necessarily destroy **natural theology**, nor did it inevitably lead to atheism.

Theistic evolutionists were quick to point out that God could have programmed the whole process from the start to ultimately produce current life-forms. So while the process may *appear* to be random and purposeless, especially to nonreligious scientists, in fact it was all in keeping with God's ultimate intention.

Among influential conservatives, Edward Hitchcock, a geologist and later president of Amherst College, regarded Darwinian evolution as a direct attack on the Christian faith. In an 1863 *Bibliotheca Sacra* article, he argued that evolution tends toward philosophical **materialism** and atheism, and thereby undermines any basis for **morality**. The Harvard professor Louis Agassiz (1807–73), one of his generation's foremost natural historians, was a convinced believer in special creation who opposed Darwinism on the basis that it was philosophically and scientifically unsupportable, while George D. Armstrong, a Princeton alumnus and a leading spokesman on science and theology among Southern Presbyterians, rejected "the hypothesis of evolution in all its forms" on purely scientific grounds. In *The Two Books of Nature and Revelation Collated* (1886), Armstrong accepted the day-age theory of an ancient earth while arguing that all life was the result of a special divine creation.

Most of the resistance against evolution came from theologians, Bible scholars, and ministers. The Reverend Gardiner Spring, an influential Presbyterian pastor in Massachusetts, was adamant that science was incapable of explaining the miracle of God's creation. The Reverend Herbert W. Morris, a professor of **mathematics** at Newington Collegiate Institution and author of the bestselling *Science and the Bible* (1871), considered **human evolution** to be "irreconcilable … with the testimony of Scripture and the facts of nature." Although he believed God had created the world in six natural days, Morris adopted the gap theory to accommodate all the various geological ages. The Reverend Luther Townsend, a Methodist minister and a graduate of Dartmouth College and Andover Theological Seminary, was one of the most influential opponents of evolutionary theory in the late nineteenth century. In works such as *Evolution or Creation* (1896), *Adam and Eve* (1904), and *The Collapse of Evolution* (1905), Townsend regarded the Genesis creation account as a simple, straightforward historical narrative of the facts "as they actually occurred." Nevertheless, he conceded that the six days of creation was figurative language for various cosmological and geological epochs.

In 1874 **Charles Hodge** (1797–1878), eminent theologian and principal of Princeton Theological Seminary, published *What Is Darwinism?* in which he claimed that the theory of natural selection and random genetic mutation was "tantamount to atheism." Hodge complained that Bible-believing

Christians were being stigmatized as "narrow-minded bigots" and "Bible worshipers," and he warned that Christianity was in "a fight for its life" against the secularizing trends of the day that elevated scientific theory above Scripture. But Hodge was no young-earth creationist. He accepted the antiquity of the earth and conceded that the Genesis genealogical tables were incomplete.

By the early 1870s, Darwinism was becoming firmly entrenched in American intellectual life, and many of the theory's earliest converts and defenders were Christian academics and clergymen. In response to fundamentalist critics, liberal Christians simply reevaluated and readjusted their interpretation of Scripture in deference to "science." Shortly after the publication of *Descent of Man*, Asa Gray (1810–88), distinguished professor of natural history at Harvard and an ardent theistic evolutionist, sought to assure not only Darwin's critics but Darwin himself that evolutionary theory allowed for "a supernatural beginning of life on earth." In response, Darwin conceded that although his theory was not necessarily "atheistical," he could not share Gray's belief in God.

Gray had many allies in academia, including James McCosh (1811–94), the president of Princeton College, who argued in *Christianity and Positivism* (1871) that natural selection was simply the product of supernatural design. Like many academics, such as the famed Vanderbilt University zoologist Alexander Winchell, McCosh was motivated by a fear that Christianity might one day be rejected for being on the wrong side of history—and thereby relegated to irrelevancy. Joseph LeConte, an eminent natural historian at the University of California, found evolutionary theory to be consistent with his understanding of "rational **theism**" and theologically unproblematic since it simply incorporated the immanent "energy of Deity."

But others such as James Dwight Dana (1813–95), America's premier geologist of the era, still drew a distinction between evolution as it applied to the animal kingdom and the special creation of humanity. (More curious was the position adopted by James Woodrow, a Presbyterian minister and professor of natural sciences at Columbia Theological Seminary, who declared that Adam's body was the result of evolutionary processes, but his **soul** and Eve's body were special divine creations.) Even a special creationist such as the respected Canadian geologist John William Dawson (1820–99) conceded in *The Story of Earth and Man* (1873) that theistic evolution could be construed in such a way as to be compatible with divine design.

Similarly, many clergymen saw no inherent contradiction between evolution and Christian theology. Most notable was Henry Ward Beecher (1813–87), one of America's best-known and beloved pastors of the era. Even staunch conservatives such as R. A. Torrey (1856–1928), who would later coedit *The Fundamentals*, acknowledged that one could believe in the infallibility of the Bible and still be "an evolutionist of a certain type"—i.e., a theistic evolutionist. Likewise, the aforementioned Charles Hodge conceded that, at least theoretically, evolution might be conceived in a way that was compatible with divine design.

Hodge's most prominent successor at Princeton Seminary was the eminent theologian **Benjamin B. Warfield** (1851–1921). Early in his career, Warfield was open to the possibility of theistic evolution, and although he conceded that Scripture could accommodate it, he was never completely convinced. In 1888 he delivered a lecture titled "Evolution or Development," which he repeated with slight modifications over subsequent years, wherein he conceived that evolution might be a secondary cause or mechanism by which God acted. But he hastened to add that this was purely conjectural, and he left it an open question.

As he put it, evolution was a "highly speculative" hypothesis that could not account for the origins of matter or the phenomenon of life, nor could it account for the human soul, self-consciousness, or our moral sensibilities. Furthermore, he reminded his audience that although a theist may see God at work in the evolutionary process, "to be a theist and a Christian are different things."

In later years he added that the whole campaign for evolution "looks amazingly like basing facts on theory rather than theory on facts" (Warfield 2000, 246).

George Frederick Wright (1838–1921), a respected geologist and theology professor at Oberlin Theological Seminary, exemplified the ambiguity of many conservative Christians in relation to Darwinism. Early in his career, Wright was a self-described "Christianized Darwinist" and close friend of Asa Gray. Wright believed in the divine inspiration of Scripture but held that it was infallible only in matters related to salvation. To bolster his position, he claimed that even Charles Hodge, the very paragon of biblical inerrancy, conceded that the biblical writers possessed no special insight when writing about history or science. However, his views began to change in the 1890s as he observed the close connection between evolutionary theory and liberal theology.

By the time he wrote his essay "The Passing of Evolution" for *The Fundamentals*, Wright was convinced that Darwinism was a purely naturalistic theory that excluded God from the creation process. Furthermore, he noted, there was no **scientific proof** for such a belief because, as far as anyone knows, life comes only from "antecedent life," and there is no evidence of any "connecting links" between man and previous life-forms.

Within 20 years of the publication of Darwin's *On the Origin of Species*, most of the American intelligentsia supported the general concept of organic evolution. Although most Christians still believed in special creation, in the late 1800s evolutionary theory was firmly established in academia as well as in most denominations and seminaries. By the early twentieth century, virtually all science textbooks taught evolutionary theory, and as William Jennings Bryan once complained, it was impossible to find "any text book on biology which does not begin with monkeys." Thus was the status of evolutionary theory at the time *The Fundamentals* addressed the issue.

Jeffrey D. Breshears

REFERENCES AND RECOMMENDED READING

Davis, Ted. 2013. "Debating Darwin: How the Church Responded to the Evolution Bombshell." BioLogos. November 22. http://biologos.org/blogs/ted-davis-reading-the-book-of-nature/debating-darwinhow-the-church-responded-to-the-evolution-bombshell.

Numbers, Ronald L. 1998. *Darwinism Comes to America*. Cambridge, MA: Harvard University Press.

———. 2006. *The Creationists: From Scientific Creationism to Intelligent Design*. Exp. ed. Cambridge, MA: Harvard University Press.

Warfield, B. B. 2000. *Evolution, Science, and Scripture: Selected Writings*. Eds. David N. Livingstone and Mark A. Noll. Grand Rapids: Baker.

SCIENCE AND THE MEDIEVAL CHURCH. Contrary to the impression given by nineteenth-century authors such as **John William Draper** and **Andrew Dickson White**, the medieval church actively encouraged the study of science as a useful adjunct to theology. Claims that the church attempted to ban **human dissection**, the number zero, or a spherical earth are untrue. No one was ever burned at the stake for beliefs that today would qualify as scientific.

The Twelfth-Century Renaissance

Up until the eleventh century, the knowledge of science in Western Europe was restricted to ancient Roman handbooks, which gave only a taste of the full achievement of Greek science. However, Catholic scholars did at least know what they were missing. Then in 1085 the Spanish city of Toledo was captured from its Islamic rulers by a Christian army. The Arabic books on Greek **mathematics** and philosophy in the city's magnificent libraries were now available for Catholics to study. The books were translated into Latin and disseminated throughout the West. At the same time, Greek books from the outposts of the Byzantine Empire were also being rendered into Latin. Within a century, almost all the surviving mathematics, medicine, and **natural philosophy** from the ancient world were available to Western readers.

As the new learning spread, theologians in France were setting out the position of natural philosophy in relation to Christian doctrine. Thinkers like William of Conches and Thierry of Chartres started from the position that the world was created by God. This meant that the study of nature was also the study of God's work. A metaphor from the time (later repeated by **Galileo**) was that both nature and the Bible were books written in the hand of God. This meant that natural philosophy was not just permitted but could be a component of Christian devotion. Nature was separate from God but followed the rules that he had ordained for it.

Determining what those rules were could also be a component of Christian study. William of Conches suggested that philosophers should seek out the secondary causes through which God acted: the Deity himself being the primary cause of everything. Thierry of Chartres noted that because nature was ordered in a rational way, it must be the product of God's wisdom. Thus science was not only permissible for a Christian; it also made rational sense to try to discover the **laws of nature** that God had decreed.

Foundation of the Universities

Following the period that saw the translation of these ancient works, the most important of the Greek authors available to the West was **Aristotle**. He had produced an entire system of philosophy that included **metaphysics**, ethics, and **physics**. Much of it was incompatible with Christian doctrine (for instance, Aristotle said the world was eternal and humans lacked individual **souls**). However, a great deal more was very useful to provide a framework for understanding how the world worked. Universities, in particular the University of Paris, provided a setting in which these questions could be considered. The university was a new kind of institution. It was self-governing and enjoyed a good deal of independence from local rulers. In Paris the university flexed its economic muscles to win concessions, while students from Oxford and Bologna founded the Universities of Cambridge and Padua respectively when they were unhappy with their treatment by local authorities.

The syllabi at the universities required students to cover mathematics and natural philosophy, as well as other subjects, in order to obtain their master of the arts degrees. Only then were they permitted to move to the theology faculty to begin a higher degree. In this way, all theologians had a solid grounding in science and math before they were even admitted to the study of Holy Scripture. While science was unquestionably a handmaiden to theology, this meant that it enjoyed a protected status and was more widely studied than it would have been in its own right.

Controversy over Aristotle

The relationship between the church and the new learning was not always smooth, however. In the early thirteenth century, a heretical sect of pantheists was uncovered in Paris that led the authorities to ban Aristotle's books on nature as potentially dangerous. The ban was overturned a few years later by the pope, who was convinced by the university's professors that the useful material in Aristotle's work outweighed any heterodox elements. A project to correct the books never came to fruition, and they rapidly became central to the university curriculum.

The elements of Aristotle's thought that were in conflict with Christian doctrine were particularly emphasized by his Arab commentator Averroës. In particular, Averroës emphasized a **determinism** in which the laws of nature were fixed by logical necessity: God had no choice about how the universe was organized. Averroists also argued that on philosophical questions, Aristotle should trump Holy Scripture.

The dispute came to a head in the 1270s when the university decreed that only qualified theologians could determine religious questions. Then in 1277 the bishop of Paris issued a list of 219 banned opinions. Among other things, this ban made it illegal to deny that humans have free will, illegal to say that God could only have created one universe, and illegal to claim that a vacuum is impossible. The essential message of the condemnations was that Aristotle was not infallible. This was important because, as we now know, most Aristotelian science was wrong, and only by condemning its more extreme conclusions could the church clear the ground for any real progress in science.

One area where the church did support Aristotle was in his rejection of **atomism**. The theory that the world is made up of tiny particles was not compatible with the doctrine of transubstantiation as far as it was understood in the Middle Ages. For this reason, Nicholas of Autrecourt, one of the few medieval atomists, was compelled to retract his ideas in 1347.

Scientific Achievements in the Middle Ages

Following the 1277 condemnations, scholars at Oxford and Paris began to criticize Aristotle's physics. In particular the Merton Calculators (named after the college in Oxford where most of them worked) developed a theory of motion called the *mean speed theorem* that was later used by Galileo as the foundation for his own mechanics.

Later in the fourteenth century, the Parisian theologian **Nicole Oresme** used graphical methods to prove the mean speed theorem and show that quantities such as acceleration and distance can be represented geometrically. **Jean Buridan**, rector of the University of Paris and Oresme's teacher, suggested early versions of the law of inertia and also that the earth might be rotating. Buridan argued that when two boats are moving relative to each other on a calm sea, it is not possible to tell which of them is actually in motion without reference to their surroundings. Likewise, standing on the earth, we cannot tell whether it or the heavens are rotating. This argument was used by **Copernicus** and Galileo when they suggested that the earth orbits the sun.

Despite these achievements, medieval science faded into obscurity during the early-modern period when Copernicus, Galileo, and others declined to give their medieval antecedents any credit. At the same time, the Protestant Reformation and humanist veneration for the ancient world further obscured medieval achievements. Modern historians have only rediscovered medieval achievements in science in the last few decades.

James Hannam

REFERENCES AND RECOMMENDED READING

Grant, Edward. 2001. *God and Reason in the Middle Ages.* Cambridge: Cambridge University Press.

Hannam, James. 2010. *The Genesis of Science: How the Medieval World Launched the Scientific Revolution.* New York: Regnery.

Lindberg, David. 2003. "The Medieval Church Encounters the Classical Tradition: Saint Augustine, Roger Bacon and the Handmaiden Metaphor." In *When Science and Christianity Meet.* Eds. David Lindberg and Ronald Numbers, 7–32. Chicago: University of Chicago Press.

———. 2008. *The Beginnings of Western Science: The European Scientific Tradition in Philosophical, Religious, and Institutional Context, Prehistory to A.D. 1450.* Chicago: University of Chicago Press.

Moody, Ernest. 1970. "Buridan, Jean." In *Dictionary of Scientific Biography.* Ed. Charles Coulston Gillispie. New York: Scribner.

Pedersen, Olaf. 1997. *The First Universities: Studium Generale and the Origins of University Education in Europe.* Cambridge: Cambridge University Press.

Thijssen, J. M. M. H. 1998. *Censure and Heresy at the University of Paris, 1200–1400.* Philadelphia: University of Pennsylvania Press.

SCIENCE AND MODERNITY. The sciences hold a preeminent place in modern Western societies. This contrasts with premodern European Christendom where Christianity held the place of honor. Modernity is sometimes simplistically conceived as the throwing off of religious shackles, with the sciences playing a leading role in pushing Christianity and other forms of **theism** aside on its way to the top of the heap (e.g., Coyne 2015; Dawkins 2008). This popularized story conceals much more than it possibly illuminates as the relationships among modernity, religion, and the sciences are far more complex (e.g., Taylor 2007; Turner 1985). Since modernity itself is a complex behemoth, the focus here will be on an important kernel of modernity—a particularly influential conception of knowledge that still dominates much of the popularized discussions of science, modernity, and religion.

Christianity, Science, and Modernity: Distinct yet Inseparable

Part of the inspiration for this "modern science pushes out religion" understanding of modern Western history comes from the way the High **Enlightenment** styled itself. But part of the inspiration came from the creation of the "warfare" metaphor for characterizing the relationship between Christianity and the sciences in the late nineteenth century (Draper 1874; White 1896).

Historians of science have demonstrated that no matter how visceral such conflict has felt over the course of the twentieth and early twenty-first century, there is little if any historical basis for such a **conflict thesis** (Brooke 1991; Lindberg and Numbers 1986). Instead of pushing Christianity and other religions out of the way, the founding and development of modern science as a distinctive approach to understanding the properties and processes of nature owes much to Christian theology and theism more generally (Bishop 2013; Brooke 1991; Turner 1985).

Enlightenment and modernity are terms fraught with misunderstanding. Nevertheless, there is something to the modern cast of **mind** that became increasingly skeptical about theistic religion while also becoming increasingly enthusiastic about the sciences. This cast of mind that is so much a part of the larger attitudes and ideals that have come to be called *modernity* provided an intellectual context for how people came to think about religion and science in the eighteenth and nineteenth centuries. Eventually this cast of mind empowered the sciences to play the role of weapon in cultural and political battles that have been going on since the late nineteenth century. One element of history lost in the popularized narratives is that clergy of various stripes played important roles in the development of modernity in

general and this cast of mind in particular (Taylor 2007; Turner 1985).

Developing the Modern Cast of Mind

One strand that played into the development of the modern cast of mind was the rise of eighteenth-century **deism**. Emphasizing God as master engineer rather than redeemer fit nicely with the conception of the universe as a divinely crafted clockworks. Such conceptions of God and creation made the idea of divine interventions in nature quite psychologically jarring (Turner 1985, chap. 2; Lindberg and Numbers 1986, 238–55). A divine engineer would make a creation that needed no such outside interventions.

Picturing God as master engineer and creation as a clockworks fit in with the seventeenth century's deep fascination with and adherence to new standards for precision for knowledge. The precisification of knowledge had been under way since the medieval period, with such developments as the invention of double-entry accounting in the mid-fourteenth century (see **Science and the Medieval Church**). The fascination with machines in the seventeenth century accelerated the pace of such precisification. Moreover, there were complicated, mutually shaping and reinforcing intellectual trends in the seventeenth and eighteenth centuries that accelerated precisification.

The drive for quantification was found not only in the scientific work of **Robert Boyle** and **Isaac Newton**, but also in the rise of mercantilism and capitalism, bureaucratization, **secularization**, and changes in the conception of persons (e.g., individualism) and society. These latter intellectual and social changes shaped much of the drive for precision in the sciences (Turner 1985, chap. 3).

By the mid-nineteenth century, a thoroughly modern and narrow conception of what counted as knowledge had emerged: Knowledge was a concrete proposition about tangible reality demonstrable via **logic** or experience. What qualified as knowledge were tangible facts, material objects, demonstrable truths, laws, and principles that were exact in the sense of logically or mathematically precise, and that were verifiable through logic, observation, and experiment. Typically we associate such features of knowledge with the sciences. However, Turner points out that in the nineteenth century, "empirical rationality fitted rather well the developing environment of commercial capitalism. A penchant for rational organization helped to bring success in an increasingly complicated and interwoven tangle of economic relationships. A sharp eye on specific concrete realities aided in taking advantage of rapidly changing markets" (1985, 132). The developing model of knowledge found inspiration and reinforcement in merchant and commercial values at least as much as it did in the sciences.

So although this characterization of knowledge sounds scientific, the sciences were only one among a number of trends contributing to the development of the modern conception of knowledge. Furthermore, this ideal was considered applicable for all knowledge whether scientific, mercantile, or theological. The sciences became the poster child for this new conception of knowledge. And combining this conception with what nonscientists mistakenly thought was the rigorously skeptical attitude of the sciences (but was, in many cases, actually the skepticism of the high Enlightenment toward organized religion), it formed the modern cast of mind that James Turner (1985) aptly calls the analytical-technical cast of mind.

Implications for Science and Religion

The implications of this cast of mind are difficult to over-estimate. For the sciences there are two important ones for science-religion relations. First, the sciences were put on a pedestal and proclaimed the model for all knowledge (not unlike **Descartes**'s privileging geometry as the model for all knowledge). Second, some took what seemed to be the logical step of developing and embracing **scientism**: scientific knowledge was the only legitimate kind of knowledge and **scientific method**s were the only legitimate means for obtaining such knowledge.

One of the earliest occurrences of the term is in John Hales and Frederick Furnivall's introduction to Bishop Thomas Percy's *Loose and Humorous Songs* (1868). However, one of the concept's most important popularizers was Herbert Spencer, who claimed that science delivered all the knowledge there is (1870, 102). Ironically, in the nineteenth century it was often those who did not understand much about scientific inquiry who were drawn to scientism (Turner 1985, 189–202). This meant that there were no such things as aesthetic, historical, spiritual, or any other kinds of knowledge outside of the scientific (hence why the Romantics and others had such vigorous responses to the development and crowning of the analytical-technical cast of mind!).

For religion there are many important implications, only two of which will be mentioned here. The first is that faith came to be viewed as being in an altogether separate category from knowledge and truth. Indeed, with respect to the analytical-technical conception of knowledge, faith was typically conceived as being a bad form of belief that lacked evidence or belief in the face of contrary evidence

(a conception of faith foreign to the Bible and which was almost unthinkable in premodern Christianity). Second, God came to be treated as an object of natural knowledge in parallel with balance sheets and chemical compounds (still on display in atheist writings such as Dawkins 2008 and Coyne 2015). Nineteenth-century clergy were more to blame than scientists for religious knowledge being reduced to this ideal (Turner 1985).

The effects of the analytical-technical cast of mind are still present, shaping much of the science-religion discussions at both popular and academic levels. Contemporary Western societies are still strongly marked by an overappraisal of scientific investigation's powers and reach. Meanwhile, religious knowledge remains suspect while faith remains largely cut off from knowledge and reason in the minds of many religious believers and nonbelievers.

Robert C. Bishop

REFERENCES AND RECOMMENDED READING

Bishop, Robert C. 2013. "God and Methodological Naturalism in the Scientific Revolution and Beyond." *Perspectives on Science and Christian Faith* 65 (1): 10–23.

Brooke, John H. 1991. *Science and Religion: Some Historical Perspectives.* Cambridge: Cambridge University Press.

Coyne, Jerry A. 2015. *Faith vs. FACT: Why Science and Religion Are Incompatible.* New York: Viking.

Dawkins, Richard. 2008. *The God Delusion.* Wilmington, MA: Mariner Books.

Draper, John W. 1874. *History of the Conflict between Religion and Science.* New York: Appleton.

Lindberg, David C., and Ronald N. Numbers, eds. 1986. *God and Nature: Historical Essays on the Encounter between Christianity and Science.* Berkeley: University of California Press.

Percy, Thomas. 1868. *Loose and Humorous Songs.* Eds. John W. Hales and Frederick J. Furnivall. London: N. Trübner.

Spencer, Herbert. 1870. "Matter, Life, and Mind." *First Principles of a New System of Philosophy.* 2nd ed. New York: Appleton.

Taylor, Charles. 2007. *A Secular Age.* Cambridge, MA: Belknap, 2007.

Turner, James. 1985. *Without God, without Creed: The Origins of Unbelief in America.* Baltimore: Johns Hopkins University Press.

White, Andrew D. 1896. *A History of the Warfare of Science with Theology in Christendom.* New York: Appleton.

SCIENCE AND THE REFORMATION. The Protestant Reformation began in the early sixteenth century with a number of near-contemporary movements for religious reform centered around Martin Luther in Wittenberg and **John Calvin** in Geneva. While these figures were not directly concerned with science, their theological writing influenced the scientific work of their followers. This has led some historians to postulate that the Protestant Reformation was one of the causes of the rise of modern science in the seventeenth century. However, while clear lines can be drawn between aspects of Protestant theology and certain scientific advances, ideas of Catholic thinkers have been just as important.

Both Luther and Calvin were recorded as making critical statements about the hypothesis of **Nicolaus Copernicus** that the earth orbits the sun. This is not evidence that they were against science, because in making these comments, they were simply echoing the consensus of educated Europeans at the time.

Lutheran Science and Astronomy

Luther's attack on Catholic theology encompassed many of the elements of scholastic philosophy and its reliance on the work of the ancient Greek philosopher **Aristotle**. For instance, Luther rejected the Aristotelian doctrine that nature had innate purposes and powers of generation because this compromised the sovereignty of God. Aristotle had said animals could be spontaneously generated from putrefying matter, but Luther insisted that only God could create life.

Luther's early follower Philipp Melanchthon took steps to reform education in Germany along Lutheran lines by downgrading scholasticism. Melanchthon emphasized the study of Greek and Latin classics, while largely ignoring the medieval commentaries on them. He also gave greater prominence to the geometry of Euclid and the **astronomy** of **Ptolemy** than had been typical at medieval universities. His reform of the syllabus at the University of Wittenberg consequently ensured there was good provision for **mathematics** and astronomy. Melanchthon also defended **astrology** as a legitimate branch of science, producing an edition of Ptolemy's astrological work *Tetrabiblios*. Although Melanchthon's enthusiasm for astrology was also not an unusual position at the time, Luther himself did not approve.

The astronomical faculty at Wittenberg attracted several important figures. Georg Joachim Rheticus taught mathematics there before he became the student of, and collaborator with, Copernicus. The *Narratio prima* (1540) of Rheticus was the first published explication of the ideas of Copernicus. Rheticus returned to Wittenberg in 1541 as professor of astronomy. His predecessor in that role was Erasmus Reinhold, who used the work of Copernicus to update the most widely used astronomical tables.

As the educational reforms of Melanchthon spread, other German universities produced Lutherans who contributed to astronomical innovation into the seventeenth century. For instance, Michael Maestlin taught at Tübingen for many years, where his most celebrated student was fellow Lutheran

Johannes Kepler. While Maestlin never accepted the theory of Copernicus, Kepler went on to develop the modern understanding of elliptical planetary orbits. He did this using the data of the Dane **Tycho Brahe**, another Lutheran educated at a German university, for whom Kepler worked in Vienna.

It goes without saying that Protestant astronomers were unaffected by the Roman Catholic Church's condemnation of Copernicanism in 1616 or by **Galileo**'s conviction by the Inquisition in 1633. While this was clearly an advantage for the new astronomy among Lutherans, historians have found that the practical effects of the Catholic prohibition were not as great as had once been assumed. In any case, widespread acceptance of heliocentricism was the result of Kepler's accurate astronomical tables rather than Galileo's polemic.

Science and Protestant Theology

John Calvin's theology included the important doctrine of accommodation in biblical interpretation. He explained that the Bible was written in the language of the common people so that it could be readily understood by all. This meant passages that could be read as imparting scientific **information** should be read instead in everyday language that accommodated the capability of the ordinary reader. In particular, Calvin defended the right of astronomers to hold to theories that conflicted with a plain reading of Scripture since the Bible describes how the heavens appear to the eye rather than their true constitution.

This doctrine allowed Reformed theologians to assume that the Bible was not to be taken literally if its language conflicted with new scientific discoveries. That said, Calvin himself did favor, for example, a straightforward literalistic reading of the six **days of creation** in Genesis 1 since this view was entirely consistent with the state of scientific knowledge at the time.

In his *Institutes of the Christian Religion*, Calvin devoted considerable attention to the relationship between God and nature. Like Luther, he was concerned to preserve the sovereignty of God over the material world. Thus he also downplayed the ability of nature to give rise to causes or to have purposes of its own.

Historians have devoted much attention to the question of how the Reformation affected the rise of science: in particular, whether Protestant theology contributed to the disenchantment of the world that made the mechanical philosophy possible. The mechanical philosophy postulated that all matter was made of inert atoms moving in the void. This meant that matter itself enjoyed no purpose or intrinsic powers. However, the atheistic taint of ancient **atomism** was avoided by subjecting the atoms to the will of God. He was thought to maintain the atoms in motion and to be responsible for creativity in nature. This increased the ongoing dependence of nature on God and enhanced his sovereignty over the world as demanded by Protestant theologians.

In 1938 Robert K. Merton suggested that Puritanism, rather than Protestantism in general, was a crucial cause of the new scientific philosophy in seventeenth-century England. Merton found that some Puritan beliefs promoted manual work. By valuing craftsmanship as much as scholarship, Puritans encouraged natural philosophers to get their hands dirty with experiments. However, critics have noted that an interest in experimentation went well beyond Puritan circles. For example, **Francis Bacon**, who was highly influential on the founders of the Royal Society and by no means a Puritan, championed an empirical approach to science and putting nature to the test.

Nonetheless, historians such as Reijer Hooykaas have made increasingly subtle arguments about how Protestant theology and biblical interpretation contributed to seventeenth-century science. Calvin's emphasis on the plain meaning of the text made Protestants skeptical of figurative and metaphorical readings of the Bible. It has been suggested that this also led them to stop looking for theological messages in nature. Medieval bestiaries had ascribed religious meaning to various animals and plants: for instance, the pelican killed its young and then restored them to life after three days, an obvious reflection of the **resurrection of Jesus**. Even before scientific observation had debunked many of the stories in the bestiaries, Protestants had dropped the religious glosses from their work on natural history. Instead of the Bible being used to understand the world, the emerging field of **natural theology** sought to find knowledge about God in the workings of nature.

Critics of the theories of Merton, Hooykaas, and their followers have noted that pioneers of the mechanical philosophy included the Catholics Pierre Gassendi and **René Descartes**; while the Protestant **Isaac Newton** reintroduced an innate power into nature with his theory of gravitation. Nonetheless, the influence of the Reformation on early-modern science remains an active field of research.

James Hannam

REFERENCES AND RECOMMENDED READING

Deason, Gary B. 1986. "Reformation Theology and the Mechanistic Conception." In *God and Science: Historical Essays on the Encounter between Christianity and Science.* Eds. David Lindberg and Ronald Numbers, 167–91. Berkeley: University of California Press.

Harrison, Peter. 1998. *The Bible, Protestantism, and the Rise of Natural Science.* Cambridge: Cambridge University Press.

Hooykaas, Reijer. 1972. *Religion and the Rise of Modern Science.* Edinburgh: Scottish Academic Press.

Merton, Robert K. 1938. "Science, Technology and Society in Seventeenth-Century England." *Osiris* 4:360–632.

Webster, Charles. 1975. *The Great Instauration: Science, Medicine and Reform, 1626–1660.* Cambridge: Duckworth.

Westman, Robert S. 1975. "The Melanchthon Circle, Rheticus, and the Wittenberg Interpretation of the Copernican Theory." *Isis* 66:164–93.

SCIENCE AND RELIGION, MODELS OF RELATING.

How science and religion relate (or should relate) is a highly complex and controversial question. For one thing, there are many religions, and some are less conducive to science than others. Thus for animists, nature is sacred and its investigation arguably sinful or taboo, while for polytheists, there is no reason to expect universal **laws of nature**. Ancient philosophy contributed the idea of universal connections, but they were discernible by reason, not observation.

Most historians of science agree that it was a biblical view of nature that supported the rise of modern empirical science. The God of the Bible is the single rational creator and sustainer of the world, so universal laws of nature can be expected. But God is also free, so the only way to discover those laws is empirical investigation. During the Reformation, theologians reemphasized **Augustine**'s distinction between God's two books, the book of Scripture and the book of nature (Harrison 2006, 118; see **Two Books Metaphor**). **Peter Harrison** (2001, 2004) argues that the Reformers' emphasis on the literal sense of Scripture (rather than on allegorical interpretations) and the priesthood of all believers (1 Peter 2:9) led scientists like **Johannes Kepler** (1571–1630) and **Robert Boyle** (1627–91) to see themselves as priests in the book of nature tasked with reading God's world.

However, even if we confine ourselves to the Judeo-Christian tradition, it remains highly controversial how best to relate God's two books because of different underlying assumptions about the relative authority of science and religion and about the best ways to interpret Scripture and nature. **Ian Barbour** (2000) helpfully sorts the various models for relating science and religion into the categories of conflict, independence, integration, and dialogue, and we will follow that rubric here.

At the extremes of fundamentalist biblical literalism and scientific **materialism**, poor exegesis may create an apparent conflict between the biblical text and the findings of modern science. To take a famous historical example, if it is assumed that Joshua 10:12–13 implies an absolutely stationary earth, the biblical literalist would have to reject Copernican **astronomy**, while a scientific materialist would have a reason to reject Scripture. However, most theologians and scientists regard such a conflict as regrettable and unnecessary.

Kepler himself, together with a significant number of both Catholic and Protestant theologians, took the view that Scripture generally expresses the way the world appears to us and is not committed to developed scientific explanations.

> Now the holy scriptures … when treating common things (concerning which it is not their purpose to instruct humanity), speak with humans in the human manner, in order to be understood by them.… Joshua meant that the sun should be held back in its place in the sky for an entire day with respect to the sense of his eyes, since for other people during the same interval of time it would remain beneath the earth.… For the gist of Joshua's petition comes to this, that it might appear so to him. (Kepler 2008, 19–20)

Some have argued that conflict between science and religion can be minimized by emphasizing their independence, reflected in their distinctive methodology or language. **Stephen Jay Gould** (1999) went further, suggesting that science and religion do not even share the same domain or subject matter, but constitute **non-overlapping magisteria** (NOMA). While science is concerned with how the world works, religion is concerned with questions of ultimate meaning and value.

Certainly there are differences between science and religion: for example, the former insists on publicly accessible data, while the latter emphasizes personal devotion. But many argue that Gould goes too far in rejecting any overlap between the domains of science and religion. To deny that God's creation makes any detectable difference to the natural world appears to imply that there is no natural knowledge of God. And the Christian religion is founded on a historical fact that can be investigated by empirical means and without which, Paul says, our faith is futile (1 Cor. 15:17).

Gould's use of NOMA also appears disingenuous, since, while he uses it to preclude religious claims about factual reality, he is happy to use science to make claims of ultimate meaning and purpose. For example, Gould claims that human beings are "a wildly improbable evolutionary event, and not the nub of universal purpose.… We are the offspring of history, and must establish our own paths" (Gould 1999,

206–7). The problem is that Gould combines the empirical data of science with a philosophy of scientific materialism that is not religiously neutral.

A more general worry about the independence model is that it fosters individuals with divided, compartmentalized minds. It encourages Christian scientists to say, "My faith is one thing, my science another," robbing them of a holistic sense of Christian vocation in their work (Pearcey 2004a, 2004b). To address this concern, some argue for integration between science and religion. One approach to integration is **natural theology** (e.g., Paley [1802] 2008), which uses scientific data to support the existence and attributes of God. Although sharply critiqued by **David Hume** ([1779] 2007) and **Charles Darwin** (1859), natural theology has recently made a major comeback (Craig and Moreland 2009). Another approach, distinguished by Barbour, is to start from a religious tradition and to develop a theology of nature in which religious doctrines (such as **providence**) are reinterpreted so that they apply to the world disclosed by modern science.

A more ambitious approach to integration is the systematic synthesis of religion and science. One example is the effort of Thomas Aquinas (1225–74) to combine biblical theology with Aristotelian philosophy. More modern examples are various attempts to understand evolution as a means of God's creation. A major concern about systematic integration is that it may implicitly give the finite and fallible theories of the human **mind** the same epistemic status as the revelation of an infinite and omniscient God. And religion may seem to be discredited if it is allied with a scientific theory that is abandoned. To avoid these problems, some argue for a more cautious, open-ended dialogue between science and religion. On this view, science and religion explore common ground, but neither of them commits to a final synthesis.

Angus J. L. Menuge

REFERENCES AND RECOMMENDED READING

Barbour, Ian G. 2000. *When Science Meets Religion*. New York: HarperOne.

Craig, William Lane, and J. P. Moreland, eds. 2009. *The Blackwell Companion to Natural Theology*. West Sussex, UK: Wiley-Blackwell.

Darwin, Charles. 2009. Reprint. *On the Origin of Species*. London and New York: John Murray.

Gould, Stephen Jay. 1999. *Rock of Ages: Science and Religion and the Fullness of Life*. New York: Penguin Classics.

Harrison, Peter. 2001. *The Bible, Protestantism, and the Rise of Natural Science*. New York: Cambridge University Press.

———. 2004. "Priests of the Most High God, with Respect to the Book of Nature." In *Reading God's World: The Scientific Vocation*. Ed. Angus Menuge, 59–84. St. Louis, MO: Concordia.

———. 2006. "The Bible and the Emergence of Modern Science." *Science and Christian Belief* 18 (2): 115–32. www.scienceandchristianbelief.org/articles/Harrison-article-18-2.pdf.

Hume, David. (1779) 2007. *Dialogues concerning Natural Religion and Other Writings.* New York: Cambridge University Press.

Kepler, Johannes. 2008. *Selections from Kepler's Astronomia Nova.* Ed. William H. Donahue. Santa Fe, NM: Green Lion.

Paley, William. (1802) 2008. *Natural Theology.* New York: Oxford World's Classics.

Pearcey, Nancy. 2004a. *Total Truth.* Wheaton, IL: Crossway.

———. 2004b. "How Science Became a Christian Vocation." In *Reading God's World: The Scientific Vocation.* Ed. Angus Menuge, 23–57. St. Louis, MO: Concordia.

SCIENCE AND THE RENAISSANCE, EARLY MODERN CHRISTIANITY.

Despite the high-profile conflict over the work of **Galileo**, both Catholics and Protestants considered science to be an ally of Christianity throughout the Renaissance and early modern periods. Many of the pioneering scientists of this era were churchmen or devout Christians.

The Renaissance

The Renaissance was characterized by a flowering of the arts and an appreciation of the literary achievements of the classical world, including in the areas of the occult and **astrology**. The main effect of the Renaissance on science was to ensure that astrology provided a market for astronomical handbooks. The church was initially sanguine about occult material, especially as its enthusiasts included such esteemed churchmen as Marsilio Ficino and Pope Pius II. Cardinal Nicholas of Cusa felt free to speculate on matters ranging from the movement of the earth to the inhabitants of other planets in his radical theological work *On Learned Ignorance.* Later the church became much more suspicious and in 1600 went so far as to burn **Giordano Bruno** at the stake for refusing to recant his magical philosophy.

Some artists, including Leonardo Da Vinci, were fascinated by the natural world and especially the formation of the human body. However, Leonardo did not publicize his findings and so made no contribution to the scientific advances of his time. In any case, his notebooks remained unpublished for centuries after his death. On the other hand, Andreas Vesalius hired artists from the school of Titian to illustrate *On the Fabric of the Human Body*, published in 1543, which certainly helped with the success of this seminal book. Contrary to myth, neither Leonardo nor Vesalius suffered persecution from the church on account of their anatomical studies.

Early Modern Astronomy

Nicolas Copernicus was a canon of Freiburg cathedral in Poland, a position that afforded him time to work on **astronomy**. He circulated early drafts of his heliocentric system in manuscript form, which led to the Cardinal Nicholas Schönberg, among others, urging him to publish. However, Copernicus was a perfectionist and could not be persuaded to release *Revolutions of the Heavenly Spheres* until he was on his deathbed in 1543. Although Copernicus himself believed the earth orbited the sun, his editor appended a prologue to the published work stating it was just a hypothesis. In any case, despite a dedication to Pope Paul III, the book had little initial impact, not least due to its heavyweight mathematical content. It was not banned, and Copernicus had not been concerned about religious persecution for his ideas.

Although it initially ignored Copernicus's heliocentrism, the Roman Catholic Church used some of his mathematical work in its own program of calendar reform, leading to the Gregorian calendar of 1582. However, in 1616 the church felt compelled to take a position on heliocentricism after theologians began to consider if the theory was compatible with the Bible. A committee of adjudicators concluded that the theory was philosophically absurd and contrary to the faith. **Copernicus**'s book was subjected to some slight corrections but not banned. In reaching their decision, the committee agreed with the vast majority of scientific opinion at the time. **Galileo Galilei**, already a famous astronomer on account of his work with the telescope, was assured that he had done nothing wrong but was admonished against supporting or teaching heliocentricism in the future.

In 1632 Galileo published his *Dialogue on Two World Systems*—a poorly disguised argument in favor of Copernicus, with the other world system discussed being the traditional geocentricism of the ancient Greeks. The book broke his previous injunction and also offended Pope Urban VIII, who felt part of it was intended to ridicule him. He insisted Galileo be put on trial for disobeying the Inquisition. On being found guilty, Galileo was sentenced to house arrest for life, and his book was suppressed.

After Galileo's sentence was promulgated throughout Catholic Europe, the French philosopher **René Descartes** decided to put aside his own cosmological work, *On the World*, since this also suggested a heliocentric cosmos. However, the accuracy of the astronomical tables of the Lutheran **Johannes Kepler** convinced astronomers that Copernicus was correct, leaving the Catholic Church in an embarrassing position it did not extract itself from until the nineteenth century.

Despite the Galileo fiasco, devout Catholic scientists such as **Blaise Pascal**, Nicholas Steno, and Marin Mersenne practiced science without offending the church. Pascal was a pioneer of pneumatics. Steno, who ended his life as an archbishop, is a founding father of **geology**. And Mersenne, despite his membership in the austere order of the Minim Friars, linked almost all the main figures of seventeenth-century science in his correspondence. These three figures also demonstrate variations in theological belief among Catholics, even at the height of the Counter-Reformation.

Jesuit Science

The Society of Jesus, founded by Ignatius Loyola in 1534, became interested in science as a result of its collective vocation in education. The Jesuit College of Rome housed many influential scientific figures, including the celebrated astronomer Christoph Clavius. They were initially strong supporters of Galileo, lionizing him on a trip to Rome in 1611. However, Galileo's dispute with the Jesuit Christoph Scheiner over sunspots led to a falling out.

The Jesuits' primary calling was as missionaries. A small group including Matteo Ricci traveled as far as China in an effort to convert the emperor. In a series of public competitions, they demonstrated the superiority of Western astronomy over the traditional Chinese methods by predicting an eclipse with enormous accuracy. Given the importance of astrology to the Imperial Court, the Jesuits were immediately placed in charge of the emperor's own observatory. However, despite making a number of converts, the missionaries were never able to convince the Chinese Empire to adopt Christianity.

Jesuit science continued to develop through the seventeenth and eighteenth centuries. They were in the front rank of experimenters and early inquirers into electricity. They also valued collaboration. The letters to and from Athanasius Kircher, a Jesuit based at the College of Rome, covered Europe and fed his prolific publication record.

Science in Early Modern Protestant Europe

Neither Martin Luther nor **John Calvin** was impressed by the theory of Copernicus, in as much as they thought about it. However, under the guidance of Philipp Melanchthon, Germany's Protestant universities, especially Wittenberg, emphasized the place of science and **mathematics** in their syllabi. A considerable amount of modern scholarship has asked whether Protestantism was more conducive to science

than Catholicism. Little conclusive evidence has been provided to support this thesis, and important early-modern scientists divide between the denominations in roughly equal numbers.

What is beyond doubt is that Protestant scientists like Johannes Kepler and **Robert Boyle**, as well as heterodox believers like **Isaac Newton**, drew enormous inspiration from the Bible. They also believed that science could be used to prove the **existence of God**. Boyle bequeathed funds for an annual lecture on **natural theology** to show how science and religion illuminate each other. Newton conceived his **physics** as a rejoinder to continental systems that he regarded as atheistic, such as that of Descartes. Newton's own denial of the divinity of Jesus, which could have warranted death at the stake a century before, was covered up to keep him in a professorship at Cambridge University. Thus, by the eighteenth century, religion was increasingly accepted as a matter of choice rather than compulsion. The direct influence of established churches over scientific practice began to wane.

James Hannam

REFERENCES AND RECOMMENDED READING

Ashworth, William B. 1986. "Catholicism and Early Modern Science. In *God and Science: Historical Essays on the Encounter between Christianity and Science*. Eds. David Lindberg and Ronald Numbers, 136–66. Berkeley: University of California Press.

Gingerich, Owen. 2004. *The Book Nobody Read: Chasing the Revolutions of Nicolaus Copernicus*. New York: Walker.

Hannam, James. 2010. *The Genesis of Science: How the Christian Middle Ages Launched the Scientific Revolution*. New York: Regnery.

Heilbron, John L. 2010. *Galileo*. Oxford: Oxford University Press.

Henry, John. 2008. *The Scientific Revolution and the Origins of Modern Science*. London: Palgrave Macmillan.

Hooykaas, Reijer. 1972. *Religion and the Rise of Modern Science*. Edinburgh: Scottish Academic Press.

Lattis, James. 1994. *Between Copernicus and Galileo: Christoph Clavius and the Collapse of Ptolemaic Cosmology*. Chicago: Chicago University Press.

McMullin, Ernan, ed. 2005. *The Church and Galileo*. Notre Dame, IN: University of Notre Dame Press.

⚓ SCIENCE AND THEOLOGY (Dialogue View).

The relation between science and theology should be one of harmony. After all, the Christian God who reveals himself in Scripture and salvation history is the same God who created the world studied by science. And yet, in the past few hundred years, with the rise of modern science, science and theology have experienced considerable tension.

This tension can take various forms. According to materialist scientists like **Richard Dawkins** (2008), theology and religion constitute a plague on humanity. Accordingly, the ultimate glory of scientists is to wield science as a weapon to destroy faith. Alternatively, according to young-earth creationists like **Ken Ham** (2013), anything other than a literalist interpretation of the Bible betrays the faith, so that much of what is called science these days is an affront to faith and needs to be abandoned. Both of these camps engage in a conflict model on the relation between science and theology. And both are misguided, elevating science or theology at the expense of the other rather than giving both their proper due.

At the other extreme are those who deny that science and theology experience any tension whatsoever. This is the approach taken by compartmentalists or complementarians. They not only deny that science and theology experience tension but go further in claiming that science and theology are inherently incapable of experiencing tension.

Though compartmentalists and complementarians come to essentially the same conclusion, they differ in the underlying rationale for keeping peace between science and theology. Compartmentalists see science and theology as belonging to fundamentally different realms of inquiry and thus as speaking to matters so different that they cannot clash. The late **Stephen Jay Gould** represented this view. On the other hand, complementarians see science and theology not so much as being about completely different things as about using radically different methods to study the same things (the world, humanity, etc.). Science and theology thus constitute different approaches to describing the same reality, with the difference between approaches cutting so deep that science and theology cannot clash.

The problem with compartmentalism and complementarianism is that they are not true to the relation between science and theology as these play out in actual conversations between real scientists and real theologians. Take Gould's compartmentalism, which he referred to by the acronym NOMA (**non-overlapping magisteria**, described in his book *Rocks of Ages*). Gould was only able to compartmentalize science and theology by tendentiously redefining the two. For Gould, science was concerned with the factual world of things and events, whereas theology was concerned with ethics and internal **religious experience**.

Given such a redefinition, the compartmentalization of science and theology follows. But theology is concerned about more than ethics and internal religious experience. Christian theologians, for instance, are also concerned about whether Jesus was truly a historical figure, whether he died in the way recounted in Scripture, and whether he arose bodily

from the dead, all of these falling in the factual world of things and events. Gould, an atheist, rejected Jesus's resurrection and did so on the grounds of a materialist science that left no room for **miracles**. Compartmentalization thus keeps peace between science and theology, but at the cost of allowing neither to be itself.

Complementarianism, as a way of keeping science and theology at peace, will strike most Christians as less offensive than compartmentalism. Compartmentalism cannot help but artificially redefine science and theology in ways that believers find unacceptable. Complementarianism, by contrast, advertises itself as being true to both science and theology. Moreover, it respects that science and theology operate as distinct forms of inquiry.

The very term *complementarianism* traces back to physicist **Niels Bohr**'s Copenhagen interpretation of quantum mechanics, in which quantum processes behave in two distinct ways, neither of which is privileged, and both of which are needed to properly understand quantum phenomena. This is sometimes referred to as wave-particle duality. Yet when complementarity is applied to the relation between science and theology, it is meant to suggest not only that the two are necessary to provide a complete account of the world but also that the two involve inherently different modes of description that are incapable of clashing.

But again, as a matter of practical experience, when real scientists and real theologians converse, their scientific and theological views can clash. Quantum mechanics itself, which was the inspiration of complementarianism, may be interpreted as yielding a world with irreducible randomness in which the future is inherently open and undetermined. Yet Christian theology, traditionally conceived, regards God as having complete knowledge of future contingent events. Quantum mechanics thus suggests a world in which such knowledge is impossible. Yet a theology that places God as transcendent over the cosmos would suggest that quantum mechanical laws ought to place no limitation on divine knowledge or power.

This tension between quantum mechanics and classical conceptions of divine omniscience is much discussed in the science and theology literature (Davis 1997). Moreover, insofar as this tension is resolved, it is not by citing complementarianism, but by weighing the competing claims of science and theology. This can lead to radically different conclusions.

Thus those who see quantum mechanics as undermining classical conceptions of divine omniscience will regard modern science as providing insights into the nature of the world closed to classical theology. In particular, because classical theology lacked the insights of modern science, its theological formulations were necessarily limited to a pre-scientific age. Accordingly, contemporary scientific insights now need to be recognized by theologians as they update and upgrade their theology, and that includes dispensing with classical divine omniscience.

Conversely, classical theologians will refuse to sacrifice so basic a doctrine as divine foreknowledge of future contingent events. As they see it, God created the **laws of nature** but is not bound by them. Thus there is no reason that limitations to knowledge that apply to us because we live in a world governed by quantum mechanical laws should also apply to God. God can know everything, even the future, because he made the laws by which the universe operates. Yet, at the same time, these laws cannot constrain God.

This example of how quantum mechanics relates to divine omniscience illustrates the importance of properly adjudicating between science and theology when they clash. A widespread tendency among thinkers adjudicating between science and theology is to play favorites and treat one as inherently superior to the other.

Thus, among more liberal theologians who, say, regard the Old and New Testaments as a hodgepodge of sources far distant from the supposed events recounted, science will seem a much securer path to knowledge, and the pronouncements of science will be accepted over any traditional claims of theology. The relation between science and theology thus becomes a one-way street, with all benefits of the doubt going to science at the expense of theology.

Of course, it is possible to reverse the direction of this one-way street, seeing in theology enduring and unchangeable truths that are so settled and perspicuous that ongoing theological growth or progress is precluded. In that case, science better get in line with theology, and insofar as it is perceived as out of line, science is false and needs to be discarded.

Treating the relation between science and theology as a one-way street is typical of the conflict model discussed earlier in this article. But a one-way street mentality can prevail even when overt conflict is absent. All that is needed is a mind-set that reflexively favors one over the other (science or theology) without trying to weigh their respective claims and without examining the particulars of the case in question.

What science and theology need is a *living dialogue* that recognizes how imperfect our knowledge is of both science and theology, and at the same time brings what clarity it can to this dialogue without betraying either science or theology. This is not to say that we don't know some things in science well and also some things in theology well. We know, as scientists (and not as theologians), that water freezes at zero degrees Celsius at sea level. And we know, as Christian theologians (and not as scientists), that Jesus is the savior of the world.

But there is much in the science-theology dialogue that we are only now beginning to appreciate, that only now makes sense given our increased understanding of the world. The street here between science and theology is two-way, with science potentially impacting our theological views and likewise with theology potentially impacting our scientific views. Moreover, if this is truly to be a living dialogue, it cannot be that science invariably trumps theology or vice versa.

The problem is that in our polarized culture, it is much easier to keep one's supporters happy by letting the one consistently trump the other. We see this with **young-earth creationism**, where no evidence from astrophysics or **geology** is ever sufficient to establish that the earth is billions rather than thousands of years old. But we also see this with certain advocates of Darwinian evolution, who see **Darwinism** as a club with which to beat religious believers and unseat religious belief.

In a living dialogue between science and theology, one recognizes that God is author of the world studied by science and that God is the main actor in the history of salvation that theology attempts to understand. Thus God is the ultimate source of true science and true theology, and the task of the thinker trying to understand their relation is not so much to resolve tensions (though this is nice when it can be had) as to gain clarity.

Indeed, Christian theology is rife with paradoxes (not least **the Trinity** and the two natures of Christology), so it should come as no surprise that the dialogue between science and theology might involve paradoxes. This is not to revel in paradoxes or to refuse to attempt to resolve them where they can be resolved. But it is to reject a simplistic mind-set that thinks the big questions in life, and notably those at the intersection of science and theology, require a tidy solution, and that such a solution can be purchased by reflexively giving priority to theology over science or vice versa.

Since theology deals with eternal truths ("the faith that was once for all delivered to the saints" according to Jude 3 ESV), whereas science deals with our best current understanding of the physical world and is subject to constant revision, shouldn't theology have priority over science? True, certain aspects of Christian theology are totally secure and nonnegotiable, such as the **incarnation** and resurrection. Get rid of these, and you don't have Christian theology. Yet likewise, certain aspects of science are totally secure and nonnegotiable, such as that we live in a physical world with certain clear features, that the world operates this way and not that (e.g., that loaded guns shoot bullets and unloaded guns don't), and that we can know enough about how the world operates to be morally responsible for our actions.

Accordingly, where science or theology is unclear, we need a living dialogue that does not privilege one over the other. Likewise, we need a living dialogue where science has recently become clear and thrown theological claims that previously we thought were clear into question. To be sure, such a living dialogue may cause discomfort. As nineteenth-century theologian **Charles Hodge** noted in his *Systematic Theology*, "It may cost the church a severe struggle to give up one interpretation and adopt another, as it did in the seventeenth century [when the Copernican system decisively displaced the Ptolemaic system of the universe], but no real evil need be apprehended. The Bible has stood, and still stands in the presence of the whole scientific world with its claims unshaken." Yet the search for truth demands a willingness to endure such discomfort.

Examples where science has caused us to revise our theological views exist, and this should come as no surprise since modern science, as a disciplined inquiry into nature using tools and methods of recent vintage, considerably postdates theology. The Copernican revolution, adverted to in the last paragraph, is a case in point. Up until then, Christian theologians had read the Bible as teaching that the earth was immovable (cf. Ps. 93:1). More recently, the widespread view among Christians that creation and humanity are considerably older than the few thousand years evident in Genesis may be credited to science.

But that raises the question whether scientific claims may ever legitimately be challenged on the basis of theology. The answer is yes, but it needs to be done right. Consider, for instance, the widespread claim, made in the name of science, that "**the singularity**" is just around the corner. This claim, trumpeted by futurist Ray Kurzweil (2005), is supposed to be based on Moore's law, the empirical finding that computer power (in terms of processing speed and memory capacity) doubles about every 18 months. At some point, this law will break down because of the limitations of matter and energy. But for the next two or so decades, Moore's law is expected to hold.

Now, according to Kurzweil, 2029 will mark a singularity at which computer power begins to match human cognition, and after that computers will completely overtake us. Once computers overtake us, the best thing we can do, according to Kurzweil, is dispense with our humanity and upload ourselves onto a computer. (If we refuse, we may, in the best of worlds, become the pets of computers; or in the worst of worlds, experience the doom of humanity as depicted in the *Terminator* films.)

Theologically, the idea that we are computers, and thus that we might need to dispense with our bodies by uploading our essence onto a computer, is repugnant and undercuts salvation in Christ. Indeed, if we are programs running on computers, then the proper role of salvation would, arguably, be to rewrite or debug the programs, not to provide a propitiatory sacrifice on a Roman cross.

Still, to resolve such tensions between science and theology, it is not enough simply to say that a scientific pronouncement is theologically objectionable. The problem is that if Kurzweil is right about us being computers and if his predictions about computers supplanting us come true, Christian theology will stand refuted. It is therefore essential to deconstruct Kurzweil's pronouncement about the singularity on its own terms.

As it is, Kurzweil is blowing smoke. He presupposes the truth of strong **artificial intelligence** (AI), that we are, literally, computers running programs (the computers, in this case, being our brains). As it is, computers give no evidence of achieving **consciousness**, being able to master natural language, or solving any number of classical problems connected with AI, notably, the frame problem (which refers to our ability to narrow down relevant background knowledge in solving problems). His argument is therefore weak.

The point to note, however, is that his argument needed to be defeated on its own terms, without appealing to theology. Only in this way can a scientific challenge to theology be effectively met. Note that I said "effectively met," not "decisively met." These debates between science and theology have an interminable vitality. Kurzweil, far from being convinced, will merely redouble his efforts to show that computers can achieve consciousness, thus making the theologian's continued task to show he is indeed still blowing smoke.

In conclusion, the only model on the relation between science and theology that works is one that acknowledges that science and theology are in living dialogue to which both parties make substantive contributions. Anything less makes for a simplistic understanding of the world in which we use science to reflexively trump theology, or vice versa, at the cost of sidestepping real issues and missing the truth.

William A. Dembski

REFERENCES AND RECOMMENDED READING

Davis, John Jefferson. 1997. "Quantum Indeterminacy and the Omniscience of God." *Science and Christian Belief* 9:129–44.

Dawkins, Richard. 2008. *The God Delusion*. New York: Mariner.

Gordon, Bruce, and William A. Dembski, eds. 2011. *The Nature of Nature: Examining the Role of Naturalism in Science*. Wilmington, DE: ISI Books.

Gould, Stephen Jay. 1999. *Rocks of Ages: Science and Religion in the Fullness of Life*. New York: Random House.

Ham, Ken. 2013. *Six Days: The Age of the Earth and the Decline of the Church*. Green Forest, AR: Master.

Kurzweil, Ray. 2005. *The Singularity Is Near: When Humans Transcend Biology*. New York: Penguin.

↬ SCIENCE AND THEOLOGY (Reconciliation View).

Most Christians recognize both science and theology as legitimate modes of inquiry. Not all agree, however, on how the findings of these disciplines ought to be related. This article explores that relationship.

I write as one who is comfortable with the label *evolutionary creationist*. That is to say, I believe that God is the Creator and that the Bible is inspired and authoritative; and I believe that contemporary science is correct in its conclusions about the vast age of the earth and the **common ancestry** of life on it. I don't have space here to defend either the theology or science behind these claims, but I will discuss and defend a way of reconciling them. Instead of moving directly to that discussion, it will be helpful first to establish some context for how scholars talk about the relationship between science and theology.

Framing the Discussion

The late **Ian Barbour** (1923–2013) was the godfather of the contemporary academic discipline of science and religion—which is more appropriately called science and *theology*, since it applies primarily to the cognitive dimensions of religion. His book *Issues in Science and Religion* (1966) is a thorough overview of the relevant topics, and it set the agenda for subsequent thinkers in the field. In that book and his *Myths, Models, and Paradigms* (1974), he began developing a classification system for how science and theology can be related to each other. His **Gifford Lectures** of 1989–90 (Barbour 1990) gave a more systematic defense of the typology.

Barbour identifies four different ways that science and

theology may be related to each other: conflict, independence, dialogue, and integration.

The first model assumes that either the scientific or the theological way of acquiring knowledge is correct, and not both; thus they are in conflict with each other. The independence view is at the other end of the spectrum: science and theology are completely separate and self-contained ways of knowing; as such, they operate in different spheres, and their claims neither conflict nor agree with each other. Barbour's third model—dialogue—assumes that science and religion do impinge on each other at certain points, such as when discussing the origin of the universe, and so they ought to recognize the insights that each brings to these questions. Finally, the integration model pushes beyond mere dialogue between distinct disciplines and tries to effect a synthesis of science and theology; this can be seen in attempts to develop a theology of nature or in process theology where explanations are developed that draw from both the sciences and theology.

As the discipline of science and religion matured, other scholars reflected on Barbour's work and offered critiques and modifications to his typology. Ted Peters (1996) expanded the list of categories, identifying eight different ways that science and religion interact. And Christian Berg (2004) reorganized the typology completely, believing it more useful to look at the relationship between science and religion under the dimensions of **metaphysics**, **epistemology**, and ethics.

For this article, I will adopt the revision of categories given by Swedish philosopher Mikael Stenmark in his "Ways of Relating Science and Religion" (2010). He gives four broad categories: irreconciliation, reconciliation, independence, and replacement. For our purposes here, we can say that his irreconciliation and independence models map closely onto Barbour's conflict and independence categories; replacement is a more radical view held by people like E. O. Wilson, who claims that science will ultimately replace religion. Most people working in the science and religion discipline would affirm some version of Stenmark's reconciliation model; so that is what I will discuss.

According to the reconciliation model, there is some conflict between science and theology, but ultimately such conflict can be reconciled (which distinguishes it from the irreconciliation model). Stenmark gives three subcategories of this, calling them the *conservative*, *traditional*, and *liberal* reconciliation models. Of course, these are abstractions and might be best considered as points on a continuum that allow for intermediate positions, but in broad strokes they can be characterized as follows. On the *conservative* version, it is primarily science that must change to come into line with traditional understandings of Christian theology. Stenmark gives as exemplars of this position **Phillip Johnson**, **William Dembski**, and perhaps **Alvin Plantinga**.

At the other end of the continuum, the *liberal reconciliation* model asserts that it is Christian theology that must change and adapt to fit with what contemporary science has discovered about the world. Here Stenmark gives Gordon Kaufman, **Arthur Peacocke**, and Sallie McFague as exemplars. And then in the middle is the position (somewhat confusingly) called *traditional reconciliation*, according to which both science and theology may need to change some of what they have claimed. **Alister McGrath**, **John Polkinghorne**, **and Francis Collins** fit somewhere within the range of traditional reconciliation.

The two positions represented in this volume map fairly closely onto the conservative and traditional models, so I won't have much to say about the liberal model here.

Reconciliation Models

I would suggest that the central distinction between the conservative and traditional models of reconciliation is their view of how Scripture functions in the reconciliation. It is important to note that the issue is not whether the Bible is authoritative—both sides accept this. Rather, there seems to be a difference in acknowledgment of the role of interpretations of Scripture. Most (but not all) in the conservative reconciliation camp will admit that their theological positions involve the interpretation of Scripture, but they hold to these interpretations more tightly. This means that they are attaching more authority to tradition than the traditional reconciliationists—an irony that can be unpacked by considering the doctrine of *sola scriptura*.

Scripture alone! This was the cry of the Protestant Reformers against the purported authority of the Roman Catholic Church to determine the content and practice of Christianity (see **Science and the Reformation**). The doctrine of *sola scriptura* began as a means of uniting Protestants against the Catholic Church, but once the right of individual interpreters was asserted, the doctrine very quickly became the grounds for endless divisions. Luther's reading of Scripture was questioned by Zwingli and **Calvin**; theirs was questioned by the Anabaptists, and so on. At last count, the number of distinct Christian denominations worldwide exceeds 33,000 (Barrett et al. 2001, 18).

Given this state of affairs in Protestant Christianity

today, it is obvious that there is more to the doctrine of *sola scriptura* than the popular and pious-sounding slogan, "The Bible says it; that settles it." The Reformers themselves—despite some quotations that could be produced—would not have advocated such an approach to the Bible. They would not have recognized the arch-individualism to Bible reading that has arisen in the American context, which is typified by a Bible study group that consists of each person saying what a passage means to her or him. The Reformers understood that our reading of Scripture must be informed and guided by church tradition and the creeds. It was just that they did not think such tradition carried the same weight as the Bible itself, and that traditions needed to be open to questioning.

But in America in the eighteenth century, the spirit of democracy permeated most of life, and the approach to science and to the Bible was no exception. Instead of being regulated by an authoritarian process, both **science and the Bible** were approached democratically. This was held to be the safest protection against the tendencies of tradition to corrupt (Noll 2009, 6). But how could you know whether your interpretation was correct? It had to be plain to see. There was an underlying assumption to this approach, namely, that the message of Scripture is clear if one would but pay attention to it.

From the time of the church fathers in the Christian tradition, there had been a multifaceted approach to the interpretation of Scripture (see **Science and the Church Fathers**). Besides the literal meaning of the words, "professional" interpreters would also discern the spiritual sense of the text, which could include an allegorical sense, a tropological or moral sense, and an anagogical or future sense. Understandably, these spiritual senses of the text were much more ambiguous; so if a clear message was desired by the Reformers, there would have to be an increased emphasis on the literal meaning of Scripture.

The problem is that by taking the literal meaning of passages, we get into all kinds of difficulties in figuring out what the "biblical" position is. Take the doctrine of salvation: what does Scripture say about it? Confining ourselves to just a few New Testament passages, we can point to Ephesians 2:8–9, where it is by grace alone we have been saved, not through works; but James 2:24 says that a person is justified by works and not by faith alone; and Jesus gives the parable of the sheep and the goats in Matthew 25 where he indicates that being saved from eternal separation from God is the result of good works we do; but he also says in John 6:29

that the work we must do is simply to believe in him. We could cite many more passages with other nuances.

The point here is not that we can't reconcile these statements and produce a clear and coherent doctrine of salvation. Rather, the point is that the clear and consistent doctrine is one of our making—not something that is read straight from Scripture. And perhaps more to the point, there are several doctrines that we humans could come up with that are clear and consistent and draw on Scripture for support. Then of course we could turn to doctrines of **eschatology**, ecclesiology, election, and eternal security (to name only the *E*'s!) and do the same thing. That's how we end up with 33,000 denominations, all thinking their understanding of the Bible is the correct one.

Sociologist Christian Smith surveyed the way the Bible functions in conservative American Protestant contexts in which a version of *sola scriptura* (biblicism) is adhered to, and he described the problem as follows: "The very same Bible—which biblicists insist is perspicuous and harmonious—gives rise to divergent understandings among intelligent, sincere, committed readers about what it says about most topics of interest. Knowledge of 'biblical' teachings, in short, is characterized by pervasive interpretive pluralism" (Smith 2011, 17).

To connect this back to the conservative reconciliation model, people who are resistant to altering their theology at all often claim that to do so would be to compromise on the authority of Scripture. But it should be clear from the foregoing that it is not the authority of Scripture that is at stake, but merely the authority of some interpretations of Scripture. The traditional reconciliation model urges that we hold these interpretations more loosely, especially as they impinge on scientific matters about which the original interpreters had no knowledge.

As an example, consider the current hot topic in science and theology: the doctrine of **the fall** and **original sin**. There is a traditional interpretation according to which **Adam and Eve**'s sin was passed to all human beings because all are descended from them. But contemporary genetics gives overwhelming evidence that there was never a single pair from whom we all descended (Venema 2014). In the face of this conflict, the conservative reconciliationists say we must come up with a different interpretation of the scientific evidence. But it is not Scripture itself that forces this. True, Paul says, "From one [blood] he made all the nations" (Acts 17:26); but Genesis 4 seems to indicate that there were other people around besides the direct decendants of Adam and Eve.

So just as we saw with the doctrine of salvation, it is possible to interpret the biblical passages in various ways, holding to the insight that humans all sin and need salvation. The traditional interpretation of the fall comes largely from the interpretation of **Augustine**. His interpretations may be very important for the history of theology, but they are not above being questioned. There are other models of the fall—including some that recognize a historical Adam and Eve—that are more consistent with the scientific data (see, e.g., Haarsma 2013).

Now, lest it be thought that the traditional reconciliation model only ever alters theology, consider also interpretations of the scientific theory of evolution. Just as with Scripture, it is possible to give different interpretations of scientific evidence. The New Atheists would have us believe that established facts like common ancestry prove that there is no plan or design to evolution and that we are accidents rather than intentional creations in the **image of God**. But this is an interpretation. A world-class paleontologist like Simon Conway Morris interprets the evidence differently, saying that there is purpose and even inevitability that we can see in the overall process of evolution (Conway Morris 2015).

According to the traditional reconciliation approach, what needs reconciling is not the Bible and the natural world. God inspired the Bible, and God created the natural world; they are not in conflict. Rather, there are interpretations of the Bible (theology) and interpretations of the natural world (science). We are the authors of both of these interpretations, and there is no good reason to think that our interpretations of the Bible are closer to infallible than are our interpretations of the natural world. So we should let these be in conversation.

Writing in 1855 (before Darwin published his work), John Henry Newman offered wise words to the person who is concerned to reconcile the "truths" delivered from the sciences and from theology: "If he has one cardinal maxim in his philosophy, it is, that truth cannot be contrary to truth; if he has a second, it is, that truth often *seems* contrary to truth; and, if a third, it is the practical conclusion, that we must be patient with such appearances, and not be hasty to pronounce them to be really of a more formidable character" (quoted in Newman 1982, 347).

When there are conflicts between theology and science, we ought to recognize that these are not conflicts between the authoritative Word of God and the created order but between our interpretations. Sorting out these interpretations is a tricky business and takes some time. Instead of immediately allowing our theology to trump science as the conservative reconciliation model does (or for science to immediately trump theology, as the liberal reconciliation model does), we ought to be patient and allow for conversations between the two disciplines. I suggest that is the approach urged by the traditional reconciliation model.

J. B. Stump

REFERENCES AND RECOMMENDED READING

Barbour, Ian. 1990. *Religion in an Age of Science.* San Francisco: HarperSan Francisco.
Barrett, David B., George T. Kurian, and Todd M. Johnson, eds. 2001. *World Christian Encyclopedia.* Oxford: Oxford University Press.
Berg, Christian. 2004. "Barbour's Way(s) of Relating Science and Theology." In *Fifty Years in Science and Religion: Ian G. Barbour and His Legacy.* Ed. Robert John Russell, 61–75. Aldershot, UK: Ashgate.
Conway Morris, Simon. 2015. *The Runes of Evolution: How the Universe Became Self-Aware.* West Conshohocken, PA: Templeton.
Haarsma, Loren. 2013. "Why the Church Needs Multiple Theories of Original Sin (Part 1)." November 25. http://biologos.org/blogs/archive/why-the -church-needs-multiple-theories-of-original-sin.
Newman, John Henry. 1982. "Christianity and Scientific Investigation." In John Henry Newman, *The Idea of a University.* Notre Dame, IN: University of Notre Dame Press.
Noll, Mark. 2009. "Evangelicals, Creation, and Scripture: An Overview." BioLogos. http://biologos.org/uploads/projects/Noll_scholarly_essay.pdf.
Peters, Ted. 1996. "Theology and Science: Where Are We?" *Zygon* 31 (2): 323–43.
Smith, Christian. 2011. *The Bible Made Impossible: Why Biblicism Is Not a Truly Evangelical Reading of Scripture.* Grand Rapids: Brazos.
Stenmark, Mikael. 2010. "Ways of Relating Science and Religion." In *The Cambridge Companion to Science and Religion.* Ed. Peter Harrison. Cambridge: Cambridge University Press.
Venema, Dennis. 2014. "Adam, Eve, and Human Population Genetics: Defining the Issues." BioLogos. November 12. http://biologos.org/blogs/dennis-venema -letters-to-the-duchess/series/adam-eve-and-human-population-genetics.

SCIENTIFIC METHOD. The scientific method is a broad term given to the process of obtaining knowledge about the universe through experimentation and observation of empirical evidence. There is no single, well-defined implementation of the scientific method common to all fields. In fact, any cursory investigation into this subject will reveal that the method can be expressed using anywhere from about 4 to 10 distinct steps. Various disciplines implement the scientific method in distinct formulations, and the exact execution may depend on the questions being explored.

A typical representation of the scientific method will include steps such as (1) observing some phenomena in nature, (2) developing a hypothesis to explain the phenomena, (3) doing experimental testing of the hypothesis, (4) analyzing data and drawing a conclusion, and (5) formulating new hypotheses based on data. Other steps often included in a formalization of the scientific method are (1) asking a question, (2) doing background research, (3) using hypotheses to make predictions about other phenomena, and (4) communicating results.

The goal of most experiments is to compare the results with the theoretical predictions to test whether a hypothesis correctly describes the phenomena or not. Most practitioners would agree that any scientific hypothesis must be falsifiable; there must be some observations or experiments that would produce results contrary to those predicted by the hypothesis. In sciences such as **physics** and chemistry, theories must make quantitative predictions that can be compared with experimental results.

Although a definitive statement of the scientific method might be valuable and informative, scientists seldom methodically follow a prescription as they perform observations and experiments and develop hypotheses. The practice of science tends to be highly creative, and the implementation of the scientific method reflects human creativity and ingenuity. For example, certain hypotheses may first be developed without observations but based on mathematical principles of symmetry or **beauty**.

Certain practical considerations must be followed to properly implement the scientific method. Experiments must be set up that, as far as possible, eliminate any experimental bias. Data must be treated impartially. A researcher must not discard data simply because it contradicts his preferred hypothesis. Statistical and systematic uncertainties must be properly treated and accounted for so that a reasonable level of confidence in the result can be achieved.

Some descriptions of the scientific method will include an explanation of the process in which an idea moves from conjecture to accepted fact. As a hypothesis is tested or a phenomenon is observed, certain patterns are seen and a model or theory is developed. A theory may be a more refined quantitative description of the phenomena than a model, but both seek to propose some underlying principle that describes the observation. As the theory is tested further and more completely, the theory may eventually develop into a law, an overarching statement about how nature behaves (Giancoli 2014, 5). In this description, a law carries more weight than a theory. Consequently, some opponents of the theory of evolution will proclaim that it can't be believed because "it is only a theory," implying that it has not yet reached the elevated status of a law.

However, the idea that only a scientific law constitutes a well-confirmed theory is an antiquated idea. Since around

1900 scientists have realized that it is impossible to test any idea in all circumstances (see **Scientific Proof** and **Laws of Nature**). Thus it is impossible to claim that any principle is an absolute law that can never be violated. Therefore in modern scientific language, even ideas for which there are no known exceptions and for which scientists don't expect any known deviations, are referred to as theories. For example, Newton's three laws of motion are known to be inadequate for describing phenomena at very small length scales or at very fast speeds, but since they were developed in the eighteenth century, they are called *laws*, while Einstein's **special theory of relativity** has no known exceptions and is expected to hold up under every circumstance, yet is still referred to as a "theory" since it was developed in the twentieth century. In modern scientific language, most "theories" are well-tested principles of physics that would probably have been labeled "laws" in previous centuries.

Throughout history many people have practiced aspects of the scientific method. In Daniel 1, Daniel tests the hypothesis that he and his fellow Jewish captives will have a better appearance if they do not eat King Nebuchadnezzar's choice food. The hypothesis was found to be correct by comparing a control group that ate the food with those who did not eat the food. Much of the modern scientific method was developed between the sixteenth and eighteenth centuries. In the early 1600s, **Francis Bacon** stressed that alternative theories should be experimentally examined to eliminate those that were not correct.

The scientific method does have limitations. These limitations are imposed on the method because it is designed to test hypotheses about the natural world that can be falsified and repeated. The scientific method cannot determine **morality** or ethics. For instance, the scientific method may develop the **technology** for a thermonuclear bomb, but it cannot determine the morality of using such a bomb. Nor can any experimental test prove the **existence of God**.

Though evidence of God may be observable in his creation, it is impossible to perform any experiment that would test for the existence of God. One reason for this is that God is transcendent and no physical experiment can accurately test any nonphysical reality. Another reason is that scientific experiments must be unbiased, but any omniscient, omnipotent deity could inject bias into any experiment meant to probe his character. Consider, for instance, studies that have attempted to test the efficacy of **prayer**. By definition, no such study can be a scientific study if God exists, because God could choose to arbitrarily bias any such study. So although the

scientific method has proven to be extremely successful in revealing the workings of the universe, it has its limitations and cannot be the sole avenue for discovering all knowledge.

Michael G. Strauss

REFERENCES AND RECOMMENDED READING

Giancoli, Douglas. 2014. *Physics: Principles with Applications.* 7th. ed. San Francisco: Pearson.
Sanford, Fernando. 1899. *The Scientific Method and Its Limitations.* Stanford, CA: Stanford University Press.

SCIENTIFIC PROOF. Merriam-Webster defines proof as "an act or process of showing that something is true." Because science cannot show that something is true in the sense that it is established as correct without exception in all circumstances, absolute scientific proof is not possible. Proofs are only possible in **logic** and in **mathematics**. In those two fields, once a proposition has been proven, that proof will remain valid forever. In contrast, scientific knowledge is the best explanation of the results of experimental observations among all the available options. If an experiment is done that contradicts the current scientific **paradigm**, then that theory is not wholly true and must be refined or discarded. Therefore scientific ideas can be disproven but never absolutely proven.

The **scientific method** is used to test hypotheses and to develop and improve scientific theories. Only empirical evidence can be considered and tested against predictions of various hypotheses. When evidence from different experiments consistently confirms a hypothesis and no experimental results conflict with the predictions of that hypothesis, then the hypothesis gains scientific credibility. The types and amount of confirming evidence will lead to different levels of scientific credibility. Theories that have a tremendous amount of confirming evidence and no contradictory observations may be said to make up a body of scientific knowledge or facts. Theories like the **conservation of energy** and the **special theory of relativity** have had so many confirming observations that they seem to be unwavering **laws of nature** or proven scientific theories. But even these apparently proven theories would be not absolutely true if a single violation were ever found.

Every theory in science has a realm of applicability. The boundaries of reliability are well known for many "laws" of nature. Some ideas, like Ohm's law, which describes the relationship between the current through a conductor and the voltage across the conductor, have very limited regions of applicability. Others, like Newton's three laws of motion, are known to work extremely well for most everyday circumstances. But these laws break down at very high speeds, near the **speed of light**, and at very small distances, approximately the size of an atom. This does not invalidate the usefulness of Newton's laws to describe observations and predict the outcome of experiments done in usual circumstances. Still others, like the conservation of energy and the special theory of relativity, are not known to have any realms where they do not apply.

What level of confidence in an experimental result is required for something to be accepted as part of the collective scientific knowledge? The answer depends somewhat on the field of science and the methods involved.

Consider as an example, the discovery of the Higgs boson (see **God Particle**) in 2012. Before the scientists involved in that discovery could be confident that they had discovered a new particle, they first assigned quantitative values to all sources of possible systematic uncertainties in their measurement. A quantitative level of confidence had to be determined that included uncertainties on the statistical fluctuations in the data and on the understanding of experimental apparatus and techniques. Only when the observed result was five standard deviations above background estimations did the experimenters declare they had discovered a Higgs boson. In other words, the discovery was announced when it was determined that there was only about a 1 in 2 million chance that this observation was not caused by the real phenomena being investigated. In experimental particle **physics**, any new discovery must meet this stringent confidence level.

Although scientific proof is not attainable, we have a high level of confidence that the body of scientific knowledge we have is extremely robust in its realm of applicability. Although theories may continue to be revised and developed, it is not expected that the major principles we understand about nature will be discarded. As was the case with Newton's laws, we may find out that certain ideas have less realm of applicability, but the principles would still be useful and applicable within well-defined boundaries.

It is not surprising that we do not have scientific proof of the **existence of God** or of the veracity of Christian beliefs. There is tremendous evidence from many areas of investigation, including scientific observations and archaeology, that the Christian God exists and that the biblical record is reliable. Yet, as with any area of investigation, scientific proof of these ideas is not possible.

Michael G. Strauss

REFERENCES AND RECOMMENDED READING

Popper, Karl. (1935) 2005. *The Logic of Scientific Discovery.* http://strangebeautiful .com/other-texts/popper-logic-scientific-discovery.pdf. Originally published as *Logik der Forschung.* Vienna: Verlag von Julius Springer. 1st Eng. ed. London, UK: Hutchinson, 1959.

———. (1963) 2012. *Conjectures and Refutations: The Growth of Scientific Knowledge.* 2nd ed. London: Routledge.

SCIENTIFIC REVOLUTION. Several important aspects of modern science emerged in Europe during the sixteenth and seventeenth centuries, a period often called the *Scientific Revolution.* The traditional narrative stressed discontinuity and **secularization**: modern science arose only when ancient and medieval **natural philosophy** were wholly discarded, leaving religious beliefs behind with the older ways of thinking.

This positivistic conception has frequently been challenged, but the opposing claim that Christianity "caused" modern science is also not wholly persuasive—major historical events can rarely be explained in terms of one or two crucial factors (Davis 1999). Nevertheless, even if the Scientific Revolution was not an inherently Christian phenomenon, it was carried out almost entirely by Christians. In what specific ways did science and Christianity interact?

A central part of the Scientific Revolution involved the gradual acceptance of **Nicolaus Copernicus**'s new theory of the heavens, which placed the sun at rest in the center of what we now call "the solar system" and put a rapidly spinning Earth circling around it at breakneck speed, utterly defying common sense. Observational evidence favoring the Copernican view would not be forthcoming for nearly 70 years after its publication in 1543, and the inability to observe annual stellar parallax at the time constituted a powerful argument against it. Consequently, only about a dozen people actually endorsed the new theory before **Galileo Galilei** first published telescopic observations in 1610.

Copernicus himself faced no ecclesiastical opposition—quite the contrary. Roman Catholic officials had long realized that the old Roman calendar was seriously flawed; the dates of the equinoxes and other annual phenomena were unstable. The Roman Catholic Church invited Copernicus to participate in efforts to find a permanent fix, and various officials urged him to publish his unorthodox astronomical ideas before Catholic bishop Tiedmann Giese and Lutheran astronomer Georg Joachim Rheticus finally persuaded him to do so.

Nevertheless, the Copernican theory was seen as contrary to Scripture by some prominent Catholic and Protestant clergy, including Martin Luther (see **Science and the Reformation**). Texts from Joshua, Ecclesiastes, and the Psalms were typically cited. The strategy that eventually proved successful was pioneered by Rheticus: invoke **Augustine**'s principle of accommodation to underscore the nontechnical nature of biblical language, thus undermining its use against scientific conclusions.

Another Lutheran astronomer, **Johannes Kepler**, made a similar argument in the early seventeenth century; so did Galileo. Kepler was keen to defend a cosmology that he found powerfully attractive theologically: its division into three parts represented **the Trinity**, with the sun in the center representing God the Father, the starry heaven at the edge representing God the Son, and the intervening space representing God the Spirit (Gingerich 2002). The bottom line was deftly stated by Galileo, quoting his acquaintance, Cardinal Cesare Baronio, "The intention of the Holy Ghost is to teach how one goes to heaven, not how heaven goes" (Galilei 1957, 186).

An identical strategy would later be used in the nineteenth century to harmonize the great age of the earth with Genesis. When Galileo used it, however, it went badly: Cardinal Roberto Bellarmine, who headed a Vatican committee charged with studying the question, concluded that the earth's motion could not be reconciled with the common understanding of the church fathers—thus violating a key hermeneutical principle from the Council of Trent. Consequently, Catholics were expected to read only censored copies of Copernicus's book until the early nineteenth century, by which time the earth's motion was no longer in doubt. Protestant acceptance of heliocentrism was not hindered by similar institutional circumstances, but still was not entirely absent of controversy.

Another challenge came from the mechanical philosophy, the view that nature is a vast, impersonal machine of moving, interacting particles. When the ancient atomists originally put forth this idea, it was accompanied by denials of divine involvement with the universe, making it difficult later for Christians to consider it. During the Scientific Revolution, however, **atomism** was effectively baptized by a Catholic priest, Pierre Gassendi, who saw atoms as the free creations of a providential God.

A devout Anglican chemist, **Robert Boyle**, went even further. In his opinion, the mechanical philosophy was theologically superior to the commonly accepted natural philosophy of **Aristotle** and Galen, which personified Nature as an intelligent, semi-divine being, intermediate between God and the creation. He feared that such a conception was "both injurious to the glory of God, and a great impediment to the solid and useful discovery of his works" (Boyle 1996, 10). Boyle argued for an alternative notion of nature as a freely created, intricately designed machine of unthinking matter, effectively denying the reality of an autonomous Nature that seemed to have a **mind** of its own. He also believed that mechanical properties are more intelligible than Aristotelian forms and qualities; by studying them, we could more effectively implement the Genesis mandate to rule over the creation for our benefit. Finally, the conception of nature as a great clockwork focused our attention on the wise and benevolent Creator who designed it, for it could not have assembled itself.

It is no accident that the rise of the mechanical philosophy overlaps with the high watermark of **natural theology**; Boyle stood at the confluence of both.

The Scientific Revolution is often said to have launched a new method of **empiricism**. In fact, what **Francis Bacon** and others gave us "was not a new method of experiment, but a new *rhetoric* of experiment, coupled with full exploitation of the possibilities of experiment in programs of scientific investigation" (Lindberg 2007, 364; italics in original). Specific theological beliefs about God's nature and human nature were often a vital part of that rhetoric. Some early modern thinkers advocated what is now called theological *voluntarism*, justifying an empirical attitude in terms of divine freedom and the limits of our created minds. Others, especially English natural philosophers, stressed the deleterious consequences of **the fall** for the intellect as well as our moral capacity (see **Fall, The**; **Evil, Problem of**).

Overall, as **Peter Harrison** has shown, "The birth of modern experimental science was not attended with a new awareness of the powers and capacities of human reason, but rather the opposite—a **consciousness** of the manifold deficiencies of the intellect, of the misery of the human condition, and of the limited scope of scientific achievement" (Harrison 2007, 258).

Edward B. Davis

REFERENCES AND RECOMMENDED READING

Boyle, Robert. 1996. *A Free Enquiry into the Vulgarly Received Notion of Nature.* Eds. Edward B. Davis and Michael Hunter. Cambridge: Cambridge University Press.

Cohen, H. Floris. 1994. *The Scientific Revolution: A Historiographical Inquiry.* Chicago: University of Chicago Press.

Davis, Edward B. 1999. "Christianity and Early Modern Science: The Foster Thesis Reconsidered." In *Evangelicals and Science in Historical Perspective.*

Eds. David N. Livingstone, D. G. Hart, and Mark A. Noll, 75–95. Oxford: Oxford University Press.

Galilei, Galileo. 1957. "Letter to the Grand Duchess Christina." In *Discoveries and Opinions of Galileo*. Trans. Stillman Drake, 173–216. Garden City, NY: Doubleday.

Gingerich, Owen. 2002. "The Copernican Revolution." In *Science and Religion: A Historical Introduction*. Ed. Gary B. Ferngren, 95–104. Baltimore: Johns Hopkins University Press.

Harrison, Peter. 2007. *The Fall of Man and the Foundations of Science*. Cambridge: Cambridge University Press.

Lindberg, David C. 2007. *The Beginnings of Western Science*. 2nd ed. Chicago: University of Chicago Press.

SCIENTISM. There are two forms of scientism: *strong* and *weak*. Strong scientism claims that some proposition is true and/or rational to believe if and only if it is a scientific proposition—that is, if and only if it is a well-established scientific proposition that, in turn, depends on its having been successfully formed, tested, and used according to appropriate scientific methodology. There are no truths apart from scientific truths, and even if there were, there would be no reason whatever to believe them.

Advocates of weak scientism allow for truths apart from science and even grant that they have some minimal, positive rationality status without the support of science. But those advocates still hold that science is the most authoritative sector of human learning. Every other intellectual activity is inferior to science. Further, there are virtually no limits to science. There is no field into which scientific research cannot shed light. To the degree that some issue outside science can be given scientific support or can be reduced to science, to that degree the issue becomes rationally acceptable. Thus we have an intellectual obligation to try to use science to solve problems in other fields that heretofore have been untouched by scientific methodology. For example, we should try to solve problems about the **mind** by the methods of neurophysiology.

Scientism suffers from three devastating criticisms. First, strong scientism is self-refuting. Strong scientism is not itself a proposition *of* science, but a second order proposition *of* philosophy *about* science to the effect that only scientific propositions are true and/or rational to believe. And strong scientism is itself offered as a true, rational belief. Self-refuting propositions (e.g., "There are no truths") don't just happen to be false but could have been true. They are necessarily false—it is not possible for them to be true. Thus no amount of scientific progress in the future will have the slightest effect on making strong scientism more acceptable.

There are two more problems that count equally against strong and weak scientism. First, scientism (in both forms) does not adequately allow for the task of stating and defending the necessary presuppositions for science itself to be practiced (assuming scientific realism). Thus scientism shows itself to be a foe and not a friend of science.

Strong scientism rules out these presuppositions because neither they nor their defense is a scientific matter. Weak scientism misconstrues their strength in its view that scientific propositions have greater cognitive authority than those of other fields like philosophy. This would mean that the conclusions of science are more certain than the philosophical presuppositions used to justify those conclusions, and that is absurd.

Finally, there is the existence of true, reasonable beliefs outside of science. Such beliefs exist in a host of fields outside of science. Strong scientism does not allow for this fact and should be rejected as an inadequate account of our intellectual enterprise.

Moreover, some propositions believed outside science (e.g., "Torturing babies for fun is wrong"; "I am now thinking about science") are better justified than some believed within science (e.g., "Evolution takes place through a series of very small steps"). Some of our currently held scientific beliefs will be rationally revised or abandoned in 100 years, but it would be hard to see how the same could be said of the extrascientific propositions just cited. Weak scientism does not account for this fact. In sum, scientism in both forms is inadequate.

J. P. Moreland

REFERENCES AND RECOMMENDED READING

Moreland, J. P. 1989. *Christianity and the Nature of Science*. Chap. 3. Grand Rapids: Baker.

Rescher, Nicholas. 1984. *The Limits of Science*. Berkeley: University of California Press.

Sorrell, Tom. 1994. *Scientism: Philosophy and the Infatuation with Science*. London: Routledge.

Williams, Richard N., and Daniel N. Robinson, eds. 2015. *Scientism: The New Orthodoxy*. London: Bloomsbury.

SCOPES TRIAL. The Scopes trial (July 10–21, 1925) was a high-profile court case in which John T. Scopes, a part-time high school teacher in Dayton, Tennessee, was charged with violating the state's recently passed statute prohibiting the teaching of evolution in public schools. Featuring celebrity combatants in the lawyers William Jennings Bryan and Clarence Darrow, the trial was portrayed in the media and in subsequent popular history as a "battle royale" between science and religion—a view perpetuated by pop chroniclers such as Frederick Lewis Allen in his 1931 bestseller, *Only Yesterday*, Broadway plays and Hollywood movies such as *Inherit the Wind*, and even many mainstream academic historians. But a closer examination reveals this interpretation to be more **mythology** than history.

In fact, the Scopes trial was more of a publicity stunt by certain local civic leaders in Dayton, Tennessee, than a serious investigation into the proper boundaries of science and religion in public schools. In 1925 the Tennessee legislature had passed a law prohibiting the teaching of "any theory that denies the story of the divine creation of man as taught in the Bible, and to teach instead that man has descended from a lower order of animals."

Immediately the American Civil Liberties Union challenged the constitutionality of the law. In Dayton, George Rappelyea, a mining engineer and an ardent evolutionist, convinced John Scopes, a 24-year-old science teacher at Central High School, to defy the law by teaching evolution to his students. Fred Robinson, the chairman of the local school board, enthusiastically supported the idea, adding that a controversial, high-profile trial would be good for business and would "put Dayton on the map."

The compliant Scopes followed the script, at which point he was arrested and put on trial for violating state law. The state's attorneys, A. T. Stuart and two brothers, Herbert and Sue Hicks, invited the three-time presidential candidate and ardent antievolutionist William Jennings Bryan to serve as an adviser to the prosecutors, hoping his celebrity status would generate media coverage.

Once the word got out that Bryan was involved, numerous lawyers offered to defend Scopes. The ACLU defense team eventually included Dudley Field Malone, Arthur Garfield Hays, and the renowned (and flamboyant) defense attorney Clarence Darrow. The ACLU defense was based on two arguments: (1) Separation of church and state, which contended that the biblical account of creation was based on religious dogma rather than science; and (2) academic freedom, which the ACLU argued is essential to quality education and a healthy democracy. It was in this context that Darrow uttered his famous declaration, "It is bigotry for public schools to teach only one theory of origins."

The trial itself was little more than a media circus, and the outcome was a foregone conclusion as the presiding judge, John Raulston, obviously favored the state. From the outset a carnival atmosphere prevailed as hundreds of reporters along with an odd mix of curiosity seekers, publicity hounds, Bible-thumping evangelists, militant atheists, and East Coast elites descended on Dayton. The trial was the first to be broadcast on the radio, and in the courtroom press photographers and motion-picture cameramen stood on tables and chairs to capture the event as though it were a championship boxing match. Throughout the proceedings the mainstream press, most notably H. L. Mencken of the *Baltimore Evening Sun*, depicted the antievolutionists as narrow-minded, uneducated simpletons.

The prosecution called three witnesses who testified that Scopes had read an offending passage from a science book, then rested its case. The defense sought to call several "expert" witnesses—mostly scientists who believed in Darwinian evolution—but Judge Raulston ruled that such testimony would be irrelevant since the trial was about whether Scopes had broken the law, not whether evolution was true. The proceedings droned on for 10 days as both sides argued technicalities until finally, on July 20, Darrow maneuvered to call Bryan to the witness stand, where he questioned him on his understanding of **science and the Bible**.

Although it has often been alleged that Darrow exposed Bryan's ignorance and subjected him to public humiliation, a reading of the transcript reveals that Bryan held his own. The interrogation ended in a heated exchange, and under pressure from state authorities who regarded the trial as an embarrassment, Judge Raulston suspended all closing arguments. The jury deliberated a few minutes before returning a guilty verdict, and Scopes was fined $100. With that, the trial abruptly ended. The ACLU promptly appealed the case, but the Tennessee Supreme Court upheld the verdict (although it overruled the $100 fine on a legal technicality).

In reality, the trial resolved nothing. However, the Darwinist side, with the overwhelming support of the media and later chroniclers, won the public relations war. In the popular imagination, William Jennings Bryan and his antievolutionist supporters had been exposed as bigoted ignoramuses. Given the inconclusive outcome of the trial, it certainly was not "the trial of the century." Nonetheless, in terms of public perception it was a watershed event that forever associated the "old-time religion" of Protestant fundamentalism with biblical literalism and an antiscience mentality.

Jeffrey D. Breshears

REFERENCES AND RECOMMENDED READING

Conlin, Joseph R. 2001. *The American Past: A Survey of American History.* 6th ed. New York: Harcourt College Publishers.

De Camp, L. Sprague. 1968. *The Great Monkey Trial*. New York: Doubleday.

Koenig, Louis W. 1975. *Bryan: A Political Biography of William Jennings Bryan*. New York: Putnam/Capricorn.

Larson, Edward J. 2006. *Summer for the Gods*. New York: Basic Books.

Levy, Leonard W., ed. 1971. *The World's Most Famous Court Trial: Tennessee v. John Thomas Scopes, 1925*. Cambridge, MA: Da Capo Press.

Olson, Steven P. 2004. *The Trial of John T. Scopes: A Primary Source Account*. New York: Rosen.

SEARLE, JOHN. American philosopher John Searle (1932–) has made important contributions to philosophy of language, philosophy of **mind**, and more recently, social philosophy. Searle received his DPhil from Oxford University and has spent most of his career teaching philosophy at the University of California–Berkeley.

A notion that runs through much of Searle's work is that of intentionality. Intentionality, for Searle, is a feature of mental phenomena and is often characterized as the of-ness or about-ness of certain mental states. A belief, for example, is an intentional state given the fact that, necessarily, there is something a belief is *about*. If one believes that God exists, then we should note that one's belief is about the **existence of God**. It is this about-ness that is the intentionality of the state. Searle sees intentionality as key to understanding language (where language has meaning insofar as it is derivatively intentional), mental phenomena (where certain mental states are intrinsically and irreducibly intentional), and even social institutions (where social constructs are analyzed in terms of collective intentionality).

Influenced by J. L. Austin, Searle's early work was in philosophy of language and, in particular, speech-act theory. A speech act is, to borrow Austin's turn of phrase, when we do things with words. There are the words we utter, but we can also *do* something with those words in communicating, such as promising or threatening. Searle argued that speech acts should be understood as utterances that are in conformity with certain constitutive rules. According to his analysis of illocutionary acts, speech acts are not a mere uttering of propositions but include a "force" that goes beyond the propositional content of the speech. The illocutionary force is determined by one's intentions in giving the utterance.

In the philosophy of mind, Searle has argued that there is a straightforward solution to the **mind-body problem**. He thinks that mental features, such as intentionality, **consciousness**, and subjectivity, are just features of the brain. So contra substance **dualism**, the mind, for Searle, is macrophenomena caused by the underlying microprocesses of the brain and nervous system. These mental properties are realized, replete with an irreducibly subjective character, contra a strict **materialism**. So although Searle is, broadly speaking, a naturalist, he is decidedly not a strict materialist. He has argued that it is a mistake to count up, as it were, the number of types of phenomena in the debates between dualists and monists (see **Soul**; **Mind**; **Mind-Body Problem**).

There are, according to Searle, many types of phenomena, and any counting will be arbitrary. Mental phenomena are as natural as any other macrofeatures that are not reducible to the underlying microstructures, such as liquidity. Liquidity is a macrofeature of water that is irreducible to the molecules constitutive of the state. Searle's view, in this way, is a more moderate philosophy of mind than, say, the eliminativist, but perhaps unmotivated if there is reason to believe in the existence of a substantial soul (see **Eliminative Materialism**).

Searle has been a vocal opponent of **artificial intelligence** (at least what he terms "strong AI"). The basic idea is that computation, even extremely sophisticated computation, need not include the features of genuine intelligence, such as consciousness, intentionality, and subjectivity. Thus digital processing is best understood as the use of syntactical rules to manipulate symbols rather than anything semantical. Searle uses his famous **Chinese Room Argument** to argue for this conclusion.

Travis M. Dickinson

REFERENCES AND RECOMMENDED READING

Austin, J. L. 1975. *How to Do Things with Words*. Cambridge, MA: Harvard University Press.

Lepore, Ernest, and Robert van Gulick. 1991. *John Searle and His Critics*. Cambridge, MA: Blackwell.

Rust, Joshua. 2009. *John Searle*. New York: Continuum.

Searle, John. 1969. *Speech Acts: An Essay in the Philosophy of Language*. New York: Cambridge University Press.

———. 1979. *Expression and Meaning: Studies in the Theory of Speech Acts*. New York: Cambridge University Press.

———. 1980. "Minds, Brains and Programs." *Behavioral and Brain Sciences* 3:417–57.

———. 1983. *Intentionality: An Essay in the Philosophy of Mind*. New York: Cambridge University Press.

———. 1984. *Minds, Brains and Science*. Cambridge, MA: Harvard University Press.

———. 1992. *The Rediscovery of the Mind*. Cambridge, MA: MIT Press.

———. 1995. *The Construction of Social Reality*. New York: Free Press.

———. 1998. *Mind, Language and Society: Philosophy in the Real World*. New York: Basic Books.

———. 2010. *Making the Social World: The Structure of Human Civilization*. New York: Oxford University Press.

Tsohatzidis, Savas L. 2007. *Intentional Acts and Institutional Acts: Essays on John Searle's Social Ontology*. Dordrecht: Springer.

———. 2007. *John Searle's Philosophy of Language: Force, Meaning and Mind*. New York: Cambridge University Press.

SECOND LAW OF THERMODYNAMICS. The second law of thermodynamics describes natural limitations inherent in the amount of useful energy produced by any system. The law has been stated in many different ways that emphasize various applications. Physicist Percy Bridgman writes, "There have been nearly as many formulations of the second law as there have been discussions of it" (Bridgman 1943, 116). Arguably the most common, and useful, formulation states that the entropy of an isolated system will never decrease. Even using this definition there is confusion about what the law means due to colloquial descriptions regarding the concept of entropy.

The mathematical definition of entropy has to do with the natural logarithm of the number of available microstates. The concept of a microstate might be best understood by considering the simple system of two six-sided dice. There is only one microstate available for the dice to roll 12: both must show a six. However, there are six possible microstates available for the dice to roll a 7. The combinations are 1 and 6, 2 and 5, 3 and 4, 4 and 3, 5 and 2, and 6 and 1. Because there are more available microstates, the dice will more often roll a 7. A macroscopic system with more available microstates has a greater entropy than one with fewer microstates. The second law of thermodynamics states that an isolated system will evolve spontaneously to the state with maximum entropy.

Other statements of the second law of thermodynamics can give a broader understanding of its meaning. The simplest statement of the law may be that heat will not naturally flow from a colder object to a hotter object. The Kelvin-Planck statement of the law says that it is impossible to make a cyclic device whose sole effect is to transform a given amount of heat completely to work. In other words, it is impossible to make an engine that operates at 100 percent efficiency. All formulations of the law convey the fact that in any process some amount of useful energy is lost or wasted. Although the total energy of an isolated system is always conserved, the amount of energy that can be used to perform work diminishes with every process.

Apart from the activity of God and supernatural beings within it, the universe is a closed, isolated system. Consequently, the second law of thermodynamics applies to the universe as a whole. The continual increase of the entropy of the universe means that over a long period of **time**, the temperature of the universe will become more uniform and the ability of any process in the universe to perform useful work will diminish. Eventually, the universe will reach an equilibrium temperature, sometimes called the *heat death* of the universe in which it will not be possible to perform any process that can do any useful work.

The term *entropy* is sometimes used to describe the amount of disorder in a system. Although not a truly accurate definition of entropy, the idea of disorder does correlate with the fact that systems with fewer microstates appear to be more ordered. However, this definition of entropy can lead to misunderstandings of the second law of thermodynamics. For instance, opponents of **biological evolution** have claimed that evolution violates the second law of thermodynamics since evolution proposes more complex systems have evolved from simpler systems. Of course, evolution does not violate the second law, and if it did, no scientists would believe it. The earth is not a closed system, so life on the earth can become more complex without any thermodynamic problems. Every human life starts very simply as a single cell and develops into a complex organism without violating the second law because the developing embryo is not an isolated system. In the same way, evolution could produce complex life without violating the second law of thermodynamics.

The second law of thermodynamics does provide **information** about the origin of the universe. Because entropy always increases, the early universe had the minimum entropy. If entropy is loosely associated with the concept of order or disorder, this means that the universe was most ordered at its beginning. Therefore the **big bang** origin of the universe requires that the "bang" is not like a random disordered explosion, but much more like a maximally ordered beginning. An ordered beginning is just one of the many aspects of the big bang that supports the biblical statement that our universe was created by a superior divine being.

Michael G. Strauss

REFERENCES AND RECOMMENDED READING

Bridgman, P. W. 1943. *The Nature of Thermodynamics.* 2nd ed. Cambridge, MA: Harvard University Press.
Giancoli, Douglas. 2014. *Physics: Principles with Applications.* 7th ed. San Francisco: Pearson.

SECULARIZATION. Secularization has become a significant trend in the latter half of the twentieth century and into the early twenty-first century, especially in Western societies. However, the term has at least a couple of meanings that are not always clearly distinguished from each other. Popular usage conveys mostly a negative meaning, highlighting the fact that the religious, especially Christian, outlook on life is losing its influence in modern Western countries because of a process of secularization that involves an emphasis on that which is "nonreligious," such as consumerism, the spread of **technology**, and a material lifestyle—in short, things of "this world."

Religion is less evident in modern life, especially in certain countries or cities: People do not attend church as frequently, do not appeal as often to their religious beliefs to tackle problems or as a guide to living. However, it is important to note that despite these trends, according to many polls, most people still remain religious believers in some type of higher being. The causes of this level of secularization are much debated and hard to pinpoint with any accuracy, though several developments are thought to contribute to the secularizing process, including the rise of the modern city as a major place of work and entertainment (which encourages a move from rural to urban life), the increased pace and **complexity** of modern living, the pervasiveness of technology, and the hegemony of science in our culture as a way of addressing human problems.

The specific connection between science and secularization in the life of the general public is hard to identify, but it has been suggested that science challenges religion in many areas, either directly or indirectly, and so this may have a deleterious effect on the influence of religion. In addition, science contributes to the rise of new developments in society (e.g., in the areas of consumer products, entertainment, medicine, travel) that encourages materialistic lifestyles dominated by comfort, escapism, the pursuit of novelty, even hedonism, all of which can be a seductive distraction from the life of the spirit.

There is, however, a deeper type of secularization taking place, again mostly in Western societies. This is the movement of *secularism*. Secularism is the view that all that exists is physical in nature, consisting of matter and energy, and that man himself must create all meaning and value. This view is a modern form of atheism, entailing no God and involving a rejection of the supernatural. Secularism is becoming a more identifiable view and is now openly argued for by prominent thinkers in Western societies, and by some politicians and political parties, and it is sometimes promoted in opposition to religion. This view is seeking more influence in the shaping of modern culture and is especially prominent in education, the media, academia, and the law courts.

Secularism is to be distinguished from "the secular," a term that retains the mostly negative connotation of "nonreligious," in the sense of not belonging to, or not promoting, a religious (especially a denominational) viewpoint, particularly at the political level (as in the concept of the "secular state," or the democratic principle of the "separation of church and state"). Secularism must now be regarded as a major influential **worldview** and one that is deliberate about shaping modern society according to its beliefs and values. As a result of the rise of secularism, contemporary social, political, and moral issues are often debated against a backdrop of the more general debate between religious and secularist views of the meaning of life.

Brendan Sweetman

REFERENCES AND RECOMMENDED READING

Berger, Peter. 1967. *The Sacred Canopy*. New York: Doubleday.

Habermas, Jürgen, and Joseph Ratzinger (Pope Benedict XVI). 2010. *The Dialectics of Secularization*. San Francisco: Ignatius.

Smith, Christian. 2003. *The Secular Revolution*. Berkeley: University of California Press.

Sweetman, Brendan. 2006. *Why Politics Needs Religion: The Place of Religious Arguments in the Public Square*. Downers Grove, IL: InterVarsity.

Taylor, Charles. 2007. *A Secular Age*. Cambridge, MA: Harvard University Press.

SELFISH GENE. The selfish gene was a term coined by Oxford zoologist **Richard Dawkins** in his 1976 book *The Selfish Gene*, as a means of expressing the view of evolution that understands the gene to be the unit of selection, as opposed to alternative views that take the organism or whole group to be the unit of selection (Dawkins [1976] 2006). Alternative views include kin selection theory (which favors an organism's relatives, even at the sacrifice of the organism's own survival and reproductive success) and group selection theory (where **natural selection** occurs at the level of the group).

Dawkins's selfish gene thesis was developed on the work of earlier writers in the 1960s, notably John Maynard Smith and W. D. Hamilton, and in particular the work of George C. Williams who, in his book *Adaptation and Natural Selection*, argued that **altruism** is based not primarily on its conferring of some benefit to the group, but is instead a result of selection that occurs at the level of the gene that is "mediated by the phenotype" (Williams 1966, 26). Moreover, Williams contended, "the natural selection of phenotypes cannot in itself produce cumulative change, because phenotypes are extremely temporary manifestations" (Williams 1966, 24).

Williams argued against group-level selection on the basis that higher-level selection is generally very weak relative to lower-level selection. He argued that sex ratios favored selection at the level of the individual rather than the group, since group-level selection would favor an uneven sex ratio (either male-dominant or female-dominant, depending on whether population growth or regulation is of benefit to the group as a whole), whereas within-group selection would favor an even sex ratio. It is now understood that there are numerous examples of extreme female-biased sex ratios, particularly in small **species** of arthropods (Hamilton 1967). Williams's rejection of group-level selection came to be generally accepted (West et al. 2007).

The gene-centric understanding of evolution argues that the gene variants (alleles) whose phenotypic effects favor their own propagation are favored by natural selection relative to other alleles, and so increase in frequency in the population. Thus, it is argued, evolution and natural selection are best understood from the perspective of genes.

The gene-centric view of evolution has been criticized by prominent biologists, including Ernst Mayr (Mayr 1997), Stephen Jay Gould (Gould 1990), and Niles Eldredge (Eldredge 2005). For example, Stephen Jay Gould pointed out that "no matter how much power Dawkins wishes to assign to genes, there is one thing that he cannot give them—direct visibility to natural selection" (Gould 1990, 90). Gould understood the unit of selection to be the phenotype, since that is what ultimately interacts with the environment.

The concept of "selfish **DNA**" also has connotations in relation to mobile DNA, elements of DNA that are thought to spread by forming copies of themselves while conferring no apparent phenotypic benefit to the host organism. As Leslie Orgel and **Francis Crick** said in 1980, "The more efficient replicators increase in number at the expense of their less efficient competitors. After a sufficient time, only the most efficient replicators survive" (Orgel and Crick 1980, 605). Many of these mobile elements are, however, now understood to be functional (e.g., Shapiro and Sternberg 2005), undermining a common argument that has been used for many years against **intelligent design**—that is, that the accumulation of so-called selfish or junk DNA is exceedingly unlikely on a design hypothesis.

Jonathan McLatchie

REFERENCES AND RECOMMENDED READING

Dawkins, Richard. (1976) 2006. *The Selfish Gene: 30th Anniversary Edition.* Oxford: Oxford University Press.

Eldredge, N. 2005. *Why We Do It: Rethinking Sex and the Selfish Gene.* New York: W. W. Norton.

Gould, S. J. 1990. "Caring Groups and Selfish Genes." In *The Panda's Thumb: More Reflections in Natural History.* London: Penguin.

Hamilton, W. D. 1967. "Extraordinary Sex Ratios. A Sex-Ratio Theory for Sex Linkage and Inbreeding Has New Implications in Cytogenetics and Entomology." *Science* 156 (3774): 477–88.

Mayr, E. 1997. "The Objects of Selection." *Proceedings of the National Academy of Sciences USA* 94:2091–94.

Orgel, L. E., and F. H. C. Crick. 1980. "Selfish DNA: The Ultimate Parasite." *Nature* 284:604–7.

Shapiro, J. A., and R. Sternberg. 2005. "Why Repetitive DNA Is Essential to Genome Function." *Biology Reviews* 80:1–24.

West, S. A., A. S. Griffin, and A. Gardner. 2007. "Social Semantics: How Useful Has Group Selection Been?" *Journal of Evolutionary Biology* 21:374–85.

Williams, G. C. 1966. *Adaptation and Natural Selection.* Princeton, NJ: Princeton University Press.

SENTIENCE. Sentience (from the Latin verb *sentire*, for feeling) is the capacity to perceive or experience. Sentient creatures are those living entities that are capable of conscious, subjective feelings, experiences, or perceptions.

On the one hand, some nonhuman animals—for example, spiders, ants, mollusks, and crustaceans—clearly respond to noxious stimuli (for instance, by recoiling when being poked with a stick), but whether they are capable of conscious, subjective feeling is doubtful. Do they say to themselves through some self-conscious inner voice, "Ouch, that hurts!" "Don't do that!" "Leave me alone"? It seems very unlikely, at least in part, because of the primitive state of their central nervous system (CNS). Animal brain studies can show that animals react either to noxious or pleasurable stimuli, but those studies cannot demonstrate a subjective state of awareness (see **Animal Pain**).

Some nonhuman animals—for example, great apes, dolphins, dogs, and cats—seem more likely to be subjective experiencers of the world and therefore sentient. Sentience, in this sense, is synonymous with conscious self-awareness. By this definition, human beings may be either sentient or nonsentient. That is, an individual human is typically a conscious, subjective experiencer of the world but may not be so, say, at the early embryonic stage of development or when permanently unconscious. Exactly when an embryonic human being becomes conscious and self-aware remains controversial, as does exactly when a previously conscious human being becomes permanently unconscious. Occasionally, for example, a patient who has been diagnosed as being in a persistent vegetative state, and therefore thought to lack conscious awareness for many years, recovers and reports that he or she was aware the entire time.

In the history of Western ethics, sentience has been viewed as a sufficient condition for the possession of rights. Enlightenment utilitarian John Stuart Mill (1806–73) maintained that all sentient creatures, including nonhuman animals, have a right not to be unnecessarily harmed, where harm is defined as causing conscious pain. For Mill, decisions about the rightness or wrongness of an action require the calculation of the pleasure and pain of all sentient creatures, including animals. An action that, on balance, results in more pain than pleasure is usually deemed immoral, while an action that results in more pleasure than pain may be morally permissible.

Philosopher and animal rights activist Peter Singer (1946–) follows Mill's lead and argues that the prevention of animal suffering requires that human beings refrain from killing and eating animals for food. Ethical treatment of animals, according to Singer, entails a vegetarian or vegan lifestyle. Furthermore, for Singer, since "a chimpanzee, dog, or pig, for instance, will have a higher degree of self-awareness and a greater capacity for meaningful relations with others than a severely retarded infant or someone in a state of advanced senility … we must grant these animals a right to life as good as, or better than, such retarded or senile humans" (Singer, *Animal Liberation*, 19).

From a naturalistic perspective, sentience or self-awareness is a function of the brain and CNS. From a Christian theological perspective, persons may be sentient even without functioning brains. For instance, both God and angels are conscious, self-aware beings. Furthermore, according to the Bible, human beings are sentient even after the **death** of the body. (See **Consciousness**; **Life after Death**; **Mind**; **Soul**.)

C. Ben Mitchell

REFERENCES AND RECOMMENDED READING

Cooper, John W. 2000. *Body, Soul and Life Everlasting: Biblical Anthropology and the Monism-Dualism Debate.* Grand Rapids: Eerdmans.
George, Robert P., and Christopher Tollefson. 2008. *Embryo: In Defense of Human Life.* New York: Doubleday.
Meilaender, Gilbert. 2009. *Neither Beast nor God: The Dignity of the Human Person.* New York: Encounter.
Moreland, J. P. 2014. *The Soul: How We Know It's Real and Why It Matters.* Chicago: Moody.
Singer, Peter. 1990. *Animal Liberation.* New York: New York Review of Books.

SERPENT, THE. Genesis 1–2 presents two narratives describing the creation of the world and the first humans (1:1–2:4a; 2:4b–25). In the second creation account (see **Creation**), we learn that God placed the first man in a garden named **Eden**, charging him to "work it and take care of it" (Gen. 2:15). A common translation of the second verb is "guard" (*shamar*), and it is likely that the command included the idea of protecting the garden against dangerous intrusion. At this point in the narrative, though, nothing has been mentioned that might present a threat to the garden or its human inhabitants. Thus first-time readers of the narrative are surprised by the appearance of a serpent in Genesis 3:1, and a walking and talking serpent at that.

The narrator informs the reader that the serpent "was more crafty (*'arum*) than any of the wild animals the LORD God had made" (Gen. 3:1). The word here translated "crafty" has a positive meaning—"prudence"—in the book of Proverbs (e.g., 1:4; 8:5, 12 NIV), but the serpent uses his "wisdom" for evil purposes as it interacts with Eve in an attempt to get her to violate God's command not to eat from the tree of the knowledge of good and evil (Gen. 2:16–17).

Instead of taking care (or guarding) the garden, Eve succumbs to the serpent's argument that rather than leading to their **death**, the fruit of the tree would make them wise. Adam, who was "with her" during her interaction with the serpent (Gen. 3:6), does not resist in the least and joins his wife in eating the fruit. Their rebellion leads to an immediate break in their relationship with God (a kind of spiritual death) and with each other. According to Paul, their sin introduced sin and death into the world (Rom. 5:12–21).

Christian interpreters differ over the genre of Genesis 3, and while some would read it as a straightforward historical account of an actual event (Beeke 2015; VanDoodewaard), others treat the story as purely symbolical (Enns 2012). Still others (Longman 2016; Walton 2015, 128–39) suggest that Genesis 3 is a figurative description of a historical event. Such a reading argues that the story tells of a time when humanity rebelled against God, thus surrendering their created moral innocence, bringing death into the human experience. This understanding takes the walking serpent not as a literal description but as a representation of evil.

In support of a symbolic interpretation of the serpent is the role played by serpents, some of them walking, in the literature of the ancient Near East. **John Walton** (2003, 2009, 2015) gives four examples. In the eleventh tablet of the ***Gilgamesh Epic***, Gilgamesh seeks to attain life by finding a plant at the bottom of the sea. Before he can consume it and attain lasting life, however, it is stolen by a snake. Second, Ningishzida (whose name means "Lord of the Productive Tree") is a serpent-shaped gatekeeper in the *Adapa Epic*, in which the main character, who gives his name to the epic,

628 SETI

is offered the bread of life but refuses it due to deceptive advice given by the god of wisdom, Ea.

Walton's third example is from Egyptian **mythology**, in which the snake represents death as well as wisdom. His final example, also from Egypt, is Apophis, the snakelike representative of chaos who must be defeated nightly by the sun god. A fifth example, and perhaps a more telling one, is Tiamat, the primeval deity sometimes represented as a sea serpent who represents the waters of chaos defeated by Marduk, the creator god in the *Enuma Elish*.

Leviathan is another name for a serpentine creature that occurs in a creation account (Ps. 74:12–17). In this poetic context, the psalmist celebrates God for crushing the many-headed Leviathan and follows that with a description of creation. The ancient Near Eastern background of Leviathan is found in Canaanite literature, where the seven-headed serpent (see also Isa. 27:1) is an ally of Yam, the god of the sea, defeated by the creator god Baal in a broken cuneiform tablet from ancient Ugarit, which in its original form almost certainly had a creation account attached to it.

The New Testament (Rom. 16:20; Rev. 12:9; 20:2, anticipated in the intertestamental Wisdom of Solomon 2:23–24) associates the serpent with Satan. Biblical scholars debate whether Satan makes any appearance in the Old Testament. English translations of the Hebrew word *satan* in 1 Chronicles 21:1; Job 1:6–12; and Zechariah 3:1–2 may be misleading, since in these contexts the Hebrew terms should probably be understood as an angelic agent of God, whom God uses to execute his will (Day 1988). Accordingly, it is unlikely that readers of Genesis 3 during the Old Testament period would have understood the serpent as Satan, but rather as the personification of evil.

That said, the New Testament serves to deepen understanding of the Old Testament (theologians speak of the progress of revelation as biblical teaching becomes clearer and clearer as God reveals more and more to his people). On this understanding, while it is important to read the Old Testament first on its own terms, interpreting Genesis 3 from the perspective of the fuller revelation of the New Testament leads to the conclusion that the serpent does represent Satan.

Tremper Longman III

REFERENCES AND RECOMMENDED READING

Beeke, J. R. 2015. "The Bible's First Word." In *God, Adam, and You: Biblical Creation Defended and Applied* Ed. R. D. Phillips, 1–14. Phillipsburg, NJ: P&R.

Day, J. 1985. *God's Conflict with the Dragon and the Sea: Echoes of a Canaanite Myth in the Old Testament.* Cambridge: Cambridge University Press.

Day, P. L. 1988. *An Adversary in Heaven: Satan in the Hebrew Bible.* Atlanta: Scholars.

Enns, P. 2012. *The Evolution of Adam: What the Bible Does and Doesn't Say about Human Origins.* Grand Rapids: Brazos.

Longman, Tremper, III . 2016. *Genesis.* Grand Rapids: Zondervan.

VanDoodewaard, W. 2015. *The Quest for the Historical Adam: Genesis, Hermeneutics, and Human Origins.* Grand Rapids: Reformation Heritage Books.

Walton, John H. 2003. "Serpent." In *Dictionary of the Old Testament: Pentateuch.* eds. T. D. Alexander and D. W. Baker, 736–39. Downers Grove, IL: InterVarsity.

———. 2009. "Genesis." In *Zondervan Illustrated Bible Backgrounds Commentary,* vol. 1. Ed. J. H. Walton, 2–159. Grand Rapids: Zondervan.

———. 2015. *The Lost World of Adam and Eve: Genesis 2–3 and the Human Origins Debate.* Downers Grove, IL: InterVarsity Press.

SETI. The search for extraterrestrial intelligence (SETI) has been pursued in various forms for the past hundred-plus years. The most common method has been to monitor incoming electromagnetic waves from space and to search for information-bearing patterns that would indicate their origin in extraterrestrial intelligence (ETI). While the term *SETI* applies broadly to this branch of scientific enquiry, it also appears as part of the name for several specific groups and activities, including the SETI Institute (www.seti.org) located in Mountain View, California; Seti@Home (http://setiathome.berkeley.edu/), a project networking thousands of personal computers to analyze signals received from radio telescopes; an interdisciplinary convention organized periodically by the SETI Institute; and Active SETI (www.activeseti.org), whose purpose is to send messages into the universe.

In the late nineteenth century, Nikola Tesla believed that contact with beings on Mars might be possible using wireless electrical transmission and detection. A few years later, he observed signals using his Tesla coil that he believed might have originated from Mars, though they were later determined to be spurious or of a natural origin. In the early years of the twentieth century, interest grew in searching for signs of life on Mars, and in August of 1924 an effort by the United States to capitalize on the close proximity of Mars resulted in a National Radio Silence Day, to enable a dedicated radio receiver at the US Naval Observatory to search for signals from Mars.

In 1960 Cornell astronomer Frank Drake began measurements of signals from space in the first modern SETI experimental effort. He used a 26-meter-diameter radio telescope in Green Bank, West Virginia, to monitor microwave signals at 1,420 MHz, a frequency corresponding to a well-understood "hyperfine" transition in cosmic hydrogen. It was thought that any intelligent beings would understand and recognize the unique importance of this transmission frequency and use it to attempt communication with other intelligent beings in the universe.

The first SETI conference was held in Green Bank, West Virginia, and participants included Frank Drake, **Carl Sagan**, and Philip Morrison. From conference discussions, Frank Drake developed his Drake Equation, which is designed to calculate the probable number of planets in the Milky Way suitable for the support of intelligent life. The equation is controversial because it depends on several variables whose values are notoriously difficult to estimate and/or measure, and so its solutions vary over an enormous range.

Carl Sagan was a very influential and outspoken proponent of SETI, cofounding the US Planetary Society and in 1982 proving instrumental in helping to reinstate congressional funding for SETI research after it was cut. Jill Tarter, the SETI Institute Research director until recently retiring, spent 35 years of her professional career searching for evidences for ETI, winning many awards and honors for her work, and is today among the most recognized figures in SETI efforts. The character Ellie Arroway in the novel *Contact* by Carl Sagan, later made into a movie with the same name, was loosely modeled on Jill Tarter and her life's work. Today some of the most well-known SETI efforts are run by Harvard University, the University of California–Berkeley, and the SETI Institute.

Humans have only been capable of receiving and interpreting electromagnetic signals from space for the past 100 years or so, whereas thousands or millions of civilizations elsewhere in the universe may have arisen and perhaps disappeared millions or billions of years ago. Also, electromagnetic waves diminish in intensity as the inverse square of the distance, meaning that signals become increasingly difficult to detect with distance from the source. Transmissions from a distant civilization of sufficient power to be detectable may already have passed by the earth long before humans were present. Therefore, given the vast span of space (over millions of light-years) and time (millions to billions of years) that could characterize the distribution of thousands or millions of ETI civilizations in the universe, the likelihood of humanity receiving a signal of sufficient strength during its very narrow 100-year "online" window is quite small.

While science cannot provide an estimate for the likelihood of life elsewhere in the universe (since we do not have a full understanding of life or its origin), significant research continues in the search for microbial life in the solar system using interplanetary probes. Additionally, the search for exo-planets, those orbiting other stars in our galaxy, is an active and fast-growing field that has already discovered thousands of planets orbiting other stars, a few of which are somewhat earthlike in size and temperature zone. The discovery of basic life elsewhere in the solar system or beyond, if it exists, would certainly advance our understanding of life, and perhaps enable us better to understand where and how to search for ETI.

Research into the detection of ETI is still in infancy, and techniques for detecting passive evidence have also been posited. Freeman Dyson, for example, proposed that civilizations far more advanced and with significantly higher energy needs than ours would very likely develop **technology** to harness energy from their own or a nearby star by surrounding it with a spherical megastructure of networked energy collectors, constituting what has come to be called a *Dyson sphere*. Structures like these would emit copious amounts of infrared radiation into the surrounding space, meaning that a search for bright objects in the infrared radiation spectrum not resembling natural astronomical sources might yield telltale signs of ETI.

Christians and non-Christians alike have been interested in the question of life elsewhere in the universe. Some have argued that discovery of ETI would undermine Christian faith and doctrine. The challenge faced by the church and humanity with the discovery of ETI would be similar to that faced several hundred years ago by the advent of the Copernican heliocentric view, or in more recent years to that faced by the evolutionary understanding of life on Earth and the discovery of the genetic interrelatedness of all life. In both of these cases, the centrality of humanity was "threatened" by new scientific **revelation**s, but the Christian gospel and the life of the church handily survived these periods of adjustment.

While the discovery of ETI could certainly set into motion a new identity crisis for humanity, God's singular and unconditional love for humanity will always remain secure in the gospel of Jesus Christ. There is no known biblical prohibition on the possibility of life elsewhere in the universe, including intelligent life. God is more than capable of creating additional life-forms to populate his universe and might delight in such creative activity. A few Christian authors have reflected on the possibility of ETI, including **C. S. Lewis**, Marie I. George, and Thomas Morris.

Warren F. Rogers

REFERENCES AND RECOMMENDED READING

Dyson, Freeman. 1981. *Disturbing the Universe*. New York: Basic Books.
George, Marie I. 2005. *Christianity and Extraterrestrials? A Catholic Perspective*. Bloomington, IN: iUniverse.
Lewis, C. S. 1990. "Dogma and the Universe." In *God in the Dock: Essays on Theology and Ethics*. Ed. Walter Hooper, 38–47. Grand Rapids: Eerdmans.
Morris, Thomas. 2001. *The Logic of God Incarnate*. Eugene, OR: Wipf and Stock.
Sagan, Carl, and Iosif Shklovskii. 1984. *Intelligent Life in the Universe*. San Francisco: Holden Day.

SHROUD OF TURIN. The famous linen artifact known as the Shroud of Turin measures 14 feet 3 inches by 3 feet 7 inches (4.4 m by 1.1 m). Its most striking and intriguing feature observed on one side of the cloth is a head-to-foot image revealing both the frontal and dorsal likenesses of a crucified male lying on his back with his arms folded at his waist. Severe whipping lacerations can be seen over essentially the entire body, along with blood flows from five major punctures in both wrists, both feet, and a more severe wound in the right side.

Debates regarding whether or not this cloth covered the body of Jesus Christ after his **death** by crucifixion account for the plethora of scientific tests and historical studies performed over the last few decades. While potential historical links to Jesus include the similar wounds featuring real human blood, the more intriguing issue is that Jesus's crucifixion as recorded in the Gospels was rather atypical. Abnormal specifics like the severity of Jesus's beating, the crown of thorns, the side wound, and the individual burial in a shroud all appear to be identical to those observed on the cloth.

A serious challenge to the view that the cloth belonged to Jesus came from the results of carbon-14 tests performed in 1988 that dated the shroud between the thirteenth and fourteenth centuries. This is frequently treated as the last word on the subject. However, subsequent microscopic chemical testing showed quite clearly that the nonimage threads from the 1988 carbon dating differed significantly from the threads from the shroud image area that were removed during the scientific testing a decade earlier—indicating that they were simply from different cloths. This has been taken by many to indicate that the material dated by the carbon-14 process was used centuries later to patch the original cloth.

The Shroud of Turin is known to have existed in Western Europe since at least the Middle Ages. But it is often argued that additional discoveries on the cloth, such as extinct pollens as well as a **species** of limestone dirt, both traceable to the area of Israel, along with leptons of Pontius Pilate placed over the eyes, all indicate a Jerusalem location from a much earlier date.

Furthermore, a trail of early paintings of Jesus Christ along with Roman coins featuring Jesus's image date from centuries prior to the medieval date suggested by the carbon-14 dating. Since many of these likenesses were seemingly copied directly from the shroud facial image in dozens of places, while dating from the sixth century AD onward, these results are taken as further challenges to the carbon-14 tests.

One popular view to arise after numerous scientific experiments on the Shroud is that the body images were caused by an X-ray-like process. Nonetheless, polarized conclusions persist regarding the Shroud of Turin.

Gary R. Habermas

REFERENCES AND RECOMMENDED READING

Antonacci, Mark. 2000. *The Resurrection of the Shroud*. New York: M. Evans.
Heller, John H. 1983. *Report on the Shroud*. Boston: Houghton Mifflin.
Rogers, Raymond N. 2005. "Studies on the Radiocarbon Sample from the Shroud of Turin." *Thermochimica Acta* 425:189–94.
Stevenson, Kenneth E., and Gary R. Habermas. 1981. *Verdict on the Shroud: Evidence for the Death and Resurrection of Jesus Christ*. Ann Arbor, MI: Servant.
Whanger, Mary, and Alan Whanger. 1998. *The Shroud of Turin: An Adventure of Discovery*. Franklin, TN: Providence House.

SINGULARITY, THE. Biology will not finally constrain human beings, according to inventor and science visionary Ray Kurzweil. Human destiny is not lashed to the deck of the human body. Through technological enhancements, humans can overcome their worst limitations and conquer **death** itself. For Kurzweil, science fiction will become science fact, and a new order of being will be introduced into earth's history. Humans and machines will merge into one dynamic new entity ("the singularity"). This vision is part of transhumanism. For such optimists, **materialism** need not be a dour philosophy that teaches that all that is living will die, and rather quickly. Humans have a glorious future.

In a description of Kurzweil's book *The Singularity Is Near: When Humans Transcend Biology*, his Web page says:

> In this new world, there will be no clear distinction between human and machine, real reality and virtual reality. We will be able to assume different bodies and take on a range of personae at will. In practical terms, human aging and illness will be reversed; pollution will be stopped; world hunger and poverty will be solved. Nanotechnology will make it possible to create virtually any physical

product using inexpensive **information** processes and will ultimately turn even death into a soluble problem.

The book was made into a docudrama in 2010.

For Kurzweil, cosmic evolution is reaching a new epoch, which radically transcends its previous stages. There are six epochs: (1) physics and chemistry, (2) biology and **DNA**, (3) brains, (4) technology, (5) merger of human technology and human intelligence, (6) the universe wakes up.

This exhilarating perspective crashes into the rocks of reality at a couple of points. First, cognition is not computation. As **John Searle** has argued in his **Chinese Room** thought experiment, computing is syntax, not semantics. Computers can arrange information in programmed ways, but they understand none of it. Digital computation exceeds the ability of humans to compute by a vast magnitude. However, the computations by even the greatest supercomputer or networked computer are not conscious of the values of what they manipulate by the syntactic rules. Therefore machine computation will never achieve **consciousness**, since consciousness involves semantic understanding (among many other things). Furthermore, if machines can never be conscious, they cannot, then, merge with conscious humans in one conscious "singularity."

Second, information cannot emerge unguided from merely material states. Kurzweil's atheism posits a grand human-machine future based on an impersonal and purposeless past. However, there is no known mechanism by which nonliving elements combine to generate genetic material. Neither **chance** nor natural law nor the combination of both is up for this metaphysical task, as **Stephen Meyer** has cogently argued in *The Signature in the Cell* (2009).

Douglas Groothuis

REFERENCES AND RECOMMENDED READING

Groothuis, Douglas. 1996. *The Soul in Cyberspace*. Grand Rapids: Baker.
Kurzweil, Ray. 2006. *The Singularity Is Near: When Humans Transcend Biology*. New York: Penguin.
Meyer, Stephen. 2009. *Signature in the Cell*. New York: HarperCollins.

SOBER, ELLIOTT. Elliott Sober (1948–) is Hans Reichenbach Professor and William F. Vilas Research Professor of Philosophy at University of Wisconsin–Madison. Besides his professorship at Wisconsin, Sober also served consecutively as Centennial and visiting professor at the London School of Economics and Political Science, and taught briefly at Stanford University. Sober received his PhD from Harvard University in 1974. His dissertation was related to "the nature of simplicity or parsimony as it features in scientific activity in general" (Callebaut 1993, 267).

Sober has written or coauthored more than 10 books and nearly 250 articles touching on numerous topics such as scientific approaches to inferring **causation**, comparing scientific model selection approaches, the roles of parsimony and simplicity in theory formation and evaluation, debates over units of **natural selection**, and clarification of (or relationships between) concepts in evolutionary theory such as fitness, selection, optimality, and adaptation.

Some of these volumes are used as textbooks, such as *Philosophy of Biology* (1993b) and *Core Questions in Philosophy* (2012). Titles focusing on various aspects of evolutionary biology theory include *The Nature of Selection* (1993a), *Evidence and Evolution* (2008), and *Did Darwin Write the Origin Backwards?* (2011a). Sober reports that he first became interested in the philosophy of evolutionary biology around 1976. Prior to that, he focused on "general questions about the nature of science as a whole" (Sober 1993a, ix).

Sober has become a consistent developer and staunch defender of neo-Darwinian theory, dealing with such concerns as the shortage of transitional fossil evidence (Sober 2009a), objections that proposed neo-Darwinian processes quickly exhaust probabilistic resources (Sober 2002, 65–74; Sober 2008, 49–51), and addressing the counterintuitive problem of how **altruism** could have evolved (Sober 1988b; Sober and Wilson 1998; 2011, 463–67; see **Darwinism**; **Fossil Record**).

As a critical tool for supporting neo-Darwinism, Sober has frequently employed a *likelihood* approach (Sober 2002, 70–71; 2004, 99–102; 2008, 8–9, 32–33), which compares rival hypotheses as to the probabilities they respectively confer on observed effects. For example, Sober has applied this approach for comparing the respective likelihoods of common versus separate ancestry (Sober 2008, 264–352; 2009b, 10050–55).

Sober's writings sometimes address questions regarding God's role in biological explanations. While not necessarily endorsing theistic evolution, he has asserted that it is not logically contradictory (Sober 2008, 110–12; 2011b, 189–90). Sober has also analyzed and objected to **design argument**s (particularly **intelligent design**) on likelihood grounds (Sober 2002, 71–78; 2004, 99–114; 2008, 118–54). Acknowledging **David Hume**'s objections to design arguments (Hume, Aiken, ed. 1948, 17–18, 23; see **Design Argument**), Sober proposes that design arguments be framed as likelihood arguments without any appeal to analogy and induction (Sober 1993b, 30–36; 2008, 139–40). Sober then claims, however, that such arguments lack independent evidential support regarding the designer's goals and abilities, thus eliminating any assessable likelihood (Sober 1999, 61–66; 2007, 5–6, 8; 2008, 143–49, 168). Consequently, Sober dismisses intelligent design from consideration as a scientific theory (Sober 2008, 190).

The present evidential landscape in science has changed drastically from Hume's day. Christian thinkers may want to revisit whether a combination of analogy and induction does not, after all, supply the independent support that, in contrast to Sober's claims, could undergird a robust likelihood for design hypotheses, which could then compete with neo-Darwinian explanations on the macrolevel of biology (see **Induction, Problem of**).

James Charles LeMaster

REFERENCES AND RECOMMENDED READING

Callebaut, Werner, ed. 1993. *Taking the Naturalistic Turn, or How Real Philosophy of Science Is Done*. Science and Its Conceptual Foundations. Chicago: University of Chicago Press.

Hume, David. 1948. *Dialogues concerning Natural Religion*. Ed. Henry D. Aiken. New York: Hafner.

LeMaster, James Charles. 2014. "A Critique of the Rejection of Intelligent Design as a Scientific Hypothesis by Elliott Sober from His Book *Evidence and Evolution*." PhD diss. Southern Baptist Theological Seminary.

Sober, Elliott. 1988a. *Reconstructing the Past: Parsimony, Evolution, and Inference*. Cambridge, MA: MIT Press.

——. 1988b. "What Is Evolutionary Altruism?" *Canadian Journal of Philosophy*, supp. vol., 14:75–99.

——. 1993a. *The Nature of Selection: Evolutionary Theory in Philosophical Focus*. Chicago: University of Chicago Press.

——. 1993b. *Philosophy of Biology*. Dimensions of Philosophy Series. Boulder, CO: Westview.

——. 1994. *From a Biological Point of View: Essays in Evolutionary Philosophy*. Cambridge Studies in Philosophy and Biology. Cambridge: Cambridge University Press.

——. 1999. "Testability." *Proceedings and Addresses of the American Philosophical Association* 73 (2): 47–76.

——. 2000. *Philosophy of Biology*. 2nd ed. Dimensions of Philosophy Series. Boulder, CO: Westview.

——. 2002. "Intelligent Design and Probability Reasoning." *International Journal for Philosophy of Religion* 52 (2): 65–80.

——. 2004. "The Design Argument." In *Debating Design: From Darwin to DNA*. Eds. William A. Dembski and Michael Ruse, 98–129. Cambridge: Cambridge University Press.

——. 2007. "What Is Wrong with Intelligent Design?" *Quarterly Review of Biology* 82 (1): 3–8.

——. 2008. *Evidence and Evolution: The Logic behind the Science*. New York: Cambridge University Press.

——. 2009a. "Absence of Evidence and Evidence of Absence: Evidential Transitivity in Connection with Fossils, Fishing, Fine-Tuning, and Firing Squads." *Philosophical Studies* 143:63–90.

——. 2009b. "Did Darwin Write the *Origin* Backwards?" *Proceedings of the National Academy of Sciences USA* 106, supp. 1:10048–55.

——. 2011a. *Did Darwin Write the Origin Backwards? Philosophical Essays on Darwin's Theory*. Amherst, NY: Prometheus.

——. 2011b. "Evolution without Naturalism." In *Oxford Studies in Philosophy of Religion*. Ed. Jonathan L. Kvanvig, 3:187–221. Oxford: Oxford University Press.

——. 2012. *Core Questions in Philosophy: A Text with Readings*. 6th ed. My Thinking Lab. Upper Saddle River, NJ: Pearson.

Sober, Elliott, and David Sloan Wilson. 1998. *Unto Others: The Evolution and Psychology of Unselfish Behavior*. Cambridge, MA: Harvard University Press.

——. 2011. "Adaptation and Natural Selection Revisited." *Journal of Evolutionary Biology* 24:462–68.

SOCIAL SCIENCES. The social sciences are a group of disciplines (e.g., **anthropology**, economics, education, history, human geography, linguistics, political science, **psychology**, and **sociology**) that are designed to study human behavior and social phenomena. Although the social sciences employ **scientific method**s (e.g., quantitative measurement), they are considered to be "soft" sciences rather than "hard" sciences such as **physics** and chemistry. The objective of the social sciences is to seek human flourishing by understanding the social behavior and phenomena of humanity through scientific methods. Thus social scientists use observation, experiments, and hypotheses to understand and interpret social phenomena and human behavior.

The social sciences emerged in the nineteenth and early twentieth centuries, although their origins can be traced back to the sixth century BC in the philosophical speculations of the Greeks. Auguste Comte (1798–1857), the founding father of sociology, is considered to be the architect of the social sciences in general in light of his attempts to systematize them. Natural science, which had emerged three centuries earlier, wielded enormous influence over the social sciences.

As natural science sought to understand the world through the lens of strictly material causes rather than a religious viewpoint, the social sciences followed suit. **Charles Darwin**'s views became influential, and many social scientists in the nineteenth and early twentieth centuries believed that human behavior was strictly biologically derived. As biological and social **Darwinism** achieved prominence, many evangelical Christians in America found themselves retreating from mainstream higher education. This marked the beginning of a schism between Christian Bible colleges and secular liberal arts colleges, as Christians came to see aspects of both natural and social science as antagonistic toward their faith.

Despite the challenges that exist between religion and the social sciences, there have been positive movements on both sides. Many social scientists have become less hostile to religion (Rolston 1987, 200–201). Similarly, some Christian scholars argue that the social sciences have been misconstrued by religious scholars. As a result, significant contributions that the social sciences can make to Christian faith have been overlooked (Moberg 1972, 120–21; Segal 2006, 312–17). Furthermore, social scientists Robert N. Bellah, Peter L. Berger, and Clifford J. Geertz have argued in various ways that the social sciences reveal religion to be an appropriate basis from which to view reality (Segal 2006, 317–19).

Theology's engagement with the social sciences has been precarious as well. Still, some theologians have incorporated social science into their work. Liberation theology, for example, is a clear attempt to "build contextual theological foundations influenced by Marxist insight" (Roberts 1997, 712). Similarly, theologian **Wolfhart Pannenberg** has incorporated anthropological theories into his theological system to argue that the credibility of Christian faith can be validated through anthropology. Further, more recently, theologian and philosopher **Nancey Murphy** has drawn on literature in psychology to defend her thesis of nonreductive **physicalism**.

Although theology and the social sciences often appear to be at odds, both are keenly interested in understanding humanity. In this regard, as Christians encounter an ever more pluralistic, globalized world, the social sciences can serve as a helpful partner that enables theology to be more explanatorily relevant and effective in confronting contemporary issues like poverty, gender, ethnicity, sexuality, and conflict.

Naomi Noguchi Reese

REFERENCES AND RECOMMENDED READING

Balswick, Jack O., Pamela E. King, and Kevin S. Reimer. 2005. *The Reciprocating Self: Human Development in Theological Perspective.* Downers Grove, IL: InterVarsity.

Brown, Warren S., Nancey Murphy, and H. Newton Malony. 1998. *Whatever Happened to the Soul? Scientific and Theological Portraits of Human Nature.* Minneapolis: Fortress.

Browning, Don. 2004. "Social Theory." In *The Blackwell Companion to Modern Theology.* Ed. Gareth Jones, 65–81. Oxford: Blackwell.

Kamm, Richey S. 1968. "The Social Sciences: A Christian Perspective." In *Christianity and the World of Thought.* Ed. Hudson T. Armerding, 11–30. Chicago: Moody.

Moberg, David O. 1972. "The Social Sciences." In *Christ and the Modern Mind.* Ed. Robert W. Smith, 109–22. Downers Grove, IL: InterVarsity.

Reimer, Kevin. 2009. "Social Sciences." In *A Science and Religion Primer.* Eds. Heidi A. Campbell and Heather Looy, 203–5. Grand Rapids: Baker Academic.

Roberts, Richard H. 1997. "Theology and the Social Sciences." In *The Modern Theologians: An Introduction to Christian Theology in the Twentieth Century.* Ed. David F. Ford, 700–719. 2nd ed. Cambridge, MA: Blackwell.

Rolston, Holmes. 1987. *Science and Religion: A Critical Survey.* New York: Random House.

Segal, Robert A. 2006. "Contributions from the Social Sciences." In *The Oxford Handbook of Religion and Science.* Eds. Philip Clayton and Zachary Simpson, 311–27. Oxford: Oxford University Press.

Van Leeuwen, Mary Stewart. 1989. "Evangelicals and the Social Sciences." *Evangelical Review of Theology* 13:246–63.

SOCIOLOGY. Sociology is a social science that emerged in the nineteenth and early twentieth centuries that seeks to study human social life in groups and societies. Although early sociological thinking was influenced by a number of individuals, Auguste Comte (1798–1857) is considered to be the founder of modern sociology. Comte, who coined the term *sociology*, regarded sociology as a science (albeit a social science) that relied on scientific evidence to uncover knowledge about society. Comte also believed that by using science, sociology could contribute to human flourishing by understanding and controlling human behavior, which had been the province of religion in Western society prior to **the Enlightenment**. However, the **objectivity** of sociology has been questioned due to the nature of its study of subjective human experience.

American sociology emerged in the late nineteenth century when American society was facing rapid social changes and in desperate need of a new science to confront growing social problems. Since its inception, however, American sociology has viewed science and religion as inherently incompatible. While sociology employs the scientific method, "fact-through-observation," to observe the world, religion relies on "superstition-through-ignorance" (Smith 2003). This Enlightenment-influenced viewpoint convinced many sociologists in the early twentieth century that religion was a "dying vestige of primitive and prescientific life" (Moberg 1968). It was thus a surprise to many sociologists when religious interest revived in the mid-twentieth century in the United States. The discipline of sociology of religion quickly developed and has demonstrated religion's significant role in modern society.

Despite continuous skepticism about the compatibility of religion and sociology, a number of Christian scholars have attempted to engage with the discipline. Indeed, an explicit "Christian sociology" has emerged involving the "systematic study of the social order that, in its theory, methodology and reporting is explicitly related to the framework of understanding that is identifiably Christian" (Barger 1982). Moreover, Christian scholars such as Christian Smith, Os Guinness, Robert Wuthnow, and others who have "practiced the public engagement of sociology for both Christian audiences, and most impressively, non-Christian audiences" have emerged (Hiebert 2008, 208). In addition, sociology has been utilized as a hermeneutical tool among biblical scholars such as Walter Brueggemann, John H. Elliot, and Robert R. Wilson.

In regard to Christian theology, interaction with sociology has resulted in scholarly work in the twentieth century. Liberation theology, which explores the relation between Christian theology and sociopolitical concerns such as human rights, social justice, and poverty, is a product of the collaboration of theology and sociology. Furthermore, a typology of five different strategies of appropriation of sociology by theologians has been recognized: (1) fundamentalist option, (2) absorption of theology into sociology (Ernst Troeltsch), (3) sociology as part of an essentially theological project (Dietrich Bonhoeffer, H. R. Niebuhr), (4) mutual mergence (Edward Farley), and (5) postmodern quasi-fundamentalism (John Milbank) (Roberts 1997).

Despite the difficulties and potential risks, the conversation between theology and sociology continues as theology aims to be relevant to modern society since "modernity is intrinsically sociological" (Roberts 1997).

Naomi Noguchi Reese

REFERENCES AND RECOMMENDED READING

Barger, George W. 1982. "A Christian Sociology?" *Journal of the American Scientific Affiliation* 34:100–104.

Bellah, Robert N. 2006. "Sociology and Theology." In *The Robert Bellah Reader*. Eds. Robert N. Bellah and Steven M. Tipton, 451–521. Durham, NC: Duke University Press.

Hiebert, Dennis. 2008. "Can We Talk? Achieving Dialogue between Sociology and Theology." *Christian Scholar's Review* 37:199–214.

Martin, David. 1997. *Reflections on Sociology and Theology.* Oxford: Clarendon.

Milbank, John. 2006. *Theology and Social Theory: Beyond Secular Reason.* 2nd ed. Malden, MA: Blackwell.

Moberg, David O. 1968. "Sociology." In *Christianity and the World of Thought.* Ed. Hudson T. Armerding, 215–32. Chicago: Moody.

Poythress, Vern Sheridan. 2011. *Redeeming Sociology: A God-Centered Approach.* Wheaton, IL: Crossway.

Roberts, Richard H. 1997. "Theology and the Social Sciences." In *The Modern Theologians: An Introduction to Christian Theology in the Twentieth Century.* Ed. David F. Ford, 700–719. 2nd ed. Cambridge, MA: Blackwell.

Rolston, Holmes, III. 1987. *Science and Religion: A Critical Survey.* New York: Random House.

Smith, Christian. 2003. "Secularizing American Higher Education: The Case of Early American Sociology." In *The Secular Revolution: Power, Interests, and Conflict in the Secularization of American Public Life.* Ed. Christian Smith, 97–159. Berkeley: University of California Press.

SOUL. Belief in the soul is primarily an immediate response to first-person experience and is thus widespread and persistent across human societies (including those of the Bible's authors). Philosophical reflection has therefore sought to articulate rather than invent an idea and to relate it to theological and scientific concerns.

Prior to **Descartes** (1596–1650) the soul was understood to be the principle or provider of **life**. **Plato** (c. 425–c. 347 BC) considered it to be the giver of life to its body while **Aristotle** (384–322 BC) distinguished distinct types of soul appropriate to different living things. For Plato a person *is* a soul and a soul is a substance: a distinct thing rather than a state of the body. Plato's concept of the soul is consistent with a Christian view of **life after death**, but his commitment to reincarnation and his negative view of embodiment are clearly not. For Aristotle the soul is an active principle providing structure and life and incapable of independent survival: it is the *form* of its body.

Plato held that the soul is *simple* in the sense that it is not composed of parts. Simplicity is important because the elements of an experience (e.g., shape and color) exist as a united whole (e.g., a colored object) for which, it seems, only a simple entity could be a suitable subject. This ancient issue is echoed today by the so-called *binding problem* within **cognitive science**: the problem of explaining how the brain could integrate distinct types of **information** that are processed separately in order to provide unified experiences (Hardcastle 1998).

In the medieval era, **Augustine** (AD 354–430) and Aquinas (AD 1225–74) were influenced by Plato and Aristotle respectively. Augustine took a soul to be an independent, immaterial substance but rejected reincarnation and held healthy embodiment to be a good and peaceful state. However, he struggled to find an account of the soul's origin consistent with his commitment to the doctrine of **original sin**. Aquinas followed Aristotle, taking a rational human soul both to be present throughout its body and to constitute a single substance with it. In order to accommodate survival of death, Aquinas claimed that the rational soul is a *subsistent* form: a soul may have independent existence, thinking and deciding but without being fully a person, perhaps in the way that an unfinished house can exist independently without yet being a house (Stump 1995, 505–31). To some, Aquinas's intriguing notion of subsistent form remains problematic or at best unclear (Kenny 1994).

With Descartes, the idea of the soul as the principle of life disappears. His famous program of doubt led him to contrast the soul as a thinking self with the body as a spatially extended, autonomous mechanism. However, Descartes nevertheless held that soul and body are united: "the self is so intermingled with [the body] that I seem to compose with it one whole" (Descartes 1986). Since the soul is nonspatial, this unity is not one of colocation, and the soul must *represent* mental events occurring in particular locations.

For Descartes, the single privileged location of interaction is the pineal gland, chosen in error but for the good reason that it is a singular, central structure within the brain and thus seemingly appropriate to the unity of experience and the self. Descartes said little about the way in which mental and physical substances interact, but the assumption that their natures are so different that interaction must be held unintelligible or impossible should be dismissed. Subsequent philosophical and scientific developments have enriched and complicated our picture of **causation** to the point that Hasker rightly considers this assumption to hold "the all-time record for overrated objections to major philosophical positions" (Hasker 1999, 150; for a serious recent argument against interaction and a reply, see Hasker 2012, 215–28).

Recent proposals about the means of interaction include Eccles's claim that interaction results from certain quantum effects at synaptic junctions and Collins's suggestive proposal based on sympathetic resonance (Collins 2011, 222–47; Eccles 1994).

A popular scientific objection to psychophysical causation holds that it is ruled out by the principle of **conservation of energy**: that in a causally isolated system the total amount of energy remains constant. However, this problem disappears if psychophysical causation excludes energy transfer or if the body is not a closed physical system (Hasker 1999; Larmer 1986, 277–85). Nor is the objection compelling if conservation principles are not found throughout modern **physics** (Collins 2011).

After Descartes, the modern shift toward talk of the **mind** as a "dynamic natural system subject to general laws of growth and development" raised the problem of how, in the soul's possible absence, a person might persist as the same individual through time. Thomas Reid (1710–96) and Joseph Butler (1692–1752) defended the soul, criticizing **John Locke**'s (1632–1704) proposal that memory can constitute personal identity by arguing that to identify a memory as genuine requires one to know beforehand that there is a single person who is both its possessor and the subject of the remembered events. In sharp contrast to Reid, **David Hume** (1711–76) denied that we can have evidence of being substances that remain identical through time.

Today widespread belief in the soul coexists with skepticism about its existence among Western intellectuals,

prompting a range of responses from Christian scholars. Issues such as simplicity and personal identity remain important, but a key theme is the compatibility of soul belief with the findings and methods of modern science. The discovery of detailed correspondences between the function of certain brain areas and specific cognitive and emotional capacities have tempted some to argue that the subject of our thoughts and feelings is in fact the brain and not an immaterial self. However, even detailed correlations between mental and physical events need not entail identity, and the functional dependence of mind on body has long been accepted.

Dualists also note that soul belief arises as an immediate response to first person awareness of the self and not as a scientific postulate to be replaced as theories develop. Methodologically, some have claimed that the success of modern science indicates that the physical world is causally closed and thus there are no souls interacting with it and no nonphysical purposes as ultimate causes of action. This gives many physicalists reason to claim that some way must be found to reduce purposes to physical entities (Kim 2005) while dualists and others respond that such reduction is incoherent, and so causal closure (which is a naturalistic rather than scientific claim) must be rejected.

Given these issues, contemporary Christian dualists defend functionally integrative or emergentist approaches (Hasker 1999; Moreland and Rae 2000; Swinburne 2013; Taliaferro 1994) while Christian monists seek to offer versions of **physicalism** that preserve the characteristics of Christian **anthropology** (Baker 2000; Murphy 2006). These varied responses are important, since the current debate over the soul reflects a wider debate between **naturalism** and **theism**.

Finally, some exponents of the **cognitive science of religion** (CSR) have claimed that the very naturalness of soul belief shows that it may be explained away as an accidental by-product of cognitive tools that evolved to function for other purposes (Bloom 2009). However, the genetic fallacy threatens, and such arguments effectively saw off the branch on which they sit. The CSR could only undercut soul belief by undercutting a wider class of by-products that would also include the very scientific beliefs on which the explanation is based (Plantinga 2009, 139–67).

Jonathan Loose

REFERENCES AND RECOMMENDED READING

Baker, Lynne Rudder. 2000. *Persons and Bodies: A Constitution View.* Cambridge: Cambridge University Press.

Baker, Mark C., and Stewart Goetz. 2011. *The Soul Hypothesis: Investigations in the Existence of the Soul.* New York: Continuum.

Bloom, Paul. 2009. "Religious Belief as an Evolutionary Accident." In *The Believing Primate: Scientific, Philosophical, and Theological Reflections on the Origin of Religion.* Oxford: Oxford University Press.

Collins, Robin. 2011. "A Scientific Case for the Soul." In *The Soul Hypothesis: Investigations in the Existence of the Soul.* Eds. Mark C. Baker and Stewart Goetz, 222–47. New York: Continuum.

Descartes, René. 1986. *Meditations on First Philosophy with Selections from the Objections and Replies.* Ed. John Cottingham. Cambridge: Cambridge University Press.

Eccles, John Carew. 1994. *How the Self Controls Its Brain.* Dordrecht: Springer.

Goetz, Stewart, and Charles Taliaferro. 2011. *A Brief History of the Soul.* Oxford: Wiley-Blackwell.

Hardcastle, V. 1998. "The Binding Problem." In *A Companion to Cognitive Science.* Eds. W. Bechtel and G. Graham. Oxford: Blackwell.

Hasker, William. 1999. *The Emergent Self.* Ithaca, NY: Cornell University Press.

———. 2012. "Jaegwon Kim's Rejection of Substance Dualism." In *Philosophy and the Christian Worldview.* Eds. David Werther and Mark D. Linville, 215–28. London: Bloomsbury Academic.

Kenny, Anthony. 1994. *Aquinas on Mind.* London: Routledge.

Kim, Jaegwon. 2005. *Physicalism, or Something Near Enough.* Princeton, NJ: Princeton University Press.

Larmer, R. 1986. "Mind-Body Interactionism and the Conservation of Energy." *International Philosophical Quarterly* 26 (September): 277–85.

Moreland, J. P., and Scott B. Rae. 2000. *Body and Soul: Human Nature and the Crisis in Ethics.* Leicester: IVP.

Murphy, Nancey C. 2006. *Bodies and Souls, or Spirited Bodies.* Current Issues in Theology. Cambridge: Cambridge University Press.

Plantinga, Alvin. 2009. "Games Scientists Play." In *The Believing Primate: Scientific, Philosophical, and Theological Reflections on the Origin of Religion.* Eds. Jeffrey P. Schloss and Michael J. Murray, 139–67. Oxford: Oxford University Press.

Stump, Eleonore. 1995. "Non-Cartesian Substance Dualism and Materialism without Reductionism." *Faith and Philosophy* 12:505–31.

Swinburne, Richard. 2013. *Mind, Brain, and Free Will.* Oxford: Oxford University Press.

Taliaferro, Charles. 1994. *Consciousness and the Mind of God.* Cambridge: Cambridge University Press.

SPACE AND TIME. The universe is constrained to a single dimension of time. Multiple independent experiments in **physics** establish that while it is possible to slow down or speed up the passage of time, it is impossible to reverse or stop the passage of time. Space, on the other hand, is not constrained to a single dimension, and space travel can be both stopped and reversed.

Scripture, astronomical observations of the past history of the universe, and the space-time theorems demonstrate that space and time had a beginning coincident with the origin of our universe. The Bible alone, among all the world's holy books and religious teachings, declares that God created space and time when he created the cosmos. Hebrews 11:3 says the universe that we can detect came from that which cannot be detected. Matter, energy, space, and time are all entities we humans can detect and measure. Thus the message of Hebrews 11 aligns with the traditional interpretation of Genesis 1:1, which says that "in the beginning" God brought into existence everything we recognize as physical reality.

The phrase in Genesis 1:1, "the heavens and the earth," is found in eight other Old Testament passages. For ancient readers as well as readers today, this phrase refers to the totality of the physical realm. The word translated "created" in Genesis 1 is the Hebrew verb *bara*. This verb occurs in 53 Old Testament passages, and in the context of God's activity, it denotes "bringing into existence" or "initiating something new" (Harris et al. 1980, 127–28), something that did not previously exist.

This understanding of the biblical creation texts serves as the basis for the historic Christian doctrine of "creation ex nihilo," or "creation out of nothing." It appears in the Nicene Creed, Belgic Confession, Scots Confession, Westminster Confession, Baptist Confession, and Heidelberg Catechism. Paul Copan and **William Lane Craig** (Copan and Craig 2004) have provided a book-length treatment of the origin, development, and evidential support for the doctrine of creation ex nihilo.

Scientific affirmations that space and time began when matter and energy began come from discoveries undergirding big bang cosmology (see **Big Bang Theory**), general relativity, and the space-time theorems. Einstein's general relativity equations, when solved, predicted that the universe is expanding from a beginning and cooling from a near infinitely hot state. The notion of ongoing expansion challenged the reigning **paradigm** of nineteenth-century cosmology, which held that the universe was vast and ancient beyond any knowable limits. However, observations later showed that the entire universe, including the space-time surface along which all its matter and energy are distributed, has indeed been expanding and cooling from a beginning, or singularity, as the general relativity equations predicted.

In the late 1960s, **George Ellis**, **Stephen Hawking**, and Roger Penrose developed the first of the space-time theorems in physics (Hawking and Penrose 1970). With this theorem, Hawking and Penrose demonstrated that *if* the universe contains mass and *if* the equations of general relativity reliably describe movements of bodies in the universe, then everything in the universe—not just the matter and energy, but also the space-time dimensions—has a past singular boundary (a beginning).

The existence of mass has never been in doubt, but researchers at the time wanted firmer evidence for general relativity. So testing ramped up. Today general relativity ranks as the most exhaustively tested and firmly established principle in physics. Meanwhile, because many scientists found the concept of a space-time beginning philosophically disturbing, several physicists invested years in searching for a loophole, some way around the beginning. Ironically, this search culminated in an even more powerful theorem (see **Borde-Guth-Vilenkin Singularity Theorem**), which concluded that whatever features the universe possesses (homogeneity, isotropy, uniformity, or lack thereof) and whatever its energy or inflationary conditions, if the universe has expanded, on average, throughout its history, then the universe did, indeed, have a space-time beginning, as the original theorem predicted.

The space-time theorems and the principles of cause-and-effect imply that a causal agent beyond space and time is responsible for creating space and time. Thus, at the very least, the space-time theorems reasonably point to a deistic interpretation of reality. As even **Lawrence Krauss** acknowledges, "One cannot rule out such a deistic view of nature" (Krauss 2013, 173). They also affirm the biblical conception of space and time while contradicting that of Eastern religions and of various philosophers, including **Immanuel Kant**.

Advancing research has shown that space and time are not wholly distinct from matter. General relativity demonstrates that space and time are intertwined, that time is an inseparable part of the cosmic space surface. Furthermore, both experiments and theory show that **quantum fluctuation**s in this space-time fabric can generate both energy and matter. One well-known example is virtual particle production. With greater understanding of black hole physics, particle physics, and the presumption that a valid unified field theory exists, physicists now postulate that the universe possesses not just three large dimensions of space, but an additional six very small ones.

Within the framework of **string theory**, nine dimensions of space are required to account for all the symmetries of quantum mechanics that coexist with gravity. Only if the universe includes nine dimensions of space does a self-consistent theory for black holes become possible. We humans do not personally interact with all nine of these spatial dimensions, because six of the nine stopped expanding when the unified field separated into two forces: gravity and the strong-electroweak force. This separation occurred when the universe was just 10^{-43} seconds old. So these six dimensions remain tightly curled. Their cross-sections measure much less than a trillionth of the diameter of an electron.

These space-time discoveries have relevance to biblical passages such as Jeremiah 23:24 and Psalm 139, which speak of God's immanence—his capacity to be present everywhere simultaneously within everything he has created. Other passages, such as 1 Kings 8:27; Job 37:23; Isaiah 55:8–9; and 1 Timothy 6:16, focus on God's transcendence—his freedom to operate beyond the boundaries of cosmic space and time, unconfined by all that he has created.

The quality of transcendence has led many theologians to assert divine timelessness, the notion that God has a timeless mode of existence (Ganssle 2001; Poe and Mattson 2005). This view, however, would seem to contradict the biblical claim that God was living and active before he created cosmic time. The Father, Son, and Holy Spirit existed in relationship with one another, an indication of some kind of "temporal" existence. And Paul writes that God put grace and hope into effect "before the beginning of time" (2 Tim. 1:9; Titus 1:2). The very act of creating the universe represents a cause that "predates" its effect.

The theory of general relativity establishes that once physical observers exist in the universe, it is impossible for the space-time manifold (surface) of the universe to touch or overlap a space-time manifold of any other possibly existing universe. This limitation, however, has not prevented theoreticians from speculating about other space-time realms. Examples of such speculations include M-theory, brane hypotheses, and various forms of the **multiverse**. In M-theory and brane hypotheses, our four-dimensional universe is presumed to exist inside a higher dimensional space often referred to as "hyperspace." In some of these cosmological models, the hyperspace is speculated to contain a very large number of branes.

Multiverse models presume the existence of an infinite number of universes. Some multiverse models also presume that the infinite number of universes manifest every imaginable set or range of physical laws, physical constants, and physical characteristics. The infinite possibilities offered by this version of the multiverse frequently are invoked to explain away the design and the fine-tuning arguments for God preparing the universe for life and humanity. However, astrophysicist Jeffrey Zweerink (Zweerink 2008) has demonstrated that while self-consistent theistic multiverse models exist, such is not the case for nontheistic multiverse models.

Hugh Ross

RESOURCES AND RECOMMENDED READING

Copan, Paul, and William Lane Craig. 2004. *Creation Out of Nothing*. Grand Rapids: Baker.

Ganssle, Gregory E., ed. 2001. *God and Time: Four Views*. Downers Grove, IL: InterVarsity.

Harris, A. Laird, Gleason L. Archer, and Bruce K. Waltke. 1980. *Theological Wordbook of the Old Testament.* Chicago: Moody, 1980.

Hawking, S. W., and R. Penrose. 1970. *Proceedings of the Royal Society of London, A* 314:520–49.

Krauss, Lawrence M. 2013. *A Universe from Nothing: Why There Is Something Rather Than Nothing.* New York: Atria.

Poe, Harry Lee, and J. Stanley Mattson. 2005. *What God Knows: Time and the Question of Divine Knowledge.* Waco, TX: Baylor University Press.

Zweerink, Jeffrey. 2008. *Who's Afraid of the Multiverse?* Covina, CA: Reasons to Believe.

SPECIES. Considered the only biologically real unit of taxonomic classification, species is connoted in binomial nomenclature—*Genus species* (e.g., *Homo sapiens*). The term was first coined by the English naturalist John Ray (1686) to describe clearly delineated types of organisms that possess "distinguishing features that perpetuate themselves in propagation from seed" and, in animals, "preserve their distinct species permanently."

This conception of the species contained both the *typological* and *biological* methods for distinguishing species. The typological method defines species as falling within particular boundaries of physical (morphological) characteristics. While variations exist within a species, all individuals conform to certain characteristics offered by the "type specimen" for which the species was named. The typological method became the basis of the modern taxonomic classification system established by Carl Linneaus in his treatise *Systema Naturae* (1758), which also instituted the binomial system for naming species.

The biological species concept relies on reproductive compatibility as the defining property of individuals within a species. If two individuals are able to produce viable offspring, they are considered members of the same species. Sterile hybrids (or those with greatly reduced fitness) connote the boundary between closely related (but separate) species (as is seen when crossing the modern horse with the donkey). More recently, the molecular revolution of the twentieth century has produced a *phylogenetic* method for defining species. Here species can be named and separated on the basis of a minimum degree of genetic similarity among individuals, as well as a threshold level of genetic difference between species. Using these definitions collectively, it is now estimated that there are 8 to 9 million species on the planet.

It should be noted that Ray's original rendering suggests fixity in the characteristics of a species and might have been used to equate biblical "kinds" with the species concept. However, it is well confirmed that species' characteristics can change over time, and (mostly through detection by genetic methods) that it is possible for new species to emerge from previously described parent species. Further, there is general scientific consensus that species diversity has increased through time (not withstanding occasional **extinction** events).

While the typological, biological, and phylogenetic methods for determining species augment one another to form a general working definition, disagreement remains around the margins. The typological method is most accessible but frequently disagrees with genetic methods. Further, numerous cases of "cryptic species" have demonstrated that the typological method fails to distinguish between closely related species (or those similar in appearance). The biological species concept is preferable but greatly limited in application. It blurs in situations where individuals from two geographically distinct populations can produce viable offspring in captivity but do not in nature because the two populations are never in contact. It also fails in cases of asexual reproduction and in cases where we simply cannot verify mating outcomes (as in very rare or geographically remote species).

As with the typological method, phylogenetic methods require agreed upon **gene** regions or **DNA** markers for comparison, as well as minimal degrees of similarity that many feel are arbitrarily established. Like the biological method, it cannot be applied to extinct taxa (where DNA is not recoverable). It has also been established that mutation rates for homologous markers differ among species. It remains unclear whether morphological (typological) or genetic traits are of equal weight or importance, but both have been used in concert to define species.

Wayne Rossiter

REFERENCES AND RECOMMENDED READING

Mora, Camilo, Derek P. Tittensor, Sina Adl, et al. 2011. "How Many Species Are There on Earth and in the Ocean?" *PLOS Biology* 9:e1001127. doi:10.1371/journal.pbio.1001127.

Shen, Yong Yi, Xiao Chen, and Robert W. Murphy. 2013. "Assessing DNA Barcoding as a Tool for Species Identification and Data Quality Control," *PLOS One* 8, no. (February 19): e57125. doi:10.1371/journal.pone.0057125.

"Species Concepts and the Definition of 'Species.'" Accessed August 13, 2014. http://science.kennesaw.edu/~rmatson/Biol%203380/3380species.html.

Taylor, Peter J. "Evolution and the Species Concept." In *Biological Science Fundamentals and Systematics*, vol. 1. Eds. Giancarlo Contrafatto and Alessandro Minelli. www.eolss.net/sample-chapters/c03/e6–71–03–03.pdf.

SPECIFIED COMPLEXITY. Consider a typical mountain. Through the effects of weathering and erosion, the mountain is highly complex. Indeed, it would take many terabytes of computer memory to record where every nook and cranny of that mountain is. But consider next Mount Rushmore. Its rock face is also complex. But unlike the typical mountain, it also matches an independently given pattern; that is, it matches the appearance of four US presidents. Mount Rushmore, unlike a typical mountain, is therefore also specified and thus exhibits specified complexity.

The term *specified complexity* is now over 40 years old, and the concept itself is even older. Biologist Leslie Orgel first used the term in his 1973 book *The Origins of Life*: "Living organisms are distinguished by their specified complexity. Crystals such as granite fail to qualify as living because they lack complexity; mixtures of random polymers fail to qualify because they lack specificity" (Orgel 1973, 189). Yet the concept is implicit in 1950s reflections by **Francis Crick** on his codiscovery with James Watson of the structure of **DNA**. And it continues to dominate reflections on the **origin of life**.

Earlier references to specified complexity were suggestive of a deeper truth but were not sufficiently developed. A rigorous formulation of specified complexity as a tool for inferring an intelligent **causation** may be credited to the work of **William Dembski**, first in his Cambridge monograph *The Design Inference* (Dembski 1998), where it took the form of "specified improbability," and then in his subsequent work.

The significance of specified complexity is that it serves as a criterion for identifying the effects of intelligence not just in human artifacts but also in nature generally. Just as the specified complexity of Mount Rushmore indicates that an intelligence is behind its formation (in this case, the artist Gutzon Borglum), so specified complexity in nature is properly ascribed to an intelligent source. Specified complexity is especially evident in the DNA and other biomacromolecules inside all living cells.

Nonetheless, materialistic scientists dispute that specified complexity is a reliable marker of intelligence. They claim that the Darwinian process of **natural selection** acting on random variations can simulate the effects of intelligence and thus produce specified complexity in nature without requiring an actual intelligence.

Several important mathematical theorems governing the origin and flow of **information**, known under the rubric "conservation of information" (summarized for a lay audience in Dembski 2014), show that specified complexity cannot be explained away by Darwinian processes. Rather, conservation of information shows that insofar as Darwinian processes output specified complexity, it is because the process itself was front-loaded with specified complexity. In general, conservation of information shows that material processes can only redistribute existing specified complexity, not create it from scratch.

Research in the **intelligent design** community since the 1990s has convincingly demonstrated that the only legitimate source of specified complexity is intelligence. Crucially important in this research has been the work of the Evolutionary Informatics Lab (http://evoinfo.org), which has developed specified complexity as a precise information-theoretic measure for quantifying the functional organization of biological structures.

William A. Dembski

REFERENCES AND RECOMMENDED READING

Dembski, William A. 1998. *The Design Inference: Eliminating Chance through Small Probabilities*. Cambridge: Cambridge University Press.
———. 2014. *Being as Communion: A Metaphysics of Information*. Surrey, UK: Ashgate.
Orgel, Leslie. 1973. *The Origins of Life*. New York: Wiley.

SPEED OF LIGHT. The "speed of light" generally refers to the speed at which light travels in a vacuum. **Einstein**'s **special theory of relativity** and experimental observations confirm that the speed of light in a vacuum has exactly the same value for light of any wavelength and for all observers in any frame of reference. Its value is now defined to be exactly 299,792,458 meters per second, denoted by c.

Because the speed of light is so fast, early attempts to measure its value could not distinguish between a finite speed and an infinite speed. **Galileo** tried to measure its speed by measuring the round-trip time it took light from a lantern that was just uncovered to travel to an assistant far away, who would then uncover his own lantern. No matter the distance of the assistant, the time required was identical to the human reaction time, and Galileo concluded that light travels either instantaneously or extremely rapidly (Galilei [1638] 1954).

In 1676 the Danish astronomer Rømer estimated the speed of light by observing the period of Jupiter's moon Io when Earth was moving toward Jupiter or away from Jupiter. His estimation that light then must take 22 minutes to cross the diameter of Earth's orbit coupled with an estimate of the size of Earth's orbit gave a result that the speed of light was 220,000,000 m/s. Direct measurement of the speed of light using rotating wheels with teeth by Hippolyte Louis Fizeau in 1849 and by using rotating mirrors by Leon Foucault in 1862 gave results of 313,300,000 m/s and 299,796,000 m/s. By 1975 the speed of light was known to 4 parts per billion, and so in 1983 the meter, whose length was not known to that accuracy, was redefined in terms of the speed of light. The meter is now defined to be 1/299,792,458 of the distance light travels in one second, so the speed of light is fixed by that definition.

Because the speed of light is finite, there is always some travel time between emission of the light and observation of the light. For instance, light from the sun takes about eight and a half minutes to reach the earth. Consequently, we see the sun not as it is the moment the light enters our eye, but rather as the sun was eight and a half minutes previously. The distance light travels in a year is called a *light-year*. The nearest visible star to our sun is Alpha Centauri, which is about 4.4 light-years away from us. When we look at Alpha Centauri, we see what that star looked like 4.4 years ago. The finite speed of light lets us actually see past events unfold. The farthest objects that we have observed from the earth are about 13 billion light-years away.

Since we can see light that was emitted from these objects, the most straightforward interpretation of the data is that the universe must be at least 13 billion years old. Some Christians have proposed alternative interpretations of the data, though there are not any nonbelieving scientists who think that the alternative ideas have any credibility or observational support. Alternatives include the idea that God created the light from distant objects already in transit, that the speed of light has changed dramatically over the history of the universe, or that the distance measurements to far-off objects are not accurate.

Some Christians have claimed that measurements of the speed of light over the last 300 years indicate that the speed of light has been decreasing, and that trend would indicate that the speed of light was much different millennia ago, so that light could have traveled from far distances in much less time than proposed (Norman and Settlefield 1987). However, careful analyses of the data using the correct uncertainties of the data points show that this conclusion is not reasonable and that there is no indication that the speed of light has changed in any significant way during the history of the universe (Aardsma 1988; Deem 2006).

The speed of light is related to other physical constants, such as the fine-structure constant, a constant that characterizes the strength of the electromagnetic force. Some experiments in the early twenty-first century seemed to indicate that the fine structure constant may have changed by a few parts in 100,000 over the last 12 billion years (Murphy et al. 2001, 2003; Webb et al. 2001). Although the uncertainty on the measurements did not require such a change, any change in the fine structure constant could imply a slight change in the speed of light of about the same percentage over the same time period. However, subsequent experiments indicate that the fine structure constant has not changed over the lifetime of the universe, which would be another observational indication of the constancy of the speed of light in a vacuum (Chand et al. 2004; Srianand et al. 2004).

Regardless of the ultimate outcome of this discrepancy, the possible small change in the speed of light over 12 billion years would not change the scientifically accepted age of the universe of 13.7 billion years old in any significant way.

Although all electromagnetic radiation travels at the same exact speed in a vacuum, different frequencies of light travel at different speeds through various materials. In general, light slows down as it travels through different media and the single frequency, or phase velocity, is less than c. However, in some special media it is possible for the phase speed of a certain frequency to travel faster than c. A light pulse composed of many frequencies may have a group velocity that can be shifted to be faster or slower than the individual phase velocities. However, in all cases it is impossible to transfer **information** faster than c, and so the special theory of relativity is not violated.

Because c is the ultimate speed limit, it is unlikely that any life-forms can travel between star systems. Unless the laws of the universe offer some way to bypass this speed limit, the distances between star systems seem to be too great to allow for reasonable travel times for living beings. Science fiction writers have proposed possible ways to circumvent the speed of light limit such as worm holes or faster-than-light travel by warping space, but there is currently no evidence that such proposals are possible.

Michael G. Strauss

REFERENCES AND RECOMMENDED READING

Aardsma, Gerald. 1988. "Has the Speed of Light Decayed?" *Acts & Facts* 17 (5). www.icr.org/article/has-speed-light-decayed.

Chand, H., R. Srianand, Patrick Petitjean, and B. Aracil. 2004. "Probing the Cosmological Variation of the Fine-Structure Constant: Results Based on VLT-UVES Sample." *Astronomy and Astrophysics* 417 (April): 853–71.

Deem, Richard. 2006. "Is the Speed of Light Decreasing?" January 16. http://godandscience.org/youngearth/speedlight.html.

Galilei, Galileo. (1638) 1954. *Dialogues concerning Two New Sciences.* Trans. H. Crew and A. de Salvio. New York: Dover.

Murphy M. T., J. K. Webb, V. V. Flambaum, et al. 2001. "Possible Evidence for a Variable Fine-Structure Constant from QSO Absorption Lines: Motivations, Analysis and Results." *Monthly Notices of the Royal Astronomical Society* 327 (4): 1208.

———. 2003. "Further Evidence for a Variable Fine-Structure Constant from Keck/HIRES QSO Absorption Spectra." *Monthly Notices of the Royal Astronomical Society* 345 (2): 609.

Norman, Trevor, and Barry Settlefield. 1987. *The Atomic Constants, Light, and Time.* Menlo Park, CA: SRI International.

"Phase, Group, and Signal Velocity." MathPages.com. Accessed October 26, 2016. www.mathpages.com/home/kmath210/kmath210.htm.

Srianand, Raghunathan, Hum Chand, Patrick Petitjean, and Bastien Aracil. 2004. "Limits on the Time Variation of the Electromagnetic Fine-Structure Constant in the Low Energy Limit from Absorption Lines in the Spectra of Distant Quasars." *Physical Review Letters* 92 (12): 121302. doi:10.1103/PhysRevLett.92.121302.

Webb, John K., Michael T. Murphy, V. V. Flambaum, et al. 2001. "Further Evidence for Cosmological Evolution of the Fine Structure Constant." *Physical Review Letters* 87 (9): 091301–4.

SPINOZA, BARUCH. Baruch Spinoza (also known as Benedito de Espinosa and Benedict de Spinoza) was born on November 24, 1632, to Portuguese Jews living in exile in the Netherlands and died in his home at the Paviljoensgracht in The Hague on February 21, 1677. Despite an early rabbinic education, he was expelled from the synagogue at Amsterdam on July 27, 1656, for defending heretical opinions.

Spinoza addressed almost every area of philosophical discourse, including **metaphysics**, **epistemology**, ethics, political philosophy, philosophy of **mind**, and **philosophy of science**. The breadth and extent of his philosophical accomplishments secured him a place within the illustrious company of influential and profound thinkers in the post-Renaissance era.

In the annals of philosophy, the importance of Spinoza's thought from the mid-eighteenth century onward is often elevated to a high, occasionally the highest, place of honor. This is, to some extent, surprising, because rationalism was not accorded an indisputably favorable acceptance among contemporaries of the Dutch philosopher. Substantially agreeing with the French rationalist **René Descartes** on a broad spectrum of ideas, Spinoza nonetheless perceived keenly the deficiencies of Cartesianism and set out to remedy them. While choosing to employ nearly the same methodology that had flung Descartes's bright star on the nightly firmament of philosophical renown, Spinoza sought to apply it differently in an attempt to avoid the conceptual incongruities that had diminished the value of the Cartesian formulas.

The enigma of what constituted the essence of true philosophy ranked high on Descartes's scale of mental tasks he set out to solve, eventually reaching the conclusion that the distinguishing mark between truth and error was conceptual clarity in contrast to confusion. On this point, Spinoza was in full agreement. Assenting to Descartes's idea of singling out geometry as a perfect model for the reasoning process in advancing logically from one proposition to the next, Spinoza identified **intuition** as the means to reach the highest plateau of certainty, namely, the immediate knowledge of God himself, thus diverging from Descartes's postulate of his own existence as the immovable ground of sure knowledge (Viljanen 2011).

The main reason the Dutch philosopher isolated the immediate knowledge of God as a more conducive guarantor of certainty was centered in his conviction that the human mind was a part of the mind of God. Continental rationalism could not advance further than Spinoza's theorem that a divine intellect was equally distributed among the entire expanse of humanity.

Three concepts encompass the essence of Spinoza's metaphysical speculations. The first was "substance," the second "attribute," and the third "mode" or "modifications of substance." "Substance" comprises "that which is in itself, and is conceived through itself: in other words, that of which a conception can be formed independently of any other conception" (the ultimately real). "Attribute" consists of "that which the intellect perceives as constituting the essence of substance" (the essential quality of the real). And "mode" entails "that which exists in, and is conceived through, something other than itself" (the essential modification of the real) (*Ethics*, pt. 1, def. 3, 4, 5).

After having defined the cardinal elements of his metaphysics, and strictly adhering to the procrustean confines of his own philosophical presuppositions, the denizen of The Hague proceeded logically to his conceptualization of god as the self-caused, self-existent, free and eternal substance; an existent entity that requires nothing but itself to exist. Unlike the Christian God, Spinoza's mental construct of the divine was in its essence an impersonal entity, thoroughly chained to the unrelenting demands of logical consistency. His god was not permitted to transcend the delimitations of the philosopher's own understanding and application of the law of noncontradiction.

Challenged to marshal evidence for the existence of this kind of god, Spinoza chose in the first 11 propositions of his *Ethics* to resort to a truncated version of the ontological argument, deliberately deviating from the position of **Augustine** and Anselm. Building on his previous case for the existence of god, Spinoza broached the idea that the ground and cause of human existence presupposes the reality of an infinite being, since humans can't produce themselves, nor are produced by others. In contrast, an infinite being, possessing unlimited power, is fully able to be the ground and cause of its own existence, while also maintaining it eternally. Put in a nutshell, Spinoza postulated that because it is not impossible for the divine substance to exist, it thus exists.

It is frequently, but erroneously, said that Spinoza was a second-generational mechanical philosopher and a proto-scientific naturalist (Nadler 1999). He distanced himself from the intellectual movement (i.e., particularly the Royal Society of his time) that conceived of the world as being merely a machine whose natural phenomena could be studied in terms of size, shape, and motion of bodies. The suitable method for the study of nature that he presented in the *Theological-Political Treatise* is markedly different from what is usually associated with the mechanical philosophy, mostly because he was skeptical of the very possibility of knowing nature accurately, if not comprehensively.

Additionally, Spinoza expressed his sympathy with those who were critical of the views of the physico-mathematicians such as **Galileo**, Huygens, Wallis, and Wren. He doubted if the application of **mathematics** to nature would prove to be successful in ascertaining an exact correspondence between theoretical thought and natural phenomena. Specifically, he questioned the unfounded confidence, as he saw it, in the all-sufficiency of measurement and the practicality of a piecemeal methodology (Gabbey 1996).

To be sure, Spinoza authored the introduction to Cartesian **physics**, without closely summarizing Descartes's *Principles* on the mechanization of the universe, in his own attempt to present genuinely novel ideas (Gabbey 1996). And yet the Newtonians of the eighteenth century keenly perceived a discontinuity between their own views on mechanics and relevant passages in Spinoza's works. The criticism (while in some ways undeserved, because Spinoza could not have anticipated later developments in Newtonian physics) singled out, in particular, Spinoza's defective conception of motion.

While being reticent, if not entirely disinterested, in articulating the **laws of nature**, Spinoza advanced the notion that the study of nature consists of two steps. He suggests, first, to create a "history" and, second, to infer from it the "definitions" of things. By "history" he meant creating lists or tables of natural events ordered by topic, similar to the method of "natural history" promoted by Bacon in *New Organon* (Gabbey 1996). In *Political Treatise* (1.4; 2.1; 3.1)

he proposes that there is, then, a deductive step that the natural philosopher needs to take after having relied on experience (induction) to reach an accurate understanding of things (i.e., definitions).

The critical issue Descartes had left unanswered was the problem of the **dualism** of mind and matter. Spinoza prided himself in his apparent success of having solved the interaction between the immaterial and material elements of existence. In accord with his metaphysical conception, the divine substance simultaneously contained both mental and physical properties, without each interfering with the other. Consequently, the universal parallelism provided a ready answer to both interactionism and **occasionalism**. On the mundane level, the mental and material aspects were two sides of the same reality, a union of two *substances, constituting* a human being. Yet in assessing the validity of this argument, some of Spinoza's later critics clearly saw that the solution to the problem of Cartesian dualism was still as elusive as before.

In truth, Spinoza's singular understanding of **pantheism**—if his view of the identity of god and nature can be called pantheistic at all—engendered more philosophical problems than it could realistically solve. The most critical of them was the issue of individuation. If there was only one reality, as described in his memorable words, "God, or Nature" (*Deus, sive Natura*; *Ethics*, pt. 4, pref., Lat. ed.), then Spinoza needed to explain why particular objects different from each other existed. Furthermore, how can a divine substance, infinite and impersonal, originate personal human beings?

In his customary fashion, Spinoza was prepared to give an answer that seemed to be sufficiently intelligible and persuasive, at least to him. He perceived god as the "naturing Nature," which, while possessing one essence, was able to bring forth individual beings, as both the immanent cause of all objects in existence and their logical ground and substance. This process brought about what Spinoza called "natured Nature" (*Ethics*, pt. 1, prop. 29 scholium), which constitutes things as humans perceive them. The stubborn fact remained, however, that Spinoza's "pantheism," in its exclusive focus on the unity of existence, did not have a sensible **explanation** for the phenomenon of particularity. The failure of rationalism, even in its most basic assumptions, to present a cogent theory of why individual objects could clearly be distinguished from one another, put Spinozism inexorably on a downward trajectory that led eventually to the morass of irrationalism and determinism.

Martin Erdmann

REFERENCES AND RECOMMENDED READING

Curley, E. M. 1985. *The Collected Works of Spinoza.* Princeton, NJ: Princeton University Press.

Della, Rocca M. 2008. *Spinoza.* London: Routledge.

Gabbey, A. 1996. "Spinoza's Natural Science and Methodology." In *The Cambridge Companion to Spinoza.* Ed. D. Garrett. Cambridge and New York: Cambridge University Press.

Huenemann, C., ed. 2008. *Interpreting Spinoza: Critical Essays.* Cambridge: Cambridge University Press, 2008.

James, Susan. 2012. *Spinoza on Philosophy, Religion, and Politics: The Theological-Political Treatise.* Oxford: Oxford University Press.

Kisner, M. J. 2011. *Spinoza on Human Freedom: Reason, Autonomy and the Good Life.* Cambridge: Cambridge University Press.

LeBuffe, M. 2010. *From Bondage to Freedom: Spinoza on Human Excellence.* Oxford: Oxford University Press.

Lord, B. 2010. *Spinoza's Ethics: An Edinburgh Philosophical Guide.* Edinburgh: Edinburgh University Press.

Melamed, Y., and M. A. Rosenthal, eds. 2010. *Spinoza's Theological-Political Treatise: A Critical Guide.* Cambridge: Cambridge University Press.

Nadler, Steven. *Spinoza: A Life.* 1999. Cambridge: Cambridge University Press.

Popkin, R. 2004. *Spinoza.* Oxford: One World.

Preus, J. S. 2001. *Spinoza and the Irrelevance of Biblical Authority.* Cambridge: Cambridge University Press.

Verbeek, T. 2003. *Spinoza's Theologico-Political Treatise: Exploring "The Will of God."* London: Ashgate.

Viljanen, V. 2011. *Spinoza's Geometry of Power.* Cambridge: Cambridge University Press.

Yovel, Y., and G. Segal, eds. 2004. *Spinoza on Reason and the "Free Man."* New York: Little Room.

STANDARD MODEL, THE. The standard model of particles and fields describes the known fundamental particles and three of the four known forces that make up the universe. It is formally a mathematical gauge quantum field theory. Although the standard model has been extremely successful in describing and predicting the results of experiments, some aspects of the universe are not included in the standard model. The force of gravity is too weak at the subatomic level to play any significant role and is not part of the standard model. In addition, **dark matter and dark energy** are features of the universe that produce observable results but of which the underlying mechanisms are unknown, and are not described by the standard model.

The particles of the standard model include six quarks, six leptons, the photon, three intermediate vector bosons (W^+, W^-, and Z^0), 8 gluons, and the Higgs boson. Each of the particles has an antiparticle with opposite quantum numbers, including electric charge. For some of the particles, including the photon and the Higgs boson, the particle is identical to the antiparticle.

Quarks and leptons are considered "matter" particles, and each is classified in three generations, with each generation consisting of two particles. Quarks and leptons all have a quantum mechanical spin that is a half integer multiple of Planck's constant and are therefore fermions. Fundamental particles like quarks and leptons are considered to be "point" particles with no size, and experimental limits put their size as less than 10^{-18} meters.

The first generation of leptons are the electron and electron neutrino; the second generation are the muon and muon neutrino; and the third generation are the tau lepton and tau neutrino. All neutrinos have zero electric charge, and the other three leptons have an electric charge of -1 times that of the proton.

The first generation of quarks are the up and down quark; the second generation are the charm and strange quarks; and the third generation are the top and bottom quarks. The mass of each generation gets successively heavier. The first quark mentioned in each generation has an electric charge of $+2/3$ that of the proton, and the second quark mentioned in each generation has a charge of $-1/3$ that of a proton. Protons and neutrons are, at a simplistic level, each made of three quarks. A proton is made of two up quarks and one down quark, with an electric charge of $+2/3 + 2/3 - 1/3 = 1$, and the neutron is made of one up quark and two down quarks, with an electric charge of $+2/3 - 1/3 - 1/3 = 0$.

Although leptons can be found as isolated particles, quarks cannot. Quarks are always bound together in groups of three (baryons), like the neutron and proton, or grouped as one quark with one antiquark (mesons). Collectively, anything made of quarks is called a *hadron*. All quarks and gluons carry a property called *color* that allows them to interact via the strong force and binds them tightly in groups. Leptons do not have color and cannot interact via the strong force.

The forces of nature are described by particles themselves that carry the force from one particle to another. An analogy to this idea would be two basketball players who are standing far apart. One player can exert a "force" on the other player by throwing him or her the basketball. Similarly, the force of electromagnetism is carried by photons when one charged particle "throws" a photon to another charged particle. The weak force is carried by the intermediate vector bosons, and the strong force is carried by gluons. These force-carrying particles have a quantum mechanical spin of 1 and are classified as bosons.

The Higgs boson (sometimes called the *God particle*; Lederman, 1993) has zero quantum mechanical spin and plays a role in giving mass to the other fundamental particles.

In the mathematical theory, fundamental particles have zero mass but acquire a mass by interacting with the Higgs boson.

Michael G. Strauss

REFERENCES AND RECOMMENDED READING

Giancoli, D. 2014. *Physics: Principles with Applications.* 7th ed. San Francisco: Pearson.
Lederman, Leon, with Dick Teresi. 1993. *The God Particle: If the Universe Is the Answer, What Is the Question?* Boston: Houghton Mifflin.

STAR OF BETHLEHEM. Three factors must be considered in any investigation of the star of Bethlehem. In order of precedence they are the text of Matthew's gospel, the magi themselves, and plausible astronomical phenomena. These considerations are related to several chronological puzzles, including the precise year of Christ's birth. Most historians place Christ's nativity around 5 BC, no later than Herod's death after a lunar eclipse in the spring of 4 BC.

Perhaps the star was miraculous, a manifestation of the "sons of the morning" (cf. Job 38:7). Matthew's curious description of the star "going before" the magi and "standing over" Bethlehem has prompted writers from John Chrysostom (fourth century) to **Bernard Ramm** (twentieth century) to regard the star as an angelic or supernatural phenomenon. Yet Matthew does not explicitly associate the star with direct angelic guidance. The magi's interpretation of the star according to their own wisdom led them to Jerusalem; Herod sent them to Bethlehem on the basis of Micah's prophecy (Mic. 5:2).

With respect to the magi, Matthew affirms neither that they were kings nor that they were three in number. According to Matthew, they came not from the Roman Empire, but from the east. Babylon at this time was the leading center for magi who were not only astrologers but also proficient astronomers. Babylonian magi were historical, not legendary, and their astronomical knowledge was sophisticated, not trivial. These magi, the "scribes of Enuma Anu Enlil," pioneered quantitative methods in ancient **astronomy** and could predict planetary cycles hundreds of years into the future (Swerdlow 1998). Few discussions of the Bethlehem star appreciate the capability of mathematical astronomy in this cuneiform tradition or delve deeply into the historical question of the magi's **astrology**, that is, how they interpreted celestial events.

In addition to the astronomy and astrology of the magi, because of the presence of a Jewish community in Babylon from the time of the exile, the magi may also have been familiar with Jewish prophecies of a coming Messiah. A chief concern of the magi was to advise the king on the rise and fall of empires. The book of Daniel, which refers to Daniel as head over the magi (e.g., Dan. 2:48; 5:11), accurately reflects this preoccupation while countering that the God of heaven, not the stars themselves, gives dominion. Daniel's vision of the Ancient of Days may describe the one whom the magi were seeking. Unlike the long succession of Mesopotamian kingdoms, the Messiah's kingdom would never be destroyed, and all nations of the world would worship him. When this everlasting kingdom arrives, divination by the stars—the way of life of the magi—would pass away. Indeed, the astronomical cuneiform tradition died out in the first century AD, only a few generations after the journey to Bethlehem.

With respect to astronomy, study of the star offers an engaging prospect, for at one time or another, practically every astronomical phenomenon has been proposed. We may group the multitude of theories according to whether they regard the star as an unexpected source of bright light or as a familiar planet moving into a significant configuration during the course of its planetary cycle.

In the first group are **explanation**s of the star as a nova, supernova, or comet. Many have imagined the star shining brightly in the sky, from Ignatius (late first century) to nativity depictions by Albrecht Dürer (sixteenth century) or Longfellow's poem "The Three Kings" (nineteenth century). Others have invoked comets to provide a commonsense explanation of how the star "stood over" the horizon of Bethlehem, from Origen (third century) to Giotto's painting *The Adoration of the Magi* (fourteenth century). Chinese records do confirm the appearance of what was either a nova or a comet in 5 BC, although ancient observers left no record of a bright star or supernova at this time. Colin Nicholl (2015) argues that the star was a different, unrecorded comet on the basis of scriptural evidence, including Revelation 12.

In the second group are explanations in which the star or "aster" refers to a planet in a significant configuration according to ancient astrology. These interpretations associate the star with the heliacal rising and retrograde motion of Jupiter, the regal planet. Matthew 2:2 and 2:9 (NASB) refer to the star "in the east," which an astronomer would understand as its heliacal rising on the eastern horizon moments before sunrise. A heliacal rising is the first appearance of a star or planet in the morning sky, just ahead of the sun, after a period of invisibility in the daytime sky. Heliacal risings were associated with birth, **death**, and transformation. Matthew's description of the star "going before" (*proēgen*, Matt. 2:9) likely refers to what is known as a planet's retrograde motion, which ancient astronomers described as "moving forward" (e.g., *proēgoumenoi*, Ptolemy 1940, 3.11, p. 312).

During retrograde motion, a planet briefly reverses its usual eastward direction and appears to travel westward against the background of fixed stars. In other words, during retrograde motion, a planet moves faster westward than, or "goes before," the nightly westward motion of the stars. Planets also appear brightest while retrograding. Matthew's description of the star "standing over" refers, in astronomical terms, to a planet's "stationary point" at the beginning or end of retrograde motion, when a planet appears to be fixed in place against the background stars. Because these planetary events are not visually striking to a casual observer, it is not surprising that Herod's court failed to notice the star, nor that Matthew's account seems confusing to readers unfamiliar with the apparent motions of the planets.

Consider the remarkable motion of the regal planet Jupiter around the time of the birth of Christ. Jupiter completed at least two interesting episodes of heliacal rising followed by retrograde motion.

The first episode, which occurred in Pisces, began with Jupiter's heliacal rising in March 7 BC. Jupiter, moving more quickly than Saturn, passed Saturn in May, making a conjunction. *Conjunction* refers to the sharing of the same coordinate with respect to the ecliptic or path of the sun (whether the two planets are in close visual proximity or appear to fuse is irrelevant). Jupiter reached its first stationary point in July, after which it began a period of retrograde motion. Jupiter then passed Saturn again in October to make a second conjunction. In November Jupiter reached its second stationary point, when its retrograde motion ended and it resumed its ordinary eastward motion. In December it passed Saturn a third time, completing a rare "triple conjunction" of a sort that recurs only every 800 years. A triple conjunction occurs when one planet passes by another three times in succession before, during, and after its retrograde loop. After this triple conjunction in January 6 BC, the two planets were joined by Mars, and then Jupiter disappeared into the daytime sky (Parpola 2001).

The Babylonian magi were deeply interested in these events and capable of predicting them. Indeed, Jupiter's stationary points and retrograde motion during the triple conjunction with Saturn in 7 BC are attested by four extant cuneiform tablets. These tablets are almanacs, which do not document how the magi interpreted the events, however (Sachs 1984). Later Rabbi Isaac Abarbanel (fifteenth century), who drew upon the astrology of Masha'allah (eighth century), attested in a commentary on the book of Daniel that triple conjunctions in Pisces were associated in Jewish tradition with the advents of Moses and the Messiah.

Johannes Kepler is the best-known exemplar of triple conjunction interpretations, although his scenario culminates with a bright star. What is now known as Kepler's supernova appeared in 1604. It followed a triple conjunction of Jupiter and Saturn in 1603 and a planetary association of Jupiter, Saturn, and Mars in 1604. Impressed by this sequence, Kepler discovered the triple conjunction in Pisces of Jupiter and Saturn in 7 BC, followed by the gathering with Mars, as noted above. Kepler then postulated that the ancient sequence would also have led to a bright star, the star of Bethlehem, as a counterpart to the supernova witnessed in 1604 (Kepler, *De stella nova*, 1606; repeated in Kepler, *De anno natali Christi*, 1614). Kepler's proposal is often adopted in popular Christmas planetarium programs. Numerous writers throughout the nineteenth and twentieth centuries have favored it, with some variations (Hughes, Kidger, Ferrari-D'Occhieppo, Parpola).

The second episode, which occurred in Aries, began with Jupiter's heliacal rising on April 17, 6 BC, with other planets in auspicious positions. On the same day, it was occulted by the moon. Jupiter then entered another period of retrograde motion between its first stationary point in August and its second stationary point in December 6 BC. Molnar demonstrates that according to Roman astrology, the planetary configuration on April 17, 6 BC, heralded an unconquerable king of the universe born in Judea. With Mercury, Venus, Mars, and Saturn auspiciously positioned, the horoscope for this date was superior to Augustus Caesar's (Molnar 1999). On this scenario, Matthew 2:2 and 2:9 refer to the heliacal rising and retrograde motion of 6 BC, rather than the heliacal rising and triple conjunction with Saturn in 7 BC.

Consequently, explanations of the star as a planetary astronomical event involving Jupiter's motion in Pisces in 7 BC or in Aries in 6 BC, which the magi interpreted as foretelling the birth of a Jewish Messiah, appear consistent with what is currently known of the magi.

The potential viability of several candidates for the star renders skepticism toward the historicity of Matthew's story unnecessary. Yet the nature and identity of the star must remain an open question at least until the magi and their ancient cuneiform tradition of mathematical astrology are better understood.

Kerry Magruder

REFERENCES AND RECOMMENDED READING

Barthel, Peter, and George Van Kooten, eds. 2015. *The Star of Bethlehem and the Magi: Interdisciplinary Perspectives from Experts on the Ancient Near East, the Greco-Roman World, and Modern Astronomy.* Leiden: Brill.

Ferrari-D'Occhieppo, Konradin. 1989. "Star of the Magi and Babylonian Astronomy." In *Chronos, Kairos, Christos.* Eds. Jerry Vardaman and Edwin M. Yamauchi, 41–54. Winona Lake, IN: Eisenbrauns.

Hughes, David. 1979. *The Star of Bethlehem: An Astronomer's Confirmation.* New York: Walker.

Kidger, Mark. 1999. *The Star of Bethlehem: An Astronomer's View.* Princeton, NJ: Princeton University Press.

Molnar, Michael. 1999. *The Star of Bethlehem: The Legacy of the Magi.* New Brunswick, NJ: Rutgers University Press.

Nicholl, Colin R. 2015. *The Great Christ Comet: Revealing the True Star of Bethlehem.* Wheaton, IL: Crossway.

Parpola, Simo. 2001. "The Magi and the Star: Babylonian Astronomy Dates Jesus' Birth." *Bible Review* 17:17–23, 52–54.

Ptolemy. 1940. *Tetrabiblos.* Trans. Frank E. Robbins. Loeb Classical Library. Cambridge, MA: Harvard University Press.

Sachs, Abraham J., and C. B. F. Walker. 1984. "Kepler's View of the Star of Bethlehem and the Babylonian Almanac for 7/6 B.C." *Iraq* 46:43–55.

Swerdlow, Noel. 1998. *The Babylonian Theory of the Planets.* Princeton, NJ: Princeton University Press.

STATISTICS. Statistics, as a field, is the science of collecting, organizing, and interpreting data. Statistics are also the techniques used for descriptions, summarizations, or making conclusions based on data analyses. Statistical techniques are classified into descriptive statistics and inferential statistics. Descriptive statistics organize and summarize data and include measures of central tendencies, frequencies, proportions, skewness, and variability. Inferential statistics use samples from populations to make inferences about those populations and include common statistical procedures such as correlations, t-tests and analysis of variance. Statistical analysis is used in many different disciplines to interpret the significance of an effect in the data. This article focuses primarily on the use of statistics in social science research to illustrate general principles of statistical analysis.

In psychological studies, entire populations can rarely be tested, therefore samples are drawn from populations. Statistical inference is the process of drawing conclusions about the population based on the results of the statistical procedures performed on the samples. Because statistics typically differ from the corresponding population parameters, **probability** theory is used to determine how accurately the sample statistics represent the population parameters.

Hypothesis testing is commonly used to draw inferences from samples to populations. Hypothesis testing presents two options for the researcher. The null hypothesis in which no significant differences exist among the treatment groups of the study, and the alternative hypothesis in which significant differences do exist among the treatment groups. Test statistics (i.e., t, z, F) are used to determine if the null or alternative hypothesis is more likely. Supporting the alternative hypothesis generally requires a finding in the extreme 5 percent of the range of possibilities (an alpha level of .05, p < .05). If the finding does not surpass the extreme 5 percent mark, then the null hypothesis is supported.

Regardless of whether the null or alternative hypothesis is supported by the analyses, a decision error is possible because statistical inferences are based on probability. A Type I error results when the alternative hypothesis is supported but there is no significant difference (false positive). A Type II error occurs when the null hypothesis is supported but there is a significant difference (false negative). Therefore any particular finding may be inaccurate even though the likelihood is that the finding is correct. Multiple studies investigating the same phenomenon help researchers to gain greater certainty about specific findings over time.

In scientific fields outside of the **social sciences**, the criteria needed to support a certain hypothesis may be much more stringent than this 5 percent level. For example, in experimental particle **physics**, a discovery is generally proclaimed only when the observed effect rules out the null hypothesis at greater than the 99.9999 percent level.

Criticisms of inferential statistics are related to assumptions underlying the use of empirical research rather than with statistical analyses per se. For instance, the decision to make **empiricism** the primary way of knowing about human thought and behavior is a philosophical commitment and may not be the best way of knowing such **information**. This being the case, statistics help to confirm or validate this epistemic commitment to quantification and therefore work against other appropriate ways of knowing about human thought and behavior. Inferential statistics help to answer important questions, but are limited in ability to inform, as with any way of knowing. To more fully investigate humanity a wider spectrum of methods should be used, specifically qualitative methods. In addition, much of what is investigated may fit better with nonlinear or dynamic models such as **chaos theory** and catastrophe theory.

Overall, quantitative statistics play an important role in the social sciences, but the explanatory power of quantitative studies would be significantly enhanced by the inclusion of qualitative methods and nonlinear models.

C. Eric Jones

REFERENCES AND RECOMMENDED READING

Frost, Nollaig. 2011. *Qualitative Research Methods in Psychology.* New York: McGraw-Hill.

Gravetter, Frederick, and Larry Wallnau. 2012. *Statistics for the Behavioral Sciences.* Belmont, CA: Wadsworth/Thomson Learning.

Vallacher, Robin, and Andrzej Nowak. 1994. *Dynamical Systems in Social Psychology.* San Diego: Academic Press.

STENGER, VICTOR J.

Victor Stenger (1935–2014) authored over a dozen books on topics related to **physics**, cosmology, and religion. The main focus of several of his books relates to attempting to undermine religious belief. Stenger received his PhD in physics from UCLA in 1963 and subsequently worked at the University of Hawaii until he retired in 2000. He also held visiting researcher positions at several universities in Europe, including Oxford. His research fields centered on particle physics and high-energy neutrino **astronomy** (*Huffington Post*).

Stenger's most popular book was *God: The Failed Hypothesis* (2007a), in which he made the contested claim that **science** disproves God. It could be noted that Stenger made a categorical mistake with his assumption that God is a "hypothesis." The monotheistic religions came to the conclusion of God not as a hypothesis but as a response to overwhelming evidence of God's existence. The evidence for God's existence has been acknowledged by billions of people throughout human history. Where Stenger did not make a mistake was in realizing that he could profit from writing books with bold titles attacking the reality of God. So, in 2012 he published *God and the Folly of Faith.*

Although raised Catholic, Stengler apparently never understood the concept of faith, either in the spiritual sense or in relation to everyday events. He says that "faith means you believe in something which you have no evidence for" (Stenger 2012, 23). However, in the everyday sense, we would assert, "I have faith the sun will rise tomorrow," based on the accumulated evidence of every morning's sunrise throughout history. Biblical faith is also based on experiential evidence and eyewitness testimony: "That which was from the beginning, which we have heard, which we have seen with our eyes, which we have looked at and our hands have touched—this we proclaim concerning the Word of life" (1 John 1:1).

Stenger narrowly focuses on examples of unanswered prayer to build his case against God (Stenger 2012). He asks a question that most honest believers have asked at one time or another: "If the Bible is true, why was my earnest prayer not answered?" Regrettably, he concluded that the Bible is wrong (see **Prayer**). He failed to conduct proper scientific protocol by refusing to consider all the evidence. How many examples of answered prayer could be related by Christians throughout history? Could their number even be counted? In addition, prayer is multipersonal activity involving the person(s) praying, the recipient(s) of prayer, and God. Each of these participants in prayer has a free will and is not bound by anything like a mechanical law of nature.

In trying to explain away the concept of a Creator to account for the numerous examples of fine-tuning of physical parameters for life in our universe, Stenger appeals to the **multiverse** concept, which supposes an unlimited number of universes with different physical properties. Unfortunately for his viewpoint, the multiverse theory has not a shred of evidence, while evidence for God permeates human experience throughout the scope of history. He attributes the **origin of life** in our universe to a principle of "self-organization," citing hurricanes and snowflakes as prominent examples. However, neither hurricanes nor snowflakes represent examples of natural forces causing an increase in **information**; their formation represents the opposite of the process required of nature in order to form the information-rich biomolecules necessary for life.

In addition to his profession as a physicist, Stenger came to be known as someone who also made something of a career of denying the existence of God.

Eric R. Hedin

REFERENCES AND RECOMMENDED READING

Stenger, Victor J. 2007a. *God: The Failed Hypothesis: How Science Shows That God Does Not Exist.* Amherst, NY: Prometheus.

———. 2007b. "Physics, Cosmology, and the New Creationism." In *Scientists Confront Intelligent Design and Creationism.* Eds. Andrew J. Petto and Laurie R. Godfrey, 131–49. New York: W. W. Norton.

———. 2012. *God and the Folly of Faith.* Amherst, NY: Prometheus.

———. 2013. *God and the Atom.* Amherst, NY: Prometheus.

———. 2014. *God and the Multiverse: Humanity's Expanding View of the Cosmos.* Amherst, NY: Prometheus.

———. "Victor Steger: Physicist, PhD, Bestselling Author." *Huffington Post.* Accessed December 28, 2015. www.huffingtonpost.com/victor-stenger/.

STRING THEORY.

String theory is a theoretical construct in **physics** that proposes that the most fundamental objects in the universe are one-dimensional objects called *strings*, and which offers the possibility of solving some challenging problems in basic physics.

In string theory, the pointlike particles of the **standard** model (including leptons, quarks, and bosons) are composed of one-dimensional objects that are described as vibrating strings. Just as different vibrational modes of a guitar string will give different musical tones, so the different vibrating modes of the primary strings give rise to different particles. String theory allows the reconciliation of quantum mechanics with a theory of gravity, and is thus a strong candidate for the ultimate theory that incorporates all the fundamental forces and particles into a theory of everything (see **Grand Unified Theory**).

The earliest string theory, called a *bosonic string theory*, was developed in the late 1960s as an attempt to explain how hadrons, particles made of quarks, interacted. The theory had fatal problems and was eventually discarded when a correct theory of hadrons was developed: quantum chromodynamics (QCD). However, in the 1980s physicists noticed that string theories naturally predicted the existence of a spin–2 fundamental particle, a required characteristic of the still undiscovered graviton, which is the quantum carrier of the gravitational force. Consequently, string theory seemed to hold out the promise of reconciling gravitational theory with quantum mechanics, and renewed interest was developed.

Eventually five independent string theories were developed, and scientists assumed that only one of the five would turn out to be correct. In the mid-1990s, however, researchers realized that the five theories could all be describing the same more fundamental theory from different perspectives. The overarching theory that has been developed and encompasses all the various string theories is called *M-theory*, where the meaning of the *M* is undefined but has had various interpretations including "membrane," "mother," and "monster."

All string theories require that the universe actually be composed of more than the four known dimensions of space-time. In general, the five modern string theories require 10 dimensions, while M-theory requires 11 dimensions and asserts that strings are actually one-dimensional projections of two-dimensional vibration entities.

The strings in string theory vibrate in different ways, and the different vibrational modes are manifest as different matter particles and force particles. Strings can be closed (meaning they form a closed loop, like a rubber band) or open (meaning the ends are not connected, like a guitar string). String theory introduces not only strings, but also the idea of "branes." A brane can be thought of as a generalization of a point into higher dimensions. A point has zero dimensions. A string is a one-dimensional object. A membrane is a two-dimensional object, like a sheet of paper with no thickness. In general, an object with p dimensions where p is some integer, is called a "p-brane." Since string theory requires dimensions beyond our known four dimensions, these branes can exist in multidimensions as well.

There are a few ideas about why we experience the world in three space dimensions and one time dimension if reality itself consists of 10 or 11 dimensions. The most prominent idea is that the other dimensions are "curled up" or "compact dimensions." An analogy of what is meant by "compact dimensions" would be an object like a hanging power cable. If you are far from the cable, it appears linear, like a one-dimensional object. The length of the cable is observable but not its diameter or thickness. However, an ant walking on the cable would be able to traverse not only its one-dimensional length, but would also be able to walk around the circumference of the cable. While the very small ant experiences the cable as a two-dimensional object, a human, who is much larger than the cable, experiences it as only a one-dimensional object, in which case the dimension of the circumference is compactified.

In string theory, it is likely that the scale of the compact dimensions is on the order of the Planck length, which is about 10^{-35} meters in size. If so, it would probably be impossible for human observers ever to experience the compact six or seven extra dimensions. Another proposal is that our universe is somehow stuck on a four-dimensional so-called D-brane of the much larger multidimensional universe. We are confined to a subspace that allows us to experience only 3 + 1 of the 10 or 11 actual dimensions.

String theory holds out the promise of solving some challenging problems in particle physics, including the development of a quantum theory of gravity. Currently **general relativity** describes the gravitational force at large scales while quantum mechanics describes the universe particularly at small scales. Scientists have not been able to develop a consistent quantum theory of gravity due to a number of difficulties, including the different frameworks used in quantum mechanics and general relativity. The most generalized **quantum physics** theory, relativistic quantum field theory, deals with particle fields in a flat space-time geometry, while general relativity models the gravity as curvatures in space-time in which the embedded particles warp the space-time geometry. String theory naturally incorporates gravity into the vibrational modes of the strings, and in fact, a consistent quantum mechanical gravitational theory that resembles general relativity at large distances is a characteristic of string theory.

String theory also offers the possibility of explaining why gravity is orders of magnitude weaker than the other three fundamental forces in nature (i.e., electromagnetism as well as strong and weak nuclear forces). One possibility is that the gravitational force operates in all the multidimensions of the universe while the other forces only operate in our 3 + 1 dimensions. Consequently, we observe only a fraction of the total gravitational force, making it appear much weaker to us.

A major challenge for scientists is determining if there are experiments that can be done to test the predictions of string theory. It is possible that strings are only evident at energies near the Planck scale, which is about 100 million joules or 10^{28} eV, or about 10^{15} times higher than the largest man-made particle accelerator, the Large Hadron Collider at CERN in Switzerland. If there are no lower energy phenomena, then string theory may not be amenable to experimental verification.

However, there are possible indirect tests, and evidence, for string theory. All of the five proposed string theories are, actually, supersymmetric string theories or superstring theories. That is, they require a whole set of yet-undiscovered supersymmetric partners for all of the known fundamental subatomic particles.

Every particle in nature is either a fermion or a boson. Fermions are particles with an intrinsic spin equal to a half integer multiple of Planck's constant. All fermions obey Fermi-Dirac statistical laws, including the Pauli exclusion principle, which states that no two identical fermions can be in the same quantum state. Bosons have integer spins and obey Bose-Einstein **statistics**. All known quarks and leptons are fermions, while force-carrying particles are bosons (see **Standard Model, The**). Supersymmetry demands that each known fermion in nature have a boson partner and vice versa. Currently, no supersymmetric partner has been discovered. However, all viable string models predict that supersymmetry must exist, so discovery of a supersymmetric particle would give indirect, circumstantial evidence for string theory.

The scale at which certain properties of string theory could become evident is unknown, and it is possible that string theory could reveal itself at scales far from the Planck scale. For instance, it is possible that one or more of the required extra dimensions could be compactified at a scale that is not as small as the Planck length but much larger, some say as large as a few microns. If so, then current or future particle accelerators could probe these scales and see evidence for multidimensions.

String theories also predict the existence of quantum mechanical black holes that could be created in accelerators but would quickly decay away through Hawking radiation. These mini black holes are not equivalent to the supermassive black holes that exist at the center of many galaxies. The microscopic black holes instantly decay without accreting any other matter. Characteristic decay signatures in particle physics experiments could signal the creation and decay of such black holes, giving possible indirect evidence for string theory.

If string theory is ever experimentally verified, it will certainly change our perception of the universe. It will confirm the existence of dimensions beyond the three known dimensions of space and one of time. For theists, who believe that God created the universe, **confirmation** of string theory may actually expand any idea of the scope of God's attributes. For instance, any minimal description of God would require that he exists in at least 11 dimensions in order to create an 11-dimensional universe. An 11-dimensional being could easily perform acts that would be described as **miracles** to us as four-dimensional humans (Ross 2010).

The classic book *Flatland* by Edwin Abbott gives a whimsical account of the interaction of a three-dimensional being with a two-dimensional world (Abbott 1884). In his account, the higher dimensional being is incomprehensible to those in the two-dimensional world. Abbott's novel gives a concrete illustration of how God, who would minimally be an 11-dimensional being if string theory is confirmed, can easily perform miracles and is incomprehensible in his fullness to humans.

Michael G. Strauss

REFERENCES AND RECOMMENDED READING

Abbott, Edwin. 1884. *Flatland: A Romance of Many Dimensions*. London: Seely & Co.
Greene, Brian. 1999. *The Elegant Universe*. New York: W. W. Norton.
Ross, Hugh. 2010. *Beyond the Cosmos: What Recent Discoveries in Astrophysics Reveal about the Glory and Love of God*. Kissimmee, FL: Signalman.

SUFFICIENT REASON, PRINCIPLE OF. Scientific activity is motivated by the belief that there are reasons why things are as they are. The polymath and inventor of the infinitesimal calculus, **Gottfried Leibniz**, was the most well-known of scholars to express this idea in a principle of sufficient reason (PSR): "Our reasonings are founded on two great principles, that of contradiction … and that of sufficient reason, in virtue of which we hold that no fact can be real or existent, no statement true, unless there be a sufficient reason why it is so and not otherwise, although most often these reasons cannot be known to us" (Rescher 1991, 31–32).

The PSR is therefore the claim that every fact, or every contingent fact, has an explanation (Pruss 2012). The scientist's conviction is validated if the PSR is true, and the view that it is self-evidently so has not been discredited (Pruss 2006). However, a true PSR achieves more, since it also figures in a valid **cosmological argument** for the **existence of God**, beginning with Leibniz's concern that if everything within the universe requires an explanation, then the universe as a whole does too: "The first question which should rightly be asked is this: Why is there something rather than nothing?" (Wiener 1951, 527–28).

The PSR tells us that Leibniz's question must have an answer. If that answer is not to lead to an infinite regress of explanations, then it must be given in terms of a being that exists necessarily, containing within itself the explanation for its own existence. Classical **theism** takes God to be just such a being (see **Existence of God**; **Natural Theology**).

Science and theism have a joint interest in the PSR. However, an important objection is that the PSR is absurd because there are contingent facts that can be shown not to have explanations. Consider the so-called big conjunctive contingent fact (BCCF). This is a single fact that is the combination (conjunction) of every other contingent fact. If the PSR is true, then the BCCF has an explanation E, and E must be either contingent or necessary. If E is contingent, then it is *part* of the BCCF by definition, rendering the BCCF self-explanatory; if E is necessary, then it *entails* the BCCF, rendering the BCCF necessary. But as a contingent fact, the BCCF can be neither self-explanatory nor necessary, and since it is not absurd, E cannot exist.

The BCCF is thus a demonstrably *inexplicable* contingent fact and hence a counterexample to the PSR showing it to be false (van Inwagen 1983, 202–4). However, Alexander Pruss has argued cogently that E could be a contingent explanation and yet not be part of BCCF if it were the free choice of a necessary being. Furthermore, E could be a necessary explanation and yet not render the BCCF necessary since an *explanans* need not always *entail* the *explanandum* (see **Explanation**). Other objections to the PSR have been raised, but versions of the principle remain alive and well, motivating both scientific endeavor and theistic belief.

Jonathan Loose

REFERENCES AND RECOMMENDED READING

Pruss, Alexander R. 2006. *The Principle of Sufficient Reason: A Reassessment.* Cambridge Studies in Philosophy. Cambridge: Cambridge University Press.
———. 2012. "The Leibnizian Cosmological Argument." In *The Blackwell Companion to Natural Theology*, 24–100. West Sussex, UK: Wiley-Blackwell.
Rescher, Nicholas. 1991. *G. W. Leibniz's Monadology [1714]: An Edition for Students.* London: Routledge.
van Inwagen, Peter. 1983. *An Essay on Free Will.* Oxford: Clarendon.
Wiener, Philip P, ed. 1951. *Leibniz Selections.* New York: Scribner.

SUPERVENIENCE. Mother Teresa was a good person, and what made her good is that she was compassionate, courageous, generous, and virtuous in other ways. The connection between goodness and character is not accidental. Any individual with a character like Mother Teresa's must be good. There could not be a person exactly like Mother Teresa in all nonmoral respects that fails to be exactly like her in moral respects. If two individuals differ with respect to their moral qualities, then there must be a corresponding difference in their nonmoral qualities that accounts for the moral difference.

Another example: An individual's being tall is determined by his particular height (relative to a comparison class). It is impossible for two individuals to be exactly the same height and differ in whether they are tall or not. Individuals with exactly similar heights must be exactly similar with respect to tallness. If two individuals differ with respect to tallness, then there must be a corresponding difference in height.

These examples illustrate how properties of one sort (moral qualities and tallness) are determined by and depend on properties of another sort (nonmoral qualities and heights). The term *supervenience* was introduced to describe this sort of relationship. At its core, supervenience is a denial of independent variation between families of properties: if properties of one sort supervene on properties of another sort, then exact similarity in properties of the second sort entails exact similarity in properties of the first sort. It is impossible for there to be a difference in properties of the first sort without a difference in properties of the second sort (Lewis 1983).

Philosophers took a keen interest in supervenience in the latter part of the twentieth century because it promised to account for how properties of different domains were related—for example, mental and physical properties and moral and nonmoral properties. While it was generally agreed that properties of the first sort could not be reduced to properties of the second sort, many philosophers held that the first depend on and are determined by the second and used supervenience to explain how this was possible. When properties of one sort, for example, A-properties, supervene on properties of another, for example, B-properties, an individual's having an A-property, A*, entails that it has some B-property, B*, that necessitates its having A* (McLaughlin 1995).

If the mental supervenes on the physical, as many philosophers think, then having a mental property, for example, being in pain, requires having some physical property, for example, a complex neural property like c-fiber activation that necessitates the individual's being in pain. Supervenience, then, could explain how the mental is thoroughly grounded in the physical without being reducible to it (see Hare 1952 and Shafer-Landau 2005 for discussions of moral supervenience; Davidson 1970 and Kim 1998 for discussions of mental supervenience).

Supervenience may also explain the tension between physicalist accounts of the **mind** and Christian **theism**. Although Christian theism is obviously inconsistent with global **physicalism** (the view that everything is physical), Christian materialists hold that human persons are purely physical things while maintaining the traditional Christian belief that God is a purely spiritual, nonphysical entity. The problem with such a combination of views is that, as a type of physicalism, Christian **materialism** is committed to holding that mental properties, by their very nature, supervene on physical properties. Yet divine mental states neither depend on nor are necessitated by any physical states, and therefore Christian theists cannot hold that mental properties always supervene on physical properties (Vallicella 1998).

Kevin Sharpe

REFERENCES AND RECOMMENDED READING

Davidson, Donald. 1970. "Mental Events." In *Experience and Theory*. Eds. L. Foster and J. W. Swanson, 79–101. New York: Humanities. Repr. in D. Davidson, *Essays on Actions and Events*. Oxford: Oxford University Press, 1980.

Hare, R. M. 1952. *The Language of Morals*. Oxford: Clarendon.

Kim, Jaegwon. 1984. "Concepts of Supervenience." *Philosophy and Phenomenological Research* 45:153–76. Repr. in J. Kim, *Supervenience and Mind*, 53–78. Cambridge: Cambridge University Press, 1993.

———. 1998. *Mind in a Physical World*. Cambridge, MA: MIT Press.

Lewis, David. 1983. "New Work for a Theory of Universals." *Australasian Journal of Philosophy* 61:343–77.

McLaughlin, Brian. 1995. "Varieties of Supervenience." In *Supervenience: New Essays*. Eds. Elias E. Savellos and Umit D. Yalçin. Cambridge: Cambridge University Press.

Shafer-Landau, Russ. 2005. *Moral Realism: A Defense*. Oxford: Oxford University Press.

Vallicella, William. 1998. "Could a Classical Theist Be a Physicalist?" *Faith and Philosophy* 15:160–80.

T

TECHNOLOGY. Technology (from the Gk. *technē*, for "craft" or "art") is, in one sense, any extension of the human body to remake the environment or to make an object. For instance, a shovel is a technology. In another sense, technology can refer to a skill or activity. So economist John Kenneth Galbraith defined technology as "the application of organized knowledge." In yet another sense, technology may refer to a volition, the will to employ knowledge in certain ways.

By nature, human beings are knowers (*Homo sapiens*) and makers or fabricators (*Homo faber*). We use tools to hunt, plant, harvest, invent, transport, communicate, and manufacture. The Bible's dominion or stewardship mandate at least implies that humanity is to develop, use, and celebrate appropriate technologies: "God blessed them and said to them, 'Be fruitful and increase in number; fill the earth and subdue it. Rule over the fish in the sea and the birds in the sky and over every living creature that moves on the ground'" (Gen. 1:28). Ruling the world that God has made sometimes requires the application of technology.

Calvin College's Stephen Monsma and colleagues have helpfully defined technology as "a distinct human cultural activity in which humans exercise freedom and responsibility in response to God by forming and transforming the natural creation, with the aid of tools and procedures, for practical ends and purposes" (Monsma 1986, 19). This way of thinking about technology underscores the necessity of stewarding technology carefully, wisely, and responsibly. Contrary to popular opinion, tools are not neutral. The development of digital technologies, for instance, demonstrates that technologies alter the way we inhabit, perceive, and interact with others in the world around us.

Essentially, technology offers two fundamental promises: efficiency and speed. Through the application of technologies, tasks are completed with less human effort and with greater speed. These are important and welcome virtues in many contexts. Great human innovations and achievements—from the invention of the wheel to lunar exploration to the mapping of human **DNA**—would not have been possible were it not for technology. However, in other contexts ease and speed may be inconsistent with the purposes of human activity. For instance, the "slow food" movement is a reaction against fast-food culture and its penchant for speed,

precisely because the current technoculture tends to erode human goods worth preserving around, say, a communal meal (e.g., long conversation, relaxation, and knowing the sources of one's food).

Technological Imperative

Another contemporary challenge of our technological age is the so-called technological imperative. This is the notion that new technologies are inevitable and will, or must, be employed once they are available. This implies a sort of technological **determinism**. Philosopher of technology David Nye argues, however, that "technologies are social constructions. Machines are not like meteors that come unbidden from outside and have an 'impact.' Rather, human beings make choices when inventing, marketing, and using a new device" (Nye 1997, 125). Despite the temptation of technological determinism, there are few but important historical examples of societies resisting certain technologies for the good of humankind, including the repudiation of certain forms of chemical warfare.

Technological Utopianism

When technological determinism is combined with an overly sanguine view of technology, a type of technological utopianism often emerges, the view that technology will solve all of humanity's problems. This perspective is nowhere more evident than in the movement known as transhumanism. Transhumanists aspire to apply emerging technologies like genetic engineering, **artificial intelligence**, robotics, pharmaceutics, and others to enhance human capacities and overcome human limitations, including the limitations of IQ, aging, and even spatiotemporal bonds. Accordingly, for transhumanists, *Homo sapiens* is seen as a transitional form on the way to being posthuman. Interestingly, for the first time humans are themselves both the technologists and the technology. Thus, once again, the question of truly human goods and a truly human future are at stake (see **Singularity**).

C. Ben Mitchell

REFERENCES AND RECOMMENDED READING

Cohen, Eric. 2009. *In the Shadow of Progress: Being Human in the Age of Technology*. New York: New Atlantis.

Lynch, Jonah. 2012. *The Scent of Lemons: Technology and Relationships in the Age of Facebook*. London: Darton, Longman and Todd.

Mitchell, C. Ben, Edmund D. Pellegrino, Jean Bethke Elshtain, John F. Kilner, and Scott B. Rae. 2006. *Biotechnology and the Human Good*. Washington, DC: Georgetown University Press.

Monsma, Stephen V., ed. 1986. *Responsible Technology*. Grand Rapids: Eerdmans.

Nye, David E. 1997. "Shaping Communication Networks: Telegraph, Telephone, Computer," in Arien Mack (ed.), *Technology and the Rest of Culture*. Columbus, OH: Ohio State University Press.

Rubin, Charles T. 2016. *Eclipse of Man: Human Extinction and the Meaning of Progress*. New York: New Atlantis.

Savulescu, Julian, Ruud ter Meulen, and Guy Kahane. 2011. *Enhancing Human Capacities*. Oxford: Wiley-Blackwell.

TEILHARD DE CHARDIN, PIERRE. Pierre Teilhard de Chardin (1881–1955) was a Christian mystic, Jesuit priest, geologist, and paleontologist. He was the fourth of 11 children and grew up outside of Clermont-Ferrand in Auvergne, France. While drawn to nature—and the volcanic history of his homeland—he was also deeply religious and entered the Jesuit seminary at Aix in 1899.

Following the Jesuit exile from France, Teilhard studied at Hastings (Sussex, England). He then taught for three years at a Jesuit school in Cairo. His subsequent studies in Paris were cut short by the First World War, where Teilhard served as a noncombatant priest in the North African regiment (Morocco). It is widely thought that his experiences as a stretcher-bearer were formative in his theology, and he wrote prolifically during this period of his life. After the war, he completed his doctorate in **geology** and accepted a position at the Institut Catholique in Paris. Inspired by an early expedition to the Ordos desert of China (1923), he would spend nearly 20 years working in the Far East, including numerous geologic expeditions. Most notably, Teilhard participated in the discovery of the Peking Man (1926).

As a process theist, Teilhard rejected the notion that creation and transformation (cosmically speaking) were distinct, and instead saw a continual evolution of creation from physical to organic, and finally to spiritual. He wrote prolifically on the evolutionary nature of God's creation, in which God should be seen not as behind creation, but ahead as the Omega point, or culmination of being. In one of his most well-known pieces, *Writings in a Time of War*, Teilhard would pen, "The world is still being created, and it is Christ who is reaching his fulfillment in it" (King 1999, 49). In *The Prayer of the Universe*, he would clarify his process **theism**, writing, "Incessantly even if imperceptibly, the world is constantly emerging a little farther above nothingness" (Haught 2001, 37).

A strong proponent of Darwinian evolution, Teilhard can be seen as an early theistic evolutionist. He felt that, while personally intuitive, the direct action of God (as in **miracles**) would be utterly undetectable. His denial of a literal **Adam and Eve** and **original sin** resulted in the censoring of his writings from the Roman Catholic Church until after his death. During his life, Teilhard's "Christic" pantheism remained problematic for the church, though his theological writings have been inspirational to many subsequent evolutionary theists (notably, Theodosius Dobzhansky). His tenuous relationship with the Roman Catholic Church resulted in a speedy transition from Paris—following the Second World War—to a research position in the United States. He died on Easter Sunday of 1955 and was buried in a Jesuit cemetery in the Hudson Valley of New York.

Wayne Rossiter

REFERENCES AND RECOMMENDED READING

Grim, John, and Mary Evelyn Tucker. "Biography." American Teilhard Association. Accessed August 13, 2014. http://teilharddechardin.org/index.php/biography.

Haught, John F. 2001. *God after Darwin: A Theology of Evolution*. Boulder, CO: Westview.

King, Ursula. 1999. *Pierre Teilhard de Chardin: Writings*. Modern Spiritual Masters Series. Maryknoll, NY: Orbis.

Teilhard de Chardin, Pierre. 1971. "On the Notion of Creative Transformation." In *Christianity and Evolution: Reflections on Science and Religion*. Ed. René Hague, 21–24. New York: Collins.

TELEOLOGY. Teleology is the study of goals, purposes, perfections, ends, and functions. Intrinsic or immanent teleology refers to things that, in virtue of their intrinsic principles, tend to an end, such as the wing of a bird existing for the purpose of flight. Extrinsic teleology refers to things that, in virtue of outside sources, tend to an end, like seed existing for the sake of nourishing birds. Teleological explanations appeal to the contribution of some thing, features, or agent toward a goal or function (intrinsic or extrinsic).

Early discussion of teleology is present in **Plato**'s *Phaedo* and more fully developed in **Aristotle**'s final **causation** as "the end, that for the sake of which a thing is done" (*Physics* 2.3 and *Metaphysics* 5.2). Teleology played a significant role in Aristotelian and medieval philosophy and science (see **Aristotle's Four Causes**; **Science and the Medieval Church**). However, the nature and legitimacy of teleology and teleological explanation have been challenged, especially in biology and **psychology**.

There are three basic accounts of teleology. According to

the *agent account*, teleology refers to an agent's contributing a purpose for something. This is most plausible in cases of artifacts. For example, the teleology of a hammer or a painting is the function for which its creator intended it. The debate here often focuses on whether or not natural objects have this, as this would imply some type of **theism**.

The *nonreductive Aristotelian account* maintains that teleological facts are grounded in the nature of an organism or substance. The purpose or end of something is produced by its tendency, its powers, to contribute to the harmony of the whole of which it is a part. This thesis is metaphysically robust as it accounts for teleological facts (normalcy, proper function) as irreducible. This view is also challenged, as the most plausible account of the origin of nonreductive teleology is theistic, and this view offers an explanation that, for principled reasons, post-Aristotelian science cannot possibly explain (Pruss 2009).

The *reductive account* maintains that teleology refers to objects possessing a proper function of doing something provided it exists because it has it. This view reduces teleology in biological things to evolution and the teleology of artifacts to agents. According to Larry Wright (1976), under the influence of Charles Taylor (1964), a feature *F* has *G* as its proper goal provided that *F* exists *because* it tends to produce *G*. More specifically, in evolutionary theory, some system has a particular goal *G* if the system was selected *because of* its propensity for achieving *G*. For example, organisms have eyes because they produce visual representations, and so the **gene**s coding for them were selected for that purpose.

Alvin Plantinga (1993) argues that Wright's account fails as it results in conditions, such as psychopathy, that become normal simply because those with the gene survive in virtue of their psychopathy. The proper function of something could be evil or destructive to the organism, which is an absurd account of teleology. Nonreductive pictures of teleology started with Aristotle and flourished in the medieval era only to be abandoned by modern science. Yet reductive accounts face difficulties.

Brandon L. Rickabaugh

REFERENCES AND RECOMMENDED READING

Aristotle. (c. mid-fourth century) 1930. *Physica*. In *The Works of Aristotle*, vol. 2. Eds. W. D. Ross and J. A. Smith, trans. R. P. Hardie and R. K. Gaye. Oxford: Oxford University Press.

Koons, Robert C. 2000. *Realism Regained: An Exact Theory of Causation, Teleology, and the Mind*. New York: Oxford University Press.

Millikan, Ruth. 1984. *Language, Thought, and Other Biological Categories*. Cambridge, MA: MIT Press. (Original defense of a biological theory of representation.)

Oderberg, David. 2008. "Teleology: Inorganic and Organic." In *Contemporary Perspectives on Natural Law*. Ed. A. M. González, 259–79. Aldershot, UK: Ashgate.

Plantinga, Alvin. 1993. *Warrant and Proper Function*. Oxford: Oxford University Press.

Pruss, Alexander R. 2009. "Altruism, Normalcy and God." In *Evolution, Games, and God*. Eds. S. Coakley and M. Nowak, 329–85. Cambridge, MA: Harvard University Press.

Taylor, Charles. 1964. *The Explanation of Behavior*. London: Routledge and Kegan Paul.

Woodfield, Andrew. 1976. *Teleology*. Cambridge: Cambridge University Press.

Wright, Larry. 1976. *Teleological Explanations*. Berkeley: University of California Press.

THEISM. Western theism — Christianity, Judaism, and Islam — understands God to be the creator and sustainer of the world and the object of religious belief and worship. While theistic thought on the nature of God derives from several distinct sources, including scriptural, experiential, and philosophical, there is broad agreement that God is a personal being that is supremely powerful, wise, good, and free. In contrast to **deism**, God is not only the creator of the initial world segment but its providential governor. In contrast to pantheism, God is not only in the world but transcends it. God's creating and sustaining activity raises at least three pressing issues with respect to science.

First, there are conceptual worries related to specifying the "causal joint" (Farrer 1967, 78) connecting God, an immaterial being, and the physical world at the moment of creation (Fales 2010). It is argued that the concept of an immaterial being bringing about a material effect is utterly mysterious and thus no sense can be given to how God creates the physical world. In response, theists point out that, while a **mystery**, this is no peculiar problem for theism. In regard to atheism, the universe came from nothing by nothing (Kenny 1969, 66). Both theists and the atheists agree that the universe had no material cause. However, theism is explanatorily superior because it posits an efficient cause of the universe, whereas atheism does not. Further, theists point out that we do have some understanding of how an immaterial being causes a physical effect in the case of the mind-body relation experienced by human persons.

Second, there is the issue of how to specify the division of labor between God and the ongoing processes of the world. On the one hand, if the world and its entire history are the sole responsibility of God, it seems **occasionalism** is true, a position that is, at best, unattractive. At worst, the physical world becomes a sham, bereft of any genuine powers. On the other hand, if **causation** is understood in terms of existence conferral, where a cause brings into being its effect, there is no obvious workable division of labor between God and nature such that God is still an active participant in the world's operations. One solution to this dilemma is to hold that secondary causation is to be understood as a *process* whereby conserved quantities of energy and momentum are transferred to produce new manifestations of what already exists (McCann 2012, chap. 2). As the primary cause, God is responsible for the existence of all, even though the products of his creation genuinely interact and exert real influence on each other.

Finally, there is the question of theism's relationship to modern science. We are often told that modern science is naturalistic (Dawkins 2006; Rosenberg 2011). In response, the theist argues (1) that it is theism, not **naturalism**, that is required for the possibility and success of science (Plantinga 2011); and (2) the deliverances of science provide evidence for theism, not naturalism.

Paul M. Gould

REFERENCES AND RECOMMENDED READING

Dawkins, Richard. 2006. *The God Delusion*. New York: Houghton Mifflin.
Fales, Evan. 2010. *Divine Intervention: Metaphysical and Epistemological Puzzles*. New York: Routledge.
Farrer, Austin. 1967. *Faith and Speculation*. London: A. & C. Black.
Kenny, Anthony. 1969. *The Five Ways: St. Thomas Aquinas' Proofs of God's Existence*. London: Routledge.
McCann, Hugh. 2012. *Creation and the Sovereignty of God*. Bloomington: Indiana University Press.
Plantinga, Alvin. 2011. *Where the Conflict Really Lies: Science, Religion, and Naturalism*. New York: Oxford University Press.
Polkinghorne, John. 1998. *Belief in God in an Age of Science*. New Haven, CT: Yale University Press.
Rosenberg, Alex. 2011. *The Atheist's Guide to Reality: Enjoying Life without Illusions*. New York: W. W. Norton.

THEODICY. A theodicy is an attempt to justify God given the fact that there is evil in the world. Unlike a defense, the aim of which is to demonstrate that the arguments from evil against reasonable belief in God are unsuccessful given a possible scenario or set of scenarios, a theodicy takes on the burden of attempting to vindicate God by providing a plausible explanation for evil. A theodicy commonly takes the following general form: God, an omnipotent, omniscient, and omnibenevolent being, will prevent or eliminate evil unless there is a good reason or set of reasons for not doing so. There is evil in the world. Therefore God must have a good reason or set of reasons for not preventing or eliminating evil.

There are various attempts to demonstrate what that reason or set of reasons is. Four of the most important attempts are theodicies that appeal to (1) the significance and value of free will, (2) the significance and value of acquiring virtuous traits of character in the midst of suffering, (3) the significance and value of a universe that is governed by natural laws, and (4) the significance of the limited nature of God.

The most widely known and used theodicy was crafted by **Augustine** (AD 354–430) over 1,500 years ago. Augustine argued that God is perfect in goodness, and the universe, God's creation, is thus also good. Since all things are good, evil must not represent the positive existence of any substantial thing. Evil must rather be a *privatio boni*—a metaphysical privation of the good.

For Augustine, both moral evil, which is evil directly brought about by a moral agent (such as rape or murder), and natural evil, which are evils in the natural world not directly brought about by a person (such as tornados and hurricanes that cause human suffering), entered into the universe through the wrongful use of free will. The theological term used to denote such actions is "sin." Since God's free creatures, both angels and humans, are finite and mutable, they have the capacity to choose evil. However, even though sin and other evils entered into the world, in a grand and aesthetic sense the whole of creation is good from God's perspective.

This Augustinian theodicy as such is problematic for many in the modern world. For one, most contemporary theologians and philosophers believe that natural evils, including disease, natural disasters, and predation, occur because of the **laws of nature**, not because of the sins of the first human beings. Thus the free will theodicy is ineffectual as a solution to natural evil.

A second type of theodicy emphasizes the value of acquiring virtuous traits of character in the midst of suffering. While also utilizing the notion of free will, the soul-making (or person-making) theodicy as developed by John Hick stands in contrast to the Augustinian free-will theodicy. According to the soul-making theodicy, God created a world that includes natural laws that allow for natural evil, suffering, and hardship, but God had a purpose in allowing this, for it fostered the development of morally and spiritually mature persons.

In summary form, first God created the world as a good place, but it was no paradise for developing human persons both spiritually and morally. Then, beginning with unconscious matter, through evolutionary means God brought about persons who have freedom of will and the capacity to mature in love and goodness. By placing human persons in this challenging environment, through their own free responses they have the opportunity to choose what is right and good and thus to grow into the mature persons that God desires them to be, exhibiting the virtues of patience, courage, generosity, and so on. The process has taken billions of years, and it will not be completed until some distant time in the future when human persons and perhaps other types of evolutionarily advanced persons will have reached moral and spiritual maturity.

Evil is the result of both the creation of the soul-making world and the human choice to sin, to rebel against God and his goodness. Nevertheless, God will continue to work with human and perhaps other persons, even in the afterlife as necessary, by allowing them opportunities to love and choose the good so that in the end everyone will be brought to a place of moral and spiritual perfection.

An objection to this theodicy is that, while it may be true that a soul-making environment cannot be a paradise, the degree and extent of pain and suffering that exist in this world are surely unjustified. Could not mature persons be developed without the sorts of horrors that exist in our world? Furthermore, some evils experienced by human beings seem to be character destroying rather than character building. Yet it could be proposed that, even though God did not intend any particular evils, for soul-making purposes God did need to create an environment where such evils were a real possibility. Thus, while each individual instance of evil may not be justified by a particular greater good, the existence of a world where evil is a real possibility may be a requisite for a world where **soul** making occurs.

Another type of theodicy begins with the notion that it is important that events occur in the universe according to regular and reliable patterns. Without such patterns it would be impossible for intelligent and morally responsible agents to learn and develop. However, some of these regular patterns or natural laws are dependent on lower-level chaotic systems, and these systems will sometimes bring about events that are destructive and harmful. Consider the chaotic systems underlying weather patterns, for instance. God's creation of these laws and systems is warranted even though they sometimes bring about natural evils. **John Polkinghorne** refers to this type of response to the **problem of evil** as a "free process defense." In rebuttal to this type of theodicy, one could ask why an omnipotent and omniscient being could not create a world that was regular and orderly without it entailing natural disasters.

A fourth approach to theodicy attempts to answer the question of why evil exists in a world created by God by proposing that God has certain limitations that make it impossible for him to eliminate the evils that exist — at least until some undetermined time in the distant future. Process theologians, for example, deny divine omnipotence. While God desires for evil to be vanquished and can lure human agents toward the good, in this view God is limited by human freedom and the laws of nature. This approach is understood by many evangelical theologians to be outside the bounds of evangelical Christianity.

There are other theodicies beyond those noted here, but this sampling of several major types provides a sense of the scope of available approaches to the subject.

Chad Meister

REFERENCES AND RECOMMENDED READING

Adams, Marilyn M. 1999. *Horrendous Evils and the Goodness of God.* Ithaca, NY: Cornell University Press.
Davis, Stephen T., ed. 2001. *Encountering Evil: Live Options in Theodicy.* New ed. Louisville, KY: Westminster John Knox.
Hick, John. 1978. *Evil and the God of Love.* 2nd ed. New York: Harper & Row.
Meister, Chad. 2012. *Evil: A Guide for the Perplexed.* New York: Bloomsbury.
Plantinga, Alvin. 1977. *God, Freedom and Evil.* Grand Rapids: Eerdmans.

THEOLOGY. Anselm of Canterbury (1033–1109) described theology as "faith seeking understanding" (*fides quaerens intellectum*). Theology is discourse ("*logos*") about God ("*theos*"), an attempt "to articulate the *content* of the gospel of Jesus Christ to the *context* of a particular culture" (Clark 2003). This entry explores how theology has been variously articulated in the context of the natural sciences.

In the modern *Zeitgeist*, science and theology are eternal enemies locked in a battle to the **death**; religious dogma retreats as science advances; Christians sacrifice their doctrinal lambs on the altar of modern science. Such images have held people captive for more than a century (Draper [1874] 1882; White [1896] 1960). They tell a tale valorized in popular media and literature (e.g., see the polemical works by the New Atheists). But this tale is largely untrue. Many early scientists professed Christian faith, including men like **Isaac Newton**, **Blaise Pascal**, **Francis Bacon**, and **Johannes Kepler**. In fact, modern science emerged in part as a result of the intellectual influence of Christian theology (e.g., Foster 1934).

Science and theology have interacted in complex ways throughout church history (Brooke 1991). The publication of **Ian Barbour**'s *Issues in Science and Religion* (1966) gave birth to the academic discipline that analyzes the interface of religion and the natural sciences. Barbour also developed a famous typology describing four ways of relating science and religion—conflict, independence, dialogue, and integration. Scientific **materialism** with its reductionist view of religion exemplifies the conflict model (e.g., sociobiology, genetic **determinism**). The independence model was embodied by Karl Barth and Rudolf Bultmann who, in different ways, cast science and theology as radically discontinuous domains of knowledge (cf. **Stephen Jay Gould**'s **non-overlapping magisteria [NOMA]**). Science and religion are more convergent in the dialogue and the integration models (Barbour 1990).

The discipline of science and theology is wide-ranging in subject matter with too many topics to list, for example, evolutionary biology and human behavior; physical cosmologies and biblical **eschatology**; **divine action** and modern **physics**; **neuroscience** and the human person; **cognitive science** and religious belief; **intelligent design** theory; science and world religions; etc. Each of these research areas has subdisciplines investigating dimensions of scientific theorizing that bear on theological or religious concerns (see Clayton 2006; Harrison 2010). Historians of science are part of this field, many of them giving sustained attention to debates that have traditionally preoccupied evangelicals, for example, the **age of the earth** and **Darwin**'s **theory of evolution** (e.g., Livingstone 1987; Numbers 2006). Emerging issues like biotechnology and environmentalism will likely loom large in future research.

In 1982 Robert John Russell established the Center for Theology and the Natural Sciences at Berkeley (CTNS); soon after, Philip Hefner in 1988 launched the Zygon Center for Religion and Science in Chicago at the Lutheran School of Theology. The Vatican Observatory has also collaborated in international conferences on science and religion. The discipline has several key journals, including *Zygon, Perspectives in Science and Christian Faith, Theology and Science, Reviews in Science and Religion*, and *Science and Christian Belief*. The Templeton Foundation and other organizations stimulate research through grants, pointing to wider cultural, political, and intellectual interests (evangelicals became more engaged in the early twenty-first century—especially through the **BioLogos Foundation**—as debates intensified over evolution and related issues). In short, science and theology promises to remain a lively, and contested, interdisciplinary field.

Hans Madueme

REFERENCES AND RECOMMENDED READING

Barbour, Ian. 1966. *Issues in Science and Religion.* New York: Harper & Row.
———. 1990. *Religion in an Age of Science.* San Francisco: Harper & Row.
———. 2000. *When Science Meets Religion: Enemies, Strangers, or Partners?* New York: HarperCollins.
Brooke, John Hedley. 1991. *Science and Religion: Some Historical Perspectives.* Cambridge: Cambridge University Press.
Clark, David K. 2003. *To Know and Love God: Method for Theology.* Wheaton, IL: Crossway.
Clayton, Philip, ed. 2006. *The Oxford Handbook of Religion and Science.* Oxford: Oxford University Press.
Cohen, I. Bernard, ed. 1990. *Puritanism and the Rise of Modern Science: The Merton Thesis.* New Brunswick, NJ: Rutgers University Press.
Dillenberger, John. 1960. *Protestant Thought and Natural Science.* Nashville: Abingdon.
Draper, John William. (1874) 1882. *History of the Conflict between Religion and Science.* London: Kegan Paul.
Foster, Michael. 1934. "The Christian Doctrine of Creation and the Rise of Modern Science." *Mind* 43:446–68.
Gould, Stephen J. 1999. *Rocks of Ages: Science and Religion in the Fullness of Life.* New York: Ballantine.
Harrison, Peter, ed. 2010. *The Cambridge Companion to Science and Religion.* Cambridge: Cambridge University Press.
Hooykas, Reijer. 1972. *Religion and the Rise of Modern Science.* Grand Rapids: Eerdmans.
Jaki, Stanley. 1979. *The Origin of Science and the Science of Its Origin.* South Bend, IN: Regnery-Gateway.
Lindberg, David C., and Ronald L. Numbers, eds. 1986. *God and Nature: Historical Essays on the Encounter between Christianity and Science.* Berkeley: University of California Press.
Livingstone, David. 1987. *Darwin's Forgotten Defenders: The Encounter between Evangelical Theology and Evolutionary Thought.* Grand Rapids: Eerdmans.
Numbers, Ronald L. 2006. *The Creationists: From Scientific Creationism to Intelligent Design.* Rev. and enl. ed. Cambridge, MA: Harvard University Press.
Pearcey, Nancy, and Charles Thaxton. *The Soul of Science: Christian Faith and Natural Philosophy.* Wheaton, IL: Crossway.
Southgate, Christopher, ed. 2005. *God, Humanity and the Cosmos.* Rev. and enl. ed. New York: T&T Clark.
White, Andrew Dickson. (1896) 1960. *A History of Warfare of Science with Theology in Christendom.* 2 vols. New York: Dover.

THEORIES OF TRUTH. The general notion of truth is massively contested. There are many theories of truth, including those with a fairly long history (the correspondence theory, the coherence theory, and the pragmatist theory) and those far more recent (the performative theory, the minimalist theory, and the disquotational view). Postmodern thought has also generated various theories of truth (or nontruth). There is massive and highly sophisticated literature on the topic, though it seems accurate to claim that the correspondence theory has been the view held by most philosophers who are confessing evangelicals.

It goes without saying that the concept of truth is crucial both to the central narrative of Scripture and to historic Christianity. As N. T. Wright claims, "The Christian is committed to the belief that certain things about the past are true"; further, Scripture itself "employs a rich and varied vocabulary of truth" (Wright 1992, 136). Kevin Vanhoozer also notes that truth is first and foremost an attribute of God that emphasizes divine reliability and steadfastness (Vanhoozer 2005, 819).

A full and comprehensive analysis of truth would critically examine all the views mentioned above as well as offering a careful discussion of the issue of truth bearers (focusing on what it is that conveys truth) and the issue of truth makers (what it is to which truth bearers refer). Given space limitations and the esoteric nature of much of the literature, this article focuses on four leading theories of truth: pragmatist, Rorty's view (as representative of a postmodern view), coherence, and correspondence. For the sake of simplicity, it will be assumed that propositions (not sentences or statements) are the primary truth bearers and that states of affairs (not facts) are the best candidate for truth makers.

The discussion below centers on what has been called the *metaphysical project of truth* (which focuses on the nature of truth) rather than the *epistemological project*, which centers on what it means for a belief to be rationally justified.

The Pragmatist View

Pragmatism has flourished in the United States since the late 1800s. **William James**, Charles Peirce, and John Dewey have all championed some version of pragmatism. James, whose remarks on truth are not easily integrated into a coherent whole, can be understood to be committed to the idea that *a proposition (P) is true if and only if holding the belief is useful to the prospective believer(s)*. We should begin by noting that James is correct in thinking that true beliefs do tend to be useful or beneficial, while false beliefs generally lack such utility.

But James's theory of truth is seriously flawed. Three of the main problems are the following. (1) Some true beliefs are not useful. We may be better off not knowing what certain people think about us. Conversely, some false beliefs may be helpful. Having an inflated view of self may contribute to one's success, even though this degree of confidence is not rooted in reality. (2) Usefulness clearly varies from person to person. Truth, on the other hand, is not person relative. This indicates that truth and usefulness are fundamentally distinct notions, while James's theory requires they be identical. (3) Finally, James errs in taking one important element of truth and absolutizing it, ignoring the obvious counterexamples mentioned above.

Rorty's View

Richard Rorty was one of the most influential philosophers of the past 50 years. He began his career in the tradition of analytic philosophy and ended it teaching comparative literature. All this is suggestive of Rorty's transformation from someone committed to objective truth to someone deeply skeptical of truth and much of the Western philosophical tradition. In his seminal *Philosophy and the Mirror of Nature* (1981), Rorty puts forward the idea that *truth is what your peers will let you get away with*.

Despite the fact that Rorty's cleverness and ingenuity are undeniable, his take on truth is fraught with danger. **Alvin Plantinga** takes Rorty to task by showing the consequences of his view of truth. If Rorty is correct, then AIDS, the Holocaust, and human suffering in general can be eliminated simply by convincing one's peers not to let one say such things happen. Whether or not Rorty is guilty of such a silly view, he does clearly avoid any sort of commitment to the idea that there is a mind-independent reality that is genuinely knowable by humans. The vast majority of modern scientists, most of them scientific realists, would see Rorty's view on truth as a nonstarter.

The Coherence View

The coherence view was fashionable in the late 1800s and early 1900s. Bradley, Blanshard, and others held this view. On this view, *a proposition (P) is true if and only if it coheres with the set of beliefs already believed*. A proposition failing to mesh with other held beliefs would be rejected as false.

If we think of our set of beliefs as a huge puzzle, in order for the proposition under consideration to be true, it must fit or mesh with the other beliefs. Both logical consistency (no two held beliefs contradict each other) and some sort of inferential relationship (belief B is somehow inferred from belief A) are central to this idea of truth. But coherence theory also runs into serious difficulties. (1) Coherence is (at best) a necessary but not a sufficient condition of truth; one's belief that the people next door are Martians may well cohere with the individual's set of beliefs, but this hardly guarantees its truth. (2) Contradictory beliefs can cohere: a proposition P may cohere with person A but not-P may cohere with person B. And on coherence grounds alone, there would be no way to settle this dispute. (3) Thus, on the coherence view, truth is relative to each person (and her particular set of beliefs).

For all these reasons, most Christian scholars have seen coherence as an inadequate theory of truth.

The Correspondence View

A good case can be made that the commonsense view of truth is the correspondence theory. The basic idea is that "truth involves a relation to reality." We can express this by claiming that *a proposition is true if and only if its content fits reality.* Consider Alfred Tarski's well-known dictum: "Snow is white if and only if snow is white." This is not a mere tautology as is sometimes thought. As **John Searle** argues, "Snow is white" specifies a particular proposition. But the right-hand side specifies the state of affairs that must be satisfied if the proposition is true. The words on the left express a timeless proposition while the right hand words describe a condition that is **mind** independent (Searle 1995). If the mind-independent conditions obtain, the proposition in question is true. If it fails to occur, then the proposition is false. That is, reality is the truth maker.

Bertrand Russell and **Ludwig Wittgenstein** believed that an extremely strong version of correspondence was defensible. Many more recent defenders (William Alston, Alvin Goldman, John Searle, and others) defend a more modest or minimalist version of correspondence. Here the idea of correspondence as correlation is explicated. Goldman develops the idea of correspondence as fittingness, and he capably defends this against both alternative theories and Russell's overly ambitious version of correspondence.

Stewart E. Kelly

REFERENCES AND RECOMMENDED READING

Alston, William. 1997. *A Realist Conception of Truth.* Ithaca, NY: Cornell University Press.

Goldman, Alvin. 1999. *Knowledge in a Social World.* New York: Oxford University Press.

Kelly, Stewart E. 2011. *Truth Considered and Applied.* Nashville: B&H Academic.

Kirkham, Richard L. 1995. *Theories of Truth.* Cambridge, MA: MIT Press.

Newton-Smith, W. H. 2002. *The Rationality of Science.* London: Routledge.

Plantinga, Alvin. 2000. *Warranted Christian Belief.* New York: Oxford University Press.

Rorty, Richard. 1981. *Philosophy and the Mirror of Nature.* Princeton, NJ: Princeton University Press.

Searle, John R. 1995. *The Social Construction of Reality.* New York: Free Press.

Vanhoozer, Kevin. 2005. "Truth." In *Dictionary for Theological Interpretation of the Bible.* Eds. Kevin J. Vanhoozer, Craig G. Bartholomew, Daniel J. Treier, and N. T. Wright. Grand Rapids: Baker.

Wright, N. T. 1992. *The New Testament and the People of God.* Minneapolis: Fortress.

THOMSON, JOSEPH JOHN.

THOMSON, JOSEPH JOHN. Sir Joseph John Thomson (1856–1940), 1906 Nobel Prize recipient in **physics**, discovered the electron at the end of the nineteenth century while investigating the nature of the mysterious rays that are emitted from the cathode of an evacuated tube, the so-called cathode rays. His discovery of the first fundamental particle ultimately revolutionized our understanding of the essential atomic nature of matter and electricity. Thomson is also credited with inventing the mass spectrometer, a device that later led to the discovery of isotopes and nuclear physics. Because of his groundbreaking work, he has been called the "father of atomic physics."

As director of the Cavendish Laboratory at Cambridge University for 35 years, J. J. Thomson exerted a profound influence on the continuing development of modern physics, both by his theoretical and experimental insights and by his leadership in the education of a generation of other pioneering atomic physicists in the early twentieth century.

Thomson, who exhibited the reserve typical of Englishmen of his day, refrained from frequent public expressions of his Christian faith but nevertheless practiced the spiritual disciplines of daily **prayer** and Bible reading. He frequented chapel and took an active interest in the local mission of his parish. He was a lifelong communicant of the Anglican Church who in his inaugural address as president of the British Association for the Advancement of Science remarked, quoting Psalm 111:2: "As we conquer peak after peak we see in front of us regions full of interest and beauty, but we do not see our goal, we do not see the horizon; in the distance tower still higher peaks, which will yield to those who ascend them still wider prospects, and deepen the feeling, the truth of which is emphasized by every advance in science, that 'Great are the Works of the Lord'" (Thomson 1909, 257).

Indeed, Thomson was echoing the motto that appears in Latin over the doors of the old Cavendish Laboratory, probably instigated by the lab's founder, **James Clerk Maxwell**, also a practicing Christian and notable scientist. The full text reads, "Great are the works of the Lord; they are pondered by all who delight in them" (Ps. 111:2). In the same psalm, the writer admonishes that "the fear of the Lord is the beginning of wisdom" (v. 10). Among the lists of devout scientists marshaled to refute the contention that a scientist of note cannot believe in the God of the Bible, Thomson's name stands out as a notable, albeit not an isolated, counterexample.

Samuel E. Matteson

REFERENCES AND RECOMMENDED READING

Navarro, Jaume. 2012. *A History of the Electron: J. J. and G. P. Thomson.* Cambridge: Cambridge University Press, 2012.

Thomson, J. J. 1909. "The British Association at Winnipeg [Inaugural Address],"
Nature 81 (August 26): 248–57.

TIME. Time is that dimension of reality whose moments are ordered by *earlier/later than* relations.

Time plays a significant role in Christian theology. Most fundamentally, there is the question of the reality of time. In contrast to some pantheistic religions, the Judeo-Christian tradition takes time to be an objective feature of the world. Moreover, time is conceived to be linear, not circular, as history moves toward God's previsioned ends. Hence **eschatology** becomes an important issue for that tradition. The doctrine of everlasting life of the redeemed implies that time will never cease.

The theological importance of time becomes most evident when we ask about God's relationship to time. One of God's essential attributes is his eternality. To say that God is eternal means minimally that God exists permanently: He never came into nor will he ever pass out of being. This minimal understanding leaves it open whether God exists timelessly or temporally; that is to say, whether God transcends the temporal dimension altogether or exists at every moment of time from the infinite past through the infinite future.

The answer to this question is likely to depend on one's view of time. On a tenseless view of time, all temporal events are equally real and existent, the distinction between past, present, and future being merely a subjective feature of human **consciousness**. By contrast, on a tensed view of time, the distinction between past, present, and future is an objective feature of reality, and things really do come into and pass out of existence.

On a tenseless view, it is natural to think of God as existing timelessly "outside" the four-dimensional space-time block, which exists coeternally with God in an asymmetrical relation of ontological dependence. But on a tensed view, it is difficult to see how God could exist atemporally. For if God is really related to the world, he stands in changing relations with things as they change and therefore must be in time. Moreover, if there are tensed facts about the world, then God, as an omniscient being, must know them. But then God's knowledge will be constantly changing as the facts change, so that God must be temporal. Theologians are increasingly attracted to understanding God to exist temporally, though philosophers of time remain deeply divided on whether time is tensed or tenseless.

On a tensed view of time, the reality of everlasting life implies that the future is potentially infinite, that is to say, the series of temporal events increases endlessly toward **infinity** as a limit. But is past time infinite or finite? If God exists temporally, either alternative poses difficulties. If time is infinite, how could God endure through an infinite number of successive, equal intervals so as to arrive at today? And why did God refrain for so long (infinity) from creating the world? On the other hand, if time had a beginning at the moment of creation, then, since God had no beginning, how does he relate to time? One possible answer is to hold that God *sans* the world exists timelessly but since the creation of the world temporally. God's temporality is thus not an essential but a contingent property of God, dependent on his free choice to create a temporal world and to enter into relations with it.

William Lane Craig

REFERENCES AND RECOMMENDED READING

Craig, William Lane. 2001. *God, Time, and Eternity.* Dordrecht: Kluwer Academic.
DeWeese, Garrett J. 2004. *God and the Nature of Time.* Aldershot, UK: Ashgate.
Ganssle, Gregory E., and David M. Woodruff, eds. 2002. *God and Time.* Oxford: Oxford University Press.
Leftow, Brian. 1991. *Time and Eternity.* Ithaca, NY: Cornell University Press.
Macey, Samuel, ed. 1994. *The Encyclopedia of Time.* New York: Garland.
Padgett, Alan G. 1992. *God, Eternity, and the Nature of Time.* New York: St. Martin's.
Sider, Theodore. 2003. *Four-Dimensionalism.* New York: Oxford University Press.

TIPLER, FRANK J. Frank J. Tipler (1947–) obtained his PhD in general relativity in 1976 from the University of Maryland. In 1979 he worked as a postdoctoral scholar for John A. Wheeler, one of the most renowned physicists of the later 1900s. Tipler holds the title of professor in the Department of Mathematics at Tulane University, New Orleans, Louisiana, where he has worked since 1981. Frank Tipler has specialized in extrapolating the concepts of cosmology and relativity theory into realms usually avoided by scientists. Tipler has published nearly 60 scientific articles in peer-reviewed journals, including eight papers in the prestigious journal *Nature*.

Two of his more controversial books include *The Physics of Immortality* (1994) and *The Physics of Christianity* (2007). Most people, even scientists and theologians, think **physics** is an odd tool to use in investigating either eternal life or religion. Some feel the same even after reading Tipler's books (Murphy and Ellis 1996, 62, 262). Tipler wrote *The Physics of Immortality* about four years before the discovery of the accelerating expansion rate of the universe (Nobel Prize). This discovery, along with a more accurate determination of the current rate of expansion of the universe, contradicts the central theory of Tipler's 1994 book. In a later work (Tipler 2007), he proposes an extravagant process to turn the universal expansion into a contraction, namely, that in the future, intelligent life will consume or annihilate all matter in the universe.

A key thesis of Tipler's ideas is that quantum mechanics implies a backward **causation** of events in the universe. He argues that God is the ultimate final state of the universe, so that every event in the history of the universe "is determined by the action of God." In *The Physics of Christianity*, Tipler remarkably attempts to extrapolate physics concepts to "explain" the central tenets of the Christian faith, such as the **virgin birth**, the **resurrection of Jesus**, and the second coming of Christ. The Christian physicist can rightly challenge the idea that God would be limited to using the physics of this universe to accomplish his divine purposes. God could certainly use means beyond scientific scrutiny to carry out his will. Are Tipler's viewpoints supportive of Christianity? To this question, the response of Jesus to his disciples could perhaps be applied: "The one who is not against us is for us" (Mark 9:40 ESV).

Together with **John Barrow**, Tipler published *The Anthropic Cosmological Principle* (1986), which has been widely influential and informative in discussions on the religious implications of scientific discoveries about the universe. Barrow and Tipler highlighted a series of "coincidences" between the values of various fundamental constants of **nature** and observed that "the possibility of our own existence seems to hinge precariously upon these coincidences." (Barrow and Tipler 1986, xi). In contrast to conclusions Tipler reached in *The Physics of Immortality*, the advance of scientific discovery has not undermined the thesis of *The Anthropic Cosmological Principle*, but has revealed further knife-edge "coincidences" in nature that render the universe congenial for life (Davies 2006).

Eric R. Hedin

REFERENCES AND RECOMMENDED READING

Barrow, John D., and Frank J. Tipler. 1986. *The Anthropic Cosmological Principle.* Oxford: Oxford University Press.

Davies, Paul. 2006. *The Goldilocks Enigma: Why Is the Universe Just Right for Life?* London: Allen Lane.

Murphy, Nancey, and George F. R. Ellis. 1996. *On the Moral Nature of the Universe: Theology, Cosmology, and Ethics.* Minneapolis: Augsburg Fortress.

Nobel Prize. 2011. "The Nobel Prize in Physics 2011." October 4. www.nobel prize.org/nobel_prizes/physics/laureates/2011/press.html.

Tipler, Frank J. 1994. *The Physics of Immortality: Modern Cosmology, God and the Resurrection of the Dead.* New York: Doubleday.

————. 2003. "Intelligent Life in Cosmology." *International Journal of Astrobiology* 2:141–48.

————. 2004. "Refereed Journals: Do They Insure Quality or Enforce Orthodoxy?" In *Uncommon Dissent: Intellectuals Who Find Darwinism Unconvincing.* Ed. William A. Dembski, 115–30. Wilmington, DE: ISI Books.

————. 2007. *The Physics of Christianity.* New York: Doubleday.

TORRANCE, THOMAS FORSYTH.

The Very Reverend Professor Thomas Forsyth Torrance (1913–2007) was professor of Christian dogmatics in the University of Edinburgh, Scotland, from 1952 to 1979. He was one of the most significant English-speaking theologians of the twentieth century. A signal feature of his work was his contribution to the discussion between theology and science, having among theologians a unique focus on the philosophy of the natural sciences.

Internationally recognized, Forsyth served as president of Académie Internationale des Sciences Religieuses from 1972 to 1981. He was a fellow of the Royal Society of Edinburgh and a fellow of the British Academy. In 1969 he won the Collins Prize for his book *Theological Science*, and he was awarded the Templeton Prize for Progress in Religion in 1978. He also served as moderator of the General Assembly of the Church of Scotland from 1976 to 1977, and he held doctorates in divinity, literature, and science. He wrote 10 books that primarily address the interrelationship of theology and science, including *God and Rationality, Theological and Natural Science, Reality and Scientific Theology, Christian Theology and Scientific Culture, Divine and Contingent Order,* and *Transformation and Convergence in the Frame of Knowledge.*

Torrance's interest in the interrelationship of theology with science was generated especially by his recognition of the interconnection between creation and the **incarnation**, grace, reconciliation, and **revelation**. He took no interest in using science to prove the **existence of God** or the **resurrection of Jesus**, nor to provide independent yet doctrinal knowledge of the nature, character, or purposes of the triune God. Rather, he believed on biblical and theological grounds that such was impossible. Only God knows God; only God reveals God. Jesus Christ is God's only self-revelation. Jesus Christ is not created but is begotten from the Father. Creation is not from the Father but is created from nothing.

Thomas was convinced that the two human disciplines of theology and science, while distinguished by their ontologically distinct objects of study, God and creation, could nevertheless mutually benefit each other in specified ways. He also demonstrated how widespread misunderstandings about the nature of theology and science had contributed to distrust and an unnecessary breakdown of constructive interaction between the two. This rift he sought to reconcile in his scholarship.

Torrance drew on biblical theology and also on early church theology, especially the works of Basil, Athanasius, Cyril of Alexandria, and the sixth-century theologian and physicist John Philoponos. In tracing the history of the **philosophy of science**, he explored and found illuminating the thought of **Blaise Pascal**, **Michael Faraday**, **James Clerk Maxwell**, **Albert Einstein**, Max Planck, Georg Cantor, Kurt Gödel, Alan Turing, Ilya Prigogine, **Bertrand Russell**, and **Michael Polanyi**. Torrance referred to his project as a "theology of the sciences" and clearly distinguished it from classical forms of **natural theology**.

Torrance thought what was needed was not so much having new ideas, but having new ways of thinking, asking new kinds of questions, ones that really comported with the nature of what we were attempting to know. He claimed that expanding our knowledge of God or of creation would require certain key correctives: (1) recognizing the contingent rationality of creation; (2) recognizing the unity and intelligibility of all created reality; (3) ordering our ways of knowing (modes of rationality) to the nature of the objects of investigation; (4) questioning assumed mechanical, logico-causal, or static and ideal closed forms of description, and pursing dynamic and ontorelational ways of describing the order of reality instead; (5) eschewing dichotomous ways of conceptualizing divine or created realities and relations; (6) recognizing the multilevel structure of reality, higher levels being more comprehensive of lower; (7) recognizing that understanding should be open and not insisting on closed, self-explanatory formulations so that beliefs of an analogous sort could operate in both theology and science.

Pursuing the knowledge of God according to revelation and to creation within such a framework, Torrance believed, would lead to advances on both fronts, healing the rifts between theory and experiment, why and how, what is and what ought to be, and the modern chasm that has grown between the sciences and humanities. In this way, a deeper knowledge of creation could arise that would be congenial with Christian faith, life, and worship, and it would enable humanity to serve as faithful stewards over creation.

Gary W. Deddo

REFERENCES AND RECOMMENDED READING

Colyer, Elmer. 2007. *How to Read T. F. Torrance*. Downers Grove, IL: InterVarsity.
Torrance, Thomas F. 1996. *Theological Science*. Edinburgh: T&T Clark.
———. 2002. *Theological and Natural Science*. Eugene, OR: Wipf and Stock.

TOWER OF BABEL. The primeval history in Genesis 1–11 gives a sweeping description of the world before the time of Abraham. The account of creation (chaps. 1–2) presents a world and its inhabitants (**Adam and Eve**) living in harmony with their Creator. This harmony is broken by Adam and Eve's rebellion and subsequent punishment (chap. 3). God, nonetheless, does not completely destroy his creatures, but rather continues to pursue them to bring about reconciliation. The remainder of the primeval history presents three additional stories (Cain and Abel [4:1–16], **the flood** [6–9], the Tower of Babel [11:1–9]) of human sin and divine judgment as well as describing tokens of grace that show God's continued involvement in the lives of his sinful human creatures (Clines 1997).

The final story of the primeval narrative is the account of the Tower of Babel. This episode is of interest to the relationship between **science and the Bible** because a straightforward reading suggests that it explains the development of multiple languages.

The story begins with the announcement that "the whole world had one language and a common speech" (11:1). Because of previous sins, God had scattered them, but now they gathered together in the plain of Shinar (Babylon) and decided to build a city with a tower that reached to the heavens. Most Old Testament scholars recognize this structure as a Babylonian ziggurat, or stepped pyramid, made out of mudbrick. The idea of a ziggurat is captured by the name given to the famous ziggurat of Babylon known from historical sources as Etemenanki, or "the house of the foundation of heaven and earth."

God, though, announces to his divine council that he will "confuse their language so they will not understand each other" (11:7). As a result, humans are unable to complete their plans and are once again scattered.

Thus the Tower of Babel story is similar to the accounts of **the fall**, Cain and Abel, and the flood in that it gives an account of human sin and divine judgment (which is always announced before its execution by a divine judgment speech). However, scholars have noted that the Babel story is missing a crucial element found in the previous three — the token of grace. God extended garments to Adam and Eve (3:21), protected Cain from violence with a mark (4:15), and allowed Noah and his family to survive the flood and begin the human race once again (6:8).

The absence of the token of grace in Genesis 11:1–9

should not cause us to miss its presence in Genesis 10, where we have a genealogy-like text that divides the sons of the three sons of Noah into a total of 70 descendants according to "their territories by their clans within their nations, each with its own language" (10:5; see also 10:20, 31). The token of grace then in the Babel story may be found in the fact that God did not eradicate the possibility of human communication in his judgment but made it much more difficult. Even so, the Babel account departs from the typical pattern found in the other postcreation stories in the primeval narrative, and indeed goes out of its way to do so, since it is clear that Genesis 10:1 – 11:9 is purposefully told out of chronological sequence. After all, Genesis 10 speaks of a diversity of languages before the story that narrates how humans moved from a single language shared by all people to many languages.

The reason for the departure for the usual pattern is likely because the tower story is the final one of the primeval narrative. The next chapter, which describes the call of Abraham (12:1 – 3), will show God working in a new direction to bring about reconciliation with his sinful human creatures.

But what are we to make of this account of the origins of multiple languages? Should it be taken at face value and provide the foundation of the modern discipline of linguistics?

Some scholars today treat the Tower of Babel story and the genealogy of Genesis 10 as an etiology of the presence of diverse languages (an explanation of origins). Not all scholars who believe that Genesis 10:1 – 11:9 is an etiology would agree that it is historically true. Indeed, many linguists today would argue that human languages did not derive from a single original language, though any treatment of the beginning of human languages is quite speculative. Most scholars, however (Longman 2016; Walton 2009), understand that Genesis 10 is a primitive linguistic map in the form of a genealogy and reflects not the immediate postflood period, but rather the perception of the known world at the time of Moses (or after) in the second half of the second millennium BC.

Though the language of father-son is used in the genealogy, Walton points out, "kinship language is sometimes used in the Bible to reflect political associations" (Walton 2009, 56). Indeed, though this chapter is in the form of a segmented genealogy (see **Genealogy**), it lists not only individuals, but also nations as part of the genealogy (i.e., "the Kittites and the Rodanites," v. 4). In any case, what is important to bear in mind is that these may be, as mentioned above, perceptions of linguistic and national relationships,

not actual relationships. (As Walton [2009, 55] points out, as one of many possible examples, Canaan is in reality Semitic, not a Hamitic language [10:6].)

It is true that when modern linguistics began some two centuries ago, it adopted its fundamental terminology from this chapter, which persists until today. We still speak of S(h)emitic, Hamitic, and Japhethic languages today. That said, modern linguistics would not make the same connections between languages that are presented in this chapter (see **Language, Origin of**). Though there is a historical reference behind the Table of Nations of Genesis 10 (it reflects political realities most likely of the second half of the second millennium), its primary purpose is theologically cataloging the further fragmentation of humanity as the result of sin.

Tremper Longman III

REFERENCES AND RECOMMENDED READING

Clines, D. J. A. 1997. *The Theme of the Pentateuch.* 2nd ed. Edinburgh: T&T Clark.
Longman, Tremper, III. 2016. *Genesis.* Story of God Bible Commentary. Grand Rapids: Zondervan.
Walton, John. "Genesis." 2009. In *Zondervan Illustrated Bible Backgrounds Commentary*, vol. 1. Ed. J. Walton. Grand Rapids: Zondervan.

TRINITY, THE. The distinctively Christian doctrine of the Trinity affirms the existence of three divine persons — Father, Son, and Holy Spirit — in one being (Torrance 2001). Thus God is not a person, but rather a personal being. The Athanasian Creed (c. AD 500) speaks of "one God in Trinity and Trinity in unity," expressing distinction ("neither confounding the Persons") while sharing in the same being ("nor dividing the substance") and avoiding polytheism ("not three Gods") and subordinationism ("equal in glory and coeternal in majesty"). This theological formulation follows the spirit of the Council of Nicea (AD 325) — the Son, contra Arius, is "of one substance" with the Father — and the Constantinopolitan Council (AD 381) that affirmed the Spirit's deity and concluded that there are three persons in one being.

Christian orthodoxy attempts to hold in tension the following three trinitarian characteristics: threeness, oneness, and equality. Threeness pertains to persons sharing divine being (though avoiding tritheism — a version of polytheism); oneness pertains to the divine being or even nature (though avoiding the heresy of modalism — a divine person revealing himself in different "modes," such as Father, Son, and Spirit). And though some theologians hold to an eternal, necessary hierarchy within the Godhead itself, we have good reason to affirm full equality in rank within the Trinity and thus to reject subordinationism (Deddo 2008; Nicole 1980).

Thomas **Aquinas** rightly asserted that the Trinity cannot be known by natural reason but only through special **revelation**. Indeed, the Scriptures affirm not only God's oneness—that is, monotheism ("the LORD/God is one": Deut. 6:4; James 2:19; cf. Isa. 46:9; Mark 12:29)—but also divine threeness (Matt. 3:16–17; 28:19; John 14:16–17, 26; 15:26; 2 Cor. 13:14; Gal. 4:6). And we have foreshadowings of trinitarian doctrine in the Old Testament with its use of "Word," "Wisdom," and "Spirit" (e.g., Gen. 1:2; 6:3; Num. 11:29; Ps. 33:6, 9; Prov. 8). Trinitarianism, along with the related doctrine of the **incarnation**, distinguishes the Christian faith from unitarian monotheistic faiths such as Judaism and Islam. Despite this Christian distinctive, theologian Karl Rahner lamented the fact that many Christians are "almost mere monotheists," that is, unitarian. Thus "Rahner's rule" affirmed that the "economic" Trinity (God as he acts in the world or salvation history) is the "immanent" Trinity (God as he is within himself without the creation), and the "immanent" Trinity is the "economic" Trinity.

What this means is that we can be confident that God's saving activity in the world informs us about the very nature of God (Rahner 1970). Though appreciating the spirit of Rahner's efforts, theologians such as Catherine Mowry LaCugna have appropriately indicated that "there remains a certain degree of disparity" between God as he is in himself and God as he is beyond the inner divine life (LaCugna 1993, 219).

Eastern Christianity has historically emphasized God's threeness—namely, the distinctiveness of each divine person, each of whom mutually indwells the other. This emphasis lends itself to a "social trinitarianism" that strongly emphasizes distinctions of the divine persons. Western Christianity, including Roman Catholicism and Protestantism, has more emphatically stressed God's oneness (e.g., **Augustine**'s analogy of three psychological faculties).

This emphasis on oneness has often been accompanied by the debated doctrine of divine simplicity, which is considered speculative and a distraction from the practical, salvific implications of trinitarian doctrine. As an aside, simplicity affirms that God has no parts. Simplicity theorists claim that God has no accidental properties and that there is ultimately no distinction of divine attributes. To this writer, such a view is problematic since (1) it appears more rooted in Greek philosophy than in the biblical text; (2) goodness and omnipotence, say, are clearly distinct properties; (3) it

apparently entails that God as "pure actuality" (and without "potentiality") cannot act freely; (4) the distinction of persons within the Godhead suggests something other than simplicity; and (5) God, upon creating or redeeming the world, in fact acquires accidental properties—say, "Creator," the Word becoming flesh, "Savior" (see Copan and Craig 2004, chap. 5).

While the Trinity is a **mystery**, it is not a contradiction, despite such a charge by Jehovah's Witnesses, Mormons, and Unitarians. Threeness pertains to person while oneness pertains to substance or being. Some Christians are content to go no further than showing that the doctrine of the Trinity contains no formal contradiction. Yet others will use analogies to help show its rational coherence, though common analogies such as water's three different states (the heresy of modalism) or an egg's three parts (the heresy of partialism) should be rejected.

What analogies prove more accurate, useful, and illuminating? Three analogies may suffice. A "constitution" view attempts to avoid part-whole relations to preserve the unity of the divine persons. Consider, say, the eighteenth-century Venetian painter Giovanni Canaletto's etching *View of a Town with a Bishop's Tomb* of an (apparently) monolithic stone structure comprised of a tomb, a canopy upheld by four Ionic pillars, atop which are statues of the four Evangelists and an angel. For our purposes, let's say we have a carved piece of solid marble that is pillar, statue, and fountain all in one column. Likewise, while not a material being, God in his nature is "formed" in a manifold way; the divine nature is constituted by Father, Son, and Spirit rather than each person possessing the divine nature (Brower and Rea 2005). Jeremy Begbie suggests the analogy of notes of a chord—say, C, E, and G. Each note alone fills the whole of the "heard" space, but when the other two notes are added, we have an integrated sound within the same space with distinctive, mutually enhancing notes (Begbie 2000).

Social trinitarians, who argue that some type of part-whole relation is inescapable, emphasize three centers of divine personal awareness and will. Thus they may use another kind of analogy, such as the mythological three-headed dog Cerberus that guards Hades' gates. Though a single organism (substance)—one dog, not three dogs—Cerberus has three distinct centers of awareness, each with the same canine nature (Moreland and Craig 2003, 574–95). In the natural world we have comparable analogies in, say, two-headed snakes or turtles. In such cases we have distinct centers of awareness within one unified organism. Likewise, God is one immaterial **soul** (substance) with three distinct centers of **consciousness**, rationality, and will (persons) who are deeply and necessarily interconnected, sharing the same unique divine nature and acting in unison in creation, redemption, resurrection, and new creation. Whichever type of analogy is used, we have three-ness and oneness without contradiction and with plausibility.

What are some implications of this rich doctrine? First, the triune God furnishes the grounding for personhood, relationality, and community. God is no isolated self. There is both union as well as distinction within God. So it can be said that God is both community and unity, distinction though not separation (Hart 2003, 174).

Second, the Trinity contributes to a resolution of the problem of "the one and the many"—what philosopher **William James** called philosophy's most central problem. The ancient philosopher Heraclitus claimed that ultimate reality is many and changing (no unity), while the philosopher Parmenides held that reality is one and unchanging (no plural-ity). The triune God furnishes us with metaphysical resources to account for both unity and plurality (Gunton 1993).

Third, the Trinity addresses many of the concerns raised by both feminist and panentheist/process theologians, who emphasize a dynamic relationality between God and the uni-verse. Some of them use the body-soul analogy to posit an eternally interdependent God-world relationship, although this is undermined by the biblical doctrine of creation out of noth-ing, which is supported by the strong scientific **confirmation** of **big bang** cosmology (Copan and Craig 2004). Moreover, the doctrine of the Trinity emphasizes God's intrinsic and necessary relationality, rendering the relational "contribution" of **panentheism** superfluous. Indeed, despite the appeal of panentheism to forge a model for—or even viable synthesis between—science and theology, the rich resources of trinitarian theology are more than adequate for this (see Cooper 2006).

Paul Copan

REFERENCES AND RECOMMENDED READING

Begbie, Jeremy. 2000. "Hearing God in C Major." In *Beholding the Glory: Incarnation through the Arts*. Grand Rapids: Baker.

Brower, Jeffrey E., and Michael C. Rea. 2005. "Understanding the Trinity." *Logos: A Journal of Catholic Thought and Culture* 8 (1): 147–57.

Cooper, John W. 2006. *Panentheism: The Other God of the Philosophers from Plato to the Present*. Grand Rapids: Eerdmans.

Copan, Paul, and William Lane Craig. 2004. *Creation Out of Nothing: A Biblical, Philosophical, and Scientific Exploration*. Grand Rapids: Baker Academic; Leicester, UK: Apollos.

Deddo, Gary W. 2008. "The Trinity and Gender: Theological Reflections on the Differences of Divine and Human Persons." *Priscilla Papers* 22, no. 4 (Autumn): 4–13.

Gunton, Colin. 1993. *The One, the Three, and the Many*. Cambridge: Cambridge University Press.

Hart, David Bentley. 2003. *The Beauty of the Infinite: The Aesthetics of Christian Truth*. Grand Rapids: Eerdmans.

Hasker, William. *Metaphysics and the Tri-Personal God*. Oxford: Oxford University Press.

LaCugna, Catherine Mowry. 1993. *God for Us: The Trinity and Christian Life*. San Francisco: HarperSanFrancisco.

Moreland, J. P., and William Lane Craig. 2003. *Philosophical Foundations for the Christian Worldview*. Downers Grove, IL: IVP Academic.

Nicole, Roger. 1980. "The Meaning of the Trinity." In *One God in Trinity*. Eds. Peter Toon and James D. Spiceland. Westchester, IL: Cornerstone.

Rahner, Karl. 1970. *The Trinity*. Trans. Joseph Donceel. New York: Herder & Herder.

Torrance, Thomas F. 2001. *The Christian Doctrine of God: One Being, Three Persons*. New York: Bloomsbury.

TURING TEST. The celebrated British mathematician Alan Turing (1912–54) sought to clarify and answer the question, "Can machines think?" (for an overview, see Oppy and Dowe 2011; for biographical context, see Hodges 2014). To that end, he replaced the question with a test, asking, "Are there imaginable digital computers which would do well in the imitation game?" (see the seminal paper, Turing 1950, 442).

The game consists of an interrogator interacting with two respondents located in a different room. Knowing that one respondent is a computer and the other a person, the interrogator's task is to determine which is which by asking questions remotely via teleprompter. The computer seeks to hinder correct identification, while the person aims to help it. Turing believed that by about the year 2000, computers would be able to play the game so well that "an average interrogator would not have more than a 70 percent chance of making the right identification after about five minutes of questioning" (Turing 1950, 442).

This criterion for passing is incomplete, failing to specify the number of trials over which success is required. However, it seems Turing understood the game probabilistically such that better performance increases the likelihood of intelli-gence (thought). Despite the supposed deceptive successes of even simple conversational programs (see, e.g., Weizenbaum 1966), this so-called Turing Test remains extremely chal-lenging given the interrogator's focus on unmasking the computer, and at the time of writing there are no uncon-troversial instances of a machine succeeding in the game in the way that Turing envisioned.

A more important concern is whether Turing was right to believe that a Turing Test-passing machine must be judged to exhibit a degree of thought. Turing lacked positive sup-port for his belief and so focused on refuting objections. One theme of these is that to be recognized as intelligent, a machine should not be required to possess capacities that are not demonstrably necessary for thought in the human case. Turing also replies to the Christian objection that thought requires a God-given **soul** by suggesting that it is logically possible that God could ensoul a Turing Test-passing machine, which would be a qualified recipient in virtue of its behavioral capacity. However, many Christians would consider severely behaviorally impaired individuals to be ensouled, rendering Turing's sop unsatisfactory.

Today Turing would likely find the missing positive support for his use of the imitation game in the functionalist claim that mental states are defined by their roles rather than their constitution (see **Functionalism**). Success in the game could then be offered in the way that many have received it: as a sufficient and perhaps necessary condition for thought. The most oft-cited objection to this stronger claim is **John Searle**'s **Chinese Room** thought experiment that describes a system equivalent to a Turing Test-passing computer, but for which thinking is obviously absent. From this the conclusion follows that digital computers are not candidates for intelligent thought (see Searle 1980). Searle's argument continues to provide a focus for debate about the relationship between human thought and computation (see **Soul**).

Jonathan Loose

REFERENCES AND RECOMMENDED READING

Hodges, Andrew. 2014. *Alan Turing: The Enigma.* London: Penguin.

Oppy, Graham, and David Dowe. 2011. "The Turing Test." In *Stanford Encyclopedia of Philosophy.* Ed. Edward N. Zalta. Spring. http://plato.stanford.edu/archives/spr2011/entries/turing-test/.

Searle, John. 1980. "Minds, Brains and Programs." *Behavioral and Brain Sciences* 3:417–57.

Turing, A. M. 1950. "Computing Machinery and Intelligence." *Mind* 59, no. 236 (October): 433–60.

Weizenbaum, Joseph. 1966. "ELIZA: A Computer Program for the Study of Natural Language Communication between Men and Machines." *Communications of the ACM* 9:36–45.

TWO BOOKS METAPHOR. The two books metaphor is a very old idea, perhaps dating as far back as Origen. **Augustine**, **Galileo**, and others used this metaphor down the centuries to characterize our knowledge of God and creation. The basic idea is that God has written two books, the book of nature and the book of Scripture.

Revelation

The two books metaphor draws on the concept of *revelation*. At its broadest, **revelation** means knowledge received

as a gift that stands in need of being understood (Gunton 1995). Although the triune God is the ultimate giver of this gift, revelation can be mediated through nature or a human being (e.g., by means of written texts or lectures).

Scientific inquiry, for example, mediates provisional knowledge about nature to us; in other words, scientific inquiry *reveals* knowledge as we study creation. Scientists do not have unmediated access to nature. The knowledge scientific inquiry produces involves the mediation of instruments, theoretical constructs, and data analysis. Furthermore, the background knowledge and presuppositions scientists carry with them play important roles in the discovery of knowledge (Gauch 2012). What data, facts, and truths mean is mediated by the experimental and theoretical practices of the various scientific communities as well as the assumptions these communities make. Creation in these domains reveals itself to scientists as they go about their normal work.

The core idea for the two books metaphor, then, is that all knowledge is revealed, whether it is disclosed through reading, discussion, controlled experiments, or any other means. Theologians usually distinguish two categories of revelation (1) general or natural revelation and (2) special or specific revelation. General revelation is typically thought of as general knowledge about God disclosed through nature (e.g., God's power and deity; cf. Rom. 1:20). In contrast, special revelation is specific, highly detailed knowledge about God, redemption, and Christ.

A third, less-discussed subcategory of general revelation is called *creation revelation*. This is specific, detailed knowledge about creation revealed through creation (Bavinck 2003, 341–42; Goheen 1996). Theologians are primarily interested in knowledge of God; so it is not too surprising that they rarely discuss creation revelation. When they focus on the book of nature, they mostly read it with respect to what can be known about God through it. On the other hand, Kepler, Galileo, Boyle, and Newton, among other natural philosophers, generally drew heavily on creation revelation (Bishop 2013). For instance, Boyle describes studying creation as reading from a scroll that is slowly being unrolled (Boyle [1772] 1965). Scientists typically read the book of nature with respect to what can be known about creation through it.

Biblical examples of creation revelation would include 1 Kings 4:29–33, which speaks of the wisdom God gave to Solomon, learning about the appropriate naming of fishes and other animals through the study of those animals, and Isaiah 28:23–29, which speaks of the farmer learning from God by working the soil. Psalm 104 articulates a considerable amount of knowledge about creation that was learned from observing and experiencing creation (cf. Job 12:7 – 8). God gives knowledge through the book of nature and the book of Scripture, and this knowledge is mediated through forms of interpretation or exegesis appropriate for each book.

Relating the Two Books

Since the Holy Spirit is the ultimate author of the two books, what they reveal about creation cannot conflict. Rather, conflicts arise from our handling of the two books. For the book of nature, scientists observe and interpret creation using systematic approaches that lead to well-confirmed theories. At each step of the way, there is the possibility for misunderstanding and error. For the book of Scripture, we work with translations, engage in exegesis, and generate doctrines and theologies. Again, at each step of the way, there is the possibility for misunderstanding and error.

Many science and religion discussions from the late nineteenth century forward assume that conflicts between the two books arise when comparing biblical statements to scientific theories. This way of framing conflicts is fundamentally misguided, however. Humans never have direct, noninterpretive access to either the Bible or nature. Instead, we are always dealing with interpretations of these two books and must ask about the quality and rigor of those interpretations when adjudicating possible conflicts.

We always read these two books with a host of background knowledge and assumptions shaping our engagement with the texts (e.g., a causal-material understanding of creation). For instance, we always already have some theological framework that mediates our reading of the Bible. In turn, as we read Scripture through that framework, our theological frame gets reworked and further articulated. Our theology always shapes our interpretation of Scripture, while our interpretation of Scripture constantly shapes our theology. Similarly for scientists, interpretation is involved in their conceptual, empirical, and analysis practices leading to the ongoing work of theory development that, in turn, guides their conceptual and empirical work.

Taking seriously our human interpretive practices and **the Trinity** as the source of both books implies that we distort science-religion conflicts when framing them in terms of "what Scripture says" versus "what science says." The historical thrust of the two books metaphor has been to avoid what might be called *Bible-first versus science-first* approaches.

A Bible-first approach demands that scientific views must be derived from biblical texts to be relevant. This privileges Scripture over scientific inquiry. A science-first approach demands that biblical interpretation must be derived from scientific inquiry to be relevant. This privileges the methods of scientific inquiry over Scripture. Since creation revelation — God's book of nature — is part of the biblical witness, choosing one of God's two books over the other is a false choice. Instead, we should consider the purposes and different foci of the two books. Special revelation primarily deals with matters of salvation, salvation-history, faith and practice; creation revelation primarily deals with the nature and workings of creation. To take the Bible seriously as authoritative is to treat both of God's books with reverence and care.

Consider this example: We would not choose what we can learn from a book about the history of World War II over a textbook on fluid dynamics when we are trying to understand fluid flow. Rather, the fluid dynamics text is the primary source for the nature of fluid flow and its applications. However, from the history of World War II we could learn about all the ways fluid flow was relevant to the course of the war. Here there is some overlap between two books that have very different purposes and treat very different domains of knowledge. Nevertheless, they can be put into conversation with each other, providing us with the opportunity to learn more than we could by focusing on one at the expense of the other.

The case of God's two books is similar. The knowledge we gain from them can mutually inform us about creation. Think of the two books as conversation partners in a relationship. As with any relationship, such conversation can be carried out well or poorly. There can be quarrels and reconciliations, mutual help and enjoyment, and so forth. Fully engaging both of God's books allows us to learn as much as we can about the totality of divine revelation.

Robert C. Bishop

REFERENCES AND RECOMMENDED READING

Bavinck, Herman. 2003. *Reformed Dogmatics.* Vol. 1, *Prolegomena.* Ed. John Bolt. Trans. John Vriend. Grand Rapids: Baker Academic.

Bishop, Robert C. 2013. "God and Methodological Naturalism in the Scientific Revolution and Beyond." *Perspectives on Science and Christian Faith* 65 (March): 10 – 23.

Boyle, Robert. (1772) 1965. *The Works of the Honorable Robert Boyle.* Ed. T. Birch. 6:796. Hildersheim, Germany: Georg Olms.

Gauch, Hugh. 2012. *Scientific Method in Brief.* Cambridge: Cambridge University Press.

Goheen, Michael. 1996. "Scriptural Revelation, Creational Revelation, and Natural Science: The Issue." In *Facets of Faith and Science*, vol. 4, *Interpreting God's Action in the World.* Ed. Jitse M. van der Meer, 331 – 43. Lanham, MD: University Press of America.

Gunton, Colin. 1995. *A Brief Theology of Revelation.* London: T&T Clark.

U

UNDERDETERMINATION. The underdetermination of theory by the evidence, stated simply, is the generally acknowledged fact that the observational data available at any given time may not be sufficient to decide among competing theories or hypotheses. A pedestrian example of this is given by considering which curve should be drawn to fit a finite collection of data points on a page. In principle, there are infinitely many different curves that pass through a finite number of data points and, in both science and everyday life, we always only have a finite number of data points. So which curve should we choose?

Another way of framing the problem is to note that any theory that posits unobservable features of the world as part of its explanatory apparatus must confront the possibility of competing theories with incompatible collections of unobservables that are equally compatible with the observational data. A standard response to underdetermination is to look for some area where rival theories make different predictions or to appeal to other cognitive virtues, like simplicity or coherence with established science, in order to decide which theory to adopt.

From a logical standpoint, this innocuous version of the underdetermination thesis follows inevitably from avoidance of a common logical fallacy. If theory T predicts observation O and O is observed to occur, scientists obviously take this to be a good thing. But on pain of committing the fallacy of affirming the consequent, observing the occurrence of O doesn't imply the truth of T, for incompatible theories $T_1, T_2,$ and so on may have the *same* observable consequence. If it's raining hard outside my house, the uncovered sidewalk will be wet, but it may also be wet when it isn't raining because I'm running the sprinkler in my yard.

We cannot infer the truth of a theory from its predictive consequences. This weak kind of underdetermination has been recognized for a long time and, from a practical standpoint, can be handled, as mentioned, by privileging the simplest theories compatible with the evidence and, where possible, extending our data collection into new ranges that allow distinctions in observation and prediction among rival theories.

But there are more pernicious forms of the underdetermination thesis to consider. Willard V. O. Quine contends

that given *any* theory T and *any* body of evidence supporting it, there is *always* another empirically equivalent theory equally well supported by the data (Quine [1953] 1980, 1960, 1969, 1975). This claim is supported—insofar as it is supportable—by Quine's argument that "our statements about the external world face the tribunal of sense experience not individually but only as a corporate body.... The unit of empirical significance is the whole of science" (Quine [1953] 1980, 41, 42). This *holism* produces a situation in which *any* theory can be held true, *regardless* of the evidence, if one is willing to alter one's other assumptions about nature (see **Duhem-Quine Thesis**; **Quine, Willard V. O.** for related discussions).

Despite its boldness, Quine's advocacy of the claim that one may retain any theory one wants in the face of any evidence whatsoever falls far short of any defense of the rationality of doing so. Indeed, his argument reduces to noting that one can always hold on to any theory, come what may, by "pleading hallucination or by amending certain statements of the kind called logical laws" ([1953] 1980, 43). But appeal to bare logical possibilities, however irrational, makes radical underdetermination a trivial consequence of Quine's holism and, as **Larry Laudan** ([1990] 2013) has argued, there is *nothing* in any of Quine's writings that would justify affirming that *every* theory, in principle, is equally well supported by *whatever* evidence is available—yet this is what a defense of the rationality of holding on to any theory whatsoever in the face of any evidence whatsoever would require.

Bruce L. Gordon

REFERENCES AND RECOMMENDED READING

Bonk, T. 2008. *Underdetermination: An Essay on Evidence and the Limits of Natural Knowledge.* Dordrecht: Springer.

Douven, Ivan. 2014. "Underdetermination." In *The Routledge Companion to Philosophy of Science.* Eds. M. Curd and S. Psillos, 336–45. 2nd ed. New York: Routledge.

Duhem, P. (1906) 1954. *The Aim and Structure of Physical Theory.* 2nd ed. Princeton, NJ: Princeton University Press.

Earman, J. 1993. "Underdetermination, Realism, and Reason." *Midwest Studies in Philosophy* 18:19–38.

Kukla, A. 1996. "Does Every Theory Have Empirically Equivalent Rivals?" *Erkenntnis* 44:137–66.

Laudan, L. (1990) 2013. "Demystifying Underdetermination." In *Philosophy of Science: The Central Issues.* Eds. M. Curd, J. A. Cover, and C. Pincock, 288–320. 2nd ed. New York: W. W. Norton.

Laudan, L., and J. Leplin. 1991. "Empirical Equivalence and Underdetermination." *Journal of Philosophy* 88:449–72.

Newton-Smith, W. H. 2000. "Underdetermination of Theory by Data." In *A Companion to the Philosophy of Science*. Ed. W. H. Newton-Smith, 532–36. Oxford: Blackwell.

Quine, W. V. O. (1953) 1980. "Two Dogmas of Empiricism." In W. V. O. Quine, *From a Logical Point of View*, 20–46. 2nd ed. Cambridge, MA: Harvard University Press.

———. 1960. *Word and Object*. Cambridge, MA: MIT Press.

———. 1969. "Ontological Relativity." In W. V. O. Quine, *Ontological Relativity and Other Essays*, 26–68. New York: Columbia University Press.

———. 1975. "On Empirically Equivalent Systems of the World." *Erkenntnis* 9:313–28.

Stanford, K. 2013. "Underdetermination of Scientific Theory." In *Stanford Encyclopedia of Philosophy*. Ed. Edward N. Zalta. September 16. http://plato.stanford.edu/entries/scientific-underdetermination/.

UNIFORMITARIANISM. Uniformitarianism is a basic principle in **geology** that presumes the uniformity of natural laws and processes throughout Earth history so that ancient rocks may be interpreted with respect to observable geologic processes. When geology emerged as a science between the middle seventeenth and late eighteenth centuries, most geological interpretations were informed by assumptions of catastrophes of magnitudes unknown in their times, corresponding with their perceptions of the narratives of creation and prehistory in Genesis.

Nineteenth-century catastrophists like Georges Cuvier (1769–1832) generally did not advocate for a recent creation but interpreted discontinuities (unconformities) in the rock record as evidence of rapid, convulsive upheavals between longer epochs of more normal activity in which the strata and fossils were deposited.

James Hutton (1726–97) introduced a new approach that eschewed catastrophic explanations and viewed Earth history in terms of steady-state cycles of known geologic processes. Charles Lyell's (1797–1875) three-volume *Principles of Geology* (1830–33) offered a definitive application of Hutton's "principle of uniformity" to the study of the Earth's crust. In reviewing *Principles*, volume 2, historian **William Whewell** (1794–1866) referred to the contrasting views of the "Uniformitarians and the Catastrophists," thus crystalizing the term that came to identify the Hutton-Lyell approach. Lyell's multipurpose applications of uniformitarianism included: (1) a *methodological* presupposition asserting spatial and temporal invariance of natural laws (*actualism*) and (2) a *substantive* assertion of uniformity of rates and material conditions throughout Earth history (Gould 1965, 1984; Rudwick, 2008). Because most observed geologic change is slow, the concept of *gradualism* (gradual formation) became associated with uniformitarianism.

By the middle of the twentieth century, geologists largely rejected Lyell's substantive assertions because of evidence for extreme-magnitude events preserved in the rock record and recognition that process rates and material conditions have indeed changed on Earth over time. Two prominent examples, now widely accepted, are the Channeled Scablands in Washington State formed by megafloods at the end of the ice age, only 18,000 to 13,000 years ago, and the mass **extinction** at the end of the Cretaceous period, 65 million years ago, related to a global catastrophe resulting from a massive asteroid impact. On a smaller scale, most sediment accumulation is now understood to be episodic, rather than gradual, such as sandstones deposited in deep water by storm activity or by gravity flows. Contemporary uniformitarianism retains the concept of actualism, which Gould affirmed as essentially a principle of simplicity or parsimony, "a warrant for inductive inference which, as Bacon showed nearly four hundred years ago, is the basic mode of reasoning in empirical science" (1965, 226).

Young-earth creationists regard uniformitarianism as incompatible with their application of the biblical record to Earth history. Throughout *The Genesis Flood* (1961), Whitcomb and Morris expounded on uniformitarianism as inadequate for most geological phenomena and as wholly unbiblical (appealing to 2 Peter 3:3–6). In contrast, **C. John Collins** (2003) concluded that uniformity of natural processes, even in the distant past, does not contradict Christian doctrine since uniformity gives us the means to recognize supernatural events. Young and Stearley (2008) observed that most flood geologists actually employ a version of methodological uniformitarianism to interpret the stratigraphic record. For example, channelized volcanic deposits at Mount St. Helens from the 1980 eruption are presented as a scaled-down model for the stratigraphy and geomorphology of the Grand Canyon. Mainstream geologists reject the analogy based on features in the Grand Canyon strata that are inconsistent with thoroughgoing catastrophic deposition (Hill and Moshier 2009).

Stephen O. Moshier

REFERENCES AND RECOMMENDED READING

Collins, C. John. 2003. *Science and Faith: Friends or Foes?* Wheaton, IL: Crossway.

Gould, Stephen J. 1965. "Is Uniformitarianism Necessary?" *American Journal of Science* 263:223–28.

———. 1984. "Toward the Vindication of Punctual Change." In *Catastrophes and Earth History: The New Uniformitarianism*. Eds. W. A. Berggren and John A. Van Couvering, 9–34. Princeton, NJ: Princeton University Press.

Hill, C. A., and S. O. Moshier. 2009. "Flood Geology and the Grand Canyon: A Critique." *Perspectives on Science and Christian Faith* 61:99–115.

Rudwick, Martin J. S. 2008. *Worlds before Adam: The Reconstruction of Geohistory in the Age of Reform.* Chicago: University of Chicago Press.

Whitcomb, John C., Jr., and Henry M. Morris. 1961. *The Genesis Flood: The Biblical Record and Its Scientific Implications.* Philadelphia: Presbyterian & Reformed.

Young, Davis A., and Ralph F. Stearley. 2008. *The Bible, Rocks and Time: Geological Evidence for the Age of the Earth.* Downers Grove, IL: IVP Academic.

UNIVERSE, ORIGIN OF THE.

UNIVERSE, ORIGIN OF THE. For millennia, humans have asked the question of how our universe came into being, or whether or not it even had a beginning. Almost every civilization throughout recorded history has a story about the origin of the universe. These usually involve a creation event by some god or gods. Until the twentieth century, there were no scientific observations that gave answers to this fundamental question.

Most scientists in the early part of the twentieth century assumed that the universe did not have a beginning and had existed forever. However, observations over the last 100 years or so give strong evidence that the universe had a beginning in an event, derisively coined by physicist **Fred Hoyle** as the **big bang**. Observations of the cosmic background radiation, the expansion of the universe, and the relative abundance of hydrogen, helium, and lithium in the universe give overwhelming evidence of an event about 13.8 billion years ago that ushered in the beginning of the universe.

Although observational and theoretical evidence can be used to understand the large-scale evolution of the universe from a fraction of a second after its origin until now, the precise cause or events leading to the actual origin of the universe are not understood, and may possibly never be understood with unambiguous observational evidence. Scientists expect that gravity acting over extremely short-distant scales was a dominant factor in the universe sometime before the first 10^{-35} seconds. But because there is currently no consistent theory of quantum gravity, there are not any reliable theoretical calculations of what occurred in that early **time** scale. In addition, if cosmic inflation occurred in the early universe, all observational evidence about the first 10^{-35} seconds or so may be permanently unobservable to us. Consequently, all postulates are, to some extent, simply a matter of speculation.

The proposition that a transcendent God created the universe is compatible with all these observations, and is arguably the best explanation for the origin of the universe (Copan and Craig 2005). Some scientists, including **Lawrence Krauss**, an astrophysicist at the University of Arizona, believe that ideas from **string theory** and **quantum physics** lead to the conclusion that the universe could be spontaneously created from nothing (Krauss 2012).

There has been much discussion about what is meant by "nothing," with most scientists and philosophers criticizing Krauss's definition, since it seems to align more with the quantum vacuum of our universe than with a philosopher's or theologian's idea of a true "nothing" (Albert 2012). Other scientists are uncomfortable with the origin of our universe being a unique event and prefer a model where universes are continually born and die. Although there are not yet any observations that support this idea, scientists such as Paul Steinhardt, a theoretical physicist at Princeton, continue to work on cyclic models with endless cycles of creation and destruction of universes with the idea that observational evidence may one day support such models.

Michael G. Strauss

REFERENCES AND RECOMMENDED READING

Albert, David. 2012. "On the Origin of Everything." *New York Times Sunday Book Review.* March 25.

Copan, P., and W. L. Craig. 2005. *Creation Out of Nothing: A Biblical, Philosophical, and Scientific Exploration.* Grand Rapids: Baker Academic.

Krauss, Lawrence. 2012. *A Universe from Nothing.* New York: Free Press.

USSHER, JAMES.

USSHER, JAMES. James Ussher (1581–1656) was the Irish archbishop of Armagh and primate of all Ireland between 1625 and 1656 and is best known today for his chronology of the Old Testament titled *The Annals of the World* (1658). Ussher was born in St. Nicholas parish in the city of Dublin, Ireland, raised by Protestant parents, and taught by his two aunts. He devoted his youth to study of the Scriptures and entered Trinity College at the age of 13. He developed his first **biblical chronology** before completing his BA at Trinity College in Dublin at the age of 16, which became the foundation for his *Annals of the World* (Lee 1899, 64–72; Usher 1658).

Ussher was ordained a priest in 1601, became a professor in 1607, earned his doctor of divinity degree in 1612, and served as vice chancellor from 1614 to 1617 at Trinity College, where he collaborated on the first confession of faith for the Church of Ireland. Ussher was a gifted scholar and considered by many to be an expert in every area of biblical investigation he endeavored (Lee 1899). Ussher became bishop of Meath in 1621, archbishop of Armagh in 1635, and primate of all Ireland in 1634. He spent his later years in England after the English Civil War started in 1642.

Ussher was respected as a scholar promoting compromise between the Parliamentarians and the Royalists, but he was ultimately influenced to side with his fellow Calvinists, the Parliamentarians.

Ussher's interests included the Scriptures, early church texts, the early church fathers, Semitic languages, Hebrew texts, the episcopacy, and writing against Roman Catholicism. He is respected today for his work on writings of early church fathers such as the epistles of Ignatius, but his chronologies may be his best-known legacy. Ussher is revered by young-earth creationists, pre- and postmillennialists, and many fundamentalists. But he is wrongly ridiculed by others. His *Annals of the World* dates the **creation** of the universe to October 23 in the year 4004 BC and the creation of Adam to Thursday, October 28, 4004 BC.

Stephen J. Gould noted that "Ussher represented the best of scholarship in his time" and was one of a large community of intellectuals during that period, including **Isaac Newton**, **Johannes Kepler**, and most notably John Lightfoot, who performed similar studies (Gould 1991). Ussher's chronology (sometimes called the *Ussher-Lightfoot chronology*) was widely accepted until the nineteenth century, included in the annotated versions of the King James Bible in 1701, and then widely distributed in the *Scofield Reference Bible*, one of the most influential evangelical theological works in the early twentieth century. Recent biographies covering the life, work, and influence of James Ussher have been written by Alan Ford (2007) and Crawford Gribben (2014), and included in *The Blackwell Companion to Protestantism* by Alister McGrath (2004).

Jonathan Howard Fisher

REFERENCES AND RECOMMENDED READING

Ford, Alan. 2007. *James Ussher: Theology, History, and Politics in Early-Modern Ireland and England.* Oxford: Oxford University Press.

Gould, Stephen Jay. 1991. "Fall in the House of Ussher." *Natural History* 100 (November): 12–21.

Gribben, Crawford. 2014. *The Irish Puritans: James Ussher and the Reformation of the Church.* Eugene, OR: Wipf and Stock.

Lee, Sidney, ed. 1899. "Ussher, James (1581–1656)." In *Dictionary of National Biography*, vol. 58. London: Smith, Elder.

McGrath, Alister E. 2004. *The Blackwell Companion to Protestantism.* Oxford: Blackwell.

O'Loughlin, Tom. "Why Study … James Ussher with Professor Alan Ford." 2011. University of Nottingham. www.youtube.com/watch?v=Dq2yFu2m4O4.

Ussher, James. 1658. *The Annals of the World.* London: E. Tyler.

———. 1864. *The Whole Works of the Most Rev. James Ussher, D.D.* 17 vols. Ed. Charles Richard Elrington. Dublin: Hodges and Smith. https://archive.org/details/wholeworksmostr00elrigoog.

V

VAN FRAASSEN, BAS C. Bastiaan Cornelius van Fraassen (1941–) is the McCosh Professor of Philosophy Emeritus at Princeton University, where he taught from 1982 to 2008. On his retirement from Princeton, he accepted an appointment as distinguished professor of philosophy at San Francisco State University, where he remains active. Born in the Netherlands, he immigrated to Canada with his family in 1956. He earned an undergraduate honors degree in philosophy from the University of Alberta in Edmonton in 1963, followed by a master's and doctorate in **philosophy of science** from the University of Pittsburgh in 1964 and 1966, respectively.

He is best known for originating and defending the constructive empiricist position in the philosophy of science and for his work in the philosophy of quantum theory. He is a member of the American Academy of Arts and Sciences, an overseas member of the Netherlands Royal Academy of Arts and Sciences, and a member of the Académie Internationale de Philosophie des Sciences. In 1986 he received the Lakatos Award for his contributions to the philosophy of science, and in 2012 the Philosophy of Science Association gave him the Hempel Award for lifetime achievement. He is also an adult convert to Catholicism and a founding member of the Kira Institute.

Van Fraassen's early philosophical work, influenced by Karel Lambert at the University of Alberta, focused on formal systems, especially free **logic** (a logic prescinding from the existence assumptions inherent in classical logic) and its metatheory (e.g., Van Fraassen 1966a, 1966b, 1968, 1969b, 1971). His early work in the philosophy of science, connected to his doctoral studies with Adolf Grünbaum, dealt with the foundations of relativity and the philosophy of space-time (e.g., Van Fraassen 1969a, 1970a); however, his interests soon turned to the articulation and defense of a formal and empiricist approach to science (Churchland and Hooker 1985; Gonzalez 2014; Monton 2007; Monton and Mohler 2012; Suppe 1989; Van Fraassen 1970b, 1972, 1980, 1981b, 1987, 1989, 2002, 2008) and to the foundations of quantum theory. His work on quantum theory has largely focused on the articulation of the modal version of the Copenhagen interpretation (see **Quantam Theory, Interpretations of**) and quantum-mechanical critiques of realism (see **Realism and Antirealism**; van Fraassen 1974, 1979a, 1979b, 1981a, 1982, 1985), culminating in his book *Quantum Mechanics: An Empiricist View* (1991).

Van Fraassen famously defines constructive **empiricism** as a form of antirealism in which empirical adequacy is the sole aim of science and acceptance of a scientific theory involves only the belief that it is empirically adequate (1980, 10). Scientific theories themselves are taken to be families of models, certain empirical substructures within which are candidates for the direct representation of observable phenomena. The structures described in experimental reports are called *appearances*, and a theory is empirically adequate if it contains a model whose empirical substructures are isomorphic to all of the relevant appearances (1980, 64). In accepting a theory, then, the only belief required is that the observational consequences of the theory are true; belief that the theory itself is true, while not prohibited, takes us out of science and into the realm of **metaphysics** and interpretation.

However, rather than trying to distinguish between observational and theoretical statements—like the logical empiricists did—and only regarding the former as truth-evaluable (see **Instrumentalism**; **Logical Positivism**), van Fraassen privileges those objects, processes, and events in the world that are directly perceivable by properly situated human observers with properly functioning sensory modalities (1980, 13–19). Since observability is strictly anthropocentric for van Fraassen, scientific instruments do not extend the realm of what is, in principle, observable; rather, they are "engines of creation" (2008, 100) that produce new phenomena that science must accommodate if it is to be empirically adequate.

As a counterpoint to his development of constructive empiricism and his critique of scientific realism, van Fraassen articulates an epistemic voluntarism that rejects traditional **epistemology** and provides a key to understanding how his austere empiricism coexists with his embrace of Catholic Christianity (van Fraassen 1973; 1984; 1988; 1989, 151–82; 1995a; 1995b; 1996; 2000; 2002; see also Jones 2011 and especially Okruhlik 2014).

Following Oliver Wendell Holmes's classification of concepts of law, van Fraassen distinguishes between Prussian and English conceptions of rationality (1989, 171–73). In the Prussian conception, anything not rationally compelled by way of belief is forbidden, whereas in the English conception, anything not rationally forbidden is permitted. There is thus considerable room for operation of the will in choosing theoretical models in science and philosophical orientations in life, for such choices are not, and could never be, uniquely determined by observational evidence and logic.

In this regard, van Fraassen (2002) speaks of his empiricism as a stance displaying an attitude (see also Fine 1986, 112–35) that takes the empirical sciences as a **paradigm** of rationality in objectifying modes of inquiry and that disregards demands for further explanations that would lead to metaphysics. But he also believes such objectifying modes are inappropriate for interactions with other persons, whether human or divine, for if we totalize objectifying inquiry, we find that "we ourselves do not seem to fit into our own world picture" (2002, 189).

His resolution of the tension for both objectifying and nonobjectifying modes of inquiry is found in an existentialist lineage of thought involving thinkers as diverse as **Blaise Pascal**, **William James**, Rudolf Bultmann, Jean-Paul Sartre, Emil Fackenheim, and **Paul Feyerabend**. Conversion to a new theory or a new outlook—representative of a new attitude toward the evidence—whether religious or scientific, is a decision problem that is only overcome through the role of emotion (2002, 103–10). Our rationality is thus only "bridled irrationality" (1989, 172), constrained by the canons of reason. Rational decisions are based on reasons that move us in the direction of greater precision, but almost never uniquely so, for "natural language is inexhaustibly rich in the possible ways of being made more precise" (2002, 114).

Bruce L. Gordon

REFERENCES AND RECOMMENDED READING

Churchland, Paul M., and Clifford A. Hooker, eds. 1985. *Images of Science: Essays on Realism and Empiricism, with a Reply from Bas C. van Fraassen.* Chicago: University of Chicago Press.

Fine, Arthur I. 1986. *The Shaky Game: Einstein, Realism, and Quantum Theory.* Chicago: University of Chicago Press.

Gonzalez, W. J., ed. 2014. *Bas van Fraassen's Approach to Representation and Models in Science.* Dordrecht: Springer.

Jones, Ward E. 2011. "Being Moved by a Way the World Is Not." *Synthese* 178:131–41.

Monton, Bradley. 2007. *Images of Empiricism: Essays on Science and Stances, with a Reply from Bas C. van Fraassen.* Oxford: Oxford University Press.

Monton, Bradley, and Chad Mohler. 2012. "Constructive Empiricism." In *Stanford Encyclopedia of Philosophy.* Ed. Edward N. Zalta. December 17. http://plato.stanford.edu/entries/constructive-empiricism/.

Okruhlik, Kathleen. 2014. "Van Fraassen's Philosophy of Science and His Epistemic Voluntarism." *Philosophy Compass* 9 (9): 653–61.

Suppe, Frederick. 1989. *The Semantic Conception of Theories and Scientific Realism.* Urbana: University of Illinois Press.

van Fraassen, Bas C. 1966a. "Singular Terms, Truth-Value Gaps, and Free Logic." *Journal of Philosophy* 63:481–94.

———. 1966b. "The Completeness of Free Logic." *Zeitschrift für mathematische Logik und Grundlagen der Mathematik* 12:219–34.

———. 1968. "A Topological Proof of the Löwenheim-Skolem, Compactness, and Strong Completeness Theorems for Free Logic." *Zeitschrift für mathematische Logik und Grundlagen der Mathematik* 14:245–54.

———. 1969a. "Conventionality in the Axiomatic Foundations of the Special Theory of Relativity." *Philosophy of Science* 36:64–73.

———. 1969b. "Presuppositions, Supervaluations, and Free Logic." In *The Logical Way of Doing Things.* Ed. Karel Lambert, 67–92. New Haven, CT: Yale University Press.

———. 1970a. *An Introduction to the Philosophy of Time and Space.* New York: Random House.

———. 1970b. "On the Extension of Beth's Semantics of Theories." *Philosophy of Science* 37:325–34.

———. 1971. *Formal Semantics and Logic.* New York: Macmillan.

———. 1972. "A Formal Approach to the Philosophy of Science." In *Paradigms and Paradoxes: Philosophical Challenges of the Quantum Domain.* Ed. R. Colodny, 303–66. Pittsburgh: University of Pittsburgh Press.

———. 1973. "Values and the Heart's Command." *Journal of Philosophy* 70:5–19.

———. 1974. "The Einstein-Podolsky-Rosen Paradox." *Synthese* 29:291–309.

———. 1979a. "Foundations of Probability: Modal Frequency Interpretation." In *Problems in the Foundation of Physics.* Ed. Toraldo Di Francia, 344–87. Amsterdam: North-Holland.

———. 1979b. "Hidden Variables and the Modal Interpretation of Quantum Statistics." *Synthese* 42:155–65.

———. 1980. *The Scientific Image.* Oxford: Clarendon.

———. 1981a. "A Modal Interpretation of Quantum Mechanics." In *Current Issues in Quantum Logic.* Eds. E. Beltrametti and B. van Fraassen, 229–58. New York: Plenum.

———. 1981b. "Theory Construction and Experiment: An Empiricist View." In *Proceedings of the 1980 Biennial Meeting of the Philosophy of Science Association.* Eds. P. Asquith and R. Giere, 663–78. East Lansing, MI: Philosophy of Science Association.

———. 1982. "The Charybdis of Realism: Epistemological Implications of Bell's Inequality." *Synthese* 52:25–38.

———. 1984. "Belief and the Will." *Journal of Philosophy* 81:235–56.

———. 1985. "EPR: When Is Correlation Not a Mystery?" In *Symposium on the Foundations of Modern Physics.* Eds. P. Lahti and P. Mittelstaedt, 113–28. Singapore: World Scientific.

———. 1987. "The Semantic Approach to Scientific Theories." In *The Process of Science.* Ed. N. J. Nersessian, 105–24. Dordrecht: Martinus Nijhoff.

———. 1988. "The Peculiar Effects of Love and Desire." In *Perspectives on Self-Deception.* Eds. Amélie Rorty and Brian McLaughlin, 123–56. Berkeley: University of California Press.

———. 1989. *Laws and Symmetry.* Oxford: Clarendon.

———. 1991. *Quantum Mechanics: An Empiricist View.* Oxford: Clarendon.

———. 1995a. "Belief and the Problem of Ulysses and the Sirens." *Philosophical Studies* 77:7–37.

———. 1995b. "Against Naturalized Epistemology." In *On Quine: New Essays.* Eds. P. Leonardi and M. Santambrogio, 68–88. Cambridge: Cambridge University Press.

———. 1996. "Science, Materialism, and False Consciousness." In *Warrant in Contemporary Epistemology: Essays in Honor of Plantinga's Theory of Knowledge.* Ed. Jonathan L. Kvanvig, 149–81. Lanham, MD: Rowman & Littlefield.

———. 2000. "The False Hopes of Traditional Epistemology." *Philosophy and Phenomenological Research* 60 (2): 253–80.

———. 2002. *The Empirical Stance.* New Haven, CT: Yale University Press.

———. 2008. *Scientific Representations: Paradoxes of Perspective.* Oxford: Clarendon.

VAN TILL, HOWARD J.

VAN TILL, HOWARD J. Howard Van Till (1938–) taught **physics** and **astronomy** for more than three decades at Calvin College after earning a PhD at Michigan State in 1965. While his scientific research focused on solid state physics and millimeter-wave astronomy, he spent much of his time researching and writing on the relationship between science and religion within the context of his evangelical, and in particular Reformed, theological framework. His book *The Fourth Day* (1986) laid out his basic approach at the time to the question of the relationship between the Bible and science, an approach that was developed and presented with even more clarity in later publications (see, e.g., Van Till 1988 as well as his contributions to Carlson 2000 and Moreland 2010).

Van Till argues that science and Christianity are "Partners in Theorizing" (Van Till in Carlson 2000, 195). He does not see them as completely independent, but rather believes that they have "differing competencies" (Van Till in Carlson 2000, 126) for addressing important questions (thus he eschews creation science of both **young-earth** and **old-earth creationism** as well as **concordism**). When it comes to creation, he argues that the Bible proclaims that God is the creator of everything and every creature, but the Bible does not tell us how God created the cosmos or human beings. Science, not the Bible, has the distinctive tools to answer the question "how," and Van Till affirms the overwhelming scientific evidence that supports the idea of cosmic and **biological evolution** (Van Till 1986).

In terms of the latter, Van Till rejects the term *theistic evolution* because it pictures God as using evolution like a tool. Rather, he speaks of God "fully gifting" creation in a way that fully affirms God as creator (his "creatonomic perspective" [1986, ix]), but he notes that God uses natural secondary causes to achieve his purposes. In this regard, he speaks of a "robust formational economy principle" at work in God's creation ("the formational economy of the universe is sufficiently robust to account for the actualization in time of all the types of physical/material structures and all the forms of life that ever existed" [Van Till in Carlson 2000, 216]), so it is in vain in his view that people look for gaps in scientific explanations that point to miraculous interjections of God (thus his criticism of the **intelligent design** movement).

Van Till vigorously resists the idea that his views are deistic, insisting that he celebrates God's intimate involvement in the creation process. Indeed, he argues that "the robust formational economy (RFE) principle" can only be accounted for by "the Creator's unfathomable creativity and unlimited generosity" (Van Till in Carlson 2000, 219).

Van Till's views have generated significant, and often harsh, pushback from critics, particularly from those who advocate for creation science and intelligent design (see responses to his contributions in Carlson 2000 and Moreland 2010).

In a speech to the Freethought Association of West Michigan (Van Till 2006), he describes how the negative response within and outside of Calvin College and its constituency made him rethink his commitment to the Calvinist tradition in which he grew up, announcing that he is on a new journey to develop a new conceptual framework. In his most recent writing, Van Till (2011) embraces what he calls "naturalistic **theism**," which affirms the **existence of God** as well as his involvement in the world through nature that has been "fully gifted" by God with all the resources, capabilities, and potentialities necessary. Theologically, he finds process theology, particularly the work of David Ray Griffin (2000 and 2004 [Van Till wrote the foreword]), most conducive to his present thinking.

Tremper Longman III

REFERENCES AND RECOMMENDED READING

Carlson, R. F. 2000. *Science and Christianity: Four Views.* Downers Grove, IL: InterVarsity.

Griffin, D. R. 2000. *Religion and Scientific Naturalism: Overcoming the Conflicts.* Albany, NY: SUNY Press.

———. 2004. *Two Great Truths: A New Synthesis of Scientific Naturalism and Christian Faith.* Louisville, KY: Westminster John Knox.

Moreland, J. P., ed. 2010. *Three Views on Creation and Evolution.* Grand Rapids: Zondervan.

Van Till, H. J. 1986. *The Fourth Day: What the Bible and the Heavens Are Telling Us about the Creation.* Grand Rapids: Eerdmans.

———. 2006. "From Calvinism to Free Thought: The Road Less Traveled." Freethought Association of West Michigan. www.freethoughtassociation.org/images/uploads/pdf/ODoRs.pdf.

———. 2011. "Cosmic Evolution, Naturalism and Divine Creativity, or Who Owns the Robust Formational Economy Principle?" In *Nature of Nature: Examining the Role of Naturalism in Science.* Eds. B. L. Gordon and W. A. Dembski. Wilmington, DE: ISI Books.

Van Till, H. J., D. A. Young, and C. Menninga. 1988. *Science Held Hostage.* Downers Grove, IL: InterVarsity.

VERIFICATION PRINCIPLE.

VERIFICATION PRINCIPLE. During the first decades of the twentieth century, logical positivists (notably Moritz Schlick, **Rudolf Carnap**, **Carl Hempel**, Otto Neurath, and A. J. Ayer) sought a method for coping with persistent philosophical problems, especially those generated by language and **logic** (see **Logical Positivism**). They required a criterion for determining the meaningfulness of linguistic expressions. A sentence is not meaningful if it does not express a proposition, something that is either true or false. There is, then, an intimate link between the meaningfulness of an expression and its truth value. If a method could be devised for ascertaining the (likely) truth value of a statement, that method would assist in determining its meaningfulness.

As strict empiricists (see **Empiricism**), the logical positivists insisted on a criterion rooted in empirical observation. Thus the formula they prescribed stipulated that a statement is meaningful if and only if it is either empirically verifiable or analytic (that is, true by definition). This they called the *principle of verifiability*.

The effect of this principle was that any "statement" that is not empirically verifiable is not even meaningful. Logical positivists called themselves *positivists* because of their emphasis on "facts" and what they took to be the nature of a "fact." That an action, described in terms of physical states and events, has occurred is a fact. That the very action has a moral quality is not a fact—there being no empirical means of detecting the alleged moral quality. So the sentence "Killing is evil" does not assert anything. It is neither true nor false. It is cognitively meaningless, pure and simple. Other casualties of this empiricist dogma include sentences of the form "God created the universe" and "The mind is an immaterial substance."

The implications for religious belief are severe. The positivist criterion for meaningfulness provided a convenient shortcut for dismissing the truth claims of Christianity. As A. C. Ewing wrote mid-twentieth century, "Today the questions most commonly asked by philosophical critics of religion, at least in this country, relate not to the truth or falsity of religious assertions but to their meaning" (1968, 223).

Common objections to verificationism include:

1. *Verificationism is dogmatic and arbitrary.* Its empiricist high-handedness entails that religious sentences, while appearing to make assertions, are not assertions at all. But this is unsympathetic to what religious believers normally intend when they utter sentences that, grammatically, seem to be assertions. This dogmatism is made worse by the unsupported arbitrariness of its general outlook. There is no general argument that empiricism is correct, nor would such an argument be plausible if it were attempted.

2. *Verificationism is self-destructive.* It enlists a criterion that cannot, when stated, satisfy its own test. The principle is not analytic; nor is it empirically verifiable.

3. *Verificationism is a metaphysical thesis, despite protestations to the contrary.* Verificationism intends the elimination of **metaphysics**. But it implies that what seem to many to be facts are not facts. Its ontology is sparing, but it is nevertheless an ontology.

4. *Verificationism is an abstruse doctrine without a clear sense.* The concepts of "*observation*" and "*verifiability*" are vague and variously construed.

The popularity of verificationism has waned, and metaphysics, moral philosophy, and philosophical theology have recovered respectability. However, this advance in the recent history of philosophy is mitigated somewhat by the retrograde dogmatism of **scientism** that, even if it acknowledges the meaningfulness of religious statements, does not take them seriously because they cannot be verified empirically.

R. Douglas Geivett

REFERENCES AND RECOMMENDED READING

Ayer, A. J. 1936. *Language, Truth and Logic.* London: V. Gollancz.
———, ed. 1959. *Logical Positivism.* New York: Free Press.
Ayer, A. J., and F. C. Copleston. 1957. "Logical Positivism—A Debate." In *A Modern Introduction to Philosophy: Readings from Classical and Contemporary Sources.* Eds. P. Edwards and A. Pap. New York: Free Press.
Carnap, Rudolf. 1936. "Testability and Meaning." *Philosophy of Science* 3 (4): 419–71.
Ewing, A. C. 1968. *Nonlinguistic Philosophy: Muirhead Library of Philosophy.* London: Allen & Unwin.
Hahn, Lewis Edwin, ed. 1992. *The Philosophy of A. J. Ayer.* La Salle, IL: Open Court.
Schlick, Moritz. 1936. "Meaning and Verification." *Philosophical Review* 45 (4).

VIRGIN BIRTH. The *virgin birth* is a term with a range of applications. First, in the strictest sense, it refers to the idea "that the actual process of Jesus' birth was so miraculous that it left Mary intact as a virgin with her hymen unruptured" (Montefiore 1992, 13). This belief, stemming from the apocryphal mid-second century "*Protoevangelium of James,*" is incorporated within the Catholic and Orthodox doctrine of Mary's perpetual virginity.

Second, the phrase stands for the biblical claim that by a unique miraculous action of God, Jesus of Nazareth was *conceived* within a virgin named Mary without any contribution from a biological human father, such that Jesus was born (c. 5 BC) to a mother who had not had sexual intercourse. Thus the Apostles' Creed states that Jesus was "conceived by the power of the Holy Spirit" and the Nicene Creed says, "For us and for our salvation he came down from heaven, was incarnate of the Holy Spirit and the Virgin Mary and became truly human." To distinguish this claim from belief in the "virgin birth," some theologians prefer to speak of Jesus's "virginal conception." Belief in the latter doesn't entail belief in the former, for as **C. S. Lewis** wrote, "If God creates a miraculous spermatozoon in the body of a virgin, it does not proceed to break any laws. The laws at once take it over. Nature is ready. Pregnancy follows, according to all the normal laws, and nine months later a child is born" (Lewis 1998, 62).

While the two are obviously related, the virginal conception isn't a necessary precondition of the **incarnation**: "Christians believe that Jesus was the incarnate Son of God not in the sense that God the father was literally the father of the man Jesus, but in the sense that the eternal Son of God assumed humanity, so that the Word became flesh and dwelt among us, and in the one person Jesus Christ there were united both divine and human nature" (Montefiore 1992, 13; cf. Moreland and Craig 2003; Swinburne 2008).

Some critics assume that the virginal conception is a myth influenced by other myths of miraculous birth. However, "there are no parallels to Jesus' conception and birth in Jewish or non-Jewish literature ..." (Montefiore 1992, 48). Nor are the gospel birth narratives nonhistorical Jewish midrash or haggadah (cf. Quarles 1998). The core historical claims concerning Jesus's virginal conception are made *independently* by the gospels of Matthew and Luke, and the virginal conception may be reflected in other biblical passages (cf. John 8:41; Gal. 4:4). Moreover, writing c. AD 108, Ignatius of Antioch confirmed that Jesus was "truly born of a virgin" (Ignatius). This claim naturally raises philosophical questions about **miracles** (cf. Larmer 2014; Lewis 1998; Moreland and Craig 2003).

Third, the phrase is colloquially inclusive of Matthew 1:1–2:23 and Luke 1:5–2:40, or at least the portions thereof that appear in the typical nativity play. In this sense, "the virgin birth" raises questions about the historicity of the relevant passages of Matthew and Luke, questions that must be considered in dialogue with academic fields including ancient history, archaeology, and **astronomy**. For example, recent astronomical studies have contributed to understanding Matthew's account of the "magi" and "the star they had seen" (cf. Humphreys 1995; Kidger 1999; Molnar 1999).

Peter S. Williams

REFERENCES AND RECOMMENDED READING

Barnett, Paul. 2003. *Is the New Testament Reliable?* 2nd ed. Downers Grove, IL: IVP.

Cabal, Ted, ed. 2007. *The Apologetics Study Bible.* Nashville: Holman.

Geisler, Norman L. 2005. "The Virgin Birth." The John Ankerberg Show. www.jashow.org/wiki/index.php?title=The_Virgin_Birth.

Howard, Jeremy Royal, ed. 2013. *The Holman Apologetics Commentary on the Bible: The Gospel and Acts.* Nashville: Holman Reference.

Humphreys, Colin J. 1992. "The Star of Bethlehem, a Comet in 5 BC and the Date of Christ's Birth." *Tyndale Bulletin* 43 (1): 31–56. http://98.131.162.170/tynbul/library/TynBull_1992_43_1_02_Humphreys_StarBethlehem.pdf.

———. 1995. "The Star of Bethlehem." *Science and Christian Belief* 5 (October): 83–101. www.asa3.org/ASA/topics/Astronomy-Cosmology/S&CB%2010–93Humphreys.html.

Humphreys, Colin J. 2008. "Science and the Star of Bethlehem." January 6. www.faraday.st-edmunds.cam.ac.uk/Multimedia.php?ItemID=210&Flash=Medium&Mode=Add&Play=Video_stream.

Ignatius (c. 108). *Ad Smyrn.* www.newadvent.org/fathers/0109.htm.

Kidger, Mark. 1999. *The Star of Bethlehem: An Astronomer's View.* Princeton, NJ: Princeton University Press.

Larmer, Robert A. 2014. *The Legitimacy of Miracle.* Lanham, MD: Lexington.

Lewis, C. S. 1998. *Miracles: A Preliminary Study.* London: Fount.

Machen, J. Gresham. 1958. *The Virgin Birth of Christ.* 2nd ed. London: James Clark.

Molnar, Michael R. 1999. *The Star of Bethlehem: The Legacy of the Magi.* London: Rutgers University Press.

Montefiore, Hugh. 1992. *The Womb and the Tomb: The Mystery of the Birth and Resurrection of Jesus.* London: Fount.

Moreland, J. P., and William Lane Craig. 2003. *Philosophical Foundations for a Christian Worldview.* Downers Grove, IL: IVP.

Quarles, L. Charles. 1998. *Midrash Criticism: Introduction and Appraisal.* Lanham, MD: University Press of America.

Ratzinger, Joseph. 2012. *Jesus of Nazareth: The Infancy Narratives.* London: Bloomsbury.

Redford, John. 2007. *Born of a Virgin: Proving the Miracle from the Gospels.* London: St. Pauls.

Swinburne, Richard. 2008. *Was Jesus God?* Oxford: Oxford University Press.

Ward, Keith. 2012. "Evidence for the Virgin Birth." http://christianevidence.org/docs/booklets/evidence_for_the_virgin_birth.pdf.

Williams, Peter S. 2016. "The Nativity." February 26. www.youtube.com/playlist?list=PLQhh3qcwVEWjXCwcSr2FYzpj5-uQrLKIR.

W

WALLACE, ALFRED RUSSEL. Alfred Russel Wallace (1823–1913) was born in Usk, Monmouthshire, a few miles north of Bristol Channel (UK). When Alfred was five years old, his family moved to Hertford, north of London. At 14 Alfred was apprenticed to his older brother William to learn the art of surveying. For the next six years, he educated himself during his spare time by reading the works of Humboldt and Lyell and Darwin's *Voyage of the Beagle*, as well as botanical treatises. Between 1844 and 1845, he was employed as a schoolteacher in Leicester, teaching drawing and mapmaking. Between 1845 and 1848, he collaborated with his brother John to run an independent, if struggling, civil engineering firm. While at Leicester, he met the young naturalist Henry Bates, who introduced Wallace to the world of beetle collecting. Wallace and Bates began to make plans for a natural history trip to South America funded by the sale of collected specimens to patrons back in England.

The spring of 1848 saw their dreams realized. With a commitment from William Hooker of the Kew Museum, who had an interest in tropical botanical specimens, Wallace and Bates set out for Brazil and the Amazon. Between 1848 and 1852, they explored, botanized, and collected natural history specimens of many types to bring back to Europe. Wallace accomplished fundamental mapping of the Rio Negro. However, during the voyage back to Britain, the vessel caught fire and all of Wallace's specimens were destroyed.

Wallace spent the next year and a half in London; during that interval he became acquainted with **Charles Darwin**. He then left on his own for the Malay Archipelago. There, during the years 1854–62, he collected more than 120,000 biological specimens. He observed the dramatic differences between the biotas of Borneo, Java, and Bali on the west versus the biotas of the Celebes, the Mollucas, and Lombok on the east; the boundary being labeled later (by T. H. Huxley) as "Wallace's Line."

While sitting out the rainy season in Sarawak during the spring of 1855, he penned a major contribution on theoretical biology, "On the Law Which Has Regulated the Introduction of a New Species." This "law" was a codification of his many observations (and those of Darwin) that similar **species** were sited near one another in space. The implication of this spatial pattern was that the two similar species

had shared a common ancestor. Wallace was catching up to Darwin in his appreciation for what today is recognized as a nested hierarchy to the organization of life.

In February 1858, after pondering what mechanism might accomplish this spatial organization to life, he arrived at a solution very similar to Darwin's concept of **natural selection**. He wrote his conclusion in a paper titled "On the Tendency of Varieties to Depart Indefinitely from the Original Type." He mailed the paper to Charles Darwin to request his opinion. Darwin was taken aback to find that Wallace had arrived at Darwin's own conclusion, to which he had devoted more than 25 years of observation and deliberation. Darwin, after consulting with friends Charles Lyell and Joseph Hooker, decided that Wallace's paper would be read simultaneously with an earlier but unpublished essay by Darwin at the meeting of the Linnean Society of London in July 1858. Wallace would not learn of this decision for several months.

When Wallace returned to England in 1862, he was widely praised as a naturalist and explorer. However, his attempts to find a position as a museum curator or university lecturer were not successful, and the majority of his income afterward was provided by book contracts and public lectures.

Wallace is today given credit as one of the preeminent founders of the discipline of biogeography. His classic work, *The Geographical Distribution of Animals* (1876), provided large lists of many taxa to delineate the world's major biogeographic regions, amplifying the prior work of the ornithologist Philip Sclater, who became a friend. Wallace wrote in a day prior to any proof that landmasses had changed their positions significantly; thus his mechanisms for organismal distributions were those of passive dispersal and/or migration. Wallace cogently linked the **fossil record** of organisms to their current distributions and probable dispersion corridors. The historical record of dispersal he explicitly linked to the principles he had adduced while in the Malay Archipelago, and they were thus highly regarded by his cohort of contemporary evolutionists, such as Joseph Hooker, T. H. Huxley, and Charles Darwin.

While Wallace's writings throughout his life reflect a firm commitment to the notion of natural selection, he concluded that human cognitive capacities in many senses transcended the purely biological. He carried this line of reasoning to what he felt was its logical conclusion: there must exist a higher **Mind**, which had effected human neural development. This conclusion was further demonstrated, he felt, by phenomena he observed at séances. Beginning in the middle 1860s he investigated spiritualism and became convinced that a psychic reality underlay these manifestations. His conclusions, expressed in several papers and summarized in *Man's Place in the Universe* (1903), disturbed his otherwise cordial relationships with Darwin, Huxley, and others.

From the late 1870s on, Wallace became increasingly involved in social reforms. He served as first president of the Land Nationalisation Society. His book *The Wonderful Century* (1898) lauded the major scientific advances of the nineteenth century, while at the same time contrasting these advances with numerous categories of social and moral ills.

Wallace married Annie Mitten, 25 years his junior, in 1866. Their marriage was a happy one and produced three children, Herbert Spencer, William, and Violet. Sadly, their eldest son, Herbert Spencer (Bertie) died at the age of six, in 1874. William and Violet lived well into the middle twentieth century.

Ralph Stearley

REFERENCES AND RECOMMENDED READING

Browne, Janet. 2002. *Charles Darwin: The Power of Place.* New York: Knopf.

Camerini, Jane R. 1993. "Evolution, Biogeography and Maps: An Early History of Wallace's Line." *Isis* 84 (4): 700–727.

Fichman, Martin. 2001. "Science in Theistic Contexts: A Case Study of Alfred Russel Wallace on Human Evolution." *Osiris*, 2nd ser., 16:227–50.

———. 2004. *An Elusive Victorian: The Evolution of Alfred Russel Wallace.* Chicago: University of Chicago Press.

McCalman, Iain. 2009. *Darwin's Armada: Four Voyages and the Battle for the Theory of Evolution.* New York: W. W. Norton.

Raby, Peter. 2001. *Alfred Russel Wallace: A Life.* Princeton, NJ: Princeton University Press.

Smith, Charles H., ed. 1991. *Alfred Russel Wallace: An Anthology of His Shorter Writings.* Oxford: Oxford University Press.

Wallace, A. R. 1853: *A Narrative of Travels on the Amazon and Rio Negro, with an Account of the Native Tribes, and Observations on the Climate, Geology, and Natural History of the Amazon Valley.* London: Reeve and Company.

———. 1855. "On the Law Which Has Regulated the Introduction of New Species." *Annals and Magazine of Natural History* 16:184–96.

———. 1858. "On the Tendency of Varieties to Depart Indefinitely from the Original Type." *Journal of the Proceedings of the Linnean Society, Zoology* 3 (20 August): 53–62.

———. 1864. "The Origin of Human Races from the Theory of Natural Selection." *Journal of the Anthropological Society of London* 2:clviii-clxx.

———. 1869. *The Malay Archipelago: The Land of the Orang-utan and the Bird of Paradise: A Narrative of Travel with Studies of Man and Nature.* 2 vols. London: Macmillan.

———. 1870. *Contributions to the Theory of Natural Selection.* London and New York: Macmillan.

———. 1876. *The Geographical Distribution of Animals: With a Study of the Relations of Living and Extinct Faunas as Elucidating the Past Changes of Earth's Surface.* 2 vols. London and New York: Macmillan.

———. 1880. *Island Life: Or, the Phenomenon and Causes of Insular Faunas and Floras, Including a Revision and Attempted Solution of the Problem of Geological Climates.* London and New York: Macmillan.

———. 1889. *Darwinism: An Exposition of the Theory of Natural Selection with Some of Its Applications.* London and New York: Macmillan.

———. 1891. *Natural Selection and Tropical Nature: Essays on Descriptive and Theoretical Biology.* London and New York: Macmillan.

———. 1903. *Man's Place in the Universe: A Study of the Results of Scientific Research in Relation to the Unity or Plurality of Worlds.* London: Chapman and Hall.

———. 1905. *My Life: A Record of Events and Opinions.* 2 vols. London: Chapman and Hall.

———. 1910. *The World of Life: A Manifestation of Creative Power, Directive Mind, and Ultimate Purpose.* London: Chapman and Hall.

———. 1913. *Social Environment and Moral Progress.* London: Cassell.

WALTON, JOHN H. John H. Walton (1952–) is professor of Old Testament at Wheaton Graduate School (since 2001) and before that was professor of Old Testament at Moody Bible Institute (1981–2001). He received his PhD from Hebrew Union College–Jewish Institute of Religion in Cincinnati, Ohio (1981), where he wrote his doctoral dissertation on the Tower of Babel. He also serves on the advisory board of the **BioLogos Foundation**.

From the start, Walton's approach to the interpretation of the Old Testament emphasized the importance of understanding it within the context of its "cognitive environment" (Walton 2011, 6–8). Thus he puts a high premium on the study of the Old Testament text in the light of ancient Near Eastern literature and culture. This approach is particularly influential in his study of the **book of Genesis** and specifically the creation accounts. While Walton recognizes "broad ideological commonalities" (2011, 194) between biblical and ancient Near Eastern creation texts, he also asserts their distinctiveness, especially in the monotheism of Israel and the different conception of humanity and its relationship with God.

Among the most important of the commonalities includes the biblical creation accounts' concern with functionality rather than material creation. Walton believes that the creation week in Genesis 1 does not describe the coming into existence of matter and the various animate and inanimate components of the cosmos, but rather their becoming functional within an ordered universe.

Walton's study of the Genesis creation account in the light of the literature of the ancient Near East also leads to his strong emphasis on the relationship between temple and cosmos. He is far from the only person to see this emphasis (Hurowitz 1992; Levenson 1988), but writing in an evangelical Protestant context, he emphasizes how again this analogy challenges readings that take the biblical accounts as straightforward descriptions of how God created creation. He notes that not only is the temple filled with imagery that indicates it is a microcosm of the cosmos, the creation accounts themselves send signals that the cosmos itself is a temple, which is a place where God rests: "Prior to day one, God's spirit was active over the nonfunctional cosmos; God was involved but had not yet taken up his residence. The establishment of the functional cosmic temple is effectuated by God taking up his residence on day seven" (Walton 2009b, 85).

Walton understands **Adam and Eve** as archetypal figures, in that they stand for every person. For example, when the author of the second creation account says that Adam was created from the dust of the ground (2:7), he is not speaking of material origins of humanity, but rather of functionality. The creation from dust means that humanity was created mortal. According to Walton, archetypes can be historical, and in the case of Adam and Eve, they are, though he denies that they are prototypes—in other words, Adam and Eve may not be the first human couple.

Walton's view of the biblical accounts of creation and cosmos emphasize the idea that they are not about material origins, and thus he does not believe that scientific theories like the **big bang theory** of the origin of the cosmos or evolutionary theory for the origin of humanity threaten biblical truth, though he himself does not explicitly endorse these ideas.

Tremper Longman III

REFERENCES AND RECOMMENDED READING

Hurowitz, V. 1992. *I Have Built You an Exalted House: Temple Building in the Bible in the Light of Mesopotamian and Northwest Semitic Writings.* Journal for the Study of the Old Testament: Supplement Series 115. Sheffield: JSOT Press.

Levenson, J. 1988. *Creation and the Persistence of Evil.* Princeton, NJ: Princeton University Press.

Walton, J. H. 2001. *Genesis.* Grand Rapids: Zondervan.

———. 2009a. "Genesis." In *Zondervan Illustrated Bible Backgrounds Commentary.* Ed. J. Walton, 1:2–159. Grand Rapids: Zondervan.

———. 2009b. *The Lost World of Genesis One: Ancient Cosmology and the Origins Debate.* Downers Grove, IL: InterVarsity.

———. 2011. *Genesis 1 as Ancient Cosmology.* Winona Lake, IN: Eisenbrauns.

———. 2013. "A Historical Adam: Archetypal Creation View." In *Four Views on the Historical Adam.* Eds. Matthew Barrett and Ardel B. Caneday. Grand Rapids: Zondervan.

———. 2015. *The Lost World of Adam and Eve.* Downers Grove, IL: InterVarsity.

WARD, KEITH. Keith Ward (1938–) is a prolific author concerned with Christian theology, philosophy, and religious studies. Within these concerns, he has written much on science and religion. He received his doctorate from Oxford and was a Regius Professor of Divinity at Oxford from 1991–2003. In 1972 he was ordained a priest in the Church of England. He has written numerous books for both academic and popular audiences as well as giving distinguished lectureships around the world. On his Web page, he describes himself as

> by nature and conviction, an Idealist philosopher, somebody who believes in the supremacy of Spirit or **Mind**, and who thinks that the material universe is an expression or creation of a Supreme Mind. I see religions as very ambiguous but probably necessary ways of giving humans some awareness of this Supreme Mind. (2016)

Ward defends a somewhat liberal form of Protestant Christianity. In *What the Bible Really Teaches* (2004), he challenges "fundamentalist" theologies concerning doctrines of salvation, the sacrifice of Jesus, the resurrection, the coming of Christ, and the afterlife. Ward has critiqued convincingly the normative religious pluralism of John Hick in *Religion and Revelation: A Theology of Revelation in the World's Religions* (1994). He challenged the supposedly science-based reasoning of the New Atheists in *Why There Is Almost Certainly a God: Doubting Dawkins* (2009). He has written several works against **materialism**, such as *More Than Matter* (2010) and *In Defense of the Soul* (2008); and he does not think that recent work in **neuroscience** refutes a spiritual understanding of humans.

Ward calls his basic position on mind and matter "dual-aspect idealism." In the world of material appearances, there is an inner reality we know as mind. "What the reality underlying those appearances may be in detail we do not know," he says. "But since minds are the only sorts of reality we know to belong to the world of things-in-themselves, it is reasonable to think that reality does not exist without mind and **consciousness**, evaluation and intention, understanding and action.... Minds are not illusory ghosts in real machines. On the contrary, machines are spectral, transitory phenomena appearing to an intelligible world of minds" (cited in Vernon 2016). He is not a physicalist with respect to the human person. He argues that uniquely human qualities cannot be exhaustively explained in physical categories.

Ward does not challenge macroevolution as an adequate account for the development of **life** on earth. He is a theistic evolutionist who holds to **methodological naturalism** and to the idea that divine design cannot be inferred from the findings of science itself, as claimed by the **intelligent** design movement, whose lead thinkers include **Michael Behe**, **William Dembski**, and **Stephen Meyer**. Ward does, however, labor to reconcile God's **providence** with current understandings of natural processes.

Douglas Groothuis

REFERENCES AND RECOMMENDED READING

Bartel, T. W., ed. 2003. *Comparative Theology: Essays for Keith Ward*. London: SPCK.

Vernon, Mark. 2016. *"More Than Matter?* by Keith Ward." *Philosophy Now* 84 (February–March). https://philosophynow.org/issues/84/More_Than_Matter_by_Keith_Ward.

Ward, Keith. 2011. *A Philosopher and the Gospels*. Oxford: Lion.

———. 2012. *By Faith and Reason: The Essential Keith Ward*. Eds. Curtis Holtzen and Roberto Sirvent. London: Darton, Longman, Todd.

———. Personal website. Accessed October 28, 2016. www.keithward.org.uk.

WARFIELD, BENJAMIN BRECKINRIDGE. Benjamin Breckinridge Warfield (1851–1921) was born near Lexington, Kentucky, the son of Christian parents whose families both had a rich legacy of devout Reformed faith. Educated first at home, in 1868 Warfield entered the sophomore class at the College of New Jersey (later Princeton University), where at age 19 he graduated with highest honors, first in his class, having received perfect scores in **mathematics** and science. He then traveled to Europe to pursue scientific studies for a time but after a year turned his attention to the Christian ministry and in 1873 returned to Princeton, this time to the already well-known bastion of the Reformed faith, Princeton Theological Seminary, where he sat under the aging and highly esteemed **Charles Hodge**.

He graduated from Princeton in 1876, and after further studies abroad and some brief stints in pulpit supply in Dayton, Ohio, and Baltimore, Maryland, in 1878 he was called to teach New Testament at Western Theological Seminary in Allegheny (Pittsburgh), Pennsylvania.

In only a few brief years, through various significant publications, he attracted the notice of scholars internationally and quickly became recognized as a uniquely equipped scholar. His 1881 landmark article "Inspiration," coauthored with A. A. Hodge (1823–86), and his 1882 "The Canonicity of Second Peter" were especially noteworthy, and in 1886 he became the first American to produce a textbook on the textual criticism of the Greek New Testament. Many at the time expressed their expectation that Warfield would become one of the most noted New Testament exegetes of the day. In 1881 he was offered but declined the chair of theology at the Theological Seminary of the Northwest in Chicago. Upon the untimely death of A. A. Hodge, the board of Princeton Seminary contacted Warfield, requesting that he consider coming on as Hodge's successor, emphasizing in the letter that he was the only man they were considering for the post and that they were eager for him at least to prayerfully consider it.

When in 1887 Warfield began his career at Princeton as professor of didactic and polemic theology (systematic theology), the congratulations were many and enthusiastic, and for the next several decades he established himself as the "brightest star" in the already bright galaxy that was Old Princeton. Known as a champion of orthodoxy in the heyday of old liberalism, he labored with a daunting breadth and depth of learning to expound and defend the historic faith of the church.

Warfield's father (William Warfield) was a cattle breeder, and due in large measure to this early and prolonged exposure, Warfield from his earliest years had a deep interest in all things scientific, which continued throughout his career. Referring to himself as a layman in scientific matters, he wrote often, usually in book reviews, on studies pertaining to the new evolutionary theories of the day.

Late in his life, Warfield acknowledged that he had held to evolution as he entered college but that he had abandoned it by around 1880. His era was a triumphing moment for evolution, and Warfield claimed that *if* evolution could be proven, the Bible could accommodate it. This openness has led many (e.g., Noll and Livingstone 2000) to assume that Warfield had, in fact, accepted evolution as established truth, but he remained skeptical. His criticisms of the theories—not just in their atheistic, Darwinistic forms, but in all their various proposals—was sometimes sarcastic, and exegetical obstacles kept him from acquiescing (Zaspel 2010a; 2010b, chap. 9; 2012).

Warfield believed deeply that because both Scripture and the created world itself are God-given, all truth (biblical and scientific) corresponds—and must correspond—perfectly. God speaks infallibly and with one voice in both volumes of his self-disclosure, natural **revelation** and special revelation. Interpreters of Scripture can err, to be sure, but then so can interpreters of the natural sciences. Interpretations may conflict, but the facts never do, and Warfield was utterly convinced that in the end this would be shown to be so. More than a scholar of wide learning, Warfield was a devout Christian devoted to discovering, expounding, and defending the truths of divine revelation. This, without question, is his leading legacy.

Fred G. Zaspel

REFERENCES AND RECOMMENDED READING

Noll, Mark A., and David N. Livingstone. 2000. *Evolution, Science, and Scripture: B. B. Warfield*. Grand Rapids: Baker.

Warfield, Benjamin Breckinridge. 2001. *Selected Shorter Writings*. 2 vols. Phillipsburg, NJ: P&R.

———. 2003. *The Works of Benjamin B. Warfield*. 10 vols. Grand Rapids: Baker.

Zaspel, Fred G. 2010a. "B. B. Warfield on Creation and Evolution." *Themelios* 35 (2): 198–211.

———. 2010b. *The Theology of B. B. Warfield: A Systematic Summary*. Wheaton, IL: Crossway.

———. 2012. "Princeton and Evolution." *Confessional Presbyterian* 8:91–98.

WEINBERG, STEVEN. Steven Weinberg (1933–) is a Nobel Prize–winning theoretical physicist regarded by many as the preeminent living practitioner of the discipline. He was born in New York and educated at the Bronx High School of Science (as was one of his fellow 1979 Nobel laureates, Sheldon Glashow), Cornell University, and Princeton University, where he received his PhD under Sam Treiman in 1957. The author of a number of respected and widely used textbooks (1972, 1995, 1996, 2000, 2008), he taught and researched at Columbia University (1957–59), the University of California–Berkeley (1959–69), the Massachusetts Institute of Technology (1969–73), and Harvard University (1973–83), and he has been the Josey Regental Chair in Science and a member of both the **physics** and **astronomy** departments at the University of Texas at Austin since 1983.

Elected to the American Academy of Arts and Sciences (1968) and the U.S. National Academy of Sciences (1972), he is the recipient of numerous awards, including the Nobel Prize in Physics in 1979 for the development of the electroweak theory and the National Medal of Science in 1991. He is the author of a number of highly regarded popular books on science (1977, 1983, 1992a, 2001, 2009, 2015) and is also widely known for his atheism, being named Humanist of the Year by the American Humanist Association in 2002.

Weinberg published a paper titled "A Model of Leptons" in 1967 that mathematically unified the force of electromagnetism with the weak force governing radioactive decay. His model, subsequently dubbed the "electroweak theory," was a significant step forward in the unification of the fundamental forces of nature (electromagnetism, the weak force, the strong nuclear force, and gravity) that physicists believe characterized the universe in its earliest moments of existence (see **Big Bang Theory**).

In modern physics, natural forces operate through the exchange of "messenger particles": photons in the case of electromagnetism, and W and Z bosons in the case of the weak force. The difficulty in trying to unify these forces is that such unification requires that both photons and the W and Z bosons belong to the same family, but the photon has zero rest mass while the weak-force bosons are more massive than the proton. Weinberg explained this mass difference in terms of spontaneous symmetry breaking. At the high energies immediately following the big bang, photons and weak-force bosons were indistinguishable, but as temperatures cooled, the symmetry among them was broken and the particles acquired different properties; most especially, the W and Z bosons acquired different masses.

Weinberg proposed that the symmetry breaking arose through interaction with the so-called Higgs boson (see **God Particle**), a particle Peter Higgs had hypothesized in 1964 to explain the origin of mass and whose existence was confirmed in 2012 at the Large Hadron Collider in Geneva, Switzerland.

Weinberg has been a prominent advocate in the public domain for scientific research and what he sees as the virtues of a scientific as opposed to a religious **worldview**. His animus toward religion seems largely motivated by questions of moral and natural evil (Weinberg 1992b, 1999; see **Evil, Problem of** and **Theodicy**), and he conceives of the universe as amoral, implacable, and utterly indifferent to humanity. In his popular book *The First Three Minutes* (1977), Weinberg famously remarked that "the more the universe seems comprehensible, the more it seems pointless." Yet at the same time he seems to recognize that "beauty" is a necessary component of viable physical theories (1992a, 132–65) and that the universe itself gives evidence of parameters that are fine-tuned for the existence of life (1999).

For the fine-tuning he is unable to discount (see **Fine-Tuning of the Universe and Solar System**), he appeals to the idea of a **multiverse** (2011), though in more technical publications he openly admits that any **contemporary cosmology** of this sort—which operates in that split second after the **big bang** and prior to matter-antimatter annihilation—is the kind of thing about which "we can only speculate" (2008, 201). In light of such considerations, Robert Koons (2011) has cogently argued that the criterion of **beauty** for scientific theories, as evinced by symmetries and invariances, can only reasonably be regarded as a guide to truth in the context of a transcendent **metaphysics** incompatible with Weinberg's **naturalism**. Furthermore, the fine-tuning of the initial conditions, laws, and constants of our universe is not easily dismissed (Collins 2013), and the very multiverse models to which Weinberg appeals are fraught with difficulties and fine-tuning issues of their own (Gordon 2011).

Bruce L. Gordon

REFERENCES AND RECOMMENDED READING

Collins, Robin. 2013. "The Fine-Tuning Evidence Is Convincing." In *Debating Christian Theism*. Eds. J. P. Moreland, C. Meister, and K. A. Sweis, 35–46. New York: Oxford University Press.

Feynman, Richard, and Steven Weinberg. 1987. *Elementary Particles and the Laws of Physics*. The 1986 Dirac Memorial Lectures. Cambridge: Cambridge University Press.

Gordon, Bruce L. 2011. "Balloons on a String: A Critique of Multiverse Cosmology." In *The Nature of Nature: Examining the Role of Naturalism in Science*. Eds. B. L. Gordon and W. A. Dembski, 558–601. Wilmington, DE: ISI Books.

Koons, Robert C. 2011. "The Incompatibility of Naturalism and Scientific Realism." In *The Nature of Nature: Examining the Role of Naturalism in Science*. Eds. B. L. Gordon and W. A. Dembski, 215–27. Wilmington, DE: ISI Books.

Weinberg, Steven. 1967. "A Model of Leptons." *Physical Review Letters* 19, no. 21 (November 20): 1264–66. http://physics.princeton.edu/~mcdonald/examples/EP/weinberg_prl_19_1264_67.pdf.

———. 1972. *Gravitation and Cosmology: Principles and Applications of the General Theory of Relativity*. New York: Wiley.

———. 1977. *The First Three Minutes: A Modern View of the Origin of the Universe*. New York: Basic Books.

———. 1979. "Conceptual Foundations of the Unified Theory of the Weak and Electromagnetic Interactions." Nobel Lecture. December 8. www.nobelprize.org/nobel_prizes/physics/laureates/1979/weinberg-lecture.pdf.

———. 1983. *The Discovery of Subatomic Particles*. Scientific American Library Edition. New York: W. H. Freeman.

———. 1992a. *Dreams of a Final Theory: The Scientist's Search for the Ultimate Laws of Nature*. New York: Pantheon.

———. 1992b. "What about God?" In Steven Weinberg, *Dreams of a Final Theory: The Scientist's Search for the Ultimate Laws of Nature*, 241–61. New York: Pantheon.

———. 1995. *The Quantum Theory of Fields*. Vol. 1, *Foundations*. Cambridge: Cambridge University Press.

———. 1996. *The Quantum Theory of Fields*. Vol. 2, *Modern Applications*. Cambridge: Cambridge University Press.

———. 1999. "A Designer Universe?" *New York Review of Books*. October 21, 1999. Reprinted with additions and modifications in Weinberg 2001, 230–42.

———. 2000. *The Quantum Theory of Fields*. Vol. 3, *Supersymmetry*. Cambridge: Cambridge University Press.

———. 2001. *Facing Up: Science and Its Cultural Adversaries*. Cambridge, MA: Harvard University Press.

———. 2008. *Cosmology*. New York: Oxford University Press.

———. 2009. *Lake Views: This World and the Universe*. Cambridge, MA: Belknap.

———. 2011. "Living in the Multiverse." In *The Nature of Nature: Examining the Role of Naturalism in Science*. Eds. B. L. Gordon and W. A. Dembski, 547–57. Wilmington, DE: ISI Books.

———. 2012. *Lectures on Quantum Mechanics*. Cambridge: Cambridge University Press.

———. 2015. *To Explain the World: The Discovery of Modern Science*. New York: Harper.

WHEWELL, WILLIAM. William Whewell (1794–1866) was born in Lancaster, England, the son of a master carpenter.

His early education included two years at Heversham Grammar School in Westmorland, which permitted him access to Cambridge University via a scholarship reserved for working-class students. He entered Trinity College, Cambridge, in 1812, and spent the entirety of his subsequent professional career at Trinity. He was ordained in 1826 to the Anglican ministry—a requirement at the time for all Cambridge faculty. He was appointed master of Trinity in 1841, serving in this capacity until his death.

Whewell's admission to Cambridge was largely due to his talent in **mathematics**, which would later yield a fellowship (1817) and a position as mathematics tutor at Trinity (1818). He established a reputation for lucid exposition of mathematically based engineering principles. An early success was the volume *An Elementary Treatise on Mechanics* (1819), which was updated through several successive editions. He then added crystallography to his expertise in mathematics and **physics**.

During the early 1820s, he studied **geology** under the tutelage of Adam Sedgwick and then from the crystallographer Friedrich Mohs. In 1828 he sought and was appointed to the vacant chair of mineralogy at Cambridge, which he held until he stepped down in favor of his student W. H. Miller in 1832. During this decade, he provided suggestions for the fundamentals of crystal organization, which would prove perceptive upon later recognition of the role of molecular bonding in crystal formation.

Whewell is most widely known for his analysis of how science works, based on his thorough background in the history of the sciences. His preparatory treatise, *The History of the Inductive Sciences* (1837), was well received in his day. The goal of his book *The Philosophy of the Inductive Sciences* (1840) was more controversial. He is often labeled as Kantian (see **Kant, Immanuel**) because he took issue with pure empiricists like John Stuart Mill. Whewell believed that humans bring an innate cognitive apparatus to their observations of nature, but he considered himself an empiricist in the lineage of **Francis Bacon**.

Whewell was confident that innate cognitive mechanisms were emplaced in humans by their Creator so that humans could flourish in the enterprise of investigating nature. Natural routes to legitimate inferences would emerge as humans more thoroughly examined natural systems and discerned real patterns (for example, the patterns of crystal organization that he had identified). The patterns themselves, as well as the mechanisms, were contingent and dependent on the choice of the Creator.

The contingency of the patterns could also be seen as evidence for the existence of a beneficent Creator. The particulars of planetary orbits, compositions of atmospheres, and the role of weather could be potentially multiplex. On earth, conditions were selected so as to coincide with the needs of living creatures. Whewell favored a weak version of the argument from design in his Bridgewater Treatise, *Astronomy and General Physics Considered with Reference to Natural Theology*, because the Creator need not create out of necessity a world such as ours (see **Design Argument**). In fact, the multiplicity of worlds in the cosmos need not be populated. Whewell compared the multiplicity of worlds to seeds broadcast by plants, of which most were not permitted to germinate (*Of the Plurality of Worlds*, chap. 11, sec. 11).

Whewell had maintained a serious engagement with ethical theory since his undergraduate years and was granted the Knightbridge Professorship of Moral Philosophy and Casuistical Divinity when it was vacated in 1838. His text *Elements of Morality Including Polity*, just like his works on mathematical physics, went through several successively modified editions. Whewell's argumentation for the foundation of ethics, as with his philosophy of natural science, depended on innate mental furniture. For this reason, his argumentation came under fire from Mill and the pure empiricists. Whewell resigned this professorship in 1855 in favor of his pupil John Grote.

Whewell, relying on Georges Cuvier and Sedgwick, was skeptical toward ideas of an organic continuum of life that could be related to a lengthy historic progression: evolution. Whewell responded to the early evolutionary work by Robert Chambers, *Vestiges of the Natural History of Creation* (1844), negatively. He promptly composed a reply, principally by extraction from his prior works, published as *Indications of the Creator* (1845).

Like many other contemporaries including Sedgwick, Whewell felt the **logic** and evidences of *Vestiges* to be sloppy and materialist. In the case of Darwin, he was gentler and more circumspect: the two had known each other for many years and had corresponded. Yet in the preface to his seventh edition (1864a) of *Astronomy and General Physics Considered with Reference to Natural Theology*, he gently objected to Darwin's evolutionary proposal, specifically with reference to the sparseness of potential transitional structures and organisms.

Whewell is characterized as a polymath. In addition to his complex writings on mathematical engineering, the history and **philosophy of science**, crystallography, and moral philosophy, he published studies of the tides, chemical nomenclature, and Gothic cathedral architecture. He also wrote poetry. He coined the words *scientist*, *physicist*, *catastrophist*, and *uniformitarian*, and he is reported to have suggested several potential terms for electrochemical phenomena to **Michael Faraday**, such as *ion*, which are in ordinary usage today. A crater on the moon is named for Whewell, as well as a mineral, Whewellite.

Whewell married twice: first in 1841 to Cordelia Marshall, who died in 1855; then to Lady Affleck, who died in 1865. No children were born from either marriage.

Ralph Stearley

REFERENCES AND RECOMMENDED READING

Fisch, Menachem. 1991. *William Whewell, Philosoher of Science.* Oxford: Oxford University Press.

Fisch, Menachem, and Simon Schaffer, eds. 1991. *William Whewell: A Composite Portrait.* Oxford: Oxford University Press. This work contains many useful chapters on aspects of Whewell's life and work, including a chapter on Whewell's natural theology by John Hedley Brook and on Whewell's philosophy of the historical sciences by M. J. S. Hodge.

Secord, James A. 2000. *Victorian Sensation: The Extraordinary Publication, Reception and Secret Authorship of* Vestiges of the Natural History of Creation. Chicago: University of Chicago Press.

Snyder, Laura J. 2012. "William Whewell." In *Stanford Encyclopedia of Philosophy*. Ed. Edward N. Zalta. Winter. http://plato.stanford.edu/archives/win2012/entries/whewell/.

Whewell's publication list extends to 150 plus items, including reviews and translations. Many of his textbooks or philosophical writings went into several editions, confusing efforts to enumerate his works.

Whewell, William. 1819. *An Elementary Treatise on Mechanics.* Cambridge: Cambridge University Press.

———. 1823. *A Treatise on Dynamics.* Cambridge: Cambridge University Press.

———. 1826. "On the Classification of Crystalline Combinations, and the Canons by Which Their Laws of Derivation May Be Investigated." *Transactions of the Cambridge Philosophical Society* 2:87–130.

———. 1828. *An Essay on Mineralogical Classification and Nomenclature, with Tables of the Orders and Species of Minerals.* Cambridge: Cambridge University Press.

———. 1831. "Review of J. Herschel's Preliminary Discourse on the Study of Natural Philosophy (1830)." *Quarterly Review* 90:374–407.

———. 1833. *Astronomy and General Physics Considered with Reference to Natural Theology.* A Bridgewater Treatise. London: Pickering.

———. 1837. *The History of the Inductive Sciences from the Earliest to the Present Time.* 3 vols. London: John W. Parker.

———. 1840. *The Philosophy of the Inductive Sciences Founded upon Their History.* 2 vols. London: John W. Parker.

———. 1842. *Architectural Notes on German Churches: With Notes Written during an Architectural Tour in Picardy and Normandy, to Which Are Added, Notes on the Churches of the Rhine, by M. F. Lassaulx, Architectural Inspector to the King of Prussia.* 3rd ed. London: Cambridge, J. and J. J. Deighton.

———. 1845. *Indications of the Creator.* London: John W. Parker.

———. 1845a. *The Elements of Morality, including Polity.* 2 vols. London: John W. Parker.

———. 1845b. *Of a Liberal Education in General and with Particular Reference to the Leading Studies of the University of Cambridge.* London: John W. Parker.

———. 1853. *Of the Plurality of Worlds: An Essay*. London: John W. Parker.

———. 1857. *History of the Inductive Sciences, from the Earliest to the Present Time*. 3rd ed., in two volumes. London: John W. Parker.

———. 1858a. *The History of Scientific Ideas*. 2 vols. London: John W. Parker.

———. 1858b. *Novum Organon Renovatum*. London: John W. Parker.

———. 1860. *On the Philosophy of Discovery*. London: John W. Parker.

———. 1862. *Six Lectures on Political Economy*. Cambridge: Cambridge University Press.

———. 1864a. *Astronomy and General Physics Considered with Reference to Natural Theology*. 7th ed. London: Pickering.

———. 1864b. *The Elements of Morality, Including Polity*. 4th ed. Cambridge: Cambridge University Press.

Edited Individual or Collections of Whewell's Works

Whewell, William. 1968. *William Whewell: Theory of Scientific Method*. Ed. with intro by Robert E. Butts. Pittsburgh: University of Pittsburgh Press. Repr., Indianapolis: Hackett, 1989.

———. 2001a. *The Collected Works of William Whewell*. 16 vols. Ed. Richard Yeo. Bristol: Thoemmes Continuum.

———. 2001b. *Of the Plurality of Worlds*. Ed. with new intro. by Michael Ruse. Chicago: University of Chicago Press.

WHITCOMB, JOHN C. John C. Whitcomb Jr. (1924–) was a professor of theology and Old Testament at Grace Theological Seminary for nearly 40 years and was a founding figure in the rise of the modern **creation science** movement in America in the 1960s. Along with Henry Morris, he coauthored *The Genesis Flood* (1961), which became the most influential book in the history of modern creationism.

Whitcomb was born in Washington, DC, the son of an army colonel, and began his undergraduate studies at Princeton University in 1943. Studying historical **geology** and **paleontology** at first, he was drafted into the army and served in the European theater of World War II from 1944 until 1946. During his first year at Princeton, he converted to evangelical Christianity. Returning to the college after the war, he graduated with a BA in ancient and European history with honors in 1948. That same year he enrolled at Grace Theological Seminary in Winona Lake, Indiana, the seminary of the Fellowship of Grace Brethren Churches. He received his MDiv in 1951 and began teaching as a professor of Old Testament while continuing his graduate studies at the school.

In 1953 the **American Scientific Affiliation** was holding its annual meeting at the school, and Whitcomb met Henry Morris there for the first time. That same year, he earned his ThM at the seminary and in 1957 completed his ThD. Stimulated and encouraged by his meeting with Morris, Whitcomb wrote his dissertation on the **Genesis flood**, presenting an exegetical, historical, and scientific basis for a universal worldwide flood. He continued teaching at the school for another 30 years, becoming one of the most popular and eloquent lecturers on campus.

Whitcomb left Grace Seminary in 1990 and presently maintains his own ministry, Whitcomb Ministries, Inc., as founder and president. He has also written on other subjects, including biblical commentaries, dispensational **eschatology**, and Darius the Mede in the book of Daniel.

With the publication of *The Genesis Flood* in 1961, Whitcomb and Morris are credited with launching the modern creation science movement. Also known as "scientific creationism," this movement seeks to provide scientific arguments for a literal reading of the Genesis narratives, including a young earth, a universal flood, and the fiat creation of humans and animal **species**.

While Whitcomb provided the biblical and interpretative argumentation for a universal flood, Morris played a key role in providing the scientific support. Henry Morris was a successful hydraulic engineer raised in Texas who had earned his PhD from the University of Minnesota. He was at one time professor and chair of the civil engineering department at Virginia Tech. Morris proceeded by reviving an earlier theory called *flood geology*, which had been advocated in the 1920s by a Seventh-day Adventist and self-taught geologist named **George McCready Price** (1870–1963). This theory argues that the fossil and geological strata used to support a very old earth can be explained by the catastrophic effects of Noah's worldwide flood. The book also advocated the idea of a vapor canopy created on the second day of creation from which the "waters above" flooded the earth.

The Genesis Flood became one of the most popular Christian books of the time, selling more than 200,000 copies in 25 years, and it is currently in its forty-ninth printing. The book led to the founding of the Creation Research Society in 1963 and the **Institute for Creation Research** in 1972.

Milton Eng

REFERENCES AND RECOMMENDED READING

Eve, Raymond A., and Francis B. Harrold. 1990. *The Creationist Movement in Modern America: Social Movements Past and Present*. Boston: Twayne.

Morris, Henry, and John C. Whitcomb. 2011. *The Genesis Flood, 50th Anniversary Edition*. Phillipsburg, NJ: P&R.

Numbers, Ronald L. (1992) 2006. *The Creationists: From Scientific Creationism to Intelligent Design*. Exp. ed. Cambridge, MA: Harvard University Press.

WHITE, ANDREW DICKSON. Educator, politician, and writer Andrew Dickson White (1832–1918) is known principally for two achievements. He cofounded Cornell University in 1865 and became its first president. Prior to its establishment, he scandalized many in Ithaca, New York, by saying that Cornell would be "an asylum for Science—where truth shall be sought for truth's sake—where it shall not be the main purpose of the Faculty to stretch or cut Science exactly to fit 'Revealed Religion'" (1862). To that end, he imposed no religious tests on faculty or students.

His second accomplishment was authoring the two-volume work *A History of the Warfare of Science with Theology in Christendom*. This was published in six non-English languages during his lifetime. Those volumes generated a conflict model between Christianity and science that still animates discussions on these topics. It is still in print as of the writing of this entry. Historians of science **David C. Lindberg** and **Ronald Numbers** write, "No work—not even **John William Draper**'s bestselling *History of the Conflict between Religion and Science* (1874)—has done more than White's to instill in the public mind a sense of the adversarial relationship between science and religion" (Lindberg and Numbers 1987).

That work declares history showed that "interference with Science in the supposed interest of religion—no matter how conscientious such interference may have been—has resulted in the direst evils both to Religion and Science, and invariably [so]" (White 1869). White seemed to mean that science and religion have their own separate spheres or domains. He claimed that religion itself suffers evil when it attempts to "interfere" with science. But, for White, the domain of religion was not that of rationally supportable truths, but of personal faith. Thus, in White's view, religion was not a source of knowledge about the most significant aspects of life. Its separate sphere was a sort of epistemological ghetto (see **Non-overlapping Magisteria**).

White's account of the historical stage for this warfare offered up **Copernicus**, **Galileo**, **Darwin**, and others as heroes who braved the ignorance of the religious authorities. Contemporary scholarship by Rodney Stark and others refutes this religion versus science model as simplistic and excessively binary. White ignored the ways in which the Christian **worldview** encourages science. These include the belief in a rational God who created a world in which humans can probe and develop nature for God's glory and the common good. Further, today we find that the best theories in **physics**, for example, can be understood to substantiate the doctrine that God created the cosmos ex nihilo and fine-tuned it for life.

Many skeptics and atheists continue to believe and propagate the conflict narrative in their quest to rationally discredit Christianity, which often harks back to White and the **conflict thesis**. The thesis can be summarized as follows:

1. Science is the best—or only—vehicle for arriving at knowledge about the most important matters (see **Scientism**).
2. Anything that undermines science should be opposed as false and irrational.
3. Christianity undermines science.
4. Therefore Christianity is false and irrational.

This argument fails for two reasons. First, science, while a vehicle for truth, cannot ground moral or metaphysical propositions necessary for the flourishing of science; thus proposition 1 is false. Second, Christianity does not undermine science, so 3 is false. Christians can agree with 2 without threatening either Christianity or scientific endeavor.

Douglas Groothuis

REFERENCES AND RECOMMENDED READING

Lindberg, David C., and Ronald L. Numbers. 1987. "Beyond War and Peace." *Perspectives on Science and Christian Faith* 39 (3): 140–49.

Stark, Rodney. 2004. *For the Glory of God: How Monotheism Led to Reformations, Science, Witch-Hunts, and the End of Slavery*. Princeton, NJ: Princeton University Press.

White, Andrew Dickson. 1862. "Letter from Andrew Dickson White to Gerrit Smith." September 1. www.math.cornell.edu/m/GeneralHistory/historyP2.

———. 1869. "The Battle-Fields of Science." *New York Daily Tribune*. 18 December.

———. (1896) 1993. *A History of the Warfare of Science with Theology in Christendom*. Amherst, NY: Prometheus.

WHITEHEAD, ALFRED NORTH. Born in Kent, England, on February 15, 1861, Whitehead (1861–1947) established his early career as a mathematician, most notably with his magisterial, three-volume *Principia Mathematica* (1910–13), coauthored with **Bertrand Russell**. Following this publication, he increasingly devoted his attention to philosophy. One of his first extended philosophical works was *The Concept of Nature* (1920), a compilation of Tarner Lectures delivered at Trinity College in November 1919. In 1929 he published his magnum opus, *Process and Reality*, regarded by Whitehead scholars David Ray Griffin and Donald W. Sherburne as "one of the major philosophical works of the modern world" (Griffin and Sherburne 1979, v). This book forms the basis of process theology.

Whitehead claimed that reality consists not of objects but of events. Thus reality is composed of episodic encounters or experiences. An "eternally real" God guides a universe of successive occasions toward value; his is a cosmology in which "all things flow." Whitehead sought to reconcile the empirical foundations of the objective universe with the subjective experiences attached to it. Here the objective and subjective are not in tension but irrevocably conjoined: "We may not pick and choose. For us the red glow of the sunset should be as much part of nature," he wrote, "as are the molecules and electric waves by which men of science would explain the phenomenon" (Whitehead 1920, 29).

As laudable as Whitehead's goal of reconciling science and religion was, his concept of God contradicted God's biblical omniscience and immutability (Pss. 90:2; 102:24–27; Mal. 3:6; 2 Tim. 2:13; Heb. 13:8). Whitehead's God is limited (dependent) and contingent on the successive occasions through which he must act, calling into question his essential sovereignty and indeed even prevenient or irresistible grace, since identity in the process model is more corporate and communal and placed within an ever-changing, ever-evolving context. The implications for a Christology rooted in a personal relationship would also appear to be problematic. Rather than putting forth the concept of a God responsible for and interacting with his creation, process theology is panentheistic (see **Pantheism**; **Panentheism**). These beliefs put process theology in tension with Christian orthodoxy.

Whitehead died in Cambridge, Massachusetts, on December 30, 1947. But process theology lives on among some liberal Christians, most notably John B. Cobb Jr., a United Methodist clergyman. Cobb has attempted to recast a Christology more compatible with process thinking by linking Jesus Christ with the embodiment of a transcendent, primordial *Logos*, but this seems to reduce Christ from God manifest and resurrected in the flesh into a vague panentheistic presence. Process theology was also developed in the years following Whitehead's death by **Charles Hartshorne** (1897–2000).

Whitehead's sophisticated analyses of age-old problems such as evil, sin, imperfection, humanity's relationship to the cosmic whole, and the intersections of science and religion have received considerable attention in academic circles, especially among clerical elites. Nevertheless, the coherence of those formulations and conclusions remains extremely problematic from an orthodox Christian perspective.

Michael A. Flannery

REFERENCES AND RECOMMENDED READING

Griffin, David Ray, and Donald W. Sherburne. 1979. "Editors' Preface." In Alfred North Whitehead, *Process and Reality*, corr. ed. New York: Free Press.
Whitehead, Alfred North. 1920. *The Concept of Nature*. Cambridge: Cambridge University Press.

WILSON, EDWARD OSBORNE.

Edward Osborne Wilson (1929–) is professor emeritus and honorary curator in entomology, Harvard University. Wilson was born in Birmingham, Alabama, to Edward and Inez Wilson. He was drawn to nature and showed interest in entomology even as a young child. He would receive both his undergraduate and master's degrees from the University of Alabama, and his doctorate from Harvard University, where he was hired as a professor in 1956. As an academic, Wilson has been wildly independent and often politely irreverent throughout his distinguished career. His contributions to the fields of entomology, **ecology**, and evolutionary biology warrant considering him among the greatest luminaries in the natural sciences.

Because of his elegant prose and even tone, Wilson has often been referred to as the "Southern gentleman." Among his many accolades, he is a member of the National Academy of Sciences and has been the recipient of the National Medal of Science, the International Prize for Biology, the Crafoord Prize, and two Pulitzer Prize awards.

The earliest of Wilson's many significant contributions was the theory of "taxon cycles," which linked **species** dispersal and range expansion and contraction to speciation. This was followed by a landmark treatise he coauthored with Robert MacArthur titled *The Theory of Island Biogeography* (1967), which provided many of the basic theories and predictions used in ecology today. Wilson's work in the area of social insect behavior and genetic **altruism** was equally groundbreaking. He argued that eusocial behavior emerges as a result of the increased shared genetics of siblings in situations of haplodiploidy. This fed Darwinian explanations of fitness-based advantages in altruistic behavior.

However, Wilson also broke away from classical Darwinian **reductionism** in arguing that **natural selection** might work at multiple scales or levels simultaneously (as opposed to the level of the **gene** or organism alone). Perhaps his most unsettling pronouncements came in an area of research he dubbed "sociobiology" (1975). Here Wilson argued that all features of human social constructs (including religion) are the products of evolutionary processes, and that individual and group behaviors can be reduced to Darwinian (fitness-based) mechanisms.

Wilson is a self-described secular humanist and is fully dedicated to the **worldview** of **naturalism**. He has been awarded the Distinguished Humanist Award from the American Humanist Association and has voiced genuine disdain for organized religion (though he was raised as a Southern Baptist). Wilson remains open to **deism**, and in his book *The Creation*, he offered an earnest olive branch to believers in an attempt to unify all parties against the common loss of species diversity on the planet. Wilson recently founded the Biodiversity Foundation and is currently working on The Encyclopedia of Life project. His extensive efforts in the area of species conservation have led to him being known as "the grandfather of biodiversity." Other major contributions include *On Human Nature* (1978, Pulitzer Prize winner), *Promethean Fire: Reflections on the Origin of Mind* (1983), *The Ants* (1990, Pulitzer Prize winner), *The Diversity of Life* (1992), and *The Future of Life* (2002).

Wayne Rossiter

REFERENCES AND RECOMMENDED READING

"E. O. Wilson (Biography): Father of Sociobiology." 2013. Academy of Achievement. June 3. www.achievement.org/autodoc/page/wil2bio–1.

MacArthur, Robert H., and Edward O. Wilson. 1967. *The Theory of Island Biogeography.* Princeton, NJ: Princeton University Press.

Nowak, Martin A., Corina E. Tarnita, and Edward O. Wilson. 2010. "The Evolution of Eusociality." *Nature* 466:1057–66.

Simberloff, Daniel S., and Edward O. Wilson. 1969. "Experimental Zoogeography of Islands: The Colonization of Empty Islands." *Ecology* 50:278–96.

Wilson, Edward O. 1971. *The Insect Societies.* Cambridge, MA: Harvard University Press.

———. 1975. *Sociobiology: The New Synthesis.* Cambridge, MA: Harvard University Press.

WITTGENSTEIN, LUDWIG. Austrian-born philosopher Ludwig Josef Johann Wittgenstein (1889–1951) was arguably the leading analytic philosopher of the twentieth century. During the span of his career, he produced two markedly different yet equally influential philosophies. His influence was not limited to philosophy but extended into disciplines such as theology, **physics**, cognitive **psychology**, **sociology**, **philosophy of science**, ethics, and literary criticism.

Wittgenstein's early philosophy was represented by his first publication, *Tractatus Logico-Philosophicus* (Wittgenstein 1922). Wittgenstein dealt with **logic**, science, math, the mystical, and the limitations of philosophy, but his primary concern was the nature of language and its relation to the world. The early Wittgenstein believed that language mirrors the world. It can express the propositions of natural science but cannot express ideas about God, ethics, or aesthetics. While one can think about God, ethics, or aesthetics, one cannot speak meaningfully about them. "Whereof we cannot speak, we must be silent" (1922, 7.0).

Just as language in general mirrors or "pictures" the world, so science forms pictures of reality. Scientific theories, however, are not determined empirically but are constructed within frameworks that Wittgenstein called "forms of representation." These forms are accepted or rejected on the basis of pragmatic considerations such as simplicity and explanatory power.

The *Tractatus* contains a discussion about scientific theory, in which Wittgenstein distinguished between three phenomena: empirical generalizations, which describe objects; **laws of nature**, which depict reality but only indirectly; and principles of specific scientific systems (1922, 6.3ff.). Principles of specific systems, such as Newton's mechanics, are inconsistent when it comes to depicting reality: some principles, such as the law of **causation**, insist that an event must be explained by a natural law; other principles, such as the law of induction, express an empirical proposition (Glock 1996, 342).

Wittgenstein's early views, as expressed in the *Tractatus*, were appropriated by the so-called Vienna Circle, a group of logical positivists including Otto Neurath (sociology), Moritz Schlick (physics), and Kurt Gödel (**mathematics**; see **Gödel's Theorem**). Members of the circle met together to read the *Tractatus* line by line and sometimes met with Wittgenstein himself. From these meetings emerged the positivists' "**verification principle**," which stated that nonanalytic sentences are insignificant unless they can be tested, and that utterances are meaningless if they are neither analytic nor empirically testable.

The later period of Wittgenstein's work, as expressed in *Philosophical Investigations*, includes the modification and/or rebuttal of many aspects of his own earlier work and signifies a departure from the mainstream of Western philosophy (Wittgenstein 1958).

(1) Against the Western tradition, he argued that philosophical method should not consist of metaphysical explanation or theory building. Instead, it should be descriptive and should function as a sort of therapy for philosophical confusion.

(2) Against his own earlier view that language mirrors the world, he now argued that language cannot mirror the world because it is a part of the world. The meaning of words is not discerned by looking at how they picture objects in reality;

rather, it is discerned by looking at a word's use within its social, behavioral, and linguistic contexts. Only by paying attention to context can people begin to understand language.

(3) In opposition to his earlier view, and against the majority tradition in Western philosophy, he rejected any attempt to separate the thinking subject from his own body and from the rest of the world. According to Wittgenstein, knowledge does not begin with **consciousness**. Knowledge does not "begin" with anything; rather, it arises from within a person's form of life. This shared form of life is the context within which he knows what he knows. Thus, in **epistemology**, just as in philosophical method and philosophy of language as described above, Wittgenstein was affirming the embodied nature of human thought and action.

In relation to science, Wittgenstein argued that scientific theories are not descriptions of objects, per se, but rather are "forms of representation" that guide the way a scientist reacts to empirical objects or evidence. When scientists lay aside an old form of representation for a new one, they do not do so because the "facts" forced them to do so but because they think the new form has better explanatory power. In this respect, Wittgenstein's forms of representation are compatible with conventionalism ("conventionalism" is the view that deep-level scientific theories are not forced on us by natural "facts" but instead are chosen by us from among various ways that we could reasonably explain the scientific phenomena), and are similar to **Thomas Kuhn**'s "paradigms" (see **Paradigm**).

Additionally, Wittgenstein's **anthropology** has influenced certain fields of science. His view of the embodied nature of human thought and action has been appropriated in philosophy of psychology (Kerr 2008; Wisdom 1991), anthropology (Geertz 1973), **neuroscience** (Bennett and Hacker 2003), and other fields.

Wittgenstein's influence on the scientific disciplines therefore consists of two different streams, including one that flows from his earlier thought and another that flows from his later thought. The earlier Wittgenstein exercised his most significant influence on the scientists and mathematicians of the Vienna Circle. The later Wittgenstein has been appropriated in philosophy of psychology, anthropology, neuroscience, and other disciplines, and continues to exercise second-hand influence through Wittgensteinian theologians, such as Fergus Kerr, David Burrell, George Lindbeck, Hans Frei, James William McClendon Jr., and their interfaces with science.

Bruce Ashford

REFERENCES AND RECOMMENDED READING

Bennett, M. R., and P. M. S. Hacker. 2003. *Philosophical Foundations of Neuroscience.* Oxford: Blackwell.
Geertz, Clifford. 1973. *The Interpretation of Cultures.* New York: Basic Books.
Glock, Hans-Johann. 1996. *A Wittgenstein Dictionary.* Oxford: Blackwell.
Hacker, P. M. S. 1972. *Insight and Illusion: Themes in the Philosophy of Wittgenstein.* Oxford: Clarendon.
Kenny, Anthony. 1973. *Wittgenstein.* Cambridge, MA: Harvard University Press.
Kerr, Fergus. 1986. *Theology after Wittgenstein.* Oxford: Basil Blackwell.
———. 2008. *"Work on Oneself": Wittgenstein's Philosophical Psychology.* Arlington, VA: Institute for the Psychological Sciences Press.
McClendon, James W., and Brad Kallenberg. 1998. "Ludwig Wittgenstein: A Christian in Philosophy." *Scottish Journal of Theology* 51, no. 2: 131–61.
Monk, Ray. (1958) 1997. *Philosophical Investigations* (German-English parallel text). 2nd. ed. Trans. G. E. M. Anscombe. Oxford: Blackwell.
———. 1990. *Wittgenstein: The Duty of Genius.* New York: Penguin.
———. 1992. *Tractatus Logico-Philosophicus* (German-English parallel text). London: Routledge and Kegan Paul. Repr. in German-English parallel text and trans. C. K. Ogden and F. P. Ramsey. London: Routledge.
Wisdom, John. 1991. *Proof and Explanation: The Virginia Lectures.* Ed. Stephen F. Barker. Lanham, MD: University Press of America.
Wittgenstein, Ludwig. 1922, repr. 1992. *Tractatus Logico-Philosophicus* [German-English parallel text]. Tr. C. K. Ogden and F. P. Ramsey. London: Routledge.
———. 1958, repr. 1997. *Philosophical Investigations* [German-English parallel text]. Tr. G. E. M. Anscombe. Oxford: Blackwell.

WORLDVIEW. In the simplest terms, a worldview may be defined as how one sees life and the world at large. A worldview functions something like a pair of glasses, as an interpretive lens through which a person makes sense of life and comprehends the world around them.

Derived from the German term *Weltanschauung*, the word *worldview* refers to the cluster of beliefs a person holds about the most significant issues of life, such as God, the cosmos, knowledge, values, humanity, and history (Naugle 2002). These beliefs, which may in reality be right or wrong or a combination thereof—not unlike the visual clarity or distortion given by glasses—form a big picture, a general outlook, or a grand perspective on life and the world.

In more technical terms, a worldview forms a mental structure that organizes one's basic or ultimate beliefs. This framework supplies a comprehensive view of what a person considers real, true, rational, good, valuable, and beautiful.

Worldview perspectives involve much more than merely a set of intellectual beliefs. However, thinking of a worldview in terms of a basic conceptual system is critical. Rather than a disconnected or disparate group of unrelated beliefs, a carefully examined and reflective worldview consists of a network of interconnected ideas that form a unified whole.

This system of beliefs then responds to the big questions of life, focusing particularly on issues central to human concern. These issues include thoughts about the human predicament (why human beings are the way they are and why they face the challenges they do) and how human beings derive meaning, purpose, and significance.

Three popular current worldviews that compete for adherents in the marketplace of ideas include secular **naturalism**, mystical pantheism, and Christian **theism**.

1. *Secular naturalism* regards the natural, material, and physical universe as the sole reality; thus no supernatural realities or entities exist (summarized as "Nature is the whole show.").
2. *Mystical pantheism* proclaims that all reality is an undifferentiated spiritual one and that unity is God or Ultimate Reality (summarized as "All is God and God is all.").
3. *Christian theism* reveals that God is an infinite, eternal, immutable, morally perfect, and tripersonal spiritual being—the transcendent Creator and sovereign Sustainer of all things (summarized as "the triune God of the Bible is the creator and redeemer of humankind"; see **Trinity, the**).

Worldviews are typically evaluated in terms of their coherence, testability, explanatory power and scope, simplicity, and livability.

Worldview and Science

The operation of science presupposes certain foundational truths not wholly derived from science itself. For science's experimental venture to work and thrive, certain nonempirical assumptions about the world must be true. In other words, it takes a certain kind of world for science to be possible. Thus science cannot function apart from worldview considerations. In particular, it was assumptions of a Christian theistic worldview that allowed science to emerge and to flourish—leading to the widely accepted development of the **scientific method**.

That method depends on a number of critical underlying assumptions or beliefs that cannot be validated by science itself. These worldview assumptions or **presuppositions of science** include:

- Objective reality of the cosmos
- Order, regularity, and uniformity of nature
- Intelligibility of the cosmos
- Validity of **mathematics** and **logic**
- Basic reliability of human cognitive faculties and sensory organs
- Congruence between the human **mind** and physical reality

Worldview considerations are therefore critical to the scientific enterprise as well as to all people who pursue meaning and truth in life.

Kenneth Richard Samples

REFERENCES AND RECOMMENDED READING

Naugle, David K. 2002. *Worldview: The History of a Concept.* Grand Rapids: Eerdmans.
Samples, Kenneth Richard. 2007. *A World of Difference: Putting Christian Truth-Claims to the Worldview Test.* Grand Rapids: Baker.

Y

YOUNG, DAVIS A. Davis A. "Dave" Young (March 5, 1941–) spent most of his early years in Philadelphia, where his father, Edward J. Young, served as professor of Old Testament at Westminster Theological Seminary (1936–68). At the age of 12, Young became interested in minerals and the study of nature in general. Young received a BS from Princeton in 1962 and an MS from Pennsylvania State University in 1965.

While at Penn State, Dave also met Dorothy "Dottie" Cairns; they were married in 1965. They then moved to Providence, Rhode Island, where Dottie worked as a teacher while Dave undertook his PhD at Brown University. His dissertation explored the petrology and structural **geology** of the Reading Prong, New Jersey. This assemblage of highly metamorphosed igneous rocks spurred him to give serious thought to the evidences for Earth's antiquity. Before he had received his PhD, Young began his first teaching assignment at New York University (1968–73).

During the mid–1960s, Young paid close examination to the founding document of the modern flood geology movement, *The Genesis Flood* (1961), by **Henry Morris** and **John Whitcomb**. Young found it initially impressive; but growing acquaintance with the Reading Prong rocks, as well as the thick sequence of metamorphosed Paleozoic sedimentary rocks exposed in central Connecticut, gave him pause. The latter sequence had been derived from an eroding mountain chain (during the mid-Paleozoic Acadian Orogeny); then buried and metamorphosed to garnet-grade schist; and then uplifted and exposed by erosion. These events could not be compressed into a single-year event, as modern-day flood geology advocates believed. Young began work on a book discussing the Earth's antiquity. This work, *Creation and the Flood: An Alternative to Flood Geology and Theistic Evolution*, would be published after his relocation to North Carolina, where Young entered his next phase of teaching (1973–78), at the University of North Carolina–Wilmington.

In 1978 Dave Young moved again to Calvin College, where he joined Clarence Menninga in the teaching of geology, later serving as department chair before his retirement in 2004.

During the 1980s, Young began to write or collaborate on several books that collectively addressed the history of geology and the relationships between historical **science** and Christian faith. These works included *Christianity and the Age of the Earth* (1982), *Science Held Hostage* (1988), and *Portraits of Creation* (1990). These books appealed to a rising generation of evangelical scientists but were not looked on with favor by the proponents of flood geology. Henry Morris, together with son John, would author a book accusing Young and several other evangelical scientists of "aiding the enemy" (1989, 82).

In the 1990s and early 2000s, Young completed studies of the mineralogy of the northern New Jersey highlands and then began to dig more deeply into the history of geology. These efforts resulted in several papers as well as a volume on N. L. Bowen and the most comprehensive single treatment of the history of igneous petrology, *Mind over Magma*. This body of work would earn him the Mary Rabbitt Award from the History of Geology section of the Geological Society of America.

Between 1995 and 2010, Young continued to author works that more comprehensively addressed the history of the thinking on Noah's flood (*The Biblical Flood*, 1995), the failure of modern flood geology to explain the rock record (*The Bible, Rocks, and Time*, with Ralph Stearley, 2008), and a thorough survey of John Calvin's writings on nature and natural science. In 2012 his book *Good News for Science*, which explains and defends Christian faith for the nonbelieving scientist, was published.

Ralph Stearley

REFERENCES AND RECOMMENDED READING

Iddings, Joseph Paxton. 2015. *Recollections of a Petrologist.* Ed. Davis Young. Boulder, CO, Geological Society of America Special Publication 512.
Morris, Henry M., and John D. Morris. 1989. *Science, Scripture and the Young Earth,* enl. and updated ed. El Cajon, CA: Institute for Creation Research.
Stearley, R. 2014. Two formal interviews. Fall.
Young, Davis A. 1971. "Precambrian Rocks of the Lake Hopatcong Area, New Jersey." *Geological Society of America Bulletin* 82:143–58.
———. 1972. "A Quartz Syenite Intrusion in the New Jersey Highlands." *Journal of Petrology* 13:511–28.
———. 1977. *Creation and the Flood: An Alternative to Flood Geology and Theistic Evolution.* Grand Rapids: Baker.
———. 1982. *Christianity and the Age of the Earth.* Grand Rapids: Zondervan.
———. 1987a. "Scripture in the Hands of Geologists (Part One)." *Westminster Theological Journal* 49:1–34.
———. 1987b. "Scripture in the Hands of Geologists (Part Two)." *Westminster Theological Journal* 49:257–304.

———. 1995a. "The Antiquity and the Unity of the Human Race Revisited." *Christian Scholar's Review* 24:380–96.

———. 1995b. *The Biblical Flood: A Case Study of the Church's Response to Extrabiblical Evidence.* Grand Rapids: Eerdmans; Carlisle: Paternoster.

———. 1998. *N. L. Bowen and Crystallization-Differentiation: The Evolution of a Theory.* Washington, DC: The Mineralogical Society.

———. 2003. *Mind over Magma: The Story of Igneous Petrology.* Princeton, NJ: Princeton University Press.

———. 2007. *John Calvin and the Natural World.* Lanham, MD: University Press of America.

———. 2012. *Good News for Science: Why Scientific Minds Need God.* Oxford, MS: Malius.

———. 2014. "How an Igneous Geologist Came to Terms with Evolution." In *Christians and Evolution.* Ed. R. J. Berry, 230–44. Oxford: Monarch.

Young, Davis A., and John Cuthbertson. 1994. "A New Ferrosilite and Fe-Pigeonite Occurrence in the Reading Prong, New Jersey, USA." *Lithos* 31:163–76.

Young, Davis A., and Ralph Stearley. 2008. *The Bible, Rocks and Time.* Downers Grove, IL: InterVarsity.

Young, Davis A., Howard J. Van Till, and Clarence Menninga. 1988. *Science Held Hostage.* Downers Grove, IL: InterVarsity.

Young, Davis A., Howard J. Van Till, Robert E. Snow, and John H. Stek. 1990. *Portraits of Creation: Biblical and Scientific Perspectives on the World's Formation.* Grand Rapids: Eerdmans.